COGNITIVE PSYCHOLOGY

Doubt everything. Find your own light.
(Buddha)

COGNITIVE PSYCHOLOGY
A Student's Handbook

Sixth Edition

MICHAEL W. EYSENCK
Royal Holloway University of London, UK

MARK T. KEANE
University College Dublin, Ireland

Psychology Press
Taylor & Francis Group

HOVE AND NEW YORK

This edition published 2010

By Psychology Press
27 Church Road, Hove, East Sussex BN3 2FA

Simultaneously published in the USA and Canada
By Psychology Press
711 Third Avenue, New York, NY 10017 (8th floor) UNITED STATES

Psychology Press is an imprint of the Taylor & Francis group,
an Informa business

© 2010 Psychology Press

British Library Cataloguing in Publication Data
A catalogue record for this book is available from the British Library

Library of Congress Cataloging in Publication Data

Eysenck, Michael W.
  Cognitive psychology : a student's handbook / Michael W. Eysenck, Mark T. Keane.
—6th ed.
    p. cm.
  Includes bibliographical references and index.
  ISBN 978-1-84169-540-2 (soft cover)—ISBN 978-1-84169-539-6 (hbk)
1. Cognition—Textbooks. 2. Cognitive psychology—Textbooks. I. Keane,
Mark T., 1961– II. Title.
  BF311.E935 2010
  153—dc22

                                                          2010017103

ISBN: 978-1-84169-539-6 (hbk)
ISBN: 978-1-84169-540-2 (pbk)

Typeset in China by Graphicraft Limited, Hong Kong
Cover design by Aubergine Design
Printed and bound in the UK by Ashford Colour Press Ltd, Gosport, Hampshire

CONTENTS

PREFACE

In the five years since the fifth edition of this textbook was published, there have been numerous exciting developments in our understanding of human cognition. Of greatest importance, large numbers of brain-imaging studies are revolutionising our knowledge rather than just providing us with pretty coloured pictures of the brain in action. As a consequence, the leading contemporary approach to human cognition involves studying the *brain* as well as *behaviour*. We have used the term "cognitive psychology" in the title of this book to refer to this approach, which forms the basis for our coverage of human cognition. Note, however, that the term "cognitive neuroscience" is often used to describe this approach.

The approaches to human cognition covered in this book are more varied than has been suggested so far. For example, one approach involves mainly laboratory studies on healthy individuals, and another approach (cognitive neuropsychology) involves focusing on the effects of brain damage on cognition. There is also computational cognitive science, which involves developing computational models of human cognition.

We have done our level best in this book to identify and discuss the most significant research and theorising stemming from the above approaches and to integrate all of this information. Whether we have succeeded is up to our readers to decide. As was the case with previous editions of this textbook, both authors have had to work hard to keep pace with developments in theory and research. For example, the first author wrote parts of the book in far-flung places including Macau, Iceland, Istanbul, Hong Kong, Southern India, and the Dominican Republic. Sadly, there have been several occasions on which book writing has had to take precedence over sightseeing!

I (Michael Eysenck) would like to express my continuing profound gratitude to my wife Christine, to whom this book (in common with the previous three editions) is appropriately dedicated. What she and our three children (Fleur, William, and Juliet) have added to my life is too immense to be captured by mere words.

I (Mark Keane) would like to thank everyone at the Psychology Press for their extremely friendly and efficient contributions to the production of this book, including Mike Forster, Lucy Kennedy, Tara Stebnicky, Sharla Plant, Mandy Collison, and Becci Edmondson.

We would also like to thank Tony Ward, Alejandro Lleras, Elizabeth Styles, Nazanin Derakhshan, Elizabeth Kensinger, Mick Power, Max Velmans, William Banks, Bruce Bridgeman, Annukka Lindell, Alan Kennedy, Trevor Harley, Nick Lund, Keith Rayner, Gill Cohen, Bob Logie, Patrick Dolan, Michael Doherty, David Lagnado, Ken Gilhooly, Ken Manktelow, Charles L. Folk who commented on various chapters. Their comments proved extremely useful when it came to the business of revising the first draft of the entire manuscript.

Michael Eysenck and Mark Keane

CHAPTER ①

APPROACHES TO HUMAN COGNITION

INTRODUCTION

We are now several years into the third millennium, and there is more interest than ever in unravelling the mysteries of the human brain and mind. This interest is reflected in the recent upsurge of scientific research within cognitive psychology and cognitive neuroscience. We will start with cognitive psychology. It is concerned with the internal processes involved in making sense of the environment, and deciding what action might be appropriate. These processes include attention, perception, learning, memory, language, problem solving, reasoning, and thinking. We can define **cognitive psychology** as involving the attempt to understand human cognition by observing the *behaviour* of people performing various cognitive tasks.

The aims of cognitive neuroscientists are often similar to those of cognitive psychologists. However, there is one important difference – cognitive neuroscientists argue convincingly that we need to study the *brain* as well as behaviour while people engage in cognitive tasks. After all, the internal processes involved in human cognition occur in the brain, and we have increasingly sophisticated ways of studying the brain in action. We can define **cognitive neuroscience** as involving the attempt to use information about behaviour and about the brain to understand human cognition. As is well known, cognitive neuroscientists use brain-imaging techniques. Note that the distinction

between cognitive psychology and cognitive neuroscience is often blurred – the term "cognitive psychology" can be used in a broader sense to include cognitive neuroscience. Indeed, it is in that broader sense that it is used in the title of this book.

There are several ways in which cognitive neuroscientists explore human cognition. First, there are brain-imaging techniques, of which PET (**positron emission tomography**) and fMRI (**functional magnetic resonance imaging**) (both discussed in detail later) are probably the best known. Second, there are electrophysiological techniques involving the recording of electrical

KEY TERMS

cognitive psychology: an approach that aims to understand human cognition by the study of behaviour.
cognitive neuroscience: an approach that aims to understand human cognition by combining information from behaviour and the brain.
positron emission tomography (PET): a brain-scanning technique based on the detection of positrons; it has reasonable spatial resolution but poor temporal resolution.
functional magnetic resonance imaging (fMRI): a technique based on imaging blood oxygenation using an MRI machine; it provides information about the location and time course of brain processes.

signals generated by the brain (also discussed later). Third, many cognitive neuroscientists study the effects of brain damage on human cognition. It is assumed that the patterns of cognitive impairment shown by brain-damaged patients can tell us much about normal cognitive functioning and about the brain areas responsible for different cognitive processes.

The huge increase in scientific interest in the workings of the brain is mirrored in the popular media – numerous books, films, and television programmes have been devoted to the more accessible and/or dramatic aspects of cognitive neuroscience. Increasingly, media coverage includes coloured pictures of the brain, showing clearly which parts of the brain are most activated when people perform various tasks.

There are four main approaches to human cognition (see the box below). Bear in mind, however, that researchers increasingly combine two or even more of these approaches. A considerable amount of research involving

---

Approaches to human cognition

1. *Experimental cognitive psychology*: this approach involves trying to understand human cognition by using behavioural evidence. Since behavioural data are of great importance within cognitive neuroscience and cognitive neuropsychology, the influence of cognitive psychology is enormous.
2. *Cognitive neuroscience*: this approach involves using evidence from behaviour and from the brain to understand human cognition.
3. *Cognitive neuropsychology*: this approach involves studying brain-damaged patients as a way of understanding normal human cognition. It was originally closely linked to cognitive psychology but has recently also become linked to cognitive neuroscience.
4. *Computational cognitive science*: this approach involves developing computational models to further our understanding of human cognition; such models increasingly take account of our knowledge of behaviour and the brain.

---

these approaches is discussed throughout the rest of this book. We will shortly discuss each of these approaches in turn, and you will probably find it useful to refer back to this chapter when reading other chapters. You may find the box on page 28 especially useful, because it provides a brief summary of the strengths and limitations of all four approaches.

EXPERIMENTAL COGNITIVE PSYCHOLOGY

It is almost as pointless to ask, "When did cognitive psychology start?" as to inquire, "How long is a piece of string?" However, the year 1956 was of crucial importance. At a meeting at the Massachusetts Institute of Technology, Noam Chomsky gave a paper on his theory of language, George Miller discussed the magic number seven in short-term memory (Miller, 1956), and Newell and Simon discussed their extremely influential model called the General Problem Solver (see Newell, Shaw, & Simon, 1958). In addition, there was the first systematic attempt to study concept formation from a cognitive perspective (Bruner, Goodnow, & Austin, 1956).

At one time, most cognitive psychologists subscribed to the information-processing approach. A version of this approach popular in the 1970s is shown in Figure 1.1. According to this version, a stimulus (an environmental event such as a problem or a task) is presented. This stimulus causes certain internal cognitive processes to occur, and these processes finally produce the desired response or answer. Processing directly affected by the stimulus input is often described as **bottom-up processing**. It was typically assumed that only one process occurs

---

KEY TERM

bottom-up processing: processing that is directly influenced by environmental stimuli; see **top-down processing**.

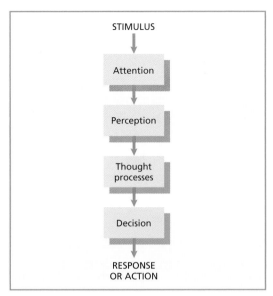

Figure 1.1 An early version of the information-processing approach.

at any moment in time. This is known as **serial processing**, meaning that the current process is completed before the next one starts.

The above approach represents a drastic oversimplification of a complex reality. There are numerous situations in which processing is not exclusively bottom-up but also involves top-down processing. **Top-down processing** is processing influenced by the individual's expectations and knowledge rather than simply by the stimulus itself. Look at the triangle shown in Figure 1.2 and read what it says. Unless you are familiar with the trick, you probably read it as, "Paris in the spring". If so, look again, and you will see that the word "the" is repeated. Your expectation that it was the well-known

Figure 1.2 Diagram to demonstrate top-down processing.

phrase (i.e., top-down processing) dominated the information actually available from the stimulus (i.e., bottom-up processing).

The traditional approach was also oversimplified in assuming that processing is typically serial. In fact, there are numerous situations in which some (or all) of the processes involved in a cognitive task occur at the same time – this is known as **parallel processing**. It is often hard to know whether processing on a given task is serial or parallel. However, we are much more likely to use parallel processing when performing a task on which we are highly practised than one we are just starting to learn (see Chapter 5). For example, someone taking their first driving lesson finds it almost impossible to change gear, to steer accurately, and to pay attention to other road users at the same time. In contrast, an experienced driver finds it easy and can even hold a conversation as well.

For many years, nearly all research on human cognition involved carrying out experiments on healthy individuals under laboratory conditions. Such experiments are typically tightly controlled and "scientific". Researchers have shown great ingenuity in designing experiments to reveal the processes involved in attention, perception, learning, memory, reasoning, and so on. As a consequence, the findings of cognitive psychologists have had a major influence on the research conducted by cognitive neuroscientists. Indeed, as we will see, nearly all the research discussed in this book owes much to the cognitive psychological approach.

An important issue that cognitive psychologists have addressed is the task impurity problem – many cognitive tasks involve the use of a complex mixture of different processes, making it hard to interpret the findings. This issue has been addressed in various ways. For example, suppose we are interested in the inhibitory processes used when a task requires us to inhibit deliberately some dominant response. Miyake, Friedman, Emerson, Witzki, Howerter, and Wager (2000) studied three tasks that require such inhibitory processes: the Stroop task; the anti-saccade task; and the stop-signal task. On the Stroop task, participants have to name the colour in which colour words are presented (e.g., RED printed in green) and avoid saying the colour word. We are so used to reading words that it is hard to inhibit responding with the colour word. On the anti-saccade task, a visual cue is presented to the left or right of the participant. The task involves *not* looking at the cue but, rather, inhibiting that response and looking in the opposite direction. On the stop-signal task, participants have to categorise words as animal or non-animal as rapidly as possible, but must inhibit their response when a tone sounds. Miyake et al. obtained evidence that these three tasks all involved similar processes. They used a statistical procedure known as latent-variable analysis to extract what was common to the three tasks, which was assumed to represent a relatively pure measure of the inhibitory process.

Cognitive psychology was for many years the engine room of progress in understanding human cognition, and all the other approaches listed in the box above have derived substantial benefit from it. For example, **cognitive neuropsychology** became an important approach about 20 years after cognitive psychology. It was only when cognitive psychologists had developed reasonable accounts of normal human cognition that the performance of brain-damaged patients could be understood properly. Before that, it was hard to decide which patterns of cognitive impairment were of theoretical importance. Similarly, the computational modelling activities of computational cognitive scientists are often informed to a large extent by pre-computational psychological theories.

Ask yourself, what colour is this stop-sign? The Stroop effect dictates that you may feel compelled to say "red", even though you see that it is green.

Finally, the selection of tasks by cognitive neuroscientists for their brain-imaging studies is influenced by the theoretical and empirical efforts of cognitive psychologists.

Limitations

In spite of cognitive psychology's enormous contributions to our knowledge of human cognition, the approach has various limitations. We will briefly consider five such limitations here. First, how people behave in the laboratory may differ from how they behave in everyday life. The concern is that laboratory research lacks **ecological validity** – the extent to which

KEY TERMS

cognitive neuropsychology: an approach that involves studying cognitive functioning in brain-damaged patients to increase our understanding of normal human cognition.
ecological validity: the extent to which experimental findings are applicable to everyday settings.

the findings of laboratory studies are applicable to everyday life. In most laboratory research, for example, the sequence of stimuli presented to the participant is based on the experimenter's predetermined plan and is not influenced by the participant's behaviour. This is very different to everyday life, in which we often change the situation to suit ourselves.

Second, cognitive psychologists typically obtain measures of the speed and accuracy of task performance. These measures provide only *indirect* evidence about the internal processes involved in cognition. For example, it is often hard to decide whether the processes underlying performance on a complex task occur one at a time (serial processing), with some overlap in time (cascade processing), or all at the same time (parallel processing). As we will see, the brain-imaging techniques used by cognitive neuro-scientists can often clarify what is happening.

Third, cognitive psychologists have often put forward theories expressed only in verbal terms. Such theories tend to be vague, making it hard to know precisely what predictions follow from them. This limitation can largely be overcome by developing computer models specifying in detail the assumptions of any given theory. This is how computational cognitive scientists (and, before them, developers of math-ematical models) have contributed to cognitive psychology.

Fourth, the findings obtained using any given experimental task or paradigm are some-times specific to that paradigm and do not generalise to other (apparently similar) tasks. This is **paradigm specificity**, and it means that some of the findings in cognitive psychology are narrow in scope. There has been relatively little research in this area, and so we do not know whether the problem of paradigm specificity is widespread.

Fifth, much of the emphasis within cognitive psychology has been on relatively specific theories applicable only to a narrow range of cognitive tasks. What has been lacking is a comprehensive theoretical architecture. Such an architecture would clarify the interrelationships among different components of the cognitive system. Various candidate cognitive architectures have been proposed (e.g., Anderson's Adaptive Control of Thought-Rational (ACT-R) model; discussed later in the chapter). However, the research community has not abandoned specific theories in favour of using cognitive architectures, because researchers are not convinced that any of them is the "one true cognitive architecture".

COGNITIVE NEUROSCIENCE: THE BRAIN IN ACTION

As indicated earlier, cognitive neuroscience involves intensive study of the brain as well as behaviour. Alas, the brain is complicated (to put it mildly!). It consists of about 50 billion neurons, each of which can connect with up to about 10,000 other neurons.

To understand research involving functional neuroimaging, we must consider how the brain is organised and how the different areas are described. Various ways of describing specific brain areas are used. We will discuss two of the main ways. First, the cerebral cortex is divided into four main divisions or lobes (see Figure 1.3). There are four lobes in each brain hemisphere: frontal, parietal, temporal, and occipital. The frontal lobes are divided from the parietal lobes by the central sulcus (**sulcus** means furrow or groove), the lateral fissure separates the temporal lobes from the parietal and frontal lobes, and the parieto-occipital sulcus and pre-occipital notch divide the occipital lobes from the parietal and temporal lobes. The main

KEY TERMS

paradigm specificity: this occurs when the findings obtained with a given paradigm or experimental task are not obtained even when apparently very similar paradigms or tasks are used.

sulcus: a groove or furrow in the brain.

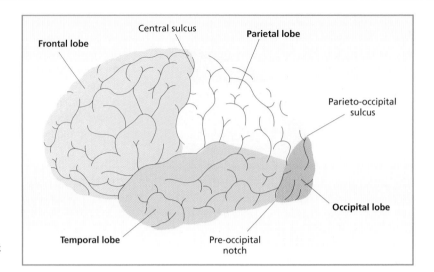

Figure 1.3 The four lobes, or divisions, of the cerebral cortex in the left hemisphere.

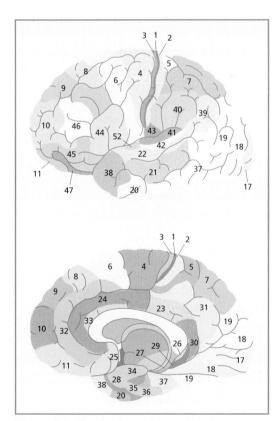

Figure 1.4 The Brodmann Areas of the brain.

gyri (or ridges; gyrus is the singular) within the cerebral cortex are shown in Figure 1.3.

Researchers use various terms to describe more precisely the area(s) of the brain activated during the performance of a given task. Some of the main terms are as follows:

dorsal: superior or towards the top
ventral: inferior or towards the bottom
anterior: towards the front
posterior: towards the back
lateral: situated at the side
medial: situated in the middle

Second, the German neurologist Korbinian Brodmann (1868–1918) produced a **cytoarchitectonic map** of the brain based on variations in the cellular structure of the tissues (see Figure 1.4). Many (but not all) of the areas identified by Brodmann correspond to functionally distinct areas. We will often refer to areas such as BA17, which simply means Brodmann Area 17.

Techniques for studying the brain

Technological advances mean we have numerous exciting ways of obtaining detailed information about the brain's functioning and structure. In principle, we can work out *where* and *when* in the brain specific cognitive processes occur. Such information allows us to determine the order in which different parts of the brain become active when someone performs a task. It also allows us to find out whether two tasks involve the same parts of the brain in the same way or whether there are important differences.

Information concerning techniques for studying brain activity is contained in the box below. Which of these techniques is the best? There is no single (or simple) answer. Each technique has its own strengths and limitations, and so researchers focus on matching the technique to the issue they want to address. At the most basic level, the various techniques vary in the precision with which they identify the brain areas active when a task is performed (spatial resolution), and the time course of such activation (temporal resolution). Thus, the techniques differ in their ability to provide precise information concerning where and

Techniques for studying brain activity

- **Single-unit recording**: This technique (also known as single-cell recording) involves inserting a micro-electrode one 110,000th of a millimetre in diameter into the brain to study activity in single neurons. This is a very sensitive technique, since electrical charges of as little as one-millionth of a volt can be detected.
- **Event-related potentials (ERPs)**: The same stimulus is presented repeatedly, and the pattern of electrical brain activity recorded by several scalp electrodes is averaged to produce a single waveform. This technique allows us to work out the timing of various cognitive processes.
- **Positron emission tomography (PET)**: This technique involves the detection of positrons, which are the atomic particles emitted from some radioactive substances. PET has reasonable spatial resolution but poor temporal resolution, and it only provides an indirect measure of neural activity.
- **Functional magnetic resonance imaging (fMRI)**: This technique involves imaging blood oxygenation using an MRI machine (described later). fMRI has superior spatial and temporal resolution to PET, but also only provides an indirect measure of neural activity.

- **Event-related functional magnetic resonance imaging (efMRI)**: This is a type of fMRI that compares brain activation associated with different "events". For example, we could see whether brain activation on a memory test differs depending on whether participants respond correctly or incorrectly.
- **Magneto-encephalography (MEG)**: This technique involves measuring the magnetic fields produced by electrical brain activity. It provides fairly detailed information at the millisecond level about the time course of cognitive processes, and its spatial resolution is reasonably good.
- **Transcranial magnetic stimulation (TMS)**: This is a technique in which a coil is placed close to the participant's head and a very brief pulse of current is run through it. This produces a short-lived magnetic field that generally inhibits processing in the brain area affected. It can be regarded as causing a very brief "lesion", a lesion being a structural alteration caused by brain damage. This technique has (jokingly!) been compared to hitting someone's brain with a hammer. As we will see, the effects of TMS are sometimes more complex than our description of it would suggest.

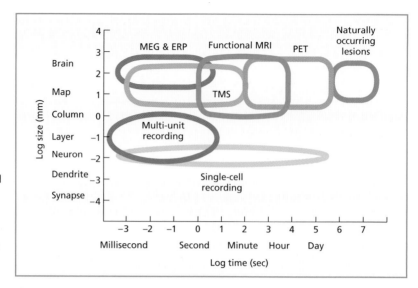

Figure 1.5 The spatial and temporal resolution of major techniques and methods used to study brain functioning. From Ward (2006), adapted from Churchland and Sejnowski (1991).

when brain activity occurs. The spatial and temporal resolutions of various techniques are shown in Figure 1.5. High spatial and temporal resolutions are advantageous if a very detailed account of brain functioning is required. In contrast, low temporal resolution can be more useful if a general overview of brain activity during an entire task is needed.

We have introduced the main techniques for studying the brain. In what follows, we consider each of them in more detail.

Single-unit recording

As indicated already, **single-unit recording** permits the study of single neurons. One of the best-known applications of this technique was by Hubel and Wiesel (1962, 1979) in research on the neurophysiology of basic visual processes in cats and monkeys. They found simple and complex cells in the primary visual cortex, both of which responded maximally to straight-line stimuli in a particular orientation (see Chapter 2). Hubel and Wiesel's findings were so clear-cut that they influenced several subsequent theories of visual perception (e.g., Marr, 1982).

The single-unit (or cell) recording technique is more fine-grain than other techniques. Another advantage is that information about neuronal activity can be obtained over time periods ranging from small fractions of a second up to several hours or even days. However, the technique can only provide information about activity at the level of single neurons, and so other techniques are needed to assess the functioning of larger cortical areas.

Event-related potentials

The **electroencephalogram** (**EEG**) is based on recordings of electrical brain activity measured at the surface of the scalp. Very small changes in electrical activity within the brain are picked up by scalp electrodes. These changes can be shown on the screen of a cathode-ray tube using an oscilloscope. However, spontaneous or background brain activity sometimes obscures the impact of stimulus processing on the EEG

KEY TERMS

single-unit recording: an invasive technique for studying brain function, permitting the study of activity in single neurons.

electroencephalogram (EEG): a device for recording the electrical potentials of the brain through a series of electrodes placed on the scalp.

recording. This problem can be solved by presenting the same stimulus several times. After that, the segment of EEG following each stimulus is extracted and lined up with respect to the time of stimulus onset. These EEG segments are then simply averaged together to produce a single waveform. This method produces **event-related potentials (ERPs)** from EEG recordings and allows us to distinguish genuine effects of stimulation from background brain activity.

ERPs have very limited spatial resolution but their temporal resolution is excellent. Indeed, they can often indicate when a given process occurred to within a few milliseconds. The ERP waveform consists of a series of positive (P) and negative (N) peaks, each described with reference to the time in milliseconds after stimulus presentation. Thus, for example, N400 is a negative wave peaking at about 400 ms.

Here is an example showing the value of ERPs in resolving theoretical controversies (discussed more fully in Chapter 10). It has often been claimed that readers take longer to detect semantic mismatches in a sentence when detection of the mismatch requires the use of world knowledge than when it merely requires a consideration of the words in the sentence. An example of the former type of sentence is, "The Dutch trains are white and very crowded" (they are actually yellow), and an example of the latter sentence type is, "The Dutch trains are sour and very crowded". Hagoort, Hald, Bastiaansen, and Petersson (2004) used N400 as a measure of the time to detect a semantic mismatch. There was no difference in N400 between the two conditions, suggesting there is no time delay in utilising world knowledge.

ERPs provide more detailed information about the time course of brain activity than most other techniques. For example, a behavioural measure such as reaction time typically provides only a *single* measure of time on each trial, whereas ERPs provide a *continuous* measure. However, ERPs do not indicate with any precision which brain regions are most involved in processing, in part because the presence of skull and brain tissue distorts the electrical fields created by the brain. In addition, ERPs

are mainly of value when stimuli are simple and the task involves basic processes (e.g., target detection) occurring at a certain time after stimulus onset. For example, it would not be feasible to study most complex forms of cognition (e.g., problem solving) with ERPs.

Positron emission tomography (PET)

Positron emission tomography is based on the detection of positrons, which are the atomic particles emitted by some radioactive substances. Radioactively labelled water (the tracer) is injected into the body, and rapidly gathers in the brain's blood vessels. When part of the cortex becomes active, the labelled water moves rapidly to that place. A scanning device next measures the positrons emitted from the radioactive water. A computer then translates this information into pictures of the activity levels in different brain regions. It may sound dangerous to inject a radioactive substance. However, tiny amounts of radioactivity are involved, and the tracer has a half-life of only 2 minutes, although it takes 10 minutes for the tracer to decay almost completely.

PET has reasonable spatial resolution, in that any active area within the brain can be located to within 5–10 millimetres. However, it suffers from various limitations. First, it has very poor temporal resolution. PET scans indicate the amount of activity in each region of the brain over a period of 30–60 seconds. PET cannot assess the rapid changes in brain activity associated with most cognitive processes. Second, PET provides only an *indirect* measure of neural activity. As Anderson, Holliday, Singh, and Harding (1996, p. 423) pointed out, "Changes in regional cerebral blood flow, reflected by changes in the spatial distribution of intravenously administered positron emitted

KEY TERM

event-related potentials (ERPs): the pattern of electroencephalograph (EEG) activity obtained by averaging the brain responses to the same stimulus presented repeatedly.

radioisotopes, are assumed to reflect changes in neural activity." This assumption may be more applicable to early stages of processing. Third, PET is an invasive technique because participants are injected with radioactively labelled water. This makes it unacceptable to some potential participants.

Magnetic resonance imaging (MRI and fMRI)

In magnetic resonance imaging (MRI), radio waves are used to excite atoms in the brain. This produces magnetic changes detected by a very large magnet (weighing up to 11 tons) surrounding the patient. These changes are then interpreted by a computer and turned into a very precise three-dimensional picture. MRI scans can be obtained from numerous different angles but only tell us about the *structure* of the brain rather than about its *functions*.

Cognitive neuroscientists are generally more interested in brain functions than brain structure. Happily enough, MRI technology can provide functional information in the form of functional magnetic resonance imaging (fMRI). Oxyhaemoglobin is converted into deoxyhaemoglobin when neurons consume oxygen, and deoxyhaemoglobin produces distortions in the local magnetic field. This distortion is assessed by fMRI, and provides a measure of the concentration of deoxyhaemoglobin in the blood. Technically, what is measured in fMRI is known as **BOLD** (blood oxygen-level-dependent contrast). Changes in the BOLD signal produced by increased neural activity take some time to occur, so the temporal resolution of fMRI is about 2 or 3 seconds. However, its spatial resolution is very good (approximately 1 millimetre). Since the temporal and spatial resolution of fMRI are both much better than those of PET, fMRI has largely superseded PET.

Suppose we want to understand why participants in an experiment remember some items but not others. This issue can be addressed by using **event-related fMRI (efMRI)**, in which we consider each participant's patterns of brain activation separately for remembered and non-remembered items. Wagner et al. (1998) recorded

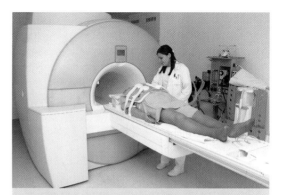

The magnetic resonance imaging (MRI) scanner has proved an extremely valuable source of data in psychology.

fMRI while participants learned a list of words. About 20 minutes later, the participants were given a test of recognition memory on which they failed to recognise 12% of the words. Did these recognition failures occur because of problems during *learning* or at *retrieval*? Wagner answered this question by using event-related fMRI, comparing brain activity during learning for words subsequently recognised with that for words not recognised. There was more brain activity in the prefrontal cortex and hippocampus for words subsequently remembered than for those not remembered. These findings suggested that forgotten words were processed less thoroughly than remembered words at the time of learning.

What are the limitations of fMRI? First, it provides a somewhat indirect measure of underlying neural activity. Second, there are distortions in the BOLD signal in some brain

KEY TERMS

BOLD: blood oxygen-level-dependent contrast; this is the signal that is measured by **fMRI**.
event-related functional magnetic imaging (efMRI): this is a form of **functional magnetic imaging** in which patterns of brain activity associated with specific events (e.g., correct versus incorrect responses on a memory test) are compared.

Can cognitive neuroscientists read our brains/minds?

There is increasing evidence that cognitive neuro-scientists can work out what we are looking at just by considering our brain activity. For example, Haxby, Gobbini, Furey, Ishai, Schouten, and Pietrini (2001) asked participants to look at pictures belonging to eight different categories (e.g., cats, faces, houses) while fMRI was used to assess patterns of brain activity. The experimenters accurately predicted the category of object being looked at by participants on 96% of the trials!

Kay, Naselaris, Prenger, and Gallant (2008) argued that most previous research on "brain reading" was limited in two ways. First, the visual stimuli were much less complex than those we encounter in everyday life. Second, the experimenters' task of predicting what people were looking at was simplified by comparing their patterns of brain activity on test trials to those obtained when the same objects or categories had been presented previously. Kay et al. overcame both limitations by presenting their two participants with 120 *novel* natural images that were reasonably complex. The fMRI data permitted correct identification of the image being viewed on 92% of the trials for one participant and on 72% of trials for the other. This is remarkable accuracy given that chance performance would be 1/120 or 0.8%!

Why is research on "brain reading" important? One reason is because it may prove very useful for identifying what people are dreaming about or imagining. More generally, it can reveal our true feelings about other people. Bartels and Zeki (2000) asked people to look at photographs of someone they claimed to be deeply in love with as well as three good friends of the same sex and similar age as their partner. There was most activity in the medial insula and the anterior cingulate within the cortex and subcortically in the caudate nucleus and the putamen when the photograph was of the loved one. This pattern of activation differed from that found previously with other emotional states, suggesting that love activates a "unique network" (Bartels & Zeki, 2000, p. 3829). In future, cognitive neuroscientists may be able to use "brain reading" techniques to calculate just how much you are in love with someone!

regions (e.g., close to sinuses; close to the oral cavity). For example, it is hard to obtain accurate measures from orbitofrontal cortex.

Third, the scanner is noisy, which can cause problems for studies involving the presentation of auditory stimuli. Fourth, some people (especially sufferers from claustrophobia) find it uncomfortable to be encased in the scanner. Cooke, Peel, Shaw, and Senior (2007) found that 43% of participants in an fMRI study reported that the whole experience was at least a bit upsetting, and 33% reported side effects (e.g., headaches).

Fifth, Raichle (1997) argued that constructing cognitive tasks for use in the scanner is "the real Achilles heel" of fMRI research. There are constraints on the kinds of stimuli that can be presented to participants lying in a scanner. There are also constraints on the kinds of responses they can be asked to produce. For example, participants are rarely asked to respond using speech because even small movements can distort the BOLD signal.

Magneto-encephalography (MEG)

Magneto-encephalography (MEG) involves using a superconducting quantum interference device (SQUID) to measure the magnetic fields produced by electrical brain activity. The technology is

KEY TERM

magneto-encephalography (MEG): a non-invasive brain-scanning technique based on recording the magnetic fields generated by brain activity.

complex, because the size of the magnetic field created by the brain is extremely small relative to the earth's magnetic field. However, MEG provides very accurate measurement of brain activity, in part because the skull is virtually transparent to magnetic fields. That means that magnetic fields are little distorted by intervening tissue, which is an advantage over the electrical activity assessed by the EEG.

Overall, MEG has excellent temporal resolution (at the millisecond level) and often has very good spatial resolution as well. However, using MEG is extremely expensive, because SQUIDs need to be kept very cool by means of liquid helium, and recordings are taken under magnetically shielded conditions.

Anderson et al. (1996) used MEG to study the properties of an area of the visual cortex known as V5 or MT (see Chapter 2). This area was responsive to motion-contrast patterns, suggesting that its function is to detect objects moving relative to their background. Anderson et al. also found using MEG that V5 or MT was active about 20 ms after V1 (primary visual cortex) in response to motion-contrast patterns. These findings suggested that some basic visual processing *precedes* motion detection.

People sometimes find it uncomfortable to take part in MEG studies. Cooke et al. (2007) found that 35% of participants reported that the experience was "a bit upsetting". The same percentage reported side effects (e.g., muscle aches, headaches).

Transcranial magnetic stimulation (TMS)

Transcranial magnetic stimulation (TMS) is a technique in which a coil (often in the shape of a figure of eight) is placed close to the participant's head, and a very brief (less than 1 ms) but large magnetic pulse of current is run through it. This causes a short-lived magnetic field that generally (but not always) leads to inhibited processing activity in the affected area (typically about 1 cubic centimetre in extent). More specifically, the magnetic field created leads to electrical stimulation in the brain. In practice, several magnetic pulses are usually administered in a fairly short period of time; this is **repetitive transcranial magnetic stimulation (rTMS)**.

What is an appropriate control condition against which to compare the effects of TMS? It might seem as if all that is needed is to compare performance on a task with and without TMS. However, TMS creates a loud noise and some twitching of the muscles at the side of the forehead, and these effects might lead to impaired performance. Applying TMS to a non-critical brain area (one theoretically not needed for task performance) is often a satisfactory control condition. The prediction is that task performance will be worse when TMS is applied to a critical area than to a non-critical one.

Why are TMS and rTMS useful? It has been argued that they create a "temporary lesion" (a lesion is a structural alteration produced by brain damage), so that the role of any given brain area in performing a given task can be assessed. If TMS applied to a particular brain area leads to impaired task performance, it is reasonable to conclude that that brain area is necessary for task performance. Conversely, if TMS has no effects on task performance, then the brain area affected by it is not needed to perform the task effectively. What is most exciting about TMS is that it can be used to show that activity in a particular brain area is *necessary* for normal levels of performance on some task. Thus, we are often in a stronger position to make causal statements about the brain areas underlying performance when we use TMS than most other techniques.

We can see the advantages of using TMS by considering research discussed more fully in Chapter 5. In a study by Johnson and Zatorre (2006), participants performed visual and auditory tasks separately or together (dual-task condition). The dorsolateral prefrontal cortex was only activated in the dual-task condition, suggesting that this condition required processes relating to task co-ordination. However, it was not clear that the dorsolateral prefrontal cortex was actually *necessary* for successful dual-task performance. Accordingly, Johnson, Strafella, and Zatorre (2007) used the same tasks as Johnson and Zatorre (2006) while administering rTMS to the dorsolateral prefrontal cortex. This caused impaired performance in the dual-task condition, thus strengthening the argument that involvement of the dorsolateral prefrontal cortex is essential in that condition.

TMS can also provide insights into *when* any given brain area is most involved in task performance. For example, Cracco, Cracco, Maccabee, and Amassian (1999) gave participants the task of detecting letters. Performance was maximally impaired when TMS was applied to occipital cortex 80–100 ms after the presentation of the letters rather than at shorter or longer delays.

Evaluation

As indicated already, the greatest advantage of TMS (and rTMS) over neuroimaging techniques is that it increases our confidence that a given brain area is necessary for the performance of some task. TMS allows us to *manipulate* or experimentally control the availability of any part of the brain for involvement in the performance of some cognitive task. In contrast, we can only establish associations or correlations between activation in various brain areas and task performance when using functional neuroimaging.

TMS can be regarded as producing a brief "lesion", but it has various advantages over research on brain-damaged patients within cognitive neuropsychology. First, the experimenter controls the brain area(s) involved with TMS. Second, it is easy to compare any given individual's performance with and without a lesion with TMS but this is rarely possible with brain-damaged patients. Third, brain damage may lead patients to develop compensatory strategies or to reorganise their cognitive system, whereas brief administration of TMS does not produce any such complications.

What are the limitations of TMS? First, it is not very clear exactly what TMS does to the brain. It mostly (but not always) *reduces* activation in the brain areas affected. Allen, Pasley, Duong, and Freeman (2007) applied rTMS to the early visual cortex of cats not engaged in any task. rTMS caused an *increase* of spontaneous brain activity that lasted up to 1 minute. However, activity in the visual cortex produced by viewing gratings was *reduced* by up to 60% by rTMS, and took 10 minutes to recover. Such differing patterns suggest that the effects of TMS are complex.

Second, TMS can only be applied to brain areas lying beneath the skull but not to areas with overlying muscle. That limits its overall usefulness.

Third, it has proved difficult to establish the precise brain area or areas affected when TMS is used. It is generally assumed that its main effects are confined to a relatively small area. However, fMRI evidence suggests that TMS pulses can cause activity changes in brain areas distant from the area of stimulation (Bohning et al., 1999). Using fMRI in combination with TMS can often be an advantage – it sheds light on the connections between the brain area stimulated by TMS and other brain areas.

Fourth, there are safety issues with TMS. For example, it has very occasionally caused seizures in participants in spite of stringent rules to try to ensure the safety of participants in TMS studies.

Fifth, it may be hard to show that TMS applied to any brain area has adverse effects on simple tasks. As Robertson, Théoret, and Pascual-Leone (2003, p. 955) pointed out, "With the inherent redundancy of the brain and its resulting high capacity to compensate for disruption caused by TMS, it is perhaps only through straining the available neuronal resources with a reasonably complex task that it becomes possible to observe behavioural impairment."

Overall evaluation

Do the various techniques for studying the brain provide the answers to all our prayers? Many influential authorities are unconvinced. For example, Fodor (1999) argued as follows: "If the mind happens in space at all, it happens somewhere north of the neck. What exactly turns on knowing how far north?" We do not agree with that scepticism. Cognitive neuroscientists using various brain techniques have contributed enormously to our understanding of human cognition. We have mentioned a few examples here, but numerous other examples are discussed throughout the book. The overall impact of cognitive neuroscience on our understanding of human cognition is increasing very rapidly.

We will now turn to six issues raised by cognitive neuroscience. First, none of the brain techniques provides magical insights into human cognition. We must avoid succumbing to "the neuroimaging illusion". This is the mistaken view that patterns of brain activation provide *direct* evidence concerning cognitive processing. Weisberg, Keil, Goodstein, Rawson, and Gray (2008; see Chapter 14) found that psychology students were unduly impressed by explanations of findings when there was neuroimaging evidence. In fact, patterns of brain activation are dependent variables. They are sources of information about human cognition but need to be interpreted within the context of other relevant information.

Second, most brain-imaging techniques reveal only *associations* between patterns of brain activation and behaviour (e.g., performance on a reasoning task is associated with activation of the prefrontal cortex). Such associations are basically correlational, and do *not* demonstrate that the brain regions activated are essential for task performance. A given brain region may be activated because participants have chosen to use a particular strategy that is not the only one that could be used to perform the task. Alternatively, some brain activation might occur because participants have worries about task performance or because they engage in unnecessary monitoring of their performance.

Transcranial magnetic stimulation offers a partial solution to the causality issue. We can show that a given brain area is necessary for the performance of a task by finding that TMS disrupts that performance. Accordingly, TMS is a technique of special importance.

Third, most functional neuroimaging research is based on the assumption of **functional specialisation**, namely, that each brain region is specialised for a different function. This notion became very popular 200 years ago with the advent of **phrenology** (the notion that individual differences in various mental faculties are revealed by bumps in the skull). Phrenology (advocated by Gall and Spurzheim) is essentially useless, but there is a grain of truth in the idea that fMRI is "phrenology with magnets" (Steve Hammett, personal communication).

The assumption of functional specialisation has some justification when we focus on relatively basic or low-level processes. For example, one part of the brain specialises in colour processing and another area in motion processing (see Chapter 2). However, higher-order cognitive functions are not organised neatly and tidily. For example, the dorsolateral prefrontal cortex is activated during the performance of an enormous range of complex tasks requiring the use of executive functions (see Chapter 5).

Cognitive neuroscientists have increasingly accepted that there is substantial *integration* and co-ordination across the brain and that

KEY TERMS

functional specialisation: the assumption that each brain area or region is specialised for a specific function (e.g., colour processing; face processing).
phrenology: the notion that each mental faculty is located in a different part of the brain and can be assessed by feeling bumps on the head.

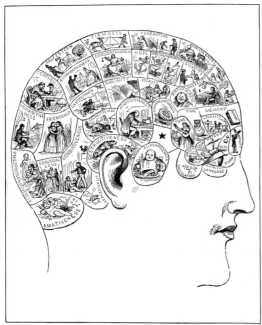

Phrenological Chart of the Faculties.

Phrenology (developed by German physician Franz Joseph Gall in 1796) is the notion that individual differences in various mental faculties are revealed by bumps in the skull. This phrenology chart, from the *People's Cyclopedia of Universal Knowledge* (1883), demarcates these areas.

functional specialisation is *not* always found. Such functional integration can be studied by *correlating* activity across different brain regions – if a network of brain areas is involved in a particular process, then activity in all of them should be positively correlated when that process occurs. Let us consider the brain areas associated with conscious perception (see Chapter 16). Melloni, Molina, Pena, Torres, Singer, and Rodriguez (2007) assessed EEG activity at several brain sites for words that were or were not consciously perceived. Conscious perception was associated with synchronised activity across large areas of the brain.

Fourth, there is the issue of whether functional neuroimaging research is *relevant* to testing cognitive theories. According to Page (2006, p. 428), "The additional dependent variable

that imaging data represents is often one about which cognitive theories make no necessary predictions. It is, therefore, inappropriate to use such data to choose between such theories." However, that argument has lost some of its force in recent years. We have increased knowledge of where in the brain many psychological processes occur, and that makes it feasible to use psychological theories to predict patterns of brain activation.

Functional neuroimaging findings are often of direct relevance to resolving theoretical controversies within cognitive psychology. Here, we will briefly discuss two examples. Our first example concerns the controversy about the nature of visual imagery (see Chapter 3). Kosslyn (1994) argued that visual imagery uses the same processes as visual perception, whereas Pylyshyn (2000) claimed that visual imagery involves making use of propositional knowledge about what things would look like in the imagined situation. Most behavioural evidence is inconclusive. However, Kosslyn and Thompson (2003) found in a meta-analysis of functional neuroimaging studies that visual imagery is generally associated with activation in the primary visual cortex or BA17 (activated during the early stages of visual perception). These findings strongly suggest that similar processes are used in imagery and perception.

Our second example concerns the processing of unattended stimuli (see Chapter 5). Historically, some theorists (e.g., Deutsch & Deutsch, 1963) argued that even unattended stimuli receive thorough processing. Studies using event-related potentials (ERPs; see Glossary) showed that unattended stimuli (visual and auditory) were less thoroughly processed than attended stimuli even shortly after stimulus presentation (see Luck, 1998, for a review). For example, in an ERP study by Martinez et al. (1999), attended visual displays produced a greater first positive wave about 70–75 ms after stimulus presentation and a greater first negative wave at 130–140 ms.

Fifth, when researchers argue that a given brain region is active during the performance of a task, they mean it is active relative to some baseline. What is an appropriate baseline? We might argue that the resting state (e.g., participant rests with his/her eyes shut) is a suitable baseline condition. This might make sense if the brain were relatively inactive in the resting state and only showed much activity when dealing with immediate environmental demands. In fact, the increased brain activity occurring when participants perform a task typically adds only a modest amount (5% or less) to resting brain activity. *Why* is the brain so active even when the environment is unstimulating? Patterns of brain activity are similar in different states of consciousness including coma, anaesthesia, and slow-wave sleep (Boly et al., 2008), suggesting that most intrinsic brain activity reflects basic brain functioning.

It is typically assumed in functional neuroimaging research that task performance produces *increased* brain activity reflecting task demands. In fact, there is often *decreased* brain activity in certain brain regions across several tasks and relative to various baseline conditions (see Raichle & Snyder, 2007, for a review). As Raichle and Synder (p. 1085) concluded, "Regardless of the task under investigation, the activity decreases almost always included the posterior cingulate and adjacent precuneus, a region we nicknamed MMPA for 'medial mystery parietal area'." Thus, brain functioning is much more complex than often assumed.

Sixth, we pointed out earlier that much research in cognitive psychology suffers from a relative lack of ecological validity (applicability to everyday life) and paradigm specificity (findings do not generalise from one paradigm to others). The same limitations apply to cognitive neuroscience since cognitive neuroscientists generally use tasks previously developed by cognitive psychologists. Indeed, the problem of ecological validity may be greater in cognitive neuroscience. Participants in studies using fMRI (the most used technique) lie on their backs in somewhat claustrophobic and noisy conditions and have only restricted movement – conditions differing markedly from those of everyday life! Gutchess and Park (2006) investigated whether participants performing a task in the distracting conditions of the fMRI environment are disadvantaged compared to those performing the same task under typical laboratory conditions. Long-term recognition memory was significantly worse in the fMRI environment. This is potentially important, because it suggests that findings obtained in the fMRI environment may not generalise to other settings.

COGNITIVE NEUROPSYCHOLOGY

Cognitive neuropsychology is concerned with the patterns of cognitive performance (intact and impaired) shown by brain-damaged patients. These patients have suffered **lesions** – structural alterations within the brain caused by injury or disease. According to cognitive neuropsychologists, the study of brain-damaged patients can tell us much about normal human cognition. We can go further. As McCloskey (2001, p. 594) pointed out, "Complex systems often reveal their inner workings more clearly when they are malfunctioning than when they are running smoothly." He described how he only began to discover much about his laser printer when it started misprinting things.

We can gain insight into the cognitive neuropsychological approach by considering a brain-damaged patient (AC) studied by Coltheart, Inglis, Cupples, Michie, Bates, and Budd (1998). AC was a 67-year-old man who had suffered several strokes, leading to severe problems with object knowledge. If we possess a *single* system for object knowledge, then AC should be severely impaired for *all* aspects of object recognition. That is not what Coltheart et al. found. AC seemed to possess practically no visual information

> **KEY TERM**
>
> **lesions:** structural alterations within the brain caused by disease or injury.

about objects (e.g., the colours of animals; whether certain species possess legs). However, AC was right 95% of the time when classifying animals as dangerous or not and had a 90% success rate when deciding which animals are normally eaten. He was also right over 90% of the time when asked questions about auditory perceptual knowledge of animals ("Does it make a sound?").

What can we conclude from the study of AC? First, there is probably no *single* object knowledge system. Second, our stored knowledge of the visual properties of objects is probably stored separately from our stored knowledge of other properties (e.g., auditory, olfactory). Most importantly, however, we have discovered something important about the organisation of object knowledge without considering *where* such information is stored. Since cognitive neuropsychology focuses on brain-damaged individuals, it is perhaps natural to assume it would relate each patient's cognitive impairments to his/her regions of brain damage. That was typically *not* the case until fairly recently. However, cognitive neuropsychologists increasingly take account of the brain, using techniques such as magnetic resonance imaging (MRI; see Glossary) to identify the brain areas damaged in any given patient.

Theoretical assumptions

Coltheart (2001) described very clearly the main theoretical assumptions of cognitive neuropsychology, and his analysis will form the basis of our account. One key assumption is that of **modularity**, meaning that the cognitive system consists of numerous modules or processors operating relatively independently of or separately from each other. It is assumed that these modules exhibit **domain specificity**, meaning they respond only to one particular class of stimuli. For example, there may be a face-recognition module that responds only when a face is presented.

The modularity assumption may or may not be correct. Fodor (1983) argued that humans possess various input modules involved in encoding and recognising perceptual inputs. As we will see in Chapter 2, the processing of various aspects of visual stimuli (e.g., colour, form, motion) occurs in specific brain areas and seems to be domain-specific.

Fodor (1983) also argued that the central system (involved in higher-level processes such as thinking and reasoning) is *not* modular. For example, attentional processes appear to be domain-independent in that we can attend to an extremely wide range of external and internal stimuli. However, some evolutionary psychologists have argued that most information-processing systems are modular – the "massive modularity hypothesis" (see Barrett & Kurzban, 2006, for a review). The argument is that, complex processing will be more efficient if we possess numerous specific modules than if we possess fewer general processing functions. The debate continues. However, we probably have some general, domain-independent processors to co-ordinate and integrate the outputs of the specific modules or processors (see Chapter 16).

The second major assumption of cognitive neuropsychology is that of *anatomical modularity*. According to this assumption, each module is located in a specific and potentially identifiable area of the brain. Why is this assumption important? In essence, cognitive neuropsychologists are likely to make most progress when studying patients having brain damage limited to a single module. Such patients may not exist if the assumption of anatomical modularity is incorrect. For example, suppose all modules were distributed across large areas of the brain.

If so, the great majority of brain-damaged patients would suffer damage to most modules, and it would be impossible to work out the number and nature of modules they possessed. There is some evidence for anatomical modularity in the visual processing system (see Chapter 2). However, there is less support for anatomical modularity with many complex tasks. For example, Duncan and Owen (2000) found that the same areas within the frontal lobes were activated when very different complex tasks were being performed.

The third major assumption is what Coltheart (2001, p. 10) called "uniformity of functional architecture across people". Suppose this assumption is actually false, and there are substantial individual differences in the arrangement of modules. We would not be able to use the findings from individual patients to draw conclusions about other people's functional architecture. We must certainly hope the assumption of uniformity of functional architecture is correct. Why is that? According to Coltheart (2001, p. 10), "This assumption is not peculiar to cognitive neuropsychology; it is widespread throughout the whole of cognitive psychology. Thus, if this assumption is false, that's not just bad news for cognitive neuropsychology; it is bad news for all of cognitive psychology."

The fourth assumption is that of *subtractivity*: "Brain damage can impair or delete existing boxes or arrows in the system, but cannot introduce new ones: that is, it can subtract from the system, but cannot add to it" (Coltheart, 2001, p. 10). (In case you are wondering, "boxes" refers to modules and "arrows" to the connections between modules.) *Why* is the subtractivity assumption important? Suppose it is incorrect and patients develop new modules to compensate for the cognitive impairments caused by brain damage. That would make it very hard to learn much about intact cognitive systems by studying brain-damaged patients. The subtractivity assumption is more likely to be correct when brain damage occurs in adulthood (rather than childhood) and when cognitive performance is assessed shortly after the onset of brain damage.

Research in cognitive neuropsychology

How do cognitive neuropsychologists set about understanding the cognitive system? Of major importance is the search for a **dissociation**, which occurs when a patient performs normally on one task (task X) but is impaired on a second task (task Y). For example, the great majority of amnesic patients perform almost normally on short-term memory tasks but are greatly impaired on many long-term memory tasks (see Chapter 6). It is tempting (but potentially dangerous!) to use such findings to argue that the two tasks involve different processing modules and that the module or modules needed on long-term memory tasks have been damaged by brain injury.

We need to avoid drawing sweeping conclusions from dissociations. A patient may perform well on one task but poorly on a second task simply because the second task is more complex than the first rather than because the second requires specific modules affected by brain damage.

The agreed solution to the above problem is to look for double dissociations. A **double dissociation** between two tasks (X and Y) is shown when one patient performs normally on task X and at an impaired level on task Y, whereas another patient performs normally on task Y and at an impaired level on task X. If a double dissociation can be shown, we cannot explain the findings away as occurring because one task is harder. Here is a concrete example of a double dissociation. Amnesic patients have severely impaired performance on many tasks involving long-term memory but essentially intact performance on tasks involving short-term memory (see Chapter 6). There are also other patients whose short-term memory is more impaired than their long-term memory (see Chapter 6). This double dissociation suggests that different modules underlie short-term and long-term memory.

The existence of double dissociations provides reasonable evidence that two systems are at work, one required for task X and the other needed for task Y. However, there are limitations with the use of double dissociations. First, as Dunn and Kirsner (2003) pointed out, here is the ideal scenario: module A is required only on task X and module B only on task Y, and there are patients having damage only to module A and others having damage only to module B. In fact, of course, reality is typically far messier than that, making it hard to interpret most findings. Second, the literature contains hundreds of double dissociations, only some having genuine theoretical relevance. It is not easy to decide *which* double dissociations are important. Third, double dissociations can provide evidence of the existence of *two* separate systems but are of little use when trying to show the existence of three or four systems.

For the sake of completeness, we will briefly consider associations. An **association** occurs when a patient is impaired on task X and is also impaired on task Y. Historically, there was much emphasis on associations of symptoms. It was regarded as of central importance to identify **syndromes**, certain sets of symptoms or impairments usually found together. A syndrome-based approach allows us to assign brain-damaged patients to a fairly small number of categories. However, there is a fatal flaw with the syndrome-based approach: associations can occur even if tasks X and Y depend on entirely separate processing mechanisms or modules if these mechanisms are adjacent in the brain. Thus, associations often tell us nothing about the functional organisation of the brain.

Groups vs. individuals

Should cognitive neuropsychologists carry out group studies (in which patients with the same symptoms or syndromes are considered together) or single-case studies? In most psychological research, we have more confidence in findings based on fairly large groups of participants. However, the group-based approach is problematic when applied to cognitive neuropsychological research because patients typically vary in their patterns of impairment. Indeed, every patient can be regarded as unique just as snowflakes are different from each other (Caramazza & Coltheart, 2006). The key problems with group studies are that, "(a) aggregating (combining) data over patients requires the assumption that the patients are homogenous (uniform) with respect to the nature of their deficits, but (b) that regardless of how patients are selected, homogeneity of deficits cannot be assumed a priori (and indeed is unlikely when deficits are characterised at the level of detail required for addressing issues of current interest in the study of normal cognition)" (McCloskey, 2001, pp. 597–598).

However, it is useful to conduct group studies in the early stages of research; they can provide a broad-brush picture, and can be followed by single-case studies to fill in the details. However, the single-case approach also has problems. As Shallice (1991, p. 433) argued, "A selective impairment found in a particular task in some patient could just reflect: the patient's idiosyncratic strategy, the greater difficulty of that task compared with the others, a premorbid lacuna (gap) in that patient, or the way a reorganised system but not the original system operates." These problems can be overcome to some extent by replicating the findings from a single case

---

> ### KEY TERMS
>
> **association:** concerning brain damage, the finding that certain symptoms or performance impairments are consistently found together in numerous brain-damaged patients.
> **syndromes:** labels used to categorise patients on the basis of co-occurring symptoms.

or patient by studying further single cases (the multiple single-patient study method).

Here is another argument in favour of single-case studies. When cognitive neuropsychologists carry out a case study, they are generally interested in testing some theory. The theory being tested is like a large and complicated jigsaw puzzle, and the individual patients are like very small jigsaw pieces. If the theory is correct, patients with very different symptoms will nevertheless fit into the jigsaw puzzle. Conversely, if the theory is incorrect, some patients (jigsaw pieces) will not fit the theory (jigsaw puzzle). However, most of the pieces are very small, and it may be a long time before we see a coherent picture. Thus, it is advantageous that patients differ from each other – it means the underlying theory is exposed to many different tests.

Limitations

What are the limitations of the cognitive neuropsychological approach? First, it is generally assumed that the cognitive performance of brain-damaged patients provides fairly direct evidence of the impact of brain damage on previously normal cognitive systems. However, some of the impact of brain damage on cognitive performance may be camouflaged because patients develop *compensatory strategies* to help them cope with their brain damage. For example, consider patients with pure alexia, a condition in which there are severe reading problems. Such patients manage to read words by using the compensatory strategy of identifying each letter separately.

Second, much research on cognitive neuropsychology is based on the seriality assumption (Harley, 2004), according to which processing is serial and proceeds from one module to another. However, the brain consists of about 50 billion *interconnected* neurons and several different brain regions are activated in an integrated way during the performance of tasks (see Chapter 16). Thus, the seriality assumption appears to be incorrect.

Third, cognitive neuropsychology would be fairly straightforward if most patients had suffered damage to only *one* module. In practice, however, brain damage is typically much more

extensive than that. When several processing modules are damaged, it is often difficult to make sense of the findings.

Fourth, there are often large differences among individuals having broadly similar brain damage in terms of age, expertise, and education. These differences may have important consequences. For example, extensive practice can produce large changes in the brain areas activated during the performance of a task (see Chapter 5). The implication is that the effects of any given brain damage on task performance would probably vary depending on how much previous practice patients had had on the task in question.

Fifth, cognitive neuropsychology has often been applied to relatively *specific* aspects of cognitive functioning. Take research on language. There has been a substantial amount of work on the reading and spelling of individual words by brain-damaged patients, but much less on text comprehension (Harley, 2004). However, cognitive neuropsychologists have recently studied more general aspects of cognition such as thinking and reasoning (see Chapter 14).

COMPUTATIONAL COGNITIVE SCIENCE

We will start by drawing a distinction between computational modelling and artificial intelligence. **Computational modelling** involves programming computers to model or mimic some aspects of human cognitive functioning. In contrast,

---

KEY TERMS

computational cognitive science: an approach that involves constructing computational models to understand human cognition. Some of these models take account of what is known about brain functioning as well as behavioural evidence.

computational modelling: this involves constructing computer programs that will simulate or mimic some aspects of human cognitive functioning; see **artificial intelligence**.

artificial intelligence involves constructing computer systems that produce intelligent outcomes but the processes involved may bear little resemblance to those used by humans. For example, consider the chess program known as Deep Blue, which won a famous match against the then World Champion Garry Kasparov on 11 May 1997. Deep Blue considered up to 200 million positions per second, which is radically different from the very small number focused on by human chess players (see Chapter 12).

Computational cognitive scientists develop computational models to understand human cognition. A good computational model shows us how a given theory can be specified and allows us to predict behaviour in new situations. Mathematical models were used in experimental psychology long before the emergence of the information-processing paradigm (e.g., in IQ testing). These models can be used to make predictions, but often lack an explanatory component. For example, having three traffic violations is a good predictor of whether a person is a bad risk for car insurance, but it is not clear why. A major benefit of the computational models developed in computational cognitive science is that they can provide an explanatory and predictive basis for a phenomenon (e.g., Costello & Keane, 2000).

In the past, many experimental cognitive psychologists stated their theories in vague verbal statements, making it hard to decide whether the evidence fitted the theory. In contrast, computational cognitive scientists produce computer programs to represent cognitive theories with all the details made explicit. Implementing a theory as a program is a good method for checking it contains no hidden assumptions or vague terms.

Many issues surround the use of computer simulations and how they mimic cognitive processes. Palmer and Kimchi (1986) argued that we should be able to decompose a theory successively through a number of levels starting with descriptive statements until we reach a written program. It should be possible to draw a line at some level of decomposition and say that everything above that line is psychologically plausible or meaningful, whereas everything below it is not. We need to do this because parts of any program are there simply because of the particular programming language being used and the machine on which the program is running. For example, to see what the program is doing, we need to have print commands in the program showing the outputs of various stages on the computer's screen.

Other issues arise about the relationship between the performance of the program and human performance (Costello & Keane, 2000). It is rarely meaningful to relate the speed of the program doing a simulated task to the reaction time taken by human participants, because the processing times of programs are affected by psychologically irrelevant features. For example, programs run faster on more powerful computers. However, the various materials presented to the program should result in differences in program operation time correlating closely with differences in participants' reaction times in processing the same materials. At the very least, the program should reproduce the same outputs as participants given the same inputs.

There are more computational models than you can shake a stick at. However, two main types are of special importance, and are outlined briefly here: production system and connectionist networks.

Production systems

Production systems consist of productions, each of which consists of an "IF...THEN" rule. Production rules can take many forms, but an everyday example is, "If the green man is lit up, then cross the road." In a typical production system model, there is a long-term memory containing numerous IF...THEN rules. There is also a working memory (i.e., a system holding information that is currently being processed). If information from the environment that "green man is lit up" reaches working memory, it will match the IF-part of the rule in long-term memory and trigger the THEN-part of the rule (i.e., cross the road).

Production systems have the following characteristics:

- They have numerous IF...THEN rules.
- They have a working memory containing information.
- The production system operates by matching the contents of working memory against the IF-parts of the rules and executing the THEN-parts.
- If information in working memory matches the IF-parts of two or more rules, there may be a conflict-resolution strategy that selects one of these rules as the best one to be executed.

Consider a very simple production system operating on lists of letters involving As and Bs. It has two rules:

(1) IF a list in working memory has an A at the end
     THEN replace the A with AB.
(2) IF a list in working memory has a B at the end
     THEN replace the B with an A.

If we input A, it will go into working memory. This A matches rule 1, and so when the THEN-part is executed, working memory will contain an AB. On the next cycle, AB doesn't match rule 1 but does match rule 2. As a result, the B is replaced by an A, leaving an AA in working memory. The system will next produce AAB, then AAAB, and so on.

Many aspects of cognition can be specified as sets of IF...THEN rules. For example, chess knowledge can readily be represented as a set of productions based on rules such as, "If the Queen is threatened, then move the Queen to a safe square." In this way, people's basic knowledge can be regarded as a collection of productions.

Newell and Simon (1972) first established the usefulness of production system models in characterising the cognitive processes involved in problem solving (see Chapter 12). However, these models have a wider applicability. For example, Anderson (1993) put forward his ACT-R theory (Adaptive Control of Thought – Rational), which can account for a wide range of findings. He distinguished among frameworks, theories, and models. Frameworks make very general claims about cognition, theories specify in some detail how frameworks operate, and models are specific kinds of theories that are applied to specific tasks and behaviour.

ACT-R

ACT-R has been systematically expanded and improved in the years since 1993. For example, Anderson et al. (2004) put forward the most comprehensive version of ACT-R (discussed more fully in Chapter 12), one that qualifies as a cognitive architecture. What are cognitive architectures? According to Sun (2007, p. 160), "Cognitive architectures are cognitive models that are domain-generic (cover many domains or areas) and encompass a wide range of cognitive applicabilities." In essence, cognitive architectures focus on those aspects of the cognitive system that remain fairly invariant across individuals, task types, and time.

The version of ACT-R described by Anderson et al. (2004) is based on the assumption that the cognitive system consists of several modules (relatively independent subsystems). These include the following: (1) a visual-object module that keeps track of what objects are being viewed; (2) a visual-location module that monitors where objects are; (3) a manual module that controls the hands; (4) a goal module that keeps track of current goals; and (5) a declarative module that retrieves relevant information.

Each module has a buffer associated with it containing a limited amount of the most important information.

How is information from all of these buffers integrated? According to Anderson et al. (p. 1058), "A central production system can detect patterns in these buffers and take co-ordinated action." If several productions could be triggered by the information contained in the buffers, then one is selected taking account of the value or gain associated with each outcome plus the amount of time or cost that would be incurred.

Connectionist networks

Books by Rumelhart, McClelland, and the PDP Research Group (1986) and by McClelland, Rumelhart, and the PDP Research Group (1986) initiated an explosion of interest in connectionist networks, neural networks, or parallel distributed processing (PDP) models, as they are variously called. **Connectionist networks** make use of elementary units or nodes connected together, and consist of various structures or layers (e.g., input; intermediate or hidden; output). Connectionist networks often (but not always) have the following characteristics (see Figure 1.6):

- The network consists of elementary or neuron-like *units* or *nodes* connected together so that a single unit has many links to other units.
- Units affect other units by exciting or inhibiting them.
- The unit usually takes the weighted sum of all of the input links, and produces a single output to another unit if the weighted sum exceeds some threshold value.
- The network as a whole is characterised by the properties of the units that make it up, by the way they are connected together, and by the rules used to change the strength of connections among units.
- Networks can have different structures or layers; they can have a layer of input links, intermediate layers (of so-called "hidden units"), and a layer of output units.

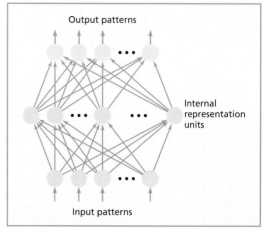

Figure 1.6 A multi-layered connectionist network with a layer of input units, a layer of internal representation units or hidden units, and a layer of output units, in a form that allows the appropriate output pattern to be generated from a given input pattern. Reproduced with permission from Rumelhart and McClelland (1986), © 1986 Massachusetts Institute of Technology, by permission of The MIT Press.

- A representation of a concept can be stored in a distributed way by an activation pattern throughout the network.
- The same network can store several patterns without disruption if they are sufficiently distinct.
- An important learning rule used in networks is called *backward propagation of errors* (*BackProp*) (see below).

In order to understand how connectionist networks work, we will consider how individual units act when activation impinges on them. Any given unit can be connected to several other units (see Figure 1.7). Each of these other units can send an excitatory or inhibitory signal to the first unit. This unit generally takes a

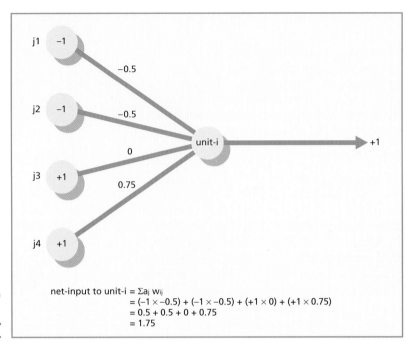

Figure 1.7 Diagram showing how the inputs from a number of units are combined to determine the overall input to unit-i. Unit-i has a threshold of 1; so if its net input exceeds 1, then it will respond with +1, but if the net input in less than 1, then it will respond with −1.

net-input to unit-i = $\Sigma a_j \, w_{ij}$
= $(-1 \times -0.5) + (-1 \times -0.5) + (+1 \times 0) + (+1 \times 0.75)$
= $0.5 + 0.5 + 0 + 0.75$
= 1.75

weighted sum of all these inputs. If this sum exceeds some threshold, it produces an output. Figure 1.7 shows a simple diagram of just such a unit, which takes the inputs from various other units and sums them to produce an output if a certain threshold is exceeded.

These networks can model cognitive performance without the explicit rules found in production systems. They do this by storing patterns of activation in the network that associate various inputs with certain outputs. The models typically make use of several layers to deal with complex behaviour. One layer consists of input units that encode a stimulus as a pattern of activation in those units. Another layer is an output layer producing some response as a pattern of activation. When the network has learned to produce a particular response at the output layer following the presentation of a particular stimulus at the input layer, it can exhibit behaviour that looks "as if" it had learned an IF…THEN rule even though no such rules exist explicitly in the model.

Networks learn the association between different inputs and outputs by modifying the weights on the links between units in the net. In Figure 1.7, the weight on the links to a unit, as well as the activation of other units, plays a crucial role in computing the response of that unit. Various learning rules modify these weights systematically until the net produces the required output patterns given certain input patterns.

One such learning rule is "backward propagation of errors" or BackProp. **Back-propagation** is a mechanism allowing a network to learn to associate a particular input pattern with a given output pattern by comparing actual responses against correct ones. The network is initially set up with random weights on the links among the units. During the early stages of learning, the output units often produce an incorrect pattern or response after the input pattern has been presented. BackProp compares the imperfect pattern with the known required response, noting the errors that occur. It then back-propagates activation through the network so the weights between the units are adjusted to produce the required pattern. This process is repeated with a given stimulus pattern until the network produces the required response pattern. Thus, the model learns the desired behaviour without being explicitly programmed to do so.

Networks have been used to produce interesting results. In a classic study, Sejnowski and Rosenberg (1987) gave a connectionist network called NETtalk 50,000 trials to learn the spelling–sound relationships of a set of 1000 words. NETtalk achieved 95% success with the words on which it had been trained. It was also 77% correct on a further 20,000 words. Thus, the network seemed to have learned the "rules of English pronunciation" without having explicit rules for combining and encoding sounds.

Several connectionist models (e.g., the parallel distributed processing approach of Rumelhart, McClelland, & The PDP Research Group, 1986) assume that representations are stored in a *distributed* fashion. This assumption is often justified by arguing that the assumption of distributed representations is biologically plausible. However, there are problems with this assumption. Suppose we try to encode two words at the same time. That would cause numerous units or nodes to become activated, but it would be hard (or even impossible) to decide which units or nodes belonged to which word (Bowers, 2002). There is also evidence that much information is stored in a given location in the brain rather than in a distributed fashion (see Bowers, 2009, for a review). For example, Quiroga, Reddy, Kreiman, Koch, and Fried (2005) discovered a neuron in the medial temporal lobe that responded strongly when pictures of the actress Jennifer Aniston were presented but not when pictures of other famous people were presented (see Chapter 3).

Some connectionist models assume there is *local* representation of knowledge. Localist connectionist models include the reading model of Coltheart, Rastle, Perry, Langdon, and Ziegler (2001; see Chapter 9); the TRACE model of word recognition (McClelland & Elman, 1986; see Chapter 9); and the models of speech production put forward by Dell (1986) and by Levelt, Roelofs, and Meyer (1999a; see Chapter 11). It is likely that some knowledge is represented locally and some is distributed (see Chapter 7).

Production systems vs. connectionism

Anderson and Lebiere (2003) evaluated connectionism and production systems (exemplified by ACT-R) with respect to 12 criteria (see Table 1.1). These ratings are within-theory: they only indicate how well a theory has done on a given criterion relative to its performance on other criteria. Thus, the ratings do *not* provide a direct comparison of the two theoretical approaches. It is nevertheless interesting to consider those criteria for which the ratings differ considerably between the two theories: operates in human time; uses language; accounts for developmental phenomena; and theoretical components map onto the brain.

We will start with operating in human time. Within ACT-R, every processing step has a time associated with it. In contrast, most connectionist models don't account for the timing effects produced by perceptual or motor aspects of a task. In addition, the number of trials to acquire an ability is generally much greater in connectionist models than in human learning.

So far as the criterion of using language is concerned, several major connectionist theories are in the area of language. In contrast, Anderson and Lebiere (2003, p. 599) admitted that, "ACT-R's treatment of natural language is fragmentary." Connectionist models have had some success in accounting for developmental phenomena by assuming that development is basically a learning process constrained by brain architecture and the timing of brain development. ACT-R has little to say about developmental phenomena.

Finally, there is the criterion of the mapping between theoretical components and the brain.

TABLE 1.1: Within-theory ratings of classical connectionism and ACT-R with respect to Newell's 12 criteria.

Criterion	Connectionism	ACT-R
1. Computationally universal (copes with very diverse environmental changes)	3	4
2. Operates in human time	2	5
3. Produces effective and adaptive behaviour	4	4
4. Uses vast amounts of knowledge	2	3
5. Copes with unexpected errors	3	4
6. Integrates diverse knowledge	2	3
7. Uses language	4	2
8. Exhibits sense of self	2	2
9. Learns from environment	4	4
10. Accounts for developmental phenomena	4	2
11. Relates to evolutionary considerations	1	1
12. Theoretical components map onto the brain	5	2

Scores range from 1 = worst to 5 = best. Based on Anderson and Lebiere (2003).

This was a weakness in the version of ACT-R considered by Anderson and Lebiere (2003), but the 2004 version (Anderson et al., 2004) has made substantial progress in that area. Connectionist theorists often claim that connectionist processing units resemble biological neurons, but this claim is hotly disputed (see below).

Evaluation

Computational cognitive science has various strengths. First, it requires theorists to think carefully and rigorously. This is so because a computer program has to contain detailed information about the processes involved in performing any given task. Second, and perhaps of greatest importance, the development of cognitive architectures offers the prospect of providing an overarching framework within which to make sense of the workings of the cognitive system. It would clearly be extremely valuable to have such a framework. This is especially the case given that much empirical research in cognitive psychology is limited in scope and suffers from paradigm specificity (see Glossary). However, there is controversy concerning the extent to which this goal has been achieved by computational cognitive scientists.

Third, it was necessary with most early computational models to program explicitly all aspects of the model, and such models did not possess any learning ability. In contrast, connectionist networks can to some extent program themselves by "learning" to produce specific outputs when certain inputs are given to them.

Fourth, many (but not all) connectionist models are based on the assumption that knowledge (e.g., about a word or concept) is represented in a *distributed* fashion in the brain rather than in a specific location. Problems with that view were discussed earlier and are discussed further in Chapter 7.

Fifth, the scope of computational cognitive science has increased progressively. Initially, computational modelling was often applied mainly to behavioural data. More recently, however, there has been the development of computational cognitive neuroscience devoted to the application of computational modelling to functional neuroimaging data. Indeed, the *Brain Research* journal in 2007 devoted a special issue to this research area (see Preface by Becker, 2007). In addition, as we have seen, Anderson et al.'s (2004) ACT-R makes considerable use of findings from functional neuroimaging. Applications of computational modelling to data in cognitive neuropsychology were considered in a special issue of the *Cognitive Neuropsychology* journal in 2008 (see Introduction by Dell and Caramazza, 2008).

Sixth, computational cognitive science (especially connectionism) is well equipped to provide powerful theoretical accounts of parallel processing systems. This is important for two reasons. First, there is convincing evidence (much of it from functional neuroimaging research) indicating that parallel processing is the rule rather than the exception. Second, making sense of parallel processing systems seems more difficult within other approaches (e.g., cognitive neuropsychology).

What are the main limitations of the computational cognitive science approach? First, computational models have only rarely been used to make new predictions. Computational cognitive scientists often develop *one* model of a phenomenon rather than exploring many models, which could then be distinguished by gathering new empirical data. Why is this the case? One reason is that there are many levels of detail at which a model can simulate people's behaviour. For example, a model can capture the direction of a difference in correct responses between two groups of people in an experiment, the specific correct and error responses of groups, general trends in response times for all response types, and so on (Costello & Keane, 2000). Many models operate at the more general end of these possible parallels, which makes them weak predictively.

Second, connectionist models that claim to have neural plausibility do not really resemble the human brain. For example, it is assumed in many connectionist models that the basic processing units are like biological neurons, and that these processing units resemble neurons in being massively interconnected. However, the resemblances are superficial. There are 100–150 billion neurons in the human brain compared to no more than a few thousand units in most connectionist networks. There are 12 different kinds of neuron in the human neocortex (Churchland & Sejnowski, 1994), and it is not clear which type or types most resemble the processing units. In addition, each cortical neuron is connected to only about 3% of neurons in the surrounding square millimetre of cortex (Churchland & Sejnowski, 1994), which does not even approximate to massive interconnectivity.

Third, many computational models contain many parameters or variables. It is often argued that theorists can adjust these parameters to produce almost any outcome they want – "parameter tweaking". However, it is important not to exaggerate the problem. In practice, the assumptions built into a computational model need to be plausible in the light of all the available evidence, and so it is not really a question of "anything goes" at all.

Fourth, human cognition is influenced by several potentially conflicting motivational and emotional factors, many of which may be operative at the same time. Most computational models ignore these factors, although ACT-R (Anderson et al., 2004) does include a motivational component in its goal module. More generally, we can distinguish between a cognitive system (the Pure Cognitive System) and a biological system (the Regulatory System) (Norman, 1980). Much of the activity of the Pure Cognitive System is determined by the various needs of the Regulatory System, including the need for survival, for food and water, and for protection of oneself and one's family. Computational cognitive science (like most of cognitive psychology) typically focuses on the Pure Cognitive System and de-emphasises the key role played by the Regulatory System.

COMPARISON OF MAJOR APPROACHES

We have discussed the major approaches to human cognition at length, and you may be wondering which one is the most useful and informative. In fact, that is not the best way of thinking about the issues for various reasons. First, an increasing amount of research involves two or more of the approaches. For example, most tasks used in cognitive neuropsychology and functional neuroimaging studies were originally developed by experimental cognitive psychologists. Another example concerns a study by Rees, Wojciulik, Clarke, Husain, Frith, and Driver (2000) on patients suffering from extinction (see Chapter 5). In this disorder, visual stimuli presented to the side of space opposite to the site of brain damage are not detected when a second stimulus is presented at the same time to the same side as the brain damage. Rees et al. found using fMRI that extinguished stimuli produced reasonable levels of activation in various areas within the visual cortex. Here, a *combination* of cognitive neuropsychology and functional neuroimaging revealed that extinguished stimuli receive a moderate amount of processing. Finally, computational modelling is being increasingly applied to data from functional neuroimaging and cognitive neuropsychology.

Second, each approach makes its own distinctive contribution, and so all are needed. In terms of an analogy, it is pointless to ask whether a driver is more or less useful than a putter to a golfer – they are both essential.

Third, as well as its own strengths, each approach also has its own limitations. This can be seen clearly in the box below. What is

Strengths and limitations of the major approaches

Experimental cognitive psychology

Strengths

1. The first systematic approach to understanding human cognition
2. The source of most of the theories and tasks used by the other approaches
3. It is enormously flexible and can be applied to any aspect of cognition
4. It has produced numerous important replicated findings
5. It has strongly influenced social, clinical, and developmental psychology

Limitations

1. Most cognitive tasks are complex and involve many different processes
2. Behavioural evidence only provides indirect evidence concerning internal processes
3. Theories are sometimes vague and hard to test empirically
4. Findings sometimes do not generalise because of paradigm specificity
5. There is a lack of an overarching theoretical framework

Functional neuroimaging + ERPs + TMS

Strengths

1. Great variety of techniques offering excellent temporal or spatial resolution
2. Functional specialisation *and* brain integration can be studied
3. TMS is flexible and permits causal inferences
4. Permits assessment of integrated brain processing, as well as specialisation
5. Resolution of complex theoretical issues

Limitations

1. Functional neuroimaging techniques provide essentially correlational data
2. Sometimes of limited relevance to cognitive theories
3. Restrictions on the tasks that can be used in brain scanners
4. Poor understanding of what TMS does to the brain
5. Potential problems with ecological validity

Cognitive neuropsychology

Strengths
1. Double dissociations have provided strong evidence for various major processing modules
2. Causal links can be shown between brain damage and cognitive performance
3. It has revealed unexpected complexities in cognition (e.g., in language)
4. It transformed memory research
5. It straddles the divide between cognitive psychology and cognitive neuroscience

Limitations
1. Patients may develop compensatory strategies not found in healthy individuals
2. Brain damage often affects several modules and so complicates interpretation of findings
3. It minimises the interconnectedness of cognitive processes
4. It is hard to interpret findings from patients differing in site of brain damage, age, expertise, and so on
5. There is insufficient emphasis on general cognitive functions

Computational cognitive science

Strengths
1. Theoretical assumptions are spelled out in precise detail
2. Comprehensive cognitive architectures have been developed
3. The notion of distributed knowledge is supported by empirical evidence
4. Computational cognitive neuroscience makes use of knowledge in cognitive neuroscience
5. The emphasis on parallel processing fits well with functional neuroimaging data

Limitations
1. Many computational models do not make new predictions
2. Claims to neural plausibility of computational models are not justified
3. Many computational models have several rather arbitrary parameters to fit the data
4. Computational models generally de-emphasise motivational factors
5. Computational models tend to ignore emotional factors

optimal in such circumstances is to make use of **converging operations** – several different research methods are used to address a given theoretical issue, with the strength of one method balancing out the limitations of the other methods. If two or more methods produce the same answer, that provides stronger evidence than could be obtained using a single method. If different methods produce different answers, then further research is needed to clarify the situation.

OUTLINE OF THIS BOOK

One problem with writing a textbook of cognitive psychology is that virtually all the processes and structures of the cognitive system are interdependent. Consider, for example, the case of a student *reading* a book to prepare for an examination. The student is *learning*, but there are several other processes going on as well. *Visual perception* is involved in the intake of information from the printed page, and there is *attention* to the content of the book. In order for the student to benefit from the book, he or she must possess considerable *language skills*, and must have considerable relevant knowledge stored in *long-term memory*. There may be an element of *problem solving* in the student's attempts to relate what is in the

KEY TERM

converging operations: an approach in which several methods with different strengths and limitations are used to address a given issue.

book to the possibly conflicting information he or she has learned elsewhere. *Decision making* may also be involved when the student decides how much time to devote to each chapter of the book. Furthermore, what the student learns will depend on his or her *emotional state*. Finally, the acid test of whether the student's learning has been effective comes during the examination itself, when the material contained in the book must be *retrieved*, and *consciously* evaluated to decide its relevance to the question being answered.

The words italicised in the previous paragraph indicate some of the main ingredients of human cognition and form the basis of our coverage. In view of the interdependence of all aspects of the cognitive system, there is an emphasis in this book on the ways in which each process (e.g., perception) depends on other processes and structures (e.g., attention, long-term memory). This should aid the task of making sense of the complexities of the human cognitive system.

CHAPTER SUMMARY

- Introduction
  Historically, cognitive psychology was unified by an approach based on an analogy between the mind and the computer. This information-processing approach viewed the mind as a general-purpose, symbol-processing system of limited capacity. Today, there are four main approaches to human cognition: experimental cognitive psychology; cognitive neuroscience; cognitive neuropsychology; and computational cognitive science. However, the four approaches are increasingly combined with information from behaviour and brain activity being integrated.

- Experimental cognitive psychology
  Cognitive psychologists assume that top-down and bottom-up processes are both involved in the performance of cognitive tasks. These processes can be serial or parallel. Various methods (e.g., latent-variable analysis) have been used to address the task impurity problem. In spite of the enormous contribution made by cognitive psychology, it sometimes lacks ecological validity, suffers from paradigm specificity, and possesses theoretical vagueness.

- Cognitive neuroscience: the brain in action
  Cognitive neuroscientists study the brain as well as behaviour. They use various techniques varying in their spatial and temporal resolution. Functional neuroimaging techniques provide basically correlational evidence, but TMS can indicate that a given brain area is necessarily involved in a particular cognitive function. Functional neuroimaging is generally most useful when the focus is on brain areas organised in functionally discrete ways. However, it is increasingly possible to study integrated processing across different brain areas. Cognitive neuroscience has contributed much to the resolution of theoretical issues. More research is needed into possible problems with ecological validity with studies using MRI scanners.

- Cognitive neuropsychology
  Cognitive neuropsychology is based on various assumptions, including modularity, anatomical modularity, uniformity of functional architecture, and subtractivity. The existence of a double dissociation provides some evidence for two separate modules or systems. Single-case studies are generally preferable to group studies, because different patients rarely have the same pattern of deficits. The multiple single-patient study method can prove more interpretable than the single-case study method. The cognitive neuropsychological

approach is limited because patients can develop compensatory strategies, because it de-emphasises co-ordinated functioning across the brain, and because the brain damage is often so extensive that it is hard to interpret the findings.

- Computational cognitive science
  Computational cognitive scientists develop computational models to understand human cognition. Production systems consist of production or "IF...THEN" rules. ACT-R is perhaps the most developed theory based on production systems, being comprehensive and taking account of functional neuroimaging findings. Connectionist networks make use of elementary units or nodes connected together. They can learn using rules such as backward propagation. Many connectionist networks focus on language and/or cognitive development. Computational cognitive science has increased in scope to provide detailed theoretical accounts of findings from functional neuroimaging and cognitive neuropsychology. Computational models often contain many parameters (so almost any outcome can be produced) and they generally de-emphasise motivational and emotional factors. Some models exaggerate the importance of distributed representations.

- Comparisons of major approaches
  The major approaches are increasingly used in combination. Each approach has its own strengths and limitations, which makes it useful to use converging operations. When two approaches produce the same findings, this is stronger evidence than can be obtained from a single approach on its own. If two approaches produce different findings, this is an indication that further research is needed to clarify what is happening.

FURTHER READING

- Cacioppo, J.T., Berntson, G.G., & Nusbaum, H.C. (2008). Neuroimaging as a new tool in the toolbox of psychological science. *Current Directions in Psychological Science, 17,* 62–67. This article provides an overview of functional neuroimaging research and introduces a special issue devoted to that area.
- Harley, T.A. (2004). Does cognitive neuropsychology have a future? *Cognitive Neuropsychology, 21,* 3–16. This article by Trevor Harley (and replies to it by Caplan et al.) provide interesting views on many key issues relating to cognitive neuropsychology, connectionism, and cognitive neuroscience. Be warned that the experts have very different views from each other!
- Page, M.P.A. (2006). What can't functional neuroimaging tell the cognitive psychologist? *Cortex, 42,* 428–443. Mike Page focuses on the limitations of the use of functional neuroimaging to understand human cognition.
- Sun, R. (2007). The importance of cognitive architectures: An analysis based on CLARION. *Journal of Experimental & Theoretical Artificial Intelligence, 19,* 159–193. This article identifies key issues in computational modelling, including a discussion of the criteria that need to be satisfied in a satisfactory model.
- Wade, J. (2006). *The student's guide to cognitive neuroscience.* Hove, UK: Psychology Press. The first five chapters of this textbook provide detailed information about the main techniques used by cognitive neuroscientists.

Visual perception is of enormous importance in our everyday lives. It allows us to move around freely, to see people with whom we are interacting, to read magazines and books, to admire the wonders of nature, and to watch films and television. It is also enormously important because we depend on visual perception being accurate to ensure our survival. For example, if we misperceive how close cars are to us as we cross the road, the consequences could be fatal. Thus, it is no surprise that far more of the cortex (especially the occipital lobes) is devoted to vision than to any other sensory modality.

We will start by considering what is meant by *perception*: "The acquisition and processing of sensory information in order to see, hear, taste, or feel objects in the world also guides an organism's actions with respect to those objects" (Sekuler & Blake, 2002, p. 621). Visual perception seems so simple and effortless that we typically take it for granted. In fact, it is very complex, and numerous processes are involved in transforming and interpreting sensory information. Some of the complexities of visual perception became clear when researchers in artificial intelligence tried to program computers to "perceive" the environment. Even when the environment was artificially simplified (e.g., consisting only of white solids) and the task was apparently easy (e.g., deciding how many objects were present), computers required very complicated programming to succeed. It remains the case that no computer can match more than a fraction of the skills of visual perception possessed by nearly every adult human.

As the authors have discovered to their cost, there is a rapidly growing literature on visual perception, especially from the cognitive neuroscience perspective. What we have tried to do over the next three chapters is to provide reasonably detailed coverage of the main issues. In Chapter 2, our coverage of visual perception focuses on a discussion of basic processes, emphasising the enormous advances that have been made in understanding the various brain systems involved. It is common-sensical to assume that the same processes that lead to object recognition also guide vision for action. However, there are strong grounds for arguing that somewhat different processes are involved. Finally, Chapter 2 contains a detailed consideration of important aspects of visual perception, including colour perception, perception without awareness, and depth and size perception.

One of the major achievements of perceptual processing is object recognition, which involves identifying the objects in the world around us. The central focus of Chapter 3 is on the processes underlying this achievement. Initially, we discuss perceptual organisation, and the ways in which we decide which parts of the visual information presented to us belong together and so form an object. We then move on to theories of object recognition, including a discussion of the relevant evidence from behavioural experiments, neuroscience, and brain-damaged patients.

Are the same recognition processes used regardless of the type of object? This is a controversial issue, but many experts have argued that face recognition differs in important ways from ordinary object recognition. Accordingly, face recognition is discussed separately. The final part of Chapter 3 is devoted to another major controversial issue, namely, whether the processes involved in visual imagery are the same as those involved in visual perception. As we will see, there are good grounds for arguing that this controversy has been resolved (turn to Chapter 3 to find out how!).

Perception is vitally important in guiding our actions, helping us to make sure we don't knock into objects or trip over when walking on rough surfaces. The processes involved in such actions are a central focus of Chapter 4. We start by considering the views of James Gibson, who argued about 60 years ago that perception and action are very closely connected. We also discuss various issues related to perception for action, including visually guided action, the processes involved in reaching and grasping, and motion perception.

There are clearly important links between visual perception and attention. The final topic discussed in Chapter 4 is concerned with the notion that we may need to *attend* to an object to perceive it consciously. Issues relating directly to attention are considered in detail in Chapter 5. In that chapter, we start by considering the processes involved in focused attention in the visual and auditory modalities. After that, we consider how we use visual processes when engaged in the everyday task of searching for some object (e.g., a pair of socks in a drawer). There has been a large increase in the amount of research concerned with disorders of visual attention, and this research has greatly increased our understanding of visual attention in healthy individuals. Finally, as we all know to our cost, it can be very hard to do two things at once. We conclude Chapter 5 by considering the factors determining the extent to which we do this successfully or unsuccessfully.

In sum, the area spanning visual perception and attention is among the most exciting and important within cognitive psychology and cognitive neuroscience. There has been tremendous progress in unravelling the complexities of perception and attention over the past decade, and some of the choicest fruits of that endeavour are set before you in the four chapters forming this section of the book.

INTRODUCTION

There has been considerable progress in understanding visual perception in recent years. Much of this is due to the efforts of cognitive neuroscientists, thanks to whom we now have a reasonable knowledge of the brain systems involved in visual perception. We start by considering the main brain areas involved in vision and the functions served by each area. After that, some theories of brain systems in vision are discussed. Next, we consider the issue of whether perception can occur in the absence of conscious awareness. Finally, there is a detailed analysis of basic aspects of visual perception (e.g., colour processing, depth processing).

Chapter 3 focuses mostly on the processes involved in object recognition and in face recognition. For purposes of exposition, we generally deal with a single aspect of visual perception in any given section. However, it is important to realise that all the processes involved in visual perception interact with each other. In that connection, Hegdé (2008) has provided a very useful overview. He emphasised the point that visual perception develops over time even though it may seem to be instantaneous. More specifically, visual processing typically proceeds in a coarse-to-fine way, so that it can take a considerable amount of time to perceive all the details in a scene.

Hegdé (2008) also pointed out that the processes involved differ considerably depending on what we are looking at and the nature of our perceptual goals. For example, we can sometimes perceive the gist of a natural scene extremely rapidly (Thorpe, Fize, & Marlot 1996). Observers saw photographs containing or not containing an animal for only 20 ms. EEG revealed that the presence of an animal was detected within about 150 ms. In contrast, have a look at the photograph shown in Figure 2.1, and try to decide how many animals are present. You probably found that it took several seconds to develop a full understanding of the picture. Bear in mind the diversity of visual perception as you read this and the two following chapters.

BRAIN SYSTEMS

In this section, we focus mainly on brain systems involved in visual perception. The visual cortex is very large, covering about 20% of the entire cortex. It includes the whole of the occipital cortex at the back of the brain and also extends well into the temporal and parietal lobes (Wandell, Dumoulin, & Brewer, 2007). However, to understand fully visual processing in the brain, we need first to consider briefly what happens between the eye and the cortex. Accordingly, we start with that before discussing cortical processing.

From eye to cortex

What happens when light from a visual stimulus reaches receptors in the retina of the eye?

Figure 2.1 Complex scene that require prolonged perceptual processing to understand fully. Study the picture and identify the animals within it. Reprinted from Hegdé (2008), Copyright © 2008, with permission from Elsevier.

There are three major consequences (Kalat, 2001). First, there is *reception*, which involves absorption of physical energy by the receptors. Second, there is *transduction*, in which the physical energy is converted into an electrochemical pattern in the neurons. Third, there is *coding*, meaning there is a direct one-to-one correspondence between aspects of the physical stimulus and aspects of the resultant nervous system activity.

Light waves from objects in the environment pass through the transparent cornea at the front of the eye and proceed to the iris (see Figure 2.2). It is just behind the cornea and gives the eye its distinctive colour. The amount of light entering the eye is determined by the pupil, which is an opening in the iris. The lens focuses light onto the retina at the back of the eye. Each lens adjusts in shape by a process of accommodation to bring images into focus on the retina.

There are two types of visual receptor cells in the retina: cones and rods. There are six million cones, mostly in the fovea or central part of the retina. The cones are used for colour vision and for sharpness of vision (see later section on colour vision). There are 125 million rods concentrated in the outer regions of the retina. Rods are specialised for vision in dim light and for movement detection. Many of these differences between cones and rods stem from the fact that a retinal ganglion cell receives input from only a few cones but from hundreds of rods. Thus, only rods produce

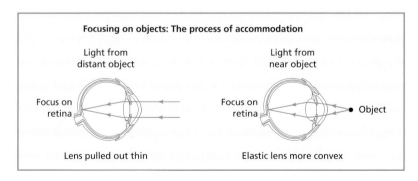

Figure 2.2 The process of accommodation.

much activity in retinal ganglion cells in poor lighting conditions.

The main pathway between the eye and the cortex is the retina–geniculate–striate pathway. It transmits information from the retina to V1 and then V2 (these are both visual areas discussed shortly) via the lateral geniculate nuclei of the thalamus. The entire retina–geniculate–striate system is organised in a similar way to the retinal system. Thus, for example, two stimuli adjacent to each other in the retinal image will also be adjacent to each other at higher levels within that system.

Each eye has its own optic nerve, and the two optic nerves meet at the optic chiasma. At this point, the axons from the outer halves of each retina proceed to the hemisphere on the same side, whereas the axons from the inner halves cross over and go to the other hemisphere. Signals then proceed along two optic tracts within the brain. One tract contains signals from the left half of each eye, and the other signals from the right half (see Figure 2.3).

After the optic chiasma, the optic tract proceeds to the lateral geniculate nucleus (LGN), which is part of the thalamus. Nerve impulses finally reach V1 in primary visual cortex within the occipital lobe at the back of the head before spreading out to nearby visual cortical areas such as V2.

There is another important feature of the retina–geniculate–striate system. There are two relatively independent channels or pathway within this system:

(1) *The parvocellular (or P) pathway*: this pathway is most sensitive to colour and to fine detail; most of its input comes from cones.
(2) *The magnocellular (or M) pathway*: this pathway is most sensitive to information about movement; most of its input comes from rods.

It is important to note (as stated above) that these two pathways are only *relatively* independent. There is plentiful evidence that there are numerous interconnections between the two pathways, and it is becoming increasingly apparent that the visual system is extremely complex (Mather, 2009). For example, there is clear evidence of intermingling of the two pathways in V1 (Nassi & Callaway, 2006, 2009).

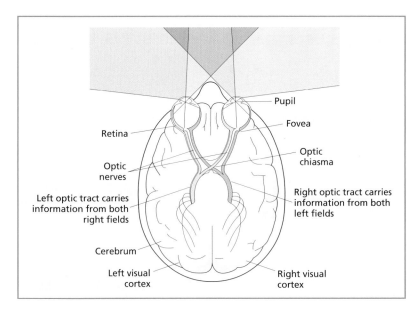

Figure 2.3 Route of visual signals. Note that signals reaching the left visual cortex come from the left sides of the two retinas, and signals reaching the right visual cortex come from the right sides of the two retinas.

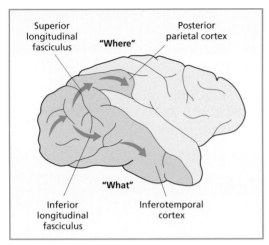

Figure 2.4 The ventral (what) and dorsal (where or how) pathways involved in vision having their origins in primary visual cortex (V1). From Gazzaniga, Ivry, and Mangun (2009). Copyright © 1998 by W.W. Norton & Company, Inc. Used by permission of W.W. Norton & Company, Inc.

Brain systems

As we have just seen, neurons from the P and M pathways mainly project to V1 in the primary visual cortex. What happens after V1? The answer is given in Figure 2.4. The P pathway associates with the ventral or "what" pathway that proceeds to the inferotemporal cortex, passing through an area (V4) involved in colour processing. In contrast, the M pathway associates with the dorsal ("where" or "how") pathway that proceeds to the posterior parietal cortex, passing through an area (V5/MT) involved in visual motion processing. Note that the assertions in the last two sentences are both only a very approximate reflection of a complex reality. For example, some parvocellular neurons project into dorsal visual areas (see Parker, 2007, for a review).

We will be considering the two pathways in much more detail later. For now, there are three points to bear in mind:

(1)   The ventral or "what" pathway that culminates in the inferotemporal cortex is mainly concerned with form and colour processing, whereas the dorsal ("where" or "how") pathway culminating in the parietal cortex is more concerned with movement processing.

(2)   There is by no means an absolutely rigid distinction between the types of information processed by the two streams. For example, Gur and Snodderly (2007) discovered a pathway by which motion-relevant information reaches the ventral stream directly without involving the dorsal stream.

(3)   The two pathways are *not* totally segregated. There are many interconnections between the ventral and dorsal pathways or streams. For example, both streams project to the primary motor cortex (Rossetti & Pisella, 2002).

As already indicated, Figure 2.4 provides only a very rough sketch map of visual processing in the brain. We can obtain more precise information from Figure 2.5, which is based on data from single-unit recordings (Schmolesky et al., 1998). This reveals three important points. First, the interconnections among the various visual cortical areas are more complicated than implied so far. Second, the brain areas forming part of the ventral pathway or stream are more than twice as large as the brain areas forming part of the dorsal pathway. Third, the figure shows that cells in the lateral geniculate nucleus respond fastest when a visual stimulus is presented followed by activation of cells in V1. However, cells are activated in several other areas (V3/V3A; MT; MST) very shortly thereafter. The take-home message is that it makes sense to think in terms of two pathways or processing streams, but these pathways are not separated in a neat and tidy way from each other.

V1 and V2

We will start with three important general points. First, to understand visual processing in primary visual cortex (V1) and in secondary

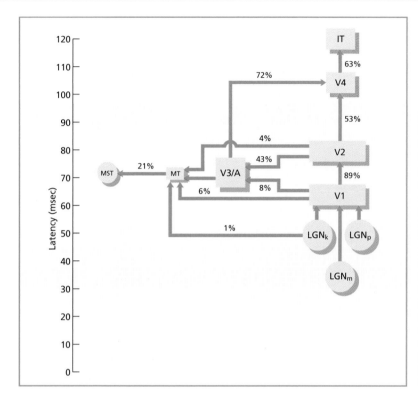

Figure 2.5 Some distinctive features of the largest visual cortical areas. The relative size of the boxes reflects the relative area of different regions. The arrows labelled with percentages show the proportion of fibres in each projection pathway. The vertical position of each box represents the response latency of cells in each area, as measured in single-unit recording studies. IT = inferotemporal cortex; MT = medial or middle temporal cortex; MST = medial superior temporal cortex. All areas are discussed in detail in the text. From Mather (2009). Copyright © George Mather.

visual cortex (V2), we must consider the notion of **receptive field**. The receptive field for any given neuron is that region of the retina in which light affects its activity.

Second, neurons often have effects on each other. For example, there is **lateral inhibition**, in which a reduction of activity in one neuron is caused by activity in a neighbouring neuron. Why is lateral inhibition useful? It increases the *contrast* at the edges of objects, making it easier to identify the dividing line between one object and another.

Third, the primary visual cortex (V1) and secondary visual cortex (V2) occupy relatively large areas within the cortex (see Figure 2.5). There is increasing evidence that early visual processing in areas V1 and V2 is more extensive than was once thought. For example, Hegdé and Van Essen (2000) studied neuronal responses to complex shapes in macaque monkeys. Approximately one-third of V2 cells responded to complex shapes and varied their

response as a function of differences in orientation and size.

Much of our knowledge of neurons (and their receptive fields) in primary and secondary visual cortex comes from the Nobel prize-winning research of Hubel and Wiesel. They used single-unit recordings (see Chapter 1) to study individual neurons. They found that many cells responded in two different ways to a spot of light depending on which part of the cell was affected:

KEY TERMS

receptive field: the region of the retina within which light influences the activity of a particular neuron.

lateral inhibition: reduction of activity in one neuron caused by activity in a neighbouring neuron.

(1)   An "on" response, with an increased rate of firing when the light was on.
(2)   An "off" response, with the light causing a decreased rate of firing.

ON-centre cells produce the on-response to a light in the centre of their receptive field and an off-response to a light in the periphery. The opposite is the case with off-centre cells.

Hubel and Wiesel (e.g., 1979) discovered two types of neuron in the receptive fields of the primary visual cortex: simple cells and complex cells. Simple cells have "on" and "off" regions, with each region being rectangular in shape. These cells respond most to dark bars in a light field, light bars in a dark field, or straight edges between areas of light and dark. Any given simple cell only responds strongly to stimuli of a particular orientation, and so the responses of these cells could be relevant to feature detection.

Complex cells resemble simple cells in that they respond maximally to straight-line stimuli in a particular orientation. However, complex cells have large receptive fields and respond more to moving contours. Each complex cell is driven by several simple cells having the same orientation preference and closely overlapping receptive fields (Alonso & Martinez, 1998). There are also end-stopped cells. The responsiveness of these cells depends on stimulus length and on orientation.

There are three final points. First, cortical cells provide *ambiguous* information because they respond in the same way to different stimuli. For example, a cell may respond equally to a horizontal line moving rapidly and a nearly horizontal line moving slowly. We need to combine information from many neurons to remove ambiguities.

Second, primary visual cortex is organised as a **retinotopic map**, which is "an array of nerve cells that have the same positions relative to one another as their receptive fields have on the surface of the retina" (Bruce, Green, & Georgeson, 2003, pp. 462–463). Note that retinotopic maps are also found in V2, V3, and posterior parietal cortex (Wandell, Dumoulin,

& Brewer, 2007). These maps are very useful because they preserve the spatial arrangement of the visual image, without which accurate visual perception would probably be impossible.

Third, V1 and V2 are both involved in the early stages of visual processing. However, that is not the complete story. In fact, there is an initial "feedforward sweep" that proceeds through the visual areas starting with V1 and then V2. In addition, however, there is a second phase of processing (recurrent processing) in which processing proceeds in the opposite direction (Lamme, 2006). There is evidence that some recurrent processing can occur in V1 within 120 ms of stimulus onset and also at later times (Boehler, Schoenfeld, Heinze, & Hopf, 2008). Observers were more likely to have visual awareness of the stimulus that had been presented on trials on which recurrent processing was strongly present. This suggests that recurrent processing may be of major importance in visual perception (see discussion in Chapter 16).

Functional specialisation

Zeki (1992, 1993) put forward a functional specialisation theory, according to which different parts of the cortex are specialised for different visual functions (e.g., colour processing, motion processing, form processing). By analogy, the visual system resembles a team of workers, each working on his/her own to solve part of a complex problem. The results of their labours are then combined to produce the solution (i.e., coherent visual perception).

Why might there be functional specialisation in the visual brain? Zeki (2005) argued that there are two main reasons. First, the attributes of objects occur in complex and unpredictable

KEY TERM

retinotopic map: nerve cells occupying the same relative positions as their respective receptive fields have on the retina.

combinations in the visual world. For example, a green object may be a car, a sheet of paper, or a leaf, and a car may be red, black, blue, or green (Zeki, 2005). We need to process *all* of an object's attributes to perceive it accurately. Second, the kind of processing required differs considerably from one attribute to another. For example, motion processing requires integrating information obtained from at least two successive points in time. In contrast, form or shape processing involves considering the relationship of elements to each other at one point in time.

Much of our early knowledge of functional specialisation in the visual brain came from research on monkeys. This is partly because certain kinds of experiments (e.g., surgical removal of parts of the visual brain) can be performed on monkeys but not humans. Some of the main areas of the visual cortex in the macaque monkey are shown in Figure 2.6. The retina connects primarily to what is known as the primary cortex or area V1. The importance of area V1 is shown by the fact that lesions at any point along the pathway to it from the retina lead to virtually total blindness within the affected part of V1. However, areas V2 to V5 are also of major significance in visual perception. It is generally assumed that the organisation of the human visual system closely resembles that of the macaque, and so reference is often made to human brain areas such as V1, V2, and so on. Technically, however, they should be referred to as analogue V1, analogue V2, and so on, because these areas are identified by analogy with the macaque brain.

Here are the main functions Zeki (1992, 2005) ascribed to these areas:

- *V1 and V2*: These areas are involved at an early stage of visual processing. They contain different groups of cells responsive to colour and form.

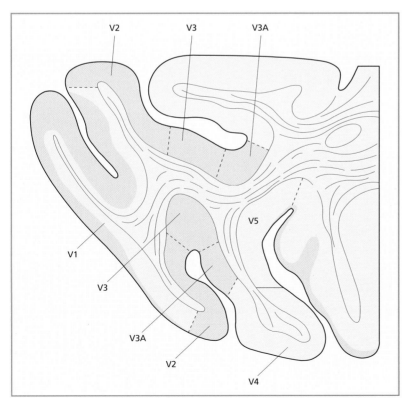

Figure 2.6 A cross-section of the visual cortex of the macaque monkey. From Zeki (1992). Reproduced with permission from Carol Donner.

- *V3 and V3A*: Cells in these areas are responsive to form (especially the shapes of objects in motion) but not to colour.
- *V4*: The overwhelming majority of cells in this area are responsive to colour; many are also responsive to line orientation. This area in monkeys is unusual in that there is much mixing of connections from temporal and parietal cortex (Baizer, Ungerleider, & Desimone, 1991).
- *V5*: This area is specialised for visual motion. In studies with macaque monkeys, Zeki found that all the cells in this area were responsive to motion but not to colour. In humans, the areas specialised for visual motion are referred to as MT and MST.

One of Zeki's central assumptions was that colour, form, and motion are processed in anatomically separate parts of the visual cortex. Much of the original evidence came from studies on monkeys. Relevant human evidence is considered below.

Form processing

Several areas are involved in form processing in humans, including areas V1, V2, V3, V4, and culminating in inferotemporal cortex. However, the cognitive neuroscience approach to form perception has focused mainly on inferotemporal cortex. For example, Sugase, Yamane, Ueno, and Kawano (1999) presented human faces, monkey faces, and simple geometrical objects (e.g., squares, circles) to monkeys. Neural activity occurring 50 ms after stimulus presentation varied as a function of the type of stimulus presented (e.g., human face vs. monkey face). Neural activity occurring several hundred milliseconds after stimulus presentation was influenced by more detailed characteristics of the stimulus (e.g., facial expression).

Zoccolan, Kouh, Poggio, and DiCarlo (2007) argued that neurons in the anterior region of the inferotemporal cortex differ in two important ways:

(1) *Object selectivity*: neurons with high object selectivity respond mainly or exclusively to specific visual objects.

(2) *Tolerance*: neurons with high tolerance respond strongly to retinal images of the same object differing due to changes in position, size, illumination, and so on.

Zoccolan et al. (2007) found in monkeys that those neurons high in object selectivity tended to be low in tolerance, and those high in tolerance were low in object selectivity. What do these findings mean? It is valuable to have neurons that are very specific in their responsiveness (i.e., high object selectivity + low tolerance) and others that respond to far more stimuli (i.e., low object selectivity + tolerance). Maximising the amount of selectivity and tolerance across neurons provides the basis for effective fine-grained identification (e.g., identifying a specific face) as well as broad categorisation (e.g., deciding whether the stimulus represents a cat).

There is much more on the responsiveness of neurons in anterior inferotemporal cortex in Chapter 3. If form processing occurs in different brain areas from colour and motion processing, we might anticipate that some patients would have severely impaired form processing but intact colour and motion processing. That does *not* seem to be the case. According to Zeki (1992), the reason is that a lesion large enough to destroy areas V3, V4, and inferotemporal cortex would probably destroy area V1 as well. As a result, the patient would suffer from total blindness rather than simply loss of form perception.

Colour processing

Studies involving brain-damaged patients and others involving techniques for studying the brain (e.g., functional neuroimaging) have been used to test the assumption that V4 is specialised for colour processing. We will consider these two kinds of study in turn.

If area V4 and related areas are specialised for colour processing, then patients with damage mostly limited to those areas should show little or no colour perception combined with fairly normal form and motion perception and ability to see fine detail. This is approximately the case in some patients with **achromatopsia** (also known as cerebral achromatopsia). Bouvier and Engel (2006) carried out a meta-analysis involving all known cases of achromatopsia. They reported three main findings:

(1) A small brain area within ventral occipital cortex in (or close to) area V4 was damaged in nearly all cases of achromatopsia.
(2) The loss of colour vision in patients with achromatopsia was often only partial, with some patients performing at normal levels on some tasks involving colour perception.
(3) Most patients with achromatopsia had substantial impairments of spatial vision.

What can we conclude from the above findings? An area in (or close to) V4 plays a major role in colour processing. However, we must not overstate its importance. The finding that some colour perception is often possible with damage to this area indicates it is not the only area involved in colour processing. The finding that patients with achromatopsia typically also have substantial deficits in spatial vision suggests that the area is not specialised just for colour processing.

Functional neuroimaging evidence that V4 plays an important role in colour processing was reported by Zeki and Marini (1998). They presented human observers with pictures of normally coloured objects (e.g., red strawberries), abnormally coloured objects (e.g., blue strawberries), and black-and-white pictures of objects. Functional magnetic resonance imaging (fMRI; see Glossary) indicated that both kinds of coloured objects activated a pathway going from V1 to V4. In addition, abnormally coloured objects (but not normally coloured ones) led to activation in the dorsolateral prefrontal cortex. A reasonable interpretation of these findings is that higher-level cognitive processes associated with the dorsolateral prefrontal cortex were involved when the object's colour was unexpected or surprising.

Similar findings were reported by Wade, Brewer, Rieger, and Wandell (2002). They used fMRI, and found that areas V1 and V2 were actively involved in colour processing in humans in addition to the involvement of area V4.

More detailed research involving single-unit recording (see Glossary) has clarified the role of V4 in colour processing. Conway, Moeller, and Tsao (2007) identified clusters of cells in V4 and adjacent areas that responded strongly to colour and also showed some responsiveness to shape. There were other cells in between these clusters showing some shape selectivity but no response to colour. These findings strengthen the argument that V4 is important for colour processing. They also help to clarify why patients with achromatopsia generally have severe problems with spatial vision – cells specialised for colour processing and for spatial processing are very close to each other within the brain.

In sum, area V4 and adjacent areas are undoubtedly involved in colour processing, as has been found in studies on patients with achromatopsia and in brain-imaging studies. However, the association between colour processing and involvement of V4 is not strong enough for us to regard it as a "colour centre". First, there is much evidence that other areas (e.g., V1, V2) are also involved in colour processing. Second, some ability to process colour is present in most individuals with achromatopsia. It is also present in monkeys with lesions to V4 (Heywood & Cowey, 1999). Third, most patients with achromatopsia have deficits in other visual processing (e.g., spatial processing) in addition to colour processing. Fourth, "The size of V4 (it is substantially the largest area beyond V2) and its anatomical position (it is the gateway to the temporal lobe) necessitate that it do more than just support colour vision" (Lennie, 1998, p. 920).

KEY TERM

achromatopsia: this is a condition involving brain damage in which there is little or no colour perception, but form and motion perception are relatively intact.

Motion processing

Area V5 (also known as MT, standing for median or middle temporal) is heavily involved in motion processing. Anderson et al. (1996) used magneto-encephalography (MEG) and fMRI (see Glossary) to assess brain activity in response to motion stimuli. They reported that, "human V5 is located near the occipito–temporal border in a minor sulcus (groove) immediately below the superior temporal sulcus" (p. 428). This is consistent with other findings. For example, Zeki, Watson, Lueck, Friston, Kennard, and Frackowiak (1991) used PET (see Glossary) and found that V5 (or MT) became very active when observers viewed moving dots relative to static ones.

Functional neuroimaging studies indicate that motion processing is associated with activity in V5 (or MT), but do not show clearly that V5 (or MT) is *necessary* for motion perception. This issue was addressed by Beckers and Zeki (1995). They used transcranial magnetic stimulation (TMS; see Glossary) to disrupt activity in V5/MT. This almost eliminated motion perception. McKeefry, Burton, Vakrou, Barrett, and Morland (2008) also used TMS. When TMS was applied to V5/MT, it produced a subjective slowing of stimulus speed and impaired the ability to discriminate between different speeds. Additional evidence that area V5/MT is of major importance in motion processing comes from studies on patients with akinetopsia. **Akinetopsia** is a condition in which stationary objects are generally perceived fairly normally but moving objects are not. Zihl, van Cramon, and Mai (1983) studied LM, a woman with akinetopsia who had suffered bilateral damage to the motion area (V5/MT). She was good at locating stationary objects by sight, she had good colour discrimination, and her binocular visual functions (e.g., stereoscopic depth) were normal, but her motion perception was grossly deficient. According to Zihl et al.:

She had difficulty . . . in pouring tea or coffee into a cup because the fluid appeared frozen, like a glacier. In addition, she could not stop pouring at the right time since she was unable to perceive the movement

Akinetopsia is a condition in which stationary objects are generally perceived fairly normally but motion perception is often deficient. Free-flowing liquids, for example, can appear to be frozen, which can make a simple task, such as pouring a glass of water, very difficult.

in the cup (or a pot) when the fluid rose. . . . In a room where more than two people were walking she felt very insecure . . . because "people were suddenly here or there but I have not seen them moving".

V5 (MT) is not the only area involved in motion processing. Another area that is involved is area MST (medial superior temporal), which is adjacent to and just above V5/MT. Vaina (1998)

KEY TERM

akinetopsia: this is a brain-damaged condition in which stationary objects are perceived reasonably well but objects in motion cannot be perceived accurately.

studied two patients with damage to MST. Both patients performed normally on some tests of motion perception, but had various problems relating to motion perception. One patient (RR) "frequently bumped into people, corners and things in his way, particularly into moving targets (e.g., people walking)" (p. 498). These findings suggest that MST is involved in the visual guidance of walking (Sekuler & Blake, 2002).

There is an important distinction between first-order and second-order motion perception (Cavanagh & Mather, 1989). With first-order displays, the moving shape differs in luminance (emitted or reflected light) from its background. For example, the shape might be dark whereas the background is light (a shadow passing over the ground). With second-order displays, there is no difference in luminance between the moving shape and the background, and we need to take account of other changes (e.g., contrast changes) to perceive motion. In everyday life, we encounter second-order displays fairly infrequently (e.g., movement of grass in a field caused by the wind).

There has been theoretical controversy concerning whether different mechanisms underlie the perception of first-order and second-order motion. There is increasing evidence that different mechanisms are involved. Ashida, Lingnau, Wall, and Smith (2007) found that repeated presentation of first-order displays led to a substantial reduction in activation in motion areas MT and MST. This is known as adaptation and occurs because many of the same neurons are activated by each display. Very similar reductions in activation in the motion areas occurred with repeated presentations of second-order displays. However, the key finding was that there was *no* evidence of adaptation in MT and MST when first-order displays were followed by second-order displays or vice versa. The implication is that the two kinds of stimuli activated *different* sets of neurons and thus probably involved different processes.

Support for the notion of different mechanisms for perception of first-order and second-order was also reported by Rizzo, Nawrot, Sparks, and Dawson (2008). They studied patients with brain damage in the visual cortex. There were 22 patients with a deficit in perception of first-order motion but not of second-order motion, and one patient with a deficit only in perception of second-order motion. This double dissociation indicates that different processes may well be involved in perception of the two types of motion. Of interest, many of the patients had brain damage not limited to the so-called motion areas, suggesting that several brain areas are involved in perception of motion.

Much of the brain research on motion perception has involved monkeys rather than humans. We need to be careful about generalising from such research to humans, because more brain areas are involved in human motion perception. Orban et al. (2003) found in an fMRI study that motion stimuli caused activation in V5/MT and surrounding areas in humans and in monkeys. However, area V3A and several other regions were more activated in humans than in monkeys. Of relevance, McKeefry et al. (2008), in a study discussed above, found that perception of stimulus speed was impaired when TMS was applied to V3A, suggesting it is involved in motion processing.

Why are there differences between species in the brain areas devoted to motion processing? Speculatively, Orban et al. (2003, p. 1766) proposed this answer: "The use of tools requires the control of motion (e.g., primitive ways of making fire) . . . this is also true for hunting with primitive weapons . . . motion processing became behaviourally much more important when humans emerged from the primate family millions of years ago."

Binding problem

Zeki's functional specialisation approach poses the obvious problem of how information about an object's motion, colour, and form is combined and integrated to produce coherent perception. This is known as the **binding problem:**

KEY TERM

binding problem: the issue of integrating different kinds of information during visual perception.

"local, spatially distributed features (e.g., colour, motion) must be grouped into coherent, global objects that are segmented from one another and from the backgrounds against which they appear" (Guttman, Gilroy, & Blake, 2007).

One approach to the binding problem is to argue that there is less functional specialisation than Zeki claimed, which reduces the complexity of the problem. For example, Kourtzi, Krekelberg, and van Wezel (2008) argued that there are numerous interactions between brain regions involved in motion and form processing, respectively. Lorteije, Kenemans, Jellema, van der Lubbe, Lommers, and van Wright (2007) studied activation to static pictures of running humans in areas of the visual cortex involved in motion processing. There was significant activation in those areas, but it was reduced when participants had previously been exposed to real motion in the same direction as the implied motion. These findings suggest that form and motion are processed in the same areas of cortex.

A different approach to the binding problem is the synchrony hypothesis (Canales, Gómez, & Maffet, 2007). According to this hypothesis, the presentation of a given object leads to widespread visual processing, and coherent visual perception depends upon a *synchronisation* of neural activity across several cortical areas. Of some relevance, there is evidence that widespread synchronisation of neural activity is associated with conscious visual awareness (e.g., Melloni et al., 2007; Rodriguez, George, Lachaux, Martinerie, Renault, & Varela, 1999; see Chapter 16). However, this association does not demonstrate that synchronisation *causes* conscious perception. Negative evidence was reported by Moutoussis and Zeki (1997) and by Bartels and Zeki (2004). Moutoussis and Zeki found that colour was perceived about 80–100 ms before motion, which suggests a lack of synchrony. Bartels and Zeki found that there was a *reduction* in synchrony across the brain when participants who had been in a resting state were presented with the Bond movie, *Tomorrow Never Dies*.

The synchrony hypothesis is oversimplified. Visual processing of an object occurs in widely distributed areas of the brain and proceeds through several stages. This makes it implausible that precise synchrony could be achieved. Another problem is that two or more objects are often presented at the same time. On the synchrony hypothesis, it would seem hard to keep the processing of these objects separate. Guttman, Gilroy, and Blake (2007) have suggested an alternative hypothesis based on the notion that perception depends on *patterns* of neural activity over time rather than on precise synchrony.

Evaluation

Zeki's functional specialisation theory has deservedly been influential. It represents an interesting attempt to provide a relatively simple overview of a remarkably complex reality. As is discussed in more detail later, there are strong grounds for agreeing with Zeki that processing of motion typically proceeds somewhat independently of other types of visual processing.

There are three major limitations with Zeki's theoretical approach. First, the various brain areas involved in visual processing are not nearly as specialised and limited in their processing as implied by the theory. Heywood and Cowey (1999) considered the percentage of cells in each visual cortical area that responded selectively to various stimulus characteristics (see Figure 2.7). Cells in several areas respond to orientation, disparity, and colour. There is reasonable evidence for specialisation only with respect to responsiveness to direction of stimulus motion.

Second, early visual processing in areas V1 and V2 is more extensive than suggested by Zeki. As we saw earlier, Hegde and Van Essen (2000) found that many V2 cells in macaque monkeys responded to complex shapes.

Third, Zeki has not addressed the binding problem satisfactorily. This problem is more tractable if we discard the functional specialisation assumption and assume instead that there are numerous interactions among the brain areas involved in visual processing (Kourtzi et al., 2008).

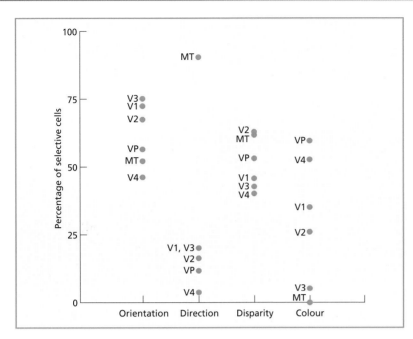

Figure 2.7 The percentage of cells in six different visual cortical areas responding selectively to orientation, direction of motion, disparity, and colour. From Heywood and Cowey (1999).

TWO VISUAL SYSTEMS: PERCEPTION AND ACTION

A fundamental question in vision research is as follows: what is the major function of vision? As Milner and Goodale (1998, p. 2) pointed out, "Standard accounts of vision implicitly assume that the purpose of the visual system is to construct some sort of internal model of the world outside." That assumption may seem reasonable but is probably inadequate.

One of the most influential answers to the above question was provided by Milner and Goodale (e.g., 1995, 1998). They argued there are *two* visual systems, each fulfilling a different function. First, there is a vision-for-perception system based on the ventral pathway; see Figure 2.4), which is the one we immediately think of when considering visual perception. It is the system we use to decide that the animal in front of us is a cat or a buffalo or to admire a magnificent landscape. In other words, it is used to identify objects.

Second, there is a vision-for-action system (based on the dorsal pathway; see Figure 2.4),

which is used for visually guided action. It is the system we use when running to return a ball at tennis or some other sport. It is also the system we use when grasping an object. When we grasp an object, it is important we calculate its orientation and position with respect to ourselves. Since observers and objects often move with respect to each other, it is important that the calculations of orientation and position are done immediately prior to initiating a movement.

Norman (2002) put forward a dual-process approach resembling the perception–action theory of Milner and Goodale (1995, 1998). He agreed with Milner and Goodale that there are separate ventral and dorsal pathways. He also agreed that the functions of each pathway were basically those proposed by Milner and Goodale. In broad terms, the functions of the two pathways or systems are as follows: "The dorsal system deals mainly with the utilisation of visual information for the guidance of behaviour in one's environment. The ventral system deals mainly with the utilisation of visual information for 'knowing' one's environment, that is, identifying and recognising items

The vision-for-perception system (based on the ventral pathway) helps this tennis player identify the incoming ball, whereas deciding where to move his hands and legs in order to return it successfully relies upon the vision-for-action system (based on the dorsal pathway).

TABLE 2.1: Eight main differences between the ventral and dorsal systems (based on Norman, 2002).

Factor	Ventral system	Dorsal system
1. Function	Recognition/identification	Visually guided behaviour
2. Sensitivity	High spatial frequencies: details	High temporal frequencies: motion
3. Memory	Memory-based (stored representations)	Only very short-term storage
4. Speed	Relatively slow	Relatively fast
5. Consciousness	Typically high	Typically low
6. Frame of reference	Allocentric or object-centred	Egocentric or body-centred
7. Visual input	Mainly foveal or parafoveal	Across retina
8. Monocular vision	Generally reasonably small effects	Often large effects (e.g., motion parallax)

previously encountered and storing new visual information for later encounters" (Norman, 2002, p. 95).

We can understand the essence of the dual-process approach if we consider the various differences assumed by Norman to exist between the two processing systems (see Table 2.1).

Norman's (2002) dual-process approach provides a more detailed account of differences between the ventral and dorsal systems than Milner and Goodale's (1995, 1998) perception–action theory. However, there is much overlap between the two theoretical approaches. Since more research has focused on perception–action theory, our focus will be on that theory.

Experimental evidence: brain-damaged patients

We can test Milner and Goodale's perception–action theory and Norman's dual-process approach by studying brain-damaged patients. We would expect to find some patients (those with damage to the dorsal pathway) having reasonably intact

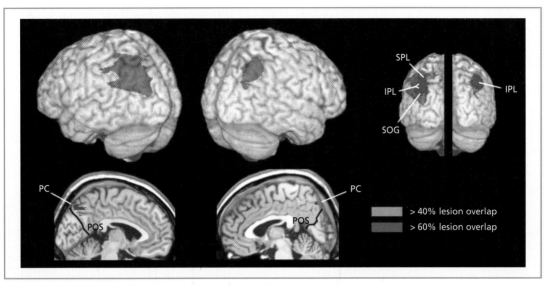

Figure 2.8 Percentage of overlapping lesions (areas of brain damage) in patients with optic ataxia (SPL = superior parietal lobule; IPL = inferior parietal lobule; SOG = superior occipital gyrus; Pc = precuneus; POS = parieto-occipital sulcus). From Karnath and Perenin (2005), by permission of Oxford University Press.

vision for perception but severely impaired vision for action. There should also be other patients (those with damage to the ventral pathway) showing the opposite pattern of intact vision for action but very poor vision for perception. There should thus be a double dissociation (see Glossary).

Of relevance to the theory are patients with optic ataxia, who have damage to the dorsal pathway, especially the intra parietal sulcus and the superior parietal lobule (see Figure 2.8). Patients with **optic ataxia** are poor at making precise visually guided movements in spite of the fact that their vision and ability to move their arms is essentially intact. Perenin and Vighetto (1988) found that patients with optic ataxia had great difficulty in rotating their hands appropriately when reaching towards (and into) a large oriented slot in front of them. These findings fit with the theory, because damage to the dorsal pathway should impair vision-for-action.

Many patients with optic ataxia do not have problems with *all* aspects of reaching for objects. More specifically, they are often better at action planning than at the subsequent production of appropriate motor movements.

Jakobson, Archibald, Carey, and Goodale (1991) studied VK, a patient with optic ataxia who had difficulty in grasping objects. Close inspection of her grip aperture at different points in grasping indicated that her *initial* planning was essentially normal.

What about patients with damage to the ventral stream only? Of relevance here are some patients with **visual agnosia**, a condition involving severe problems with object recognition even though visual information reaches the cortex (see Chapter 3). Perhaps the most studied visual agnosic is DF. James, Culham, Humphrey, Milner, and Goodale (2003) found that her

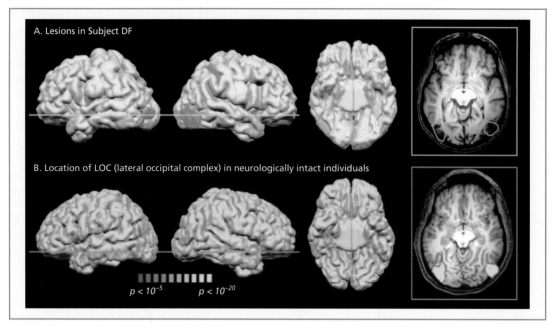

Figure 2.9 A: damage to DF's lateral occipital complex within the ventral stream is shown in pale blue; B: location of the lateral occipital complex in healthy individuals. From James et al. (2003), by permission of Oxford University Press.

brain damage was in the ventral pathway or stream (see Figure 2.9). DF showed no greater activation in the ventral stream when presented with drawings of objects than when presented with scrambled line drawings. However, she showed high levels of activation in the dorsal stream when grasping for objects.

In spite of having reasonable visual acuity, DF could not identify any of a series of drawings of common objects. However, as pointed out by Milner et al. (1991, p. 424), DF "had little difficulty in everyday activity such as opening doors, shaking hands, walking around furniture, and eating meals . . . she could accurately reach out and grasp a pencil orientated at different angles."

In a study by Goodale and Milner (1992), DF held a card in her hand and looked at a circular block into which a slot had been cut. She was unable to orient the card so it would fit into the slot, suggesting that she had very poor perceptual skills. However, DF performed well when asked to move her hand forward and insert the card into the slot.

Dijkerman, Milner, and Carey (1998) assessed DF's performance on various tasks when presented with several differently coloured objects. There were two main findings. First, DF could not distinguish accurately between the coloured objects, suggesting problems with object recognition due to damage to the ventral stream. Second, DF reached out and touched the objects as accurately as healthy individuals using information about their positions relative to her own body. This suggests that her ability to use visual information to guide action using the dorsal stream was largely intact.

Some other studies on brain-damaged patients produced findings less consistent with the original version of perception–action theory. We will consider those findings shortly.

Experimental evidence: visual illusions

There have been hundreds of studies of visual illusions over the years. The Müller–Lyer

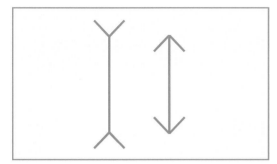

Figure 2.10 Müller–Lyer illusion.

illusion (see Figure 2.10) is one of the most famous. The vertical line on the left looks longer than the one on the right. In fact, however, they are the same length, as can be confirmed by using a ruler! Another well-known illusion is the Ebbinghaus illusion (see Figure 2.11). In this illusion, the central circle surrounded by smaller circles looks larger than

a central circle of the same size surrounded by larger circles. In fact, the two central circles are the *same* size.

There are hundreds of other visual illusions. Their existence leaves us with an intriguing paradox. How has the human species been so successful given that our visual perceptual processes are apparently very prone to error? Milner and Goodale (1995, 2006) provided a neat explanation. According to them, most studies on visual illusions have involved the vision-for-perception system. However, we use mostly the vision-for-action system when avoiding walking too close to a precipice or dodging cars as we cross the road. Milner and Goodale argued that the vision-for-action system provides accurate information about our position with respect to objects. These ideas produce an exciting prediction: grasping for objects using the vision-for-action system should be unaffected by the Müller–Lyer, the Ebbinghaus, and many other visual illusions.

Numerous studies support the above prediction. For example, Haart, Carey, and Milne (1999) used a three-dimensional version of the Müller–Lyer illusion. There were two tasks:

(1) A matching task in which participants indicated the length of the shaft on one figure by the size of the gap between their index finger and thumb. This task was designed to require the vision-for-perception system.
(2) A grasping task, in which participants rapidly grasped the target figure lengthwise using their index finger and thumb. This task was designed to use the vision-for-action system.

What Haart et al. (1999) found is shown in Figure 2.12. There was a strong illusion effect when the matching task was used. More interestingly, there was *no* illusory effect at all with the grasping task.

Bruno, Bernardis, and Gentilucci (2008) carried out a meta-analysis of 33 studies involving

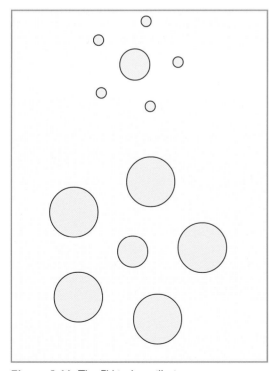

Figure 2.11 The Ebbinghaus illusion.

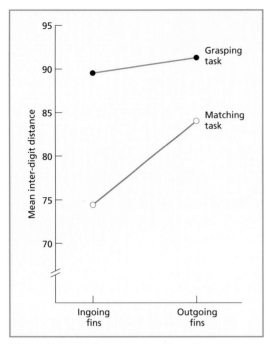

Figure 2.12 Performance on a three-dimensional version of the Müller–Lyer illusion as a function of task (grasping vs. matching) and type of stimulus (ingoing fins vs. outgoing fins). Based on data in Haart et al. (1999).

the Müller–Lyer or related illusions in which observers had to point rapidly at the figure. These studies were designed to involve the vision-for-action system, and the mean illusion effect was 5.5%. For comparison purposes, they considered 11 studies using standard procedures (e.g., verbal estimations of length) and designed to involve the vision-for-perception system. Here, the mean illusion effect was 22.4%. The finding that the mean illusion effect was *four* times greater in the former studies clearly supports the perception–action model. However, it could be argued that the model predicts no illusion effect at all with rapid pointing.

Action: planning + motor responses

A study by Króliczak et al. (2006; see Box) found that some motor movements (slow pointing) were much more affected by the hollow-face illusion than were different motor movements (fast flicking). How can we best explain this difference? The starting point is to realise that the processes involved in producing different actions can vary substantially.

The hollow-face illusion

Many studies have shown that visual illusion effects are reduced (or disappear altogether) when observers make rapid reaching or grasping movements towards illusory figures. This is as predicted by the perception–action theory. However, the magnitude of such effects is typically relatively small, and there have been several failures to obtain the predicted findings. Króliczak, Heard, Goodale, and Gregory (2006) tested the theory using the hollow-face illusion in which a realistic hollow mask looks like a normal convex face (see Figure 2.13; visit the website: www.richardgregory.org/experiments/index/htm). They did this because this illusion is especially strong.

There were three stimuli: (1) a normal convex face mask perceived as a normal face; (2) a hollow mask perceived as convex (projecting outwards) rather than hollow; and (3) a hollow mask perceived as hollow. There were also three tasks involving a target (small cylindrical magnet) placed on the face mask:

(1) Drawing the target position on paper. This task was designed to involve the ventral stream and thus the vision-for-perception system.
(2) Fast flicking finger movements were made to targets presented on the face. This task was designed to involve the dorsal stream and thus the vision-for-action system.
(3) Slow pointing finger movements were made to targets on the face. Previous research had suggested this task might provide time for the vision-for-perception system to influence performance.

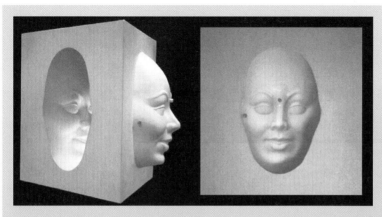

Figure 2.13 Left: normal and hollow faces with small target magnets on the forehead and cheek of the normal face; right: front view of the hollow mask that appears as an illusory face projecting forwards. Reprinted from Króliczak et al. (2006), Copyright © 2006, with permission from Elsevier.

What happened? When participants drew the target position, there was a strong illusion effect (see Figure 2.14). The target was perceived as being much closer to the observer than was actually the case with the illusory hollow face. Indeed, the target was perceived as being almost as close as when presented on the normal face, and about 8 cm closer than the non-illusory hollow face.

The findings with the flicking task were very different (see Figure 2.14). The flicking response was very accurate – the flicking response to the illusory hollow face treated it as a hollow face and very different to the normal face. Here, the

difference between the response to the illusory and non-illusory hollow faces was less than 1 cm. Thus, the strong illusion of reversed depth almost disappeared when participants made rapid flicking responses to the hollow mask.

Finally, there are the findings with slow pointing (see Figure 2.14). The pointing response to the illusory hollow face was very different to that to the non-illusory hollow face, indicating the illusory effect was fairly strong in this condition. The most plausible interpretation of this finding is that the vision-for-perception influenced the slow pointing response. For evidence supporting that conclusion, return to the text.

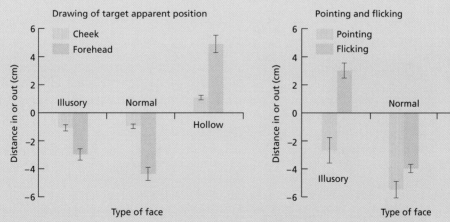

Figure 2.14 Left: performance on drawing task with participants drawing illusory hollow face as if it projected forwards like the obviously hollow face; right: performance on fast flicking task was very accurate, treating the illusory hollow face as if it were hollow; performance on the slow pointing task treated the illusory hollow face as if it were projecting forwards. Reprinted from Króliczak et al. (2006), Copyright © 2005, with permission from Elsevier.

For example, most of your actions probably occur rapidly and with little or nothing in the way of conscious planning. In contrast, if you have ever eaten a Chinese meal using chopsticks, you probably found yourself laboriously working out what to do to get any food into your mouth. The take-home message is that our actions often involve the ventral, vision-for-perception system as well as the dorsal, vision-for-action system. This makes much sense given that the dorsal and ventral streams both project to the primary motor cortex (Rossetti & Pisella, 2002). (There is additional coverage of some of these issues in Chapter 4 in the section on Glover's (2004) planning–control model.)

Evidence suggesting the ventral stream can be involved in perception for action was reported by Creem and Proffitt (2001). They argued that we should distinguish between *effective* and *appropriate* grasping. For example, we can grasp a toothbrush effectively by its bristles, but appropriate grasping involves picking it up by the handle. The key assumption is that appropriate grasping involves accessing stored knowledge about the object; with the consequence that appropriate grasping depends in part on the ventral stream.

Creem and Proffitt tested the above hypothesis by asking participants to pick up various familiar objects with distinct handles

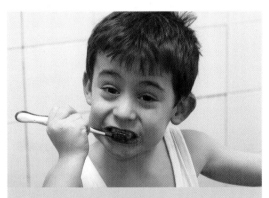

Creem and Proffitt (2001) found that appropriate grasping of an object requires the retrieval of object knowledge from long-term memory.

(e.g., toothbrush, hammer, knife). The handle always pointed away from the participant, and the measure of interest was the percentage of occasions on which the objects were grasped appropriately. The grasping task was performed on its own (control condition), while learning a list of paired associates, or while performing a spatial imagery task.

What was predicted by Creem and Proffitt (2001)? If appropriate grasping requires the retrieval of object knowledge from long-term memory, then paired-associate learning (which involves retrieving words from long-term memory) should greatly impair people's ability to grasp objects appropriately. That is precisely what was found. Thus, retrieval of object knowledge (*not* involving the dorsal stream) is necessary for appropriate grasping.

Milner and Goodale (2008) argued that most tasks in which observers grasp an object involve some processing in the ventral stream as well as in the dorsal stream. Involvement of the ventral, vision-for-perception system is especially likely in the following circumstances: (1) memory is required (e.g., there is a time lag between the offset of the stimulus and the start of the grasping movement); (2) time is available to plan the forthcoming movement (e.g., Króliczak et al., 2006); (3) planning which movement to make is necessary; or (4) the action is unpractised or awkward. As a rule of thumb, actions are most likely to involve the ventral stream when they are *not* automatic but involve conscious cognitive processes. It is assumed theoretically that the dorsal stream is *always* involved in carrying out actions even if the ventral stream has been much involved in prior action planning.

Milner, Dijkerman, McIntosh, Rossetti, and Pisella (2003) studied two patients with optic ataxia. As discussed earlier, this is a condition in which there are severe deficits in reaching and grasping due to damage to the dorsal stream. These patients made reaching and grasping movements immediately or a few seconds after the offset of the target object. Surprisingly, the patients' performance was *better* when they relied on memory. How can we explain this finding?

According to Milner et al., the patients did reasonably well in the memory condition because they could make use of their intact ventral stream. They did poorly when immediate responses were required because they could not use the ventral stream in that condition.

Van Doorn, van der Kamp, and Savelsbergh (2007) provided evidence that the ventral stream is involved in the planning of action. Participants were presented with a rod of various lengths forming part of a Müller–Lyer figure (see Figure 2.10). They had to decide whether to pick the rod up end-to-end using a one-handed or a two-handed grip, a decision which clearly involved planning. The key finding was that participants chose a two-handed grip at shorter rod lengths when the fins pointed outwards than when they pointed inwards. However, their maximal grip size was unaffected by the illusion. The visual processes guiding action selection (planning) seemed to involve the ventral stream whereas those guiding motor programming did not.

Finally, we consider findings difficult to account for on the revised version of the perception–action theory. Coello, Danckert, Blangero, and Rossetti (2007) tested a patient, IG, with optic ataxia involving extensive damage to the dorsal stream. This patient was presented with visual illusions, and made perceptual judgements or actions (pointing or grasping). It was assumed that IG would rely on her intact ventral stream to perform both kinds of task, and so would always be affected by the visual illusions. In fact, however, she was *not* affected by the illusions when she used pointing or grasping actions. This is surprising, because showing no illusory effect in those conditions is supposed theoretically to depend on use of information from the dorsal stream. Coello et al. argued that IG may have used a visual system independent of the dorsal stream (and possibly running through the inferior parietal lobule) to provide visual guidance of her actions.

Evaluation

The perception–action theory has been very influential. The central assumption that there are two rather separate visual systems (one mostly concerned with perception for recognition and the other with perception for action) is probably broadly correct. This assumption has received strong support from two types of research. First, there are studies on patients with optic ataxia (damage to the dorsal stream) and on visual agnosia (damage to the ventral stream) that have produced the predicted double dissociation. Second, there are studies involving several visual illusions. These studies have produced the surprising (but theoretically predicted) finding that action-based performance (e.g., grasping, pointing) is often immune to the illusory effects. More recently, Milner and Goodale (2008) have clarified the circumstances in which the ventral stream is involved in grasping and pointing. This is an important development of the theory because it was never likely that vision for action depended solely on the dorsal stream.

What are the limitations of the perception–action theory? First, there is much evidence that the ventral stream is more likely to influence reaching and grasping responses when those responses are not immediate (Milner & Goodale, 2008). That makes sense given that cortical responses to visual stimulation are typically much faster in dorsal areas than in ventral ones (Mather, 2009). The implication is that reaching and grasping are typically influenced by both processing streams provided that there is sufficient time for the ventral stream to make its contribution.

Second, it is generally the case that any given theory is most likely to be discarded when someone suggests a superior theory. That has not happened with Milner and Goodale's theory. However, Chen et al. (2007) have suggested a promising approach that can be described as a "frame and fill" theory (Mather, 2009). According to this theory, rapid, coarse processing in the dorsal stream provides the "frame" for slower and more precise ventral stream processing that supplies the "fill". One of the advantages of this theory is that it helps to make sense of the findings discussed below under point six.

Third, the emphasis within the theory is on the *separate* contributions of the dorsal and ventral streams to vision and action. In fact, however, the two visual systems typically *interact* with each other. Kourtzi et al. (2008) discussed some of these interactions. For example, Kourtzi and Kanwisher (2000) found that photographs of an athlete running produced strong responses in human MT/MST (specialised for motion processing) in the dorsal stream. Thus, visual perception can have a direct impact on processing in the dorsal stream. Much additional research provides evidence that there are numerous reciprocal connections between the two visual streams (Mather, 2009).

Fourth, the notion that dorsal and ventral streams process very different kinds of information is too extreme. As we saw earlier, there is evidence that motion-relevant information can reach the ventral stream without previously having been processed within the dorsal stream. Some of the complex interactions between the two processing streams can be inferred from Figure 2.5.

Fifth, it is often difficult to make firm predictions from the theory. This is because most visual tasks require the use of both processing streams, and there are individual differences in the strategies used to perform these tasks.

Sixth, there has been some scepticism (e.g., Pisella, Binkofski, Lasek, Toni, & Rossetti 2006) as to whether clear double dissociations between optic ataxia and visual agnosia have been demonstrated. For example, patients with optic ataxia are supposed theoretically to have impaired reaching for visual objects but intact visual perception. However, some of them have impaired visual perception for stimuli presented to peripheral vision (see Pisella et al., 2006, for a review).

Seventh, there is much exciting research to be done by studying visual illusions in brain-damaged patients. Such research has hardly started, but early findings (e.g., Coello et al., 2007) seem somewhat inconsistent with predictions of perception–action theory.

COLOUR VISION

Why has colour vision developed? After all, if you see an old black-and-white movie on television, you can easily understand the moving images. One reason is that colour often makes an object stand out from its background, making it easier to distinguish figure from ground. As is well known, the ability of chameleons to change colour to blend in with their immediate environment reduces their chances of being attacked by predators. Another reason is that colour helps us to recognise and categorise objects. For example, colour perception is useful when deciding whether a piece of fruit is under-ripe, ripe, or over-ripe.

Before going any further, we need to consider the meaning of the word "colour". There are three main qualities associated with colour. First, there is *hue*, which is what distinguishes red from yellow or blue. Second, there is *brightness*, which is the perceived intensity of light. Third, there is *saturation*, which allows us to determine whether a colour is vivid or pale. We saw earlier that the cones in the retina are specialised for colour vision, and we turn now to a more detailed consideration of their role.

Trichromacy theory

Cone receptors contain light-sensitive photo-pigment allowing them to respond to light. According to trichromatic (three-coloured) theory, there are three different kinds of cone receptors. One type of cone receptor is most sensitive to short-wavelength light, and generally responds most to stimuli perceived as blue. A second type of cone receptor is most sensitive to medium-wavelength light, and responds greatly to stimuli generally seen as yellow-green. The third type of cone receptor responds most to long-wavelength light such as that coming from stimuli perceived as orange-red.

How do we see other colours? According to the theory, most stimuli activate two or all three cone types. The colour we perceive is determined by the relative levels of stimulation of

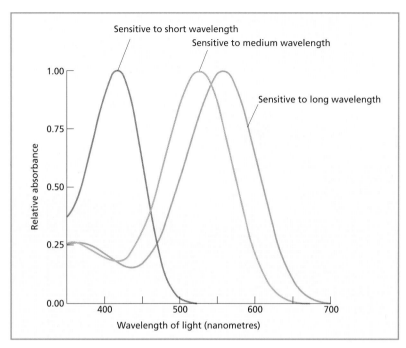

Sensitive to short wavelength
Sensitive to medium wavelength
Sensitive to long wavelength

Figure 2.15 Three types of colour receptors or cones identified by microspectrophotometry. From Bowmaker and Dartnell (1980). Reprinted with permission of Wiley-Blackwell.

each cone type, with activation of all three cone types leading to the perception of whiteness.

Bowmaker and Dartnall (1980) obtained support for trichromatic theory using **microspectrophotometry**, a technique permitting measurement of the light absorbed at different wavelengths by individual cone receptors. This revealed three types of cones or receptors responding maximally to different wavelengths (see Figure 2.15). Each cone type absorbs a wide range of wavelengths, and so it would be wrong to equate one cone type directly with perception of blue, one with yellow-green, and one with orange-red. There are about 4 million long-wavelength cones, over 2 million medium-wavelength cones, and under 1 million short-wavelength cones (Cicerone & Nerger, 1989).

Roorda and Williams (1999) found that all three types of cone are distributed fairly randomly within the human eye. However, there are few cones responsive to short-wavelength light within the fovea or central part of the retina. More recent research has indicated that the ratio of long-wavelength to medium-wavelength cones increases dramatically in the extreme periphery of the human retina (Kuchenbecker, Sahay, Tait, Neitz, & Neitz, 2008). Since long-wavelength cones are maximally responsive to stimuli perceived as red, this may help to explain why matadors use red capes while engaged in bull-fighting.

Many forms of colour deficiency are consistent with trichromacy theory. Most individuals with colour deficiency have **dichromacy**, in which one cone class is missing. In deuteranomaly, the medium-wavelength (green) cones are missing; in protanomaly, the long-wavelength (red) cones are missing; and in tritanopia, the short-wavelength (blue) cones are missing.

Why has evolution equipped us with three types of cone? It is clearly a very efficient system – we can discriminate literally millions of colours even with such a limited number of cone types.

Opponent-process theory

Trichromatic theory provides a reasonable account of what happens at the receptor level. However, it does not explain what happens *after* the cone receptors have been activated. In addition, it cannot account for **negative afterimages**. If you stare at a square of a given colour for several seconds and then shift your gaze to a white surface, you will see a negative afterimage in the complementary colour (complementary colours produce white when combined). For example, a green square produces a red afterimage, whereas a blue square produces a yellow afterimage.

The mysteries of negative afterimages were solved by Ewald Hering (1878) with his opponent-process theory. He assumed there are three types of opponent processes in the visual system. One opponent process (red–green channel) produces perception of green when it responds in one way and of red when it responds in the opposite way. A second type of opponent process (blue–yellow channel) produces perception of blue or yellow in the same fashion. The third type of process (achromatic channel) produces the perception of white at one extreme and of black at the other.

There is convincing evidence supporting opponent-process theory. DeValois and DeValois (1975) discovered opponent cells in the geniculate nucleus of monkeys. These cells showed increased activity to some wavelengths of light but decreased activity to others. For red-green cells, the transition point between increased and decreased activity occurred between the green and red parts of the spectrum. In contrast, blue-yellow cells had a transition point between the yellow and blue parts of the spectrum.

According to opponent-process theory, it is impossible to see blue and yellow together or red and green, but the other colour combinations can be seen. That is precisely what Abramov and Gordon (1994) found when observers indicated the percentage of blue, green, yellow, and red they perceived when presented with single wavelengths.

Opponent-process theory explains negative afterimages. Prolonged viewing of a given colour (e.g., red) produces one extreme of activity in the relevant opponent process. When attention is then directed to a white surface, the opponent process moves to its other extreme, thus producing the negative afterimage.

The theory is of relevance in explaining some types of colour deficiency. Red-green deficiency (the most common form of colour blindness) occurs when the high- or medium-wavelength cones are damaged or missing, and so the red–green channel cannot be used. Blue-yellow deficiency occurs when individuals lacking the short-wavelength cones cannot make effective use of the blue–yellow channel.

Dual-process theory

The trichromacy and opponent-process theories are both partially correct. Hurvich and Jameson (1957) developed a dual-process theory that provided a synthesis of the two earlier theories. According to their theory, signals from the three cone types identified by trichromacy theory are sent to the opponent cells described in the opponent-process theory (see Figure 2.16). There are three channels. The achromatic (non-colour) channel combines the activity of the medium- and long-wavelength cones. The blue–yellow channel represents the difference between the sum of the medium- and long-wavelength cones, on the one hand, and the short-wavelength cones, on the other. The direction of difference determines

KEY TERM

negative afterimages: the illusory perception of the complementary colour to the one that has just been fixated for several seconds; green is the complementary colour to red, and blue is complementary to yellow.

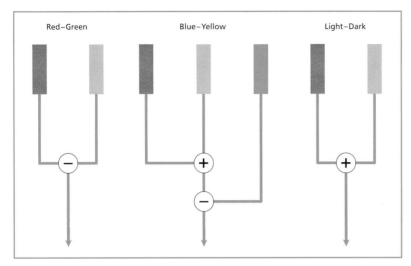

Figure 2.16 Schematic diagram of the early stages of neural colour processing. Three cone classes (red = long; green = medium; blue = short) supply three "channels". The achromatic (light–dark) channel receives nonspectrally opponent input from long and medium cone classes. The two chromatic channels receive spectrally opponent inputs to create the red–green and blue–yellow channels. From Mather (2009), Copyright © 2009, George Mather. Reproduced with permission.

whether blue or yellow is seen. Finally, the red–green channel represents the difference between activity levels in the medium- and long-wavelength cones. The direction of this difference determines whether red or green is perceived.

Evaluation

As we have seen, there is plentiful support for the dual-process theory. However, it is becoming increasingly clear that it is oversimplified (see Solomon & Lennie, 2007, for a review). For example, Solomon and Lennie identify two findings that are puzzling from the perspective of dual-process theory. First, the proportions of different cone types vary considerably across individuals, but this has very little effect on colour perception. Second, the arrangement of cone types in the eye is fairly *random* (e.g., Roorda & Williams, 1999). This seems odd because it presumably makes it difficult for colour-opponent mechanisms to work effectively. What such findings suggest is that the early processes involved in colour vision are much more complicated than was previously believed to be the case. Solomon and Lennie discuss some of these complications in their review article.

Colour constancy

Colour constancy is the tendency for a surface or object to be perceived as having the same colour when there is a change in the wavelengths contained in the illuminant (the light illuminating the surface or object). The phenomenon of colour constancy indicates that colour vision does not depend solely on the wavelengths of the light reflected from objects. What is the importance of colour constancy? We can answer that question by considering what would happen if we lacked colour constancy. The apparent colour of familiar objects would change dramatically as a function of changes in the lighting conditions, and this would make it very difficult to recognise objects rapidly and accurately.

How good is our colour constancy? Granzier, Brenner, and Smeets (2009) addressed this issue in a study in which they assessed colour constancy under natural conditions. Observers were initially presented with six uniformly coloured papers that were similar in colour and learned to name them. After that, the observers tried to identify individual papers presented at various indoor and outdoor

KEY TERM

colour constancy: the tendency for any given object to be perceived as having the same colour under widely varying viewing conditions.

locations differing substantially in term of lighting conditions. The key finding was that 55% of the papers were identified correctly. This may not sound very impressive, but represents a good level of performance given the similarities among the papers and the large differences in viewing conditions.

A crucial problem we have when identifying the colour of an object is that the wavelengths of light reflected from it are greatly influenced by the nature of the illuminant. Indeed, if you observe a piece of paper in *isolation*, you cannot tell the extent to which the wavelengths of light reflected from it are due to the illuminant. Many factors are involved in allowing us to show reasonable colour constancy most of the time in spite of this problem. However, what is of central importance is *context* – according to Land's (1977, 1986) retinex theory, we decide the colour of a surface by comparing its ability to reflect short, medium, and long wavelengths against that of adjacent surfaces. Land argued that colour constancy breaks down when such comparisons cannot be made effectively.

Foster and Nascimento (1994) developed some of Land's ideas into an influential theory based on cone-excitation ratios. They worked out cone excitations from various surfaces viewed under different conditions of illumination. We can see what their big discovery was by considering a simple example. Suppose there were two illuminants and two surfaces. If surface 1 led to the long-wavelength or red cones responding *three* times as much with illuminant 1 as illuminant 2, then the same *threefold* difference was also found with surface 2. Thus, the ratio of cone responses was essentially invariant with different illuminants, and thus displayed reasonably high constancy. As a result, we can use information about cone-excitation ratios to eliminate the effects of the illuminant and so assess object colour accurately.

There is considerable support for the notion that cone-excitation ratios are important. Nascimento, De Almeida, Fiadeiro, and Foster (2004) obtained evidence suggesting that the level of colour constancy shown in different conditions could be predicted on the basis of cone-excitation ratios.

Reeves, Amano, and Foster (2008) argued that it is important to distinguish between our subjective experience and our judgements about the world. We can see the difference clearly if we consider feelings of warmth. As you walk towards a fire, it feels subjectively to get progressively hotter, but how hot the fire is judged to be is unlikely to change. Reeves et al. found high levels of colour constancy when observers made judgements about the *objective* similarity of two stimuli seen under different illuminants. Observers were also very good at deciding whether differences between two stimuli resulted from a change in material or a change in illumination. However, low levels of colour constancy were obtained when observers rated the *subjective* similarity of the hue and saturation of two stimuli. Colour constancy was high when observers took account of the context to distinguish between the effects of material change and illumination change, but it was low when they focused only on the stimuli themselves. More generally, the findings show that we can use our visual system in very *flexible* ways.

Shadows create apparent colour changes, yet we interpret the colour as remaining constant under a variety of conditions despite this. In this example, we perceive a continuous green wall with a sun streak, rather than a wall painted in different colours.

Other factors

One of the reasons we show colour constancy is because of **chromatic adaptation**, in which sensitivity to light of any given colour or hue decreases over time. If you stand outside after dark, you may be struck by the yellowness of the artificial light in people's houses. However, if you have been in a room illuminated by artificial light for some time, the light does not seem yellow. Thus, chromatic adaptation can enhance colour constancy. Uchikawa, Uchikawa, and Boynton (1989) carried out a study in which observers looked at isolated patches of coloured paper. When the observer and the paper were both illuminated by red light, there was chromatic adaptation – the perceived colour of the paper only shifted slightly towards red. The findings were different when the observer was illuminated by white light and the paper by red light. In this condition, there was little chromatic adaptation, and the perceived colour of the paper shifted considerably towards red.

Kraft and Brainard (1999) set up a visual environment in a box. It included a tube wrapped in tin foil, a pyramid, a cube, and a Mondrian stimulus (square shapes of different colours). When all the objects were visible, colour constancy was as high as 83% even with large changes in illumination. However, it decreased when the various cues were progressively eliminated. The most important factor in colour constancy was *local contrast*, which involves comparing the retinal cone responses from the target surface with those from the immediate background (cone-excitation ratios). When local contrast could not be used, colour constancy dropped from 83 to 53%. Another important factor was *global contrast*, in which retinal cone responses from the target surface are compared with the average cone responses across the entire visual scene. When the observers could not use global contrast, colour constancy dropped from 53 to 39%. When all the non-target objects were removed, the observers were denied valuable information in the form of reflected highlights from glossy surfaces (e.g., tube wrapped in tin foil). This caused colour constancy to drop to 11%.

Top-down influences (e.g., knowledge, familiar colour) can have a strong effect on colour constancy. Suppose that light from a strongly coloured surface reflects onto a nearby white surface. We all know that will affect the light reflected from the white surface, and take that into account when judging the colour of the white surface. Bloj, Kersten, and Hurlbert (1999) set up a visual display in which observers judged the colour of a white surface. In one condition, observers were presented with a three-dimensional display that created the *false* impression that a strongly coloured surface reflected onto that white surface. This misled the observers and produced a substantial reduction in colour constancy.

Colour constancy is influenced by our knowledge of the familiar colours of objects (e.g., bananas are yellow; tomatoes are red). This was shown in a study by Hansen, Olkkonen, Walter, and Gegenfurtner (2006). Observers viewed digitised photographs of fruits and adjusted their colour until they appeared grey. The key finding was a general over-adjustment. For example, a banana still looked yellowish to the observers when it was actually grey, causing them to adjust its colour to a slightly bluish hue. Thus, objects tend to be perceived in their typical colour.

Zeki (1983) found in monkeys that cells in area V4 (specialised for colour processing) responded strongly to a red patch illuminated by red light. However, these cells did not respond when the red patch was replaced by a green, blue, or white patch, even though the dominant reflected wavelength would generally be perceived as red. Thus, these cells responded to the *actual* colour of a surface rather than simply to the wavelengths reflected from it. In similar fashion, Kusunoki, Moutoussis, and Zeki (2006) found that cells in V4 continued

KEY TERM

chromatic adaptation: reduced sensitivity to light of a given colour or hue after lengthy exposure.

to respond to a given colour even though there were large changes in the background colour. Thus, cells in V4 (but not earlier in visual processing) exhibit colour constancy.

Barbur and Spang (2008) studied instantaneous colour constancy, in which there is high colour constancy following a sudden change in illuminant. Use of fMRI revealed, as expected, that the computations involved in instantaneous colour constancy involved V4. Less expectedly, V1 (primary visual cortex) was equally involved, and there was also significant activation in V2 and V3. These findings suggest that areas other than V4 play an important role in colour constancy.

There is a final point. We should not regard colour processing as being entirely separate from other kinds of object processing. For example, colour can influence perceived shape. Imagine looking at a garden fairly late on a sunny day with strong shadows cast by the trees. It is easier to work out object boundaries (e.g., of the lawn) by using differences in colour or chromaticity than in luminance. Kingdom (2003) found that gratings that look almost flat can be made to look corrugated in depth by the addition of appropriate colour.

Evaluation

Colour constancy is a complex achievement, and observers often fall well short of complete constancy. In view of its complexity, it is unsurprising that the visual system adopts an "all hands on deck" approach in which many factors make a contribution. The most important factors are those relating to the visual environment, especially context (local contrast, global contrast). Of special importance are cone-excitation ratios that remain almost invariant across changes in illumination. In addition, top-down factors such as our knowledge and memory of the familiar colour of common objects also play a role. Our understanding of the brain mechanisms underlying colour constancy has been enhanced by the discovery of cells in V4 responding to colour constancy.

What are the limitations of research on colour constancy? First, we lack a comprehen-

sive theory of how the various factors combine to produce colour constancy. Second, there is much to be discovered about the brain mechanisms involved in colour perception and colour constancy. For example, we do not have a clear understanding of why the cone types in the eye are distributed fairly randomly rather than systematically. Third, there is evidence (e.g., Reeves et al., 2008) indicating that the extent to which we show colour constancy depends greatly on the precise instructions used. Little is known of the factors producing these large differences.

PERCEPTION WITHOUT AWARENESS

It is tempting to assume that visual perception is a conscious process. However, that is not always the case. For example, there are patients with severe damage to VI (primary visual cortex) who suffer from **blindsight**. Such patients can respond appropriately to visual stimuli in the absence of conscious visual experience. After we have considered blindsight patients, we will discuss evidence from healthy individuals relating to **unconscious perception** or **subliminal perception** (perception occurring below the level of conscious awareness).

Blindsight

Numerous British soldiers in the First World War who had received head wounds were treated by an Army doctor called George Riddoch. He found something fascinating in many of those

---

KEY TERMS

blindsight: the ability to respond appropriately to visual stimuli in the absence of conscious vision in patients with damage to the primary visual cortex.

unconscious perception: perceptual processes occurring below the level of conscious awareness.

subliminal perception: processing that occurs in the absence of conscious awareness.

with injuries to the primary visual cortex (BA 17) at the back of the occipital area of the brain (see Figure 1.3). This area is involved in the early stages of visual processing, so it was unsurprising that these patients had a loss of perception in parts of the visual field. Much more surprising was that they responded to motion in those parts of the visual field in which they claimed to be blind (Riddoch, 1917)! Such patients are said to suffer from blindsight, which neatly captures the apparently paradoxical nature of their condition.

Blindsight patients typically have extensive damage to V1. However, their loss of visual awareness in the blind field is probably *not* due directly to the V1 damage. Damage to V1 has knock-on effects throughout the visual system, leading to greatly reduced activation of subsequent visual processing areas (Silvanto, 2008).

There are at least ten pathways from the eye to the brain, many of which can be used by blindsight patients (Cowey, 2004). It appears that cortical mechanisms are not essential. Köhler and Moscovitch (1997) found that blindsight patients who had had an entire cortical hemisphere removed nevertheless showed evidence of blindsight for stimulus detection, stimulus localisation, form discrimination, and motion detection for stimuli presented to their removed hemisphere. However, those having a cortical visual system (apart from primary visual cortex) can perform more perceptual tasks than those lacking a cerebral hemisphere (Stoerig & Cowey, 1997). There is evidence that blindsight patients can often make use of a tract linking the lateral geniculate nucleus to the ipsilateral (same side of the body) human visual motion area V5/MT that bypasses V1.

Blindsight patients vary in their residual visual abilities. Danckert and Rossetti (2005) identified three sub-types:

(1) *Action-blindsight*: these patients have some ability to grasp or point at objects in the blind field because they can make some use of the dorsal stream of processing. Baseler, Morland, and Wandell (1999) found that GY showed activation in the dorsal stream (but not the ventral stream) to visual stimuli presented in the blind field. This is the most studied sub-type.

(2) *Attention-blindsight*: these patients can detect objects and motion and have a vague conscious feeling of objects in spite of reporting that they cannot see them. They can make some use of the dorsal stream and the motion area (MT). Danckert et al. (2003) found that an intact posterior parietal cortex in the dorsal stream was essential for showing action-blindsight.

(3) *Agnosopsia*: these patients deny any conscious awareness of visual stimuli. However, they exhibit some ability to discriminate form and wavelength and to use the ventral stream.

The phenomenon of blindsight becomes somewhat less paradoxical if we consider how it is assessed in more detail. There are generally two measures. First, there are patients' subjective reports that they cannot see some stimulus presented to their blind region. Second, there is a forced-choice test in which patients guess (e.g., stimulus present or absent?) or point at the stimulus they cannot see. Blindsight is defined by an absence of self-reported visual perception accompanied by above-chance performance on the forced-choice test. Note that the two measures are very different from each other. Note also that we could try to account for blindsight by assuming that subjective reports provide a less sensitive measure of visual perception than does a forced-choice test. This is an issue to which we will return.

There is one final point. As Cowey (2004, p. 588) pointed out, "The impression is sometimes given, however unwittingly, that blindsight . . . (is) like normal vision stripped of conscious visual experience. Nothing could be further from the truth, for blindsight is characterised by severely impoverished discrimination of visual stimuli."

Evidence
The most thoroughly studied blindsight patient is DB. He underwent surgical removal of the

right occipital cortex including most of the primary visual cortex. He showed some perceptual skills, including an ability to detect whether a visual stimulus had been presented to the blind area and to identify its location. However, he reported no conscious experience in his blind field. According to Weiskrantz, Warrington, Sanders, and Marshall (1974, p. 721), "When he was shown a video film of his reaching and judging orientation of lines (by presenting it to his intact visual field), he was openly astonished."

Suppose you fixate on a red square for several seconds, after which you look away at a white surface. The surface will appear to have the complementary colour (i.e., green). This is a negative after-effect (discussed earlier in the chapter). Weiskrantz (2002) found to his considerable surprise that DB showed this negative after-effect. This is surprising, because there was conscious perception of the after-image but not of the stimulus responsible for producing the afterimage! DB showed other afterimages found in healthy individuals. For example, he reported an apparent increase in the size of visual afterimages when viewed against a nearby surface and then against a surface further away (**Emmert's law**). Thus, DB's perceptual processing is more varied and thorough than previously believed.

Impressive findings were reported by de Gelder, Vroeman, and Pourtois (2001), who discovered GY could discriminate whether an unseen face had a happy or a fearful expression. He was probably responding to some distinctive facial feature (e.g., fearful faces have wide-open eyes), since it is improbable that he processed the subtleties of facial expression. The ability of blindsight patients to distinguish among emotional expressions in the absence of visual awareness is known as affective blindsight (see Chapter 15).

It would be useful to study the perceptual abilities of blindsight patients *without* relying on their subjective (and possibly inaccurate) reports of what they can see in the blind field. This was done by Rafal, Smith, Krantz, Cohen, and Brennan (1990). Blindsight patients performed at chance level when trying to detect a light presented to the blind area of the visual field. However, the time they took to direct their eyes at a light presented to the *intact* part of the visual field increased when a light was presented to the blind area at the same time. Thus, blindsight patients processed the light in the blind area even though they showed no evidence of detecting it when deciding whether it was present or absent.

One of the central issues is whether blindsight patients genuinely lack conscious visual perception. Some blindsight patients may have residual vision, claiming that they are aware that *something* is happening even though they cannot see anything. Weiskrantz (e.g., 2004) used the term blindsight Type 1 (similar to Danckert and Rossetti's, 2005, agnosopsia) to describe patients with no conscious awareness. He used the term blindsight Type 2 (similar to attention-blindsight) to describe those with awareness that something was happening. An example of Type 2 blindsight was found in patient EY, who "sensed a definite pinpoint of light", although "it does not actually look like a light. It looks like nothing at all" (Weiskrantz, 1980). Type 2 blindsight sounds suspiciously like residual conscious vision. However, patients who have been tested many times may start to rely on indirect evidence (Cowey, 2004). For example, the performance of patients with some ability to guess whether a stimulus is moving to the left or the right may depend on some vague awareness of their own eye movements.

Evidence that blindsight can be very unlike normal conscious vision was reported by Persaud and Cowey (2008). The blindsight patient GY was presented with a stimulus in the upper or lower part of his visual field. On some trials (inclusion trials), he was instructed to report the part of the visual field to which the stimulus had been presented. On other

> ### KEY TERM
>
> **Emmert's law:** the size of an afterimage appears larger when viewed against a far surface than when viewed against a near one.

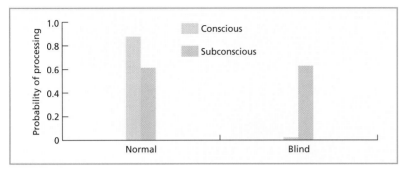

Figure 2.17 Estimated contributions of conscious and subconscious processing to GY's performance in exclusion and inclusion conditions in his normal and blind fields. Reprinted from Persaud and Cowey (2008), Copyright © 2008, with permission from Elsevier.

trials (exclusion trials), GY was told to report the opposite of its actual location (e.g., "Up" when it was in the lower part). GY tended to respond with the *real* rather than the *opposite* location on exclusion trials as well as inclusion trials when the stimulus was presented to his blind field. This suggests that he had access to location information but lacked any conscious awareness of that information. In contrast, GY showed a large difference in performance on inclusion and exclusion trials when the stimulus was presented to his normal or intact field, indicating he had conscious access to location information. Persaud and Cowey used the findings from inclusion and exclusion trials to conclude that conscious processes were involved when stimuli were presented to GY's normal field but not to his blind field (see Figure 2.17).

Overgaard et al. (2008) pointed out that researchers often ask blindsight patients to indicate on a yes/no basis whether they have seen a given stimulus. That opens up the possibility that blindsight patients have some conscious vision but simply set a high threshold for reporting awareness. Overgaard et al. used a four-point scale of perceptual awareness: "clear image", "almost clear image", "weak glimpse", and "not seen". Their blindsight patient, GR, was given a visual discrimination task (deciding whether a triangle, circle, or square had been presented). There was a strong association between the level of perceptual awareness and the accuracy of her performance when stimuli were presented to her blind field. She was correct 100% of the time when she had a clear image, 72% of the time when her

image was almost clear, 25% of the time when she had a weak glimpse, and 0% when the stimulus was not seen. Thus, the use of a sensitive method to assess conscious awareness suggests that degraded conscious vision sometimes underlies blindsight patients' ability to perform at above-chance levels on visual tasks.

Evaluation

There are various reasons for accepting blindsight as a genuine phenomenon. First, there are studies indicating blindsight in which potential problems with the use of subjective (and possibly distorted) verbal reports have apparently been overcome (e.g., Persaud & Cowey, 2008). Second, there are studies in which evidence for blindsight did not depend on subjective verbal reports (e.g., Rafal et al., 1990). Third, there are functional neuroimaging studies showing that many blindsight patients have activation predominantly or exclusively in the dorsal stream (see Danckert & Rossetti, 2005, for a review). This is important evidence because conscious visual perception is primarily associated with activation in the ventral stream (Norman, 2002).

What are the problems with research on blindsight? First, there are considerable differences among blindsight patients, which led Danckert and Rossetti (2005) to identify three subtypes. As a result, it is hard to draw any general conclusions.

Second, there is evidence (e.g., Danckert & Rossetti, 2005; Overgaard, Fehl, Mouridsen, Bergholt, & Cleermans, 2008; Weiskrantz, 2004) that a few blindsight patients possess some conscious visual awareness in their allegedly

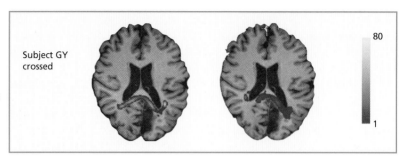

Figure 2.18 Contralateral tracts connecting the left geniculate lateral geniculate (GLN) to the right visual motion area (MT+/V5 and the right GLN to the left MT+/V5; this is absent in healthy individuals. From Bridge et al. (2008) by permission of Oxford University Press.

blind field. It is doubtful whether such patients fulfil all the criteria for blindsight.

Third, consider one of the most-studied blindsight patients, GY, whose left V1 was destroyed. He has a tract connecting the undamaged right lateral geniculate nucleus to the *contralateral* (opposite side of the body) visual motion area V5/MT (Bridge, Thomas, Jbabdi, & Cowey, 2008) (see Figure 2.18). This tract is *not* present in healthy individuals. The implication is that some visual processes in blindsight patients may be specific to them and so we cannot generalise from such patients to healthy individuals.

Fourth, Campion, Latto, and Smith (1983) argued that stray light may fall into the intact visual field of blindsight patients. As a result, their ability to show above-chance performance on various detection tasks could reflect processing within the intact visual field. However, blindsight is still observed when attempts are made to prevent stray light affecting performance (see Cowey, 2004). If blindsight patients are actually processing within the intact visual field, it is unclear why they lack conscious awareness of such processing.

Unconscious perception

In 1957, a struggling market researcher called James Vicary reported powerful evidence for unconscious perception. He claimed to have flashed the words EAT POPCORN and DRINK COCA-COLA for 1/300th of a second (well below the threshold of conscious awareness) numerous times during showings of a film called *Picnic* at a cinema in Fort Lee, New Jersey.

This caused an increase of 18% in the cinema sales of Coca-Cola and a 58% increase in popcorn sales. Alas, Vicary admitted in 1962 that the study was a fabrication. In addition, Trappery (1996) reported in a meta-analysis that stimuli presented below the conscious threshold had practically no effect on consumer behaviour.

In spite of early negative findings, many researchers have carried out studies to demonstrate the existence of unconscious perception. There are three main ways in which they present visual stimuli below the level of conscious awareness. First, the stimuli can be very weak or faint. Second, the stimuli can be presented very briefly. Third, the target stimulus can be immediately followed by a masking stimulus (one that serves to inhibit processing of the target stimulus).

How can we decide whether an observer has consciously perceived certain visual stimuli? According to Merikle, Smilek, and Eastwood (2001), there are two main thresholds or criteria:

(1) *Subjective threshold*: this is defined by an individual's failure to report conscious awareness of a stimulus.
(2) *Objective threshold*: this is defined by an individual's inability to make accurate forced-choice decisions about a stimulus (e.g., guess at above-chance level whether it is a word or not).

Two issues arise with these threshold measures. First, as Reingold (2004, p. 882) pointed out, "A valid measure must index *all* of the perceptual information available for consciousness . . . and *only* conscious, but not unconscious information." That is a tall order. Second, it is hard to show that either measure indicates zero conscious awareness given the difficulty (or impossibility) of proving the null hypothesis.

In practice, observers often show "awareness" of a stimulus assessed by the objective threshold even when the stimulus does not exceed the subjective threshold. The objective threshold may seem unduly stringent. However, many psychologists argue that it is more valid than a reliance on people's possibly inaccurate or biased reports of their conscious experience.

Evidence

Naccache, Blandin, and Dehaene (2002) carried out various experiments in which participants decided rapidly whether a clearly visible target digit was smaller or larger than 5. Unknown to them, an invisible, masked digit was resented for 29 ms immediately before the target. The masked digit was congruent with the target (both digits on the same side of 5) or incongruent. In one experiment (Experiment 2), a cue signalling the imminent presentation of the target digit was either present or absent.

Naccache et al. (2002) reported three main findings. First, there was no evidence of conscious perception of the masked digits: no participants reported seeing any of them (subjective measure) and their performance when guessing whether the masked digit was below or above 5 was at chance level (objective measure). Second, performance with the target digits was faster on congruent than on incongruent trials when cueing was present, indicating that some unconscious perceptual processing of the masked digits had occurred. Third, this congruency effect disappeared when there was no cueing, indicating that attention was necessary for unconscious perception to occur.

It is generally assumed that information perceived with awareness can be used to control our actions, whereas information perceived without awareness cannot. If so, there should be situations in which perceiving with or without awareness has very different effects on behaviour. Supporting evidence was reported by Persaud and McLeod (2008). They presented the letter "b" or "h" for 10 ms (short interval) or 15 ms (long interval). In the key condition, participants were instructed to respond with the letter that had *not* been presented. The rationale for doing this was that participants who were consciously aware of the letter would be able to inhibit saying the letter actually presented. In contrast, those who were not consciously aware of it would be unable to inhibit saying the presented letter.

What did Persaud and McLeod (2008) find? With the longer presentation interval, participants responded correctly with the non-presented letter on 83% of trials. This suggests that there was some conscious awareness of the stimulus in that condition. With the shorter presentation interval, participants responded correctly on only 43% of trials, which was significantly below chance. This finding indicates there was some processing of the stimulus. However, the below-chance performance strongly suggests that participants lacked conscious awareness of that processing.

The above conclusion was supported in a further similar experiment by Persaud and McLeod (2008). The main difference was that participants had to decide whether to wager £1 or £2 on the correctness of each of their responses. With the shorter presentation interval, participants wagered the smaller amount on 90% of trials on which their response was correct (i.e., saying the letter not presented). Presumably they would have wagered the larger amount if they had had conscious awareness of the stimulus that had been presented.

Dehaene et al. (2001) used fMRI and event-related potentials (ERPs; see Glossary) to identify brain areas active during the processing of masked words that were not consciously perceived and unmasked words that were consciously perceived. In one condition, a masked word was followed by an unmasked presentation of the same word. There were two main findings. First, there was detectable brain activity when masked words were presented. However, it was much less than when unmasked words were presented, especially in prefrontal and parietal areas. Second, the amount of brain activity produced by presentation of an unmasked word was reduced when preceded by the same word presented masked. This repetition suppression effect suggests that some of the processing typically found when a word is presented occurs even when it is presented below the conscious threshold.

Findings consistent with those of Dehaene et al. (2001) were reported by Melloni et al. (2007; see Chapter 16). They used EEG (see Glossary) to compare brain activity associated with the processing of consciously perceived words and those not consciously perceived. Only the former were associated with synchronised neural activity involving several brain areas including prefrontal cortex. However, and most importantly in the present context, even words not consciously perceived were associated with sufficient EEG activation to produce reasonably thorough processing. Additional research on brain activation associated with subliminal perception is discussed in Chapter 16.

Snodgrass, Bernat, and Shevrin (2004) carried out meta-analyses involving nine studies on unconscious perception. In their first meta-analysis, there was no significant evidence of above-chance performance on measures of conscious perception. However, in their second meta-analysis, there was very highly significant evidence of above-chance performance on objective measures designed to assess unconscious perception.

Evaluation

The entire notion of unconscious or subliminal perception used to be regarded as very controversial. However, there is now reasonable evidence for its existence. Some of the evidence is behavioural (e.g., Naccache et al., 2002; Persaud & McLeod, 2008). Recently, there has been a substantial increase in functional neuro-imaging evidence (e.g., Dehaene et al., 2001; see Chapter 16). This evidence indicates that there can be substantial processing of visual stimuli up to and including the semantic level in the absence of conscious visual awareness. The findings on unconscious or subliminal

perception in healthy individuals taken in conjunction with the findings on blindsight patients discussed earlier clearly suggest that considerable visual processing can occur in the absence of conscious awareness.

The main task for the future is to develop detailed theoretical accounts of unconscious perception. Erdelyi (1974) argued that we should think of perception as involving multiple processing stages or mechanisms with consciousness possibly representing the final stage of processing. Thus, a stimulus can receive sufficient perceptual processing to influence at least some aspects of behaviour without conscious perceptual experience. Other theoretical ideas have emerged in the cognitive neuroscience area (see Chapter 16).

DEPTH AND SIZE PERCEPTION

A major accomplishment of visual perception is the transformation of the two-dimensional retinal image into perception of a three-dimensional world seen in depth. There are more than a dozen cues to visual depth, with a cue being defined as "any sensory information that gives rise to a sensory estimate" (Ernst & Bülthoff, 2004, p. 163). All cues provide ambiguous information (Jacobs, 2002). In addition, different cues often provide conflicting information. For example, when you watch a film at the cinema or on television, some cues (e.g., stereo ones) indicate that everything you see is at the same distance from you, whereas other cues (e.g., perspective, shading) indicate that some objects are closer to you than others.

In real life, cues to depth are often provided by movement of the observer or objects in the visual environment. Some of the cues we use are not visual (e.g., based on touch or on hearing). However, the major focus here will be on visual depth cues available even if the observer and environmental objects are static. These cues can conveniently be divided into monocular, binocular, and oculomotor cues. **Monocular**

cues are those requiring only the use of one eye, although they can be used readily when someone has both eyes open. Such cues clearly exist, because the world still retains a sense of depth with one eye closed. **Binocular cues** are those involving both eyes being used together. Finally, **oculomotor cues** are kinaesthetic, depending on sensations of muscular contraction of the muscles around the eye.

Monocular cues

Monocular cues to depth are sometimes called *pictorial cues*, because they are used by artists trying to create the impression of three-dimensional scenes while painting on two-dimensional canvases. One such cue is *linear perspective*. Parallel lines pointing directly away from us seem progressively closer together as they recede into the distance (e.g., the edges of a motorway). This convergence of lines creates a powerful impression of depth in a two-dimensional drawing.

Another cue related to perspective is aerial perspective. Light is scattered as it travels through the atmosphere (especially if it is dusty), making more distant objects lose contrast and seem hazy. O'Shea, Blackburn, and Ono (1994) mimicked the effects of aerial perspective by reducing the contrast of features within a picture. This led those features to appear more distant.

Another monocular cue is *texture*. Most objects (e.g., carpets, cobble-stoned roads) possess texture, and textured objects slanting away from us have a texture gradient (Gibson, 1979; see Figure 2.19). This is a gradient (rate of change) of texture density as you look from the front to the back of a slanting object. If you were unwise enough to stand between the rails of a railway track and look along it, the details would become less clear as you looked into the distance. In addition, the distance between the connections would appear to reduce. Sinai, Ooi, and He (1998) found that observers were good at judging the distance of objects within seven metres of them when the ground in-between was uniformly textured.

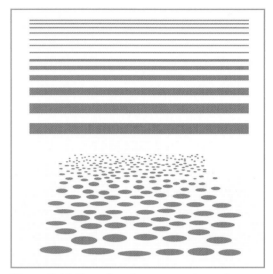

Figure 2.19 Examples of texture gradients that can be perceived as surfaces receding into the distance. From Bruce et al. (2003).

However, distances were systematically overestimated when there was a gap (e.g., a ditch) in the texture pattern.

A further cue is *interposition*, in which a nearer object hides part of a more distant one from view. The strength of this cue can be seen in Kanizsa's (1976) illusory square (see Figure 2.20). There is a strong impression of a yellow square in front of four purple circles even though many of the contours of the yellow square are missing.

Shading provides another monocular cue to depth. Flat, two-dimensional surfaces do not cast shadows, and so the presence of shading indicates the presence of a three-dimensional

---

KEY TERMS

monocular cues: cues to depth that can be used with one eye, but can also be used with both eyes.
binocular cues: cues to depth that require both eyes to be used together.
oculomotor cues: kinaesthetic cues to depth produced by muscular contraction of the muscles around the eye.

Figure 2.20 Kanizsa's (1976) illusory square.

object. Ramachandran (1988) presented observers with a visual display consisting of numerous very similar shaded circular patches, some illuminated by one light source and the remainder illuminated by a different light source. The observers incorrectly assumed that the visual display was lit by a single light source above the display. This led them to assign different depths to different parts of the display (i.e., some "dents" were misperceived as bumps).

Another useful monocular cue is *familiar size*. If we know the actual size of an object, we can use its retinal image size to provide an accurate estimate of its distance. However, we can be misled if an object is *not* in its familiar size. Ittelson (1951) had observers look at playing cards through a peephole restricting them to monocular vision and largely eliminated depth cues other than familiar size. There were three playing cards (normal size, half size, and double size) presented one at a time at a distance of 2.28 metres. The actual judged distances were determined almost entirely by familiar size – the half-size card was seen as 4.56 metres away and the double-size card as 1.38 metres away.

The final monocular cue we will discuss is **motion parallax**. This refers to the movement of an object's image over the retina due to

movement of the observer's head, with that movement being greater for the closer of two objects. If you look into the far distance through the windows of a moving train, the apparent speed of objects passing by seems faster the nearer they are to you. Rogers and Graham (1979) found that motion parallax can generate depth information in the absence of all other cues. Observers looked with only one eye at a display containing about 2000 random dots. When there was relative motion of part of the display (motion parallax) to simulate the movement produced by a three-dimensional surface, observers reported a three-dimensional surface standing out in depth from its surroundings.

Oculomotor and binocular cues

The pictorial cues we have discussed could all be used as well by one-eyed people as by those with normal vision. Depth perception also depends on oculomotor cues based on perceiving contractions of the muscles around the eyes. One such cue is **convergence**, which refers to the fact that the eyes turn inwards more to focus on a very close object than one farther away. Another oculomotor cue is **accommodation**. It refers to the variation in optical power produced by a thickening of the lens of the eye when focusing on a close object. Each of these cues only produces a single value in any situation. That means it can only provide information about the distance of one object at a time.

If you look into the distance through the windows of a moving train, distant objects seem to move in the same direction as the train whereas nearby ones apparently move in the opposite direction. This is motion parallax.

Depth perception also depends on binocular cues that are only available when both eyes are used. **Stereopsis** involves binocular cues. It is based on **binocular disparity**, which is the difference or disparity in the images projected on the retinas of the two eyes when you view a scene. Convergence, accommodation, and stereopsis are only effective in facilitating depth perception over relatively short distances. The usefulness of convergence as a cue to distance has been disputed. However, it is clearly of no use at distances greater than a few metres, and negative findings have been reported when real objects are used (Wade & Swanston, 2001). Accommodation is also of limited use. Its potential value as a depth cue is limited to the region of space immediately in front of you. However, distance judgements based on accommodation are fairly inaccurate even with nearby objects (Künnapas, 1968). With respect to stereopsis, the disparity or discrepancy in the retinal images of an object decreases by a factor of 100 as its distance increases from 2 to 20 metres (Bruce et al., 2003). Thus, stereopsis rapidly becomes less effective at greater distances.

It has sometimes been assumed that stereoscopic information is available early in visual perception and is of use in object recognition. However, contrary evidence was reported by Bülthoff, Bülthoff, and Sinha (1998). Observers' recognition of familiar objects was *not* adversely affected when stereoscopic information was scrambled and thus incongruous. Indeed, the observers seemed unaware the depth information was scrambled! What seemed to happen was that observers' expectations about the structure of familiar objects were more important than the misleading stereoscopic information.

A key process in stereopsis is to match features in the input presented to the two eyes. Sometimes we make mistakes in doing this, which can lead to various visual illusions. For example, suppose you spend some time staring at wallpaper having a regular pattern. You may find that parts of the wallpaper pattern seem

KEY TERMS

stereopsis: one of the binocular cues; it is based on the small discrepancy in the retinal images in each eye when viewing a visual scene (**binocular disparity**).
binocular disparity: the slight discrepancy in the retinal images of a visual scene in each eye; it forms the basis for **stereopsis**.

to float in front of the wall – this is the **wall-paper illusion**.

Something similar occurs with the auto-stereograms found in the Magic Eye books. An **autostereogram** is a two-dimensional image containing depth information so that it appears three-dimensional when viewed appropriately (you can see an autostereogram of a shark if you access the *Wikipedia* entry for autostereo-gram). What happens with autostereograms is that repeating two-dimensional patterns are presented to each eye. If you do not match the patterns correctly, then two adjacent patterns will form an object that appears to be at a different depth from the background. If you only glance at an autostereogram, all you can see is a two-dimensional pattern. However, if you stare at it and strive *not* to bring it into focus, you can (sooner or later) see a three-dimensional image. Many people still have problems in seeing the three-dimensional image – what often helps is to hold the autostereo-gram very close to your face and then move it very slowly away while preventing it from coming into focus.

Studies of the brain have indicated that most regions of the visual cortex contain neurons responding strongly to binocular disparity. This suggests that the dorsal and ventral processing streams are both involved in stereopsis. Their respective roles have recently been clarified after a period of some controversy (Parker, 2007). We start by distinguishing between absolute disparity and relative disparity. Absolute disparity is based on the differences in the images of a *single* object presented to both eyes. In contrast, relative disparity is based on differences in the absolute disparities of *two* objects. It allows us to assess the spatial relationship between the two objects in three-dimensional space.

The dorsal and ventral streams both process absolute and relative disparity. However, there is incomplete processing of relative disparity in the dorsal stream, but it is sufficient to assist in navigation. In contrast, there is more complete processing of relative disparity in the ventral stream. This processing is of great importance in analysing the shape and curvature of three-dimensional objects. In general terms, processing of disparity information is relatively basic in the dorsal stream and more sophisticated in the ventral stream.

Integrating cue information

Most of the time we have access to several depth cues. This raises the question of how we *combine* these different sources of information to make judgements about depth or distance. Two possibilities are additivity (adding together information from all cues) and selection (only using information from a single cue) (Bruno and Cutting, 1988). In fact, cues are sometimes combined in more complex ways.

Jacobs (2002) argued that, when we combine information from multiple visual cues, we assign more weight to *reliable* cues than to *unreliable* ones. Since cues that are reliable in one context may be less so in another context, we need to be *flexible* in our assessments of cue reliability. These notions led Jacobs to propose two hypotheses:

(1) Less ambiguous cues (e.g., ones that provide consistent information) are regarded as more reliable than more ambiguous ones. For example, binocular disparity provides inconsistent information because its value is much less for distant objects than for close ones.
(2) A cue is regarded as reliable if inferences based on it are consistent with those based on other available cues.

KEY TERMS

wallpaper illusion: a visual illusion in which staring at patterned wallpaper makes it seem as if parts of the pattern are floating in front of the wall.

autostereogram: a complex two-dimensional image that is perceived as three-dimensional when it is *not* focused on for a period of time.

Experimentation in this area has benefited from advances in virtual reality technologies. These advances permit researchers to control visual cues very precisely and to provide observers with virtual environments that could not exist in the real world.

Evidence

Bruno and Cutting (1988) studied relative distance in studies in which three untextured parallel flat surfaces were arranged in depth. Observers viewed the displays monocularly, and there were four sources of depth information: relative size; height in the projection plane; interposition; and motion parallax. The findings supported the additivity notion.

Bruno and Cutting (1988) did not study what happens when two or more cues provide *conflicting* information about depth. In such circumstances, observers sometimes use the selection strategy and ignore some of the available depth cues. For example, consider the "hollow face" illusion (Gregory, 1973), in which stereoscopic information is ignored (discussed earlier in the chapter). When a hollow mask of a face is viewed from a few feet away, it is perceived as a normal face because of our familiarity with such faces.

A common situation in which we experience a substantial conflict among cues is at the movies. We use the selection strategy: perspective and texture cues are used, whereas we ignore the binocular disparity and motion parallax cues indicating that everything we can see is the same distance from us.

Evidence supporting Jacobs' (2002) first hypothesis was reported by Triesch, Ballard, and Jacobs (2002). They used a virtual reality situation in which observers tracked an object defined by the visual attributes of colour, shape, and size. On each trial, two of these attributes were unreliable (their values changed frequently). The observers attached increasing weight to the reliable cue and less to the unreliable cues during the course of each trial.

Evidence supporting Jacobs' (2002) second hypothesis was reported by Atkins, Fiser, and Jacobs (2001). They used a virtual reality environment in which observers viewed and grasped elliptical cylinders. There were three cues to cylinder depth: texture, motion, and **haptic** (relating to the sense of touch). When the haptic and texture cues indicated the same cylinder depth but the motion cue indicated a different depth, observers made increasing use of the texture cue and decreasing use of the motion cue. When the haptic and motion cues indicated the same cylinder depth but the texture cue did not, observers increasingly relied on the motion cue and tended to disregard the texture cue. Thus, whichever visual cue correlated with the haptic cue was preferred, and this preference increased with practice.

Where in the brain is information about different depth cues integrated? Tsutsui, Taira, and Sakata (2005) considered this issue. They discussed much research suggesting that integration occurs in the caudal intraparietal sulcus. More specifically, they argued that this is the brain area in which a three-dimensional representation of objects is formed on the basis of information from several depth cues.

Conclusions

Information from different depth cues is typically combined to produce accurate depth perception, and this often happens in an additive fashion. However, there are several situations (especially those in which different cues conflict strongly with each other) in which one cue is dominant over others. This makes sense. If, for example, one cue suggests an object is 10 metres away and another cue suggests it is 90 metres away, splitting the difference and deciding it is 50 metres away is unlikely to be correct! However, such situations are probably much more likely to occur in the virtual environments created by scientists than in the real world.

There is much support for Jacobs' (2002) view that we attach more weight to cues that provide reliable information and that provide

---

KEY TERM

haptic: relating to the sense of touch.

information consistent with that provided by other cues. There is also good support for his contention that the weight we attach to any given cue is flexible – we sometimes learn that a cue that was reliable in the past is no longer so. More remains to be discovered about the ways in which we combine and integrate information from different cues in depth perception.

Size constancy

Size constancy is the tendency for any given object to appear the same size whether its size in the retinal image is large or small. For example, if someone walks towards you, their retinal image increases progressively but their size seems to remain the same.

Why do we show size constancy? Many factors are involved. However, an object's apparent distance is especially important when judging its size. For example, an object may be judged to be large even though its retinal image is very small if it is a long way away. The reason why size constancy is often not shown when we look at objects on the ground from the top of a tall building may be because it is hard to judge distance accurately. These ideas were incorporated into the size–distance invariance hypothesis (Kilpatrick & Ittelson, 1953). According to this hypothesis, for a given size of retinal image, the perceived size of an object is proportional to its perceived distance. As we will see, this hypothesis is more applicable to unfamiliar objects than to familiar ones.

Evidence

Findings consistent with the size–distance invariance hypothesis were reported by Holway and Boring (1941). Observers sat at the intersection of two hallways. A test circle was presented in one hallway and a comparison circle in the other. The test circle could be of various sizes and at various distances, and the observers' task was to adjust the comparison circle to make it the same size as the test circle. Their performance was very good when depth cues were available. However, it became poor when depth cues were removed by placing curtains in the hallway and requiring observers to look through a peephole. Lichten and Lurie (1950) removed all depth cues, and found that observers relied totally on retinal image size in their judgements of object size.

If size judgements depend on perceived distance, then size constancy should not be found when the perceived distance of an object differs considerably from its actual distance. The Ames room provides a good example (Ames, 1952; see Figure 2.21). It has a peculiar shape: the floor slopes and the rear wall is not at right angles to the adjoining walls. In spite of this, the Ames room creates the same retinal image as a normal rectangular room when viewed through a peephole. The fact that one end of the rear wall is much farther from the viewer is disguised by making it much higher. The cues suggesting that the rear wall is at right angles to the viewer are so strong that observers mistakenly assume that two adults standing in the corners by the rear wall are at the same distance from them. This leads them to estimate the size of the nearer adult as much greater than that of the adult who is farther away.

The illusion effect with the Ames room is so great than an individual walking backwards and forwards in front of the rear wall seems to grow and shrink as he/she moves! Thus, perceived distance seems to drive perceived size. However, observers are more likely to realise what is going on if the individual is someone they know very well. There is an anecdote about a researcher's wife who arrived at the laboratory to find him inside the Ames room. She immediately said, "Gee, honey, that room's distorted!" (Ian Gordon, personal communication).

Similar (but more dramatic) findings were reported by Glennerster, Tcheang, Gilson, Fitzgibbon, and Parker (2006). Participants

---

KEY TERM

size constancy: objects are perceived to have a given size regardless of the size of the retinal image.

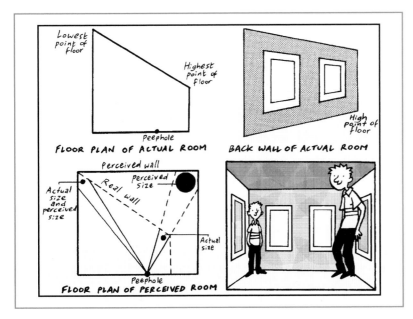

Figure 2.21 The Ames room.

walked through a virtual-reality room as it expanded or contracted considerably. Even though they had considerable information from motion parallax and motion to indicate that the room's size was changing, no participants noticed the changes! There were large errors in participants' judgements of the sizes of objects at longer distances. The powerful expectation that the size of the room would not alter caused the perceived distance of the objects to be very inaccurate.

Several factors not discussed so far influence size judgements. We will briefly discuss some of them, but bear in mind that we do not have a coherent theoretical account indicating *why* these factors are relevant. Higashiyama and Adachi (2006) persuaded observers to estimate the size of objects while standing normally or when viewed upside-down through their legs. There was less size constancy in the upside-down condition, so you are advised not to look at objects through your legs. Of relevance to the size–distance invariance hypothesis, perceived size in this condition did not correlate with perceived distance.

Luo et al. (2007) considered the effects of scene complexity, binocular disparity, and motion parallax on size constancy in a virtual environment. Scene complexity and binocular disparity both contributed to size constancy. However, motion parallax (whether produced by movement of the virtual environment or of the observer) did not.

Bertamini, Yang, and Proffitt (1998) argued that the horizon provides useful information because the line connecting the point of observation to the horizon is virtually parallel to the ground. For example, if your eyes are 1.5 metres above the ground, then an object appearing to be the same height as the horizon is 1.5 metres tall. Size judgements were most accurate when objects were at about eye level, whether observers were standing or sitting (Bertamini et al., 1998).

Haber and Levin (2001) argued that size perception of objects typically depends on *memory* of their familiar size rather than solely on perceptual information concerning their distance from the observer. They initially found that participants estimated the sizes of common objects with great accuracy purely on the basis

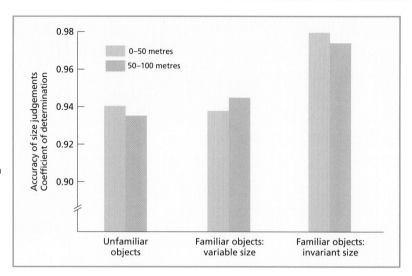

Figure 2.22 Accuracy of size judgements as a function of object type (unfamiliar; familiar variable size; familiar invariant size) and viewing distance (0–50 metres vs. 50–100 metres). Based on data in Haber and Levin (2001).

of memory. In another experiment, they presented observers with various objects at close viewing range (0–50 metres) or distant viewing range (50–100 metres) and asked them to make size judgements. The objects belonged to three categories: (1) those most invariant in size or height (e.g., tennis racquet, bicycle); (2) those varying in size (e.g., television set, Christmas tree); and (3) unfamiliar stimuli (e.g., ovals, triangles).

What findings would we expect? If familiar size is of major importance, then size judgements should be better for objects of invariant size than those of variable size, with size judgements worst for unfamiliar objects. What if distance perception is all-important? Distances are estimated more accurately for nearby objects than for more distant ones, so size judgements should be better for all categories of objects at close than at distant viewing range.

Haber and Levin's (2001) findings indicated the importance of familiar size to accuracy of size judgements (see Figure 2.21). However, we obviously cannot explain the fairly high accuracy of size judgements with unfamiliar objects in terms of familiar size. It can also be seen in Figure 2.22 that the viewing distance had practically no effect on size judgements.

Witt, Linkenauger, Bakdash, and Proffitt (2008) asked good golfers and not-so-good golfers to judge the size of the hole when putting. As you may have guessed, the better golfers perceived the hole to be larger. Witt et al. also found that golfers who had a short putt perceived the hole's size to be larger than golfers who had a long putt. They concluded that objects look larger when we have the ability to act effectively with respect to them. That would explain why the hole always looks remarkably small to the first author when he is playing a round of golf!

Evaluation
Size perception and size constancy depend mainly on perceived distance. Some of the strongest evidence for this comes from studies in which misperceptions of distance (e.g., in the Ames room) produce systematic distortions in perceived size. Several other factors, including the horizon, scene complexity, familiar size, and purposeful interactions, also contribute to size judgements.

What is lacking so far are comprehensive theories of size judgements. Little is known about the relative importance of the factors influencing size judgements or of the circumstances in which any given factor is more or less influential. In addition, we do not know how the various factors combine to produce size judgements.

CHAPTER SUMMARY

- Brain systems
  In the retina, there are cones (specialised for colour vision) and rods (specialised for movement detection). The main route between the eye and the cortex is the retina–geniculate–striate pathway, which is divided into partially separate P and M pathways. The dorsal pathway terminates in the parietal cortex and the ventral pathway terminates in the inferotemporal cortex. According to Zeki's functional specialisation theory, different parts of the cortex are specialised for different visual functions. This is supported by findings from patients with selective visual deficits (e.g., achromatopsia, akinetopsia), but there is much less specialisation than claimed by Zeki. One solution to the binding problem (integrating the distributed information about an object) is the synchrony hypothesis. According to this hypothesis, coherent visual perception requires synchronous activity in several brain areas. It is doubtful whether precise synchrony is achievable.

- Two visual systems: perception and action
  According to Milner and Goodale, there is a vision-for-perception system based on the ventral pathway and a vision-for-action system based on the dorsal pathway. Predicted double dissociations have been found between patients with optic ataxia (damage to the dorsal stream) and visual agnosia (damage to the ventral stream). Illusory effects found with visual illusions when perceptual judgements are made (ventral stream) are greatly reduced when grasping or pointing responses (dorsal stream) are used. Grasping or reaching for an object also involves the ventral stream when memory or planning is involved or the action is awkward. The two visual systems interact and combine with each more than is implied by Milner and Goodale.

- Colour vision
  Colour vision helps us to detect objects and to make fine discriminations among them. According to dual-process theory (based on previous research), there are three types of cone receptor and also three types of opponent processes (green–red, blue–yellow, and white–black). This theory explains the existence of negative afterimages and several kinds of colour deficiency. Colour constancy occurs when a surface seems to have the same colour when there is a change in the illuminant. A theory based on cone-excitation ratios provides an influential account of colour constancy. Chromatic adaptation and top-down factors (e.g., knowledge, familiarity of object colour) are also involved in colour constancy. Local contrast and global contrast are of particular importance, but reflected highlights from glossy objects and mutual reflections are additional factors. Cells in V4 demonstrate colour constancy.

- Perception without awareness
  Patients with extensive damage to V1 sometimes suffer from blindsight – they can respond to visual stimuli in the absence of conscious visual awareness. There are three subtypes: action-blindsight, attention-blindsight, and agnosopsia. The visual abilities of most blindsight patients seem to involve primarily the dorsal stream of processing. Subliminal perception can be assessed using a subjective threshold or a more stringent objective threshold. There is strong evidence for subliminal perception using both types of threshold. Functional neuroimaging studies indicate that extensive visual processing in the absence of conscious awareness is possible.

- Depth and size perception
  There are many monocular cues to depth (e.g., linear perspective, texture, familiar size), as well as oculomotor and binocular cues. Sometimes cues are combined in an additive fashion in depth perception. However, cues are often weighted, with more weight being attached to cues that provide consistent information and/or provide information that correlates highly with that provided by other cues. The weighting that any given cue receives changes if experience indicates that it has become more or less reliable as a source of information about depth. Size judgements depend mostly on perceived distance. However, several other factors (e.g., familiar size, purposeful interactions) are also important. As yet, the ways in which different factors combine to produce size judgements remain unknown.

FURTHER READING

- **Cowey, A.** (2004). Fact, artefact, and myth about blindsight. *Quarterly Journal of Experimental Psychology, 57A,* 577–609. This article by a leading researcher on blindsight gives a balanced and comprehensive account of that condition.
- **Goldstein, E.B.** (2007). *Sensation and perception* (7th ed.). Belmont, CA: Thomson. Most of the topics discussed in this chapter are covered in this American textbook.
- **Hegdé, J.** (2008). Time course of visual perception: Coarse-to-fine processing and beyond. *Progress in Neurobiology, 84,* 405–439. This article contains a very good overview of the main processes involved in visual perception.
- **Mather, G.** (2009). *Foundations of sensation and perception* (2nd ed.). Hove, UK: Psychology Press. George Mather provides good introductory coverage of some of the topics discussed in this chapter. For example, depth perception is covered in Chapter 10 of his book.
- **Milner, A.D., & Goodale, M.A.** (2008). Two visual systems re-viewed. *Neuropsychologia, 46,* 774–785. An updated version of the perception–action theory, together with relevant evidence, is presented in this article.
- **Shevell, S.K., & Kingdom, F.A.A.** (2008). Colour in complex scenes. *Annual Review of Psychology, 59,* 143–166. This article contains a good overview of our current understanding of the factors involved in colour perception.
- **Solomon, S.G., & Lennie, P.** (2007). The machinery of colour vision. *Nature Reviews Neuroscience, 8,* 276–286. This review article provides an up-to-date account of the neuroscience approach to colour processing and pinpoints limitations in earlier theories.

CHAPTER 3

OBJECT AND FACE RECOGNITION

INTRODUCTION

Tens of thousands of times every day we identify or recognise objects in the world around us. At this precise moment, you are aware that you are looking at a book (possibly with your eyes glazed over). If you raise your eyes, perhaps you can see a wall, windows, and so on in front of you. Object recognition typically occurs so effortlessly it is hard to believe it is actually a rather complex achievement. Here are some of the reasons why object recognition is complex:

(1) If you look around you, you will find many of the objects in the environment overlap. You have to decide where one object ends and the next one starts.

(2) We can nearly all recognise an object such as a chair without any apparent difficulty. However, chairs (and many other objects) vary enormously in their visual properties (e.g., colour, size, shape), and it is not immediately clear how we manage to assign such diverse stimuli to the same category.

(3) We recognise objects accurately over a wide range of viewing distances and orientations. For example, most plates are round but we can still identify a plate when it is seen from an angle and so appears elliptical. We are also confident that the ant-like creatures we can see from the window of a plane during our descent are actually people.

In spite of the above complexities, we can go beyond simply identifying objects in the visual environment. For example, we can generally describe what an object would look like if viewed from a different angle, and we also know its uses and functions. All in all, there is much more to object recognition than might initially be supposed (than meets the eye?).

What is covered in this chapter? The overarching theme is to unravel some of the mysteries involved in object recognition. We start by considering how we see which parts of the visual world belong together and thus form separate objects. This is a crucial early stage in object recognition. After that, we consider more general theories of object recognition. These theories are evaluated in the light of behavioural experiments, neuroimaging studies, and studies on brain-damaged patients. There is much evidence suggesting that face recognition (which is vitally important in our everyday lives) differs in important ways from ordinary object recognition. Accordingly, we discuss face recognition in a separate section. Finally, we address the issue of whether the processes involved in visual *imagery* of objects resemble those involved in visual *perception* of objects. Note that some other issues relating to object recognition (e.g., depth perception, size constancy) were discussed in Chapter 2.

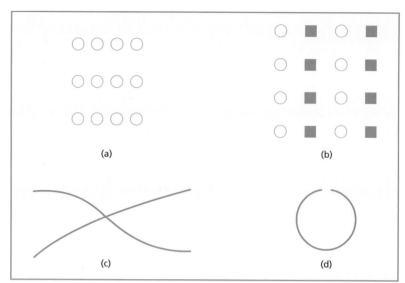

Figure 3.1 Examples of the Gestalt laws of perceptual organisation: (a) the law of proximity; (b) the law of similarity; (c) the law of good continuation; and (d) the law of closure.

PERCEPTUAL ORGANISATION

A basic issue in visual perception is **perceptual segregation**, which involves working out which parts of the presented visual information form separate objects. It seems reasonable to assume that perceptual segregation is completed before object recognition occurs. Thus, we work out *where* the object is before deciding *what* it is. In fact, that is an oversimplified view.

The first systematic attempt to study perceptual segregation (and the perceptual organisation to which it gives rise) was made by the Gestaltists. They were German psychologists (including Koffka, Köhler, and Wertheimer) who emigrated to the United States between the two world wars. Their fundamental principle was the law of Prägnanz: "Of several geometrically possible organisations that one will actually occur which possesses the best, simplest and most stable shape" (Koffka, 1935, p. 138).

Most of the Gestaltists' other laws can be subsumed under the law of Prägnanz. Figure 3.1a illustrates the law of proximity, according to which visual elements close in space tend to be grouped together. Figure 3.1b illustrates the

law of similarity, according to which similar elements tend to be grouped together. We see two crossing lines in Figure 3.1c because, according to the law of good continuation, we group together those elements requiring the fewest changes or interruptions in straight or smoothly curving lines. Figure 3.1d illustrates the law of closure: the missing parts of a figure are filled in to complete the figure (here, a circle). The Gestaltists claimed no learning is needed for us to use these various laws.

Evidence supporting the Gestalt approach was reported by Pomerantz (1981). Observers viewed four-item visual arrays and tried to identify rapidly the one different from the others. When the array was simple but could not easily be organised, it took an average of 1.9 seconds to perform the task. However, when the array was more complex but more

---

KEY TERM

perceptual segregation: human ability to work out accurately which parts of presented visual information belong together and thus form separate objects.

easily organised, it took only 0.75 seconds on average. This beneficial effect of organisation is known as the *configural superiority effect*.

Other Gestalt laws are discussed in Chapter 4. For example, there is the law of common fate, according to which visual elements moving together are grouped together. Johansson (1973) attached lights to the joints of an actor wearing dark clothes, and then filmed him moving around a dark room. Observers perceived a moving human figure when he walked around, although they could only see the lights.

The Gestaltists emphasised **figure–ground segregation** in perceptual organisation. One part of the visual field is identified as the figure, whereas the rest of the visual field is less important and so forms the ground. The Gestaltists claimed that the figure is perceived as having a distinct form or shape, whereas the ground lacks form. In addition, the figure is perceived as being in front of the ground, and the contour separating the figure from the ground belongs to the figure. Check the validity of these claims by looking at the faces–goblet illusion (see Figure 3.2). When the goblet is the figure, it seems to be in front of a dark background; in contrast, the faces are in front of a light background when forming the figure.

There is more attention to (and processing of) the figure than of the ground. Weisstein and Wong (1986) flashed vertical lines and slightly tilted lines onto the faces–goblet illusion, and gave observers the task of deciding whether the line was vertical. Performance on this task was three times better when the line was presented to what the observers perceived as the figure than the ground. In addition, processing of the ground representation is suppressed. Stimuli with clear figure–ground organisation were associated with suppression of the ground representation in early visual areas V1 and V2 (Likova & Tyler, 2008). The combination of greater attention to the figure and active suppression of the ground helps to explain why the figure is perceived much more clearly than the ground.

Evidence

What happens when different laws of organisation are in conflict? This issue was de-emphasised by the Gestaltists but investigated by Quinlan and Wilton (1998). For example, they presented a display such as the one in Figure 3.3a, in which there is a conflict between proximity and similarity. About half the participants grouped the stimuli by proximity and half by similarity. Quinlan and Wilton also used more complex displays like those shown in Figure 3.3b and 3.3c. Their findings led them to propose the following notions:

- The visual elements in a display are initially grouped or clustered on the basis of proximity.
- Additional processes are used if elements provisionally clustered together differ in one or more features (within-cluster mismatch).

Figure 3.2 An ambiguous drawing that can be seen as either two faces or as a goblet.

Figure 3.3 (a) Display involving a conflict between proximity and similarity; (b) display with a conflict between shape and colour; (c) a different display with a conflict between shape and colour. All adapted from Quinlan and Wilton (1998).

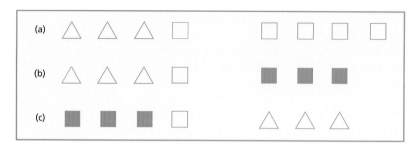

- If there is a within-cluster mismatch on features but a between-cluster match (e.g., Figure 3.3a), then observers choose between grouping based on proximity or on similarity.
- If there are within-cluster and between-cluster mismatches, then proximity is ignored, and grouping is often based on colour. In the case of the displays shown in Figures 3.3b and 3.3c, most observers grouped on the basis of common colour rather than common shape.

The Gestaltists' approach was limited in that they mostly studied artificial figures, making it important to see whether their findings apply to more realistic stimuli. Geisler, Perry, Super, and Gallogly (2001) used pictures to study in detail the contours of flowers, a river, trees, and so on. The contours of objects could be worked out very well using two principles different from those emphasised by the Gestaltists:

(1) Adjacent segments of any contour typically have very similar orientations.
(2) Segments of any contour that are further apart generally have somewhat different orientations.

Geisler et al. (2001) presented observers with two complex patterns at the same time; they decided which pattern contained a winding contour. Task performance was predicted very well from the two key principles described above. These findings suggest that we use our extensive knowledge of real objects when making decisions about contours.

Elder and Goldberg (2002) also used pictures of natural objects in their study. However, they obtained more support for the Gestalt laws. Proximity was a very powerful cue when deciding which contours belonged to which objects. In addition, the cue of good continuation also made a positive contribution.

Palmer and Rock (1994) proposed a new principle of visual organisation termed **uniform connectedness**. According to this principle, any connected region having uniform visual properties (e.g., colour, texture, lightness) tends to be organised as a single perceptual unit. Palmer and Rock argued that uniform connectedness can be more powerful than Gestalt grouping laws such as proximity and similarity. They also argued that it occurs *prior* to the operation of these other laws. This argument was supported by findings that grouping by uniform connectedness dominated over proximity and similarity when these grouping principles were in conflict.

Uniform connectedness may be less important than assumed by Palmer and Rock (1994). Han, Humphreys, and Chen (1999) assessed discrimination speed for visual stimuli, with the elements of the stimuli being grouped by proximity, by similarity, or by uniform connectedness. They found that grouping by similarity of shapes was perceived relatively slowly, but grouping by proximity was as rapid as grouping by uniform connectedness. These findings suggest that grouping by uniform connectedness does not occur prior to grouping by proximity. In subsequent research, Han and Humphreys (2003) found that grouping by proximity was as fast as grouping by uniform connectedness when one or two objects were presented. However, grouping by uniform connectedness was faster than grouping by proximity when more objects were presented. Thus, uniform connectedness may be especially important when observers are presented with multiple objects.

The Gestaltists argued that the various laws of grouping typically operate in a bottom-up (or stimulus-driven) way to produce perceptual organisation. If so, figure–ground segregation should not be affected by past knowledge or attentional processes. If, as mentioned earlier, we decide where an object is before we work out what it is, then figure–ground segregation must occur before object recognition. As we will see, the evidence does not support the Gestaltist position.

Kimchi and Hadad (2002) found that past experience influenced speed of perceptual grouping. Students at an Israeli university were presented with Hebrew letters upright or upside down and with their lines connected or disconnected. Perceptual grouping occurred within 40 ms for all types of stimuli except disconnected letters presented upside down, for which considerably more time was required. Perceptual grouping occurred much faster for disconnected upright letters than disconnected upside-down letters because it was much easier for participants to apply their past experience and knowledge of Hebrew letters with the former stimuli.

The issue of whether attentional processes can influence figure–ground segregation was addressed by Vecera, Flevaris, and Filapek (2004). Observers were presented with displays consisting of a convex region (curving outwards) and a concave region (curving inwards) (see Figure 3.4), because previous research had

Figure 3.4 Sample visual display in which the convex region is shown in black and the concave region in white. From Vecera et al. (2004). Reprinted with permission of Wiley-Blackwell.

shown that convex regions are much more likely than concave ones to be perceived as the figure. In addition, a visual cue (a small rectangle) was sometimes presented to one of the regions to manipulate attentional processes. After that, two probe shapes were presented, and observers decided rapidly which shape had appeared in the previous display.

What did Vecera et al. (2004) find? The effect of convexity on figure–ground assignment was 40% smaller when the visual cue was in the concave region than when it was in the convex region (see Figure 3.5). This indicates that spatial attention can occur *before* the completion of figure–ground processes. However, attention is not *always* necessary for figure–ground segmentation. When observers were presented with very simple stimuli, they processed information about figure and ground even when their attention was directed to a separate visual task (Kimchi & Peterson, 2008). It is likely that figure–ground processing can occur in the absence of attention provided that the stimuli are relatively simple and do not require complex processing.

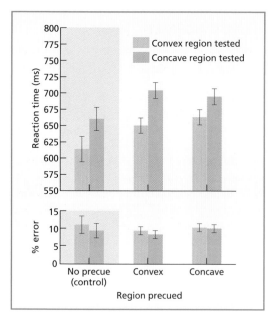

Figure 3.5 Mean reaction times (in ms) and error rates for figure–ground assignment. Performance speed was consistently faster when the convex region was tested rather than the concave region. However, this advantage was less when attention (via precuing) had been directed to the concave region. From Vecera et al. (2004). Reprinted with permission of Wiley-Blackwell.

The assumption that figure–ground segregation always precedes object recognition was tested by Grill-Spector and Kanwisher (2005). Photographs were presented for between 17 ms and 167 ms followed by a mask. On some trials, participants performed an object detection task based on deciding whether the photograph contained an object to assess figure–ground segregation. On other trials, participants carried out an object categorisation task (e.g., deciding whether the photograph showed an object from a given category such as "car"). Surprisingly, reaction times and error rates on both tasks were extremely similar. In another experiment, Grill-Spector and Kanwisher asked participants to perform the object detection and categorisation tasks on each trial. When the object was not detected, categorisation performance was at chance level; when the object was not categorised accurately, detection performance was at chance.

The above findings imply that top-down processes are important in figure–ground segregation. They also imply that the processes involved in figure–ground segregation are very similar to those involved in object recognition. Indeed, Grill-Spector and Kanwisher (2005, p. 158) concluded that, "Conscious object segmentation and categorisation are based on the same mechanism."

Mack, Gauthier, Sadr, and Palmeri (2008) cast doubt on the above conclusion. Like Grill-Spector and Kanwisher (2005), they compared performance on object detection (i.e., is an object there?) and object categorisation (i.e., what object is it) tasks. However, they used conditions in which objects were inverted or degraded to make object categorisation more difficult. In those conditions, object categorisation performance was significantly worse than object detection, suggesting that object categorisation is more complex and may involve somewhat different processes.

Evaluation

The Gestaltists discovered several important aspects of perceptual organisation. As Rock and Palmer (1990, p. 50) pointed out, "The laws of grouping have withstood the test of time. In fact, not one of them has been refuted." In addition, the Gestaltists focused on key issues: it is of fundamental importance to understand the processes underlying perceptual organisation.

There are many limitations with the Gestalt approach. First, nearly all the evidence the Gestaltists provided for their principles of perceptual organisation was based on two-dimensional line drawings. Second, they produced *descriptions* of interesting perceptual phenomena, but failed to provide adequate *explanations*. Third, the Gestaltists did not consider fully what happens when different perceptual laws are in conflict (Quinlan & Wilton, 1998). Fourth, the Gestaltists did not identify all the principles of perceptual organisation. For example, uniform connectedness may be as important as the Gestalt principles (e.g.,

Han & Humphreys, 2003; Han et al., 1999). Fifth, and most importantly, the Gestaltists were incorrect in claiming that figure–ground segregation depends very largely on bottom-up or stimulus factors. (Note, however, that Wertheimer (1923/1955) admitted that past experience was sometimes of relevance.) In fact, top-down processes are often involved, with figure–ground segregation being influenced by past experience and by attentional processes (Kimchi & Hadad, 2002; Vecera et al., 2004).

In sum, top-down processes (e.g., based on knowledge of objects and their shapes) and bottom-up or stimulus-driven processes are typically both used to maximise the efficiency of figure–ground segregation. Top-down processes may have been unnecessary to produce figure–ground segregation with the typically very simple shapes used by the Gestaltists, as is suggested by the findings of Kimchi and Peterson (2008). However, natural scenes are often sufficiently complex and ambiguous that top-down processes based on object knowledge are very useful in achieving satisfactory figure–ground segregation. Instead of figure–ground segregation based on bottom-up processing preceding object recognition involving top-down processing, segregation and recognition may involve similar bottom-up and top-down processes (Grill-Spector & Kanwisher, 2005). However, this conclusion is disputed by Mack et al. (2008). Theoretical ideas concerning the ways in which bottom-up and top-down processes might combine to produce figure–ground segregation and object recognition are discussed by Ullman (2007).

THEORIES OF OBJECT RECOGNITION

Object recognition (identifying objects in the visual field) is of enormous importance to us. As Peissig and Tarr (2007, p. 76) pointed out, "Object identification is a primary end state of visual processing and a critical precursor to interacting with and reasoning about the world.

Thus, the question of how we recognise objects is both perceptual and cognitive."

Numerous theories of object recognition have been put forward over the years (see Peissig & Tarr, 2007, for a historical review). The most influential theorist in this area has probably been David Marr, whose landmark book, *Vision: A computational investigation into the human representation and processing of visual information*, was published in 1982. He put forward a computational theory of the processes involved in object recognition. He proposed a series of representations (i.e., descriptions) providing increasingly detailed information about the visual environment:

- *Primal sketch*: this provides a two-dimensional description of the main light-intensity changes in the visual input, including information about edges, contours, and blobs.
- *2.5-D sketch*: this incorporates a description of the depth and orientation of visible surfaces, making use of information provided by shading, texture, motion, binocular disparity, and so on. Like the primal sketch, it is observer-centred or viewpoint dependent.
- *3-D model representation*: this describes three-dimensionally the shapes of objects and their relative positions independent of the observer's viewpoint (it is thus viewpoint invariant).

Irving Biederman's (1987) recognition-by-components theory represents a development and extension of Marr's theory. We start by considering Biederman's approach before moving on to more recent theories.

Biederman's recognition-by-components theory

The central assumption of Biederman's (1987, 1990) recognition-by-components theory is that objects consist of basic shapes or components known as "geons" (geometric ions). Examples of geons are blocks, cylinders, spheres, arcs, and wedges. According to Biederman (1987), there are approximately 36 different geons. That may seem suspiciously few to provide descriptions of all the objects we can recognise and identify. However, we can identify enormous numbers of spoken English words even though there are only approximately 44 phonemes (basic sounds) in the English language. This is because these phonemes can be arranged in almost endless combinations. The same is true of geons: part of the reason for the richness of the object descriptions provided by geons stems from the different possible spatial relationships among them. For example, a cup can be described by an arc connected to the side of a cylinder, and a pail can be described by the same two geons, but with the arc connected to the top of the cylinder.

The essence of recognition-by-components theory is shown in Figure 3.6. The stage we have discussed is that of the determination of the components or geons of a visual object and their relationships. When this information is available, it is matched with stored object representations or structural models containing information about the nature of the relevant geons, their orientations, sizes, and so on. The identification of any given visual object is determined by whichever stored object representation provides the best fit with the component- or geon-based information obtained from the visual object.

As indicated in Figure 3.6, the first step in object recognition is edge extraction. Biederman (1987, p. 117) described this as follows: "[There is] an early edge extraction stage, responsive to differences in surface characteristics, namely, luminance, texture, or colour, providing a line drawing description of the object."

The next step is to decide how a visual object should be segmented to establish its parts or components. Biederman (1987) argued that the concave parts of an object's contour are of particular value in accomplishing the task of segmenting the visual image into parts. The importance of concave and convex regions was discussed earlier (Vecera et al., 2004).

The other major element is to decide which edge information from an object possesses the important characteristic of remaining invariant across different viewing angles. According to Biederman (1987), there are five such invariant properties of edges:

- *Curvature*: points on a curve
- *Parallel*: sets of points in parallel
- *Cotermination*: edges terminating at a common point
- *Symmetry*: versus asymmetry
- *Collinearity*: points sharing a common line

According to the theory, the components or geons of a visual object are constructed from these invariant properties. For example, a cylinder has curved edges and two parallel edges connecting the curved edges, whereas a brick has three parallel edges and no curved edges. Biederman (1987, p. 116) argued that the five properties:

have the desirable properties that they are invariant over changes in orientation and can be determined from just a few

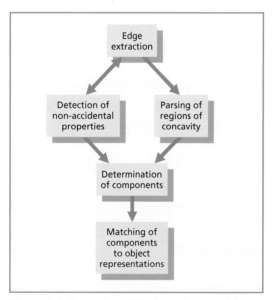

Figure 3.6 An outline of Biederman's recognition-by-components theory. Adapted from Biederman (1987).

points on each edge. Consequently, they allow a primitive (component or geon) to be extracted with great tolerance for variations of viewpoint, occlusions (obstructions), and noise.

This part of the theory leads to the key prediction that object recognition is typically viewpoint-invariant, meaning an object can be recognised equally easily from nearly all viewing angles. (Note that Marr (1982) assumed that the three-dimensional model representation was viewpoint-invariant.) Why is this prediction made? Object recognition depends crucially on the identification of geons, which can be identified from a great variety of viewpoints. It follows that object recognition from a given viewing angle would be difficult only when one or more geons were hidden from view.

An important part of Biederman's (1987) theory with respect to the invariant properties is the "non-accidental" principle. According to this principle, regularities in the visual image reflect actual (or non-accidental) regularities in the world rather than depending on accidental characteristics of a given viewpoint. Thus, for example, a two-dimensional symmetry in the visual image is assumed to indicate symmetry in the three-dimensional object. Use of the non-accidental principle occasionally leads to error. For example, a straight line in a visual image usually reflects a straight edge in the world, but it might not (e.g., a bicycle viewed end on).

How do we recognise objects when conditions are suboptimal (e.g., an intervening object obscures part of the target object)? Biederman (1987) argued that the following factors are important in such conditions:

- The invariant properties (e.g., curvature, parallel lines) of an object can still be detected even when only parts of edges are visible.
- Provided the concavities of a contour are visible, there are mechanisms allowing the missing parts of the contour to be restored.

- There is generally much *redundant* information available for recognising complex objects, and so they can still be recognised when some geons or components are missing. For example, a giraffe could be identified from its neck even if its legs were hidden from view.

Evidence

The central prediction of Biederman's (1987, 1990) recognition-by-components theory is that object recognition is viewpoint-invariant. Biederman and Gerhardstein (1993) obtained support for that prediction in an experiment in which a to-be-named object was preceded by a prime. Object naming was priming as well when there was an angular change of 135° as when the two views of the object and when the two views were identical. Biederman and Gerhardstein used *familiar* objects, which have typically been encountered from multiple viewpoints, and this facilitated the task of dealing with different viewpoints. Not surprisingly, Tarr and Bülthoff (1995) obtained different findings when they used novel objects and gave observers extensive practice at recognising these objects from certain specified viewpoints. Object recognition was viewpoint-dependent, with performance being better when familiar viewpoints were used rather than unfamiliar ones.

It could be argued that developing expertise with given objects produces a shift from viewpoint-dependent to viewpoint-invariant recognition. However, Gauthier and Tarr (2002) found no evidence of such a shift. Observers received seven hours of practice in learning to identify Greebles (artificial objects belonging to various "families"; see Figure 3.7). Two Greebles were presented in rapid succession, and observers decided whether the second Greeble was the same as the first. The second Greeble was presented at the same orientation as the first, or at various other orientations up to 75°.

Gauthier and Tarr's (2002) findings are shown in Figure 3.8. There was a general increase in speed as expertise developed. However,

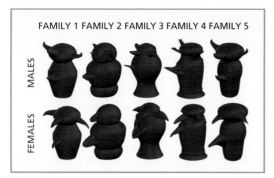

Figure 3.7 Examples of "Greebles". In the top row five different "families" are represented. For each family, a member of each "gender" is shown. Images provided courtesy of Michael. J. Tarr (Carnegie Mellon University, Pittsburgh, PA), see www.tarrlab.org

performance remained strongly viewpoint-dependent throughout the experiment. Such findings are hard to reconcile with Biederman's emphasis on viewpoint-invariant recognition.

Support for recognition-by-components theory was reported by Biederman (1987). He presented observers with degraded line drawings of objects (see Figure 3.9). Object recognition was much harder to achieve when parts of the

contour providing information about concavities were omitted than when other parts of the contour were deleted. This confirms that concavities are important for object recognition.

Support for the importance of geons was obtained by Cooper and Biederman (1993) and Vogels, Biederman, Bar, and Lorincz (2001). Cooper and Biederman (1993) asked observers to decide whether two objects presented in rapid succession had the same name (e.g., hat). There were two conditions in which the two objects shared the same name but were not identical: (1) one of the geons was changed (e.g., from a top hat to a bowler hat); and (2) the second object was larger or smaller than the first. Task performance was significantly worse when a geon changed than when it did not. Vogels et al. (2001) assessed the response of individual neurons in inferior temporal cortex to changes in a geon compared to changes in the size of an object with no change in the geon. Some neurons responded more to geon changes than to changes in object size, thus providing some support for the reality of geons.

According to the theory, object recognition depends on edge information rather than on surface information (e.g., colour). However,

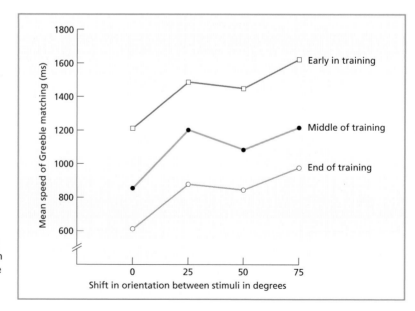

Figure 3.8 Speed of Greeble matching as a function of stage of training and difference in orientation between successive Greeble stimuli. Based on data in Gauthier and Tarr (2002).

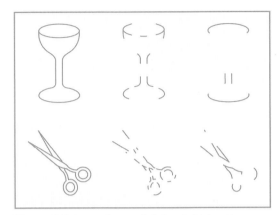

Figure 3.9 Intact figures (left-hand side), with degraded line drawings either preserving (middle column) or not preserving (far-right column) parts of the contour providing information about concavities. Adapted from Biederman (1987).

Sanocki, Bowyer, Heath, and Sarkar (1998) pointed out that edge-extraction processes are less likely to lead to accurate object recognition when objects are presented in the context of other objects rather than on their own. This is because it can be difficult to decide which edges belong to which object when several objects are presented together. Sanocki et al. presented observers briefly with objects in the form of line drawings or full-colour photographs, and these objects were presented in isolation or in context. Object recognition was much worse with the edge drawings than with the colour photographs, especially when objects were presented in context. Thus, Biederman (1987) exaggerated the role of edge-based extraction processes in object recognition.

Look back at Figure 3.6. It shows that recognition-by-components theory strongly emphasises bottom-up processes. Information extracted from the visual stimulus is used to construct a geon-based representation that is then compared against object representations stored in long-term memory. According to the theory, top-down processes depending on factors such as expectation and knowledge do not influence the early stages of object recognition. In fact, however, top-down processes are often very important (see Bar et al., 2006, for a

review). For example, Palmer (1975) presented a picture of a scene (e.g., a kitchen) followed by the very brief presentation of the picture of an object. This object was either appropriate to the context (e.g., a loaf) or inappropriate (e.g., a mailbox or drum). There was also a further condition in which no contextual scene was presented. The probability of identifying the object correctly was greatest when the object was appropriate to the context, intermediate with no context, and lowest when the object was contextually inappropriate.

Evaluation

A central puzzle is how we manage to identify objects in spite of substantial differences among the members of any given category in shape, size, and orientation. Biederman's (1987) recognition-by-components theory provides a reasonably plausible account of object recognition explaining how this is possible. The assumption that geons or geon-like components are involved in visual object recognition seems plausible. In addition, there is evidence that the identification of concavities and edges is of major importance in object recognition.

Biederman's theoretical approach possesses various limitations. First, the theory focuses primarily on bottom-up processes triggered directly by the stimulus input. By so doing, it de-emphasises the importance of top-down processes based on expectations and knowledge. This important limitation is absent from several recent theories (e.g., Bar, 2003; Lamme, 2003).

Second, it only accounts for fairly unsubtle perceptual discriminations. Thus, it explains how we decide whether the animal in front of us is a dog or cat, but not how we decide whether it is *our* dog or cat. We can easily make discriminations *within* categories such as identifying individual faces, but Biederman, Subramaniam, Bar, Kalocsai, and Fiser (1999) admitted that his theory is not applicable to face recognition.

Third, it is assumed within recognition-by-components theory that object recognition generally involves matching an object-centred representation *independent* of the observer's viewpoint with object information stored in long-term memory. However, as discussed below, there is considerable evidence for viewpoint-dependent object recognition (e.g., Gauthier & Tarr, 2002; Tarr & Bülthoff, 1995). Thus, the theory is oversimplified.

Fourth, Biederman's theory assumes that objects consist of invariant geons, but object recognition is actually much more *flexible* than that. As Hayward and Tarr (2005, p. 67) pointed out, "You can take almost any object, put a working light-bulb on the top, and call it a *lamp* ... almost *anything* in the image might constitute a feature in appropriate conditions." The shapes of some objects (e.g., clouds) are so variable that they do not have identifiable geons.

Object recognition is rather flexible. As Hayward and Tarr (2005) pointed out, you could put a working light-bulb on top of almost any object, and perceive it to be a lamp.

Viewpoint-dependent vs. viewpoint-invariant approaches

We have discussed Biederman's (1987) viewpoint-invariant theory, according to which ease of object recognition is unaffected by the observer's viewpoint. In contrast, viewpoint-dependent theories (e.g., Tarr & Bülthoff, 1995, 1998) assume that changes in viewpoint reduce the speed and/or accuracy of object recognition. According to such theories, "Object representations are collections of views that depict the appearance of objects from specific viewpoints" (Tarr & Bülthoff, 1995). As a consequence, object recognition is easier when an observer's view of an object corresponds to one of the stored views of that object.

Object recognition is sometimes viewpoint-dependent and sometimes viewpoint-invariant. According to Tarr and Bülthoff (1995), viewpoint-invariant mechanisms are typically used when object recognition involves making easy categorical discriminations (e.g., between cars and bicycles). In contrast, viewpoint-dependent mechanisms are more important when the task requires difficult within-category discriminations (e.g., between different makes of car).

Evidence consistent with the above general approach was reported by Tarr, Williams, Hayward, and Gauthier (1998). They considered recognition of the same three-dimensional objects under various conditions across nine experiments. Performance was close to viewpoint-invariant when the object recognition task was easy (e.g., detailed feedback after each trial). However, it was viewpoint-dependent when the task was difficult (e.g., no feedback provided).

Vanrie, Béatse, Wagemans, Sunaert, and van Hecke (2002) also found that task complexity influenced whether object recognition was viewpoint-dependent or viewpoint-invariant. Observers saw pairs of three-dimensional block figures in different orientations, and decided whether they represented the same figure (i.e., matching or non-matching). Non-matches were produced in two ways:

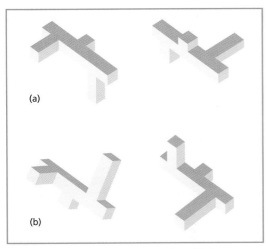

(a)

(b)

Figure 3.10 Non-matching stimuli in (a) the invariance condition and (b) the rotation condition. Reprinted from Vanrie et al. (2002), Copyright © 2002, with permission from Elsevier.

(1) An invariance condition, in which the side components were tilted upward or downward by 10°.
(2) A rotation condition, in which one object was the mirror image of the other (see Figure 3.10).

Vanrie et al. predicted that object recognition would be viewpoint-invariant in the much simpler invariance condition, but would be viewpoint-dependent in the more complex rotation condition.

What did Vanrie et al. (2002) find? As predicted, performance in the invariance condition was not influenced by the angular difference between the two objects (see Figure 3.11). Also as predicted, performance in the rotation condition was strongly viewpoint-dependent because it was greatly affected by alteration in angular difference (see Figure 3.11).

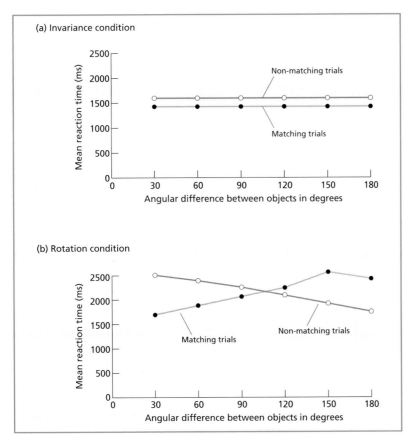

Figure 3.11 Speed of performance in (a) the invariance condition and (b) the rotation condition as a function of angular difference and trial type (matching vs. non-matching). Based on data in Vanrie et al. (2002).

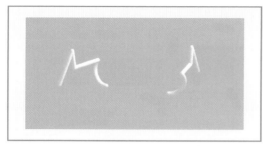

Figure 3.12 Example images of a "same" pair of stimulus objects. From Foster and Gilson (2002) with permission from The Royal Society London.

Blais, Arguin, and Marleau (2009) argued that some kinds of visual information about objects are processed in the same way, regardless of rotation. In contrast, the processing of other kinds of visual information does depend on rotation. They obtained support for that argument in studies on visual search. Some visual processing (e.g., conjunctions of features) was viewpoint-invariant, whereas other visual processing (e.g., depth processing) was viewpoint-dependent.

Some theorists (e.g., Foster & Gilson, 2002; Hayward, 2003) argue that viewpoint-dependent and viewpoint-invariant information are combined co-operatively to produce object recognition. Supporting evidence was reported by Foster and Gilson (2002). Observers saw pairs of simple three-dimensional objects constructed from connected cylinders (see Figure 3.12), and decided whether the two images showed the same object or two different ones. When two objects were different, they could differ in a viewpoint-invariant feature (i.e., number of parts) and/or various viewpoint-dependent features (e.g., part length, angle of join between parts). The key finding was that observers used both kinds of information together. This suggests that we make use of *all* available information in object recognition.

Evaluation

We know now that it would be a gross over-simplification to argue that object recognition is *always* viewpoint-dependent or viewpoint-invariant. The extent to which object recognition is primarily viewpoint-dependent or viewpoint-invariant depends on several factors, such as whether between- or within-category discriminations are required, and more generally on task complexity. The notion that *all* the available information (whether viewpoint-dependent or viewpoint-invariant) is used in parallel to facilitate object recognition has received some support.

Most of the evidence suggesting that object recognition is viewpoint-dependent is rather indirect. For example, it has sometimes been found that the time required to identify two objects as the same increases as the amount of rotation of the object increases (e.g., Biederman & Gerhardstein, 1993). All that really shows is that *some* process is performed more slowly when the angle of rotation is greater (Blais et al., 2009). That process may occur early in visual processing. If so, the increased reaction time might be of little or no relevance to the theoretical controversy between viewpoint-dependent and viewpoint-invariant theories. In the next section, we consider an alternative approach to object recognition based on cognitive neuroscience.

COGNITIVE NEUROSCIENCE APPROACH TO OBJECT RECOGNITION

In recent years, there has been remarkable progress in understanding the brain processes involved in object recognition. This is all the more impressive given their enormous complexity. Consider, for example, our apparently effortless ability to recognise Robert de Niro when we see him in a film. It actually involves numerous interacting processes at all levels from the retina through to the higher-level visual areas in the brain.

As we saw in Chapter 2, the ventral visual pathway is hierarchically organised. Visual processing basically proceeds from the retina, through several areas including the lateral geniculate nucleus V1, V2, and V4, culminating in the inferotemporal cortex (see Figure 2.4). The stimuli causing the greatest neuronal activation become progressively more complex as processing moves along the ventral stream. At the same time, the receptive fields of cells increase progressively in size. Note that most researchers assume that the ventral pathway is specialised for object recognition, whereas the dorsal pathway is specialised for spatial vision and visually guided actions (e.g., Milner & Goodale, 2008; see Chapter 2).

Inferotemporal cortex (especially its anterior portion) is of crucial importance in visual object recognition (Peissig & Tarr, 2007). Suppose we assess neuronal activity in inferotemporal cortex while participants are presented with several different objects, each presented at various angles, sizes, and so on. There are two key dimensions of neuronal responses in such a situation: *selectivity* and *invariance* or tolerance (Ison & Quiroga, 2008). Neurons responding strongly to one visual object but weakly (or not at all) to other objects possess high selectivity. Neurons responding almost equally strongly to a given object regardless of its orientation, size, and so on possess high invariance or tolerance.

We need to be careful when relating evidence about neuronal selectivity and tolerance to the theories of object recognition discussed earlier in the chapter. In general terms, however, inferotemporal neurons having high invariance or tolerance seem consistent with theories claiming that object recognition is viewpoint-invariant. In similar fashion, inferotemporal neurons having low invariance appear to fit with theories claiming object recognition is viewpoint-dependent.

When we move on to discuss the relevant evidence, you will notice that the great majority of studies have used monkeys. This has been done because the invasive techniques involved can only be used on non-human species. It is generally (but perhaps incorrectly) assumed that basic visual processes are similar in humans and monkeys.

Evidence

Evidence that inferotemporal cortex is especially important in object recognition was provided by Leopold and Logothetis (1999) and Blake and Logothetis (2002). Macaque monkeys were presented with a different visual stimulus to each eye and trained to indicate which stimulus they perceived. This is known as binocular rivalry (see Glossary). The key finding was that the correlation between neural activity and the monkey's perception was greater at later stages of visual processing. For example, the activation of only 20% of neurons in V1 was associated with perception, whereas it was 90% in higher visual areas such as inferotemporal cortex and the superior temporal sulcus.

The above findings reveal an *association* between neuronal activation in inferotemporal cortex and perception, but this falls short of demonstrating a *causal* relationship. This gap was filled by Afraz, Kiani, and Esteky (2006). They trained two macaque monkeys to decide whether degraded visual stimuli were faces or non-faces. On some trials, the experimenters applied microstimulation to face-selective neurons within the inferotemporal cortex. This microstimulation caused the monkeys to make many more face decisions than when it was not applied. Thus, this study shows a causal relationship between activity of face-selective neurons in inferotemporal cortex and face perception.

We turn now to the important issue of neuronal selectivity and intolerance in object recognition. There is greater evidence of both selectivity *and* invariance at higher levels of visual processing (e.g., Rousselet, Thorpe, & Fabre-Thorpe, 2004). We first consider selectivity before discussing invariance. fMRI research suggests that regions of inferotemporal cortex are specialised for different categories of object. Examples include areas for faces, places, cars, birds, chess boards, cats, bottles, scissors, shoes, and chairs (Peissig & Tarr, 2007). However, most of the associations between object categories and brain regions are not neat and tidy. For example, the fusiform face area (see Figure 3.19 below) has often been identified as a crucial area for face recognition (discussed more fully later). However, Grill-Spector, Sayres, and Ress (2006) found that small parts of that area responded mostly to animals, cars, or sculptures rather than faces.

The above evidence relates to regions rather than individual neurons. However, Tsao, Freiwald, Tootell, and Livingstone (2006) studied neurons within face-responsive regions of the superior temporal sulcus in macaque monkeys. The key finding was that 97% of the visually responsive neurons responded strongly to faces but not other objects. This indicates that neurons can exhibit strong object specificity (at least for faces).

Striking findings were reported by Quiroga, Reddy, Kreiman, Koch, and Fried (2005). They found a neuron in the medial temporal lobe that responded strongly to pictures of Jennifer Aniston (the actress from *Friends*), but hardly responded to pictures of other famous faces or other objects. Surprisingly, this neuron did not respond to Jennifer Aniston with Brad Pitt! Other neurons responded specifically to a different famous person (e.g., Julia Roberts) or a famous building (e.g., Sydney Opera House). Note, however, that only a very limited number of neurons were studied out of the 2 to 5 million neurons activated by any given visual stimulus. It is utterly improbable that only a single neuron in the medial temporal lobe responds to Jennifer Aniston. Note also that the neurons were in an area of the brain mostly concerned with memory and so these neurons are not just associated with visual processing.

Do neurons in the temporal cortex have high or low invariance? Some have high invariance and others have low invariance. Consider, for example, a study by Booth and Rolls (1998). Monkeys initially spent time playing with novel objects in their cages. After that, Booth and Rolls presented photographs of these objects taken from different viewpoints while recording neuronal activity in the superior temporal sulcus. They found that 49% of the neurons responded mostly to specific views and only 14% produced viewpoint-invariant responses. However, the viewpoint-invariant neurons may be more important to object perception than their limited numbers might suggest. Booth and Rolls showed there was potentially enough information in the patterns of activation of these neurons to discriminate accurately among the objects presented.

What is the relationship between selectivity and invariance or tolerance in inferotemporal neurons? The first systematic attempt to provide an answer was by Zoccolan, Kouh, Poggio, and DiCarlo (2007). There was a moderate *negative* correlation between object selectivity and tolerance. Thus, some neurons respond to many objects in several different sizes and orientations, whereas others respond mainly to a single object in a limited range of views. *Why* are selectivity and invariance negatively correlated? Perhaps our ability to perform visual tasks ranging from very precise object identification to very broad categorisation of objects is facilitated by having neurons with very different patterns of responsiveness to changing stimuli.

It is generally assumed that the processes involved in object recognition occur mainly in the ventral stream, whereas the dorsal stream is involved in visually guided actions (see Chapter 2). However, that may well be an oversimplification. Substantial evidence for processes associated with object recognition in the dorsal stream as well as the ventral one was found in a recent study on humans (Konen & Kastner, 2008). There was clear object selectivity at several stages of visual processing in both streams. In addition, there was increased invariance at higher levels of processing (e.g., posterior parietal cortex) than at intermediate ones (e.g., V4, MT). Overall, the findings suggested that object information is processed in parallel in both streams or pathways.

Suppose we discover neurons in inferotemporal cortex that respond strongly to photographs of giraffes but not other animals. It would be tempting to conclude that these neurons are object-selective for giraffes. However, it is also possible that they are responding instead to an important feature of giraffes (i.e., their long necks) rather than to the object as a whole. Some neurons in the inferotemporal cortex of macaque monkeys respond to specific features of objects rather than the objects themselves (Sigala, 2004). The take-home message is that many of the neurons labelled "object-selective" in other studies may actually be "feature-selective".

Evaluation

There is convincing evidence that inferotemporal cortex is of major importance in object recognition. Some inferotemporal neurons exhibit high invariance, whereas others have low invariance. The existence of these different kinds of neuron is consistent with the notion that object recognition can be viewpoint-invariant or viewpoint-dependent. It has also been established that various inferotemporal areas are somewhat specialised for different categories of object.

Top-down processes in object recognition

Most cognitive neuroscientists (and cognitive psychologists) studying object recognition have focused on bottom-up processes as processing proceeds along the ventral pathway. However, top-down processes not directly involving the ventral pathway are also important. A crucial issue is whether top-down processes (probably involving the prefrontal cortex) occur *prior* to object recognition and are necessary for recognition or whether they occur *after* object recognition and relate to semantic processing of already recognised objects.

Bar et al. (2006) presented participants with drawings of objects presented briefly and then masked to make them hard to recognise. Activation in orbitofrontal cortex (part of the prefrontal cortex) occurred 50 ms before activation in recognition-related regions in the temporal cortex (see Figure 3.13). This orbitofrontal activation predicted successful object recognition,

and so seemed to be important for recognition to occur. Bar et al. concluded that top-down processes in orbitofrontal cortex facilitate object recognition when recognition is difficult. There was less involvement of orbitofrontal cortex in object recognition when recognition was easy (longer, unmasked presentations). This makes sense – top-down processes are less important when detailed information is available to bottom-up processes.

Stronger evidence that top-down processes in the prefrontal cortex play a direct role in object recognition was reported by Viggiano et al. (2008). They presented participants with blurred photographs of animals for object recognition under four conditions: (1) repetitive transcranial magnetic stimulation (rTMS: see Glossary) applied to the left dorsolateral prefrontal cortex; (2) rTMS applied to the right dorsolateral prefrontal cortex; (3) sham rTMS (there was no magnetic

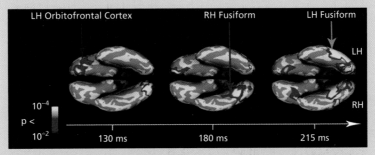

Figure 3.13 Brain activation associated with successful object recognition at 130 ms after stimulus onset in left orbitofrontal cortex, at 180 ms in right temporal cortex (fusiform area), and at 215 ms in left and right temporal cortex (fusiform area). Copyright © 2006 National Academy of Sciences, USA. Reprinted with permission.

field); and (4) baseline (no rTMS at all). The key finding was that rTMS (whether applied to the left or the right dorsolateral prefrontal cortex) slowed down object-recognition time (see Figure 3.14). However, rTMS had no effect on object-recognition time when the photographs were not blurred. These findings suggest that top-down processes are directly involved in object recognition when the sensory information available to bottom-up processes is limited.

In sum, we are starting to obtain direct evidence of the involvement of prefrontal cortex (and top-down processes) in object recognition. That involvement is greater when sensory information is limited, as is likely to be the case much of the time in the real world. Some issues remain to be resolved. For example, the respective roles played by orbitofrontal and dorsolateral prefrontal cortex in object recognition need clarification.

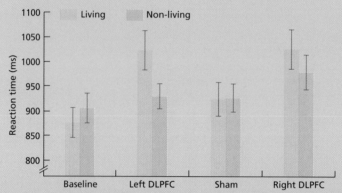

Figure 3.14 Mean object recognition times (in ms) for living (green columns) and non-living objects (purple columns) in four conditions: baseline = no rTMS; left DLPFC = rTMS applied to left dorsolateral prefrontal cortex; sham = "pretend" rTMS applied to left dorsolateral prefrontal cortex; right DLPFC = rTMS applied to right dorsolateral prefrontal cortex. Reprinted from Viggiano et al. (2008), Copyright © 2008, with permission from Elsevier.

What are the limitations of research in this area? First, we must be cautious about generalising findings from monkeys to humans. However, some studies on humans (e.g., Konen & Kastner, 2008) have produced findings closely resembling those obtained from monkeys. Second, the research emphasis has been on the role of the ventral stream in object recognition. However, the dorsal stream may play a more active role in object recognition than generally assumed (Konen & Kastner, 2008). Third, it is often assumed that neurons responding only to certain objects are necessarily object-selective. However, detailed experimentation is needed to distinguish between object-selective and feature-selective neurons (e.g., Sigala, 2004). Fourth, it has typically been assumed that the

processes involved in object recognition proceed along the ventral stream from the retina through to the inferotemporal cortex. This de-emphasises the role of top-down processes in object recognition (e.g., Bar et al., 2006; Viggiano et al., 2008).

COGNITIVE NEUROPSYCHOLOGY OF OBJECT RECOGNITION

Information from brain-damaged patients has enhanced our understanding of the processes involved in object recognition. In this section, we will focus on **visual agnosia** (see Glossary), which is "the impairment of visual object recognition in people who possess sufficiently preserved visual fields, acuity and other elementary forms of visual ability to enable object recognition, and in whom the object recognition impairment cannot be attributed to…loss of knowledge about objects.…[Agnosics'] impairment is one of visual recognition rather than naming, and is therefore manifest on naming and non-verbal tasks alike" (Farah, 1999, p. 181).

Historically, a distinction was often made between two forms of visual agnosia:

(1) *Apperceptive agnosia*: object recognition is impaired because of deficits in perceptual processing.

(2) *Associative agnosia*: perceptual processes are essentially intact. However, object recognition is impaired because of difficulties in accessing relevant knowledge about objects from memory.

How can we distinguish between apperceptive agnosia and associative agnosia? One way is to assess patients' ability to copy objects they cannot recognise. Patients who can copy objects are said to have associative agnosia, whereas those who cannot have apperceptive agnosia. A test often used to assess apperceptive agnosia is the Gollin picture test. On this test, patients are presented with increasingly complete drawings of an object. Those with apperceptive agnosia require more drawings than healthy individuals to identify the objects.

The distinction between apperceptive and associative agnosia is oversimplified. Patients suffering from various perceptual problems can all be categorised as having apperceptive agnosia. In addition, patients with apperceptive agnosia and associative agnosia have fairly *general* deficits in object recognition. However, many patients with visual agnosia have relatively specific deficits. For example, later in the chapter we discuss prosopagnosia, a condition involving *specific* problems in recognising faces.

Riddoch and Humphreys (2001; see also Humphreys & Riddoch, 2006) argued that the problems with visual object recognition ex-perienced by brain-damaged patients can be accounted for by a hierarchical model of object recognition and naming (see Figure 3.15):

- *Edge grouping by collinearity*: this is an early processing stage during which the edges of an object are derived (collinear means having a common line).
- *Feature binding into shapes*: during this stage, object features that have been extracted are combined to form shapes.
- *View normalisation*: during this stage, processing occurs to allow a viewpoint-invariant representation to be derived. This stage is optional.
- *Structural description*: during this stage, individuals gain access to stored knowledge about the structural descriptions of objects.
- *Semantic system*: the final stage involves gaining access to stored knowledge relevant to an object.

What predictions follow from this model? The most obvious one is that we might expect to find different patients with visual agnosia having object-recognition problems at each of these stages of processing. That would show very clearly the limitations in distinguishing only between apperceptive and associative agnosia.

Evidence

In our discussion of the evidence, we will follow Riddoch and Humpreys (2001) in considering each stage in the model in turn. Many patients have problems with edge grouping or form perception. For example, Milner et al. (1991) studied a patient, DF, who had very severely impaired object recognition (this patient is discussed in detail in Chapter 2). She recognised only a few real objects and could not recognise any objects shown in line drawings. She also had poor performance when making judgements about simple patterns grouped on the basis of various properties (e.g., collinearity, proximity). Other patients have shown similar problems with edge grouping (see Riddoch & Humphreys, 2001).

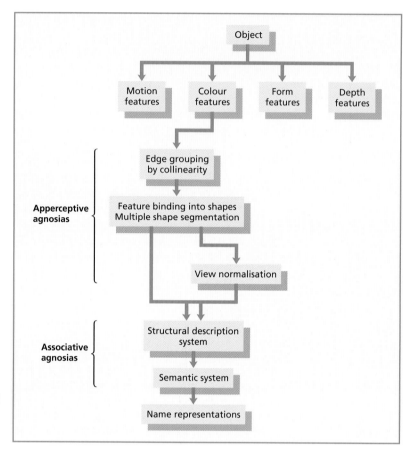

Figure 3.15 A hierarchical model of object recognition and naming, specifying different component processes which, when impaired, can produce varieties of apperceptive and associative agnosia. From Riddoch and Humphreys (2001).

Humphreys (1999) discussed what he termed **integrative agnosia**, a condition in which the patient experiences great difficulty in integrating or combining an object's features during object recognition. Humphreys and Riddoch (1987) studied HJA. He produced accurate drawings of objects he could not recognise and could draw objects from memory. However, he found it very hard to integrate visual information. In his own words, "I have come to cope with recognising many common objects, if they are standing alone. When objects are placed together, though, I have more difficulties. To recognise one sausage on its own is far from picking one out from a dish of cold foods in a salad" (Humphreys & Riddoch, 1987).

Giersch, Humphreys, Boucart, and Kovacs (2000) presented HJA with an array of three geometric shapes that were spatially separated, superimposed, or occluded (covered) (see Figure 3.16). Then, a second array was presented, which was either the original array or a distractor array in which the positions of the shapes had been re-arranged. HJA performed reasonably well in deciding whether the two arrays were the same with separated shapes but not with superimposed or occluded shapes. Thus, HJA has poor ability for shape segregation.

Behrmann, Peterson, Moscovitch, and Suzuki (2006) studied SM, a man with integrative

> **KEY TERM**
>
> **integrative agnosia:** a form of **visual agnosia** in which patients have problems in integrating or combining an object's features in object recognition.

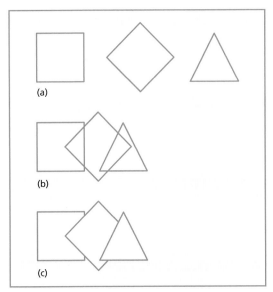

Figure 3.16 Examples of (a) separated, (b) superimposed, and (c) occluded shapes used by Giersch et al. (2000). From Riddoch and Humphreys (2001).

agnosia. He was trained to identify simple objects consisting of two parts, and could correctly reject distractors having a mismatching part. Of greatest importance, SM was poor at rejecting distractors having the same parts as objects on which he had been trained but with the spatial arrangement of the parts altered. Behrmann et al. concluded that separate mechanisms are involved in identifying the shapes of individual parts of objects and in perceiving the spatial arrangements of those parts. SM has much more severe problems with the latter mechanism than the former one.

Riddoch, Humphreys, Akhtar, Allen, Bracewell, and Scholfield (2008) compared two patients, one of whom (SA) has problems with edge grouping (form agnosia) and the other of whom (HJA) has integrative agnosia. Even though both patients have apperceptive agnosia, there are important differences between them. SA was worse than HJA at some aspects of early visual processing (e.g., contour tracing) but was better than HJA at recognising familiar objects. SA has inferior bottom-up processes to HJA but is better able to use top-down

processes for visual object recognition. The problems that integrative agnosics have with integrating information about the parts of objects may depend in part on their limited top-down processing abilities. The fact that the areas of brain damage were different in the two patients (dorsal lesions in SA versus more ventral medial lesions in HJA) is also consistent with the notion that there are at least two types of apperceptive agnosia.

One way of determining whether a given patient can produce structural descriptions of objects is to give him/her an object-decision task. On this task, patients are presented with pictures or drawings of objects and non-objects, and decide which are the real objects. Some patients perform well on object-decision tasks but nevertheless have severe problems with object recognition. Fery and Morais (2003) studied DJ, who has associative agnosia. He recognised only 16% of common objects when presented *visually*, but his performance was normal when recognising objects presented *verbally*. Thus, DJ finds it very hard to use the information in structural descriptions to *access* semantic knowledge about objects. However, he performed well on tasks involving shape processing, integration of parts, and copying and matching objects. For example, DJ was correct on 93% of trials on a difficult animal-decision task in which the non-animals were actual animals with one part added, deleted, or substituted (see Figure 3.17). This indicates that several of the processes relating to object recognition are essentially intact in DJ.

Finally, some patients have severe problems with object recognition because they have damage to the semantic memory system containing information about objects. Patients whose object-recognition difficulties depend *only* on damaged semantic memory are not regarded as visual agnosics because their visual processes are essentially intact (see Chapter 7). However, some visual agnosics have partial damage to semantic memory. Peru and Avesani (2008) studied FB, a woman who suffered damage to the right frontal region and the left posterior temporal lobe as the result of a skiing accident.

Figure 3.17 Examples of animal stimuli with (from top to bottom) a part missing, the intact animal, with a part substituted, and a part added. From Fery and Morais (2003).

Her basic visual processes were intact, but she was very poor at identifying drawings of animate and inanimate objects. This pattern of findings suggested she had associative agnosia. However, she differed from DJ in that she had some damage to semantic memory rather than simply problems in accessing knowledge in semantic memory. When asked verbally, she

was largely unable to access information about objects' perceptual features, although she was reasonably good at indicating the uses of objects when asked.

Evaluation

The hierarchical model put forward by Riddoch and Humphreys (2001) provides a useful framework within which to discuss the problems with object recognition shown by visual agnosics. The evidence from brain-damaged patients is broadly consistent with the model's predictions. What is very clear is that the model represents a marked improvement on the simplistic distinction between apperceptive and associative agnosia.

What are the limitations of the hierarchical model? First, it is based largely on the assumption that object recognition occurs primarily in a bottom-up way. In fact, however, top-down processes are also important, with processes associated with later stages influencing processing at early stages (e.g., Bar et al., 2006; Viggiano et al., 2008). Second, and related to the first point, the processing associated with object recognition may not proceed in the neat, stage-by-stage way envisaged within the model. Third, the model is more like a framework than a complete theory. For example, it is assumed that each stage of processing uses the output from the previous stage, but the details of how this is accomplished remain unclear.

FACE RECOGNITION

There are several reasons for devoting a separate section to face recognition. First, the ability to recognise faces is of huge significance in our everyday lives. As you may have found to your cost, people are offended if you fail to recognise them. In certain circumstances, it can be a matter of life or death to recognise whether someone is a friend or enemy. It is significant that robbers try to conceal their identity by covering their faces. In addition, it is important to be able to recognise the expressions on other people's faces to judge your impact on them.

Second, face recognition differs in important ways from other forms of object recognition. As a result, theories of object recognition are of only limited value in explaining face recognition, and theories specifically devoted to accounting for face recognition are needed.

Third, we now have a reasonably good understanding of the processes involved in face recognition. One reason for this is the diversity of research – it includes behavioural studies, studies on brain-damaged patients, and neuro-imaging studies.

How does face recognition differ from the recognition of other objects? An important part of the answer is that face recognition involves more **holistic processing** or configural process-ing (processing involving strong integration across the whole object). Information about specific features of a face can be unreliable because different individuals share similar facial features (e.g., eye colour) or because an individual's features are subject to change (e.g., skin shade, mouth shape). In view of the unreli-ability of feature information, it is desirable for us to use holistic or configural processing of faces.

Evidence that holistic processing is used much more often with faces than other objects comes from studies on the inversion, part–whole, and composite effects (see McKone, Kanwisher, & Duchaine, 2007, for a review). In the **inversion effect**, faces are much harder to identify when presented inverted or upside-down rather than upright. McKone (2004) asked participants to decide which of two faces had been presented briefly to them centrally or at various locations towards the periphery of vision. Identification accuracy was consistently much higher when the faces were presented upright rather than inverted. In contrast, adverse effects of inversion on object recognition are much smaller with non-face objects and generally disappear rapidly with practice (see McKone, 2004, for a review).

The inversion effect does not assess holistic processing directly, unlike the part–whole and composite effects. In the **part–whole effect**, memory for a face part is more accurate when it is presented within the whole face rather than on its own. Farah (1994) studied this effect. Participants were presented with draw-ings of faces or houses, and associated a name with each face and each house. After that, they were presented with whole faces and houses or with only a single feature (e.g., mouth, front door). Recognition performance for face parts was much better when the whole face was presented rather than only a single feature (see Figure 3.18). This is the part–whole effect. In contrast, recognition performance for house features was very similar in whole- and single-feature conditions.

The part–whole effect indicates that faces are stored in *memory* in holistic form, but does not directly show that faces are *perceived* holistically. Farah, Wilson, Drain, and Tanaka (1998) filled this gap. Participants were pre-sented with a face followed by a mask and then a second face, and decided whether the second face was the same as the first. The mask consisted of a face arranged randomly or of a whole face. Face-recognition performance was better when part masks were used rather than whole masks, presumably because the first face was processed as a whole. With house or word stimuli, the beneficial effects of part masks over whole masks were much less than with faces.

In the composite effect, participants are presented with two half faces of different individuals and these two half faces are aligned or unaligned. Performance on tasks requiring

KEY TERMS

holistic processing: processing that involves integrating information from an entire object.
inversion effect: the finding that faces are considerably harder to recognise when presented upside down; the effect is less marked with other objects.
part–whole effect: the finding that it is easier to recognise a face part when it is presented within a whole face rather than in isolation.

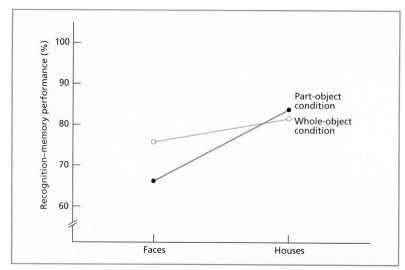

Figure 3.18 Recognition memory for features of houses and faces when presented with whole houses or faces or with only features. Data from Farah (1994).

perception of only one half face is impaired when the half faces are aligned compared to when they are unaligned (e.g., Young, Hellawell, & Hay, 1987). The composite effect is typically *not* found with inverted faces or with non-face objects (see McKone et al., 2007, for a review).

Evaluation

The inversion, part–whole, and composite effects all provide evidence that faces are subject to holistic or configural processing. Of importance, all these effects are generally absent in the processing of non-face objects. Thus, there are major differences between face and object recognition. However, the inversion effect does not provide a direct assessment of holistic processing, and so provides weaker evidence than the other effects that face processing is holistic. Most people have much more experience at processing faces than other objects and have thus developed special expertise in face processing (Gauthier & Tarr, 2002). It is thus possible that holistic or configural processing is found for any category of objects for which an individual possesses expertise. That would mean that there is nothing special about faces. As we will see later, most of the evidence fails to support this alternative explanation.

The inversion, part-whole, and composite effects all provide evidence that faces are subject to holistic processing. This helps explain why we are able to recognise Giuseppe Arcimboldo's (circa 1590) painting as that of a face, rather than simply a collection of fruit.

Prosopagnosia

If face processing differs substantially from object processing, we might expect to find some brain-damaged individuals with severely impaired face processing but not object processing. Such individuals exist. They suffer from a condition known as **prosopagnosia**, coming from the Greek words meaning "face" and "without knowledge". Patients with prosopagnosia ("face-blindness") can generally recognise most objects reasonably well in spite of their enormous problems with faces. JK, a woman in her early thirties, described an embarrassing incident caused by her prosopagnosia: "I went to the wrong baby at my son's daycare and only realised that he was not my son when the entire daycare staff looked at me in horrified disbelief" (Duchaine & Nakayama, 2006, p. 166).

In spite of their poor conscious recognition of faces, prosopagnosics often show evidence of covert recognition (i.e., processing of faces without conscious awareness). In one study, prosopagnosics decided rapidly whether names were familiar or unfamiliar (Young, Hellawell, & de Haan, 1988). They performed the task more rapidly when presented with a related priming face immediately before the target name, even though they could not recognise the face at the conscious level. Covert recognition can sometimes be turned into overt or conscious recognition if the task is very easy. In one study, prosopagnosics showed evidence of overt recognition when several faces were presented and they were informed that all belonged to the same category (Morrison, Bruce, and Burton, 2003).

There are three points to bear in mind before discussing the evidence. First, prosopagnosia is a heterogeneous or diverse condition in which the precise problems of face and object recognition vary from patient to patient. Second, the origins of the condition also vary. In acquired prosopagnosia, the condition is due to brain damage. In contrast, developmental prosopagnosics have no obvious brain damage but never acquire the ability to recognise faces. Third, there are various reasons why prosopagnosics find it much harder to recognise faces than objects. The obvious explanation is that acquired prosopagnosics have suffered damage to a part of the brain specialised for processing faces. However, an alternative interpretation is that face recognition is simply much harder than object recognition – face recognition involves distinguishing among members of the same category (i.e., faces), whereas object recognition generally only involves identifying the category to which an object belongs (e.g., cat, car).

Strong support for the notion that face recognition involves different processes from object recognition would come from the demonstration of a double dissociation (see Glossary). In this double dissociation, some prosopagnosics would show severely impaired face recognition but intact object recognition, whereas other patients would show the opposite pattern. Convincing evidence that some prosopagnosics have intact object recognition was reported by Duchaine and Nakayama (2005). They tested seven developmental prosopagnosics on various tasks involving memory for faces, cars, tools, guns, horses, houses, and natural landscapes. Of importance, participants tried to recognise exemplars *within* each category to make the task of object recognition comparable to face recognition. Some of them performed in the normal range on all (or nearly all) of the non-face tasks.

Duchaine (2006) carried out an exceptionally thorough study on a developmental prosopagnosic called Edward, a 53-year-old married man with two PhDs. He did very poorly on several tests of face memory. Indeed, he performed no better with upright faces than with inverted ones, suggesting he could not engage in holistic face processing. In contrast, he performed slightly *better* than healthy controls on most memory tasks involving non-face objects, even when the task involved recognising exemplars within categories. Virtually all healthy individuals and

---

KEY TERM

prosopagnosia: a condition caused by brain damage in which the patient cannot recognise familiar faces but can recognise familiar objects.

most developmental prosopagnosics have voxels (very small three-dimensional volume elements) that respond more strongly to faces than to objects, but none was found in Edward's brain.

The opposite pattern of intact object recognition but impaired face recognition has also been reported. Moscovitch, Winocur, and Behrmann (1997) studied CK, a man with object agnosia (impaired object recognition). He performed as well as controls on face-recognition tasks regardless of whether the face was a photograph, a caricature, or a cartoon provided it was upright and the internal features were in the correct locations. McMullen, Fisk, Phillips, and Mahoney (2000) tested HH, who has severe problems with object recognition as a result of a stroke. However, his face-recognition performance was good.

In sum, while most prosopagnosics have somewhat deficient object recognition, some have essentially intact object recognition even when difficult object-recognition tasks are used. Surprisingly, a few individuals have reasonably intact face recognition in spite of severe problems with object recognition. This double dissociation is most readily explained by assuming that different processes (and brain areas) underlie face and object recognition.

Prosopagnosics have problems recognising familiar faces. Imagine the distress it would cause to be unable to recognise your own father.

Fusiform face area

If faces are processed differently to other objects, we would expect to find brain regions specialised for face processing. The fusiform face area in the lateral fusiform gyrus (see Figure 3.19) has (as its name strongly implies!) been identified as such a brain region (see Kanwisher & Yovel, 2006, for a review). One reason is that this area is frequently damaged in patients with acquired prosopagnosia (Barton, Press, Keenan, & O'Connor, 2002). In addition, there is substantial support for the importance of the fusiform face area in face processing from brain-imaging studies: this area typically responds at least twice as strongly to faces as to other objects (McKone et al., 2007). Downing, Chan, Peelen, Dodds, and Kanwisher (2006) presented participants with faces, scenes, and 18 object categories (e.g., tools, fruits,

vegetables). The fusiform face area responded significantly more strongly to faces than to any other stimulus category. In a study discussed earlier, Tsao et al. (2006) identified a region within the monkey equivalent of the fusiform face area in which 97% of visually responsive neurons responded much more strongly to faces than to objects (e.g., fruits, gadgets).

Yovel and Kanwisher (2004) tried to force participants to process houses in the same way as faces. Houses and faces were constructed so they varied in their parts (windows and doors versus eyes and mouth) or in the spacing of those parts. The stimuli were carefully adjusted so that performance on deciding whether successive stimuli were the same or different was equated for faces and houses. Nevertheless,

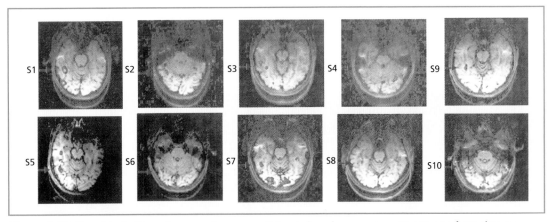

Figure 3.19 The right fusiform face area for ten participants based on greater activation to faces than to non-face objects. From Kanwisher McDermott, and Chun (1997) with permission from Society of Neuroscience.

responding in the fusiform face area was three times stronger to faces than to houses.

In spite of strong evidence that the fusiform face area is much involved in face processing, three points need to be made. First, the fusiform face area is not the *only* brain area involved in face processing. Other face-selective areas are the occipital face area and the superior temporal sulcus. Rossion, Caldara, Seghier, Schuller, Lazayras, and Mayer (2003) considered a prosopagnosic patient, PS. Her right fusiform face area was intact, but she had damage to the occipital face area. Rossion et al. suggested that normal face processing depends on integrated functioning of the right fusiform face area *and* the right occipital face area. The superior temporal sulcus is sometimes activated during processing of changeable aspects of faces (e.g., expression) (see Haxby, Hoffman, & Gobbini, 2000, for a review).

Second, the fusiform face area is more complicated than generally assumed. Grill-Spector et al. (2006) in a study discussed earlier found, using high-resolution fMRI, that the fusiform face area has a diverse structure. Observers saw faces and three categories of object (animals, cars, and abstract sculptures). More high-resolution **voxels** (small volume elements in the brain) in the fusiform face area were selective to faces than to any of the object categories. However, the differences were not dramatic. The average number of voxels selective to faces

was 155 compared to 104 (animals), 63 (cars), and 63 (sculptures). As Grill-Spector et al. (p. 1183) concluded, "The results challenge the prevailing hypothesis that the FFA (fusiform face area) is a uniform brain area in which all neurons are face-selective."

Third, there has been a major theoretical controversy concerning the finding that the fusiform face area is face-selective. Gauthier and Tarr (2002) assumed we have much more expertise in recognising faces than individual members of other categories. They argued that the brain mechanisms claimed to be specific to faces are also involved in recognising the members of *any* object category for which we possess expertise. This issue is discussed at length below.

Are faces special?

According to Gauthier and Tarr (2002), many findings pointing to major differences between face and object processing should not be taken at face value (sorry!). According to them (as mentioned above), it is of crucial importance that most people have far more expertise in

---

KEY TERM

voxels: these are small, volume-based units in the brain identified in neuroimaging research; short for volume elements.

recognising individual faces than the individual members of other categories. Most findings interpreted as being specific to faces may actually apply to *any* object category for which the observer possesses real expertise. Three major predictions follow from this theoretical approach. First, holistic or configural processing is not unique to faces but characterises any categories for which observers possess expertise. Second, the fusiform face area should be highly activated when observers recognise the members of *any* category for which they possess expertise. Third, prosopagnosics have damage to brain areas specialised for processing of objects for which they possess expertise. Accordingly, their ability to recognise non-face objects of expertise should be impaired.

So far as the first prediction is concerned, Gauthier and Tarr (2002) found supporting evidence in a study (discussed earlier) in which participants spent several hours learning to identify families of artificial objects called Greebles (see Figure 3.7). There was a progressive increase in sensitivity to configural changes in Greebles as a function of developing expertise. However, these findings are discrepant with most other research. McKone et al. (2007) reviewed studies on the influence of expertise for non-face objects on the inversion, part–whole, and composite effects discussed earlier, all of which are assumed to require holistic or configural processing. Expertise typically failed to lead to any of these effects.

So far as the second hypothesis is concerned, Gauthier, Behrmann, and Tarr (1999) gave participants several hours' practice in recognising Greebles. The fusiform face area was activated when participants recognised Greebles, especially as their expertise with Greebles increased. Gauthier, Skudlarski, Gore, and Anderson (2000) assessed activation of the fusiform face area during recognition tasks involving faces, familiar objects, birds, and cars. Some participants were experts on birds, and the others were experts on cars. Expertise influenced activation of the fusiform face area: there was more activation to cars when recognised by car experts than by bird experts, and to birds when recognised

by bird experts than by car experts. While it appears that expertise directly influenced activation in the fusiform face area, it is possible that experts simply paid more attention to objects relating to their expertise.

McKone et al. (2007) reviewed eight studies testing the hypothesis that the fusiform face area is more activated by objects of expertise than by other objects. Three studies reported small but significant effects of expertise, whereas the effects were non-significant in the others. Five studies considered whether any expertise effects are greatest in the fusiform face area. Larger effects were reported *outside* the fusiform face area than *inside* it (McKone et al., 2007). Finally, there are a few recent studies (e.g., Yue, Tjan, & Biederman 2006) in which participants received extensive training to discriminate between exemplars of novel categories of stimuli. Against the expertise theory, activation in the fusiform face area was no greater for trained than for untrained categories.

According to the third hypothesis, prosopagnosics should have impaired ability to recognise the members of non-face categories for which they possess expertise. Some findings are inconsistent with this hypothesis. Sergent and Signoret (1992) studied a prosopagnosic, RM, who had expertise for cars. He had very poor face recognition but recognised considerably more makes, models and years of car than healthy controls. Another prosopagnosic, WJ, acquired a flock of sheep. Two years later, his ability to recognise individual sheep was as good as that of healthy controls with comparable knowledge of sheep.

Evaluation

As assumed by the expertise theory, most people possess much more expertise about faces than any other object category. It is also true that we have more experience of identifying individual faces than individual members of most other categories. However, none of the specific hypotheses of the expertise theory has been supported. Of crucial importance is recognition of objects belonging to categories for which the individual possesses expertise. According to the expertise theory, such objects should show the same effects associated with faces (i.e., configural processing; activation of the fusiform face area; impaired recognition in prosopagnosics). None of these effects has been obtained reliably. Instead, non-face objects of expertise typically show the same effects as objects for which individuals have no expertise. Thus, faces have special and unique characteristics not shared by other objects.

Models of face recognition

We now turn to models of face recognition, most of which have emphasised the sheer variety of information we extract from faces. The model considered in most detail is that of Bruce and Young (1986). Why is that? It has been easily the most influential theoretical approach to face recognition. Indeed, most subsequent models incorporate many ideas taken from the Bruce and Young model.

The model consists of eight components (see Figure 3.20):

(1) *Structural encoding*: this produces various representations or descriptions of faces.
(2) *Expression analysis*: other people's emotional states are inferred from their facial expression.
(3) *Facial speech analysis*: speech perception is assisted by observing a speaker's lip movements (lip-reading – see Chapter 9).
(4) *Directed visual processing*: specific facial information is processed selectively.
(5) *Face recognition nodes*: these contain structural information about known faces.
(6) *Person identity nodes*: these provide information about individuals (e.g., occupation, interests).
(7) *Name generation*: a person's name is stored separately.
(8) *Cognitive system*: this contains additional information (e.g., most actors and actresses have attractive faces); it influences which other components receive attention.

What predictions follow from the model? First, there should be major differences in the

processing of familiar and unfamiliar faces. Recognising familiar faces depends mainly on structural encoding, face recognition units, person identity nodes, and name generation. In contrast, the processing of unfamiliar faces involves structural encoding, expression analysis, facial speech analysis, and directed visual processing.

Second, consider the processing of facial identity (who is the person?) and the processing of facial expression (e.g., what is he/she feeling?). According to the model, *separate* processing routes are involved in the two cases, with the key component for processing facial expression being the expression analysis component.

Third, when we look at a familiar face, familiarity information from the face recognition unit should be accessed first, followed by information about that person (e.g., occupation)

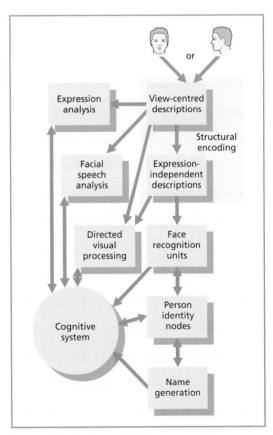

Figure 3.20 The model of face recognition put forward by Bruce and Young (1986).

from the person identity node, followed by that person's name from the name generation component. Thus, familiarity decisions about a face should be made faster than decisions based on person identity nodes, and the latter decisions should be made faster than decisions concerning the individual's name.

If you found it a struggle to come to grips with the complexities of the Bruce and Young (1986) model, help is at hand. Duchaine and Nakayama (2006) have provided a modified version of that model including an additional face-detection stage (see Figure 3.21). At this initial stage, observers decide whether the stimulus they are looking at is a face. Duchaine (2006), in a study discussed earlier, found that a prosopag-

nosic called Edward detected faces as rapidly as healthy controls in spite of his generally very poor face recognition.

Evidence

It is self-evident that the processing of familiar faces differs from that of unfamiliar ones, because we only have access to relevant stored knowledge (e.g., name, occupation) with familiar faces. If the two types of face are processed very differently, we might find a double dissociation in which some patients have good recognition for familiar faces but poor recognition for unfamiliar faces, whereas other patients show the opposite pattern. Malone, Morris, Kay, and Levin (1982) obtained this double dissociation. One patient recognised the photographs of 82% of famous statesmen but was extremely poor at matching unfamiliar faces. A second patient performed normally at matching unfamiliar faces but recognised the photographs of only 23% of famous people. However, Young, Newcombe, de Haan, Small, and Hay (1993) reported less clear findings with 34 brain-damaged men. There was only weak evidence for selective impairment of either familiar or unfamiliar face recognition.

Much research supports the assumption that separate routes are involved in the processing of facial identity and facial expression. Young et al. (1993) reported a double dissociation in which some patients showed good performance on face recognition but poor performance on identifying facial expression, whereas others showed the opposite pattern. Humphreys, Avidan, and Behrmann (2007) reported very clear findings in three participants with developmental prosopagnosia. All three had poor ability to recognise faces, but their ability to recognise facial expressions (even the most subtle ones) was comparable to that of healthy individuals.

Many patients with intact face recognition but facial expression impairments have other emotional impairments (e.g., poor memory for emotional experience; impaired subjective emotional experience – Calder & Young, 2005). As Calder and Young (p. 647) pointed out, "It seems likely that at least some facial expression

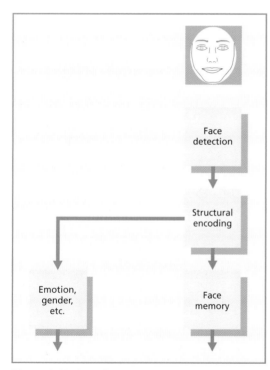

Figure 3.21 Simplified version of the Bruce and Young (1986) model of face recognition. Face detection is followed by processing of the face's structure, which is then matched to a memory representation (face memory). The perceptual representation of the face can also be used for recognition of facial expression and gender discrimination. Reprinted from Duchaine and Nakayama (2006), Copyright © 2006, with permission from Elsevier.

impairments reflect damage to emotion systems rather than to face-specific mechanisms."

It has often been argued that different brain regions are involved in the processing of facial expressions and facial identity. Haxby et al. (2000) argued that the processing of changeable aspects of faces (especially expressions) occurs mainly in the superior temporal sulcus. Other areas associated with emotion (e.g., the amygdala) are also involved in the processing of facial expression. The evidence provides modest support for this theory. Winston, Vuilleumier, and Dolan (2003) found that repeating facial *identity* across face pairs affected activation within the fusiform face area, whereas repeating facial *expression* affected an area within the superior temporal sulcus not influenced by repeated facial identity. In general, however, the evidence much more consistently implicates the fusiform face area in processing of facial identity than the superior temporal sulcus in processing of facial expression (Calder & Young, 2005).

Calder, Young, Keane, and Dean (2000) constructed three types of composite stimuli based on the top and bottom halves of faces of two different people:

(1) The same person posing two different facial expressions.
(2) Two different people posing the same facial expression.
(3) Two different people posing different facial expressions.

The participants' task was to decide rapidly the facial identity or the facial expression of the person shown in the bottom half of the composite picture.

What would we predict if *different* processes are involved in recognition of facial identity and facial expression? Consider the task of deciding on the facial expression of the face shown in the bottom half. Performance should be slower when the facial expression is different in the top half, but there should be *no* additional cost when the two halves also differ in facial identity. In similar fashion, facial identity decisions should not be slower when

the facial expressions differ in the two face halves. The predicted findings were obtained (see Figure 3.22).

According to the Bruce and Young (1986) model, when we look at a familiar face we first access familiarity information, followed by personal information (e.g., the person's occupation), followed by the person's name. As predicted, Young, McWeeny, Hay, and Ellis (1986) found the decision as to whether a face was familiar was made faster than the decision as to whether it was a politician's face. Kampf, Nachson, and Babkoff (2002) found as predicted that participants categorised familiar faces with respect to occupation faster than they could name the same faces.

The Bruce and Young model assumes that the name generation component can be accessed *only* via the appropriate person identity node.

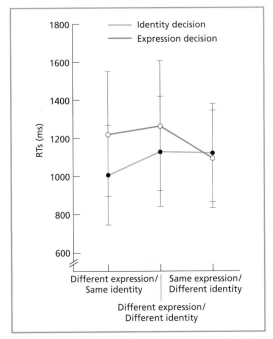

Figure 3.22 Participants' reaction times to identify the expression displayed (expression decision) or identity (identity decision) in the bottom segment of three types of composite images (different expression–same identity; same expression–different identity; and different expression–different identity). From Calder et al., 2000. Copyright © 2000 American Psychological Association. Reproduced with permission.

Thus, we should never be able to put a name to a face without also having available other information about that person (e.g., his/her occupation). Young, Hay, and Ellis (1985) asked people to keep a diary record of problems they experienced in face recognition. There were 1008 incidents in total, but people *never* reported putting a name to a face while knowing nothing else about that person. If the appropriate face recognition unit is activated but the person identity node is not, there should be a feeling of familiarity but an inability to think of any relevant information about that person. In the incidents collected by Young et al., this was reported on 233 occasions.

Most published studies comparing speed of recall of personal information and names have focused exclusively on famous faces. As Brédart, Brennen, Delchambre, McNeill, and Burton (2005) pointed out, we name famous faces less often than our personal friends and acquaintances. If the frequency with which we use people's names influences the speed with which we can recall them, findings with faces with which we are personally familiar might differ from those obtained with famous faces. Brédart et al. presented members of a Cognitive Science Department with the faces of close colleagues and asked them to name the face or to indicate the highest degree the person had obtained. Naming times were faster than the times taken to provide the person information about educational level (832 ms versus 1033 ms, respectively), which is the opposite to the predictions of the model. The probable reason why these findings differed from those of previous researchers is because of the high frequency of exposure to the names of close colleagues.

Evaluation

Bruce and Young's (1986) model has deservedly been highly influential. It identifies the wide range of information that can be extracted from faces. The assumption that separate processing routes are involved in the processing of facial identity and facial expression has received empirical support. Key differences in the processing of familiar and unfamiliar faces are identified. Finally, as predicted by the model, the processing of familiar faces typically leads first to accessing of familiarity information, followed by personal information, and then finally name information.

The model possesses various limitations, mostly due to the fact it is oversimplified. First, the model omits the first stage of processing, during which observers detect that they are looking at a face (Duchaine & Nakayama, 2006).

Second, the assumption that facial identity and facial expression involve separate processing routes may be too extreme (Calder & Young, 2005). The great majority of prosopagnosics have severe problems with processing facial expression as well as facial identity, and the two processing routes are probably only partially separate.

Third, patients with impaired processing of facial expression sometimes have much greater problems with one emotional category (e.g., fear, disgust) than others. This suggests there may not be a single system for facial expressions, and that the processing of facial expressions involves emotional systems to a greater extent than assumed by the model.

Fourth, the assumption that the processing of names always occurs after the processing of other personal information about faces is too rigid (Brédart et al., 2005). What is needed is a more flexible approach, one that has been provided by various models (e.g., Burton, Bruce, & Hancock, 1999).

VISUAL IMAGERY

In this chapter (and Chapter 2), we have focused on the main processes involved in visual perception. We turn now to visual imagery, which "occurs when a visual short-term memory (STM) representation is present but the stimulus is not actually being viewed; visual imagery is accompanied by the experience of 'seeing with the mind's eye'" (Kosslyn & Thompson, 2003, p. 723). It is often assumed that imagery and perception are very similar, which is probably consistent with your personal experience of imagery.

If visual imagery and perception are very similar, why don't we confuse images and perceptions? In fact, a few people show such confusions, suffering from hallucinations in which what is regarded as visual perception occurs in the absence of the appropriate environmental stimulus. Hallucinations are common in individuals with **Charles Bonnet syndrome**, a condition associated with eye disease in which detailed visual hallucinations not under the patient's control are experienced. One sufferer reported the following hallucination: "There's heads of 17th century men and women, with nice heads of hair. Wigs, I should think. Very disapproving, all of them. They never smile" (Santhouse, Howard, & ffytche, 2000). ffytche found using fMRI that patients with Charles Bonnet syndrome had increased activity in brain areas specialised for visual processing when hallucinating. In addition, hallucinations in colour were associated with increased activity in brain areas specialised for colour processing, hallucinations of faces were related to increased activity in regions specialised for face processing, and so on.

Very few people experience hallucinations. Indeed, anyone (other than those with eye disease) suffering from numerous hallucinations is unlikely to remain at liberty for long! Why don't most of us confuse images with perceptions? One reason is that we are often aware that we have *deliberately* constructed images, which is not the case with perception. Another reason is that images typically contain much less detail than perception, as was reported by Harvey (1986). Participants rated their visual images of faces as most similar to photographs of the same faces from which the sharpness of the edges and borders had been removed.

Perceptual anticipation theory

Kosslyn (e.g., 1994, 2005) proposed an extremely influential approach to mental imagery. It is known as perceptual anticipation theory because the mechanisms used to generate images involve processes used to anticipate perceiving stimuli. Thus, the theory assumes there are close similarities between visual imagery and visual perception. Visual images are **depictive representations** – they are like pictures or drawings in that the objects and parts of objects contained in them are arranged in space. More specifically, information within an image is organised spatially in the same way as information within a percept. Thus, for example, a visual image of a desk with a computer on top of it and a cat sleeping beneath it would be arranged so that the computer was at the top of the image and the cat at the bottom.

Where in the brain are these depictive representations formed? Kosslyn argues that such representations must be formed in a topographically organised brain area, meaning that the spatial organisation of brain activity resembles that of the imagined object. According to Kosslyn and Thompson (2003), depictive representations are created in early visual cortex, which consists of primary visual cortex (also known as BA17 or V1) and secondary visual cortex (also known as BA18 or V2) (see Figure 3.23). They used the term **visual buffer** to refer to the brain areas in which the depictive representations are formed, among which Areas 17 and 18 are of special importance. This visual buffer is used in visual perception as well as visual imagery; indeed, Areas 17 and 18 are of great importance in the early stages of visual processing. In perception, processing in the visual buffer depends primarily

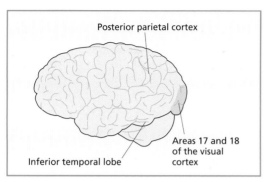

Figure 3.23 The approximate locations of the visual buffer in BA17 and BA18 of long-term memories of shapes in the inferior temporal lobe, and of spatial representations in posterior parietal cortex, according to Kosslyn and Thompson's (2003) anticipation theory.

on external stimulation. In contrast, visual images in the visual buffer depend on non-pictorial, propositional information stored in long-term memory. Visual long-term memories of shapes are stored in the inferior temporal lobe, whereas spatial representations are stored in posterior parietal cortex (see Figure 3.23).

We can compare Kosslyn's perceptual anticipation theory against the propositional theory of Pylyshyn (e.g., 2002, 2003a). According to Pylyshyn, performance on mental imagery tasks does not involve depictive or pictorial representations. Instead, what is involved is tacit knowledge (knowledge not generally accessible to conscious awareness). More specifically, tacit knowledge is "knowledge of *what things would look like* to subjects in situations like the ones in which they are to imagine themselves" (Pylyshyn, 2002, p. 161). Thus, participants given an imagery task base their performance on relevant stored knowledge rather than on visual images.

The exact nature of the tacit knowledge allegedly involved in visual imagery seems puzzling, because Pylyshyn has not provided a very explicit account. However, there is no reason within his theory to assume that early visual cortex would be involved when someone forms a visual image.

Imagery resembles perception

If visual perception and visual imagery depend on the same visual buffer, we would expect perception and imagery to influence each other. More specifically, there should be *facilitative* effects if the content of the perception and the image is the same but *interference* effects if the content is different. As we will see, both predictions have been supported.

So far as facilitation is concerned, we will consider a study by Pearson, Clifford, and Tong (2008). Observers initially perceived or imagined a green vertical grating or a red horizontal grating. After that, they saw a visual display in which a green grating was presented to one eye and a red grating to the other eye at various orientations. When two different stimuli are presented one to each eye there is binocular rivalry (see Glossary), with only *one* of the stimuli being consciously perceived. There was a facilitation effect, in that under binocular rivalry conditions the stimulus originally perceived or imagined was more likely to be perceived. This facilitation effect was greatest when the orientation of the grating under binocular rivalry conditions was the same as the initial orientation and least when there was a large difference in orientation (sees Figure 3.24). Note that the pattern of findings was remarkably similar regardless of whether the repeated grating was initially perceived or imagined. The overall findings suggest that visual imagery involves similar processes to visual perception. They also suggest that visual images contain detailed orientation-specific information as predicted by perceptual anticipation theory.

Baddeley and Andrade (2000) obtained an interference effect. Participants rated the vividness of visual or auditory images under control conditions (no additional task) or while performing a second task. This second task involved the visuo-spatial sketchpad (tapping a pattern on a keypad) or it involved the phonological loop (counting aloud repeatedly from 1 to 10) (see Chapter 6 for accounts of the visuo-spatial sketchpad and phonological loop).

According to Kosslyn's theory, visual imagery and spatial tapping tasks both involve use of

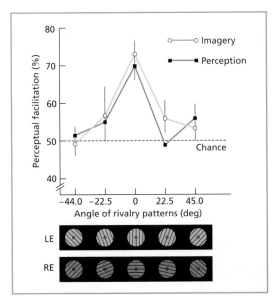

Figure 3.24 Perceptual facilitation (no facilitation = 50%) in a binocular rivalry task for previously seen or imagined patterns sharing the same orientation (0°) as the test figure or differing in orientation (−45°, −22.5°, 22.5°, or 45°). Reprinted from Pearson et al. (2008), Copyright © 2008, with permission from Elsevier.

the visual buffer, and so there should be an interference effect. This is precisely what was found (see Figure 3.25), since spatial tapping reduced the vividness of visual imagery more

than the vividness of auditory imagery. The counting task reduced the vividness of auditory imagery more than that of visual imagery, presumably because auditory perception and auditory imagery use the same mechanisms.

According to Kosslyn (1994, 2005), much processing associated with visual imagery occurs in early visual cortex (BA17 and BA18), although several other brain areas are also involved. Kosslyn and Thompson (2003) considered 59 brain-imaging studies in which activation of early visual cortex had been assessed. Tasks involving visual imagery were associated with activation of early visual cortex in about half the studies reviewed. Kosslyn and Thompson identified three factors jointly determining the probability of finding that early visual cortex is activated during visual imagery:

(1) *The nature of the task*: Imagery tasks requiring participants to inspect fine details of their visual images are much more likely to be associated with activity in early visual cortex than are other imagery tasks.

(2) *Sensitivity of brain-imaging technique*: Early visual cortex is more likely to be involved in visual imagery when more sensitive brain-imaging techniques (e.g.,

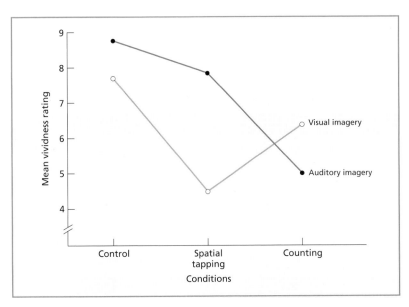

Figure 3.25 Vividness of auditory and visual imagery as a function of additional task (none in the control condition, spatial tapping, or counting). Data from Baddeley and Andrade (2000).

fMRI) are used than when less sensitive ones (e.g., PET) are used.

(3) *Shape-based vs. spatial/movement tasks*: Early visual cortex is more likely to be involved when the imagery task requires processing of an object's shape than when the emphasis is on imaging an object in motion. Motion or spatial processing often involves posterior parietal cortex (e.g., Aleman et al., 2002).

The finding that activation in early visual cortex is associated with visual imagery provides no guarantee that it is *essential* for visual imagery. More convincing evidence was reported by Kosslyn et al. (1999). Participants memorised a stimulus containing four sets of stripes, after which they formed a visual image of it and compared the stripes (e.g., in terms of their relative width). Immediately before performing the task, some participants received repetitive transcranial magnetic stimulation (rTMS; see Glossary) applied to Area 17 (V1). rTMS significantly impaired performance on the imagery task, thus showing it is causally involved in imagery.

Sceptics might argue that showing that the brain areas involved in visual imagery are often the same as those involved in visual perception does not prove that imagery and perception involve the same *processes*. The findings of Klein et al. (2004) provide reassurance. Participants were presented with flickering black-and-white, bow-tie shaped stimuli with a horizontal or a vertical orientation in the perceptual condition. In the imagery condition, they imagined the same bow-tie shaped stimuli. Unsurprisingly, there was more activation within early visual cortex in the vertical direction when the stimulus was in the vertical orientation and more in the horizontal direction when it was in the horizontal orientation. Dramatically, the same was also the case in the imagery condition, thus providing powerful evidence that the processes involved in visual imagery closely approximate to those involved in visual perception (see Figure 3.26).

Ganis, Thompson, and Kosslyn (2004) used fMRI to compare patterns of activation across most of the brain in visual perception and imagery. Participants visualised or saw faint drawings of objects and then made judgements about them (e.g., contains circular parts). There were two main findings. First, there was extensive overlap in the brain areas associated with perception and imagery. This was especially so in the frontal and parietal areas, perhaps because perception and imagery both involve similar cognitive control processes. Second, the brain areas activated during imagery formed a *subset* of those activated during perception, especially in temporal and occipital regions. This suggests that visual imagery involves some (but not all) of the processes involved in visual perception.

Imagery does not resemble perception

In spite of the findings discussed above, there is evidence suggesting important differences between visual imagery and visual perception. For example, imagine a cube balanced on one corner and then cut across the equator. What is the shape of the cut surface when the top is cut off? Most students say it is a square (Ian Gordon, personal communication), but in fact it is a regular hexagon. The implication is that images often consist of simplified structural descriptions that omit important aspects of the object being imagined.

Slezak (1991, 1995) also found that images can be seriously deficient when compared against visual percepts. Participants memorised an image resembling one of those shown in Figure 3.27. They then rotated the image by 90 degrees clockwise and reported what they saw. No participants reported seeing the objects that are clearly visible if you rotate the book. This was *not* really a deficiency in memory – participants who sketched the image from memory and then rotated it did see the new object. It seems that information contained in images cannot be used as flexibly as visual information.

If perception and imagery involve the same mechanisms, we might expect that brain damage would often have similar effects on perception and on imagery. This expectation has only sometimes been supported (see Bartolomeo, 2002).

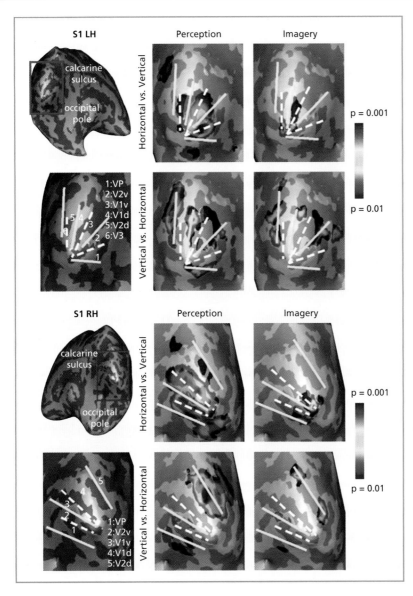

Figure 3.26 Differing patterns of activation in V1 to horizontal and vertical stimuli that were visually perceived or imagined (LH = left hemisphere; RH = right hemisphere). Note the great similarity between the patterns associated with perception and imagery. Reprinted from Klein et al. (2004), Copyright © 2004, with permission from Elsevier.

In considering this evidence, bear in mind the main differences between perception and imagery. Processing in the visual buffer depends mainly on external stimulation in perception, whereas non-pictorial information stored in long-term memory within the inferior temporal lobe is of crucial importance in imagery (see Figure 3.28).

Some brain-damaged patients have essentially intact visual perception but impaired visual imagery. According to Bartolomeo (2002, p. 362), "In the available cases of (relatively) isolated deficits of visual mental imagery, the left temporal lobe seems always extensively damaged." For example, Sirigu and Duhamel (2001) studied a patient, JB, who had extensive damage to both temporal lobes. JB initially had severe problems with visual perception, but these problems disappeared subsequently. However, JB continued to have a profound

Figure 3.27 Slezak (1991, 1995) asked participants to memorise one of the above images. They then imagined rotating the image 90° clockwise and reported what they saw. None of them reported seeing the figures that can be seen clearly if you rotate the page by 90° clockwise. Left image from Slezak (1995), centre image from Slezak (1991), right image reprinted from Pylyshyn (2003a), reprinted with permission from Elsevier and the author.

impairment of visual imagery. Kosslyn (e.g., 1994) argued that visual imagery differs from visual perception in that there is a process of *generation* – visual images are constructed from object information stored in the temporal lobe. The notion that object information is stored in the temporal lobe was supported by Lee, Hong, Seo, Tae, and Hong (2000). They applied electrical cortical stimulation to epileptic patients, and found that they only had conscious visual experience of complex visual forms (e.g., animals, people) when the temporal lobe was stimulated. In sum, the co-existence of intact visual perception but impaired visual imagery may occur because stored object knowledge is more important in visual imagery.

The opposite pattern of intact visual imagery but impaired visual perception has also been reported (see Bartolomeo, 2002). Some people suffer from **Anton's syndrome** ("blindness denial"), in which a blind person is unaware that he/she is blind and may confuse imagery for actual perception. Goldenburg, Müllbacher, and Nowak (1995) described the case of a patient with Anton's syndrome, nearly all of whose primary visual cortex had been destroyed. In spite of that, the patient generated visual images so vivid they were mistaken for real visual perception.

Bartolomeo et al. (1998) studied a patient, D, with brain damage to parts of early visual cortex (BA18) and to temporal cortex. She had severe perceptual impairment for object recognition, colour identification, and face recognition. However, "Madame D performed the imagery tasks…in such a rapid and easy way as to suggest that her imagery resources were relatively spared by the lesions."

How can we account for intact visual imagery combined with impaired visual perception? There is no clear answer. Perhaps such patients actually have impairments of visual imagery which would become apparent if they were given imagery tasks requiring focusing on high-resolution details. If so, that would preserve Kosslyn's theory. Alternatively, it may simply be that early visual cortex is more important for visual perception than for visual imagery.

Evaluation
Considerable progress has been made in understanding the relationship between visual

Figure 3.28 Structures and processes involved in visual perception and visual imagery. Based on Bartolomeo (2002).

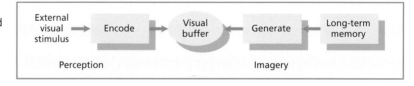

imagery and visual perception. The central assumption of Kosslyn's perceptual anticipation theory, namely, that very similar processes are involved in imagery and perception, has attracted considerable support. The predictions that perceptual and imagery tasks will have facilitatory effects on each other if the content is the same, but will interfere with each other otherwise, have been supported. Of most importance, visual imagery involving attention to high-resolution details consistently involves early visual cortex, a finding much more in line with Kosslyn's theory than Pylyshyn's.

On the negative side, the evidence from brain-damaged patients is harder to evaluate. In particular, the existence of patients with intact visual imagery but severely impaired visual perception is puzzling from the perspective of Kosslyn's theory. More generally, we need an increased understanding of *why* dissociations occur between perception and imagery. Finally, we know that different brain areas are involved in imagery for object shapes and imagery for movement and spatial relationships. However, these forms of imagery are presumably often used together, and we do not know how that happens.

CHAPTER SUMMARY

- Perceptual organisation
  The Gestaltists put forward several laws of perceptual organisation that were claimed to assist in figure–ground segregation. There is much evidence supporting these laws, but they generally work better with artificial stimuli than with natural scenes. The Gestaltists provided descriptions rather than explanations, and they incorrectly argued that the principles of visual organisation do not depend on experience and learning. Subsequent research has indicated that top-down processes are important in perceptual organisation, and there is evidence that the processes involved in object recognition are similar to those involved in figure–ground segregation. In addition, the principle of uniform connectedness seems to be important in perceptual grouping.

- Theories of object recognition
  Biederman assumed that objects consist of basic shapes known as geons. An object's geons are determined by edge-extraction processes focusing on invariant properties of edges, and the resultant geonal description is viewpoint-invariant. However, edge information is often insufficient to permit object identification. Biederman's theory was designed to account for easy categorical discriminations, and the viewpoint-invariant processes emphasised by him are generally replaced by viewpoint-dependent processes for hard within-category discriminations. The processes involved in object recognition are more varied and flexible than assumed by Biederman, and it is likely that viewpoint-invariant and viewpoint-dependent information is combined in object recognition.

- Cognitive neuroscience approach to object recognition
  Inferotemporal cortex plays a major role in object recognition. Some inferotemporal neurons have high invariance (consistent with viewpoint-invariant theories of object recognition), whereas others have low invariance (consistent with viewpoint-dependent theories). Regions of inferotemporal cortex seem to exhibit some specialisation for different categories of object. Most research has focused on the ventral stream and on bottom-up processes. However, the dorsal stream contributes to object recognition, and top-down processes often have an important influence on object recognition.

- Cognitive neuropsychology of object recognition
  Visual agnosia can be divided into apperceptive agnosia and associative agnosia, but this is an oversimplification. Much of the evidence is consistent with a hierarchical model in which object recognition proceeds through several stages, with different agnosic patients having special problems at different processing stages. This hierarchical model is based on the assumption that processing stages occur in a serial, bottom-up fashion. However, it is likely that there are some top-down influences during object recognition, and that processing often does not proceed neatly from one stage to the next.

- Face recognition
  Face recognition involves more holistic processing than object recognition, as is shown by the inversion, part–whole, and composite effects. Prosopagnosic patients often show covert face recognition in spite of not recognising familiar faces overtly. There is a double dissociation in which some individuals have severe problems with face recognition but not with object recognition, and others have the opposite pattern. The fusiform face area (typically damaged in prosopagnosics) plays a major role in face recognition but is not used exclusively for that purpose. The hypothesis that faces only appear special because we have much expertise with them has not received much support. According to Bruce and Young's model, there are major differences in the processing of familiar and unfamiliar faces, and processing of facial identity is separate from processing of facial expression. There is broad support for the model, but it is clearly oversimplified.

- Visual imagery
  According to Kosslyn's perceptual anticipation theory, there are close similarities between visual imagery and visual perception, with images being depictive representations. It is assumed that these depictive representations are created in early visual cortex. In contrast, Pylyshyn proposed a propositional theory, according to which people asked to form images make use of tacit propositional knowledge. There is strong evidence from fMRI and rTMS studies that early visual cortex is of central importance in visual imagery. Many brain-damaged patients have comparable impairments of perception and imagery. However, the existence of dissociations between perception and imagery in such patients poses problems for Kosslyn's theory.

FURTHER READING

- Blake, R., & Sekuler, R. (2005). *Perception* (5th ed.). New York: McGraw-Hill. Chapter 6 of this American textbook provides good coverage of topics relating to object recognition.
- Ganis, G., Thompson, W.L., & Kosslyn, S.M. (2009). Visual mental imagery: More than "seeing with the mind's eye". In J.R. Brockmole (ed.), *The visual world in memory*. Hove, UK: Psychology Press. This chapter provides an up-to date perspective on visual imagery.
- Goldstein, E.B. (2007). *Sensation and perception* (7th ed.). Belmont, CA: Thomson. This textbook contains various chapters covering topics discussed in this chapter.
- Humphreys, G.W., & Riddoch, M.J. (2006). Features, objects, action: The cognitive neuro-psychology of visual object processing, 1984–2004. *Cognitive Neuropsychology, 23,*

156–183. What has been learned about object recognition from the study of brain-damaged patients is discussed in detail in this comprehensive article.

- Mather, G. (2009). *Foundations of sensation and perception* (2nd ed.). Hove, UK: Psychology Press. This textbook contains excellent coverage of the key topics in perception; object recognition is discussed in Chapter 9.
- McKone, E., Kanwisher, N., & Duchaine, B.C. (2007). Can generic expertise explain special processing for faces? *Trends in Cognitive Sciences, 11*, 8–15. Three experts in face recognition present an excellent and succinct account of our current knowledge.
- Morgan, M. (2003). *The space between our ears: How the brain represents visual space.* London: Weidenfeld & Nicolson. Much of this entertaining book is devoted to the topics discussed in this chapter.
- Peissig, J.J., & Tarr, M.J. (2007). Visual object recognition: Do we know more now than we did 20 years ago? *Annual Review of Psychology, 58*, 75–96. Thankfully, the answer to the question the authors pose is positive! This article provides a good overview of developments in our understanding of object recognition over the past 20 years.

CHAPTER 4

PERCEPTION, MOTION, AND ACTION

INTRODUCTION

Several issues considered in this chapter hark back to earlier discussions in Chapter 2. The first major theme addressed in this chapter is perception for action, or how we manage to act appropriately on the environment and the objects within it. Of relevance here are theories (e.g., the perception–action theory; the dual-process approach) distinguishing between processes and systems involved in vision-for-perception and those involved in vision-for-action. Those theories are discussed in Chapter 2. Here we will consider theories providing more detailed accounts of vision-for-action and/or the workings of the dorsal pathway allegedly underlying vision-for-action.

The second theme addressed is perception of movement. Again, this issue was considered to some extent in Chapter 2, to which reference should be made. In this chapter, we focus specifically on perception of biological movement.

Finally, we consider the extent to which visual perception depends on attention. We will see there is convincing evidence that attention plays an important role in determining which aspects of the environment are consciously perceived. This issue is discussed at the end of the chapter because it provides a useful bridge between the areas of visual perception and attention (the subject of the next chapter).

DIRECT PERCEPTION

James Gibson (1950, 1966, 1979) put forward a radical theoretical approach to visual perception that was largely ignored for many years. It was generally assumed until about 25 years ago that the central function of visual perception is to allow us to identify or recognise objects in the world around us. This involves extensive cognitive processing, including relating information extracted from the visual environment to our stored knowledge about objects (see Chapter 3). Gibson argued that this approach is of limited relevance to visual perception in the real world. In our evolutionary history, vision initially developed to allow our ancestors to respond appropriately to the environment (e.g., killing animals for food; avoiding falling over precipices). Even today, perceptual information is used mainly in the organisation of action, and so perception and action are closely intertwined. As Wade and Swanston (2001, p. 4) pointed out, Gibson "incorporated the time dimension into perception, so that all perception becomes motion perception."

Gibson argued that perception influences our actions without any need for complex cognitive processes to occur. The reason is because the information available from environmental stimuli is much greater than had previously been assumed. There are clear links between Gibson's views on the nature of perception and the vision-for-action system proposed by

Milner and Goodale (1995, 1998; see Chapter 2). According to both theoretical accounts, there is an intimate relationship between perception and action. In addition, perception influences action rapidly and with minimal involvement of conscious awareness. Support for this position was reported by Chua and Enns (2005). Their participants could not gain conscious access to the information they used in pointing, even though they could see and feel their own hands.

Gibson (1979) regarded his theoretical approach as *ecological*, emphasising that the central function of perception is to facilitate interactions between the individual and his/her environment. More specifically, he put forward a direct theory of perception:

> *When I assert that perception of the environment is direct, I mean that it is not mediated by* retinal *pictures,* neural *pictures, or* mental *pictures.* Direct perception *is the activity of getting information from the ambient array of light. I call this a process of* information pickup *that involves…looking around, getting around, and looking at things* (p. 147).

We will briefly consider some of Gibson's theoretical assumptions:

- The pattern of light reaching the eye is an **optic array**; this structured light contains all the visual information from the environment striking the eye.
- The optic array provides unambiguous or invariant information about the layout of objects in spaces. This information comes in many forms, including texture gradients, optic flow patterns, and affordances (all described below).
- Perception involves "picking up" the rich information provided by the optic array directly via resonance with little or no information processing.

Gibson was given the task in the Second World War of preparing training films describing the problems experienced by pilots taking off and landing. This led him to wonder what information pilots have available to them while performing these manoeuvres. There is **optic flow** (Gibson, 1950), which consists of the changes in the pattern of light reaching an observer that are created when he/she moves or parts of the visual environment move. The typical perceptual experience produced by optic flow can be illustrated by considering a pilot approaching a landing strip. The point towards which the pilot is moving (the **focus of expansion** or pole) appears motionless, with the rest of the visual environment apparently moving away from that point (see Figure 4.1). The further away any part of the landing strip is from that point, the greater is its apparent speed of movement. Over time, aspects of the environment at some distance from the focus of expansion pass out of the visual field and are replaced by new aspects emerging at the focus of expansion. A shift in the centre of the outflow indicates a change in the plane's direction.

Evidence that optic flow is important was reported by Bruggeman, Zosh, and Warren (2007). Participants walked through a virtual environment to reach a goal with their apparent heading direction displaced 10 degrees to the right of the actual walking direction. The visual environment either provided rich optic flow information or none at all. Participants' performance was much better when they had access to optic-flow information. However, the two

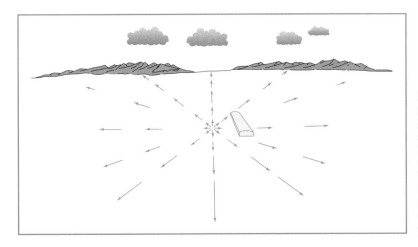

Figure 4.1 The optic flow field as a pilot comes in to land, with the focus of expansion in the middle. From Gibson (1950). Copyright © 1950 Wadsworth, a part of Cengage Learning, Inc. Reproduced with permission www.cengage.com/permissions.

environments differed in other ways as well. As Rushton (2008) pointed out, if you are walking towards a target in a richly textured environment, objects initially to the left of the target will remain to the left, and those to the right will remain to the right. Participants may have used that information rather than optic flow.

According to Gibson (1950), optic flow provides pilots with unambiguous information about their direction, speed, and altitude. Gibson was so impressed by the wealth of sensory information available to pilots in optic flow fields that he devoted himself to an analysis of the information available in other visual environments. For example, **texture gradients** provide very useful information. As we saw in Chapter 2, objects slanting away from you have a gradient (rate of change) of texture density as you look from the near edge to the far edge. Gibson (1966, 1979) claimed that observers "pick up" this information from the optic array, and so some aspects of depth are perceived directly.

Gibson (1966, 1979) argued that certain higher-order characteristics of the visual array (**invariants**) remain unaltered as observers move around their environment. The fact that they remain the same over different viewing angles makes invariants of particular importance. The lack of apparent movement of the point towards which we are moving (the focus of expansion) is an invariant feature of the optic array (discussed earlier). Another invariant is useful in terms of maintaining size constancy: the ratio of an object's height to the distance between its base and the horizon is invariant regardless of its distance from the viewer. This invariant is known as the horizon ratio relation.

Affordances

How did Gibson account for the role of meaning in perception? Gibson (1979) claimed that all potential uses of objects (their **affordances**) are directly perceivable. For example, a ladder "affords" ascent or descent, and a chair "affords" sitting. The notion of affordances was even applied (implausibly) to postboxes (p. 139):

KEY TERMS

texture gradient: the rate of change of texture density from the front to the back of a slanting object.

invariants: properties of the **optic array** that remain constant even though other aspects vary; part of Gibson's theory.

affordances: the potential uses of an object, which Gibson claimed are perceived directly.

"The postbox...affords letter-mailing to a letter-writing human in a community with a postal system. This fact is perceived when the postbox is identified as such." Most objects give rise to more than one affordance, with the particular affordance influencing behaviour depending on the perceiver's current psychological state. Thus, an orange can have the affordance of edibility to a hungry person but a projectile to an angry one.

Gibson had little to say about the processes involved in learning which affordances will satisfy particular goals. However, as Gordon (1989, p. 161) pointed out, Gibson assumed that, "the most important contribution of learning to perception is to educate attention."

Most objects give rise to more than one affordance, depending on the perceiver's current psychological state. Would you want to eat this satsuma right now, or throw it at someone?

More generally, Gibson was determined to show that all the information needed to make sense of the visual environment is directly present in the visual input.

Gibson's notion of affordances has received some support from empirical research. Di Stasi and Guardini (2007) asked observers to judge the affordance of "climbability" of steps varying in height. The step height that was judged the most "climbable" was the one that would have produced the minimum expenditure of energy.

Gibson argued that an object's affordances are perceived directly. Pappas and Mack (2008) presented images of objects so briefly that they were not consciously perceived. In spite of that, each object's main affordance produced motor priming. Thus, for example, the presentation of a hammer caused activation in those parts of the brain involved in preparing to use a hammer.

Resonance

How exactly do human perceivers "pick up" the invariant information supplied by the visual world? According to Gibson, there is a process of **resonance**, which he explained by analogy to the workings of a radio. When a radio set is turned on, there may be only a hissing sound. However, if it is tuned in properly, speech or music will be clearly audible. In Gibson's terms, the radio is now resonating with the information contained in the electromagnetic radiation.

The above analogy suggests that perceivers can pick up information from the environment in a relatively automatic way if attuned to it. The radio operates in a holistic way, in the sense that damage to any part of its circuitry would prevent it from working. In a similar way, Gibson assumed that the nervous system works in a holistic way when perceiving.

KEY TERM

resonance: the process of automatic pick-up of visual information from the environment in Gibson's theory.

Evaluation

The ecological approach to perception has proved successful in various ways. First, Gibson was right to emphasise that visual perception evolved in large part to allow us to move successfully around the environment.

Second, Gibson was far ahead of his time. It is now often accepted (e.g., Milner & Goodale, 1995, 1998; Norman, 2002) that there are two visual systems, a vision-for-perception system and a vision-for-action system. Gibson argued that our perceptual system allows us to respond rapidly and accurately to environmental stimuli without making use of memory, and these are all features of the vision-for-action system. This system was largely ignored prior to his pioneering research and theorising.

Third, Gibson was correct that visual stimuli provide much more information than had previously been believed. Traditional laboratory research had generally involved static observers looking at impoverished visual displays. In contrast, Gibson correctly emphasised that we spend much of our time in motion. The moment-by-moment changes in the optic array provide much useful information (discussed in detail shortly).

Fourth, Gibson was correct to argue that inaccurate perception often depends on the use of very artificial situations and a failure to focus on the important role of visual perception in guiding behaviour. For example, many powerful illusory effects present when observers make judgements about visual stimuli disappear when observers grasp the stimuli in question (see Chapter 2).

What are the limitations of Gibson's approach? First, the processes involved in perception are much more complicated than implied by Gibson. Many of these complexities were discussed in detail in Chapters 2 and 3.

Second, Gibson largely ignored the vision-for-perception system. We can approach this issue by considering a quotation from Fodor and Pylyshyn (1981, p. 189): "What you see when you see a thing depends upon what the thing you see is. But what you see the thing as depends upon what you know about what you are seeing." That sounds like mumbo jumbo. However, Fodor and Pylyshyn illustrated their point by considering someone called Smith who is lost at sea. Smith sees the Pole Star, but what matters for his survival is whether he sees it as the Pole Star or as simply an ordinary star. If it is the former, this will be useful for navigational purposes; if it is the latter, Smith remains as lost as ever. Gibson's approach is relevant to "seeing" but has little to say about "seeing as".

Third, Gibson's argument that we do not need to assume the existence of internal representations (e.g., object memories) to understand perception is seriously flawed. It follows from the logic of Gibson's position that, "There are invariants specifying a friend's face, a performance of Hamlet, or the sinking of the *Titanic*, and no knowledge of the friend, of the play, or of maritime history is required to perceive these things" (Bruce, Green, & Georgeson, 2003, p. 410).

Fourth, as discussed in the next section, Gibson's views are oversimplified when applied to the central issue with which he was concerned. For example, when moving towards a goal we use many more sources of information than suggested by Gibson.

VISUALLY GUIDED ACTION

From an ecological perspective, it is very important to understand how we move around the environment. For example, what information do we use when walking towards a given target? If we are to avoid premature death, we must ensure we are not hit by cars when crossing the road, and when driving we must avoid hitting cars coming the other way. Visual perception plays a major role in facilitating human locomotion and ensuring our safety. Some of the main processes involved are discussed below.

Heading and steering: optic flow and future path

When we want to reach some goal (e.g., a gate at the end of a field), we use visual information to move directly towards it. Gibson (1950) emphasised the importance of optic flow. When someone is moving forwards in a straight line, the point towards which he/she is moving (the point of expansion) appears motionless. In contrast, the point around that point seems to be expanding. Various aspects of optic flow might be of crucial importance to an observer's perception of heading (the point towards which he/she is moving at any given moment). Gibson (1950) proposed a global radial out-flow hypothesis, according to which the overall or global outflow pattern specifies an observer's heading. If we happen not to be moving directly towards our goal, we can resolve the problem simply by using the focus of expansion and optic flow to bring our heading into alignment with our goal.

Gibson's views make reasonable sense when applied to an individual moving straight from point A to point B. However, complications occur when we start considering what happens when we cannot move directly to our goal (e.g., going around a bend in the road; avoiding obstacles). There are also issues concerning head and eye movements. The **retinal flow field** (changes in the pattern of light on the retina) is determined by two factors:

(1) Linear flow containing a focus of expansion.
(2) Rotary flow (rotation in the retinal image) produced by following a curved path and by eye and head movements.

Thus, it is often difficult for us to use information from retinal flow to determine our direction of heading. One possible way of doing this would be by using extra-retinal information about eye and head movements (e.g., signals from stretch receptors in the eye muscles) to remove the effects of rotary flow.

Evidence

There have been several attempts to locate the brain areas most involved in processing optic-flow and heading information (see Britten, 2008, for a review). Most of the evidence implicates the dorsal medial superior temporal cortex and the ventral intraparietal area. For example, Britten and van Wezel (1998) found they could produce biases in heading perception in monkeys by stimulating parts of the medial superior temporal area. This finding suggests that that area plays an important role in processing direction of heading. Smith, Wall, Williams, and Singh (2006) found that the human medial superior temporal area was strongly and selectively responsive to optic flow (see Figure 4.2). In contrast, the human medial temporal area was not selective for optic flow because it also responded to random motion.

Warren and Hannon (1988) produced two films consisting of patterns of moving dots. Each film simulated the optic flow that would be produced if someone moved in a given direction. In one condition, observers generated retinal flow by making an eye movement to pursue a target in the display. In the other condition, observers fixated a point in the display and rotary flow was added to the display. The same retinal flow information was available in both conditions, but additional extra-retinal information to calculate rotary flow was available only in the first condition. The accuracy of heading judgments was unaffected by the extra-retinal information, suggesting that observers may use optic flow on its own.

Subsequent research has indicated that extra-retinal information about eye and head movements often influences heading judgements. Wilkie and Wann (2003) had observers watch films simulating brisk walking or steady cycling/slow driving along a linear path while fixating a target offset from the direction of

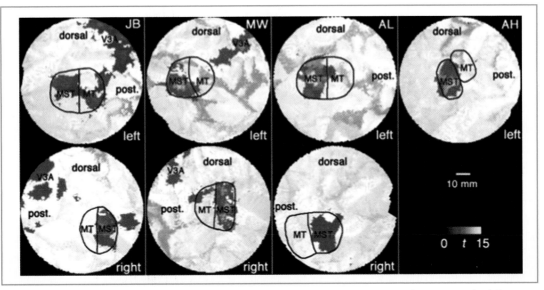

Figure 4.2 Activity in the MT (medial temporal) and MST (medial superior temporal) regions in the left and right hemispheres elicited by optic flow after subtraction of activity elicited by random motion. Data are from four participants. From Smith et al. (2006). Reprinted by permission of Wiley-Blackwell.

movement. Extra-retinal information (e.g., based on head- and eye-movement signals) consistently influenced heading judgements.

We often use factors over and above optic-flow information when making heading judgements, which is not surprising given the typical richness of the available environmental information. Van den Berg and Brenner (1994) pointed out that we only need one eye to use optic-flow information. However, they found that heading judgements were more accurate when observers used both eyes rather than only one. Binocular disparity in the two-eye condition probably provided useful additional information about the relative depths of objects in the display.

Gibson assumed that optic-flow patterns generated by motion are of fundamental importance when we head towards a goal. However, Hahn, Andersen, and Saidpour (2003) found that motion is *not* essential for accurate perception of heading. Observers viewed two photographs of a real-world scene in rapid succession. When the two photographs were presented 50 ms apart, apparent motion was perceived. When they were presented 1000 ms apart, no apparent motion was perceived. The camera position moved by 7.5, 15, 22.5, or 30 cm between photographs, and the observers' task in each case was to identify the direction of heading.

Hahn et al.'s (2003) findings are shown in Figure 4.3. Judgements of heading direction were generally more accurate when the changes in camera position between photographs were relatively great. However, the key finding was that performance was reasonably good even when apparent motion information was *not* available (1000 ms condition). Indeed, the absence of apparent motion (and thus of optic-flow information) had no effect on accuracy of heading judgements when the change in camera position was 22.5 or 30 cm.

Perhaps the simplest explanation of how we move towards a particular goal is that we use information about perceived target location.

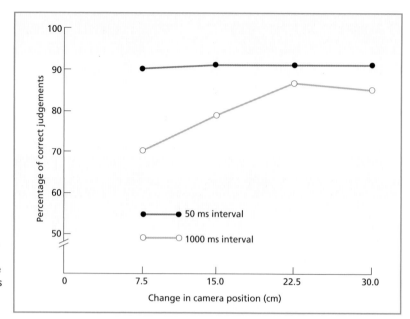

Figure 4.3 Percentage of correct judgements on heading direction as a function of extent of change in camera position (7.5, 15, 22.5, and 30 cm) and of time interval between photographs (50 vs. 1000 ms). Based on data in Hahn et al. (2003).

More specifically, we may use the cue of **visual direction** (the angle between a target and the front–back body axis) to try to walk directly to the target. Wilkie and Wann (2002) used a simulated driving task in which participants steered a smooth curved path to approach a gate under various lighting conditions designed to resemble daylight, twilight, and night. This is a task in which participants rotate their gaze from the direction in which they are heading to fixate the target (i.e., the gate). Wilkie and Wann argued that three sources of information might be used to produce accurate steering:

(1) Visual direction: the direction of the gate with respect to the front–back body axis.
(2) Extra-retinal information in the form of head- and eye-movement signals to take account of gaze rotation.
(3) Retinal flow.

What did Wilkie and Wann (2002) find? First, all three sources of information were used in steering. Second, when information about visual direction was available, it was generally the dominant source of information.

Third, there was less reliance on retinal flow information and more on head- and eye-movement signals when the lighting conditions were poor.

Rushton, Harris, Lloyd, and Wann (1998) carried out a fascinating experiment designed to put optic-flow information and visual direction in conflict. Observers walked towards a target about 10 metres away while wearing prisms displacing the apparent location of the target and thus providing misleading information about visual direction. However, the prisms should have had no effect on optic-flow information. The observers tried to walk directly to the target, but the displacing prisms caused them to walk along a curved path as predicted if they were using the misleading information about visual direction available to

KEY TERM

visual direction: the angle between a visual object or target and the front–back body axis.

them. The findings are at variance with the prediction from the optic-flow hypothesis that the prisms would have no effect on the direction of walking.

It could be argued that Rushton et al.'s (1998) findings are inconclusive. The prisms greatly reduced the observer's visual field and thus limited access to optic-flow information. Harris and Carré (2001) replicated Rushton et al.'s findings, and did not find that limited access to optic-flow information influenced walking direction. However, observers wearing displacing prisms moved more directly to the target when required to crawl rather than walk, indicating that visual direction is not always the sole cue used.

Evidence: future path

Wilkie and Wann (2006) argued that judgements of heading (the direction in which someone is moving at a given moment) are of little relevance if someone is moving along a curved path. According to them, path judgements (i.e., identifying future points along one's path) are more important. Observers made accurate heading and path judgements when travelling along straight paths. With curved paths, however, path judgements were considerably more accurate than heading judgements (mean errors 5 and 13 degrees, respectively). The errors with heading judgements were so large that drivers and cyclists would be ill-advised to rely on them. Supporting evidence comes from Wilkie and Wann (2003), who found that observers steered less accurately when told to fixate their heading rather than their path.

The notion that separate processes underlie heading and path judgements received support in a study by Field, Wilkie, and Wann (2007). Processing future path information was associated with activation in the superior parietal lobe. This is distinct from the brain areas typically associated with processing of optic-flow and heading information (dorsal medial superior temporal and ventral intraparietal areas; Britten, 2008).

We can find out more about the information being used by people approaching bends or proceeding along curved paths by examining where they look. Drivers approaching a bend tend to look ahead some distance, which is consistent with the notion that they are making use of information about the future path (see Wilkie, Wann, & Allison, 2008, for a review). However, such evidence does *not* show that advanced fixation is necessary for accurate steering. Wilkie et al. provided stronger evidence in a study in which participants sitting on a bicycle trainer in a simulator had to steer through several slalom gates. Participants typically fixated the most immediate gate until it was 1.5 metres away, and then switched their gaze to the next gate. Of more importance, there were significant increases in steering errors when the situation was changed so that participants could not use their normal looking patterns. Thus, efficient steering along a complex route requires that people engage in advanced fixation to plot their future path.

It has often been suggested (e.g., Land & Lee, 1994) that drivers approaching a bend focus on the **tangent point**. This is the point at which the direction of the inside edge of the road appears to reverse (see Figure 4.4). Note that the tangent point is not fixed but keeps moving over time. It is assumed that the tangent point is important because it allows drivers to estimate accurately the curvature of the road. Mars (2008) found that drivers often fixated the tangent point when allowed to look wherever they wanted. However, there is nothing magical about the tangent point. Mars used conditions in which drivers fixated a moving target at the tangent point or offset to the left or right. The drivers' steering performance was comparable in all conditions, indicating that road curvature can be estimated accurately *without* fixating the tangent point.

KEY TERM

tangent point: from a driver's perspective, the point on a road at which the direction of its inside edge appears to reverse.

Figure 4.4 A video frame from a study by Mars (2008), in which drivers were instructed to track the blue target as they drove on the right-hand side of the road around a bend. Here, the blue target is on the tangent point, which is the point at which the direction of the inside edge line seems to a driver to reverse. As such, it moves along the edge of the road as the driver goes around a bend. From Mars (2008).

Evaluation

Gibson's views concerning the importance of optic-flow information are oversimplified. Such information is most useful when individuals can move straight towards their goal without needing to take account of obstacles or other problems, as was the case with the pilots studied by Gibson. It is now very clear that numerous factors can influence visually guided movement. In addition to optic flow, these factors include extra-retinal information, relative depth of objects, visual direction, retinal flow, and information about the future path (e.g., based on the tangent point).

What are the limitations of research in this area? First, when we move through a typical visual environment, we are exposed to a bewildering amount of information that could potentially be used to allow us to arrive efficiently at our goal. It requires considerable experimental ingenuity to decide which information is actually used by individuals on the move.

Second, the role of learning has been under-researched. Fajen (2008) gave participants the task of using a foot pedal to come to a stop at a target. There were two conditions differing in the factors determining the responsiveness of the foot pedal. Participants in both groups learned the task effectively, but they used optic flow in different ways. Thus, we can adapt *flexibly* to the particular circumstances in which we find ourselves. Third, while several aspects of the visual environment that influence movement towards a goal have been identified, we still know relatively little about the ways in which these aspects *interact* and combine to determine our actions.

Time to contact

Everyday life is full of numerous situations in which we want to know the moment at which there is going to be contact between us and some object. These situations include ones in which we are moving towards some object (e.g., a wall) and those in which an object (e.g., a ball) is approaching us. We could calculate the time to contact by estimating the initial distance away from us of the object, estimating our speed, and then combining these two estimates into an overall estimate of the *time to contact* by dividing distance by speed. However, combining the two kinds of information would be fairly complicated.

Lee (1976) argued that it is unnecessary to perceive the distance or speed of an approaching object to work out the time to contact, provided that we are approaching it (or it is approaching us) with constant velocity. Lee defined tau as the size of an object's retinal image divided by its rate of expansion. Tau specifies the time to contact with an approaching object – the faster the rate of expansion of the image, the less time there is to contact. When driving, the rate of decline of tau over time (tau–dot) indicates whether there is sufficient braking to stop at the target. Lee's tau–dot hypothesis is in general agreement with Gibson's approach, because information about time to contact is directly available from optic flow.

We will shortly consider the relevant experimental evidence. Before doing so, however, we will consider four basic limitations of tau as a source of information about time to contact that were identified by Tresilian (1999):

(1) Tau ignores acceleration in object velocity.
(2) Tau can only provide information about the time to contact with the eyes. A driver using tau when braking to avoid an obstacle might find the front of his/her car smashed in!
(3) Tau is only accurate when applied to objects that are spherically symmetrical. It would be less useful when trying to catch a rugby ball.
(4) Tau requires that the image size and expansion of the object are both detectable.

Tresilian (1999) argued that estimates of time to contact are arrived at by combining information from several different cues (probably including tau). The extent to which any particular cue is used depends on the observer's task.

In our discussion of the evidence, we will focus on two main lines of research. First, we consider the processes involved in catching a moving ball. Second, we turn our attention to studies of drivers' braking in order to stop at a given point.

Evidence: catching balls

Suppose you try to catch a ball that is coming towards you. Lee (1976) assumed that your judgement of the time to contact depends crucially on the rate of expansion of the ball's retinal image. Supporting evidence was obtained by Benguigui, Ripoli, and Broderick (2003). Their participants were presented with a horizontal moving stimulus that was accelerating or decelerating. The stimulus was hidden from view shortly before reaching a specified position, and participants estimated its time of arrival. The prediction from the tau hypothesis (according to which observers assume that stimulus velocity is constant) was that time to contact should have been *over-estimated* when the stimulus accelerated and *under-estimated* when it decelerated. That is precisely what Benguigui et al. found.

Savelsbergh, Whiting, and Bootsma (1991) argued that Lee's hypothesis could be tested fairly directly by manipulating the rate of expansion. They achieved this by requiring participants to catch a deflating ball swinging towards them on a pendulum. The rate of expansion of the retinal image is less for a deflating than a non-deflating ball. Thus, on Lee's hypothesis, participants should have assumed the deflating ball would take longer to reach them than was actually the case. Savelsbergh et al. found the peak grasp closure was 5 ms later with the deflating ball than a non-deflating ball, and Savelsbergh, Pijpers, and van Santvoord (1993) obtained similar findings. However, these findings only superficially support Lee's hypothesis. Strict application of the hypothesis to Savelsbergh et al.'s (1993) data indicated that the peak grasp closure should have occurred 230 ms later to the deflating ball than to the non-deflating one. In fact, the average difference was only 30 ms.

When we try to catch a ball falling vertically towards us, it accelerates due to the force of gravity. Evidence that we take account of gravity was reported by Lacquaniti, Carozzo, and Borghese (1993). They studied observers catching balls dropped from heights of under 1.5 metres. The observers' performance was better than predicted by the tau hypothesis, presumably because they took account of the ball's acceleration.

McIntyre, Zago, Berthoz, and Lacquaniti (2001) found that astronauts showed better timing when catching balls on earth than in zero-gravity conditions during a space flight. The authors concluded that the astronauts incorrectly anticipated gravitational acceleration under zero-gravity conditions. Zago, McIntyre, Senot, and Lacquaniti (2008) discussed findings from several of their studies. Overall, 85% of targets were correctly intercepted at the first attempt on earth compared with only 14% under zero-gravity conditions. Baurès, Benguigui, Amorim, and Siegler (2007) pointed out that astronauts would have made much greater timing errors when catching balls than they actually did if they had simply misapplied their knowledge of gravity in zero-gravity conditions. There are probably two reasons why the errors were relatively modest:

(1) The astronauts had only vague knowledge of the effects of gravity.
(2) The astronauts changed their predictions of when the ball would arrive as they saw it approaching them.

According to the tau hypothesis, the rate of expansion of an object's retinal image is estimated from changes in optic flow. However, as Schrater, Knill, and Simoncelli (2001) pointed out, rate of expansion could also be estimated from changes in the size or scale of an object's features. They devised stimuli in which there were gradual increases in the scale of object features but the optic-flow pattern was random. Expansion rates could be estimated fairly accurately from scale-change information in the *absence* of useful optic-flow information.

Another factor influencing our estimates of when a ball will arrive is binocular disparity (see Glossary). Rushton and Wann (1999) used a virtual reality situation involving catching balls, and manipulated tau and binocular disparity independently. When tau indicated contact with the ball 100 ms *before* binocular disparity, observers responded about 75 ms earlier. When tau indicated contact 100 ms *after* disparity, the response was delayed by 35 ms. Thus, information about tau is combined with information about binocular disparity. According to Rushton and Wann, the source of information specifying the shortest time to contact is given the greatest weight in this combination process.

López-Moliner, Field, and Wann (2007) found that observers' judgement of time to contact of a ball was determined in part by their knowledge of its size. When the ball was slightly larger or smaller than expected, this reduced the accuracy of observers' performance. The influence of familiar size may help to explain why professional sportspeople can respond with amazing precision to balls travelling at high speed.

Finally, note that people are very adaptable – the strategy they use to catch a ball depends on the circumstances. Mazyn, Savelsbergh, Montagne, and Lenoir (2007) compared people's movements when catching a ball under normal conditions with their performance in a condition in which all the lights went out within 3 ms of their initial movement. The lights-out condition caused the participants to delay the onset of any movement and to engage in much advance planning of their movements.

Evidence: braking by drivers

In everyday life, it is important for drivers to make accurate decisions about when to brake and how rapidly they should decelerate to avoid cars in front of them. According to Lee (1976), drivers use tau when braking to a stop at a given point. More specifically, they brake so as to hold constant the rate of change of tau. This is an efficient strategy in principle because it involves relatively simple calculations and only requires constant braking. Yilmaz and Warren (1995) obtained some support for Lee's position. Participants were told to stop at a stop sign in a simulated driving task. There was generally a linear reduction in tau during braking, but sometimes there were large changes in tau shortly before stopping.

Terry, Charlton, and Perrone (2008) gave participants a simulated driving task in which they braked when the vehicle in front of them decelerated. This task was performed on its own or at the same time as the secondary task of searching for pairs of identical road-side signs. Tau (estimated time to contact) was significantly less in the condition with the distracting secondary task. Thus, the calculation of tau requires attentional processes.

Rock, Harris, and Yates (2006) reported findings inconsistent with Lee's hypothesis. Drivers performed a real-world driving task requiring them to brake to stop at a visual target. Braking under real-world conditions was smoother and more consistent than braking in most previous laboratory-based studies. Of most importance, there was very little support for the tau–dot hypothesis. The findings of

Rock et al. suggested that the drivers were estimating the constant ideal deceleration based on tau plus additional information (e.g., the global optical flow rate).

Evaluation

Much has been learned about the information we use when engaged in tasks such as catching a ball or braking to stop at a given point. In addition to tau, other factors involved in ball catching include binocular disparity, knowledge of object size, and our knowledge of gravity. Braking depends in part on trying to hold constant the rate of change in tau, but also seems to involve estimating the constant ideal deceleration.

What are the limitations of research in this area? First, it remains unclear how the various relevant factors are combined to permit ball catching or accurate braking. Second, it is known that the tau and tau–dot hypotheses are inadequate. However, no comprehensive theory has replaced those hypotheses. Third, the behaviour of drivers when braking in the real world and in simulated conditions in the laboratory is significantly different (Rock et al., 2006). More research is needed to clarify the reasons for such differences.

PLANNING–CONTROL MODEL

Glover (2004) was interested in explaining how visual information is used in the production of action (e.g., reaching for a pint of beer). In his planning–control model, he argued that we initially use a planning system followed by a control system, but with the two systems overlapping somewhat in time. Here are the main characteristics of the planning and control systems:

(1) Planning system
  • It is used mostly *before* the initiation of movement.
  • It selects an appropriate target (e.g., pint of beer), decides how it should be grasped, and works out the timing of the movement.
  • It is influenced by factors such as the individual's goals, the nature of the target object, the visual context, and various cognitive processes.
  • It is relatively slow because it makes use of much information and is influenced by conscious processes.
  • Planning depends on a visual representation located in the inferior parietal lobe together with motor processes in the frontal lobes and basal ganglia (see Figure 4.5). More specifically, the inferior parietal lobe is involved in integrating information about object identification and context with motor planning to permit tool and object use.

(2) Control system
  • It is used during the carrying out of a movement.
  • It ensures that movements are accurate, making adjustments if necessary based on visual feedback.
  • It is influenced only by the target object's spatial characteristics (e.g., size, shape, orientation) and not by the surrounding context.
  • It is fairly fast because it makes use of little information and is not susceptible to conscious influence.
  • Control depends on a visual representation located in the superior parietal lobe combined with motor processes in the cerebellum (see Figure 4.5).

Glover's planning–control model helps us understand the factors determining whether perception is accurate or inaccurate. Of crucial importance, most errors and inaccuracies in perception and action stem from the planning system, whereas the control system typically ensures that human action is accurate and achieves its goal. Many visual illusions occur because of the influence of the surrounding visual context. According to the planning–control model, information about visual context is used by the planning system but not by the control

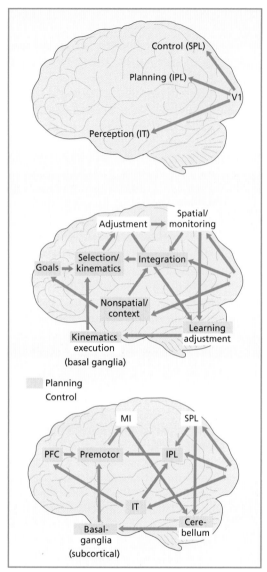

Figure 4.5 Brain areas involved in the planning and control systems within Glover's theory. IPL = inferior parietal lobe; IT = inferotemporal lobe; MI = primary motor; PFC = prefrontal cortex; SPL = superior parietal lobe. From Glover (2004). Copyright © Cambridge University Press. Reproduced with permission.

system. Accordingly, responses to visual illusions should typically be inaccurate if they depend on the planning system but accurate if they depend on the control system.

Glover (2004) argued that the inferior parietal lobe plays a crucial role in human motor planning. Through the course of evolution, humans have become very good at using tools and objects, so it is very important for us to integrate information about object identification and context into our motor planning. Such integration occurs in the inferior parietal lobe.

There are some similarities between Glover's (2004) planning–control model and Milner and Goodale's (1995) theory based on two visual systems (this theory is discussed thoroughly in Chapter 2). According to Milner and Goodale, our vision-for-action system permits fast, accurate movements, and thus resembles Glover's control system. However, Milner and Goodale (e.g., 2008) have increasingly accepted that our movements also often involve the vision-for-perception system. We use this system when remembering which movement to make or when planning which particular movement to make. Thus, there are similarities between their vision-for-perception system and Glover's planning system. However, Glover's approach has three advantages over that of Milner and Goodale. First, he has considered planning processes in more detail. Second, he has focused more on the *changes* occurring during the performance of an action. Third, he has identified the brain areas underlying the planning and control systems.

Evidence

According to the planning–control model, our initial actions towards an object (determined by the planning system) are often less accurate than our subsequent actions (influenced by the control system). Suppose you tried to grasp the central object in the Ebbinghaus illusion (see Figure 2.12). According to the model, accuracy of performance as assessed by grip aperture (trying to adjust one's grip so it is appropriate for grasping the target) should increase as your hand approaches the target. That was precisely what Glover and Dixon (2002a) found, presumably because only the initial planning process was influenced by the illusion.

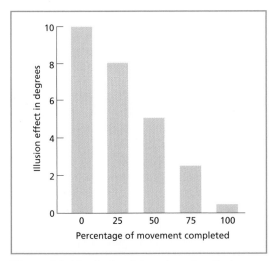

Figure 4.6 Magnitude of the orientation illusion as a function of time into the movement. Based on data in Glover and Dixon (2001).

Glover and Dixon (2001) presented a small bar on a background grating which caused the bar's orientation to be misperceived. The participants were instructed to pick up the bar. The effects of the illusion on hand orientation were relatively large early on but almost disappeared as the hand approached the bar (see Figure 4.6).

The hypothesis that action planning involves conscious processing followed by rapid, nonconscious processing during action control was tested by Liu, Chua, and Enns (2008). The main task involved participants pointing at (and identifying) a peripheral target stimulus. This task was sometimes accompanied by the secondary task of identifying a central stimulus. The secondary task interfered with the planning of the pointing response but did not interfere with the pointing response itself. These findings are consistent with the hypothesis. The conscious processes involved in planning were affected by task interference, but the more automatic processes involved in producing the pointing response were not.

Related findings were reported by Creem and Proffitt (2001) in a study discussed in Chapter 2. They distinguished between effective grasping (in which an object is grasped successfully) and appropriate grasping (in which knowledge of the object is used to grasp it at the most suitable point, e.g., the handle). According to Glover's model, only appropriate grasping involves the planning system, because only appropriate grasping requires people to take account of the nature of the object. Performing a secondary demanding task at the same time impaired appropriate grasping more than effective grasping, which is consistent with the planning–control model.

According to the model, cognitive processes are involved much more within the planning system than the control system. Evidence supporting this hypothesis was reported by Glover and Dixon (2001). Participants reached for an object that had the word "LARGE" or the word "SMALL" written on it. It was assumed that any impact of these words on grasping behaviour would reflect the involvement of the cognitive system. Early in the reach (when movement was directed by the planning system), participants showed an illusion effect in that their grip aperture was greater for objects with the word "LARGE" on them. Later in the reach (when movement was directed by the control system), the illusion effect decreased, as predicted by the model.

A central assumption of the planning–control model is that visual context influences the planning system but not the control system. Mendoza, Elliott, Meegan, Lyons, and Walsh (2006) tested this assumption in a study based on the Müller–Lyer illusion (see Figure 2.11). Participants pointed at the end of a horizontal line presented on its own, with arrowheads pointing inwards or with arrowheads pointing outwards. Of crucial importance, this visual stimulus generally *changed* between participants' initial planning and their movements towards it. It was predicted from Glover's model that the arrowheads would lead to movement errors when present during planning but not when present during online control of movement. These predictions were based on the notion that visual context (e.g., arrowheads) only influences planning. In fact, however, the arrowheads led to movement errors regardless of when they were present, suggesting the processes involved in planning and control are less different than assumed theoretically.

What brain areas are involved in planning and control? Evidence supporting Glover's (2004) assumptions, that planning involves the inferior parietal lobe whereas control involves the superior parietal lobe, was reported by Krams, Rushworth, Deiber, Frackowiak, and Passingham (1998). Participants copied a hand posture shown on a screen under three conditions:

(1) *Control only*: participants copied the movement immediately.
(2) *Planning and control*: participants paused before copying the movement.
(3) *Planning only*: participants prepared the movement but did not carry it out.

What did Krams et al. (1998) find? There was increased activity in the inferior parietal lobe, the premotor cortex, and the basal ganglia in the condition with more emphasis on planning. In contrast, there was some evidence of increased activity in the superior parietal lobe and cerebellum in conditions emphasising control.

Relevant evidence has also come from studies using transcranial magnetic stimulation (TMS; see Glossary) to produce "temporary lesions" in a given brain area. Rushworth, Ellison, and Walsh (2001) applied TMS to the left inferior parietal lobe and found this led to a lengthening of planning time. Desmurget, Gréa, Grethe, Prablanc, Alexander, and Grafton (1999) applied TMS to an area bordering the inferior parietal lobe and the superior parietal lobe. There were no effects of this stimulation on the accuracy of movements to stationary targets, but there was significant disruption when movements needed to be corrected because the target moved. This finding suggests there was interference with control rather than planning.

Further TMS evidence of the involvement of parietal cortex in visually guided action was reported by Davare, Duque, Vandermeeren, Thonnard, and Oliver (2007). They administered TMS to the anterior intraparietal area while participants prepared a movement. TMS disrupted hand shaping and grip force scaling designed to prepare for the shape and the weight of the to-be-grasped object.

Additional relevant information about the brain areas involved in planning and control has come from studies on brain-damaged patients. Patients with damage to the inferior parietal lobe should have problems mainly with the planning of actions. Damage to the left inferior parietal lobe often produces **ideomotor apraxia**, in which patients find it hard to carry out learned movements. Clark et al. (1994) studied three patients with ideomotor apraxia who showed some impairment when slicing bread even when both bread and knife were present. However, such patients are often reasonably proficient at simple pointing and grasping movements. This pattern of performance suggests they have impaired planning (as shown by the inability to slice bread properly) combined with a reasonably intact control system (as shown by adequate pointing and grasping).

Jax, Buxbaum, and Moll (2006) gave patients with ideomotor apraxia various tasks in which they made movements towards objects with unimpeded vision or while blindfolded. There were three main findings. First, the patients' overall level of performance was much worse than that of healthy controls. Second, the adverse effect of blindfolding was greater on the patients than on healthy controls, suggesting the patients were very poor at planning their actions accurately. Third, as predicted by the planning–control model, poor performance on the movement tasks was associated with damage to the inferior parietal lobe. Thus, patients with damage to the inferior parietal lobe have an impaired planning system.

Patients with damage to the superior parietal lobe should have problems mainly with the control of action. Damage to the superior and posterior parietal cortex often produces optic ataxia (see

---

KEY TERM

ideomotor apraxia: a condition caused by brain damage in which patients have difficulty in carrying out learned movements.

Glossary), in which there are severe impairments in the ability to make accurate movements in spite of intact visual perception (see Chapter 2). Some optic ataxics have relatively intact velocity and grip aperture early in the making of a reaching and grasping movement but not thereafter (e.g., Binkofski et al., 1998), a pattern suggesting greater problems with control than with planning.

Grea et al. (2002) studied IG, a patient with optic ataxia. She performed as well as healthy controls when reaching out and grasping a stationary object. However, she had much poorer performance when the target suddenly jumped to a new location. These findings suggest IG had damage to the control system. Blangero et al. (2008) found that CF, a patient with optic ataxia, was very slow to correct his movement towards a target that suddenly moved location. CF also had slowed performance when pointing towards stationary targets presented in peripheral vision. Blangero et al. concluded that CF was deficient in processing hand location and in detecting target location for peripheral targets.

Evaluation

Glover's (2004) planning–control model has proved successful in several ways. First, the notion that cognitive processes are involved in the planning of actions (especially complex ones) has received much support. For example, Serrien, Ivry, and Swinnen (2007) discussed evidence indicating that brain areas such as dorsolateral prefrontal cortex, the anterior cingulate, and the pre-supplementary motor area are involved in planning and monitoring action as well as in cognition. Second, there is plentiful evidence that somewhat different processes are involved in the online control of action than in action planning. Third, the evidence from neuroimaging and transcranial magnetic stimulation (TMS) studies has supported the assumption that areas within the inferior and superior parietal cortex are important for planning and control, respectively.

What are the limitations with the planning–control model? First, the planning and control systems undoubtedly interact in complex ways when an individual performs an action. Thus,

the proposed sequence of planning followed by control is too neat and tidy (Mendoza et al., 2006). Second, various processes occur within both the planning and control systems, and we have as yet only a limited understanding of the number and nature of those processes. Third, the model is concerned primarily with body movements rather than eye movements. However, co-ordination of eye and body movements is very important for precise and accurate movements.

PERCEPTION OF HUMAN MOTION

Most people are very good at interpreting the movements of other people. They can decide very rapidly whether someone is walking, running, or limping. This is unsurprising in view of how important it is for us to make sense of others' movements. Our focus here will be on two key issues. First, how successful are we at interpreting biological movement with very limited visual information? Second, do the processes involved in perception of biological motion differ from those involved in perception of motion in general? We will consider the second issue later in the light of findings from cognitive neuroscience.

Johansson (1975) addressed the first issue using point-light displays. Actors were dressed entirely in black with lights attached to their joints (e.g., wrists, knees, ankles). They were filmed moving around a darkened room so that only the lights were visible to observers subsequently watching the film (see Figure 4.7). Reasonably accurate perception of a moving person was achieved with only six lights and a short segment of film. Most observers described accurately the position and movements of the actors, and it almost seemed as if their arms and legs could be seen. More dramatic findings were reported by Johansson, von Hofsten, and Jansson (1980): observers who saw a point-light display for only one-fifth of a second perceived biological motion with no apparent difficulty.

Observers can make precise discriminations when viewing point-light displays. Runeson and Frykholm (1983) asked actors to carry out

Figure 4.7 Johansson (1975) attached lights to an actor's joints. While the actor stood still in a darkened room, observers could not make sense of the arrangement of lights. However, as soon as he started to move around, they were able to perceive the lights as defining a human figure.

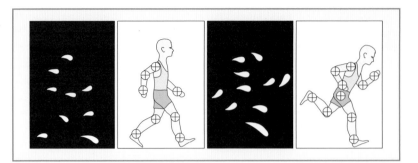

a sequence of actions naturally or as if they were a member of the opposite sex. Observers guessed the gender of the actor correctly 85.5% of the time when he/she acted naturally and there was only a modest reduction to 75.5% correct in the deception condition.

Kozlowki and Cutting (1977) found that observers were correct 65% of the time when guessing the sex of someone walking. Judgements were better when joints in both the upper and lower body were illuminated. Cutting, Proffitt, and Kozlowski (1978) pointed out that men tend to show relatively greater side-to-side motion (or swing) of the shoulders than of the hips, whereas women show the opposite. This happens because men typically have broad shoulders and narrow hips in comparison to women. The shoulders and hips move in opposition to each other, i.e., when the right shoulder is forward, the left hip is forward. We can identify the centre of moment in the upper body, which is the neutral reference point around which the shoulders and hips swing. The position of the centre of moment is determined by the relative sizes of the shoulders and hips, and is typically lower in men than in women. Cutting et al. found that the centre of moment correlated well with observers' sex judgements.

There are two correlated cues that may be used by observers to decide whether they are looking at a man or a woman in point-light displays:

(1) Structural cues based on width of shoulders and hips; these structural cues form the basis of the centre of moment.

(2) Dynamic cues based on the tendency for men to show relatively greater body sway with the upper body than with the hips when walking, whereas women show the opposite.

Sex judgements were based much more on dynamic cues than on structural ones when the two cues were in conflict. Thus, the centre of moment may be less important than claimed by Cutting et al. (1978).

Bottom-up or top-down processes?

Johansson (1975) argued that the ability to perceive biological motion is innate. He described the processes involved as "spontaneous" and "automatic". Support for that argument was reported by Simion, Regolin, and Bulf (2008), in a study on newborns aged between one and three days. These babies preferred to look at a display showing biological motion than one that did not. In addition, the babies looked longer at upright displays of biological motion than upside-down ones. What was remarkable was that Simion et al. used point-light displays of chickens, and it was impossible that the newborns had any visual experience of moving chickens. These findings led them to conclude that, "Detection of motion is an intrinsic capacity of the visual system" (p. 809). These findings are consistent with the notion that the perception of biological motion involves relatively basic, bottom-up processes.

Thornton, Rensink, and Shiffrar (2002) argued that perception of biological motion can be less straightforward and effortless than suggested by Johansson (1975). They presented observers on each trial with a point-light walker figure embedded in masking elements. There were two mask conditions: (1) scrambled mask, in which each dot mimicked the motion of a dot from the walker figure; and (2) random mask, in which the dots moved at random. It was assumed that it would be more difficult to perceive the walker in the scrambled condition. As a result, observers would have to attend more closely to the display to decide the direction in which the walker was moving. This hypothesis was tested by having the observers perform the task on its own or at the same time as a second, attentionally-demanding task.

What did Thornton et al. (2002) find? Observers' ability to identify correctly the walker's direction of movement was greatly impaired by the secondary task when scrambled masks were used (see Figure 4.8). However, the secondary task had only a modest effect when random masks were used. These findings indicate that top-down

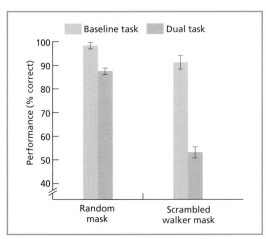

Figure 4.8 Percentage correct detections of a walker's direction of movement (left or right) as a function of the presence of a random mask or a scrambled walker mask and the presence (dual-task condition) or absence (baseline task) of a demanding secondary task. Performance was worst with a scrambled walker mask in the dual-task condition. From Thornton et al. (2002). Reprinted with permission of Pion Limited, London.

processes (e.g., attention) can be of major importance in detection of biological motion, but the extent of their involvement varies considerably from situation to situation. Note that direction-detection performance in the scrambled and random mask conditions was very good (over 90%) when there was no secondary task. In sum, efficient detection of biological motion can depend mainly on bottom-up processes (random-mask condition) or on top-down processes (scrambled-mask condition).

Cognitive neuroscience

Suppose the processes involved in perceiving biological motion differ from those involved in perceiving object motion generally. If so, we might expect to find some patients who can detect one type of motion reasonably but have very impaired ability to detect the other type of motion. There is support for this prediction. There have been studies on "motion-blind" patients with damage to the motion areas MT and MST who have severely impaired ability to perceive motion in general (see Chapter 2). Such patients are often reasonably good at detecting biological motion (e.g., Vaina, Cowey, LeMay, Bienfang, & Kinkinis, 2002). In contrast, Saygin (2007) found in stroke patients that lesions in the superior temporal and premotor frontal areas were most associated with impaired perception of biological motion (see Figure 4.9). However, patients' deficits in biological motion perception did not correlate with their ability to detect coherence of directional motion. This suggests that different brain areas underlie perception of biological motion and motion in general.

Several neuroimaging studies are of relevance. Similar brain areas to those identified in stroke patients are active when healthy participants perceive biological motion (Saygin, 2007). Saygin reviewed previous neuroimaging research, which had most consistently identified the posterior superior temporal gyrus and sulcus as being activated during observation of point-light displays. For example, Grossman et al. (2000) found that point-light displays of biological motion activated an area in the superior temporal sulcus,

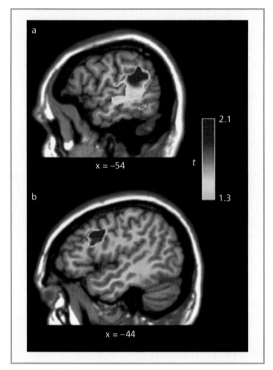

Figure 4.9 Brain areas damaged in patients having impaired biological motion perception: (a) damaged area in temporo-parietal cortex; (b) damaged area in frontal cortex. From Saygin (2007), by permission of Oxford University Press.

whereas displays of other forms of motion did not. However, we must not exaggerate the differences between perception of biological motion and perception of object motion. Virji-Babul, Cheung, Weeks, Kerns, and Shiffrar (2008) used magneto-encephalography (MEG; see Glossary) while observers watched point-light displays of human and object motion. For both kinds of motion, brain activity started in the posterior occipital and mid-parietal areas, followed by activation in the parietal, sensory-motor, and left temporal regions. However, only perception of human motion was associated with activation of the right temporal area.

Imitation and the mirror neuron system

One explanation of our ability to perceive (and to make sense of) the movements of other people is based on imitation. Some theorists (e.g., Gallese, Keysers, & Rizzolatti, 2004) have argued that many neurons in the brain activated when we perform an action are also activated when we see someone else perform the same action. It is claimed that these neurons play a central role in our understanding of others' intentions.

Initial evidence was reported by Gallese, Fadiga, Fogassi, and Rizzolatti (1996). They assessed brain activity in monkeys in two different situations: (1) the monkeys performed a particular action (e.g., grasping); and (2) the monkeys observed another monkey performing a similar action. Gallese et al. discovered that 17% of the neurons in area F5 of the premotor cortex were activated in both situations. They labelled these neurons "mirror neurons".

Findings such as those of Gallese et al. (1996) led theorists to put forward the notion of a mirror neuron system. This **mirror neuron system** is formed of neurons that are activated when animals perform an action *and* when they observe another animal perform the same action. This system allegedly facilitates imitation and understanding of the actions of others. Subsequent research confirmed the importance of area F5 and also indicated that the superior temporal sulcus forms part of the mirror neuron system in monkeys. There is some evidence for a similar mirror neuron system in humans (see review by Rizzolatti and Craighero, 2004). According to Gallese et al. (2004, p. 396), this system is of huge importance: "The fundamental mechanism that allows us a direct experiential grasp of the minds of others is...direct simulation of observed events through the mirror mechanism (mirror neuron system).

How can we show that mirror neurons are involved in working out *why* someone else is

KEY TERM

mirror neuron system: a system of neurons that respond to actions whether performed by oneself or by someone else.

The mirror neuron system is formed of neurons that are activated when we perform an action, and when we observe another perform the same action, thereby perhaps facilitating imitation of the actions of others.

performing certain actions as well as deciding *what* those actions are? One way is to demonstrate that mirror neurons discharge when the participant cannot see the action but can infer what it is likely to be. Precisely this was done by Umiltà et al. (2001). They used two main conditions. In one condition, the experimenter's action directed towards an object was fully visible to the monkey participants. In the other condition, the monkeys saw the same action but the most important part of the action was hidden from them behind a screen. Before each trial, the monkeys saw the experimenter place some food behind the screen so they knew what the experimenter was reaching for.

What did Umiltà et al. (2001) find? First, over half of the mirror neurons tested discharged in the hidden condition. Second, about half of the mirror neurons that discharged in the hidden condition did so as strongly in that condition as in the fully visible condition. Third, Umiltà et al. used a third condition, which was the same as the hidden condition except that the monkeys knew no food had been placed behind the screen. In terms of what the monkeys could see of the experimenter's actions, this condition was identical to the hidden condition. However, mirror neurons that discharged in the hidden condition did *not* discharge in this third condition. Thus, it was the *meaning* of the observed actions that determined activity within the mirror neuron system.

Is there a mirror neuron system in humans? Much research is consistent with the notion that we have such a system. Dinstein, Hasson, Rubin, and Heeger (2007) assessed activation in many brain areas while human participants observed the same movement being made repeatedly or repeatedly performed that movement. Some brain areas showed reduced responses only to repeated observed movements; some exhibited reduced responses only to repeated performed movements. However, six brain areas (including ventral premotor cortex, anterior intraparietal cortex, and superior intraparietal cortex) were affected in similar fashion by both tasks (see Figure 4.10). These brain areas may form a human mirror neuron system.

There is an important limitation with the findings reported by Dinstein et al. (2007). All they found was that neurons within the same brain *areas* responded on both tasks. Convincing evidence for a mirror neuron system in humans requires that the same *neurons* are activated whether observing a movement or performing it. Turella, Pierno, Tubaldi, and Castiello (2009) recently reviewed brain-imaging studies in this area, and found that none of them satisfied that requirement. They concluded that the available evidence is only weakly supportive of the notion of a mirror neuron system in humans.

Iacoboni, Molnar-Szakacs, Gallese, Buccino, Mazziotta, and Rizzolatti (2005) argued that our understanding of the intentions behind

Figure 4.10 Brain areas responding less to repeated than non-repeated movement observation (green) or to movement execution (orange) and thus associated with initial detection of these types of movement. Areas in the left hemisphere have overlap (yellow) or close proximity of reduced activation to observed and to executed movements. aIFS = anterior intraparietal sulcus; vPM = ventral premotor cortex; aIPS = anterior intraparietal sulcus; sIPS = superior intraparietal cortex; pIPS = posterior intraparietal sulcus; LO = area within lateral occipital cortex. From Dinstein et al. (2007). Copyright © 2007 American Psychological Association. Reproduced with permission.

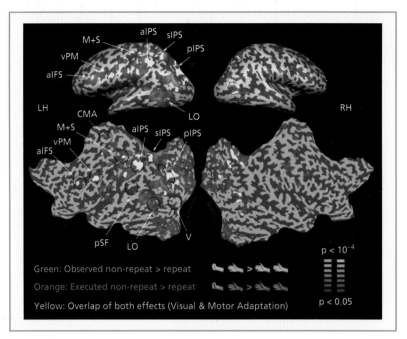

someone else's actions is often helped by taking account of the context. For example, someone may shout loudly at another person because they are angry or because they are acting in a play. Iacoboni et al. investigated whether the mirror neuron system in humans was sensitive to context using three conditions:

(1) *Intention condition*: There were film clips of two scenes involving a teapot, mug, biscuits, a jar, and so on – one scene showed the objects before being used (drinking context) and the other showed the object after being used (cleaning context). A hand was shown grasping a cup in a different way in each scene.

(2) *Action condition*: The same grasping actions were shown as in the intention condition. However, the context was not shown, so it was not possible to understand the intention of the person grasping the cup.

(3) *Context condition*: The same two contexts were shown as in the intention condition, but no grasping was shown.

There was more activity in areas forming part of the mirror neuron system in the inten-

tion condition than the action condition. This suggests that the mirror neuron system is involved in understanding the intentions behind observed actions, because it was only in the intention condition that the participants could work out *why* the person was grasping the cup.

Overall evaluation

Our ability to perceive biological motion with very limited visual information is impressive. There is reasonable evidence that our ability to perceive biological motion depends on a combination of bottom-up and top-down processes. Evidence from brain-imaging studies and from brain-damaged patients suggests that the brain areas involved in perception of biological motion differ from those used in perceiving motion in general.

Recent research has suggested that we use a mirror neuron system to make sense of the movements of other people.

What are the limitations of research in this area? First, relatively little is known about the ways in which bottom-up and top-down processes interact when we perceive biological motion. Second, the similarities and differences between the processes underlying perception of biological motion and motion in general remain somewhat unclear. Third, most of the research on the human mirror neuron system has involved functional magnetic resonance imaging (fMRI; see Glossary). This is not precise enough to identify activity at the level of individual neurons, making it unwise to speculate on what is happening at that level. Indeed, according to Agnew, Bhakoo, and Puri (2007, p. 288), "There is no direct evidence of human neurons that respond to action." Fourth, when we try to understand someone else's intentions, we often take account of their stable characteristics (e.g., personality). It seems improbable that the mirror neuron system takes account of these stable characteristics.

CHANGE BLINDNESS

We feel we have a clear and detailed visual representation of the world around us. As Mack (2003, p. 180) pointed out, "Our subjective impression of a coherent and richly detailed world leads most of us to assume that we see what there is to be seen by merely opening our eyes and looking." As a result, we are confident we could immediately detect any change in the visual environment provided it was sufficiently great. In fact, our ability to detect such changes is often far less impressive than we think. **Change blindness** (the failure to detect that an object has moved, changed, or disappeared) is the phenomenon we will be discussing.

Change blindness is an important phenomenon for various reasons. First, whereas most studies of perception consider visual processes applied to *single* stimuli, those on change blindness are concerned with dynamic processes in visual perception over time applied to two or more stimuli. Second, as we will see, studies on change blindness have greatly clarified the role of attention in scene perception. That explains why change blindness is discussed at the end of the final chapter on perception and just before

the chapter on attention. Third, experiments on change blindness have shed light on the processes underlying our conscious awareness of the visual world. Fourth, as already implied, studies on change blindness have produced findings that are striking and counterintuitive.

The existence of change blindness means that we rarely spot unintended changes in films when the same scene has been shot more than once. For example, in *Grease*, while John Travolta is singing "Greased Lightning", his socks change colour several times between black and white. In the film *Diamonds Are Forever*, James Bond tilts his car on two wheels to drive through a narrow alleyway. As he enters the alleyway, the car is balanced on its *right* wheels, but when it emerges it is miraculously on its *left* wheels!

Magicians have profited over the years from the phenomenon of change blindness (Kuhn, Amlani, & Rensink, 2008). It is often thought that magicians baffle us because the hand is quicker than the eye. That is not the main reason. Most magic tricks involve misdirection, in which the magician directs spectators' attention away from some action crucial to the success of the trick. When this is done skilfully, spectators fail to see how the magician is doing his/her tricks while thinking they have seen everything that is going on.

We often greatly overestimate our ability to detect visual changes. In one study, participants saw various videos involving two people having a conversation in a restaurant (Levin, Drivdahl, Momen, & Beck, 2002). In one video, the plates on their table changed from red to white, and in another a scarf worn by one of them disappeared. These videos had previously been used by Levin and Simons (1997), who found that none of their participants detected any of the changes. Levin et al. asked their participants whether they thought they would have noticed the changes if they had not been forewarned about them.

KEY TERM

change blindness: failure to detect changes in the visual environment.

Magicians (like this street performer) rely on the phenomenon of change blindness where misdirection is used to direct spectators' attention away from the action that is crucial to the success of the trick.

Figure 4.11 Frame showing a woman in a gorilla suit in the middle of a game of passing the ball. From Simons and Chabris (1999). Copyright © 1999 Daniel J. Simons. Reproduced with permission of the author.

Forty-six per cent claimed they would have noticed the change in the colour of the plates, and 78% the disappearing scarf. Levin et al. used the term change blindness to describe our wildly optimist beliefs about our ability to detect visual changes.

Inattentional blindness (the failure to notice an unexpected object in a visual display) is a phenomenon closely resembling change blindness blindness. Evidence for inattentional blindness was reported in a famous experiment by Simons and Chabris (1999; see Figure 4.11). Observers watched a film in which students *passed* a ball to each other. At some point, a woman in a gorilla suit walks right into camera shot, looks at the camera, thumps her chest, and then walks off. Imagine yourself as one of the observers – wouldn't you be very confident of spotting the woman dressed up as a gorilla

almost immediately? Surprisingly, 50% of the observers did not notice the woman's presence at all, even though she was on the screen for nine seconds!

In the real world, we are often aware of changes in the visual environment because we detect motion signals accompanying the change. Accordingly, various techniques have been used to ensure that observers' ability to detect visual changes is not simply due to the detection of motion (Rensink, 2002). These techniques include making the change during a saccade (rapid movement of the eyes), making the change during a short temporal gap between the original and altered stimuli, or making the change during an eyeblink.

Sparce representations?

An obvious way of explaining many of the findings on change blindness and inattentional blindness is to assume that the visual representations we form when viewing a scene are sparse and incomplete because they depend on our limited

> **KEY TERM**
>
> **inattentional blindness:** failure to detect an unexpected object appearing in a visual display; see **change blindness**.

attentional focus. Indeed, that assumption was made by several early researchers in the area (e.g., Rensink, O'Regan, & Clark 1997; Simons & Levin, 1997). However, as Simons and Rensink (2005) pointed out, there are various alternative explanations. First, detailed and complete representations exist initially but may either decay rapidly or be overwritten by a subsequent stimulus. Second, visual representations of the pre-change stimulus may exist but be inaccessible to consciousness. Third, visual representations of the pre-change and post-change stimuli may exist but the two representations may not be compared and so the change is not detected.

Change blindness depends on overwriting rather than simply attention

As we have seen, it has often been assumed that change blindness occurs because our limited attentional focus only allows us to form visual representations of a very small number of objects. Convincing evidence that this assumption is oversimplified was reported by Landman, Spekreijse, and Lamme (2003), who argued that there is more information in the pre-change visual representation than generally supposed. Eight rectangles (some horizontal and some vertical) were presented for 400 ms, followed 1600 ms later by a second array of eight rectangles. The task was to decide whether any of the rectangles had changed orientation from horizontal or vertical or vice versa. When there was no cue, participants' detection performance suggested that their storage capacity for the pre-change display was only three items. This is consistent with the notion that attentional limitations greatly restrict our storage capacity.

More importantly, the findings were very different when a cue indicating the location of any change was presented up to 900 ms after the offset of the first display. When this happened, the apparent storage capacity was approximately seven items, and it was about 4.5 items when a cue was presented 1500 ms after offset of the first display (see Figure 4.12). Thus, there is a considerable amount of information in the pre-change visual representation that can be accessed provided that attention is directed rapidly to it (e.g., via cueing). That means that our sense that we can see most of the visual scene in front of us is more accurate than seemed to be the case based on most research on change blindness.

What can we conclude from this study? According to Landman et al. (2003), change blindness does not result directly from attentional limitations. Instead, the explanation is as follows: "Change blindness involves overwriting of a large capacity representation by the post-change display" (p. 149). Our visual system is designed so that what we currently perceive is not disrupted by what we last perceived. This is achieved by overwriting or replacing the latter with the former.

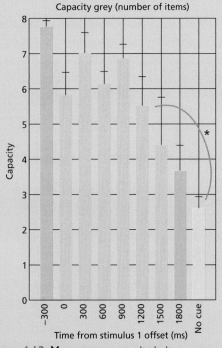

Figure 4.12 Mean storage capacity in items over an interval of 1600 ms with a cue presented at various times after offset of the first display. There was also a no-cue control condition. Reprinted from Landman et al. (2003), Copyright © 2003, with permission from Elsevier.

The notion that self-report measures of change blindness may *underestimate* people's ability to detect changes was supported by Laloyaux, Destrebecqz, and Cleeremans (2006). They presented participants with an initial array of eight black rectangles, half vertical and half horizontal. In the second array of black rectangles, one of them might have a changed orientation. The third array (presented for only 40 ms) was the same as the second one except that one of the rectangles (the probe) was in white. Participants indicated whether they had detected a change in orientation between the first and second arrays, and whether the white rectangle was horizontal or vertical. Congruent trials were those on which the probe's orientation matched that of the changed rectangle and incongruent trials were those with no match. When participants showed change blindness, they nevertheless identified the probe's orientation more accurately and faster on congruent trials than on incongruent ones. Thus, changes not detected consciously can nevertheless influence conscious decisions about the orientation of a subsequent object.

In related research, Fernandez-Duque, Grossi, Thornton, and Neville (2003) compared event-related potentials (ERPs; see Glossary) on trials in which a change in a scene was not detected versus trials in which there was no change. Undetected changes triggered a positive response between 240–300 ms, suggesting that they trigger certain brain processes, although they do not produce conscious awareness of change.

In sum, there is a danger of assuming that observers' failure to report detecting a change in a scene means that they engaged in little or no processing of the changed object. As we have seen, several different kinds of evidence indicate that that assumption is often incorrect.

Attentional processes

There is universal agreement that attentional processes play an important role in change blindness. Evidence suggesting that attention is important comes from studies in which participants have to detect target stimuli. It is

reasonable to assume that unexpected stimuli similar to target stimuli will be more likely to attract attention than those that are dissimilar and so should be detected more often. Most, Simons, Scholl, Jimenez, Clifford, and Chabris (2001) asked observers to count the number of white shapes or the number of black shapes bouncing off the edges of a display window. What was of interest was the percentage of observers noticing an unexpected object that could be white, light grey, dark grey, or black. The detection rates for unexpected objects were much higher when they were similar in luminance or brightness to the target objects (see Figure 4.13), presumably because those resembling target objects were most likely to receive attention.

Earlier we discussed the surprising finding of Simons and Chabris (1999) that 50% of observers failed to detect a woman dressed as a gorilla. Similarity was a factor, in that the gorilla was black whereas the members of the team whose passes the observers were counting were dressed in white. Simons and Chabris carried out a further experiment in which observers counted the passes made by members of the team dressed in white or the one dressed in black. The gorilla's presence was detected by only 42% of observers when the attended team was the one dressed in white, thus replicating the previous findings. However, the gorilla's presence was detected by 83% of observers when the attended team was the one dressed in black. This shows the impact of similarity between the unexpected stimulus (gorilla) and task-relevant stimuli (members of attended team).

Hollingworth and Henderson (2002) assessed the role played by attention in change blindness. Eye movements were recorded while observers looked at a visual scene (e.g., kitchen; living room) and pressed a button if they detected any change in the scene. There were two possible kinds of change:

(1) *Type* change, in which the object was replaced by an object from a different category (e.g., knife replaced by fork).
(2) *Token* change, in which the object was replaced by another object from the same

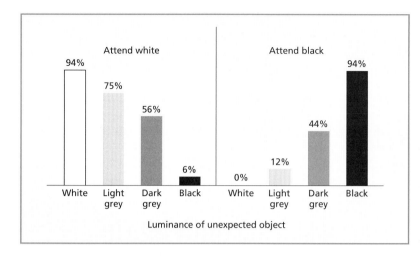

Figure 4.13 Percentage of participants detecting unexpected objects as a function of similarity between their luminance or brightness and that of target objects. From Most et al. (2001). Copyright © Blackwell Publishing. Reprinted with permission of Wiley-Blackwell.

category (e.g., one knife replaced by a different knife).

Finally, there was a test of long-term memory between 5 and 30 minutes after each scene had been viewed. On this test, participants saw two scenes: (1) the original scene with a target object marked with a green arrow; and (2) a distractor scene identical to the original scene except that there was a different object in the location of the target object. The task was to decide which was the original object.

What did Hollingworth and Henderson (2002) find? First, they considered the probability of reporting a change as a function of whether the changed object had been fixated *prior* to the change. Change detection was much greater when the changed object had been fixated before the change (see Figure 4.14a). Since observers mistakenly claimed to have detected a change on 9% of trials in which there was no change (false alarm rate), there was no real evidence that observers could accurately detect change in objects not fixated prior to change. These findings suggest that attention to the to-be-changed object is necessary (but not sufficient) for change detection, because there was change blindness for about 60% of objects fixated before they were changed.

Second, Hollingworth and Henderson (2002) studied the fate of objects fixated some time prior to being changed. As can be seen in Figure 4.14b, the number of fixations on other objects occurring after the last fixation on the to-be-changed object had no systematic effect on change detection. Thus, the visual representations of objects that are the focus of attention last for some time after they have been formed.

Third, as can be seen in Figures 4.14a and 4.14b, change detection was much better when there was a change in the type of object rather than merely swapping one member of a category for another (token change). This makes sense given that type changes are more dramatic and obvious than token ones.

How much long-term memory do we have for objects fixated and attended to several minutes earlier? Hollingworth and Henderson (2002) found that 93% of type changes and 81% of token changes were detected on a test 5–30 minutes later. Hollingworth (2004) used a "follow-the-dot" method in which observers fixated a dot moving from object to object. On a test of change detection, the original object and a token change were presented. Change-detection performance was good even when 402 objects were fixated between the original presentation of an object and its second presentation.

Triesch, Ballard, Hayhoe, and Sullivan (2003) argued that detection of change blindness does *not* merely involve fixating the object that is changed. According to them, we typically focus

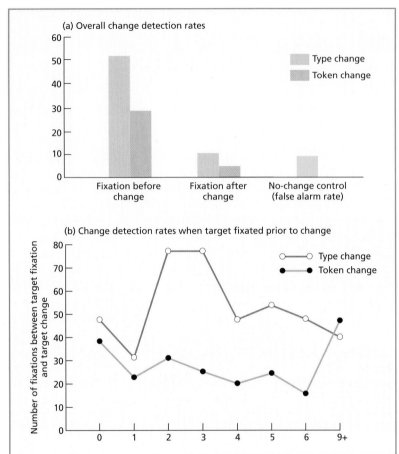

Figure 4.14 (a) Percentage of correct change detection as a function of form of change (type vs. token) and time of fixation (before vs. after change); also false alarm rate when there was no change. (b) Mean percentage correct change detection as a function of the number of fixations between target fixation and change of target and form of change (type vs. token). Both from Hollingworth and Henderson (2002). Copyright © 2002 American Psychological Association. Reproduced with permission.

only on information that is directly relevant to our current task. They tested this hypothesis using a virtual reality set-up in which participants sorted bricks of different heights onto two conveyor belts. There were three conditions differing in instructions for picking up the bricks and placing them on the conveyor belt. Brick size was irrelevant for both tasks in one condition. In a second condition, it was relevant only for the picking-up stage, and in a third condition, it was relevant at both stages. On 10% of pick-and-place actions, the height of the brick changed while the participant moved it from the pick-up area to the conveyor belts.

What did Triesch et al. (2003) find? Change detection (assessed by spontaneous reporting and a questionnaire administered at the end of the experiment) was greatest when brick size was relevant for picking up and placing and least when it was not relevant to either task (see Figure 4.15). However, the three groups did not differ in their pattern of eye fixations or the number of trials on which participants fixated the brick during the change. These findings led Triesch et al. (p. 92) to the following conclusion: "In everyday tasks only a very limited amount of visual information is 'computed' – just enough to solve the current sensori-motor micro-task."

Evaluation

Inattentional blindness and change blindness are important phenomena. The discovery that

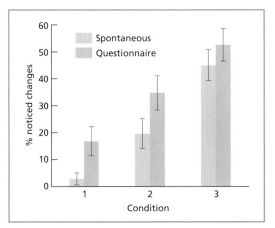

Figure 4.15 Changes reported spontaneously and on a questionnaire in three conditions: 1 (brick size irrelevant for both tasks); 2 (brick size relevant only for picking-up task); and 3 (brick size relevant for both tasks). From Triesch et al. (2003). Reprinted with permission of Pion Limited, London.

these phenomena can be obtained with naturalistic stimuli under naturalistic conditions indicates that they are of general importance, and their exploration has revealed much about the dynamics of visual perception over time.

It has been assumed from the outset of research on change blindness that attentional processes are important: in crude terms, we are much more likely to detect changes in objects attended to prior to change (e.g., Hollingworth & Henderson, 2002). However, prior attention to the object is often *not* sufficient when the change is relatively modest (i.e., a token change) or is not of direct relevance to an ongoing task (e.g., Triesch et al., 2003).

The greatest limitation of early theorising was the assumption that sparse visual representations of pre-change stimuli or objects were important in causing change blindness. In fact, we typically form fairly detailed visual representations of stimuli, but much of the detail becomes inaccessible unless attention is directed to it soon after the disappearance of the stimuli. Thus, our belief that we have a clear-detailed representation of the visual environment is approximately correct, but we are mistaken in assuming that our attention will automatically be drawn to important events. It has also been found that changes not detected at the conscious level can nevertheless influence cognitive processing and behaviour.

CHAPTER SUMMARY

- **Direct perception**
  Gibson argued that perception and action are closely intertwined, with the main purpose of perception being to assist in the organisation of action. According to his direct theory, movement of an observer creates optic flow, which provides useful information about the direction of heading. Of particular importance are invariants, which remain the same as individuals move around their environment, and which are detected by resonance. The uses of objects (their affordances) were claimed to be perceived directly. Gibson's approach was very original and anticipated recent theoretical ideas about a vision-for-action system. However, he underestimated the complexity of visual processing, he minimised the importance of stored visual knowledge when grasping objects appropriately, and he de-emphasised those aspects of visual perception concerned with object recognition.

- **Visually guided action**
  According to Gibson, our perception of heading depends on optic-flow information. However, the retinal flow field is determined by eye and head movements as well as by optic flow. Heading judgements are also influenced by binocular disparity and visual direction, and optic-flow information is not essential for accurate judgements. Accurate

steering on curved paths involves focusing on the future path rather than immediate heading. According to the tau hypothesis, observers assume that moving objects have constant velocity and use tau to estimate time to contact. In addition, observers take some account of gravity, use binocular disparity, and utilise their knowledge of object size. It has been argued that drivers who brake in order to stop at a target point do this by holding constant the rate of change of tau. However, it seems likely that they are estimating the constant ideal deceleration.

- Planning–control model
  In his planning–control model, Glover distinguished between a slow planning system used mostly before the initiation of movement and a fast control system used during movement execution. According to the model, planning is associated with the inferior parietal lobe, whereas control depends on the superior parietal lobe. As predicted by the model, action errors mostly stem from the planning system rather than the control system. There is support for the model from neuroimaging studies and studies on brain-imaging patients. The processes of the planning system need to be spelled out in more detail, as do the complex interactions between the two systems.

- Perception of human motion
  Biological motion is perceived even when only impoverished visual information is available. Perception of biological motion involves bottom-up and top-down processes. Evidence from brain-damaged patients suggests that different brain areas are associated with perception of biological motion and motion in general. Neuroimaging studies suggest that the posterior superior temporal gyrus and sulcus are associated specifically with processing of biological motion. Our ability to perceive (and to make sense of) the movements of other people may involve the mirror neuron system. However, the existence of such a system in humans remains somewhat controversial.

- Change blindness
  There is convincing evidence for the phenomena of inattentional blindness and change blindness. Much change blindness occurs because there is a rapid overwriting of a previous visual representation by a current one. However, perhaps the single most important factor determining change blindness is whether the changed object was attended to prior to the change. There is often very good long-term visual memory for objects that have previously been fixated. Change blindness is also more likely when there is only a small change in the object and when the nature of the change is irrelevant to the individual's ongoing task.

FURTHER READING

- Blake, R., & Sekuler, R. (2005). Perception (5th ed.). New York: McGraw-Hill. Several issues relating to motion perception and perception for action are discussed in an accessible way in this American textbook.
- Blake, R., & Shiffrar, M. (2007). Perception of human motion. *Annual Review of Psychology, 58,* 47–73. This chapter provides a good review of research on biological motion and related areas.

- Britten, K.H. (2008). Mechanisms of self-motion perception. *Annual Review of Neuroscience, 31*, 389–410. This review article considers the brain mechanisms associated with visually guided motion.
- Lavie, N. (2007). Attention and consciousness. In M. Velmans & S. Schneider (eds.), *The Blackwell companion to consciousness*. Oxford: Blackwell. Nilli Lavie provides a detailed account of the involvement of attentional processes in change blindness.
- Mather, G. (2009). *Foundations of sensation and perception* (2nd ed.). Hove, UK: Psychology Press. Visual motion perception is discussed in Chapter 11 of this introductory textbook.
- Rensink, R.A. (2008). On the applications of change blindness. *Psychologia, 51*, 100–116. In this article, Rensink discusses how the change blindness paradigm has shed light on several important issues in perception and attention.

ATTENTION AND PERFORMANCE

INTRODUCTION

Attention is invaluable in everyday life. We use attention to avoid being hit by cars as we cross the road, to search for missing objects, and to perform two tasks at the same time. Psychologists use the term "attention" in several ways. However, attention typically refers to selectivity of processing, as was emphasised by William James (1890, pp. 403–404) many years ago:

> Attention is...the taking into possession of the mind, in clear and vivid form, of one out of what seem several simultaneously possible objects or trains of thought. Focalisation, concentration, of consciousness are of its essence.

William James (1890) distinguished between "active" and "passive" modes of attention. Attention is active when controlled in a top-down way by the individual's goals or expectations but passive when controlled in a bottom-up way by external stimuli (e.g., a loud noise). This distinction, which remains important in recent theorising and research (e.g., Corbetta & Shulman, 2002; Yantis, 2008), is discussed in detail later.

There is another important distinction between focused and divided attention. **Focused attention** (or selective attention) is studied by presenting individuals with two or more stimulus inputs at the same time and instructing them

to respond only to one. Work on focused or selective attention tells us how effectively we can select certain inputs rather than others. It also allows us to study the nature of the selection process and the fate of unattended stimuli.

Divided attention is also studied by presenting at least two stimulus inputs at the same time, but with instructions that individuals must

Divided attention is also known as multi-tasking; a skill that most of us regard as important in today's hectic world.

KEY TERMS

focused attention: a situation in which individuals try to attend to only one source of information while ignoring other stimuli; also known as selective attention.
divided attention: a situation in which two tasks are performed at the same time; also known as multi-tasking.

attend to (and respond to) *all* stimulus inputs. Divided attention is also known as multi-tasking, a skill that is increasingly important in today's 24/7 world! Studies of divided attention or multi-tasking provide useful information about an individual's processing limitations. They also tell us something about attentional mechanisms and their capacity.

Much attentional research suffers from two limitations. First, we can attend to the external environment (e.g., our friend walking towards us) or to the internal environment (e.g., our plans for tomorrow). However, there has been far more research on the former than on the latter because it is much easier to identify and control environmental stimuli.

Second, what we attend to in the real world is largely determined by our current goals and emotional states. In most research, however, what people attend to is determined by the experimenter's instructions rather than their own motivational or emotional states. Some exceptions are discussed in Chapter 15.

Two important topics related to attention are discussed in other chapters. The phenomenon of change blindness, which shows the close links between attention and perception, is considered in Chapter 4. Consciousness (including its relationship to attention) is discussed in Chapter 16.

FOCUSED AUDITORY ATTENTION

The British scientist Colin Cherry became fascinated by the "cocktail party" problem, i.e., how can we follow just one conversation when several people are talking at once? Cherry (1953) found that this ability involved using physical differences (e.g., sex of speaker; voice intensity; speaker location) to maintain attention to a chosen auditory message. When Cherry presented two messages in the same voice to both ears at once (thus eliminating these physical differences), listeners found it hard to separate out the two messages on the basis of meaning alone.

Cherry also carried out studies in which one auditory message was shadowed (i.e., repeated back out loud) while a second auditory message was played to the other ear. Very little information seemed to be extracted from the second or non-attended message. Listeners seldom noticed when that message was spoken in a foreign language or reversed speech. In contrast, physical changes (e.g., a pure tone) were nearly always detected. The conclusion that unattended auditory information receives practically no processing was supported by finding there was very little memory for unattended words even when presented 35 times each (Moray, 1959).

Broadbent's theory

Broadbent (1958) argued that the findings from the shadowing task were important. He was also impressed by data from a memory task in which three pairs of digits were presented dichotically. On this task, three digits were presented one after the other to one ear at the same time as three different digits were presented to the other ear. Most participants chose to recall the digits ear by ear rather than pair by pair. Thus, if 496 were presented to one ear and 852 to the other ear, recall would be 496852 rather than 489562.

Broadbent (1958) accounted for the various findings as follows (see Figure 5.1):

- Two stimuli or messages presented at the same time gain access in parallel (at the same time) to a sensory buffer.
- One of the inputs is then allowed through a filter on the basis of its physical characteristics, with the other input remaining in the buffer for later processing.
- This filter prevents overloading of the limited-capacity mechanism beyond the filter, which processes the input thoroughly (e.g., in terms of its meaning).

This theory handles Cherry's basic findings, with unattended messages being rejected by the filter and thus receiving minimal processing.

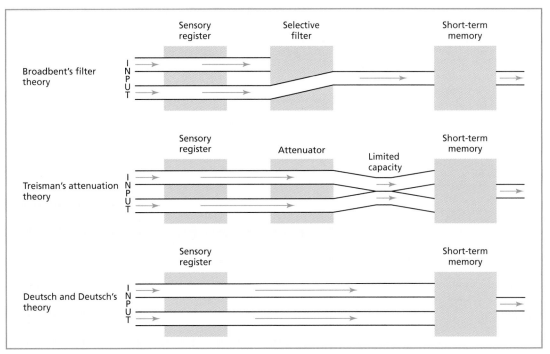

Figure 5.1 A comparison of Broadbent's theory (top); Treisman's theory (middle); and Deutsch and Deutsch's theory (bottom).

It also accounts for performance on Broadbent's dichotic task. The filter selects one input on the basis of the most prominent physical characteristic(s) distinguishing the two inputs (i.e., the ear of arrival). However, the assumption that the unattended message is typically rejected at an early stage of processing (unless attended to rapidly) is dubious. The original shadowing experiments used participants with very little experience of shadowing messages, so nearly all their available processing resources had to be allocated to shadowing. Underwood (1974) found that naïve participants detected only 8% of the digits on the non-shadowed message but an experienced researcher in the area (Neville Moray) detected 67%.

In most early work on the shadowing task, the two messages were rather similar (i.e., auditorily presented verbal messages). Allport, Antonis, and Reynolds (1972) found that the degree of *similarity* between the two messages had a major impact on memory for the non-shadowed message. When shadowing of audi-torily presented messages was combined with auditory presentation of words, memory for the words was very poor. However, when shadowing was combined with picture presentation, memory for the pictures was very good (90% correct). If two inputs are dissimilar, they can both be processed more fully than assumed by Broadbent.

In the early studies, it was assumed there was no processing of the meaning of unattended messages because the participants had no conscious awareness of hearing them. However, meaning can be processed without awareness. Von Wright, Anderson, and Stenman (1975) presented two lists of words auditorily, with instructions to shadow one list and ignore the other. When a word previously associated with electric shock was presented on the non-attended list, there was sometimes a physiological reaction (galvanic skin response). The same effect was produced by presenting a word very similar in sound or meaning to the shocked word. Thus, information on the unattended message was sometimes processed for sound and meaning even though the participants were not consciously aware that a word related to the previously shocked word had been presented.

When the participant's own name is presented on the unattended message, about one-third of them report hearing it (Moray, 1959). This finding is hard to account for in Broadbent's theory. Conway, Cowan, and Bunting (2001) found the probability of detecting one's own name on the unattended message depended on individual differences in working memory capacity (see Chapter 6). Individuals with low working memory capacity were more likely than those with high working memory capacity to detect their own name (65% versus 20%, respectively). This probably occurred because those low in working memory capacity are less able to control their focus of attention and so ignore the unattended message. This interpretation was supported by Colflesh and Conway (2007). Participants shadowed one message but were told *explicitly* to try to detect their own name in the other message. Those high in working memory capacity performed this task much better than those with low capacity (67% versus 34%).

Evaluation

Broadbent (1958) proposed a somewhat *inflexible* system of selective attention, which apparently cannot account for the great variability in the amount of analysis of the non-shadowed message. The same inflexibility of the filter theory is shown in its assumption that the filter selects information on the basis of physical features. This assumption is supported by people's tendency to recall dichotically presented digits ear by ear. However, Gray and Wedderburn (1960) used a version of the dichotic task in which "Who 6 there?" might be presented to one ear as "4 goes 1" was presented to the other ear. The preferred order of report was determined by meaning (e.g., "Who goes there?" followed by "4 6 1"). The fact that selection can be based on the meaning of presented information is inconsistent with filter theory.

In spite of these various problems with Broadbent's theory, it has recently received reasonable support in research by Lachter, Forster, and Ruthruff (2004). We will consider their research a little later.

Alternative theories

Treisman (1960) found with the shadowing task that participants sometimes said a word that had been presented on the unattended channel. Such "breakthroughs" typically occurred when the word on the unattended channel was highly probable in the context of the attended message. Even in those circumstances, however, Treisman only observed breakthrough on 6% of trials. Such findings led Treisman (1964) to argue that the filter reduces or attenuates the analysis of unattended information (see Figure 5.1). Treisman claimed that the location of the bottleneck was more flexible than Broadbent had suggested. She proposed that stimulus analysis proceeds systematically through a hierarchy, starting with analyses based on physical cues, syllable pattern and specific words, and moving on to analyses based on grammatical structure and meaning. If there is insufficient processing capacity to permit full stimulus analysis, tests towards the top of the hierarchy are omitted.

Treisman (1964) argued that the thresholds of all stimuli (e.g., words) consistent with current expectations are lowered. As a result, partially processed stimuli on the unattended channel sometimes exceed the threshold of conscious awareness. This aspect of the theory helps to account for breakthrough.

Treisman's theory accounted for the extensive processing of unattended sources of information that was embarrassing for Broadbent. However, the same facts were also explained by Deutsch and Deutsch (1963). They argued that all stimuli are fully analysed, with the most important or relevant stimulus determining the response (see Figure 5.1). This theory places the bottleneck in processing much nearer the response end of the processing system than Treisman's attenuation theory.

Treisman and Riley (1969) had participants shadow one of two auditory messages, but they were told to stop shadowing and to tap when they detected a target in either message. According to Treisman's theory, there should be attenuated processing of the non-shadowed message and so fewer targets should be detected on that message. According to Deutsch and Deutsch (1963), there is complete perceptual analysis of all stimuli, and so there should be no difference in detection rates between the two messages. In fact, many more target words were detected on the shadowed message.

Neurophysiological studies provide evidence against Deutsch and Deutsch's theory (see Lachter et al., 2004, for a review). Coch, Sanders, and Neville (2005) used a dichotic listening task in which participants attended to one of two auditory messages. Their task was to detect probe targets presented on the attended or unattended message. Event-related potentials (ERPs; see Glossary) were recorded. ERPs 100 ms after probe presentation were greater when the probe was presented on the attended message than the unattended one, suggesting there was more processing of attended than of unattended probes. No difference in these ERPs would be the natural prediction from Deutsch and Deutsch's theory.

Broadbent returns!

The evidence discussed so far suggests that Deutsch and Deutsch's theory is the least adequate of the three theories and Treisman's theory the most adequate. However, we must not dismiss Broadbent's approach too readily. Broadbent argued that there is a sensory buffer or immediate memory that briefly holds relatively unprocessed information. We now know that there are separate sensory buffers for the auditory modality (echoic memory) and the visual modality (iconic memory) (see Chapter 6). If we could switch our attention rapidly to the information in the appropriate sensory buffer, we would be able to process "unattended" stimuli thoroughly. Broadbent (1958)

was pessimistic about the possibility of doing that because he believed it took 500 ms to shift attention. In fact, involuntary shifts of attention can occur in 50 ms (Tsal, 1983). The crucial point is that shifting attention to information in a sensory buffer can be almost as effective as shifting attention to the actual object.

We now have *two* contrasting explanations for the occasional semantic processing of "unattended" stimuli. According to Treisman, this depends on a leaky filter. According to Broadbent's modified theory, it depends on what Lachter et al. (2004) called "slippage", meaning that attention is shifted to allegedly "unattended" stimuli so they are not really unattended.

Slippage may be more important than leakage. Von Wright et al. (1975), in a study discussed earlier, found heightened physiological responses to shock-associated words on the "unattended" message. Dawson and Schell (1982) replicated that finding, but most of the enhanced physiological responses occurred on trials in which it seemed likely that listeners had shifted attention.

Lachter et al. (2004) tested the slippage account. They used a lexical-decision task in which participants decided whether a letter string formed a word. This letter string was immediately preceded by a prime word the same as (or unrelated to) the target word presented for lexical decision. In the crucial condition, this prime word was presented for 55 ms, 110 ms, or 165 ms to the unattended location. According to the slippage account, participants would need to shift attention to the "unattended" prime to show a priming effect. Since attentional shifting takes at least 50 ms, there should be no priming effect when the prime word was presented for 55 ms. However, there should be a priming effect when it was presented for 110 ms or 165 ms because that would give sufficient time for attention to shift. That is precisely what happened. Thus, there was no evidence that the "unattended" prime word was processed when stringent steps were taken to prevent slippage but not to prevent leakage.

Evaluation

The three theories discussed in this section have all been very influential in the development of our understanding of focused auditory attention. Much of the evidence indicates that there is reduced processing of unattended stimuli compared to attended ones and is thus consistent with Treisman's theoretical approach. However, Lachter et al.'s (2004) research has revived interest in Broadbent's approach. Later in the chapter we discuss a theory put forward by Lavie (e.g., 2005). She argued that sometimes there is early selection (as claimed by Broadbent, 1958) and sometimes there is late selection (as claimed by Deutsch and Deutsch, 1963).

What are the limitations of research in this area? First, it is very hard to control the onset and offset of auditory stimuli with as much precision as can be done with visual stimuli. This helps to explain why Lachter et al. (2004) tested Broadbent's theory using visual stimuli. Second, all three theories are expressed sufficiently vaguely that it is difficult to provide definitive tests of them. Third, as Styles (1997, p. 28) pointed out, "Finding out *where* selection takes places may not help to understand *why* or *how* this happens."

FOCUSED VISUAL ATTENTION

Over the past 30 years or so, most researchers have studied visual rather than auditory attention. Why is this? There are several reasons. First, vision is probably our most important sense modality, with more of the cortex devoted to vision than to any other sensory modality. Second, it is easier to control precisely the presentation times of visual stimuli than auditory stimuli. Third, we can explore a wider range of issues in the visual than in the auditory modality.

There are more studies on focused visual attention than you can shake a stick at. Accordingly, we will consider only a few key issues. First, what are the major systems involved in visual attention? Second, what is selected in selective or focused visual attention? Third, what happens to unattended stimuli?

Major attentional systems

Several theorists (e.g., Corbetta & Shulman, 2002; Posner, 1980; Yantis, 2008) have argued that two major systems are involved in visual attention. One attentional system has been described as voluntary, endogenous, or goal-directed, whereas the other system is regarded as involuntary, exogenous, or stimulus-driven.

Posner (1980) carried out classic research in this area. His research involved **covert attention**, in which attention shifts to a given spatial location in the absence of an eye movement. In his studies, participants responded as rapidly as possible when they detected the onset of a light. Shortly before light onset, they were presented with a central cue (arrow pointing to the left or right) or a peripheral cue (brief illumination of a box outline). These cues were mostly valid (i.e., they indicated accurately where the target light would appear), but sometimes were invalid (i.e., they provided inaccurate information about the location of the target light).

What did Posner (1980) find? Valid cues produced faster responding to light onset than did neutral cues (a central cross), whereas invalid cues produced slower responding than neutral cues. The findings were comparable for central and peripheral cues, and were obtained in the absence of eye movements. When the cues were valid on only a small fraction of trials, they were ignored when they were central cues. However, they affected performance when they were peripheral cues.

KEY TERM

covert attention: attention to an object or sound in the absence of overt movements of the relevant receptors (e.g., looking at an object in the periphery of vision without moving one's eyes).

The above findings led Posner (1980) to distinguish between two systems:

(1) An *endogenous system*: This is controlled by the individual's intentions and expectations, and is involved when peripheral cues are presented.

(2) An *exogenous system*: This system automatically shifts attention and is involved when uninformative peripheral cues are presented. Stimuli that are salient or that differ from other stimuli (e.g., in colour; in motion) are most likely to be attended to via this system (Beck & Kastner, 2005).

Corbetta and Shulman (2002) identified a goal-directed or top-down attentional system (the dorsal network) resembling Posner's endogenous system and consisting of a dorsal fronto-parietal network (see Figure 5.2). The functioning of this system is influenced by expectations, knowledge, and current goals. Thus, this system is involved if people are given a cue predicting the location, motion, or other characteristic of a forthcoming visual stimulus.

Corbetta and Shulman also identified a stimulus-driven or bottom-up system (the ventral network) resembling Posner's exogenous system. This system is used when an unexpected and potentially important stimulus (e.g., flames appearing under the door of your room) is presented. This system has a "circuit-breaking" function, meaning that visual attention is redirected from its current focus. According to Corbetta and Shulman, this system consists of a right-hemisphere ventral fronto-parietal network (see Figure 5.3).

The goal-directed (dorsal network) and stimulus-driven (ventral network) systems often influence and interact with each other. According to Corbetta and Shulman (2002), connections between the temporo-parietal junction and the intraparietal sulcus interrupt goal-directed attention when unexpected stimuli are detected. More specifically, information concerning the significance of unexpected stimuli passes from the intraparietal sulcus to the temporo-parietal junction.

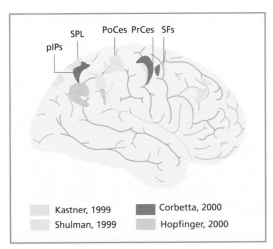

Figure 5.2 The brain network involved in the goal-directed attentional system, based on findings from various brain-imaging studies in which participants were expecting certain visual stimuli. The full names of the brain areas are in the text. Reprinted by permission from Macmillan Publishers Ltd: *Nature Reviews Neuroscience* (Corbetta & Shulman, 2002), Copyright © 2002.

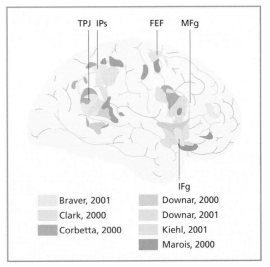

Figure 5.3 The brain network involved in the stimulus-driven attentional system, based on findings from various brain-imaging studies in which participants detected low-frequency target stimuli. The full names of the brain areas are in the text. Reprinted by permission from Macmillan Publishers Ltd: *Nature Reviews Neuroscience* (Corbetta & Shulman, 2002), Copyright © 2002.

Corbetta, Patel, and Shulman (2008) developed Corbetta and Shulman's (2002) argument that the ventral network has a "circuit-breaking" function. What stimuli trigger this circuit-breaking? The most obvious answer is that salient or distinctive stimuli attract attention to themselves. However, Corbetta et al. disputed that answer, claiming that *task-relevant* stimuli are much more likely to attract attention from the ventral network than are salient or distinctive stimuli. We will shortly discuss the relevant evidence.

Evidence

Corbetta and Shulman (2002) carried out meta-analyses of brain-imaging studies on the goal-directed system (dorsal network). The brain areas most often activated while individuals expect a stimulus that has not yet been presented are the posterior intraparietal sulcus (pIPs), the superior parietal lobule (SPL), the postcentral sulcus (PoCes), and precentral sulcus (PrCes), and the superior frontal sulcus (SFs) (see Figure 5.2). Somewhat different areas were activated from one study to the next, presumably because *what* participants expected varied across studies. They expected a stimulus at a given location in the Corbetta et al. (2000) and Hopfinger et al. (2000) studies, they expected a given direction of motion in the Shulman et al. (1999) study, and they expected a complex visual array in the Kastner (1999) study.

Corbetta and Shulman (2002) also carried out a meta-analysis of brain studies in which participants detected low-frequency targets using the stimulus-driven system (ventral network). The brain areas in this attentional network include the temporo-parietal junction (TPJ), the intraparietal sulcus (IPs), the frontal eye field (FEF), and the middle frontal gyrus (Mfg) (see Figure 5.3). There was substantial overlap in the brain areas activated across studies, especially in areas like the temporo-parietal junction. Note that activation was mainly present in the *right* hemisphere in all the studies contributing to the meta-analysis.

There are two reasons why it is somewhat difficult to interpret the evidence reported by Corbetta and Shulman (2002). First, the tasks used to assess the brain areas activated by the goal-directed attentional system generally differed from those used to assess activation associated with the stimulus-driven system. Second, most studies considered only one of the attentional systems and so failed to provide direct *comparisons* of patterns of brain activation in the two systems.

Hahn, Ross, and Stein (2006) attempted to eliminate these problems. Participants fixated a central circle and then detected a target presented to any of four peripheral locations. Cues varying in how informative they were concerning the location of the next target were presented in the central circle. It was assumed that top-down processes would be used most extensively when the cue was very informative. In contrast, bottom-up processes would occur *after* the target stimulus had been presented, and would be most used when the cue was relatively uninformative.

What did Hahn et al. (2006) discover? First, there was practically no overlap in the brain areas associated with top-down and bottom-up processing. This strengthens the argument that the two systems are separate. Second, the brain regions associated with top-down processing overlapped considerably with those identified by Corbetta and Shulman (2002). Third, the brain areas associated with stimulus-driven processing corresponded reasonably well to those emerging from Corbetta and Shulman's meta-analysis.

The neuroimaging evidence discussed so far is essentially correlational. For example, there is an association between individuals' expectations about imminent stimuli and activation of the goal-directed system. However, that does not demonstrate that the goal-directed or dorsal system has a *causal* influence on visual attention and perception. More convincing evidence was reported by Ruff et al. (2006) in a study in which participants decided which of two stimuli had greater contrast. When transcranial magnetic stimulation (TMS; see Glossary) was applied to the ventral system, it produced systematic and predicted effects on patterns of brain activation in several visual areas (e.g., V1) and on perceptual performance. Such findings strengthen the case for claiming that the ventral system influences attention in a top-down fashion.

Most patients with persistent neglect ignore or neglect visual stimuli presented to the left side of the visual field. According to Corbetta et al. (2008), this occurs because they have suffered damage to the stimulus-driven system. As we will see later, neglect patients vary in the areas of brain damage. However, the stimulus-driven system (especially the temporo-parietal junction) is typically damaged, and so the findings from neglect patients provide support for Corbetta et al.'s theory.

Evidence that involuntary or stimulus-driven attention is captured more by distractors resembling task-relevant stimuli than by salient or distinctive distractor stimuli was reported by Folk, Remington, and Johnston (1992). They used targets defined by colour or abrupt onset and the same was true of the distractors. When the participants looked for abrupt-onset targets, abrupt-onset distractors captured attention but colour distractors did not. In contrast, when the participants looked for colour targets, colour distractors captured attention but abrupt-onset distractors did not.

Indovina and Macaluso (2007) used functional magnetic resonance imaging (fMRI; see Glossary) to assess the effects of different types of distractor on activation within the stimulus-driven system or ventral network. Participants reported the orientation of a coloured letter T in the presence of a letter T in a different colour (task-relevant distractor) or a flickering draughtboard (salient distractor). The ventral network (e.g., the temporo-parietal junction) was activated by task-relevant distractors but not by salient ones.

Evaluation

Corbetta and Shulman (2002) and Corbetta et al. (2008) used the distinction between stimulus-driven and goal-directed attentional systems as the basis for an impressive cognitive neuroscience theory of visual attention. The neuroimaging evidence supports the notion of somewhat separate ventral and dorsal attention systems. This notion also receives support from research on neglect patients, who have damage primarily to the stimulus-driven system. In addition, the hypothesis that the stimulus-driven system is more responsive to task-relevant than to salient distractors has been supported empirically.

What are the limitations of this theoretical approach? First, we know little about how the two visual attention systems interact. Light will be shed on this issue if we can obtain more detailed information about the timing of activation in each system in various situations. Second, attentional processes are involved in the performance of numerous tasks. It is unlikely that all these processes can be neatly assigned to one or other of Corbetta and Shulman's (2002) attention systems. Third, attentional processes are influenced by several substances such as adrenaline, noradrenaline, and dopamine (Corbetta et al., 2008). However, *how* these substances influence the two attention systems is unclear.

Spotlight, zoom-lens, or multiple spotlights?

What is focused visual attention like? You may well agree with Posner (1980) and others that it is like a spotlight. Thus, visual attention illuminates a small part of the visual space around you, little can be seen outside its beam, and it can be redirected flexibly to focus on any object of interest. Eriksen and St. James (1986) developed the spotlight notion in their zoom-lens model, in which they compared focused attention to a zoom lens. They argued that we can increase or decrease the area of focal attention at will, just as a zoom lens can be adjusted. This certainly makes sense. For example, when driving a car it is generally a good idea to attend to as much of the visual field as possible to anticipate danger. However, when drivers detect a potential hazard, they focus specifically on it to avoid having a crash.

LaBerge (1983) reported findings supporting the zoom-lens model. Five-letter words

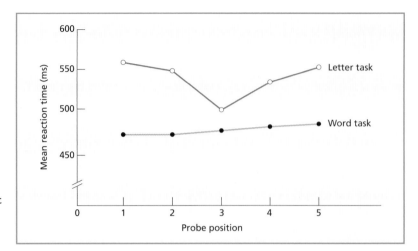

Figure 5.4 Mean reaction time to the probe as a function of probe position. The probe was presented at the time that a letter string would have been presented. Data from LaBerge (1983).

were presented, and a probe requiring a rapid response was occasionally presented instead of (or immediately after) the word. This probe could appear in the spatial position of any of the five letters. In one condition, an attempt was made to focus participants' attention on the middle letter of the five-letter word by asking them to categorise that letter. In another condition, participants categorised the entire word. It was expected that this would lead them to adopt a broader attentional beam.

Focused visual attention can be likened to a spotlight – a small area is brightly illuminated, everything outside its beam is poorly illuminated, and it can be moved around flexibly to illuminate any object of interest.

The findings on speed of detection of the probe are shown in Figure 5.4. LaBerge (1983) assumed that the probe would be responded to faster when it fell within the central attentional beam than when it did not. On this assumption, the attentional spotlight or zoom lens can have a very narrow (letter task) or fairly broad (word task) beam.

Müller, Bartelt, Donner, Villringer, and Brandt (2003) also supported the zoom-lens theory. On each trial, participants were presented with four squares in a semi-circle. They were cued to focus their attention on one specific square, or two specific squares, or on all four squares. After that, four objects were presented (one in each square), and participants decided whether a target (e.g., white circle) was among them. When a target was present, it was always in one of the cued squares. Müller et al. used functional magnetic resonance imaging (fMRI; see Glossary) to assess brain activation.

There were two key findings. First, as predicted by the zoom-lens theory, targets were detected fastest when the attended region was small (i.e., only one square) and slowest when it was large (i.e., all four squares). Second, activation in early visual areas was most widespread when the attended region was large and was most limited when the attended region was small (see Figure 5.5). This finding supports

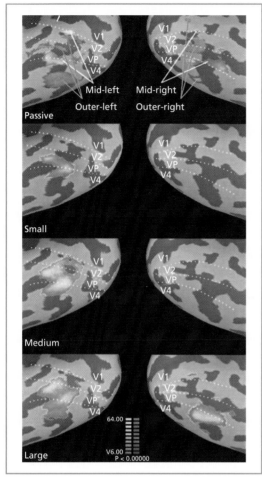

Figure 5.5 Top row: activation associated with passive viewing of stimuli at the four single locations. Following rows: activation when only the middle left location (small, second row), both left locations (medium, third row), or all four locations (large, fourth row) were cued. Left hemisphere on the right. From Müller et al. (2003) with permission from Society of Neuroscience.

the notion of an attentional beam that can be wide or narrow.

The zoom-lens model sounds plausible. However, the multiple spotlights theory (e.g., Awh & Pashler, 2000; Morawetz, Holz, Baudewig, Treue, & Dechent 2007) provides a superior account of visual attention. According to this theory, visual attention is even more flexible than assumed within the zoom-lens model. It

is assumed that we can show **split attention**, in which attention is directed to two or more regions of space *not* adjacent to each other. Split attention could save processing resources because we would avoid attending to irrelevant regions of visual space lying between two relevant areas.

Evidence of split attention was reported by Awh and Pashler (2000). Participants were presented with a 5 × 5 visual display containing 23 letters and two digits, and reported the identity of the two digits. Just before the display was presented, participants were given two cues indicating the probable locations of the two digits. These cues were invalid on 20% of trials. Part of what was involved is shown in Figure 5.6a. The crucial condition was one in which the cues were invalid, with one of the digits being presented in between the cued locations (the near location).

How good would we expect performance to be for a digit presented *between* the two cued locations? If the spotlight or zoom-lens theory is correct, focal attention should include the two cued locations *and* the space in between. In that case, performance should have been high for that digit because it would have received full attention. If the multiple spotlights theory is correct, performance should have been poor for that digit because only the cued locations would have received full attention. In fact, performance was much lower for digits presented *between* cued locations than for digits presented *at* cued locations (see Figure 5.6b). Thus, attention can apparently be shaped like a doughnut with nothing in the middle.

Morawetz et al. (2007) presented letters and digits at five locations simultaneously: one in the centre of the visual field and one in each quadrant of the visual field. In one condition, participants were instructed to attend to the

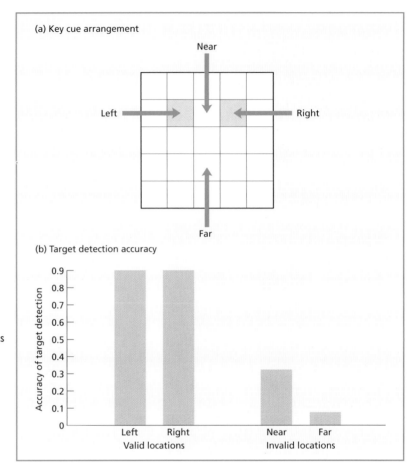

Figure 5.6 (a) Shaded areas indicate the cued locations and the near and far locations are not cued. (b) Probability of target detection at valid (left or right) and invalid (near or far) locations. Both based on information in Awh and Pashler (2000).

visual stimuli at the upper-left and bottom-right locations and to ignore the other stimuli. There were two peaks of brain activation in and close to primary visual cortex, indicating enhancement of cortical areas representing visual space. However, there was less activation corresponding to the region in between. This pattern of activation is as predicted by multiple spotlights theory.

What is selected?

What is selected by the zooms lens or multiple spotlights? There are various possibilities. First, we may selectively attend to an area or region of space, as when we look behind us to identify the source of a sound. Second, we may attend to a given object or objects. This seems likely given that visual perception is mainly concerned with specific objects of interest to us (see Chapters 2 and 3). Third, our processing system may be so flexible that we can attend to an area of space *or* a given object. We consider these possibilities in turn. Note, however, that it is hard to distinguish between attention to a location and attention to an object given that any object has to be present in some location.

Location-based attention

O'Craven, Downing, and Kanwisher (1999) obtained findings supporting the notion that attention can be location-based. Participants were presented with two ovals of different colours, one to the left of fixation and one to the right, and indicated the orientation of the one in a given colour. Each oval was superimposed on a task-irrelevant face or house. They made use of the fact that the fusiform face area is selectively activated when faces are processed, whereas the parahippocampal place area is selectively activated when houses are processed. As predicted on the assumption that attention is location-based, fMRI indicated that there was more processing of the stimulus superimposed on the attended oval than of the stimulus superimposed on the unattended oval.

Object-based attention

Visual attention is often directed to objects rather than a particular region of space. Neisser and Becklen (1975) superimposed two moving scenes on top of each other. Their participants could easily attend to one scene while ignoring the other. These findings suggest that objects can be the main focus of visual attention.

O'Craven, Downing, and Kanwisher (1999) presented participants with two stimuli (a face and a house) transparently overlapping at the same location, with one of the objects moving slightly. Participants attended to the direction of motion of the moving stimulus or the position of the stationary stimulus. Suppose attention is location-based. In that case, participants would have to attend to both stimuli, because they were both in the same location. In contrast, suppose attention is object-based. In that case, processing of the attended stimulus should be more thorough than processing of the unattended stimulus.

O'Craven et al. (1999) tested the above competing predictions by using fMRI to assess activity in brain areas involved in processing faces (fusiform face area) or houses (parahippocampal place area). There was more activity in the fusiform face area when the face stimulus was attended than unattended, and more activity in the parahippocampal place area when the house stimulus was attended than unattended. Thus, attention was object- rather than location-based.

There is evidence for object-based selection from studies on patients with persistent neglect, who typically fail to attend to stimuli presented to the left visual field. Marshall and Halligan (1994) presented a neglect patient with ambiguous displays that could be seen as a black shape against a white background or a white shape on a black background. There was a jagged edge dividing the two shapes at the centre of each display. The patient copied this jagged edge when drawing the shape on the left side of the display, but could not copy exactly the same edge when drawing the shape on the right side. Thus, the patient attended to objects rather than simply to a region of visual space.

Evaluation

It is not surprising that visual attention is often object-based, given that the goal of visual perception is generally to identify objects in the environment. It is also relevant that the grouping processes (e.g., law of similarity; law of proximity) occurring relatively early in visual perception help to segregate the visual environment into figure (central object) and ground (see Chapter 2). However, attention can also be location-based.

Location- and object-based attention

Egly, Driver, and Rafal (1994) found evidence for both location- and object-based attention. They used displays like those shown in Figure 5.7. The task was to detect a target stimulus as rapidly as possible. A cue was presented before the target, and this cue was valid (same location as the target) or invalid (different location from target). Of key importance, invalid cues were in the same object as the target or in a different object. Target detection was slower on invalid trials than on valid trials. On invalid trials, target detection was slower when the cue was in a different object, suggesting that attention was at least partially object-based. Egly et al. (1994) used the same displays to test patients suffering from brain damage to the right parietal area. When the cue was presented to the same side as the brain damage but the target was presented to the opposite side, the patients showed considerable slowing of target detection. This occurred

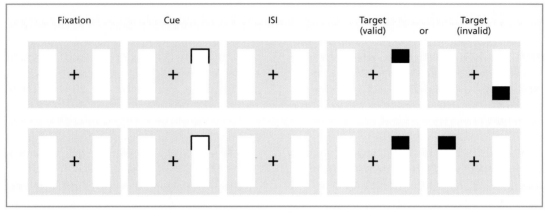

Figure 5.7 Examples of the displays used by Egly et al. (1994). The heavy black lines in the panels of the second column represent the cue. The filled squares in the panels of the fourth and fifth columns represent the target stimulus. In the fifth column, the top row shows a within-object invalid trial, whereas the bottom row shows a between-object invalid trial. From Umiltà (2001).

because they had impairment of the location-based component of visual attention and so could not switch attention rapidly from one part of visual space to another.

When we are searching the visual environment, it would be inefficient if we repeatedly attended to any given location. This could be avoided if we possess inhibitory processes reducing the probability of that happening. Of direct relevance here is the phenomenon of **inhibition of return**, "a reduced perceptual priority for information in a region that recently enjoyed a higher priority" (Samuel & Kat, 2003, p. 897). A central issue is whether inhibition of return applies to locations or to objects.

Posner and Cohen (1984) provided the original demonstration of inhibition of return. There were two boxes, one on each side of the fixation point. An uninformative cue was presented in one of the boxes (e.g., its outline brightened). This was followed by a target stimulus (e.g., an asterisk) in one of the boxes, with the participant's task being to respond as rapidly as possible when it was detected. When the time interval between cue and target was under 300 ms, targets in the cued location were detected faster than those in the non-cued location. However, when the time interval exceeded 300 ms, there was inhibition of return

– targets in the cued location were responded to more slowly than those in the non-cued location.

List and Robertson (2007) addressed the issue of whether inhibition of return applies to locations or to objects using the paradigm previously employed by Egly et al. (1994; see Figure 5.7). They found some evidence for object-based inhibition of return. However, object-based effects were "slow to emerge, small in magnitude, and susceptible to minor changes in procedure" (List & Robertson, 2007, p. 1332). In contrast, location- or space-based inhibition of return occurred rapidly, was of much greater magnitude, and was found consistently.

Leek, Reppa, and Tipper (2003) argued that object-based and location-based inhibition of return both exist. Thus, the magnitude of the inhibitory effect in standard conditions (with an object present) is a *combination* of location- and object-based inhibition of return.

KEY TERM

inhibition of return: a reduced probability of visual attention returning to a previously attended location or object.

Leek et al. compared inhibition of return under conditions in which an object was absent or present. They expected to find that the inhibitory effect would be stronger in the standard condition (location-based + object-based inhibition) than in a condition in which the object was absent. That is precisely what they found.

What underlies inhibition of return? Two main answers have been suggested: inhibition of perceptual/attentional processes and inhibition of motor processes. The findings have been inconsistent. Prime and Ward (2004) used event-related potentials (ERPs; see Glossary) to clarify the processes involved in inhibition of return. Early visual processing of targets presented to the location previously cued was reduced (or inhibited) compared to that of targets presented to a different location. In contrast, the ERP evidence failed to indicate any difference in motor processes between the two types of target. However, Pastötter, Hanslmayr, and Bäuml (2008) found, using EEG, that response inhibition was important in producing inhibition of return. Finally, Tian and Yao (2008) found, using ERPs, that "both sensory inhibition processes and response inhibition processes are involved in the behavioural IOR (inhibition of return) effect" (p. 177).

In sum, visual attention can be object- or location-based, and so can be used flexibly. In similar fashion, inhibition of return can be object- or location-based, although some evidence (e.g., List & Robertson, 2007) suggests that location-based inhibition effects are generally stronger. Presumably the individual's goals determine whether visual attention is focused on objects or locations, but the precise processes involved remain unclear.

What happens to unattended visual stimuli?

Not surprisingly, unattended stimuli receive less processing than attended ones. For example, Wojciulik, Kanwisher, and Driver (1998) presented displays containing two faces and two houses. A same–different task was applied in separate blocks to the faces or to the houses, with the other type of stimulus being unattended. Activity in the fusiform face area that responds selectively to faces was significantly greater when the faces were attended than when they were not. However, there was still some activity within the fusiform face area in response to unattended faces.

Evidence that there can be more processing of unattended visual stimuli than initially seems to be the case was reported by McGlinchey-Berroth, Milber, Verfaellie, Alexander, and Kilduff (1993). Neglect patients (who typically ignore visual stimuli presented to the left visual field) decided which of two drawings matched a drawing presented immediately beforehand to the left or the right visual field. The patients performed well when the initial drawing was presented to the right visual field but at chance level when presented to the left visual field (see Figure 5.8a). The latter finding suggests that the stimuli in the left visual field were not processed. In a second study, however, neglect patients decided whether letter strings formed words. Decision times were faster on "yes" trials when the letter string was preceded by a semantically related object rather than an unrelated one. This effect was the same size regardless of whether the object was presented to the left or the right visual field (see Figure 5.8b), indicating that there was some semantic processing of left-field stimuli by neglect patients.

We saw earlier that task-relevant distracting stimuli are often more disruptive of task performance than salient or distinctive distractors (e.g., Folk et al., 1992). However, other factors are also important in determining whether we can maintain our attentional focus on the task in hand. Lavie (e.g., 2005) developed a theory in which the emphasis is on two major assumptions:

(1) Susceptibility to distraction is greater when the task involves low *perceptual load* than when it involves high perceptual load. Perceptual load depends on factors such as the number of task stimuli that need to be perceived or the processing

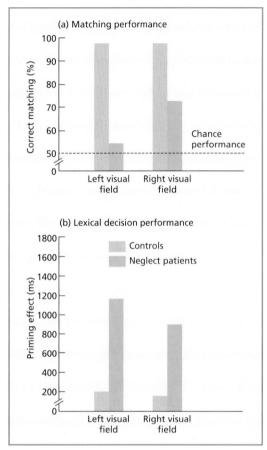

Figure 5.8 Effects of prior presentation of a drawing to the left or right visual field on matching performance and lexical decision in neglect patients. Data from McGlinchey-Berroth et al. (1993).

demands of each stimulus. The argument is that, "High perceptual load that engages full capacity in relevant processing would leave no spare capacity for perception of task-irrelevant stimuli" (p. 75).

(2) Susceptibility to distraction is greater when there is a high load on *executive cognitive control functions* (e.g., working memory) than when there is a low load. The reason for this assumption is that, "Cognitive control is needed for actively maintaining the distinction between targets and distractors" (p. 81). This is especially likely when it is hard to discriminate between target and distractor stimuli.

Most of the evidence supports this theory. Lavie (1995) carried out an experiment in which participants detected a target letter (an "x" or a "z") appearing in one of six positions arranged in a row. In the high perceptual-load condition, the other five positions were occupied by non-target letters, whereas none of those positions was occupied in the low perceptual load condition. Finally, a large distractor letter was also presented. On some trials, it was incompatible (i.e., it was "x" when the target was "z" or vice versa) and on other trials it was neutral. According to the theory, the nature of the distractor should have more effect on time to identify target stimuli when perceptual load is low than when it is high. That is precisely what happened (see Figure 5.9).

Forster and Lavie (2008) pointed out that people in everyday life are often distracted by stimuli obviously irrelevant to their current task. For example, more than 10% of drivers hospitalised after car accidents reported that they had been distracted by irrelevant stimuli such as a person outside the car or an insect inside it (McEvoy, Stevenson, & Woodward, 2007). Participants searched for a target letter and the distractor was another letter or a cartoon character (e.g., Mickey Mouse; Donald Duck). There were two key findings. First, the completely task-irrelevant distractors interfered with task performance as much as the task-relevant distractors. Second, the interfering effects of both kinds of distractor were eliminated when there was high perceptual load on the task.

Neuroimaging studies have provided additional evidence of the importance of perceptual load. Schwartz, Vuilleumier, Hutton, Marouta, Dolan, and Driver (2005) assessed brain activation to distractor flickering draughtboards while participants carried out a task involving low or high perceptual load. As predicted, the draughtboard distractors produced less activation in several brain areas related to visual processing (e.g., V1, V2, and V3) when there was high perceptual load (see Figure 5.10).

The prediction that the effects of distractors should be more disruptive when the load on working memory is high than when it is low, was tested by de Fockert, Rees, Frith, and Lavie

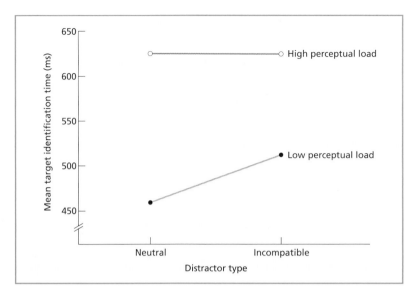

Figure 5.9 Mean target identification time as a function of distractor type (neutral vs. incompatible) and perceptual load (low vs. high). Based on data in Lavie (1995).

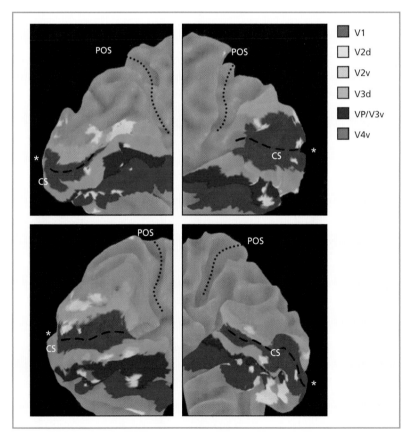

Figure 5.10 Areas of medial occipital cortex (shown in white) in which the activation associated with distractors was significantly less when the central task involved high rather than low perceptual load. Data are from four representative participants (two left and two right hemispheres). CS = calcarine sulcus; POS = parieto-occipital sulcus. From Schwartz et al. (2005), by permission of Oxford University Press.

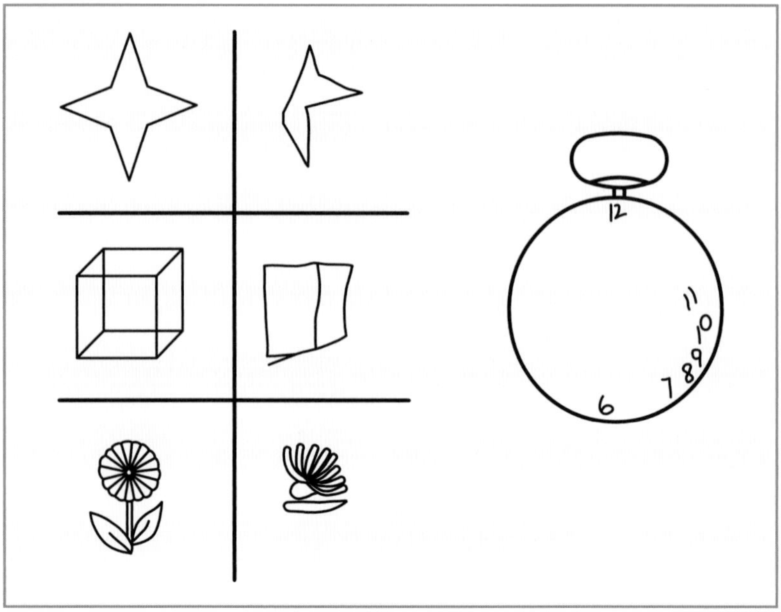

Figure 5.11 Left is a copying task in which a patient with unilateral neglect distorted or ignored the left side of the figures to be copied (shown on the left). Right is a clock-drawing task in which the patient was given a clock face and told to insert the numbers into it. Reprinted from Danckert and Ferber (2006), Copyright © 2006, with permission from Elsevier.

(2001). Participants classified famous written names as pop stars or politicians under conditions of low or high working memory load (involving remembering strings of digits). Distraction was provided by famous faces. Task performance was more adversely affected by the distracting faces when there was high working memory load. In addition, there was more face-related activity in the visual cortex in the high load condition than the low load condition.

In sum, the effects of distracting stimuli depend on perceptual load and on the load on executive control. High perceptual load *decreases* the impact of distracting stimuli on task performance, whereas high executive control load *increases* the impact of distracting stimuli. Thus, there is no simple relationship between load and susceptibility to distraction – it all depends on the nature of the load.

DISORDERS OF VISUAL ATTENTION

We can learn much about attentional processes by studying brain-damaged individuals suffering from various attentional disorders. Here, we consider two of the main attentional disorders: neglect and extinction. **Neglect** (or unilateral neglect) is a condition in which there is a lack of awareness of stimuli presented to the side of space on the opposite side of the brain (the contralesional side). In the great majority of cases of persistent neglect, the brain damage is in the right hemisphere (involving the inferior parietal lobe), and there is little awareness of stimuli on the left side of the visual field. This occurs because of the nature of the visual system, with information from the left side of the visual field proceeding to the right hemisphere of the brain. When neglect patients draw an object or copy a drawing, they typically leave out most of the details from the left side of it (see Figure 5.11).

KEY TERM

neglect: a disorder of visual attention in which stimuli or parts of stimuli presented to the side opposite the brain damage are undetected and not responded to; the condition resembles **extinction** but is more severe.

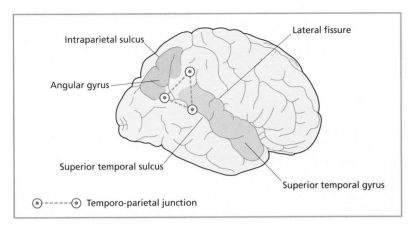

Figure 5.12 The areas within the parietal and temporal association cortex probably involved in unilateral neglect (adapted from Duvernoy, 1999). The region of the angular gyrus is outlined in light green and that of the superior temporal gyrus in pale orange. The region of the temporo-parietal junction is shown by the circles joined by dotted lines. Reprinted from Danckert and Ferber (2006), Copyright © 2006, with permission from Elsevier.

Some neglect patients show personal neglect (e.g., failing to shave the left side of their face), whereas others show neglect for far space but not for near space. Buxbaum et al. (2004) found 12 different patterns of deficit. Thus, neglect is *not* a single disorder.

We can test for the presence of neglect in various ways (e.g., tasks in which patients copy figures). Neglect patients typically distort or neglect the left side of any figure they copy (see Figure 5.11). Then there is the line bisection task in which patients try to put a mark through the line at its centre, but typically put it to the right of the centre.

Which brain areas are damaged in neglect patients? There is controversy on this issue. Some findings suggest that the superior temporal gyrus is crucial, whereas others point to the temporo-parietal junction or the angular gyrus (Danckert & Ferber, 2006; see Figure 5.12). Fierro et al. (2000) found that they could produce neglect-like performance on the line bisection task by administering transcranial magnetic stimulation (TMS; see Glossary) to the angular gyrus, which strengthens the argument that damage to this area is involved in neglect. Bartolomeo, Thiebaut de Schotten, and Doricchi (2007) reviewed the literature and concluded that neglect is due to the disconnection of large-scale brain networks rather than damage to a single cortical region. More specifically, they argued that damage to connections between parietal and frontal cortex

is of central importance to neglect. Most of the evidence indicates that Corbetta and Shulman's (2002) stimulus-driven system is damaged in neglect patients.

Extinction is often found in patients suffering from neglect. Extinction involves the inability to detect a visual stimulus on the side opposite that of the brain damage in the presence of a second visual stimulus on the same side as the brain damage. Extinction is a serious condition, because multiple stimuli are typically present at the same time in everyday life.

How can we explain neglect? Driver and Vuilleumier (2001, p. 40) argued that what happens in neglect patients is a more extreme form of what happens in healthy individuals. According to them, "Perceptual awareness is not determined solely by the stimuli impinging on our senses, but also by which of these stimuli we choose to attend. This choice seems pathologically limited in neglect patients, with their attention strongly biased towards events

KEY TERM

extinction: a disorder of visual attention in which a stimulus presented to the side opposite the brain damage is not detected when another stimulus is presented at the same time to the same side as the brain damage.

on the ipsilesional side [same side as the lesion]." Thus, there are important similarities between neglect in patients and inattention in healthy individuals.

How can we explain extinction? Marzi et al. (2001, p. 1354) offered the following explanation:

> *The presence of extinction only during bilateral stimulation is strongly suggestive of a competition mechanism, whereby the presence of a more salient stimulus presented on the same side of space as that of the brain lesion (ipsilesional side) captures attention and hampers the perception of a less salient stimulus on the opposite (contralesional) side.*

Driver and Vuilleumier (2001, p. 50) provided a similar account: "While extinction is by no means the whole story for neglect, it encapsulates a critical general principle that applies for most aspects of neglect, namely, that the patient's spatial deficit is most apparent in competitive situations."

As we saw earlier, Corbetta and Shulman (2002) argued that the attentional problems of neglect patients are due mainly to impairment of the stimulus-driven system. Bartolomeo and Chokron (2002, p. 217) proposed a similar hypothesis: "A basic mechanism leading to left neglect behaviour is an impaired exogenous [originating outside the individual] orienting towards left-sided targets. In contrast, endogenous processes [originating inside the individual] seem to be relatively preserved, if slowed, in left unilateral neglect." In simpler terms, bottom-up processes are more impaired than top-down ones in neglect patients.

There is reasonable overlap among the various theoretical accounts. For example, impaired functioning of a competition mechanism in patients with neglect and extinction may be due in large measure to damage to the stimulus-driven system. However, what is distinctive about Bartolomeo and Chokron's (2002) theory is the notion that the goal-directed system is reasonably intact in neglect patients.

Evidence

Neglect patients often process stimuli on the neglected side of the visual field fairly thoroughly even though they lack conscious awareness of those stimuli (e.g., the study by McGlinchey-Berroth et al., 1993, discussed earlier). Marshall and Halligan (1988) presented a neglect patient with two drawings of a house identical except that the house presented to the left visual field had flames coming out of its windows. The patient could not report any differences between the two drawings but indicated she would prefer to live in the house on the right.

Vuilleumier, Armony, Clarke, Husain, Driver, and Dolan (2002) presented pictures of objects briefly to the left visual field, the right visual field, or to both visual fields to patients with neglect and extinction. When two pictures were presented together, patients only reported the picture presented to the right visual field. They also showed very little memory for the pictures presented to the left visual field. Finally, the patients identified degraded pictures. There was a facilitation effect for pictures that had been presented to the neglected visual field, indicating that they had been processed.

Further evidence that extinguished stimuli are processed was reported by Rees et al. (2000) in an fMRI study. Extinguished stimuli produced moderate levels of activation in the primary visual cortex and some nearby areas. This suggested that these stimuli of which the patient was unaware were nonetheless processed reasonably thoroughly.

Evidence that competition is important in extinction was reported by Marzi et al. (1997). Extinction patients detected contralesional stimuli (presented to the side opposite the brain damage) more slowly than ipsilesional ones (presented to the same side as the brain damage) when only one stimulus was presented at a time. Those patients showing the greatest difference in detecting contralesional and ipsilesional stimuli had the greatest severity of extinction. What do these findings mean? According to Marzi et al., extinction occurs in part because the contralesional stimuli cannot *compete* successfully for attention;

the slower the processing of contralesional stimuli compared to ipsilesional stimuli, the less their ability to compete for attention.

Under what circumstances is extinction reduced or eliminated? Theoretically, we could reduce competition by presenting two stimuli integrated in some way. For example, an extinction patient showed extinction when black circles with quarter-segments removed were presented to the contralesional side at the same time as similar stimuli were presented to the ipsilateral side (Mattingley, Davis, & Driver, 1997). However, extinction was much reduced when the stimuli were altered slightly to form Kanizsa's illusory square (see Figure 2.20). Rather similar finding were found with neglect patients by Conci, Matthias, Keller, Muller, and Finke (2009).

Riddoch, Humphreys, Hickman, Daly, and Colin (2006) extended the above research. Two stimuli were presented briefly either side of the fixation point. They represented objects often used together, less often used together, and never used together (control condition) (see Figure 5.13). Extinction patients identified both items most frequently when both objects are often used together (65% correct), followed by objects less often used together (55%), and control items (40%). Thus, extinction patients can avoid extinction when two stimuli can be combined rather than competing with each other.

In sum, patients with neglect and extinction can group visual stimuli from both sides of the visual field. This reduces attentional competition and allows them to gain conscious access to stimuli presented to the contralesional side.

What evidence indicates that neglect involves impaired exogenous orienting (or stimulus-driven processing) rather than problems with endogenous orienting (or goal-directed attention)? Bartolomeo, Siéroff, Decaix, and Chokron (2001) carried out an experiment in which a visual cue predicted the target would probably be presented to the other side. Endogenous orienting or goal-directed attention is required to shift attention away from the cue to the probable target locations. Neglect patients resembled healthy controls by responding rapidly when

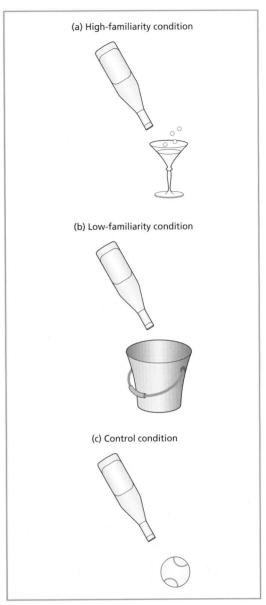

Figure 5.13 Pairs of items that are: (a) often used together (high-familiarity condition); (b) occasionally used together (low-familiarity condition); and (c) never used together (control condition). From Riddoch et al. (2006).

the cue was presented to the right side and the target to the left side.

Duncan, Bundesen, Olson, Humphreys, Chavda, Shibuya (1999) presented arrays of letters briefly, and asked neglect patients to recall all the letters or to recall only those in a pre-specified colour. It was assumed that endogenous orienting was possible *only* in the latter condition. As expected, recall of letters presented to the left side was much worse than that of letters presented to the right side when all letters had to be reported. However, neglect patients resembled healthy controls in showing equal recall of letters presented to each side of visual space when target letters were defined by colour.

It has generally been assumed that attentional selection for ipsilesional stimuli (i.e., those presented to the "good" side) is essentially normal in neglect and extinction patients. Evidence that this is *not* the case was reported by Snow and Mattingley (2006). Patients with right-hemisphere lesions (presumably a mixture of neglect and extinction patients) made speeded judgements about a central target item. To-be-ignored stimuli presented to the *right* field interfered with task performance for the patients regardless of their relevance to the task. These stimuli only interfered with task performance for healthy controls when relevant to the task. The take-home message is that patients have deficient top-down or goal-driven attentional control even for stimuli presented to the "good" or ipsilesional side, and thus their attentional problems are greater than is generally assumed.

How can we reduce the symptoms of neglect? Rossetti, Rode, Pisella, Boisson, and Perenin (1998) came up with an interesting answer. When neglect patients in the dark are asked to point straight ahead, they typically point several degrees off to the right. This led Rossetti et al. to ask neglect patients to wear prisms that shifted the visual field 10 degrees to the right. After adaptation, patients in the dark pointed almost directly ahead. They also performed significantly better on other tasks (e.g., the line-bisection task) and produced more symmetrical drawings of a daisy for up to two hours after prism removal. Subsequent research (reviewed by Chokron, Dupierrix, Tabert, & Bartolomeo, 2007) has confirmed the effectiveness of prism adaptation up to five weeks after prism removal.

Why does prism adaptation have such beneficial effects? Nijboer, McIntosh, Nys, Dijkerman, and Milner (2008) found that prism adaptation in neglect patients improved their ability to orient attention leftwards following an endogenous (internal) cue but not following an exogenous (external) one. They concluded that prism adaptation made it easier for neglect patients to engage in voluntary orienting to compensate for their habitual rightward bias.

Evaluation
The study of neglect and extinction patients has produced several important findings. First, such patients can process unattended visual stimuli, and this processing is sometimes at the semantic level (McGlinchey-Berroth et al., 1993). Second, such patients provide evidence about the range of preattentive processing, which can include grouping of visual stimuli (e.g., Mattingley et al., 1997; Riddoch et al., 2006). Third, neglect patients have several impairments of exogenous orienting (stimulus-driven processing) but much milder impairments of endogenous orienting (top-down processing). Fourth, the success of prism adaptation as a form of treatment for neglect is likely to lead to an enhanced understanding of the underlying mechanisms of neglect.

What are the limitations of research on neglect and extinction? First, the precise symptoms and regions of brain damage vary considerably across patients. Thus, it is difficult to produce a theoretical account applicable to all patients with neglect or extinction. Second, it has generally been assumed that patients' problems centre on the contralesional side of the visual field. The findings of Snow and Mattingley (2006) suggest that patients may also have unexpected problems with attentional control on the ipsilesional side of the visual field. Third, while it is clear that attentional processes are important to an understanding of neglect and extinction, the precise nature of those processes has not been established.

Three attentional abilities
Posner and Petersen (1990) proposed a theoretical framework representing a development

of his earlier notion of separate endogenous and exogenous systems (Posner, 1980; see earlier in chapter). According to Posner and Petersen, three separate abilities are involved in controlling attention:

- *Disengagement* of attention from a given visual stimulus.
- *Shifting* of attention from one target stimulus to another.
- *Engaging* or locking attention on a new visual stimulus.

These three abilities are all functions of the posterior attention system (resembling the stimulus-driven system of Corbetta and Shulman, 2002). In addition, there is an anterior attention system (resembling Corbetta and Shulman's goal-directed system). It is involved in co-ordinating the different aspects of visual attention, and resembles the central executive component of working memory (see Chapter 6). According to Posner and Petersen (1990, p. 40), there is "a hierarchy of attentional systems in which the anterior system can pass control to the posterior system when it is not occupied with processing other material." In what follows, we will briefly consider the three attentional abilities identified by Posner and Petersen (1990) in the light of evidence from brain-damaged patients.

Disengagement of attention

According to Posner and Petersen (1990), damage to the posterior parietal region is most associated with impaired disengagement of attention. As we have seen, neglect patients have suffered damage to the parietal region of the brain. Losier and Klein (2001) found, in a meta-analysis, that problems of disengagement of attention were greater in patients suffering from neglect than in other brain-damaged patients. However, there is evidence that neglect patients only have problems of disengagement when they need to shift attention *between* rather than *within* objects (Schindler et al., 2009). This suggests that it is hard to disengage from objects but not necessarily from a given point in space. Petersen, Corbetta, Miezin, and Shulman (1994) found, using PET scans, that there was much activation within the parietal area when attention shifted from one spatial location to another.

Problems with disengaging attention are found in patients suffering from **simultanagnosia**. In this condition, only one object (out of two or three) can be seen at any one time even when the objects are close together. Michel and Henaff (2004) found that AT, a patient with simultanagnosia, had an almost normal visual field but a substantially restricted attentional visual field. The presence of a restricted attentional field probably explains why patients with simultanagnosia have "sticky" fixations and find it hard to disengage attention.

Tyler (1968) described a patient whose visual exploration was limited to "the point in the picture where her eye accidentally was, when the picture was projected." Nyffeler et al. (2005) studied a 53-year-old woman with simultanagnosia. She was asked to name four overlapping objects presented horizontally so that two were presented to the left and two to the right of the initial fixation point. She had great difficulty in disengaging attention from the objects presented to the left side: 73% of her eye fixations were on one of those objects. As a result, she totally failed to fixate almost one-quarter of the objects. In contrast, healthy participants fixated virtually 100% of the objects.

Shifting of attention

Posner, Rafal, Choate, and Vaughan (1985) examined problems of shifting attention in patients with progressive supranuclear palsy. Such patients have damage to the midbrain and find it very hard to make voluntary eye movements, especially in the vertical direction. Posner et al. presented cues to the locations of forthcoming targets followed at varying intervals

> **KEY TERM**
>
> **simultanagnosia:** a brain-damaged condition in which only one object can be seen at a time.

by a target. Patients made reasonable use of valid cues (cues providing accurate information about target location) when the targets were presented to the left or right of the cue. However, they had difficulty in shifting their attention appropriately in the vertical direction in response to the cues.

Part of the midbrain known as the superior colliculus is involved in the top-down control of attention and is important in attentional shifting. For example, Bell and Munoz (2008) studied a monkey's ability to use a cue to shift attention to the valid location. There was a greater increase in activity within the superior colliculus when the monkey shifted attention appropriately than when it did not.

Further evidence of the role of the superior colliculus in the shifting of attention was reported by Sereno, Briand, Amador, and Szapiel (2006). A patient with damage to the superior colliculus showed a complete absence of inhibition of return (discussed earlier; see Glossary). Since the great majority of healthy individuals show inhibition of return, it seems damage to the superior colliculus disrupts processes associated with shifting of attention.

Engaging attention

According to Posner and Petersen (1990), the pulvinar nucleus of the thalamus plays an important role in engaging attention to an appropriate stimulus and suppressing attention to irrelevant stimuli. Rafal and Posner (1987) carried out a study in which patients with pulvinar damage responded to visual targets preceded by cues. They responded faster after valid than invalid cues when the target stimulus was presented to the same side as the brain damage. However, they responded rather slowly following both kinds of cues when the target stimulus was presented to the side opposite to the brain damage. These findings suggest the patients had a problem in engaging attention to such stimuli.

Ward, Danziger, Owen, and Rafal (2002) studied TN, who had suffered damage to the pulvinar. She was asked to report the identity and colour of a target letter while ignoring a distractor letter in a different colour. TN typically identified the target letter correctly. However, she often mistakenly assigned the colour of the distractor letter to it, especially when the two letters were close together. This suggests a difficulty in effective attentional engagement with the target letter.

Additional evidence that the pulvinar nucleus of the thalamus is involved in controlling focused attention was obtained by LaBerge and Buchsbaum (1990). PET scans indicated increased activation in the pulvinar nucleus when participants ignored a given stimulus. Thus, the pulvinar nucleus is involved in preventing attention from being focused on an unwanted stimulus as well as in directing attention to significant stimuli.

Evaluation

Several fairly specific attentional problems have been found in brain-damaged patients. Thus, it makes sense to assume that the attentional system consists of various components. In general terms, we can distinguish among disengaging of attention from a stimulus, shifting of attention, and engaging of attention on a new stimulus. Posner and Petersen (1990) went a step further and tentatively identified brain areas especially associated with each process.

The main limitation of theorising in this area is that it oversimplifies a complex reality. For example, it has been argued that the pulvinar is involved in orienting to feature changes (Michael & Buron, 2005) as well as attentional engagement. Evidence that different parts of the pulvinar are involved in somewhat different processes was reported by Arend, Rafal, and Ward (2008). A patient with damage to the anterior of the pulvinar found it harder to engage spatial than temporal attention, whereas another patient with posterior pulvinar damage showed the opposite pattern.

VISUAL SEARCH

As Peterson, Kramer, Wang, Irwin, and McCarley (2001, p. 287) pointed out, "We spend a good deal of each day searching the environment…in the office we may look for a coffee cup, the manuscript we were working on several days ago, or a phone number of a colleague." The processes involved in such activities have been examined in studies on **visual search**, in which a specified target within a visual display must be detected as rapidly as possible. On visual search tasks, participants are typically presented with a visual display containing a variable number of items (the set or display size). A target (e.g., red G) is presented on half the trials, and participants decide rapidly whether the target is present.

Feature integration theory

Treisman (e.g., 1988, 1992) and Treisman and Gelade (1980) put forward feature integration theory, a very influential approach to understanding visual search. Here are its main assumptions:

- There is an important distinction between the features of objects (e.g. colour, size, lines in particular orientation) and the objects themselves.
- There is a rapid parallel process in which the visual features of objects in the environment are processed together; this does not depend on attention.
- There is then a serial process in which features are combined to form objects.
- The serial process is slower than the initial parallel process, especially when the set size is large.
- Features can be combined by focused attention to the location of the object, in which case focused attention provides the "glue" forming unitary objects from the available features.
- Feature combination can be influenced by stored knowledge (e.g., bananas are usually yellow).
- In the absence of focused attention or relevant stored knowledge, features from different objects will be combined randomly, producing "illusory conjunctions".

Treisman and Gelade (1980) provided support for this theory. Participants searched

for a target in a visual display having a set or display size of between one and 30 items. The target was either an object based on a conjunction of features (a green letter T) or consisted of a single feature (a blue letter or an S). When the target was a green letter T, all non-targets shared one feature with the target (i.e., they were either the brown letter T or the green letter X). The prediction was that focused attention would be needed to detect the conjunctive target (because it was defined by a combination or conjunction of features), but would not be required to detect single-feature targets.

The findings were as predicted (see Figure 5.14). Set or display size had a large effect on detection speed when the target was defined by a combination or conjunction of features (i.e., a green letter T), presumably because focused attention was required. However, there was very little effect of display size when the target was defined by a single feature (i.e., a blue letter or an S).

Feature integration theory assumes that lack of focused attention can produce illusory conjunctions (random combinations of features). Friedman-Hill, Robertson, and Treisman (1995) studied a brain-damaged patient who had problems with the accurate location of visual stimuli. He produced many illusory conjunctions, combining the shape of one stimulus with the colour of another.

According to feature integration theory, illusory conjunctions occur because of problems in combining features to form objects at a relatively late stage of processing. Evidence partially consistent with the theory was reported by Braet and Humphreys (2009). Transcranial magnetic stimulation (TMS; see Glossary), which typically disrupts processing, was administered at different intervals of time after the onset of a visual display. There were more illusory

> **KEY TERM**
>
> **visual search:** a task involving the rapid detection of a specified target stimulus within a visual display.

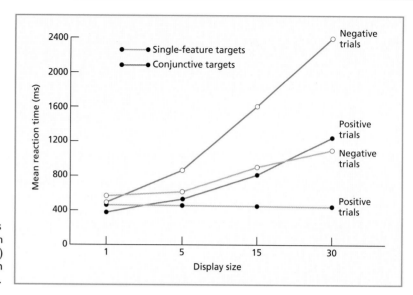

Figure 5.14 Performance speed on a detection task as a function of target definition (conjunctive vs. single feature) and display size. Adapted from Treisman and Gelade (1980).

conjunctions when TMS was applied relatively late rather than relatively early, suggesting that the processes involved in combining features occur at a late stage.

Treisman (1993) put forward a more complex version of feature integration theory in which there are four kinds of attentional selection. First, there is selection by *location* involving a relatively broad or narrow attention window. Second, there is selection by *features*. Features are divided into surface-defining features (e.g., colour; brightness; relative motion) and shape-defining features (e.g., orientation; size). Third, there is selection on the basis of *object-defined locations*. Fourth, there is selection at a late stage of processing that determines the *object file* controlling the individual's response. Thus, attentional selectivity can operate at various levels depending on task demands.

Duncan and Humphreys (1989, 1992) identified two factors influencing visual search times not included in the original version of feature integration theory. First, there is similarity among the distractors, with performance being faster when the distractors are very similar (e.g., Humphreys, Riddoch, & Quinlan, 1985). Second, there is similarity between the target and the distractors. Duncan and Humphreys (1989) found a large effect of set

on visual search times when the target was very similar to the distractors even when the target was identified by a single feature. Treisman and Sato (1990) conceded that this factor was important. They found that visual search for an object target defined by more than one feature was typically limited to those distractors sharing at least one of the target's features. For example, if you were looking for a blue circle in a display containing blue triangles, red circles, and red triangles, you would ignore red triangles.

Duncan and Humphreys (1989, 1992) found that visual search times for a given target are faster when there is similarity among the distractors.

Guided search theory

Wolfe (1998, 2003) developed feature integration theory in his guided search theory. He replaced Treisman's assumption that the initial feature processing is necessarily parallel and subsequent processing is serial with the notion that processes are more or less efficient. Why did he do this? According to Wolfe (p. 20), "Results of visual search experiments run from flat to steep RT [reaction time] × set size functions.…The continuum [continuous distribution] of search slopes does make it implausible to think that the search tasks, themselves, can be neatly classified as serial or parallel." More specifically, there should be no effect of set size on target-detection times if parallel processing is used, but a substantial effect of set size if serial processing is used. However, findings typically fall between these two extremes.

Guided search theory is based on the assumption that the initial processing of basic features produces an activation map, with every item in the visual display having its own level of activation. Suppose someone is searching for red, horizontal targets. Feature processing would activate all red objects and all horizontal objects. Attention is then directed towards items on the basis of their level of activation, starting with those most activated. This assumption explains why search times are longer when some distractors share one or more features with targets (e.g., Duncan & Humphreys, 1989).

A central problem with the original version of feature integration theory is that targets in large displays are typically detected faster than predicted. The activation-map notion provides a plausible way in which visual search can be made more efficient by ignoring stimuli not sharing any features with the target.

Evaluation

Feature integration theory has been very influential because it was the first systematic attempt to understand the processes determining speed of visual search. However, its influence extends well beyond that. As Quinlan (2003, p. 643) pointed out: "FIT [feature integration theory] has influenced thinking on processes that range from the early stages of sensory encoding to higher order characteristics of attentional control.….FIT was one of the most influential and important theories of visual information."

Feature integration theory (especially the original version) possesses several limitations. First, as we will see, conjunction searches do *not* typically involve parallel processing followed by serial search. Second, the search for targets consisting of a conjunction or combination of features is typically faster than predicted by the theory. Factors causing fast detection that are missing from the theory (e.g., grouping of distractors; distractors sharing no features with targets) are incorporated into guided search theory. Third, and related to the second point, it was originally assumed that effects of set size on visual search depend mainly on the nature of the target (single feature or conjunctive feature). In fact, the nature of the distractors (e.g., their similarity to each other) is also important. Fourth, the theory seems to predict that the attentional deficits of neglect and extinction patients should disrupt their search for conjunctive but not single-feature targets. In fact, such patients often detect both types of target more slowly than healthy individuals even though the impairment is greater with conjunctive targets (Umiltà, 2001).

Decision integration hypothesis

According to feature integration theory, processing in visual search varies considerably depending on whether the targets are defined by single features or by conjunctions of features. In contrast, Palmer and his associates (e.g., Eckstein, Thomas, Palmer, & Shimozaki, 2000; Palmer, Verghese, & Pavel, 2000) argued, in their decision integration hypothesis, that parallel processing is involved in both kinds of search.

Palmer et al. (2000) argued that observers form internal representations of target and distractor stimuli. These representations are noisy because the internal response to any given item varies from trial to trial. Visual search involves decision making based on the *discriminability* between target and distractor items

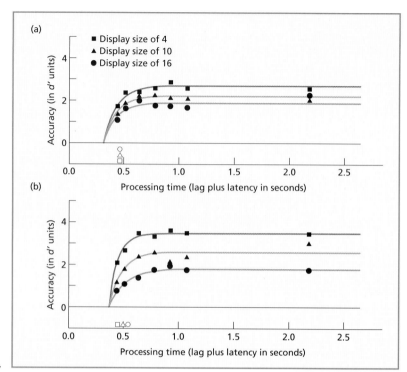

Figure 5.15 Accuracy of performance as assessed by d' (sensitivity) with display signs of 4, 10, or 16 items viewed for 150 ms for feature (a) and conjunction (b) searches. Open symbols at the bottom of each figure indicate when each function reached two-thirds of its final value. From McElree and Carrasco (1999). Copyright © 1999 American Psychological Association. Reproduced with permission.

regardless of whether the targets are defined by single features or by conjunctions of features. Why is visual search less efficient with conjunction searches than feature searches? Conjunction searches are harder because there is less discriminability between target and distractor stimuli. Visual search is typically slower with larger set sizes because the complexity of the decision-making process is greater when there are numerous items in the visual display.

McElree and Carrasco (1999) reported findings consistent with the decision integration hypothesis. They pointed out that the usual practice of assessing visual search performance only by reaction time is limited, because speed of performance depends in part on participants' willingness (or otherwise) to accept errors. Accordingly, they controlled speed of performance by requiring participants to respond rapidly following a signal. Each visual display contained 4, 10, or 16 items, and targets were defined by a single feature or by a conjunction of features.

What did McElree and Carrasco (1999) find? First, the patterns for performance accuracy were much more similar for feature and conjunction search than would be predicted in feature integration theory (see Figure 5.15). Second, set size had more effect on conjunction search than on feature search. This is as predicted by feature integration theory. However, it could also be due to increasing set size reducing the discriminability between target and distractor items more for conjunction searches than for feature searches. Third, the effects of set size on conjunction search were much smaller than expected on most serial processing models (including feature integration theory). Overall, the findings suggested that parallel processing was used for feature and conjunction searches.

Leonards, Sunaert, Van Hecke, and Orban (2000) carried out an fMRI study to assess the brain areas involved in feature and conjunction search. They concluded that, "The cerebral networks in efficient (feature) and inefficient (conjunction) search overlap almost completely." These findings suggest that feature and conjunction searches involve very similar processes, as assumed by the decision integration hypothesis. Anderson et al. (2007) reported that there was some overlap in the brain regions activated during the two kinds of search, especially within the superior frontal cortex. However, there was more activation of the inferior and middle frontal cortex with conjunction search than with feature search, probably because the former type of search placed more demands on attentional processes.

Multiple-target visual search

Nearly all the research on visual search discussed so far has involved a *single* target presented among distractors. It has generally been assumed that progressive lengthening of target-detection time with increasing number of distractors indicates serial processing. However, as Townsend (e.g., 1990) pointed out, the same pattern of findings could result from a parallel process incurring costs of divided attention. Thornton and Gilden (2007) argued that we can clarify the crucial issue of whether visual search is serial or parallel by using multiple targets. Consider what happens when all the stimuli in a visual display are targets. If processing is serial, the first item analysed will *always* be a target and so target-detection time should not vary as a function of set size. In contrast, suppose that target-detection time *decreases* as the number of targets increases. That would indicate parallel processing, because such processing would allow individuals to take in information from all the targets at the same time.

Thornton and Gilden used a combination of single-target and multiple-target trials with 29 visual search tasks in which the set size was 1, 2, or 4. Across these tasks, there were three basic patterns in the data. One pattern strongly suggested parallel processing. It consisted of target-detection times increasing only modestly with increasing set size on single-target trials and decreasing with increasing set size when all the stimuli were targets. This pattern was found with search tasks in which targets and distractors only differed along a single feature dimension (e.g., colour; size; orientation). This makes sense given that parallel processes in early visual cortex seem to detect such features very rapidly (Kandel, Schwartz, & Jessell, 2005).

Another data pattern strongly suggested serial processing. It consisted of target-detection times increasing rapidly with increasing set size on single-target trials and also increasing with increasing set size when all the stimuli were targets. This pattern was found with complex visual tasks involving the detection of a specific direction of rotation (e.g., pinwheels rotating clockwise; textures rotating clockwise).

Finally, there was an intermediate pattern consisting of moderate increases of set size on target-detection times with single targets and no effect of set size when all the stimuli were targets. Conjunction search tasks in which targets were defined by a conjunction of features (e.g., white verticals) exhibited this pattern. On balance, this pattern of findings was more consistent with parallel models than serial ones.

What conclusions can we draw from the above research? First, Thornton and Gilden (2007) have provided perhaps the strongest evidence yet that some visual search tasks involve parallel search whereas others involve serial search. Second, they found that 72% of the tasks seemed to involve parallel processing and only 28% serial processing. Thus, parallel processing models account for more of the data than do serial processing models. Third, the relatively few tasks that involved parallel processing were especially complex and had the longest average target-detection times.

Overall evaluation

There has been much progress in understanding the processes involved in visual search. Even though it has proved difficult to decide whether serial, parallel, or a mixture of serial and parallel processes are used on any given task, several factors influencing the search process have been identified. Developments such as the use of multiple targets have clarified the situation. It appears that parallel processing is used on most visual search tasks other than those that are very complicated and so have especially long times to detect targets.

What are the limitations of research in this area? First, much of it is of dubious relevance to our everyday lives. As Wolfe (1998, p. 56) pointed out, "In the real world, distractors are very heterogeneous [diverse]. Stimuli exist in many size scales in a single view. Items are probably defined by conjunctions of many features. You don't get several hundred trials with the same targets and distractors."

Second, in most research, a target is presented on 50% of trials. In contrast, targets are very rare in several very important situations such as airport security checks. Does this matter? Evidence that it does was reported by Wolfe, Horowitz, Van Wert, Kenner, Place, and Kibbi (2007). Participants were shown X-ray images of packed bags and the targets were weapons (knives or guns). When targets appeared on 50% of trials, 80% of them were detected. When targets appeared on 2% of the trials, the detection rate fell to only 54%. This poor performance was due to excessive caution in reporting a target rather than a lack of attention.

Third, most researchers have used reaction-time measures of visual search performance. This is unfortunate because there are many ways of interpreting such data. As McElree and Carrasco (1999, p. 1532) pointed out, "RT [reaction time] data are of limited value... because RT can vary with either differences in discriminability, differences in processing speed, or unknown mixtures of the two effects." In that connection, the speed–accuracy trade-off procedure used by McElree and Carrasco is a definite improvement.

CROSS-MODAL EFFECTS

The great majority of the research discussed so far is limited in that the visual modality was studied on its own. In similar fashion, research on auditory attention typically ignores visual perception. This approach has been justified on the grounds that attentional processes in each sensory modality (e.g., vision; hearing) operate *independently* from those in all other modalities. In fact, that assumption is wrong. In the real world, we often combine or integrate information from different sense modalities at the same time (**cross-modal attention**). For example, when listening to someone speaking, we often observe their lip movements at the same time. Information from the auditory and visual modalities is combined to facilitate our understanding of what they are saying (lip-reading – see Chapter 9).

Before turning to research on cross-modal effects, we need to distinguish between endogenous spatial attention and exogenous spatial attention (see the earlier discussion of Posner's endogenous and exogenous attention systems). **Endogenous spatial attention** involves an individual voluntarily directing his/her visual attention to a given spatial location. This generally happens because he/she anticipates that a target stimulus will be presented at that location. In contrast, **exogenous spatial attention** involves the "involuntary" direction of visual attention to a given spatial location determined by aspects of the stimulus there (e.g., its intensity or its threat value). Cross-modal effects occur when directing visual attention to a given location also attracts auditory and/or tactile (touch-based) attention to the same location. Alternatively, directing auditory tactile attention to a given location can attract visual attention to the same place.

Evidence

We will start by considering the **ventriloquist illusion**. In this illusion, which everyone who has been to the movies or seen a ventriloquist will have experienced, sounds are misperceived as coming from their apparent visual source. Ventriloquists try to speak without moving their lips while at the same time manipulating the mouth movements of a dummy. It seems as if the dummy rather than the ventriloquist is speaking. Something very similar happens at the movies. We look at the actors and actresses on the screen, and see their lips moving. The sounds of their voices are actually coming from loudspeakers to the side of the screen, but we hear those voices coming from their mouths.

Bonath et al. (2007) shed light on what happens in the brain to produce the ventriloquist illusion. They combined event-related potentials (ERPs; see Glossary) with functional magnetic resonance imaging (fMRI; see Glossary)

In the ventriloquist illusion, we make the mistake of misperceiving the sounds we hear as coming from their apparent visual source (the dummy) rather than the ventriloquist.

to show that the ventriloquist illusion involves processing within the auditory cortex matching the apparent visual source of the sound. *Why* does vision dominate sound? The location of environmental events is typically indicated more precisely by visual than auditory information, and so it makes sense for us to rely more heavily on vision.

We turn now to endogenous or "voluntary" spatial attention. Suppose we present participants with two streams of light (as was done by Eimer and Schröger, 1998), with one stream of light being presented to the left and the other to the right. At the same time, we also present participants with two streams of sound, with one stream of sound being presented to each side. In one condition, participants are instructed to detect deviant *visual* events (e.g., longer than usual stimuli) presented to one side only. In the other condition, participants have to detect deviant *auditory* events in only one of the streams.

Event-related potentials (ERPs) were recorded to obtain information about the allocation of attention. Not surprisingly, Eimer and Schröger (1998) found that ERPs to deviant stimuli in the *relevant* modality were greater to stimuli presented on the to-be-attended side than those on the to-be-ignored side. This finding simply shows that participants allocated their attention as instructed. What is of more interest is what happened to the allocation of attention in the *irrelevant* modality. Suppose participants had to detect *visual* targets on the left side. In that case, ERPs to deviant *auditory* stimuli were greater on the left side than on the right side. This is a cross-modal effect in which the voluntary or endogenous allocation of visual attention also affected the allocation of auditory attention. In similar fashion, when participants had to detect *auditory* targets on one side, ERPs to deviant *visual* stimuli on the same

> ### KEY TERM
>
> **ventriloquist illusion:** the mistaken perception that sounds are coming from their apparent visual source, as in ventriloquism.

side were greater than ERPs to those on the opposite side. Thus, the allocation of auditory attention influenced the allocation of visual attention as well.

Eimer, van Velzen, Forster, and Driver (2003) pointed out that nearly all cross-modal studies on endogenous spatial attention had used situations in which the locations of auditory and tactile targets were visible. As a result, it is possible the cross-modal effects obtained depended heavily on the visual modality. However, Eimer et al. found that visual–tactile cross-modal effects were very similar in lit and dark environments. The findings can be interpreted by assuming that endogenous spatial attention is controlled for the most part by a high-level system that influences attentional processes within each sensory modality.

We now turn to exogenous or "involuntary" spatial attention. Clear evidence of cross-modal effects was reported by Spence and Driver (1996). Participants fixated straight ahead with hands uncrossed, holding a small cube in each hand. There were two light-emitting diodes, with one light at the top and one at the bottom of each diode. In one condition, loudspeakers were placed directly above and below each hand close to the light sources. There was a sound from one of the loudspeakers shortly before one of the four lights was illuminated. Visual judgements were more accurate when the auditory cue was on the *same* side as the subsequent visual target even though the cue did *not* predict which light would be illuminated. Thus, "involuntary" or exogenous auditory attention influenced the allocation of visual attention.

Spence and Driver (1996) also had a condition in which the roles of the visual and auditory modalities were reversed. In other words, a light was illuminated shortly before a sound was presented, and the task involved making auditory judgements. Auditory judgements were more accurate when the non-predictive visual cue was on the *same* side as the subsequent auditory target. Thus, involuntary visual attention influenced the allocation of auditory attention.

We have seen that voluntary and involuntary visual attention can influence auditory attention, and vice versa. In addition, visual attention to a given location can influence attention to tactile stimuli (involving touch) and attention to tactile stimuli at a given location can influence visual attention (Driver & Spence, 1998).

What light has cognitive neuroscience shed on cross-modal effects? The effects depend in part on multi-modal neurons, which are responsive to stimuli in various modalities. These neurons respond strongly to multi-modal stimulation at a given location. However, they show reduced responding when there is multi-modal stimulation involving more than one location (see Stein & Meredith, 1993, for a review).

Molholm, Martinez, Shpanker, and Foxe (2007) carried out a study using event-related potentials (ERPs; see Glossary) in which participants attended to the visual or auditory features of an object. There was brain activation of object features in the task-irrelevant sensory modality, especially when the task required attending to an object's visual features.

Driver and Noesselt (2008) reviewed the neuroscience evidence. Neurons responding to visual or auditory input are often found in close proximity in several areas of the brain, including the midbrain and the cerebral cortex. What Driver and Noesselt describe as "multi-sensory interplay" also happens in and around auditory cortex. Such interplay is much more prevalent than was assumed by traditional approaches that regarded each sensory system as being independent of the others.

Evaluation

Studies of exogenous spatial attention, endogenous spatial attention, and the ventriloquist illusion indicate clearly that there are numerous links between the sense modalities. The same conclusion emerges from neuroscience research, and that research has increased our understanding of some of the brain mechanisms involved. Of most importance, these findings demonstrate the falsity of the traditional assumption (generally implicit) that attentional processes in each sensory modality operate independently of those in all other modalities.

What are the limitations of research on cross-modal effects? First, there has been much more research on cross-modal effects in spatial attention than on such effects in the *identification* of stimuli and objects. Thus, we know little about how information from different modalities is combined to facilitate object recognition. Second, our theoretical understanding has lagged behind the accumulation of empirical findings. For example, it is generally not possible to predict ahead of time how strong any cross-modal effects are likely to be. Third, much of the research has involved complex, artificial tasks and it would be useful to investigate cross-modal effects in more naturalistic conditions.

DIVIDED ATTENTION: DUAL-TASK PERFORMANCE

Our lives are becoming busier and busier. As a consequence, we spend much time multi-tasking: trying to do two (or even more!) things at the same time. How successful we are at multi-tasking obviously depends very much on the two "things" or tasks in question. Most of us can easily walk and have a conversation at the same time, but find it surprisingly difficult to rub our stomach with one hand while patting our head with the other.

There has been a huge amount of research using the dual-task approach to assess our ability (or inability!) to perform two tasks at the same time. In essence, we can ask people to perform two tasks (a and b) together or separately. What generally happens is that performance on one or both tasks is worse when they are performed together (dual-task condition) than separately (single-task condition). In what follows, we will be considering the main factors influencing dual-task performance. Note that the dual-task approach is also considered towards the end of this chapter (in much of the section on automatic processing) and in the section on working memory in Chapter 6.

When we consider multi-tasking in everyday life, an issue of great importance is whether the ability to drive a car is impaired when the driver uses a mobile phone. More than 20 countries have passed laws restricting the use of mobile phones by drivers, which suggests it is a dangerous practice. The relevant research evidence is discussed in the box.

Factors determining dual-task performance

What determines how well we can perform two activities at the same time? Three important factors will be discussed in this section: task similarity, practice, and task difficulty. With respect to task similarity, two tasks can be similar in stimulus modality or the required responses. Treisman and Davies (1973) found that two monitoring tasks interfered with each other much more when the stimuli on both tasks were in the same sense modality (visual or auditory). McLeod (1977) found that response similarity was important. His participants performed a continuous tracking task with manual responding together with a tone-identification task. Some participants responded vocally to the tones, whereas others responded with the hand not involved in the tracking task. Performance on the tracking task was worse with high response similarity (manual responses on both tasks) than with low response similarity (manual responses on one task and vocal ones on the other). An issue that is hard to resolve is how to measure similarity. For example, how similar are piano playing and poetry writing?

We all know the saying, "Practice makes perfect". Support for this commonsensical saying was reported by Spelke, Hirst, and Neisser (1976). Two students (Diane and John) received five hours' training a week for four months on various tasks. Their first task was to read short stories for comprehension while writing down words to dictation, which they initially found very hard. After six weeks of training, however, they could read as rapidly and with as much comprehension when taking dictation as when

Can we think and drive?

Strayer and Johnston (2001) studied the potential dangers of drivers using mobile phones with a simulated-driving task in which the participants braked as rapidly as possible when they detected a red light. This task was carried out on its own or while the participants conducted a conversation using a hand-held or hands-free mobile phone.

What did Strayer and Johnston (2001) find? First, performance on the driving task was the same in the hand-held and hands-free conditions. Second, participants missed more red lights when using a mobile phone at the same time (7% versus 3%, respectively). Third, the mean response time to the red light was 50 ms longer in the mobile-phone conditions. This may sound trivial. However, it translates into travelling an extra 5 feet (1.5 metres) before stopping for a motorist doing 70 mph (110 kph). This could mean the difference between stopping just short of a child in the road or killing that child.

Further evidence that driving performance is very easily disrupted was reported by Levy, Pashler, and Boer (2006) in a study involving simulated driving. Participants pressed a brake pedal when the brake lights of the car in front came on. This task was performed on its own or at the same time as a secondary task. In the latter, dual-task conditions, participants responded manually or vocally to the number of times (one or two) that a visual or auditory stimulus was presented. The addition of this apparently very simple second task increased the time taken to press the brake by 150 ms. Levy et al. argued that some of the processing of each task was done in a serial fashion because of the existence of a central-processing bottleneck (discussed in more detail later).

Strayer and Drews (2007) investigated the effects of hands-free mobile-phone use on driving performance. They hypothesised that mobile-phone use by drivers produces a form of inattentional blindness (discussed in Chapter 4) in which objects are simply not seen. In one experiment, 30 objects of varying importance to drivers (e.g., pedestrians; advertising hoardings) were clearly in view as participants performed a simulated driving task. This task was followed by an unexpected test of recognition memory for the objects. Participants who had used a mobile phone on the driving task performed much worse on the recognition-memory task regardless of the importance of the objects. Strikingly, these findings were obtained even for objects fixated during the driving task. This suggests the problem was one of inattentional blindness rather than simply a question of not looking at the objects.

Strayer and Drews (2007) obtained additional evidence that mobile-phone use interferes with attention in another experiment. Participants responded as rapidly as possible to the onset of the brake lights on the car in front. Strayer and Drews recorded event-related potentials (ERPs; see Glossary), focusing mainly on P300. This is a positive wave occurring 300 ms after stimulus onset that is sensitive to attention. The key finding was that the magnitude of the P300 was reduced by 50% in mobile-phone users.

In sum, the various findings indicate that it is surprisingly difficult for people to perform two tasks at the same time even when the tasks are apparently very different (verbal processing versus visual processing). That is still the case when one of the tasks is extremely simple and only involves deciding whether a stimulus has been presented once or twice. Theoretical explanations of such findings are discussed in the main text.

---

only reading. After further training, Diane and John learned to write down the names of the categories to which the dictated words belonged while maintaining normal reading speed and comprehension.

Spelke et al. (1976) found that practice can produce a dramatic improvement in people's ability to perform two tasks together. However, it is not clear how to interpret their findings, for two reasons. First, they focused on accuracy

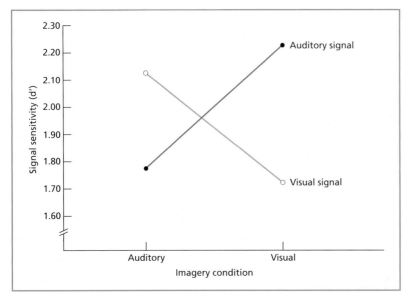

Figure 5.16 Sensitivity (d') to auditory and visual signals as a function of concurrent imagery modality (auditory vs. visual). Adapted from Segal and Fusella (1970).

measures which can be less sensitive than speed measures to dual-task interference (Lien, Ruthruff, & Johnston, 2006). Second, the reading task gave Diane and John flexibility in terms of *when* they attended to the reading matter, and such flexibility means they may well have alternated attention between tasks. More controlled research on the effects of practice on dual-task performance is discussed later in the chapter.

Not surprisingly, the ability to perform two tasks together depends on their difficulty. Sullivan (1976) used the tasks of shadowing (repeating back out loud) an auditory message and detecting target words on a non-shadowed message at the same time. When the shadowing task was made harder by using a less redundant message, fewer targets were detected on the non-shadowed message.

Sometimes the effects of task similarity swamp those of task difficulty. Segal and Fusella (1970) combined image construction (visual or auditory) with signal detection (visual or auditory). The auditory image task impaired detection of auditory signals more than the visual task did (see Figure 5.16), suggesting that the auditory image task was more demanding. However, the auditory image task was less disruptive than the visual image task when each

task was combined with a task requiring detection of visual signals, suggesting the opposite conclusion. Thus, performance was determined much more by task similarity than by task difficulty.

Central capacity vs. multiple resources

How can we explain the typical finding that performance levels are lower when tasks are paired than when they are performed separately? A simple (dangerously simple!) approach (e.g., Kahneman, 1973) is to assume that some central capacity (e.g., central executive; attention) can be used flexibly across a wide range of activities. This central capacity has strictly limited resources. The extent to which two tasks can be performed together depends on the demands each task makes on those resources. We could potentially explain why driving performance is impaired when drivers use a mobile phone by assuming that both tasks require use of the same central capacity.

Bourke, Duncan, and Nimmo-Smith (1996) tested central capacity theory. They used four tasks designed to be as different as possible and to vary in their demands on central capacity:

(1) *Random generation*: generating letters at random.
(2) *Prototype learning*: working out the features of two patterns or prototypes from seeing various exemplars.
(3) *Manual task*: screwing a nut down to the bottom of a bolt and back up to the top, and then down to the bottom of a second bolt and back up, and so on.
(4) *Tone test*: detecting the occurrence of a target tone.

Participants performed two of these tasks together, with one task being identified as more important. Bourke et al. (1996) predicted that the task making greatest demands on central capacity (the random generation task) would interfere most with all the other tasks. They also predicted that the least demanding task (the tone task) would interfere least with all the other tasks. The findings largely confirmed these predictions regardless of whether the instructions identified these tasks as more or less important than the task with which they were paired.

Hegarty, Shah, and Miyake (2000) also used a dual-task paradigm, but their findings were less consistent with central capacity theory. They had previous evidence suggesting that a paper-folding task (imagining the effect of punching a hole through a folded piece of paper) required more central capacity than an identical-pictures task (deciding which test figure was identical to a target figure). They predicted that requiring participants to perform another task at the same time (e.g., random number generation) would disrupt performance on the paper-folding task more than on the identical-pictures task. In fact, the findings were the opposite. According to Hegarty et al., tasks involving much response selection are more readily disrupted than ones that do not. The identical-figures task involved much more response selection than the paper-folding task, and that was why its performance suffered much more under dual-task conditions.

The notion of a central capacity is consistent with many findings, such as those of Bourke et al. (1996). In addition, we will shortly see that brain-imaging studies have supported the view that dual-task performance depends in part on some central capacity. However, central capacity theory possesses various limitations. First, there is a danger of circularity. We can "explain" dual-task interference by assuming the resources of some central capacity have been exceeded, and we can account for a lack of interference by assuming the two tasks did not exceed those resources. However, this is often simply a re-description of the findings rather than an explanation. Second, evidence for the existence of a central capacity does not necessarily clarify the nature of that central capacity (e.g., Bourke et al., 1996). Third, interference effects in dual-task situations can be caused by response selection (Hegarty et al., 2000) or by task similarity (e.g., Segal & Fusella, 1970), as well as by task demands on central capacity. Fourth, this theoretical approach implicitly assumes that all participants use the same strategies in dual-task situations. This assumption is probably wrong. Lehle, Steinhauser, and Hubner (2009) trained participants to engage in serial or parallel processing when performing two tasks at the same time. Participants using serial processing performed better than those using parallel processing. However, they found the tasks more effortful, and this was supported by heart-rate measures.

Some theorists (e.g., Wickens, 1984) have argued that the processing system consists of independent processing mechanisms in the form of multiple resources. If so, it is clear why the degree of similarity between two tasks is so important. Similar tasks compete for the same specific resources, and thus produce interference, whereas dissimilar tasks involve different resources and so do not interfere.

Wickens (1984) put forward a three-dimensional structure of human processing resources (see Figure 5.17). According to his model, there are three successive stages of processing (encoding, central processing, and responding). Encoding involves the perceptual processing of stimuli, and typically involves the visual or auditory modality. Encoding and

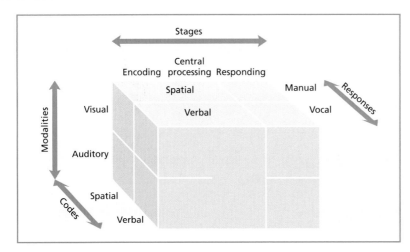

Figure 5.17 A proposed three-dimensional structure of human processing resources. From Wickens (1984). Copyright © Elsevier 1984.

central processing can involve spatial or verbal codes. Finally, responding involves manual or vocal responses. There are two key theoretical assumptions:

(1) There are several pools of resources based on the distinctions among stages of processing, modalities, codes, and responses.
(2) If two tasks make use of different pools of resources, then people should be able to perform both tasks without disruption.

What is the definition of a "resource"? According to Wickens (2002), there are three main criteria. First, each resource should have an identifiable manifestation within the brain. Second, there should be evidence from real-world dual-task situations that each resource accounts for some interference effects. Third, each resource should be easily identifiable by system designers trying to change systems to reduce resource competition.

There is much support for this multiple-resource model and its prediction that several kinds of task similarity influence dual-task performance. For example, there is more interference when two tasks share the same modality (Treisman & Davies, 1973) or the same type of response (McLeod, 1977). In addition, brain-imaging research indicates that tasks very different from each other often involve activation in widely separated brain areas. This suggests they are making use of different resources. However, the model has some limitations. First, it focuses only on visual and auditory inputs or stimuli, but tasks can be presented in other modalities (e.g., touch). Second, there is often some disruption to performance even when two tasks involve different modalities (e.g., Treisman & Davies, 1973). Third, the model implicitly assumes that a given strategy is used when individuals perform two tasks at the same time. However, as we saw earlier, there is evidence that performance and effort both depend on whether individuals engage in serial or parallel processing (Lehle et al., 2009). Fourth, Wickens' model assumes several tasks could be performed together without interference providing each task made use of different pools of resources. This assumption minimises the problems associated with the higher-level processes of co-ordinating and organising the demands of tasks being carried out at the same time. Relevant brain-imaging research is discussed in the next section.

Synthesis

Some theorists (e.g., Baddeley, 1986, 2001) have argued for an approach involving a synthesis of the central capacity and multiple-resource notions (see Chapter 6). According to Baddeley, the processing system has a hierarchical structure. The central executive (involved in attentional control) is at the top of the hierarchy and is involved in the co-ordination and control of behaviour. Below this level are specific processing mechanisms (phonological loop; visuo-spatial sketchpad) operating relatively independently of each other.

Cognitive neuroscience

The simplest approach to understanding dual-task performance is to assume that the demands for resources of two tasks performed together equal the sum of the demands of the two tasks performed separately. We can apply that assumption to brain-imaging research in which participants perform tasks x and y on their own or together. If the assumption is correct, we might expect that brain activation in the dual-task condition would simply be the sum of the activations in the two single-task conditions. As we will see, actual findings rarely correspond closely to that expectation.

Just, Carpenter, Keller, Emery, Zajac, and Thulborn (2001) used two tasks performed together or on their own. One task was auditory sentence comprehension and the other task involved mentally rotating three-dimensional figures to decide whether they were the same. These tasks were selected deliberately in the expectation that they would involve different processes in different parts of the brain.

What did Just et al. (2001) find? First, performance on both tasks was impaired under dual-task conditions compared to single-task conditions. Second, the language task mainly activated parts of the temporal lobe, whereas the mental rotation task mostly activated parts of the parietal lobe. Third, and most importantly, Just et al. compared the brain activation associated with each task under single- and dual-task conditions. Brain activation in regions associated with the language task decreased by 53% under dual-task conditions compared to single-task conditions. In similar fashion, brain activation in regions involved in the mental rotation task decreased by 29% under dual-task conditions. Finding that brain activity in dual-task conditions is less than the total of the activity in the two tasks performed on their own is known as **underadditivity**.

What do the above findings mean? They suggest that the need to distribute a limited central capacity (e.g., attention) across two tasks meant the amount each could receive was reduced compared to the single-task condition. Newman, Keller, and Just (2007) used similar tasks to Just et al. (2001) and obtained similar findings. They explained their findings as follows: "There is an interdependence among cortical regions in how much activation they can sustain at a given time, probably because of the resource demands that they conjointly make during the performance of a cognitive task" (Newman et al., 2007, p. 114). We can see this most clearly with respect to the comprehension task. There was much activation within both temporal lobes when this task was performed on its own, but there was a dramatic reduction in right-hemisphere temporal activation under dual-task conditions. This probably happened because participants did not have the resources to engage in elaborative processing of the sentences in the dual-task condition.

Executive functioning

Some theorists (e.g., Collette, Hogge, Salmon, & van der Linden, 2006) have argued that dual-task performance often involves executive functioning. They defined executive functioning as, "high-level processes, the main function of which is to facilitate adaptation to new or complex situations." Examples of executive processes in dual-task situations are co-ordination of task demands, attentional control, and dual-task management generally. Collette and van der Linden (2002) found evidence in a literature review that some regions within prefrontal cortex (BA9/46, BA10, and anterior cingulated) are activated by numerous executive tasks. How-

> ## KEY TERM
>
> **underadditivity:** the finding that brain activation when two tasks are performed together is less than the sum of the brain activations when they are performed singly.

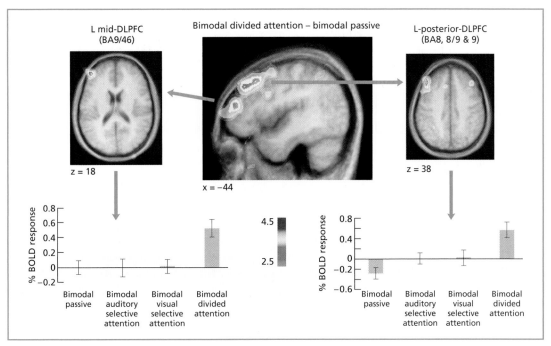

Figure 5.18 Regions of dorsolateral prefrontal cortex (DLPFC) activated in the bimodal (auditory task + visual task) divided attention condition compared to the bimodal passive condition (no task performed). These regions were not activated in single-task conditions. Reprinted from Johnson and Zatorre (2006), Copyright © 2006, with permission from Elsevier.

ever, they did not consider dual-task research directly.

It is puzzling from the above perspective that the brain-imaging studies considered so far have not shown that executive functioning is important in dual-task situations. However, what was actually found was that activation within the prefrontal cortex was no greater in dual-task than in single-task conditions. Thus, it is possible that there were relatively high levels of prefrontal activation with single tasks. Evidence that executive functioning within the prefrontal cortex is important in dual-task situations might be obtained if the two tasks individually made minimal demands on such functioning. This strategy was adopted by Johnson and Zatorre (2006). They carried out an experiment in which participants were presented with auditory (melodies) and visual (abstract shapes) stimuli at the same time. There was a divided attention condition in which participants attended to both sensory modalities

and a selective attention condition in which they attended to only one modality.

What did Johnson and Zatorre (2006) discover? Only divided attention was associated with activation of the dorsolateral prefrontal cortex (see Figure 5.18). That suggests that this brain area (known to be involved in various executive processes) is needed to handle the demands of co-ordinating two tasks at the same time but is not required for selective attention. However, the findings do not show that the dorsolateral prefrontal cortex is *required* for dual-task performance. More direct evidence was reported by Johnson, Strafella, and Zatorre (2007) using the same auditory and visual tasks as Johnson and Zatorre (2006). They used transcranial magnetic stimulation (TMS; see Glossary) to disrupt the functioning of the dorsolateral prefrontal cortex. As predicted, this impaired the ability of participants to divide their attention between the two tasks. Johnson et al. speculated that the dorsolateral prefrontal cortex is needed to manipulate information in working memory in dual-task situations.

Collette, Oliver, van der Linden, Laureys, Delfiore, Luxen, and Salmon (2005) presented participants with simple visual and auditory discrimination tasks. There was a dual-task condition in which both tasks were performed and single-task conditions in which only the visual or auditory task was performed. Performance was worse under dual-task than single-task conditions. There was no evidence of prefrontal activation specifically in response to the single tasks. In the dual-task condition, however, there was significant activation in various prefrontal and frontal areas (e.g., BA9/46, BA10/47, BA6), and the inferior parietal gyrus (BA40). Finally, the brain areas activated during single-task performance were less activated during dual-task performance.

Evaluation

The cognitive neuroscience approach has shown that there are substantial differences between processing two tasks at the same time versus processing them singly. More specifically, brain-imaging research has uncovered two reasons why there are often interference effects in dual-task situations. First, there is a ceiling on the processing resources that can be allocated to two tasks even when they seem to involve very different processes. This is shown by the phenomenon of underadditivity. Second, dual-task performance often involves processing demands (e.g., task co-ordination) absent from single-task performance. This is shown by studies in which various prefrontal areas are activated under dual-task but not single-task conditions.

What are the limitations of the cognitive neuroscience approach? First, it is not entirely clear why prefrontal areas are sometimes very important in dual-task performance and sometimes apparently unimportant. Second, prefrontal areas are activated in many complex cognitive processes, and it has proved difficult to identify the *specific* processes responsible for activation with any given pair of tasks. Third, underadditivity is an important phenomenon, but as yet *why* it happens has not been established.

Attentional blink

One of the main limitations with much dual-task research is that the tasks used do not permit detailed assessment of the underlying processes (e.g., attention). This has led to the development of various tasks, including the attentional blink task. On this task, observers are presented with a series of rapidly presented visual stimuli. In the crucial condition, observers try to detect two different targets. There is an **attentional blink**, which is a reduced ability to perceive and respond to the second visual target when it is presented very shortly after the first target. More specifically, the second target often goes undetected when it follows the first target by 200–500 ms, with distractor stimuli being presented during the interval.

What causes the attentional blink? It has generally been assumed that observers devote most of their available attentional resources to the first target and thus have insufficient remaining resources to devote to the second target (see Olivers, 2007, for a review). However, Olivers (p. 14) identified a problem with this explanation: "Humans probably would not have survived for long if our attention had been knocked out for half a second each time we saw something relevant." According to Olivers, what is crucial is the presence of distractors. When someone is attending to the first target and a distractor is presented, he/she strongly suppresses processing of further input to keep irrelevant information out of conscious awareness. This suppression effect can be applied mistakenly to the second target and thus cause the attentional blink.

How can we distinguish between the limited capacity and suppression accounts? Suppose we present three targets in succession with no intervening distractors. According to the limited capacity account, participants should show an

KEY TERM

attentional blink: a reduced ability to detect a second visual target when it follows closely the first visual target.

attentional blink because of the allocation of attentional resources to the first target. According to the suppression account, in contrast, there should be no suppression effect in the absence of distractors and thus no attentional blink. Olivers, van der Stigchel, and Hulleman (2007) obtained findings as predicted by the suppression account.

Nieuwenstein, Potter, and Theeuwes (2009) carried out a more direct test of the suppression account. They compared detection of the second target when distractors were presented during the time interval between the two targets and when the interval was blank. According to the suppression account, there should have been no attentional blink in the no-distractor condition. In fact, there was an attentional blink in that condition, although it was less than in the distractor condition (see Figure 5.19). Thus, the suppression account is only partially correct. Nieuwenstein et al. (2009, p. 159) concluded that, "The root cause of the [attentional] blink lies in the difficulty of engaging attention twice within a short period of time for 2 temporally discrete target events." Attention only has to be engaged once when two targets are presented one after the other, which explains why there is no attentional blink in that condition (Olivers et al., 2007). More generally, our limited ability to engage attention twice in a short time period helps to explain the difficulties we typically have when allocating attention to two tasks that are being performed at the same time.

AUTOMATIC PROCESSING

A key finding in studies of divided attention is the dramatic improvement practice often has on performance. This improvement has been explained by assuming that some processing activities become automatic through prolonged practice. There was a strong emphasis on the notion of automatic processes in classic articles by Shiffrin and Schneider (1977) and Schneider and Shiffrin (1977). They drew a theoretical distinction between controlled and automatic processes:

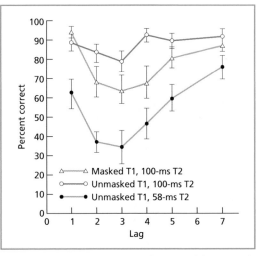

Figure 5.19 Percentage identification of the second target (T2) on trials when the first target was identified when the interval between targets was filled with distractors (masked condition) or with no distractors (unmasked conditions). The time interval between onset of the two target stimuli varied between 100 ms (lag 1) and 700 ms (lag 7). There was a strong attentional blink effect in the masked condition and the unmasked condition when the second target was presented for only 58 ms but a much smaller effect when it was presented for 100 ms. From Nieuwenstein et al. (2009), Copyright © 2000 American Psychological Association. Reproduced with permission.

- Controlled processes are of limited capacity, require attention, and can be used flexibly in changing circumstances.
- Automatic processes suffer no capacity limitations, do not require attention, and are very hard to modify once learned.

This theoretical distinction greatly influenced many other theorists (see Moors & de Houwer, 2006, for a review), and we will use the term "traditional approach" to describe their shared views.

Schneider and Shiffrin (1977) used a task in which participants memorised up to four letters (the memory set) and were then shown a visual display containing up to four letters. Finally, participants decided rapidly whether any of the items in the visual display were the same as any of the items in the memory set. The crucial manipulation was the type of mapping

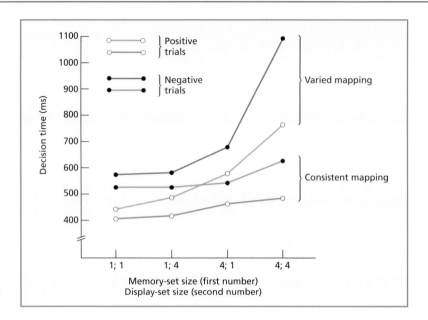

Figure 5.20 Response times on a decision task as a function of memory-set size, display-set size, and consistent versus varied mapping. Data from Shiffrin and Schneider (1977).

used. With *consistent* mapping, only consonants were used as members of the memory set and only numbers were used as distractors in the visual display (or vice versa). Thus, a participant given only consonants to memorise would know that any consonant detected in the visual display must be an item from the memory set. With *varied* mapping, a mixture of numbers and consonants was used to form the memory set and to provide distractors in the visual display.

The mapping manipulation had dramatic effects (see Figure 5.20). The numbers of items in the memory set and visual display greatly affected decision speed *only* in the varied mapping conditions. According to Schneider and Shiffrin (1977), a controlled process was used with varied mapping. This involves serial comparisons between each item in the memory set and each item in the visual display until a match is achieved or every comparison has been made. In contrast, performance with consistent mapping involved automatic processes operating independently and in parallel. According to Schneider and Shiffrin (1977), these automatic processes evolve through years of practice in distinguishing between letters and numbers.

The notion that automatic processes develop through practice was tested by Shiffrin and

Schneider (1977). They used consistent mapping with the consonants B to L forming one set and the consonants Q to Z forming the other set. As before, items from only one set were always used in the construction of the memory set, and the distractors in the visual display were all selected from the other set. There was a great improvement in performance over 2100 trials, reflecting the growth of automatic processes.

The greatest limitation with automatic processes is their *inflexibility*, which disrupts performance when conditions change. This was confirmed in the second part of the study. The initial 2100 trials with one consistent mapping were followed by a further 2100 trials with the *reverse* consistent mapping. This reversal of the mapping conditions greatly disrupted performance. Indeed, it took nearly 1000 trials before performance recovered to its level at the very start of the experiment!

Shiffrin and Schneider (1977) carried out further experiments in which participants initially located target letters anywhere in a visual display. Subsequently, they detected targets in one part of the display and ignored targets elsewhere. Participants were less able to ignore part of the visual display when they had developed automatic processes than when they had made use of controlled search processes.

In sum, automatic processes function rapidly and in parallel but suffer from inflexibility. Controlled processes are flexible and versatile but operate relatively slowly and in a serial fashion.

Problems with the traditional approach

It was sometimes assumed within the traditional approach (e.g., Shiffrin & Schneider, 1977) that any given process is controlled or automatic. It was also assumed that automatic processes generally possess various features (e.g., they do not require attention; they are fast; they are unavailable to consciousness). In other words, the main features co-occur when participants performing a given task are using automatic processes.

Problems with the traditional approach can be seen in some of Shiffrin and Schneider's findings. According to their theory, automatic processes operate in parallel and place no demands on attentional capacity. Thus, there should be a slope of zero (i.e., a horizontal line) in the function relating decision speed to the number of items in the memory set and/or in the visual display when automatic processes are used. In fact, decision speed was slower when the memory set and the visual display both contained several items (see Figure 5.20).

The **Stroop effect**, in which the naming of the colours in which words are printed is slowed down by using colour words (e.g., the word YELLOW printed in red) has often been assumed to involve automatic processing of the colour words. According to the traditional approach, that would imply that attentional processes are irrelevant to the Stroop effect. Contrary evidence was reported by Kahneman and Chajczyk (1983). They used a version of the Stroop test in which a colour word was presented close to a strip of colour, and the colour had to be named. This reduced the Stroop effect compared to a condition in which the colour word and the colour strip were in the same location.

A final problem with the traditional approach is that it is descriptive rather than explanatory. For example, Shiffrin and Schneider's (1977) assumption that some processes become automatic with practice is uninformative about what is actually happening. More specifically, *how* does the serial processing associated with controlled processing turn into the parallel processing associated with automatic processing?

Moors and De Houwer

Moors and De Houwer (2006) argued that we should define "automaticity" in terms of various features distinguishing it from non-automaticity. They initially considered eight possible features: unintentional; goal independent; uncontrolled/ uncontrollable; autonomous (meaning "uncontrolled in terms of every possible goal" (p. 307)); purely stimulus driven; unconscious; efficient (consuming little attentional capacity or few processing resources); and fast. However, a theoretical and conceptual analysis suggested that several features (i.e., unintentional; goal independent; uncontrolled; autonomous; and purely stimulus driven) overlapped considerably with each other in that they all implied being goal-unrelated. Accordingly, their four features for "automaticity" are as follows: goal-unrelated; unconscious; efficient (i.e., using few resources); and fast.

Moors and De Houwer argued that the above four features associated with automaticity are not always found together: "It is dangerous to draw inferences about the presence or absence of one feature on the basis of the presence or absence of another" (p. 320). They also argued that there is no firm dividing line between automaticity and non-automaticity. The features are gradual rather than all-or-none (e.g., a

> ### KEY TERM
>
> **Stroop effect:** the finding that naming of the colours in which words are printed is slower when the words are conflicting colour words (e.g., the word RED printed in green).

process can be fairly fast or fairly slow; it can be partially conscious). As a result, most processes involve some blend of automaticity and non-automaticity. This entire approach is rather imprecise in that we generally cannot claim that a given process is 100% automatic or non-automatic. However, as Moors and De Houwer pointed out, we can make relative statements (e.g., process *x* is more/less automatic than process *y*).

Cognitive neuroscience

Suppose we consider the behavioural findings in relation to the four features of automaticity identified by Moors and De Houwer (2006). Increasing automaticity is nearly always associated with faster responses. However, it has often been harder to provide behavioural evidence indicating that automatic processes are goal-unrelated, unconscious, and efficient in the sense of using little attentional capacity. In that connection, research within cognitive neuroscience has provided valuable information. No *single* brain area is uniquely associated with consciousness (see Chapter 16) and the same is true of attention. However, the prefrontal cortex is of special significance with respect to both consciousness and attention. If automatic processes are unconscious and efficient, we can predict that the development of automaticity should be associated with reduced activation in the prefrontal cortex.

Jansma, Ramsey, Slagter, and Kahn (2001) used fMRI to identify the changes taking place during the development of automatic processing in the consistent mapping condition. Automatic processing was associated with reduced usage of working memory (see Chapter 6), especially its attention-like central executive component. Jansma et al. concluded that increased automaticity, "was accompanied by a decrease in activation in regions related to working memory (bilateral but predominantly left dorsolateral prefrontal cortex, right superior frontal cortex, and right frontopolar area), and the supplementary motor area" (p. 730).

Poldrack et al. (2005) had participants perform a serial reaction time task under single-

and dual-task conditions. There was a gradual increase in automaticity with practice, as indexed by faster performance and the elimination of dual-task interference. There was considerable activation in the lateral and dorsolateral regions of the prefrontal cortex when participants initially performed in dual-task conditions, but this reduced substantially with practice. However, there was some increase in activation within the basal ganglia.

Saling and Phillips (2007) reviewed neuroimaging studies of automaticity. Most studies found reduced brain activation associated with the development of automaticity, and no study reported an increase in brain activation. There were variations from study to study in the precise changes in brain activation as a result of practice. However, the growth of automaticity is generally associated with a relative shift away from cortical activation and towards subcortical activation (e.g., basal ganglia). As Saling and Phillips concluded, "The acquisition of automaticity can be conceptualised as a shift from cortical consideration and hence selection where there is a degree of uncertainty to solved, simple, direct routing through the basal ganglia" (p. 15).

Instance theory

We have seen that there is evidence that automaticity is associated with a gradual reduction in the use of attentional resources. However, most theories have not specified a learning mechanism explaining *how* this happens. Logan (1988) and Logan, Taylor, and Etherton (1999) filled this gap by putting forward instance theory based on the following assumptions:

- *Obligatory encoding*: "Whatever is attended is encoded into memory" (Logan et al., 1999, p. 166).
- *Obligatory retrieval*: "Retrieval from long-term memory is a necessary consequence of attention. Whatever is attended acts as a retrieval cue that pulls things associated with it from memory" (Logan et al., 1999, p. 166).

- *Instance representation*: "Each encounter with a stimulus is encoded, stored, and retrieved separately, even if the stimulus has been encountered before" (Logan et al., 1999, p. 166).
- The increased storage of information in long-term memory when a stimulus is encountered many times produces automaticity: "Automaticity is memory retrieval: performance is automatic when it is based on a single-step direct-access retrieval of past solutions from memory" (Logan, 1988, p. 493).
- In the absence of practice, responding to a stimulus requires the application of rules and is time-consuming. It involves multi-step memory retrieval rather than single-step retrieval.

These theoretical assumptions make coherent sense of several characteristics of automaticity. Automatic processes are fast because they require only the retrieval of past solutions from long-term memory. They make few demands on attentional resources because the retrieval of heavily over-learned information is relatively effortless. Finally, there is no conscious awareness of automatic processes because no significant processes intervene between the presentation of a stimulus and the retrieval of the appropriate response.

Logan (1988, p. 519) summarised instance theory as follows: "Novice performance is limited by a lack of knowledge rather than a lack of resources.... Only the knowledge base changes with practice." However, the acquisition of knowledge means that fewer attentional or other resources are needed to perform a task.

Logan, Taylor, and Etherton (1996) argued that knowledge stored in memory as a result of prolonged practice may or may not be produced automatically depending on the precise conditions of retrieval. Participants were given 512 training trials during which any given word was always presented in the same colour (red or green). The task required them to process its colour. After that, there were 32 transfer trials on which the colour of each word was *reversed* from the training trials. When the task on these transfer trials required colour processing, performance was disrupted, suggesting that there was an automatic influence of colour information.

Would we expect colour reversal to disrupt performance when the task on the transfer trials did *not* require colour processing? Information about colour had been thoroughly learned during training, and so might produce disruption via automatic processes. In fact, there was no disruption. As predicted, colour information only exerted an automatic influence on performance when it was relevant to the current task.

It has often been assumed that automaticity mainly reflects processes occurring during learning or encoding. In contrast, the findings of Logan et al. (1996) suggest that automaticity is also a memory phenomenon. More specifically, automatic performance depends on the relationship between learned information and retrieval.

In sum, the greatest strength of instance theory is that it specifies a learning mechanism that produces automaticity, and that helps to explain the various features associated with automaticity (e.g., fast responding; few demands on attentional resources). However, there is some danger of circularity in Logan's argument: single-step retrieval is his definition of automaticity and it is also his preferred explanation of the phenomenon of automaticity.

Cognitive bottleneck theory

Earlier we discussed research (e.g., Hirst, Spelke, Reaves, Caharack, & Neisser, 1980; Spelke et al., 1976) suggesting that two complex tasks could be performed very well together with minimal disruption. However, the participants in those studies had considerable flexibility in terms of *when* and *how* they processed the two tasks. Thus, it is entirely possible that there were interference effects that went unnoticed because of insensitivity of measurement.

We turn now to what is probably the most sensitive type of experiment for detecting dual-task interference. In studies on the psychological refractory period, there are two stimuli (e.g., two lights) and two responses (e.g., button presses). Participants respond to each stimulus as rapidly as possible. When the second stimulus is presented very shortly after the first one, there is generally a marked slowing of the response to the second stimulus. This is known as the **psychological refractory period (PRP) effect** (see Pashler et al., 2001). This effect does *not* occur simply because people have little previous experience in responding to two immediately successive stimuli. Pashler (1993) discussed one of his studies in which the PRP effect was still observable after more than 10,000 practice trials.

How can we explain this effect? According to the central bottleneck theory of Welford (1952) and Pashler, Johnston, and Ruthroff (2001), there is a bottleneck in the processing system. This bottleneck makes it impossible for two decisions about the appropriate responses to two different stimuli to be made at the same time. Thus, response selection inevitably occurs in a serial fashion, and this creates a bottleneck in processing even after prolonged practice. According to Pashler et al. (2001, p. 642), "The PRP effect arises from the postponement of central processing stages in the second task – a processing bottleneck…central stages in task 2 cannot commence until corresponding stages of the first task have been completed, whereas perceptual and motoric stages in the two tasks can overlap without constraint."

Evidence that the PRP effect occurs because response selection requires serial processing was reported by Sigman and Dehaene (2008). Participants performed an auditory and a visual task at the same time, and performance revealed a PRP effect. Data from fMRI and EEG suggested that this effect was due to processes occurring at the time of response selection. More specifically, the timing of activation in a bilateral parieto-frontal network involved in response selection correlated with the delay in responding to the second stimulus (i.e., the PRP effect). In contrast, brain activation associated with early visual and auditory processes of the task stimuli was not correlated with the PRP effect. These findings suggested that perceptual processing on two tasks can occur in parallel, but subsequent response selection must occur in a serial fashion.

The notion of a processing bottleneck implies that a PRP effect will *always* be obtained. However, Greenwald (2003) found that two tasks can be performed at the same time with no disruption or interference. One task involved vocal responses to auditory stimuli: saying "A" or "B" in response to hearing those letter names. The other task involved manual responses to visual stimuli: moving a joystick to the left to an arrow pointing left and moving it to the right to an arrow pointing right. Both tasks used by Greenwald possess a very direct relationship between stimuli and responses (e.g., saying "A" when you hear "A" and saying "B" when you hear "B"). According to Greenwald (2004), two tasks can readily be performed together if they both involve *direct* stimulus–response relationships. It could be argued that, in those circumstances, there is little or no need for response selection (Spence, 2008).

Findings that are more problematic for the notion of a bottleneck were reported by Schumacher et al. (2001). They used two tasks: (1) say "one", "two", or "three" to low-, medium-, and high-pitched tones, respectively; (2) press response keys corresponding to the position of a disc on a computer screen. These two tasks were performed together for a total of 2064 trials, at the end of which some participants performed them as well together as singly. Schumacher et al. found substantial individual differences in the amount of dual-task interference. In one experiment, there was a correlation of +0.81 between dual-task

---

KEY TERM

psychological refractory period (PRP) effect: the slowing of the response to the second of two stimuli when they are presented close together in time.

interference and mean reaction time on single-task trials. Thus, those who performed each task on its own particularly well were least affected by dual-task interference.

The experiment by Schumacher et al. (2001) was exceptional in finding an absence of disruption, even though neither task involved direct stimulus–response relationships. However, this atypical finding only occurred after very extensive practice – there was substantial disruption under dual-task conditions early in practice.

One limitation in the study by Schumacher et al. was that their second task (pressing keys to discs) was so simple it did not require the use of central processes. Hazeltine, Teague, and Ivry (2000) replicated and extended the findings of Schumacher et al. that were obtained some time previously but published in 2001. Of special importance, they found very little dual-task interference even when the disc–key press task was made more difficult.

Evaluation

The evidence from most (but not all) studies of the psychological refractory period indicates that there is a bottleneck and that response selection occurs in a serial fashion. However, the size of the PRP effect is typically not very large, suggesting that many processes (e.g., early sensory processes; response execution) do *not* operate in a serial fashion.

We have seen that some studies (e.g., Schumacher et al., 2001) have reported no PRP effect. For the most part, such studies have used simple tasks involving direct stimulus–response relationships (Greenwald, 2003, 2004), which presumably minimised response selection. The jury is still out on the question of whether there are any circumstances in which we can perform two tasks involving response selection at the same time *without* incurring significant costs. The studies by Schumacher et al. (2001) and by Hazeltine et al. (2000) suggest it may be possible, but we need more research.

CHAPTER SUMMARY

- Focused auditory attention
  Initial research on focused auditory attention with the shadowing task suggested that there was very limited processing of unattended stimuli. However, there can be extensive processing of unattended stimuli, especially when they are dissimilar to the attended ones. There has been a controversy between early- and late-selection theorists as to the location of a bottleneck in processing. More evidence favours early-selection theories with some flexibility as to the stage at which selection occurs.

- Focused visual attention
  There are two attentional systems. One is stimulus-driven and is located in a right-hemisphere ventral fronto-parietal network, and the other is goal-directed and is located in a dorsal fronto-parietal network. The two systems interact. For example, salient task-irrelevant stimuli are most likely to attract attention when they resemble task-relevant stimuli. Visual attention has been compared to a spotlight or zoom lens, but can resemble multiple spotlights. Visual attention can be location-based or object-based, and the same is true of inhibition of return. Unattended visual stimuli are often processed fairly thoroughly, with some of the strongest evidence coming from neglect patients. According to Lavie, we are more susceptible to distraction when our current task involves low perceptual load and/or high load on executive cognitive control functions (e.g., working memory).

- Disorders of visual attention
  Neglect is often attributed to an impairment of the stimulus-driven system. Extinction occurs mostly when an ipsilesional stimulus captures attention in competition with a contralesional stimulus. Extinction is reduced when two stimuli are integrated and so do not compete with each other. Prisms that shift the visual field to the right reduce the symptoms of neglect. Research on brain-damaged patients has provided evidence for three components of visual attention: disengagement, shifting, and engagement. Posner and Petersen (1990) have identified the brain areas associated with each component.

- Visual search
  According to feature integration theory, object features are processed in parallel and are then combined by focused attention. Factors (e.g., grouping of distractors; distractors sharing no features with targets) associated with fast detection are missing from feature integration theory but are included in guided search theory. Thornton and Gilden (2007) found evidence of parallel processing when targets and distractors differed in only one feature dimension and of serial processing on complex tasks involving the detection of a specific direction of rotation. Visual search tasks used in the laboratory often differ in important ways from everyday situations in which visual search is used.

- Cross-modal effects
  In the real world, we often need to co-ordinate information from two or more sense modalities. Convincing evidence of cross-modal effects has been obtained in studies of exogenous and endogenous spatial attention. The ventriloquist illusion shows that vision can dominate sound, probably because an object's location is typically indicated more precisely by vision. There is much "multi-sensory interplay" within the brain because neurons responding to input from different modalities are in close proximity.

- Divided attention: dual-task performance
  Driving performance is impaired substantially by a secondary task (e.g., mobile-phone use). Dual-task performance is influenced by task similarity, practice, and task difficulty. Central-capacity and multiple-resource theories have been proposed to explain dual-task performance. Some neuroimaging studies have found underadditivity under dual-task conditions, suggesting problems in distributing a limited central capacity across the tasks. Dual-task conditions can also introduce new processing demands of task co-ordination associated with activation within the dorsolateral prefrontal cortex. The attentional blink suggests that impaired dual-task performance is due in part to difficulties in engaging attention twice within a short period of time.

- Automatic processing
  Shiffrin and Schneider distinguished between slow, controlled processes and fast, automatic processes. Automatic processes are typically goal-unrelated, unconscious, efficient, and fast. Neuroimaging studies suggest that the development of automaticity is associated with reduced activation within the prefrontal cortex (e.g., dorsolateral prefrontal cortex). According to instance theory, automatic processes are fast because they require only the retrieval of past solutions from long-term memory. The great majority of relevant dual-task studies have found a psychological refractory period effect, which suggests the existence of a processing bottleneck. However, the effect is sometimes not found when both tasks involve direct stimulus–response relationships.

FURTHER READING

- Bartolomeo, P. (2007). Visual neglect. *Current Opinion in Neurology, 20,* 381–386. Paulo Bartolomeo's article gives us a succinct account of research and theory on visual neglect.
- Corbetta, M., Patel, G., & Shulman, G.L. (2008). The reorienting system of the human brain: From environment to theory of mind. *Neuron, 58,* 306–324. This article presents an updated version of Corbetta and Shulman's (2002) influential cognitive neuroscience theory of visual attention.
- Lavie, N. (2005). Distracted and confused? Selective attention under load. *Trends in Cognitive Sciences, 9,* 75–82. Nilli Lavie provides an overview of her theoretical approach to attention and the research that supports it.
- Logan, G.D. (2004). Cumulative progress in formal theories of attention. *Annual Review of Psychology, 55,* 207–234. Major theoretical approaches to important phenomena in attention are considered in an authoritative way in this chapter.
- Moors, A., & De Houwer, J. (2006). Automaticity: A theoretical and conceptual analysis. *Psychological Bulletin, 132,* 297–326. The main issues and controversies surrounding the topic of automaticity are discussed at length in this excellent article.
- Styles, E.A. (2006). *The psychology of attention* (2nd ed.). Hove, UK: Psychology Press. The second edition of this textbook by Elizabeth Styles provides excellent coverage of most of the topics discussed in this chapter.

How important is memory? Imagine if we were without it. We wouldn't recognise anyone or anything as familiar. We would be unable to talk, read, or write, because we would remember nothing about language. We would have extremely limited personalities, because we would have no recollection of the events of our own lives and therefore no sense of self. In sum, we would have the same lack of knowledge as newborn babies.

We use memory for numerous purposes throughout every day of our lives. It allows us to keep track of conversations, to remember telephone numbers while we dial them, to write essays in examinations, to make sense of what we read, to recognise people's faces, and to understand what we read in books or see on television.

The wonders of human memory are discussed in Chapters 6–8. Chapter 6 deals mainly with key issues that have been regarded as important from the very beginnings of research into memory. For example, we consider the overall architecture of human memory and the distinction between short-term and long-term memory. We also consider the uses of short-term memory in everyday life. Another topic discussed in that chapter is learning, including evidence suggesting that some learning is implicit (i.e., does not depend on conscious processes). Finally, we deal with forgetting. Why is it that we tend to forget information as time goes by?

When we think about long-term memory, it is obvious that its scope is enormous. We have long-term memories for personal information about ourselves and those we know, knowledge about language, much knowledge about psychology (hopefully!), and knowledge about thousands of objects in the world around us. The key issue addressed in Chapter 7 is how to account for this incredible richness. At one time, many psychologists proposed theories in which there was a single long-term memory store. However, it is now almost universally acknowledged that there are several long-term memory systems. As we will see in Chapter 7, some of the most convincing evidence supporting that position has come from patients whose brain damage has severely impaired their long-term memory.

Memory is important in everyday life in ways that historically have not been the focus of much research. For example, autobiographical memory is of great significance to all of us. Indeed, we would lose our sense of self and life would lose most of its meaning if we lacked memory for the events and experiences that have shaped our personalities. Autobiographical memory is one of the topics discussed in Chapter 8. Other topics on everyday memory considered in that chapter are eyewitness testimony and prospective memory. Research into eyewitness testimony is of considerable importance with respect to the legal system. It has revealed that many of the assumptions we make about the accuracy of eyewitness testimony are mistaken. This matters because hundreds or even thousands of innocent people have been imprisoned solely on the basis of eyewitness testimony.

When we think about memory, we naturally focus on memory for what has happened in the past. However, most of us have to remember numerous future commitments (e.g., meeting a friend as arranged; turning up for a lecture), and such remembering involves prospective memory. We will consider the ways in which people try to ensure that they carry out their future intentions.

As will become apparent in the next three chapters, the study of human memory is fascinating and a substantial amount of progress has been made. However, human memory is undoubtedly complex. It depends on several different factors. According to Jenkins (1979) and Roediger (2008), at least four kinds of factor are important in memory research: events, participants, encoding, and retrieval. Events are the stimuli, and can range from words and pictures to texts and life events. The participants can vary in age, expertise, memory-specific disorders, and so on.

What happens at encoding varies as a function of task instructions, the immediate context, participants' strategies, and many other factors. Finally, memory performance at retrieval often varies considerably depending on the nature of the memory task (e.g., free recall; cued recall; recognition).

The crucial message of the above approach is that memory findings are context-sensitive – they depend on interactions among the four factors. In other words, the effects of manipulating, say, what happens at encoding depend on the participants used, the events to be remembered, and on the conditions of retrieval. As a result, we should not expect to find many (if any) laws of memory that hold under all circumstances. How, then, do we make progress? As Baddeley (1978, p. 150) pointed out, what is required is "to develop ways of separating out and analysing more deeply the complex underlying processes."

CHAPTER 6

LEARNING, MEMORY, AND FORGETTING

INTRODUCTION

This chapter and the next two are concerned with human memory. All three chapters deal with intact human memory, but Chapter 7 also considers amnesic patients. Traditional laboratory-based research is the focus of this chapter, with more naturalistic research being discussed in Chapter 8. As we will see, there are important links among these different types of research. Many theoretical issues are relevant to brain-damaged and healthy individuals whether tested in the laboratory or in the field.

Theories of memory generally consider both the architecture of the memory system and the processes operating within that structure. Architecture refers to the way in which the memory system is organised and processes refer to the activities occurring within the memory system.

Learning and memory involve a series of stages. Processes occurring during the presentation of the learning material are known as "encoding" and involve many of the processes involved in perception. This is the first stage. As a result of encoding, some information is stored within the memory system. Thus, storage is the second stage. The third (and final) stage is retrieval, which involves recovering or extracting stored information from the memory system.

We have emphasised the distinctions between architecture and process and among encoding, storage, and retrieval. However, we cannot have architecture without process, or retrieval without previous encoding and storage.

ARCHITECTURE OF MEMORY

Throughout most of the history of memory research, it has been assumed that there is an important distinction between short-term memory and long-term memory. It seems reasonable that the processes involved in briefly remembering a telephone number are very different from those involved in long-term memory for theories and research in psychology. This traditional view is at the heart of multi-store models, which are discussed initially. In recent times, however, some theorists have argued in favour of unitary-store models in which the distinction between short-term and long-term memory is much less clear-cut than in the traditional approach. We will consider unitary-store models shortly.

Multi-store model

Several memory theorists (e.g., Atkinson & Shiffrin, 1968) have described the basic architecture of the memory system. We can identify a multi-store approach based on the common features of their theories. Three types of memory store were proposed:

- Sensory stores, each holding information very briefly and being modality specific (limited to one sensory modality).
- Short-term store of very limited capacity.
- Long-term store of essentially unlimited capacity holding information over very long periods of time.

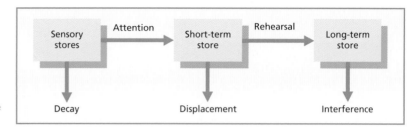

Figure 6.1 The multi-store model of memory.

The basic multi-store model is shown in Figure 6.1. Environmental stimulation is initially received by the sensory stores. These stores are modality-specific (e.g., vision, hearing). Information is held very briefly in the sensory stores, with some being attended to and processed further by the short-term store. Some information processed in the short-term store is transferred to the long-term store. Long-term storage of information often depends on rehearsal. There is a direct relationship between the amount of rehearsal in the short-term store and the strength of the stored memory trace. There is much overlap between the areas of attention and memory. Broadbent's (1958) theory of attention (see Chapter 5) was the main influence on the multi-store approach to memory. For example, Broadbent's buffer store resembles the notion of a sensory store.

Sensory stores

The visual store is often known as the iconic store. In Sperling's (1960) classic work on this store, he presented a visual array containing three rows of four letters each for 50 ms. Participants could usually report only 4–5 letters, but claimed to have seen many more. Sperling assumed this happened because visual information had faded before most of it could be reported. He tested this by asking participants to recall only *part* of the information presented. Sperling's results supported his assumption, with part recall being good provided that the information to be recalled was cued very soon after the offset of the visual display.

Sperling's (1960) findings suggested that information in iconic memory decays within about 0.5 seconds, but this may well be an underestimate. Landman, Spekreijse, and Lamme (2003) pointed out that the requirement to verbally identify and recall items in the part-recall condition may have interfered with performance. They imposed simpler response demands on participants (i.e., is a second stimulus the same as the first one?) and found that iconic memory lasted for up to about 1600 ms (see Figure 4.12).

Iconic storage is very useful for two reasons. First, the mechanisms responsible for visual perception always operate on the icon rather than directly on the visual environment. Second, information remains in iconic memory for upwards of 500 ms, and we can shift our attention to aspects of the information within iconic memory in approximately 55 ms (Lachter, Forster, & Ruthruff, 2004; see Chapter 5). This helps to ensure we attend to important information.

The transient auditory store is known as the **echoic store**. In everyday life, you may sometimes have been asked a question while your mind was on something else. Perhaps you replied, "What did you say?", just before realising that you do know what had been said. This "playback" facility depends on the echoic store. Estimates of the duration of information in the echoic store are typically within the range of 2–4 seconds (Treisman, 1964).

KEY TERM

echoic store: a sensory store in which auditory information is briefly held.

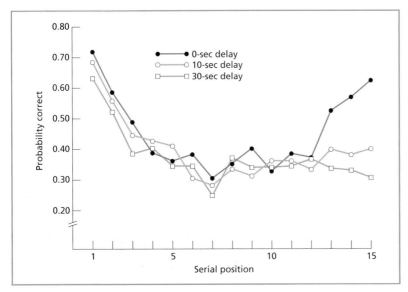

Figure 6.2 Free recall as a function of serial position and duration of the interpolated task. Adapted from Glanzer and Cunitz (1966).

Short- and long-term stores

The capacity of short-term memory is very limited. Consider digit span: participants listen to a random series of digits and then repeat them back immediately in the correct order. Other span measures are letter span and word span. The maximum number of units (e.g., digits) recalled without error is usually "seven plus or minus two" (Miller, 1956). However, there are two qualifications concerning that finding. First, Miller (1956) argued that the capacity of short-term memory should be assessed by the number of **chunks** (integrated pieces or units of information). For example, "IBM" is one chunk for those familiar with the company name International Business Machines but three chunks for everyone else. The capacity of short-term memory is often seven chunks rather than seven items. However, Simon (1974) found that the span in chunks was less with larger chunks (e.g., eight-word phrases) than with smaller chunks (e.g., one-syllable words).

Second, Cowan (2000, p. 88) argued that estimates of short-term memory capacity are often inflated because participants' performance depends in part on rehearsal and on long-term memory. When these additional factors are largely eliminated, the capacity of short-term memory is typically only about four chunks. For example, Cowan et al. (2005) used the running memory task – a series of digits ended at an unpredictable point, with the participants' task being to recall the items from the end of the list. The digits were presented very rapidly to prevent rehearsal, and the mean number of items recalled was 3.87.

The **recency effect** in free recall (recalling the items in any order) refers to the finding that the last few items in a list are usually much better remembered in immediate recall than those from the middle of the list. Counting backwards for 10 seconds between the end of list presentation and start of recall mainly affects the recency effect (Glanzer & Cunitz, 1966; see Figure 6.2). The two or three words susceptible to the recency effect may be in the short-term store at the end of list presentation and so especially vulnerable. However, Bjork

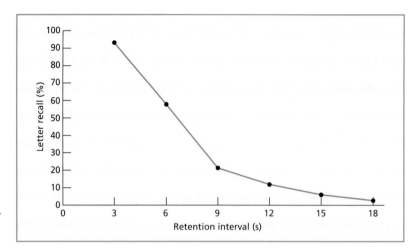

Figure 6.3 Forgetting over time in short-term memory. Data from Peterson and Peterson (1959).

and Whitten (1974) found that there was still a recency effect when participants counted backwards for 12 seconds after each item in the list was presented. According to Atkinson and Shiffrin (1968), this should have eliminated the recency effect.

The above findings can be explained by analogy to looking along a row of telephone poles. The closer poles are more distinct than the ones farther away, just as the most recent list words are more discriminable than the others (Glenberg, 1987).

Peterson and Peterson (1959) studied the duration of short-term memory by using the task of remembering a three-letter stimulus while counting backwards by threes followed by recall in the correct order. Memory performance reduced to about 50% after 6 seconds and forgetting was almost complete after 18 seconds (see Figure 6.3), presumably because unrehearsed information disappears rapidly from short-term memory through decay (see Nairne, 2002, for a review). In contrast, it is often argued that forgetting from long-term memory involves different mechanisms. In particular, there is much cue-dependent forgetting, in which the memory traces are still in the memory system but are inaccessible (see later discussion).

Nairne, Whiteman, and Kelley (1999) argued that the rate of forgetting observed by Peterson and Peterson (1959) was especially rapid for

two reasons. First, they used all the letters of the alphabet repeatedly, which may have caused considerable interference. Second, the memory task was difficult in that participants had to remember the items themselves and the presentation order. Nairne et al. presented different words on each trial to reduce interference, and tested memory only for order information and not for the words themselves. Even though there was a rehearsal-prevention task (reading aloud digits presented on a screen) during the retention interval, there was remarkably little forgetting even over 96 seconds (see Figure 6.4).

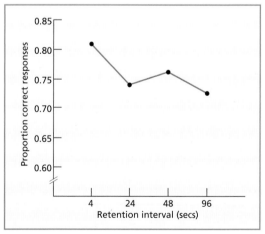

Figure 6.4 Proportion of correct responses as a function of retention interval. Data from Nairne et al. (1999).

This finding casts doubt on the notion that decay causes forgetting in short-term memory. However, reading digits aloud may not have totally prevented rehearsal.

Finally, we turn to the strongest evidence that short-term and long-term memory are distinct. If short-term and long-term memory are separate, we might expect to find some patients with impaired long-term memory but intact short-term memory and others showing the opposite pattern. This would produce a double dissociation. The findings are generally supportive. Patients with amnesia (discussed in Chapter 7) have severe impairments of many aspects of long-term memory, but typically have no problem with short-term memory (Spiers, Maguire, & Burgess, 2001). Amnesic patients have damage to the medial temporal lobe, including the hippocampus (see Chapter 7), which primarily disrupts long-term memory (see Chapter 7).

A few brain-damaged patients have severely impaired short-term memory but intact long-term memory. For example, KF had no problems with long-term learning and recall but had a very small digit span (Shallice & Warrington, 1970). Subsequent research indicated that his short-term memory problems focused mainly on recall of letters, words, or digits rather than meaningful sounds or visual stimuli (e.g., Shallice & Warrington, 1974). Such patients typically have damage to the parietal and temporal lobes (Vallar & Papagno, 2002).

Evaluation

The multi-store approach has various strengths. The conceptual distinction between three kinds of memory store (sensory store, short-term store, and long-term store) makes sense. These memory stores differ in several ways:

- temporal duration
- storage capacity
- forgetting mechanism(s)
- effects of brain damage

Finally, many subsequent theories of human memory have built on the foundations of the multi-store model, as we will see later in this chapter.

However, the multi-store model possesses several serious limitations. First, it is very oversimplified. It was assumed that the short-term and long-term stores are both *unitary*, i.e., each store always operates in a single, uniform way. As we will see shortly, Baddeley and Hitch (1974) proposed replacing the concept of a single short-term store with a working memory system consisting of *three* different components. That is a more realistic approach. In similar fashion, there are several long-term memory systems (see Chapter 7).

Second, it is assumed that the short-term store acts as a gateway between the sensory stores and long-term memory (see Figure 6.1). However, the information processed in the short-term store has already made contact with information stored in long-term memory (Logie, 1999). For example, consider the phonological similarity effect: immediate recall of visually presented words in the correct order is worse when they are phonologically similar (sounding similar) (e.g., Larsen, Baddeley, & Andrade, 2000). Thus, information about the sounds of words stored in long-term memory affects processing in short-term memory.

Third, Atkinson and Shiffrin (1968) assumed that information in short-term memory represents the "contents of consciousness". This implies that only information processed consciously can be stored in long-term memory. However, learning without conscious awareness of what has been learned (implicit learning) appears to exist (see later in the chapter).

Fourth, multi-store theorists assumed that most information is transferred to long-term memory via rehearsal. However, the role of rehearsal in our everyday lives is very limited. More generally, multi-store theorists focused too much on structural aspects of memory rather than on memory processes.

Unitary-store models

In recent years, various theorists have argued that the entire multi-store approach is misguided and should be replaced by a unitary-store model (see Jonides, Lewis, Nee, Lustig, Berman, &

Moore, 2008, for a review). Unitary-store models assume that, "STM [short-term memory] consists of temporary activations of LTM [long-term memory] representations or of representations of items that were recently perceived" (Jonides et al., 2008, p. 198). Such activations will often occur when certain representations are the focus of attention.

Unitary-store models would seem to have great difficulty in explaining the consistent finding that amnesic patients have essentially intact short-term memory in spite of having severe problems with long-term memory. Jonides et al. (2008) argued that amnesic patients have special problems in forming novel relations (e.g., between items and their context) in both short-term and long-term memory. Amnesic patients apparently have no problems with short-term memory because short-term memory tasks typically do not require relational memory. This leads to a key prediction: amnesic patients should have impaired short-term memory performance on tasks requiring relational memory.

According to Jonides et al. (2008), the hippocampus and surrounding medial temporal lobes (typically damaged in amnesic patients) play a crucial role in forming novel relations (sometimes called binding) (see Chapter 7). Multi-store theorists assume that these structures are much more involved in long-term memory than in short-term memory. However, it follows from unitary-store models that the hippocampus and medial temporal lobes would be involved if a short-term memory task required forming novel relations.

Evidence

Evidence supporting the unitary-store approach was reported by Hannula, Tranel, and Cohen (2006). They studied patients who had become amnesic as the result of an anoxic episode (involving deficient oxygen supply). In one experiment, scenes were presented for 20 seconds. Some scenes were repeated exactly, whereas others were repeated with one object having been moved spatially. Participants decided whether each scene had been seen previously. It was assumed that short-term memory was involved

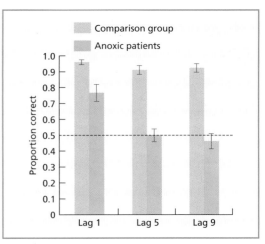

Figure 6.5 Proportion of correct responses for healthy controls (comparison group) and amnesics (anoxic patients). The dashed line represents chance performance. From Hannula et al. (2006) with permission from Society of Neuroscience.

when a given scene was repeated in its original or slightly modified form immediately after its initial presentation (Lag 1) but that long-term memory was involved at longer lags.

The findings are shown in Figure 6.5. Amnesic patients performed much worse than healthy controls in short-term memory (Lag 1) and the performance difference between the two groups was even larger in long-term memory. The crucial issue is whether performance at Lag 1 was *only* due to short-term memory. The finding that amnesics' performance fell to chance level at longer lags suggests that they may well have relied almost exclusively on short-term memory at Lag 1. However, the finding that controls' performance changed little over lags suggests that they formed strong long-term relational memories, and these long-term memories may well account for their superior performance at Lag 1.

Further support for the unitary-store approach was reported by Hannula and Ranganath (2008). They presented four objects in various locations and instructed participants to rotate the display mentally. Participants were then presented with a second display, and decided whether second display matched or failed to match their mental representation of the rotated display. This task involved relational memory. The key finding was that the amount of activation in the anterior and posterior regions of the left hippocampus predicted relational memory performance.

Shrager, Levy, Hopkins, and Squire (2008) pointed out that a crucial issue is whether memory performance at short retention intervals actually depends on short-term memory rather than long-term memory. They argued that a distinguishing feature of short-term memory is that it involves active maintenance of information throughout the retention interval. Tasks that mostly depend on short-term memory are vulnerable to distraction during the retention interval because distraction disrupts active maintenance. Shrager et al. divided their memory tasks into those susceptible to distraction in healthy controls and those that were not. Amnesic patients with medial temporal lobe lesions had essentially normal levels of performance on distraction-sensitive memory tasks but were significantly impaired on distraction-insensitive memory tasks. Shrager et al. concluded that short-term memory processes are intact in amnesic patients. Amnesic patients only show impaired performance on so-called "short-term memory tasks" when those tasks actually depend substantially on long-term memory.

Evaluation

The unitary-store approach has made memory researchers think deeply about the relationship between short-term and long-term memory. There are good reasons for accepting the notion that activation of part of long-term memory plays an important role in short-term memory. According to the unitary-store approach (but not the multi-store approach), amnesic patients can exhibit impaired short-term memory under some circumstances. Some recent evidence (e.g., Hannula et al., 2006) supports the prediction of the unitary-store approach. Functional neuroimaging evidence (e.g., Hannula & Ranganath, 2008) also provides limited support for the unitary-store approach.

What are the limitations of the unitary-store approach? First, it is oversimplified to argue that short-term memory is *only* activated by long-term memory. We can manipulate activated long-term memory in flexible ways and such manipulations go well beyond simply activating some fraction of long-term memory. Two examples of ways in which we can manipulate information in short-term memory are backward digit recall (recalling digits in the opposite order to the presentation order) and generating novel visual images (Logie & van der Meulen, 2009). Second, there is no convincing evidence that amnesic patients have impaired performance on relational memory tasks dependent primarily on short-term memory. It seems likely that amnesic patients only perform poorly on "short-term memory" tasks that depend to a large extent on long-term memory (Shrager et al., 2008). Third, there is no other evidence that decisively favours the unitary-store approach over the multiple-store approach. However, the search for such evidence only recently started in earnest.

WORKING MEMORY

Baddeley and Hitch (1974) and Baddeley (1986) replaced the concept of the short-term store with that of working memory. Since then, the conceptualisation of the working memory system has become increasingly complex. According to Baddeley (2001) and Repovš and Baddeley (2006), the working memory system has four components (see Figure 6.6):

- A modality-free **central executive** resembling attention.
- A **phonological loop** holding information in a phonological (speech-based) form.

KEY TERMS

central executive: a modality-free, limited capacity, component of **working memory**.
phonological loop: a component of **working memory**, in which speech-based information is held and subvocal articulation occurs.

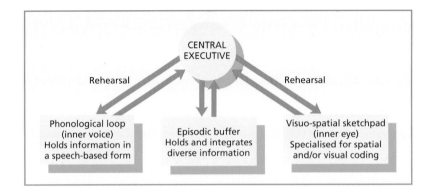

Figure 6.6 The major components of Baddeley's working memory system. Figure adapted from Baddeley (2001).

- A **visuo-spatial sketchpad** specialised for spatial and visual coding.
- An **episodic buffer**, which is a temporary storage system that can hold and integrate information from the phonological loop, the visuo-spatial sketchpad, and long-term memory. This component (added 25 years after the others) is discussed later.

The most important component is the central executive. It has limited capacity, resembles attention, and deals with any cognitively demanding task. The phonological loop and the visuo-spatial sketchpad are slave systems used by the central executive for specific purposes. The phonological loop preserves the order in which words are presented, and the visuo-spatial sketchpad stores and manipulates spatial and visual information. All three components have limited capacity and are relatively independent of each other. Two assumptions follow:

(1) If two tasks use the same component, they cannot be performed successfully together.
(2) If two tasks use different components, it should be possible to perform them as well together as separately.

Numerous dual-task studies have been carried out on the basis of these assumptions. For example, Robbins et al. (1996) considered the involvement of the three original components of working memory in the selection of chess moves by weaker and stronger players. The players selected continuation moves from various chess positions while also performing one of the following tasks:

- *Repetitive tapping*: this was the control condition.
- *Random number generation*: this involved the central executive.
- *Pressing keys on a keypad in a clockwise fashion*: this used the visuo-spatial sketchpad.
- *Rapid repetition of the word "see-saw"*: this is **articulatory suppression** and uses the phonological loop.

Robbins et al. (1996) found that selecting chess moves involved the central executive and the visuo-spatial sketchpad but not the phonological loop (see Figure 6.7). The effects of the various additional tasks were similar on stronger and weaker players, suggesting that

KEY TERMS

visuo-spatial sketchpad: a component of **working memory** that is involved in visual and spatial processing of information.
episodic buffer: a component of **working memory** that is used to integrate and to store briefly information from the **phonological loop**, the **visuo-spatial sketchpad**, and **long-term memory**.
articulatory suppression: rapid repetition of some simple sound (e.g., "the, the, the"), which uses the articulatory control process of the **phonological loop**.

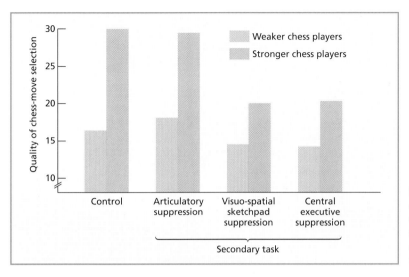

Figure 6.7 Effects of secondary tasks on quality of chess-move selection in stronger and weaker players. Adapted from Robbins et al. (1996).

According to Robbins et al. (1996), selecting good chess moves requires use of the central executive and the visuo-spatial sketchpad, but not of the phonological loop.

both groups used the working memory system in the same way.

Phonological loop

Most early research on the phonological loop focused on the notion that verbal rehearsal (i.e., saying words over and over to oneself) is of central importance. Two phenomena providing support for this view are the phonological similarity effect and the word-length effect. The **phonological similarity effect** is found when a short list of visually presented words is recalled immediately in the correct order. Recall performance is worse when the words are phonologically similar (i.e., having similar sounds) than when they are phonologically dissimilar. For example, FEE, HE, KNEE, LEE, ME, and SHE form a list of phonologically similar words, whereas BAY, HOE, IT, ODD, SHY, and UP form a list of phonologically dissimilar words. Larsen, Baddeley, and Andrade (2000) used those word lists, finding that recall of the words in order was 25% worse with the phonologically similar list. This phonological similarity effect occurred because participants used speech-based rehearsal processes within the phonological loop.

The **word-length effect** is based on memory span (the number of words or other items recalled immediately in the correct order). It is defined by the finding that memory span is lower for words taking a long time to say than for

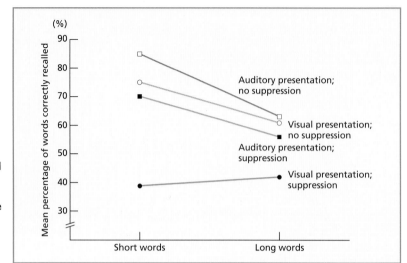

Figure 6.8 Immediate word recall as a function of modality of presentation (visual vs. auditory), presence versus absence of articulatory suppression, and word length. Adapted from Baddeley et al. (1975).

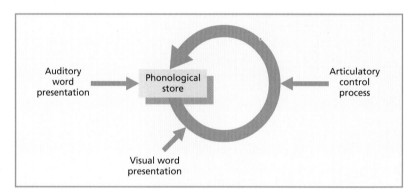

Figure 6.9 Phonological loop system as envisaged by Baddeley (1990).

those taking less time. Baddeley, Thomson, and Buchanan (1975) found that participants recalled as many words presented visually as they could read out loud in 2 seconds. This suggested that the capacity of the phonological loop is determined by temporal duration like a tape loop. Service (2000) argued that these findings depend on phonological complexity rather than on temporal duration. Reassuringly, Mueller, Seymour, Kieras, and Meyer (2003) found with very carefully chosen words that memory span depended on the articulatory duration of words rather than their phonological complexity.

In another experiment, Baddeley et al. (1975) obtained more direct evidence that the word-length effect depends on the phonological loop. The number of visually presented words (out of five) that could be recalled was assessed.

Some participants were given the articulatory suppression task of repeating the digits 1 to 8 while performing the main task. The argument was that the articulatory suppression task would involve the phonological loop and so prevent it being used on the word-span task. As predicted, articulatory suppression eliminated the word-length effect (see Figure 6.8), suggesting it depends on the phonological loop.

As so often in psychology, reality is more complex than was originally thought. Note that the research discussed so far involved the *visual* presentation of words. Baddeley et al. (1975) obtained the usual word-length effect when there was auditory presentation of word lists. Puzzlingly, however, there was still a word-length effect with auditorily presented words even when articulatory suppression was used (see Figure 6.8). This led

Baddeley (1986, 1990; see Figure 6.9) to argue that the phonological loop has two components:

* A passive phonological store directly concerned with speech perception.
* An articulatory process linked to speech production that gives access to the phonological store.

According to this account, words presented auditorily are processed differently from those presented visually. Auditory presentation of words produces *direct* access to the phonological store regardless of whether the articulatory control process is used. In contrast, visual presentation of words only permits *indirect* access to the phonological store through subvocal articulation.

The above account makes sense of many findings. Suppose the word-length effect observed by Baddeley et al. (1975) depends on the rate of articulatory rehearsal (see Figure 6.8). Articulatory suppression eliminates the word-length effect with visual presentation because access to the phonological store is prevented. However, it does *not* affect the word-length effect with auditory presentation because information about the words enters the phonological store directly.

Progress has been made in identifying the brain areas associated with the two components of the phonological loop. Some brain-damaged patients have very poor memory for auditory-verbal material but essentially normal speech production, indicating they have a damaged phonological store but an intact articulatory control process. These patients typically have damage to the left inferior parietal cortex (Vallar & Papagno, 1995). Other brain-damaged patients have an intact phonological store but a damaged articulatory control process shown by a lack of evidence for rehearsal. Such patients generally have damage to the left inferior frontal cortex.

Similar brain areas have been identified in functional neuroimaging studies on healthy volunteers. Henson, Burgess, and Frith (2000) found that a left inferior parietal area was associated with the phonological store, whereas left prefrontal cortex was associated with rehearsal.

Logie, Venneri, Della Sala, Redpath, and Marshall (2003) gave their participants the task of recalling letter sequences presented auditorily in the correct order. All participants were instructed to use subvocal rehearsal to ensure the involvement of the rehearsal component of the phonological loop. The left inferior parietal gyrus and the inferior and middle frontal gyri were activated.

Evaluation

Baddeley's theory accounts for the word-length effects and for the effects of articulatory suppression. In addition, evidence from brain-damaged patients and from functional neuroimaging studies with healthy participants indicates the existence of a phonological store and an articulatory control process located in different brain regions. Our understanding of the phonological loop is greater than that for the other components of the working memory system.

What is the value of the phonological loop? According to Baddeley, Gathercole, and Papagno (1998, p. 158), "The function of the phonological loop is not to remember familiar words but to learn new words." Supporting evidence was reported by Papagno, Valentine, and Baddeley (1991). Native Italian speakers learned pairs of Italian words and pairs of Italian–Russian words. Articulatory suppression (which reduces use of the phonological loop) greatly slowed the learning of foreign vocabulary but had little effect on the learning of pairs of Italian words.

Several studies have considered the relationship between children's vocabulary development and their performance on verbal short-term memory tasks involving the phonological loop. The capacity of the phonological loop generally predicts vocabulary size (e.g., Majerus, Poncelet, Elsen, & van der Linden, 2006). Such evidence is consistent with the notion that the phonological loop plays a role in the learning of vocabulary. However, much of the evidence is correlational – it is also possible that having a large vocabulary increases the effective capacity of the phonological loop.

Trojano and Grossi (1995) studied SC, a patient with extremely poor phonological functioning. SC showed reasonable learning ability in most situations but was unable to learn auditorily presented word–nonword pairs. Presumably SC's poorly functioning phonological loop prevented the learning of the phonologically unfamiliar nonwords.

Visuo-spatial sketchpad

The visuo-spatial sketchpad is used for the temporary storage and manipulation of visual patterns and spatial movement. It is used in many situations in everyday life (e.g., finding the route when walking; playing computer games). Logie, Baddeley, Mane, Donchin, and Sheptak (1989) studied performance on a complex computer game called Space Fortress, which involves manoeuvring a space ship around a computer screen. Early in training, performance on Space Fortress was severely impaired when participants had to perform a secondary visuo-spatial task. After 25 hours' training, the adverse effects on the computer game of carrying out a visuo-spatial task at the same time were greatly reduced, being limited to those aspects directly involving perceptuo-motor control. Thus, the visuo-spatial sketchpad was used throughout training on Space Fortress, but its involvement decreased with practice.

The most important issue is whether there is a *single* system combining visual and spatial processing or whether there are partially or completely *separate* visual and spatial systems. According to Logie (1995; see Figure 6.10), the visuo-spatial sketchpad consists of two components:

- **Visual cache:** This stores information about visual form and colour.
- **Inner scribe:** This processes spatial and movement information. It is involved in the rehearsal of information in the visual cache and transfers information from the visual cache to the central executive.

Recent developments in theory and research on the visuo-spatial sketchpad are discussed by Logie and van der Meulen (2009).

Klauer and Zhao (2004) explored the issue of whether there are separate visual and spatial systems. They used two main tasks – a spatial task (memory for dot locations) and a visual task (memory for Chinese ideographs). There were also three secondary task conditions:

- A movement discrimination task (spatial interference).
- A colour discrimination task (visual interference).
- A control condition (no secondary task).

What would we expect if there are somewhat separate visual and spatial systems? First, the spatial interference task should disrupt performance more on the spatial main task than on the visual main task. Second, the visual interference task should disrupt performance more on the visual main task than on the spatial main task. Both predictions were supported (see Figure 6.11).

Additional evidence supporting the notion of separate visual and spatial systems was reported by Smith and Jonides (1997) in an ingenious study. Two visual stimuli were presented together, followed by a probe stimulus.

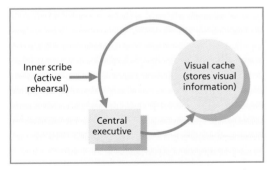

Figure 6.10 The visuo-spatial sketchpad or working memory as envisaged by Logie. Adapted from Logie (1995), Baddeley, Mane, Donchin, and Sheptak.

KEY TERMS

visual cache: according to Logie, the part of the visuo-spatial sketchpad that stores information about visual form and colour.

inner scribe: according to Logie, the part of the **visuo-spatial sketchpad** that deals with spatial and movement information.

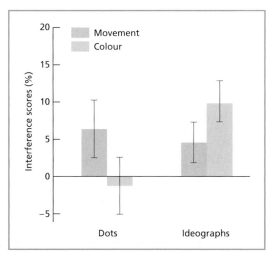

Figure 6.11 Amount of interference on a spatial task (dots) and a visual task (ideographs) as a function of secondary task (spatial: movement vs. visual: colour discrimination). From Klauer and Zhao (2004), Copyright © 2000 American Psychological Association. Reproduced with permission.

Participants decided whether the probe was in the same location as one of the initial stimuli (spatial task) or had the same form (visual task). Even though the stimuli were identical in the two tasks, there were clear differences in patterns of brain activation. There was more activity in the right hemisphere during the spatial task than the visual task, but more activity in the left hemisphere during the visual task than the spatial task.

Several other studies have indicated that different brain regions are activated during visual and spatial working-memory tasks (see Sala, Rämä, & Courtney, 2003, for a review). The ventral prefrontal cortex (e.g., the inferior and middle frontal gyri) is generally activated more during visual working-memory tasks than spatial ones. In contrast, more dorsal prefrontal cortex (especially an area of the superior prefrontal sulcus) tends to be more activated during spatial working-memory tasks than visual ones. This separation between visual and spatial processing is consistent with evidence that rather separate pathways are involved in visual and spatial perceptual processing (see Chapter 2).

Evaluation

Various kinds of evidence support the view that the visuo-spatial sketchpad consists of somewhat separate visual (visual cache) and spatial (inner scribe) components. First, there is often little interference between visual and spatial tasks performed at the same time (e.g., Klauer & Zhao, 2004). Second, functional neuroimaging data suggest that the two components of the visuo-spatial sketchpad are located in different brain regions (e.g., Sala et al., 2003; Smith & Jonides, 1997). Third, some brain-damaged patients have damage to the visual component but not to the spatial component. For example, NL found it very hard to describe details from the left side of scenes in visual imagery even though his visual perceptual system was essentially intact (Beschin, Cocchini, Della Sala, & Logie, 1997).

Many tasks require both components of the visuo-spatial sketchpad to be used in combination. It remains for the future to understand more fully how processing and information from the two components are combined and integrated on such tasks. In addition, much remains unknown about interactions between the workings of the visuo-spatial sketchpad and the episodic buffer (Baddeley, 2007).

Central executive

The central executive (which resembles an attentional system) is the most important and versatile component of the working memory system. Every time we engage in any complex cognitive activity (e.g., reading a text; solving a problem; carrying out two tasks at the same time), we make considerable use of the central executive. It is generally assumed that the prefrontal cortex is the part of the brain most involved in the functions of the central executive. Mottaghy (2006) reviewed studies using repetitive transcranial magnetic stimulation (rTMS; see Glossary) to disrupt activity within the dorsolateral prefrontal cortex. Performance on many complex cognitive tasks was impaired by this manipulation, indicating that dorsolateral prefrontal cortex is of importance in central executive functions. However, we need to be careful about associating the central executive too directly with prefrontal cortex. As Andrés (2003) pointed out, patients with damage to prefrontal cortex do not always show executive deficits, and some patients with no damage to prefrontal cortex nevertheless have executive deficits.

One way of trying to understand the importance of the central executive in our everyday functioning is to study brain-damaged individuals whose central executive is impaired. Such individuals suffer from **dysexecutive syndrome** (Baddeley, 1996), which involves problems with planning, organising, monitoring behaviour, and initiating behaviour. Patients with dysexecutive syndrome typically have damage within the frontal lobes at the front of the brain (adverse effects of damage to the prefrontal cortex on problem solving are discussed in Chapter 12). However, some patients seem to have damage to posterior (mainly parietal) rather than to frontal regions (e.g., Andrés, 2003). Brain-damaged patients are often tested with the Behavioural Assessment of the Dysexecutive Syndrome (BADS; Wilson, Alderman, Burgess, Emslie, & Evans, 1996). This consists of various tests assessing the ability to shift rules, to devise and implement a solution to a practical problem, to divide time effectively among various tasks, and so on. Individuals with dysexecutive syndrome as assessed by the BADS typically have great problems in holding down a job and functioning adequately in everyday life (Chamberlain, 2003).

The conceptualisation of the central executive has changed over time. As Repovš and Baddeley (2006, p. 12) admitted, it was originally "a convenient ragbag for unanswered questions related to the control of working memory and its two slave subsystems." In the original model, the central executive was *unitary*, meaning that it functioned as a single unit. In recent years, theorists have increasingly argued that the central executive is more complex. Baddeley (1996) suggested that four of the functions of the central executive were as follows: switching of retrieval plans; timesharing in dual-task studies; selective attention to certain stimuli while ignoring others; and temporary activation of long-term memory. These are examples of **executive processes,** which are processes that serve to organise and co-ordinate the functioning of the cognitive system to achieve current goals.

Miyake et al. (2000) identified three executive processes or functions overlapping partially with those of Baddeley (1996). They assumed these functions were related but separable:

* *Inhibition function*: This refers to "one's ability to deliberately inhibit dominant, automatic, or prepotent responses when necessary" (p. 55). Friedman and Miyake (2004) extended the inhibition function to include resisting distractor interference. For example, consider the **Stroop task,** on which participants have to name the colours in which words are printed. In the most difficult condition, the words are conflicting colour words (e.g., the word BLUE printed in red). In this condition, performance is slowed down and there are often many errors. The inhibition function is needed to minimise the distraction effect created by the conflicting colour word. It is useful in preventing us from thinking and behaving in habitual ways when such ways are inappropriate.
* *Shifting function*: This refers to "shifting back and forth between multiple tasks, operations, or mental sets" (p. 55). It is used when you switch attention from one task to another. Suppose, for example, you are presented with a series of trials, on each of which two numbers are presented. In one

> **KEY TERMS**
>
> **dysexecutive syndrome:** a condition in which damage to the frontal lobes causes impairments to the **central executive** component of **working memory**.
> **executive processes:** processes that organise and co-ordinate the functioning of the cognitive system to achieve current goals.
> **Stroop task:** a task in which the participant has to name the colours in which words are printed.

condition, there is task switching: on some trials you have to multiply the two numbers and on other trials you have to divide one by the other. In the other condition, there are long blocks of trials on which you always multiply the two numbers and there are other long blocks of trials on which you always divide one number by the other. Performance is slower in the task-switching condition, because attention has to be switched backwards and forwards between the two tasks. Task switching involves the shifting function, which allows us to shift attention rapidly from one task to another. This is a very useful ability in today's 24/7 world.

- *Updating function*: This refers to "updating and monitoring of working memory representations" (p. 55). It is used when you update the information you need to remember. For example, the updating function is required when participants are presented with members of various categories and have to keep track of the most recently presented member of each category. Updating is useful if you are preparing a meal consisting of several dishes or, more generally, if you are trying to cope with changing circumstances.

Evidence

Various kinds of evidence support Miyake et al.'s (2000) identification of three executive functions. First, there are the findings from their own research. They argued that most cognitive tasks involve various processes, which makes it difficult to obtain clear evidence for any single process. Miyake et al. administered several tasks to their participants and then used latent-variable analysis. This form of analysis focuses on positive correlations among tasks as the basis for identifying the common process or function involved. Thus, for example, three tasks might all involve a common process (e.g., the shifting function) but each task might also involve additional specific processes. Latent-variable analysis provides a useful way of identifying the common process. Miyake et al.

found evidence for three separable executive functions of inhibition, shifting, and monitoring, but also discovered that these functions were positively correlated with each other.

Second, Collette et al. (2005) administered several tasks designed to assess the same three executive processes, and used positron emission tomography (PET; see Glossary) to compare brain activation associated with each process. There were two main findings. First, each executive process or function was associated with activation in a different region within the prefrontal cortex. Second, all the tasks produced activation in the right intraparietal sulcus, the left superior parietal sulcus, and the left lateral prefrontal cortex. Collette et al. suggested that the right intraparietal sulcus is involved in selective attention to relevant stimuli plus the suppression of irrelevant information; the left superior parietal sulcus is involved in switching and integration processes; and the lateral prefrontal cortex is involved in monitoring and temporal organisation.

Are there executive processes or functions not included within Miyake et al.'s (2000) theory? According to Baddeley (1996), one strong contender relates to the dual-task situation, in which people have to perform two different tasks at the same time. Executive processes are often needed to co-ordinate processing on the two tasks. Functional neuroimaging studies focusing on dual-task situations have produced somewhat variable findings (see Chapter 5). However, there is sometimes much activation in prefrontal areas (e.g., dorsolateral prefrontal cortex) when people perform two tasks at the same time but not when they perform only one of the tasks on its own (e.g., Collette et al., 2005; Johnson & Zatorre, 2006). Such findings suggest that co-ordination of two tasks can involve an executive process based mainly in the prefrontal cortex.

Further support for the notion that there is an executive process involved specifically in dual-task processing was reported by Logie, Cocchini, Della Sala, and Baddeley (2004). Patients with Alzheimer's disease were compared with healthy younger and older people on digit recall and tracking tasks, the latter of which involved keeping a pen on a red oval that moved randomly. The Alzheimer's patients were much more sensitive than the healthy groups to dual-task demands, but did not differ in their ability to cope with single-task demands. These findings suggest that Alzheimer's patients have damage to a part of the brain involved in dual-task co-ordination. MacPherson, Della Sala, Logie, and Wilcock (2007) reported very similar findings using verbal memory and visuo-spatial memory tasks.

Dysexecutive syndrome

Stuss and Alexander (2007) argued that the notion of a dysexecutive syndrome is flawed because it implies that brain damage to the frontal lobes typically damages *all* central executive functions of the central executive. They accepted that patients with widespread damage to the frontal lobes have a global dys-executive syndrome. However, they claimed there are three executive processes based in different parts of the frontal lobes:

- *Task setting*: This involves planning and was defined as "the ability to set a stimulus–response relationship . . . necessary in the early stages of learning to drive a car or planning a wedding" (p. 906).
- *Monitoring*: This was defined as "the process of checking the task over time for 'quality control' and the adjustment of behaviour" (p. 909).
- *Energisation*: This involves sustained attention or concentration and was defined as "the process of initiation and sustaining of any response. . . . Without energisation . . . maintaining performance over prolonged periods will waver" (pp. 903–904).

All three executive processes are very general in that they are used across an enormous range of tasks. They are not really independent, because they are typically all used when you deal with a complex task. For example, if you have to give a speech in public, you would first plan roughly what you are going to say (task setting), concentrate through the delivery of the speech (energisation), and check that what you are saying is what you intended (monitoring).

Stuss and Alexander (2007) tested their theory of executive functions on patients having fairly specific lesions within the frontal lobes. In view of the possibility that there may be reorganisation of cognitive structures and processes following brain damage, the patients were tested within a few months of suffering brain damage. A wide range of cognitive tasks was administered to different patient groups to try to ensure that the findings would generalise.

Public speaking involves all three of Stuss and Alexander's (2007) executive functions: planning what you are going to say (task setting); concentrating on delivery (energisation); and checking that what you say is as intended (monitoring).

Stuss and Alexander found evidence for the three hypothesised processes of energisation, task setting, and monitoring. They also discovered that each process was associated with a different region within the frontal cortex. Energisation involves the superior medial region of the frontal cortex, task setting involves the left lateral frontal region, and monitoring involves the right lateral frontal region. Thus, for example, patients with damage to the right lateral frontal region generally fail to detect the errors they make while performing a task and so do not adjust their performance.

Why do the processes identified by Stuss and Alexander (2007) differ from those identified by Miyake et al. (2000)? The starting point in trying to answer that question is to remember that Stuss and Alexander based their conclusions on studies with brain-damaged patients, whereas Miyake et al. studied only healthy individuals. Nearly all executive tasks involve common processes (e.g., energisation, task setting, monitoring). These common processes are positively correlated in healthy individuals and so do not emerge clearly as separate processes. However, the differences among energisation, task setting, and monitoring become much clearer when we consider patients with very specific frontal lesions. It remains for future research to show in more detail how the views of Stuss and Alexander and of Miyake et al. can be reconciled.

Evaluation

There has been real progress in understanding the workings of the central executive. The central executive consists of various related but separable executive processes. There is accumulating evidence that inhibition, updating, shifting, and dual-task co-ordination may be four major executive processes. It has become clear that the notion of a dysexecutive syndrome is misleading in that it suggests there is a *single* pattern of impairment. Various executive processes associated with different parts of frontal cortex are involved.

Two issues require more research. First, the executive processes suggested by behavioural and functional neuroimaging studies on healthy individuals do not correspond precisely with those suggested by studies on patients with damage to the frontal cortex. We have speculated on the reasons for this, but solid evidence is needed. Second, while we have emphasised the differences among the major executive processes or functions, there is plentiful evidence suggesting that these processes are fairly closely related to each other. The reasons for this remain somewhat unclear.

Episodic buffer

Baddeley (2000) added a fourth component to the working memory model. This is the **episodic buffer,** in which information from various sources (the phonological loop, the visuo-spatial sketchpad, and long-term memory) can be integrated and stored briefly. According to Repovš and Baddeley (2006, p. 15), the episodic buffer, "is episodic by virtue of holding information that is integrated from a range of systems including other working memory components and long-term memory into coherent complex structures: scenes or episodes. It is a buffer in that it serves as an intermediary between subsystems with different codes, which it combines into multi-dimensional representations."

In view of the likely processing demands involved in integrating information from different modalities, Baddeley (2000, 2007) suggested that there would be close links between the episodic buffer and the central executive. If so, we would expect to find prefrontal activation on tasks involving the episodic buffer, because there are associations between use of the central executive and prefrontal cortex.

KEY TERM

episodic buffer: a component of **working memory** that is used to integrate and to store briefly information from the **phonological loop**, the **visuo-spatial sketchpad**, and **long-term memory**.

Why did Baddeley add the episodic buffer to the working memory model? The original version of the model was limited because its various components were too separate in their functioning. For example, Chincotta, Underwood, Abd Ghani, Papadopoulou, and Wresinki (1999) studied memory span for Arabic numerals and digit words, finding that participants used both verbal and visual encoding while performing the task. This suggests that participants combined information from the phonological loop *and* the visuo-spatial sketchpad. Since these two stores are separate, this combination and integration process must take place elsewhere, and the episodic buffer fits the bill.

Another finding hard to explain within the original working memory model is that, in immediate recall, people can recall about five unrelated words but up to 16 words presented in sentences (Baddeley, Vallar, & Wilson, 1987). The notion of an episodic buffer is useful, because this is where information from long-term memory could be integrated with information from the phonological loop and the visuo-spatial sketchpad.

Evidence

Zhang et al. (2004) obtained evidence consistent with the notion that the episodic buffer is often used in conjunction with the central executive. Their participants had to recall a mixture of digits and visual locations, a task assumed to require the episodic buffer. As predicted, there was greater right prefrontal activation in this condition than one in which digits and visual locations were not mixed during presentation.

Baddeley and Wilson (2002) provided support for the notion of an episodic buffer. They pointed out that it had generally been assumed that good immediate prose recall involves the ability to store some of the relevant information in long-term memory. According to this view, amnesic patients with very impaired long-term memory should have very poor immediate prose recall. In contrast, Baddeley and Wilson argued that the ability to exhibit good immediate prose recall depends on two factors: (1) the capacity of the episodic buffer; and (2) an efficiently

functioning central executive creating and maintaining information in the buffer. According to this argument, even severely amnesic patients with practically no delayed recall of prose should have good immediate prose recall provided they have an efficient central executive. As predicted, immediate prose recall was much better in amnesics having little deficit in executive functioning than in those with a severe executive deficit.

Other studies suggest that the episodic buffer can operate independently of the central executive. Gooding, Isaac, and Mayes (2005) failed to replicate Baddeley and Wilson's (2002) findings in a similar study. Among their amnesic patients (who were less intelligent than those studied by Baddeley and Wilson), there was a non-significant correlation between immediate prose recall and measures of executive functioning. It is possible that using the central executive to maintain reasonable immediate prose recall requires high levels of intelligence. Berlingeri et al. (2008) found in patients with Alzheimer's disease that 60% of those having almost intact performance on tasks requiring the central executive nevertheless had no immediate prose recall. This finding also casts doubt on the importance of the central executive on tasks involving the episodic buffer.

Rudner, Fransson, Ingvar, Nyberg, and Ronnberg (2007) used a task involving combining representations based on sign language and on speech. This episodic buffer task was not associated with prefrontal activation, but was associated with activation in the left hippocampus. This is potentially important because the hippocampus plays a key role in binding together different kinds of information in memory (see Chapter 7). An association between use of the episodic buffer and the hippocampus was also reported by Berlingeri et al. (2008). They found among patients with Alzheimer's disease that those with most atrophy of the anterior part of the hippocampus did worst on immediate prose recall.

Evaluation

The addition of the episodic buffer to the working memory model has proved of value. The original three components of the model were too separate from each other and from long-term memory to account for our ability to combine different kinds of information (e.g., visual, verbal) on short-term memory tasks. The episodic buffer helps to provide the "glue" to integrate information within working memory.

Some progress has been made in tracking down the brain areas associated with the episodic buffer. The hippocampus is of central importance in binding and integrating information during learning, and so it is unsurprising that it is associated with use of the episodic buffer. The evidence suggests that use of the episodic buffer is sometimes associated with the central executive, but we do not know as yet what determines whether there is an association.

It is harder to carry out research on the episodic buffer than on the phonological loop or the visuo-spatial sketchpad. We have to use complex tasks to study the episodic buffer because it involves the complicated integration of information. In contrast, it is possible to devise relatively simple tasks to study the phonological loop or the visuo-spatial sketchpad. In addition, there are often close connections between the episodic buffer and the other components of the working memory system. That often makes it difficult to distinguish clearly between the episodic buffer and the other components.

Overall evaluation

The working memory model has several advantages over the short-term memory store proposed by Atkinson and Shiffrin (1968). First, the working memory system is concerned with both active processing and transient storage of information, and so is involved in all complex cognitive tasks, such as language comprehension (see Chapter 10) and reasoning (see Chapter 14).

Second, the working memory model explains the partial deficits of short-term memory observed in brain-damaged patients. If brain damage affects only one of the three components of working memory, then selective deficits on short-term memory tasks would be expected.

Third, the working memory model incorporates verbal rehearsal as an optional process within the phonological loop. This is more realistic than the enormous significance of rehearsal within the multi-store model of Atkinson and Shiffrin (1968).

What are the limitations of the working memory model? First, it has proved difficult to identify the number and nature of the main executive processes associated with the central executive. For example, disagreements on the nature of executive functions have emerged from approaches based on latent-variable analyses of executive tasks (Miyake et al., 2000) and on data from brain-damaged patients (Stuss & Alexander, 2007). One reason for the lack of clarity is that most complex tasks involve the use of more than one executive process, making it hard to establish the contribution that each has made.

Second, we need more research on the relationship between the episodic buffer and the other components of the working memory system. As yet, we lack a detailed account of how the episodic buffer integrates information from the other components and from long-term memory.

LEVELS OF PROCESSING

What determines how well we remember information over the long term? According to Craik and Lockhart (1972), what is crucial is how we process that information during learning. They argued in their levels-of-processing approach that attentional and perceptual processes at learning determine what information is stored in long-term memory. There are various levels of processing, ranging from shallow or physical analysis of a stimulus (e.g., detecting specific letters in words) to deep or semantic analysis; the greater the extent to which meaning is processed, the deeper the level of processing. They implied that processing nearly always proceeds in a serial fashion from shallow sensory levels to deeper semantic ones. However, they subsequently (Lockhart & Craik, 1990) admitted that that was an oversimplification and that processing is often parallel.

Craik and Lockhart's (1972) main theoretical assumptions were as follows:

- The level or depth of processing of a stimulus has a large effect on its memorability.
- Deeper levels of analysis produce more elaborate, longer lasting and stronger memory traces than do shallow levels of analysis.

Craik and Lockhart (1972) disagreed with Atkinson and Shiffrin's (1968) assumption that rehearsal *always* improves long-term memory. They argued that rehearsal involving simply repeating previous analyses (**maintenance rehearsal**) does not enhance long-term memory. In fact, however, maintenance rehearsal typically has a rather small (but beneficial) effect on long-term memory (Glenberg, Smith, & Green, 1977).

Evidence

Numerous studies support the main assumptions of the levels-of-processing approach. For example, Craik and Tulving (1975) compared recognition performance as a function of the task performed at learning:

- *Shallow graphemic task*: decide whether each word is in uppercase or lowercase letters.
- *Intermediate phonemic task*: decide whether each word rhymes with a target word.
- *Deep semantic task*: decide whether each word fits a sentence containing a blank.

Depth of processing had impressive effects on memory performance, with performance more than three times higher with deep than with shallow processing. In addition, performance was generally much better for words associated with "Yes" responses on the processing task than those associated with "No" responses. Craik and Tulving used incidental learning – the participants did not realise at the time of learning that there would be a memory test. They argued that the nature of task processing

rather than the intention to learn is crucial.

Craik and Tulving (1975) assumed that the semantic task involved deep processing and the uppercase/lowercase task involved shallow processing. However, it would be preferable to assess depth. One approach is to use brain-imaging to identify the brain regions involved in different kinds of processing. For example, Wagner, Maril, Bjork, and Schacter (2001) found there was more activation in the left inferior frontal lobe and the left lateral and medial temporal lobe during semantic than perceptual processing. However, the findings have been somewhat inconsistent. Park and Rugg (2008b) presented word pairs and asked participants to rate the extent to which they shared a semantic theme (deep processing) or sounded similar (shallow processing). Memory was better following semantic processing than phonological processing. However, successful memory performance was associated with activation in the left ventrolateral prefrontal cortex regardless of the encoding task. This finding suggests that there is no simple relationship between processing task and patterns of brain activation.

Craik and Tulving (1975) argued that elaboration of processing (i.e., the amount of processing of a particular kind) is important as well as depth of processing. Participants were presented on each trial with a word and a sentence containing a blank, and decided whether the word fitted into the blank space. Elaboration was manipulated by using simple (e.g., "She cooked the ____") and complex "The great bird swooped down and carried off the struggling ____") sentence frames. Cued recall was twice as high for words accompanying complex sentences.

Long-term memory depends on the *kind* of elaboration as well as the *amount*. Bransford, Franks, Morris, and Stein (1979) presented either minimally elaborated similes (e.g., "A mosquito

KEY TERM

maintenance rehearsal: processing that involves simply repeating analyses which have already been carried out.

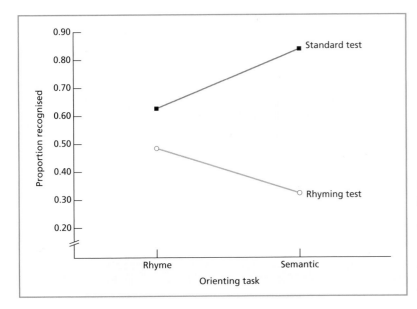

Figure 6.12 Mean proportion of words recognised as a function of orienting task (semantic or rhyme) and of the type of recognition task (standard or rhyming). Data are from Morris et al. (1977), and are from positive trials only.

is like a doctor because they both draw blood") or multiply elaborated similes (e.g., "A mosquito is like a raccoon because they both have heads, legs, jaws"). Recall was much better for the minimally elaborated similes than the multiply elaborated ones, indicating that the nature of semantic elaborations needs to be considered.

Eysenck (1979) argued that distinctive or unique memory traces are easier to retrieve than those resembling other memory traces. Eysenck and Eysenck (1980) tested this notion using nouns having irregular grapheme–phoneme correspondence (i.e., words not pronounced in line with pronunciation rules, such as "comb" with its silent "b"). In one condition, participants pronounced these nouns as if they had regular grapheme–phoneme correspondence, thus producing distinctive memory traces. Other nouns were simply pronounced normally, thus producing non-distinctive memory traces. Recognition memory was much better in the former condition, indicating the importance of distinctiveness.

Morris, Bransford, and Franks (1977) argued that stored information is remembered only if it is of *relevance* to the memory test. Participants answered semantic or shallow (rhyme) questions for lists of words. Memory was tested by a standard recognition test, in which list and non-list words were presented, or by a rhyming recognition test. On this latter test, participants selected words that rhymed with list words: the words themselves were *not* presented. With the standard recognition test, the predicted superiority of deep over shallow processing was obtained (see Figure 6.12). However, the *opposite* result was reported with the rhyme test, which disproves the notion that deep processing always enhances long-term memory.

Morris et al. (1977) argued that their findings supported transfer-appropriate processing theory. According to this theory, different kinds of learning lead learners to acquire different kinds of information about a stimulus. Whether the stored information leads to subsequent retention depends on the *relevance* of that information to the memory test. For example, storing semantic information is essentially irrelevant when the memory test requires the identification of words rhyming with list words. What is required for this kind of test is shallow rhyme information. Further evidence supporting transfer-appropriate theory is discussed later in the chapter.

Nearly all the early research on levels-of-processing theory used standard memory tests (e.g., recall, recognition) involving explicit memory (conscious recollection). It is also important to consider the effects of level of processing on implicit memory (memory not involving conscious recollection; see Chapter 7). Challis, Velichkovsky, and Craik (1996) asked participants to learn word lists under various conditions: judging whether the word was related to them (self-judgement); simple intentional learning; judging whether it referred to a living thing (living judgement); counting the number of syllables (syllable task); or counting the number of letters of a certain type (letter type). The order of these tasks reflects decreasing depth of processing. There were four explicit memory tests (recognition, free recall, semantic cued recall involving a word related in meaning to

a list word, and graphemic cued recall involving a word with similar spelling to a list word), and two implicit memory tests. One of these tests involved answering general knowledge questions in which the answers corresponded to list words, and the other involved completing word fragments (e.g., c _ pp _ _).

For the four explicit memory tests, there was an overall tendency for performance to increase with increasing depth of processing, but there are some hard-to-interpret differences as well (see Figure 6.13). We turn now to the implicit memory tests. The word-fragment test failed to show any levels-of-processing effect, whereas level of processing had a significant

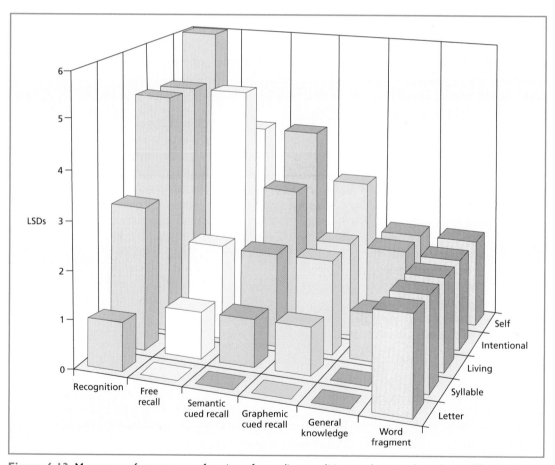

Figure 6.13 Memory performance as a function of encoding conditions and retrieval conditions. The findings are presented in units of least significant differences (LSDs) relative to baseline performance, meaning that columns of differing heights are significantly different. Reprinted from Roediger (2008), based on data in Challis et al. (1996), Copyright © 1996, with permission from Elsevier.

effect on the general knowledge memory test. The general knowledge memory test is a conceptual implicit memory test based on meaning. As a result, it seems reasonable that it would be affected by level of processing, even though the effects were much smaller than with explicit memory tests. In contrast, the word-fragment test is a perceptual implicit memory test not based on meaning, which helps to explain why there was no levels-of-processing effect with this test.

In sum, levels-of-processing effects were generally greater in explicit memory than implicit memory. In addition, there is some support for the predictions of levels-of-processing theory with all memory tests other than the word-fragment test. Overall, the findings are too complex to be explained readily by levels-of-processing theory.

Evaluation

Craik and Lockhart (1972) argued correctly that processes during learning have a major impact on subsequent long-term memory. This may sound obvious, but surprisingly little research before 1972 focused on learning processes and their effects on memory. Another strength is the central assumption that perception, attention, and memory are all closely interconnected, and that learning and remembering are by-products of perception, attention, and comprehension. In addition, the approach led to the identification of elaboration and distinctiveness of processing as important factors in learning and memory.

The levels-of-processing approach possesses several limitations. First, it is generally difficult to assess processing depth. Second, Craik and Lockhart (1972) greatly underestimated the importance of the retrieval environment in determining memory performance. As Morris et al. (1977) showed, the typical levels effect can be reversed if stored semantic information is irrelevant to the requirements of the memory test. Third, long-term memory is influenced by depth of processing, elaboration of processing, and distinctiveness of processing. However, the relative importance of these factors (and how they are inter-related) remains unclear. Fourth, findings from amnesic patients (see Chapter 7) cannot be explained by the levels-of-processing approach. Most amnesic patients have good semantic or deep processing skills, but their long-term memory is extremely poor, probably because they have major problems with consolidation (fixing of newly learned information in long-term memory) (Craik, 2002; see Chapter 7). Fifth, Craik and Lockhart (1972) did not explain precisely *why* deep processing is so effective, and it is not clear why there is a much smaller levels-of-processing effect in implicit than in explicit memory.

IMPLICIT LEARNING

Do you think you could learn something without being aware of what you have learned? It sounds improbable. Even if we do acquire information without any conscious awareness, it might seem somewhat pointless and wasteful – if we do not realise we have learned something, it seems unlikely that we are going to make much use of it. What we are considering here is **implicit learning**, which is, "learning without conscious awareness of having learned" (French & Cleeremans, 2002, p. xvii). Implicit learning has been contrasted with explicit learning, which involves conscious awareness of what has been learned.

Cleeremans and Jiménez (2002, p. 20) provided a fuller definition of implicit learning: "Implicit learning is the process through which we become sensitive to certain regularities in the environment (1) in the absence of intention to learn about these regularities, (2) in the absence of awareness that one is learning, and (3) in such a way that the resulting knowledge

KEY TERM

implicit learning: learning complex information without the ability to provide conscious recollection of what has been learned.

Implicit learning is "learning without conscious awareness of having learned". Bike riding is an example of implicit learning in which there is no clear conscious awareness of what has been learned.

is difficult to express." You probably possess skills that are hard to express in words. For example, it is notoriously difficult to express what we know about riding a bicycle.

There are clear similarities between implicit learning and implicit memory, which is memory not depending on conscious recollection (see Chapter 7). You may wonder why implicit learning and implicit memory are not discussed together. There are three reasons. First, there are some differences between implicit learning and implicit memory. As Buchner and Wippich (1998) pointed out, implicit learning refers to "the [incidental] acquisition of knowledge about the structural properties of the relations between [usually more than two] objects or events." In contrast, implicit memory refers to "situations in which effects of prior experiences can be observed despite the fact that the participants are not instructed to relate their current performance to a learning episode" (Buchner & Wippich, 1998). Second, studies of implicit learning have typically used relatively complex, novel stimulus materials, whereas most studies of implicit memory have used simple, familiar stimulus materials. Third, relatively few researchers have considered the relations between implicit learning and implicit memory.

How do the systems involved in implicit learning differ from those involved in explicit learning and memory? Reber (1993) proposed five such characteristics (none has been established definitively):

- *Robustness*: Implicit systems are relatively unaffected by disorders (e.g., amnesia) affecting explicit systems.
- *Age independence*: Implicit learning is little influenced by age or developmental level.
- *Low variability*: There are smaller individual differences in implicit learning and memory than in explicit learning and memory.
- *IQ independence*: Performance on implicit tasks is relatively unaffected by IQ.
- *Commonality of process*: Implicit systems are common to most species.

We can identify three main types of research on implicit learning. First, there are studies to see whether healthy participants can learn fairly complex material in the absence of conscious awareness of what they have learned. According to Reber (1993), individual differences in such learning should depend relatively little on IQ. It is often assumed that implicit learning makes minimal demands on attentional resources. If so, the requirement to perform an additional attentionally-demanding task at the same time should not impair implicit learning.

Second, there are brain-imaging studies. If implicit learning depends on different cognitive processes to explicit learning, the brain areas associated with implicit learning should differ from those associated with explicit learning. More specifically, brain areas associated with conscious experience and attentional control (e.g., parts of the prefrontal cortex) should be much less activated during implicit learning than explicit learning.

Third, there are studies on brain-damaged patients, mostly involving amnesic patients having severe problems with long-term memory. Amnesic patients typically have relatively intact implicit memory even though their explicit memory is greatly impaired (see Chapter 7). If amnesic patients have intact implicit learning but impaired explicit learning, this would provide evidence that the two types of learning are very different.

You might imagine it would be relatively easy to decide whether implicit learning has occurred – we simply ask participants to perform a complex task without instructing them to engage in deliberate learning. Afterwards, they indicate their conscious awareness of what they have learned. Implicit learning has been demonstrated if learning occurs in the absence of conscious awareness of the nature of that learning. Alas, there are several reasons why participants fail to report conscious awareness of what they have learned. For example, there is the "retrospective problem" (Shanks & St. John, 1994): participants may be consciously aware of what they are learning at the time, but have forgotten it when questioned at the end of the experiment. Shanks and St. John proposed two criteria for implicit learning to be demonstrated:

- *Information criterion*: The information participants are asked to provide on the awareness test must be the information responsible for the improved level of performance.
- *Sensitivity criterion*: "We must be able to show that our test of awareness is sensitive to all of the relevant knowledge" (p. 374). People may be consciously aware of more task-relevant knowledge than appears on an insensitive awareness test, leading us to underestimate their consciously accessible knowledge.

Complex learning

Much early research on implicit learning involved artificial grammar learning. On this task, participants initially memorise meaningless letter strings (e.g., PVPXVPS; TSXXTVV). After that, they are told that the memorised letter strings all follow the rules of an artificial grammar, but are not told the nature of these rules. Next, the participants classify *novel* strings as grammatical or ungrammatical. Finally, they describe the rules of the artificial grammar. Participants typically perform significantly above chance level on the classification task, but cannot describe the grammatical rules (e.g., Reber, 1967). Such findings are less impressive than they appear. As several researchers have found (e.g., Channon, Shanks, Johnstone, Vakili, Chin, & Sinclair, 2002), participants' decisions on the grammaticality of letter strings do *not* depend on knowledge of grammatical rules. Instead, participants classify letter strings as grammatical when they share letter pairs with the letter strings memorised initially and as ungrammatical when they do not. Thus, above-chance performance depends on conscious awareness of two-letter fragments, and provides little or no evidence of implicit learning.

The most commonly used implicit learning task involves serial reaction time. On each trial, a stimulus appears at one out of several locations on a computer screen, and participants respond rapidly with the response key corresponding to its location. There is typically a complex, repeating sequence over trials in the various stimulus locations, but participants are not told this. Towards the end of the experiment, there is typically a block of trials conforming to a novel sequence, but this information is not given to participants. Participants speed up during the course of the experiment but respond much slower during the novel sequence (see Shanks, 2005, for a review). When questioned at the end of the experiment, participants usually show no conscious awareness that there was a repeating sequence or pattern in the stimuli presented to them.

One strength of the serial reaction time task is that the repeating sequence (which is crucial to the demonstration of implicit learning) is incidental to the explicit task of responding to the stimuli as rapidly as possible. However, we need to satisfy the information and sensitivity criteria (described above) with this task. It seems reasonable to make the awareness test very similar to the learning task, as was done by Howard and Howard (1992). An asterisk appeared in one of four locations on a screen, under each of which was a key. The task was to press the key corresponding to the position of the asterisk as rapidly as possible. Participants showed clear evidence of learning the underlying sequence by responding faster and faster to the asterisk. However, when given the awareness test of predicting where the asterisk would appear next, their performance was at chance level. These findings suggest there was implicit learning – learning occurred in the absence of conscious awareness of what had been learned.

Contrary evidence that participants have some conscious awareness of what they have learned on a serial reaction time task was reported by Wilkinson and Shanks (2004). Participants were given either 1500 trials (15 blocks) or 4500 trials (45 blocks) on the task and showed strong evidence of sequence learning. Then they were told there was a repeated sequence in the stimuli, following which they were presented on each of 12 trials with part of the sequence under one of two conditions. In the *inclusion* condition, they guessed the next location in the sequence. In the *exclusion* condition, they were told they should avoid guessing the next location in the sequence. If sequence knowledge is wholly implicit, then performance should not differ between the inclusion and exclusion conditions because participants would be unable to control how they used their sequence knowledge. In contrast, if it is partly explicit, then participants should be able to exert intentional control over their sequence knowledge. If so, the guesses generated in the inclusion condition should be more likely to conform to the repeated sequence than those in the exclusion condition. The findings indicated that explicit knowledge was acquired on the serial reaction time task (see Figure 6.14).

Similar findings were reported by Destrebecqz et al. (2005) in another study using the serial reaction time task. The interval of time between the participant's response to one stimulus and the presentation of the next one was either 0 ms or 250 ms, it being assumed that explicit learning would be more likely with the longer interval. Participants responded progressively faster over trials with both response-to-stimulus intervals. As Wilkinson and Shanks (2004) had done, they used inclusion and exclusion conditions. Participants' responses were significantly closer

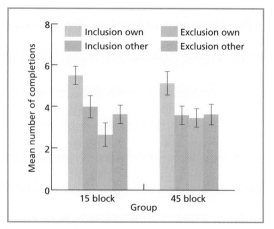

Figure 6.14 Mean number of completions (guessed locations) corresponding to the trained sequence (own) or the untrained sequence (other) in inclusion and exclusion conditions as a function of number of trials (15 vs. 45 blocks). From Wilkinson and Shanks (2004). Copyright © 2004 American Psychological Association. Reproduced with permission.

to the training sequence in the inclusion condition than in the exclusion condition, suggesting that some explicit learning occurred, especially when the response-to-stimulus interval was long. In addition, as discussed below, brain-imaging findings from this study suggested that explicit learning occurred.

If the serial reaction time task genuinely involves implicit learning, performance on that task might well be unaffected by the requirement to perform a second, attentionally-demanding task at the same time. This prediction was tested by Shanks, Rowland, and Ranger (2005). Four different target stimuli were presented across trials, and the main task was to respond rapidly to the location at which a target was presented. Half the participants performed only this task, and the remainder also carried out the attentionally-demanding task of counting targets. Participants with the additional task performed much more slowly than those with no additional task, and also showed significantly inferior sequence learning. Thus, attentional resources were needed for effective learning of the sequence on the serial reaction time task, which casts doubt on the notion that such learning is implicit. In addition, both groups of participants had significantly more accurate performance under inclusion than exclusion instructions, further suggesting the presence of explicit learning.

As mentioned above, Reber (1993) assumed that individual differences in intelligence have less effect on implicit learning than on explicit learning. Gebauer and Mackintosh (2007) carried out a thorough study using various implicit learning tasks (e.g., artificial grammar learning; serial reaction time). These tasks were given under standard implicit instructions or with explicit rule discovery instructions (i.e., indicating explicitly that there were rules to be discovered). The mean correlation between implicit task performance and intelligence was only +0.03, whereas it was +0.16 between explicit task performance and intelligence. This supports the hypothesis. It is especially important that intelligence (which is positively associated with performance on the great majority of cognitive tasks) failed to predict implicit learning performance.

Brain-imaging studies

Different areas of the brain should be activated during implicit and explicit learning if they are genuinely different. Conscious awareness is associated with activation in many brain regions, but the main ones are the anterior cingulate and the dorsolateral prefrontal cortex (Dehaene & Naccache, 2001; see Chapter 16). Accordingly, these areas should be more active during explicit than implicit learning. In contrast, it has often been assumed that the striatum is associated with implicit learning (Destrebecqz et al., 2005). The **striatum** is part of the basal ganglia; it is located in the interior areas of the cerebral hemispheres and the upper region of the brainstem.

Functional neuroimaging studies have provided limited support for the above predictions. Grafton, Hazeltine, and Ivry (1995) found that explicit learning was associated with activation in the anterior cingulate, regions in the parietal cortex involved in working memory, and areas in the parietal cortex concerned with voluntary

attention. Aizenstein et al. (2004) found that there was greater activation in the prefrontal cortex and anterior cingulate during explicit rather than implicit learning. However, they did not find any clear evidence that the striatum was more activated during implicit than explicit learning.

Destrebecqz et al. (2005) pointed out that most so-called explicit or implicit learning tasks probably involve a mixture of explicit and implicit learning. As mentioned before, they used inclusion and exclusion conditions with the serial reaction time task to distinguish clearly between the explicit and implicit components of learning. Activation in the striatum was associated with the implicit component of learning, and the mesial prefrontal cortex and anterior cingulate were associated with the explicit component.

In sum, failure to discover clear differences in patterns of brain activation between explicit and implicit learning can occur because the tasks used are not pure measures of these two forms of learning. It is no coincidence that the study distinguishing most clearly between explicit and implicit learning (Destrebecqz et al., 2005) is also the one producing the greatest support for the hypothesised associations of prefrontal cortex with explicit learning and the striatum with implicit learning.

Brain-damaged patients

As discussed in Chapter 7, amnesic patients typically perform very poorly on tests of explicit memory (involving conscious recollection) but often perform as well as healthy individuals on tests of implicit memory (on which conscious recollection is not needed). The notion that separate learning systems underlie implicit learning and explicit learning would be supported

---

KEY TERM

striatum: it forms part of the basal ganglia of the brain and is located in the upper part of the brainstem and the inferior part of the cerebral hemispheres.

if amnesic patients showed intact levels of implicit learning combined with impaired explicit learning. Explicit learning in amnesics is often severely impaired, but amnesics' performance on tasks allegedly involving implicit learning is variable (see Vandenberghe, Schmidt, Fery, & Cleeremans, 2006, for a review). For example, Knowlton, Ramus, and Squire (1992) found that amnesics performed as well as healthy controls on an implicit test on which participants distinguished between grammatical and ungrammatical letter strings (63% versus 67% correct, respectively). However, they performed significantly worse than the controls on an explicit test (62% versus 72%, respectively).

Meulemans and Van der Linden (2003) pointed out that amnesics' performance on Knowlton et al.'s (1992) implicit test may have depended on explicit fragment knowledge (e.g., pairs of letters found together). Accordingly, they used an artificial grammar learning task in which fragment knowledge could not influence performance on the test of implicit learning. They also used a test of explicit learning in which participants wrote down ten letter strings they regarded as grammatical. The amnesic patients performed as well as the healthy controls on implicit learning. However, their performance was much worse than that of the controls on explicit learning.

There is evidence of implicit learning in amnesic patients in studies on the serial reaction time task. The most thorough such study was carried out by Vandenberghe et al. (2006). Amnesic patients and healthy controls were given two versions of the task: (1) deterministic sequence (fixed repeating sequence); and (2) probabilistic sequence (repeating sequence with some deviations). The healthy controls showed clear evidence of learning with both sequences. The use of inclusion and exclusion instructions indicated that healthy controls showed explicit learning with the deterministic sequence but not with the probabilistic one. The amnesic patients showed limited learning of the deterministic sequence but not of the probabilistic sequence. Their performance was comparable with inclusion and exclusion instructions, indicating that this learning was implicit.

Earlier we discussed the hypothesis that the striatum is of major importance in implicit learning. Patients with Parkinson's disease (the symptoms of which include limb tremor and muscle rigidity) have damage to the striatum, and so we could predict that they would have impaired implicit learning. The evidence generally supports that prediction (see Chapter 7 for a fuller discussion). Siegert, Taylor, Weatherall, and Abernethy (2006) carried out a meta-analysis of six studies investigating the performance of patients with Parkinson's disease on the serial reaction time task. Skill learning on this task was consistently impaired in the patients relative to healthy controls. Wilkinson and Jahanshahi (2007) obtained similar findings with patients having Parkinson's disease using a different version of the serial reaction time task. In addition, they reported convincing evidence that patients' learning was implicit (i.e., lacked conscious awareness). The patients performed at chance level when trying to recognise old sequences. In addition, their knowledge was not under intentional control, as was shown by their inability to suppress the expression of what they had learned when instructed to do so.

We have seen that there is some evidence that amnesic patients have poor explicit learning combined with reasonably intact implicit learning. We would have evidence of a double dissociation (see Glossary) if patients with Parkinson's disease had poor implicit learning combined with intact explicit learning. This pattern has occasionally been reported with patients in the early stages of the disease (e.g., Saint-Cyr, Taylor, & Lang, 1988). However, Parkinson's patients generally have impaired explicit learning, especially when the learning task is fairly complex and involves organisation of the to-be-learned information (see Vingerhoets, Vermeule, & Santens, 2005, for a review).

Evaluation

There has been a considerable amount of recent research on implicit learning involving three different approaches: behavioural studies on healthy participants; functional neuroimaging studies on healthy participants; and studies on amnesic patients. Much of that research suggests that implicit learning should be distinguished from explicit learning. Some of the most convincing evidence has come from studies on brain-damaged patients. For example, Vanderberghe et al. (2006) found, using the serial reaction time task, that amnesic patients' learning seemed to be almost entirely at the implicit level. Other convincing evidence has come from functional neuroimaging studies. There is accumulating evidence that explicit learning is associated with the prefrontal cortex and the anterior cingulate, whereas implicit learning is associated with the striatum.

What are the limitations of research on implicit learning? First, it has proved hard to devise tests of awareness that can detect *all* the task-relevant knowledge of which people have conscious awareness. Second, some explicit learning is typically involved on the artificial grammar learning task and the serial reaction time task (e.g., Destrebecqz et al., 2005; Shanks et al., 2005; Wilkinson & Shanks, 2004). Third, the brain areas underlying what are claimed to be explicit and implicit learning are not always clearly different (e.g., Schendan, Searl, Melrose, & Stern, 2003).

What conclusions can we draw about implicit learning? It is too often assumed that finding that explicit learning plays some part in explaining performance on a given task means that *no* implicit learning occurred. It is very likely that the extent to which learners are consciously aware of what they are learning varies from individual to individual and from task to task. One possibility is that we have greatest conscious awareness when the representations of what we have learned are stable, distinctive, and strong, and least when those representations are unstable, non-distinctive, and weak (Kelly, 2003). All kinds of intermediate position are also possible.

Sun, Zhang, and Mathews (2009) argued that learning nearly always involves implicit and explicit aspects, and that the balance between these two types of learning changes over time. On some tasks, there is initial implicit learning based on the performance of successful actions followed by explicit learning of the rules apparently explaining why those actions are successful.

On other tasks, learners start with explicit rules and then engage in implicit learning based on observing their actions directed by those rules.

THEORIES OF FORGETTING

Forgetting was first studied in detail by Hermann Ebbinghaus (1885/1913). He carried out numerous studies with himself as the only participant (not a recommended approach!). Ebbinghaus initially learned a list of nonsense syllables lacking meaning. At various intervals of time, he recalled the nonsense syllables. He then re-learned the list. His basic measure of forgetting was the **savings method**, which involved seeing the reduction in the number of trials during re-learning compared to original learning. Forgetting was very rapid over the first hour after learning but slowed down considerably after that (see Figure 6.15). These findings suggest that the forgetting function is approximately logarithmic.

Rubin and Wenzel (1996) analysed the forgetting functions taken from 210 data sets involving numerous memory tests. They found (in line with Ebbinghaus (1885/1913) that a logarithmic function most consistently described the rate of forgetting (for alternative possibilities, see Wixted, 2004). The major exception was autobiographical memory, which showed slower forgetting. One of the possible consequences of a logarithmic forgetting function is Jost's (1897) law: if two memory traces differ in age but are of equal strength, the older one will decay more slowly over any given time period.

Most studies of forgetting have focused on declarative or explicit memory (see Chapter 7), which involves conscious recollection of

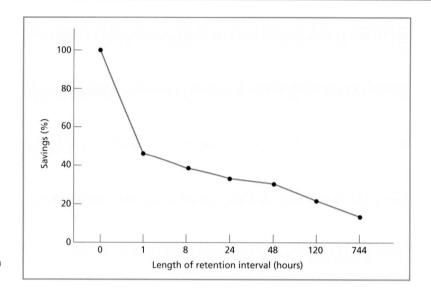

Figure 6.15 Forgetting over time as indexed by reduced savings. Data from Ebbinghaus (1885/1913).

previously learned information. Comparisons of forgetting rates in explicit and implicit memory (in which conscious recollection is not required) suggest that forgetting is slower in implicit memory. Tulving, Schacter, and Stark (1982) carried out a study in which participants initially learned a list of relatively rare words (e.g., "toboggan"). One hour or one week later, they received a test of explicit memory (recognition memory) or a word-fragment completion test of implicit memory. Word fragments (e.g., _ O _ O _ GA _) were presented and participants filled in the blanks to form a word without being told that any of the words came from the list studied previously. Recognition memory was much worse after one week than one hour, whereas word-fragment completion performance was unchanged.

Dramatic evidence of long-lasting implicit memories was reported by Mitchell (2006). His participants tried to identify pictures from fragments having seen some of them before in a laboratory experiment 17 years previously. They did significantly better with the pictures seen before; thus providing strong evidence for implicit memory after all those years! In contrast, there was rather little explicit memory for the experiment 17 years earlier. A 36-year-old male participant confessed, "I'm sorry – I don't really remember this experiment at all."

In what follows, we will be discussing the major theories of forgetting in turn. As you read about these theories, bear in mind that they are not mutually exclusive. Thus, it is entirely possible that all the theories discussed identify some of the factors responsible for forgetting.

Interference theory

The dominant approach to forgetting during much of the twentieth century was interference theory. According to this theory, our ability to remember what we are currently learning can be disrupted (interfered with) by previous learning (proactive interference) or by future learning (retroactive interference) (see Figure 6.16).

Interference theory dates back to Hugo Munsterberg in the nineteenth century. For many years, he kept his pocket-watch in one particular pocket. When he moved it to a different pocket, he often fumbled about in confusion when asked for the time. He had learned an association between the stimulus, "What time is it, Hugo?", and the response of removing the watch from his pocket. Later on, the stimulus remained the same. However, a different response was now associated with it, thus causing proactive interference.

Research using methods such as those shown in Figure 6.16 revealed that proactive

	Proactive interference		
Group	Learn	Learn	Test
Experimental	A–B (e.g. Cat–Tree)	A–C (e.g. Cat–Dirt)	A–C (e.g. Cat–Dirt)
Control	–	A–C (e.g. Cat–Dirt)	A–C (e.g. Cat–Dirt)

	Retroactive interference		
Group	Learn	Learn	Test
Experimental	A–B (e.g. Cat–Tree)	A–C (e.g. Cat–Dirt)	A–B (e.g. Cat–Tree)
Control	A–B (e.g. Cat–Tree)	–	A–B (e.g. Cat–Tree)

Note: for both proactive and retroactive interference, the experimental group exhibits interference. On the test, only the first word is supplied, and the participants must provide the second word.

Figure 6.16 Methods of testing for proactive and retroactive interference.

and retroactive interference are both maximal when two different responses are associated with the same stimulus and minimal when two different stimuli are involved (Underwood & Postman, 1960). Strong evidence of retroactive interference has been obtained in studies of eyewitness testimony in which memory of an event is interfered with by post-event information (see Chapter 8).

Proactive interference

Proactive interference can be very useful when circumstances change. For example, if you have re-arranged everything in your room, it is a real advantage to forget where your belongings used to be.

Most research on proactive interference has involved declarative or explicit memory. An exception was a study by Lustig and Hasher (2001). They used a word-fragment completion task (e.g., A _ L _ _ GY), on which participants wrote down the first appropriate word coming to mind. Participants previously exposed to words almost fitting the fragments (e.g., ANALOGY) showed evidence of proactive interference.

Jacoby, Debner, and Hay (2001) argued that proactive interference might occur for two reasons. First, it might be due to problems in retrieving the correct response (discriminability). Second, it might be due to the great strength of the incorrect response learned initially (bias or habit). Thus, we might show proactive interference because the correct response is very weak or because the incorrect response is very strong. Jacoby et al. found consistently that proactive interference was due more to strength of the incorrect first response than to discriminability.

At one time, it was assumed that individuals *passively* allow themselves to suffer from interference. Suppose you learn something but find your ability to remember it is impaired by proactive interference from something learned previously. It would make sense to adopt active strategies to minimise any interference effect. Kane and Engle (2000) argued that individuals with high working-memory capacity (correlated with intelligence) would be better able to resist proactive interference than those with low capacity. However, even they would be unable to resist proactive interference if performing an attentionally demanding task at the same time as the learning task. As predicted, the high-capacity participants with no additional task showed the least proactive interference (see Figure 6.17).

The notion that people use active control processes to reduce proactive interference has

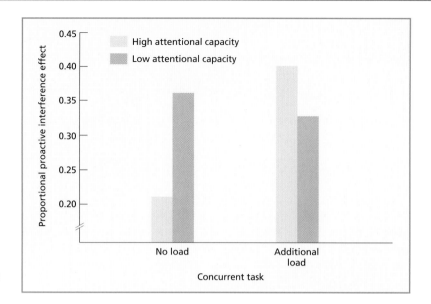

Figure 6.17 Amount of proactive interference as a function of attentional capacity (low vs. high) and concurrent task (no vs. additional load). Data from Kane and Engle (2000).

been tested in several studies using the Recent Probes task. A small set of items (target set) is presented, followed by a recognition probe. The task is to decide whether the probe is a member of the target set. On critical trials, the probe is *not* a member of the current target set but was a member of the target set used on the previous trial. There is clear evidence of proactive interference on these trials in the form of lengthened reaction times and increased error rates.

Which brain areas are of most importance on proactive interference trials with the Recent Probes task? Nee, Jonides, and Berman (2007) found that the left ventrolateral prefrontal cortex was activated on such trials. The same brain area was also activated on a directed forgetting version of the Recent Probes task (i.e., participants were told to forget some of the target set items). This suggests that left ventrolateral prefrontal cortex may play an important role in suppressing unwanted information.

Nee et al.'s (2007) study could not show that left ventrolateral prefrontal cortex actually controls the effects of proactive interference. More direct evidence was reported by Feredoes, Tononi, and Postle (2006). They administered transcranial magnetic stimulation (TMS; see Glossary) to left ventrolateral prefrontal cortex.

This produced a significant increase in the error rate on proactive interference trials, suggesting that this brain area is directly involved in attempts to control proactive interference.

Retroactive interference

Numerous laboratory studies using artificial tasks such as paired-associate learning (see Figure 6.16) have produced large retroactive interference effects. Such findings do not necessarily mean that retroactive interference is important in everyday life. However, Isurin and McDonald (2001) argued that retroactive interference explains why people forget some of their first language when acquiring a second one. Bilingual participants fluent in two languages were first presented with various pictures and the corresponding words in Russian or Hebrew. Some were then presented with the same pictures and the corresponding words in the other language. Finally, they were tested for recall of the words in the first language. There was substantial retroactive interference – recall of the first-language words became progressively worse the more learning trials there were with the second-language words.

Retroactive interference is generally greatest when the new learning resembles previous learning. However, Dewar, Cowan, and Della

Sala (2007) found retroactive interference even when no new learning occurred during the retention interval. In their experiment, participants learned a list of words and were then exposed to various tasks during the retention interval before list memory was assessed. There was significant retroactive interference even when the intervening task involved detecting differences between pictures or detecting tones. Dewar et al. concluded that retroactive interference can occur in two ways: (1) expenditure of mental effort during the retention interval; or (2) learning of material similar to the original learning material. The first cause of retroactive interference probably occurs more often than the second in everyday life.

Lustig, Konkel, and Jacoby (2004) identified two possible explanations for retroactive interference in paired-associate learning. First, there may be problems with controlled processes (active searching for the correct response). Second, there may be problems with automatic processes (high accessibility of the incorrect response). They identified the roles of these two kinds of processes by assessing retroactive interference in two different ways. One way involved direct instructions (i.e., deliberately retrieve the correct responses) and the other way involved indirect instructions (i.e., rapidly produce the first response coming to mind when presented with the cue). Lustig et al. assumed that direct instructions would lead to the use of controlled and automatic processes, whereas indirect instructions would primarily lead to the use of automatic processes.

What did Lustig et al. (2004) find? First, use of direct instructions was associated with significant retroactive interference on an immediate memory test (cued recall) but not one day later. Second, the interference effect found on the immediate test depended mainly on relatively automatic processes (i.e., accessibility of the incorrect response). Third, the disappearance of retroactive interference on the test after one day was mostly due to reduced accessibility of the incorrect responses. Thus, relatively automatic processes are of major importance in retroactive interference.

Evaluation

There is strong evidence for both proactive and retroactive interference. There has been substantial progress in understanding interference effects in recent years, mostly involving an increased focus on underlying processes. For example, automatic processes make incorrect responses accessible, and people use active control processes to minimise interference effects.

What are the limitations of interference theory? First, the emphasis has been on interference effects in declarative or explicit memory, and detailed information about interference effects in implicit memory is lacking. Second, interference theory explains why forgetting occurs but not directly why the rate of forgetting decreases over time. Third, more needs to be done to understand the brain mechanisms involved in interference and attempts to reduce interference.

Repression

One of the best-known theories of forgetting owes its origins to the bearded Austrian psychologist Sigmund Freud (1856–1939). He claimed that very threatening or traumatic memories are often unable to gain access to conscious awareness, using the term **repression** to refer to this phenomenon. According to Freud (1915/1963, p. 86), "The essence of repression lies simply in the function of rejecting and keeping something out of consciousness." However, Freud sometimes used the concept to refer merely to the inhibition of the capacity for emotional experience (Madison, 1956). Even though it is often believed that Freud regarded repression as unconscious, Erdelyi (2001) showed convincingly that Freud accepted that repression is sometimes an active

KEY TERM

repression: motivated forgetting of traumatic or other threatening events.

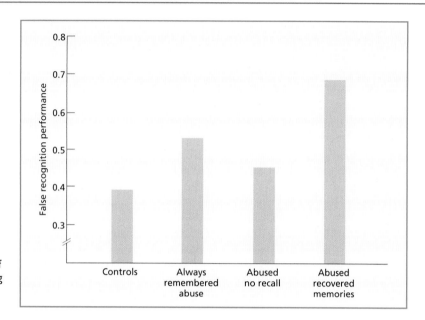

Figure 6.18 False recognition of words not presented in four groups of women with lists containing eight associates. Data from Clancy et al. (2000).

and intentional process. It is harder to test the notion of repression if it can be either unconscious or conscious.

Most evidence relating to repression is based on adult patients who have apparently recovered repressed memories of childhood sexual and/or physical abuse in adulthood. As we will see, there has been fierce controversy as to whether these recovered memories are genuine or false. Note that the controversy centres on *recovered* memories – most experts accept that continuous memories (i.e., ones constantly accessible over the years) are very likely to be genuine.

Evidence

Clancy, Schacter, McNally, and Pitman (2000) used the Deese–Roediger–McDermott paradigm, which is known to produce false memories. Participants are given lists of semantically related words and are then found to falsely "recognise" other semantically related words not actually presented. Clancy et al. compared women with recovered memories of childhood sexual abuse with women who believed they had been sexually abused but could not recall the abuse, women who had always remem-

bered being abused, and female controls. Women reporting recovered memories showed higher levels of false recognition than any other group (see Figure 6.18), suggesting that these women might be susceptible to developing false memories.

Lief and Fetkewicz (1995) found that 80% of adult patients who admitted reporting false recovered memories had therapists who made direct suggestions that they had been the victims of childhood sexual abuse. This suggests that recovered memories recalled *inside* therapy may be more likely to be false than those recalled *outside* therapy (see box).

Motivated forgetting

Freud, in his repression theory, focused on some aspects of motivated forgetting. However, his approach was rather narrow, with its emphasis on repression of traumatic and other distressing memories and his failure to consider the cognitive processes involved. In recent years, a broader approach to motivated forgetting has been adopted.

Motivated forgetting of traumatic or other upsetting memories could clearly fulfil a useful

Memories of abuse recovered inside and outside therapy

Geraerts, Schooler, Merckelbach, Jelicic, Haner, and Ambadar (2007) carried out an important study to test whether the genuineness of recovered memories depends on the context in which they were recovered. They divided adults who had suffered childhood sexual abuse into three groups: (1) those whose recovered memories had been recalled inside therapy; (2) those whose recovered memories had been recalled outside therapy; and (3) those who had continuous memories. Geraerts et al. discovered how many of these memories had corroborating evidence (e.g., someone else had also reported being abused by the same person; the perpetrator had confessed) to provide an approximate assessment of validity.

What did Geraerts et al. (2007) find? There was corroborating evidence for 45% of the individuals in the continuous memory group, for 37% of those who had recalled memories outside therapy, and for 0% of those who had recalled memories inside therapy. These findings suggest that recovered memories recalled outside therapy are much more likely to be genuine than those recalled inside therapy. In addition, those individuals whose memories were recalled outside therapy reported being much more surprised at the existence of these memories than did those whose memories were recalled inside therapy. Presumably those whose recovered memories emerged inside therapy were unsurprised at these memories because they had previously been led to expect them by their therapist.

Geraerts et al. (2008) asked various groups of adults who claimed memories of childhood sexual abuse to recall the most positive and the most anxiety-provoking event they had experienced during the past two years. The participants were then told to try to suppress thoughts relating to these events, and to keep a diary record of any such thoughts over the following week. Adults who had recovered memories outside therapy were much better at this than control participants, those who had recovered memories inside therapy, and those who had continuous memories.

In sum, it appears that many of the traumatic memories recovered by women outside therapy are genuine. The finding that such women are especially good at suppressing emotional memories under laboratory conditions helps to explain why they were unaware of their traumatic memories for long periods of time prior to recovery.

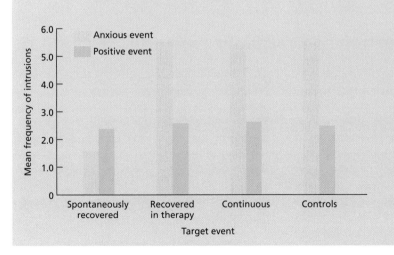

Figure 6.19 Mean numbers of intrusions of anxious and positive events over seven days for patients who had recovered traumatic memories outside therapy (spontaneously recovered), inside therapy (recovered in therapy), or who had had continuous traumatic memories (continuous), and non-traumatised controls. Based on data in Geraerts et al. (2008).

function. In addition, much of the information we have stored in long-term memory is outdated or irrelevant, making it useless for present purposes. For example, if you are looking for your car in a car park, there is no point in remembering where you have parked the car previously. Thus, motivated or intentional forgetting can be adaptive (e.g., by reducing proactive interference).

Directed forgetting

Directed forgetting is a phenomenon involving impaired long-term memory caused by an instruction to forget some information presented for learning (see Geraerts & McNally, 2008, for a review). Directed forgetting has been studied in two ways. First, there is the item method. Several words are presented, each followed immediately by an instruction to remember or to forget it. After all the words have been presented, participants are tested for their recall or recognition of *all* the words. Memory performance on recall and recognition tests is typically worse for the to-be-forgotten words than for the to-be-remembered words.

Second, there is the list method. Here, participants receive two lists of words. After the first list has been presented, participants are told to remember or forget the words. Then the second list is presented. After that, memory is tested for the words from both lists. Recall of the words from the first list is typically impaired when participants have been told to forget those words compared to when they have been told to remember them. However, there is typically no effect when a recognition memory test is used.

Why does directed forgetting occur? Directed forgetting with the item method is found with both recall and recognition, suggesting that the forget instruction has its effects during learning. For example, it has often been suggested that participants may selectively rehearse remember items at the expense of forget items (Geraerts & McNally, 2008). This explanation is less applicable to the list method, because participants have had a substantial opportunity to rehearse the to-be-forgotten list

items before being instructed to forget them. The finding that directed forgetting with the list method is not found in recognition memory suggests that directed forgetting in recall involves retrieval inhibition or interference (Geraerts & McNally, 2008).

Inhibition: executive deficit hypothesis

A limitation with much of the research is that the precise reasons *why* directed forgetting has occurred are unclear. For example, consider directed forgetting in the item-method paradigm. This could occur because to-be-forgotten items receive much less rehearsal than to-be-remembered items. However, it could also occur because of an active process designed to inhibit the storage of words in long-term memory. Wylie, Foxe, and Taylor (2007) used fMRI with the item-method paradigm to test these rival hypotheses. In crude terms, we might expect *less* brain activity for to-be-forgotten items than to-be-remembered ones if the former simply attract less processing. In contrast, we might expect *more* brain activity for to-be-forgotten items if active processes are involved. In fact, intentional forgetting when compared with intentional remembering was associated with *increased* activity in several areas (e.g., medial frontal gyrus (BA10) and cingulated gyrus (BA31)) known to be involved in executive control.

Anderson and Green (2001) developed a variant of the item method known as the think/no-think paradigm. Participants first learn a list of cue-target word pairs (e.g., Ordeal–Roach). Then they are presented with cues studied earlier (e.g., Ordeal) and instructed to think of the associated word (Roach) (respond condition) or to prevent it coming to mind (suppress condition). Some of the cues were not presented at this stage (baseline condition).

KEY TERM

directed forgetting: impaired long-term memory resulting from the instruction to forget information presented for learning.

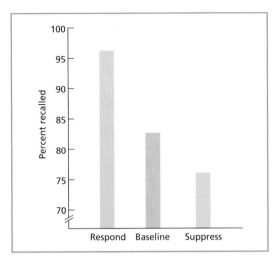

Figure 6.20 Meta-analysis of final recall performance in the think/no-think procedure as a function of whether participants had earlier tried to recall the item (respond), suppress the item (suppress), or had had no previous reminder (baseline). Reprinted from Levy and Anderson (2008), Copyright © 2008, with permission from Elsevier.

Finally, all the cues are presented and participants provide the correct target words. Levy and Anderson (2008) carried out a meta-analysis of studies using the think/no-think paradigm. There was clear evidence of directed forgetting (see Figure 6.20). The additional finding that recall was worse in the suppress condition than in the baseline condition indicates that inhibitory processes were involved in producing directed forgetting in this paradigm.

What strategies do participants use in the suppress condition? They report using numerous strategies, including forming mental images, thinking of an alternative word or thought, or repeating the cue word (Levy & Anderson, 2008). Bergstrom, de Fockert, and Richardson-Klavehn (2009) manipulated the strategy used. Direct suppression of the to-be-forgotten words was more effective than producing alternative thoughts.

Anderson et al. (2004) focused on individual differences in memory performance using the think/no-think paradigm. Their study was designed to test the executive deficit hypothesis, according to which the ability to

suppress memories depends on individual differences in executive control abilities. Recall for word pairs was worse in the suppress condition than in the respond and baseline conditions. Of special importance, those individuals having the greatest activation in bilateral dorsolateral and ventrolateral prefrontal cortex were most successful at memory inhibition. Memory inhibition was also associated with reduced hippocampal activation – this is revealing because the hippocampus plays a key role in episodic memory (see Chapter 7). These findings suggest that successful intentional forgetting involves an executive control process in the prefrontal cortex that disengages hippocampal processing.

Additional support for the executive deficit hypothesis was reported by Bell and Anderson (in preparation). They compared individuals high and low in working memory capacity (see Chapter 10), a dimension of individual differences strongly related to executive control and intelligence. As predicted, memory suppression in the think/no-think paradigm was significantly greater in the high capacity group.

Is research using the think/no-think paradigm relevant to repression? There are encouraging signs that it is. First, Depue, Banich, and Curran (2006, 2007) had participants learn to pair unfamiliar faces with unpleasant photographs (e.g., a badly deformed infant; a car accident) using the paradigm. The findings were very similar to those of Anderson et al. (2004). There was clear evidence for suppression of unwanted memories and suppression was associated with increased activation of the lateral prefrontal cortex and reduced hippocampal activity. Second, Anderson and Kuhl (in preparation) found that individuals who had experienced several traumatic events showed superior memory inhibition abilities than those who had experienced few or none. This suggests that the ability to inhibit or suppress memories improves with practice.

Evaluation

Directed forgetting is an important phenomenon. The hypothesis that it involves executive control processes within the frontal lobes has received much empirical support. The extension of this hypothesis to account for individual differences in directed forgetting has also been well supported. In addition, the notion that research on directed forgetting may be of genuine relevance to an understanding of repression is important. A major implication of directed forgetting research is that suppression or repression occurs because of deliberate attempts to control awareness rather than occurring unconsciously and automatically, as suggested by Freud.

Directed forgetting is clearly one way in which forgetting occurs. However, most forgetting occurs in spite of our best efforts to remember, and so the directed forgetting approach is not of general applicability. The suppression effect in the think/no-think paradigm (baseline–suppression conditions) averages out at only 6% (see Figure 6.20), suggesting it is rather weak. However, participants spent an average of only 64 seconds trying to suppress each item, which is presumably massively less than the amount of time many individuals devote to suppressing traumatic memories. Most research on directed forgetting has used neutral and artificial learning materials, and this limits our ability to relate the findings to Freud's ideas about repression.

Cue-dependent forgetting

Forgetting often occurs because we lack the appropriate cues (cue-dependent forgetting). For example, suppose you are struggling to think of the name of the street on which a friend of yours lives. If someone gave you a short list of possible street names, you might have no difficulty in recognising the correct one.

Tulving and Psotka (1971) showed the importance of cues. They presented between one and six word lists, with four words in six different categories in each list. After each list, participants free recalled as many words as possible (original learning). After all the lists had been presented, participants free recalled the words from all the lists (total free recall). Finally, all the category names were presented

and the participants tried again to recall all the words from all the lists (free cued recall).

There was strong evidence for retroactive interference in total free recall, since word recall from any given list decreased as the number of other lists intervening between learning and recall increased. However, there was essentially *no* retroactive interference or forgetting when the category names were available to the participants. Thus, the forgetting observed in total free recall was basically cue-dependent forgetting (due to a lack of appropriate cues).

Tulving (1979) developed the notion of cue-dependent forgetting in his **encoding specificity principle**: "The probability of successful retrieval of the target item is a monotonically increasing function of *informational overlap* between the information present at retrieval and the information stored in memory" (p. 408; emphasis added). If you are bewildered by that sentence, note that "monotonically increasing function" refers to a generally rising function that does not decrease at any point. Tulving also assumed that the memory trace for an item generally consists of the item itself plus information about context (e.g., the setting; current mood state). It follows that memory performance should be best when the context at test is the same as that at the time of learning.

The encoding specificity principle resembles the notion of transfer-appropriate processing (Morris et al., 1977; see earlier in chapter). The central idea behind transfer-appropriate processing is that long-term memory is best when the processing performed at the time of test closely resembles that at the time of learning. The main difference between these two notions is that transfer-appropriate processing focuses more directly on the processes involved.

KEY TERM

encoding specificity principle: the notion that retrieval depends on the overlap between the information available at retrieval and the information in the memory trace.

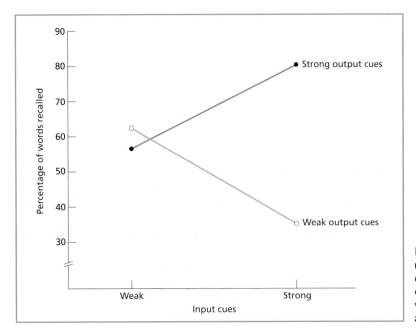

Figure 6.21 Mean word recall as a function of input cues (strong or weak) and output cues (strong or weak). Data from Thomson and Tulving (1970).

Evidence

Many attempts to test the encoding specificity principle involve two learning conditions and two retrieval conditions. This allows the researcher to show that memory depends on the information in the memory trace *and* the information available in the retrieval environment. Thomson and Tulving (1970) presented pairs of words in which the first was the cue and the second was the to-be-remembered word. The cues were weakly associated with the list words (e.g., "Train–BLACK") or strongly associated (e.g., "White–BLACK"). Some of the to-be-remembered items were tested by weak cues (e.g., "Train–?"), and others were tested by strong cues (e.g., "White–?").

Thomson and Tulving's (1970) findings are shown in Figure 6.21. As predicted, recall performance was best when the cues provided at recall *matched* those provided at learning. Any change in the cues reduced recall, even when the shift was from weak cues at input to strong cues at recall. Why were strong cues associated with relatively poor memory performance when learning had involved weak cues? Tulving assumed that participants found it easy to gen-

erate the to-be-remembered words to strong cues, but failed to recognise them as appropriate. However, that is not the whole story. Higham and Tam (2006) found that participants given strong cues at test after weak cues at learning found it harder to generate the target words than other participants given strong cues at test who had not previously engaged in any learning! This happened because participants given weak cues at learning had formed a mental set to generate mainly weak associates to cues.

Context is important in determining forgetting. For example, information about current mood state is often stored in the memory trace, and there is more forgetting if the mood state at the time of retrieval is different. The notion that there should be less forgetting when the mood state at learning and retrieval is the same is known as mood-state-dependent memory. There is reasonable evidence for mood-state-dependent memory (see Chapter 15). However, the effect is stronger when participants are in a positive rather than negative mood because they are motivated to alter negative moods.

Mood-state dependent memory refers to the enhanced ease in recalling events that have an emotional tone similar to our current mood. If we're feeling happy and content, we are more likely to recall pleasant memories; when depressed we are likely to retrieve unpleasant ones.

Other kinds of context are also important. Marian and Neisser (2000) studied the effects of linguistic context. Russian–English bilinguals recalled personal memories when prompted with cues presented in the Russian or English language. The participants generated Russian memories (based on experiences in a Russian-speaking context) to 64% of the cues in Russian compared to only 35% when the cues were in English.

The effects of context are often stronger in recall than recognition memory. Godden and Baddeley (1975) asked participants to learn a list of words on land or 20 feet underwater, followed by a test of free recall on land or under water. Those who had learned on land recalled more on land and those who learned underwater did better when tested underwater. Overall, recall was about 50% higher when learning and recall took place in the same environment. However, there was no effect of context when Godden and Baddeley (1980) repeated the experiment using recognition memory rather than recall.

We all know that recognition is generally better than recall. For example, we may be unable to recall the name of an acquaintance but if someone mentions their name we in-

stantly recognise it. One of the most dramatic predictions from the encoding specificity principle is that recall should sometimes be better than recognition. This should happen when the information in the recall cue overlaps more than the information in the recognition cue with the information stored in the memory trace. Muter (1978) presented participants with people's names (e.g., DOYLE, THOMAS) and asked them to circle those they "recognised as a person who was famous before 1950". They were then given recall cues in the form of brief descriptions plus first names of the famous people whose surnames had appeared on the recognition test (e.g., author of the Sherlock Holmes stories: Sir Arthur Conan ____; Welsh poet: Dylan ____). Participants recognised only 29% of the names but recalled 42% of them.

Brain-imaging evidence supporting the encoding specificity principle and transfer-appropriate processing was reported by Park and Rugg (2008a). Participants were presented with pictures and words and then on a subsequent recognition test each item was tested with a congruent cue (word–word and picture–picture conditions) or an incongruent cue (word–picture and picture–word conditions). As predicted by the encoding specificity principle, memory performance was better in the congruent than in the incongruent conditions.

Park and Rugg (2008) carried out a further analysis based on brain activity at learning for items subsequently recognised. According to transfer-appropriate processing, it is more important for successful recognition for words to be processed at learning in a "word-like" way if they are tested by picture cues than by word cues. In similar fashion, successful recognition of pictures should depend more on "picture-like" processing at study if they are tested by pictures cues than by word cues. Both predictions were supported, suggesting that long-term memory is best when the processing at the time of learning is similar to that at the time of retrieval.

Rugg, Johnson, Park, and Uncapher (2008) reported similar findings supporting transfer-appropriate processing. However, they pointed out that the similarity in patterns of brain activation at learning and retrieval was never very great. This probably happened because only some of the processing at the time of learning directly influenced what information was stored. In addition, only some of the processing at retrieval directly determined what was retrieved.

Evaluation

The overlap between the information stored in the memory trace and that available at the time of retrieval often plays an important role in determining whether retrieval occurs. Recent neuroimaging evidence supports both the encoding specificity principle and transfer-appropriate processing. The emphasis placed on the role of contextual information in retrieval is also valuable. As we have seen, several different kinds of context (e.g., external cues; internal mood states; linguistic context) influence memory performance.

What are the limitations of Tulving's approach? First, it is most directly applicable to relatively simple memory tasks. Tulving assumed that the information at the time of test is compared in a simple and direct way with the information stored in memory to assess informational overlap. That is probably often the case, as when we effortlessly recall autobiographical memories when in the same place as the original event (Berntsen & Hall, 2004). However, if you tried to answer the question, "What did you do six days ago?, you would probably use complex problem-solving strategies not included within the encoding specificity principle.

Second, the encoding specificity principle is based on the assumption that retrieval occurs fairly automatically. However, that is not always the case. Herron and Wilding (2006) found that active processes can be involved in retrieval. People found it easier to recollect episodic memories relating to when and where an event occurred when they adopted the appropriate mental set or frame of mind beforehand. Adopting this mental set was associated

with increased brain activity in the right frontal cortex.

Third, there is a danger of circularity (Eysenck, 1978). Memory is said to depend on "informational overlap", but this is rarely measured. It is tempting to infer the amount of informational overlap from the level of memory performance, which is circular reasoning.

Fourth, as Eysenck (1979) pointed out, what matters is not only the informational overlap between retrieval information and stored information but also the extent to which retrieval information allows us to *discriminate* the correct responses from the incorrect ones. Consider the following thought experiment (Nairne, 2002b). Participants read aloud the following list of words: write, right, rite, rite, write, right. They are then asked to recall the word in the third serial position. We increase the informational overlap for some participants by providing them with the sound of the item in the third position. This increased informational overlap is totally unhelpful because it does not allow participants to discriminate the correct spelling of the sound from the wrong ones.

Fifth, Tulving assumed that context influences recall and recognition in the same way. However, the effects of context are often greater on recall than on recognition memory (e.g., Godden & Baddeley, 1975, 1980).

Consolidation

None of the theories considered so far provides a wholly convincing account of forgetting over time. They identify factors causing forgetting, but do not indicate clearly why forgetting is greater shortly after learning than later on. Wixted (2004a, 2005) argued that the secret of forgetting may lie in consolidation theory. **Consolidation** is a process lasting for a long

> ### KEY TERM
>
> **consolidation:** a process lasting several hours or more which fixes information in **long-term memory**.

time (possibly years) that fixes information in long-term memory. More specifically, it is assumed that the hippocampus plays a vital role in the consolidation of memories (especially episodic memories for specific events and episodes), with many memories being stored ultimately in various parts of the neocortex, including the temporal lobes. A key assumption is that recently formed memories still being consolidated are especially vulnerable to interference and forgetting. Thus, "New memories are clear but fragile and old ones are faded but robust" (Wixted, 2004a, p. 265).

According to some versions of consolidation theory (e.g., Eichenbaum, 2001), the process of consolidation involves two major phases. The first phase occurs over a period of hours and centres on the hippocampus. The second phase takes place over a period of time ranging from days to years and involves interactions between the hippocampal region, adjacent entorhinal cortex and the neocortex. This second phase only applies to episodic memories and semantic memories (stored knowledge about the world). It is assumed that such memories are stored in the lateral neocortex of the temporal and other lobes.

Consolidation theory is relevant to two of the oldest laws of forgetting (Wixted, 2004b). First, there is Jost's (1897) law (mentioned earlier), according to which the older of two memories of the same strength will decay slower. According to the theory, the explanation is that the older memory has undergone more consolidation and so is less vulnerable. Second, there is Ribot's (1882) law, according to which the adverse effects of brain injury on memory are greater on newly formed memories than older ones. This is temporally graded retrograde amnesia. It can be explained on the basis that newly formed memories are most vulnerable to disruption because they are at an early stage of consolidation.

Evidence

Several lines of evidence support consolidation theory. First, consider the form of the forgetting curve. A decreasing rate of forgetting over time since learning follows from the notion that recent memories are vulnerable due to an ongoing process of consolidation. Consolidation theory also provides an explanation of Jost's law.

Second, there is research on Ribot's law, which claims that brain damage adversely affects recently-formed memories more than older ones. Such research focuses on patients with **retrograde amnesia**, which involves impaired memory for events occurring before the onset of the amnesia. Many of these patients have suffered damage to the hippocampus as the result of an accident, and this may have a permanently adverse effect on consolidation processes. As predicted by consolidation theory, numerous patients with retrograde amnesia show greatest forgetting for those memories formed very shortly before the onset of amnesia (Manns, Hopkins, & Squire, 2003). However, retrograde amnesia can in extreme cases extend for periods of up to 40 years (Cipolotti et al., 2001).

Third, consolidation theory predicts that newly-formed memories are more susceptible to retroactive interference than are older memories. On the face of it, the evidence is inconsistent. The amount of retroactive interference generally does not depend on whether the interfering material is presented early or late in the retention interval (see Wixted, 2005, for a review). However, the great majority of studies have only considered specific retroactive interference (i.e., two responses associated with the same stimulus). Consolidation theory actually claims that newly-formed memories are more susceptible to interference from *any* subsequent learning. When the interfering material is dissimilar, there is often more retroactive interference when it is presented early in the retention interval (Wixted, 2004a).

KEY TERM

retrograde amnesia: impaired memory for events occurring before the onset of amnesia.

Fourth, consider the effects of alcohol on memory. People who drink excessive amounts of alcohol sometimes suffer from "blackout", an almost total loss of memory for all events occurring while they were conscious but very drunk. These blackouts probably indicate a failure to consolidate memories formed while intoxicated. An interesting (and somewhat surprising) finding is that memories formed shortly *before* alcohol consumption are often better remembered than those formed by individuals who do not subsequently drink alcohol (Bruce & Pihl, 1997). Alcohol probably prevents the formation of new memories that would interfere with the consolidation process of the memories formed just before alcohol consumption. Thus, alcohol protects previously formed memories from disruption.

Fifth, Haist, Gore, and Mao (2001) obtained support for the assumption that consolidation consists of two phases. Participants identified faces of people famous in the 1980s or 1990s. Selective activation of the hippocampus for famous faces relative to non-famous ones was only found for those famous in the 1990s. In contrast (and also as predicted), there was greater activation in the entorhinal cortex connected to widespread cortical areas for famous faces from the 1980s than from the 1990s.

Evaluation

Consolidation theory has various successes to its credit. First, it explains *why* the rate of forgetting decreases over time. Second, consolidation theory successfully predicts that retrograde amnesia is greater for recently formed memories and that retroactive interference effects are greatest shortly after learning. Third, consolidation theory identifies the brain areas most associated with the two phases of consolidation.

What are the limitations of consolidation theory? First, we lack strong evidence that consolidation processes are responsible for all the effects attributed to them. For example, there are various possible reasons why newly formed memories are more easily disrupted than older ones. Second, consolidation theory indicates in a *general* way why newly formed memory traces are especially susceptible to interference effects, but not the more *specific* finding that retroactive interference is greatest when two different responses are associated with the same stimulus. Third, forgetting can involve several factors other than consolidation. For example, forgetting is greater when there is little informational overlap between the memory trace and the retrieval environment (i.e., encoding specificity principle), but this finding cannot be explained within consolidation theory. Fourth, consolidation theory ignores cognitive processes influencing forgetting. For example, as we have seen, the extent to which forgetting due to proactive interference occurs depends on individual differences in the ability to inhibit or suppress the interfering information.

CHAPTER SUMMARY

- Architecture of memory
  According to the multi-store model, there are separate sensory, short-term, and long-term stores. Much evidence (e.g., from amnesic patients) provides general support for the model, but it is clearly oversimplified. According to the unitary-store model, short-term memory is the temporarily activated part of long-term memory. There is support for this model in the finding that amnesics' performance on some "short-term memory" tasks is impaired. However, it is likely that long-term memory plays an important role in determining performance on such tasks.

- Working memory
  Baddeley replaced the unitary short-term store with a working memory system consisting of an attention-like central executive, a phonological loop holding speech-based information, and a visuo-spatial sketchpad specialised for spatial and visual coding. More recently, Baddeley has added a fourth component (episodic buffer) that integrates and holds information from various sources. The phonological loop and visuo-spatial sketchpad are both two-component systems, one for storage and one for processing. The central executive has various functions, including inhibition, shifting, updating, and dual-task co-ordination. Some brain-damaged patients are said to suffer from dysexecutive syndrome, but detailed analysis indicates that different brain regions are associated with the functions of task setting, monitoring, and energisation.

- Levels of processing
  Craik and Lockhart (1972) focused on learning processes in their levels-of-processing theory. They identified depth of processing (the extent to which meaning is processed), elaboration of processing, and distinctiveness of processing as key determinants of long-term memory. Insufficient attention was paid to the relationship between processes at learning and those at retrieval. In addition, the theory isn't explanatory, it is hard to assess processing depth, and shallow processing can lead to very good long-term memory.

- Implicit learning
  Much evidence supports the distinction between implicit and explicit learning, and amnesic patients often show intact implicit learning but impaired explicit learning. In addition, the brain areas activated during explicit learning (e.g., prefrontal cortex) differ from those activated during implicit learning (e.g., striatum). However, it has proved hard to show that claimed demonstrations of implicit learning satisfy the information and sensitivity criteria. It is likely that the distinction between implicit and explicit learning is oversimplified, and that more complex theoretical formulations are required.

- Theories of forgetting
  Strong proactive and retroactive interference effects have been found inside and outside the laboratory. People use active control processes to minimise proactive interference. Much retroactive interference depends on automatic processes making the incorrect responses accessible. Most evidence on Freud's repression theory is based on adults claiming recovered memories of childhood abuse. Such memories when recalled outside therapy are more likely to be genuine than those recalled inside therapy. There is convincing evidence for directed forgetting, with executive control processes within the prefrontal cortex playing a major role. Forgetting is often cue-dependent, and the cues can be external or internal. However, decreased forgetting over time is hard to explain in cue-dependent terms. Consolidation theory provides an explanation for the form of the forgetting curve, and for reduced forgetting rates when learning is followed by alcohol.

FURTHER READING

- Baddeley, A.D. (2007). *Working memory: Thought and action*. Oxford: Oxford University Press. Alan Baddeley, who has made massive contributions to our understanding of working memory, has written an excellent overview of current knowledge in the area.
- Baddeley, A.D., Eysenck, M.W., & Anderson, M.C. (2009). *Memory*. Hove, UK: Psychology Press. Several chapters in this book provide additional coverage of the topics discussed in this chapter (especially forgetting).
- Jonides, J., Lewis, R.L., Nee, D.E., Lustig, C.A., Berman, M.G., & Moore, K.S. (2008). The mind and brain of short-term memory. *Annual Review of Psychology, 59*, 193–224. This chapter discusses short-term memory at length, and includes a discussion of the multi-store and unitary-store models.
- Repovš, G., & Baddeley, A. (2006). The multi-component model of working memory: Explorations in experimental cognitive psychology. *Neuroscience, 139*, 5–21. This article provides a very useful overview of the working memory model, including a discussion of some of the most important experiment findings.
- Roediger, H.L. (2008). Relativity of remembering: Why the laws of memory vanished. *Annual Review of Psychology, 59*, 225–254. This chapter shows very clearly that learning and memory are more complex and involve more factors than is generally assumed to be the case.
- Shanks, D.R. (2005). Implicit learning. In K. Lamberts & R. Goldstone (eds.), *Handbook of cognition*. London: Sage. David Shanks puts forward a strong case for being critical of most of the evidence allegedly demonstrating the existence of implicit learning.
- Wixted, J.T. (2004). The psychology and neuroscience of forgetting. *Annual Review of Psychology, 55*, 235–269. A convincing case is made that neuroscience has much to contribute to our understanding of forgetting.

INTRODUCTION

We have an amazing variety of information stored in long-term memory. For example, long-term memory can contain details of our last summer holiday, the fact that Paris is the capital of France, information about how to ride a bicycle or play the piano, and so on. Much of this information is stored in the form of schemas or organised packets of knowledge, and is used extensively during language comprehension. The relationship between schematic knowledge and language comprehension is discussed in Chapter 10.

In view of the variety of information in long-term memory, Atkinson and Shiffrin's (1968) notion that there is a single long-term memory store seems improbable (see Chapter 6). As we will see, it is generally accepted that there are several major long-term memory systems. For example, Schacter and Tulving (1994) argued that there are four major long-term memory systems (episodic memory, semantic memory, the perceptual representation system, and procedural memory), and their approach will be discussed. However, there has been some controversy about the precise number and nature of long-term memory systems.

What do we mean by a memory system? According to Schacter and Tulving (1994) and Schacter, Wagner, and Buckner (2000), we can use three criteria to identify a memory system:

(1) *Class inclusion operations*: Any given memory system handles various kinds of information within a given class or domain. For example, semantic memory is concerned with general knowledge of different kinds.

(2) *Properties and relations*: The properties of a memory system, "include types of information that fall within its domain, rules by which the system operates, neural substrates, and functions of the system (what the system is 'for')" (Schacter et al., 2000, p. 629).

(3) *Convergent dissociations*: Any given memory system should differ clearly in various ways from other memory systems.

Amnesia

Convincing evidence that there are several long-term memory systems comes from the study of brain-damaged patients with amnesia. Such patients have problems with long-term memory, but if you are a movie fan you may have mistaken ideas about the nature of amnesia (Baxendale, 2004). In the movies, serious head injuries typically cause characters to forget the past while still being fully able to engage in new learning. In the real world, however, new learning is generally greatly impaired. In the movies, amnesic individuals often suffer a profound loss of identity or their personality changes completely. For example, consider the film *Overboard* (1987). In that film, Goldie Hawn falls from her yacht, and immediately switches from being a rich, spoilt socialite into a loving mother. Such personality shifts are extremely rare. Most bizarrely,

The famous case HM

HM was the most-studied amnesic patient of all time. He suffered from very severe epilepsy starting at the age of ten. This eventually led to surgery by William Beecher Scoville, involving removal of the medial temporal lobes including the hippocampus. HM had his operation on 23 August 1953, and since then he "forgets the events of his daily life as fast as they occur" (Scoville & Milner, 1957). More dramatically, Corkin (1984, p. 255) reported many years after the operation that HM, "does not know where he lives, who cares for him, or where he ate his last meal....In 1982 he did not recognise a picture of himself that had been taken on his fortieth birthday in 1966." When shown faces of individuals who had become famous after the onset of his amnesia, HM could only identify John Kennedy and Ronald Reagan. In spite of everything, HM still had a sense of humour. When Suzanne Corkin asked him how he tried to remember things, he replied, "Well, that I don't know 'cause I don't remember [laugh] what I tried" (Corkin, 2002, p. 158).

It would be easy to imagine that all HM's memory capacities were destroyed by surgery. In fact, what was most striking (and of greatest theoretical importance) was that he retained the ability to form many kinds of long-term memory as well as having good short-term mem-ory (e.g., on immediate span tasks; Wickelgren, 1968). For example, HM showed reasonable learning on a mirror-tracing task (drawing objects seen only in reflection), and he retained some of this learning for one year (Corkin, 1968). He also showed learning on the pursuit rotor, which involves manual tracking of a moving target. HM showed normal performance on a perceptual identification task in which he had to identify words presented very briefly. He identified more words previously studied than words not previously studied, thus showing evidence for long-term memory.

Some reports indicated that his language skills were reasonably well preserved. However, Mackay, James, Taylor, and Marian (2007) reported that he was dramatically worse than healthy controls at language tasks such as detecting grammatical errors or answering questions about who did what to whom in sentences.

HM died on 2 December 2008 at the age of 82. He was known only as HM to protect his privacy, but after his death it was revealed that his real name was Henry Gustav Molaison.

Researchers have focused on the patterns of intact and impaired memory performance shown by HM and other amnesic patients. The theoretical insights they have produced will be considered in detail in this chapter.

the rule of thumb in the movies is that the best cure for amnesia caused by severe head injury is to suffer another massive blow to the head!

We turn now to the real world. Amnesic patients are sometimes said to suffer from the "amnesic syndrome" consisting of the following features:

- *Anterograde amnesia*: a marked impairment in the ability to remember new information learned after the onset of amnesia. HM is a famous example of anterograde amnesia (see box).
- *Retrograde amnesia*: problems in remembering events occurring prior to the onset of amnesia (see Chapter 6).

- Only slightly impaired short-term memory on measures such as digit span (the ability to repeat back a random string of digits).
- Some remaining learning ability after the onset of amnesia.

The reasons why patients have become amnesic are very varied. Bilateral stroke is one

KEY TERM

anterograde amnesia: reduced ability to remember information acquired after the onset of amnesia.

factor causing amnesia, but closed head injury is the most common cause. However, patients with closed head injury often have several cognitive impairments, which makes interpreting their memory deficit hard. As a result, most experimental work has focused on patients who became amnesic because of chronic alcohol abuse (Korsakoff's syndrome; see Glossary). There are two problems with using Korsakoff patients to study amnesia. First, the amnesia usually has a gradual onset, being caused by an increasing deficiency of the vitamin thiamine associated with chronic alcoholism. That makes it hard to know whether certain past events occurred before or after the onset of amnesia. Second, brain damage in Korsakoff patients is often rather widespread. Structures within the diencephalon (e.g., the hippocampus and the amygdala) are usually damaged. There is often damage to the frontal lobes, and this can produce various cognitive deficits not specific to the memory system. It would be easier to interpret findings from Korsakoff patients if the brain damage were more limited. Other cases of amnesia typically have damage to the hippocampus and adjacent areas in the medial temporal lobes. The brain areas associated with amnesia are discussed more fully towards the end of the chapter.

Why have amnesic patients contributed substantially to our understanding of human memory? The study of amnesia provides a good *test-bed* for existing theories of healthy memory. For example, strong evidence for the distinction between short- and long-term memory comes from studies on amnesic patients (see Chapter 6). Some patients have severely impaired long-term memory but intact short-term memory, whereas a few patients show the opposite pattern. The existence of these opposite patterns forms a double dissociation (see Glossary) and is good evidence for separate short- and long-term stores.

The study of amnesic patients has also proved very valuable in leading to various theoretical developments. For example, distinctions such as the one between declarative or explicit memory and non-declarative or implicit memory (discussed in the next section) were originally proposed in part because of data collected from amnesic patients. Furthermore, such patients have provided some of the strongest evidence supporting these distinctions.

Declarative vs. non-declarative memory

The most important distinction between different types of long-term memory is that between declarative memory and non-declarative memory. **Declarative memory** involves conscious recollection of events and facts – it refers to memories that can be "declared" or described. Declarative memory is sometimes referred to as **explicit memory**, defined as memory that "requires conscious recollection of previous experiences" (Graf & Schacter, 1985, p. 501).

In contrast, **non-declarative memory** does not involve conscious recollection. Typically, we obtain evidence of non-declarative memory by observing changes in behaviour. For example, consider someone learning how to ride a bicycle. We would expect their cycling performance (a form of behaviour) to improve over time even though they could not consciously recollect what they had learned about cycling. Non-declarative memory is also known as **implicit memory**, which involves enhanced performance in the absence of conscious recollection.

KEY TERMS

declarative memory: a form of long-term memory that involves knowing that something is the case and generally involves conscious recollection; it includes memory for facts (**semantic memory**) and memory for events (**episodic memory**).

explicit memory: memory that involves conscious recollection of information; see **implicit memory**.

non-declarative memory: forms of long-term memory that influence behaviour but do not involve conscious recollection; **priming** and **procedural memory** are examples of non-declarative memory.

implicit memory: memory that does not depend on conscious recollection; see **explicit memory**.

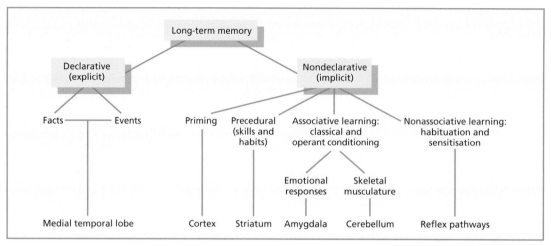

Figure 7.1 The main forms of long-term memory, all of which can be categorised as declarative (explicit) or nondeclarative (implicit). The brain regions associated with each form of long-term memory are also indicated. From Kandel, Kupferman, and Iverson (2000) with permission from McGraw Hill.

Declarative memory and non-declarative memory seem to be very different. Evidence for the distinction comes from amnesic patients. They seem to have great difficulties in forming declarative memories but their ability to form non-declarative memories is intact or nearly so. In the case of HM, he had extremely poor declarative memory for personal events occurring after the onset of amnesia and for faces of those who had become famous in recent decades (see Box on p. 252). However, he had reasonable learning ability on tasks such as mirror tracing, the pursuit rotor, and perceptual identification. What these otherwise different tasks have in common is that they all involve non-declarative memory. As we will see later in the chapter, the overwhelming majority of amnesic patients have very similar patterns of memory performance to HM.

Functional imaging evidence also supports the distinction between declarative and non-declarative memory. Schott, Richardson-Klavehn, Henson, Becker, Heinze, and Duzel (2006) found that brain activation during learning that predicted subsequent declarative memory performance occurred in the bilateral medial temporal lobe and the left prefrontal cortex. In contrast, brain activation predicting subsequent non-declarative memory performance occurred in the bilateral extrastriate cortex, the left fusiform gyrus, and bilateral inferior prefrontal cortex, areas that are involved in stimulus identification.

Schott et al. (2005) found that different brain areas were associated with memory *retrieval* on declarative memory and non-declarative tasks. Declarative retrieval was associated with bilateral parietal and temporal and left frontal increases in activation, whereas non-declarative retrieval was associated with decreases in activation in the left fusiform gyrus and bilateral frontal and occipital regions. Thus, the brain areas associated with declarative memory and non-declarative memory are different both at the time of encoding or learning and at the time of retrieval. In addition, retrieval from declarative memory is generally associated with *increased* brain activation, whereas retrieval from non-declarative memory is associated with *decreased* brain activation.

For the rest of the chapter, we will discuss the various forms of declarative and non-declarative memory. Figure 7.1 provides a sketch map of the ground we are going to be covering.

Declarative memory

We all have declarative or explicit memory for many different kinds of memories. For example, we remember what we had for breakfast this morning or that "le petit déjeuner" is a French expression meaning "breakfast". Tulving (1972) argued that these kinds of memories are very different, and he used the terms "episodic memory" and "semantic memory" to refer to the difference. **Episodic memory** involves storage (and retrieval) of specific events or episodes occurring in a given place at a given time. According to Wheeler, Stuss, and Tulving (1997, p. 333), the main distinguishing characteristic of episodic memory is, "its dependence on a special kind of awareness that all healthy human adults can identify. It is the type of awareness experienced when one thinks back to a specific moment in one's personal past and consciously recollects some prior episode or state as it was previously experienced."

In contrast, **semantic memory** "is the aspect of human memory that corresponds to general knowledge of objects, word meanings, facts and people, without connection to any particular time or place" (Patterson, Nestor, & Rogers, 2007, p. 976). Wheeler et al. (1997) shed further light on the distinction between semantic and episodic memory. They pointed out that semantic memory involves "knowing awareness" rather than the "self-knowing" associated with episodic memory.

Semantic memory goes beyond the meaning of words and extends to sensory attributes such as taste and colour; and to general knowledge of how society works, such as how to behave in a supermarket.

There are similarities between episodic and semantic memory. Suppose you remember meeting your friend yesterday afternoon at Starbuck's. That clearly involves episodic memory, because you are remembering an event at a given time in a given place. However, semantic memory is also involved – some of what you remember depends on your general knowledge about coffee shops, what coffee tastes like, and so on.

Tulving (2002, p. 5) clarified the relationship between episodic and semantic memory: "Episodic memory…shares many features with semantic memory, out of which it grew,…but also possesses features that semantic memory does not.…Episodic memory is a recently evolved, late-developing, and early-deteriorating past-oriented memory system, more vulnerable than other memory systems to neuronal dysfunction."

What is the relationship between episodic memory and autobiographical memory (discussed in Chapter 8)? They are similar in that both forms of memory are concerned with personal experiences from the past, and there is no clear-cut distinction between them. However, there are some differences. Much information in episodic memory is relatively trivial and is remembered for only a short period of time. In contrast, autobiographical memory stores information for long periods of time about events and experiences of some importance to the individual concerned.

Non-declarative memory

A defining characteristic of non-declarative memory is that it is expressed by behaviour and does not involve conscious recollection. Schacter et al. (2000) identified two non-declarative memory systems: the perceptual representation system and procedural memory: the **perceptual representation system** "can be viewed as a collection of domain-specific modules that operate on perceptual information about the form and structure of words and objects" (p. 635). Of central importance within this system is **repetition priming** (often just called priming): stimulus processing occurs faster and/or more easily on the second and successive presentations of a stimulus. For example, we may *identify* a stimulus more rapidly the second time it is presented than the first time. What we have here is learning related to the *specific* stimuli used during learning. Schacter, Wig, and Stevens (2007, p. 171) provided a more technical definition: "Priming refers to an improvement or change in the identification, production, or classification of a stimulus as a result of a prior encounter with the same or a related stimulus." The fact that repetition priming has been obtained in the visual, auditory, and touch modalities supports the notion that there is a perceptual representation system.

In contrast, **procedural memory** "refers to the learning of motor and cognitive skills, and is manifest across a wide range of situations. Learning to ride a bike and acquiring reading skills are examples of procedural memory" (Schacter et al., 2000, p. 636). The term "skill learning" has often been used to refer to what Schacter et al. defined as procedural memory. It is shown by learning that *generalises* to several stimuli other than those used during training. On the face of it, this seems quite different from the very specific learning associated with priming.

Reference back to Figure 7.1 will indicate that there are other forms of non-declarative memory: classical conditioning, operant conditioning, habituation, and sensitisation. We will refer to some of these types of memory later in the chapter as and when appropriate.

There is one final point. The distinction between declarative or explicit memory and non-declarative or implicit memory has been hugely influential and accounts for numerous findings on long-term memory. As you read through this chapter, you will see that some doubts have been raised about the distinction. Towards the end of this chapter, an alternative approach is discussed under the heading, "Beyond declarative and non-declarative memory: amnesia". Much of that section focuses on research suggesting that the notion that amnesic patients have deficient declarative memory but intact non-declarative memory is oversimplified.

EPISODIC VS. SEMANTIC MEMORY

If episodic and semantic memory form separate memory systems, there should be several important differences between them. We will consider three major areas of research here.

The first major area of research involves testing the ability of amnesic patients to acquire episodic and semantic memories after the onset of amnesia. In other words, the focus was on the extent of anterograde amnesia. Spiers, Maguire, and Burgess (2001) reviewed 147 cases of amnesia involving damage to the hippocampus or fornix. There was impairment of episodic memory in *all* cases, whereas many of the patients had only modest problems with semantic memory. Thus, the impact of brain damage was much greater on episodic than on semantic memory, suggesting that the two types of memory are distinctly different. Note that

---

KEY TERMS

perceptual representation system: an implicit memory system thought to be involved in the faster processing of previously presented stimuli (e.g., **repetition priming**).
repetition priming: the finding that stimulus processing is faster and easier on the second and successive presentations.
procedural memory/knowledge: this is concerned with knowing how, and includes the ability to perform skilled actions; see **declarative memory**.

the memory problems of amnesic patients are limited to long-term memory. According to Spiers et al. (p. 359), "None of the cases was reported to have impaired short-term memory (typically tested using digit span – the immediate recall of verbally presented digits)."

We would have stronger evidence if we could find amnesic patients with very poor episodic memory but *intact* semantic memory. Such evidence was reported by Vargha-Khadem, Gadian, Watkins, Connelly, Van Paesschen, and Mishkin (1997). They studied three patients, two of whom had suffered bilateral hippocampal damage at an early age before they had had the opportunity to develop semantic memories. Beth suffered brain damage at birth, and Jon did so at the age of four. Jon suffered breathing problems which led to anoxia and caused his hippocampus to be less than half the normal size. Both of these patients had very poor episodic memory for the day's activities, television programmes, and telephone conversations. In spite of this, Beth and Jon both attended ordinary schools, and their levels of speech and language development, literacy, and factual knowledge (e.g., vocabulary) were within the normal range.

Vargha-Khadem, Gadian, and Mishkin (2002) carried out a follow-up study on Jon at the age of 20. As a young adult, he had a high level of intelligence (IQ = 120), and his semantic memory continued to be markedly better than his episodic memory. Brandt, Gardiner, Vargha-Khadem, Baddeley, and Mishkin (2006) obtained evidence suggesting that Jon's apparent recall of information from episodic memory actually involved the use of semantic memory. Thus, Jon's episodic memory may be even worse than was previously assumed.

How can we explain the ability of Beth and Jon to develop fairly normal semantic memory in spite of their grossly deficient episodic memory? Vargha-Khadem et al. (1997) argued that episodic memory depends on the hippocampus, whereas semantic memory depends on the underlying entorhinal, perihinal, and parahippocampal cortices. The brain damage suffered by Beth and Jon was centred on the hippocampus. Why do so many amnesics have great problems with both episodic and semantic memory? The answer may be that they have damage to the hippocampus *and* to the underlying cortices. This makes sense given that the two areas are adjacent.

Some support for the above hypothesis was reported by Verfaellie, Koseff, and Alexander (2000). They studied a 40-year-old woman (PS), who, as an adult, suffered brain damage to the hippocampus but not the underlying cortices. In spite of her severe amnesia and greatly impaired episodic memory, she managed to acquire new semantic memories (e.g., identifying people who only became famous after the onset of her amnesia).

We have seen that some amnesic patients perform relatively better on tasks involving semantic memory than on those involving episodic memory. However, there is a potential problem of interpretation, because the opportunities for learning are generally greater with semantic memory (e.g., acquiring new vocabulary). Thus, one reason why these patients do especially poorly on episodic memory tasks may be because of the limited time available for learning.

The second main area of research involves amnesic patients suffering from retrograde amnesia (i.e., impaired memory for learning occurring before the onset of amnesia; see also Chapter 6). If episodic and semantic memory form different systems, we would expect to find some patients showing retrograde amnesia only for episodic or semantic memory. For example, consider KC, who suffered damage to several cortical and subcortical brain regions, including the medial temporal lobes. According to Tulving (2002, p. 13), "[KC's] retrograde amnesia is highly asymmetrical: He cannot recollect any personally experienced events..., whereas his semantic knowledge acquired before the critical accident is still reasonably intact. His knowledge of mathematics, history, geography, and other 'school subjects', as well as his general knowledge of the world is not greatly different from others' at his educational level."

The opposite pattern was reported by Yasuda, Watanabe, and Ono (1997), who studied an amnesic patient with bilateral lesions to the temporal lobe. She had very poor ability to remember public events, cultural items, historical figures, and some items of vocabulary from the time prior to the onset of amnesia. However, she was reasonably good at remembering personal experiences from episodic memory dating back to the pre-amnesia period.

Kapur (1999) reviewed studies on retrograde amnesia. There was clear evidence for a double dissociation: some patients showed more loss of episodic than semantic memory, whereas others showed the opposite pattern.

Which brain regions are involved in retrograde amnesia? The hippocampal complex of the medial temporal lobe (including the hippocampus proper, dentate gyrus, the perirhinal, enterorhinal, and parahippocampal cortices) is of special importance. According to multiple trace theory (e.g., Moscovitch, Nadel, Winocur, Gilboa, & Rosenbaum, 2006), every time an episodic memory is retrieved, it is re-encoded. This leads to multiple episodic traces of events distributed widely throughout the hippocampal complex. Of key importance, it is assumed theoretically that detailed episodic or autobiographical memories of the past always depend on the hippocampus. Semantic memories initially depend heavily on the hippocampus, but increasingly depend on neocortex.

Multiple trace theory has received support from studies on healthy individuals as well as patients with retrograde amnesia. For example, Gilboa, Ramirez, Kohler, Westmacott, Black, and Moscovitch (2005) studied people's personal recollections of recent and very old events going back several decades. Activation of the hippocampus was associated with the vividness of their recollections rather than the age of those recollections.

There is reasonable support for predictions following from multiple trace theory. First, the severity of retrograde amnesia in episodic memory is fairly strongly related to the amount of damage to the hippocampal complex, although frontal areas are also often damaged (Moscovitch et al., 2006). Second, damage to the hippocampal complex generally has less effect on semantic memory than on episodic memory, with any

effects being limited to a period of about ten years. Third, damage to the neocortex impairs semantic memory. Westmacott, Black, Freedman, and Moscovitch (2004) studied retrograde amnesia in patients suffering from **Alzheimer's disease** (a progressive disease in which cognitive abilities including memory are gradually lost). The severity of retrograde amnesia for vocabulary and famous names in these patients increased with the progress of the disease. This suggests that the impairment in semantic memory was related to the extent of degeneration of neocortex.

The third main area of research involves functional neuroimaging. Studies in this area indicate that episodic and semantic memory involve activation of somewhat different parts of the brain. In a review, Wheeler et al. (1997) reported that the left prefrontal cortex was more active during episodic than semantic encoding. What about brain activation during retrieval? Wheeler et al. reported that the right prefrontal cortex was more active during episodic memory retrieval than during semantic memory retrieval in 25 out of 26 neuroimaging studies.

Further neuroimaging evidence was reported by Prince, Tsukiura, and Cabeza (2007). The left hippocampus was associated with episodic encoding but not with semantic memory retrieval, whereas the lateral temporal cortex was associated with semantic memory retrieval but not with episodic encoding. The greater involvement of the hippocampus with episodic than with semantic memory is consistent with the research on brain-damaged patients discussed above (Moscovitch et al., 2006). In addition, Prince et al. (2007) found within the left inferior prefrontal cortex that a posterior region was involved in semantic retrieval, a mid-region was associated with both semantic retrieval and episodic encoding, and a more anterior region was associated with episodic encoding only

> **KEY TERM**
>
> **Alzheimer's disease:** a condition involving progressive loss of memory and mental abilities.

when semantic retrieval was also involved. These various findings suggested that, "episodic and semantic memory depend on different but closely interacting memory systems" (Prince et al., 2007, p. 150).

Evaluation

There is convincing evidence for separate episodic and semantic memory systems. The relevant evidence is of various kinds, and includes studies of anterograde and retrograde amnesia as well as numerous neuroimaging studies.

It should be emphasised that the episodic and semantic memory systems typically *combine* in their functioning. For example, suppose you retrieve an episodic memory of having an enjoyable picnic in the countryside. To do this, you need to retrieve semantic information about the concepts (e.g., picnic; grass) contained in your episodic memory. We have just seen that Prince et al. (2007) found evidence that some of the same brain regions are associated with episodic and semantic memory. In similar fashion, Nyberg et al. (2003) found that four regions of prefrontal cortex were activated during episodic and semantic memory tasks: left fronto-polar cortex, left mid-ventrolateral prefrontal cortex, left mid-dorsolateral prefrontal cortex, and dorsal anterior cingulate cortex. Nyberg et al. also found that the same areas were activated during various working-memory tasks, which raises the possibility that these regions of prefrontal cortex are involved in executive processing or cognitive control.

EPISODIC MEMORY

As we saw in Chapter 6, most episodic memories exhibit substantial and progressive forgetting over time. However, there are some exceptions. For example, Bahrick, Bahrick, and Wittlinger (1975) made use of photographs from high-school yearbooks dating back many years. Ex-students showed remarkably little forgetting of information about their former classmates at retention intervals up to 25 years. Performance was 90% for recognising a name as being that of a classmate, for recognising a classmate's photograph, and for matching a classmate's name to his/her school photograph. Performance remained very high on the last two tests even at a retention interval of almost 50 years, but performance on the name recognition task declined.

Bahrick, Hall, and Da Costa (2008) asked American ex-college students to recall their academic grades. Distortions in recall occurred shortly after graduation but thereafter remained fairly constant over retention intervals up to 54 years. Perhaps not surprisingly, the great

Bahrick et al. (1975) found that adults were remarkably good at recognising the photographs of those with whom they had been at school almost so years later.

majority of distortions involved inflating the actual grade.

Bahrick (1984) used the term permastore to refer to very long-term stable memories. This term was based on permafrost, which is the permanently frozen subsoil found in polar regions. It seems probable that the contents of the permastore consist mainly of information that was very well-learned in the first place.

We turn now to a detailed consideration of how we can assess someone's episodic memory. Recognition and recall are the two main types of episodic memory test. The basic recognition-memory test involves presenting a series of items, with participants deciding whether each one was presented previously. As we will see, however, more complex forms of recognition-memory test have also been used. There are three basic forms of recall test: free recall, serial recall, and cued recall. Free recall involves producing to-be-remembered items in any order in the absence of any specific cues. Serial recall involves producing to-be-remembered items in the order in which they were presented originally. Cued recall involves producing to-be-remembered items in the presence of cues. For example, 'cat–table' might be presented at learning and the cue, 'cat–?' might be given at test.

Recognition memory

Recognition memory can involve recollection or familiarity (e.g., Mandler, 1980). According to Diana, Yonelinas, and Ranganath (2007, p. 379), "Recollection is the process of recognising an item on the basis of the retrieval of specific contextual details, whereas familiarity is the process of recognising an item on the basis of its perceived memory strength but without retrieval of any specific details about the study episode."

We can clarify the distinction with the following anecdote. Several years ago, the first author walked past a man in Wimbledon, and was immediately confident that he recognised him. However, he simply could not think of the situation in which he had seen the man previously. After some thought (this is the kind

of thing academic psychologists think about!), he realised the man was a ticket-office clerk at Wimbledon railway station. Thus, initial recognition based on familiarity was replaced by recognition based on recollection.

There are various ways of distinguishing between these two forms of recognition memory. Perhaps the simplest is the remember/know task, in which participants indicate subjectively whether their positive recognition decisions were based on recollection of contextual information (remember responses) or solely on familiarity (know responses). The crucial issue here is deciding whether recollection and familiarity involve different processes – sceptics might argue that the only real difference is that strong memory traces give rise to recollection judgements and weak memory traces give rise to familiarity judgements. Dunn (2008) is one such sceptic. He carried out a meta-analysis of 37 studies using the remember–know task, and found that the findings could be explained in terms of a single process based on memory strength. However, as we will see, there is much support for dual-process models.

We saw earlier that the medial temporal lobe and adjacent areas are of crucial importance in episodic memory. There is now reasonable support for a more precise account of the brain areas involved in recognition memory provided by the binding-of-item-and-context model (Diana et al., 2007) (see Figure 7.2):

(1) Perirhinal cortex receives information about specific items ("what" information needed for familiarity judgements).
(2) Parahippocampal cortex receives information about context ("where" information useful for recollection judgements).
(3) The hippocampus receives what and where information (both of great importance to episodic memory), and binds them together to form item-context associations that permit recollection.

Functional neuroimaging studies provide support for the binding-of-item-and-context model. Diana et al. (2007) combined findings

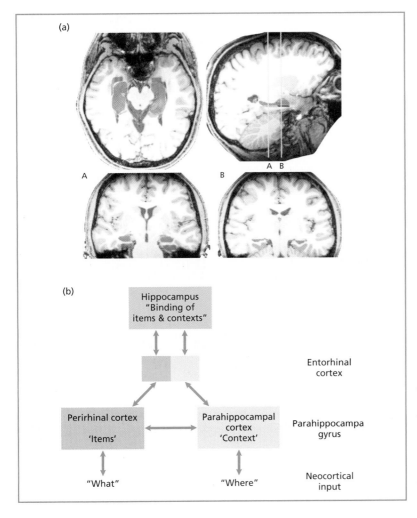

Figure 7.2 (a) locations of the hippocampus (red), the perirhinal cortex (blue), and the parahippocampal cortex (green); (b) the binding-of-item-and-context model. Reprinted from Diana et al. (2007), Copyright © 2007, with permission from Elsevier.

from several studies of recognition memory that considered patterns of brain activation during encoding and retrieval (see Figure 7.2). As predicted, recollection was associated with more activation in parahippocampal cortex and the hippocampus than in the perirhinal cortex. In contrast, familiarity was associated with more activation in the perirhinal cortex than the parahippocampal cortex or hippocampus.

It is a reasonable prediction from the above model that amnesic patients (who nearly always have extensive hippocampal damage) should have greater problems with recognition based on recollection than recognition based on familiarity. Skinner and Fernandes (2007) carried out a meta-analysis of recognition-memory studies involving amnesic patients with and without lesions in the medial temporal lobes (including the hippocampus). Of central interest was the memory performance of these two groups on measures of recollection and familiarity (see Figure 7.3). Both groups performed consistently worse than healthy controls. Most importantly, however, the patient group with medial temporal lobe lesions only had significantly worse performance than the other patient group with recollection and not with familiarity. This suggests that the hippocampus and adjacent regions are especially important in supporting recollection.

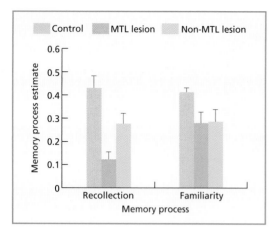

Figure 7.3 Mean recollection and familiarity estimates for healthy controls, patients with medial temporal lobe (MTL) lesions, and patients with non-MTL lesions. Reprinted from Skinner and Fernandes (2007), Copyright © 2007, with permission from Elsevier.

Recall memory

Some research on recall is discussed in Chapter 6. Here, we will focus on whether the processes involved in free recall are the same as those involved in recognition memory. In an important study, Staresina and Davachi (2006) used three memory tests: free recall, item recognition (familiarity), and associative recognition (recollection). Successful memory performance on all three tests was associated with increased activation in the left hippocampus and left ventrolateral prefrontal cortex at the time of encoding. This was most strongly the case with free recall and least strongly the case with item recognition. In addition, only successful subsequent free recall was associated with increased activation in the dorsolateral prefrontal cortex and posterior parietal cortex. The most likely explanation of this finding is that successful free recall involves forming associations (in this case between items and the colours in which they were studied), something that is not required for successful recognition memory.

What conclusions can we draw? First, the finding that similar brain areas are associated with successful free recall and recognition suggests that there are important similarities between the two types of memory test. Second,

successful free recall is associated with higher levels of brain activity in several areas at encoding and at retrieval than successful recognition memory. This suggests that free recall is in some sense more "difficult" than recognition memory. Third, Staresina and Davachi's (2006) finding that some brain areas are associated with successful free recall but not recognition memory suggests that free recall involves processes additional to those involved in recognition memory. As indicated above, inter-item processing is the most obvious requirement specific to free recall.

Is episodic memory constructive?

We use episodic memory to remember past events that have happened to us. You might imagine that our episodic memory system would work like a video recorder, providing us with accurate and detailed information about past events. That is *not* the case. As Schacter and Addis (2007, p. 773) pointed out, "Episodic memory is...a fundamentally constructive, rather than reproductive process that is prone to various kinds of errors and illusions." Plentiful evidence for this constructive view of episodic memory is discussed in other chapters. In Chapter 8, we discuss research showing how the constructive nature of episodic memory leads eyewitnesses to produce distorted memories of what they have seen. In Chapter 10, we discuss the influential views of Bartlett (1932). His central assumption was that the knowledge we possess can produce systematic distortions and errors in our episodic memories, an assumption that has been supported by much subsequent research.

Why are we saddled with an episodic memory system that is so prone to error? Schacter and Addis (2007) identified three reasons. First, it would require an incredible amount of processing to produce a semi-permanent record of all our experiences. Second, we generally want to access the gist or essence of our past experiences; thus, we want our memories to be *discriminating* by omitting the trivial details. Third, imagining possible future events and scenarios is important to us for various reasons (e.g., forming plans for the future). Perhaps the constructive processes involved in episodic memory are also used to imagine the future.

Evidence

We typically remember the gist of what we have experienced previously, and our tendency to remember gist increases with age. Consider a study by Brainerd and Mojardin (1998). Children aged 6, 8, and 11 listened to sets of three sentences (e.g., "The coffee is hotter than the tea"; "The tea is hotter than the cocoa"; "The cocoa is hotter than the soup"). On the subsequent recognition test, participants decided whether the test sentences had been presented initially in precisely that form. The key condition was one in which sentences having the same meaning as original sentences were presented (e.g., "The cocoa is cooler than the tea"). False recognition on these sentences increased steadily with age.

We turn now to the hypothesis that imagining future events involves the same processes as those involved in remembering past events. On that hypothesis, individuals with very poor episodic memory (e.g., amnesic patients) should also have impaired ability to imagine future events. Hassabis, Kumaran, Vann, and Maguire (2007) asked amnesic patients and healthy controls to imagine future events (e.g., "Imagine you are lying on a white sandy beach in a beautiful tropical bay"). The amnesic patients produced imaginary experiences consisting of isolated fragments of information lacking the richness and spatial coherence of the experiences imagined by the controls.

Addis, Wong, and Schacter (2007) compared brain activity when individuals generated past and future events and then elaborated on them. There was considerable overlap in patterns of brain activity during the elaboration phase. The areas activated during elaboration of past and future events included the left anterior temporal cortex (associated with conceptual and semantic information about one's life) and the left frontopolar cortex (associated with self-referential processing). There was some overlap during the generation phase as well. However, there were higher levels of activity in several areas (e.g., the right frontopolar cortex; the left inferior frontal gyrus) during the generation of future than of past events. This suggests that more intensive constructive processes are required to imagine future events than to retrieve past events.

Evaluation

It has been assumed by many theorists, starting with Bartlett (1932), that episodic memory relies heavily on constructive processes, and there is convincing evidence to support that assumption (see Chapters 8 and 10). The further assumption by Schacter and Addis (2007) that the same constructive processes involved in episodic memory for past events are also involved in imaging the future is an exciting development. The initial findings from amnesic patients and functional neuroimaging studies are supportive. However, further research is needed to clarify the reasons why there are higher levels of brain activation when individuals imagine future events than when they recall past events.

SEMANTIC MEMORY

Our organised general knowledge about the world is stored in semantic memory. The content of such knowledge can be extremely varied, including information about the French language, the rules of hockey, the names of capital cities, and the authors of famous books. How is information organised within semantic memory? Most is known about the organisation of **concepts,** which are mental representations of categories of objects or items. We will start by considering influential models focusing on the ways in which concepts are interconnected. After that, we will consider the storage of information about concepts within the brain.

KEY TERM

concepts: mental representations of categories of objects or items.

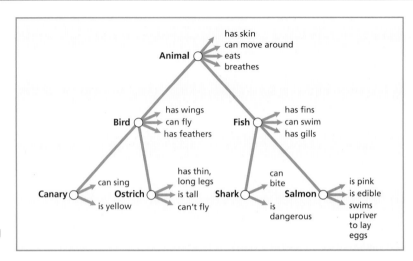

Figure 7.4 Collins and Quillian's (1969) hierarchical network.

Network models

We can answer numerous simple questions about semantic memory very rapidly. For example, it takes about one second to decide a sparrow is a bird, or to think of a fruit starting with p. This great efficiency suggests that semantic memory is highly organised or structured.

The first systematic model of semantic memory was put forward by Collins and Quillian (1969). Their key assumption was that semantic memory is organised into hierarchical networks (see Figure 7.4). The major concepts (e.g., animal, bird, canary) are represented as nodes, and properties or features (e.g., has wings; is yellow) are associated with each concept. You may wonder why the property "can fly" is stored with the bird concept rather than with the canary concept. According to Collins and Quillian, those properties possessed by nearly all birds (e.g., can fly; has wings) are stored only at the bird node or concept. The underlying principle is one of cognitive economy: property information is stored as high up the hierarchy as possible to minimise the amount of information stored.

According to the model of Collins and Quillian (1969), it should be possible to decide very rapidly that the sentence, "A canary is yellow", is true because the concept (i.e., "canary") and the property (i.e., "is yellow") are stored together at the same level of the hierarchy. In contrast, the sentence, "A canary can fly", should take longer because the concept and property are separated by one level in the hierarchy. The sentence, "A canary has skin", should take even longer because two levels separate the concept and the property. As predicted, the time taken to respond to true sentences became progressively slower as the separation between the subject of the sentence and the property became greater.

The model is right in its claim that we often use semantic memory successfully by *inferring* the right answer. For example, the information that Leonardo da Vinci had knees is not stored directly in semantic memory. However, we know Leonardo da Vinci was a human being, and that human beings have knees, and so we confidently infer that Leonardo da Vinci had knees. This is the kind of inferential process proposed by Collins and Quillian (1969).

In spite of its successes, the model suffers from various problems. A sentence such as, "A canary is yellow", differs from, "A canary has skin", not only in the hierarchical distance between the concept and its property, but also in familiarity. Indeed, you have probably never encountered the sentence, "A canary has skin", in your life before! Conrad (1972) found that hierarchical distance between the subject and the property had little effect on verification time when familiarity was controlled.

The typicality effect determines that it will take longer to decide that a penguin is a bird than that a canary is a bird. A penguin is an example of a relatively atypical member of the category to which it belongs, whereas the canary – being a more representative bird – can be verified more quickly.

There is another limitation. Consider the following statements: "A canary is a bird" and "A penguin is a bird". On their theory, both statements should take the same length of time to verify, because they both involve moving one level in the hierarchy. In fact, however, it takes longer to decide that a penguin is a bird. Why is that so? The members of most categories vary considerably in terms of how typical or representative they are of the category to which they belong. For example, Rosch and Mervis (1975) found that oranges, apples, bananas, and peaches were rated as much more typical fruits than olives, tomatoes, coconuts, and dates. Rips, Shoben, and Smith (1973) found that verification times were faster for more typical or representative members of a category than for relatively atypical members (the **typicality effect**).

More typical members of a category possess more of the characteristics associated with that category than less typical ones. Rosch (1973) produced a series of sentences containing the word "bird". Sample sentences were as follows: "Birds eat worms"; "I hear a bird singing"; "I watched a bird fly over the house"; and "The bird was perching on the twig". Try replacing the word *bird* in each sentence in turn with *robin*, *eagle*, *ostrich*, and *penguin*. *Robin* fits all the sentences, but *eagle*, *ostrich*, and *penguin* fit progressively less well. Thus, penguins and ostriches are less typical birds than eagles, which in turn are less typical than robins.

What does this tell us about the structure of semantic memory? It strongly implies that Collins and Quillian (1969) were mistaken in assuming that the concepts we use belong to rigidly defined categories. Convincing evidence that many concepts in semantic memory are fuzzy rather than neat and tidy was reported by McCloskey and Glucksberg (1978). They gave 30 people tricky questions such as, "Is a stroke a disease?" and "Is a pumpkin a fruit?" They found that 16 said a stroke is a disease, but 14 said it was not. A pumpkin was regarded as a fruit by 16 participants but not as a fruit by the remainder. More surprisingly, when McCloskey and Glucksberg tested the same participants a month later, 11 of them had changed their minds about "stroke" being a disease, and eight had altered their opinion about "pumpkin" being a fruit!

Collins and Loftus (1975) put forward a spreading activation theory. They argued that

KEY TERM

typicality effect: the finding that objects can be identified faster as category members when they are typical or representative members of the category in question.

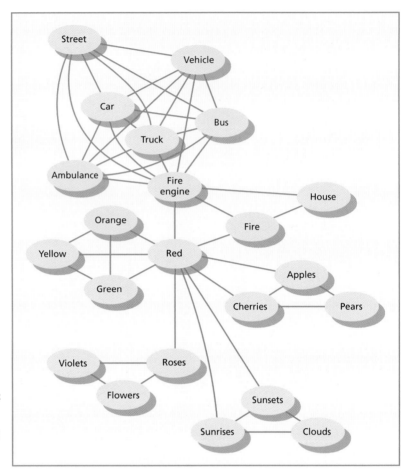

Figure 7.5 Example of a spreading activation semantic network. From Collins and Loftus (1975). Copyright © 1975 American Psychological Association. Reproduced with permission.

the notion of logically organised hierarchies was too inflexible. They assumed instead that semantic memory is organised on the basis of semantic relatedness or semantic distance. Semantic relatedness can be measured by asking people to decide how closely related pairs of words are. Alternatively, people can list as many members as they can of a particular category. Those members produced most often are regarded as most closely related to the category.

You can see part of the organisation of semantic memory assumed by Collins and Loftus in Figure 7.5, with the length of the links between two concepts indicating their degree of semantic relatedness. Thus, for example, *red* is more closely related to *orange* than to *sunsets*.

According to spreading activation theory, whenever a person sees, hears, or thinks about a concept, the appropriate node in semantic memory is activated. This activation then spreads most strongly to other concepts closely related semantically, and more weakly to those more distant semantically. For example, activation would pass strongly and rapidly from "robin" to "bird" in the sentence, "A robin is a bird", because "robin" and "bird" are closely related semantically. However, it would pass more weakly and slowly from "penguin" to "bird" in the sentence, "A penguin is a bird". As a result, the model predicts the typicality effect.

Other predictions of the spreading activation model have been tested experimentally. For example, Meyer and Schvaneveldt (1976) had participants decide as rapidly as possible whether a string of letters formed a word. In the key condition, a given word (e.g., "butter") was immediately preceded by a semantically related word (e.g., "bread") or by an unrelated word (e.g., "nurse"). According to the model, activation should have spread from the first word to the second only when they were semantically related and this activation should have made it easier to identify the second word. Thus, "butter" should have been identified as a word faster when preceded by "bread" than by "nurse". Indeed, there was a facilitation (or semantic priming) effect for semantically related words.

McNamara (1992) used the same basic approach as Meyer and Schvaneveldt (1976). Suppose the first word was "red". This was sometimes followed by a word one link away (e.g., "roses"), and sometimes by a word two links away (e.g., "flowers"). More activation should spread from the activated word to words one link away than those two links away, and so the facilitation effect should have been greater in the former case. That is what McNamara (1992) found.

Schacter, Alpert, Savage, Rauch, and Albert (1996) used the Deese–Roediger–McDermott paradigm described in Chapter 6. Participants received word lists constructed in a particular way. An initial word (e.g., "doctor") was selected, and then several words closely associated with it (e.g., "nurse", "sick", "hospital", "patient") were selected. All these words (excluding the initial word) were presented for learning, followed by a test of recognition memory. When the initial word was presented on the recognition test, it should theoretically have been highly activated because it was so closely related to all the list words. Schacter et al. compared brain activation on the recognition test when participants falsely recognised the initial word and when they correctly recognised list words. The pattern and intensity of brain activation were very similar in both cases, indicating that there was substantial activation of the initial word, as predicted by the model.

The spreading activation model has generally proved more successful than the hierarchical network model. An important reason is that it is a much more flexible approach. However, flexibility means that the model typically does not make very precise predictions. This makes it difficult to assess its overall adequacy.

Organisation of concepts in the brain

It is often assumed (e.g., Bartlett, 1932; Bransford, 1979) that we have schemas (organised packets of knowledge) stored in semantic memory. For example, our schematic knowledge leads us to expect that most kitchens will have an oven, a refrigerator, a sink, cupboards, and so on. What is known about the organisation of schematic knowledge in the brain is discussed in Chapter 10.

In this section, we focus on our semantic knowledge of concepts and objects. How is that knowledge organised in the brain? One obvious possibility is that all information we possess about any given object or concept is stored in *one* location in the brain. Another possibility is that different kinds of information (features) about a given object are stored in different locations in the brain. This notion is incorporated in feature-based theories. According to such theories, "Object concepts may be represented in the brain as distributed networks of activity in the areas involved in the processing of perceptual or functional knowledge" (Canessa et al., 2008, p. 740). As we will see, both of these possibilities capture part of what is actually the case.

Perceptual–functional theories

An influential feature-based approach was put forward by Warrington and Shallice (1984) and Farah and McClelland (1991). According to this approach, there is an important distinction between visual or perceptual features (e.g., what does the object look like?) and functional features (e.g., what is the object used for?). Our semantic knowledge of living things is mostly based on perceptual information. In contrast, our knowledge of non-living things (e.g., tools) mainly involves functional information.

An additional assumption of the perceptual–functional approach is that semantic memory contains far more information about perceptual properties of objects than of functional properties. Farah and McClelland (1991) examined the descriptors of living and non-living objects given in the dictionary. Three times more of the descriptors were classified as visual than as functional. As predicted, the ratio of visual to functional descriptors was 7.7:1 for living objects but only 1.4:1 for non-living objects.

Two major predictions follow from the perceptual–functional approach. First, brain damage should generally impair knowledge of living things more than non-living things. Brain damage is likely to destroy more information about perceptual features than functional features because more such information is stored in the first place. Second, neuroimaging should reveal that different brain areas are activated when perceptual features of an object are processed than functional features.

We turn now to a consideration of the relevant evidence. Some research has focused on brain-damaged patients who have problems with semantic memory and other research has used neuroimaging while healthy participants engage in tasks that involve semantic memory.

Evidence

Many brain-damaged patients exhibit **category-specific deficits,** meaning they have problems with specific categories of object. For example, Warrington and Shallice (1984) studied a patient (JBR). He had much greater difficulty in identifying pictures of living than of non-living things (success rates of 6% and 90%, respectively). This pattern is common. Martin and Caramazza (2003) reviewed the evidence. More than 100 patients with a category-specific deficit for living but not for non-living things have been studied compared to approximately 25 with the opposite pattern. These findings are as predicted by perceptual–functional theories.

Why do some patients show greater impairment in recognising non-living than living things? Gainotti (2000) reviewed the evidence

from 44 patients. Of the 38 patients having a selective impairment for knowledge of living things, nearly all had damage to the anterior, medial, and inferior parts of the temporal lobes. In contrast, the six patients having a selective impairment for knowledge of man-made objects had damage in fronto-parietal areas extending further back in the brain than the areas damaged in the other group.

Support for perceptual–functional theories has also come from neuroimaging studies. Lee, Graham, Simons, Hodges, Owen, and Patterson (2002) asked healthy participants to retrieve perceptual or non-perceptual information about living or non-living objects or concepts when presented with their names. Processing of perceptual information from both living and non-living objects was associated with activation of left posterior temporal lobe regions. In contrast, processing of non-perceptual information (e.g., functional attributes) was associated with activation of left posterior inferior temporal lobe regions. Comparisons between living and non-living objects indicated that the same brain regions were activated for *both* types of concept. Thus, what determined which brain areas were activated was whether perceptual or non-perceptual information was being processed.

Similar findings were reported by Marques, Canessa, Siri, Catricala, and Cappa (2008). Participants were presented with statements about the features (e.g., form, colour, size, motion) of living and non-living objects, and patterns of brain activity were assessed while they decided whether the statements were true or false. Their findings largely agreed with those of Lee et al. (2002): "The results…highlighted that feature type rather than concept domain [living versus non-living] is the main organisational factor of the brain representation of conceptual knowledge" (Marques et al., 2008, p. 95).

KEY TERM

category-specific deficits: disorders caused by brain damage in which **semantic memory** is disrupted for certain semantic categories.

Multiple-property approach

The findings discussed so far are mostly consistent with perceptual–functional theories. However, there is increasing evidence that such theories are oversimplified. For example, many properties of living things (e.g., carnivore; lives in the desert) do not seem to be sensory or functional. In addition, the definition of functional feature has often been very broad and included an object's uses as well as how it is manipulated. Buxbaum and Saffran (2002) have shown the importance of distinguishing between these two kinds of knowledge. Some of the patients they studied suffered from **apraxia**, a disorder involving the inability to make voluntary bodily movements. Apraxic patients with frontoparietal damage had preserved knowledge of the uses of objects but loss of knowledge about how to manipulate objects. In contrast, non-apraxic patients with damage to the temporal lobe showed the opposite pattern. Functional knowledge should probably be divided into "what for" and "how" knowledge (Canessa et al., 2008).

Canessa et al. (2008) reported functional magnetic resonance imaging (fMRI; see Glossary) findings supporting the above distinction. Healthy participants were presented with pictures of pairs of objects on each trial. They decided whether the objects were used in the same context (functional or "what for" knowledge) or involved the same manipulation pattern (action or "how" knowledge). Processing action knowledge led to activation in a left frontoparietal network, whereas processing functional knowledge activated areas within the lateral anterior inferotemporal cortex. The areas associated with these two kinds of knowledge were generally consistent with those identified by Buxbaum and Saffran (2002) in brain-damaged patients.

Cree and McRae (2003) showed that the distinction between perceptual and functional properties of objects is oversimplified. They argued that functional features should be divided into entity behaviours (what a thing does) and functional information (what humans use it for). Perceptual properties should be divided into visual (including colour), auditory, taste, and tactile. For example, there are similarities among fruits, vegetables, and foods because sensory features associated with taste are important to all three categories.

Cree and McRae (2003) identified seven different patterns of category-specific deficits occurring following brain damage (see Table 7.1). They pointed out that no previous theory could account for all these patterns. However, their multiple-feature approach can do so. When brain damage reduces stored knowledge for one or more properties of objects, semantic memory for all categories relying strongly on those properties is impaired.

The multiple-property approach is promising for various reasons. First, it is based on a recognition that most concepts consist of several properties and that these properties determine similarities and differences among them. Second, the approach provides a reasonable account of several different patterns of deficit in conceptual knowledge observed in brain-damaged patients. Third, it is consistent with brain-imaging findings suggesting that different object properties are stored in different parts of the brain (e.g., Martin & Chao, 2001).

Distributed-plus-hub theory vs. grounded cognition

As we have seen, there is general agreement that much of our knowledge of objects and concepts is widely distributed in the brain. Such knowledge is modality-specific (e.g., visual or auditory) and relates to perception, language, and action. This knowledge is probably stored in brain regions overlapping with those involved in perceiving, using language, and acting.

Does semantic memory also contain relatively abstract amodal representations not associated directly with any of the sensory

---

KEY TERM

apraxia: a neurological condition in which patients are unable to perform voluntary bodily movements.

TABLE 7.1: Cree and McRae's (2003) explanation of why brain-damaged patients show various patterns of deficit in their knowledge of different categories. From Smith and Kosslyn (2007). Copyright © Pearson Education, Inc. Reproduced with permission.

Deficit pattern	Shared properties
1. Multiple categories consisting of living creatures	Visual motion, visual parts, colour
2. Multiple categories of non-living things	Function, visual parts
3. Fruits and vegetables	Colour, function, taste, smell
4. Fruits and vegetables with living creatures	Colour
5. Fruits and vegetables with non-living things	Sound, colour
6. Inanimate foods with living things (especially fruits and vegetables)	Function, taste, smell
7. Musical instruments with living things	Function

modalities? There has been much recent controversy on this issue. Barsalou (2008) argued that the answer is, "No". He argued in favour of theories of grounded cognition which, "reject the standard view that amodal symbols represent knowledge in semantic memory…[they] focus on the roles of simulation in cognition.…Simulation is the re-enactment of perceptual, motor, and introspective states acquired during experience (p. 618).

According to the distributed-plus-hub theory (Patterson et al., 2007; Rogers et al., 2004), the answer is, "Yes". There is a hub for each concept or object in addition to distributed modality-specific information. Each hub is a unified conceptual representation that "supports the interactive activation of [distributed] representations in all modalities" (Patterson et al., 2007, p. 977). According to Patterson et al., concept hubs are stored in the anterior temporal lobes. Why do we have hubs? First, they provide an efficient way of integrating our knowledge of any given concept. Second, they make it easier for us to detect semantic similarities across concepts differing greatly in their modality-specific attributes. As Patterson et al. pointed out, scallops and prawns are conceptually related even though they have different shapes, colours, shell structures, forms of movement, names, and so on.

Evidence

As predicted by theories of grounded cognition, modality-specific information is very important in our processing of concepts. Consider a study by Hauk, Johnsrude, and Pulvermüller (2004). Tongue, finger, and foot movements produced different patterns of activation along the motor strip. When they presented participants with words such as "lick", "pick", and "kick", these verbs activated parts of the motor strip overlapping with (or very close to) the corresponding part of the motor strip. Thus, for example, the word "lick" activated areas associated with tongue movements.

The findings of Hauk et al. (2004) show that the motor system is *associated* with the processing of action words. However, these findings do not necessarily mean that the motor and premotor cortex *influence* the processing of action words. More convincing evidence was reported by Pulvermüller, Hauk, Nikulin, and Ilmoniemi (2005). Participants performed a lexical decision task in which they decided whether strings of letters formed words. Different parts of the motor system were stimulated with transcranial magnetic stimulation (TMS; see Glossary) while this task was performed. The key conditions were those in which arm-related or leg-related words were presented while TMS was applied to parts of the left-hemisphere

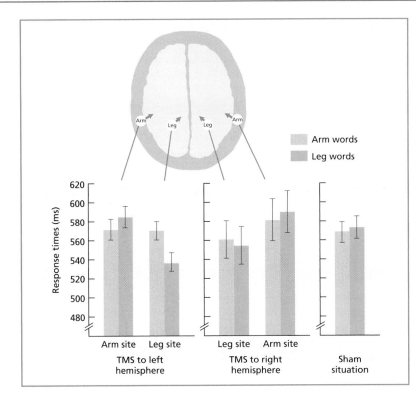

Figure 7.6 Top: sites to which TMS was applied. Bottom left: response times to make lexical (word vs. non-word) decisions on arm- and leg-related words when TMS was applied to the left language-dominant hemisphere. Bottom middle and right: findings from control experiments with TMS to the right hemisphere and during sham stimulation. From Pulvermüller et al. (2005). © 2005 Federation of European Neuroscience Societies. Reprinted with permission of Wiley-Blackwell.

motor strip associated with arm or leg movements. There was a facilitation effect: arm-related words were processed faster when TMS was applied to the arm site than to the leg site, and the opposite was the case with leg-related words (see Figure 7.6).

Evidence that perceptual information is involved in our use of concepts was reported by Solomon and Barsalou (2001). Participants decided whether concepts possessed certain properties. The key issue was whether verification times would be speeded up when the same property was linked to two different concepts. There was a facilitation effect *only* when the shape of the property was similar in both cases, indicating that perceptual information influenced task performance. For example, verifying that "mane" is a property of "pony" was facilitated by previously verifying "mane" for "horse" but not by verifying "mane" for "lion".

The grounded cognition approach is clearly useful in understanding our knowledge of concrete concepts or objects that we can see and interact with. On the face of it, the approach seems less useful when applied to abstract concepts such as "truth", "freedom", and "invention". However, Barsalou and Wiemer-Hastings (2005) argued that abstract concepts can potentially be understood within the grounded cognition approach. Participants indicated the characteristic properties of various abstract concepts. Many properties referred to settings or events associated with the concept (e.g., scientists working in a laboratory for "invention"), and others referred to relevant mental states. Thus, much of the knowledge we have of abstract concepts is relatively concrete.

According to the distributed-plus-hub theory, hubs or amodal conceptual representations are stored in the anterior temporal lobes. What would happen if someone suffered brain damage to these lobes? Theoretically, this should lead to impaired performance on all tasks requiring semantic memory. Thus, performance would be poor regardless of the modality of input (e.g., objects; words; sounds) and the modality of output (e.g., object naming; object drawing).

The above predictions have been tested using patients with semantic dementia. **Semantic dementia** involves loss of concept knowledge even though most cognitive functions are reasonably intact early in the disease. It always involves degeneration of the anterior temporal lobes. As predicted by the distributed-plus-hub theory, patients with semantic dementia perform very poorly on tests of semantic memory across all semantic categories regardless of the modalities of input and output (see Patterson et al., 2007, for a review). Patients with semantic dementia are unable to name objects when relevant pictures are presented or when they are given a description of the object (e.g., "What do we call the African animal with black and white stripes?"). They are also unable to identify objects when listening to their characteristic sounds (e.g., a phone ringing; a dog barking).

Theoretically, we would expect functional neuroimaging studies to indicate strong activation in the anterior temporal lobes when healthy participants perform semantic memory tasks. In fact, most studies have found no evidence for such activation! Rogers et al. (2006) identified two likely reasons. First, most studies used fMRI, which is poor at detecting activation in the anterior frontal lobes. Second, the semantic memory tasks used in most fMRI studies have not required objects to be classified with much precision or specificity, but patients with semantic dementia have greater problems with more precise categories. Rogers et al. carried out a study on healthy participants using PET rather than fMRI. Their task involved deciding whether an object belonged to the category specified by a previous word. The category was *specific* (e.g., BMW; labrador) or more *general* (e.g., car; dog). There was activation in the anterior temporal lobes when the task involved specific categories. Thus, we finally have solid evidence of the involvement of the anterior temporal lobes in semantic memory from a functional neuroimaging study.

Evaluation

Much progress has been made in understanding the organisation of semantic memory (see also Chapter 10). The distributed-plus-hub theory provides a more comprehensive account of semantic memory than previous theories. The evidence from brain-damaged patients with category-specific deficits indicates that different object properties are stored in different brain areas. In addition, patients with semantic dementia provide evidence for the existence of concept hubs stored in the anterior temporal lobes.

What are the limitations of distributed-plus-hub theory? First, more remains to be discovered about the information contained within concept hubs. For example, is more information stored in the hubs of very familiar concepts than of less familiar ones? Second, how do we combine or integrate concept hub information with distributed modality-specific information? It would seem that complex processes are probably involved, but we do not as yet have a clear sense of how these processes operate.

NON-DECLARATIVE MEMORY

The essence of non-declarative memory is that it does not involve conscious recollection but instead reveals itself through behaviour. As discussed earlier, repetition priming (facilitated processing of repeated stimuli) and procedural memory (mainly skill learning) are two of the major types of non-declarative memory. There are several differences between repetition priming and procedural memory. First, priming often occurs rapidly, whereas procedural memory or skill learning is typically slow and gradual

> **KEY TERM**
>
> **semantic dementia:** a condition in which there is widespread loss of information about the meanings of words and concepts but executive functioning is reasonably intact in the early stages.

(Knowlton & Foerde, 2008). Second, there is stimulus specificity. Priming is tied to specific stimuli whereas skill learning typically generalises to numerous stimuli. For example, it would not be much use if you learned how to hit backhands at tennis very well, but could only do so provided that the ball came towards you from a given direction at a given speed! Third, there is increasing evidence that different brain areas are involved in repetition priming and skill learning (Knowlton & Foerde, 2008).

If repetition priming and skill learning involve different memory systems, then there is no particular reason why individuals who are good at skill learning should be good at priming. There is often practically no correlation between performance on these two types of task. Schwartz and Hashtroudi (1991) used a word-identification task to assess priming and an inverted-text reading task to assess skill learning. There was no correlation between priming and skill learning. However, the interpretation of such findings is open to dispute. Gupta and Cohen (2002) developed a computational model based on the assumption that skill learning and priming depend on a *single* mechanism. This model accounted for zero correlations between skill learning and priming.

It is probable that priming and skill learning involve separate memory systems. However, most of the evidence is not clear-cut because the tasks assessing skill learning and repetition priming have been very different. This led Poldrack, Selco, Field, and Cohen (1999) to compare skill learning and priming within a *single* task. Participants entered five-digit numbers as rapidly as possible into a computer keypad. Priming was assessed by performance on repeated digit strings, whereas skill learning was assessed by performance on non-repeated strings. Skill learning and the increase in speed with repetition priming were both well described by a power function, leading Poldrack et al. to conclude that they both involve the same learning mechanism.

Poldrack and Gabrieli (2001) studied skill learning and repetition priming using a mirror-reading task in which words and pronounceable non-words presented in a mirror were read as fast as possible. Activity in different areas of the brain was assessed by fMRI. The findings were reasonably clear-cut:

> [Skill] learning...was associated with increased activation in left inferior temporal, striatal, left inferior prefrontal and right cerebellar regions and with decreased activity in the left hippocampus and left cerebellum. Short-term repetition priming was associated with reduced activity in many of the regions active during mirror reading and...long-term repetition priming resulted in a virtual elimination of activity in those regions. (p. 67)

The finding that very similar areas were involved in skill learning and priming is consistent with the hypothesis that they involve the same underlying memory system. However, evidence less supportive of that hypothesis is discussed later.

Repetition priming

We can draw a distinction between perceptual priming and conceptual priming. **Perceptual priming** occurs when repeated presentation of a stimulus leads to facilitated processing of its perceptual features. For example, it is easier to identify a word presented in a degraded fashion if it has recently been encountered. In contrast, **conceptual priming** occurs when repeated presentation of a stimulus leads to facilitated processing of its meaning. For example, people can decide faster whether an object is living or nonliving if they have seen it recently.

KEY TERMS

perceptual priming: a form of repetition priming in which repeated presentation of a stimulus facilitates perceptual processing of it.
conceptual priming: a form of **repetition priming** in which there is facilitated processing of stimulus meaning.

Perceptual priming occurs when repeated presentation of a stimulus leads to facilitated processing of its perceptual features. For example, it would be easier to identify words that had been eroded and had faded in the sand, if they had previously been seen when freshly etched.

Much evidence supports the distinction between perceptual and conceptual priming. Keane, Gabrieli, Mapstone, Johnson, and Corkin (1995) studied perceptual and conceptual priming in LH, a patient with bilateral brain damage within the occipital lobes. LH had an absence of perceptual priming but intact conceptual priming. In contrast, patients with Alzheimer's disease have the opposite pattern of intact perceptual priming but impaired conceptual priming (see Keane et al., 1995, for a review). According to Keane et al., the impaired conceptual priming shown by Alzheimer's patients is due to damage within the temporal and parietal lobes. The findings suggest the existence of a double dissociation (see Glossary), which provides reasonable support that different processes underlie the two types of priming.

Evidence

If repetition priming involves non-declarative memory, then amnesic patients should show intact repetition priming. This prediction has been supported many times. Cermak, Talbot, Chandler, and Wolbarst (1985) compared the performance of amnesic patients and non-amnesic alcoholics on perceptual priming. The patients were presented with a list of words followed by a priming task. This task was perceptual identification, and involved presenting the words at the minimal exposure time needed to identify them. The performance of the amnesic patients resembled that of control participants, with identification times being faster for the primed list words than for the unprimed ones. Thus, the amnesic patients showed as great a perceptual priming effect as the controls. Cermak et al. also used a conventional test of recognition memory (involving episodic memory) for the list words. The amnesic patients did significantly worse than the controls on this task.

Graf, Squire, and Mandler (1984) studied a different perceptual priming effect. Word lists were presented, with the participants deciding how much they liked each word. The lists were followed by one of four memory tests. Three tests involved declarative memory (free recall, recognition memory, and cued recall), but the fourth test (word completion) involved priming. On this last test, participants were given three-letter word fragments (e.g., STR ____) and simply wrote down the first word they thought of starting with those letters (e.g., STRAP; STRIP). Priming was assessed by the extent to which the word completion corresponded to words from the list previously presented. Amnesic patients did much worse than controls on all the declarative memory tests, but the groups did not differ on the word-completion test.

Levy, Stark, and Squire (2004) studied conceptual priming and recognition memory (involving declarative memory) in amnesic patients with large lesions in the medial temporal lobe, amnesic patients with lesions limited to the hippocampus, and healthy controls. The conceptual priming task involved deciding whether words previously studied or not studied belonged to given categories. The findings were striking. All three groups showed very similar amounts of conceptual priming. However, both amnesic groups performed poorly on recognition memory (see Figure 7.7). Indeed, the amnesic patients with large lesions showed no evidence of any declarative memory at all.

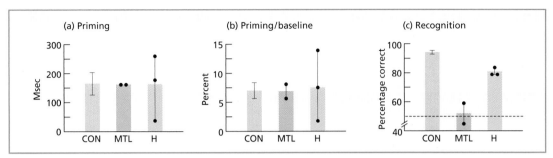

Figure 7.7 Performance of healthy controls (CON), patients with large medial temporal lobe lesions (MTL), and patients with hippocampal damage only (H) on: (a) priming in terms of reaction times; (b) priming in terms of percentage priming effect; and (c) recognition performance. From Levy et al. (2004). Reprinted with permission of Wiley-Blackwell.

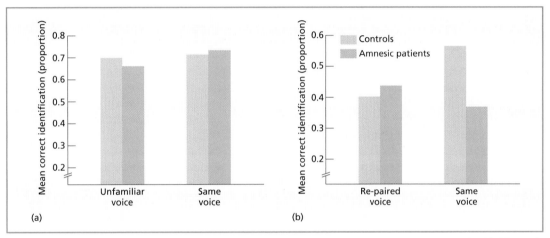

Figure 7.8 Auditory word identification for previously presented words in amnesics and controls. (a) All words originally presented in the same voice; data from Schacter and Church (1995). (b) Words originally presented in six different voices; data from Schacter et al. (1995).

The notion that priming depends on memory systems different from those involved in declarative memory would be strengthened if we could find patients having intact declarative memory but impaired priming. This would be a double dissociation, and was achieved by Gabrieli, Fleischman, Keane, Reminger, and Morell (1995). They studied a patient, MS, who had right occipital lobe lesion. MS had normal levels of performance on the declarative memory tests of recognition and cued recall but impaired performance on perceptual priming.

Further evidence that amnesics have intact perceptual priming was reported by Schacter and Church (1995). Participants initially heard words spoken in the same voice. After that, they tried to identify the same words passed through an auditory filter; the words were spoken in the same voice or an unfamiliar voice. Amnesic patients and healthy controls both showed perceptual priming, with word-identification performance being better when the words were spoken in the same voice (see Figure 7.8a).

The findings discussed so far seem neat and tidy. However, complications arose in research by Schacter, Church, and Bolton (1995). Their study resembled that of Schacter and Church (1995) in that perceptual priming based on auditory word identification was investigated. However, it differed in that the words were initially presented in *six* different voices. On the word-identification test, half the words were presented in the same voice and half were spoken by one of the other voices (re-paired condition). The healthy controls showed more priming for words presented in the same voice, but the amnesic patients did not (see Figure 7.8b).

How can we explain the above findings? In both the same voice and re-paired voice conditions, the participants were exposed to words and voices they had heard before. The only advantage in the same voice condition was that the pairing of word and voice was the same as before. However, only those participants who had linked or associated words and voices at the original presentation would benefit from that fact. The implication is that amnesics are poor at binding together different kinds of information even on priming tasks apparently involving non-declarative memory (see discussion later in the chapter).

What processes are involved in priming? One popular view is based on perceptual fluency: repeated presentation of a stimulus means it can be processed more efficiently using fewer resources. It follows from this view that priming should be associated with *reduced* levels of brain activity (known as neural priming). There is considerable evidence for this prediction (e.g., Poldrack & Gabrieli, 2001). The precise brain regions showing reduced activation vary somewhat depending on the task and whether perceptual or conceptual priming is being studied. Early visual areas in the occipital lobe often show reduced activity with perceptual priming, whereas the inferior frontal gyrus and left inferior temporal cortex show reduced activity with conceptual priming (see Schacter et al., 2007, for a review).

The finding that repetition of a stimulus causes priming and reduced brain activity does not show there is a *causal* link between patterns of brain activation and priming. More direct evidence was reported by Wig, Grafton, Demos, and Kelley (2005). They studied conceptual priming using a task in which participants classified objects as living or nonliving. Wig et al. tested the involvement of the left inferior

frontal gyrus in conceptual priming by delivering transcranial magnetic stimulation to that area. The subsequent classification of objects that had been accompanied by TMS showed an absence of both conceptual and neural priming. These findings suggest that the left inferior temporal cortex plays a causal role in producing conceptual priming.

Evaluation

There are important similarities and differences between perceptual and conceptual priming. They are similar in that most amnesic patients typically show essentially intact perceptual and conceptual priming, suggesting that both types of priming involve non-declarative memory. However, the finding of a double dissociation in which some patients are much better at perceptual than at conceptual priming, whereas others show the opposite pattern, suggests there are some important differences between them. The consistent finding that repetition priming is associated with reduced brain activation suggests that people become more efficient at processing repeated stimuli. Recent research has supported the hypothesis that there is a causal link between patterns of brain activation and priming performance.

Future research needs to establish more clearly that reduced brain activation during repetition priming is causally related to enhanced priming. There is also a need to identify more precisely the different processes involved in perceptual and conceptual priming.

Procedural memory or skill learning

What exactly is skill learning? According to Poldrack et al. (1999, p. 208), "Skill learning refers to the gradual improvement of performance with practice that generalises to a range of stimuli within a domain of processing." Motor skills are important in everyday life. For example, they are needed in word processing, writing, and playing a musical instrument.

Foerde and Poldrack (2009) identified numerous types of skill learning or procedural memory, including the following: motor skill learning; sequence learning, mirror tracing; perceptual skill learning; mirror reading; probabilistic classification learning; and artificial grammar learning. Some of these forms of skill learning are discussed at length in Chapter 6.

Here, we will address the issue of whether the above tasks involve non-declarative or procedural memory, and thus involve different memory systems from those underlying episodic and semantic memory. This issue has been addressed in various ways. However, we will mostly consider research on skill learning in amnesic patients. The rationale for doing this is simple: if amnesic patients have essentially intact skill learning but severely impaired declarative memory that would provide evidence that different memory systems are involved.

We will shortly turn to the relevant evidence. Before doing so, however, we need to consider an important issue. It is easy to imagine that some tasks involve only non-declarative or procedural memory, whereas others involve declarative memory. In fact, matters are rarely that simple (see Chapter 6). For example, consider the probabilistic classification task. Participants predict whether the weather will be sunny or rainy on the basis of various cues. Reber, Knowlton, and Squire (1996) found that amnesics learned this task as rapidly as healthy controls, suggesting that the task involves procedural memory.

Foerde, Knowlton, and Poldrack (2006) obtained evidence suggesting that learning on the probabilistic classification task can depend on either procedural or declarative memory. Participants performed the task on its own or with a demanding secondary task. Performance was similar in the two conditions. However, important differences emerged between the conditions when the fMRI data were considered. Task performance in the dual-task condition correlated with activity in the striatum (part of the basal ganglia), a part of the brain associated with procedural learning and memory. In contrast, task performance in the single-task performance correlated with activity in the medial temporal lobe, an area associated with

declarative memory. Thus, the involvement of procedural and declarative memory on the probabilistic classification task seemed to depend on the precise conditions under which the task was performed.

Evidence
Amnesics often have normal (or nearly normal) rates of skill learning across numerous tasks. Spiers et al. (2001), in a review discussed earlier, considered the memory performance of numerous amnesic patients. They concluded as follows: "None of the cases was reported to…be impaired on tasks which involved learning skills or habits, priming, simple classical conditioning and simple category learning" (p. 359).

Corkin (1968) reported that the amnesic patient HM (see p. 252) was able to learn mirror drawing, in which the pen used in drawing a figure is observed in a mirror rather than directly. He also showed learning on the pursuit rotor, which involves manual tracking of a moving target. HM's rate of learning was slower than that of healthy individuals on the pursuit rotor. In contrast, Cermak, Lewis, Butters, and Goodglass (1973) found that amnesic patients learned the pursuit rotor as rapidly as healthy participants. However, the amnesic patients were slower than healthy individuals at learning a finger maze.

Tranel, Damasio, Damasio, and Brandt (1994) found in a study on 28 amnesic patients that all showed comparable learning on the pursuit rotor to healthy controls. Of particular note was a patient, Boswell, who had unusually extensive brain damage to areas (e.g., medial and lateral temporal lobes) strongly associated with declarative memory. In spite of this, his learning on the pursuit rotor and retention over a two-year period were both at the same level as healthy controls.

The typical form of the serial reaction time task involves presenting visual targets in one of four horizontal locations, with the participants pressing the closest key as rapidly as possible (see Chapter 6). The sequence of targets is sometimes repeated over 10 or 12 trials, and skill learning is shown by improved performance on these repeated sequences. Nissen, Willingham, and Hartman (1989) found that amnesic patients and healthy controls showed comparable performance on the serial reaction time task during learning and also on a second test one week later. Vandenberghe et al. (2006) obtained more complex findings. They had a deterministic condition in which there was a repeating sequence and a probabilistic condition in which there was a repeating sequence but with some deviations. Amnesic patients failed to show skill learning in the probabilistic condition, but exhibited some implicit learning in the deterministic condition. Thus, amnesic patients do not always show reasonable levels of skill learning.

Mirror tracing involves tracing a figure with a stylus, with the figure to be traced being seen reflected in a mirror. Performance on this task improves with practice in healthy participants, and the same is true of amnesic patients (e.g., Milner, 1962). The rate of learning is often similar in both groups.

In mirror reading we can distinguish between *general* improvement in speed of reading produced by practice and more *specific* improvement produced by re-reading the same groups of words or sentences. Cohen and Squire (1980) reported general and specific improvement in reading mirror-reversed script in amnesics, and there was evidence of improvement even after a delay of three months. Martone, Butters, Payne, Becker, and Sax (1984) also obtained evidence of general and specific improvement in amnesics.

Cavaco, Anderson, Allen, Castro-Caldas, and Damasio (2004) pointed out that most tasks used to assess skill learning in amnesics require learning far removed from that occurring in everyday life. Accordingly, Cavaco et al. used five skill-learning tasks requiring skills similar to those needed in the real world. For example, there was a weaving task and a control stick task requiring movements similar to those involved in operating machinery. Amnesic patients showed comparable rates of learning to those of healthy individuals on all five tasks, in spite of having significantly impaired declarative memory for the tasks assessed by recall and recognition tests.

In sum, amnesic patients show reasonably good skill or procedural learning and memory in spite of very poor declarative memory. That provides reasonable evidence that there are major differences between the two forms of memory. Shortly, we will consider evidence indicating that the brain areas associated with procedural memory differ from those associated with declarative memory. However, we must not think of declarative and procedural memory as being entirely separate. Brown and Robertson (2007) gave participants a procedural learning task (the serial reaction time task) and a declarative learning task (free recall of a word list). Procedural memory was disrupted when declarative learning occurred during the retention interval. In a second experiment, declarative memory was disrupted when procedural learning occurred during the retention interval. Thus, there can be *interactions* between the two memory systems.

BEYOND DECLARATIVE AND NON-DECLARATIVE MEMORY: AMNESIA

Most memory researchers have argued that there is a very important distinction between declarative/explicit memory and non-declarative/implicit memory. As we have seen, this distinction has proved very useful in accounting for most of the findings (especially those from amnesic patients). However, there are good grounds for arguing that we need to move beyond that distinction. We will focus our discussion on amnesia, but research on healthy individuals also suggests that the distinction between declarative and non-declarative memory is limited (see Reder, Park, & Kieffaber, 2009, for a review).

According to the traditional viewpoint, amnesic patients should have intact performance on declarative memory tasks and impaired performance on non-declarative tasks. There is an alternative viewpoint that has attracted increasing interest (e.g., Reder et al., 2009; Ryan, Althoff, Whitlow, & Cohen, 2000; Schacter et al., 1995). According to Reder et al. (2009, p. 24), "The critical feature that distinguishes tasks that are impaired from those that are spared under amnesia hinges on whether the task requires the formation of an association (or binding) between the two concepts." We will briefly consider research relevant to adjudicating between these two viewpoints. Before we do so, note that the binding-of-item-and-context model (Diana et al., 2007; discussed earlier in the chapter) identifies the hippocampus as of central importance in the binding process. The relevance of that model here is that amnesic patients typically have extensive damage to the hippocampus.

Evidence

Earlier in the chapter we discussed a study by Schacter et al. (1995) on perceptual priming. Amnesic patients and healthy controls identified words passed through an auditory filter having previously heard them spoken by the same voice or one out of five different voices. The measure of perceptual priming was the extent to which participants were better at identifying words spoken in the same voice than those spoken in a different voice. Since six different voices were used altogether, successful perceptual priming required binding or associating the voices with the words when the words were presented initially. In spite of the fact that Schacter et al. used a non-declarative memory task, amnesic patients showed no better performance for words presented in the same voice than in a different voice (see Figure 7.8b). This finding is inconsistent with the traditional viewpoint but is as predicted by the binding hypothesis.

More evidence that amnesic patients sometimes have deficient implicit memory was reported by Chun and Phelps (1999). Amnesic patients and healthy controls carried out a visual search task in which the target was a rotated T and the distractors were rotated Ls. Half the displays were new and the remainder were old or repeated. There were two main findings with the healthy controls. First, their performance improved progressively throughout the experiment (skill learning). Second, they improved significantly

more with practice on the old displays than on the new ones. This involved implicit learning, because they had no ability to discriminate old displays from new ones on a recognition test. The amnesic patients showed general improvement with practice, and thus some implicit learning. However, there was no difference between their performance on new and old displays. This failure of implicit learning probably occurred because the amnesic patients could not bind the arrangement of the distractors to the location of the target in old displays.

There have been some failures to replicate the above findings (see Reder et al., 2009, for a review), perhaps because amnesic patients differ so much in their precise brain damage and memory impairments. Park, Quinlan, Thornton, and Reder (2004) argued that a useful approach is to use drugs that mimic the effects of amnesia. They administered midazolam, a benzodiazepine that impairs performance on explicit memory tasks but not implicit tasks (e.g., repetition priming). They carried out a study very similar to that of Chun and Phelps (1999), and obtained similar findings. Their key result was that healthy individuals given midazolam failed to perform better on old displays than new ones, in contrast to individuals given a placebo (saline) (see Figure 7.9). Thus, midazolam-induced amnesia impairs implicit learning because it disrupts binding with old displays.

A study by Huppert and Piercy (1976) on declarative memory supports the binding hypothesis. They presented large numbers of pictures on day 1 and on day 2. Some of those presented on day 2 had been presented on day 1 and others had not. Ten minutes after the day-2 presentation, there was a recognition-memory test, on which participants decided which pictures had been presented on day 2. Successful performance on this test required binding of picture and temporal context at the time of learning. Healthy controls performed much better than amnesic patients in correctly identifying day-2 pictures and rejecting pictures presented only on day 1 (see Figure 7.10a). Thus, amnesic patients were at a great disadvantage when binding was necessary for memory.

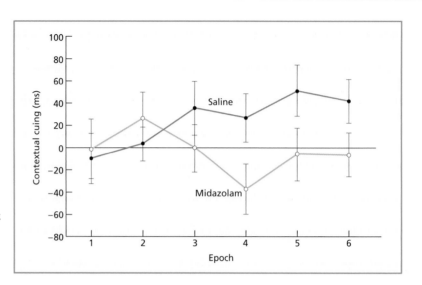

Figure 7.9 The difference between visual search performance with old and new displays (i.e., contextual cueing effect) as a function of condition (Midazolam vs. placebo/saline) and stage of practice (epochs). From Park et al. (2004), Copyright © 2004 National Academy of Sciences, USA. Reprinted with permission.

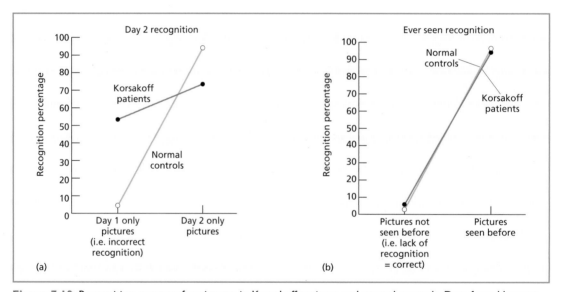

Figure 7.10 Recognition memory for pictures in Korsakoff patients and normal controls. Data from Huppert and Piercy (1976).

Huppert and Piercy (1976) also used a familiarity-based recognition memory test. Participants decided whether they had ever seen the pictures before. Here, no prior binding of picture and temporal context was necessary. On this test, the amnesic patients and healthy controls performed the task extremely well (see Figure 7.10b). Thus, as predicted by the binding hypothesis, amnesic patients can perform declarative memory tasks successfully provided that binding is not required.

Evaluation

Since declarative memory tasks generally require the formation of associations and non-declarative memory tasks do not, it is often hard to decide which viewpoint is preferable. However, there is increasing support for the binding hypothesis. More specifically, we now have studies showing that amnesic patients sometimes fail to show non-declarative/implicit memory when binding of information (e.g., stimulus + context) is required (e.g., Chun & Phelps, 1999; Schacter et al., 1995). In addition, amnesic patients sometimes show essentially intact declarative/explicit memory when binding of information is not required (e.g., Huppert & Piercy, 1976).

What is needed for the future? First, we need more research in which the predictions based on the traditional viewpoint differ from those based on the binding hypothesis. Second, we should look for tasks that differ more clearly in their requirements for binding than most of those used hitherto. Third, it is important to specify more precisely what is involved in the binding process.

LONG-TERM MEMORY AND THE BRAIN

Our understanding of long-term memory has been greatly enhanced by functional imaging studies and research on brain-damaged patients. It is clear that encoding and retrieval in long-term memory involve several processes and are more complex than was previously thought. In this section, we will briefly consider how different brain regions contribute to long-term memory, with an emphasis on the *major* brain areas associated with each memory system. As we will see, each memory system is associated with different brain areas. This strengthens the argument that the various memory systems are indeed somewhat separate. In what follows, we will discuss some of the evidence. The role of the anterior temporal lobes in semantic memory (e.g., Patterson et al., 2007), early visual areas in the occipital lobe in perceptual priming (Schacter et al., 2007), and left inferior temporal cortex in conceptual priming (e.g., Wig et al., 2005) were discussed earlier in the chapter.

Medial temporal lobe and medial diencephalon

The medial temporal lobe including the hippocampal formation is of crucial importance in anterograde amnesia and in declarative memory generally. However, we have a problem because chronic alcoholics who develop Korsakoff's syndrome have brain damage to the diencephalon including the mamillary bodies and various thalamic nuclei (see Figure 7.11). Aggleton (2008) argued persuasively that temporal lobe amnesia and diencephalic amnesia both reflect damage to the same integrated brain system involving the temporal lobes and the medial diencephalon. Aggleton pointed out

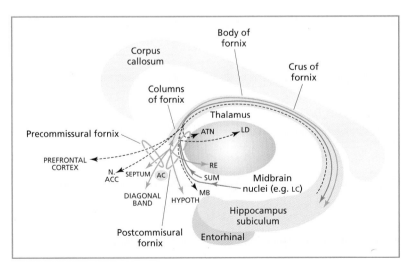

Figure 7.11 The main interconnected brain areas involved in amnesia: AC = anterior commissure; ATN = anterior thalamic nuclei; HYPOTH = hypothalamus; LC = locus coeruleus; LD = thalamic nucleus lateralis dorsalis; MB = mammillary bodies; RE = nucleus reuniens; SUM = supramammillary nucleus. From Aggleton (2008).

that the anterior thalamic nuclei and the mammillary bodies differ from the rest of the medial diencephalon in that they both receive direct inputs from the hippocampal formation via the fornix (see Figure 7.11). Thus, these areas are likely to be of major importance within the hypothesised integrated system. Aggleton and Brown (1999) proposed that an "extended hippocampal system" consisting of the hippocampus, fornix, mammillary bodies, and the anterior thalamic nuclei is crucial for episodic memory.

There is much support for the notion of an extended hippocampal system. Harding, Halliday, Caine, and Kril (2000) studied the brains of alcoholics with Korsakoff's syndrome and those of alcoholics without amnesia. The only consistent difference between the two groups was that the Korsakoff patients had degeneration of the anterior thalamic nuclei. There is also evidence for the importance of the fornix. Patients with benign brain tumours who suffer atrophy of the fornix as a consequence consistently exhibit clear signs of anterograde amnesia (Gilboa et al., 2006).

We have focused on anterograde amnesia in this section. However, the hippocampal formation and medial temporal lobe are also very important in retrograde amnesia (Moscovitch et al., 2006). In addition, the hippocampus (and the prefrontal cortex) are of central importance in autobiographical memory (Cabeza & St. Jacques, 2007; see Chapter 8).

Striatum and cerebellum

Which brain areas are involved in skill learning or procedural memory? Different types of skill learning involve different brain areas depending on characteristics of the task (e.g., auditory versus visual input). However, two brain areas are most closely associated with procedural memory: the striatum (part of the basal ganglia) in particular but also the cerebellum. The evidence implicating those brain areas comes from studies on brain-damaged patients and from neuroimaging research.

Much research has made use of brain-damaged patients suffering from Parkinson's disease, which is associated with damage to the striatum. **Parkinson's disease** is a progressive disorder characterised by tremor of the limbs, muscle rigidity, and mask-like facial expression. Siegert, Taylor, Weatherall, and Abernethy (2006) reported a meta-analysis of learning on the serial reaction time task (discussed above) by patients with Parkinson's disease (see Chapter 6). Skill learning by Parkinson's patients was consistently slower than that by healthy controls.

Strong evidence that the basal ganglia are important in skill learning was reported by Brown, Jahanshahi, Limousin-Dowsey, Thomas, Quinn, and Rothwell (2003). They studied patients with Parkinson's disease who had had posteroventral pallidotomy, a surgical form of treatment that disrupts the output of the basal ganglia to the frontal cortex. These patients showed no implicit learning at all on the serial reaction time task.

Not all the evidence indicates that Parkinson's patients show deficient procedural learning and memory. Osman, Wilkinson, Beigi, Castaneda, and Jahanshahi (2008) reviewed several studies in which Parkinson's patients performed well on procedural learning tasks. In their own experiment, participants had to learn about and control a complex system (e.g., water-tank system). Patients with Parkinson's disease showed the same level of procedural learning as healthy controls on this task, which suggests that the striatum is not needed for all forms of procedural learning and memory.

Neuroimaging studies have produced somewhat variable findings (see Kelly & Garavan, 2005, for a review). However, practice in skill learning is often associated with decreased activation in the prefrontal cortex but increased activation in the basal ganglia. It is likely that the decreased activation in the prefrontal cortex occurs because attentional and control processes

---

KEY TERM

Parkinson's disease: it is a progressive disorder involving damage to the basal ganglia; the symptoms include rigidity of the muscles, limb tremor, and mask-like facial expression.

are important early in learning but become less so with extensive practice. Debaere et al. (2004) found, during acquisition of a skill requiring co-ordination of hand movements, that there were decreases in activation within the right dorso-lateral prefrontal cortex, the right premotor cortex, and the bilateral superior parietal cortex. At the same time, there were increases in activation within the cerebellum and basal ganglia.

In sum, the striatum (and to a lesser extent the cerebellum) are important in procedural learning and memory. However, we must avoid oversimplifying a complex reality. The neuro-imaging findings indicate clearly that several other areas (e.g., the prefrontal cortex; the posterior parietal cortex) are also involved.

Prefrontal cortex

As discussed in Chapter 5, the prefrontal cortex is extremely important in most (or all) executive processes involving attentional control. As we have seen in this chapter, it is also of signi-ficance in long-term memory. Two relatively small regions on the lateral or outer surface of the frontal lobes are of special importance: the dorsolateral prefrontal cortex (roughly BA9 and B46) and the ventrolateral prefrontal cortex (roughly BA45 and BA47) (see Figure 1.4).

Dorsolateral prefrontal cortex

What is the role of dorsolateral prefrontal cortex in declarative memory? One idea is that this area is involved in relational encoding (forming links between items or between an item and its context). Murray and Ranganath (2007) carried out a study in which unrelated word pairs were presented. In one condition, the task involved a comparison between the two words (relational encoding) and in the other it did not (item-specific encoding). Activation of the dorsolateral prefrontal cortex was greater during relational than item-specific encoding. More importantly, the amount of dorsolateral activity at encoding predicted successful performance on a recogni-tion test of relational memory.

Another possible role of dorsolateral pre-frontal cortex in memory is to evaluate the relevance of retrieved information to current task requirements (known as post-retrieval monitor-ing). The more information that is retrieved, the more likely the individual will engage in monitoring. Achim and Lepage (2005) manipu-lated the amount of information likely to be retrieved in two recognition-memory tests. As predicted, activity within the dorsolateral pre-frontal cortex was greater when there was more demand for post-retrieval monitoring.

In sum, dorsolateral prefrontal cortex plays a role at encoding and at retrieval. First, it is involved in relational encoding at the time of learning. Second, it is involved in post-retrieval monitoring at the time of retrieval. In general terms, dorsolateral prefrontal cortex is often activated when encoding and/or retrieval is relatively complex.

Ventrolateral prefrontal cortex

Badre and Wagner (2007) discussed a two-process account of the involvement of the ventrolateral prefrontal cortex in declarative memory. There is a controlled retrieval process used to activate goal-relevant knowledge. There is also a post-retrieval selection process that deals with competition between memory repre-sentations active at the same time.

Evidence that both of the above processes involve the ventrolateral prefrontal cortex was reported by Badre, Poldrack, Pare-Blagoev, Insler, and Wagner (2005). A cue word and two or four target words were presented on each trial, and the task was to decide which target word was semantically related to the cue word. It was assumed that the controlled retrieval process would be involved when the target word was only weakly associated with the cue (e.g., cue = candle; target word = halo). It was also assumed that the post-retrieval selection process would be needed when one of the incorrect target words was non-semantically associated with the cue word (e.g., cue = ivy; incorrect target word = league). As predicted, there was increased activation within the ventrolateral prefrontal cortex when the task required the use of controlled retrieval or post-retrieval selection.

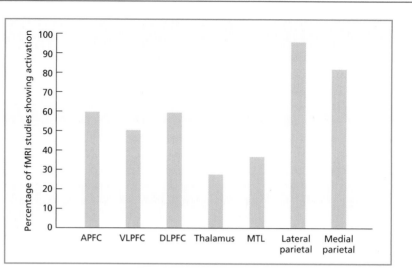

Figure 7.12 Percentages of fMRI studies of episodic memory showing activation in various brain regions. APFC = anterior prefrontal cortex; VLPFC = ventrolateral prefrontal cortex; DLPFC = dorsolateral prefrontal cortex; MTL = medial temporal lobe. Reprinted from Simons et al. (2008), Copyright © 2008, with permission from Elsevier.

Kuhl, Kahn, Dudukovic, and Wagner (2008) studied the post-retrieval selection process. There was activation of the right ventrolateral prefrontal cortex and the anterior cingulate when memories that had previously been selected against were successfully retrieved. It was assumed that an effective post-retrieval selection process was needed to permit previously selected-against memories to be retrieved.

Parietal lobes

What is the involvement of the parietal lobes in long-term memory? Simons et al. (2008) carried out a meta-analysis of functional neuro-imaging studies on episodic memory in which brain activation was assessed during successful recollection of the context in which events had occurred. Lateral and medial areas within the parietal lobes were more consistently activated than any other areas in the entire brain (see Figure 7.12).

The picture seems to be very different when we consider patients with damage to the parietal lobes. For the most part, these patients do not seem to have severe episodic memory deficits (see Cabeza, 2008, for a review). However, some deficits have been found in such patients. In one study (Berryhill, Phuong, Picasso, Cabeza, & Olson, 2007), patients with ventral parietal damage freely recalled events from their own

lives. The memories recalled were less vivid and contained less detail than those of healthy controls. However, the same patients performed normally when they were probed for specific details of their memories.

Cabeza (2008) explained this and other findings in his dual attentional processes hypothesis. According to this hypothesis, ventral parietal cortex is associated with bottom-up attentional processes captured by the retrieval output. These attentional processes were damaged in the patients studied by Berryhill et al. (2007). In contrast, dorsal parietal cortex is associated with top-down attentional processes influenced by retrieval goals. The hypothesis is supported by two findings (see Cabeza, 2008, for a review):

(1) There is greater ventral parietal activation when memory performance is high due to greater capture of bottom-up attention by relevant stimuli.
(2) There is greater dorsal parietal activation when memory performance is low due to greater demands on top-down attention.

Evaluation

Considerable progress has been made in understanding the involvement of different brain areas in the major memory systems. The findings from cognitive neuroscience are generally consistent with those from cognitive psychology. As a result, we have an increasingly clear overall picture of how memory works.

What are the limitations of research in this area? First, the findings from brain-damaged patients and from functional neuroimaging sometimes seem inconsistent. Thus, for example, the importance of the parietal cortex in human memory seems greater in neuroimaging studies than in studies on brain-damaged patients.

Second, even when we have established that a given brain area is important with respect to some memory system, its role is not always very clear. A brain area might be important because it is needed for initial encoding, for subsequent storage of information, for control of memory-relevant processes, or for retrieval of stored information. Finding that a given brain area is activated during a particular memory task does not immediately indicate *why* it is activated.

Third, a major task for the future is to understand how different brain areas interact and combine during learning and memory. Learning and memory undoubtedly depend upon networks consisting of several brain regions, but as yet we know relatively little about the structure or functioning of such networks.

CHAPTER SUMMARY

- **Introduction**
  There are several long-term memory systems. However, the crucial distinction is between declarative and non-declarative memory. Strong evidence for that distinction comes from amnesic patients having severely impaired declarative memory but almost intact non-declarative memory and from functional neuroimaging. Declarative memory can be divided into episodic and semantic memory. Non-declarative memory can be divided into repetition priming and procedural memory or skill learning.

- **Episodic vs. semantic memory**
  Virtually all amnesic patients have severe problems with forming new episodic memories but many have only modest problems in forming new semantic memories. Some amnesic patients have retrograde amnesia mainly for episodic memory, whereas others have retrograde amnesia mainly for semantic memory. Damage to the hippocampal complex has less effect on semantic memory than on episodic memory, whereas damage to the neocortex impairs semantic memory. Functional neuroimaging also indicates that different brain areas are associated with episodic and semantic memory.

- **Episodic memory**
  There is an important distinction between familiarity and recollection in recognition memory. According to the binding-of-item-and-context model, familiarity judgements depend on perirhinal cortex, whereas recollection depends on binding what and where information in the hippocampus. Free recall involves similar brain areas to recognition memory. However, it is associated with higher levels of brain activity, and it also involves some brain areas not needed for recognition memory. Episodic memory is basically constructive rather than reproductive, and so we remember the gist or essence of our past experiences. We use the constructive processes associated with episodic memory to imagine future events.

- Semantic memory
Collins and Quillian (1969) argued that semantic memory is organised into hierarchical networks with concept properties stored as high up the hierarchy as possible. This inflexible approach was superseded by spreading activation theory, in which activation of one concept causes activation to spread to semantically related concepts. Perceptual–functional theories assume that the visual or perceptual features of an object are stored in different locations from its functional features. Such theories are oversimplified. The distributed-plus-hub theory provides the most comprehensive approach to semantic memory. There are hubs (unified abstract conceptual representations) for concepts as well as distributed modality-specific information. Evidence from patients with semantic dementia indicates that these hubs are stored in the anterior temporal lobes.

- Non-declarative memory
Amnesic patients typically have intact repetition priming but impaired declarative memory, whereas a few patients with other disorders show the opposite pattern. Priming is associated with perceptual fluency and increased neural efficiency. Amnesic patients generally (but not always) have high levels of procedural learning and memory. This is the case whether standard motor-skill tasks are used or tasks requiring skills similar to those needed in the real world.

- Beyond declarative and non-declarative memory: amnesia
Several theorists have argued that the distinction between declarative and non-declarative memory is oversimplified and is inadequate to explain the memory deficits of amnesic patients. According to an alternative viewpoint, amnesic patients are deficient at binding or forming associations of all kinds. The evidence mostly supports this binding hypothesis over the traditional viewpoint that amnesic patients are deficient at declarative or explicit memory.

- Long-term memory and the brain
Research on amnesic patients has shown that an extended hippocampal system is crucial for episodic memory. Skill learning or procedural memory involves the striatum and the cerebellum. Patients with Parkinson's disease have damage to the striatum and are generally impaired at procedural learning. Neuroimaging studies suggest that the prefrontal cortex is often involved in the early stages of procedural learning and the striatum at later stages. The dorsolateral prefrontal cortex is involved in relational encoding and post-retrieval monitoring. The ventrolateral prefrontal cortex is involved in controlled retrieval and a process dealing with competing memory representations. The parietal cortex is involved in various attentional processes of relevance to learning and memory.

FURTHER READING

- Baddeley, A.D., Eysenck, M.W., & Anderson, M.C. (2009). *Memory*. Hove, UK: Psychology Press. Several chapters (especially 5, 6, and 11) are of direct relevance to the topics covered in this chapter.

- Foerde, K., & Poldrack, R.A. (2009). Procedural learning in humans. In *Encyclopedia of neuroscience*. New York: Elsevier. This chapter gives an excellent overview of theory and research on procedural learning and procedural memory.
- Patterson, K., Nestor, P.J., & Rogers, T.T. (2007). Where do you know what you know? The representation of semantic knowledge in the human brain. *Nature Reviews Neuroscience*, 8, 976–987. The authors provide a succinct overview of our current understanding of how semantic memory is organised within the brain.
- Reder, L.M., Park, H., & Kieffaber, P.D. (2009). Memory systems do not divide on consciousness: Re-interpreting memory in terms of activation and binding. *Psychological Bulletin*, 135, 23–49. The distinction between explicit/declarative and implicit/non-declarative memory systems is evaluated in the light of the evidence and an alternative theoretical perspective is proposed.
- Schacter, D.L., & Addis, D.R. (2007). The cognitive neuroscience of constructive memory: Remembering the past and imagining the future. *Philosophical Transactions of the Royal Society B: Biological Sciences, 362*, 773–786. Interesting new perspectives on episodic memory are offered in this article by Schacter and Addis.
- Schacter, D.L., Wig, G.S., & Stevens, W.D. (2007). Reductions in cortical activity during priming. *Current Opinion in Neurobiology, 17*, 171–176. Schacter and his co-authors discuss the main mechanisms underlying priming.

CHAPTER 8

EVERYDAY MEMORY

INTRODUCTION

When most of us think about memory, we consider it in the context of our own everyday experience. For example, we wonder why our memory is so fallible and how we might improve it. Perhaps we also wonder why we remember some aspects of our lives much better than others, or why we sometimes forget to carry out tasks like buying a birthday present for a friend or turning up for a dental appointment.

It is obviously important to study memory in the real world (often known as everyday memory). However, for nearly 100 years, most research on human memory was carried out under laboratory conditions and often used artificial learning materials such as lists of nonsense syllables or unrelated words. This led Ulric Neisser (1978, p. 4) to argue in despair, "If X is an interesting or socially significant aspect of memory, then psychologists have hardly ever studied X." In fact, more memory research prior to 1978 was of relevance to the phenomena of everyday memory than Neisser realised. For example, there was Bartlett's (1932) very influential research on the ways in which our prior knowledge can distort our memory for stories (see Chapter 10). In any case, Neisser's argument helped to produce a dramatic increase in research concerned explicitly with everyday memory. Some highlights of that research are discussed in this chapter.

Traditional memory research vs. everyday memory research

What are the main differences between the traditional approach to memory research and the one based on everyday memory phenomena? Koriat and Goldsmith (1996) argued that traditional memory research is based on the storehouse metaphor. According to this metaphor, items of information are stored in memory and what is of interest is the *number* of items accessible at retrieval. In contrast, the correspondence metaphor is more applicable to everyday memory research. According to this metaphor, what is important is the correspondence or goodness of fit between an individual's report and the actual event. Consider eyewitness testimony about a crime. According to the storehouse metaphor, what matters is simply how many items of information can be recalled. In contrast, what matters on the correspondence metaphor is whether the crucial items of information (e.g., facial characteristics of the criminal) are remembered. Thus, the *content* of what is remembered is more important within the correspondence metaphor.

Cohen (2008) identified other differences between the two types of memory research. For example, everyday memories are often of events that happened a long time ago and have frequently been thought about or rehearsed during that time. As a result, "Naturally occurring memories are very often memories of memories rather than memories of the originally perceived objects and events" (p. 2). In contrast, participants in laboratory studies usually remember information presented shortly beforehand.

Original learning in most everyday memory research is incidental (i.e., not deliberate), and individuals learn information relevant to their goals or interests. In most traditional memory research, in contrast, learning is intentional, and what individuals learn is determined largely by the instructions they are given.

We turn now to what is probably the most crucial difference between memory as traditionally studied and memory in everyday life. Participants in traditional memory studies are generally motivated to be as accurate as possible in their memory performance. In contrast, everyday memory research is typically based on the notion that, "remembering is a form of purposeful action" (Neisser, 1996, p. 204). This approach involves three assumptions about everyday memory:

(1) It is purposeful.
(2) It has a personal quality about it, meaning it is influenced by the individual's personality and other characteristics.
(3) It is influenced by situational demands (e.g., the wish to impress one's audience).

The essence of Neisser's (1996) argument is this: what we remember in everyday life is determined by our personal goals, whereas what we remember in traditional memory research is mostly determined by the experimenter's demands for accuracy. There are occasions in everyday life when we strive for maximal accuracy in our recall (e.g., during an examination; remembering a shopping list), but accuracy is typically *not* our main goal.

Relevant research was reported by Marsh and Tversky (2004). Students recorded information about their retelling of personal memories to other people over a period of one month. The students admitted that 42% of these retellings were inaccurate. In addition, one-third of the retellings they classified as accurate nevertheless contained distortions.

Neisser (1996) argued that what we remember in everyday life is determined by our personal goals. A desire to impress our date, for example, may introduce inaccuracies into the retelling of an anecdote, and may even distort our subsequent long-term memory of the event.

Dudukovic, Marsh, and Tversky (2004) asked participants to read a story and then retell it three times accurately (as in traditional memory research) or entertainingly (as in the real world). Not surprisingly, entertaining retellings contained more affect but fewer sensory references than accurate retellings. The key issue was whether the requirement to retell a story in an entertaining way impaired participants' ability to recall it accurately subsequently. The evidence was clear: those who had previously provided entertaining retellings recalled fewer story events, fewer details, and were less accurate than those who had provided accurate retellings. Thus, the goals we have in remembering can distort our subsequent long-term memory even after those goals have changed. As Marsh (2007, p. 19) pointed out, "What people remember about events may be the story they last told about those events."

What should be done?

Research on human memory should ideally possess ecological validity (i.e., applicability to real life; see Glossary). Kvavilashvili and Ellis (2004) argued that ecological validity consists of two aspects: (1) *representativeness*; and (2) *generalisability*. Representativeness refers to the naturalness of the experimental situation, stimuli, and task, whereas generalisability refers to the extent to which a study's findings are applicable to the real world. Generalisability is more important than representativeness. It is often (but mistakenly) assumed that everyday memory research always has more ecological validity than traditional laboratory research. Research possessing high ecological validity can be carried out by devising naturalistic experiments in which the task and conditions resemble those found in real life, but the experiment is well-controlled.

It used to be argued that traditional memory research and everyday memory research are mutually antagonistic. That argument is incorrect in two ways. First, the distinction between these two types of research is blurred and indistinct. Second, there is increasing *cross-fertilisation*, with the insights from both kinds of memory research producing a fuller understanding of human memory.

AUTOBIOGRAPHICAL MEMORY

Of all the hundreds of thousands of memories we possess, those relating to our own past, to the experiences we have had, and to people important to us have special significance. Our own autobiographical memories are of consuming interest because they relate to our major life goals, to our most powerful emotions, and to our personal meanings. As Conway, Pleydell-Pearce, and Whitecross (2001, p. 493) pointed out, autobiographical knowledge has the function of "defining identity, linking personal history to public history, supporting a network of personal goals and projects across the life span, and ultimately in grounding the self in experience."

It is worth distinguishing between auto-biographical memory and episodic memory. **Autobiographical memory** is memory for the events of one's own life, whereas episodic memory is concerned with personal experiences or events that happened at a given time in a specific place (discussed in Chapter 7). The fact that autobiographical and episodic memory both relate to personally experienced events indicates that there is substantial overlap. However, there are various differences. First, autobiographical memory is concerned with events of personal significance, whereas episodic memory often relates to trivial events (e.g., was the word "chair" in the first or the second list?). Second, autobiographical memory extends back over years or decades, whereas episodic memory (at least for events in the laboratory) often extends back only for minutes or hours. Third, autobiographical memory typically deals with complex memories selected from a huge collection of personal experiences, whereas episodic memory is much more limited in scope.

Gilboa (2004) discussed brain-imaging evidence that autobiographical and episodic memory are different. He carried out a meta-analysis of studies on autobiographical memory and episodic memory (mostly involving memory for word lists, word pairs, and so on). There were some clear differences in patterns of activation within the prefrontal cortex between the two forms of memory (see Figure 8.1). There was substantially more activation in the right mid-dorsolateral prefrontal cortex in episodic memory than in autobiographical memory. This probably occurs because episodic memory requires conscious monitoring to avoid errors. In contrast, there was much more activation in the left ventromedial prefrontal cortex in autobiographical memory than in episodic memory. This probably happens because autobiographical memory involves monitoring the accuracy of retrieved memories in relation to activated knowledge of the self.

Burianova and Grady (2007) carried out a study in which the same pictures were used

> ## KEY TERM
>
> **autobiographical memory:** memory for the events of one's own life.

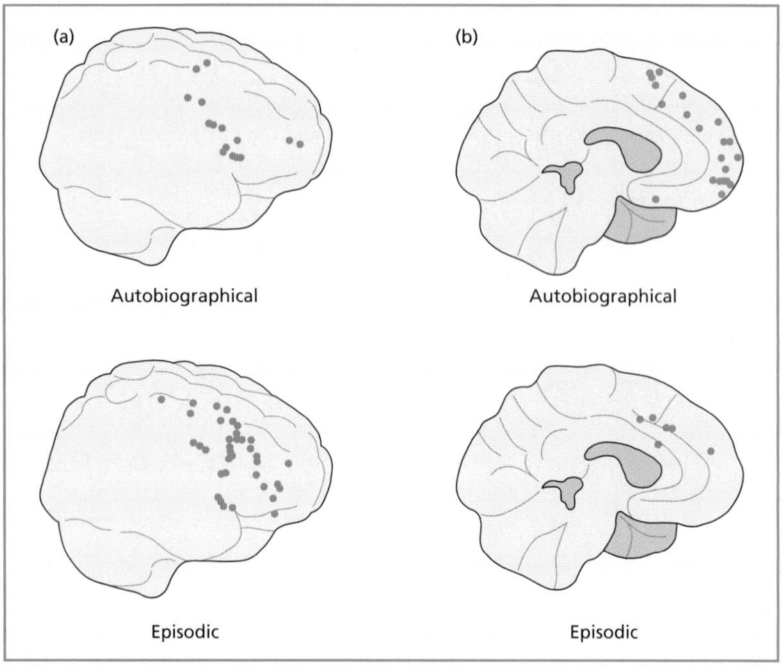

Figure 8.1 (a) Shows more activation in the right mid-dorsolateral (top and to the side) prefrontal cortex in episodic than in autobiographical memory; (b) shows more activation in the left ventromedial (bottom middle) prefrontal cortex in autobiographical than in episodic memory. Both reprinted from Gilboa (2004), Copyright © 2004, with permission from Elsevier.

in all conditions, but the retrieval demands were varied to require autobiographical, episodic, or semantic memory. All three forms of memory shared some brain regions including the inferior frontal gyrus, the middle frontal gyrus, and the caudate nucleus. In addition, each form of memory was associated with some unique activation: only autobiographical memory involved medial frontal activation, only episodic memory involved right middle frontal activation, and only semantic memory involved right inferior temporal activation. These findings strengthen the case for distinguishing among these three forms of declarative memory.

Flashbulb memories

Most people think they have very clear and long-lasting autobiographical memories for important, dramatic, and surprising public events such as the terrorist attacks on the United States on 11 September 2001 or the death of Princess Diana. Such memories were termed **flashbulb memories** by Brown and Kulik (1977). They argued that dramatic events perceived by an individual as surprising and as having real consequences for his/her life activate a special neural mechanism. This mechanism "prints" the details of such events permanently in the memory system. According to Brown and Kulik, flashbulb memories often include the following information:

- Informant (person who supplied the information).
- Place where the news was heard.
- Ongoing event.
- Individual's own emotional state.
- Emotional state of others.
- Consequences of the event for the individual.

KEY TERMS

flashbulb memories: vivid and detailed memories of dramatic events.
Proust phenomenon: the finding that odours are especially powerful cues for the recall of very old and emotional autobiographical memories.
olfaction: the sense of smell.

Proust nose best: the Proust phenomenon

Many people believe that odours provide very powerful cues to remind us of vivid and emotional personal experiences that happened a very long time ago. The notion that odours are especially good at allowing us to recall very old and emotional personal memories is known as the **Proust phenomenon** in honour of the French novelist Marcel Proust (1871–1922). He described how the smell and taste of a tea-soaked pastry evoked childhood memories:

> I raised to my lips a spoonful of the tea in which I had soaked a morsel of the cake. No sooner had the warm liquid, and the crumbs with it, touched my palate than a shudder ran through my entire body ... it was connected with the taste of tea and cake.... The smell and taste of things remain poised for a long time ... and bear unfaltering ... the vast structure of recollection.

Laird (1935) surveyed 254 eminent men and women; 76% of the women and 47% of the men claimed that memories triggered by odours were among their most vivid. Only 7% of the women and 16% of the men said their odour-triggered memories were emotionally neutral. Maylor, Carter, and Hallett (2002) found that odour cues were strong in young (mean age = 21 years) and older (mean age = 84 years) individuals. Both groups recalled twice as many autobiographical memories when appropriate odour cues were presented.

Chu and Downes (2000, 2004) investigated the role of **olfaction** (the sense of smell) in the recall of autobiographical memories. One feature of the Proust phenomenon is that the memories triggered by odours are generally very old. Chu and Downes found that more odour-cued autobiographical memories came from the period when participants were between the ages of six and ten than any other period. In contrast, the peak period for memories triggered by verbal cues was between the ages of 11 and 25. Willander and Larsson (2006) presented their participants with odour, word, or picture cues for autobiographical memories. Most memories triggered by odour cues related to events occurring before the age of ten, whereas the peak age for autobiographical memories triggered by visual and verbal cues was between 11 and 20. In addition, the odour-triggered memories produced stronger feelings of being brought back in time.

Chu and Downes (2000) asked participants to think of autobiographical events triggered by verbal cues corresponding to the names of odorous objects. After that, they were presented with the appropriate odour, an inappropriate odour, a picture of the odorous object, or its verbal label and recall further details. The appropriate odour triggered recall of more additional details than any other cue. In addition, the appropriate odour led to a greater increase in the rated emotionality of the autobiographical memories than did any other cue.

Why do odours have such powerful effects? First, information about the smell and the taste of food and drink is combined in the orbitofrontal cortex (Doop et al., 2006), which may produce stronger memory traces. The association with taste may be important – one of the first author's strongest early autobiographical memories involves intensely disliking eating beetroot that had been soaked in vinegar. Second, most people have far fewer autobiographical memories in the olfactory modality than in other modalities (e.g., vision). This may help to make odour-related memories distinctive and protect them from interference. Third, language probably plays a smaller role in odour-related autobiographical memories than in other autobiographical memories. Since we are bombarded with visually and auditorily presented language all day long, the relative lack of linguistic information in odour-related memories may reduce interference effects.

Brown and Kulik's (1977) central point was that flashbulb memories are very different from other memories in their longevity, accuracy, and reliance on a special neural mechanism. Many other theorists disagree. Finkenauer, Luminet, Gisle, El-Ahmadi, and van der Linden (1998) argued that flashbulb memories depend on several factors, including relevant prior knowledge, personal importance, surprise, overt rehearsal, the novelty of the event, and the individual's affective attitude towards the central person or persons in the event. All these factors can be involved in the formation of *any* new memory.

Evidence

If flashbulb memories involve permanent storage of information about dramatic world events, they should show *consistency* (lack of change) over time. Conway, Anderson, Larsen, Donnelly, McDaniel, and McClelland (1994) studied flashbulb memories for the unexpected resignation of the British Prime Minister Margaret Thatcher in 1990, which was regarded as surprising and consequential by most British people. Memory for this event was tested within a few days, after 11 months, and after 26 months. Flashbulb memories were found in 86% of British participants after 11 months, and remained consistent even after 26 months. However, most research on flashbulb memories suggests they are not special. For example, Bohannon (1988) found that many people remembered the explosion of the space shuttle *Challenger* because they had often rehearsed their memories.

Flashbulb memories can be surprisingly inaccurate. If you think your memories of 11 September are accurate, try answering the following question: "On September 11, did you see the videotape on television of the first plane striking the first tower?" Among American students, 73% said, "Yes" (Pezdek, 2003). In fact, only the videotape of the *second* tower being hit was available on that day. In similar fashion, Ost, Vrij, Costall, and Bull (2002) asked British people whether they had seen the film of the car crash in which Princess Diana was killed. There is no film, but 45% claimed to have seen it!

Inaccuracies in flashbulb memories are especially likely at long retention intervals. Cubelli and Della Sala (2008) assessed Italians' memories for a bomb explosion in Bologna that killed 85 people 24 years after the event. Of the small number of personal memories relating to the explosion that could be checked, *all* were inaccurate!

Talarico and Rubin (2003) pointed out that we do not really know whether flashbulb memories are better remembered than everyday memories because very few studies have assessed both kinds of memory. They provided the missing evidence. On 12 September 2001, they assessed students' memories for the terrorist attacks of the previous day and also their memory for a very recent everyday event. The students were tested again 7, 42, or 224 days later. There were two main findings (see Figure 8.2). First, the reported vividness of flashbulb memories remained very high throughout. Second, flashbulb memories showed no more consistency over time than did everyday memories.

Winningham, Hyman, and Dinnel (2000) studied memory for the unexpected acquittal of O. J. Simpson (a retired American football star) accused of murdering his ex-wife and her friend. Participants' memories changed considerably in the first few days after hearing about the acquittal before becoming consistent. This finding threatens the notion that flashbulb memories are fully formed at the moment when individuals learn about a dramatic event. It also makes sense of the literature. Conway et al. (1994) found consistent memories over time, but they first tested participants several days after Mrs Thatcher's resignation. In contrast, Talarico and Rubin (2003) found inconsistent memories over time with an initial memory test the day after September 11. Thus, our memories of dramatic world events are often constructed over the first few days after the event.

In sum, the great majority of flashbulb memories contain inaccurate information and involve reconstructive processes based on what was likely to have been experienced. Why do we think that flashbulb memories are special? They are distinctive and do not

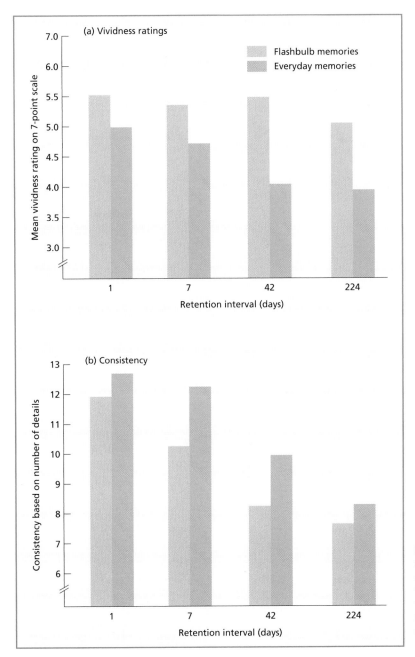

Figure 8.2 (a) Vividness ratings and (b) consistency of memory as a function of type of memory (flashbulb vs. everyday) and length of retention interval. Based on data in Talarico and Rubin (2003).

suffer interference from similar events (Cubelli & Della Sala, 2008). Flashbulb memories that are well remembered over a long period of time may benefit from having been retrieved many times (Bob Logie, personal communication). There is strong evidence for the importance of repeated retrieval in the testing effect (Roediger & Karpicke, 2006). This is the finding that there is much better long-term memory for information that is retrieved repeatedly than for information that is merely studied repeatedly.

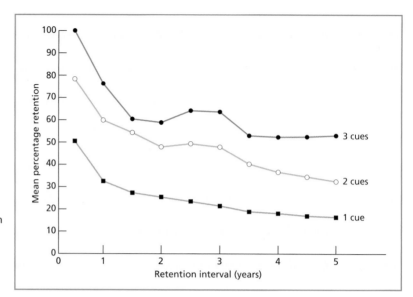

Figure 8.3 Memory for personal events as a function of the number of cues available and the length of the retention interval. Adapted from Wagenaar (1986).

Diary studies

How can we tell whether the memories produced by participants are genuine? If you have read an autobiography recently, you probably wondered whether the author provided an unduly positive view of him/herself. Evidence for distorted autobiographical memory was reported by Karney and Frye (2002). Spouses often recalled their past contentment as lower than their present level of satisfaction because they underestimated their past contentment.

We can establish the accuracy of autobiographical memories by carrying out a diary study. Wagenaar (1986) kept a diary record of over 2000 events over a six-year period. For each event, he recorded information about who, what, where, and when, plus the rated pleasantness, emotionality, and salience or rarity of each event. He then tested his memory by using the who, what, where, and when pieces of information singly or in combination. "What" information provided easily the most useful retrieval cue, probably because our autobiographical memories are organised in categories. "What" information was followed in order of decreasing usefulness by "where", "who", and "when" information, which was almost useless. The probability of recall

increased as more cues were presented (see Figure 8.3). However, even with three cues, almost half the events were forgotten over a five-year period. When these forgotten events involved another person, that person provided additional information. This was typically sufficient for Wagenaar to remember the event, suggesting that the great majority of life events may be stored in long-term memory. Finally, high levels of salience, emotional involvement, and pleasantness were all associated with high levels of recall.

There is a significant limitation with diary studies such as that of Wagenaar (1986). As Burt, Kemp, and Conway (2003) pointed out, the emphasis is on specific on-one-day events. However, most autobiographical events we remember are more general. For example, Barsalou (1988) asked college students to recall events of the previous summer. The students recalled relatively few on-one-day memories but numerous general events extended in time.

Memories across the lifetime

Suppose we ask 70 year olds to recall personal memories suggested by cue words (e.g., nouns referring to common objects). From which

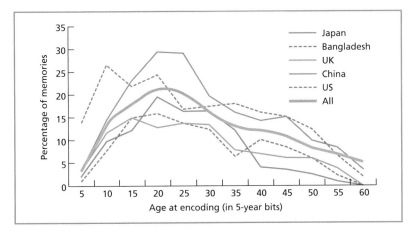

Figure 8.4 Lifespan retrieval curves from five countries. From Conway et al. (2005), Copyright © 2005 SAGE Publications. Reprinted by permission of SAGE publications.

parts of their lives would most of the memories come? Rubin, Wetzler, and Nebes (1986) answered this question by combining findings from various studies. There were two findings of theoretical interest:

- **Infantile amnesia** (or childhood amnesia) shown by the almost total lack of memories from the first three years of life.
- A **reminiscence bump**, consisting of a surprisingly large number of memories coming from the years between 10 and 30, and especially between 15 and 25.

A possible limitation of Rubin et al.'s findings is that they were based mainly on American participants. This issue was addressed by Conway, Wang, Hanyu, and Haque (2005), who studied participants from China, UK, Bangladesh, and America. Reassuringly, there was clear evidence of childhood amnesia and a reminiscence bump in all five cultures (see Figure 8.4).

Rubin, Rahhal, and Poon (1998) discussed other evidence that 70 year olds have especially good memories for early childhood. This effect was found for the following: particularly memorable books; vivid memories; memories the participants would want included in a book about their lives; names of winners of Academy awards; and memory for current events. Note, however, that the reminiscence bump has not

generally been found in people younger than 30 years of age, and has not often been observed in 40 year olds. There is a detailed discussion of factors accounting for the reminiscence bump after the next section on infantile amnesia.

Infantile amnesia

Adults may find it hard to recall the events of early childhood because young children find it hard to form long-term memories. There is some support for this view. Autobiographical memory is a type of declarative memory depending heavily on the hippocampus (see Chapter 7). The dentate gyrus within the hippocampal formation has only about 70% of the adult number of cells at birth, and continues to develop through the first year of life. Other parts of the hippocampal formation may not be fully developed until the child is between two and eight years of age (Richmond & Nelson, 2007).

KEY TERMS

infantile amnesia: the inability of adults to recall autobiographical memories from early childhood.

reminiscence bump: the tendency of older people to recall a disproportionate number of autobiographical memories from the years of adolescence and early adulthood.

The prefrontal cortex is known to be involved in long-term memory (Bauer, 2004). Of relevance here, the density of synapses in the prefrontal cortex increases substantially at about eight months of age, and continues to increase until the infant is 15–24 months of age (Bauer, 2004).

In spite of the fact that brain development is incomplete in young children, they still show clear evidence of forming numerous long-term memories. For example, Fivush, Gray, and Fromhoff (1987) studied young children with a mean age of 33 months. They were asked questions about various significant events (e.g., a trip to Disneyland) that had happened some months previously. The children responded to over 50% of the events, and produced on average 12 items of information about each event.

The most famous (or notorious) account of childhood or infantile amnesia is the one provided by Sigmund Freud (1915/1957). He argued that infantile amnesia occurs through repression, with threat-related thoughts and experiences (e.g., sexual feelings towards one's parents) being consigned to the unconscious. Freud claimed that such threatening memories are changed into more innocuous memories (screen memories). This is a dramatic theory. However, it fails to explain why adolescents and adults cannot remember *positive* and *neutral* events from early childhood.

Howe and Courage (1997) emphasised the role played by the development of the cognitive self. They argued that infants can only form autobiographical memories *after* developing a sense that events having *personal* significance can occur. This sense of self develops towards the end of the second year of life. For example, Lewis and Brooks-Gunn (1979) carried out a study in which infants who had a red spot applied surreptitiously to their nose were held up to a mirror. Those recognising their own reflection and so reaching for their own nose were claimed to show at least some self-awareness. Practically no infants in the first year of life showed clear evidence of self-awareness, but 70% of infants between 21 and 24 months did so.

The crucial assumption of Howe and Courage's (1997, p. 499) theory is as follows:

The development of the cognitive self late in the second year of life (as indexed by visual self-recognition) provides a new framework around which memories can be organised. With this cognitive advance..., we witness the emergence of autobiographical memory and the end of infantile amnesia.

The finding that the cognitive self appears shortly before the onset of autobiographical memory around or shortly after children's second birthday (see review by Peterson, 2002) fits the theory. However, it does not show that the former plays any role in *causing* the latter. Stronger evidence comes in a study by Howe, Courage, and Edison (2003). Among infants aged between 15 and 23 months, self-recognisers had better memory for personal events than infants who were not self-recognisers. More strikingly, not a single child showed good performance on a memory test for personal events *before* achieving self-recognition.

The social–cultural–developmental theory (e.g., Fivush & Nelson, 2004) provides another plausible account of childhood amnesia. According to this theory, language and culture are both central in the early development of autobiographical memory. Language is important in part because we use language to communicate our memories. Experiences occurring before children develop language are difficult to express in language later on.

Fivush and Nelson (2004) argued that parents vary along a dimension of elaboration when discussing the past with their children. Some parents discuss the past in great detail when talking to their children whereas others do not. According to the theory, children whose parents have an elaborative reminiscing style will report more and fuller childhood memories. There are important cultural differences here, because mothers from Western cultures talk about the past in a more elaborated and emotional way than those from Eastern cultures (Leichtman, Wang, & Pillemer, 2003).

As predicted by the social–cultural–developmental theory, the mother's reminiscing style is an important factor. Children's very early ability to talk about the past was much better among those whose mothers had an elaborative reminiscing style (Harley & Reese, 1999). Perhaps the simplest explanation is that children whose mothers talk in detail about the past are being provided with good opportunities to rehearse their memories.

The language skills available to children at the time of an experience determine what they can recall about it subsequently. Simcock and Hayne (2002) asked two- and three-year-old children to describe their memories for complex play activities at periods of time up to 12 months later. The children *only* used words they had already known at the time of the event. This is impressive evidence given that they had acquired hundreds of new words during the retention interval.

Cross-cultural research reveals that adults from Eastern cultures have a later age of first autobiographical memory than those from Western cultures (Pillemer, 1998). In addition, the reported memories of early childhood are much more elaborated and emotional in American children than in those from Korea or China (Han, Leichtman, & Wang, 1998). These findings are predictable on the basis of cultural differences in mothers' reminiscing style. However, American children may be more inclined to report their personal experiences than are those from Eastern cultures.

Evaluation

Three points need to be emphasised. First, the two theories just discussed are *not* mutually exclusive. The *onset* of autobiographical memory in infants may depend on the emergence of the self, with its subsequent expression being heavily influenced by social factors, cultural factors, and infants' development of language. Second, *all* the main factors identified in the two theories seem to be involved in the development of autobiographical memory. Third, while the research evidence is supportive, most of it only shows an *association* in time between,

for example, the mother's reminiscing style and autobiographical memory performance in her child. This does not demonstrate that the memory performance was *caused* by the reminiscing style.

Reminiscence bump

As we saw earlier, a reminiscence bump has been found in several different cultures (see Figure 8.4). How can we explain its existence? Rubin, Rahhal, and Poon (1998) argued that stability and novelty are both involved. Most adults have a period of stability starting in early adulthood because a sense of adult identity develops at that time. This provides a cognitive structure serving as a stable organisation to cue events. Many memories from early adulthood are novel (e.g., first-time experiences) in that they are formed shortly after the onset of adult identity. Novelty is an advantage because it produces distinctive memories and there is a relative lack of proactive interference (interference from previous learning).

There is limited support for the views of Rubin et al. (1998). Pillemer, Goldsmith, Panter, and White (1988) asked middle-aged participants to recall four memories from their first year at college more than 20 years earlier. They found that 41% of those autobiographical memories came from the first month of the course.

Berntsen and Rubin (2002) found that older individuals showed a reminiscence bump for *positive* memories but not for *negative* ones. This means that the reminiscence bump is more limited in scope than had been believed previously. How can we interpret this finding? One interpretation is based on the notion of a **life script**, which consists of cultural expectations concerning the major life events in a typical person's life (Rubin, Berntsen, & Hutson, 2009). Examples of such events are falling in love,

KEY TERM

life scripts: cultural expectations concerning the nature and order of major life events in a typical person's life.

The reminiscence bump applies to a period when many important life events – such as falling in love, getting married, and having children – tend to happen.

marriage, and having children. Most of these events are emotionally positive and generally occur between the ages of 15 and 30. Rubin et al.'s key finding was that the major life events that individuals recalled from their own lives had clear similarities with those included in their life script.

Glück and Bluck (2007, p. 1935) adopted a similar viewpoint: "The reminiscence bump consists largely of...events in which the individual made consequential life choices....Such choices are characterised by positive valence and by a high level of perceived control." Thus,

our strongest autobiographical memories are associated with a real sense of development and progress in our lives.

Glück and Bluck (2007) tested their ideas in a study on individuals aged between 50 and 90 who thought of personally important autobiographical memories. These memories were categorised as being positive or negative emotionally and as involving high or low perceived control. The key finding was that a reminiscence bump was present *only* for memories that were positive and involved high perceived control (see Figure 8.5).

Self-memory system

Conway and Pleydell-Pearce (2000) put forward an influential theory of autobiographical memory. According to this theory, we possess a self-memory system with two major components:

(1) *Autobiographical memory knowledge base*: This contains personal information at three levels of specificity:
   - *Lifetime periods*: These generally cover substantial periods of time defined by major ongoing situations (e.g., time spent living with someone).
   - *General events*: These include repeated events (e.g., visits to a sports club) and single events (e.g., a holiday in South

Figure 8.5 Distribution of autobiographical memories for participants who were over 40 years old. Only positive memories show the reminiscence bump. From Glück and Bluck (2007). Copyright © The Psychonomic Society. Reproduced with permission.

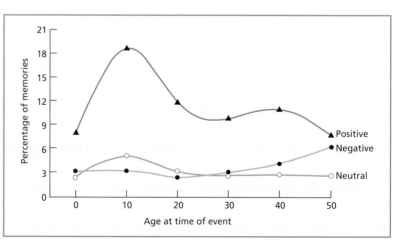

Africa). General events are often related to each other as well as to lifetime periods.

- *Event-specific knowledge*: This knowledge consists of images, feelings, and other details relating to general events, and spanning time periods from seconds to hours. Knowledge about an event is usually organised in the correct temporal order.

(2) *Working self*: This is concerned with the self, what it may become in the future and with the individual's current set of goals. The goals of the working self influence the kinds of memories stored within the autobiographical memory knowledge base. They also partially determine which autobiographical memories we recall. The goals of the working self influence the kinds of memories stored in the autobiographical memory knowledge base. As a result, "Autobiographical memories are primarily records of success or failure in goal attainment" (p. 266).

According to the theory, autobiographical memories can be accessed through generative or direct retrieval. We use **generative retrieval** when we deliberately construct autobiographical memories by combining the resources of the working self with information contained in the autobiographical knowledge base. As a result, autobiographical memories produced via generative retrieval often relate to the individual's goals as contained within the working self. In contrast, direct retrieval does not involve the working self. Autobiographical memories produced by **direct retrieval** are triggered by specific cues (e.g., hearing the word "Paris" on the radio may produce direct retrieval of a memory of a holiday there). Remembering autobiographical memories via generative retrieval is more effortful and involves more active involvement by the rememberer than does direct retrieval.

Conway (2005) developed the above theory (see Figure 8.6). The knowledge structures in autobiographical memory divide into the conceptual self and episodic memories (previously called event-specific knowledge). At the top of the hierarchy, the life story and themes have been added. The life story consists of very general factual and evaluative knowledge we possess about ourselves and themes refer to major life domains such as work and relationships.

Conway (2005) argued that we want our autobiographical memories to exhibit coherence (consistency with our current goals and beliefs). However, we also often want our autobiographical memories to exhibit correspondence (being accurate). In the battle between coherence and correspondence, coherence tends to win out over correspondence over time.

Evidence

Studies of brain-damaged patients suggest that there are three types of autobiographical knowledge. Of particular importance are cases of retrograde amnesia in which there is widespread forgetting of events preceding the brain injury (see Chapter 7). Many patients have great difficulty in recalling event-specific knowledge but their ability to recall general events and lifetime periods is less impaired (Conway & Pleydell-Pearce, 2000). Even KC, who has no episodic memories, possesses some general autobiographical knowledge about his life (Rosenbaum et al., 2005).

Autobiographical memory and the self are closely related. Woike, Gershkovich, Piorkowski, and Polo (1999) distinguished between two types of personality:

KEY TERMS

generative retrieval: deliberate or voluntary construction of autobiographical memories based on an individual's current goals; see **direct retrieval**.

direct retrieval: involuntary recall of autobiographical memories triggered by a specific retrieval cue (e.g., being in the same place as the original event); see **generative retrieval**.

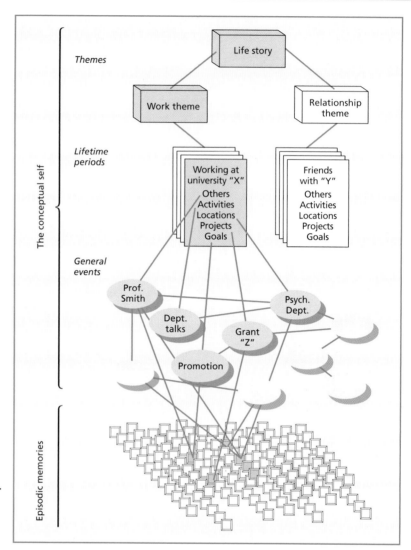

Figure 8.6 The knowledge structures within autobiographical memory, as proposed by Conway (2005). Reprinted from Conway (2005), Copyright © 2005, with permission from Elsevier.

(1) *Agentic personality type*, with an emphasis on independence, achievement, and personal power.

(2) *Communal personality type*, with an emphasis on interdependence and similarity to others.

In their first study, Woike et al. (1999) asked participants with agentic and communal personality types to write about a positive or negative personal experience. When the experience was positive, 65% of the agentic participants recalled agentic memories (e.g., involving success), whereas 90% of the communal participants recalled communal memories (e.g., involving love or friendship). The same pattern was found for negative personal experiences: 47% of the agentic individuals recalled agentic memories (e.g., involving failure), but 90% of the communal individuals recalled communal memories (e.g., involving betrayal of trust).

In a second study, Woike et al. (1999) asked participants to recall autobiographical memories associated with six different emotions (happiness, pride, relief, anger, fear, and sadness). Those with an agentic personality recalled more autobiographical memories concerned with agency (e.g., success, absence of failure, failure) than those with a communal personality. In contrast, individuals with a communal personality recalled more memories concerned with communion (e.g., love, friendship, betrayal of trust) than those with an agentic personality.

Evidence supporting the distinction between generative or voluntary retrieval of autobiographical memories and direct or involuntary retrieval was reported by Berntsen (1998) and Berntsen and Hall (2004). Berntsen (1998) compared memories produced by voluntary retrieval (i.e., elicited by cues) and by involuntary retrieval (i.e., coming to mind with no attempt to recall them). More of the latter memories were of specific events (89% versus 63%, respectively). Berntsen and Hall (2004) repeated these findings. In addition, the cues most associated with direct retrieval of autobiographical memories were specific ones, such as being in the same place as the original event (61% of cases) or being in the same place engaged in the same activity (25% of cases).

Conway and Pleydell-Pearce (2000) argued that generative retrieval initially involves the control processes of the working self followed by activation of parts of the autobiographical knowledge base. They speculated that processes within the working self involve activation in the frontal lobes, whereas processes within the autobiographical knowledge base involve activation in more posterior areas of the brain. Conway, Pleydell-Pearce, and Whitecross (2001) found extensive activation in the left frontal lobe during the initial stages of generative retrieval of autobiographical memories. After that, when an autobiographical memory was being held in conscious awareness, there was activation in the temporal and occipital lobes, especially in the right hemisphere.

Conway, Pleydell-Pearce, Whitecross, and Sharpe (2003) replicated and extended the findings of Conway et al. (2001) by comparing memory for experienced events with memory for imagined events. What differences might we find? First, if construction and maintenance are more effortful for imagined memories than for experienced ones, there should be greater activation of prefrontal cortex for imagined memories. Second, if experienced memories depend on the retrieval of more detailed and specific information, there should be more activation in occipito-temporal regions for experienced memories than for imagined ones. Both of these predictions were confirmed.

Evaluation

Conway and Pleydell-Pearce (2000) and Conway (2005) put forward a reasonably comprehensive theory of autobiographical memory. Several of their major theoretical assumptions (e.g., the hierarchical structure of autobiographical memory; the intimate relationship between autobiographical memory and the self; and the importance of goals in autobiographical memory) are well supported by the evidence. In addition, the fact that several brain regions are involved in the generative retrieval of autobiographical memories is consistent with the general notion that such retrieval is complex.

What are the limitations of the theory? First, autobiographical memory may involve more processes and more brain areas than assumed within the theory (Cabeza & St. Jacques, 2007; discussed below). Second, we need to know more about *how* the working self interacts with the autobiographical knowledge base to produce recall of specific autobiographical memories. Third, it remains to be seen whether there is a clear distinction between generative and direct retrieval. It may well be that the recall of autobiographical memories often involves elements of both modes of retrieval. Fourth, autobiographical memories vary in the extent to which they contain episodic information (e.g., contextual details) and semantic information (e.g., schema-based), but this is not fully addressed within the theory.

Cognitive neuroscience: Cabeza and St. Jacques (2007)

There is considerable evidence that the prefrontal cortex plays a major role in the retrieval of autobiographical memories. Svoboda, McKinnon, and Levine (2006) found, in a meta-analysis of functional neuroimaging studies, that the medial and ventromedial prefrontal cortex were nearly always activated during autobiographical retrieval, as were medial and lateral temporal cortex. Summerfield, Hassabis, and Maguire (2009) provided a more detailed picture of the involvement of the prefrontal cortex. Participants recalled autobiographical and non-autobiographical (e.g., from television news clips) events that were either real or imagined. Recollection of real autobiographical events (compared to recall of imagined autobiographical events) was associated with activation in the ventromedial prefrontal cortex as well as the posterior cingulate cortex.

Cabeza and St. Jacques (2007) agreed that the prefrontal cortex is of major importance in autobiographical retrieval. They produced a comprehensive theoretical framework within which to understand autobiographical memory from the perspective of cognitive neuroscience (see Figure 8.7). The six main processes assumed to be involved in retrieval of autobiographical memories are as follows:

(1) *Search and controlled processes*: These processes are associated with generative retrieval. Steinvorth, Corkin, and Halgren

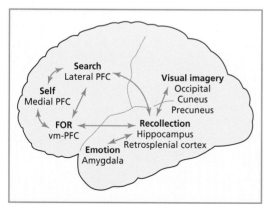

Figure 8.7 The main components of the autobiographical memory retrieval network and their interconnections. FOR = feeling-of-rightness monitoring; vm-PFC = ventromedial prefrontal cortex. Reprinted from Cabeza and St. Jacques (2007), Copyright © 2007, with permission from Elsevier.

(2006) found that there was more activation in lateral prefrontal cortex during retrieval of autobiographical than of laboratory-formed memories, and much of this activation continued through most of the retrieval period. This is consistent with the notion that the construction of auto-biographical memories requires almost continuous search and controlled processes.

(2) *Self-referential processes*: Evidence that self-referential processes involve medial prefrontal cortex was reported by Cabeza et al. (2004). That brain region was more activated when participants recognised photographs taken by themselves than photographs taken by other people.

(3) *Recollection*: The retrieval of basic auto-biographical memories involves the hippo-campus and parts of the medial temporal lobes. Gilboa et al. (2005) found that loss of autobiographical memory in patients with Alzheimer's disease correlated with the amount of damage to the medial temporal lobes including the hippocampus.

(4) *Emotional processing*: Autobiographical memories are generally more emotional than laboratory-formed memories, and involve processing within the amygdala. Buchanan, Tranel, and Adolphs (2006) found that patients with damage to the amygdala as well as the medial temporal lobes had greater impairment in retrieving emotional autobiographical memories than patients with damage to the medial temporal lobes but not the amygdala.

(5) *Visual imagery*: Autobiographical memories are generally more vivid than laboratory-formed memories, in part because of the use of imagery associated with occipital and cuneus/precuneus areas. Evidence that the processes involved in imagery and vividness differ from those involved in emotional processing was reported by LaBar et al. (2005). Emotion ratings for autobiographical memories correlated with amygdala activity early in retrieval, whereas vividness ratings correlated with subsequent occipital activity.

(6) *Feeling-of-rightness monitoring*: This is a rapid, preconscious process to check the accuracy of retrieved autobiographical memories and involves the ventrolateral prefrontal cortex. Gilboa et al. (2006) reported that patients with damage in the ventrolateral prefrontal cortex unintentionally produce false autobiographical memories, which suggests a failure of monitoring.

Evaluation

Cabeza and St. Jacques (2007) provide an impressive overview of the major processes involved in the retrieval of autobiographical memories and the associated brain regions. There is reasonably strong evidence for all of the processes they identify, and they have gone further than previous theorists in coming to grips with the complexities of autobiographical memory. An exciting implication of their theoretical framework is that brain-damaged patients could have several different patterns of autobiographical memory impairment depending on which brain regions are damaged.

The next step would appear to be to establish more clearly *interactions* among the six processes. For example, the process of recollection affects (and is affected by) four other processes, but the bi-directional arrows in Figure 8.7 are not very informative about the details of what is happening.

EYEWITNESS TESTIMONY

Many innocent people have been found guilty of a crime and sent to prison. In the United States, for example, approximately 200 people have been shown to be innocent by DNA tests, and more than 75% of them were found guilty on the basis of mistaken eyewitness identification. For example, in early 2008, DNA testing led to the release of Charles Chatman, who had spent nearly 27 years in prison in Dallas County, Texas. He was 20 years old when a young woman who had been raped picked him out from a line-up. Her eyewitness testimony led to Chatman being sentenced to 99 years in prison. On his last night in prison, Chatman said to the press: "I'm bitter, I'm angry. But I'm not angry or bitter to the point where I want to hurt anyone or get revenge."

You might assume that most jurors and judges would be knowledgeable about potential problems with eyewitness testimony. However, that assumption is wrong. Benton, Ross, Bradshaw, Thomas, and Bradshaw (2006) asked judges, jurors, and eyewitness experts 30 questions concerned with eyewitness issues. Judges disagreed with the experts on 60% of the issues and jurors disagreed with the experts on 87%!

Eyewitness testimony can be distorted via **confirmation bias**, i.e., event memory is influenced by the observer's expectations. For example, consider a study by Lindholm and Christianson (1998). Swedish and immigrant students saw a videotaped simulated robbery in which the perpetrator seriously wounded a cashier with a knife. After watching the video, participants were shown colour photographs of eight men – four Swedes and the remainder immigrants. Both Swedish and immigrant participants were twice as likely to select an innocent immigrant as an innocent Swede. Immigrants are over-represented in Swedish crime statistics, and this influenced participants' expectations concerning the likely ethnicity of the criminal.

Bartlett (1932) explained *why* our memory is influenced by expectations. He argued that we possess numerous schemas or packets of knowledge stored in long-term memory. These schemas lead us to form certain expectations and can distort our memory by causing us to reconstruct an event's details based on "what must have been true" (see Chapter 10). Tuckey and Brewer (2003a) found that most people's bank-robbery schema includes information that

> ### KEY TERM
>
> **confirmation bias:** a greater focus on evidence apparently confirming one's hypothesis than on disconfirming evidence.

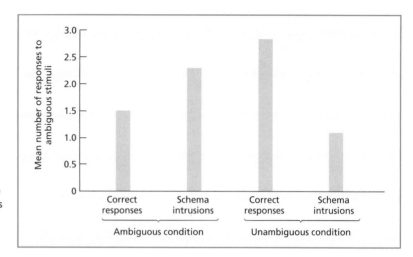

Figure 8.8 Mean correct responses and schema-consistent intrusions in the ambiguous and unambiguous conditions with cued recall. Data from Tuckey and Brewer (2003b).

Eyewitness testimony has been found by psychologists to be extremely unreliable, as it can be distorted by several factors – yet jurors tend to find such testimony highly believable.

robbers are typically male, wear disguises and dark clothes, make demands for money, and have a getaway car with a driver in it. Tuckey and Brewer showed eyewitnesses a video of a simulated bank robbery followed by a memory test. As predicted by Bartlett's theory, eyewitnesses recalled information relevant to the bank-robbery schema better than information irrelevant to it (e.g., the colour of the getaway car).

Tuckey and Brewer (2003b) focused on how eyewitnesses remembered ambiguous information about a simulated crime. For example, some eyewitnesses saw a robber's head covered by a balaclava (ski mask) so that the robber's gender was ambiguous. As predicted, eyewitnesses mostly interpreted the ambiguous information as being consistent with their bank-robbery schema (see Figure 8.8). Thus, their recall was systematically distorted by including information from their bank-robbery schema even though it did not correspond to what they had observed.

Violence and anxiety

What are the effects of violence and anxiety on the accuracy of eyewitness memory? Much of the relevant research has been concerned with **weapon focus**, in which eyewitnesses attend to the weapon, which reduces their memory for other information. In one study, Loftus, Loftus, and Messo (1987) asked participants to watch one of two sequences: (1) a person pointing a gun at a cashier and receiving some cash; (2) a person handing a cheque to the cashier and receiving some cash. The participants looked more at the gun than at the

> **KEY TERM**
>
> **weapon focus:** the finding that eyewitnesses pay so much attention to some crucial aspect of the situation (e.g., the weapon) that they tend to ignore other details.

cheque. As predicted, memory for details un-related to the gun/cheque was poorer in the weapon condition.

Pickel (1999) pointed out that the weapon focus effect may occur because the weapon poses a threat or because it attracts attention because it is unexpected in most of the contexts in which it is seen by eyewitnesses. Pickel produced four videos involving a man approaching a woman while holding a handgun to compare these explanations:

(1) *Low threat, expected*: gun barrel pointed at the ground + setting was a shooting range.
(2) *Low threat, unexpected*: gun barrel pointed at the ground + setting was a baseball field.
(3) *High threat, expected*: gun pointed at the woman who shrank back in fear + setting was a shooting range.
(4) *High threat, unexpected*: gun pointed at the woman who shrank back in fear + setting was a baseball field.

The findings were clear-cut (see Figure 8.9). Eyewitnesses' descriptions of the man were much better when the gun was seen in an expected setting (a shooting range) than one in which it was unexpected (a baseball field). However, the level of threat had no effect on eyewitnesses' memory.

Weapon focus may be less important with real line-ups or identification parades than in the laboratory. Valentine, Pickering, and Darling (2003) found in over 300 real line-ups that the presence of a weapon had no effect on the probability of an eyewitness identifying the suspect (but bear in mind that the suspect wasn't always the culprit!). However, Tollestrup, Turtle, and Yuille (1994) found evidence for the weapon focus effect in their analysis of police records of real-life crimes.

What are the effects of stress and anxiety on eyewitness memory? In a study by Peters (1988), students received an inoculation and had their pulse taken two minutes later. Two groups were formed: (1) those whose heart rate

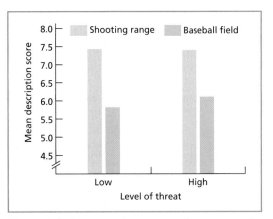

Figure 8.9 Accuracy of eyewitness descriptions of the man with the gun as a function of setting (shooting range vs. baseball field) and level of threat (low vs. high). From Pickel (1999). Reproduced with kind permission from Springer Science + Business Media.

was much higher during inoculation than two minutes later (high reactive); and (2) those whose heart rate was similar on both occasions (low reactive). Identification accuracy for the in-oculating nurse was 31% for the high-reactive group and 59% for the low-reactive group. Thus, participants regarding the inoculation as a stressful and anxiety-provoking procedure showed much worse memory than those re-garding it as innocuous.

Deffenbacher, Bornstein, Penroad, and McGorthy (2004) carried out two meta-analyses. In the first meta-analysis, they found that culprits' faces were identified 54% of the time in low anxiety or stress conditions compared to 42% for high anxiety or stress conditions. In a second meta-analysis, Deffenbacher et al. considered the effects of anxiety and stress on recall of culprit details, crime scene details, and the actions of the central characters. The average percentage of details recalled correctly was 64% in low stress conditions and 52% in high stress conditions. Thus, stress and anxiety generally impair eyewitness memory.

Ageing and memory
You would probably guess that the eyewitness memory of older adults would be less accurate

than that of younger adults. That is, indeed, the case. Dodson and Krueger (2006) showed a video to younger and older adults, who later completed a questionnaire that misleadingly referred to events not shown on the video. The older adults were more likely than the younger ones to produce false memories triggered by the misleading suggestions. Worryingly, the older adults tended to be very confident about the correctness of their false memories. In contrast, the younger adults were generally rather uncertain about the accuracy of their false memories.

The effects of misinformation are sometimes much greater on older than on younger adults. Jacoby, Bishara, Hessels, and Toth (2005) presented misleading information to younger and older adults. On a subsequent recall test, the older adults had a 43% chance of producing false memories compared to only 4% for the younger adults.

Wright and Stroud (2002) considered differences between younger and older adults who tried to identify the culprits after being presented with crime videos. They found an "own age bias", with both groups being more accurate at identification when the culprit was of a similar age to themselves. Thus, older adults' generally poorer eyewitness memory was less so when the culprit was an older person, perhaps because they paid more attention to the facial and other features of someone of similar age to themselves.

In sum, older adults very often produce memories that are genuine in the sense that they are based on information or events to which they have been exposed. However, they often misremember the context or circumstances in which the information was encountered. Thus, it is essential in detailed questioning with older adults to decide whether remembered events actually occurred at the time of the crime or other incident.

Remembering faces

Information about the culprit's face is very often the most important information that eyewitnesses may or may not remember. We will consider factors determining whether culprits' faces are remembered (see also Chapter 3).

Eyewitnesses sometimes remember a face but fail to remember the precise circumstances in which they saw it. In one study (Ross, Ceci, Dunning, & Toglia, 1994), eyewitnesses observed an event in which a bystander was present as well as the culprit. Eyewitnesses were three times more likely to select the bystander than someone else they had not seen before from a line-up including the bystander but not the culprit. This effect is known as **unconscious transference** – a face is correctly recognised as having been that of someone seen before but incorrectly judged to be responsible for a crime. Ross et al. found there was no unconscious transference effect when eyewitnesses were informed before seeing the line-up that the bystander and the culprit were not the same person.

You might imagine that an eyewitness's ability to identify the culprit of a crime would be increased if he/she were asked initially to provide a verbal description of the culprit. In fact, eyewitnesses' recognition memory for faces is generally *worse* if they have previously provided a verbal description! This is known as **verbal overshadowing**, and was first demonstrated by Schooler and Engstler-Schooler (1990). After eyewitnesses had watched a film of a crime, they provided a detailed verbal report of the criminal's appearance or performed an unrelated task. The eyewitnesses who had provided the detailed verbal report performed worse.

Why does verbal overshadowing occur? Clare and Lewandowsky (2004) argued that providing a verbal report of the culprit can

KEY TERMS

unconscious transference: the tendency of eyewitnesses to misidentify a familiar (but innocent) face as belonging to the person responsible for a crime.
verbal overshadowing: the reduction in recognition memory for faces that often occurs when eyewitnesses provide verbal descriptions of those faces before the recognition-memory test.

The cross-race effect

The accuracy of eyewitness identification depends in part on the **cross-race effect**, in which same-race faces are recognised better than cross-race faces. For example, Behrman and Davey (2001) found, from an analysis of 271 actual criminal cases, that the suspect was much more likely to be identified when he/she was of the same race as the eyewitness rather than a different race (60% versus 45%, respectively).

How can we explain the cross-race effect? According to the expertise hypothesis, we have had much more experience at distinguishing among same-race than cross-race faces and so have developed expertise at same-race face recognition. According to the social-cognitive hypothesis, we process the faces of individuals with whom we identify (our ingroup) more thoroughly than those of individuals with whom we don't identify (outgroups).

Much evidence seems to support the expertise hypothesis. For example, eyewitnesses having the most experience with members of another race often show a smaller cross-race effect than others (see review by Shriver, Young, Hugenberg, Bernstein, & Lanter, 2008). However, the effects of expertise or experience are generally modest. Shriver et al. studied the cross-race effect in middle-class white students at the University of Miami. They saw photographs of black or white college-aged males in impoverished contexts (e.g., dilapidated housing; run-down public spaces) or in wealthy contexts (e.g., large suburban homes; golf courses). They then received a test of recognition memory.

What did Shriver et al. (2008) find? There were three main findings (see Figure 8.10). First, there was a cross-race effect when white and black faces had been seen in wealthy contexts. Second, this effect disappeared when white and black faces had been seen in impoverished contexts. Third, the white participants recognised white faces much better when they had been seen in wealthy rather than impoverished contexts. Thus, as predicted by the social-cognitive hypothesis, *only* ingroup faces (i.e., white faces seen in wealthy contexts) were well recognised. The precise relevance of these findings for eyewitness identification needs to be explored. However, it is clear that the context in which a face is seen can influence how well it is remembered.

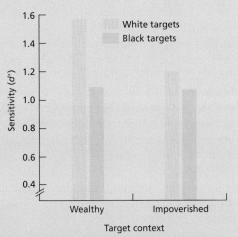

Figure 8.10 Mean recognition sensitivity as a function of target race (white vs. black) and target context (wealthy vs. impoverished). From Shriver et al. (2008). Copyright © 2008 Society for Personality and Social Psychology, Inc. Reprinted by permission of SAGE Publications.

make eyewitnesses more reluctant to identify anyone on a subsequent line-up. The verbal overshadowing effect disappeared when eyewitnesses were forced to select someone from the line-up and so could not be cautious. Excessive caution may be the main explanation

KEY TERM

cross-race effect: the finding that recognition memory for same-race faces is generally more accurate than for cross-race faces.

of the verbal overshadowing effect when eye-witnesses provide a fairly brief verbal description of the culprit. However, verbal overshadowing can depend on other factors (see Chin & Schooler, 2008, for a review). For example, eyewitnesses tend to focus on specific facial features when producing a verbal description, but face recognition is typically best when eyewitnesses process the face as a whole (Chin & Schooler, 2008; see Chapter 3).

Post- and pre-event information

The most obvious explanation for the inaccurate memories of eyewitnesses is that they often fail to pay attention to the crime and to the criminal(s). After all, the crime they observe typically occurs suddenly and unexpectedly. However, Loftus and Palmer (1974) argued that what happens *after* observing the crime (e.g., the precise questions eyewitnesses are asked) can easily distort eyewitnesses' fragile memories. They showed eyewitnesses a film of a multiple car accident. After viewing the film, eyewitnesses described what had happened, and then answered specific questions. Some were asked, "About how fast were the cars going when they smashed into each other?" For other participants, the verb "hit" was substituted for "smashed into". Control eyewitnesses were not asked a question about car speed. The estimated speed was affected by the verb used in the question, averaging 41 mph when the verb "smashed" was used versus 34 mph when "hit" was used. Thus, the information implicit in the question affected how the accident was remembered.

One week later, all the eyewitnesses were asked, "Did you see any broken glass?" In fact, there was no broken glass in the accident, but 32% of those previously asked about speed using the verb "smashed" said they had seen broken glass (see Figure 8.11). In contrast, only 14% of those asked using the verb "hit" said they had seen broken glass, and the figure was 12% for controls. Thus, our memory for events is sometimes so fragile it can be distorted by changing one word in one question!

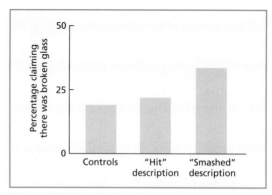

Figure 8.11 Results from Loftus and Palmer's (1974) study showing how the verb used in the initial description of a car accident affected recall of the incident after one week.

The tendency for eyewitness memory to be influenced by misleading post-event information is very strong. Eakin, Schreiber, and Sergent-Marshall (2003) showed participants slides of a maintenance man repairing a chair in an office and stealing some money and a calculator. Eyewitness memory was impaired by misleading post-event information. Of key importance, there was often memory impairment even when the eyewitnesses were warned immediately about the presence of misleading information.

We have seen that information acquired between original learning (at the time of the event) and the subsequent memory test can disrupt memory performance. This is retroactive interference, defined as disruption of memory by the learning of other material during the retention interval (see Chapter 6). Can eyewitness memory also be distorted by proactive interference (i.e., learning occurring *prior* to observing the critical event?). Evidence that the answer is positive was reported by Lindsay, Allen, Chan, and Dahl (2004). Participants were shown a video of a museum burglary. On the previous day, they listened to a narrative either thematically similar (a palace burglary) or thematically dissimilar (a school field-trip to a palace) to the video. Eyewitnesses made many more errors when recalling information from the video when the narrative was thematically similar.

The discovery that eyewitnesses' memory can be systematically distorted by information presented before or after observing a crime is worrying. However, such distorting effects may be less damaging than might be imagined. Most research has focused on distortions for peripheral or minor details (e.g., presence of broken glass) and has not considered distortions for central features. Dalton and Daneman (2006) carried out a study in which eyewitnesses watched a video clip of an action sequence and were then presented with misinformation about central and peripheral features. Memory distortions were much more common following misinformation about peripheral features than following misinformation about central features. However, eyewitnesses showed some susceptibility to misinformation even about central features.

Theoretical explanations

How does misleading post-event information distort what eyewitnesses report? One possibility is that there is source misattribution (Johnson, Hashtroudi, & Lindsay, 1993). The basic idea is that a memory probe (e.g., a question) activates memory traces overlapping with it in terms of the information they contain. Any memory probe may activate memories from various sources. The individual decides on the *source* of any activated memory on the basis of the information it contains. Source misattribution is likely when the memories from one source resemble those from a second source. Allen and Lindsay (1998) presented two narrative slide shows describing two different events with different people in different settings. However, some details in the two events were similar (e.g., a can of Pepsi versus a can of Coke). When eyewitnesses were asked to recall the first event, some details from the second event were mistakenly recalled.

Wright and Loftus (2008) identified several factors in addition to source misattribution that can lead eyewitnesses to be misled by post-event information. First, there is the *vacant slot explanation*: misinformation is likely to be accepted when related information from the original event was not stored in memory. Second, there is the *coexistence explanation*: memory representations from the original event and the post-event information both exist and the post-event information is selected because eyewitnesses think they are supposed to or because of source misattribution. Third, there is the *blend explanation*: post-event information and information from the original event are combined together in memory. Fourth, there is the *response bias explanation*: the way a study is conducted may bias eyewitnesses towards reporting the misinformation rather than information from the original event.

From laboratory to courtroom

You may be wondering whether we can safely apply findings from laboratory studies to real-life crimes. There are several important differences. First, in the overwhelming majority of laboratory studies, the event in question is observed by eyewitnesses rather than the victim or victims. This is quite different to real-life crimes, where evidence is much more likely to be provided by the victim than by eyewitnesses. Second, it is much less stressful to watch a video of a violent crime than to experience one in real life (especially if you are the victim). Third, laboratory eyewitnesses generally observe the event passively from a single perspective. In contrast, eyewitnesses to a real-life event are likely to move around and may be forced to interact with those committing the crime. Fourth, in laboratory research the consequences of an eyewitness making a mistake are trivial (e.g., minor disappointment at his/her poor memory), but can literally be a matter of life or death in an American court of law.

Do the above differences between observers' experiences in the laboratory and in real life have large and systematic effects on the accuracy of eyewitness memory? Lindsay and Harvie (1988) had eyewitnesses watch an event via slide shows, video films, or live staged events. The accuracy of culprit identification was very similar across these three conditions, suggesting that artificial laboratory conditions do not distort findings.

Ihlebaek, Løve, Eilertsen, and Magnussen (2003) used a staged robbery involving two robbers armed with handguns. In the live condition, eyewitnesses were ordered repeatedly to "Stay down". A video taken during the live condition was presented to eyewitnesses in the video condition. There were important similarities in memory in the two conditions. Participants in both conditions exaggerated the duration of the event, and the patterns of memory performance (i.e., what was well and poorly remembered) were similar. However, eyewitnesses in the video condition recalled more information. They estimated the age, height, and weight of the robbers more closely, and also identified the robbers' weapons more accurately.

Ihleback et al.'s (2003) findings suggest that witnesses to real-life events are more inaccurate in their memories of those events than those observing the same events under laboratory conditions. That finding (if confirmed) is important. It implies that the inaccuracies and distortions in eyewitness memory obtained under laboratory conditions provide an *underestimate* of eyewitnesses' memory deficiencies for real-life events. If so, it is legitimate to regard laboratory research as providing evidence of genuine relevance to the legal system. This conclusion receives support from Tollestrup et al. (1994), who analysed police records concerning the identifications by eyewitnesses to crimes involving fraud and robbery. Factors found to be important in laboratory studies (e.g., weapon focus; retention interval) were also important in real-life crimes.

Eyewitness identification

The police often ask eyewitnesses to identify the person responsible for a crime from various people either physically present or shown in photographs. Eyewitness identification from such identification parades or line-ups is often very fallible (see Wells & Olson, 2003, for a review). For example, Valentine et al. (2003) studied the evidence from 640 eyewitnesses who tried to identify suspects in 314 real line-ups. About 20% of witnesses identified a non-suspect, 40% identified the suspect, and 40% failed to make an identification.

There has been a dramatic increase in the number of closed-circuit television (CCTV) cameras in many countries. It seems reasonable to assume that it would be easy to identify someone on the basis of CCTV images. In fact, that is not necessarily the case. Bruce, Henderson, Greenwood, Hancock, Burton, and Miller (1999) presented people with a target face taken from a CCTV video together with an array of ten high-quality photographs (see Figure 8.12). Their task was to select the matching face or to indicate that the target face was *not* present. Performance was poor. When the target face was present, it was selected only 65% of the time. When it was *not* present, 35% of participants nevertheless claimed that one of the faces in the array matched the target face. Allowing the participants to watch a five-second video segment of the target person as well as a photograph of their face had no effect on identification performance.

Improving matters

How can we increase the effectiveness of eyewitness identification procedures? It is often assumed that warning eyewitnesses that the culprit may not be in a line-up reduces the chances of mistaken identification. Steblay (1997) carried out a meta-analysis. Such warnings reduced mistaken identification rates in culprit-absent line-ups by 42%, while reducing accurate identification rates in culprit-present line-ups by only 2%.

Line-ups can be simultaneous (the eyewitness sees everyone at the same time) or sequential (the eyewitness sees only one person at a time). Steblay, Dysart, Fulero, and Lindsay (2001) found, in a meta-analysis, that the chance of an eyewitness mistakenly selecting someone when the line-up did not contain the culprit was 28% with sequential line-ups and 51% with simultaneous line-ups. However, sequential line-ups were less effective than

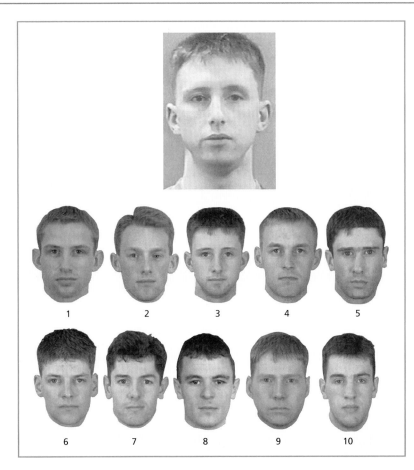

Figure 8.12 Example of full-face neutral target with an array used in the experiments. You may wish to attempt the task of establishing whether or not the target is present in this array and which one it is. The studio and video images used are from the Home Office Police Information Technology Organisation. Target is number 3. From Bruce et al. (1999), Copyright © 1999 American Psychological Association. Reprinted with permission.

simultaneous ones when the line-up did contain the culprit: the culprit was selected only 35% of the time with sequential line-ups compared to 50% of the time with simultaneous line-ups. These findings indicate that eyewitnesses adopt a more stringent criterion for identification with sequential than with simultaneous line-ups.

Is it preferable to use sequential or simultaneous line-ups? The answer depends on two factors (Malpass, 2006). First, you must decide how important it is to avoid identifying an innocent person as the culprit. Second, the probability that the actual culprit is in the line-up is important. Evidence cited by Malpass suggests that, on average, the probability is about 0.8. Malpass concluded that simultaneous line-ups are often preferable unless you think it is totally unacceptable for innocent people to be identified as potential culprits.

Douglass and Steblay (2006) carried out a meta-analysis on studies in which feedback was given to eyewitnesses after they had made an identification. Eyewitnesses who received confirming feedback (e.g., "Good, you identified the suspect") believed mistakenly that they had been very confident in the accuracy of their identification before receiving the feedback. This finding suggests that witnesses' reports should be recorded immediately after making an identification and that no feedback of any kind should be provided.

Cognitive interview

It is obviously important for police to interview eyewitnesses so as to maximise the amount of accurate information they can provide. According to Geiselman, Fisher, MacKinnon, and Holland (1985), effective interviewing techniques need to be based on the following notions:

* Memory traces are usually complex and contain various kinds of information.
* The effectiveness of a retrieval cue depends on its informational overlap with information stored in the memory trace; this is the encoding specificity principle (see Chapter 6).
* Various retrieval cues may permit access to any given memory trace; if one is ineffective, find another one. For example, if you can't think of someone's name, form an image of that person, or think of the first letter of their name.

Geiselman et al. (1985) used the above notions to develop the **cognitive interview**:

* The eyewitness recreates the context existing at the time of the crime, including environmental and internal (e.g., mood state) information.
* The eyewitness reports everything he/she can remember about the incident even if the information is fragmented.
* The eyewitness reports the details of the incident in various orders.
* The eyewitness reports the events from various perspectives, an approach that Anderson and Pichert (1978; see Chapter 10) found effective.

Geiselman et al. (1985) found that eyewitnesses produced 40% more correct statements with the cognitive interview than with a standard police interview. This was promising, but Fisher, Geiselman, Raymond, Jurkevich, and Warhaftig (1987) devised an enhanced cognitive interview which added the following aspects to the original cognitive interview (Roy, 1991, p. 399):

Investigators should minimise distractions, induce the eyewitness to speak slowly, allow a pause between the response and next question, tailor language to suit the individual

eyewitness, follow up with interpretive comment, try to reduce eyewitness anxiety, avoid judgmental and personal comments, and always review the eyewitness's description of events or people under investigation.

Evidence

Fisher et al. (1987) found the enhanced cognitive interview was more effective than the original cognitive interview. Eyewitnesses produced an average of 57.5 correct statements when given the enhanced interview compared to 39.6 with the basic interview.

Fisher et al.'s (1987) findings were obtained under artificial conditions. Fisher, Geiselman, and Amador (1990) used the enhanced cognitive interview in field conditions. Detectives working for the Robbery Division of the Metro-Dade Police Department in Miami were trained in the techniques of the enhanced interview. Police interviews with eyewitnesses and the victims of crime were tape-recorded and scored for the number of statements obtained and the extent to which these statements were confirmed by a second eyewitness. Training produced an increase of 46% in the number of statements. Where confirmation was possible, over 90% of the statements were accurate.

Köhnken, Milne, Memon, and Bull (1999) reported a meta-analysis based on over 50 studies. The cognitive interview on average led to the recall of 41% more correct details than standard police interviews. However, there was a small cost in terms of reduced accuracy. The average eyewitness given a cognitive interview produced 61% more errors than those given a standard interview.

KEY TERM

cognitive interview: an approach to improving the memory of eyewitness recall based on the assumption that memory traces contain many features.

Is it essential to use all of the ingredients of the cognitive interview? It has often been found that the effectiveness of the cognitive interview was scarcely reduced when eyewitnesses did not recall in different orders or from various perspectives (see Ginet & Verkampt, 2007, for a review). In their own study, Ginet and Verkampt showed eyewitnesses a video of a road accident. They then used a cognitive interview omitting recalling in different orders and from different perspectives or a structured interview without the social components of the cognitive interview. About 17% more correct details were recalled with the cognitive interview.

Does the cognitive interview reduce the adverse effects of misleading information provided after witnessing an incident? This question was addressed by Centofanti and Reece (2006). Eyewitnesses watched a video of a bank robbery followed by neutral or misleading information. Overall, 35% more correct details were remembered with the cognitive interview than with the structured interview with no increase in errors. However, the adverse effects of misleading information on eyewitness memory were as great with the cognitive interview as with the structured interview.

Evaluation

The cognitive interview has proved itself to be more effective than other interview techniques in obtaining as much accurate information as possible from eyewitnesses. Its effectiveness provides support for the underlying principles that led to its development. However, the cognitive interview possesses several limitations. First, the increased amount of incorrect information recalled by eyewitnesses (even though small) can lead detectives to misinterpret the evidence. Second, recreating the context at the time of the incident is a key ingredient in the cognitive interview. However, context has less effect on recognition memory than on recall (see Chapter 6), and so does not improve person identification from photographs or line-ups (Fisher, 1999).

Third, the cognitive interview is typically less effective at enhancing recall when used at longer retention intervals (Geiselman & Fisher, 1997). Thus, eyewitnesses should be interviewed as soon as possible after the event.

Fourth, there are several components to the cognitive interview (especially in its enhanced form), and it remains somewhat unclear which components are more and less important. There is some evidence that recreating the context and reporting everything no matter how fragmented are more important than recalling in different orders and from different perspectives.

Fifth, some of the evidence (e.g., Centofanti & Reece, 2006) suggests that the cognitive interview is ineffective in reducing the negative effects of misleading information. Thus, it is very important to ensure that eyewitnesses are not exposed to misleading information even if they are going to be questioned by a cognitive interview.

PROSPECTIVE MEMORY

Most studies of human memory have been on **retrospective memory**. The focus has been on the past, especially on people's ability to remember events they have experienced or knowledge they have acquired previously. In contrast, **prospective memory** involves remembering to carry out intended actions. We can see its importance by considering a tragic case of prospective memory failure discussed by Einstein and McDaniel (2005, p. 286):

After a change in his usual routine, an adoring father forgot to turn toward the daycare centre and instead drove his usual route to work at the university.

KEY TERMS

retrospective memory: memory for events, words, people, and so on encountered or experienced in the past; see **prospective memory**.
prospective memory: remembering to carry out intended actions.

Several hours later, his infant son, who had been quietly asleep in the back seat, was dead.

According to Ellis and Freeman (2008), prospective memory involves five stages:

(1) *Encoding*: The individual stores away information about *what* action needs to be performed, *when* the action needs to be performed, and the *intention* to act.
(2) *Retention*: The stored information has to be retained over a period of time.
(3) *Retrieval*: When a suitable opportunity presents itself, the intention has to be retrieved from long-term memory.
(4) *Execution*: When the intention is retrieved, it needs to be acted upon.
(5) *Evaluation*: The outcome of the preceding stages is evaluated. If prospective memory has failed, there is re-planning.

How different are prospective and retrospective memory? As Baddeley (1997) pointed out, retrospective memory generally involves remembering *what* we know about something and can be high in informational content. In contrast, prospective memory typically focuses on *when* to do something, and has low informational content. The low informational content helps to ensure that any failures to perform the prospective memory task are *not* due to retrospective memory failures. In addition, prospective memory (but not retrospective memory) is relevant to the plans or goals we form for our daily activities. A further difference is that there are generally more external cues available in the case of retrospective memory. Finally, as Moscovitch (2008, p. 309) pointed out, "Research on prospective memory is about the only major enterprise in memory research in which the problem is not memory itself, but the uses to which memory is put."

Remembering and forgetting often involve a mixture of prospective and retrospective memory. For example, suppose you agree to buy various goods at the supermarket for yourself and the friends with whom you share an apartment. Two things need to happen. First, you have to remember your intention to go to the supermarket (prospective memory). Even if you remember to go to the supermarket, you then have to remember precisely what you had agreed to buy (retrospective memory).

Smith, Della Sala, Logie, and Maylor (2000) devised the Prospective and Retrospective Memory Questionnaire (PRMQ). A sample item on prospective memory is as follows: "Do you decide to do something in a few minutes' time and then forget to do it?", and here is a sample item on retrospective memory: "Do you fail to recognise a place you have visited before?" When Crawford, Smith, Maylor, Della Sala, and Logie (2003) re-analysed data from this questionnaire obtained by Smith et al. (2000), they found evidence for separate prospective and retrospective memory factors. In addition, however, there was also a general memory factor incorporating elements of prospective and retrospective memory.

Event-based vs. time-based prospective memory

There is an important distinction between time-based and event-based prospective memory. **Time-based prospective memory** is assessed by tasks that involve remembering to perform a given action at a particular time (e.g., arriving at the cafe at 8.00pm). In contrast, **event-based prospective memory** is assessed by tasks that involve remembering to perform an action in the appropriate circumstances (e.g., passing on a message when you see someone).

> **KEY TERMS**
>
> **time-based prospective memory:** remembering to carry out an intended action at the right time; see **event-based prospective memory**.
> **event-based prospective memory:** remembering to perform an intended action when the circumstances are suitable; see **time-based prospective memory**.

Sellen, Lowie, Harris, and Wilkins (1997) compared time-based and event-based prospective memory in a work environment in which participants were equipped with badges containing buttons. They were told to press their button at pre-arranged times (time-based task) or when in a pre-specified place (event-based task). Performance was better in the event-based task than in the time-based task (52% versus 33% correct, respectively). Sellen et al. argued that event-based prospective memory tasks are easier than time-based tasks because the intended actions are more likely to be triggered by external cues.

Kim and Mayhorn (2008) compared time-based and event-based prospective memory in naturalistic settings and in the laboratory over a one-week period. Event-based prospective memory was superior to time-based prospective memory, especially under laboratory conditions. In addition, there was a general tendency for prospective memory to be better under naturalistic conditions, perhaps because participants were more motivated to remember intentions under such conditions than in the laboratory. The importance of motivation was shown on an event-based task by Meacham and Singer (1977). People were instructed to send postcards at one-week intervals, and performance was better when a financial incentive was offered.

How similar are the strategies used during the retention interval by individuals given event- and time-based prospective memory tasks? Time-based tasks are more difficult than event-based ones and often lack external cues. As a result, we might imagine that people performing time-based tasks would be more likely to use deliberate self-initiated processes to rehearse intended actions. In fact, Kvavilashvili and Fisher (2007) found the strategies were remarkably similar. Participants made a phone call at a particular time after an interval of one week (time-based task) or as soon as they received a certain text message (event-based task) which arrived after one week. Participants had a mean of nine rehearsals over the week with the time-based task and seven with the

event-based task. About 50% of the rehearsals with both tasks occurred automatically (i.e., the task simply popped into the participant's head without any apparent reason) and very few (6% with the time-based task and 3% with the event-based task) involved deliberate self-initiated retrieval of the task. Performance was better on the event-based task than on the time-based task (100% versus 53% reasonably punctual phone calls), presumably because the text message in the event-based task provided a useful external cue.

Hicks, Marsh, and Cook (2005) argued that it is too simple to argue that event-based tasks are always less demanding than time-based ones. They hypothesised that the specificity of the prospective memory task is more important than its type (event-based versus time-based). In their study, there was a central lexical decision task (i.e., deciding as rapidly as possible whether each letter string formed a word). There were two event-based tasks, one of which was well-specified (detect the words "nice" and "hit") and the other of which was ill-specified (detect animal words). There were also two time-based tasks which were well-specified (respond after 4 and 8 minutes) or ill-specified (respond after 3–5 minutes and 7–9 minutes). The extent to which these tasks slowed down performance on the lexical decision task was taken as a measure of how demanding they were.

What did Hicks et al. (2005) find? First, the adverse effects of event-based tasks on lexical decision times were less than those of time-based tasks (see Figure 8.13). Second, ill-specified tasks (whether event-based or time-based) disrupted lexical decision performance more than well-specified tasks. Thus, more processing resources are required when an individual's intentions on a prospective memory task are ill-specified.

Everyday life

Prospective memory is essential in everyday life if we are to keep our various social and work appointments. How good are we at remembering to act on our intentions? Marsh,

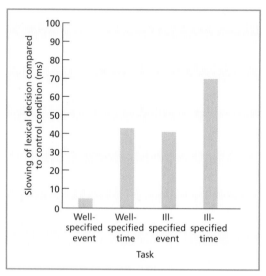

Figure 8.13 The effects of specification specificity (well-specified vs. ill-specified) and task type (event-based vs. time-based) on slowing of lexical decision time. Based on data in Hicks et al. (2005).

Dismukes and Nowinski's (2006) study showed that although airline pilots have excellent knowledge and memory of all the operations needed to fly a plane, their training provides less protection against failures of prospective memory.

Hicks, and Landau (1998) found that people reported an average of 15 plans for the forthcoming week, of which 25% were not completed. The main reasons for these non-completions were rescheduling and re-prioritisation, with only 3% being forgotten.

Evidence that prospective memory is of major importance in real life was reported by Dismukes and Nowinski (2006) in a study on pilot errors. They sampled 20% of all air carrier reports submitted to the Aviation Safety Reporting System (ASRS) over a one-year period to study in detail those involving memory failures. Out of 75 incidents or accidents, there were failures of prospective memory in 74 cases! There was only one failure of retrospective memory because air pilots have excellent knowledge and memory of all the operations needed to fly a plane.

Dismukes and Nowinski (2006) found that pilots were most likely to show failures of prospective memory if *interrupted* while carrying out a plan of action. They argued that interruptions often occur so rapidly and so forcefully that individuals do not think explicitly about producing a new plan or intention to deal with the changed situation. Dodhia and Dismukes (2005) found that interruptions can seriously impair prospective memory. Participants answered questions arranged in blocks (e.g., vocabulary questions; analogy questions). If an interrupting block of questions was presented before they had finished answering all the questions in a given block, they were to return to the interrupted block after completing the interrupting block.

What did Dodhia and Dismukes (2005) find? When there was no explicit prompt to return to the interrupted block, only 48% of the participants resumed the interrupted block (see Figure 8.14). Some participants were given a reminder lasting four seconds at the time of the interruption ("Please remember to return to the block that was just interrupted"), and 65% of them resumed the interrupted block. However, 65% of participants receiving no reminder but who spent four seconds staring at a blank screen immediately after being interrupted resumed the interrupted block. In a further condition, there was a delay of ten seconds between the end of the interrupted task and the start of the next block. In this condition, 88% of participants resumed the interrupted task. When there was a ten-second

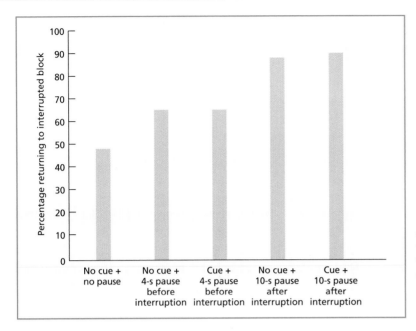

Figure 8.14 Percentage of participants returning to an interrupted task as a function of cuing and pause duration before or after interruption. Based on data in Dodhia and Dismukes (2005).

delay but participants were given a reminder – "End of interruption" – 90% resumed the interrupted task.

The above findings indicate that the provision of explicit reminders is not always very effective when people are interrupted on a task. It is important that people have a few seconds in which to formulate a new plan when an interruption changes the situation. It is also important to have a few seconds at the end of the interruption to retrieve the intention of returning to the interrupted task.

Theoretical perspectives

As we saw in Chapter 6, the working memory system is involved in numerous tasks requiring people to process and store information at the same time. It thus seems likely that it would often be involved in the performance of prospective memory tasks. This issue was addressed by Marsh and Hicks (1998). Participants performed an event-based prospective memory task at the same time as another task requiring one of the components of working memory (see Chapter 6). A task involving the attention-like central executive (e.g., random number generation) impaired prospective memory performance relative to the control condition. However, tasks involving the phonological loop or the visuo-spatial sketchpad did not. Thus, the prospective memory task used by Marsh and Hicks involved the central executive but not the other components of the working memory system.

Preparatory attentional and memory processes (PAM) theory

Does successful prospective memory performance *always* involve active and capacity-consuming monitoring (e.g., attention)? According to some theorists (e.g., Smith & Bayen, 2005), the answer is "Yes", whereas others (e.g., Einstein & McDaniel, 2005) claim that the answer is "Sometimes". We will start with Smith and Bayen's PAM theory, according to which prospective memory requires two processes:

(1) A capacity-consuming monitoring process starting when an individual forms an intention which is maintained until the required action is performed.

(2) Retrospective memory processes that ensure we remember what action is to be performed on the prospective memory task.

According to the PAM theory, performance on a prospective memory task should be superior when participants can devote their full attentional resources to it. There is much support for this prediction. For example, McDaniel, Robinson-Riegler, and Einstein (1998) had participants perform a prospective memory task under full or divided attention. Prospective memory performance was much better with full attention than with divided attention, indicating that attentional processes were needed on the prospective memory task.

Are prospective-memory tasks attentionally demanding even during periods of time in which no target stimuli are presented? Smith (2003) addressed this issue. The main task was lexical decision (deciding whether strings of letters form words). The prospective memory task (performed by half the participants) involved pressing a button whenever a target word was presented. When the target word was not presented, lexical decision was almost 50% slower for those participants performing the prospective memory task. Thus, a prospective memory task can utilise processing resources (and so impair performance on another task) even when no target stimuli are presented.

In spite of the support for the PAM theory, it seems somewhat implausible that we *always* use preparatory attentional processes when trying to remember some future action. Indeed, there is much evidence that remembering to perform a pre-determined action simply "pops" into our minds. For example, Kvavilashvili and Fisher (2007) studied the factors triggering rehearsals of a future action on an event-based prospective memory task. The overwhelming majority of rehearsals (97%) either had no obvious trigger or were triggered by some incidental external stimulus or internal thought. Reese and Cherry (2002) interrupted participants performing a prospective memory task

to ask them what they were thinking about. Only 2% of the time did they report thinking about the prospective memory task, which seems inconsistent with the notion that we maintain preparatory attentional processes.

Smith, Hunt, McVay, and McConnell (2007) modified their theory somewhat to accommodate the above points. They accepted that we are not constantly engaged in preparatory attentional processing over long periods of time. For example, someone who has the intention of buying something at a shop on their way home from work will probably not use preparatory attentional processing until they are in their car ready to drive home. However, they argued that retrieval of intentions on prospective memory tasks always incurs a cost and is never automatic.

Multi-process theory

Einstein and McDaniel (2005) put forward a multi-process theory, according to which various cognitive processes (including attentional processes) can be used to perform prospective memory tasks. However, the detection of cues for response will typically be automatic (and thus not involve attentional processes) when some or all of the following criteria are fulfilled:

(1) The cue and the to-be-performed target action are highly associated.
(2) The cue is conspicuous or salient.
(3) The ongoing processing on another task being performed at the same time as the prospective memory task directs attention to the relevant aspects of the cue.
(4) The intended action is simple.

The processing demands of prospective memory tasks often depend on the four factors identified above (see Einstein & McDaniel, 2005, for a review). However, even prospective memory tasks that theoretically should be performed automatically and without monitoring nevertheless involve processing costs. Einstein et al. (2005) investigated this issue. Participants received sentences such as the following:

The warrior's armour makes him _____ to any blows that he may undergo in battle. IMPERVIOUS. Their main task was to decide whether the final word in capital letters correctly completed the sentence. This task was performed on its own or at the same time as a prospective memory task (detecting a target word in the sentence).

Just over half of the participants performed the main task slower when combined with the prospective memory task, suggesting they may have engaged in monitoring on the latter task. However, the remaining participants performed the main task as rapidly when combined with the prospective memory task as when performed on its own. Thus, a substantial proportion of the participants apparently performed the prospective memory task automatically without using monitoring.

Einstein et al. (2005) compared the PAM and multi-process theories further in another experiment. Participants were presented with the following sequence on each trial:

(1) A target item was presented for the prospective memory task.
(2) Seven items were rated for imagery.
(3) Lexical decisions (word versus non-word) were made for 18 items.
(4) Seven additional items were rated for imagery.

Participants pressed a key whenever they detected the target word (prospective memory task) while performing the imagery rating task. However (and this is crucial), participants were told to ignore the prospective memory task while performing the lexical-decision task.

What happened when the target word from the prospective memory task was presented during the lexical-decision task? According to the PAM theory, participants should not have engaged in deliberate monitoring, and so the target word should not have disrupted performance on the lexical-decision task. According to the multi-process theory, in contrast, the target word should have activated automatic processes, which would produce disruption of

lexical-decision performance. The findings favoured the multi-process view.

Smith et al. (2007) argued that the findings reported by Einstein et al. (2005) were not convincing because of limitations of experimental design and the small size of some of their effects. They pointed out that no previous experiments fulfilled all four of the criteria for automaticity. Accordingly, they carried out an experiment in which the criteria were all satisfied. Their prospective memory task involved pressing the "P" key on a keyboard when a pink stimulus was presented. In spite of the simplicity of this task, it had a disruptive effect on performance speed of the central task being carried out at the same time. This finding strongly supports the PAM theory and its assumption that prospective memory always requires some processing capacity.

In sum, successful performance of prospective memory tasks often involves extensive monitoring, and this seems to be the case even when all of the theoretical criteria for automatic processing are present (Smith et al., 2007). However, monitoring is less likely when people remember intentions over long periods of time (as often happens in real life) than over short periods of time (as in the laboratory). As assumed by multi-process theory, the processes we use on prospective memory tasks vary between those that are very demanding (e.g., monitoring) and those imposing very few demands depending upon the precise task requirements. However, it remains a matter of controversy whether intentions on prospective memory tasks can ever be retrieved automatically with no processing cost.

Cognitive neuroscience

Which parts of the brain are most important in prospective memory? The notion that prospective memory consists of five stages suggests that several brain areas should be involved. However, most research focus has been on the frontal lobes, which are known to be involved in many executive functions (see Chapter 6). Burgess, Veitch, Costello, and Shallice (2000) considered 65 brain-damaged patients having problems with prospective memory, finding that various frontal regions were damaged. They argued that the right dorsolateral prefrontal cortex is involved in planning and the creation of intentions. BA10 (also known as rostral prefrontal cortex), which is located just behind the forehead, is involved in the maintenance of intentions. In contrast, the retrospective memory component of prospective memory tasks (i.e., remembering which action needs to be carried out) is based in the anterior and posterior cingulated.

Burgess et al. (2000) argued that BA10 is the area of greatest relevance to prospective memory. It is a large and somewhat mysterious area. It is mysterious in the sense that damage to this area often seems to have remarkably little effect on tests of intelligence, language, memory, or many types of problem solving. Burgess et al. suggested a solution to the mystery. According to their **gateway hypothesis**, "BA10 supports a mechanism that enables us to either maintain thoughts in our head...while doing something else, or switch between the thoughts in our head and attending to events in the environment...[it acts] as an attentional gateway between inner mental life and the external world as experienced through the senses" (p. 251). Most prospective memory tasks involve switching between external stimuli and internal thoughts, and so it follows from the gateway hypothesis that BA10 should be activated during prospective memory tasks.

The gateway hypothesis was tested by Gilbert, Frith, and Burgess (2005). Participants performed a task either "in their heads" or with the task stimuli present. There was BA10 activation when participants switched between the two ways of performing the task. Okuda et al. (2007) found that there was activation in BA10 in both time- and event-based prospective memory tasks but the precise pattern of activation varied between the two tasks.

Gilbert, Spengler, Simons, Frith, and Burgess (2006) carried out a meta-analysis of over 100 studies on BA10 activations. They identified the regions within BA10 associated with three pro-cesses of relevance to prospective memory. First, episodic memory retrieval was associated with lateral BA10 activations. Second, co-ordinating two processing demands involved very anterior [at the front] BA10. Third, self-reflection involved activation within medial BA10. Thus, there is reasonable evidence that several cognitive processes involved in prospective memory depend on BA10.

The available research indicates that BA10 is involved when people retain and act on intentions over short periods of time. Sometimes we need to store information about intended actions over long periods of time, and it is implausible that BA10 is involved in such storage. Thus, a complete neuroscience account of prospective memory would need to include a consideration of the brain areas in which intentions are stored.

Evaluation

Research interest in prospective memory started fairly recently, and the progress since then has been impressive in several ways. First, we have a reasonable understanding of the similarities and differences between event- and time-based prospective memory. Second, there is real-world evidence that serious failures of prospective memory are more likely when someone is interrupted while carrying out a plan of action. Third, we are beginning to understand the roles of attentional, monitoring, and automatic processes in prospective memory. Fourth, the ways in which the prefrontal cortex is involved in prospective memory are becoming clearer.

What are the limitations of research on prospective memory? First, in the real world, we typically form intentions to perform some

---

KEY TERM

gateway hypothesis: the assumption that BA10 in the prefrontal cortex acts as an attentional gateway between our internal thoughts and external stimuli.

future action because we hope to achieve some goal (e.g., establishing a friendship with someone). In contrast, as Gollwitzer and Cohen (2008, p. 438) pointed out, "Most laboratory prospective memory studies involve instructions that are fairly arbitrary with no clearly specified goal." As a result, many participants in laboratory studies may exhibit poor prospective memory mainly because they lack any real incentive to remember to perform intended actions as instructed by the experimenter.

Second, it is sometimes assumed too readily that the processes involved in prospective memory are very different from those involved in retrospective memory. In fact, there is evidence for a general memory factor including both prospective and retrospective memory (Crawford, Smith, Maylor, Della Sala, & Logie, 2003). Prospective and retrospective memory seem to share some common features (e.g., responding in the light of what has been learned previously), and many prospective memory tasks clearly also involve retrospective memory. Thus, we need more focus on the similarities as well as the differences between the two types of memory.

Third, it is generally accepted that prospective memory involves several stages such as encoding, retention, retrieval, execution, and evaluation. However, much research fails to distinguish clearly among these stages. For example, failures of prospective memory are often attributed to retrieval failure without considering the possibility of execution failure.

Fourth, a final weakness is that the great majority of studies of prospective memory have used relatively short retention intervals between the establishment of a prospective memory and the circumstances in which it should be used. Attentional and monitoring processes are likely to be more important (and long-term memory much less important) when the retention interval is short than when it is long.

CHAPTER SUMMARY

- Introduction
  What we remember in traditional memory research is largely determined by the experimenter's demands for accuracy, whereas what we remember in everyday life is determined by our personal goals. All kinds of memory research should strive for ecological validity, which involves generalisability and representativeness. In most respects, the distinction between traditional and everyday memory research is blurred, and there has been much cross-fertilisation between them.

- Autobiographical memory
  There is overlap between autobiographical and episodic memories, but the former tend to have greater personal significance. Odours can provide powerful retrieval cues for long-distant autobiographical memories (the Proust phenomenon). Flashbulb memories often seem to be unusually vivid and accurate, but actually show poor consistency and accuracy. Childhood amnesia occurs because the cognitive self only emerges towards the end of the second year of life and its extent depends on social and cultural factors and infants' development of language. The reminiscence bump consists mainly of positive memories involving high perceived control associated with progress in life. According to Conway (2005), autobiographical information is stored hierarchically at four levels: themes, lifetime periods, general events, and episodic memories. Conway also argues that the goals of the working self influence the storage and retrieval of autobiographical memories. Most recall of autobiographical memories involves the control processes of the working self within the frontal lobes, followed by activation of parts of the knowledge base in more posterior regions.

- Eyewitness testimony
Eyewitness memory is influenced by many factors, including confirmation bias, weapon focus, misleading post-event information, and proactive interference. Memory for culprits' faces and details of the crime scene is impaired by stress and anxiety. Eyewitnesses' memory for faces is influenced by unconscious transference, verbal overshadowing, and the cross-race effect. Various explanations have been offered for the finding that misleading post-event information can distort what eyewitnesses report: vacant slot, coexistence (e.g., source misattribution), blending of information, and response bias. Culprits are more likely to be selected from simultaneous than from sequential line-ups but there are more false alarms when the culprit is absent with simultaneous line-ups. The cognitive interview (based on the assumptions that memory traces are complex and can be accessed in various ways) leads eyewitnesses to produce many more accurate memories at the expense of a small increase in inaccurate memories.

- Prospective memory
Prospective memory involves successive stages of encoding, retention, retrieval, execution, and evaluation, and it can be event- or time-based. Event-based prospective memory is often better because the intended actions are more likely to be triggered by external cues. Many prospective memory failures occur when individuals are interrupted while carrying out a plan of action and have insufficient time to form a new plan. Some theorists argue that people always use a capacity-consuming monitoring process during the retention interval and that the retrieval of intentions always requires some capacity. Others claim that the involvement of attention and/or automatic processes depends on the nature of the cue and the task in prospective memory. Evidence from brain-damaged patients and from functional neuroimaging indicates that the frontal lobes have a central role in prospective memory. Several processes (e.g., episodic memory retrieval, co-ordination of task demands, and self-reflection) of relevance to prospective memory involve BA10 within the prefrontal cortex.

FURTHER READING

- Baddeley, A., Eysenck, M.W., & Anderson, M.C. (2009). *Memory*. Hove, UK: Psychology Press. This textbook provides detailed coverage of research and theory on all the main topics discussed in this chapter.
- Cohen, G., & Conway, M.A. (eds.) (2008). *Memory in the real world* (3rd ed.). Hove, UK: Psychology Press. Most of the topics discussed in this chapter are explored in depth in this excellent edited book (see the Williams, Conway, and Cohen reference below).
- Kliegel, M., McDaniel, M.A., & Einstein, G.O. (eds.) (2008). *Prospective memory: Cognitive, neuroscience, developmental, and applied perspectives*. London: Lawrence Erlbaum Associates Ltd. This edited book has chapters by all the world's leading researchers on prospective memory. It provides a comprehensive overview of the entire field.
- Lindsay, R.C.L., Ross, D.F., Read, J.D., & Toglia, M.P. (eds.) (2007). *The handbook of eyewitness psychology: Volume II: Memory for people*. Mahwah, NJ: Lawrence Erlbaum Associates, Inc. This edited book contains contributions from the world's leading experts on eyewitness memory for people.

- Toglia, M.P., Read, J.D., Ross, D.F., & Lindsay, R.C.L. (eds.) (2007). *The handbook of eyewitness psychology: Volume I: Memory for events*. Mahwah, NJ: Lawrence Erlbaum Associates, Inc. This book is an invaluable source of information on eyewitness memory for events, with contributions from leading researchers in several countries.
- Williams, H.L., Conway, M.A., & Cohen, G. (2008). Autobiographical memory. In G. Cohen & M. Conway (eds.), *Memory in the real world* (3rd ed.). Hove, UK: Psychology Press. This chapter provides a comprehensive review of theory and research on autobiographical memory.

Our lives would be remarkably limited without language. Our social interactions rely very heavily on language, and a good command of language is vital for all students. We are considerably more knowledgeable than people of previous generations because knowledge is passed on from one generation to the next via language.

What is language? According to Harley (2008, p. 5), language "is a system of symbols and rules that enable us to communicate. Symbols are things that stand for other things: Words, either written or spoken, are symbols. The rules specify how words are ordered to form sentences." It is true that communication is the primary function of language, but it is not the only one. Crystal (1997) identified eight functions of language, of which communication was one. In addition, we can use language for thinking, to record information, to express emotion (e.g., "I love you"), to pretend to be animals (e.g., "Woof! Woof!"), to express identity with a group (e.g., singing in church), and so on.

Can other species acquire language? The most important research here has involved trying to teach language to apes. Some of the most impressive evidence came from the research of Savage-Rumbaugh with a bonobo chimpanzee called Panbanisha (see Leake, 1999), who was born in 1985. Panbanisha has spent her entire life in captivity receiving training in the use of language. She uses a specially designed keypad with about 400 geometric patterns, or lexigrams, on it. When she presses a sequence of keys, a computer translates the sequence into a synthetic voice. Panbanisha learned a vocabulary of 3000 words by the age of 14 years, and became very good at combining a series of symbols in the grammatically correct order. For example, she can construct sentences such as, "Please can I have an iced coffee?", and, "I'm thinking about eating something."

Panbanisha's achievements are considerable. However, her command of language is much less than that of young children. For example, she does not produce many novel sentences, she only rarely refers to objects that are not visible, and the complexity of her sentences is generally less than that of children. As Noam Chomsky (quoted in Atkinson, Atkinson, Smith, & Bem, 1993) remarked, "If animals had a capacity as biologically advantageous as language but somehow hadn't used it until now, it would be an evolutionary miracle, like finding an island of humans who could be taught to fly."

IS LANGUAGE INNATE?

There has been fierce controversy over the years concerning the extent to which language is innate. A key figure in this controversy is Chomsky (1965). He argued that humans possess a language acquisition device consisting of innate knowledge of grammatical structure. Children require some exposure to (and experience with) the language environment provided by their parents and other people to develop language. Such experience determines *which* specific language any given child will learn.

One of the reasons why Chomsky put forward the notion of a language acquisition device was that he was so impressed by the breathtaking speed with which most young children acquire language. From the age of about 16 months onwards, children often acquire upwards of ten new words every day. By the age of five, children have mastered most of the grammatical rules of their native language.

It should be pointed out that many experts regard the entire notion of an innate grammar as implausible. For example, Bishop (1997, p. 123) argued as follows: "What makes an innate grammar a particularly peculiar idea is the fact that innate knowledge must be general enough to account for acquisition of Italian, Japanese, Turkish, Malay, as well as sign language acquisition by deaf children."

Bickerton (1984) put forward the language bioprogramme hypothesis, which is closely related to Chomsky's views. According to this hypothesis, children will create a grammar even if not exposed to a proper language during their early years. Some of the strongest support for this hypothesis comes from the study of pidgin languages. These are new, primitive languages created when two or more groups of people having different native languages are in contact with each other. Pinker (1984) discussed research on labourers from China, Japan, Korea, Puerto Rico, Portugal, and the Philippines who were taken to the sugar plantations of Hawaii 100 years ago. These labourers developed a pidgin language that was very simple and lacked most grammatical structures. Here is an example: "Me cape buy, me check make." The meaning is, "He bought my coffee; he made me out a cheque." The offspring of these labourers developed a language known as Hawaiian Creole, which is a proper language and fully grammatical.

We do not know the extent to which the development of Hawaiian Creole depended on the labourers' prior exposure to language. Clearer evidence that a language can develop in

groups almost completely lacking in exposure to a developed language was reported by Senghas, Kita, and Özyürek (2004). They studied deaf Nicaraguan children at special schools. Attempts (mostly unsuccessful) were made to teach them Spanish. However, these deaf children developed a new system of gestures that expanded into a basic sign language passed on to successive groups of children who joined the school. Since Nicaraguan Sign Language bore very little relation to Spanish or to the gestures made by hearing children, it appears that it is a genuinely new language owing remarkably little to other languages.

What do the above findings mean? They certainly suggest that humans have a strong innate motivation to acquire language (including grammatical rules) and to communicate with others. However, the findings do *not* provide strong support for the notion of a language acquisition device.

The genetic approach is another way of showing that innate factors are important in language (see Grigorenko, 2009, for a review). There are huge individual differences in language ability, some of which depend on genetic factors. Of particular importance is research on the KE family in London. Across three generations of this family, about 50% of its members suffer from severe language problems (e.g., difficulties in understanding speech, slow and ungrammatical speech, and a poor ability to decide whether sentences are grammatical).

Detailed genetic research indicated that the complex language disorder found in members of the KE family was controlled by a specific gene named FOXP2 (Lai, Fisher, Hurst, Vargha-Khadem, & Monaco, 2001). More specifically, mutations of this gene were found in affected members of the family but not in unaffected members. In a subsequent study on other patients with similar language problems (MacDermot et al., 2005), other mutations of FOXP2 were discovered.

What is the role of FOXP2 in language? It is probably involved in the brain mechanisms underlying the development of language. The fact that affected members of the KE family find it difficult to control their tongues and to make speech sounds suggests that the gene may be relevant to precise movements within the articulatory system. However, we must not exaggerate the importance of FOXP2. Studies on individuals suffering from a range of language disorders more common than those experienced by members of the KE family have consistently failed to find evidence of the involvement of FOXP2 in those disorders (Grigorenko, 2009).

In sum, there is convincing evidence that some aspects of language are innate. However, there is also overwhelming evidence that numerous environmental factors are incredibly important. Of particular importance is child-directed speech, which is the simplified sentences spoken by mothers and other adults when talking to young children. This book is primarily about adult cognition (including language), but Chapter 4 in Harley (2008) provides a detailed account of language development in children.

WHORFIAN HYPOTHESIS

The best-known theory about the interrelationship between language and thought was put forward by Benjamin Lee Whorf (1956). He was a fire prevention officer for an insurance company who spent his spare time working in linguistics. According to his hypothesis of linguistic relativity (the **Whorfian hypothesis**), language determines or influences thinking. Miller and McNeill (1969) distinguished three versions of the Whorfian hypothesis. According to the strong hypothesis, language determines thinking. Thus, any language imposes constraints on what can be thought, with those constraints varying from one language to another. The weak hypothesis states that language influences perception. Finally, the weakest hypothesis claims only that language influences memory.

Evidence

Casual inspection of the world's languages indicates significant differences among them. For example, the Hanuxoo people in the Philippines have 92 different names for various types of rice, and there are hundreds of camel-related words in Arabic. These differences may influence thought. However, it is more plausible that different environmental conditions influence the things people think about, and this in turn influences their linguistic usage. Thus, these differences occur because thought influences language rather than because language influences thought.

According to the Whorfian hypothesis, colour categorisation and memory should vary as a function of the participants' native language. In early research, Heider (1972) compared colour memory in Americans and members of the Dani, a "Stone Age" agricultural people in Indonesian New Guinea. The Dani language has only two basic colour terms: "mola" for bright-warm hues and "mili" for dark, cold hues. Heider found that colour memory was comparable in both groups. She concluded that colour categories are universal, and that the Whorfian hypothesis was not supported. However, Roberson et al. (2000) was unable to replicate these findings in a study comparing English participants with members of the Berinmo, who live in Papua New Guinea and whose language contains only five basic colour terms.

Roberson, Davies, and Davidoff (2000) carried out further research on the Berinmo. In one study, they considered categorical perception, meaning that it is easier to discriminate between stimuli belonging to *different* categories than stimuli within the *same* category (see Chapter 9). In the English language, we have categories of green and blue, whereas Berinmo has categories of nol (roughly similar to green) and wor (roughly similar to yellow). Roberson et al. presented participants with three coloured stimuli, and asked them to select the two most similar. Suppose two of the stimuli would

---

KEY TERM

Whorfian hypothesis: the notion that language determines, or at least influences, thinking.

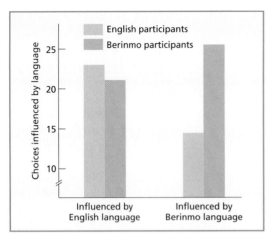

Figure III.I Influence of language (English vs. Berinmo) on choice of similar pairs of stimuli by English and Berinmo participants. Data from Roberson et al. (2000).

normally be described as green in English and the third one as blue. According to the notion of categorical perception, English speakers should regard the two green stimuli as being more similar. However, there is no reason to expect Berinmo speakers to do the same, because their language does not distinguish between blue and green. In similar fashion, Berinmo speakers presented with two nol stimuli and a wor stimulus should select the two nol stimuli but there is no good reason why English-speaking participants should do the same.

What did Roberson et al. (2000) find? Language determined performance: both groups showed categorical perception based on their own language (see Figure III.1). This is good support for the Whorfian hypothesis. In another study, Roberson et al. studied the effects of categorical perception on memory. Participants decided on a test of recognition memory which of two test stimuli matched a target stimulus that had been presented previously. According to the Whorfian hypothesis, English speakers should have had good recognition memory when the test stimuli were on opposite sides of the green–blue boundary, but this should have been irrelevant to the Berinmo. In contrast, Berinmo speakers should have performed

well when the test stimuli were on opposite sides of the nol–wor boundary, but this should have been irrelevant to the English participants. All these predictions were supported.

It could be argued that at least some of the findings obtained from the Berinmo were due to their lack of experience with man-made colours rather than their limited colour vocabulary. However, this explanation does not account for findings from a study on Russian participants (Winawer, Witthoft, Frank, Wade, & Boroditsky, 2007). The Russian language is unique in that it has separate words for dark blue (siniy) and light blue (goluboy). Winawer et al. carried out a study in which Russian participants had to select which of two test colours matched a siniy (dark blue) target that remained visible. There was clear evidence of categorical perception – the participants performed faster when the distractor was goluboy than when it was a different shade of siniy. English speakers, who would simply describe all the stimuli as "blue", did not show this effect.

Evidence that language can influence thinking was reported by Hoffman, Lau, and Johnson (1986). Bilingual English-Chinese speakers read descriptions of individuals, and then provided free interpretations of the individuals described. The descriptions conformed to Chinese or English stereotypes of personality. For example, in English there is a stereotype of the artistic type (e.g., moody and intense temperament; bohemian lifestyle), but this stereotype does not exist in Chinese. Bilinguals thinking in Chinese used Chinese stereotypes in their free interpretations, whereas those thinking in English used English stereotypes. Thus, the inferences we draw can be influenced by the language in which we are thinking.

Casasanto (2008) pointed out that English speakers generally used *distance* metaphors to describe the duration of an event (e.g., long meeting; short discussion). In contrast, Greek speakers use *amount* metaphors (e.g., *synantisis pou diekese poli*, meaning "meeting that lasts much"). Casasanto discussed his own research with English and Greek speakers using two tasks involving the estimation of brief intervals of time. On one task, participants saw a line "growing" across the screen, and estimated how long it had been on the screen. The length of the line was unrelated to its duration. On the other task, participants viewed a drawing of a container filling gradually with liquid, and estimated how long the filling had taken. The amount of filling was unrelated to its duration.

Casasanto (2008) predicted that English speakers' duration estimates would be strongly biased by distance (i.e., the length of the line) but not by amount (i.e., the extent of the fill). He assumed that English speakers naturally think of duration in terms of distance, and so would produce longer estimates when the line was long than when it was short. In contrast, he predicted that Greek speakers' duration estimates would be strongly biased by amount but not by distance, because they naturally think of duration in terms of amount. All these predictions were supported by the findings.

Evaluation

Recent years have seen increased support for the Whorfian hypothesis on several kinds of task (e.g., colour discrimination; colour memory; temporal estimation). The available evidence supports the weakest and the weak versions of the Whorfian hypothesis. When tasks are used giving participants flexibility in the approach they adopt (e.g., Hoffman et al., 1986), there is even modest evidence favouring the strong version of the hypothesis.

What is lacking is a detailed specification of the ways in which language influences cognition. Hunt and Agnoli (1991) assumed that an individual's estimate of computational costs or mental effort helps to determine whether language influences cognition. However, these costs have rarely been assessed.

It is important to establish whether the limiting effects of language on cognition are relatively easy to remove. Whorf (1956) assumed that it would be hard to change the effects of language on cognition, whereas Hunt and Agnoli (1991) assumed that it would be rela-

tively easy. Only future research will provide the answer.

LANGUAGE CHAPTERS

There are four main language skills (listening to speech, reading, speaking, and writing). It is perhaps natural to assume that any given person will have generally strong or weak language skills. That assumption may often be correct with respect to first-language acquisition, but is very frequently not so with second-language acquisition. For example, the first author spent ten years at school learning French, and he has spent his summer holidays there most years over a long period of time. He can just about read newspapers and easy novels in French, and he can write coherent (if somewhat ungrammatical) letters in French. However, in common with many British people, he finds it agonisingly difficult to understand rapid spoken French, and his ability to speak French is poor.

The next three chapters (Chapters 9–11) focus on the four main language skills. Chapter 10 deals with the basic processes involved in reading and in listening to speech. There is an emphasis in this chapter on the ways in which readers and listeners identify and make sense of individual words that they read on the printed page or hear in speech. As we will see, the study of brain-damaged patients has helped to reveal the complexity of the processes underlying reading and speech recognition.

Chapter 10 is concerned mainly with the processes involved in the comprehension of sentences and discourse (connected text or speech). There are some important differences between understanding text and understanding speech (e.g., it is generally easier to refer back to what has gone before with text than with speech). However, it is assumed that comprehension processes are broadly similar for text and for speech, and major theories of language comprehension are considered in detail.

Chapter 11 deals with the remaining two main language abilities: speaking and writing.

Speech production takes up much more of our time than does writing. It may be no coincidence that we know much more about speech production than we do about writing. Research on writing has been somewhat neglected until recently, which is a shame given the importance of writing skills in most cultures.

The processes discussed in these three chapters are *interdependent*. As we will see, speakers use comprehension processes to monitor what they are saying (Levelt, 1989). In addition, listeners use language production processes to predict what speakers are going to say next (Pickering & Garrod, 2007).

CHAPTER 9

READING AND SPEECH PERCEPTION

INTRODUCTION

Humanity excels in its command of language. Indeed, language is of such enormous importance that this chapter and the following two are devoted to it. In this chapter, we consider the basic processes involved in reading words and in recognising spoken words. It often does not matter whether a message is presented to our eyes or to our ears. For example, you would understand the sentence, "You have done exceptionally well in your cognitive psychology examination", in much the same way whether you read or heard it. Thus, many comprehension processes are very similar whether we are reading a text or listening to someone talking.

However, reading and speech perception differ in various ways. In reading, each word can be seen as a whole, whereas a spoken word is spread out in time and is transitory. More importantly, it is much harder to tell where one word ends and the next starts with speech than with text. Speech generally provides a more ambiguous signal than does printed text. For example, when words were spliced out of spoken sentences and presented on their own, they were recognised only half of the time (Lieberman, 1963).

There are other significant differences. The demands on memory are greater when listening to speech than reading a text, because the words already spoken are no longer accessible. So far we have indicated ways in which listening to speech is harder. However, there is one major way in which listening to speech can be easier than reading. Speech often contains prosodic cues (discussed in Chapter 11; see Glossary). Prosodic cues are hints to sentence structure and intended meaning via the speaker's pitch, intonation, stress, and timing (e.g., questions have a rising intonation on the last word in the sentence). In contrast, the main cues to sentence structure specific to text are punctuation marks (e.g., commas, semi-colons). These are often less informative than prosodic cues in speech.

The fact that reading and listening to speech differ considerably can be seen by considering children and brain-damaged patients. Young children often have good comprehension of spoken language, but struggle to read even simple stories. Part of the reason may be that reading is a relatively recent invention in our evolutionary history, and so lacks a genetically programmed specialised processor (McCandliss, Cohen, & Dehaene, 2003). Some adult brain-damaged patients can understand spoken language but cannot read, and others can read perfectly well but cannot understand the spoken word.

Basic processes specific to reading are dealt with first in this chapter. These processes are involved in recognising and reading individual words and in guiding our eye movements during reading. After that, we consider basic processes specific to speech, including those required to divide the speech signal into separate words and to recognise those words.

In Chapter 10, we discuss comprehension processes common to reading and listening. In contrast to this chapter, the emphasis will be on larger units of language consisting of several sentences. Bear in mind, however, that the processes discussed in this chapter play an important role in our comprehension of texts or long speech utterances.

READING: INTRODUCTION

It is important to study reading because adults without effective reading skills are at a great disadvantage. Thus, we need to understand the processes involved in reading to help poor readers. In addition, reading requires several perceptual and other cognitive processes as well as a good knowledge of language and of grammar. Thus, reading can be regarded as visually guided thinking.

Research methods

Several methods are available for studying reading. These methods have been used extensively in research, and so it is important to understand what they involve as well as their limitations. For example, consider ways of assessing the time taken for word identification or recognition (e.g., deciding a word is familiar; accessing its meaning). The **lexical decision task** involves deciding rapidly whether a string of letters forms a word. The **naming task** involves saying a printed word out loud as rapidly as possible. These techniques ensure certain processing has been performed but possess clear limitations. Normal reading times are disrupted by the requirement to respond to the task, and it is hard to know precisely what processes are reflected in lexical decision or naming times.

Recording eye movements during reading is useful. It provides an unobtrusive and detailed on-line record of attention-related processes. The only important restriction on readers whose eye movements are being recorded is that they must keep their heads fairly still. The main problem is the difficulty of deciding precisely *what* processing occurs during each fixation (period of time during which the eye remains still).

Balota, Paul, and Spieler (1999) argued that reading involves several kinds of processing: **orthography** (the spelling of words); **phonology** (the sound of words); **semantics** (word meaning); syntax; and higher-level discourse integration. The various tasks differ in the involvement of these kinds of processing:

> *In naming, the attentional control system would increase the influence of the computations between orthography and phonology…the demands of lexical decision performance might place a high priority on the computations between orthographic and meaning level modules [processors]…if the goal…is reading comprehension, then attentional control would increase the priority of computations of the syntactic-, meaning-, and discourse-level modules (p. 47).*

Thus, performance on naming and lexical decision tasks may not reflect accurately normal reading processes.

Next, there is **priming**, in which a prime word is presented very shortly before the target word. The prime word is related to the target word (e.g., in spelling, meaning, or sound). What is of interest is to see the effects of the prime on processing of (and response to) the target word. For example, when reading the

Reading is a complex skill. It involves processing information about word spellings, the sounds of words, and the meanings of words, as well as higher-level comprehension processes.

word "clip", do you access information about its pronunciation? We will see shortly that the most likely answer is, "Yes". If the word is preceded by a non-word having identical pronunciation ("klip") presented below the level of conscious awareness, it is processed faster (see Rastle & Brysbaert, 2006, for a review).

Finally, there is brain imaging. In recent years, there has been increasing interest in identifying the brain areas associated with various language processes. Some of the fruits of such research will be discussed in this chapter and the next two.

Phonological processes in reading

You are currently reading this sentence. Did you access the relevant sounds when identifying the words in the previous sentence? The most common view (e.g., Coltheart, Rastle, Perry, Langdon, & Ziegler, 2001) is that phonological processing of visual words is relatively slow and inessential for word identification. This view (the weak phonological model) differs from the strong phonological model in which phonology has a much more central role:

A phonological representation is a necessary product of processing printed words, even though the explicit

pronunciation of their phonological structure is not required. Thus, the strong phonological model would predict that phonological processing will be mandatory [obligatory], perhaps automatic (Frost, 1998, p. 76).

Evidence

The assumption that phonological processing is important when identifying words was supported by van Orden (1987). Some of the words he used were **homophones** (words having one pronunciation but two spellings). Participants made many errors when asked questions such as, "Is it a flower? ROWS", than when asked, "Is it a flower? ROBS". The problem with "ROWS" is that it is homophonic with "ROSE", which of course is a flower. The participants made errors because they engaged in phonological processing of the words.

We now move on to the notion of phonological neighbourhood. Two words are phonological neighbours if they differ in only one phoneme (e.g., "gate" has "bait" and "get" as neighbours). If phonology is used in visual word recognition, then words with many phonological neighbours should have an advantage. Yates (2005) found support for this assumption using various tasks (e.g., lexical decision; naming). Within sentences, words having many phonological neighbours are fixated for less time than those with few neighbours (Yates, Friend, & Ploetz, 2008).

Many researchers have used masked phonological priming to assess the role of phonology in word processing (mentioned earlier). A word (e.g., "clip") is immediately preceded by a phonologically identical non-word prime (e.g., "klip"). This prime is masked and presented very briefly so it is not consciously perceived. Rastle and Brysbaert (2006) carried out a meta-analysis.

Words were processed faster on various tasks (e.g., lexical decision task; naming task) when preceded by such primes than by primes similar to them in terms of spelling but not phonology (e.g., "plip"). These findings strongly imply that phonological processing occurs rapidly and automatically, as predicted by the strong phonological model. However, findings with masked phonological priming do not prove that visual word recognition *must* depend on prior phonological processing.

In a study on proof-reading and eye movements, Jared, Levy, and Rayner (1999) found that the use of phonology depended on the nature of the words and participants' reading ability. Eye-movement data suggested that phonology was used in accessing the meaning of low-frequency words (those infrequently encountered) but not high-frequency ones. In addition, poor readers were more likely than good ones to access phonology.

Does phonological processing occur *before* or *after* a word's meaning has been accessed? In one study (Daneman, Reingold, and Davidson, 1995), readers fixated homophones longer when they were incorrect (e.g., "He was in his stocking *feat*") than when they were correct (e.g., "He was in his stocking *feet*"). That would not have happened if the phonological code had been accessed before word meaning. However, there were many backward eye movements (regressions) after incorrect homophones had been fixated. These findings suggest that the phonological code may be accessed *after* word meaning is accessed.

Reasonably convincing evidence that word meaning can be accessed without access to phonology was reported by Hanley and McDonnell (1997). They studied a patient, PS, who understood the meanings of words while reading even though he could not pronounce them accurately. PS did not even seem to have access to an internal phonological representation of words. He could not gain access to the other meaning of homophones when he saw one of the spellings (e.g., "air"). The fact that PS could give accurate definitions of printed words in spite of his impairments suggests strongly that he had full access to the meanings of words for which he could not supply the appropriate phonology.

One way of finding out when phonological processing occurs is to use event-related potentials (ERPs; see Glossary). When Ashby and Martin (2008) did this, they found that syllable information in visually presented words was processed 250–350 ms after word onset. This is rapidly enough to influence visual word recognition.

Evaluation

Phonological processing typically occurs rapidly and automatically during visual word recognition. Thus, the weak phonological model may have underestimated the importance of phonological processing. As Rastle and Brysbaert (2006) pointed out, the fact that we develop phonological representations years before we learn to read may help to explain why phonology is so important.

What are the limitations of the strong phonological model? There is as yet little compelling evidence that phonological information has to be used in visual word recognition. In several studies (e.g., Hanley & McDonnell, 1997; Jared et al., 1999), evidence of phonological processing was limited or absent. There is also phonological dyslexia (discussed in detail shortly). Phonological dyslexics have great difficulties with phonological processing but can nevertheless read familiar words. This is somewhat puzzling if phonological processing is essential for reading. Even when there is clear evidence of phonological processing, this processing may occur after accessing word meaning (Daneman et al., 1995).

In sum, the strong phonological model is probably too strong. However, phonological processing often plays an important role in visual word recognition even if word recognition can occur in its absence.

WORD RECOGNITION

College students typically read at about 300 words per minute, thus averaging only 200 ms to recognise each word. How long does word recognition take? That is hard to say, in part because of imprecision about the meaning of "word recognition". The term can refer to deciding that a word is familiar, accessing a word's name, or accessing its meaning. We will see that various estimates of the time taken for word recognition have been produced.

Automatic processing

Rayner and Sereno (1994) argued that word recognition is generally fairly automatic. This makes intuitive sense given that most college students have read between 20 and 70 million words in their lifetimes. It has been argued that automatic processes are unavoidable and unavailable to consciousness (see Chapter 5). Evidence that word identification may be unavoidable in some circumstances comes from the Stroop effect (see Glossary), in which naming the colours in which words are printed is slowed when the words themselves are different colour names (e.g., the word RED printed in green). The Stroop effect suggests that word meaning can be extracted even when people try *not* to process it. Cheesman and Merikle (1984) found that the Stroop effect could be obtained even when the colour name was presented below the level of conscious awareness. This latter finding suggests that word recognition or identification does not necessarily depend on conscious awareness.

Letter and word processing

It could be argued that the recognition of a word on the printed page involves two *successive* stages:

(1) Identification of the individual letters in the word.
(2) Word identification.

In fact, however, the notion that letter identification must be complete before word identification can begin is wrong. For example, consider the **word superiority effect** (Reicher, 1969). A letter string is presented very briefly, followed by a pattern mask. Participants decide which of two letters was presented in a particular position (e.g., the third letter). The word superiority effect is defined by the finding that performance is better when the letter string forms a word than when it does not.

The word superiority effect suggests that information about the word presented can facilitate identification of the letters of that word. However, there is also a pseudoword superiority effect: letters are better recognised when presented in **pseudowords** (pronounceable nonwords such as "MAVE") than in unpronounceable nonwords (Carr, Davidson, & Hawkins, 1978).

Interactive activation model

McClelland and Rumelhart (1981) proposed an influential interactive activation model of visual word processing to account for the word superiority effect. It was based on the assumption that bottom-up and top-down processes interact (see Figure 9.1):

* There are recognition units at three levels: the feature level at the bottom; the letter level in the middle; and the word level at the top.
* When a feature in a letter is detected (e.g., vertical line at the right-hand side of a letter), activation goes to all letter units containing that feature (e.g., H, M, N), and inhibition goes to all other letter units.
* Letters are identified at the letter level. When a letter within a word is identified, activation is sent to the word level for all four-letter word units containing that letter in that position within the word, and inhibition is sent to all other word units.

KEY TERMS

word superiority effect: a target letter is more readily detected in a letter string when the string forms a word than when it does not.
pseudoword: a pronounceable nonword (e.g., "tave").

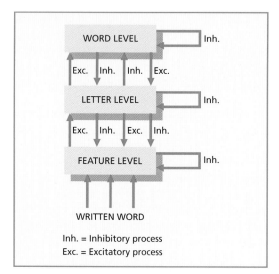

Figure 9.1 McClelland and Rumelhart's (1981) interactive activation model of visual word recognition. Adapted from Ellis (1984).

- Words are recognised at the word level. Activated word units increase the level of activation in the letter-level units for the letters forming that word.

According to the model, top-down processing is involved in the activation and inhibition processes going from the word level to the letter level. The word superiority effect occurs because of top-down influences of the word level on the letter level. Suppose the word SEAT is presented, and participants decide whether the third letter is an A or an N. If the word unit for SEAT is activated at the word level, this will increase activation of the letter A at the letter level and inhibit activation of the letter N, leading to stronger activation of SEAT.

How can the pseudoword superiority effect be explained? When letters are embedded in pronounceable nonwords, there will generally be some overlap of spelling patterns between the pseudoword and genuine words. This overlap can produce additional activation of the letters presented in the pseudoword and lead to the pseudoword superiority effect.

According to the model, time to identify a word depends in part on its **orthographic neighbours**, the words that can be formed by changing just one of its letters. Thus, for example, the word "stem" has words including "seem", "step", and "stew" as orthographic neighbours. When a word is presented, these orthographic neighbours become activated and increase the time taken to identify it. Theoretically, this inhibitory effect is especially great when a word's orthographic neighbours are higher in frequency in the language than the word itself. This is because high-frequency words (words encountered frequently in our everyday lives) have greater resting activation levels than low-frequency ones. It has proved very difficult to find this predicted inhibitory effect of higher frequency neighbours in studies using English words (e.g., Sears, Campbell, & Lupker, 2006). Interestingly, there is much stronger evidence for an inhibitory effect in other languages (e.g., French, Dutch, Spanish; see Sears et al., 2006, for a review). English has many more short words with several higher frequency neighbours than these other languages. As a result, inhibitory effects in English might make it extremely difficult to identify many low-frequency words.

The model predicts that the word superiority effect should be greater for high-frequency words than for low-frequency ones. The reason is that high-frequency words have a higher resting level of activation and so should generate more top-down activation from the word level to the letter level. In fact, however, the size of the word superiority effect is unaffected by word frequency (Gunther, Gfoerer, & Weiss, 1984).

Evaluation

The interactive activation model has been very influential. It was one of the first examples of how a connectionist processing system (see Chapter 1) can be applied to visual word processing. It apparently accounts for phenomena such as the word superiority effect and the pseudoword superiority effect.

KEY TERM

orthographic neighbours: with reference to a given word, those other words that can be formed by changing one of its letters.

The model was not designed to provide a comprehensive account of word recognition. Accordingly, it is not surprising that it has little to say about various factors that play an important role in word recognition. For example, we have seen that phonological processing is often involved in word recognition, but this is not considered within the model. In addition, the model does not address the role of meaning. As we will see, the meaning of relevant context often influences the early stages of word recognition (e.g., Lucas, 1999; Penolazzi, Hauk, & Pulvermüller, 2007).

Context effects

Is word identification influenced by context? This issue was addressed by Meyer and Schvaneveldt (1971) in a study in which participants decided whether letter strings formed words (lexical decision task). The decision time for a word (e.g., DOCTOR) was shorter when the preceding context or prime was semantically related (e.g., NURSE) than when it was semantically unrelated (e.g., LIBRARY) or there was no prime. This is known as the **semantic priming effect**.

Why does the semantic priming effect occur? Perhaps the context or priming word automatically activates the stored representations of all words related to it due to massive previous learning. Another possibility is that controlled processes may be involved, with a prime such as NURSE leading participants to *expect* that a semantically related word will follow.

Neely (1977) distinguished between the above explanations. The priming word was a category name (e.g., "Bird"), followed by a letter string at one of three intervals: 250, 400, or 700 ms. In the key manipulation, participants expected a particular category name would usually be followed by a member of a *different* pre-specified category (e.g., "Bird" followed by the name of part of a building). There were two kinds of trial with this manipulation:

(1) The category name was followed by a member of a different (but expected) category (e.g., Bird–Window).

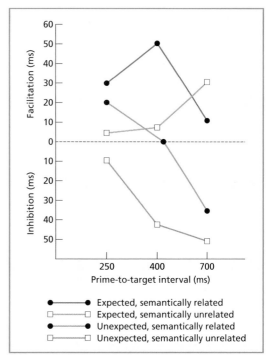

Figure 9.2 The time course of inhibitory and facilitatory effects of priming as a function of whether or not the target word was related semantically to the prime, and of whether or not the target word belonged to the expected category. Data from Neely (1977).

(2) The category name was followed by a member of the same (but unexpected) category (e.g., Bird–Magpie).

There were two priming or context effects (see Figure 9.2). First, there was a rapid, automatic effect based only on semantic relatedness. Second, there was a slower-acting attentional effect based only on expectations. Subsequent research has generally confirmed Neely's (1977) findings except that automatic processes can cause inhibitory effects at short intervals (e.g., Antos, 1979).

Do context effects occur *before* or *after* the individual has gained access to the internal **lexicon** (a store containing several kinds of information about words)? In other words, do context effects precede or follow **lexical access**? Lucas (1999) addressed this issue in a meta-analysis. In most of the studies, each context sentence contained an ambiguous word (e.g., "The man spent the entire day fishing on the *bank*"). The ambiguous word was immediately followed by a target word on which a naming or lexical decision task was performed. The target word was appropriate (e.g., "river") or inappropriate (e.g., "money") to the meaning of the ambiguous word in the sentence context. Overall, the appropriate interpretation of a word produced more priming than the inappropriate one.

Further support for the notion that context can influence lexical access was reported by Penolazzi et al. (2007) using event-related potentials (ERPs). The target word (shown here in bold) was expected (when "around" was in the sentence) or not expected (when "near" was in the sentence): "He was just around/near the **corner**." There was a difference in the ERPs within 200 ms of the onset of the target word depending on whether the word was expected or unexpected. The finding that the meaning of the context affected the processing of the target word so rapidly suggests (but does not prove) that context affects lexical access to the target word.

We have seen that context has a rapid impact on processing. However, that does *not* mean that word meanings inconsistent with the context are always rejected very early on. Chen and Boland (2008) focused on the processing of homophones. They selected homophones having a dominant and a non-dominant meaning (e.g., "flower" is dominant and "flour" is non-dominant). Participants listened to sentences in some of which the context biased the interpretation towards the non-dominant meaning of the homophones. Here is an example:

The baker had agreed to make several pies for a large event today, so he started by taking out necessary ingredients like milk, eggs, and flour.

At the onset of the homophone at the end of the sentence, participants were presented with four pictures. In the example given, one of the pictures showed flour and another picture showed an object resembling a flower. The participants showed a tendency to fixate the flower-like picture even though the context made it very clear that was *not* the homophone's intended meaning.

In sum, context often has a rapid influence on word processing. However, this influence is less than total. For example, word meanings that are inappropriate in a given context can be activated when listening to speech or reading (Chen & Boland, 2008).

READING ALOUD

Read out the following words and pseudowords (pronounceable nonwords):

CAT FOG COMB PINT MANTINESS FASS

Hopefully, you found it a simple task even though it involves hidden complexities. For example, how do you know the "b" in "comb" is silent and that "pint" does not rhyme with "hint"? Presumably you have specific information stored in long-term memory about how to pronounce these words. However, this cannot explain your ability to pronounce nonwords such as "mantiness" and "fass". Perhaps pseudowords are pronounced by analogy with real words (e.g., "fass" is pronounced to rhyme with "mass"). Another possibility is that rules governing the translation of letter strings into sounds are used to generate a pronunciation for nonwords.

> **KEY TERMS**
>
> **lexicon:** a store of detailed information about words, including orthographic, phonological, semantic, and syntactic knowledge.
> **lexical access:** entering the **lexicon** with its store of detailed information about words.

The above description of the reading of individual words is oversimplified. Studies on brain-damaged patients suggest that there are different reading disorders depending on which parts of the language system are damaged. We turn now to two major theoretical approaches that have considered reading aloud in healthy and brain-damaged individuals. These are the dual-route cascaded model (Coltheart et al., 2001) and the distributed connectionist approach or triangle model (Plaut, McClelland, Seidenberg, & Patterson, 1996).

At the risk of oversimplification, we can identify various key differences between the two approaches as follows. According to the dual-route approach, the processes involved in reading words and nonwords differ from each other.

These processes are relatively neat and tidy, and some of them are rule-based. According to the connectionist approach, in contrast, the various processes involved in reading are used more *flexibly* than assumed within the dual-route model. In crude terms, it is a matter of "all hands to the pump": all the relevant knowledge we possess about word sounds, word spellings, and word meanings is used in parallel whether we are reading words or nonwords.

Dual-route cascaded model

Coltheart and his colleagues have put forward various theories of reading, culminating in their dual-route cascaded model (2001; see Figure 9.3). This model accounts for reading

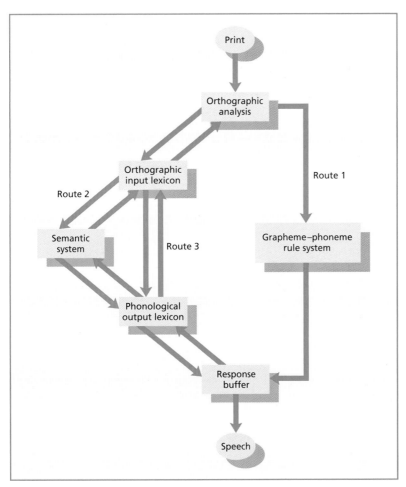

Figure 9.3 Basic architecture of the dual-route cascaded model. Adapted from Coltheart et al. (2001).

aloud and for silent reading. There are two main routes between the printed word and speech, both starting with orthographic analysis (used for identifying and grouping letters in printed words). The crucial distinction is between a lexical or dictionary lookup route and a non-lexical route (Route 1), which involves converting letters into sounds. In Figure 9.3, the non-lexical route is Route 1, and the lexical route is divided into two sub-routes (Routes 2 and 3).

It is assumed that healthy individuals use both routes when reading aloud, and that these two routes are not independent in their functioning. However, naming visually presented words typically depends mostly on the lexical route rather than the non-lexical route, because the former route generally operates faster.

It is a **cascade model** because activation at one level is passed on to the next level before processing at the first level is complete. Cascaded models can be contrasted with thresholded models in which activation at one level is only passed on to other levels after a given threshold of activation is reached.

Earlier we discussed theoretical approaches differing in the importance they attach to phonological processing in visual word identification. Coltheart et al. (2001) argued for a weak phonological model in which word identification generally does not depend on phonological processing.

Route 1 (grapheme–phoneme conversion)

Route 1 differs from the other routes in using grapheme–phoneme conversion, which involves converting spelling (graphemes) into sound (phonemes). A grapheme is a basic unit of written language and a phoneme is a basic unit of spoken language. According to Coltheart et al. (2001, p. 212), "By the term 'grapheme' we mean a letter or letter sequence that corresponds to a single phoneme, such as the *i* in *pig*, the *ng* in *ping*, and the *igh* in *high*." In their computational model, "For any grapheme, the phoneme assigned to it was the phoneme most commonly associated with that grapheme in the set of English monosyllables that contain that grapheme" (p. 216).

If a brain-damaged patient used only Route 1, what would we find? The use of grapheme–phoneme conversion rules should permit accurate pronunciation of words having regular spelling–sound correspondences but not of irregular words not conforming to the conversion rules. For example, if an irregular word such as "pint" has grapheme–phoneme conversion rules applied to it, it should be pronounced to rhyme with "hint". This is known as regularisation. Finally, grapheme–phoneme conversion rules can provide pronunciations of nonwords.

Patients adhering most closely to exclusive use of Route 1 are surface dyslexics. **Surface dyslexia** is a condition involving particular problems in reading irregular words. McCarthy and Warrington (1984) studied KT, who had surface dyslexia. He read 100% of nonwords accurately, and 81% of regular words, but was successful with only 41% of irregular words. Over 70% of the errors KT made with irregular words were due to regularisation.

If patients with surface dyslexia exclusively use Route 1, their reading performance should not depend on lexical variables (e.g., word frequency). That is not true of some surface dyslexics. Bub, Cancelliere, and Kertesz (1985) studied MP, who read 85% of irregular high-frequency words accurately but only 40% of low-frequency ones. Her ability to read many irregular words and her superior performance with high-frequency words indicate she could make some use of the lexical route.

According to the model, the main reason patients with surface dyslexia have problems

---

KEY TERMS

cascade model: a model in which information passes from one level to the next before processing is complete at the first level.

surface dyslexia: a condition in which regular words can be read but there is impaired ability to read irregular words.

when reading irregular words is that they rely primarily on Route 1. If they can also make reasonable use of Route 3, then they might be able to read aloud correctly nearly all the words they know in the absence of any knowledge of the meanings of those words stored in the semantic system. Thus, there should not be an association between impaired semantic knowledge and the incidence of surface dyslexia. Woollams, Lambon Ralph, Plaut, & Patterson (2007) studied patients with semantic dementia (see Glossary). This is a condition in which brain damage impairs semantic knowledge (see Chapter 7), but typically has little effect on the orthographic or phonological systems. There was a strong association between impaired semantic knowledge and surface dyslexia among these patients. The implication is that damage to the semantic system is often a major factor in surface dyslexia.

Route 2 (lexicon + semantic knowledge) and Route 3 (lexicon only)

The basic idea behind Route 2 is that representations of thousands of familiar words are stored in an orthographic input lexicon. Visual presentation of a word leads to activation in the orthographic input lexicon. This is followed by obtaining its meaning from the semantic system, after which its sound pattern is generated by the phonological output lexicon. Route 3 also involves the orthographic input and phonological output lexicons, but it bypasses the semantic system.

How could we identify patients using Route 2 or Route 3 but not Route 1? Their intact orthographic input lexicon means they can pronounce familiar words whether regular or irregular. However, their inability to use grapheme–phoneme conversion should mean they find it very hard to pronounce unfamiliar words and nonwords.

Phonological dyslexics fit this predicted pattern fairly well. **Phonological dyslexia** involves particular problems with reading unfamiliar words and nonwords. The first case of phonological dyslexia reported systematically was RG (Beauvois & Dérouesné, 1979). RG successfully read 100% of real words but only 10% of nonwords. Funnell (1983) studied a patient, WB. His ability to use Route 1 was very limited because he could not produce the sound of any single letters or nonwords. He could read 85% of words, and seemed to do this by using Route 2. He had a poor ability to make semantic judgements about words, suggesting he was bypassing the semantic system when reading words.

According to the dual-route model, phonological dyslexics have *specific* problems with grapheme–phoneme conversion. However, Coltheart (1996) discussed 18 patients with phonological dyslexia, all of whom had *general* phonological impairments. Subsequent research has indicated that some phonological dyslexics have impairments as specific as assumed within the dual-route model. Caccappolo-van Vliet, Miozzo, and Stern (2004) studied two phonological dyslexics. IB was a 77-year-old woman who had worked as a secretary, and MO was a 48-year-old male accountant. Both patients showed the typical pattern associated with phonological dyslexia – their performance on reading regular and irregular words exceeded 90% compared to under 60% with nonwords. Crucially, the performance of IB and MO on various phonological tasks (e.g., deciding whether two words rhymed; finding a rhyming word) was intact (above 95%).

Deep dyslexia

Deep dyslexia occurs as a result of brain damage to left-hemisphere brain areas involved in language. Deep dyslexics have particular problems in reading unfamiliar words, and an inability to read nonwords. However, the most striking symptom is semantic reading errors (e.g., "ship" read as "boat"). Deep dyslexia may result from damage to the grapheme–phoneme conversion and semantic systems. Deep dyslexia resembles a more severe form of phonological dyslexia. Indeed, deep dyslexics showing some recovery of reading skills often become phono-logical dyslexics (Southwood & Chatterjee, 2001). Sato, Patterson, Fushimi, Maxim, and Bryan (2008) studied a Japanese woman, YT. She had problems with the Japanese script *kana* (each symbol represents a syllable) and the Japanese script *kanji* (each symbol stands for a morpheme, which is the smallest unit of meaning). YT showed deep dyslexia for kanji but phonological dyslexia for kana. Sato et al. concluded that YT's impaired reading performance was due mainly to a general phonological deficit.

The notion that deep dyslexia and phono-logical dyslexia involves similar underlying mech-anisms is an attractive one. Jefferies, Sage, and Lambon Ralph (2007) found that deep dyslexics performed poorly on various phonologically-based tasks (e.g., phoneme addition; phoneme subtraction). They concluded that deep dyslexics have a general phonological impairment, as do phonological dyslexics.

Computational modelling
Coltheart et al. (2001) produced a detailed computational model to test their dual-route cascaded model. They started with 7981 one-syllable words varying in length between one and eight letters. They used McClelland and Rumelhart's (1981) interactive activation model (discussed earlier) as the basis for the ortho-graphic component of their model, and the output or response side of the model derives from the theories of Dell (1986) and Levelt et al. (1999) (see Chapter 11). The pronunciation most activated by processing in the lexical and non-lexical routes is the one determining the naming response.

Evidence
Coltheart et al. (2001) presented their com-putational model with all 7981 words and found

that 7898 (99%) were read accurately. When the model was presented with 7000 one-syllable nonwords, it read 98.9% of them correctly.

It follows from the model that we might expect different brain regions to be associated with each route. What has been done in several studies is to compare the brain activation when participants name irregular words and pseudo-words (pronounceable nonwords). The assump-tion is that the lexical route is of primary importance with irregular words, whereas the non-lexical route is used with pseudowords. Seghier, Lee, Schofield, Ellis, and Price (2008) found that the left anterior occipito-temporal region was associated with reading irregular words. In contrast, the left posterior occipito-temporal region was associated with reading pseudowords. These findings are consistent with the notion of separate routes in reading.

Zevin and Balota (2000) argued that the extent to which we use the lexical and non-lexical routes when naming words depends on attentional control. Readers named low-frequency irregular words or pseudowords before naming a target word. They predicted that naming irregular words would cause readers to attend to lexical information, whereas naming pseudo-words would lead them to attend to non-lexical information. As predicted, the relative roles of the lexical and non-lexical routes in reading the target word were affected by what had been read previously.

According to the model, regular words (those conforming to the grapheme–phoneme rules in Route 1) can often be named faster than irregular words. According to the distributed connectionist approach (Plaut et al., 1996; discussed shortly), what is important is con-sistency. Consistent words have letter patterns that are always pronounced the same in all words in which they appear and are assumed to be faster to name than inconsistent words. Irregular words tend to be inconsistent, and so we need to decide whether *regularity* or *consistency* is more important. Jared (2002) compared directly the effects of regularity and of consistency on word naming. Her findings were reasonably clear-cut: word naming times

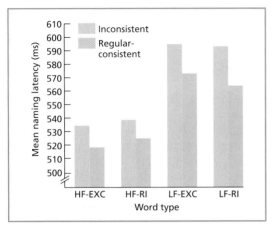

Figure 9.4 Mean naming latencies for high-frequency (HF) and low-frequency (LF) words that were irregular (exception words: EXC) or regular and inconsistent (RI). Mean naming latencies of regular consistent words matched with each of these word types are also shown. The differences between consistent and inconsistent words were much greater than those between regular and irregular words (EXC compared to RI). Reprinted from Jared (2002), Copyright 2002, with permission from Elsevier.

were affected much more by consistency than by regularity (see Figure 9.4). This finding, which is contrary to the dual-route model, has been replicated in other studies (Harley, 2008).

Evaluation

The dual-route cascaded model represents an ambitious attempt to account for basic reading processes in brain-damaged and healthy individuals. Its explanation of reading disorders such as surface dyslexia and phonological dyslexia has been very influential. The model has also proved useful in accounting for the naming and lexical-decision performance of healthy individuals, and has received some support from studies in cognitive neuroscience (e.g., Seghier et al., 2008). Perry, Ziegler, and Zorzi (2007) developed a new connectionist dual process model (the CDP+ model) based in part on the dual-route cascaded model. This new model includes a lexical and a sublexical route, and eliminates some of the problems with the dual-route cascaded model (e.g., its inability to learn; its inability to account for consistency effects).

What are the model's limitations? First, the assumption that the time taken to pronounce a word depends on its regularity rather than its consistency is incorrect (e.g., Glushko, 1979; Jared, 2002). This is serious because the theoretical significance of word regularity follows directly from the central assumption that the non-lexical route uses a grapheme–phoneme rule system.

Second, as Perry et al. (2007, p. 276) pointed out, "A major shortcoming of DRC [dual-route cascaded model] is the absence of learning. DRC is fully hardwired, and the nonlexical route operates with a partially hard-coded set of grapheme–phoneme rules."

Third, the model assumes that only the non-lexical route is involved in pronouncing nonwords. As a consequence, similarities and differences between nonwords and genuine words are irrelevant. In fact, however, we will see shortly that prediction is incorrect, because consistent nonwords are faster to pronounce than inconsistent ones (Zevin & Seidenberg, 2006).

Fourth, the model assumes that the phonological processing of visually presented words occurs fairly slowly and has relatively little effect on visual word recognition. In fact, however, such phonological processes generally occur rapidly and automatically (Rastle & Brysbaert, 2006).

Fifth, it is assumed that the semantic system can play an important role in reading aloud (i.e., via Route 2). In practice, however, "The semantic system of the model remains unimplemented" (Woollams et al., 2007, p. 317). The reason is that it is assumed within the model that individuals can read all the words they know without accessing the meanings of those words.

Sixth, as Coltheart et al. (2001, p. 236) admitted, "The Chinese, Japanese, and Korean writing systems are structurally so different from the English writing system that a model like the DRC [dual-route cascaded] model would simply not be applicable: for example, monosyllabic nonwords cannot even be written in the Chinese script or in Japanese kanji, so the distinction between a lexical and non-lexical route for reading cannot even arise."

Distributed connectionist approach

Within the dual-route model, it is assumed that pronouncing irregular words and nonwords involves different routes. This contrasts with the connectionist approach pioneered by Seidenberg and McClelland (1989) and developed most notably by Plaut et al. (1996). According to Plaut et al. (p. 58), their approach

> *eschews [avoids] separate mechanisms for pronouncing nonwords and exception [irregular] words. Rather, all of the system's knowledge of spelling–sound correspondences is brought to bear in pronouncing all types of letter strings [words and nonwords]. Conflicts among possible alternative pronunciations of a letter string are resolved…by co-operative and competitive interactions based on how the letter string relates to all known words and their pronunciations.*

Thus, Plaut et al. (1996) assumed that the pronunciation of words and nonwords is based on a highly *interactive* system.

This general approach is known as the distributed connectionist approach or the triangle model (see Figure 9.5). The three sides of the triangle are orthography (spelling), phonology (sound), and semantics (meaning). There are two routes from spelling to sound: (1) a direct pathway from orthography to phonology; and (2) an indirect pathway from orthography to phonology that proceeds via word meanings.

Plaut et al. (1996) argued that words (and nonwords) vary in consistency (the extent to which their pronunciation agrees with those of similarly spelled words). Highly consistent words and nonwords can generally be pronounced faster and more accurately than inconsistent words and nonwords, because more of the available knowledge supports the correct pronunciation of such words. In contrast, the dual-route cascaded model divides words into two categories: words are regular (conforming to grapheme–phoneme rules) or irregular (not

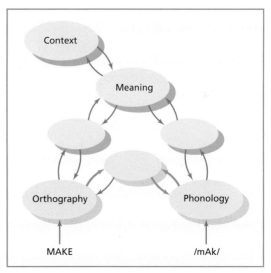

Figure 9.5 Seidenberg and McClelland's (1989) "triangle model" of word recognition. Implemented pathways are shown in blue. Reproduced with permission from Harm and Seidenberg (2001).

conforming to those rules). As we have seen, the evidence favours the notion of consistency over regularity (Jared, 2002).

Plaut et al. (1996) developed a successful simulation of reading performance. Their network learned to pronounce words accurately as connections developed between the visual forms of letters and combinations of letters (grapheme units) and their corresponding phonemes (phoneme units). The network learned via back-propagation, in which the actual outputs or responses of the system are compared against the correct ones (see Chapter 1). The network received prolonged training with 2998 words. At the end of training, the network's performance resembled that of adult readers in various ways:

(1) Inconsistent words took longer to name than consistent ones.
(2) Rare words took longer to name than common ones.
(3) There was an interaction between word frequency and consistency, with the effects of consistency being much greater for rare words than for common ones.

(4) The network pronounced over 90% of nonwords "correctly", which is comparable to adult readers. This is impressive given that the network received no direct training on nonwords.

What role does semantic knowledge of words play in Plaut et al.'s (1996) model? It is assumed that the route from orthography to phonology via meaning is typically slower than the direct route proceeding straight from orthography to phonology. Semantic knowledge is most likely to have an impact for inconsistent words – they take longer to name, and this provides more opportunity for semantic knowledge to have an effect.

Evidence

How does the distributed connectionist approach account for surface dyslexia, phonological dyslexia, and deep dyslexia? It is assumed that surface dyslexia (involving problems in reading irregular or inconsistent words) occurs mainly because of damage to the semantic system. We saw earlier that patients with semantic dementia (which involves extensive damage to the semantic system) generally exhibit the symptoms of surface dyslexia. Plaut et al. (1996) damaged their model to reduce or eliminate the contribution from semantics. The network's reading performance remained very good on regular high- and low-frequency words and on nonwords, worse on irregular high-frequency words, and worst on irregular low-frequency words. This matches the pattern found with surface dyslexics.

It is assumed that phonological dyslexia (involving problems in reading unfamiliar words and nonwords) is due to a general impairment of phonological processing. The evidence is mixed (see earlier discussion). On the one hand, Coltheart (1996) found many cases in which phonological dyslexia was associated with a general phonological impairment. On the other hand, Caccappolo-van Vliet et al. (2004) studied phonological dyslexics whose phonological processing was almost intact. Phonological dyslexics may also suffer from an orthographic impairment in addition to the phonological one. Howard and Best (1996) found that their patient, Melanie-Jane, was better at reading pseudohomophones whose spelling resembled the related word (e.g., "gerl") than those whose spellings did not (e.g., "phocks"). Finally, Nickels, Biedermann, Coltheart, Saunders, and Tree (2008) used a combination of computer modelling and data from phonological dyslexics. No *single* locus of impairment (e.g., the phonological system) could account for the various impairments found in patients.

What does the model say about deep dyslexia? Earlier we discussed evidence (e.g., Jefferies et al., 2007) suggesting that a general phonological impairment is of major importance in deep dyslexia. Support for this viewpoint was provided by Crisp and Lambon Ralph (2006). They studied patients with deep dyslexia or phonological dyslexia. There was no clear dividing line between the two conditions, with the two groups sharing many symptoms. Patients with both conditions had a severe phonological impairment, but patients with deep dyslexia were more likely than those with phonological dyslexia to have severe semantic impairments as well.

According to the model, semantic factors can be important in reading aloud, especially when the words (or nonwords) are irregular or inconsistent and so are more difficult to read. McKay, Davis, Savage, and Castles (2008) decided to test this prediction directly by training participants to read aloud nonwords (e.g., "bink"). Some of the nonwords had consistent (or expected) pronunciations whereas others had inconsistent pronunciations. The crucial manipulation was that participants learned the meanings of some of these nonwords but not of others.

The findings obtained by McKay et al. (2008) were entirely in line with the model. Reading aloud was faster for nonwords in the semantic condition (learning pronunciations) than in the non-semantic condition when the nonwords were inconsistent (see Figure 9.6). However, speed of reading aloud was the same in the semantic and non-semantic conditions when the nonwords were consistent.

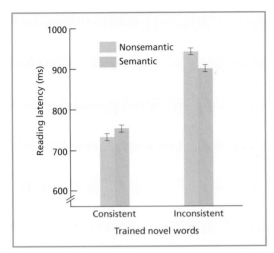

Figure 9.6 Mean reading latencies in ms for consistent and inconsistent novel words (nonwords) that had been learned with meanings (semantic) or without meanings (nonsemantic). From McKay et al. (2008), Copyright © 2008 American Psychological Association. Reproduced with permission.

According to the triangle model, the time taken to pronounce nonwords should depend on whether they are consistent or not. For example, the word body "–ust" is very consistent because it is always pronounced in the same way in monosyllabic words, and so the nonword "nust" is consistent. In contrast, the word body "–ave" is inconsistent because it is pronounced in different ways in different words (e.g., "save" and "have"), and so the nonword "mave" is inconsistent. The prediction is that inconsistent nonwords will take longer to pronounce. According to the dual-route cascaded model, in contrast, nonwords are pronounced using non-lexical pronunciation rules and so there should be no difference between consistent and inconsistent nonwords.

The findings are clear-cut. Inconsistent nonwords take longer to pronounce than consistent ones (Glushko, 1979; Zevin & Seidenberg, 2006). Such findings provide support for the triangle model over the dual-route model. Zevin and Seidenberg obtained further support for the triangle model over the dual-route model. According to the dual-route model, the pronunciation rules should generate only *one* pronunciation for each nonword. According

to the triangle model, however, the pronunciations of inconsistent nonwords should be more variable than those of consistent ones, and that is what was found.

Evaluation

The distributed connectionist approach has several successes to its credit. First, the overarching assumption that the orthographic, semantic, and phonological systems are used in parallel in an interactive fashion during reading has received much support. Second, much progress has been made in understanding reading disorders by assuming that a general phonological impairment underlies phonological dyslexia, whereas a semantic impairment underlies surface dyslexia. Third, the assumption that the semantic system is often important in reading aloud appears correct (e.g., McKay et al., 2008). Fourth, the assumption that consistency is more important than word regularity (emphasised within the dual-route cascaded model) in determining the time taken to name words has received strong support. Fifth, the distributed connectionist approach is more successful than the dual-route model in accounting for consistency effects with nonwords and for individual differences in nonword naming (Zevin & Seidenberg, 2006). Sixth, the distributed connectionist approach includes an explicit mechanism to simulate how we learn to pronounce words, whereas the dual-route model has less to say about learning.

What are the triangle model's limitations? First, as Harley (2008) pointed out, connectionist models have tended to focus on the processes involved in reading relatively simple, single-syllable words.

Second, as Plaut et al. (1996, p. 108) admitted, "The nature of processing within the semantic pathway has been characterised in only the coarsest way." However, Harm and Seidenberg (2004) largely filled that gap within the triangle model by implementing its semantic component to map orthography and phonology onto semantics.

Third, the model's explanations of phonological dyslexia and surface dyslexia are somewhat oversimplified. Phonological dyslexia is supposed to be due to a general phonological impairment, but some phonological dyslexics do not show that general impairment (e.g., Caccappolo-van Vliet et al., 2004; Tree & Kay, 2006). In similar fashion, surface dyslexia is supposed to be due to a general semantic impairment, but this is not always the case (Woollams et al., 2007).

Fourth, we saw earlier that the processes involved in naming words can be influenced by attentional control (Zevin & Balota, 2000). However, this is not a factor explicitly considered within the triangle model.

READING: EYE-MOVEMENT RESEARCH

Eye movements are of fundamental importance to reading. Most of the information that we process from a text at any given moment relates to the word that is currently being fixated, although some information may be processed from other words close to the fixation point.

Our eyes seem to move smoothly across the page while reading. In fact, they actually move in rapid jerks (**saccades**), as you can see if you look closely at someone else reading. Saccades are ballistic (once initiated, their direction cannot be changed). There are fairly frequent regressions in which the eyes move backwards in the text, accounting for about 10% of all saccades. Saccades take 20–30 ms to complete, and are separated by fixations lasting for 200–250 ms. The length of each saccade is approximately eight letters or spaces. Information is extracted from the text only during each fixation and not during the intervening saccades (Latour, 1962).

The amount of text from which useful information can be obtained in each fixation has been studied using the "moving window" technique (see Rayner & Sereno, 1994). Most of the text is mutilated except for an experimenter-defined area or window surrounding the reader's fixation point. Every time the reader moves his/her eyes, different parts of the text are mutilated to permit normal reading only within the window region. The effects of different-sized windows on reading performance can be compared.

The **perceptual span** (effective field of view) is affected by the difficulty of the text and print size. It extends three or four letters to the left of fixation and up to 15 letters to the right. This asymmetry is clearly learned. Readers of Hebrew, which is read from right to left, show the opposite asymmetry (Pollatsek, Bolozky, Well, & Rayner, 1981). The size of the perceptual span means that parafoveal information (from the area surrounding the central or foveal region of high visual acuity) is used in reading. Convincing evidence comes from use of the boundary technique, in which there is a preview word just to the right of the point of fixation. As the reader makes a saccade to this word, it changes into the target word, although the reader is unaware of the change. The fixation duration on the target word is less when that word is the same as the preview word. The evidence using this technique suggests that visual and phonological information can be extracted (see Reichle, Pollatsek, Fisher, & Rayner, 1998) from parafoveal processing.

Readers typically fixate about 80% of content words (nouns, verbs, and adjectives), whereas they fixate only about 20% of function words (articles such as "a" and "the"; conjunctions such as "and", "but", and "or"); and pronouns such as "he", "she", and "they"). Words not fixated tend to be common, short, or predictable. Thus, words easy to process are most likely to be skipped. Finally, there is the **spillover effect:**

KEY TERMS

saccades: fast eye movements that cannot be altered after being initiated.
perceptual span: the effective field of view in reading (letters to the left and right of fixation that can be processed).
spillover effect: any given word is fixated longer during reading when preceded by a rare word rather than a common one.

the fixation time on a word is longer when it is preceded by a rare word.

E-Z Reader model

Reichle et al. (1998), Reichle, Rayner, and Pollatsek (2003), and Pollatsek, Reichle, and Rayner (2006) have accounted for the pattern of eye movements in reading in various versions of their E-Z Reader model. The name is a spoof on the title of the movie *Easy Rider*. However, this is only clear if you know that Z is pronounced "zee" in American English!

How do we use our eyes when reading? The most obvious model assumes that we fixate on a word until we have processed it adequately, after which we immediately fixate the next word until it has been adequately processed. Alas, there are two major problems with such a model. First, it takes 85–200 ms to execute an eye-movement programme. If readers operated according to the simple model described above, they would waste time waiting for their eyes to move to the next word. Second, as we have seen, readers sometimes skip words. It is hard to see how this could happen within the model, because readers would not know anything about the next word until they had fixated it. How,

then, could they decide which words to skip?

The E-Z Reader model provides an elegant solution to the above problems. A crucial assumption is that the next eye movement is programmed after only *part* of the processing of the currently fixated word has occurred. This assumption greatly reduces the time between completion of processing on the current word and movement of the eyes to the next word. There is typically less spare time available with rare words than common ones, and that accounts for the spillover effect described above. If the processing of the next word is completed rapidly enough (e.g., it is highly predictable in the sentence context), it is skipped.

According to the model, readers can attend to two words (the currently fixated one and the next word) during a single fixation. However, it is a *serial* processing model, meaning that at any given moment only *one* word is processed. This can be contrasted with *parallel* processing models such as the SWIFT (Saccade-generation With Inhibition by Foveal Targets) model put forward by Engbert, Longtin, and Kliegl (2002) and Engbert, Nuthmann, Richter, and Kliegl (2005). It is assumed within the SWIFT model that the durations of eye fixations in reading are influenced by the previous and the next word as well as the one currently fixated. As Kliegl (2007) pointed out, the typical perceptual span of about 18 letters is large enough to accommodate all three words (prior, current, and next) provided they are of average length. We will discuss evidence comparing serial and parallel models later.

Here are the major assumptions of the E-Z Reader model:

(1) Readers check the familiarity of the word currently fixated.
(2) Completion of frequency checking of a word (the first stage of lexical access) is the signal to initiate an eye-movement programme.
(3) Readers then engage in the second stage of lexical access (see Glossary), which involves accessing the current word's semantic and phonological forms. This

According to the E-Z Reader model (a spoof on the title of the movie *Easy Rider*) readers can attend to two words (the currently fixated one and the next word) during a single fixation.
© John Springer Collection/CORBIS.

stage takes longer than the first one.

(4) Completion of the second stage is the signal for a shift of covert (internal) attention to the next word.

(5) Frequency checking and lexical access are completed faster for common words than rare ones (more so for lexical access).

(6) Frequency checking and lexical access are completed faster for predictable than for unpredictable words.

The above theoretical assumptions lead to various predictions (see Figure 9.7). Assumptions (2) and (5) together predict that the time spent fixating common words will be less than rare words: this has been found repeatedly. According to the model, readers spend the time between completion of lexical access to one word and the next eye movement in parafoveal processing of the next word. There is less parafoveal processing when the fixated word is rare (see Figure 9.7). Thus, the word following a rare word needs to be fixated longer than the word following a common word (the spillover effect described earlier).

Why are common, predictable, or short words most likely to be skipped or not fixated? A word is skipped when its lexical access has been completed while the current word is being fixated. This is most likely to happen with common, predictable, or short words because lexical access is fastest for these words (assumptions 5 and 6).

Evidence

Reichle et al. (2003) compared 11 models of reading in terms of whether each one could account for each of eight phenomena (e.g., frequency effects; spillover effects; costs of skipping). E-Z Reader accounted for all eight phenomena, whereas eight of the other models accounted for no more than two.

One of the model's main assumptions is that information about word frequency is accessed rapidly during word processing. There is support for that assumption. For example, Sereno, Rayner, and Posner (1998) observed effects of word frequency on event-related potentials (ERPs; see Glossary) within 150 ms.

The model was designed to account for the eye fixations of native English speakers reading English texts. However, English is unusual in some respects (e.g., word order is very important), and it is possible that the reading strategies used by readers of English are not universal. This issue was addressed by Rayner, Li, and Pollatsek (2007), who studied eye movements in Chinese readers reading Chinese text. Chinese differs from English in that it is written without spaces between successive characters and consists of words mostly made up of two characters. However, the pattern of eye movements was similar to that previously found for readers of English.

According to the model, word frequency and word predictability are *independent* factors determining how long we fixate on a word during reading. However, McDonald and

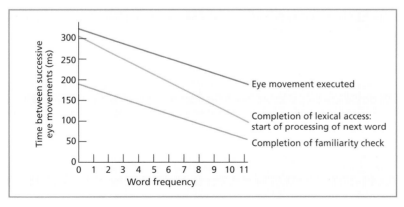

Figure 9.7 The effects of word frequency on eye movements according to the E-Z Reader model. Adapted from Reichle et al. (1998).

Shillcock (2003) found that common words were more predictable than rare ones on the basis of the preceding word. When the effects of word frequency and word predictability were disentangled, the effects of word frequency on word fixation time disappeared.

It is assumed within the model that fixations should be shortest when they are on the centre of words rather than towards either end. The reason is because word identification should be easiest when that happens. In fact, fixations tend to be much *longer* when they are at the centre of words than towards one end (Vitu, McConkie, Kerr, & O'Regan, 2001). Why is this? Some fixations at the end of a word are short because readers decide to make a second fixation closer to the middle of the word to facilitate its identification.

We turn finally to the controversial assumption that words are processed serially (one at a time), which is opposed by advocates of parallel processing models such as SWIFT (Engbert et al., 2002, 2005). We will focus on **parafoveal-on-foveal effects** – it sounds complicated but simply means that characteristics of the *next* word influence the fixation duration on the *current* word. If such effects exist, they suggest that the current and the next word are both processed at the same time. In other words, these effects suggest the existence of parallel processing, which is predicted by the SWIFT model but not by the E-Z Reader model.

The findings are mixed (see Rayner et al. (2007) for a review). However, Kennedy, Pynte, and Ducrot (2002) obtained convincing evidence of parafoveal-on-foveal effects in a methodologically sound study. White (2008) varied the orthographic familiarity and word frequency of the next word. There were no parafoveal-on-foveal effects when word frequency was manipulated and only a very small effect (6 ms) when orthographic familiarity was manipulated. These findings suggest there may be a limited amount of parallel processing involving low-level features (i.e., letters) of the next word, but not lexical features (i.e., word frequency).

According to the E-Z Reader model, readers fixate and process words in the "correct" order

(although occasional words may be skipped). If readers deviate from the "correct" order, it would be expected that they would struggle to make sense of what they are reading. In contrast, a parallel processing model such as SWIFT does not assume that words have to be read in the correct order or that deviation from that order necessarily creates any problems. Kennedy and Pynte (2008) found that readers only rarely read texts in a totally orderly fashion. In addition, there was practically no evidence that a failure to read the words in a text in the correct order caused any significant disruption to processing.

Evaluation

The model has proved very successful. It specifies many of the major factors determining eye movements in reading, and has performed well against rival models. At a very general level, the model has identified close connections between eye fixations and cognitive processes during reading. In addition, the model has identified various factors (e.g., word frequency; word predictability) influencing fixation times.

What are the limitations of the model? First, its emphasis is very much on the early processes involved in reading (e.g., lexical access). As a result, the model has little to say about higher-level processes (e.g., integration of information across the words within a sentence) that are important in reading. Reichle et al. (2003) defended their neglect of higher-level processes as follows: "We posit [assume] that higher-order processes intervene in eye-movement control only when 'something is wrong' and either send a message to stop moving forward or a signal to execute a regression."

Second, doubts have been raised concerning the model's assumptions that attention is allocated in a serial fashion to only one word at

> **KEY TERM**
>
> **parafoveal-on-foveal effects:** the finding that fixation duration on the current word is influenced by characteristics of the next word.

a time and that words are processed in the "correct" order. The existence of parafoveal-on-foveal effects (e.g., Kennedy et al., 2002; White, 2008) suggests that parallel processing can occur, but the effects are generally small. The finding that most readers fail to process the words in a text strictly in the "correct" order is inconsistent with the model.

Third, the emphasis of the model is perhaps too much on explaining eye-movement data rather than other findings on reading. As Sereno, Brewer, and O'Donnell (2003, p. 331) pointed out, "The danger is that in setting out to establish a model of eye-movement control, the result may be a model of eye-movement experiments." What is needed is to integrate the findings from eye-movement studies more closely with general theories of reading.

Fourth, the model attaches great importance to word frequency as a determinant of the length of eye fixations. However, word frequency generally correlates with word predictability, and some evidence (e.g., McDonald & Shillcock, 2003) suggests that word predictability may be more important than word frequency.

LISTENING TO SPEECH

Understanding speech is much less straightforward than one might imagine. Some idea of the processes involved in listening to speech is provided in Figure 9.8. The first stage involves *decoding* the auditory signal. As Liberman, Cooper, Shankweiler, and Studdert-Kennedy (1967) pointed out, speech can be regarded as a code, and we as listeners possess the key to understanding it. However, before starting to do that, we often need to select out the speech signal from other completely irrelevant auditory input

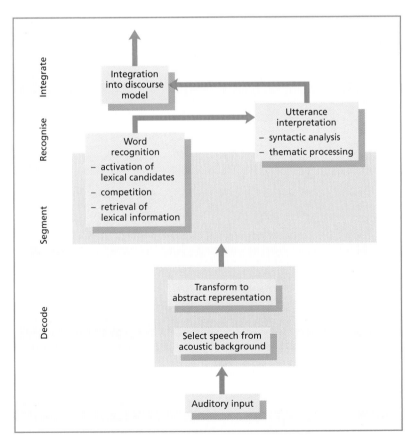

Figure 9.8 The main processes involved in speech perception and comprehension. From Cutler and Clifton (1999) by permission of Oxford University Press.

(e.g., traffic noise). Decoding itself involves extracting discrete elements from the speech signal. Cutler and Clifton (1999, p. 126) provide a good account of what is involved: "Linguists describe speech as a series of phonetic segments; a phonetic segment (**phoneme**) is simply the smallest unit in terms of which spoken language can be sequentially described. Thus, the word *key* consists of two segments /ki/, and *sea* of the two segments /si/; they differ in the first phoneme."

It is generally assumed that the second stage of speech perception involves identifying the syllables contained in the speech signal. However, there is some controversy as to whether the phoneme or the syllable is the basic unit (or building block) in speech perception. Goldinger and Azuma (2003) argued that there is no basic unit of speech perception. Instead, the perceptual unit varies flexibly depending on the precise circumstances. They presented listeners with lists of two-syllable nonwords and asked them to decide whether each nonword contained a target. The target was a phoneme or a syllable. The volunteers who recorded the lists of nonwords were told that phonemes are the basic units of speech perception or that syllables are the basic units. These instructions influenced how they read the nonwords, and this in turn affected the listeners' performance. Listeners detected phoneme targets faster than syllable targets when the speaker believed phonemes are the fundamental units in speech perception. In contrast, they detected syllable targets faster than phoneme targets when the speaker believed syllables are the basic perceptual units. Thus, either phonemes or syllables can form the perceptual units in speech perception.

The third stage of speech perception (word identification) is of particular importance. Some of the main problems in word identification are discussed shortly. However, we will mention one problem here. Most people know tens of thousands of words, but these words (in English at least) are constructed out of only about 35 phonemes. The obvious consequence is that the great majority of spoken words resemble many other words at the phonemic level, and so are hard for listeners to distinguish.

The fourth and fifth stages both emphasise speech comprehension. The focus in the fourth stage is on interpretation of the utterance. This involves constructing a coherent meaning for each sentence on the basis of information about individual words and their order in the sentence. Finally, in the fifth stage, the focus is on integrating the meaning of the current sentence with preceding speech to construct an overall model of the speaker's message.

Speech signal

Useful information about the speech signal has been obtained from the **spectrograph**. Sound enters this instrument through a microphone, and is then converted into an electrical signal. This signal is fed to a bank of filters selecting narrow-frequency bands. Finally, the spectrograph produces a visible record of the component frequencies of speech over time; this is known as a spectrogram (see Figure 9.9). This provides information about **formants**, which are frequency bands emphasised by the vocal apparatus when saying a phoneme. Vowels have three formants numbered first, second, and third, starting with the formant of lowest frequency. The sound frequency of vowels is generally lower than that of consonants.

Spectrograms may seem to provide an accurate picture of those aspects of the sound wave having the greatest influence on the human auditory system. However, this is not necessarily so. For example, formants look important in a spectrogram, but this does not prove they are of value in human speech perception. Evidence that the spectrogram is of value has been provided by using a *pattern*

> **KEY TERMS**
>
> **phonemes:** basic speech sounds conveying meaning.
> **spectrograph:** an instrument used to produce visible records of the sound frequencies in speech.
> **formants:** peaks in the frequencies of speech sounds; revealed by a **spectrograph**.

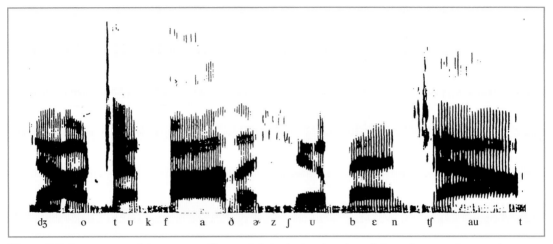

dʒ   o   t   ʊ   k   f   a   ð   ɚ   z   ʃ   ʊ   b   ɛ   n   tʃ   au   t

Figure 9.9 Spectrogram of the sentence "Joe took father's shoe bench out". From *Language Processes* by Vivian C. Tartter (1986, p. 210). Reproduced with permission of the author.

playback or *vocoder*, which allows the spectrogram to be played back (i.e., reconverted into speech). Liberman, Delattre, and Cooper (1952) constructed "artificial" vowels on the spectrogram based only on the first two formants of each vowel. These vowels were easily identified when played through the vocoder, suggesting that formant information is used to recognise vowels.

Problems faced by listeners
Listeners are confronted by several problems when understanding speech:

(1) Language is spoken at about ten phonemes (basic speech sounds) per second, and so requires rapid processing. Amazingly, we can understand speech artificially speeded up to 50–60 sounds or phonemes per second (Werker & Tees, 1992).

(2) There is the **segmentation problem**, which is the difficulty of separating out or distinguishing words from the pattern of speech sounds. This problem arises because speech typically consists of a continuously changing pattern of sound with few periods of silence. This can make it hard to know when one word ends and the next word

begins. Ways in which listeners cope with the segmentation problem are discussed shortly.

(3) In normal speech, there is **co-articulation**, which is "the overlapping of adjacent articulations" (Ladefoged, 2001, p. 272). More specifically, the way a phoneme is produced depends on the phonemes preceding and following it. The existence of co-articulation means that the pronunciation of any given phoneme is not invariant, which can create problems for the listener. However, co-articulation means that listeners hearing one phoneme are provided with some information about the surrounding phonemes. For example, "The /b/ phonemes in 'bill', 'bull', and 'bell' are all slightly different acoustically,

and tell us about what is coming next" (Harley, 2008, p. 259).

(4) There are significant individual differences from one speaker to the next. For example, speakers vary considerably in their rate of speaking. Sussman, Hoemeke, and Ahmed (1993) asked various speakers to say the same short words starting with a consonant. There were clear differences across speakers in their spectrograms. Wong, Nusbaum, and Small (2004) studied brain activation when listeners were exposed to several speakers or to only one. When exposed to several speakers at different times, listeners had increased attentional processing in the major speech areas (e.g., posterior superior temporal cortex) and in areas associated with attentional shifts (e.g., superior parietal cortex). Thus, listeners respond to the challenge of hearing several different voices by using active attentional and other processes.

(5) Mattys and Liss (2008) pointed out that listeners in everyday life have to contend with degraded speech. For example, there are often other people talking at the same time and/or there are distracting sounds (e.g., noise of traffic or aircraft). It is of some concern that listeners in the laboratory are rarely confronted by these problems in research on speech perception. This led Mattys and Liss (p. 1235) to argue that, "Laboratory-generated phenomena reflect what the speech perception system *can* do with highly constrained input."

We have identified several problems that listeners face when trying to make sense of spoken language. Below we consider some of the main ways in which listeners cope with these problems.

Lip-reading: McGurk effect

Listeners (even those with normal hearing) often make extensive use of lip-reading to provide them with additional information. McGurk and MacDonald (1976) provided

Listeners often have to contend with degraded speech; for example: interference from a crackly phone line; street noise; or other people nearby talking at the same time. How do we cope with these problems?

a striking demonstration. They prepared a videotape of someone saying "ba" repeatedly. The sound channel then changed so there was a voice saying "ga" repeatedly in synchronisation with lip movements still indicating "ba". Listeners reported hearing "da", a blending of the visual and auditory information. Green, Kuhl, Meltzoff, and Stevens (1991) showed that the so-called McGurk effect is surprisingly robust – they found it even with a female face and a male voice.

It is generally assumed that the McGurk effect depends primarily on bottom-up processes triggered directly by the discrepant visual and auditory signals. If so, the McGurk effect should not be influenced by top-down processes based on listeners' expectations. However, expectations are important. More listeners produced the McGurk effect when the crucial word (based on blending the discrepant visual and auditory cues) was presented in a semantically congruent than a semantically incongruent sentence (Windmann, 2004). Thus, top-down processes play an important role.

Addressing the segmentation problem

Listeners have to divide the speech they hear into its constituent words (i.e., segmentation)

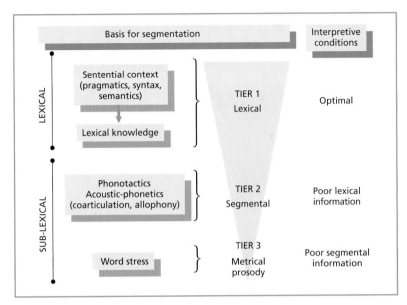

Figure 9.10 A hierarchical approach to speech segmentation involving three levels or tiers. The relative importance of the different types of cue is indicated by the width of the purple triangle. From Mattys et al. (2005). Copyright © 2005 American Psychological Association.

and decide what words are being presented. There has been controversy as to whether segmentation precedes and assists word recognition or whether it is the product of word recognition. We will return to that controversy shortly. Before doing so, we will consider various non-lexical cues used by listeners to facilitate segmentation. First, certain sequences of speech sounds (e.g., <m,r> in English) are never found together within a syllable, and such sequences suggest a likely boundary between words (Dumay, Frauenfelder, & Content, 2002).

Second, Norris, McQueen, Cutler, and Butterfield (1997) argued that segmentation is influenced by the possible-word constraints (e.g., a stretch of speech lacking a vowel is not a possible word). For example, listeners found it hard to identify the word "apple" in "fapple" because the /f/ could not possibly be an English word. In contrast, listeners found it relatively easy to detect the word "apple" in "vuffapple", because "vuff" could conceivably be an English word.

Third, there is stress. In English, the initial syllable of most content words (e.g., nouns, verbs) is typically stressed. When listeners heard strings of words without the stress on the first syllable (e.g., "conduct ascents uphill") presented faintly, they often misheard them (Cutler & Butterfield, 1992). For example, "conduct ascents hill" was often misperceived as the meaningless, "A duck descends some pill."

Fourth, the extent of co-articulation provides a useful cue to word boundaries. As mentioned above, co-articulation can help the listener to anticipate the kind of phoneme that will occur next. Perhaps more importantly, there is generally more co-articulation within words than between them (Byrd & Saltzman, 1998).

Mattys, White, and Melhorn (2005) argued persuasively that we need to go beyond simply describing the effects of individual cues on word segmentation. He put forward a hierarchical approach, according to which there are three main categories of cue: lexical (e.g., syntax, word knowledge); segmental (e.g., coarticulation); and metrical prosody (e.g., word stress) (see Figure 9.10). We prefer to use lexical cues (Tier 1) when all cues are available. When lexical information is lacking or is impoverished, we make use of segmental cues such as co-articulation and **allophony** (one phoneme may be associated

KEY TERM

allophony: an allophone is one of two or more similar sounds belonging to the same **phoneme**.

with two or more similar sounds or allophones) (Tier 2). For example, Harley (2008) gives this example: the phoneme /p/ can be pronounced differently as in "pit" and "spit". Finally, if it is difficult to use Tier 1 or Tier 2 cues, we resort to metrical prosody cues (e.g., stress) (Tier 3).

Why do we generally prefer not to use stress cues? As Mattys et al. (2005) pointed out, stress information is misleading for words in which the initial syllable is not stressed (cf., Cutler & Butterfield, 1992).

There is reasonable support for the above hierarchical approach. Mattys (2004) found that co-articulation (Tier 2) was more useful than stress (Tier 3) for identifying word boundaries when the speech signal was phonetically intact. However, when the speech signal was impoverished so that it was hard to use Tier 1 or Tier 2 cues, stress was more useful than co-articulation. Mattys et al. (2005) found that lexical cues (i.e., word context versus non-word context) were more useful than stress in facilitating word segmentation in a no-noise condition. However, stress was more useful than lexical cues in noise.

Categorical perception

Speech perception differs from other kinds of auditory perception. For example, there is a definite left-hemisphere advantage for perception of speech but not other auditory stimuli. There is **categorical perception** of phonemes: speech stimuli intermediate between two phonemes are typically categorised as one phoneme or the other, and there is an abrupt boundary between phoneme categories. For example, the Japanese language does not distinguish between /l/ and /r/. These sounds belong to the same category for Japanese listeners, and so they find it very hard to discriminate between them (Massaro, 1994).

The existence of categorical perception does *not* mean we cannot distinguish at all between slightly different sounds assigned to the same phoneme category. Listeners decided faster that two syllables were the same when the sounds were identical than when they were not (Pisoni & Tash, 1974).

Raizada and Poldrack (2007) presented listeners with auditory stimuli ranging along a continuum from the phoneme /ba/ to the phoneme /da/. Two similar stimuli were presented at the same time, and participants decided whether they represented the same phoneme. Listeners were more sensitive to the differences between the stimuli when they straddled the category boundary between /ba/ and /da/. The key finding was that differences in brain activation of the two stimuli being presented were strongly *amplified* when they were on opposite sides of the category boundary. This amplification effect suggests that categories are important in speech perception.

Context effects: sound identification

Spoken word recognition involves a mixture of bottom-up or data-driven processes triggered by the acoustic signal, and top-down or conceptually driven processes generated from the linguistic context. Finding that the identification of a sound or a word is influenced by the context in which it is presented provides evidence for top-down effects. However, there has been much controversy concerning the interpretation of most context effects. We will consider context effects on the identification of sounds in this section, deferring a discussion of context effects in word identification until later. We start by considering context in the form of an adjacent sound, and then move on to discuss sentential context (i.e., the sentence within which a sound is presented). We will see that the processes underlying different kinds of context effect probably differ.

KEY TERM

categorical perception: perceiving stimuli as belonging to specific categories; found with **phonemes**.

Lexical identification shift

We have seen that listeners show categorical perception, with speech stimuli intermediate between two phonemes being categorised as one phoneme or the other. Ganong (1980) wondered whether categorical perception of phonemes would be influenced by context. Accordingly, he presented listeners with various sounds ranging between a word (e.g., *dash*) and a non-word (e.g., *tash*). There was a context effect – an ambiguous initial phoneme was more likely to be assigned to a given phoneme category when it produced a word than when it did not (the **lexical identification shift**).

There are at least two possible reasons why context might influence categorical perception. First, context may have a *direct* influence on perceptual processes. Second, context may influence decision or other processes occurring *after* the perceptual processes are completed but *prior* to a response being made. Such processes can be influenced by providing rewards for correct responses and penalties for incorrect ones. Pitt (1995) found that rewards and penalties had *no* effect on the lexical identification shift, suggesting that it depends on perceptual processes rather than ones occurring subsequently.

Connine (1990) found that the identification of an ambiguous phoneme is influenced by the meaning of the sentence in which it is presented (i.e., by sentential context). However, the way in which this happened differed from the lexical identification shift observed by Ganong (1980). Sentential context did *not* influence phoneme identification during initial speech perception, but rather affected processes occurring *after* perception.

In sum, the standard lexical identification shift depends on relatively early perceptual processes. In contrast, the effects of sentence context on the identification of ambiguous phonemes involve later processes following perception.

Phonemic restoration effect

Evidence that top-down processing based on the sentence context can be involved in speech perception was apparently reported by Warren and Warren (1970). They studied the **phonemic restoration effect**. Listeners heard a sentence in which a small portion had been removed and replaced with a meaningless sound. The sentences used were as follows (the asterisk indicates a deleted portion of the sentence):

- It was found that the *eel was on the axle.
- It was found that the *eel was on the shoe.
- It was found that the *eel was on the table.
- It was found that the *eel was on the orange.

The perception of the crucial element in the sentence (e.g., *eel) was influenced by the sentence context. Participants listening to the first sentence heard "wheel", those listening to the second sentence heard "heel", and those exposed to the third and fourth sentences heard "meal" and "peel", respectively. The crucial auditory stimulus (i.e., "*eel") was always the same, so all that differed was the contextual information.

What causes the phonemic restoration effect? According to Samuel (1997), there are two main possibilities:

(1) There is a *direct* effect on speech processing (i.e., the missing phoneme is processed almost as if it were present).
(2) There is an *indirect* effect with listeners guessing the identity of the missing phoneme *after* basic speech processing has occurred.

KEY TERMS

lexical identification shift: the finding that an ambiguous phoneme tends to be perceived so as to form a word rather than a nonword.
phonemic restoration effect: an illusion in which the listener "perceives" a phoneme has been deleted from a spoken sentence.

The findings appear somewhat inconsistent. Samuel (e.g., 1981, 1987) added noise to the crucial phoneme or replaced the missing phoneme with noise. If listeners processed the missing phoneme as usual, they would have heard the crucial phoneme plus noise in both conditions. As a result, they would have been unable to tell the difference between the two conditions. In fact, the listeners could readily distinguish between the conditions, suggesting that sentence context affects processing occurring following perception.

Samuel (1997) used a different paradigm in which there was no sentential context. Some listeners repeatedly heard words such as "academic", "confidential", and "psychedelic", all of which have /d/ as the third syllable. The multiple presentations of these words reduce the probability of categorising subsequent sounds as /d/ because of an adaptation effect. In another condition, listeners were initially exposed to the same words with the key phoneme replaced by noise (e.g., aca*emic; confi*entail; psyche*elic). In a different condition, the /d/ phoneme was replaced by silence. Listeners could have guessed the missing phoneme in both conditions. However, perceptual processes could only have been used to identify the missing phoneme in the noise condition.

What did Samuel (1997) find? There was an adaptation effect in the noise condition but not in the silence condition. These findings seem to rule out guessing as an explanation. They suggest that there was a direct effect of lexical or word activation on perceptual processes in the noise condition leading to an adaptation effect.

In sum, it is likely that the processes underlying the phonemic restoration effect vary depending on the precise experimental conditions. More specifically, there is evidence for direct effects (Samuel, 1997) and indirect effects (Samuel, 1981, 1987).

THEORIES OF SPOKEN WORD RECOGNITION

There are several theories of spoken word recognition, three of which are discussed here.

We start with a brief account of the motor theory of speech perception originally proposed over 40 years ago. However, our main focus will be on the cohort and TRACE models, both of which have been very influential in recent years. The original cohort model (Marslen-Wilson & Tyler, 1980) emphasised interactions between bottom-up and top-down processes in spoken word recognition. However, Marslen-Wilson (e.g., 1990) subsequently revised his cohort model to increase the emphasis on bottom-up processes driven by the auditory stimulus. In contrast, the TRACE model argues that word recognition involves interactive top-down and bottom-up processes. Thus, a crucial difference is that top-down processes (e.g., context-based effects) play a larger role in the TRACE model than in the cohort model.

Motor theory

Liberman, Cooper, Shankweiler, and Studdert-Kennedy (1967) argued that a key issue in speech perception is to explain how listeners perceive words accurately even though the speech signal provides variable information. In their motor theory of speech perception, they proposed that listeners mimic the articulatory movements of the speaker. The motor signal thus produced was claimed to provide much less variable and inconsistent information about what the speaker is saying than the speech signal itself. Thus, our recruitment of the motor system facilitates speech perception.

Evidence

Findings consistent with the motor theory were reported by Dorman, Raphael, and Liberman (1979). A tape was made of the sentence, "Please say shop", and a 50 ms period of silence was inserted between "say" and "shop". As a result, the sentence was misheard as, "Please say chop". Our speech musculature forces us to pause between "say" and "chop" but not between "say" and "shop". Thus, the evidence from internal articulation would favour the wrong interpretation of the last word in the sentence.

Fadiga, Craighero, Buccino, and Rizzolatti (2002) applied transcranial magnetic stimulation (TMS; see Glossary) to the part of the motor cortex controlling tongue movements while Italian participants listened to Italian words. Some of the words (e.g., "terra") required strong tongue movements when pronounced, whereas others (e.g., "baffo") did not. The key finding was that there was greater activation of listeners' tongue muscles when they were presented with words such as "terra" than with words such as "baffo".

Wilson, Saygin, Sereno, and Iacoboni (2004) had their participants say aloud a series of syllables and also listen to syllables. As predicted by the motor theory, the motor area activated when participants were speaking was also activated when they were listening. This activated area was well away from the classical frontal lobe language areas.

The studies discussed so far do not show that activity in motor areas is linked *causally* to speech perception. This issue was addressed by Meister, Wilson, Deblieck, Wu, and Iacobini (2007). They applied repetitive transcranial magnetic stimulation (rTMS) to the left premotor cortex while participants performed a phonetic discrimination or tone discrimination task. Only the former task requires language processes. TMS adversely affected performance *only* on the phonetic discrimination task, which involved discriminating stop consonants in noise. These findings provide reasonable evidence that speech perception is facilitated by recruitment of the motor system.

Evaluation

There has been an accumulation of evidence supporting the motor theory of speech perception in recent years (see reviews by Galantucci, Fowler, and Turvey, 2006, and Iacoboni, 2008). Speech perception is often associated with activation of the motor area and motor processes can facilitate speech perception. However, we must be careful not to exaggerate the importance of motor processes in speech perception.

What are the limitations of the motor theory? First, the underlying processes are not spelled out. For example, it is not very clear *how* listeners use auditory information to mimic the speaker's articulatory movements. More generally, the theory doesn't attempt to provide a comprehensive account of speech perception.

Second, many individuals with very severely impaired speech production nevertheless have reasonable speech perception. For example, some patients with Broca's aphasia (see Glossary) have effective destruction of the motor speech system but their ability to perceive speech is essentially intact (Harley, 2008). In addition, some mute individuals can perceive spoken words normally (Lenneberg, 1962). However, the motor theory could account for these findings by assuming the motor movements involved in speech perception are fairly abstract and do not require direct use of the speech musculature (Harley, 2008).

Third, it follows from the theory that infants with extremely limited expertise in articulation of speech should be very poor at speech perception. In fact, however, 6- to 8-month-old infants perform reasonably well on syllable detection tasks (Polka, Rvachew, & Molnar, 2008).

Cohort model

The cohort model was originally put forward by Marslen-Wilson and Tyler (1980), and has been revised several times since then. We will consider some of the major revisions later, but for now we focus on the assumptions of the original version:

- Early in the auditory presentation of a word, words conforming to the sound sequence heard so far become active; this set of words is the "word-initial cohort".
- Words belonging to this cohort are then eliminated if they cease to match further information from the presented word, or because they are inconsistent with the semantic or other context. For example, the words "crocodile" and "crockery" might both belong to a word-initial cohort, with the latter word being excluded when the sound /d/ is heard.

- Processing of the presented word continues until contextual information and information from the word itself are sufficient to eliminate all but one of the words in the word-initial cohort. The uniqueness point is the point at which the initial part of a word is consistent with only one word. However, words can often be recognised earlier than that because of contextual information.
- Various sources of information (e.g., lexical, syntactic, semantic) are processed in parallel. These information sources *interact* and combine with each other to produce an efficient analysis of spoken language.

Marslen-Wilson and Tyler tested their theoretical notions in a word-monitoring task in which listeners identified pre-specified target words presented within spoken sentences. There were normal sentences, syntactic sentences (grammatically correct but meaningless), and random sentences (unrelated words). The target was a member of a given category, a word rhyming with a given word, or a word identical to a given word. The dependent variable was the speed with which the target was detected.

According to the original version of the cohort model, sensory information from the target word and contextual information from the rest of the sentence are both used at the same time. As predicted, complete sensory analysis was not needed with adequate contextual information (see Figure 9.11). It was only necessary to listen to the entire word when the sentence context contained no useful syntactic or semantic information (i.e., random condition).

Evidence that the uniqueness point is important in speech perception was reported by Marslen-Wilson (1984). Listeners were presented with words and nonwords and decided on a lexical decision task whether a word had been presented. The key finding related to nonwords. The later the position of the phoneme at which the sound sequence deviated from all English words, the more time the listeners took to make nonword decisions.

O'Rourke and Holcomb (2002) also addressed the assumption that a spoken word is identified when the uniqueness point is reached (i.e., the point at which only *one* word is consistent with the acoustic signal). Listeners heard spoken words and pseudowords and decided as rapidly as possible whether each stimulus was a word. Some words had an early uniqueness point (average of 427 ms after word onset), whereas others had a late uniqueness point (average of 533 ms after word onset). The N400 (a negative-going wave assessed by

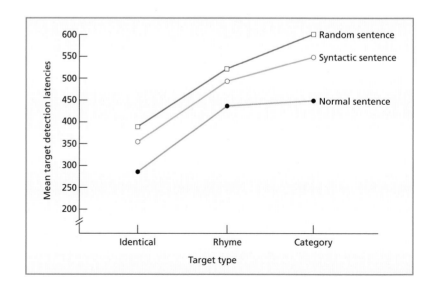

Figure 9.11 Detection times for word targets presented in sentences. Adapted from Marslen-Wilson and Tyler (1980).

ERPs; see Glossary) was used as a measure of the speed of word processing.

O'Rourke and Holcomb (2002) found that the N400 occurred about 100 ms earlier for words having an early uniqueness point than for those having a late uniqueness point. This is important, because it suggests that the uniqueness point may be significant. The further finding that N400 typically occurred shortly after the uniqueness point had been reached supports the assumption of cohort theory that spoken word processing is highly efficient.

Radeau, Morais, Mousty, and Bertelson (2000) cast some doubt over the general importance of the uniqueness point. Listeners were presented with French nouns having early or late uniqueness points. The uniqueness point influenced performance when the nouns were presented at a slow rate (2.2 syllables/second) or a medium rate (3.6 syllables/second) but not when presented at a fast rate (5.6 syllables/second). This is somewhat worrying given that the fast rate is close to the typical conversational rate of speaking!

There is considerable emphasis in the cohort model on the notion of *competition* among candidate words when a listener hears a word. Weber and Cutler (2004) found that such competition can include more words than one might imagine. Dutch students with a good command of the English language identified target pictures corresponding to a spoken English word. Even though the task was in English, the Dutch students activated some Dutch words – they fixated distractor pictures having Dutch names that resembled phonemically the English name of the target picture. Overall, Weber and Cutler's findings revealed that lexical competition was greater in non-native than in native listening.

Undue significance was given to the initial part of the word in the original cohort model. It was assumed that a spoken word will generally not be recognised if its initial phoneme is unclear or ambiguous. Evidence against that assumption has been reported. Frauenfelder, Scholten, and Content (2001) found that French-speaking listeners activated words even when the initial phoneme of spoken words was distorted (e.g.,

hearing "focabulaire" activated the word "vocabulaire"). However, the listeners took some time to overcome the effects of the mismatch in the initial phoneme. Allopenna, Magnuson, and Tanenhaus (1998) found that the initial phoneme of a spoken word activated other words sharing that phoneme (e.g., the initial sounds of "beaker" caused activation of "beetle"). Somewhat later, there was a weaker tendency for listeners to activate words rhyming with the auditory input (e.g., "beaker" activated "speaker"). The key point in these studies is that some words not sharing an initial phoneme with the auditory input were *not* totally excluded from the cohort as predicted by the original cohort model.

Revised model

Marslen-Wilson (1990, 1994) revised the cohort model. In the original version, words were either in or out of the word cohort. In the revised version, candidate words vary in their level of activation, and so membership of the word cohort is a matter of degree. Marslen-Wilson (1990) assumed that the word-initial cohort may contain words having similar initial phonemes rather than being limited *only* to words having the initial phoneme of the presented word.

There is a second major difference between the original and revised versions of cohort theory. In the original version, context influenced word recognition early in processing. In the revised version, the effects of context on word recognition occur only at a fairly late stage of processing. More specifically, context influences only the integration stage at which a selected word is integrated into the evolving representation of the sentence. Thus, the revised cohort model places more emphasis on bottom-up processing than the original version. However, other versions of the model (e.g., Gaskell & Marslen-Wilson, 2002) are less explicit about the late involvement of context in word recognition.

Evidence

The assumption that membership of the word cohort is gradated rather than all-or-none is clearly superior to the previous assumption that membership is all-or-none. Some research causing problems for the original version of the model (e.g., Allopenna et al., 1998; Frauenfelder et al., 2001) is much more consistent with the revised assumption.

Some of the strongest support for the assumption that context influences only the later stages of word recognition was reported by Zwitserlood (1989). Listeners performed a lexical decision task (deciding whether visually presented letter strings were words) immediately after hearing part of a spoken word. For example, when only "cap___" had been presented, it was consistent with various possible words (e.g., "captain", "capital"). Performance on the lexical decision task was faster when the word on that task was related in meaning to either of the possible words (e.g., "ship" for "captain" and "money" for "capital"). Of greatest importance was what happened when the part word was preceded by a biasing context (e.g., "With dampened spirits the men stood around the grave. They mourned the loss of their *captain*." Such context did not prevent the activation of competitor words (e.g., "capital").

So far we have discussed Zwitserlood's (1989) findings when only part of the spoken word was presented. What happened when enough of the word was presented for listeners to be able to guess its identity correctly? According to the revised cohort model, we should find effects of context at this late stage of word processing. That is precisely what Zwitserlood found.

Friedrich and Kotz (2007) carried out a similar study to that of Zwitserlood (1989).

They presented sentences ending with incomplete words (e.g., "To light up the dark she needed her can ___". Immediately afterwards, listeners saw a visual word matched to the incomplete word in form and meaning (e.g., "candle"), in meaning only (e.g., "lantern"), in form only (e.g., "candy"), or in neither ("number"). Event-related potentials (ERPs; see Glossary) were recorded to assess the early stages of word processing. There was evidence for a form-based cohort 250 ms after presentation of the visual word, and of a meaning-based cohort 220 ms after presentation. The existence of a form-based cohort means that "candy" was activated even though the context strongly indicated that it was not the correct word. Thus, context did not constrain the words initially processed as predicted by the revised cohort model.

In spite of the above findings, sentence context can influence spoken word processing some time *before* a word's uniqueness point has been reached. Van Petten, Coulson, Rubin, Plante, and Parks (1999) presented listeners with a spoken sentence frame (e.g., "Sir Lancelot spared the man's life when he begged for _____"), followed after 500 ms by a final word congruent (e.g., "mercy") or incongruent (e.g., "mermaid") with the sentence frame. Van Petten et al. used ERPs to assess processing of the final word. There were significant differences in the N400 (a negative wave occurring about 400 ms after stimulus presentation) to the contextually congruent and incongruent words 200 ms *before* the uniqueness point was reached. Thus, very strong context influenced spoken word processing earlier than expected within the revised cohort model.

Immediate effects of context on processing of spoken words

One of the most impressive attempts to show that context can have a very rapid effect during speech perception was reported by Magnuson, Tanenhaus, and Aslin (2008). Initially, they taught participants an artificial lexicon consisting of nouns referring to shapes and adjectives referring to textures. After that, they presented visual displays consisting of four objects, and participants were instructed to click on one of the objects (identified as "the (adjective)" or as "the (noun)"). The dependent variable of interest was the eye fixations of participants.

On some trials, the display consisted of four different shapes, and so *only* a noun was needed to specify uniquely the target object. In other words, the visual context allowed participants to predict that the target would be accurately described just by a noun. On every trial, there was an incorrect competitor word starting with the same sound as the correct word. This competitor was a noun or an adjective. According to the cohort model, this competitor should have been included in the initial cohort regardless of whether it was a noun or an adjective. In contrast, if listeners could use context very rapidly, they would have *only* included the competitor when it was a noun.

The competitor was considered until 800 ms after word onset (200 ms after word offset) when it was a noun (see Figure 9.12). Dramatically, however, the competitor was eliminated within 200 ms of word onset (or never considered at all) when it was an adjective.

What do these findings mean? They cast considerable doubt on the assumption that context effects occur only after an initial cohort of possible words has been established. If the context allows listeners to predict accurately which words are relevant and which are irrelevant, then the effects of context can occur more rapidly than is assumed by the cohort model. According to Magnuson et al. (2008), delayed effects of context are found when the context only weakly predicts which word is likely to be presented.

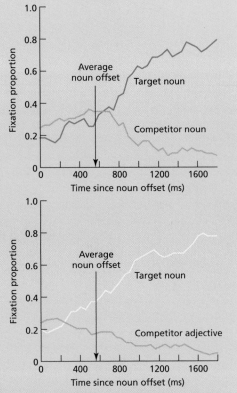

Figure 9.12 Eye fixation proportions to noun targets and noun competitors (top figure) and to noun targets and adjective competitors (bottom figure) over time after noun onset. The time after noun onset at which the target attracted significantly more fixations than the competitor occurred much later with a noun than an adjective competitor. Based on data in Magnuson et al. (2008).

Overall evaluation

The theoretical approach represented by the cohort model possesses various strengths. First, the assumption that accurate perception of a spoken word involves processing and rejecting several competitor words is generally correct. However, previous theories had typically paid little or no attention to the existence of substantial competition effects. Second, there is the assumption that the processing of spoken words is sequential and changes considerably during the course of their presentation. The speed with which spoken words are generally identified and the importance of the uniqueness point indicate the importance of sequential processing. Third, the revised version of the model has two advantages over the original version:

(1) The assumption that membership of the word cohort is a matter of degree rather than being all-or-none is more in line with the evidence.

(2) There is more scope for correcting errors within the revised version of the model

because words are less likely to be eliminated from the cohort at an early stage.

What are the limitations of the cohort model? First, there is the controversial issue of the involvement of context in auditory word recognition. According to the revised version of the cohort model, contextual factors only exert an influence late in processing at the integration stage. This is by no means the whole story. It may be correct when context only moderately constrains word identity but strongly constraining context seems to have an impact much earlier in processing (e.g., Magnuson et al., 2008; Van Petten et al., 1999). However, Gaskell and Marslen-Wilson (2002) emphasised the notion of "continuous integration" and so can accommodate the finding that strong context has early effects.

Second, the modifications made to the original version of the model have made it less precise and harder to test. As Massaro (1994, p. 244) pointed out, "These modifications…make it more difficult to test against alternative models."

Third, the processes assumed to be involved in processing of speech depend heavily on identification of the starting points of individual words. However, it is not clear within the theory *how* this is accomplished.

TRACE model

McClelland and Elman (1986) and McClelland (1991) produced a network model of speech perception based on connectionist principles (see Chapter 1). Their TRACE model of speech perception resembles the interactive activation model of visual word recognition put forward by McClelland and Rumelhart (1981; discussed earlier in the chapter). The TRACE model assumes that bottom-up and top-down processes interact flexibly in spoken word recognition. Thus, *all* sources of information are used at the same time in spoken word recognition.

The TRACE model is based on the following theoretical assumptions:

- There are individual processing units or nodes at three different levels: features (e.g., voicing; manner of production), phonemes, and words.
- Feature nodes are connected to phoneme nodes, and phoneme nodes are connected to word nodes.
- Connections *between* levels operate in both directions, and are only facilitatory.
- There are connections among units or nodes at the *same* level; these connections are inhibitory.
- Nodes influence each other in proportion to their activation levels and the strengths of their interconnections.
- As excitation and inhibition spread among nodes, a pattern of activation or trace develops.
- The word recognised or identified by the listener is determined by the activation level of the possible candidate words.

The TRACE model assumes that bottom-up and top-down processes *interact* throughout speech perception. In contrast, most versions of the cohort model assume that top-down processes (e.g., context-based effects) occur relatively late in speech perception. Bottom-up activation proceeds upwards from the feature level to the phoneme level and on to the word level, whereas top-down activation proceeds in the opposite direction from the word level to the phoneme level and on to the feature level.

Evidence

Suppose we asked listeners to detect target phonemes presented in words and nonwords. According to the TRACE model, performance should be better in the word condition. Why is that? In that condition, there would be activation from the word level proceeding to the phoneme level which would facilitate phoneme detection. Mirman, McClelland, Holt, and Magnuson (2008) asked listeners to detect a target phoneme (/t/ or /k/) in words and nonwords. Words were presented on 80% or 20% of the trials. The argument was that attention to (and activation at) the word level would be

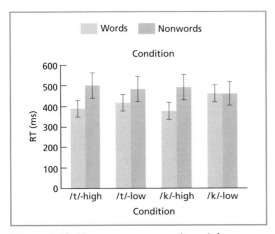

Figure 9.13 Mean reaction times (in ms) for recognition of /t/ and /k/ phonemes in words and nonwords when words were presented on a high (80%) or low (20%) proportion of trials. From Mirman et al. (2008). Reprinted with permission of the Cognitive Science Society Inc.

greater when most of the auditory stimuli were words, and that this would increase the word superiority effect.

What did Mirman et al. (2008) find? First, the predicted word superiority effect was found in most conditions (see Figure 9.13). Second, the magnitude of the effect was greater when 80% of the auditory stimuli were words than when only 20% were. These findings provide strong evidence for the involvement of top-down processes in speech perception.

The TRACE model can easily explain the lexical identification shift (Ganong, 1980). In this effect (discussed earlier), there is a bias towards perceiving an ambiguous phoneme so that a word is formed. According to the TRACE model, top-down activation from the word level is responsible for the lexical identification shift.

McClelland, Rumelhart, and the PDP (Parallel Distributed Processing) Research Group (1986) applied the TRACE model to the phenomenon of categorical speech perception discussed earlier. According to the model, the discrimination boundary between phonemes becomes sharper because of mutual inhibition between phoneme units at the phoneme level. These inhibitory processes produce a "winner takes all" situation in which one phoneme becomes increasingly

activated while other phonemes are inhibited. McClelland et al.'s computer simulation based on the model successfully produced categorical speech perception.

Norris, McQueen, and Cutler (2003) obtained convincing evidence that phoneme identification can be directly influenced by top-down processing. Listeners were initially presented with words ending in the phoneme /f/ or /s/. For different groups, an ambiguous phoneme equally similar to /f/ and /s/ replaced the final /f/ or /s/ in these words. After that, listeners categorised phonemes presented *on their own* as /f/ or /s/. Listeners who had heard the ambiguous phonemes in the context of /s/-ending words strongly favoured the /s/ categorisation. In contrast, those who had heard the same phoneme in the context of /f/-ending words favoured the /f/ categorisation. Thus, top-down learning at the word level affected phoneme categorisation as predicted by the TRACE model.

According to the TRACE model, high-frequency words (those often encountered) are processed faster than low-frequency ones partly because they have higher resting activation levels. Word frequency is seen as having an important role in the word-recognition process and should influence even early stages of word processing. Support for these predictions was reported by Dahan, Magnuson, and Tanenhaus (2001) in experiments using eye fixations as a measure of attentional focus. Participants were presented with four pictures (e.g., bench, bed, bell, lobster), three of which had names starting with the same phoneme. They clicked on the picture corresponding to a spoken word (e.g., "bench") while ignoring the related distractors (bed, bell) and the unrelated distractor (lobster). According to the model, more fixations should be directed to the related distractor having a high-frequency name (i.e., bed) than to the one having a low-frequency name (i.e., bell). That was what Dahan et al. found. In addition, frequency influenced eye fixations very early in processing, which is also predicted by the TRACE model.

We turn now to research revealing problems with the TRACE model. One serious limitation is that it attaches too much importance to the influence of top-down processes on spoken word recognition. Frauenfelder, Segui, and Dijkstra (1990) gave participants the task of detecting a given phoneme. The key condition was one in which a nonword closely resembling an actual word was presented (e.g., "vocabutaire" instead of "vocabulaire"). According to the model, top-down effects from the word node corresponding to "vocabulaire" should have inhibited the task of identifying the "t" in "vocabutaire". They did not.

The existence of top-down effects depends more on stimulus degradation than predicted by the model. McQueen (1991) presented ambiguous phonemes at the end of stimuli, and participants categorised them. Each ambiguous phoneme could be perceived as completing a word or a nonword. According to the model, top-down effects from the word level should have produced a preference for perceiving the phonemes as completing words. This prediction was confirmed *only* when the stimulus was degraded. It follows from the TRACE model that the effects should be greater when the stimulus is degraded. However, the absence of effects when the stimulus was not degraded is inconsistent with the model.

Imagine you are listening to words spoken by someone else. Do you think that you would activate the spellings of those words? It seems unlikely that orthography (information about word spellings) is involved in speech perception, and there is no allowance for its involvement in the TRACE model. However, orthography *does* play a role in speech perception. Perre and Ziegler (2008) gave listeners a lexical decision task (deciding whether auditory stimuli were words or nonwords). The words varied in terms of the consistency between their phonology and their orthography or spelling. This should be irrelevant if orthography isn't involved in speech perception. In fact, however, listeners performed the lexical decision task slower when the words were inconsistent than when they were consistent. Event-related potentials (ERPs; see Glossary) indicated that inconsistency between phonology and orthography was detected rapidly (less than 200 ms).

Finally, we consider a study by Davis, Marslen-Wilson, and Gaskell (2002). They challenged the TRACE model's assumption that recognising a spoken word is based on identifying its *phonemes*. Listeners heard only the first syllable of a word, and decided whether it was the *only* syllable of a short word (e.g., "cap" or the *first* syllable of a longer word (e.g., "captain"). The two words between which listeners had to choose were cunningly selected so that the first phoneme was the same for both words. Since listeners could not use phonemic information to make the correct decision, the task should have been very difficult according to the TRACE model. In fact, however, performance was good. Listeners used non-phonemic information (e.g., small differences in syllable duration) ignored by the TRACE model to discriminate between short and longer words.

Evaluation

The TRACE model has various successes to its credit. First, it provides reasonable accounts of phenomena such as categorical speech recognition, the lexical identification shift, and the word superiority effect in phoneme monitoring. Second, a significant general strength of the model is its assumption that bottom-up and top-down processes both contribute to spoken word recognition, combined with explicit assumptions about the processes involved. Third, the model predicts accurately some of the effects of word frequency on auditory word processing (e.g., Dahan et al., 2001). Fourth, "TRACE...copes extremely well with noisy input – which is a considerable advantage given the noise present in natural language." (Harley, 2008, p. 274). Why does TRACE deal well with noisy and degraded speech? TRACE emphasises the role of top-down processes, and such processes become more important when bottom-up processes have to deal with limited stimulus information.

What are the limitations of the TRACE model? First, and most importantly, the model exaggerates the importance of top-down effects on speech perception (e.g., Frauenfelder et al., 1990; McQueen, 1991). Suppose listeners hear a mispronunciation. According to the model, top-down activation from the word level will generally lead listeners to perceive the word best fitting the presented phonemes rather than the mispronunciation itself. In fact, however, mispronunciations have a strong adverse effect on speech perception (Gaskell & Marslen-Wilson, 1998).

Second the TRACE model incorporates many different theoretical assumptions, which can be regarded as an advantage in that it allows the model to account for many findings. However, there is a suspicion that it makes the model so flexible that, "it can accommodate any result" (Harley, 2008, p. 274).

Third, tests of the model have relied heavily on computer simulations involving a small number of one-syllable words. It is not entirely clear whether the model would perform satisfactorily if applied to the vastly larger vocabularies possessed by most people.

Fourth, the model ignores some factors influencing auditory word recognition. As we have seen, orthographic information plays a significant role in speech perception (Perre & Ziegler, 2008). In addition, non-phonemic information such as syllable duration also helps to determine auditory word perception (Davis et al., 2002).

COGNITIVE NEUROPSYCHOLOGY

We have been focusing mainly on the processes permitting spoken words to be identified, i.e., word recognition. This is significant because word recognition is of vital importance as we strive to understand what the speaker is saying. In this section, we consider the processes involved in the task of repeating a spoken word immediately after hearing it. A major goal of research using this task is to identify some of the main processes involved in speech perception. However, the task also provides useful information about speech production (discussed in Chapter 11).

In spite of the apparent simplicity of the repetition task, many brain-damaged patients experience difficulties with it even though audiometric testing reveals they are not deaf. Detailed analysis of these patients suggests various processes can be used to permit repetition of a spoken word. As we will see, the study of such patients has shed light on issues such as the following: Are the processes involved in repeating spoken words the same for familiar and unfamiliar words? Can spoken words be repeated without accessing their meaning?

Information from brain-damaged patients was used by Ellis and Young (1988) to propose a theoretical account of the processing of spoken words (see Figure 9.14; a more complete figure of the whole language system is provided by Harley, 2008, p. 467). This theoretical account (a framework rather than a complete theory) has five components:

- The *auditory analysis system* extracts phonemes or other sounds from the speech wave.
- The *auditory input lexicon* contains information about spoken words known to the listener but not about their meaning.
- Word meanings are stored in the *semantic system* (cf., semantic memory discussed in Chapter 7).
- The *speech output lexicon* provides the spoken form of words.
- The *phoneme response buffer* provides distinctive speech sounds.
- These components can be used in various combinations so there are several routes between hearing a spoken word and saying it.

The most striking feature of the framework is the assumption that saying a spoken word can be achieved using *three* different routes varying in terms of which stored information about heard spoken words is accessed. We will consider these three routes after discussing the role of the auditory analysis system in speech perception.

Auditory analysis system

Suppose a patient had damage only to the auditory analysis system, thereby producing a

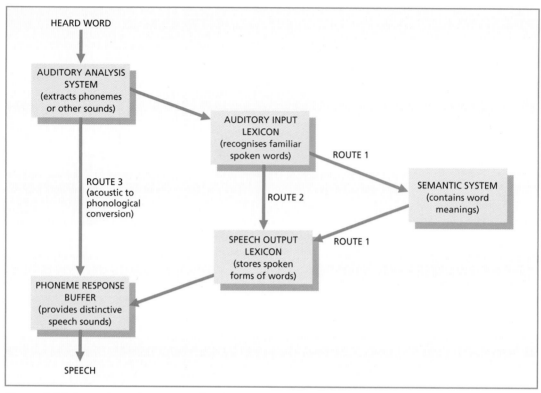

Figure 9.14 Processing and repetition of spoken words. Adapted from Ellis and Young (1988).

deficit in phonemic processing. Such a patient would have impaired speech perception for words and nonwords, especially those containing phonemes that are hard to discriminate. However, such a patient would have generally intact speech production, reading, and writing, would have normal perception of non-verbal environmental sounds not containing phonemes (e.g., coughs; whistles), and his/her hearing would be unimpaired. The term **pure word deafness** describes patients with these symptoms. There would be evidence for a double dissociation if we could find patients with impaired perception of non-verbal sounds but intact speech perception. Peretz et al. (1994) reported the case of a patient having a functional impairment limited to perception of music and prosody.

A crucial part of the definition of pure word deafness is that auditory perception problems are highly selective to speech and do *not* apply to non-speech sounds. Many patients seem to display the necessary selectivity. However, Pinard, Chertkow, Black, and Peretz (2002) identified impairments of music perception and/or environmental sound perception in 58 out of 63 patients they reviewed.

Speech perception differs from the perception of most non-speech sounds in that coping with rapid change in auditory stimuli is much more important in the former case. Jörgens et al.

(2008) studied a 71-year-old woman with pure word deafness, who apparently had no problems in identifying environmental sounds in her everyday life. However, when asked to count rapid clicks, she missed most of them. This suggests she had problems in dealing with rapid changes in auditory input. Other patients with pure word deafness have problems in perceiving rapid changes in non-speech sounds with complex pitch patterns (see Martin, 2003). Thus, impaired ability to process rapidly changing auditory stimuli may help to explain the poor speech perception of patients with pure word deafness.

Three-route framework

Unsurprisingly, the most important assumption of the three-route framework is that there are three different ways (or routes) that can be used when individuals process and repeat words they have just heard. As you can see in Figure 9.14, these three routes differ in terms of the number and nature of the processes used by listeners. All three routes involve the auditory analysis system and the phonemic response buffer. Route 1 involves three additional components of the language system (the auditory input lexicon, the semantic system, and the speech output lexicon), Route 2 involves two additional components (auditory input lexicon and the speech output lexicon), and Route 3 involves an additional rule-based system that converts acoustic information into words that can be spoken. We turn now to a more detailed discussion of each route.

According to the three-route framework, Routes 1 and 2 are designed to be used with familiar words, whereas Route 3 is designed to be used with unfamiliar words and non-words. When Route 1 is used, a heard word activates relevant stored information about it, including its meaning and its spoken form. Route 2 closely resembles Route 1 except that information about the meaning of heard words is *not* accessed. As a result, someone using Route 2 would say familiar words accurately but would not know their meaning. Finally, Route 3 involves using rules about the con-

version of the acoustic information contained in heard words into the appropriate spoken forms of those words. It is assumed that such conversion processes must be involved to allow listeners to repeat back unfamiliar words and nonwords.

Evidence

If patients could use Route 2 but Routes 1 and 3 were severely impaired, they should be able to understand familiar words but would not understand their meaning (see Figure 9.14). In addition, they should have problems with unfamiliar words and nonwords, because nonwords cannot be dealt with via Route 2. Finally, since such patients would make use of the input lexicon, they should be able to distinguish between words and nonwords.

Patients suffering from **word meaning deafness** fit the above description. The notion of word meaning deafness has proved controversial and relatively few patients with the condition have been identified. However, a few fairly clear cases have been identified. For example, Jacquemot, Dupoux, and Bachoud-Lévi (2007) claimed that a female patient, GGM, had all of the main symptoms of word meaning deafness.

Franklin, Turner, Ralph, Morris, and Bailey (1996) studied Dr O, who was another clear case of word meaning deafness. He had impaired auditory comprehension but intact written word comprehension. His ability to repeat words was dramatically better than his ability to repeat nonwords (80% versus 7%, respectively). Finally, Dr O had a 94% success rate at distinguishing between words and nonwords.

Dr O seemed to have reasonable access to the input lexicon as shown by his greater ability to repeat words than nonwords, and by his almost perfect ability to distinguish between

> **KEY TERM**
>
> **word meaning deafness:** a condition in which there is a selective impairment of the ability to understand spoken (but not written) language.

words and nonwords. He clearly has some problem relating to the semantic system. However, the semantic system itself does not seem to be damaged, because his ability to understand written words is intact. He probably has damage to parts of Route 1. Tyler and Moss (1997) argued that Dr O might also have problems earlier in processing (e.g., in extracting phonemic features from speech). For example, when he was asked to repeat spoken words as rapidly as possible, he made 25% errors.

According to the theoretical framework, we would expect to find some patients who make use primarily or exclusively of Route 3, which involves converting acoustic information from heard words into the spoken forms of those words. Such patients would be reasonably good at repeating spoken words and nonwords but would have very poor comprehension of these words. Some patients with **transcortical sensory aphasia** exhibit precisely this pattern of symptoms (Coslett, Roeltgen, Rothi, & Heilman, 1987; Raymer, 2001). These patients typically have poor reading comprehension in addition to impaired auditory comprehension, suggesting they have damage within the semantic system.

Some brain-damaged patients have extensive problems with speech perception and production. For example, patients with **deep dysphasia** make semantic errors when asked to repeat spoken words by saying words related in meaning to those spoken (e.g., saying "sky" when they hear "cloud"). In addition, they find it harder to repeat abstract words than concrete ones, and have a very poor ability to repeat nonwords.

How can we explain deep dysphasia? With reference to Figure 9.14, it could be argued that none of the routes between heard words and speech is intact. Perhaps there is a severe impairment to the non-lexical route (Route 3) combined with an additional impairment in (or near) the semantic system. Other theorists (e.g., Jefferies et al., 2007) have argued that the central problem in deep dysphasia is a general phonological impairment (i.e., problems in processing word sounds). This leads to semantic errors because it increases patients' reliance on word meaning when repeating spoken words.

Jefferies et al. (2007) found that patients with deep dysphasia suffered from poor phonological production on word repetition, reading aloud, and spoken picture naming. As predicted, they also performed very poorly on tasks involving the manipulation of phonology such as the phoneme subtraction task (e.g., remove the initial phoneme from "cat"). Furthermore, they had problems with speech perception, as revealed by their poor performance in deciding whether two words rhymed with each other. In sum, Jefferies et al. provided good support for their phonological impairment hypothesis.

Evaluation

The three-route framework is along the right lines. Patients vary in the precise problems they have with speech perception (and speech production), and some evidence exists for each of the three routes. At the very least, it is clear that repeating spoken words can be achieved in various different ways. Furthermore, conditions such as pure word deafness, word meaning deafness and transcortical aphasia can readily be related to the framework.

What are the limitations of the framework? First, it is often difficult to decide precisely how patients' symptoms relate to the framework. For example, deep dysphasia can be seen as involving impairments to all three routes or alternatively as mainly reflecting a general phonological impairment. Second, some conditions (e.g., word meaning deafness; auditory phonological agnosia) have only rarely been reported and so their status is questionable.

KEY TERMS

transcortical sensory aphasia: a disorder in which words can be repeated but there are many problems with language.

deep dysphasia: a condition in which there is poor ability to repeat spoken words and especially nonwords, and there are semantic errors in repeating spoken words.

CHAPTER SUMMARY

- Reading: introduction
  Several methods are available to study reading. Lexical decision, naming, and priming tasks have been used to assess word identification. Recording eye movements provides detailed on-line information, and is unobtrusive. Studies of masked phonological priming suggest that phonological processing occurs rapidly and automatically in reading. However, phonological activation is probably not essential for word recognition.

- Word recognition
  According to the interactive activation model, bottom-up and top-down processes interact during word recognition. It seems to account for the word-superiority effect, but ignores the roles of phonological processing and meaning in word recognition. Sentence context often has a rapid influence on word processing, but this influence is less than total.

- Reading aloud
  According to the dual-route cascaded model, lexical and non-lexical routes are used in reading words and nonwords. Surface dyslexics rely mainly on the non-lexical route, whereas phonological dyslexics use mostly the lexical route. The dual-route model emphasises the importance of word regularity, but consistency is more important. The model also ignores consistency effects with nonwords and minimises the role of phonological processing. The triangle model consists of orthographic, phonological, and semantic systems. Surface dyslexia is attributed to damage within the semantic system, whereas phonological dyslexia stems from a general phonological impairment. Deep dyslexia involves phonological and semantic impairments. The triangle model has only recently considered the semantic system in detail, and its accounts of phonological and surface dyslexia are oversimplified.

- Reading: eye-movement research
  According to the E-Z Reader model, the next eye-movement is planned when only part of the processing of the currently fixated word has occurred. Completion of frequency checking of a word is the signal to initiate an eye-movement programme, and completion of lexical access is the signal for a shift of covert attention to the next word. The model provides a reasonable account of many findings. However, it exaggerates the extent of serial processing, and mistakenly predicts that readers will read words in the "correct" order or suffer disruption if they do not.

- Listening to speech
  Listeners make use of prosodic cues and lip-reading. Among the problems faced by listeners are the speed of spoken language, the segmentation problem, co-articulation, individual differences in speech patterns, and degraded speech. Listeners prefer to use lexical information to achieve word segmentation, but can also use co-articulation, allophony, and syllable stress. There is categorical perception of phonemes, but we can discriminate unconsciously between sounds categorised as the same phoneme. The lexical identification shift and the phonemic restoration effect show the effects of context on speech perception.

- Theories of spoken word recognition
  According to the motor theory, listeners mimic the articulatory movements of the speaker. There is reasonable evidence that motor processes can facilitate speech perception. However, some patients with severely impaired speech production have reasonable speech perception. Cohort theory is based on the assumption that perceiving a spoken word involves rejecting competitors in a sequential process. However, contextual factors can influence speech perception earlier in processing than assumed by the model. The TRACE model is highly interactive and accounts for several phenomena (e.g., word superiority effect in phoneme monitoring). However, it exaggerates the importance of top-down effects.

- Cognitive neuropsychology
  It has been claimed that there are three routes between sound and speech. Patients with pure word deafness have problems with speech perception that may be due to impaired phonemic processing. Patients with word meaning deafness have problems in acoustic-to-phonological conversion and with using the semantic system. Patients with transcranial sensory aphasia seem to have damage to the semantic system but can use acoustic-to-phonological conversion. The central problem in deep dysphasia is a general phonological impairment.

FURTHER READING

- Diehl, R.L., Lotto, A.J., & Holt, L.L. (2004). Speech perception. *Annual Review of Psychology, 55,* 149–179. The authors discuss major theoretical perspectives in terms of their ability to account for key phenomena in speech perception.
- Gaskell, G. (ed.) (2007). *Oxford handbook of psycholinguistics.* Oxford: Oxford University Press. This large edited volume contains several chapters dealing with basic processes in reading and speech perception. This is especially the case with Part 1, which is devoted to word recognition.
- Harley, T.A. (2008). *The psychology of language: From data to theory* (3rd ed.). Several chapters (e.g., 6, 7, and 9) of this excellent textbook contain detailed information about the processes involved in recognising visual and auditory words.
- Pisoni, D.B., & Remez, R.E. (eds.) (2004). *The handbook of speech perception.* Oxford: Blackwell. This edited book contains numerous important articles across the entire field of speech perception.
- Rayner, K., Shen, D., Bai, X., & Yan, G. (eds.) (2009). *Cognitive and cultural influences on eye movements.* Hove, UK: Psychology Press. Section 2 of this edited book is devoted to major contemporary theories of eye movements in reading.
- Smith, F. (2004). *Understanding reading: A psycholinguistic analysis of reading and learning to read.* Mahwah, NJ: Lawrence Erlbaum Associates, Inc. This textbook provides a thorough account of theory and research on reading.

CHAPTER 10

LANGUAGE COMPREHENSION

INTRODUCTION

Basic processes involved in the initial stages of reading and listening to speech were discussed in the previous chapter. The focus there was on the identification of individual words. In this chapter, we discuss the ways in which phrases, sentences, and entire stories are processed and understood during reading and listening.

The previous chapter dealt mainly with those aspects of language processing *differing* between reading and listening to speech. In contrast, the higher-level processes involved in comprehension are somewhat similar whether a story is being listened to or read. There has been much more research on comprehension processes in reading than in listening to speech, and so our emphasis will be on reading. However, what is true of reading is also generally true of listening to speech.

What is the structure of this chapter? At a general level, we start by considering comprehension processes at the level of the sentence and finish by focusing on comprehension processes with larger units of language such as complete texts. A more specific indication of the coverage of this chapter is given below.

There are two main levels of analysis in sentence comprehension. First, there is an analysis of the syntactical (grammatical) structure of each sentences (**parsing**). What exactly is grammar? It is concerned with the way in which words are combined. However, as Altmann (1997, p. 84) pointed out, "It [the way in which words are combined] is important, and has meaning, only

insofar as both the speaker and the hearer (or the writer and the reader) share some common knowledge regarding the significance of one combination or another. This shared knowledge is *grammar*."

Second, there is an analysis of sentence meaning. The intended meaning of a sentence may differ from its literal meaning (e.g., saying, "Well done!", when someone drops the plates) as in irony, sarcasm, and metaphor. The study of intended meaning is known as **pragmatics**. The context in which a sentence is spoken can also influence its intended meaning in various ways. Issues concerning pragmatics are discussed immediately following the section on parsing.

Most theories of sentence processing have ignored individual differences. In fact, however, individuals differ considerably in their comprehension processes, and it is important to consider such individual differences. The issue of individual differences in language comprehension is considered in the third section of the chapter. Our focus will be on individual differences in working memory capacity, which relates to the ability to process and store information at the same time. Not surprisingly,

---

> ### KEY TERMS
>
> **parsing:** an analysis of the syntactical or grammatical structure of sentences.
> **pragmatics:** the study of the ways in which language is used and understood in the real world, including a consideration of its intended meaning.

individuals with high working memory capacity exhibit superior language comprehension skills to those with low capacity.

In the fourth section of the chapter, we consider some of the processes involved when people are presented with a text or speech consisting of several sentences. Our focus will be mainly on the inferences readers and listeners draw during comprehension. We will be considering the following important theoretical issue: what determines which inferences are and are not drawn during language comprehension?

In the fifth and final section of the chapter, we consider processing involving larger units of language (e.g., texts or stories). When we read a text or story, we typically try to *integrate* the information within it. Such integration often involves drawing inferences, identifying the main themes in the text, and so on. These integrative processes (and the theories put forward to explain them) are discussed in this section.

PARSING

This section is devoted to parsing, and the processes used by readers and listeners to comprehend the sentences they read or hear. The most fundamental issue is to work out *when* different types of information are used. Much of the research on parsing concerns the relationship between syntactic and semantic analysis. There are at least four major possibilities:

(1) Syntactic analysis generally precedes (and influences) semantic analysis.
(2) Semantic analysis usually occurs *prior* to syntactic analysis.
(3) Syntactic and semantic analysis occur at the same time.
(4) Syntax and semantics are very closely associated, and have a hand-in-glove relationship (Altmann, personal communication).

The above possibilities will be addressed shortly. Note, however, that most studies on parsing have considered only the English language. Does this

matter? Word order is more important in English than in inflectional language such as German (Harley, 2008). As a result, parsing English sentences may differ in important ways from parsing German sentences.

Grammar or syntax

An infinite number of sentences is possible in any language, but these sentences are nevertheless systematic and organised. Linguists such as Noam Chomsky (1957, 1959) have produced rules to account for the productivity and regularity of language. A set of rules is commonly referred to as a grammar. Ideally, a grammar should be able to generate all the permissible sentences in a given language, while at the same time rejecting all the unacceptable ones. For example, our knowledge of grammar allows us to be confident that, "Matthew is likely to leave", is grammatically correct, whereas the similar sentence, "Matthew is probable to leave", is not.

Syntactic ambiguity

You might imagine that parsing or assigning grammatical structure to sentences would be easy. However, numerous sentences in the English language (e.g., "They are flying planes") have an ambiguous grammatical structure. Some sentences are syntactically ambiguous at the *global* level, in which case the whole sentence has two or more possible interpretations. For example, "They are cooking apples", is ambiguous because it may or may not mean that apples are being cooked. Other sentences are syntactically ambiguous at the *local* level, meaning that various interpretations are possible at some point during parsing.

Much research on parsing has focused on ambiguous sentences. *Why* is that the case? Parsing operations generally occur very rapidly, making it hard to study the processes involved. However, observing the problems encountered by readers struggling with ambiguous sentences can provide revealing information about parsing processes.

One way listeners work out the syntactic or grammatical structure of spoken language is by using **prosodic cues** in the form of stress, intonation, and duration. When listeners are confronted by speech in which each syllable is spoken with equal weight in a monotone (i.e., no prosodic cues are present), they find it hard to understand what is being said (Duffy & Pisoni, 1992).

Prosodic cues are most likely to be used (and are of most value) when spoken sentences are ambiguous. For example, in the ambiguous sentence, "The old men and women sat on the bench", the women may or may not be old. If the women are not old, the spoken duration of the word "men" will be relatively long, and the stressed syllable in "women" will have a steep rise in pitch contour. Neither of these prosodic features will be present if the sentence means the women are old.

Implicit prosodic cues seem to be used during silent reading. In one study (Steinhauer & Friederici, 2001), participants listened to or read various sentences. These sentences contained intonational boundaries (speech) or commas (text), and event-related potentials (ERPs; see Glossary) were similar in both cases. Other aspects of prosody (e.g., syllable structure; number of stressed syllables in a word) influence eye movements and reading time (e.g., Ashby & Clifton, 2005).

Frazier, Carlson, and Clifton (2006) argued that the overall *pattern* of prosodic phrasing is important rather than simply what happens at *one* particular point in a sentence. For example, consider the following ambiguous sentence:

> I met the daughter (#1) of the colonel (#2) who was on the balcony.

There was an intermediate phrase boundary at (#2), and the phrase boundary at (1#) was larger, the same size, or smaller. What determined how the sentence was interpreted was the *relationship* between the two phrase boundaries. Listeners were most likely to assume that the colonel was on the balcony when the first boundary was greater than the second one,

and least likely to do so when the first boundary was smaller than the second.

The above findings conflict with the traditional view. According to this view, the presence of a prosodic boundary (#2) immediately before the ambiguously-attached phrase (i.e., who was on the balcony) indicates that the phrase should not be attached to the most recent potential candidate (i.e., the colonel). This view exaggerates the importance of a single local phrase boundary and minimises the importance of the pattern of boundaries.

Snedeker and Trueswell (2003) found that listeners rapidly used prosodic cues to attend to the relevant objects mentioned by the speaker. Indeed, listeners' interpretations of ambiguous sentences were influenced by prosodic cues *before* the start of the ambiguous phrase. Thus, prosodic cues can be used to predict to-be-presented information.

In sum, prosody is important in language comprehension. As Frazier et al. (2006, p. 248) concluded, "Perhaps prosody provides the structure within which utterance comprehension takes place (in speech and even in silent reading)."

THEORIES OF PARSING

There are more theories of parsing than you can shake a stick at. However, we can categorise theories or models on the basis of *when* semantic information influences parsing choices. The garden-path model is the most influential theoretical approach based on the assumption that the initial attempt to parse a sentence involves using *only* syntactic information. In contrast, constraint-based models (e.g., Mac-Donald, Pearlmutter, & Seidenberg, 1994)

KEY TERM

prosodic cues: features of spoken language such as stress, intonation, and duration that make it easier for listeners to understand what is being said.

assume that *all* sources of information (syntactic and semantic) are used from the outset to construct a syntactic model of sentences. After discussing these models, we turn to the unrestricted race model, which attempts to combine aspects of the garden-path and constraint-based models.

Garden-path model

Frazier and Rayner (1982) put forward a two-stage, garden-path model. It was given that name because readers or listeners can be misled or "led up the garden path" by ambiguous sentences such as, "The horse raced past the barn fell." The model is based on the following assumptions:

- Only *one* syntactical structure is initially considered for any sentence.
- Meaning is *not* involved in the selection of the initial syntactical structure.
- The simplest syntactical structure is chosen, making use of two general principles: minimal attachment and late closure.
- According to the principle of minimal attachment, the grammatical structure producing the fewest nodes (major parts of a sentence such as noun phrase and verb phrase) is preferred.
- The principle of late closure is that new words encountered in a sentence are attached to the current phrase or clause if grammatically permissible.
- If there is a conflict between the above two principles, it is resolved in favour of the minimal attachment principle.
- If the syntactic structure that a reader constructs for a sentence during the first stage of processing is incompatible with additional information (e.g., semantic) generated by a thematic processor, then there is a second stage of processing in which the initial syntactic structure is revised.

The principle of minimal attachment can be illustrated by the following example taken from Rayner and Pollatsek (1989). In the sentences, "The girl knew the answer by heart", and, "The girl knew the answer was wrong", the minimal attachment principle leads a grammatical structure in which "the answer" is regarded as the direct object of the verb "knew". This is appropriate only for the first sentence.

The principle of late closure produces the correct grammatical structure in a sentence such as, "Since Jay always jogs a mile this seems like a short distance to him". However, use of this principle would lead to an inaccurate syntactical structure in the following sentence: "Since Jay always jogs a mile seems like a short distance". The principle leads "a mile" to be placed in the preceding phrase rather than at the start of the new phrase. Of course, there would be less confusion if a comma were inserted after the word "jogs". In general, readers are less misled by garden-path sentences that are punctuated (Hills & Murray, 2000).

Evidence

There is much evidence that readers typically follow the principles of late closure and minimal attachment (see Harley, 2008). However, the crucial assumption is that semantic factors do *not* influence the construction of the initial syntactic structure. Ferreira and Clifton (1986) provided support for this assumption in a study in which eye movements were recorded while readers read sentences such as the following:

Garden-path sentences, such as "The horse raced past the barn fell", are favourite tools of researchers interested in parsing.

- The defendant examined by the lawyer turned out to be unreliable.
- The evidence examined by the lawyer turned out to be unreliable.

According to the principle of minimal attachment, readers should initially treat the verb "examined" as the main verb, and so experience ambiguity for both sentences. However, if readers initially make use of semantic information, they would experience ambiguity only for the first sentence. This is because the defendant could possibly examine something, but the evidence could not. The eye-movement data suggested that readers experienced ambiguity equally for both sentences, implying that semantic information did *not* influence the initial syntactic structure.

Readers' use of late closure was shown by Van Gompel and Pickering (2001). Consider the following sentence: "After the child had sneezed the doctor prescribed a course of injections". Eye-movement data indicated that readers experienced a difficulty after the word "sneezed" because they mistakenly used the principle of late closure to try to make "the doctor" the direct object of "sneezed". This shows the powerful influence exerted by the principle of late closure, given that the verb "sneezed" cannot take a direct object.

It seems inefficient that readers and listeners often construct incorrect grammatical structures for sentences. However, Frazier and Rayner (1982) claimed that the principles of minimal attachment and late closure *are* efficient because they minimise the demands on short-term memory. They measured eye movements while participants read sentences such as those about jogging given earlier. Their crucial argument was as follows: if readers construct both (or all) possible syntactic structures, then there should be additional processing time at the point of disambiguation (e.g., "seems" in the first jogging sentence and "this" in the second one). According to the garden-path model, in contrast, there should be increased processing time *only* when the actual grammatical structure conflicts with the one produced by application of the principles of minimal attachment and late closure (e.g., the first jogging sentence). The eye-movement data consistently supported the model's predictions.

Breedin and Saffran (1999) studied a patient, DM, who had a very severe loss of semantic knowledge because of dementia. However, he performed at essentially normal levels on tasks involving the detection of grammatical violations or selecting the subject and object in a sentence. These findings suggest that the syntactic structure of most sentences can be worked out correctly in the almost complete absence of semantic information. However, the fact that DM made very little use of semantic information when constructing syntactic structures does not necessarily mean that healthy individuals do the same.

Readers do not *always* follow the principle of late closure. Carreiras and Clifton (1993) presented English sentences such as, "The spy shot the daughter of the colonel who was standing on the balcony". According to the principle of late closure, readers should interpret this as meaning that the colonel was standing on the balcony. In fact, they did not strongly prefer either interpretation. When an equivalent sentence was presented in Spanish, there was a clear preference for assuming that the daughter was standing on the balcony (early rather than late closure). This is also contrary to theoretical prediction.

Semantic information often influences sentence processing earlier than assumed within the garden-path model. In some studies, this semantic information is contained within the sentence being processed, whereas in others it takes the form of prior context. Here, we will briefly consider each type of study, with additional relevant studies being considered in connection with other theories.

We saw earlier that Ferreira and Clifton (1986) found that semantic information did not influence readers' initial processing of sentences. Trueswell, Tanenhaus, and Garnsey (1994) repeated their experiment using sentences with stronger semantic constraints. Semantic information was used at an early stage to identify the correct syntactic structure. However, Clifton, Traxler, Mohamed, Williams, Morris, and Rayner (2003) used the same sentences as Trueswell et al. but found that semantic information was of relatively little use in removing ambiguity!

According to the garden-path model, *prior context* should not influence the initial parsing of an ambiguous sentence. However, contrary evidence was reported by Tanenhaus, Spivey-Knowlton, Eberhard, and Sedivy (1995), who presented participants auditorily with the ambiguous sentence, "Put the apple on the towel in the box". They recorded eye movements to assess how the sentence was interpreted. According to the model, "on the towel" should initially be understood as the place where the apple should be put, because that is the simplest syntactic structure. That is what was found when the context did not remove the ambiguity. However, when the visual context consisted of two apples, one on a towel and the other on a napkin, the participants rapidly used that context to identify which apple to move.

Spivey, Tanenhaus, Eberhard, and Sedivy (2002) carried out a similar experiment but used pre-recorded digitised speech to prevent speech intonation from influencing participants' interpretations. There were far fewer eye movements

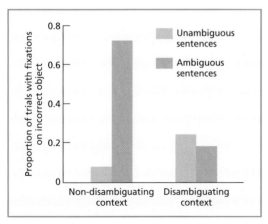

Figure 10.1 Proportion of trials with eye fixations on the incorrect object as a function of sentence type (unambiguous vs. ambiguous) and context (non-disambiguating vs. disambiguating). Based on data in Spivey et al. (2002).

to the incorrect object (e.g., towel on its own) when the context disambiguated the sentence (see Figure 10.1), indicating that context had a rapid effect on sentence interpretation.

Evaluation

The model provides a simple and coherent account of key processes in sentence processing. There is evidence indicating that the principles of minimal attachment and late closure often influence the selection of an initial syntactic structure for sentences.

What are the model's limitations? First, the assumption that the meanings of words within sentences do not influence the initial assignment of grammatical structure is inconsistent with some of the evidence (e.g., Trueswell et al., 1994). As we will see later, studies using event-related potentials (ERPs; see Glossary) have provided strong evidence that semantic information about word meanings and about world knowledge influences sentence processing very early in processing (e.g., Hagoort et al., 2004).

Second, prior context often seems to influence the interpretation of sentences much earlier in processing than assumed by the model. Further evidence for that was obtained in an ERP study by Nieuwland and van Berkum (2006), which is discussed later.

Third, the notion that the initial choice of grammatical structure depends only on the principles of minimal attachment and late closure seems too neat and tidy. For example, decisions about grammatical structure are also influenced by punctuation when reading and by prosodic cues when listening to speech.

Fourth, the model does not take account of differences among languages. For example, there is a preference for early closure rather than late closure in various languages including Spanish, Dutch, and French.

Fifth, it is hard to provide a definitive test of the model. Evidence that semantic information is used early in sentence processing seems inconsistent with the model. However, it is possible that the second stage of parsing (which includes semantic information) starts very rapidly.

Constraint-based theories

There are substantial differences between constraint-based theories and the garden-path model. According to constraint-based theories, the initial interpretation of a sentence depends on multiple sources of information (e.g., syntactic, semantic, general world knowledge) called constraints. These constraints limit the number of possible interpretations. There are several constraint-based theories. However we will focus on the influential theory put forward by MacDonald et al. (1994).

MacDonald et al.'s theory is based on a connectionist architecture. It is assumed that all relevant sources of information are available immediately to the parser. Competing analyses of the current sentence are activated at the same time and are ranked according to activation strength. The syntactic structure receiving most support from the various constraints is highly activated, with other syntactic structures being less activated. Readers become confused when reading ambiguous sentences if the correct syntactic structure is less activated than one or more incorrect structures.

According to the theory, the processing system uses four language characteristics to resolve ambiguities in sentences:

(1) Grammatical knowledge constrains possible sentence interpretations.
(2) The various forms of information associated with any given word are typically not independent of each other.
(3) A word may be less ambiguous in some ways than in others (e.g., ambiguous for tense but not for grammatical category).
(4) The various interpretations permissible according to grammatical rules generally differ considerably in frequency and probability on the basis of past experience.

Evidence

Pickering and Traxler (1998) presented participants with sentences such as the following:

(1) As the woman edited the magazine amused all the reporters.

(2) As the woman sailed the magazine amused all the reporters.

These two sentences are identical syntactically, and both are likely to lead readers to identify the wrong syntactic structure initially. However, the semantic constraints favouring the wrong structure are greater in sentence (1) than (2). As predicted by the constraint-based theory, eye-movement data indicated that eye fixations in the verb and post-verb regions were longer for those reading sentence (1).

According to the model, the assignment of syntactic structure to a sentence is influenced by **verb bias**. Many verbs can occur within various syntactic structures, but are found more often in some syntactic structures than others. For example, as Harley (2008) pointed out, the verb "read" is most often followed by a direct object e.g., "The ghost read the book during the plane journey"), but can also be used with a sentence complement (e.g., "The ghost read the book had been burned"). Garnsey, Pearlmutter, Myers, and Lotocky (1997) found that readers resolved ambiguities and identified the correct syntactic structure more rapidly when the sentence structure was consistent with the verb bias. This is inconsistent with the garden-path model, according to which verb bias should not influence the initial identification of syntactic structure.

Boland and Blodgett (2001) used noun/verb homographs (e.g., duck, train) – words that can be used as a noun or a verb. For example, if you read a sentence that started, "She saw her duck and…", you would not know whether the word "duck" was being used as a noun ("…and chickens near the barn") or a verb "…and stumble near the barn"). According to the constraint-based approach, readers should initially construct a syntactic structure in which the homograph is used as its more common part of speech (e.g., "duck" is mostly a verb and "train" is mostly a noun). As predicted, readers rapidly experienced problems (revealed by eye movements) when noun/verb homographs were used in their less common form.

Other studies discussed previously provide additional support for constraint-based theory. For example, there is evidence (e.g., Spivey et al., 2002; Tanenhaus et al., 1995) indicating that prior context influences sentence processing at an early stage.

Evaluation

The assumption that there can be varying degrees of support for different syntactic interpretations of a sentence is plausible. It seems efficient that readers should use all relevant information from the outset when trying to work out the syntactic structure of a sentence. As we will see, much of the evidence from cognitive neuroscience indicates that semantic information is used very early on in sentence processing, which seems more consistent with the constraint-based theory than the garden-path model. Finally, the constraint-based model assumes there is some *flexibility* in parsing decisions because several sources of information are involved. In contrast, there is little scope for flexibility within the garden-path model. Brysbaert and Mitchell (1996) found that there were substantial individual differences among Dutch people in their parsing decisions, which is much more consistent with the constraint-based model.

What are the limitations of constraint-based theory? First, it is not entirely correct that all relevant constraints are used immediately (e.g., Boland & Blodgett, 2001). Second, little is said within the theory about the detailed processes involved in generating syntactic structures for complex sentences. Third, it is assumed that various representations are formed in parallel, with most of them subsequently being rejected. However, there is little direct evidence for the existence of these parallel representations. Fourth, as Harley (2008, p. 308) pointed out, "Proponents of the garden path model argue that the effects that are claimed to support constraint-based models arise because the second stage of parsing begins very quickly, and that many experiments that are supposed to be looking at the first stage are in fact looking at the second stage of parsing."

Unrestricted race model

Van Gompel, Pickering, and Traxler (2000) put forward the unrestricted race model that combined aspects of the garden-path and constraint-based models. Its main assumptions are as follows:

(1) All sources of information (semantic as well as syntactic) are used to identify a syntactic structure, as is assumed by constraint-based models.
(2) All other possible syntactic structures are ignored unless the favoured syntactic structure is disconfirmed by subsequent information.
(3) If the initially chosen syntactic structure has to be discarded, there is an extensive process of re-analysis before a different syntactic structure is chosen. This assumption makes the model similar to the garden-path model, in that parsing often involves two distinct stages.

Evidence

Van Gompel, Pickering, and Traxler (2001) compared the unrestricted race model against the garden-path and constraint-based models. Participants read three kinds of sentence (sample sentences provided):

(1) *Ambiguous sentences*: The burglar stabbed only the guy with the dagger during the night. (This sentence is ambiguous because it could be either the burglar or the guy who had the dagger.)
(2) *Verb-phrase attachment*: The burglar stabbed only the dog with the dagger during the night. (This sentence involves verb-phrase attachment because it must have been the burglar who stabbed with the dagger.)
(3) *Noun-phrase attachment*: The burglar stabbed only the dog with the collar

during the night. (This sentence involves noun-phrase attachment because it must have been the dog that had the collar.)

According to the garden-path model, the principle of minimal attachment means that readers should always adopt the verb-phrase analysis. This will lead to rapid processing of sentences such as (2) but slow processing of sentences such as (3). It allows readers to interpret the ambiguous sentences as rapidly as verb-phrase sentences, because the verb-phrase analysis provides an acceptable interpretation. According to the constraint-based theory, sentences such as (2) and (3) will be processed rapidly, because the meanings of the words support only the correct interpretation. However, there will be serious competition between the two possible interpretations of sentence (1) because both are reasonable. As a result, processing of the ambiguous sentences will be slower than for either type of unambiguous sentence.

In fact, the ambiguous sentences were processed *faster* than either of the other types of sentence, which did not differ (see Figure 10.2). Why was this? According to van Gompel et al. (2001), the findings support the unrestricted race model. With the ambiguous sentences, readers rapidly use syntactic and semantic information to form a syntactic structure. Since both syntactic structures are possible, no re-analysis is necessary. In contrast, re-analysis is sometimes needed with noun-phrase and verb-phrase sentences.

Van Gompel, Pickering, Pearson, and Liversedge (2005) pointed out that the study by van Gompel et al. (2001) was limited. More specifically, sentences such as (2) and (3) were disambiguated some time after the initial point of ambiguity. As a result, competition between possible interpretations during that interval may have slowed down sentence processing. Van Gompel et al. (2005) carried out a study similar to that of van Gompel et al. (2001) but ensured that disambiguation occurred immediately to minimise any competition. Their findings were similar to those of van Gompel et al. (2001), and thus provided strong support for the unrestricted race model.

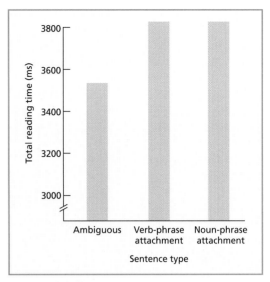

Figure 10.2 Total sentence processing time as a function of sentence type (ambiguous; verb-phrase attachment; noun-phrase attachment). Data from van Gompel et al. (2001).

Evaluation

The unrestricted race model is an interesting attempt to combine the best features of the garden-path and constraint-based models. It seems reasonable that all sources of information (including world knowledge) are used from the outset to construct a syntactic structure, which is then retained unless subsequent evidence is inconsistent with it. As we will see shortly, there is reasonable cognitive neuroscience evidence (e.g., Hagoort et al., 2004) that world knowledge influences sentence processing at a very early stage.

Sentence processing is somewhat more flexible than assumed within the unrestricted race model. As we will see shortly, the thoroughness of sentence processing depends in part on the reader's comprehension goals. In addition, ambiguous sentences may be read faster than non-ambiguous ones when an easy comprehension test is expected but not when a more detailed test of comprehension is expected (Swets, Desmet, Clifton, & Ferreira, 2008). The rapid processing of ambiguous sentences found by van Gompel et al. (2001) might not have occurred if they had used a more detailed comprehension test.

Good-enough representations

Nearly all theories of sentence processing (including those we have discussed) have an important limitation. Such theories are based on the assumption that the language processor "generates representations of the linguistic input that are complete, detailed, and accurate" (Ferreira, Bailey, & Ferraro, 2002, p. 11). An alternative viewpoint is based on the assumption of "good-enough" representations. According to this viewpoint, the typical goal of comprehension is "to get a parse of the input that is 'good enough' to generate a response given the current task" (Swets et al., 2008, p. 211).

The Moses illusion (e.g., Erickson & Mattson, 1981) is an example of inaccurate comprehension. When asked, "How many animals of each sort did Moses put on the ark?", many people reply, "Two", but the correct answer is, "None" (think about it!). Ferreira (2003) presented sentences aurally, and found that our representations of sentences are sometimes inaccurate rather than rich and complete. For example, a sentence such as, "The mouse was eaten by the cheese", was sometimes misinterpreted as meaning the mouse ate the cheese. A sentence such as, "The man was visited by the woman", was sometimes mistakenly interpreted to mean the man visited the woman.

It follows from the good-enough approach of Swets et al. (2008) that readers should process sentences more thoroughly if they anticipate detailed comprehension questions rather than superficial comprehension questions. As predicted, participants read sentences (especially syntactically ambiguous ones) more slowly in the former case than in the latter. Ambiguous sentences were read *more* rapidly than non-ambiguous ones when superficial questions were asked. However, this ambiguity advantage disappeared when more challenging comprehension questions were anticipated.

Why are people so prone to error when processing sentences (especially passive ones)?

According to Ferreira (2003), we use heuristics or rules of thumb to simplify the task of understanding sentences. A very common heuristic (the NVN strategy) is to assume that the subject of a sentence is the agent of some action, whereas the object of the sentence is the patient or theme. This makes some sense because a substantial majority of English sentences conform to this pattern.

Cognitive neuroscience

Cognitive neuroscience is making substantial contributions to our understanding of parsing and sentence comprehension. Since the precise *timing* of different processes is so important, much use has been made of event-related potentials (ERPs; see Glossary). As we will see, semantic information of various kinds is actively processed very early on, which is broadly consistent with predictions from the constraint-based theory and the unrestricted race model. The evidence is reviewed by Hagoort and van Berkum (2007).

The N400 component in the ERP waveform is of particular importance in research on sentence comprehension. It is a negative wave with an onset at about 250 ms and a peak at about 400 ms, which is why it is called N400. The presence of a large N400 in sentence processing typically indicates that there is a *mismatch* between the meaning of the word currently being processed and its context. Thus, N400 reflects aspects of semantic processing.

The traditional view assumes that contextual information is processed *after* information concerning the meanings of words within a sentence. Evidence against this view was reported by Nieuwland and van Berkum (2006). Here is an example of the materials they used:

> A woman saw a dancing peanut who had a big smile on his face. The peanut was singing about a girl he had just met. And judging from the song, the peanut was totally crazy about her. The woman thought it was really cute to see the

Word meanings and world knowledge in sentence comprehension

How does meaning influence initial sentence construction? The traditional view (e.g., Sperber & Wilson, 1986) is that initially we take account only of the meanings of the words in the sentence. Other aspects of meaning that go beyond the sentence itself (e.g., our world knowledge) are considered subsequently. Convincing evidence against that view was reported by Hagoort, Hald, Bastiaansen, and Petersson (2004) in a study in which they measured the N400 component in the ERP waveform. They asked their Dutch participants to read sentences such as the following (the critical words are in italics):

(1) The Dutch trains are *yellow* and very crowded. (This sentence is true.)
(2) The Dutch trains are *sour* and very crowded. (This sentence is false because of the meaning of the word "sour".)
(3) The Dutch trains are *white* and very crowded. (This sentence is false because of world knowledge – Dutch trains are yellow.)

According to the traditional view, the semantic mismatch in a sentence such as (3) should have taken longer to detect than the mismatch in a sentence such as (2). In fact, however, the effects of these different kinds of semantic mismatch on N400 were very similar (see Figure 10.3).

What do these findings mean? First, "While reading a sentence, the brain retrieves and integrates word meanings and world knowledge at the same time" (Hagoort et al., 2004, p. 440). Thus, the traditional view that we process word meaning before information about world knowledge appears to be wrong. Second, it is noteworthy that word meaning and world knowledge are both accessed and integrated into the reader's sentence comprehension within about 400 ms. The speed with which this happens suggests that sentence processing involves making immediate use of all relevant information, as is assumed by the constraint-based theory of MacDonald et al. (1994).

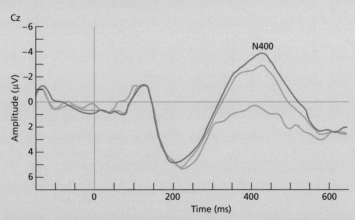

Figure 10.3 The N400 response to the critical word in a correct sentence ("The Dutch trains are yellow...": green line), a sentence incorrect on the basis of world knowledge ("The Dutch trains are white...": yellow line), and a sentence incorrect on the basis of word meanings ("The Dutch trains are sour...": red line). The N400 response was very similar with both incorrect sentences. From Hagoort et al. (2004). Reprinted with permission from AAAS.

peanut singing and dancing like that.
The peanut was salted/in love, *and by the*
sound of it, this was definitely mutual.

Some listeners heard "salted", which was appropriate in terms of word meanings but inappropriate in the context of the story. Others heard "in love", which was appropriate in the story context but inappropriate in terms of word meanings. The key finding was that the N400 was greater for "salted" than for "in love". Thus, contextual information can have a very rapid major impact on sentence processing.

Hagoort and van Berkum (2007) discussed an unpublished experiment of theirs in which participants listened to sentences. Some of these sentences included a word inconsistent with the apparent characteristics of the speaker (e.g., someone with an upper-class accent saying, "I have a large tattoo on my back"). There was a large N400 to the inconsistent word ("tattoo"). As Hagoort and van Berkum (p. 806) concluded, "By revealing an immediate impact of what listeners infer about the speaker, the present results add a distinctly social dimension to the mechanisms of online language interpretation."

Evaluation

Behavioural measures (e.g., time to read a sentence) generally provide rather indirect evidence concerning the nature and timing of the underlying processes involved in sentence comprehension. In contrast, research using event-related potentials has indicated clearly that we make use of our world knowledge, knowledge of the speaker, and contextual knowledge at an early stage of processing. Such findings are more supportive of constraint-based theories than of the garden-path model.

PRAGMATICS

Pragmatics is concerned with practical language use and comprehension, especially those aspects going beyond the literal meaning of what is said and taking account of the current social context. Thus, pragmatics relates to the *intended*

rather than *literal* meaning as expressed by speakers and understood by listeners, and often involves drawing inferences. The literal meaning of a sentence is often not the one the writer or speaker intended to communicate. For example, we assume that someone who says, "The weather's really great!", when it has been raining non-stop for several days, actually thinks the weather is terrible.

We will start by discussing a few examples in which the intended meaning of a sentence differs from the literal meaning. For example, when a speaker gives an indirect and apparently irrelevant answer to a question, the listener often tries to identify the speaker's goals to understand what he/she means. Consider the following (Holtgraves, 1998, p. 25):

Ken: Did Paula agree to go out with you?
Bob: She's not my type.

Holtgraves found that most people interpreted Bob's reply in a negative way as meaning that Paula had not agreed to go out with him but he wanted to save face. Suppose Bob gave an indirect reply that did not seem to involve face saving (e.g., "She's my type"). Listeners took almost 50% longer to comprehend such indirect replies than to comprehend typical indirect replies (e.g., "She's not my type"), presumably because it is hard to understand the speaker's motivation.

Figurative language is language not intended to be taken literally. Speakers and writers often make use of metaphor, in which a word or phrase is used figuratively to mean something it resembles. For example, here is a well-known metaphor from Shakespeare's *Richard III*:

Now is the winter of our discontent
Made glorious summer by this sun of
York.

KEY TERM

figurative language: forms of language (e.g., metaphor) not intended to be taken literally.

Theoretical approaches

Much theorising has focused on figurative language in general and metaphor in particular. According to the standard pragmatic model (e.g., Grice, 1975), three stages are involved:

(1) The literal meaning is accessed. For example, the literal meaning of "David kicked the bucket", is that David struck a bucket with his foot.
(2) The reader or listener decides whether the literal meaning makes sense in the context in which it is read or heard.
(3) If the literal meaning seems inadequate, the reader or listener searches for a non-literal meaning that does make sense in the context.

According to the standard pragmatic model, literal meanings should be accessed faster than non-literal or figurative ones. This is because literal meanings are accessed in stage one of processing, whereas non-literal ones are accessed only in stage three. Another prediction is that literal interpretations are accessed automatically, whereas non-literal ones are optional. In contrast, Glucksberg (2003) argued that literal and metaphoric meanings are processed in parallel and involve the same mechanisms.

Giora (1997, 2002) put forward the graded salience hypothesis, according to which initial processing is determined by salience or prominence rather than by type of meaning (literal versus non-literal). According to this hypothesis, "Salient messages are processed initially, regardless of either literality [whether the intended meaning is the literal one] or contextual fit. Salience is…determined primarily by frequency of exposure and experiential familiarity with the meaning in question.…Salient meanings are assumed to be accessed immediately upon encounter of the linguistic stimuli via a direct lookup in the mental lexicon. Less-salient meanings require extra inferential processes, and for the most part strong contextual support" (Giora, 2002, pp. 490–491).

Kintsch (2000) put forward a predication model of metaphor understanding designed to identify the underlying mechanisms. This model has two components:

(1) *The Latent Semantic Analysis component*: This represents the meanings of words based on their relations with other words in a 300-dimension space.
(2) *The Construction–integration component*: This uses the information from the first component to construct interpretations of statements with an "ARGUMENT is a PREDICATE" structure (e.g., "Lawyers are sharks"). More precisely, this component selects features of the *predicate* that are relevant to the argument and *inhibits* irrelevant predicate features. For example, features of sharks such as vicious and aggressive are relevant whereas having fins and swimming are not.

Evidence

Most evidence fails to support the standard pragmatic model. According to the model, figurative or metaphorical meanings are not accessed automatically. Opposing evidence was reported by Glucksberg (2003). The task was to decide whether various sentences were literally true or false, and so participants should not have accessed the figurative meaning of metaphors (e.g., "Some surgeons are butchers"). In fact, however, participants took a long time to judge metaphor sentences as false because there was competition between their "true" non-literal meaning and their false literal meaning (Figure 10.4).

The standard pragmatic model also predicts that non-literal meanings should take longer to comprehend than literal ones. In fact, however, non-literal or metaphorical meanings are typically understood as rapidly as literal ones (see Glucksberg, 2003). For example, Blasko and Connine (1993) presented participants with relatively unfamiliar metaphors (e.g., "Jerry first knew that loneliness was a desert when he was very young"). The metaphorical meanings of such sentences were understood as rapidly as the literal ones.

Arzouan, Goldstein, and Faust (2007) gave participants the task of deciding whether

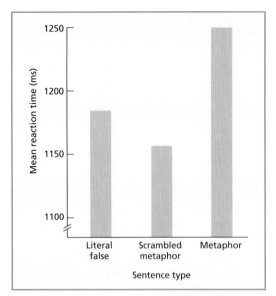

Figure 10.4 Time to decide that a sentence was literally false as a function of sentence type (literal false; scrambled metaphor (e.g., "some jobs are butchers"); metaphor). Adapted from Glucksberg (2003).

expressions were meaningful. Reaction times were as fast for conventional metaphors (e.g., "lucid mind") as for literal expressions (e.g., "burning fire"). Event-related potentials (ERPs; see Glossary) indicated that the pattern of brain activation was similar for both types of expression except that the N400 (a wave at 400 ms reflecting semantic processing) was greater in magnitude with conventional metaphors than with literal expressions. These findings suggest that the same comprehension mechanisms were used in both cases (as suggested by Glucksberg, 2003), but that the processing of conventional metaphors was more difficult.

Arzouan et al. (2007) found that reaction times were slower for novel metaphors (e.g., "ripe dream") than for conventional metaphors or literal expressions. In addition, the amplitude of the N400 was greatest for novel metaphors and they were the only expressions associated with a late negative wave. These findings are consistent with the graded salience hypothesis – novel metaphors are less salient and familiar than conventional metaphors and so require additional processing.

Giora and Fein (1999) tested the graded salience hypothesis more directly using familiar metaphors (having salient literal and metaphorical meanings) and less-familiar metaphors (having a salient literal meaning only). These metaphors were presented in a context biasing their metaphorical or literal meaning. If salience is what matters, then the literal and metaphorical meanings of familiar metaphors should be activated regardless of context. In contrast, the literal meaning of less-familiar metaphors should be activated in both contexts, but the non-salient metaphorical meaning should not be activated in the literal context. The findings were exactly as predicted by the hypothesis.

More support for the graded salience hypothesis was reported by Laurent, Denhières, Passerieux, Iakamova, and Hardy-Baylé (2006). ERPs were smaller to the last word of strongly salient idioms than weakly salient idioms. In addition, participants rapidly understood the idiomatic meanings of highly salient idioms and the literal interpretations of less salient idioms. These findings are consistent with the assumption that salient meanings (even of idioms) are accessed automatically.

The non-reversibility of metaphors is an important phenomenon (see Chiappe & Chiappe, 2007, for a review). For example, "My surgeon is a butcher" has a very different meaning to, "My butcher is a surgeon". This phenomenon can be accounted for with Kintsch's (2000) predication model. According to the model, only those features of the predicate (second noun) relevant to the argument (first noun) are selected, and so changing the argument changes the features selected.

Kintsch's predication model also explains an interesting finding reported by McGlone and Manfredi (2001). Suppose we ask people to understand a metaphor such as, "My lawyer was a shark". According to the model, it should take longer to understand that metaphor when literal properties of sharks (e.g., "has fins"; "can swim") irrelevant to its metaphorical meaning have recently been activated. As predicted, McGlone and Manfredi found that the above metaphor took longer to understand when preceded by a contextual sentence emphasising the literal meaning of "shark" (e.g., "Sharks can swim").

According to Kintsch's predication model, our understanding of metaphors depends on our ability to *inhibit* semantic properties of the predicate that are irrelevant to the argument. There is much evidence that individuals high in working memory capacity (discussed later in the chapter) are better than those low in working memory capacity at inhibiting potentially distracting information (see Chiappe & Chiappe, 2007, for a review). As predicted, Chiappe and Chiappe found that participants with high working memory capacity interpreted metaphors 23% faster than those with low working memory capacity, and their interpretations were of superior quality.

Evaluation

There has been reasonable progress in understanding the processes involved in metaphor comprehension. The traditional notion that literal meanings are always accessed before non-literal ones is inadequate. What actually happens is far more *flexible* than was assumed in the standard pragmatic model. Selection of the appropriate features of the predicate is crucial for metaphor understanding. It depends on various factors such as salience, prior experience, immediate context, and individual differences in working memory capacity.

An important limitation of much research on metaphor comprehension is that insufficient attention has been paid to individual differences. For example, the finding that it takes longer to decide that sentences are literally false with metaphors than with scrambled metaphors (Glucksberg, 2003) suggests that metaphorical meanings are accessed automatically. Kazmerski, Blasko, and Dessalegn (2003) found that high-IQ individuals accessed metaphorical meanings automatically but low-IQ ones did not.

Common ground

Grice (1975) argued that speakers and listeners generally conform to the co-operativeness principle – they work together to ensure mutual understanding. In that connection, it is important for speakers and listeners to share a common ground (shared knowledge and beliefs between speaker and listener). Listeners expect that speakers will mostly refer to information and knowledge that is in the common ground, and they may experience comprehension difficulties if that is not the case.

Keysar (e.g., Keysar, Barr, Balin, & Brauner, 2000) argued for a different theoretical approach in his perspective adjustment model. He assumed that it can be very effortful for listeners to keep working out the common ground existing between them and the speaker. Instead, listeners use a rapid and non-effortful **egocentric heuristic**, which is "a tendency to consider as potential referents [what is being referred to] objects that are not in the common ground, but are potential referents from one's own perspective" (p. 32). Information about common ground is calculated more slowly and is used to correct misunderstandings resulting from use of the egocentric heuristic.

Listeners expect that speakers will mostly refer to information and knowledge that is in the common ground. They may experience comprehension difficulties if that is not the case. © Don Hammond/Design Pics/Corbis.

Evidence

Keysar et al. (2000) used a set-up in which a speaker and a listener were on opposite sides of a vertical array containing 16 slots arranged in a 4×4 pattern. Some slots contained objects (e.g., candles, toy cars) and the listener's task was to obey the speaker's instructions to move one of the objects. Some slots were blocked so the listener could see the objects in them but the speaker could not. For example, in one display, the listener could see three candles of different sizes but the speaker could see only two, with the smallest candle blocked from view. What will happen when the speaker says, "Now put the small candle above it?" If the listener uses only common ground information, he/she will move the smaller of the two candles that the speaker can see. However, if the listener uses the egocentric heuristic, he/she may initially consider the candle the speaker cannot see.

Keysar et al.'s findings supported the perspective adjustment model. The initial eye movements were often directed to the object they could see but the speaker could not, indicating that they did not consider only the common ground. In addition, listeners reached for the object only they could see on 20% of trials, and actually picked it up on 75% of those trials.

Subsequent research has suggested that we rarely make use of the egocentric heuristic. Heller, Grodner, and Tanenhaus (2008) pointed out that there was a systematic bias in the study by Keysar et al. (2000), in that the object only the listener could see was a better fit to the speaker's instructions than was the intended target object. Heller et al. carried out a similar study eliminating that bias. Their participants rapidly fixated the target object regardless of the presence of an object only the listener could see. Thus, the participants seemed to have no trouble in making use of the common ground.

Barr (2008) found that listeners expected speakers to refer to objects in the common ground. However, listeners took longer to fixate the target object when there was a competitor object visible only to them. How can we interpret these findings? According to Barr, listeners' apparent egocentrism reflects processing limitations rather than neglect of the speaker's perspective. The processing limitations can cause brief interference effects, but listeners rapidly focus on the common ground.

Shintel and Keysar (2007) discussed evidence that listeners expect speakers to use the same term repeatedly when referring to a given object. For example, if a speaker describes an object to us as an "elephant rattle" on one occasion we expect him/her to use the same description in future. This could occur because listeners expect speakers to maximise the common ground between them by using the same terms repeatedly and so adhering to the co-operativeness principle. However, there is an alternative explanation. Perhaps listeners simply expect speakers to be *consistent* in their utterances regardless of any considerations of the common ground.

Shintel and Keysar (2007) tested the above hypotheses by having participants watch a video of the experimenter describing a given object as an "elephant rattle" or a "baby rattle" to another participant in the absence of the experimenter (the no-knowledge condition). Other participants watched the video in the presence of the experimenter (knowledge condition). After that, the participants were instructed by the experimenter to move the same object that was described in the same way as on the video or in a different way. The key finding was that it took listeners longer to fixate the target object when it was described differently in both the knowledge and no-knowledge conditions (see Figure 10.5). Thus, listeners expected the experimenter to be consistent whether or not common ground had been established between them and the experimenter.

Evaluation

There has been theoretical progress in this area. We now know that the distinction between common ground and egocentric heuristic accounts is oversimplified and masks a complex reality. Listeners generally expect that speakers will make use of the common ground and the co-operativeness principle. However, processing limitations sometimes prevent listeners from focusing only on the common ground. In addition, findings that seem to suggest that listeners

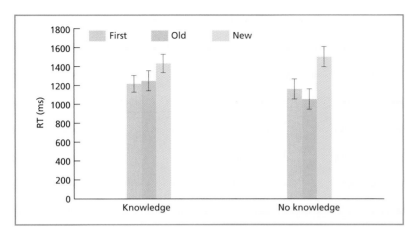

Figure 10.5 Latencies (in ms) of first fixations on the target stimulus as a function of whether it was described as previously (old vs. new) and whether or not the experimenter was present when they heard the target described before (knowledge vs. no knowledge). There were two control conditions (first) in which the target stimulus had not previously been described. From Shintel and Keysar (2007), Copyright © 2007 American Psychological Association. Reproduced with permission.

expect speakers to adhere to the co-operativeness principle are sometimes better explained in terms of an expectation that speakers will be consistent (Shintel & Keysar, 2007).

What are the limitations of research in this area? First, the situations used in several studies are highly artificial. For example, it is unusual in everyday life for objects present immediately in front of a speaker and a listener to differ in their perceptual accessibility, as happened in the studies by Keysar et al. (2000) and Heller et al. (2008). Such situations may make it hard for listeners to focus on the common ground. Second, we probably make more use of the common ground and less of the egocentric heuristic when listening to someone whose beliefs are very familiar to us (e.g., a good friend) than a stranger in the laboratory. Third, it is plausible to assume that listeners typically make as much use of the common ground as their processing limitations will permit, but this assumption has not been tested directly.

INDIVIDUAL DIFFERENCES: WORKING MEMORY CAPACITY

There are considerable individual differences in almost all complex cognitive activities. Accordingly, theories based on the assumption that everyone comprehends text in the same way are unlikely to be correct. One of the most influential theories of individual differences in comprehension was put forward by Just and Carpenter (e.g., 1992). They assumed that there are individual differences in the capacity of working memory, by which they meant a system used for both storage and processing (see Chapter 6). Within the theory, working memory is used for both storage and processing during comprehension. Storage and processing demands can be heavy, and working memory has strictly limited capacity. As a consequence, individuals high in working memory capacity perform better on comprehension tasks than those low in working memory capacity.

The most used method of assessing working memory capacity is a task devised by Daneman and Carpenter (1980). Participants read a number of sentences for comprehension, and then try to recall the final word of each sentence. The largest number of sentences for which a participant can recall all the final words more than 50% of the time is his/her **reading span**,

KEY TERM

reading span: the largest number of sentences read for comprehension from which an individual can recall all the final words more than 50% of the time.

which is a measure of working memory capacity. It is assumed that the processes used in comprehending the sentences require a smaller proportion of the available working memory capacity of those with a large capacity. As a result, they have more capacity for retaining the last words of the sentences.

Operation span is another measure of working memory capacity. Participants are presented with a series of items (e.g., IS (4 × 2) − 3 = 5? TABLE), and have to answer each arithmetical question and remember all the last words. **Operation span** is the maximum number of items for which participants can remember all the last words. It correlates as highly with language comprehension as does reading span. These findings suggest that reading span and operation span both assess individual differences in general processing resources needed for text comprehension (and other cognitive tasks).

What accounts for individual differences in working memory capacity? One of the most influential theories was put forward by Barrett, Tugade, and Engle (2004). They discussed a range of research findings suggesting that an important difference between individuals low and high in working memory capacity is that the latter have greater capacity to control attention. Support for that hypothesis was reported by Kane, Brown, McVay, Silvia, Myin-Germeys, and Kwapil (2007). Their participants were contacted eight times a day, and reported immediately whether their thoughts had strayed from their current activity. During challenging activities requiring much concentration, individuals high in working memory capacity reported more ability to maintain on-task thoughts and to avoid mind wandering.

Evidence

How well do reading span and operation span predict comprehension performance? This issue was addressed by Daneman and Merikle (1996) in a meta-analysis of data from 77 studies. There were two key findings. First, measures of working memory capacity (e.g., reading span; operation span) predicted comprehension

performance better than measures of storage capacity (e.g., digit span; word span). Second, comprehension performance was predicted as well by operation span as by reading span. Thus, the ability of reading span to predict comprehension performance is not simply due to the fact that reading span itself involves sentence comprehension.

Just and Carpenter (1992) found that whether the initial syntactic parsing of a sentence is affected by meaning depends on working memory capacity. They examined reading times for sentences such as, "The evidence examined by the lawyer shocked the jury", and, "The defendant examined by the lawyer shocked the jury". "The evidence" (an inanimate noun) is unlikely to be doing the examining, whereas "the defendant" (an animate noun) might well. Accordingly, the actual syntactic structure of the sentence should come as more of a surprise to readers given the second sentence if they attend rapidly to meaning. Gaze durations on the crucial phrase (e.g., "by the lawyer") were affected by the animate/inanimate noun manipulation for readers with high working memory capacity but not those with low working memory capacity.

Later in the chapter we discuss the controversy concerning the extent to which readers draw elaborative inferences (those that add details not contained in the text). Calvo (2001) considered the role of individual differences in working memory capacity. Target sentences (e.g., "The pupil studied for an hour approximately") followed a relevant sentence (predicting sentence) or an irrelevant sentence (control sentence). It was assumed that individuals who form elaborative inferences would find it easier to process the target sentence when it was preceded by a predicting sentence. Individuals with high working memory capacity spent less

KEY TERM

operation span: the maximum number of items (arithmetical questions + words) from which an individual can recall all the last words.

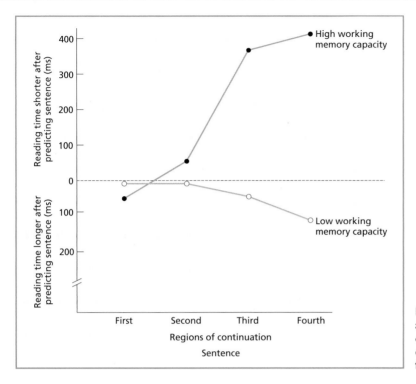

Figure 10.6 Effect of a predicting sentence on reading time of a continuation sentence. Data from Calvo (2001).

time on integrating information from the target sentence when it followed a predicting sentence, whereas those with low working memory capacity did not (see Figure 10.6). The implication is that high-capacity individuals rapidly drew elaborative inferences but low-capacity individuals did not.

Working memory capacity is related to the ability to inhibit or suppress unwanted information (Barrett et al., 2004). The importance of this ability was shown by Gernsbacher, Varner, and Faust (1990). Participants decided whether a given word was related to a previous sentence. The crucial condition was one in which the word was related to an inappropriate meaning of one of the words in the sentence (e.g., "ace" following "He dug with the spade"). When the word followed the sentence by 850 ms, only individuals with low comprehension skills showed an interference effect. Thus, individuals with high comprehension skills can suppress irrelevant information more efficiently than those with low comprehension skills.

Sachez and Wiley (2006) considered the role of working memory capacity in the ability to inhibit irrelevant processing. They studied the seductive details effect, which is exemplified in the tendency for comprehension of a text to be reduced if accompanied by irrelevant illustrations. Individuals low in working memory capacity showed a greater seductive details effect on text comprehension. In addition, their eye fixations indicated that they looked at the irrelevant illustrations more often and for longer periods of time.

Additional evidence that those high in working memory capacity are better at focusing attention on relevant information was reported by Kaakinen, Hyönä, and Keenan (2003). Participants read a text on rare diseases containing a mixture of relevant and irrelevant information, and only those with high working memory capacity allocated extra time to reading the relevant information during the initial reading of the text.

Prat, Keller, and Just (2007) carried out a neuroimaging study in which individuals low and high in working memory capacity (assessed by reading span) read sentences of varying complexity for comprehension. Those high in working memory capacity were generally faster and more accurate in their comprehension performance. In addition, the neuroimaging evidence revealed three important differences between those low and high in working memory capacity:

(1) *Efficiency*: High-capacity individuals were more efficient. They had less activation in bilateral middle frontal and right lingual gyri, suggesting that their planning abilities were more efficient than those of low-capacity individuals.

(2) *Adaptability*: The effects of word frequency on brain activation were greater in high-capacity individuals in several brain areas (e.g., middle frontal; inferior occipital).

(3) *Synchronisation*: High-capacity individuals had greater synchronisation of brain activation across several brain regions (e.g., left temporal; left inferior frontal; left parietal; right occipital). This was especially the case when the sentences presented on the comprehension task were complex.

What do these findings mean? Individuals high in working memory capacity process sentences in a more adaptable and synchronised way, which is associated with greater efficiency. As a result, their comprehension abilities are greater.

Evaluation

One of the greatest strengths of Just and Carpenter's (1992) theoretical approach is that it emphasised that there are substantial individual differences in the processes used in language comprehension. For example, whether meaning affects initial syntactic parsing (Just & Carpenter, 1992) or whether elaborative inferences are drawn (Calvo, 2001) can depend on individual differences in working memory capacity. For reasons that are not clear to us,

most theorists have studiously avoided incorporating individual differences into their theories. Of particular importance for the future is the cognitive neuroscience approach (e.g., Prat et al., 2007). It offers the prospect of clarifying the processing differences between low- and high-capacity individuals.

What are the limitations of research in this area? First, individuals low and high in working memory capacity also differ in other ways (e.g., reading span correlates about +0.6 with verbal intelligence (Just & Carpenter, 1992)). As a result, differences between low- and high-capacity individuals may reflect verbal intelligence rather than simply working memory capacity.

Second, the cognitive processing of low- and high-capacity individuals differs in several ways (Baddeley, 2007). We have focused on differences in attentional control and ability to inhibit irrelevant information. However, high-capacity individuals also have larger vocabularies than low-capacity individuals (Chiappe & Chiappe, 2007), and it is often hard to know precisely why high-capacity individuals' comprehension performance surpasses that of low-capacity individuals.

DISCOURSE PROCESSING

So far we have focused mainly on the processes involved in understanding individual sentences. In real life, however, we are generally presented with connected **discourse** (written text or speech at least several sentences in length). What are the main differences? According to Graesser, Millis, and Zwaan (1997, p. 164), "A sentence out of context is nearly always ambiguous, whereas a sentence in a discourse context is rarely ambiguous. . . . Both stories and everyday experiences include people performing actions in pursuit of goals, events that present obstacles

> **KEY TERM**
>
> **discourse:** connected text or speech generally at least several sentences long.

to these goals, conflicts between people, and emotional reactions."

We draw inferences most of the time when reading or listening to someone, even though we are generally unaware of doing so. Indeed, if a writer or speaker spelled everything out in such detail that there was no need to draw any inferences, you would probably be bored to tears! Here is an example of inference drawing taken from Rumelhart and Ortony (1977):

(1)   Mary heard the ice-cream van coming.
(2)   She remembered the pocket money.
(3)   She rushed into the house.

You probably made various inferences while reading the story. For example, Mary wanted to buy some ice-cream; buying ice-cream costs money; Mary had some pocket money in the house; and Mary had only a limited amount of time to get hold of some money before the ice-cream van appeared. Note that none of these inferences is explicitly stated.

There are three main types of inferences: logical inferences, bridging inferences, and elaborative inferences. **Logical inferences** depend only on the meanings of words. For example, we can infer that anyone who is a widow is female. **Bridging inferences** establish coherence between the current part of the text and the preceding text, and so are also known as backward inferences. **Elaborative inferences** embellish or add details to the text by making use of our world knowledge. They are sometimes known as forward inferences because they often involve anticipating the future. As Harley (2008) pointed out, a major theoretical problem is to work out how we typically manage to access *relevant* information from our huge store of world knowledge when forming elaborative inferences.

Readers generally draw logical and bridging inferences because they are essential for understanding. What is more controversial is the extent to which non-essential or elaborative inferences are drawn automatically. Singer (1994) compared the time taken to verify a test sentence (e.g., "A dentist pulled a tooth") following one of three contexts: (1) the information had already been explicitly presented; (2) a bridging inference was needed to understand the test sentence; and (3) an elaborative inference was needed. Verification times in conditions (1) and (2) were fast and the same, suggesting that the bridging inference was drawn automatically during comprehension. However, verification times were significantly slower in condition (3), presumably because the elaborative inference was not drawn automatically.

Garrod and Terras (2000) studied the processes involved in bridging inferences. For a start, let us consider the following two sentences:

Keith drove to London yesterday.
The car kept overheating.

You had no trouble (hopefully!) in linking these sentences based on the assumption that Keith drove to London in a car that kept overheating. Garrod and Terras argued that there are two possible explanations for the way in which the bridging inference could be made. First, reading the verb "drove" in the first sentence may activate concepts relating to driving (especially "car"). Second, readers may form a representation of the entire situation described in the first sentence, and then relate information in the second sentence to that representation. The crucial difference is that the sentential context is irrelevant in the first explanation but is highly relevant in the second explanation.

Garrod and Terras (2000) tried to distinguish between these two possibilities. They recorded eye movements while participants read a sentence such as, "However, she was disturbed by a loud scream from the back of the class and the pen dropped on the floor". This sentence was preceded by a sentence about a teacher writing a letter or writing on a blackboard. If context is important, participants should have found it harder to process the word "pen" when the previous sentence was about writing on a blackboard rather than writing a letter. In fact, the initial fixation on the word "pen" was uninfluenced by context. However, participants spent longer going back over the sentence containing the word "pen" when the preceding context was inappropriate.

What do the above findings mean? According to Garrod and Terras, there are *two* stages in forming bridging inferences. The first stage is *bonding*, a low-level process involving the automatic activation of words from the preceding sentence. The second stage is *resolution*, which involves making sure the overall interpretation is consistent with the contextual information. Resolution is influenced by context but bonding is not.

Anaphor resolution

Perhaps the simplest form of bridging inference is **anaphor resolution**, in which a pronoun or noun has to be identified with a previously mentioned noun or noun phrase. Here is an example: "Fred sold John his lawnmower, and then he sold him his garden hose". It requires a bridging inference to realise that "he" refers to Fred rather than John. How do people make the appropriate anaphoric inference? Sometimes gender makes the task very easy (e.g., "Juliet sold John her lawnmower, and then she sold him her garden hose"). Sometimes the number of the noun (singular versus plural) provides a useful cue (e.g., "Juliet and her friends sold John their lawnmower, and then they sold him their garden hose").

Evidence that gender information makes anaphor resolution easier was reported by Arnold, Eisenband, Brown-Schmidt, and Trueswell (2000). Participants looked at pictures while listening to text. Gender information ("he" or "she") was used more rapidly to look at the appropriate picture when it contained a male and a female character than when it contained two same-sex characters.

Anaphor resolution is also easier when pronouns are in the expected order. Harley (2001) provided the following example:

(1) Vlad sold Dirk his broomstick because he hated it.
(2) Vlad sold Dirk his broomstick because he needed it.

The first sentence is easy to understand because "he" refers to the first-named man (i.e., Vlad). In contrast, the second sentence is relatively hard to understand because "he" refers to the second-named man (i.e., Dirk).

Nieuwland and van Berkum (2006) asked participants low and high in working memory capacity to read sentences varying in the extent to which the context biased one interpretation of the pronoun:

(1) *No bias*: Anton forgave Michael the problem because his car was a wreck.
(2) *Strong bias*: The businessman called the dealer just as he left the trendy club.

Nieuwland and van Berkum used event-related potentials (ERPs; see Glossary) to assess pronoun processing. There were two main findings (see Figure 10.7). First, individuals high in working memory capacity were more likely to take account of the two possible interpretations of the pronoun, indicating that they were more sensitive to subtleties of language. Second, there was a smaller probability of processing both

KEY TERM

anaphor resolution: working out the referent of a pronoun or noun by relating it to some previously mentioned noun or noun phrase.

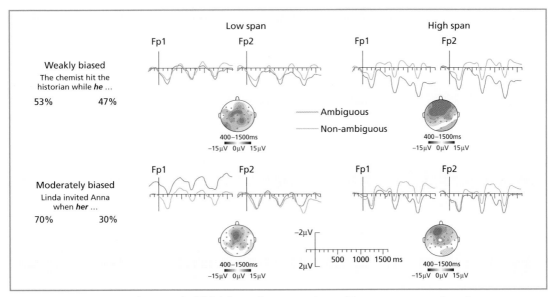

Figure 10.7 Event-related potentials (ERPs) for ambiguous and unambiguous pronouns when the context was weakly or strongly biased with individuals high or low in working memory capacity (high vs. low span). The impact of ambiguity on ERPs was greatest with high span individuals and a weakly biased context (top right of figure). Fp1 and Fp2 are electrode positions. From Nieuwland and van Berkum (2006). Reproduced with permission from MIT Press.

interpretations when the contextual bias was strong.

How do we go about the business of interpreting anaphors? According to Badecker and Straub's (2002) interactive parallel constraint model, we use several different sources of information at the same time. It is more difficult to decide on the most appropriate interpretation of an anaphor when competing interpretations create conflict (e.g., they involve the correct gender and fit with the sentence context).

Constructionist approach

Everyone agrees that various elaborative inferences are made while we read text or listen to speech. However, there has been much theoretical controversy concerning the number and nature of the elaborative inferences typically drawn. The constructionist approach originally proposed by Bransford (e.g., Bransford, Barclay, & Franks, 1972) represents a major theoretical position that influenced subsequent theoretical accounts (e.g., the construction–integration model, the event-indexing model, and the experiential-simulations approach discussed later). Bransford argued that readers typically construct a relatively complete "mental model" of the situation and events referred to in the text. A key implication of the constructionist approach is that numerous elaborative inferences are typically drawn while reading a text.

Most early research supporting the constructionist position involved using memory tests to assess inference drawing. For example, Bransford et al. (1972) presented participants with sentences such as, "Three turtles rested on a floating log, and a fish swam beneath them". They argued that participants would draw the inference that the fish swam under the log. To test this, some participants on a subsequent recognition-memory test were given the sentence, "Three turtles rested on a floating log, and a fish swam beneath it". Most participants were confident this inference was the original sentence. Indeed, their level of confidence was as high as it was when the original sentence was re-presented on the memory test!

Bransford et al. concluded that inferences from text are typically stored in memory just like information actually presented in the text.

Memory tests provide only an *indirect* measure of inferential processes. The potential problem is that any inferences found on a memory test may be made at the time of test rather than during reading. Indeed, many inferences found on memory tests reflect reconstructive processes occurring during retrieval. Evidence that elaborative inferences are often not drawn during initial reading is discussed in the next section in connection with the minimalist hypothesis. Before proceeding, however, note that the extent to which elaborative inferences are drawn depends very much on the reader's goals. Calvo, Castillo, and Schmalhofer (2006) instructed some participants to read sentences for comprehension, whereas others were explicitly told to try to anticipate what might happen next. Participants in the latter condition drew more elaborative inferences than those in the former condition. Even when participants reading for comprehension drew elaborative inferences, they did so more slowly than those in the anticipation condition.

Minimalist hypothesis

The constructionist position has come under increasing attack over the years. McKoon and Ratcliff (1992) challenged this approach with their *minimalist hypothesis*: "In the absence of specific, goal-directed strategic processes, inferences of only two kinds are constructed: those that establish locally coherent representations of the parts of a text that are processed concurrently and those that rely on information that is quickly and easily available" (p. 440).

Here are the main assumptions made by McKoon and Ratcliff (1992):

- Inferences are either automatic or strategic (goal directed).
- Some automatic inferences establish local coherence (two or three sentences making sense on their own or in combination with easily available general knowledge). These

inferences involve parts of the text in working memory at the same time (this is working memory in the sense of a general-purpose capacity rather than the Baddeley multiple-component working memory system discussed in Chapter 6).
- Other automatic inferences rely on information readily available because it is explicitly stated in the text.
- Strategic inferences are formed in pursuit of the reader's goals; they sometimes serve to produce local coherence.
- Most elaborative inferences are made at recall rather than during reading.

The greatest difference between the minimalist hypothesis and the constructionist position concerns the number of automatic inferences formed. Constructionists claim that numerous automatic inferences are drawn in reading. In contrast, those favouring the minimalist hypothesis argue that there are strong constraints on the number of inferences generated automatically.

Evidence

Dosher and Corbett (1982) obtained evidence supporting the distinction between automatic and strategic inferences. They focused on instrumental inferences (e.g., "Mary stirred her coffee" has "spoon" as its instrumental inference). In order to decide whether participants generated these instrumental inferences during reading, Dosher and Corbett used an unusual procedure. The time taken to name the colour in which a word is printed is slowed down if the word has recently been activated. Thus, if presentation of the sentence, "Mary stirred her coffee", activates the word "spoon", this should increase the time taken to name the colour in which the word "spoon" is printed. There was no evidence that the instrumental inferences had been formed with normal reading instructions. However, those inferences were formed when the participants guessed the instrument in each sentence as it was presented.

What do the above findings mean? First, whether an inference is drawn can depend on the reader's intentions or goals, which is one of the central assumptions of the minimalist hypothesis. In other words, strategic inferences were formed but automatic ones were not. Second, the findings go against the constructionist position. We need to infer the instrument used in stirring coffee to achieve full understanding, but such instrumental inferences were *not* drawn under normal reading conditions. The findings of Calvo et al. (2006) discussed earlier also support the hypothesis that the reader's goals influence whether elaborative inferences are drawn.

McKoon and Ratcliff (1992) assumed that automatic inferences are drawn to establish local coherence for information contained in working memory. However, global inferences (inferences connecting widely separated pieces of textual information) are not drawn automatically. They presented short texts containing a global goal (e.g., assassinating a president) and one or two local or subordinate goals (e.g., using a rifle; using hand grenades). Active use of local and global inferences was tested by presenting a test word after each text, with participants instructed to decide rapidly whether it had appeared in the text.

What did McKoon and Ratcliff (1992) find? Local inferences were drawn automatically, but global inferences were not. These findings are more consistent with the minimalist hypothesis than with the constructionist position, in which no distinction is drawn between local and global inferences.

McKoon and Ratcliff (1992) pointed out that most studies reporting large numbers of elaborative inferences had used memory tests to assess inference drawing. Thus, the inferences may have been drawn at the time of the memory test rather than during reading. Supporting evidence was reported by Dooling and Christiaansen (1977). Some participants read a story about a ruthless dictator called Gerald Martin, and one week later were given a test of recognition memory. They were told just before the memory test that the story had really been about Adolf Hitler. This led them mistakenly to "recognise" sentences relevant to Hitler that

had not appeared in the original story. The inferences about Hitler leading to false recognition could not have been drawn while the story was being read but must have been drawn just before or during the memory test. A somewhat similar study by Sulin and Dooling (1974) is discussed shortly.

Readers sometimes draw more inferences during reading than predicted by the minimalist hypothesis. For example, it is assumed by the minimalist hypothesis that readers do not generally infer the main goals. Poynor and Morris (2003) compared texts in which the goal of the protagonist [principal character] was explicitly stated or only implied. Later in the text there was a sentence in which the protagonist carried out an action consistent or inconsistent with his/her goal. Readers took longer to read a sentence describing an inconsistent action than one describing a consistent action, regardless of whether the goal was explicit or implicit. Thus, readers inferred the protagonist's goal even when it was only implied.

According to the minimalist hypothesis, readers do not draw predictive inferences, which involve inferring what will happen next on the basis of the current situation. Contrary evidence was reported by Campion (2004), who presented readers with texts such as the following:

> It was a pitch black night and a gigantic iceberg floated in the ocean, emerging by only five metres. The helmsman was attentive, but the ship advanced towards the iceberg and ran into it, causing a terrible noise.

What do you think happened next? Campion found that readers drew the predictive inference that the ship sank. However, this inference was made somewhat tentatively. This was shown by the additional finding that readers were slow to read the follow-up sentence: "What a big mistake, as the ship went down at sea." Campion pointed out that predictive inferences were not drawn in previous research when predictable events were only weakly associated with text information in the reader's knowledge.

Individual differences have been ignored in most of the research. Murray and Burke (2003) considered inference drawing in participants with high, moderate, or low reading skill. They were tested on predictive inferences (e.g., inferring "break" when presented with a sentence such as "The angry husband threw the fragile vase against the wall"). All three groups showed some evidence of drawing these predictive inferences. However, these inferences were only drawn automatically by participants with high reading skill. The existence of such individual differences points to a limitation of the minimalist and constructionist approaches.

Evaluation

The minimalist hypothesis clarifies which inferences are drawn automatically when someone is reading a text. In contrast, constructionist theorists often argue that inferences needed to understand fully the situation described in a text are drawn automatically. This is rather vague, as there could be differences in opinion over exactly what information needs to be encoded for full understanding. There is evidence that the distinction between automatic and strategic inferences is an important one. Another strength of the minimalist hypothesis is the notion that many inferences will be drawn only if consistent with the reader's goals. Finally, many of the studies reporting more elaborative inferences than predicted by the minimalist hypothesis are flawed because of their reliance on memory tests, which provide a very indirect assessment of processing during reading.

What are the limitations of the minimalist hypothesis? First, we cannot always predict accurately from the hypothesis *which* inferences will be drawn. For example, automatic inferences are drawn if the necessary information is "readily available", but how do we establish the precise degree of availability of some piece of information? Second, the minimalist hypothesis is *too* minimalist and somewhat underestimates

the inferences drawn from text (e.g., Campion, 2004; Poynor & Morris, 2003). Third, neither the minimalist nor the constructionist approach provides an adequate account of individual differences in inference drawing (e.g., Murray & Burke, 2003).

We end this evaluation section with the following reasonable conclusion proposed by Graesser et al. (1997, p. 183): "The minimalist hypothesis is probably correct when the reader is very quickly reading the text, when the text lacks global coherence, and when the reader has very little background knowledge. The constructionist theory is on the mark when the reader is attempting to comprehend the text for enjoyment or mastery at a more leisurely pace."

STORY PROCESSING

If someone asks us to describe a story or book we have read recently, we discuss the major events and themes and leave out the minor details. Thus, our description is highly *selective*, depending on the meaning extracted from the story while reading it and on selective processes operating at retrieval. Imagine our questioner's reaction if our description were *not* selective, but simply involved recalling random sentences from the story!

Gomulicki (1956) showed how selectively stories are comprehended and remembered. One group of participants wrote a précis (a summary) of a story visible in front of them, and a second group recalled the story from memory. A third group was given each précis and recall, and found it very hard to tell them apart. Thus, story memory resembles a précis in that people focus on important information.

Our processing of stories or other texts involves relating the information in the text to relevant structured knowledge stored in long-term memory. What we process in stories, how we process information in stories, and what we remember from stories we have read all depend in part on such stored information. We will initially consider theories emphasising the importance of **schemas**, which are well-integrated packets of knowledge about the world, events, people, and actions. After that, we will turn to theories identifying in more detail the processes occurring when someone reads or listens to a story.

Schema theories

The schemas stored in long-term memory include what are often referred to as *scripts* and *frames*. Scripts deal with knowledge about events and consequences of events. For example, Schank and Abelson (1977) referred to a restaurant script, which contains information about the usual sequence of events involved in having a restaurant meal. In contrast, frames are knowledge structures relating to some aspect of the world (e.g., building). They consist of fixed structural information (e.g., has floors and walls) and slots for variable information (e.g., materials from which the building is constructed). Schemas are important because they contain much of the knowledge used to facilitate understanding of what we hear and read.

Schemas allow us to form *expectations*. In a restaurant, for example, we expect to be shown to a table, to be given a menu by the waiter or waitress, to order food and drink, and so on. Schemas help us to make the world relatively predictable, because our expectations are generally confirmed.

Evidence that schemas can influence story comprehension was reported by Bransford and Johnson (1972, p. 722). Here is part of the story they used:

The procedure is quite simple. First, you arrange items into different groups. Of course one pile may be sufficient depending on how much there is to do. If you have to go somewhere else due to lack of facilities, that is the next step; otherwise, you are pretty well set. It is important not to overdo things. That is, it is better to do too few things at once than too many.

What on earth was that all about? Participants hearing the passage in the absence of a title rated it as incomprehensible and recalled an average of only 2.8 idea units. In contrast, those supplied beforehand with the title "Washing clothes" found it easy to understand and recalled 5.8 idea units on average. Relevant schema knowledge helped passage comprehension rather than simply acting as a retrieval cue. We know this because participants receiving the title *after* hearing the passage but *before* recall recalled only 2.6 idea units on average.

Bartlett's theory

Bartlett (1932) was the first psychologist to argue persuasively that schemas play an important role in determining what we remember from stories. According to him, memory is affected not only by the presented story but also by the participant's store of relevant prior schematic knowledge. Bartlett had the ingenious idea of presenting people with stories producing a *conflict* between what was presented to them and their prior knowledge. If, for example, people read a story taken from a different culture, prior knowledge might produce distortions in the remembered version of the story, making it more conventional and acceptable from the standpoint of their own cultural background. Bartlett's findings supported his predictions. A substantial proportion of the recall errors made the story read more like a conventional English story. He used the term **rationalisation** to refer to this type of error.

Bartlett (1932) assumed that memory for the precise material presented is forgotten over time, whereas memory for the underlying

> ### KEY TERMS
>
> **schemas:** organised packets of information about the world, events, or people stored in long-term memory.
> **rationalisation:** in Bartlett's theory, the tendency in recall of stories to produce errors conforming to the cultural expectations of the rememberer.

schemas is not. As a result, rationalisation errors (which depend on schematic knowledge) should increase at longer retention intervals. Bartlett investigated this prediction using stories from the North American Indian culture, including the famous story, 'The War of the Ghosts'. There were numerous rationalisation errors. However, Bartlett failed to give very specific instructions: "I thought it best, for the purposes of these experiments, to try to influence the subjects' procedure as little as possible" (p. 78). As a result, some distortions observed by Bartlett were due to conscious guessing rather than deficient memory. This was shown by Gauld and Stephenson (1967) using 'The War of the Ghosts'. Instructions stressing the need for accurate recall (and thus presumably reducing deliberate guessing) eliminated almost half the errors usually obtained.

In spite of problems with Bartlett's procedures, evidence from well-controlled studies has confirmed his major findings. This was done by Bergman and Roediger (1999) using 'The War of the Ghosts'. They found that participants had more rationalisation errors in their recall of the story after six months than after one week or 15 minutes.

Sulin and Dooling (1974) also supported Bartlett's findings. They presented some participants with a story about Gerald Martin: "Gerald Martin strove to undermine the existing government to satisfy his political ambitions.... He became a ruthless, uncontrollable dictator. The ultimate effect of his rule was the downfall of his country" (p. 256). Other participants were given the same story, but the main character was called Adolf Hitler. Those participants presented with the story about Adolf Hitler were much more likely than the other participants to believe incorrectly that they had read the sentence, "He hated the Jews particularly and so persecuted them." Their schematic knowledge about Hitler distorted their recollections of what they had read (see Figure 10.8). As Bartlett (1932) predicted, this type of distortion was more common at a long than a short retention interval, because schematic information is more long-lasting than information contained in the text.

In Sulin and Dooling's (1974) study, participants used their schematic knowledge of Hitler to incorrectly organise the information about the story they had been told. The study revealed how schematic organisation can lead to errors in recall. Photo from the National Archives and Records Administration.

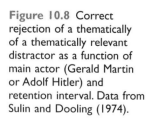

Figure 10.8 Correct rejection of a thematically of a thematically relevant distractor as a function of main actor (Gerald Martin or Adolf Hitler) and retention interval. Data from Sulin and Dooling (1974).

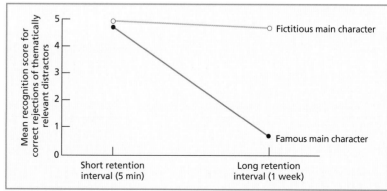

Figure 10.9 The "graduate student's" room used by Brewer and Treyens (1981) in their experiment. Photo reproduced with kind permission of Professor Brewer.

Most of the research discussed so far used artificially constructed texts and the participants deliberately learned the material. Brewer and Treyens (1981) wondered whether schemas influence memory when information is acquired incidentally in a naturalistic situation. Their participants spent 35 seconds in a room resembling a graduate student's office before the experiment proper took place (see Figure 10.9). The room contained schema-consistent objects you would expect to find in a graduate student's office (e.g., desk, calendar, eraser, pencils) and schema-inconsistent objects (e.g., a skull, a toy top). Some schema-consistent objects (e.g., books) were omitted.

After the participants moved to another room, they were unexpectedly tested on their memory for the objects in the first room. Many of them initially provided written free recall of all the objects they could remember, followed by a recognition memory test including words referring to objects, some of which had been present in the room and some of which had not. There were three main findings:

(1) Participants recalled more schema-consistent than schema-inconsistent objects for those

that had been present and for those that had not.

(2) Objects that had *not* been present in the room but were "recognised" with high confidence were nearly all highly schema-consistent (e.g., books, filing cabinet). This is clear evidence for schemas leading to errors in memory.

(3) Most participants recognised many more objects than they recalled. The objects recognised with high confidence that were most likely to have been recalled were ones very consistent with the room schema (e.g., typewriter). This suggests that the schema was used as a retrieval mechanism to facilitate recall.

Bartlett (1932) assumed that memorial distortions occur mainly because of schema-driven reconstructive processes operating at retrieval. However, we have seen that schemas can influence comprehension processes (Bransford & Johnson, 1972) when a story is very difficult to understand. In addition, as Bartlett predicted, schemas often influence the retrieval of information from long-term memory. For example, Anderson and Pichert (1978) asked participants to read a story from the perspective of a burglar or of someone interested in buying a home. After they had recalled the story, they shifted to the alternative perspective and recalled the story again. On the second recall, participants recalled more information that was important only to the second perspective or schema than they had done on the first recall (see Figure 10.10).

Altering the perspective produced a shift in the schematic knowledge accessed by the participants (e.g., from knowledge of what burglars are interested in to knowledge of what potential house buyers are interested in). Accessing different schematic knowledge enhanced recall, and thus provides support for the notion of schema-driven retrieval.

Disorders of schema-based memory

Schema theories assume that the information stored in semantic memory is hierarchically

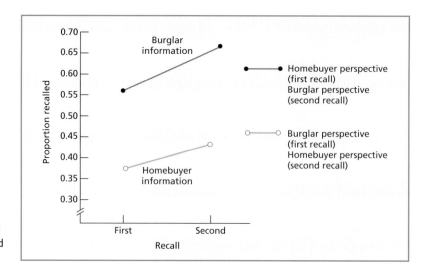

Figure 10.10 Recall as a function of perspective at the time of retrieval. Based on data from Anderson and Pichert (1978).

organised. At the upper level of the hierarchy, there are relatively large structures involving schemas and scripts. At the lower level, there are more specific units of information. If that assumption is correct, we might expect some brain-damaged patients would have greater problems with accessing lower-level information than schema- or script-based information. There should also be others who find it harder to use schema or script information than lower-level information.

Which brain-damaged patients have special problems with accessing concept-based information? Many are patients with semantic dementia (see Glossary and Chapter 7). This is a condition involving severe problems accessing the meanings of words and objects but good executive functioning in the early stages of deterioration. Funnell (1996) found that EP, a patient with semantic dementia, retained reasonable access to script knowledge. For example, when the next research appointment was being arranged, EP went to the kitchen and collected her calendar and a ballpoint pen. EP also used a needle correctly when given a button to sew on to a shirt. However, her performance was extremely poor when tested on the meanings of common objects (e.g., ballpoint pen, needle, scissors). On one task, each object was presented with two additional objects, one of which was functionally associated with

the use of the target objects (e.g., the ballpoint pen was presented with a pad of writing paper and a small printed book). She performed at chance level when instructed to select the functionally-associated object.

Similar findings with another semantic dementia patient, KE, were reported by Snowden, Griffiths, and Neary (1994). KE found it difficult to identify and use her own objects when they moved to an unusual location in her home. However, she showed evidence of script memory by carrying out everyday tasks appropriately and by using objects (e.g., clothes pegs) correctly when in their usual location (e.g., her own peg-bag). Other patients with semantic dementia show impaired script memory for relatively simple tasks (e.g., knowing how to cook; cutting the lawn) (Hodges & Patterson, 2007).

What brain-damaged patients have greater problems with accessing script-related information than lower-level knowledge? Scripts typically have a goal-directed quality (e.g., to achieve the goal of having an enjoyable restaurant meal), and executive functioning within the prefrontal cortex is very useful in constructing and implementing goals. Sirigu, Zalla, Pillon, Grafman, Agid, and Dubois (1995) asked patients with prefrontal damage to generate and evaluate several types of script relating to various events. These patients produced as many events as patients with posterior lesions and healthy controls. They also retrieved the relevant actions as rapidly as members of the other two groups. These findings suggested that the prefrontal patients had as much stored information about actions relevant to various events as the other patients and healthy controls. However, they made many mistakes in *ordering* actions within a script and deciding which actions were of most importance to goal achievement. Thus, they had particular problems in *assembling* the actions within a script in the optimal sequence.

Cosentino, Chute, Libon, Moore, and Grossman (2006) studied patients with **fronto-temporal dementia**. This is a condition involving degeneration of the frontal lobe of the brain and often also parts of the temporal lobe, and is generally associated with poor complex planning and sequencing. These patients (as well as those with semantic dementia and healthy controls) were presented with various scripts. Some scripts contained sequencing errors (e.g., dropping fish in a bucket occurring *before* casting the fishing line), whereas others contained semantic or meaning errors (e.g., placing a flower on the hook in a story about fishing). Patients with semantic dementia and healthy controls both made as many sequencing errors as semantic ones (see Figure 10.11). In contrast, the temporo-frontal patients with poor executive functioning failed to detect almost twice as many sequencing errors as semantic ones. Thus, these patients had relatively intact lower-level semantic knowledge of concepts combined with severe impairment of script-based knowledge.

Overall evaluation

Our organised schematic knowledge of the world is used to help text comprehension and recall. In addition, many of the errors and distortions that occur when we try to remember texts or stories are due to the influence of schematic information. There is plentiful evidence of schema-based memory distortions in the laboratory, and such distortions may be even more common in everyday life. For example, we often describe personal events to other people in distorted and exaggerated ways influenced

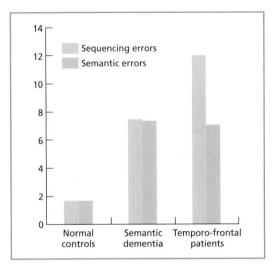

Figure 10.11 Semantic and sequencing errors made by patients with semantic dementia, temporo-frontal patients, and normal controls. Data from Cosentino et al. (2006).

by our schematic knowledge of ourselves or how we would like to be (see Marsh, 2007, for a review).

There is evidence suggesting that some patients have more severely impaired upper-level (schema-based) knowledge than lower-level knowledge, whereas others show the opposite pattern. This double dissociation is consistent with the notion that the knowledge stored in semantic memory is hierarchically organised.

What are the limitations of schema research? First, it has proved hard to identify the characteristics of schemas. For example, there is no straightforward way to work out how much information is contained in a schema or the extent to which that information is integrated.

Second, most versions of schema theory are sadly lacking in testability. If we want to explain text comprehension and memory in terms of the activation of certain schemas, we need *independent* evidence of the existence (and appropriate activation) of those schemas. However, such evidence is generally not available. As Harley (2008, p. 384) pointed out, "The primary accusation against schema and script-based approaches is that they are nothing more than re-descriptions of the data."

Third, the conditions determining *when* a given schema will be activated are unclear. According to schema theory, top-down processes should lead to the generation of numerous inferences during story comprehension. However, as we have seen, such inferences are often not drawn.

Fourth, there are many complexities associated with the double dissociation apparently found in brain-damaged patients. Much more research is needed before such evidence can be fully evaluated.

Kintsch's construction–integration model

Walter Kintsch (1988, 1998) put forward a construction–integration model specifying in some detail the processes involved in comprehending and remembering story information. It incorporates aspects of schema-based theories and Johnson-Laird's mental model approach (see Chapter 14). Kintsch's model assumes story comprehension involves forming propositions. A **proposition** is a statement making an assertion or denial; it can be true or false.

There is much evidence for the importance of propositions. Kintsch and Keenan (1973) varied the number of propositions in sentences while holding the number of words approximately constant. An example of a sentence with four propositions is: "Romulus, the legendary founder of Rome, took the women of the Sabine by force." In contrast, the following sentence contains eight propositions: "Cleopatra's downfall lay in her foolish trust of the fickle political figures of the Roman world." The reading time increased by about one second for each additional proposition. This suggests

that the sentences were processed proposition by proposition almost regardless of the number of words per proposition.

Ratcliff and McKoon (1978) also provided evidence for the existence of propositions. They presented sentences (e.g., "The mausoleum that enshrined the tsar overlooked the square"), followed by a recognition test in which participants decided whether test words had been presented before. For the example given, the test word "square" was recognised faster when the preceding test word was from the same proposition (e.g., "mausoleum") than when it was closer in the sentence but from a different proposition (e.g., "tsar").

The basic structure of Kintsch's construction–integration model is shown in Figure 10.12. According to the model, the following states occur during comprehension:

- Sentences in the text are turned into propositions representing the meaning of the text.
- These propositions are entered into a short-term buffer and form a *propositional net*.
- Each proposition constructed from the text retrieves a few associatively related propositions (including inferences) from long-term memory.
- The propositions constructed from the text plus those retrieved from *long-term memory* jointly form the *elaborated propositional net*. This net usually contains many irrelevant propositions.
- A spreading activation process then selects propositions for the text representation. Clusters of highly interconnected propositions attract most activation and have the greatest probability of inclusion in the text representation. In contrast, irrelevant propositions are discarded. This is the *integration process*.

KEY TERM

proposition: a statement making an assertion or denial and which can be true or false.

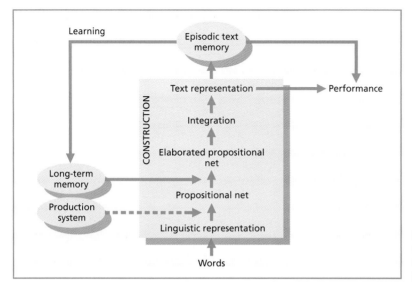

Figure 10.12 The construction–integration model. Adapted from Kintsch (1992).

- The *text representation* is an organised structure stored in *episodic text memory*; information about the relationship between any two propositions is included if they were processed together in the short-term buffer. Within the text representation, it is hard to distinguish between propositions based directly on the text and propositions based on inferences.
- As a result of these various processes, three levels of representation are constructed:
  - Surface representation (the text itself).
  - Propositional representation or text-base (propositions formed from the text).
  - Situation representation (a mental model describing the situation referred to in the text; schemas can be used as building blocks for the construction of situational representations or models).

The construction–integration model may sound rather complex, but its key assumptions are straightforward. The processes involved in the construction of the elaborated propositional net are relatively *inefficient*, with many irrelevant propositions being included. This is basically a bottom-up approach, in that the elaborated propositional net is constructed without taking account of the context provided by the overall theme of the text. After that, the integration process uses contextual information from the text to weed out irrelevant propositions.

How do the assumptions of the construction–integration model differ from those of other models? According to Kintsch, Welsch, Schmalhofer, and Zimny (1990, p. 136), "Most other models of comprehension attempt to specify strong, 'smart' rules which, guided by schemata, arrive at just the right interpretations, activate just the right knowledge, and generate just the right inferences." These strong rules are generally very complex and insufficiently flexible. In contrast, the weak rules incorporated into the construction–integration model are robust and can be used in virtually all situations.

Evidence

Kintsch et al. (1990) tested the assumption that text processing produces three levels of representation ranging from the surface level based directly on the text, through the propositional level, to the situation or mental model level (providing a representation similar to the one that would result from actually experiencing the situation described in the text). Participants read brief descriptions of various situations, and then their recognition memory was tested immediately or at times ranging up to four days later.

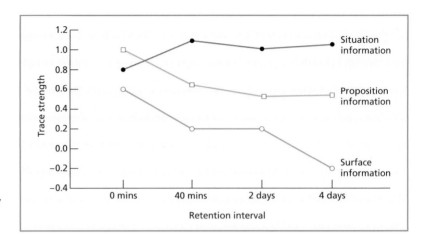

Figure 10.13 Forgetting functions for situation, proposition, and surface information over a four-day period. Adapted from Kintsch et al. (1990).

The forgetting functions for the surface, propositional, and situational representations were distinctively different (see Figure 10.13). There was rapid and complete forgetting of the surface representation, whereas information from the situational representation showed no forgetting over four days. Propositional information differed from situational information in that there was forgetting over time, and it differed from surface information in that there was only partial forgetting. As predicted, the most complete representation of the text's meaning (i.e., the situation representation) was best remembered, and the least complete representation (i.e., the surface representation) was the worst remembered.

Another prediction of the model is that readers with more relevant knowledge should construct deeper levels of representation of a text than less knowledgeable ones. Caillies, Denhière, and Kintsch (2002) presented texts describing the use of software packages to individuals whose knowledge ranged from non-existent to advanced. As predicted, intermediate and advanced individuals showed superior text comprehension to the beginners. However, on another memory test (recognition memory for parts of the text), the beginner group actually performed *better* than the other groups. Why was this? The beginners had focused mainly on forming a surface representation which was perfectly adequate for good recognition memory.

The reader's goals help to determine which representations are formed. Zwaan (1994) argued that someone reading an excerpt from a novel may focus on the text itself (e.g., the wording; stylistic devices) and so form a strong surface representation. In contrast, someone reading a newspaper article may focus on updating his/her representation of a real-world situation, and so form a strong situation representation. As predicted, memory for surface representations was better for stories described as literary, whereas memory for situation representations was better for stories described as newspaper reports (see Figure 10.14).

It is assumed within the model that inference processing involves a generation process (in which possible inferences are produced) and a subsequent integration process (in which the most appropriate inference is included in the text representation). Mason and Just (2004) obtained support for this part of the model in a brain-imaging study. When the generation process increased in difficulty, there was increased activity in the dorsolateral prefrontal cortex, suggesting that this brain area is involved in generating inferences. In contrast, increased difficulty in the integration process was associated with increased activity in the right-hemisphere language area including the inferior, middle, and superior temporal gyri and the angular gyrus. Thus, different brain areas are associated with the generation and integration processes.

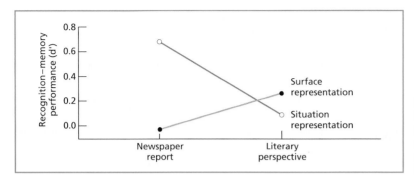

Figure 10.14 Memory for surface and situation representations for stories described as literary or as newspaper reports. Data from Zwaan (1994).

According to the construction–integration model, textual information is first linked with general world or semantic knowledge. After that, it is linked to contextual information from the rest of the text. Cook and Myers (2004) tested this assumption using various passages. Here is an excerpt from one passage:

The movie was being filmed on location in the Sahara Desert. It was a small independent film with a low budget and small staff, so everyone involved had to take on extra jobs and responsibilities. On the first day of filming, "Action!" was called by the actress so that shooting could begin . . .

What was of interest was how long the readers fixated the word "actress". This word is inappropriate in terms of our knowledge, which tells us it is the director who says, "Action!" However, the context of the passage (in italics) provides a reason why it might not be the director who is in charge. According to the construction–integration model, readers' knowledge that actresses do not direct films should have caused them to dwell a long time on the unexpected word "actress". In fact, the word was *not* fixated for long. Presumably readers immediately used the contextual justification for someone other than the director being in charge. Thus, in opposition to the model, contextual information can be used *before* general world knowledge during reading. Similar findings were reported by Nieuwland and van Berkum (2006) in a study discussed earlier.

As Kaakinen and Hyönä (2007, p. 1323) pointed out, it is assumed within the construction–integration model that, "During the construction phase, the text input launches a dumb bottom-up process in the reader's knowledge base . . . top-down factors, such as reading perspective or reading goal, exert their influence at the integration phase." It seems implausible that this is what *always* happens. Suppose you read a text that discusses four rare diseases. You are asked to imagine that a close friend has been diagnosed with one of those diseases, and your task is to inform common friends about it. It seems likely that this reading goal would cause you to spend a relatively long time processing relevant sentences (i.e., dealing with your friend's disease) and relatively little time processing irrelevant sentences. This is precisely what Kaakinen and Hyönä found. The finding that reading goal influenced the early stages of text processing suggests strongly that top-down factors can influence the construction phase as well as the integration phase, which is inconsistent with the model.

Evaluation
The construction–integration model has the advantage over previous theories that the ways in which text information combines with the reader's related knowledge are spelled out in more detail. For example, the notion that propositions for the text representation are selected on the basis of a spreading activation process operating on propositions drawn from the text and from stored knowledge is an interesting one. Another strength is that

there is reasonable evidence for the three levels of representation (surface, propositional, and situation) specified in the model. Finally, it is predicted accurately that readers will often find it hard to discriminate between information actually presented in a text and inferences based on that information (as in the study by Bransford et al., 1972). The reason is that very similar propositions are formed in either case.

What are the model's limitations? First, the assumption that only bottom-up processes are used during the construction phase of text processing is dubious. One implication of that assumption is that readers only engage in *selective* processing based on top-down processes at the subsequent integration phase. The finding that readers' goals can lead them to allocate visual attention selectively very early in text processing (Kaakinen and Hyönä, 2007) indicates that text processing is more flexible than assumed by Kintsch.

Second, it is assumed that only general world and semantic knowledge is used in addition to text information during the formation of propositions in the construction phase. However, the notion that other sources of information (e.g., contextual information) are used *only* at the integration phase was disproved by Cook and Myers (2004).

Third, the assumption that readers invariably construct several propositions when reading a text has not received strong support. We will see later that some theorists (e.g., Kaup, Yaxley, Madden, Zwaan, & Lüdtke, 2007) argue that the only meaningful representation formed is a perceptual simulation resembling a situation representation.

Fourth, Graesser et al. (1997) argued that Kintsch ignored two levels of discourse representation. One is the *text genre level*, which is concerned with the nature of the text (e.g., narrative, description, jokes, exposition). The other is the *communication level*, which refers to the ways in which the writer communicates with his/her readers. For example, some writers present themselves as invisible story-tellers.

Fifth, the model is not specific about the processes involved in the construction of situ-

ation models. This omission was remedied in the event-indexing model, to which we next turn.

Event-indexing model

According to the event-indexing model (Zwaan & Radvansky, 1998), readers monitor five aspects or indexes of the evolving situation model at the same time when they read stories:

(1) *The protagonist*: the central character or actor in the present event compared to the previous one.
(2) *Temporality*: the relationship between the times at which the present and previous events occurred.
(3) *Causality*: the causal relationship of the current event to the previous one.
(4) *Spatiality*: the relationship between the spatial setting of the current event and a previous event.
(5) *Intentionality*: the relationship between the character's goals and the present event.

As readers work through a text, they continually update the situation model to reflect accurately the information presented with respect to all five aspects or indexes. *Discontinuity* (unexpected changes) in any of the five aspects

According to the event-indexing model (Zwaan & Radvansky, 1998), readers monitor five aspects of the evolving situation model at the same time when they read stories: the protagonist; temporality; causality; spatiality; and intentionality.

of a situation (e.g., a change in the spatial setting; a flashback in time) requires more processing effort than when all five aspects or indexes remain the same. It is also assumed that the five aspects are monitored *independently* of each other. It follows that processing effort should be greater when two aspects change at the same time rather than only one.

Zwaan and Madden (2004) distinguished between two views on updating situation models. One is the *here-and-now view*, in which the most current information is more available than outdated information. The other is the *resonance view*, according to which new information in a text resonates with *all* text-related information stored in memory. As a result, outdated or incorrect information can influence the comprehension process. The here-and-now view forms part of the event-indexing model.

Evidence

Support for the prediction that reading a sentence involving discontinuity in one aspect takes longer than one with no discontinuity was reported by Rinck and Weber (2003). They considered shifts (versus continuity) in the protagonist, temporality, and spatiality. The reading time per syllable was 164 ms with no shifts and 220 with one shift. This increased to 231 ms with two shifts and 248 ms with three shifts.

Support for the here-and-now view of updating was reported by Zwaan and Madden (2004). In one of their stories, all participants read the following target sentence: "Bobby began pounding the boards together with the hammer." In different conditions, the preceding sentences indicated that the hammer was always available (enablement condition), was never available because it was lost (disablement condition), or had been unavailable because it was lost but had now been found (re-enablement condition). What was of most theoretical importance was the time taken to read the target sentence in the re-enablement condition. According to the here-and-now view, the time should be the same as in the enablement condition because use of the hammer is consistent with the current situation. According to the

resonance view, the time should be longer in the re-enablement condition than in the enablement condition because outdated information interferes with processing the target sentence. The findings were as predicted by the here-and-now view.

Claus and Kelter (2006) found that readers often update their knowledge even when it is effortful. Participants were presented with passages describing four events that occurred in a given chronological order. In some passages, the events were not presented in the correct order – the first event was presented *after* the second and third events. Thus, the first event was a flashback. The duration of the second event was short (e.g., "For half an hour they fly above the countryside") or it was long (e.g., "For five hours they fly above the countryside"). The key finding was that the duration of the second event (and thus the apparent distance in time of the first event) influenced the speed with which information about the first event could be accessed. This strongly suggests that readers put the four events in the correct chronological order.

Evaluation

The greatest strength of the event-indexing model is that it identifies key processes involved in creating and updating situation models. As predicted, reading times increase when readers respond to changes in any of the five indexes or aspects. The model's emphasis on the construction of situation models is probably well placed. As Zwaan and Radvansky (1998, p. 177) argued, "Language can be regarded as a set of processing instructions on how to construct a mental representation of the described situation." In addition, the here-and-now view of situation-model updating has received support.

What are the limitations of the event-indexing model? First, it is not entirely correct to regard the various aspects of a situation as entirely separate. Consider the following sentence from Zwaan and Radvansky (p. 180): "Someone was making noise in the backyard. Mike had left hours ago." This sentence provides information about temporality but also permits the causal inference that Mike was not the person making the noise.

Second, situation models are not always constructed. Zwaan and van Oostendorp (1993) found that most readers failed to construct a situation model when reading a complex account of the details of a murder scene. This probably happened because it was cognitively demanding to form a situation model – participants explicitly instructed to form such a model read the text very slowly.

Third, the event-indexing model claims that readers update their situation model to take account of new information. However, this generally did not happen when people read stories in which their original impression of an individual's personality was refuted by subsequent information (Rapp & Kendeou, 2007).

Fourth, the event-indexing model has relatively little to say about the *internal representations* of events that readers and listeners form when engaged in language comprehension. Progress in understanding such internal representations has emerged from the experiential-simulations approach, which is discussed next. As Zwaan (2008) argued, the two approaches are complementary: the focus of the event-indexing model is at a fairly general level, whereas that of the experiential-simulations approach is at a more specific level.

Experiential-simulations approach

The experiential-simulations approach has been advocated by several theorists (e.g., Kaup, Yaxley, Madden, Zwaan, & Lüdtke, 2007; Zwaan, Stanfield, & Yaxley, 2002). Its crucial assumption was expressed by Kaup et al. (2007, p. 978): "Comprehension is tied to the creation of representations that are similar in nature to the representations created when directly experiencing or re-experiencing the respective situations and events." Thus, situation models contain many perceptual details that would be present if the described situation were actually perceived.

The experiential-simulations approach is more *economical* than the construction–

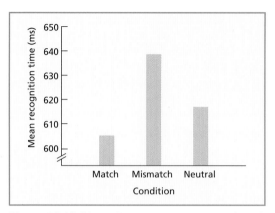

Figure 10.15 Mean object recognition times (in ms) in the match, mismatch, and neutral conditions. Based on data in Zwaan et al. (2002).

integration model. It is assumed that the *only* meaningful representation that is formed is a perceptual simulation, which contrasts with the three representations assumed within the construction–integration model.

Evidence

Support for the experiential-simulations approach was reported by Zwaan et al. (2002). Participants read sentences such as the following: "The ranger saw an eagle in the sky" or "The ranger saw an eagle in the nest". They were then presented with a picture, and decided rapidly whether the object in the picture had been mentioned in the sentence. On "Yes" trials, the picture was a match for the implied shape of the object (e.g., an eagle with outstretched wings after the "in the sky" sentence) or was not a match (e.g., an eagle with folded wings after the "in the sky" sentence). Participants responded significantly faster when the object's shape in the picture matched that implied by the sentence (see Figure 10.15). This suggests that people construct a perceptual simulation of the situation described by sentences.

What happens when people are presented with negated sentences such as, "There was no eagle in the sky" or "There was no eagle in the nest"? Do they continue to create experiential simulations in the same way as when presented with sentences describing what is the case? Kaup et al. (2007) used the same paradigm as

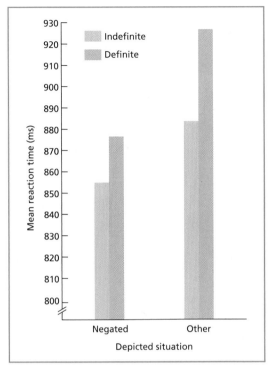

Figure 10.16 Mean correct response times (in ms) to decide that a picture had been presented in the preceding sentence. The sentences were definite (e.g., "the eagle was not in the sky") or indefinite (e.g., "there was no eagle in the sky"), and the pictured object's shape was appropriate (negated condition) or inappropriate (other condition). Based on data in Kaup et al. (2007).

Zwaan et al. (2002) but using only negated sentences. The findings resembled those of Zwaan et al. (2002) – participants decided more rapidly that an object in a picture (e.g.,

eagle) had been presented in the preceding sentence when its shape was appropriate in the context of the sentence (see Figure 10.16). The similarity in the findings of Kaup, Lüdtke, and Zwaan (2006) and Zwaan et al. (2002) suggests that the processing of negative sentences involves very similar initial experiential simulations to those produced by corresponding affirmative sentences.

If readers simply created the same experiential simulation whether the situation in question had actually occurred or had been negated, chaos and error would result! Kaup et al. (2006) found that readers presented with negative sentences initially simulate the negated situation but then rapidly create an experiential simulation of the correct meaning of the sentence. This second simulation is produced within about 1.5 seconds or so.

Evaluation

The notion that the comprehension process involves constructing a perceptual simulation of the situation described is an exciting one. However, what is needed is more systematic research to identify the circumstances in which the experiential-simulations approach is applicable. For example, constructing perceptual simulations is likely to be cognitively demanding so that individuals often lack sufficient processing resources to construct them. In addition, the experiential-simulations approach has little to say about the processes involved in comprehending abstract material.

CHAPTER SUMMARY

• Parsing
Sentence processing involves parsing and the assignment of meaning. The garden-path model is a two-stage model in which the simplest syntactic structure is selected at the first stage using the principles of minimal attachment and late closure. In fact, semantic information is often used earlier in sentence processing than proposed by the model. According to the constraint-based theory, all relevant sources of information are available immediately to someone processing a sentence. Competing analyses of a sentence are activated in parallel, with several language characteristics (e.g., verb bias) being used to resolve ambiguities. In fact, it is not clear that several possible syntactic structures are formed at

the same time. According to the unrestricted race model, all sources of information are used to identify a single syntactic structure for a sentence. If this structure is disconfirmed, there is extensive re-analysis. Studies using ERPs support the view that several sources of information (including word meanings and context) influence sentence processing at a very early stage. The common assumption that sentences are eventually interpreted correctly is often wrong – we actually use heuristics and are prone to error.

- Pragmatics
  The notion that the literal meaning of metaphors is accessed before the non-literal meaning is incorrect. Non-literal meanings are often accessed as rapidly as literal ones. There is support for the graded salience hypothesis, according to which salient messages (whether literal or non-literal) are processed initially. According to the predication model, understanding metaphors involves selecting features of the predicate that are relevant to the argument and inhibiting irrelevant predicate features. Individuals high in working memory capacity are better at such inhibition. Listeners generally try to use their knowledge of the common ground when understanding what a speaker is saying. However, processing limitations often prevent them from doing this fully, which sometimes makes it appear that they are using the egocentric heuristic.

- Individual differences: working memory capacity
  Reading span and operation span have been used as measures of working memory capacity. There is evidence that individuals having high working memory capacity are better at sentence comprehension than those with low capacity, in part because they have greater attentional control and can suppress irrelevant information. Functional neuroimaging research has suggested that comprehension processes of high-capacity individuals are characterised by greater efficiency, adaptability, and synchronisation of brain activation than are those of low-capacity individuals.

- Discourse processing
  We typically make logical and bridging inferences (e.g., anaphor resolution). According to the constructionist approach, numerous elaborative inferences are typically drawn when we read a text. According to the minimalist hypothesis, only a few inferences are drawn automatically; additional strategic inferences depend on the reader's goals. The evidence is generally more supportive of the minimalist hypothesis than the constructionist approach. However, the minimalist hypothesis is too minimalist and readers sometimes make more elaborative inferences than expected by the hypothesis.

- Story processing
  According to schema theory, schemas or organised packets of knowledge influence what we remember of stories. Schema influence comprehension and retrieval processes. There is some evidence of a double dissociation between schema knowledge and concept knowledge in brain-damaged patients. According to Kintsch's construction–integration model, three levels of representation of a text are constructed. Top-down processes occur earlier in comprehension than assumed by the model. According to the event-indexing model, readers monitor five aspects of the evolving situational model, with discontinuity in any aspect creating difficulties in situation-model construction. According to the experiential-simulations approach, we construct perceptual simulations during comprehension.

FURTHER READING

- Gaskell, G. (ed.) (2007). *Oxford handbook of psycholinguistics*. Oxford: Oxford University Press. Part Three of this edited handbook is devoted to chapters on language comprehension by leading experts.
- Hagoort, P., & van Berkum, J. (2007). Beyond the sentence given. *Philosophical Transactions of the Royal Society B, 362*, 801–811. This article provides comprehensive coverage of the authors' outstanding research on sentence comprehension.
- Harley, T. (2008). *The psychology of language from data to theory* (3rd ed.). Hove, UK: Psychology Press. Chapters 10 and 12 of this outstanding textbook contain detailed coverage of most of the topics discussed in this chapter.
- Schmalhofer, F., & Perfetti, C.A. (eds.) (2007). *Higher level language processes in the brain: Inference and comprehension processes*. Hove, UK: Psychology Press. Major researchers in the area of language comprehension contribute overviews in this edited book.

CHAPTER 11

LANGUAGE PRODUCTION

INTRODUCTION

We know more about language comprehension than language production. Why is this? We can control the material to be comprehended, but it is harder to constrain an individual's production of language. A further problem in accounting for language production (shared with language comprehension) is that more than a theory of language is needed. Language production is basically a goal-directed activity having communication as its main goal. People speak and write to impart information, to be friendly, and so on. Thus, motivational and social factors need to be considered in addition to purely linguistic ones.

The two major topics considered in this chapter are speech production and writing, including coverage of the effects of brain damage on these language processes. More is known about speech production than about writing. Nearly everyone spends more time talking than writing, and so it is of more practical value to understand the processes involved in talking. However, writing is an important skill in most societies.

There is much controversy concerning the extent to which the psychological processes involved in spoken and written language are the same or different. They are similar in that both have as their central function the communication of information about people and the world and both depend on the same knowledge base. However, children and adults often find writing much harder than speaking, which suggests that there are important differences between them. The main similarities and differences between speaking and writing will now be considered.

Similarities

The view that speaking and writing are similar receives some support from theoretical approaches to speech production and writing. It is assumed there is an initial attempt to decide on the overall meaning to be communicated (e.g., Dell, Burger, & Svec, 1997, on speech production; Hayes & Flower, 1986, on writing). At this stage, the actual words to be spoken or written are not considered. This is followed by the production of language, which often proceeds on a clause-by-clause basis.

Hartley, Sotto, and Pennebaker (2003) studied an individual (Eric Sotto) who dictated word-processed academic letters using a voice-recognition system or simply word processed them. Eric Sotto had much less experience of dictating word-processed letters than word processing them, but the letters he produced did not differ in readability or in typographical and grammatical errors. However, there were fewer long sentences when dictation was used, because Eric Sotto found it harder to change the structure of a sentence when dictating it.

Gould (1978) found that even those highly practised at dictation rarely dictated more than 35% faster than they wrote. This is notable given that people can speak five or six times faster than they can write. Gould (1980) video-taped people while they composed letters. Planning took up two-thirds of the total composition time for both dictated and written letters, which explains why dictation was only slightly faster than writing.

More evidence suggesting that speech production and writing involve similar processes comes from the study of patients with Broca's aphasia (see later in the chapter), whose speech is grammatically incorrect and lacking fluency. Most such patients have deficits in sentence production whether speaking or writing (Benson & Ardila, 1996). However, Assal, Buttet, and Jolivet (1981) reported an exceptional case of a patient whose writing was very ungrammatical but whose speech was largely unaffected.

Differences

There are several differences between speaking and writing (see Cleland & Pickering, 2006, for a review). Written language uses longer and more complex constructions, as well as longer words and a larger vocabulary. Writers make more use than speakers of words or phrases signalling what is coming next (e.g., but; on the other hand). This helps to compensate for the lack of prosody (rhythm, intonation, and so on, discussed shortly) that is important in spoken language.

Five differences between speaking and writing are as follows:

(1) Speakers know precisely who is receiving their messages.
(2) Speakers generally receive moment-by-moment feedback from the listener or listeners (e.g., expressions of bewilderment) and adapt what they say in response to verbal and non-verbal feedback from listeners.
(3) Speakers generally have much less time than writers to plan their language production, which helps to explain why spoken language is generally shorter and less complex.

(4) Writers typically have direct access to what they have produced so far, whereas speakers do not. However, Olive and Piolat (2002) found no difference in the quality of the texts produced by writers having (or not having) access to visual feedback of what they had written.
(5) "Writing is in essence a more conscious process than speaking...spontaneous discourse is usually spoken, self-monitored discourse is usually written" (Halliday, 1987, pp. 67–69).

What are the consequences of the above differences between speaking and writing? Spoken language is often informal and simple in structure, with information being communicated rapidly. In contrast, written language is more formal and has a more complex structure. Writers need to write clearly because they do not receive immediate feedback, and this slows down the communication rate.

Some brain-damaged patients have writing skills that are largely intact in spite of an almost total inability to speak and a lack of inner speech. For example, this pattern was observed in EB, who had suffered a stroke (Levine, Calvanio, & Popovics, 1982). Other patients can speak fluently but find writing very difficult. However, the higher-level processes involved in language production (e.g., planning; use of knowledge) may not differ between speaking and writing.

SPEECH AS COMMUNICATION

For most people (unless there is something seriously wrong with them), speech nearly always occurs as conversation in a social context. Grice (1967) argued that the key to successful communication is the Co-operative Principle, according to which speakers and listeners must try to be co-operative.

In addition to the Co-operative Principle, Grice proposed four maxims the speaker should heed:

- *Maxim of quantity*: the speaker should be as informative as necessary, but not more so.
- *Maxim of quality*: the speaker should be truthful.
- *Maxim of relation*: the speaker should say things that are relevant to the situation.
- *Maxim of manner*: the speaker should make his/her contribution easy to understand.

What needs to be said (maxim of quantity) depends on what the speaker wishes to describe (the referent). It is also necessary to know the object from which the referent must be distinguished. It is sufficient to say, "The boy is good at football", if the other players are all men, but not if some of them are also boys. In the latter case, it is necessary to be more specific (e.g., "The boy with red hair is good at football").

Those involved in a conversation typically exhibit co-operation in terms of smooth switches between speakers. Two people talking at once occurs less than 5% of the time in conversation, and there is typically a gap of under 500 ms between the end of one speaker's turn and the start of the next speaker's turn (Ervin-Tripp, 1979). How does this happen? Sacks, Schegloff, and Jefferson (1974) found that those involved in a conversation tend to follow certain rules. For example, when the speaker gazes at the listener, this is often an invitation to the listener to become the speaker. If the speaker wishes to continue speaking, he/she can indicate this by hand gestures or filling pauses with meaningless sounds (e.g., "Errrrr").

Brennan (1990) argued that one common way in which a conversation moves from one speaker to another is via an *adjacency pair*. What the first speaker says provides a strong invitation to the listener to take up the conversation. A question followed by an answer is a very common example of an adjacency pair. If the first speaker completes what he/she intended to say without producing the first part of an adjacency pair, then the next turn goes to the listener.

Sacks et al. (1974) found that those involved in a conversation tend to follow certain rules. For example, if the speaker wishes to continue speaking, he/she can indicate this by using hand gestures.

Common ground

It is often assumed that speakers try hard to ensure that their message is understood. According to Clark (e.g., Clark & Krych, 2004), speakers and listeners typically work together to maximise **common ground**, i.e., mutual beliefs, expectations, and knowledge. In other words, speakers and listeners try to get "on the same wavelength".

To what extent do speakers pay attention to the common ground? Horton and Keysar (1996) distinguished between two theoretical positions:

(1) *The initial design model*: this is based on the principle of optimal design, in which the speaker's initial plan for an utterance takes full account of the common ground with the listener.
(2) *The monitoring and adjustment model*: according to this model, speakers plan their utterances initially on the basis of information available to them *without* considering the listener's perspective.

KEY TERM

common ground: the mutual knowledge and beliefs shared by a speaker and listener.

These plans are then monitored and corrected to take account of the common ground.

Horton and Keysar asked participants to describe moving objects so the listener could identify them. These descriptions were produced rapidly (speeded condition) or slowly (unspeeded condition). There was a shared-context condition in which the participants knew the listener could see the same additional objects they could see, and a non-shared-context condition in which the participants knew the listener could *not* see the other objects. If the participants made use of the common ground, they should have utilised contextual information in their descriptions only in the shared-context condition.

Participants in the unspeeded condition used the common ground in their descriptions. However, those in the speeded condition included contextual information in their descriptions regardless of its appropriateness. These findings fit the predictions of the monitoring and adjustment model better than those of the initial design model. Presumably the common ground was not used properly in the speeded condition because there was insufficient time for the monitoring process to operate. Thus, the processing demands involved in always taking account of the listener's knowledge when planning utterances can be excessive (see Figure 11.1).

Ferreira (2008, p. 209) argued along similar lines: "Speakers seem to choose utterances that are especially easy for them to say, specifically by producing more accessible, easy-to-think-of material sooner, and less accessible, harder-to-think-of material later." He reviewed evidence indicating that speakers often produce ambiguous sentences even though such sentences pose special difficulties for listeners. This approach often works well in practice, because listeners are typically provided with enough information to understand ambiguous sentences.

The study by Horton and Keysar (1996) was limited in that the listeners did not speak. Common ground can be achieved much more easily in a situation involving interaction and dialogue (Clark & Krych, 2004). There were pairs of participants, with one being a director who instructed the other member (the builder) how to construct Lego models. Errors in the constructed model were made on 39% of trials when no interaction was possible compared to only 5% when the participants could interact. In addition, directors often very rapidly altered what they said to maximise the common ground between them and the builders in the interactive condition. For example, when Ken (one of the builders) held a block over the right location while Jane (one of the directors) was speaking, she almost instantly took advantage by interrupting herself to say, "Yes, and put it on the right-hand half of the – yes – of the green rectangle."

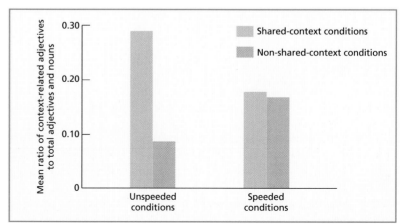

Figure 11.1 Mean ratio of context-related adjectives to adjectives plus nouns in speeded vs. unspeeded conditions and shared vs. non-shared-context conditions. Adapted from Horton and Keysar (1996).

How do speakers deal with the common ground?

Bard, Anderson, Chen, Nicholson, Havard, and Dalzel-Job (2007) agreed with Horton and Keysar (1996) that speakers typically fail to take full account of the common ground. They identified two possible strategies speakers might take with respect to the common ground:

(1) Shared responsibility: the speaker may expect the listener to volunteer information if he/she perceives there to be a problem with the common ground.
(2) Cognitive overload: the speaker may try to keep track of his/her own knowledge as well as that of the listener, but generally finds that this requires excessive cognitive processing.

Bard et al. (2007) asked speakers to describe the route on a map so another person could reproduce it. Unknown to the speaker, the other person was a confederate of the experimenter. Each speaker had two kinds of information indicating that the confederate was having difficulties in reproducing the route: (1) the confederate said he/she had a problem; or (2) the confederate's fake eye movements were focused away from the correct route.

What would we expect to find? According to the shared responsibility account, the speaker should pay more attention to what the confederate said than to his/her direction of gaze. Only the former involves the confederate volunteering information. According to the cognitive overload account, the speaker should focus more on the gaze feedback than on what the confederate said because it is easier to process gaze information. In fact, speakers took much more account of what the confederate said than his/her gaze pattern (see Figure 11.2).

The take-home message is that speakers generally focus mainly on their own knowledge rather than their listener's. Presumably they do this to make life easier for themselves. However, speakers do attend to the listener's lack of knowledge when he/she says something is amiss.

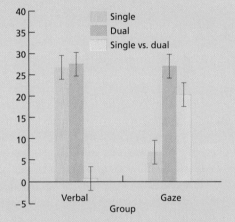

Figure 11.2 Rate of advice from speaker to the confederate to change direction as a function of verbal and gaze feedback from the confederate. Feedback was provided in one modality (single condition) or both modalities (dual condition). Reprinted from Bard et al. (2007), Copyright © 2007, with permission from Elsevier.

Evaluation

Communication would be most effective if speakers took full account of listeners' knowledge and the common ground, but this is often too cognitively demanding to do. In practice, speakers make more use of the common ground when time is not limited, when interaction is possible between speakers and listeners, and when listeners state that they have a problem.

One limitation of most research in this area is that speakers and listeners do not know each other beforehand. It is more demanding to keep track of the other person's knowledge in such situations than when two long-term friends have a conversation. Another limitation in most studies is that the common ground relates to information presented in visual displays. In everyday life, the common ground often refers to past events, knowledge of mutual acquaintances, knowledge of the world, and so on, as well as information directly present.

Interactive alignment model

Pickering and Garrod (2004) accepted in their interactive alignment model that speakers and listeners often lack the processing resources to maximise the common ground. As a consequence, two people involved in a conversation often do not *deliberately* try to infer the other person's representation of the current situation. However, these situation representations often overlap substantially as a result of various fairly automatic processes. Thus, speakers and listeners can frequently achieve common ground in a relatively effortless way. For example, speakers often copy phrases and even sentences they heard when the other person was speaking. Thus, the other person's words serve as a prime or prompt. In addition, speakers often make extensive use of the ideas communicated by the other person.

One of the ways in which speakers and listeners get on the same wavelength is via syntactic priming. **Syntactic priming** occurs when a previously experienced syntactic structure influences current processing. Here is a concrete example. If you have just heard a passive sentence (e.g., "The man was bitten by the dog"), this increases the chance that you will produce a passive sentence yourself. This occurs even when you are not consciously aware of copying a previous syntactic structure (see Pickering & Ferreira, 2008, for a review).

Evidence of syntactic priming was reported by Cleland and Pickering (2003). A confederate of the experimenter described a picture to participants using an adjective–noun order (e.g., "the red sheep") or a noun–relative-clause order (e.g., "the sheep that's red"). Participants tended to use the syntactic structure they had heard even when the words in the two sentences were very different. However, there was stronger syntactic priming when the noun remained the same (e.g., sheep–sheep) than when it did not (e.g., sheep–knife). Syntactic priming makes it easier for those involved in a conversation to co-ordinate information.

What happens when syntactic priming and other processes fail to achieve common ground? According to the model, speakers expect the other person to sort the problem out. This can be done in various ways. For example, the speaker can repeat what the previous speaker said with a rising intonation or with an additional question (Pickering & Garrod, 2004). The approach here is consistent with the notion of shared responsibility emphasised by Bard et al. (2007).

PLANNING OF SPEECH

The first stage in speech production generally involves deciding what message you want to communicate. Most of the time, you plan some of what you are going to say before speaking. However, there has been much controversy concerning the *amount* of forward planning that occurs. Several theorists (e.g., Garrett, 1980) have argued that the planning of speech may extend over an entire **clause**, a part of a sentence containing a subject and a verb. There is support for this view from the study of speech errors (see Garrett, 1980). For example, word-exchange errors (discussed later) involve two words changing places. Of importance, the words exchanged often come from different phrases but the same clause (e.g., "My chair seems empty without my room").

Additional evidence that planning may be at the clause level was reported by Holmes (1988). Speakers talked spontaneously about various topics, and then other participants read the utterances produced. Speakers (but not readers) often had hesitations and pauses before the start of a clause, suggesting they were planning the forthcoming clause.

Other evidence suggests that speech planning may be at the level of the **phrase**, a group of

---

KEY TERMS

syntactic priming: the tendency for the syntactic structure of a spoken or written sentence to correspond to that of a recently processed sentence.
clause: part of a sentence that contains a subject and a verb.
phrase: a group of words expressing a single idea; it is smaller in scope than a **clause**.

words expressing a single idea and smaller in scope than a clause. Martin, Miller, and Vu (2004) asked participants to describe moving pictures. The sentences had a simple initial phrase (e.g., "The ball moves above the tree and the finger") or a complex initial phrase (e.g., "The ball and the tree move above the finger"). Speakers took longer to initiate speech when using complex initial phrases, suggesting they were planning the initial phrase before starting to speak.

In contrast, Griffin (2001) argued that speech planning is extremely limited. Participants were presented with displays containing three pictured objects and responded according to the following sentence frame: "The A and the B are above the C." The time taken to start speaking was influenced by the difficulty in finding the right word to describe the first object (i.e., A), but was *not* affected by the difficulty in finding the right words to describe the second and third objects (i.e., B and C). Thus, participants started talking when they had prepared a name for only *one* object, suggesting that speech planning is very limited.

Flexibility

How can we account for the apparently inconsistent findings? The amount of planning preceding speech is *flexible*, and varies according to situational demands. Support for this viewpoint was reported by Ferreira and Swets (2002). Participants answered mathematical problems varying in difficulty level, and the time taken to start speaking and the length of time spent speaking were recorded. If there were complete planning before speaking, the time taken to start speaking should have been longer for more difficult problems than for easier ones, but the time spent speaking would not vary. In contrast, if people started speaking before planning their responses, then the time taken to start speaking should be the same for all problems. However, the duration of speaking should be longer with more difficult problems.

Ferreira and Swets (2002) found that task difficulty affected the time taken to start speaking but not the time spent speaking. This suggested that participants fully planned their responses before speaking. However, the findings differed in a second experiment in which participants had to start producing their answers to mathematical problems very rapidly for them to be counted. In these circumstances, some planning occurred before speaking, with additional planning occurring during speaking. Thus, speakers did only as much prior planning as was feasible in the time available before starting to speak.

Spieler and Griffin (2006) also found evidence of flexibility in a study on individual differences. Speakers who spoke the fastest tended to be the ones whose speech was least fluent. The implication is that fast speakers engaged in less planning of speech than slow speakers, and this relative lack of planning time impaired the fluency of what they said.

Evaluation

Progress has been made in discovering the factors determining the amount of forward planning in which speakers engage. In general, studies in which speakers are free from constraints as to *what* to say and *when* to say it (e.g., Garrett, 1980; Holmes, 1988) indicate that speech planning is fairly extensive and probably includes entire phrases or clauses. However, when the task is more artificial and the same sentence frame is used repeatedly (e.g., Griffin, 2001; Martin, Miller, & Vu, 2004), planning is more limited. Not surprisingly, there is less forward planning when speakers are under time pressure (e.g., Ferreira & Swets, 2002). Finally, there are substantial individual differences among speakers (e.g., Spieler & Griffin, 2006) – some people seem unable to follow the advice to "keep your mouth closed until your mind is in gear".

What are the limitations of research in this area? First, many studies have used very artificial tasks, and so findings are unlikely to generalise to more naturalistic situations. Second, the main dependent variable is typically the time to speech onset or the length of the pause between successive utterances. It is hard to know what speakers are doing during such time intervals or to assess the precise extent of their forward planning.

BASIC ASPECTS OF SPOKEN LANGUAGE

On the face of it (by the sound of it?), speech production is straightforward. It seems almost effortless as we chat with friends or acquaintances. We typically speak at 2–3 words a second or about 150 words a minute, and this rapid speech rate fits the notion that speaking is very undemanding of processing resources.

The reality of speech production is often very different from the above account. We use various strategies when talking to reduce processing demands while we plan what to say next (see Smith, 2000, for a review). One example is **preformulation**, which involves reducing processing costs by producing phrases used before. About 70% of our speech consists of word combinations we use repeatedly (Altenberg, 1990). Kuiper (1996) analysed the speech of two groups of people (auctioneers and sports commentators) who often need to speak very rapidly. Speaking quickly led them to make very extensive use of preformulations (e.g., "They are on their way"; "They are off and racing now").

Another strategy we use to make speech production easier is **underspecification**, which involves using simplified expressions in which the full meaning is not expressed explicitly. Smith (2000) illustrated underspecification with the following: "Wash and core six cooking apples. Put them in an oven." In the second sentence, the word "them" underspecifies the phrase "six cooking apples".

Discourse markers

There are important differences between spontaneous conversational speech and prepared speech (e.g., a public talk). As Fox Tree (2000) pointed out, several words and phrases (e.g., well; you know; oh; but anyway) are far more common in spontaneous speech. These **discourse markers** do not contribute directly to the content of utterances but are nevertheless of value. Flowerdew and Tauroza (1995) found that participants understood a videotaped lecture better when the discourse markers were left in rather than edited out. However, the lecture was in the participants' second language and so the findings may not be relevant to first-language listening.

Bolden (2006) considered the discourse markers speakers use when embarking on a new conversational topic. More specifically, she focused on the discourse markers "so" and "oh". The word "oh" was used 98.5% of the time when the new topic directly concerned the speaker, whereas "so" was used 96% of the time when it was of most relevance to the listener. You almost certainly do the same, but you probably do not realise that that is what you do.

Discourse markers fulfil various other functions. For example, "anyway" and "be that as it may" indicate that the speaker is about to return to the topic he/she had previously been talking about. The context is also important. Fuller (2003) found that the discourse markers "oh" and "well" were used more often in casual conversations than in interviews, whereas "you know", "like", "yeah", and "I mean" were not. These differences may occur because speakers need to respond more to what the other person has said in conversations than in interviews.

Prosodic cues

Prosodic cues (see Glossary) include rhythm, stress, and intonation, and make it easier for listeners to understand what speakers are trying to say (see Chapter 10). The extent to which

---

KEY TERMS

preformulation: this is used in speech production to reduce processing costs by saying phrases often used previously.
underspecification: a strategy used to reduce processing costs in speech production by producing simplified expressions.
discourse markers: spoken words and phrases that do not contribute directly to the content of what is being said but still serve various functions (e.g., clarification of the speaker's intentions).

speakers use prosodic cues varies considerably from study to study. Speakers are less likely to use prosodic cues if they simply read aloud ambiguous sentences rather than communicating spontaneously. For example, Keysar and Henly (2002) asked participants to read ambiguous sentences to convey a specific meaning, with listeners deciding which of two meanings was intended. The speakers did not use prosodic cues (or used them ineffectively), because the listeners only guessed correctly 61% of the time. Speakers failed to make their meaning clearer because they overestimated how much of the time listeners understood the intended meaning.

Snedeker and Trueswell (2003) argued that prosodic cues are much more likely to be provided when the context fails to clarify the meaning of an ambiguous sentence. Speakers said ambiguous sentences (e.g., "Tap the frog with the flower": you either use the flower to tap the frog or you tap the frog that has the flower). They provided many more prosodic cues when the context was consistent with both interpretations of the sentence.

Suppose we discover in some situation that speakers generally provide prosodic cues that resolve syntactic ambiguities. Does that necessarily mean that speakers are responsive to the needs of their listener(s)? According to Kraljic and Brennan (2005), it does not. Speakers producing spontaneous sentences made extensive use of prosodic cues, and listeners successfully used these cues to disambiguate what they heard. However, speakers consistently produced prosodic cues regardless of whether the listener needed them and regardless of whether they realised that the listener needed disambiguating cues. Thus, speakers' use of prosodic cues did not indicate any particular responsiveness to their listener.

Gesture

When two people have a conversation, the person who is speaking generally makes various gestures co-ordinated in timing and in meaning with the words being spoken. It is natural to assume that these gestures serve a communicative function by providing visual cues that make the speaker's message easier for the listener to understand. However, that is not the whole story. As you may have noticed, speakers often gesture during telephone conversations, even though these gestures are not visible to the listener.

Bavelas, Gerwing, Sutton, and Prevost (2008) found that speakers make any gestures while talking to someone face-to-face than over the telephone, which suggests that gestures *are* often used for communication purposes. Why do speakers make any gestures when on the telephone? Perhaps it has become habitual for them to use gestures while speaking, and they maintain this habit even when it is not useful. However, Bavelas et al. found that the nature of the gestures differed in the two conditions – they tended to be larger and more expressive in the face-to-face condition. Speakers on the telephone probably find that using gestures makes it easier for them to communicate what they want to say through speech.

Why do speakers make gestures when on the telephone? Perhaps they have simply become accustomed to using gestures while speaking, or perhaps the use of gestures facilitates communication.

SPEECH ERRORS

Our speech is imperfect and prone to various kinds of error. Many psychologists have argued that we can learn much about the processes involved in speech production by studying the types of error made and their relative frequencies. There are various reasons why the study of speech errors is important. First, we can gain insights into how the complex cognitive system involved in speech production works by focusing on what happens when it malfunctions.

Second, speech errors can shed light on the extent to which speakers plan ahead. For example, there are *word-exchange errors* in which two words in a sentence switch places (e.g., "I must let the house out of the cat" instead of "I must let the cat out of the house"). The existence of word-exchange errors suggests that speakers engage in forward planning of their utterances.

Third, comparisons between different speech errors can be revealing. For example, we can compare word-exchange errors with *sound-exchange errors* in which two sounds exchange places (e.g., "barn door" instead of "darn bore"). Of key importance, the two words involved in word-exchange errors are typically further apart in the sentence than the two words involved in sound-exchange errors. This suggests that planning of the words to be used occurs at an earlier stage than planning of the sounds to be spoken.

How do we know what errors are made in speech? The evidence consists mainly of those personally heard by the researcher concerned. You might imagine this would produce distorted data since some errors are easier to detect than others. However, the types and proportions of speech errors obtained in this way are very similar to those obtained from analysing tape-recorded conversations (Garnham, Oakhill, & Johnson-Laird, 1982). In recent years, there has been an increase in laboratory studies designed to produce certain kinds of speech error.

Types of error

There are several types of speech error other than those mentioned already. One type of error is the **spoonerism**, which occurs when the initial letter or letters of two words are switched. It is named after the Reverend William Archibald Spooner, who is credited with several memorable examples (e.g., "You have hissed all my mystery lectures"). Alas, most of the Reverend Spooner's gems were the result of much painstaking effort.

One of the most famous kinds of speech error is the **Freudian slip**, which reveals the speaker's true desires. Motley (1980) studied Freudian slips by trying to produce sex-related spoonerisms. Male participants said out loud pairs of items such as *goxi furl* and *bine foddy*. The experimenter was a male or a female "who was by design attractive, personable, very provocatively attired, and seductive in behaviour" (p. 140). Motley predicted (and found) that the number of spoonerisms (e.g., *goxi furl* turning into *foxy girl*) was greater when the passions of the male participants were inflamed by the female experimenter. In other experiments (see Motley, Baars, & Camden, 1983), male participants were given word pairs such as *tool kits* and *fast luck*. There were more sexual spoonerisms (e.g., *cool tits*) when the situation produced sexual arousal.

Semantic substitution errors occur when the correct word is replaced by a word of similar meaning (e.g., "Where is my tennis bat" instead of "Where is my tennis racquet?"). In 99% of cases, the substituted word is of the same form class as the correct word (e.g., nouns substitute for nouns). Verbs are much less likely than nouns, adjectives, or adverbs

> ### KEY TERMS
>
> **spoonerism:** a speech error in which the initial letter or letters of two words are switched.
> **Freudian slip:** a motivated error in speech (or action) that reveals the individual's underlying thoughts and/or desires.

to undergo semantic substitution (Hotopf, 1980).

Morpheme-exchange errors involve inflections or suffixes remaining in place but attached to the wrong words (e.g., "He has already trunked two packs"). An implication of morpheme-exchange errors is that the positioning of inflections is dealt with by a rather separate process from the one responsible for positioning word stems (e.g., "trunk"; "pack"). The word stems (e.g., trunk; pack) seem to be worked out *before* the inflections are added. This is the case because the spoken inflections or suffixes are generally altered to fit with the new word stems to which they are linked. For example, the "s" sound in the phrase "the forks of a prong" is pronounced in a way appropriate within the word "forks". However, this is different to the "s" sound in the original word "prongs" (Smyth, Morris, Levy, & Ellis, 1987).

Finally, we consider *number-agreement errors*, in which singular verbs are mistakenly used with plural subjects or vice versa. We are prone to making such errors in various circumstances. For example, we have problems with collective nouns (e.g., government; team) that are actually singular but have characteristics of plural nouns. We should say, "The government has made a mess of things" but sometimes say, "The government have made a mess of things". We also make errors when we make a verb agree with a noun close to it rather than with the subject of the sentence. For example, we complete the sentence fragment, "The player on the courts" with "*were* very good". Bock and Eberhard (1993) found frequent number-agreement errors with such sentences, but practically none at all when participants completed word fragments such as, "The player on the court…".

Why do we make number-agreement errors? According to Haskell and MacDonald (2003), we use several sources of information. For example, consider the two sentence fragments, "The family of mice…" and "The family of rats…". Strictly speaking, the verb should be singular in both cases. However, many participants used a plural verb with such sentences because family is a collective noun. This tendency was greater when the noun closest to the verb was more obviously plural (e.g., *rats* ends in –s, which is a strong predictor of a plural noun).

McDonald (2008) asked participants to decide whether various sentences were grammatically correct. This was done with or without an externally imposed load on working memory. Participants with this load found it especially difficult to make accurate decisions concerning subject–verb agreement. This suggests that we need to use considerable processing resources to avoid number-agreement errors.

THEORIES OF SPEECH PRODUCTION

Theorists agree that speech production involves various general processes, but there are disagreements concerning the nature of these processes and how they interact. In this section, we will discuss two of the most influential theories of speech production. First, there is spreading-activation theory (Dell, 1986). According to this theory, the processes involved in speech production occur in parallel (at the same time) and very different kinds of information can be processed together. These assumptions suggest that the processes involved in speech production are very flexible or even somewhat chaotic. Second, there is the WEAVER++ model (Levelt, Roelofs, & Meyer, 1999). According to this model, processing is serial and proceeds in an orderly fashion. These assumptions imply that the processes involved in speech production are highly regimented and structured. As we will see, both theoretical approaches have much to recommend them and some compromise between them is probably appropriate.

Spreading-activation theory

Dell (1986) argued in his spreading-activation theory that speech production consists of four levels:

- *Semantic level*: the meaning of what is to be said or the message to be communicated.
- *Syntactic level*: the grammatical structure of the words in the planned utterance.
- *Morphological level*: the **morphemes** (basic units of meaning or word forms) in the planned sentence.
- *Phonological level*: the phonemes (basic units of sound).

As mentioned already, it is assumed within Dell's spreading-activation theory that processing occurs in parallel (at the same time) at all levels (e.g., semantic; syntactic). In addition, processing is *interactive*, meaning that processes at any level can influence those at any other level. In practice, however, Dell (1986) accepted that processing is generally more advanced at some levels (e.g., semantic) than others (e.g., phonological).

Unsurprisingly, the notion of **spreading activation** is central to Dell's (1986) spreading-activation model. It is assumed that the nodes within a network (many corresponding to words) vary in their activation or energy. When a node or word is activated, activation or energy spreads from it to other related nodes. For example, strong activation of the node corresponding to "tree" may cause some activation of the node corresponding to "plant". According to the theory, spreading activation can occur for sounds as well as for words and there are *categorical rules* at the semantic, syntactic, morphological, and phonological levels of speech production. These rules are constraints on the categories of items and combinations of categories that are acceptable. The rules at each level define categories appropriate to that level. For example, the categorical rules at the syntactic level specify the syntactic categories of items within the sentence.

In addition to the categorical rules, there is a *lexicon* (dictionary) in the form of a connectionist network. It contains nodes for concepts, words, morphemes, and phonemes. When a node is activated, it sends activation to all the nodes connected to it (see Chapter 1).

Insertion rules select the items for inclusion in the representation of the to-be-spoken sentence according to the following criterion: the most highly activated node belonging to the appropriate category is chosen. For example, if the categorical rules at the syntactic level dictate that a verb is required at a particular point within the syntactic representation, then the verb whose node is most activated will be selected. After an item has been selected, its activation level immediately reduces to zero, preventing it from being selected repeatedly.

Dell, Oppenheim, and Kittredge (2008) focused on why we tend to replace a noun with a noun and a verb with a verb when we make mistakes when speaking. They argued that, through learning, we possess a "syntactic traffic cop". It monitors what we intend to say, and inhibits any words not belonging to the appropriate syntactical category.

According to spreading-activation theory, speech errors occur because an incorrect item is sometimes more activated than the correct one. The existence of spreading activation means that numerous nodes are *all* activated at the same time, which increases the likelihood of errors being made in speech.

Evidence

What kinds of error are predicted by the theory? First, and of particular importance, there is the **mixed-error effect**, which occurs when an incorrect word is both semantically and phonemically related to the correct word. Dell

---

KEY TERMS

morphemes: the smallest units of meaning within words.
spreading activation: the notion that activation of a given node (often a word) in long-term memory leads to activation or energy spreading to other related nodes or words.
mixed-error effect: speech errors that are semantically and phonologically related to the intended word.

(1986) quoted the example of someone saying, "Let's stop", instead of, "Let's start", where the word "stop" is both semantically and phonemically related to the correct word (i.e., "start"). The existence of this effect suggests that the various levels of processing *interact* flexibly with each other. More specifically, the mixed-error effect suggests that semantic and phonological factors can both influence word selection at the same time.

It is hard with the mixed-error effect to work out how many incorrect words would be phonemically related to the correct word by chance. Stronger evidence was provided by Ferreira and Griffin (2003). In their key condition, participants were presented with an incomplete sentence such as, "I thought that there would still be some cookies left, but there were…" followed by picture naming (e.g., of a priest). Participants tended to produce the wrong word "none". This was due to the semantic similarity between *priest* and *nun* combining with the phonological identity of *nun* and *none*.

Second, errors should belong to the appropriate category because of the operation of the categorical rules and the syntactic traffic cop. As expected, most errors *do* belong to the appropriate category (e.g., nouns replacing nouns; Dell, 1986). We might predict that some patients would suffer damage to the syntactic traffic cop and so make numerous syntactic errors. Precisely that was found by Berndt, Mitchum, Haendiges, and Sandson (1997) in a study on patients with **aphasia** (impaired language abilities due to brain damage). The patients were given the task of naming pictures and videos of objects (noun targets) and actions (verb targets). The errors made by some of the patients nearly always involved words belonging to the correct syntactic category, whereas those made by other patients were almost randomly distributed across nouns and verbs. It seems reasonable to argue that the latter patients had an impaired syntactic traffic cop.

Third, many errors should be anticipation errors, in which a word is spoken earlier in the sentence than appropriate (e.g., "The sky is in the sky"). This happens because all the words in the sentence tend to become activated during speech planning.

Fourth, anticipation errors should often turn into exchange errors, in which two words within a sentence are swapped (e.g., "I must write a wife to my letter"). Remember that the activation level of a selected item immediately reduces to zero. Therefore, if "wife" has been selected too early, it is unlikely to be selected in its correct place in the sentence. This allows a previously unselected and highly activated item such as "letter" to appear in the wrong place. Many speech errors are of the exchange variety.

Fifth, anticipation and exchange errors generally involve words moving only a relatively short distance within the sentence. Those words relevant to the part of the sentence under current consideration will tend to be more activated than those relevant to more distant parts of the sentence. Thus, the findings are in line with the predictions of spreading-activation theory.

Sixth, speech errors should tend to consist of actual words rather than nonwords (the **lexical bias effect**). The reason is that it is easier for words than nonwords to become activated because they have representations in the lexicon. This effect was shown by Baars, Motley, and MacKay (1975). Word pairs were presented briefly, and participants had to say both words rapidly. The error rate was twice as great when the word pair could be re-formed to create two new words (e.g., "lewd rip" can be turned into "rude lip") than when it could not (e.g., "Luke risk" turns into "ruke lisk"). The explanation of the lexical bias effect is more complicated than is assumed within the spreading-activation

KEY TERMS
aphasia: impaired language abilities as a result of brain damage.
lexical bias effect: the tendency for speech errors to consist of words rather than nonwords.

theory. Hartsuiker, Corley, and Martensen (2005) found that the effect depends in part on a self-monitoring system that inhibits nonword speech errors.

According to spreading-activation theory, speech errors occur when the wrong word is more highly activated than the correct one, and so is selected. Thus, there should be numerous errors when incorrect words are readily available. Glaser (1992) studied the time taken to name pictures (e.g., a table). Theoretically, there should have been a large increase in the number of errors made when each picture was accompanied by a semantically related distractor word (e.g., chair). In fact, however, there was only a modest increase in errors.

Evaluation

Spreading-activation theory has various strengths. First, the mixed-error effect indicates that the processing associated with speech production can be highly interactive, as predicted theoretically. Second, several other types of speech error can readily be explained by the theory. Third, the theory's emphasis on spreading activation provides links between speech production and other cognitive activities (e.g., word recognition; McClelland & Rumelhart, 1981). Fourth, our ability to produce novel sentences may owe much to the widespread activation between processing levels assumed within the theory.

What are the limitations of the theory? First, it has little to say about the processes operating at the semantic level. In other words, it de-emphasises issues relating to the construction of a message and its intended meaning. Second, while the theory predicts many of the speech errors that occur in speech production, it is not designed to predict the *time* taken to produce spoken words. Third, the theory focuses very much on the types of error made in speech. However, the interactive processes emphasised by the theory are more apparent in speech-error data than in error-free data (Goldrick, 2006). Fourth, an interactive system such as proposed within spreading-activation theory seems likely to produce many more errors than are actually observed in speech.

For example, the theory seems to predict too many errors in situations in which two or more words are all activated simultaneously (e.g., Glaser, 1992).

Anticipatory and perseveration errors

Dell, Burger, and Svec (1997) developed spreading-activation theory, arguing that most speech errors belong to two categories:

(1) *Anticipatory*: sounds or words are spoken ahead of their time (e.g., "cuff of coffee" instead of "cup of coffee"). These errors mainly reflect inexpert planning.
(2) *Perseveratory*: sounds or words are spoken later than they should be (e.g., "beef needle" instead of "beef noodle"). These errors reflect failure to monitor what one is about to say or planning failure.

Dell et al.'s key assumption was that expert speakers plan ahead more than non-expert speakers, and so a higher proportion of their speech errors will be anticipatory. In their own words, "Practice enhances the activation of the present and future at the expense of the past. So, as performance gets better, perseverations become relatively less common." The activation levels of sounds and words that have already been spoken are little affected by practice. However, the increasing activation levels of present and future sounds and words with practice prevent the past from intruding into present speech.

Dell et al. (1997) assessed the effects of practice on the anticipatory proportion (the proportion of total errors [anticipation + perseveration] that is anticipatory). In one study, participants were given extensive practice at saying several tongue twisters (e.g., five frantic fat frogs; thirty-three throbbing thumbs). As expected, the number of errors decreased as a function of practice. However, the anticipatory proportion increased from 0.37 early in practice to 0.59 at the end of practice, in line with prediction.

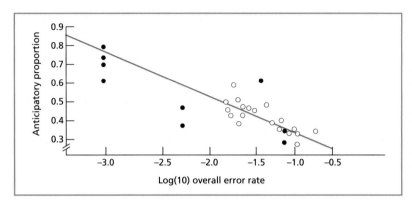

Figure 11.3 The relationship between overall error rate and the anticipatory proportion. The filled circles come from studies reported by Dell et al. (1997) and unfilled circles come from other studies. Adapted from Dell et al. (1997).

Dell et al. (1997) argued that speech errors are most likely when the speaker has not formed a coherent speech plan. In such circumstances, there will be relatively few anticipatory errors, and so the anticipatory proportion will be low. Thus, the overall error rate (anticipatory + perseverative) should correlate *negatively* with the anticipatory proportion. Dell et al. worked out the overall error rate and the anticipatory proportion for several sets of published data. The anticipatory proportion decreased from about 0.75 with low overall error rates to about 0.40 with high overall error rates (see Figure 11.3).

Vousden and Maylor (2006) tested the theory by assessing speech errors in eight-year-olds, 11-year-olds, and young adults who said tongue twisters aloud at a slow or fast rate. There were main findings. First, the anticipatory proportion increased as a function of age. This is predicted by the theory, because older children and young adults have had more practice at producing language. Second, fast speech produced a higher error rate than slow speech and also resulted in a lower antici-patory proportion. This is in agreement with the prediction that a higher overall error rate should be associated with a reduced anticipatory proportion.

Levelt's theoretical approach and WEAVER++

Levelt et al. (1999) put forward a computational model called WEAVER++, with WEAVER standing for Word-form Encoding by Activation and VERification (see Figure 11.4). It focuses on the processes involved in producing individual spoken words. The model is based on the following assumptions:

- There is a feed-forward activation-spreading network, meaning that activation proceeds forwards through the network but not backwards. Of particular importance, processing proceeds from meaning to sound.
- There are three main levels within the network:
  - At the highest level are nodes representing lexical concepts.
  - At the second level are nodes each representing a **lemma** from the mental lexicon. Lemmas are representations of words that "are specified syntactically and semantically but not phonologically" (Harley, 2008, p. 412). Thus, if you know the meaning of a word you are about to say and that it is a noun but you do not know its pronunciation, you have accessed its lemma.
  - At the lowest level are nodes representing word forms in terms of morphemes (basic units of meaning) and their phonemic segments.

KEY TERM

lemmas: abstract words possessing syntactic and semantic features but not phonological ones.

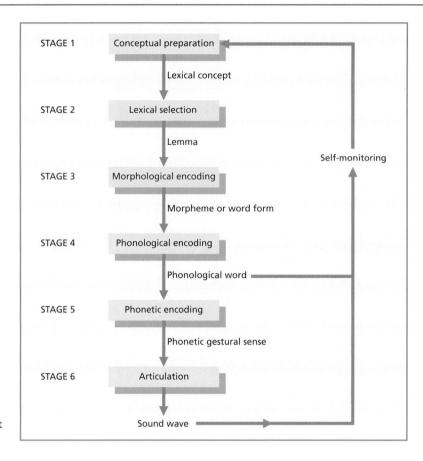

Figure 11.4 The WEAVER++ computational model. Adapted from Levelt et al. (1999).

- Speech production involves various processing stages following each other in *serial* fashion (one at a time).
- Speech errors are avoided by means of a checking mechanism.

It is easy to get lost in the complexities of this model. However, it is mainly designed to show how word production proceeds from meaning (lexical concepts and lemmas) to sound (e.g., phonological words). There is a stage of lexical selection, at which a lemma (representing word meaning + syntax) is selected. A given lemma is generally selected because it is more activated than any other lemma. After that, there is morphological encoding, during which the basic word form of the selected lemma is activated. This is followed by phonological encoding, during which the syllables of the word are computed.

What happens is known as **lexicalisation**, which is "the process in speech production whereby we turn the thoughts underlying words into sounds. We translate a semantic representation (the meaning of a content word) into its phonological representation or form (its sound)" (Harley, 2008, p. 412).

In sum, WEAVER++ is a discrete, feed-forward model. It is discrete, because the speed-production system completes its task of identifying the correct lemma or abstract word before starting to work out the sound of the selected word. It is feed-forward, because

---

KEY TERM

lexicalisation: the process of translating the meaning of a word into its sound representation during speech production.

processing proceeds in a strictly forward (from meaning to sound) direction.

Evidence

We can see the distinction between a lemma and the word itself in the "tip-of-the-tongue" state. We have all had the experience of having a concept or idea in mind while searching in vain for the right word to describe it. This frustrating situation defines the tip-of-the-tongue state. As Harley (2008) pointed out, it makes much sense to argue that the tip-of-the-tongue state occurs when semantic processing is successful (i.e., we activate the correct lemma or abstract word) but phonological processing is unsuccessful (i.e., we cannot produce the sound of the word).

The most obvious explanation for the tip-of-the-tongue state is that it occurs when the links between the semantic and phonological systems are relatively weak. Evidence consistent with that view was reported by Harley and Bown (1998). Words sounding unlike nearly all other words (e.g., apron; vineyard) were much more susceptible to the tip-of-the-tongue state than words sounding like several other words (e.g., litter; pawn). The unusual phonological forms of words susceptible to the tip-of-the-tongue state make them hard to retrieve.

The tip-of-the-tongue state is an extreme form of pause, where the word takes a noticeable time to come out – although the speaker has a distinct feeling that they know exactly what they want to say. © image100/Corbis.

Abrams (2008) discussed her research designed to test the notion that the tip-of-the-tongue state occurs because individuals find it hard to assess the phonological representation of the correct word. When participants in the tip-of-the-tongue state were presented with words sharing the first syllable with the correct word, their performance improved significantly.

Levelt et al. (1999) assumed that the lemma includes syntactic as well as semantic information (syntactic information indicates whether the word is a noun, a verb, adjective, and so on). Accordingly, individuals in the tip-of-the-tongue state should have access to syntactic information. In many languages (e.g., Italian and German), part of the syntactic information about nouns is in the form of grammatical gender (e.g., masculine, feminine). Vigliocco, Antonini, and Garrett (1997) carried out a study on Italian participants who guessed the grammatical gender of words they could not produce. When in the tip-of-the-tongue state, they guessed the grammatical gender correctly 85% of the time.

Findings less supportive of WEAVER++ were reported by Biedermann, Ruh, Nickels, and Coltheart (2008), in a study in which German speakers guessed the grammatical gender and initial phoneme of nouns when in a tip-of-the-tongue state. Theoretically, access to grammatical gender information precedes access to phonological information. As a result, participants should have been more successful at guessing the first phoneme when they had access to accurate gender information. That was *not* the case, thus casting doubt on the notion that syntactic information is available before phonological information.

The theoretical assumption that speakers have access to semantic and syntactic information about words *before* they have access to phonological information has been tested in studies using event-related potentials (ERPs; see Glossary). For example, van Turennout, Hagoort, and Brown (1998) measured ERPs while their Dutch participants produced noun phrases (e.g., "rode tafel" meaning "red table").

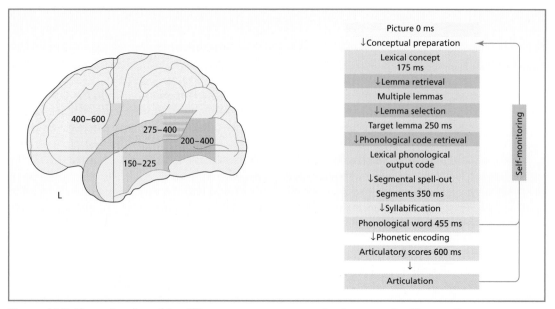

Figure 11.5 Time taken (in ms) for different processes to occur in picture naming. The specific processes are shown on the right and the relevant brain regions are shown on the left. Reprinted from Indefrey and Levelt (2004), Copyright © 2004 reproduced with permission from Elsevier.

Syntactic information about the noun's gender was available 40 ms before its initial phoneme.

Indefrey and Levelt (2004) used the findings from dozens of imaging studies involving picture naming to carry out a meta-analysis. Lexical selection occurs within about 175 ms of picture presentation, with the appropriate phonological (sound) code being retrieved between 250 and 300 ms of stimulus presentation. After that, a phonological word is generated at about 455 ms. Finally, after a further 145 ms or so, the sensori-motor areas involved in word articulation become active (see Figure 11.5). These timings are all consistent with predictions from WEAVER++.

According to WEAVER++, abstract word or lemma selection is completed before phonological information about the word is accessed. In contrast, it is assumed within Dell's spreading-activation theory that phonological processing can start *before* lemma or word selection is completed. Most of the evidence is inconsistent with predictions from WEAVER++. Meyer and Damian (2007) asked participants to name target pictures while ignoring simultaneously presented distractor pictures. The names of the objects in the pictures were phonologically related (e.g., dog–doll; ball–wall) or unrelated. According to Levelt et al.'s model, the phonological features of the names for distractor pictures should not have been activated. Thus, speed of naming target pictures should not have been influenced by whether the names of the two pictures were phonologically related. In fact, the naming of target pictures was faster when accompanied by phonologically related distractors. These findings are consistent with spreading-activation theory.

More problems for WEAVER++ come from a study on bilinguals by Costa, Caramazza, and Sebastian-Galles (2000). Bilinguals who spoke Catalan and Spanish named pictures in Spanish. The main focus was on words that look and sound similar in both languages (e.g., "cat" is "gat" in Catalan and "gato" in Spanish). According to WEAVER++, bilinguals should only access *one* lemma or abstract word at a time, and so it should be irrelevant that the Catalan word is very similar to the Spanish one. In fact, however, the naming times for such words were significantly faster for bilinguals than for monolinguals.

The tasks used in most of the research discussed up to this point have required the production of single words and so are far removed from speech production in everyday life. Can similar findings to those with single words be obtained when people have to produce entire sentences? Evidence that the answer is, "Yes", was reported by Smith and Wheeldon (2004). Participants described a moving scene presented to them. On some trials, they produced sentences involving two semantically related nouns (e.g., "The saw and the axe move apart"). On other trials, the sentences to be produced involved two phonologically related nouns (e.g., "The cat and the cap move up"). On still other trials, the two nouns were semantically and phonologically unrelated (e.g., "The saw and the cat move down").

What did Smith and Wheeldon (2004) find? First, there was a semantic interference effect even when the two nouns were in different phrases within the sentence. Second, there was a phonological facilitation effect, but only when the two nouns were in the same phrase. Both findings suggest strongly that there is more parallel processing of words within to-be-spoken sentences than assumed within WEAVER++, and this is more so with semantic processing than with phonological processing. The same conclusion follows from a consideration of several of the speech errors discussed earlier in the chapter. Of particular relevance here are word-exchange and sound-exchange errors – the two words involved in word-exchange errors tend to be further apart than those involved in sound-exchange errors. The take-home message is that planning of words (in terms of their meaning) precedes planning of sounds.

Evaluation

WEAVER++ has various successes to its credit. First, the notion that word production involves a series of stages moving from lexical selection to morphological encoding to phonological encoding provides a reasonable approximation

to what typically happens. That conclusion emerges from Indefrey and Levelt's (2004) meta-analysis of studies on the timing of different processes in word production. Second, the development of Levelt's theoretical approach had the advantage of shifting the balance of research away from speech errors and towards precise timing of word-production processes under laboratory conditions. As Levelt, Schriefers, Vorberg, Meyer, Pechman, and Havinga (1991, p. 615) pointed out, "An exclusively error-based approach to…speech production is as ill-conceived as an exclusively illusion-based approach in vision research." Third, WEAVER++ is a simple and elegant model making many testable predictions. It is probably easier to test WEAVER++ than more interactive theories such as Dell's spreading-activation theory.

What are the limitations of WEAVER++? First, it has a rather narrow focus, with the emphasis being on the production of single words. As a result, several of the processes involved in planning and producing entire sentences are not considered in detail.

Second, extensive laboratory evidence indicates that there is much more interaction between different processing levels than assumed within WEAVER++. Relevant studies include those by Costa et al. (2000) and Meyer and Damian (2007). There is also evidence (e.g., Smith & Wheeldon, 2004) that processing within sentences is more interactive than can be accounted for on WEAVER++.

Third, much of the evidence concerning speech errors suggests there is considerable parallel processing during speech production. Speech errors such as word-exchange errors, sound-exchange errors, the mixed-error effect, and the lexical bias effect are all somewhat difficult to explain on WEAVER++. Rapp and Goldrick (2000, p. 478) carried out a computer simulation and found that, "A simulation incorporating the key assumptions of a discrete feedforward theory of spoken naming did not exhibit either mixed error or lexical bias effects."

Fourth, as Harley (2008, p. 416) pointed out, "It is not clear that the need for lemmas is strongly motivated by the data. Most of the evidence really only demands a distinction between the semantic and the phonological levels."

COGNITIVE NEUROPSYHOLOGY: SPEECH PRODUCTION

The cognitive neuropsychological approach to aphasia started in the nineteenth century. It has been claimed that some aphasic or language-disordered patients have relatively intact access to syntactic information but impaired access to content words (e.g., nouns, verbs), whereas other aphasic patients show the opposite pattern. The existence of such a pattern (a double dissociation) would support the notion that speech production involves separable stages of syntactic processing and word finding, and would be consistent with theories such as spreading-activation theory and WEAVER++.

There is a historically important distinction between Broca's and Wernicke's aphasia. Patients with **Broca's aphasia** have slow, non-fluent speech. They also have a poor ability to produce syntactically correct sentences, although their speech comprehension is relatively intact. In contrast, patients with **Wernicke's aphasia** have fluent and apparently grammatical speech which often lacks meaning, and they have severe problems with speech comprehension.

According to the classical view, these two forms of aphasia involve different brain regions within the left hemisphere (see Figure 11.6). Broca's aphasia arises because of damage within a small area of the frontal lobe (Broca's area). In contrast, Wernicke's aphasia involves damage within a small area of the posterior temporal lobe (Wernicke's area).

There is some truth in the classical view. McKay et al. (2008) studied a patient, MJE, who had suffered a minor stroke that affected a relatively small part of Broca's area. He had impaired production of grammatical sentences, motor planning of speech, and some aspects

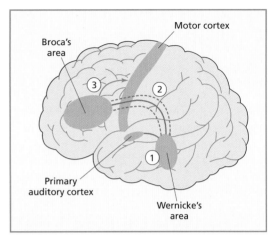

Figure 11.6 The locations of Wernicke's area (1) and Broca's area (3) are shown. When someone speaks a heard word, activation proceeds from Wernicke's area through the arcuate fasciculus (2) to Broca's area.

of sentence production. Of particular interest, when blood flow was restored to Broca's area, MJE showed immediate recovery of his language abilities. Yang, Zhao, Wang, Chen, and Zhang (2008) found, in a large sample of stroke patients, that the main determinant of their language difficulties was the brain location of the lesion. Most patients with damage to Broca's area had the language deficits associated with Broca's aphasia and those with damage to Wernicke's area had the language problems associated with Wernicke's aphasia. However, a few patients had damage to one of these areas without any obvious language impairment.

Other studies have produced findings less consistent with the classical view. For example, De Bleser (1988) studied six very clear cases of Wernicke's aphasia. They all had damage to Wernicke's area but two also had damage

KEY TERMS

Broca's aphasia: a form of **aphasia** involving non-fluent speech and grammatical errors.
Wernicke's aphasia: a form of **aphasia** involving impaired comprehension and fluent speech with many content words missing.

to Broca's area. De Bleser also studied seven very clear cases of Broca's aphasia. Four had damage to Broca's area but the others had damage to Wernicke's area.

According to Dick, Bates, Wulfeck, Utman, Dronkers, and Gernsbacher (2001), the notion that patients with Broca's aphasia have much greater problems in speaking grammatically than patients with Wernicke's aphasia may be incorrect. They pointed out that this finding has been obtained in studies involving English-speaking patients. In contrast, studies on patients who speak richly inflected languages (e.g., Italian and German) indicate that Wernicke's aphasia patients make comparable numbers of grammatical errors to patients with Broca's aphasia (Dick et al., 2001). How can we explain these findings? In most languages, grammatical changes to nouns and verbs are indicated by changes to the words themselves (e.g., the plural of "houses" is "houses"; the past tense of "see" is "saw"). This is known as inflection. English is a less inflected language than most. According to Dick et al. (2001), this is important. The fact that English is not a very inflected language means that the grammatical limitations of English-speaking patients with Wernicke's aphasia are less obvious than those of patients speaking other languages.

Evaluation

The distinction between Broca's aphasia and Wernicke's aphasia has become less popular for various reasons. First, both forms of aphasia are commonly associated with grammatical errors and word-finding difficulties or anomia (discussed shortly), thus blurring the distinction.

Second, the terms Broca's aphasia and Wernicke's aphasia imply that numerous brain-damaged patients all have similar patterns of language impairment. In fact, however, patients exhibit very different symptoms.

Third, the emphasis has shifted away from descriptions of broad patterns of language impairment towards systematic attempts to understand relatively specific cognitive impairments. These more specific impairments include anomia, agrammatism, and jargon aphasia (see following sections).

Anomia

Most aphasic patients suffer from **anomia**, which is an impaired ability to name objects. This is often assessed by giving patients a picture-naming task. Unsurprisingly, the speech of most patients is low in content and lacking in fluency. However, Crutch and Warrington (2003) studied a patient with anomia, FAV, who described most scenes with normal fluency. It seemed as if he had a feedback mechanism allowing him to predict in advance which words would be retrievable, and so avoid constructing sentences requiring non-retrievable ones.

According to Levelt et al.'s (1999a) WEAVER++ model, patients might have difficulties in naming for two reasons. First, there could be a problem in lemma or abstract word selection, in which case naming errors would be similar in meaning to the correct word. Second, there could be a problem in word-form selection, in which case patients would be unable to find the appropriate phonological form of the word.

Evidence

A case of anomia involving a semantic impairment (deficient lemma selection?) was reported by Howard and Orchard-Lisle (1984). When the patient, JCU, named objects shown in pictures, she would often produce the wrong answer when given the first phoneme or sound of a word closely related to the target object. However, if she produced a name very different in meaning from the object depicted, she rejected it 86% of the time. JCU had access to *some* semantic information but this was often insufficient for accurate object naming.

KEY TERM

anomia: a condition caused by brain damage in which there is an impaired ability to name objects.

Kay and Ellis (1987) studied a patient, EST, who could apparently select the correct abstract word or lemma but not the phonological form of the word. He seemed to have no significant impairment to his semantic system, but had great problems in finding words other than very common ones. Kay and Ellis argued that his condition resembled, in greatly magnified form, that of the rest of us when in the tip-of-the-tongue state.

Lambon Ralph, Moriarty, and Sage (2002) argued that the evidence on anomia could be explained without recourse to lemmas or abstract words. They assessed semantic/conceptual functioning, phonological functioning, and lemma functioning in aphasics. Their key finding was that the extent of anomia shown by individual aphasics was predicted well simply by considering their general semantic and phonological impairments. Thus, severe anomia was found in patients who had problems in accessing the meaning and the sounds of words. There was no evidence to indicate a role for an abstract lexical level of representation (i.e., the lemma).

Findings apparently inconsistent with those of Lambon Ralph were reported by Ingles, Fisk, Passmore, and Darvesh (2007). They studied a patient, MT, who had severe anomia with *no* apparent semantic or phonological impairment. Ingles et al. suggested that she might have an impairment in mapping semantic representations onto phonological ones even though both systems were intact. The fact that MT used the strategy of reciting the phonemes of the alphabet as cues to assist her retrieval of words is consistent with that suggestion.

Evaluation

Most research on anomia is consistent with Levelt et al.'s (1999) notion that problems with word retrieval can occur at two different stages: (1) abstract word selection or lemma selection; and (2) accessing the phonological form of the word. However, a simpler explanation may well be preferable. According to this explanation, anomia occurs in patients as a fairly direct consequence of their semantic and phonological impairments.

Agrammatism

It is generally assumed theoretically that there are separate stages for working out the syntax or grammatical structure of utterances and for producing the content words to fit that grammatical structure (e.g., Dell, 1986). Patients who can apparently find the appropriate words but not order them grammatically suffer from **agrammatism** or non-fluent aphasia, a condition traditionally associated with Broca's area. In the next section, we discuss patients with jargon aphasia, who allegedly have much greater problems with word finding than with producing grammatical sentences. If such a double dissociation (see Glossary) could be found, it would support the view that there are separable stages of processing of grammar and word finding.

Patients with agrammatism tend to produce short sentences containing content words (e.g., nouns, verbs) but lacking function words (e.g., the, in, and) and word endings. This makes good sense because function words play a key role in producing a grammatical structure for sentences. Finally, patients with agrammatism often have problems with the comprehension of syntactically complex sentences.

Evidence

Saffran, Schwartz, and Marin (1980a, 1980b) studied patients with agrammatism. One patient produced the following description of a woman kissing a man: "The kiss…the lady kissed…the lady is…the lady and the man and the lady…kissing." In addition, Saffran et al. found that agrammatic aphasics had great difficulty in putting the two nouns in the correct order when describing pictures containing two living creatures.

KEY TERM

agrammatism: a condition in which speech production lacks grammatical structure and many function words and word endings are omitted; often also associated with comprehension difficulties.

Evidence that agrammatic patients have particular problems in processing function words was reported by Biassou, Obler, Nespoulous, Dordain, and Harris (1997). Agrammatic patients given the task of reading words made significantly more phonological errors on function words than on content words. Guasti and Luzzatti (2002) found that agrammatic patients often failed to adjust the form of verbs to take account of person or number, and mostly used only the present tense of verbs.

Beeke, Wilkinson, and Maxim (2007) argued that the artificial tasks (e.g., picture description) used in most research may have led researchers to *underestimate* the grammatical abilities of agrammatic patients. They supported this argument in a study on a patient with agrammatism who completed tests of spoken sentence construction and was videotaped having a conversation at home with a family member. His speech appeared more grammatical in the more naturalistic situation.

There is considerable variation across agrammatic patients in their precise symptoms (Harley, 2008). Some of this variation can be explained with reference to a model proposed by Grodzinsky and Friederici (2006), who argued that different aspects of syntactic processing occur in different brain areas. They used evidence mainly from functional neuro-imaging to identify three phases of syntactic processing, together with the brain areas involved (see Figure 11.7):

(1) At this phase, local phrase structures are formed after word category information (e.g., noun; verb) has been identified. The frontal operculum and anterior superior temporal gyrus are involved.

(2) At this phase, dependency relationships among the various sentence elements are calculated (i.e., who is doing what to whom?). Broca's area (BA44/45) is involved. For example, Friederici, Fiebach, Schlewesky, Bornkessel, and von Cramon (2006) found that activation in Broca's area was greater with syntactically complex sentences than with syntactically simple ones. This is the phase of most relevance to agrammatism.

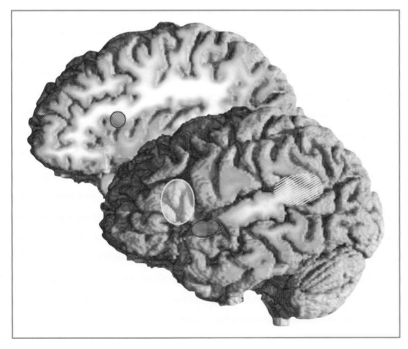

Figure 11.7 The main brain areas involved in syntactic processing. Pink areas (frontal operculum and anterior superior temporal gyrus) are involved in the build-up of local phrase structures; the yellow area (BA33/45) is involved in the computation of dependency relations between sentence components; the striped area (posterior superior temporal gyrus and sulcus) is involved in integration processes. Reprinted from Grodzinsky and Friederici (2006), Copyright © 2006, with permission from Elsevier.

(3) At this phase, there is integration of syntactic and lexical information, especially when ungrammatical word strings are encountered. The posterior superior temporal gyrus and sulcus are involved (including Wernicke's area).

Burkhardt, Avrutin, Piñango, and Ruigendijk (2008) argued that agrammatic patients have limited processing capacity specifically affecting syntactic processing. Agrammatics were reasonably successful at resolving syntactic complexities in sentences, but took a considerable amount of time to do so. The implication was that they had a processing limitation rather than loss of the necessary syntactic knowledge. Within the context of Grodzinsky and Friederici's (2006) model, this effect would be mainly at the second phase of syntactic processing.

Evaluation
Research on agrammatism supports the notion that speech production involves a syntactic level at which the grammatical structure of a sentence is formed. Progress has been made in identifying reasons why individuals with agrammatism have problems in syntactic comprehension and grammatical speech. They often seem to have reduced resources for syntactic processing. Evidence that different brain areas are involved in different aspects of syntactic processing may prove of lasting value in developing an understanding of the various symptoms associated with agrammatism.

What are the limitations of research on agrammatism? First, as Harley (2008, p. 438) pointed out, "If it [i.e., agrammatism] is a meaningful syndrome, we should find that the sentence construction deficit, grammatical element loss, and a syntactic comprehension deficit should always co-occur. A number of single case studies have found dissociations between these impairments." Second, it has proved difficult to account theoretically for the impairments in agrammatism. Some kind of processing deficit is often involved, but we do not as yet know the precise nature of that deficit.

Jargon aphasia

Patients with agrammatism can find the content words they want to say but cannot produce grammatically correct sentences. Patients suffering from **jargon aphasia** apparently show the opposite pattern. They seem to speak fairly grammatically, leading many experts to assume they have a largely intact syntactic level of processing. Unlike patients with agrammatism, jargon aphasics experience great difficulty in finding the right words. They often substitute one word for another and also produce **neologisms** (made-up words; see below). Finally, jargon aphasics typically seem unaware that their speech contains numerous errors, and can become irritated when others do not understand them (see Marshall, 2006, for a review).

We can illustrate the speech errors made by jargon aphasics by considering RD (Ellis, Miller, and Sin, 1983). Here is his description of a picture of a scout camp (the words he seemed to be searching for are given in brackets):

> *A b-boy is swi'ing (SWINGING) on the bank with his hand (FEET) in the stringt (STREAM). A table with ostrum (SAUCEPAN?) and...I don't know...and a three-legged stroe (STOOL) and a strane (PAIL) – table, table...near the water.*

RD, in common with most jargon aphasics, produced more neologisms or invented words when the word he wanted was not a common one.

It is easy to conclude that jargon aphasics communicate very poorly. However, as Marshall (2006, p. 406) pointed out, "Even the most

---

KEY TERMS

jargon aphasia: a brain-damaged condition in which speech is reasonably correct grammatically but there are great problems in finding the right words.
neologisms: made-up words produced by individuals suffering from **jargon aphasia**.

impaired jargon aphasic can still communicate a great deal. They can convey anger, delight, puzzlement, surprise, and humour."

Evidence

How grammatical is the speech of jargon aphasics? The fact that they produce numerous neologisms makes it hard to answer this question. However, the neologisms they produce are often imbedded within phrase structures (Marshall, 2006). If jargon aphasics have some ability to engage in syntactic processing, their neologisms or made-up words might possess appropriate prefixes or suffixes to fit into the syntactic structure of the sentence. For example, if the neologism refers to the past participle of a verb, it might end in –ed. Evidence that jargon aphasics do modify their neologisms to make them fit syntactically was reported by Butterworth (1985).

Some of the problems in assessing jargon aphasics' grammaticality can be seen if we consider the following utterance (taken from Butterworth & Howard, 1987): "Isn't look very dear, is it?" The sentence certainly looks ungrammatical. However, Butterworth and Howard argued that the patient had blended or combined two syntactic options (i.e., "doesn't look very dear" and "isn't very dear").

Why do jargon aphasics produce neologisms? Some of their neologisms are phonologically related to the target word, whereas others are almost unrelated phonologically, and it is unclear whether the same mechanisms are involved. Olson, Romani, and Halloran (2007) studied VS, an 84-year-old woman with jargon aphasia. Her neologisms (regardless of how phonologically related to target words) were affected in similar ways by factors such as word frequency, imageability, and length, suggesting that there might be a single underlying deficit. Olson et al. concluded that this deficit may occur at a level of phonological encoding that follows immediately after lexical access.

What determines the phonemes found in the neologisms of jargon aphasics? We will consider three factors. First, as we have seen, some of the phonemes often resemble those in

the target word. Second, a jargon aphasic, LT, had a strong tendency to produce consonants common in the English language regardless of whether they were correct when he was picture naming (Robson, Pring, Marshall, & Chiat, 2003). Third, Goldman, Schwartz, and Wilshire (2001) found evidence suggesting that jargon aphasics tend to include recently used phonemes in neologisms, presumably because they still retained some activation.

Why are jargon aphasics poor at monitoring and correcting their own speech? Several answers have been suggested (Marshall, 2006). One possibility is that jargon aphasics find it hard to speak and to monitor their own speech at the same time. Some support for that hypothesis was reported by Shuren, Hammond, Maher, Roth, and Heilman (1995). A jargon aphasic indicated whether his responses on a picture naming test were correct. His judgements were right 90% of the time when he listened to a tape of his own voice some time after performing the test compared to only 6.7% right when he made immediate judgements.

Another possibility was suggested by Marshall, Robson, Pring, and Chiat (1998). They studied a jargon aphasic, CM, who named pictures and repeated words he had produced on the naming task. He was much better at detecting neologisms on the repetition task than on the naming task (95% versus 55%, respectively). Marshall et al. (p. 79) argued that, "His [CM's] monitoring difficulties arise when he is accessing phonology from semantics." This ability was required when naming pictures because he had to access the meaning of each picture (semantics) before deciding how to pronounce its name (phonology).

Evaluation

We have an increased understanding of the processes underlying the neologisms produced by jargon aphasics. However, it is unclear whether the same processes are responsible for neologisms resembling the target word phonologically closely or not at all. In addition, there are several possible reasons why jargon aphasics fail to monitor their own speech effectively for errors, and the relative importance of these reasons has not been established. There is some controversy concerning the grammaticality of the sentences produced by jargon aphasics, and this reduces the relevance of findings from jargon aphasics for evaluating theories of speech production.

WRITING: THE MAIN PROCESSES

Writing involves the retrieval and organisation of information stored in long-term memory. In addition, it involves complex thought processes. This has led several theorists (e.g., Kellogg, 1994; Oatley & Djikic, 2008) to argue that writing is basically a form of thinking. According to Kellogg (1994, p. 13), "I regard thinking and writing as twins of mental life. The study of the more expressive twin, writing, can offer insights into the psychology of thinking, the more reserved member of the pair." Thus, although writing is an important topic in its own right (no pun intended!), it is *not* separate from other cognitive activities.

The development of literacy (including writing skills) can enhance thinking ability. Luria (1976) studied two groups in Uzbekistan in the early 1930s, only one of which had received brief training in literacy. Both groups were asked various questions including the following: "In the Far North, where there is snow, all bears are white. Novaya Zemlya is in the Far North. What colour are the bears there?" Only 27% of those who were illiterate produced the right answer compared to 100% of those who had partial literacy.

Key processes
Hayes and Flower (1986) identified three key writing processes:

(1) The *planning process*: this involves producing ideas and organising them into a writing plan to satisfy the writer's goals.

One of the three key processes in writing is the revision process, in which we evaluate what we have written. This can occur at all levels from individual words to the entire structure of our writing.

(2) The *sentence-generation process*: this involves turning the writing plan into the actual writing of sentences.
(3) The *revision process*: this involves evaluating what has been written. Its focus ranges between individual words and the overall structural coherence of the writing.

The "natural" sequence of the three processes is obviously planning, sentence generation, and revision. However, writers often deviate from this sequence if, for example, they spot a problem with what they are writing before producing a complete draft.

Evidence
We can identify the processes involved in writing by using **directed retrospection**. Writers are stopped at various times during the writing process and categorise what they were just doing (e.g., planning, sentence generation, revision).

> ### KEY TERM
>
> **directed retrospection:** a method of studying writing in which writers are stopped while writing and categorise their immediately preceding thoughts.

Kellogg (1994) discussed studies involving directed retrospection. On average, writers devoted about 30% of their time to planning, 50% to sentence generation, and 20% to revision.

Levy and Ransdell (1995) analysed writing processes systematically. As well as asking their participants to verbalise what they were doing, Levy and Ransdell obtained videorecordings as they wrote essays on computers. The percentage of time devoted to planning decreased from 40 to 30% during the course of the study. Surprisingly, the length of time spent on each process before moving on to another process was often very short. In the case of text generation, the median time was 7.5 seconds, and it was only 2.5 seconds for planning, reviewing, and revising. These findings suggest that the various processes involved in writing are heavily interdependent and much less separate than we might imagine.

Levy and Ransdell (1995) reported a final interesting finding – writers were only partially aware of how they allocated time. Most overestimated the time spent on reviewing and revising, and underestimated the time spent on generating text. The writers estimated that they spent just over 30% of their time reviewing and revising, but actually devoted only 5% of their time to those activities!

Kellogg (1988) considered the effects of producing an outline (focus on the main themes) on subsequent letter writing. Producers of outlines spent more time in sentence generation than no-outline participants, but less time in planning and reviewing or revising. Producing an outline increased the quality of the letter. Why was this? Producers of outlines did not have to devote so much time to planning, which is the hardest process in writing.

Planning

Writing depends heavily on the writer's knowledge. Alexander, Schallert, and Hare (1991) identified three kinds of relevant knowledge:

(1) *Conceptual knowledge*: information about concepts and schemas stored in long-term memory.

(2) *Socio-cultural knowledge*: information about the social background or context.

(3) *Metacognitive knowledge*: knowledge about what one knows.

Hayes and Flower (1986) also identified strategic knowledge as important. This concerns ways of organising the goals and sub-goals of writing to construct a coherent writing plan. Good writers use strategic knowledge flexibly to change the structure of the writing plan if problems arise.

Sentence generation

Kaufer, Hayes, and Flower (1986) found that essays were always at least eight times longer than outlines or writing plans. The technique of asking writers to think aloud permitted Kaufer et al. to explore the process of sentence generation. Expert and average writers accepted about 75% of the sentence parts they verbalised. The length of the average sentence part was 11.2 words for the expert writers compared to 7.3 words for the average writers. Thus, good writers use larger units or "building blocks".

Revision

Revision is a key (and often underestimated) process in writing. Expert writers devote more of their writing time to revision than non-expert ones (Hayes & Flower, 1986). Of importance, expert writers focus more on the coherence and structure of the arguments expressed. Faigley and Witte (1983) found that 34% of revisions by experienced adult writers involved a change of meaning against only 12% of the revisions by inexperienced college writers.

Evaluation

No one denies that planning, sentence generation, and revision are all important processes in writing. However, these three processes cannot be neatly separated. We saw that in the study by Levy and Ransdell (1995). In addition, the processes of planning and sentence generation are almost inextricably bound up with each other.

Another issue is that Hayes and Flower (1986) de-emphasised the social aspect of much writing. As is discussed shortly, writers need to take account of the intended readership for the texts they produce. This is one of the most difficult tasks faced by writers, especially when the readership is likely to consist of individuals having very different amounts of relevant knowledge.

Writing expertise

Why are some writers more skilful than others? As with any complex cognitive skill, extensive and deliberate practice over a prolonged period of time is very important (see Chapter 12). Practice can help to provide writers with additional relevant knowledge, the ability to write faster (e.g., using word processing), and so on. We will see shortly that the working memory system (see Chapter 6) plays a very important role in writing. All of the components of working memory have limited capacity, and it is likely that writing demands on these components decrease with practice. That would provide experienced writers with spare processing capacity to enhance the quality of what they are writing.

Individual differences in writing ability probably depend mostly on planning and revision processes. Bereiter and Scardamalia (1987) argued that two major strategies are used in the planning stage:

(1) A knowledge-telling strategy.
(2) A knowledge-transforming strategy.

The knowledge-telling strategy involves writers simply writing down everything they know about a topic with minimal planning. The text already generated provides retrieval cues for generating the rest of the text. In the words of a 12-year-old child who used the knowledge-telling strategy (Bereiter & Scardamalia, 1987, p. 9), "I have a whole bunch of ideas and write them down until my supply of ideas is exhausted."

With increasing writing expertise, most adolescents shift from the knowledge-telling strategy to the knowledge-transforming strategy. This involves use of a *rhetorical problem space* and a content problem space. Rhetorical problems relate to the achievement of the goals of the writing task (e.g., "Can I strengthen the argument?"), whereas content problems relate to the specific information to be written down (e.g., "The case of Smith vs. Jones strengthens the argument"). There should be movement of information in both directions between the content space and the rhetorical space. This happens more often with skilled writers.

Bereiter, Burtis, and Scardamalia (1988) argued that knowledge-transforming strategists would be more likely than knowledge-telling strategists to produce high-level main points capturing important themes. Children and adults wrote an essay. Those producing a high-level main point used on average 4.75 different knowledge-transforming processes during planning. In contrast, those producing a low-level main point used only 0.23 knowledge-transforming processes on average.

Successful use of the planning process also depends on the writer's relevant knowledge. Adults possessing either much knowledge or relatively little on a topic were compared by Hayes and Flower (1986). The experts produced more goals and sub-goals, and so constructed a more complex overall writing plan. In addition, the experts' various goals were much more interconnected.

Expert writers also differ from non-expert ones in their ability to use the revision process. Hayes, Flower, Schriver, Stratman, and Carey (1985) found that expert writers detected 60% more problems in a text than non-experts. The expert writers correctly identified the nature of the problem in 74% of cases against only 42% for the non-expert writers.

Levy and Ransdell (1995) found that writers who produced the best essays spent 40% more of their time reviewing and revising them than those producing the essays of poorest quality. Revisions made towards the end of the writing session were especially important.

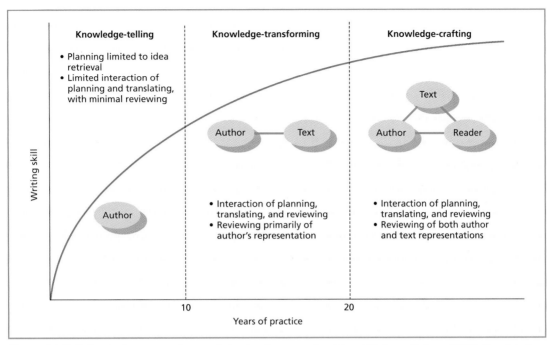

Figure 11.8 Kellogg's three-stage theory of the development of writing skill. From Kellogg (2008). Reprinted with permission of *Journal of Writing Research* www.jowr.org

Knowledge-crafting: focus on the reader

Kellogg (2008) argued that really expert writers attain the knowledge-crafting stage. This is an advance on the knowledge-transforming stage: "In…knowledge-crafting, the writer is able to hold in mind the author's ideas, the words of the text itself, and the imagined reader's interpretation of the text" (p. 5). As can be seen in Figure 11.8, the distinctive feature of the knowledge-crafting stage is its focus on the reader's needs.

It is important to consider the reader because of the **knowledge effect** – the tendency to assume that other people share the knowledge we possess. Hayes and Bajzek (2008) found that individuals familiar with technical terms greatly overestimated the knowledge other people would have of these terms (this is a failing that may have afflicted the authors of this book!). Hayes and Bajzek found that providing feedback to improve writers' predictions

of the knowledge possessed by others made their texts more understandable.

Instructing writers explicitly to consider the reader's needs often produces beneficial results. Holloway and McCutcheon (2004) found that the revisions made to a text by students aged about 11 or 15 were improved by the instruction to "read-as-the-reader". However, *feedback* from readers is especially effective. Schriver (1984) asked students to read an imperfect text and predict the comprehension problems another reader would have. Then the students read a reader's verbal account produced while he/she tried to understand that text. After the students had been given various texts plus readers' accounts, they became better at predicting the problems readers would have with new texts.

Sato and Matsushima (2006) found the quality of text writing by 15-year-old students was not improved by instructing them to attend to potential readers, perhaps because the instructions were not sufficiently detailed. However, feedback from the readers about the comprehension problems they encountered was effective, and the benefits transferred to subsequent writing.

Carvalho (2002) used a broader approach based on procedural facilitation. In this technique, writers evaluate what they have written for relevance, repetition, missing details, and clarity to readers after writing each sentence. Student participants exposed to this technique wrote more effectively and were more responsive to readers' needs subsequently.

In sum, non-expert writers typically focus on producing text they find easy to understand without paying much attention to the problems that other readers are likely to encounter with it. In contrast, expert writers engage in knowledge-crafting: they focus explicitly on the needs of their potential readers. Expert writers writing on topics on which they possess considerable knowledge are liable to overestimate the amount of relevant knowledge possessed by their readers. Most writing problems (including the knowledge effect) can be reduced by providing writers with detailed feedback from readers.

Working memory

Most people find writing difficult and effortful, because it involves several different cognitive processes such as attention, thinking, and memory. According to Kellogg (2001a, p. 43), "Many kinds of writing tasks impose considerable demands on working memory, the system responsible for processing and storing information on a short-term basis." The key component of the working memory system (discussed at length in Chapter 6) is the central executive, an attention-like process involved in organising and co-

ordinating cognitive activities. Other components of the working memory system are the visuo-spatial sketchpad (involved in visual and spatial processing) and the phonological loop (involved in verbal rehearsal). All of these components have limited capacity. As we will see, writing can involve any or all of these working memory components (see Olive, 2004, for a review).

Evidence

According to Kellogg's working memory theory, all the main processes involved in writing depend on the central executive component of working memory. As a consequence, writing quality is likely to suffer if *any* writing process is made more difficult. As predicted, the quality of the written texts was lower when the text had to be written in capital letters rather than in normal handwriting (Olive & Kellogg, 2002).

How can we assess the involvement of the central executive in writing? One way is to measure reaction times to auditory probes presented in isolation (control condition) or while participants are engaged on a writing task. If writing uses much of the available capacity of working memory (especially the central executive), then reaction times should be longer in the writing condition. Olive and Kellogg used this probe technique to work out the involvement of the central executive in the following conditions:

(1) *Transcription*: a prepared text was simply copied, so no planning was required.
(2) *Composition*: a text had to be composed, i.e., the writer had to plan and produce a coherent text. There was a pause in writing when the auditory signal was presented.
(3) *Composition + transcription*: a text had to be composed, and the participant continued writing when the auditory signal was presented.

Olive and Kellogg (2002) found that composition was more demanding than transcription (see Figure 11.9), because composition involves planning and sentence generation. In

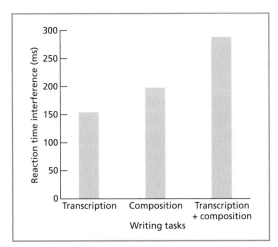

Figure 11.9 Interfering effects of writing tasks (transcription; composition; transcription + composition) on reaction time to an auditory signal. Adapted from Olive and Kellog (2002).

addition, composition + transcription is more demanding than composition. Thus, writers can apparently engage in higher-level processes (e.g., planning) *and* lower-level processes (writing words) at the same time.

Kellogg (2001a) assumed that writers with much relevant knowledge about an essay topic would have large amounts of well-organised information stored in long-term memory. This knowledge should reduce the effort involved in writing an essay. He asked students with varying degrees of relevant knowledge to write an essay about baseball, and used the probe technique to assess processing demands. As predicted, processing demands were lower in those students with the most background knowledge.

Kellogg (2001b) used the probe technique to assess the processing demands of planning, translating, and reviewing during the production of texts in longhand or on a word processor. It was assumed that students would find use of a word processor more demanding than writing in longhand because of their lesser familiarity with word processing. There were three main findings. First, probe reaction times were much slower for planning, translating, and reviewing than under control conditions,

indicating that all three writing processes are very demanding. Second, reviewing was more demanding than planning and translating. Third, word processing was more demanding than writing in longhand.

Why is reviewing/revising the text that has been produced so demanding? According to Hayes (2004), text reviewing or revision involves language comprehension processes plus additional processes (e.g., problem solving and decision making). Roussey and Piolat (2008) used the probe technique, and found that reviewing was more demanding of processing resources than comprehension. This was more so for participants low in working memory capacity (see Chapter 10), suggesting that text reviewing or revising is especially demanding for such individuals.

Vanderberg and Swanson (2007) adopted an individual-difference approach to assess the involvement of the central executive in writing. They considered writing performance at the *general* (e.g., planning, sentence generation, revision) and at the *specific* (e.g., grammar, punctuation) levels. Individuals with the most effective central executive functioning had the best writing performance at both levels.

What about the other components of working memory? Chenoweth and Hayes (2003) asked participants to perform the task of typing sentences to describe cartoons on its own or while repeating a syllable continuously (syllable repetition uses the phonological loop and is known as articulatory suppression). Articulatory suppression caused writers to produce shorter sequences of words in rapid succession, suggesting that it suppressed their "inner voice". It could be argued that the reason why articulatory suppression impaired writing performance was because the writing task was a fairly complex one. Hayes and Chenoweth (2006) investigated this issue by asking their participants to transcribe or copy texts from one computer window to another. In spite of the apparent simplicity of this writing task, participants transcribed more slowly and made more errors when the task was accompanied by articulatory suppression.

We turn now to the visuo-spatial sketchpad. Levy and Ransdell (2001) found that a visuo-spatial task (detecting when two consecutive characters were in the same place or were similar in colour) increased writers' initial planning time. Kellogg, Oliver, and Piolat (2007) asked students to write descriptions of concrete (e.g., house; pencil) and abstract (e.g., freedom; duty) nouns while performing a detection task. The writing task slowed detection times for visual stimuli *only* when concrete words were being described. Thus, the visuo-spatial sketchpad is more involved when writers are thinking about concrete objects than abstract ones.

Evaluation

The main writing processes are very demanding or effortful and make substantial demands on working memory (especially the central executive). The demands on the central executive may be especially great during revision or reviewing (Kellogg, 2001b; Roussey & Piolat, 2008). The phonological loop and the visuo-spatial sketchpad are also both involved in the writing process. However, the involvement of the visuo-spatial sketchpad depends on the type of text being produced (Kellogg et al., 2007). It is not clear that writing performance *necessarily* depends on the involvement of the phonological loop. Some patients with a severely impaired phonological loop nevertheless have essentially normal written language (Gathercole & Baddeley, 1993).

The main limitation of Kellogg's theoretical approach is that it does not indicate clearly *why* processes such as planning or sentence generation are so demanding. We need a more fine-grain analysis of writers' strategies during the planning process. The theory focuses on the effects of writing processes on working memory. However, working memory limitations probably influence *how* we allocate our limited resources during writing. For example, we may shift rapidly from one writing process to another when our processing capacity is in danger of being exceeded. It would be useful to know more about the ways in which the various components of working memory *interact* in the writing process. Finally, we would expect that individual differences in working memory capacity would have a large impact on the quality of writing and on the processes used during writing. However, research to date has barely addressed these issues (e.g., Roussey & Piolat, 2008).

Word processing

There has been a substantial increase in the use of word processors in recent years. Most evidence suggests that this is a good thing. Goldberg, Russell, and Cook (2003) carried out meta-analyses (combining findings from many studies) to compare writing performance when students used word processors or wrote in longhand. Here are their conclusions: "Students who use computers when learning to write are not only more engaged in their writing but they produce work that is of greater length and higher quality" (p. 1). One reason why word processing leads to enhanced writing quality is because word-processed essays tend to be better organised than those written in longhand (Whithaus, Harrison, & Midyette, 2008).

Kellogg and Mueller (1993) compared text produced by word processor and by writing in longhand. There were only small differences in writing quality or the speed at which text was produced. However, use of the probe technique indicated that word processing involved more effortful planning and revision (but not sentence generation) than writing in longhand. Those using word processors were much less likely than those writing in longhand to make notes (12% versus 69%, respectively), which may explain the findings.

In sum, we should not expect word processing to have a dramatic impact on writing quality. Factors such as access to relevant knowledge, skill at generating sentences, and ability to revise text effectively are essential to high-quality writing, and it is not clear whether these factors are much influenced by the way in which the text is written.

SPELLING

Spelling is an important aspect of writing, and has been the subject of considerable research interest. We will base our discussion on a theoretical sketch map of the main processes and structures involved in spelling heard words according to Goldberg and Rapp (2008; see Figure 11.10):

- There are two main routes between hearing a word and spelling it: (1) the lexical route (left-hand side of Figure 11.10) and the non-lexical route (right-hand side). There are some similarities here with the dual-route cascaded model of reading (Coltheart et al., 2001, see Chapter 9).
- The lexical route contains the information needed to relate phonological (sound), semantic (meaning), and orthographic (spelling) representations of words to each other.

Thus, this route to spelling a heard word involves accessing detailed information about all features of the word. It is the main route we use when spelling familiar words whether the relationship between the sound units (phonemes) and units of written language (graphemes) is regular (e.g., "cat") or irregular (e.g., "yacht").

- The non-lexical route does *not* involve gaining access to detailed information about the sound, meaning, and spelling of heard words. Instead, this route uses stored rules to convert sounds or phonemes into groups of letters or graphemes. We use this route when spelling unfamiliar words or nonwords. It produces correct spellings when the relationship between phonemes and graphemes is regular or common (e.g., "cat"). However, it produces systematic spelling errors when the relationship is irregular or uncommon (e.g., "yacht"; "comb").

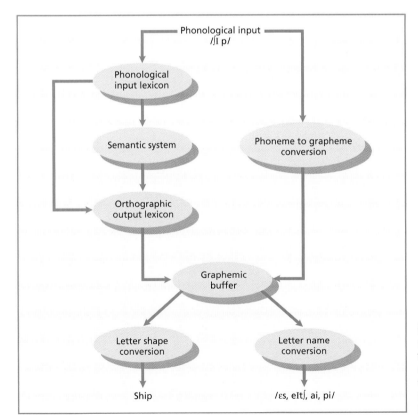

Figure 11.10 A two-route model of the spelling system with the lexical route (based on words) on the left and the non-lexical route on the right. From Goldberg and Rapp (2008).

- Both routes make use of a **graphemic buffer**. This briefly holds graphemic representations consisting of abstract letters or letter groups just before they are written or typed.

Lexical route: phonological dysgraphia

What would happen if a brain-damaged patient could make very little use of the non-lexical route but the lexical route was essentially intact? He/she would spell known words accurately, because their spellings would be available in the orthographic output lexicon. However, there would be great problems with unfamiliar words and nonwords for which relevant information is *not* contained in the orthographic output lexicon. The term **phonological dysgraphia** is applied to patients with these symptoms. Several patients with phonological dysgraphia have been studied. Shelton and Weinrich (1997) studied a patient, EA, who could not write correctly any of 55 nonwords to dictation. However, the patient wrote 50% of regular words and 45% of irregular words correctly.

A simpler hypothesis to explain the spelling problems of patients with phonological dysgraphia is that they have a severe deficit with phonological processing (processing involving the sounds of words). According to this hypothesis, such patients should have problems on *any* task involving phonological processing even if it did not involve spelling at all. Rapcsak et al. (2009) obtained support for this hypothesis. Patients with phonological dysgraphia performed poorly on phonological tasks such as deciding whether two words rhymed or producing a word rhyming with a target word.

Non-lexical route: surface dysgraphia

If a patient had damage to the lexical route and so relied largely on the phoneme–grapheme conversion system in spelling, what would happen? Apart from producing misspellings sounding like the relevant word, such a patient would have some success in generating appropriate spellings of nonwords. In addition, he/she would be more accurate at spelling regular words (i.e., words where the spelling can be worked out from the sound) than irregular words. Patients with these symptoms suffer from **surface dysgraphia**. Macoir and Bernier (2002) studied a patient, MK, who spelled 92% of regular words correctly but only 52% of irregular words. Her overall word spelling was much better for words about which she could access semantic information than those about which she could not (85% versus 19%, respectively). This makes sense given that the semantic system forms part of the lexical route.

Strong evidence that patients with surface dysgraphia often have poor access to lexical information about words was reported by Bormann, Wallesch, Seyboth, and Blanken (2009). They studied MO, a male German patient. When he heard two words (e.g., "lass das" meaning "leave it"), he often wrote them as a single meaningless word (e.g., "lasdas").

Are the two routes independent?

We have seen that an important distinction exists between lexical and non-lexical routes to spelling. Do these two routes operate independently or do they interact with each other? There is increasing evidence that they often interact. Rapp, Epstein, and Tainturier (2002) studied LAT, a patient with Alzheimer's disease. He made many errors in spelling, but used the phoneme–grapheme system reasonably well. He showed

KEY TERMS

graphemic buffer: a store in which graphemic information about the individual letters in a word is held immediately before spelling the word.
phonological dysgraphia: a condition caused by brain damage in which familiar words can be spelled reasonably well but nonwords cannot.
surface dysgraphia: a condition caused by brain damage in which there is poor spelling of irregular words, reasonable spelling of regular words, and some success in spelling nonwords.

good spelling of nonwords and most of his spelling errors on real words were phonologically plausible (e.g., "pursuit" spelled PERSUTE; "leopard" spelled LEPERD). Such findings indicate that LAT was using the non-lexical route.

Rapp et al. found that LAT made other errors suggesting he was using the lexical route. For example, he spelled "bouquet" as BOUKET and "knowledge" as KNOLIGE. These spellings suggest some use of the non-lexical route. However, some features of these spellings could not have come directly from the sounds of the words. LAT could only have known that "bouquet" ends in "t" and that "knowledge" starts with "k" by using information in the orthographic output lexicon, which forms part of the lexical route. Thus, LAT sometimes integrated information from lexical and non-lexical processes when spelling familiar words.

Suppose we asked healthy participants to spell various words and nonwords. If the two routes are independent, we would expect the spelling of nonwords to involve *only* the phoneme–grapheme conversion system within the non-lexical route. In fact, there are lexical influences on nonword spelling (Campbell, 1983; Perry, 2003). For example, an ambiguous spoken nonword (vi:m in the international phonetic alphabet) was more likely to be spelled as VEAM after participants had heard the word "team", as VEEM after the word "deem", and as VEME after the word "theme".

Delattre, Bonin, and Barry (2006) compared speed of written spelling of regular and irregular words in healthy participants. A key difference between these two categories of words is that irregular words produce a *conflict* between the outputs of the lexical and non-lexical routes, whereas regular ones do not. Thus, finding that it takes longer to write irregular than regular words would provide evidence that the two routes interact with each other. That is precisely what Delattre et al. found.

Deep dysgraphia

If only partial semantic information about a heard word was passed on from the semantic system to the orthographic output lexicon, then a word similar in meaning to the correct word might be written down. Precisely this has been observed in individuals with **deep dysgraphia**. For example, Bub and Kertesz (1982) studied JC, a young woman with deep dysgraphia. She made numerous semantic errors, writing "sun" when the word "sky" was spoken, writing "chair" when "desk" was spoken, and so on.

Bormann, Wallesch, and Blanken (2008) studied MD, a man with deep dysgraphia. He made a few semantic errors, and his spelling was affected by word concreteness and word class (e.g., noun; verb). Of particular importance, he (along with other deep dysgraphics) produced "fragment errors", which involved omitting two or more letters when writing a word. This may have happened because the letter information reaching his graphemic buffer was degraded.

Graphemic buffer

The lexical and non-lexical routes both lead to the graphemic buffer (see Figure 11.10). It is a memory store in which graphemic information about the letters in a word is held briefly prior to spelling it. Suppose a brain-damaged patient had damage to the graphemic buffer so that information in it decayed unusually rapidly. As a result, spelling errors should increase with word length. This is what has been found (see Glasspool, Shallice, & Cipolotti, 2006, for a review). In addition, individuals with damage to the graphemic buffer make more spelling errors in the middle of words than at the start and end of words. Many of these spelling errors involve transposing letters because it is especially difficult to keep track of the correct sequence of letters in the middle of words.

KEY TERM

deep dysgraphia: a condition caused by brain damage in which there are semantic errors in spelling and nonwords are spelled incorrectly.

Evaluation

What is perhaps most impressive is the way in which research has revealed a surprising degree of complexity about the processes involved in spelling. There is reasonable evidence that the spelling of heard words can be based on a lexical route or a non-lexical route. Some of the strongest support comes from studies on individuals with surface dysgraphia having a severely impaired lexical route and from those with phonological dysgraphia having a severely impaired non-lexical route. The lexical route, with its phonological input lexicon, semantic system, and orthographic input lexicon, is much more complex than the non-lexical route, and it is not surprising that some individuals (e.g., those with deep dysgraphia) have a partially intact and partially impaired lexical route.

What are the limitations of theory and research in this area? First, the notion that phonological dysgraphia is due to a *specific* problem with turning sounds into groups of letters may be incorrect. It is entirely possible that phonological dysgraphia involves a much more *general* problem with phonological processing. Second, we need to know more about the interactions between the two routes assumed to be involved in spelling. Third, the precise rules used in phoneme–grapheme conversion have not been clearly identified. Fourth, much remains to be discovered about the ways in which the three components of the lexical route combine to produce spellings of heard words.

How many orthographic lexicons are there?

Knowledge of word spellings is important in reading and writing. The simplest assumption is that there is a *single* orthographic lexicon used for both reading and spelling. An alternative assumption is that an input orthographic lexicon is used in reading and a separate orthographic output lexicon is used in spelling.

Evidence

What evidence suggests that there are two orthographic lexicons? Much of it comes from the study of brain-damaged patients. For example, Tainturier, Schiemenz, and Leek (2006) reported the case of CWS, a 58-year-old man who had had a stroke. His ability to spell words was severely impaired, but his ability to read words was almost intact. For example, he was very good at deciding which of two homophones (e.g., obey–obay) was correct. There are many other similar cases (see Tainturier & Rapp, 2001, for a review). The limitation with such evidence is that full knowledge of the letters in a word is essential for spelling but is often not needed for accurate reading. Thus, there may be many patients with poorer spelling than reading simply because spelling is a harder task. For example, MLB was a French woman whose ability to spell irregular words was very poor. However, she performed at chance level on the difficult reading task of deciding which letter strings formed words when the nonwords were pronounced the same as actual words (e.g., BOATH; SKOOL) (Tainturier, 1996).

What findings suggest that there is only one orthographic lexicon? First, most brain-damaged patients with a reading impairment (dyslexia) generally also have a spelling impairment (dysgraphia), and the reverse is often also the case. In addition, patients having particular problems with reading nonwords typically also have specific problems in spelling nonwords, and those who find it hard to read irregular words generally have difficulties in spelling such words (see Tainturier & Rapp, 2001). Some patients even show great similarity between the specific words they can read and those they can spell (Berhmann & Bub, 1992).

Second, Holmes and Carruthers (1998) presented normal participants with five versions of words they could not spell: the correct version; their own misspelling; the most popular misspelling (if it differed from their own misspelling); and two or three other misspellings. The participants showed *no* ability to select the correct spelling over their own misspelling regardless of their confidence in their decisions (see Figure 11.11).

Third, Holmes, Malone, and Redenbach (2008) focused on a group of students whose

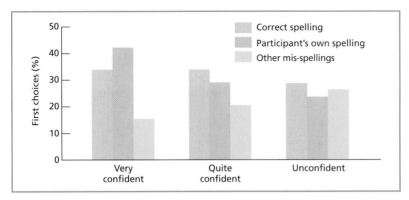

Figure 11.11 Ability to select the correct spelling of a word from various mis-spellings as a function of confidence in correctness of decision. Based on data in Holmes and Carruthers (1998).

spelling ability was much worse than their reading ability (unexpectedly poor spellers), suggesting that the processes involved in spelling and reading are different. They were compared to another group of students having comparable reading ability but better spelling. When both groups were given a more difficult reading test (e.g., deciding whether "pilrgim"; "senrty" were words), the two groups did not differ. Thus, the discrepancy between the reading and spelling performance of the unexpectedly poor spellers was more apparent than real and disappeared when the complex reading task was used.

Fourth, Philipose et al. (2007) carried out a study on patients who had very recently suffered a stroke. Impaired performance on reading and spelling tasks for words and pseudo-words was associated with damage in a shared network in the left hemisphere. This suggests that common brain areas are involved in reading and spelling words, and is consistent with the notion of a single orthographic lexicon.

Evaluation

It is very hard to obtain definitive evidence on the issue of one versus two orthographic lexicons. However, most evidence from normal and from brain-damaged individuals supports the assumption that there is a single orthographic lexicon. This makes sense given that it is presumably more efficient for us to have only one orthographic lexicon.

CHAPTER SUMMARY

• **Introduction**
The same knowledge base and similar planning skills are used in speaking and writing. However, spoken language is typically more informal and simple than written language, in part because there is less time for planning and it is more interactive. Some brain-damaged patients can speak well although their spelling and writing are poor, whereas others can write accurately but can hardly speak, suggesting that there are important differences between speaking and writing.

• **Speech as communication**
The key to successful communication in a conversation involves use of the Co-operative Principle. Common ground is easier to achieve when speakers and listeners interact with each other. Speakers' failures to use the common ground seem to depend more on notions of shared responsibility than on cognitive overload. According to the interactive alignment model, speakers and listeners often achieve common ground fairly effortlessly by copying aspects of what the other person has just said.

- Planning of speech
  There has been controversy as to whether speech planning extends over a phrase or a clause. Forward planning is fairly extensive when speakers have relative freedom about what to say and when to say it. However, there is much less planning when the same sentence frame is used repeatedly or speakers are under time pressure.

- Basic aspects of spoken language
  The demands on speech production are reduced by preformulation and underspecification. The existence of syntactic priming suggests that speakers form syntactic representations separate from meaning and phonology. Discourse markers (commonly found in spontaneous speech) assist listeners' comprehension (e.g., by signalling shifts of topic). Speakers often use prosodic cues, but their use does not seem to indicate any particular responsiveness of speakers to the listener.

- Speech errors
  Speech errors provide insights into the processes involved in speech production. They suggest that planning of the words to be used occurs earlier than the planning of the sounds to be spoken. Number-agreement errors are common when we are faced with conflicting information because avoiding them requires considerable processing resources.

- Theories of speech production
  According to Dell's spreading-activation theory, speech production involves semantic, syntactic, morphological, and phonological levels, with processing being parallel and interactive. The theory accounts for most speech errors, but predicts more errors than are actually found. The proportion of speech errors that are anticipatory is greater among individuals who make relatively few errors. WEAVER++ is a discrete, feed-forward model based on the assumption of serial processing. Neuroimaging evidence provides some support for the processing sequence assumed within the model. WEAVER++ cannot account for the extensive interactions involving words within a sentence or different processing levels for individual words.

- Cognitive neuropsychology: speech production
  There is a traditional distinction between Broca's aphasia (slow, ungrammatical, and non-fluent speech) and Wernicke's aphasia (fluent speech often lacking meaning), but it is not clear-cut. Anomia seems to depend mainly on semantic and phonological impairments and may not involve problems with lemma selection. Patients with agrammatism produce sentences lacking grammatical structure and with few function words, which supports the notion that there is a syntactic level of processing. Agrammatics seem to have reduced resources for syntactic processing, but the range of deficits they show precludes any sweeping generalisations. The speech of jargon aphasics is reasonably grammatical. They produce many neologisms but are generally unaware of doing so. Their neologisms often include phonemes from the target word and consonants common in the English language.

- Writing: the main processes
  Writing involves planning, sentence generation, and revision processes, but these processes cannot be separated neatly. On average, writers devote about 30% of their time to planning,

50% to sentence generation, and 20% (or less) to revision. Good writers use a knowledge-transforming rather than knowledge-telling strategy; this helps them to produce high-level main points. Good writers also spend more time revising than do other writers. Expert writers attain the knowledge-crafting stage in which the focus is on the reader's needs. Reviewing places more demands on the central executive component of working memory than planning or translating. The phonological loop and the visuo-spatial sketchpad are also involved in writing. Writing performance tends to be better when essays are word processed rather than written in longhand.

- Spelling
It is generally assumed that there are separate lexical and non-lexical routes in spelling, with the former being used to spell familiar words and the latter being used to spell unfamiliar words and nonwords. Both routes make use of a graphemic buffer that briefly holds graphemic representations. Patients with phonological dysgraphia have damage to the lexical route, whereas those with surface dysgraphia have damage to the non-lexical route. However, there is some evidence that phonological dysgraphia involves a very general impairment in phonological processing. The two routes often interact with each other. The evidence suggests that a single orthographic lexicon is used in reading and spelling.

FURTHER READING

- Alario, F.-X., Costa, A., Ferreira, V., & Pickering, M. (eds.) (2006). *Language production: First international workshop on language production*. Hove, UK: Psychology Press. This edited book contains contributions on several topics in language production, including the ways in which the language production system is organised.
- Gaskell, G. (ed.) (2007). *Oxford handbook of psycholinguistics*. Oxford: Oxford University Press. Part IV of this excellent handbook contains chapters by leading experts on major topics in language production.
- Goldrick, M., Costa, A., & Schiller, N. (eds.) (2008). *Language production: third international workshop on language production*. Hove, UK: Psychology Press. This is the third volume in a well-established series in which prominent researchers in language production discuss theoretical and empirical advances. This volume focuses on control processes in speech production and speech production in dialogue.
- Harley, T.A. (2008). *The psychology of language: From data to theory* (3rd ed.). Hove, UK: Psychology Press. Chapter 13 in this truly excellent textbook gives a comprehensive account of the main factors involved in language production.
- Olive, T. (2004). Working memory in writing: Empirical evidence from the dual-task technique. *European Psychologist*, 9, 32–42. This article represents an impressive attempt to identify the role played by the working memory system in writing.
- Schiller, N.O., Ferreira, V., & Alario, F.-X. (eds.) (2007). *Language production: Second international workshop on language production*. Hove, UK: Psychology Press. This edited volume contains contributions by leading experts on topics including word selection in speech production and the factors influencing pausing during speech.

Our ability to reflect in a complex way on our lives, to plan and solve problems that arise on a daily basis, is the bedrock of thinking behaviour. However, as in all things human, the ways in which we think (and reason and make decisions) are many and varied. They range from solving puzzles in the newspaper to troubleshooting (or not!) when our car breaks down to developing a new theory of the universe. Below we consider a sample of the sorts of things to which we apply the term "thinking".

First, a fragment of Molly Bloom's sleepy thoughts from James Joyce's *Ulysses* (1922/1960, pp. 871–872), about Mrs Riordan:

> *God help the world if all women in the world were her sort down on bathingsuits and lownecks of course nobody wanted her to wear I suppose she was pious because no man would look at her twice I hope I'll never be like her a wonder she didn't want us to cover our faces but she was a well educated woman certainly and her gabby talk about Mr. Riordan here and Mr. Riordan there I suppose he was glad to get shut of her.*

Next, a person (S) answering an experimenter's (E) question about regulating the thermostat on a home-heating system (Kempton, 1986, p. 83):

E: Let's say you're in the house and you're cold.... Let's say it's a cold day, you want to do something about it.

S: Oh, what I might do is, I might turn the thing up high to get out, to get a lot of air out fast, then after a little while turn it off or turn it down.

E: Uh-huh.

S: So, there also, you know, these issues about, um, the rate at which the thing produces heat, the higher the setting is, the more heat that's produced per unit of time, so if you're cold, you want to get warm fast, um, so you turn it up high.

Finally, here is the first author trying to use PowerPoint:

> *Why has the Artwork put the title in the wrong part of the slide? Suppose I try to put a frame around it so I can drag it up to where I want it. Ah-ha, now if I just summon up the arrows I can move the top bit up, and then I do the same with the bottom bit. If I move the bottom bit up more than the top bit, then the title will fit in okay.*

These three samples illustrate several general aspects of thinking. First, all the pieces involve individuals being *conscious* of their thoughts. Clearly, thinking typically involves conscious awareness. However, we tend to be conscious of the products of thinking rather than the processes themselves (see Chapter 16). Furthermore, even when we can introspect on our thoughts, our recollections of them are often inaccurate. Joyce reconstructs well the character of idle, associative thought in Molly Bloom's internal monologue. However, if we asked her to tell us her thoughts from the previous five minutes, little of it would be recalled.

Second, thinking varies in the extent to which it is directed. It can be relatively undirected, as in the case of Molly Bloom letting one thought slide into another as she is on the point of slipping into a dream. In the other two cases, the goal is much clearer and more well-defined.

Third, the amount and nature of the knowledge used in different thinking tasks varies enormously. For example, the knowledge required in the PowerPoint case is quite limited, even though it took the author concerned a fair amount of time to acquire it. In contrast, Molly Bloom is using a vast amount of her knowledge of people and of life.

The next three chapters (12–14) are concerned with the higher-level cognitive processes involved in thinking and reasoning (see the Box below). Bear in mind that we use the *same* cognitive system to deal with all these types of thinking. As a result, many distinctions among different forms of thinking and reasoning are rather arbitrary and camouflage underlying similarities in cognitive processes. It is not surprising that the same (or similar) brain areas are typically involved in most problem-solving and reasoning tasks (see Chapter 14).

We will briefly describe the structure of this section of the book. Chapter 12 is concerned primarily with the processes involved in problem solving. We include research concentrating on the role of learning in problem solving, with a particular emphasis on the knowledge and skills possessed by experts.

Chapter 13 deals with the important topics of judgement and decision making. Among the questions posed (and answered!) in this chapter are the following: What are the main factors influencing our decisions? Why do we sometimes ignore relevant information? What kinds of biases impair our judgement and our decision making? A central theme is that we use heuristics, or rules of thumb, that are simple to use but prone to error.

Chapter 14 deals mainly with deductive reasoning but with some coverage of inductive reasoning. We discuss major theories of reasoning, and also address broader issues that span the three chapters in this section. First, we consider the extent to which the same brain areas are involved in various forms of higher-level cognition. Second, we discuss the key question, "Are humans rational?" As you might expect from psychologists, the answer is, "Yes and no", rather than a definite "Yes" or "No"!

Forms of thinking

Problem solving	Cognitive activity that involves moving from the recognition that there is a problem through a series of steps to the solution. Most other forms of thinking involve some problem solving.
Decision making	Selecting one out of a number of presented options or possibilities, with the decision having personal consequences.
Judgement	A component of decision making that involves calculating the likelihood of various possible events; the emphasis is on accuracy.
Deductive reasoning	Deciding what conclusions follow necessarily provided that various statements are assumed to be true.
Inductive reasoning	Deciding whether certain statements or hypotheses are true on the basis of the available information. It is used by scientists and detectives but is not guaranteed to produce valid conclusions.

CHAPTER 12

PROBLEM SOLVING AND EXPERTISE

INTRODUCTION

We often find ourselves in situations in which we need to solve a problem. We will consider three examples here. First, you have an urgent meeting in another city and so must get there rapidly. However, the trains generally run late, your car is old and unreliable, and the buses are slow. Second, you are struggling to work out the correct sequence of operations on your computer to perform a given task. You try to remember what you needed to do with your previous computer. Third, you are an expert chess player in the middle of a competitive match against a strong opponent. The time clock is ticking away, and you have to decide on your move in a complicated position.

The above examples relate to the three main topics of this chapter. The first topic is problem solving, which Mayer (1990, p. 284) defined as "cognitive processing directed at transforming a given situation into a goal situation when no obvious method of solution is available to the problem solver." As we will see, most problems studied by psychologists are such that it is clear when the goal has been reached.

The second topic is transfer, which is concerned with the beneficial (or adverse) effects of previous learning and problem solving on some current task or problem. This is a very important topic (yes, it is!) because we constantly make use of past experience and knowledge to assist us in our current task. There is reasonable overlap between the areas of problem solving and transfer. However, transfer is more con-

cerned with the effects of learning than is most research on problem solving. In addition, the knowledge transferred from the past to the present extends beyond that directly relevant to problem solving.

The third topic is expertise. There are overlaps between expertise and problem solving, in that experts are very efficient at solving numerous problems in their area of expertise. However, there are also some important differences. First, most traditional research on problem solving involved problems requiring no special training or knowledge for their solution. In contrast, studies on expertise have typically involved problems requiring considerable knowledge. Second, there is more focus on individual differences in research on expertise than in research on problem solving. Indeed, a central issue in expertise research is to identify the main differences (e.g., in knowledge; in strategic processing) between experts and novices.

There is also overlap between the areas of transfer and expertise. One of the key reasons why experts perform at a much higher level than novices is because they can transfer or make use of their huge stock of relevant knowledge. What is of fundamental importance to both areas is an emphasis on understanding the processes involved in learning.

In sum, there are important similarities among the areas of problem solving, transfer, and expertise. For example, they all involve problems requiring individuals to generate their own options (possible answers), and then to use their ability and knowledge to select the best choice from those options. However, as we will see, there are also good reasons why rather separate bodies of theory and research have built up around each of the three areas.

PROBLEM SOLVING

There are three major aspects to problem solving:

(1) It is purposeful (i.e., goal-directed).
(2) It involves controlled processes and is not totally reliant on automatic processes.
(3) A problem only exists when someone lacks the relevant knowledge to produce an immediate solution. Thus, a problem for most people (e.g., a mathematical calculation) may not be so for someone with relevant expertise (e.g., a professional mathematician).

There is an important distinction between well-defined and ill-defined problems. **Well-defined problems** are ones in which all aspects of the problem are clearly specified: these include the initial state or situation, the range of possible moves or strategies, and the goal or solution. The goal is well-specified, meaning it is clear when the goal has been reached. A maze is a well-defined problem in which escape from it (or reaching the centre, as in the Hampton Court maze) is the goal. Mind you, the first author has managed to get completely lost on the way out from the centre of the Hampton Court maze on more than one occasion! Chess can also be regarded as a well-defined problem, although obviously an extremely complex one. It is well-defined in the sense that there is a standard initial state, the rules specify all legitimate rules, and the goal is to achieve checkmate.

In contrast, **ill-defined problems** are under-specified. Suppose you have locked your keys inside your car, and want to get into it without causing any damage. However, you have urgent business elsewhere, and there is no one around to help you. In such circumstances, it may be very hard to identify the best solution to the problem. For example, breaking a window will solve the immediate problem but will obviously create additional problems.

Escaping from, or reaching the middle of, a maze is an example of a well-defined problem. It is clear when a solution is reached.

Most everyday problems are ill-defined problems. In contrast, psychologists have focused mainly on well-defined problems. Why is this? One important reason is that well-defined problems have an optimal strategy for their solution. Another reason is that the investigator knows the right answer. As a result, we can identify the errors and deficiencies in the strategies adopted by human problem solvers.

There is a further distinction between knowledge-rich and knowledge-lean problems. **Knowledge-rich problems** can only be solved by individuals possessing a considerable amount of specific knowledge. In contrast, **knowledge-lean problems** do not require the possession of such

KEY TERMS

well-defined problems: problems in which the initial state, goal, and methods available for solving them are clearly laid out; see **ill-defined problems**.
ill-defined problems: problems in which the definition of the problem statement is imprecisely specified; the initial state, goal state, and methods to be used to solve the problem may be unclear; see **well-defined problems**.
knowledge-rich problems: problems that can only be solved through the use of considerable amounts of prior knowledge; see **knowledge-lean problems**.
knowledge-lean problems: problems that can be solved without the use of much prior knowledge, with most of the necessary information being provided by the problem statement; see **knowledge-rich problems**.

The Monty Hall problem

We can illustrate key issues in problem solving with the notorious Monty Hall problem. It is named after the host of an American television show, and is a well-defined and knowledge-lean problem:

> *Suppose you're on a game show and you're given the choice of three doors. Behind one door is a car, behind the others, goats. You pick a door, say, Number 1, and the host, who knows what's behind the doors, opens another door, say Number 3, which has a goat. He then says to you, "Do you want to switch to door Number 2?" Is it to your advantage to switch your choice?*

If you stayed with your first choice, you are in good company. About 85% of people make that decision (Burns & Wieth, 2004). Unfortunately, it is wrong! There is actually a two-thirds chance of being correct if you switch your choice.

Many people (including you?) furiously dispute this answer. We will use two ways to convince you that switching doubles your chances of winning the car. First, when you made your initial choice of picking one door out of three at random, you clearly only had a one-third chance of winning the car. Regardless of whether your initial choice was correct, the host can open a door that does not have the prize behind it. Thus, the host's action sheds *no light at all* on the correctness of your initial choice.

Second, there are only three possible scenarios with the Monty Hall problem (Krauss & Wang, 2003; see Figure 12.1). With scenario 1, your first choice was incorrect, and so Monty Hall opens the only remaining door with a goat behind it. Here, switching is certain to succeed. With scenario 2, your first choice was incorrect, and Monty Hall opens the only remaining door with a goat behind it. As with scenario 1, switching is certain to succeed. With scenario 3, your

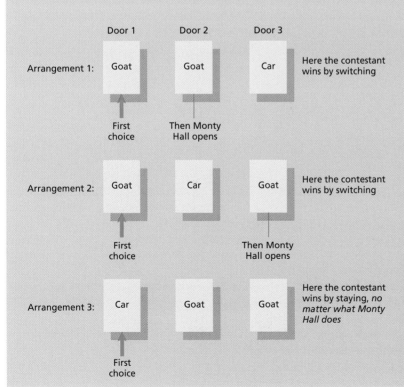

Figure 12.1 Explanation of the solution to the Monty Hall problem: in two out of three possible car–goat arrangements, the contestant would win by switching; therefore she should switch. From Krauss and Wang, 2003. Copyright © 2003 American Psychological Association. Reproduced with permission.

first choice was correct, and you would win by refusing to switch. Thus, switching succeeds with two out of three scenarios (2 and 3) and fails with only scenario (1), thus producing a two-thirds chance that switching will succeed.

Why do people fail on this problem? We will focus on three reasons. First, many people use the number-of-cases heuristic or rule of thumb ("If the number of alternatives is N, then the probability of each one is 1/N") (Shimojo & Ichikawa, 1989). Second, De Neys and Verschueren (2006) argued that the Monty Hall problem places substantial demands on the central executive, an attention-like component of working memory (see Chapter 6). There were 22% correct responses on the problem when presented on its own but only 8% when participants had to perform a demanding task at the same time.

Third, Burns and Wieth (2004) argued that the central problem is that people make errors when thinking about *causality* – the host's actions may seem random but are actually not so.

Accordingly, they made the problem's causal structure clearer. In their version, there are three boxers, one of whom is so good he is certain to win any bout. You select one boxer and then the other two boxers fight each other. The winner of the first fight then fights the boxer initially selected, and you win if you choose the winner of this second bout. You decide whether to stay with your initial choice or switch to the winner of the first bout. Fifty-one per cent of the participants made the correct decision to switch compared to only 15% with the standard three-door version. This difference occurred because it is easy to see that the boxer who won the first bout did so because of skill rather than random factors.

In sum, the Monty Hall problem shows our fallibility as problem solvers. We produce wrong answers because we use heuristics or rules of thumb, because our processing capacity is limited, and because we misrepresent problems (e.g., misunderstanding their causal structure).

knowledge, because most of the necessary information is given in the problem statement. Most traditional research on problem solving has involved the use of knowledge-lean problems. In contrast, research on expertise (discussed later) has typically involved knowledge-rich problems.

Gestalt approach

The American psychologist Thorndike (1898) carried out early research on problem solving. Hungry cats in closed cages could see a dish of food outside the cage. The cage doors opened when a pole inside the cage was hit. Initially, the cats thrashed about and clawed the sides of the cage. After some time, however, the cat hit the pole inside the cage and opened the door. On repeated trials, the cats gradually learned what was required. Eventually, they would hit the pole almost immediately and so

gain access to the food. Thorndike was unimpressed by the cats' performance, referring to their apparently almost random behaviour as **trial-and-error learning**.

The Gestaltists (German psychologists flourishing in the 1930s) objected to the fact that there was a purely arbitrary relationship between the cats' behaviour (hitting the pole) and the desired consequence (the opening of the cage door) in Thorndike's research. A key difference between Thorndike's approach and that of the Gestaltists is captured in the distinction between reproductive and productive thinking.

KEY TERM

trial-and-error learning: a type of learning in which the solution is reached by producing fairly random responses rather than by a process of thought.

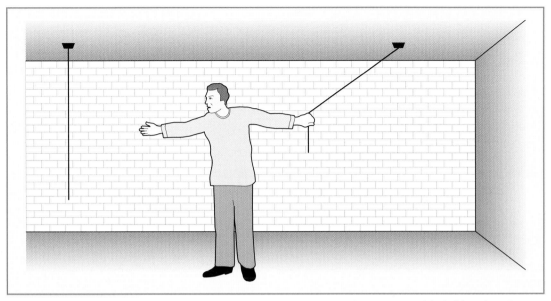

Figure 12.2 The two-string problem in which it is not possible to reach one string while holding the other.

Reproductive thinking involves the re-use of previous experiences, and was the focus of Thorndike's research. In contrast, **productive thinking** involves a novel restructuring of the problem and is more complex than reproductive thinking.

Köhler (1925) showed that animals can engage in productive problem solving. A caged ape called Sultan could only reach a banana outside the cage by joining two sticks together. The ape seemed lost at first. However, after Sultan had put two sticks together by accident, he rapidly joined the sticks together. According to Köhler, the ape had shown **insight**, which involves a sudden restructuring of a problem and is often accompanied by the "ah-ha experience". However, Sultan had spent the early months of his life in the wild and so could have previously learned how sticks can be combined. Birch (1945) found that apes raised in captivity showed little evidence of the kind of insightful problem solving observed by Köhler (1925). Thus, the apparent insight shown by Sultan may have been due to a slow learning process rather than a sudden flash of insight.

Maier (1931) used the "pendulum problem" to study insight in humans. Participants were brought into a room containing various objects (e.g., poles, pliers, extension cords), plus two strings hanging from the ceiling (see Figure 12.2). The task was to tie together the two strings, but they were too far apart for the participants to reach one string while holding the other. The most "insightful" (but rare) solution was to tie the pliers to one of the strings and then to swing the string like a pendulum. In this way, it was possible to hold one string and to catch the other on its upswing.

Maier found that insight and problem solution could be facilitated by having the experimenter apparently accidentally brush against the string to set it swinging. Maier claimed that

---

KEY TERMS

reproductive thinking: re-use of previous knowledge to solve a current problem; see **productive thinking**.
productive thinking: solving a problem by developing an understanding of the problem's underlying structure; see **reproductive thinking**.
insight: the experience of suddenly realising how to solve a problem.

the participants were not consciously aware of being influenced by the experimenter's action. However, there is evidence for a *conscious* cue effect. Battersby, Teuber, and Bender (1953) found that the experimenter could greatly speed up solution times on the pendulum problem by highlighting objects that might be relevant to the problem.

Does insight exist?

The Gestaltists did not provide convincing evidence that insight really exists. Subsequent research, however, has filled that gap. One approach is based on introspective evidence. For example, Metcalfe and Weibe (1987) recorded participants' feelings of "warmth" (closeness to solution) while engaged in problems assumed to involve or not to involve insight. Warmth increased progressively during non-insight problems, as expected if they involve a sequence of processes. With insight problems, in contrast, the warmth ratings remained at the same low level until suddenly increasing dramatically just before the solution was reached.

It is somewhat misleading to categorise problems as involving or not involving insight because any given problem can be solved in various ways. For example, Bowden, Jung-Beeman, Fleck, and Kounios (2005) used Compound Remote Associate problems. On each problem, three words were presented (e.g., "fence", "card", and "master"), and participants had to think of a word (e.g., "post") that would go with each of them to form a compound word. The participants indicated that insight (i.e., the answer suddenly popped into their mind) was involved on some trials but not on others.

In one experiment, Bowden et al. (2005) used fMRI. Differences in brain activity between insight and non-insight trials centred on the right hemisphere. More specifically, the anterior superior temporal gyrus (ridge) in the right hemisphere (see Figure 12.3) was activated only when solutions involved insight. This is a brain area involved in processing distant semantic relations between words and more specifically in re-interpretation and semantic integration.

In a second experiment, Bowden et al. recorded event-related potentials (ERPs; see Glossary). There was a burst of high-frequency brain activity one-third of a second before participants indicated that they had achieved an insightful solution. This brain activity was centred on the right anterior superior temporal gyrus.

Bowden and Beeman (1998) had previously found that the right hemisphere plays an important role in insight. Participants were presented with problems similar to those found on the Remote Associates Test. Before solving each problem, they were shown the solution word or an unrelated word and decided whether the word provided the solution. The word was presented to the left or the right hemisphere. Participants responded much faster when the word (solution or unrelated) was presented to the right hemisphere.

Why is the right hemisphere more associated with insight than the left hemisphere? According to Bowden and Jung-Beeman (2007), integration of weakly active and distant associations occurs mostly in the right hemisphere. Thus, for example, connecting weakly related sentences occurs mainly in the right-hemisphere temporal areas (e.g., Mason & Just, 2004). These processing activities are very relevant for producing insight. In contrast, strong activation of closely connected associations occurs mostly in the left hemisphere.

Insight involves replacing one way of thinking about a problem with a new and more efficient way. This implies that cognitive conflict is involved, and there is much evidence that the anterior cingulate cortex is activated during the processing of cognitive conflict. Jing Luo and his associates have carried out much relevant research (see Luo & Knoblich, 2007, for a review). Some of this research has involved the presentation of mystifying sentences (e.g., "The haystack was important because the cloth ripped") followed by a cue designed to produce insight (e.g., "parachute"). Processing of this "insight cue" was associated with increased activity in the anterior cingulate cortex.

Kounios et al. (2006) studied brain activity *before* verbal problems were presented. Problems

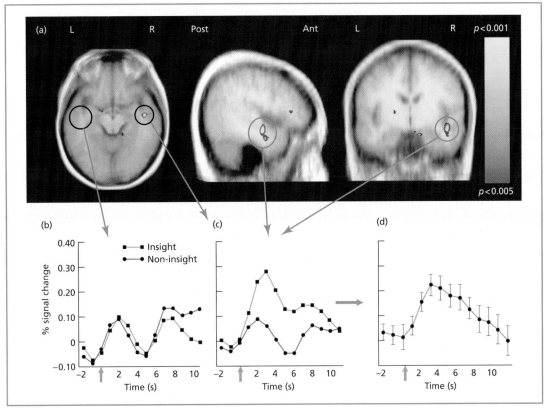

Figure 12.3 Activation in the right hemisphere anterior superior temporal gyrus (RH-aSTG). (a) Areas within the aSTG showing greater activation for insight than non-insight problems; (b) mean signal change following solution for insight and non-insight solutions in left hemisphere (b) and right hemisphere (c); (d) difference between changes shown in (c). Reprinted from Bowden et al. (2005), Copyright © 2005, with permission from Elsevier.

solved using insight were preceded by increased activity in medial frontal areas including the anterior cingulate cortex as well as temporal areas associated with semantic processing. These findings suggest preparation for engaging in conflict resolution and for semantic processing. In contrast, problems solved without the use of insight were preceded by increased activity in the occipital area, suggestive of an increase in visual attention.

One criterion for insight is that it occurs suddenly and unexpectedly and is consistent with our subjective experience. Novick and Sherman (2003) addressed the crucial issue of whether what is true of our subjective experience is also true of the underlying process. Anagrams and non-anagrams were presented very briefly (469 or 953 ms), after which the participants (expert and non-expert anagram solvers) indicated very rapidly whether each letter string could be re-arranged to form an English word. Both groups had above-chance levels of performance, with the experts out-performing the non-experts.

What can we conclude from Novick and Sherman's (2003) research? Much *relevant* processing apparently occurs before insight anagram solutions, as is shown by the above-chance performance. However, people have no conscious awareness of such processing. How, then, can we account for the fact that insight solutions differ from non-insightful solutions in speed and subjective experience? Perhaps insight solutions are based on parallel processing (several processes occurring at the same time), whereas non-insightful solutions are based on serial processing (only one process at a time).

In sum, there is reasonable (but not over-whelming) evidence to suggest that insight does exist. Subjective report, behavioural evidence, and neuroimaging evidence all support a dis-tinction between problem solutions based on insight and those based on more deliberate thought processes. The mechanisms underlying insight remain unclear. However, the notion that there are parallel processes operating below the level of conscious awareness is plausible.

Past experience

Past experience generally increases our ability to solve problems. However, Duncker (1945) argued that this is not always the case. He studied functional fixedness, in which we fail to solve problems because we assume from past experience that any given object has only a limited number of uses. Note in passing that Maier's (1931) pendulum problem involves functional fixedness – participants failed to realise that pliers can be used as a pendulum weight.

Duncker gave his participants a candle, a box of nails, and several other objects. Their task was to attach the candle to a wall next to a table so it did not drip onto the table below. Most participants tried to nail the candle directly to the wall or to glue it to the wall by melting it. Only a few decided to use the inside of the nail-box as a candle holder, and to nail it to the wall. Duncker argued that the parti-cipants "fixated" on the box's function rather than its use as a platform. More correct solutions were produced when the nail-box was empty at the start of the experiment, presumably because that situation made the box appear less like a container.

Duncker (1945) argued that functional fixedness occurred in his study because of his participants' past experience with boxes. Using that argument, German and Defeyter (2000) suggested that young children with very limited past experience with boxes might be immune to functional fixedness. They used a set-up similar to that of Duncker with five, six, and

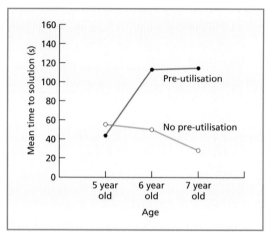

Figure 12.4 Mean time to solution as a function of condition (pre-utilisation: box previously used as a container vs. no pre-utilisation) and age (5, 6, or 7). From German and Defeyter (2000). Reprinted with permission of Psychonomic Society Publications.

seven year olds initially shown a box functioning or not functioning as a container. After that, the time taken to use the box as a support was measured. There were two key findings (see Figure 12.4). First, only the performance of the five year olds was unaffected by having previ-ously been shown the box used as a container. Second, the five year olds actually outperformed the older groups of children when the box's containment function had been shown.

Luchins (1942) and Luchins and Luchins (1959) *manipulated* participants' past experi-ence to provide stronger evidence of its relevance. They used water-jar problems involving three water jars of varying capacity. The task was to imagine pouring water from one jar to another to finish up with a specified amount in one of the jars. Here is a sample problem: Jar A can hold 28 quarts of water, Jar B 76 quarts, and Jar C 3 quarts. You must end up with exactly 25 quarts in one of the jars. The solution is not hard: Jar A is filled, and then Jar C is filled from it, leaving 25 quarts in Jar A. Of parti-cipants who had previously been given similar problems, 95% solved it. Other participants were trained on a series of problems all having the same complex three-jar solution (fill Jar B and use the contents to fill Jar C twice and

Jar A once). Of these participants, only 36% managed to solve this comparatively easy problem!

What do the above findings mean? Luchins (1942) emphasised the notion of **Einstellung** or mental set. The basic idea is that people tend to use a well-practised strategy on problems even when it is inappropriate or sub-optimal. In the words of Luchins (p. 15), "One...is led by a mechanical application of a used method."

Representational change theory

Ohlsson (1992) incorporated key aspects of the Gestalt approach into his representational change theory based on the following assumptions:

- The way in which a problem is currently represented or structured in the problem solver's mind serves as a memory probe to retrieve related knowledge from long-term memory (e.g., operators or possible actions).
- The retrieval process is based on spreading activation among concepts or items of knowledge in long-term memory.
- An impasse or block occurs when the way a problem is represented does not permit retrieval of the necessary operators or possible actions.
- The impasse is broken when the problem representation is changed. The new mental representation acts as a memory probe for relevant operators in long-term memory. Thus, it extends the information available to the problem solver.
- Changing the problem representation can occur in various ways:
  - Elaboration or addition of new problem information.
  - Constraint relaxation, in which inhibitions on what is regarded as permissible are removed.
  - Re-encoding, in which some aspect of the problem representation is re-interpreted (e.g., a pair of pliers is re-interpreted as a weight in the pendulum problem).

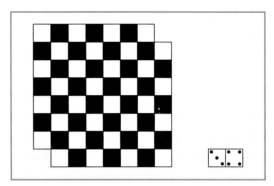

Figure 12.5 The mutilated draughtboard problem.

- Insight occurs when an impasse is broken, and the retrieved knowledge operators are sufficient to solve the problem.

Ohlsson's theory is based squarely on Gestalt theory. Changing the problem representation in Ohlsson's theory is very similar to restructuring in the Gestalt approach, and both theories emphasise the role of insight in producing problem solution. The main difference is that Ohlsson specified in more detail the processes leading to insight.

Evidence

Changing the problem representation often leads to solution. Consider the mutilated draughtboard problem (see Figure 12.5). Initially, the board is completely covered by 32 dominoes occupying two squares each. Then two squares from diagonally opposite corners are removed. Can the remaining 62 squares be filled by 31 dominoes? Kaplan and Simon (1990) asked participants to think aloud while trying to solve the problem. They all started by mentally covering squares with dominoes. However, this strategy is not terribly effective because there are

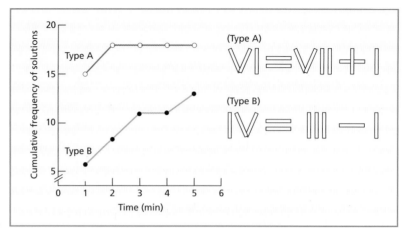

Figure 12.6 Two of the matchstick problems used by Knoblich et al. (1999), and the cumulative solution rates produced to these types of problem in their study. Copyright © 1999. American Psychological Association. Reproduced with permission.

758,148 possible permutations of the dominoes! What is needed is to represent each domino as an object covering one white and one black square (re-encoding) and to represent the draughtboard as having lost two black (or two white) squares (elaboration). It then becomes clear that the 31 dominoes cannot cover the mutilated board.

Knoblich, Ohlsson, Haider, and Rhenius (1999) showed the importance of constraints in reducing the likelihood of insight. Participants were given problems such as those shown in Figure 12.6. As you can see, you would need to know all about Roman numerals to solve the problems! The task involved moving a *single* stick to produce a true statement in place of the initial false one. Some problems (Type A) only required changing two of the values in the equation (e.g., VI = VII + I becomes VII = VI + I). In contrast, other problems (Type B) involved a less obvious change in the representation of the equation (e.g., IV = III – I becomes IV – III = I).

Knoblich et al. argued that our experience of arithmetic tells us that many operations change the values (numbers) in an equation (as is the case with Type A problems). In contrast, relatively few operations change the operators (i.e., +, –, and = signs) as is required in Type B problems. As predicted, it was much harder for participants to relax the normal constraints of arithmetic (and thus to show insight) for

Type B problems than for Type A ones (see Figure 12.6).

Knoblich et al.'s (1999) study does not provide *direct* evidence about the underlying processes causing difficulties with Type B problems. Accordingly, Knoblich et al. (2001) recorded eye movements while participants were solving matchstick arithmetic problems. Participants initially spent much more time fixating the values than the operators for both types of problem. Thus, participants' initial representation was based on the assumption that values rather than operators needed to be changed.

Reverberi, Toraldo, D'Agostini, and Skrap (2005) argued that the lateral frontal cortex is the part of the brain involved in imposing constraints on individuals' processing when confronted by an insight problem. It follows that patients with damage to that brain area would *not* impose artificial constraints and so might perform better than healthy controls. That is exactly what they found. Brain-damaged patients solved 82% of the most difficult matchstick arithmetic problems compared to only 43% of healthy controls.

Evaluation

Ohlsson's view that changing the problem representation (the Gestaltists' restructuring) often allows people to solve problems is correct. Constraint reduction is of major importance

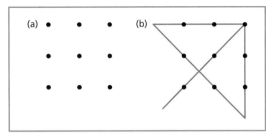

Figure 12.7 The nine-dot problem (a) and its solution (b).

in solving insight problems, as was shown most dramatically by Reverberi et al. (2005). Ohlsson's theory is an improvement on the Gestalt approach because the mechanisms underlying insight are specified more precisely. In general terms, the theory involves a fruitful combination of Gestalt ideas with the information-processing approach.

What are the limitations of representational change theory? First, it is often not possible to predict when (or in what way) the representation of a problem will change. Second, the theory is basically a single-factor theory, in that it is assumed that constraint relaxation is crucial to successful solution of insight problems. However, Kershaw and Ohlsson (2004) found with the nine-dot problem (see Figure 12.7) that multiple factors were involved, and that hints to produce constraint relaxation had only a modestly beneficial effect. Third, Ohlsson de-emphasised important individual differences in problem-solving skills (e.g., those based on IQ differences).

Incubation

The emphasis within representational change theory is on factors that permit people to overcome a block or impasse in problem solving. Wallas (1926) suggested that one important factor was **incubation**, in which a problem is solved more easily by simply ignoring it for some time. His basic idea was that the subconscious mind continues to work towards a solution while the conscious mind focuses on other activities. Research on incubation has

often involved comparing an experimental group having an incubation period away from an unsolved problem with a control group working continuously.

Sio and Ormerod (2009) carried out a meta-analysis of 117 studies on incubation, and reported three main findings. First, there was a fairly small but highly significant overall incubation effect, with positive effects being reported in 85 of the studies. Second, there was a stronger incubation effect with creative problems having multiple solutions than with linguistic and verbal problems having a single solution. Incubation often leads to a widening of the search for knowledge, and this may well be more useful with multiple-solution problems than with single-solution ones. Third, the effects were greater when there was a relatively long preparation time prior to incubation. This may have occurred because an impasse or block in thinking is more likely to develop when the preparation time is long.

It is often claimed that "sleeping on a problem" can be a very effective form of incubation. For example, the dreams of August Kekulé led to the discovery of a simple structure for benzene. Wagner, Gais, Haider, Verleger, and Born (2004) tested the value of sleep in a study in which participants performed a complex mathematical task and were then re-tested several hours later. The mathematical problems were designed so that they could be solved in a much simpler way than the one used initially by nearly all the participants. Of those who slept between training and testing, 59% found the short cut, compared to only 25% of those who did not.

How can we explain incubation effects? As we have seen, Wallas (1926) argued that subconscious processes were responsible. In contrast, Simon (1966) argued that incubation involves a special type of forgetting. More specifically, what tends to be forgotten over time

---

KEY TERM

incubation: the finding that a problem is solved more easily when it is put aside for some time.

is control information relating to the strategies tried by the problem solver. This forgetting makes it easier for problem solvers to adopt a new approach to the problem after the incubation period.

Support for Simon's (1966) approach was reported by Vul and Pashler (2007). They used the Remote Associates Test (e.g., finding a word "*top*" that links *tank*, *hill*, and *secret*). In the crucial interference condition, associated clue words were presented that emphasised the *differences* in meanings of the three words (*water* was paired with *tank*, *ant* with *hill*, and *hideout* with secret). There was also a control condition with no misleading clue words. Participants solved the anagrams with or without a five-minute break to play a video game in the middle to permit incubation. Participants in the interference condition given an incubation period solved 67% of the problems compared to only 54% in the interference condition. In contrast, there was no incubation effect at all in the control condition without the misleading associates. Thus, there was an incubation effect only when the break allowed misleading information to be forgotten.

General Problem Solver

Allen Newell and Herb Simon (1972) argued that it is possible to produce systematic computer simulations of human problem solving. They achieved this with their General Problem Solver, a computer program designed to solve numerous well-defined problems. Newell and Simon's starting assumptions were that information processing is serial (one process at a time), that people possess limited short-term memory capacity, and that they can retrieve relevant information from long-term memory.

Newell and Simon (1972) started by asking people to solve problems while thinking aloud. They then used these verbal reports to decide what general strategy was used on each problem. Finally, they specified the problem-solving strategy in sufficient detail for it to be programmed as a **problem space**. This problem space consists of the initial stage of the problem, the

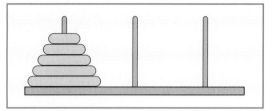

Figure 12.8 The initial state of the five-disc version of the Tower of Hanoi problem.

goal state, all of the possible mental operators (e.g., moves) that can be applied to any state to change it into a different state, and all of the intermediate states of the problem.

The above notions can be illustrated by considering the Tower of Hanoi problem (see Figure 12.8). The initial state of the problem consists of up to five discs piled in decreasing size on the first of three pegs. When all the discs are piled in the same order on the last peg, the goal state has been reached. The rules state that only one disc can be moved at a time, and a larger disc cannot be placed on top of a smaller disc.

How do problem solvers cope with their limited processing capacities? According to Newell and Simon (1972), the complexity of most problems means that we rely heavily on heuristics or rules of thumb. **Heuristics** can be contrasted with **algorithms,** which are generally complex methods or procedures guaranteed to lead to problem solution. The most important of the various heuristic methods is **means–ends analysis:**

KEY TERMS

problem space: an abstract description of all the possible states that can occur in a problem situation.
heuristics: rules of thumb that are cognitively undemanding and often produce approximately accurate answers.
algorithm: a computational procedure providing a specified set of steps to a solution.
means–ends analysis: a **heuristic** method for solving problems based on creating a subgoal to reduce the difference between the current state and the goal state.

- Note the difference between the current problem state and the goal state.
- Form a subgoal that will reduce the difference between the current and goal states.
- Select a mental operator that will permit attainment of the subgoal.

Means–ends analysis is a heuristic rather than an algorithm because, while useful, it is not guaranteed to lead to problem solution.

The way in which means–ends analysis is used can be illustrated with the Tower of Hanoi problem. A reasonable subgoal in the early stages of the problem is to try to place the largest disc on the last peg. If a situation arises in which the largest disc must be placed on either the middle or the last peg, then means–ends analysis will lead to that disc being placed on the last peg.

Another important heuristic is hill climbing. **Hill climbing** involves changing the present state within the problem into one closer to the goal or problem solution, in the same way that someone climbing a hill feels he/she is making progress if they keep moving upwards. As Robertson (2001, p. 38) pointed out, "Hill climbing is a metaphor for problem solving in the dark." Thus, hill climbing is a simpler heuristic than means–ends analysis.

Newell and Simon (1972) applied the General Problem Solver to 11 rather different problems (e.g., letter-series completions; missionaries and cannibals; the Tower of Hanoi). The General Problem Solver managed to solve all the problems, but it did not do so in the same way as people.

Evidence

Thomas (1974) argued that people should experience difficulties in solving a problem at those points at which it is necessary to make a move that temporarily *increases* the distance between the current state and the goal state. In other words, problem solvers should struggle when heuristics are inadequate. He used a variant of the missionaries and cannibals problem based on hobbits and orcs. In the standard version, three missionaries and three cannibals need to be transported across a river in a boat that can hold only two people. The number of cannibals can never exceed the number of missionaries, because then the cannibals would eat the missionaries. One move involves transferring one cannibal and one missionary back to the starting point. This move seems to be going away from the goal or solution, and so is inconsistent with the hill-climbing heuristic. As predicted, it was at this point that participants experienced severe difficulties. However, General Problem Solver didn't find this move especially difficult.

Thomas (1974) also obtained evidence that participants set up subgoals. They would often perform a block of several moves at increasing speed, followed by a long pause before embarking on another rapid sequence of moves. This suggested that participants were dividing up the problem into three or four major subgoals.

According to the theory, people generally make extensive use of means–ends analysis. Dramatic evidence that people sometimes persist with that heuristic even when it severely impairs performance was reported by Sweller and Levine (1982). Participants were given the maze shown in Figure 12.9, but most of it wasn't visible to them. All participants could see the current problem state (where they were in the problem). Some could also see the goal state (goal-information group), whereas the others could not (no-goal-information group).

What do you think happened on this relatively simple problem (simple because its solution only involved alternating left and right moves)? Use of means–ends analysis requires knowledge of the location of the goal, so only the goal-information group could have used that heuristic. However, the problem was designed so that means–ends analysis would not be useful, because every move involved turning *away* from the goal. As predicted,

> **KEY TERM**
>
> **hill climbing:** a **heuristic** involving changing the present state of a problem into one apparently closer to the goal.

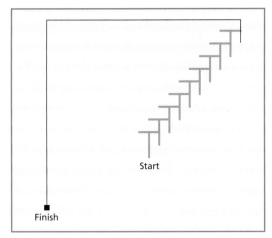

Figure 12.9 The maze used in the study by Sweller and Levine (1982). Adapted from Sweller and Levine (1982).

participants in the goal-information group performed very poorly – only 10% solved the problem in 298 moves! In contrast, participants in the no-goal-information group solved the problem in a median of only 38 moves.

Why do most people engage in only a modest amount of planning when engaged in problem solving? According to Newell and Simon (1972), the main problem is our limited short-term memory capacity. However, another possibility is that planning incurs costs in terms of time and effort, and is often unnecessary because simple heuristics suffice. Evidence favouring the latter possibility was reported by Delaney, Ericsson, and Knowles (2004) using water-jar problems in which the task was to finish up with specified amounts of water in each of three water jars. Half the participants were instructed to generate the complete solution before making any moves, whereas the other half (control group) were free to adopt whatever strategy they wanted.

Delaney et al. (2004) found the control participants showed little evidence of planning. However, the key finding was that those in the planning group showed very clear evidence of being able to plan, and they solved the problem in far fewer moves than the control participants. Thus, we have a greater ability to plan than is usually assumed, but often choose not to plan unless required to do so.

Newell and Simon (1972) assumed that people would shift strategies or heuristics if the ones they were using proved ineffective. This idea was developed by MacGregor, Ormerod, and Chronicle (2001). They argued that people use a heuristic known as **progress monitoring**: the rate of progress towards a goal is assessed, and criterion failure occurs if progress is too slow to solve the problem within the maximum number of moves. The basic idea is that criterion failure acts as a "wake-up call", leading people to change strategy.

MacGregor et al. (2001) obtained evidence of progress monitoring in a study on the nine-dot problem (see Figure 12.10(a)). In this problem, you must draw four straight lines connecting all nine dots without taking your pen off the paper. The solution is shown in Figure 12.10(b). One reason why many people fail to solve this problem is because they mistakenly assume the lines must stay within the square. The key conditions used by MacGregor et al. (2001) are shown in Figure 12.10(c) and (d). We might expect participants given (c) to perform better than those given (d) because it is clearer in (c) that the lines must go outside the square. In contrast, MacGregor et al. argued that individuals given Figure 12.10(c) can cover more dots with the next two lines than those given Figure 12.10(d) while remaining within the square. As a result, they are less likely to experience criterion failure, and so will be less likely to shift to a superior strategy.

The findings supported the prediction. Only 31% of those given Figure 12.10(c) solved the nine-dot problem compared to 53% of those given Figure 12.10(d). The take-home message is that, if the strategy you are using

KEY TERM

progress monitoring: a **heuristic** used in problem solving in which insufficiently rapid progress towards solution leads to the adoption of a different strategy.

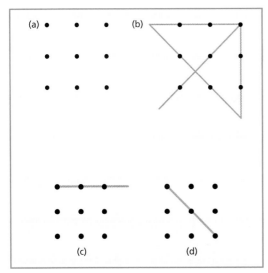

Figure 12.10 The nine-dot problem (a) and its solution (b); two variants of the nine-dot problem (c) and (d) presented in MacGregor et al. (2001). Copyright © 2001 American Psychological Association. Reproduced with permission.

cannot allow you to solve the problem, the sooner you realise that is the case the better.

Evaluation

The Newell and Simon approach works reasonably well with many well-defined problems. Their theoretical approach also has the advantage that it allows us to specify the shortest sequence of moves from the initial state to the goal state. Thus, we can see exactly *when* and *how* an individual participant's performance deviates from the ideal. The General Problem Solver is broadly consistent with our knowledge of human information processing. For example, we have limited working memory capacity (see Chapter 6), which helps to explain why we use heuristics or rules of thumb such as means–ends analysis and hill climbing.

What are the limitations of Newell and Simon's approach? First, the General Problem Solver is better than humans at remembering what has happened on a problem, but it is inferior to humans at planning future moves. It focuses on only a single move, whereas humans can plan several moves ahead. Second,

most problems in everyday life are ill-defined and so differ considerably from those studied by Newell and Simon. Third, the theoretical approach is best suited to multiple-move problems requiring serial processing (e.g., missionaries-and-cannibals problem). It is less able to account for performance on insight problems. Fourth, Newell and Simon de-emphasised individual differences in strategy and speed of problem solving. Handley, Capon, Copp, and Harper (2002) found that individual differences in spatial working memory capacity (see Chapter 6) predicted performance on the Tower of Hanoi task, but this is not predicted by General Problem Solver.

Problem solving: brain systems

Several studies have indicated that the frontal cortex is heavily involved in problem solving. We will start by considering the evidence from brain-damaged patients and then move on to neuroimaging studies on healthy individuals. Owen, Downes, Sahakian, Polkey, and Robbins (1990) used a computerised version of the Tower of London problem resembling the Tower of Hanoi problem. Patients with left frontal damage, right frontal damage, and healthy controls did not differ in time to plan the first move. After that, however, both patient groups were much slower than the healthy controls and required more moves to solve the problem. There were no differences between the left and right frontal damage patients. In similar fashion, Goel and Grafman (1995) found that patients with prefrontal damage performed worse than healthy controls on the Tower of Hanoi even though both groups used basically the same strategy. The patients were especially at a disadvantage compared to the controls with respect to a difficult move involving moving away from the goal. The implication is that patients with prefrontal damage find it harder to plan ahead.

Similar findings using Luchins' (1942) water-jar problems were reported by Colvin, Dunbar, and Grafman (2001). Patients with prefrontal damage and healthy controls used a relatively unsophisticated hill-climbing strategy. However, the patients performed worse because they found it harder to make moves in conflict with the strategy. Patients with damage to the left dorsolateral prefrontal cortex performed worse than those with right damage. Why was this? According to Colvin et al. (p. 1129), "Patients with left dorsolateral prefrontal cortex lesions have difficulty making a decision requiring the conceptual comparison of non-verbal stimuli, manipulation of select representations of potential solutions, and are unable to appropriately inhibit a response in keeping with the final goal."

Neuroimaging studies have provided findings broadly consistent with those from brain-damaged patients. Dagher, Owen, Boecker, and Brooks (1999) used PET scans while healthy participants performed the Tower of London task in various versions varying in complexity. The more complex versions of the task were associated with increased activity in several brain areas compared to simpler versions. Of particular note, the dorsolateral prefrontal cortex was more active when participants were engaged in solving complex versions of the Tower of London task.

Fincham, Carter, van Veen, Stenger, and Anderson (2002) used a modified version of the Tower of Hanoi problem. Engaging in problem solving was associated with activation in several brain regions, including the right dorsolateral prefrontal cortex, bilateral parietal cortex, and bilateral premotor cortex. These areas are associated with use of the working memory system and attentional processes (see Chapter 6).

Unterrainer et al. (2004) considered brain activity while strong and weak problem solvers attempted several Tower of London problems. There were two main findings. First, the right dorsolateral prefrontal cortex was highly activated during strategy planning and performance execution. Second, performance on the Tower of London problems was positively associated with the extent of activity in the right dorsolateral prefrontal cortex, especially BA9. It is worth noting that Burgess et al. (2000) found that frontal lobe patients with damage in the right dorsolateral prefrontal cortex found it harder than those with left damage to generate plans in a multi-tasking experiment.

In sum, several interesting findings have emerged from research in this area. First, the frontal lobes (especially the dorsolateral prefrontal cortex) are more consistently activated than other parts of the brain during problem solving. Second, research on brain-damaged patients also indicates the importance of the frontal lobes in problem solving. More specifically, patients with prefrontal damage seem to be especially impaired in making difficult moves. Third, the right dorsolateral prefrontal cortex seems to be more important than the left dorsolateral prefrontal cortex with the Tower of London or Tower of Hanoi problems, whereas the opposite is the case with water-jar problems.

What are the psychological implications of the above findings? First, the involvement of the prefrontal cortex suggests that problem solvers engage in complex cognitive processing and do not totally rely on simple heuristics. However, some heuristics may involve the prefrontal cortex. Second, the finding that the dorsolateral prefrontal cortex is activated in different forms of problem solving suggests that they may involve common cognitive processes. Third, patients with prefrontal damage experience particular difficulties when a simple heuristic proves inadequate because they find it hard to inhibit dominant responses. Evidence that response inhibition is important for successful performance on the Tower of London problem was reported by Asato, Sweeney, and Luna (2006). Improvements in performance on this problem during adolescence were strongly associated with improved performance on the antisaccade task. This task involves inhibiting an eye movement or saccade to a cue and instead making an eye movement in the opposite direction.

Adaptive control of thought – rational (ACT-R)

Anderson et al. (2004) put forward a very influential theoretical approach known as the adaptive control of thought – rational (ACR-R) theory (also discussed in Chapter 1). ACT-R

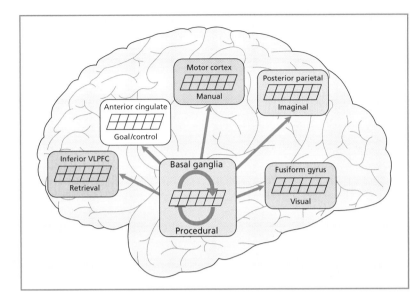

Figure 12.11 The main modules of the ACT-R (Adaptive Control of Thought – Rational) cognitive architecture with their locations within the brain. Reprinted from Anderson et al. (2008), Copyright © 2008, with permission from Elsevier.

was subsequently developed by Anderson, Fincham, Qin, and Stocco (2008), and we will be focusing on this version. ACT-R is intended to apply very generally to human cognition, but in practice much of the research designed to test it has involved problem solving.

Earlier versions of ACT-R emerged from within computational cognitive science, and so consisted of complex computational models. More recent versions have combined computational cognitive science with cognitive neuroscience. Here are the major assumptions of ACT-R:

• The cognitive system consists of seven modules. Each module performs its own specialised operations fairly independently of the other modules.
• Four of the modules are of particular importance to human cognition, including problem solving (see Figure 12.11):
  – *Retrieval module*: it maintains the retrieval cues needed to access information. Functional neuroimaging studies (e.g., Badre & Wagner, 2007) suggest it is located in the inferior ventrolateral prefrontal cortex (VLPFC).
  – *Imaginal module*: it transforms problem representations (e.g., a change to a

planned state in the Tower of Hanoi task). Functional neuroimaging studies suggest it is located in the posterior parietal cortex.
  – *Goal module*: it keeps track of an individual's intentions and controls information processing. It is located in the anterior cingulate cortex.
  – *Procedural module*: it uses production (IF…THEN) rules (see Chapter 1) to determine what action will be taken next. It is located at the head of caudate nucleus within the basal ganglia.
• The brain regions corresponding to the four modules just described are generally all activated by complex cognitive tasks. However, it is assumed that each region responds to somewhat different factors.
• Each module has a buffer associated with it containing a limited amount of information. According to Anderson et al. (2004, p. 1058), "A central production system can detect patterns in these buffers and take co-ordinated action."

There are two important features of functional neuroimaging research designed to test predictions of ACT-R. First, the emphasis has been on identifying factors that influence activity of one of the modules but not the others. Second, the same well-defined regions corresponding to the various modules are the focus of interest. This theory-driven approach is preferable to the blunderbuss approach of searching around for brain areas that are especially responsive to some manipulation.

Evidence

Anderson, Albert, and Fincham (2005) used fMRI with the Tower of Hanoi to address two main issues. First, they predicted that there would be least activity in the ventrolateral prefrontal cortex (retrieval module) when participants were producing sequences of moves that placed minimal demands on memory retrieval. That prediction was supported. Anderson et al. also predicted that there would be the greatest activation of the posterior parietal region (imaginal module) when planning on the Tower of Hanoi problem was most intense. That prediction was also supported.

Qin et al. (2004) carried out a study in which children aged 11–14 spent one hour a day for six days learning to solve equations of varying levels of difficulty. All four brain regions identified within ACT-R showed an effect of task complexity. However, there were two key findings. First, the area associated with the retrieval module (ventrolateral prefrontal cortex) showed almost no response in a task condition in which virtually nothing had to be retrieved. In contrast, the other three regions were activated in that condition. Second, practice led to substantial reductions in activation in the brain areas associated with the retrieval, imaginal, and procedural modules. However, the anterior cingulate (associated with the goal module) showed practically no effect of practice. Theoretically, this happened because the problem-solving strategy remained the same with practice.

Similar results with adults using a different task were reported by Fincham and Anderson (2006). Participants were given extensive practice in learning and applying rules associated with each of eight sports. At the end of practice, a change was introduced in the task to increase the demands on decision making. The findings

were dramatic. Practice was associated with a substantial decrease in activation of the ventrolateral prefrontal cortex (retrieval module) because retrieval of relevant information became easier with practice. However, practice was associated with a significant increase in activation of the anterior cingulate (goal module) because the change in the task introduced additional control demands.

Evaluation

ACT-R is an impressive theory in several ways. First, it is an ambitious attempt to provide a theoretical framework for understanding information processing and performance on numerous very different cognitive tasks. Second, it represents the most thorough attempt to date to combine computational cognitive science with cognitive neuroscience. As such, it provides a theory-driven approach to functional neuroimaging research. Third, the fact that several brain regions all tend to be activated during the performance of a complex cognitive task makes it hard to identify the specific functions served by any given region. The research generated by ACT-R has made progress in achieving this difficult goal.

What are the limitations of ACT-R? First, it is assumed within the theory that only small areas of prefrontal cortex are of crucial importance in human information processing. It seems probable that several other areas play important roles. For example, we saw earlier that many studies have found evidence that dorsolateral prefrontal cortex is strongly involved in problem solving.

Second, the central ganglia are assumed to have major significance in co-ordinating processing within various cortical regions and in action selection. This minimises the numerous direct connections between different brain regions that have been found in functional neuroimaging studies.

Third, the various modules within the theory may not be as distinct as assumed. Danker and Anderson (2007) used a multi-step algebra task in which transformation was required initially, followed later by retrieval. It was predicted that there would be initial activation of the posterior parietal cortex followed by activation of the inferior ventrolateral prefrontal cortex. In fact, both areas were activated at both stages, suggesting that it is hard to disentangle transformation and retrieval processes in mathematical problem solving.

TRANSFER OF TRAINING AND ANALOGICAL REASONING

Suppose you have solved a given problem in the past, and are now confronted by a similar problem. You would probably assume your previous experience would allow you to solve the current problem faster and more easily than would otherwise have been the case. In the jargon of psychologists, this is **positive transfer**. However, solving a given problem in the past sometimes disrupts our ability to solve a similar current problem. This state of affairs is **negative transfer**. We encountered examples of negative transfer earlier in studies on functional fixedness (e.g., Duncker, 1945; Luchins, 1942).

Why is transfer of training of practical interest and importance? Nearly everyone involved in education firmly believes that what students learn at school and at university facilitates learning in their future lives. **Far transfer** (positive transfer to a dissimilar context) is of special interest because of its direct relevance to everyday life. In fact, however, most research has focused on **near transfer** (positive transfer to a similar context). In such research, the focus is on the immediate application of knowledge and skills from one situation to a similar one. This approach differs from most real-life situations in that participants on the transfer task are not permitted to make use of external support (e.g., texts, friends, feedback from others). Bransford and Schwartz (1999) argued that a preferable approach is preparation for future learning, in which the emphasis is on participants' ability to learn in new, support-rich situations. Within this approach, learning is regarded as an active and constructive process, and the importance of **metacognition** (beliefs and knowledge about one's own cognitive processes) is emphasised.

Chen and Klahr (2008) identified three dimensions determining the transfer distance between a current problem and a relevant past problem:

(1) *Task similarity*: similarities between the problems in superficial (objects and their properties) and structural (i.e., underlying relations) features.
(2) *Context similarity*: similarities in physical context (location) and social context (e.g., people).
(3) *Time interval*: the period of time between the past and present problems.

Transfer is generally greatest when two problems are similar, the contexts are similar, and the time interval is short (see Chen & Klahr, 2008, for a review).

In what follows, we will first consider far transfer. Dunbar (2001) identified the "analogical paradox" – it is generally believed that far transfer is common in the real world but it has often proved elusive in the laboratory. After that, we will discuss analogical problem solving, which has proved a rich source of information

KEY TERMS

positive transfer: past experience of solving one problem makes it easier to solve a similar current problem.

negative transfer: past experience in solving one problem disrupts the ability to solve a similar current problem.

far transfer: beneficial effects of previous problem solving on current problem solving in a dissimilar context; a form of **positive transfer**.

near transfer: beneficial effects of previous problem solving on current problem solving; a form of **positive transfer**.

metacognition: an individual's beliefs and knowledge about his/her own cognitive processes and strategies.

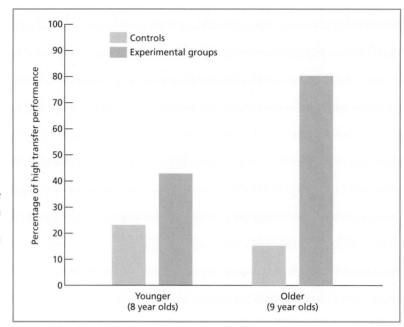

Figure 12.12 Percentage of children performing at a high level on the transfer test (13 or more out of 15) given 7 months after learning as a function of age (8 vs. 9) and previous relevant training (control vs. experimental). Based on data from Chen and Klahr (1999).

on the factors (e.g., cognitive processes) increasing or decreasing near transfer.

Far transfer

Evidence of large far transfer effects was reported by Chen and Klahr (1999). Children aged between seven and ten years of age were trained to design and evaluate experiments in the domain of physical science. Of central importance in the children's learning was the control of variables strategy involving the ability to create sound experiments and to distinguish between confounded and unconfounded experiments.

Chen and Klahr carried out a test of far transfer seven months after training. This test assessed mastery of the control of variables strategy in five new domains, including plant growth, biscuit making, and drink sales. Children who had received the previous training performed much better on the test than did control children who had not received training (see Figure 12.12).

Evidence of the importance of task similarity for far transfer was shown by Chen, Mo, and Honomichl (2004). They used a statue problem,

in which the chief of a riverside village needs to measure an amount of gold equal in weight to a statue without using a weighing machine. The solution involves putting the statue in a tub (mentioned in the problem), placing the tub in the river, and observing how much lower the tub sits in the water when the statue is in it.

Chen et al. found that 69% of Chinese students but only 8% of American students solved the statue problem. The explanation of this huge difference is that there is a Chinese story (weigh the elephant) that closely resembles the statue problem in that an elephant has to be weighed but the largest weighing machine available is much too small. The solution involves putting the elephant in a boat and marking the water level on the boat. After that, the elephant is replaced with small stones until the water level is the same as it was with the elephant. Finally, the small stones are weighed individually. The high level of performance of the Chinese students was based on far transfer based on their childhood exposure to the weigh-the-elephant problem.

Chen et al. (2004) argued that successful far transfer involves several different processing

The high level of performance of the Chinese students in Chen et al.'s (2004) statue problem was based on far transfer resulting from their childhood exposure to the weigh-the-elephant problem.

stages. These include accessing (retrieving the weigh-the-elephant tale), mapping (selection of goal object and solution tool), and executing (finding the correct strategy to solve the problem). Chen et al. manipulated the difficulty of the target problem by varying the similarity of the goal object (elephant versus asteroid) and solution tool (boat versus spring platform) to the original tale. Chinese participants performed worst when the goal object and solution were both dissimilar to the tale (i.e., asteroid + spring platform). This low level of performance was due to problems in accessing, mapping, and executing.

Effects of context similarity were obtained by Spencer and Weisberg (1986). Students solved an initial problem in a laboratory or a classroom and subsequently solved a related problem in a classroom or a laboratory. There was more transfer when the context was the same for both problems.

Effects of time interval on far transfer have nearly always been obtained. For example, Chen and Klahr (2008) discussed one of their studies in which transfer of hypothesis-testing strategies was tested one or two years after first testing. Children initially aged five or six showed some transfer of these strategies to problems with different perceptual and contextual features, but there was more transfer after one year than after two.

How can we enhance far transfer? De Corte (2003) found that metacognition is useful. Students studying business economics were provided with training over a seven-month period in two metacognitive skills: orienting and self-judging. Orienting involves preparing oneself to solve problems by thinking about possible goals and cognitive activities. Self-judging is a motivational activity designed to assist students to assess accurately the effort required for successful task completion.

De Corte found on the subsequent learning of statistics that students who had received the training performed better than those who had not. Within the group that had been trained, orienting and self-judging were both positively correlated with academic performance in statistics.

Evaluation

The approach adopted by Chen, Klahr, and their colleagues is a valuable one. Far transfer is important in the real world, but had previously been under-researched. There is good support for Chen and Klahr's (2008) assumption that transfer depends on task similarity, context similarity, and time interval (see next section).

What are the limitations of Chen and Klahr's (2008) theoretical and experimental approach? First, there are relatively few studies in which context similarity has been manipulated, and social context in particular has not been considered in detail.

Second, we still do not know much about the underlying mechanisms. For example, *why* exactly does changing the context between initial and subsequent problem solving lead to reduced transfer?

Third, individual differences in intelligence are de-emphasised in Chen and Klahr's approach. For example, Davidson and Sternberg (1984) found that children of high intelligence performed at the same level as those of average intelligence on logical-mathematical problems when they had not been given any previous examples. However, gifted children (but not average children) showed substantial positive transfer when exposed to a *single* previous example. In a study discussed earlier, De Corte (2003) found that training in metacognitive skills produced more transfer among the most intelligent students.

Analogical problem solving

Much research on positive and negative transfer (especially near transfer) has involved analogical problem solving, in which the solver uses similarities between the current problem and one or more problems solved in the past. Analogical problem solving has proved important in the history of science. For example, the New Zealand physicist, Ernest Rutherford, used a solar system analogy to understand the structure of the atom. More specifically, he argued that electrons revolve around the nucleus in the same way that the planets revolve around the sun. Other examples include the computer model of human information processing, the billiard-ball model of gases, and the hydraulic model of the blood circulation system. Thus, when people do not have knowledge directly relevant to a problem, they apply knowledge indirectly by *analogy* to the problem.

Under what circumstances do people make successful use of previous problems to solve a current problem? What is crucial is that they notice (and make use of) similarities between the current problem and a previous one. Chen (2002) identified *three* main types of similarity between problems:

(1) *Superficial similarity*: solution-irrelevant details (e.g., specific objects) are common to both problems.
(2) *Structural similarity*: causal relations among some of the main components are shared by both problems.
(3) *Procedural similarity*: procedures for turning the solution principle into concrete operations are common to both problems.

Initially, we will consider some factors determining whether people use relevant analogies when solving a problem. After that, we will consider the processes involved when people are given an explicit analogical problem to solve. Analogical reasoning performance has been found to correlate approximately +0.7 with intelligence (Spearman, 1927), which suggests that higher-level cognitive processes are involved. More specifically, it has been argued that the central executive component of the working memory system (see Chapter 6) plays an important role (Morrison, 2005).

Evidence

Gick and Holyoak (1980) studied Duncker's radiation problem, in which a patient with a malignant tumour in his stomach can only be saved by a special kind of ray. However, a ray of sufficient strength to destroy the tumour will also destroy the healthy tissue, whereas a ray that does not harm healthy tissue will be too weak to destroy the tumour.

Only 10% of participants given the radiation problem on its own managed to solve it. The correct answer is to direct several low-intensity rays at the tumour from different directions. Other participants were given three stories to memorise, one of which was structurally similar to the radiation problem. This story was about a general capturing a fortress by having his army converge at the same time on the fortress along several different roads. When participants were told this story was relevant to solving the radiation problem, 80% of them solved it (see Figure 12.13). When no hint was offered, only 40% solved the problem, presumably because

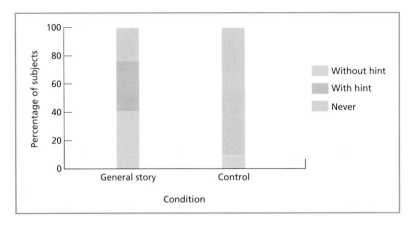

Figure 12.13 Some of the results from Gick and Holyoak (1980, Experiment 4) showing the percentage of participants who solved the radiation problem when they were given an analogy (general-story condition) or were just asked to solve the problem (control condition). Note that just under half of the subjects in the general-story condition had to be given a hint to use the story analogy before they solved the problem.

many of the participants failed to use the analogy provided by the story. Thus, the fact that relevant information is stored in long-term memory is no guarantee that it will be used.

Why did Gick and Holyoak's (1980) participants fail to make spontaneous use of the relevant story they had memorised? Keane (1987) suggested that the lack of superficial similarities between the story and the problem may have been important. He presented students with a semantically close story (about a surgeon using rays on a cancer) or a semantically remote story (the general-and-fortress story). They were given this story during a lecture, and then took part in an experiment involving the radiation problem several days later. Of those students given the close analogy, 88% spontaneously retrieved it when given the radiation problem. In contrast, only 12% of those who had been given the remote analogy spontaneously retrieved it.

Blanchette and Dunbar (2000) argued that we should not conclude that most people focus mainly on the superficial similarities between problems at the expense of structural similarities. Most laboratory studies use a "reception paradigm" in which participants are provided with detailed information about one or more possible analogies before being presented with a current problem. In contrast, what typically happens in everyday life is that people produce their own analogies rather than being given them. Blanchette and Dunbar compared performance using the standard reception paradigm and the more realistic "production paradigm" in which people generated their own analogies. As in previous research, people in the reception paradigm often selected analogies based on superficial similarities. However, those in the production paradigm tended to produce analogies sharing structural features with the current problem.

Dunbar and Blanchette (2001) studied what leading molecular biologists and immunologists said during laboratory meetings when they were fixing experimental problems and formulating hypotheses. When the scientists used analogies to fix experimental problems, the previous problem was often superficially similar to the current one. When scientists were generating hypotheses, the analogies they used involved fewer superficial similarities and considerably more structural similarities. The take-home message is that the types of analogy that people use depend importantly on their current goals.

It has often been assumed that individuals who realise that a current problem has important similarities with a previous problem are almost certain to solve it. Chen (2002) disagreed. He argued that people may perceive important similarities between a current and previous problem but may still be unable to solve it if the two problems do not share *procedural* similarity. Chen presented participants with an initial story resembling the weigh-the-elephant problem discussed earlier. Those provided with an initial story resembling the weigh-the-elephant problem in both structural and procedural similarity performed much better on the problem than those provided with an initial story containing only structural similarity to the problem. Many of those in the latter condition grasped the general solution based on weight equivalence, but could not find appropriate procedures to solve the problem. Thus, effective analogies often need to possess procedural as well as structural similarity to a current problem.

Morrison, Holyoak, and Truong (2001) studied the processes involved in analogical problem solving. Participants were presented with verbal analogies (e.g., BLACK: WHITE:: NOISY: QUIET) and decided whether they were true or false. They were also presented with picture-based analogies involving cartoon characters. The analogies were either solved on their own or while participants performed an additional task imposing demands on the central executive, the phonological loop (a rehearsal-based system), or the visuo-spatial sketchpad (see Glossary).

What did Morrison et al. (2001) find? First, performance on both verbal and pictorial analogies was impaired when the additional task involved the central executive. This finding suggests that solving analogies requires use of the central executive, which has limited capacity. Second, performance on verbal analogies was impaired when the additional task involved the phonological loop. This occurred because both tasks involved verbal processing. Third, performance on pictorial analogies suffered when the additional task involved the visuo-spatial sketchpad.

Krawczyk et al. (2008) argued that analogical problem solving depends in part on executive processes that inhibit responding to relevant distractors. For example, consider a picture analogy as follows:

sandwich: lunchbox:: hammer: ?????

The task is to choose one of the following options: toolbox (correct); nail (semantic distractor); gavel (auctioneer's hammer: perceptual distractor); and ribbon (irrelevant distractor).

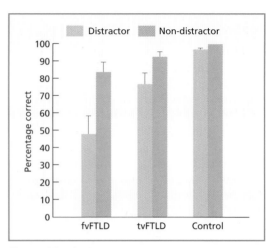

Figure 12.14 Mean percentage correct responses on analogical problems with and without relevant distractors. fvFTLD = frontotemporal lobar degeneration; tvFTLD = temporal-variant frontotemporal lobar degeneration. Reprinted from Krawczyk et al. (2008), Copyright © 2008, with permission from Elsevier.

According to Krawczyk et al., inhibitory executive processes involve the prefrontal cortex. Accordingly, they used a group of patients with damage to the prefrontal cortex, another group with damage to the temporal area, and a control group of healthy individuals.

What did Krawcyzk et al. (2008) find? First, the frontal damage patients were more likely than the temporal damage patients to give incorrect responses involving relevant semantic or perceptual distractors. Second, only the frontal patients had enhanced performance on pictorial analogies when no relevant distractors were present (see Figure 12.14). These findings suggest that an intact prefrontal cortex is needed to inhibit related but incorrect answers in analogical problem solving.

How can we improve analogical problem solving? Kurtz and Loewenstein (2007) argued that individuals would find it easier to grasp the underlying structure of a problem if they compared it *directly* with another problem sharing the same structure. The target problem for all participants was the radiation problem used by Gick and Holyoak. One group (control group) received the problem about the general and the fortress initially, followed by the radiation problem. Another group received the problem about the general and another analogous problem initially, and considered similarities between them. After that, they received the radiation problem. A third group received the problem about the general initially. After that, they were presented with the radiation problem and another analogous problem, and told to look for similarities between them.

What happened in the above experiment? The radiation problem was rarely solved by members of the control group. Performance was much better in both of the other two groups. Directly comparing the structure of two analogous problems promotes understanding of the underlying structure and leads to greatly improved analogical problem solving.

Evaluation

Much has been learned about the factors determining whether individuals will use relevant past knowledge in analogical problem solving. For example, superficial, structural, and procedural similarity between past problems and a current problem are all important. In addition, the nature of the individual's task and the goals they have set themselves both influence analogical thinking. The central executive component of the working memory system is heavily involved in analogical problem solving, as is the visuo-spatial sketchpad with pictorial problems or the phonological loop with verbal problems. Inhibitory executive processes are needed to prevent interference from distractors.

What are the limitations of research on analogical problem solving? First, analogical problems in the laboratory can often be solved by using an appropriate analogy provided earlier in the experiment. In everyday life, in contrast, the fit or match between previous knowledge and the current problem is typically imprecise. Second, individuals in the laboratory generally focus on superficial similarities between past problems and a current one, whereas structural similarities are often more important in more realistic situations (Blanchette & Dunbar, 2000; Dunbar & Blanchette, 2001). Third, some

people are much better than others at finding and using analogies. As yet, however, there has been little research focused on individual differences in performance.

EXPERTISE

So far in this chapter we have mostly discussed studies in which the time available for learning has been short, the tasks involved relatively limited, and prior specific knowledge is not required. In the real world, however, people sometimes spend several years acquiring knowledge and skills in a given area (e.g., psychology, law, medicine, journalism). The end point of such long-term learning is the development of expertise, which is "highly skilled, competent performance in one or more task domains [areas]" (Sternberg & Ben-Zeev, 2001, p. 365). We can, of course, study the processes involved on the road to achieving expertise. This is the area of **skill acquisition**:

> When we speak of a "skill" we mean an ability that allows a goal to be achieved within some domain with increasing likelihood as a result of practice. When we speak of "acquisition of skill" we refer to the attainment of those practice-related capabilities that contribute to the increased likelihood of goal achievement.

The development of expertise resembles problem solving, in that experts are extremely efficient at solving numerous problems in their area of expertise. However, as mentioned in the Introduction, most traditional research on problem solving involved "knowledge-lean" problems, meaning no special training or knowledge is required for the solution. In

KEY TERM

skill acquisition: developing abilities through practice so as to increase the probability of goal achievement.

contrast, studies on expertise have typically used "knowledge-rich" problems requiring much knowledge beyond that presented in the problem itself.

In this section, we will first consider in detail one specific domain of expertise, namely, chess expertise. There are several advantages to studying chess playing (Gobet, Voogt, & Retschitzki, 2004). First, the ELO ranking system provides a precise and valid assessment of individual players' level of expertise. Second, expert chess players develop specific cognitive skills (e.g. pattern recognition; selective search) that are useful in other areas of expertise. Third, information about chess experts' remarkable memory for chess positions generalises very well to most other forms of expertise.

After discussing chess expertise, we turn to the important issue of medical expertise, especially as it applies to medical diagnosis. Finally, we will analyse Ericsson's theoretical approach, according to which deliberate practice is the main requirement for the development of expertise.

Chess expertise

Why do some people excel at playing chess? According to Chase and Simon (1973b), no one can become an international chess master without devoting at least one decade to intensive practice. This ten-year rule is generally accepted as a reasonable estimate of the practice period needed to develop chess-playing excellence.

What benefits occur as a result of practice? Expert chess players have very detailed knowledge about chess positions stored in long-term memory. This allows them to relate the position in the current game to those in previous games. De Groot (1965) assessed individual differences in such knowledge. Participants received brief presentations (between 2 and 15 seconds) of board positions from actual games. After removing the board, De Groot asked them to reconstruct the positions. Chess masters recalled the positions very accurately (91% correct), whereas less expert players made many more errors (41% correct). This difference reflected differences in stored chess information rather than differences in memory ability because there were no group differences in remembering random board positions.

Chase and Simon (1973a) argued that chess players memorising chess positions break them down into about seven **chunks** or units. Their key assumption was that the chunks formed by expert players contain more information than those of other players. They asked three chess players to look at the position of the pieces on one board, and to reconstruct it on a second board with the first board still visible. Chase and Simon argued that the number of pieces placed on the second board after each glance at the first board provided a measure of chunk size. The most expert player had chunks averaging 2.5 pieces, whereas the novice had chunks averaging only 1.9 pieces. In fact, however, these are substantial underestimates (Gobet & Simon, 1998).

Chase and Simon (1973b) argued, in their chunking theory, that a major advantage held by chess experts is that they have very large numbers of chess chunks stored in long-term memory. Simon and Gilmartin (1973) estimated that chess experts have between 10,000 and 100,000 chunks stored in their memories, and computer simulations have suggested a figure of 300,000 chunks (Gobet & Simon, 2000). However, we should not assume that the *only* advantage that chess experts have over novices is that they have stored information about tens of thousands of chess pieces. That would be like arguing that the only advantage Shakespeare had over other writers was a larger vocabulary!

The strategies used by human expert chess players do not resemble those used by chess-playing computers, which do almost unimaginable amounts of search. For example, the computer Deep Blue processed about 200 million positions per second, and considered up to

> **KEY TERM**
>
> **chunk:** a stored unit formed from integrating smaller pieces of information.

Chase and Simon (1973a) argued that chess players memorising chess positions, break them down into about seven chunks or units, and that these chunks contain much more information than those of other players.

about six moves ahead. This vast amount of search allowed it to beat the then World Chess Champion, Garry Kasparov, in May 1997. In order to understand human chess playing, we need to turn from computers to template theory, which represents a major development of chunking theory.

Template theory

Gobet and Waters (2003) identified two major weaknesses with chunking theory. First, it fails to relate mechanisms at the chunk level with the higher-level representations used by expert chess players. Second, the theory predicts that

it will take longer than is actually the case to encode chess positions.

Template theory overcomes the above weaknesses with chunking theory. According to template theory, chunks that are used frequently develop into more complex data structures known as templates. A **template** is a schematic structure that is more general than an actual board position. Each template consists of a *core* (very similar to the fixed information stored in chunks) plus *slots* (which contain variable information about pieces and locations). A template is larger than a chunk and is a more complex and abstract representation. It typically stores information relating to about ten pieces, although it can be larger than that. The fact that templates contain slots means that templates are more flexible and adaptable than chunks.

Template theory makes several testable predictions. First, it predicts that the chunks into which information about chess positions is organised are larger and fewer in number than is assumed by chunking theory. More specifically, it is assumed that chess positions are stored in three templates, with some of these templates being relatively large.

Second, it is assumed that outstanding chess players owe their excellence mostly to their superior template-based knowledge of chess rather than their use of slow, strategy-based processes. It is assumed that their knowledge can be accessed rapidly, and allows them to narrow down the possible moves they need to consider. If these assumptions are correct, then the performance of outstanding players should remain extremely high even when making their moves under considerable time pressure.

Third, it is assumed that expert chess players generally store away the precise board locations of pieces after studying a board position. In addition, it is assumed that chess pieces close together are most likely to be found in the same template (Gobet & Simon, 2000).

Fourth, it is predicted that expert chess players will have better recall of apparently random chess positions than non-experts. The reason is that some patterns occur by chance even in random positions, and these patterns relate to template-based information.

Fifth, the emphasis within template theory is very much on the notion that chess-playing expertise depends on domain-specific expertise rather than on more general abilities (e.g., intelligence). Thus, individuals of high intelligence should have only a modest advantage at chess compared to those of lower intelligence.

Evidence

Gobet and Clarkson (2004) provided strong support for the first prediction. They started by pointing out two limitations in the research of Chase and Simon (1973a). Chase and Simon used only three players, and their master was in his forties and out of practice. More importantly, the players in their study had to move the pieces physically, and the limited capacity of the hand for holding chess pieces may have made chunk size seem smaller than is actually the case. Gobet and Clarkson removed these problems by using 12 chess players and a computer display so that chess pieces could be moved using a mouse.

Gobet and Clarkson (2004) found that the superior recall of chess board positions by expert players was due to the larger size of their templates. The maximum template size was about 13–15 for masters compared to only about six for beginners. The number of templates did not vary as a function of playing strength and averaged out at about two. That is much closer to the prediction of template theory (i.e., three) than to that of chunking theory (i.e., seven).

There is mixed support for the second prediction. Charness, Reingold, Pomplun, and Stampe (2001) asked expert and intermediate chess players to study chess positions and identify the best move. Their first five eye fixations (lasting in total only about one second) were recorded.

Even at this early stage, the experts were more likely than the intermediate players to fixate on tactically relevant pieces (80% versus 64% of fixations, respectively).

Burns (2004) considered chess performance in normal competitive games and in blitz chess, in which the entire game must be completed in five minutes (less than 5% of the time available in normal chess). The basic assumption was that players' performance in blitz chess must depend mainly on their template-based knowledge, because there is so little time to engage in slow searching through possible moves. If template theory is correct, then players who perform best in normal chess should also tend to perform best in blitz chess. The reason is that the key to successful chess (i.e., template-based knowledge) is available in both forms of chess.

What did Burns (2004) find? The key finding was that performance in blitz chess correlated highly (between +0.78 and +0.90) with performance in normal chess, which accords with theoretical prediction. However, it was emphatically not the case that slow search processes were irrelevant. The same players playing chess under normal conditions and under blitz conditions made superior moves in the former condition, which provided much more time for slow searching.

Van Harreveld, Wagenmakers, and van der Maas (2007) also considered the effects of reducing the time available for chess moves. Skill differences between players were less predictive of game outcomes as the time available decreased. As they concluded, "This result indicates that slow processes are at least as important for strong players as they are for weak players" (p. 591).

More evidence that search processes are important was reported by Charness (1981). Experts and grand masters considered about five moves ahead by each player. In contrast, class D players (who have a low level of skill) considered an average of only 2.3 moves ahead by each player.

We turn now to the third prediction. Most of the available evidence indicates that chess players typically recall the precise squares on

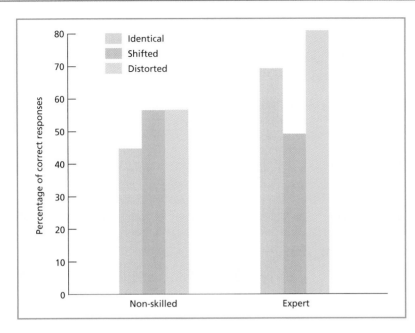

Figure 12.15 Percentage of correct responses on a recognition test as a function of skill group (non-skilled vs. expert) and condition (identical, shifted, or distorted). Data from McGregor and Howes (2002).

the board occupied by given pieces and the pieces contained within a template are close together on the board (e.g., Gobet & Simon, 1996a). However, McGregor and Howes (2002) identified an important limitation with previous findings. The participants were generally asked to *memorise* board positions, whereas actual chess playing focuses much more on the need to *evaluate* board positions. McGregor and Howes argued that chess players evaluating a board position would probably remember the attack/defence relations among pieces rather than their precise locations.

McGregor and Howes (2002) asked expert and non-skilled players to evaluate 30 chess positions (decide which colour was winning or if there was no advantage). After that, there was a test of recognition memory on which the players decided whether or not they had seen each board position before. Some board positions were *identical* to those presented previously, others were *shifted* (all pieces moved one square horizontally), and others were *distorted* (only one piece was moved one square, but this changed the attack/defence relations). Expert players had much better memory for attack/defence relations than for the precise

board locations of the pieces (see Figure 12.15). In another experiment, McGregor and Howes found that the structure of chunks is determined more by attack/defence relations among pieces than by proximity of pieces.

The fourth prediction is that expert players will have better recall than non-experts of random chess positions. This contrasts with chunking theory, according to which there should be no effects of chess expertise on the ability to remember random chess positions. Gobet and Simon (1996b) carried out a meta-analysis and found there was a small effect of skill on random board positions. However, Gobet and Waters (2003) pointed out that the random board positions used in these studies were not totally random. More specifically, the positions of the pieces were random, but the pieces placed on the board were not selected at random (e.g., two kings were always present). Gobet and Waters used truly random positions and pieces. The findings were as predicted theoretically by template theory: the number of pieces recalled varied from 14.8 for the most expert players to 12.0 for the least expert.

The fifth prediction is that individual differences in chess-playing expertise depend relatively little on general abilities such as intelligence. This prediction seems somewhat counterintuitive given that chess is a complex and intellectually demanding game. In fact, chess-playing ability has often been found to be almost unrelated to intelligence (see Gobet et al., 2004, for a review). However, individual differences in intelligence were moderately predictive of chess-playing level in a study by Grabner, Stern, and Neubauer (2007) on adult tournament chess players. They obtained a correlation of +0.35 between general intelligence and ELO ranking (a measure of playing ability). In addition, they found that numerical intelligence correlated +0.46 with ELO ranking. However, as predicted by template theory, players' chess experience (e.g., amount of practice) was an even better predictor of ELO ranking.

Evaluation

Template theory has several successes to its credit. First, as the theory assumes, there is evidence that much of the information that experts store from a board position is in the form of a few large templates rather than a larger number of chunks (Gobet & Clarkson, 2004). Second, outstanding chess players possess much more knowledge about chess positions than do non-experts, and this gives them a substantial advantage when playing chess. For example, template-based knowledge explains why expert players can identify key pieces in a board position in under one second (Charness et al., 2001). Third, the tendency of experts to win at blitz chess is due mainly to their superior template-based knowledge. Fourth, as predicted theoretically, experts have better recall than non-experts of board positions even when the positions and the pieces are truly random (Gobet & Waters, 2003).

What are the limitations of template theory? First, slow search processes are more important to expert players than is assumed by the theory. For example, they look ahead more moves than non-expert ones (Charness, 1981) and skill level is less predictive of outcome with reduced time available per move (van Harreveld et al., 2007). Bilalić, McLeod, and Gobet (2008)

reported interesting findings. Chess players were presented with a chess problem that could be solved in five moves using a familiar strategy but in only three moves using a less familiar solution. The players were told to look for the shortest way to win. They found that 50% of the International Masters found the shorter solution compared to 0% of the Candidate Masters. Precisely why the International Masters exhibited flexibility of thought and avoided the familiar, template-based solution is unclear.

Second, there is a reduction in performance level for all chess players under severe time pressure (Burns, 2004), suggesting that all players rely to some extent on slow search processes. The distinction between routine and adaptive expertise (Hatano & Inagaki, 1986) may be relevant here. **Routine expertise** is involved when a player can solve familiar problems rapidly and efficiently. In contrast, **adaptive expertise** is involved when a player has to develop strategies for deciding what to do when confronted by a novel board position. Template theory provides a convincing account of what is involved in routine expertise. However, it is less clear that it sheds much light on adaptive expertise.

Third, the precise information stored in long-term memory remains controversial. It is assumed within the theory that templates consist mainly of pieces that were close together on the board, and that the precise locations of individual pieces are stored. However, attack/defence relations seem to be more important (McGregor & Howes, 2002).

Fourth, there has been a tendency within template theory to exaggerate the importance of the sheer amount of time devoted to practice

KEY TERMS

routine expertise: using acquired knowledge to solve familiar problems efficiently.
adaptive expertise: using acquired knowledge to develop strategies for dealing with novel problems.

and to minimise the role of individual differences. For example, the finding by Grabner et al. (2007) that intelligence (especially numerical intelligence) is moderately predictive of chess-playing expertise seems unexpected from the perspective of template theory.

Medical expertise

We turn now to medical expertise, specifically the ability of medical experts to make rapid and accurate diagnoses. This involves complex decision making, which is discussed in more general terms in Chapter 13.

Medical decision making is often literally a matter of life-or-death, and even experts make mistakes. The number of deaths per year in the United States attributable to preventable medical error is between 44,000 and 98,000. This makes it extremely important to understand medical expertise. Of course, medical experts with many years of training behind them generally make better decisions than novice doctors. However, what is less obvious is precisely *how* the superior knowledge of medical experts translates into superior diagnoses and decision making.

Several theorists have argued that the medical reasoning of experts differs considerably from that of novices and does not simply involve using the same strategies more effectively. There are important differences among these theorists. However, as Engel (2008) pointed out, there is an important distinction between explicit reasoning and implicit reasoning. Explicit reasoning is relatively slow, deliberate, and is associated with conscious awareness, whereas implicit reasoning is fast, automatic, and is not associated with conscious awareness. The crucial assumption is that medical novices engage mainly in explicit reasoning, whereas medical experts engage mainly in implicit reasoning.

Theorists differ in the terms they use to refer to the above distinction. For example, Norman, Young, and Brooks (2007) distinguishes between analytic reasoning strategies (explicit reasoning) and non-analytic reasoning strategies (implicit reasoning). In contrast, Kundel, Nodine,

Conant, and Weinstein (2007) distinguished between focal search (explicit reasoning) and global impression (implicit reasoning). Note that a distinction very similar to those just discussed has been very influential in reasoning research generally (see Chapter 14) and in research on judgement and decision making (see Chapter 13).

We should note three qualifications on the notion that the development of medical expertise leads from a reliance on explicit reasoning to one on implicit reasoning. First, as we will see, that is only approximately correct. For example, medical experts may start with fast, automatic processes but generally cross-check their diagnoses with slow, deliberate processes. Second, it is likely that fast, automatic processing strategies are used considerably more often in *visual* specialities such as pathology, radiology, and dermatology than in more *technical* specialities such as surgery or anaesthesiology (Engel, 2008). Third, while we have emphasised the similarities in the views of different theorists, we must avoid assuming that there are no important differences.

Evidence

How can we identify the diagnostic strategies used by medical novices and experts? One interesting approach is to track eye movements while doctors examine case slides. This was done by Krupinsky et al. (2006) and Kundel et al. (2007). Krupinsky et al. recorded eye movements while medical students, pathology residents, and fully trained pathologists examined slides relating to breast biopsy cases. The fully trained pathologists spent least time examining each slide (4.5 seconds versus 7.1 seconds for residents and 11.9 seconds for students). Of more importance, greater expertise was associated with more information being extracted from the initial fixation. In the terminology used by Krupinsky et al., experts relied heavily on global impression (implicit reasoning), whereas novices made more use of focal search (explicit reasoning), in which several different parts of each slide were attended to in turn.

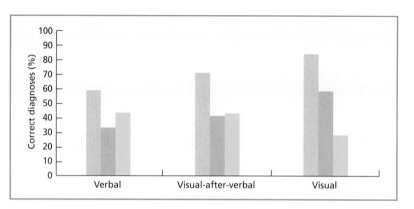

Figure 12.16 Percentage correct diagnoses in the verbal only, visual-after-verbal, and visual only conditions. Green = experts (dermatologists); purple = general practitioners; orange = residents. From Kulatunga-Moruzi et al. (2004), Copyright © 2004. American Psychological Association. Reproduced with permission.

Kundel et al. (2007) presented difficult mammograms showing or not showing breast cancer to doctors experienced in mammography. The mean search time for the mammograms showing cancer was 27 seconds. However, the median time to fixate a cancer was 1.13 seconds, and was typically less than one second for the experts. There was a strong negative correlation of about –0.9 between time of first fixation on the cancer and performance, meaning that fast fixation was an excellent predictor of high performance. The most expert doctors typically fixated almost immediately on the cancer, suggesting that they used holistic or global processes. In contrast, the least expert doctors seemed to rely on a slower, more analytic search-to-find processing strategy.

Convincing evidence that the processing strategies of medical experts differ from those of non-experts was reported by Kulatunga-Moruzi, Brooks, and Norman (2004) in a study on skin lesions. They argued that non-experts use an analytic, rule-based strategy in which the various clinical features are considered carefully before any diagnoses are entertained. In contrast, experts use an automatic exemplar-based strategy in which they rapidly search for a stored exemplar that closely resembles any given case photograph. There were three groups: expert dermatologists; moderately expert general practitioners; and less knowledgeable resident doctors. In one condition, they were shown case photographs and made diagnoses. In another condition, they were initially given a comprehensive verbal description followed by the

relevant case photograph, and made a diagnosis after the photograph.

What findings would we expect to find? If non-experts (i.e., resident doctors) base their diagnoses mostly on clinical features, they should have found the verbal descriptions to be valuable. If experts (i.e., the dermatologists) base their diagnoses mostly on an exemplar-based strategy, they might have found that the verbal descriptions interfered with effective use of that strategy. These predictions were supported by the findings (see Figure 12.16). The diagnostic accuracy of the non-experts was higher when their diagnoses were based on verbal descriptions as well as photographs. In striking contrast, the more expert groups performed better when they weren't exposed to the verbal descriptions.

Are there circumstances in which experts perform *worse* than non-experts? Adam and Reyna (2005) argued that the answer is, "Yes". According to fuzzy-trace theory, experts are more likely than non-experts to make use of gist-based processing. This has various advantages. It generally means that experts are very *discriminating*: they base their decisions on crucial information while largely ignoring less important details. However, gist-based processing involves simplifying the issues, and this can sometimes impair performance through oversimplification.

Relevant evidence was reported by Adam and Reyna (2005). They asked health professionals with relevant expertise various questions relating to sexually transmitted infections. As expected, experts in the field generally displayed more knowledge of the risks of various sexually transmitted infections. However, there were some exceptions. Most sexually transmitted infections are fluid-borne. Accordingly, gist-based representations would focus on those infections rather than the rarer infections that are transmitted through skin-to-skin contact. For example, the experts greatly underestimated the prevalence of human papillomavirus (which is transmitted through skin-to-skin contact) compared to sexually transmitted infections that are fluid-borne. In addition, experts' de-emphasis on infections caused by skin-to-skin contact led them to overestimate the effectiveness of condoms in preventing sexually transmitted infections.

Reyna and Lloyd (2006) presented doctors possessing varying degrees of relevant expertise with information about hypothetical patients at different levels of cardiac risk. There were three main findings, all consistent with the assumption that experts tend to use gist-based processing:

(1) The most expert doctors (cardiologists and nationally recognised experts in cardiology) were better than the less expert ones at discriminating among different levels of risk.
(2) The experts processed *less* information than the non-experts.
(3) The coherence or consistency of experts' judgements on any given patient was no better than that of non-experts, presumably because they relied on gist-based processing.

Evaluation

Much progress has been made in understanding medical expertise. There is convincing evidence that the processes used by medical experts and non-experts in diagnosis often differ qualitatively. It is approximately the case that medical experts compared to non-experts rely more on fast, automatic processes in diagnosis and less on slow, conscious ones, but there are many exceptions to that generalisation. Unsurprisingly,

Medical experts often make use of fast, automatic processes in diagnosis, whereas non-experts rely more on slow, conscious processes.

medical experts typically outperform non-experts. However, there is interesting evidence that experts' reliance on gist-based processes can impair their performance.

What are the limitations of theory and research on medical expertise? First, nearly all studies have involved comparing experts and non-experts. This approach has provided much useful information, but suffers from the disadvantage that it is uninformative about the specific learning processes responsible for the development of expertise. We need studies in which the impact of different learning strategies on the development of expertise is studied over time.

Second, there is a danger of underestimating the value of analytic processing, which is sometimes regarded as "an optional extra in information processing" (McLaughlin, Remy, & Schmidt, 2008). As McLaughlin et al. pointed out, the relationship between expertise, information processing, and diagnostic performance is more complex than is often assumed. This relationship is affected by several factors, including task difficulty, clinical domain, context, and experimental conditions. The optimal strategy is for experts to use automatic and analytic processes flexibly depending on the specific details of any given diagnostic task.

Third, we need research to compare the various theories. For example, some theories emphasise experts' use of stored exemplars, whereas others focus on experts' use of gist. It would seem that exemplars are more specific and less abstract than gist, but research designed to compare these theoretical accounts has not been carried out as yet.

Chess expertise vs. medical expertise

We will conclude this section with a brief comparison of chess and medical expertise. The two kinds of expertise share several similarities, although it is important not to exaggerate them. First, several years of intensive training are needed to attain genuine expertise. Second, the years of training lead to the acquisition of huge amounts of relevant stored knowledge that can be accessed rapidly. Third, those with expertise in either area are better able than non-experts to make use of rapid (possibly "automatic") processes. Fourth, experts have the ability to make flexible use of analytic or strategy-based processes as and when required.

What are the differences between chess expertise and medical expertise? First, there is suggestive evidence that the form in which knowledge is stored differs between the two kinds of expertise. More specifically, much of the knowledge of chess experts is stored in the form of fairly abstract templates. In contrast, the knowledge of medical experts is perhaps less abstract and is stored in the form of exemplars. Second, there are important differences in the ways in which chess and medical experts use their expertise. Chess experts have to relate a current chess position to their stored knowledge and then think deeply about the implications for their subsequent moves and those of their opponent. In contrast, the task of medical experts is more narrowly focused on relating the information they have to their stored knowledge.

DELIBERATE PRACTICE

Everyone knows that prolonged and carefully organised practice is essential in the develop-ment of almost any kind of expertise. That is a useful starting point. However, what we really need is a theory in which the details of what is involved in effective practice are spelled out. Precisely that was done by Ericsson, Krampe, and Tesch-Römer (1993) and Ericsson and Lehmann (1996), who argued that a wide range of expertise can be developed through deliberate practice. **Deliberate practice** has four aspects:

(1) The task is at an appropriate level of difficulty (not too easy or hard).
(2) The learner is given informative feedback about his/her performance.
(3) The learner has adequate chances to repeat the task.
(4) The learner has the opportunity to correct his/her errors.

According to Ericsson et al. (1993, p. 368), "The amount of time an individual is engaged in deliberate practice activities is monotonically [never decreasingly] related to that individual's acquired performance."

What exactly happens as a result of prolonged deliberate practice? According to Ericsson and Kintsch (1995), experts can get round the limited capacity of working memory. They proposed the notion of **long-term working memory**: experts learn how to store relevant information in long-term memory so that it can be accessed readily through retrieval cues held in working memory. This does not mean that experts have greater working memory capacity than everyone else. Instead, they are

---

KEY TERMS

deliberate practice: this form of practice involves the learner being provided with informative feedback and having the opportunity to correct his/her errors.
long-term working memory: this is used by experts to store relevant information in long-term memory and to access it through retrieval cues in **working memory**.

more efficient at combining the resources of long-term memory and working memory. There are three requirements for long-term working memory to function effectively (Robertson, 2001):

(1) The individual must have extensive knowledge of the relevant information.

(2) The activity in which the individual is engaged must be very familiar so that he/she can predict what information will subsequently need to be retrieved.

(3) The information that is stored must be associated with appropriate retrieval cues so that subsequent presentation of the retrieval cues leads to retrieval of the stored information.

Finally, we come to the most controversial theoretical assumption, namely, that deliberate practice is *all* that is needed to develop expert performance. It follows from that assumption that innate talent or ability has practically no influence on expert performance, a conclusion that seems implausible.

Evidence

There is support for the notion that experts make use of long-term working memory to enhance their ability to remember information. Ericsson and Chase (1982) studied SF, a student at Carnegie-Mellon University in the United States. He was given extensive practice on the digit-span task on which random digits have to be recalled immediately in the correct order. Initially, his digit span was about seven digits. He was then paid to practise the digit-span task for one hour a day for two years. At the end of that time, he reached a digit span of 80 digits, which is about ten times the average level of performance.

How did SF do it? He reached a digit span of about 18 items by using his extensive knowledge of running times. For example, if the first few digits presented were "3594", he would note that this was Bannister's world-record time for the mile, and so these four digits would be stored as a single unit or chunk. He then increased his digit span by organising these chunks into a hierarchical retrieval structure. Thus, SF made effective use of long-term working memory by using meaningful encoding, developing a retrieval structure, and taking advantage of speed-up produced by extensive practice.

Experts in many areas have excellent long-term working memory (see Ericsson & Kintsch, 1995). For example, the first author is constantly surprised by how expert bridge players can recall nearly every detail of hands that have just been played. Norman, Brooks, and Allen (1989) found that medical experts were much better than novices when unexpectedly asked to recall medical information. This is consistent with the notion that they had superior long-term working memory.

Evidence that retrieval structures are important was reported by Ericsson and Chase (1982). Highly practised participants learned digit matrices consisting of 25 digits in 5×5 displays, setting up retrieval structures so they could recall the digits row by row. When recalling the digits column by column, their performance was much slower because their retrieval structures did not match the requirements of the task.

According to Ericsson and Lehmann (1996), what is important in acquiring expertise is the amount of *deliberate* practice rather than simply the sheer amount of practice. Charness, Tuffiash, Krampe, Reingold, and Vasyukova (2005) found among tournament-rated chess players that time spent on serious study alone, tournament play, and formal instruction all predicted chess-playing expertise. Of those factors, serious study alone was the strongest predictor correlating approximately +0.50 with current playing level. Grandmasters had spent an average of 5000 hours on serious study alone during their first ten years of playing chess, nearly five times as much as the amount of time spent by intermediate players.

Deliberate practice has also been shown to be important in the development of expertise in other contexts. Ericsson, Krampe, and Tesch-Römer (1993) reported a study on violinists in a German music academy. The key difference

Ericsson et al. (1993) suggested that deliberate practice was key in the development of expertise.

between 18-year-old students having varying levels of expertise on the violin was the amount of deliberate practice they had had over the years. The most expert violinists had spent on average nearly 7500 hours engaged in deliberate practice compared to the 5300 hours clocked up by the good violinists.

The above study only showed that there is a correlation or association between amount of deliberate practice and level of performance. Perhaps those musicians with the greatest innate talent and/or musical success decide to spend more time practising than those with less talent or previous success. However, contrary evidence was reported by Sloboda, Davidson, Howe, and Moore (1996), who compared highly successful young musicians with less successful ones. The two groups did not differ in the amount of practice they required to achieve a given level of performance. This suggests that the advantage possessed by the very successful musicians is not due to their greater level of natural musical ability.

Tuffiash, Roring, and Ericsson (2007) obtained evidence for the importance of deliberate practice among 40 tournament-rated Scrabble players. The main comparisons were between elite and average players having comparable levels of verbal ability. The elite players spent more time than the average players on deliberate practice activities (e.g., analysis of their own previous games; solving anagrams), but the two groups did not differ with respect to other forms of practice (e.g., playing Scrabble for fun; playing in Scrabble tournaments). In addition, lifetime accumulated study of Scrabble was a reasonable predictor of Scrabble-playing expertise.

What role does innate ability or intelligence play in the development of expertise? High intelligence is not required to acquire expertise in narrow domains. For example, consider individuals known patronisingly as **idiots savants** (knowledgeable idiots). They have mental retardation and low IQs but possess some special expertise. For example, some idiots savants can work out in a few seconds the day of the week corresponding to any specified date in the past or the future (calendar calculating). Others can perform multiplications at high speed or know what *pi* is to thousands of places of decimals.

In spite of the great feats of idiots savants, their abilities are often very restricted. For example, Howe and Smith (1988) studied a 14-year-old boy who was very good at subtraction problems expressed in terms of calendar dates (e.g., "If a man was born in 1908, how old would he have been in 1934?"). However, when essentially the same subtraction problem was expressed as, "What is 34 minus 8?", he took much longer to produce an answer and the answer was often wrong!

More evidence that high intelligence is not needed for narrow forms of expertise was reported by Ceci and Liker (1986). They studied individuals with considerable expertise about harness racing, in which horses pull a sulky (a light two-wheeled cart). They identified 14 experts whose IQs ranged from 81 to 128, with four of them having IQs in the low 80s. These experts worked out probable odds which involved taking account of complex interactions among up to seven variables (e.g., each horse's lifetime speed; track size). The experts' high level of performance did not depend at all on a high IQ – the correlation between performance and IQ was –0.07.

There is much stronger evidence for the importance of intelligence in the development of very broad expertise. For most people, the broadest expertise they are likely to acquire is in their career, especially those involving complex skills. Gottfredson (1997) discussed the literature on intelligence and occupational success. The correlation between intelligence and work performance was only +0.23 with low-complexity jobs (e.g., shrimp picker; corn-husking machine operator), but rose to +0.58 for high-complexity jobs (e.g., biologist; city circulation manager). The mean IQ of those in very complex occupations (e.g., accountants; lawyers; doctors) is approximately 120–130, which is much higher than the population mean of 100 (see Mackintosh, 1998).

There is a moderate correlation between intelligence and socio-economic status (Mackintosh, 1998), and so some of the effects of intelligence on job performance may actually be due to socio-economic status and related factors such as school quality or neighbourhood. However, this possibility was convincingly disproved by Murray (1998). He used a sample of male full biological siblings in intact families, thereby controlling for socio-economic status, schools, neighbourhood, and so on. The siblings with higher intelligence had more prestigious occupations plus higher income. When they were in their late twenties, a person with average intelligence earned on average nearly $18,000 (£10,500) less per annum than his sibling with an IQ of at least 120 but over $9,000 (£5,000) more than his sibling with an IQ of 80 or less.

Why is job performance well predicted by intelligence? Hunter and Schmidt (e.g., 1996) answered this question with a theory based on four main assumptions:

(1) Work performance depends to a moderate extent on job-relevant learning and knowledge.
(2) Highly intelligent individuals learn more rapidly than less intelligent ones.
(3) Successful job performance sometimes requires that workers respond in an innovative or adaptive fashion.
(4) More intelligent workers respond more adaptively than less intelligent ones.

Hunter (1983) reported the findings from 14 studies on civilian and military groups supporting this theory. First, there was a high correlation between intelligence and job knowledge. Second, learning (i.e., job knowledge) was strongly associated with job performance. Third, there was a direct influence of intelligence on job performance not dependent on job knowledge.

Evaluation

There is much support for the notion that memory in a domain of expertise can be developed via the use of long-term working memory. Most (or all) experts seem to develop superior long-term working memory, which serves to reduce limitations on processing capacity. The evidence also indicates that deliberate practice is more important than non-deliberate practice for the development of high levels of expertise; indeed, it appears to be *necessary* for the achievement of outstanding performance.

What are the limitations of deliberate practice theory? First, much evidence indicates that deliberate practice is *not* the only important factor in the development of expertise. For example, innate ability or intelligence predicts level of expertise as reflected in occupational success (Gottfredson, 1997) or chess-playing performance (Grabner et al., 2007).

Second, the notion that innate talent is unimportant is unconvincing. As Sternberg and Ben-Zeev (2001, p. 302) argued, "Is one to believe that anyone could become a Mozart if only he or she put in the time? ... Or that becoming an Einstein is just a matter of deliberate practice?" Why, then, does intelligence often fail to predict level of expertise? One reason may be that most experts are highly talented or intelligent, thus making it difficult for individual differences in intelligence to predict performance. For example, Bilalić, McLeod, and Gobet (2008) found that there was a *negative* correlation between intelligence and chess-playing expertise among elite young chess players. However, the mean IQ of this elite sample was 133, which is at approximately the 97th or 98th percentile.

Third, there are real methodological inadequacies in most of the research, which has shown only that the amount of deliberate practice is positively correlated with level of expertise. What generally happened was that individual participants themselves decided how much time to devote to deliberate practice, and so the amount of deliberate practice was not under experimental control. Perhaps those individuals having high levels of innate talent or who encounter early success in a given domain (e.g., chess playing) are the ones most likely to engage in substantial amounts of deliberate practice.

Fourth, and related to the third point, there is an important issue that has not received enough attention. *Why* do some individuals decide to devote hundreds or thousands of hours to effortful deliberate practice to achieve very high levels of expertise? Deliberate practice theory has identified some of the important cognitive factors involved in the development of expertise. However, it has been strangely silent on the crucial motivational factors that must also be involved.

Fifth, deliberate practice theory is less applicable to the development of broad and complex skills (e.g., becoming an outstanding lawyer) than the development of narrow and less complex skills (e.g., calendar calculating). That would explain why individual differences in intelligence are more predictive of the former type of expertise than the latter.

CHAPTER SUMMARY

- Introduction
  This chapter is devoted to problem solving, transfer of training, and expertise. Most research on problem solving focuses on problems requiring no special knowledge. In contrast, research on expertise typically involves problems requiring considerable background knowledge. Transfer and expertise research both focus on learning processes. Transfer research focuses on the effects of previous learning on current performance, whereas expertise research is concerned with the issue of what differentiates experts from novices in a given area.

- Problem solving
  Problem solving is goal directed. The problems studied by psychologists are mostly well-defined and knowledge-lean, which is the opposite of those generally encountered in everyday life. The Gestalt psychologists argued that problems often require insight and that past experience often disrupts current problem solving. Insight seems to involve parts

of the right hemisphere, and probably depends on parallel processes below the conscious level. Ohlsson's representational change theory emphasises the importance of changing representations through elaboration, constraint relaxation, and re-encoding for insight to occur. The beneficial effects of incubation on problem solving seem to depend on forgetting misleading information or ineffective strategies. The General Problem Solver assumes that processing is serial, people have limited processing capacity, and problem solvers make extensive use of heuristics. The General Problem Solver has better memory than (but inferior planning ability to) humans. The dorsolateral prefrontal cortex plays a central role in problem solving. ACT-R theory claims that retrieval, imaginal, goal, and procedural modules are all important in problem solving, and the brain areas associated with each module are identified.

• Transfer of training and analogical reasoning
Transfer of training between a past task and a current one depends on task similarity, context similarity, and time interval. Far transfer has been shown many times. It is enhanced by metacognitive skills such as orienting and self-judging, and can also be increased by self-explanation. Transfer in analogical problem solving depends on three kinds of similarity: superficial, structural, and procedural. The kind of similarity used by experts when problem solving depends on their specific goals. Analogical problem solving can be improved by direct comparisons of the characteristics of two problems. Much laboratory research on analogical problem solving differs considerably from real life in that analogies between problems are typically imprecise in real life. The central executive plays a major role in analogical problem solving, and executive processes that inhibit responding to relevant distractors may be of special importance.

• Expertise
Expertise is typically assessed by using knowledge-rich problems. Expert chess players differ from non-expert players in possessing far more templates containing knowledge of chess positions. These templates allow expert players to identify good moves rapidly and to remember even random chess positions better than non-experts. The precise information contained in templates remains unclear and template theory does not fully account for the adaptive expertise of outstanding players. It is generally agreed that medical experts tend to rely on fast, automatic processes in diagnosis whereas non-experts rely on slow, conscious processes. However, this is only approximately correct, and experts generally cross-check their diagnoses with slow, deliberate processes. Medical experts often rely on gist-based processes, which can impair their performance in some circumstances.

• Deliberate practice
According to Ericsson, the development of expertise depends on deliberate practice involving informative feedback and the opportunity to correct errors. Deliberate practice is necessary for the development of expertise, but it is rarely sufficient except in narrow domains. Individual differences in innate ability are also important, especially in broad domains (e.g., career success). It may be mainly individuals of high innate ability who are willing to devote hundreds or thousands of hours to deliberate practice. At any rate, the deliberate practice approach has relatively little to say about crucial motivational factors.

FURTHER READING

- Davidson, J.E., & Sternberg, R.J. (eds.) (2003). *The psychology of problem solving*. New York: Cambridge University Press. This edited book has contributions covering most of the major areas within problem solving.
- Ericsson, K.A., Charness, N., Feltovich, P., & Hoffman, R.R. (eds.) (2006). *Cambridge handbook of expertise and expert performance*. Cambridge: Cambridge University Press. This edited handbook contains contributions by the world's leading authorities on expertise.
- Norman, G. (2005). From theory to application and back again: Implications of research on medical expertise for psychological theory. *Canadian Journal of Experimental Psychology, 59*, 35–40. This article contains an excellent overview of theory and research on medical expertise.
- Robertson, S.I. (2001). *Problem solving*. Hove, UK: Psychology Press. This book remains a very accessible introduction to the field of problem solving.
- Sio, U.N., & Ormerod, T.C. (2009). Does incubation enhance problem solving? A meta-analytic review. *Psychological Bulletin, 135*, 94–120. The authors show that there is convincing evidence that problem solving can benefit from incubation.

CHAPTER 13

JUDGEMENT AND DECISION MAKING

INTRODUCTION

In this chapter, our focus is on the overlapping areas of judgement and decision making. Judgement researchers focus on the ways in which individuals make use of various cues (which may be ambiguous) to draw inferences about situations and events. In contrast, decision making involves choosing among various options. Decision-making researchers address the question, "How do people choose what action to take to achieve labile [changeable], sometimes conflicting goals in an uncertain world?" (Hastie, 2001, p. 657).

There are other differences between judgement and decision making. For example, judgements are evaluated in terms of their *accuracy*. In contrast, the value of decisions is typically assessed in terms of the *consequences* of those decisions (Harvey, 2001).

Decision making involves some problem solving, since individuals try to make the best possible choice from a range of options. However, there are some differences. First, the options are generally present in decision making, whereas problem solvers typically have to generate their own options. Second, decision making tends to be concerned with preferences, whereas problem solving is concerned with solutions. As a result, the focus in decision making is on the factors influencing preference. With problem solving, in contrast, the focus is on factors influencing the choice of strategies (successful or unsuccessful).

Finally, we turn to the relationship between judgement and decision making. According to Hastie (2001, p. 657), "Decision making refers to the entire process of choosing a course of action. Judgement refers to the components of the larger decision-making process that are concerned with assessing, estimating, and inferring what events will occur and what the decision-maker's evaluative reactions to those outcomes will be."

What does research on judgement and decision making tell us about human rationality? That issue is part of a broader one concerning human rationality and logicality in general. That broader issue (which includes consideration of research on judgement and decision making) is discussed at length at the end of Chapter 14.

JUDGEMENT RESEARCH

We often change our opinion of the likelihood of something based on new information. Suppose you are 90% confident someone has lied to you. However, their version of events is later confirmed by another person, leading you to believe there is only a 60% chance you have been lied to. Everyday life is full of cases in which the strength of our beliefs is increased or decreased by new information.

The Reverend Thomas Bayes provided a precise way of thinking about such cases. He focused on situations in which there are two possible beliefs or hypotheses (e.g., X is lying versus X is not lying), and he showed how new data or information change the probabilities of each hypothesis being correct.

According to Bayes' theorem, we need to assess the relative probabilities of the two hypotheses *before* the data are obtained (prior odds). We also need to calculate the relative probabilities of obtaining the observed data under each hypothesis (likelihood ratio). Bayesian methods evaluate the probability of observing the data, D, if hypothesis A is correct, written $p(D/H_A)$, and if hypothesis B is correct, written $p(D/H_B)$. Bayes' theorem is expressed in the form of an odds ratio as follows:

$$\frac{p(H_A/D)}{p(H_B/D)} = \frac{p(H_A)}{p(H_B)} \times \frac{p(D/H_A)}{p(D/H_B)}$$

The above formula may look intimidating and offputting, but is not really so (honest!). On the left side of the equation are the relative probabilities of hypotheses A and B in the light of the new data. These are the probabilities we want to work out. On the right side of the equation, we have the prior odds of each hypothesis being correct *before* the data were collected multiplied by the likelihood ratio based on the probability of the data given each hypothesis.

We can clarify Bayes' theorem by considering the taxi-cab problem used by Kahneman and Tversky (1972). In this problem, a taxi-cab was involved in a hit-and-run accident one night. Of the taxi-cabs in the city, 85% belonged to the Green company and 15% to the Blue company. An eyewitness identified the cab as a Blue cab. However, when her ability to identify cabs under appropriate visibility conditions was tested, she was wrong 20% of the time. The participants had to decide the probability that the cab involved in the accident was Blue. Before proceeding, what is your answer to this problem?

The hypothesis that the cab was Blue is H_A and the hypothesis that it was Green is H_B. The prior probability for H_A is 0.15 and for H_B it is 0.85, because 15% of the cabs are blue and 85% are green. The probability of the

eyewitness identifying the cab as Blue when it was Blue, $p(D/H_A)$, is 0.80. Finally, the probability of the eyewitness saying the cab was Blue when it was Green, $p(D/H_B)$ is 0.20. According to the formula:

$$\frac{0.15}{0.85} \times \frac{0.80}{0.20} = \frac{0.12}{0.17}$$

Thus, the odds ratio is 12:17, and there is a 41% (12/29) probability that the taxi-cab was Blue compared to a 59% probability that it was Green. As we will see very shortly, this is *not* the answer produced by most people given the problem.

Neglecting base rates

People often take less account of the prior odds (base-rate information) than they should according to Bayes' theorem. **Base-rate information** was defined by Koehler (1996, p. 1) as, "the relative frequency with which an event occurs or an attribute is present in the population". In the taxi-cab problem discussed above, Kahneman and Tversky (1972) found that most participants ignored the base-rate information about the relative numbers of Green and Blue cabs. They focused only on the evidence of the witness, and maintained there was an 80% likelihood that the taxi was blue rather than green. In fact, the correct answer based on Bayes' theorem is 41%.

Here is another example of people failing to take account of base-rate information in the way they should according to Bayes' theorem. Kahneman and Tversky (1973, p. 241) presented participants with the following description:

> *Jack is a 45-year-old man. He is married and has four children. He is generally*

conservative, careful, and ambitious. He shows no interest in political and social issues and spends most of his free time on his many hobbies, which include home carpentry, sailing, and numerical puzzles.

The participants had to decide the probability that Jack was an engineer or a lawyer. They were all told that the description had been selected at random from a total of 100 descriptions. Half of the participants were told 70 of the descriptions were of engineers and 30 of lawyers, and the other half were told there were descriptions of 70 lawyers and 30 engineers. On average, the participants decided that there was a 0.90 probability that Jack was an engineer regardless of whether most of the 100 descriptions were of lawyers or of engineers. Thus, participants took no account of the base-rate information (i.e., the 70:30 split of the 100 descriptions). If they had used base-rate information, the estimated probability that Jack was an engineer would have been less when the description was selected from a set of descriptions mainly of lawyers.

Heuristics and biases

Danny Kahneman and the late Amos Tversky have been the most influential psychologists working in the area of human judgement. They have focused on explaining why we seem so prone to error on many judgement problems. They argued that we typically rely on simple heuristics (see Glossary) or rules of thumb when confronted by problems such as those of the taxi-cab or engineer/lawyer just discussed. According to Kahneman and Tversky, we use heuristics even though they can cause us to make errors because they are cognitively undemanding and can be used very rapidly. In this section, we consider their heuristics-and-biases approach.

Why do we fail to make proper use of base-rate information? According to Kahneman and Tversky (1973), we often use a simple heuristic or rule of thumb known as the **representativeness**

heuristic. When people use this heuristic, "Events that are representative or typical of a class are assigned a high probability of occurrence. If an event is highly similar to most of the others in a population or class of events, then it is considered representative" (Kellogg, 1995, p. 385).

The representativeness heuristic is used when people judge the probability that an object or event A belongs to a class or process B. Suppose you are given the description of an individual and estimate the probability he/she has a certain occupation. You would probably estimate that probability in terms of the *similarity* between the individual's description and your stereotype of that occupation. Indeed (the argument goes), you will do this even when it means ignoring other relevant information. That was precisely what happened in the study by Kahneman and Tversky (1973) discussed above. Participants focused on the fact that the description of Jack resembled the stereotype of an engineer and largely ignored the base-rate information.

Further evidence indicating use of the representativeness heuristic was reported by Tversky and Kahneman (1983). They studied the **conjunction fallacy,** which is the mistaken belief that the conjunction or combination of two events (A and B) is more likely than one of the two events on its own. This fallacy seems to involve the representativeness heuristic. Tversky and Kahneman used the following description:

Linda is 31 years old, single, outspoken, and very bright. She majored in

We use the representativeness heuristic to judge the probability that an object or event A belongs to a class or process B. For example, you would estimate the probability that the woman in the picture has a certain occupation based on the similarity between her appearance and your stereotype of that occupation. You are more likely, for example, to state that she is a lawyer, than a fitness instructor.

philosophy. As a student, she was deeply concerned with issues of discrimination and social justice, and also participated in anti-nuclear demonstrations.

Participants rank ordered eight possible categories in terms of the probability that Linda belonged to each one. Three of the categories were bank teller, feminist, and feminist bank teller. Most participants ranked feminist bank teller as more probable than bank teller or feminist. This is incorrect, because *all* feminist bank tellers belong to the larger categories of bank tellers and of feminists!

Availability heuristic

Tversky and Kahneman (1974) argued that some judgement errors depend on use of the **availability heuristic**. This heuristic involves estimating the frequencies of events on the basis of how easy or difficult it is to retrieve relevant information from long-term memory. For example, Lichtenstein, Slovic, Fischhoff, Layman, and Coombs (1978) asked people to judge the relative likelihood of different causes of death. Those causes of death attracting considerable publicity (e.g., murder) were judged more likely than those that do not (e.g., suicide), even when the opposite is the case. These findings suggest that people used the availability heuristic.

Hertwig, Pachur, and Kurzenhäuser (2005) argued that we can interpret Lichtenstein et al.'s (1978) findings in two ways. We can distinguish between two different mechanisms associated with use of the availability heuristic. First, there is the availability-by-recall mechanism: this is based on the number of people that an individual recalls having died from a given risk (e.g., a specific disease). Second, there is the fluency mechanism: this involves judging the number of deaths from a given risk by deciding how easy it would be to bring relevant instances to mind but without retrieving them.

Hertwig, Pachur, and Kurzenhäuser (2005) used a task in which pairs of risks were presented and participants judged which claims more lives each year. Performance on this task was predicted moderately well by both mechanisms. Some individuals apparently used the availability-by-recall mechanism most of the time, whereas others used it more sparingly.

Oppenheimer (2004) provided convincing evidence that we do not always use the availability heuristic. He presented American participants with pairs of names (one famous, one non-famous), and asked them to indicate which

KEY TERM

availability heuristic: the assumption that the frequencies of events can be estimated accurately by the accessibility in memory.

surname was more common in the United States. For example, one pair consisted of the names "Bush" and "Stevenson" – which name do you think is more common? Here is another one: which surname is more common: "Clinton" or "Woodall"? If participants had used the availability heuristic, they would have said "Bush" and "Clinton". In fact, however, only 12% said Bush and 30% Clinton. They were correct to avoid these famous names because the non-famous name is slightly more common.

How did participants make their judgements in the above study? According to Oppenheimer (p. 100), "People not only spontaneously recognise when familiarity of stimuli comes from sources other than frequency (e.g., fame), but also overcorrect."

Support theory

Tversky and Koehler (1994) put forward their support theory based in part on the availability heuristic. Their key assumption was that any given event will appear more or less likely depending on how it is described. Thus, we need to distinguish between events themselves and the descriptions of those events. You would almost certainly assume that the probability you will die on your next summer holiday is extremely low. However, it might seem more likely if you were asked the following question: "What is the probability that you will die on your next summer holiday from a disease, a car accident, a plane crash, or from any other cause?"

Why is the subjective probability of death on holiday greater in the second case? According to support theory, a more explicit description of an event is regarded as having greater subjective probability than the same event described in less explicit terms. There are two main reasons (related to the availability heuristic) behind this theoretical assumption:

(1) An explicit description may draw attention to aspects of the event that are less obvious in the non-explicit description.
(2) Memory limitations may mean that people do not remember all the relevant information if it is not supplied.

It follows from support theory that the subjective probability of any given possibility will increase when it is mentioned explicitly and so becomes salient or conspicuous. Relevant evidence is discussed below.

Evidence

Mandel (2005) carried out a study during the first week of the 2003 Iraq war. Some participants assessed the risk of at least one terrorist attack over the following six months, whereas others assessed the risk of an attack plotted by al Quaeda or not plotted by al Quaeda. The mean estimated probabilities were 0.30 for a terrorist attack, 0.30 for an al Quaeda attack, and 0.18 for a non-al Quaeda attack. Thus, as predicted by support theory, the overall estimated probability of a terrorist attack was greater (0.30 + 0.18 = 0.48) when the two major possibilities were made explicit than when they were not (0.30). Similar findings were reported by Rottenstreich and Tversky (1997). Estimates of the probability that an accidental death is due to murder were higher when different categories of murder were considered explicitly (e.g., by an acquaintance versus by a stranger).

We have seen that there is evidence for the phenomenon of higher subjective probability for an explicitly described event than for a less explicit one. We might imagine that experts would not show this phenomenon, since experts provided with a non-explicit description can presumably fill in the details from their own knowledge. However, Redelmeier, Koehler, Liberman, and Tversky (1995) found that expert doctors *did* show the effect. The doctors were given a description of a woman with abdominal pain. Half assessed the probabilities of two specified diagnoses (gastroenteritis and ectopic pregnancy) and of a residual category of everything else; the other half assigned probabilities to five specified diagnoses (including gastroenteritis and ectopic pregnancy). The key comparison was between the subjective probability of the residual category for the former group and the combined probabilities of the three additional diagnoses plus the residual category in the latter group.

Since both subjective probabilities cover the same range of diagnoses, they should have been the same. However, the former probability was 0.50 but the latter was 0.69, indicating that subjective probabilities are higher for explicit descriptions even with experts.

Evaluation

The main predictions of support theory have often been supported with various tasks. Another strength of support theory is that it helps us to understand more clearly how the availability heuristic can lead to errors in judgement. It is also impressive (and somewhat surprising) that experts' judgements are influenced by the explicitness of the information provided.

On the negative side, it is not very clear why people often overlook information that is well known to them. It is also not entirely clear *why* focusing on a given possibility typically increases its perceived support. Thus, the *mechanisms* underlying the obtained biases have not been identified with any precision (Keren & Teigen, 2004).

Overall evaluation of heuristics-and-biases approach

Kahneman and Tversky have shown that several general heuristics or rules of thumb (e.g., representativeness heuristic; availability heuristic) underlie judgements in many different contexts. They were instrumental in establishing the field of judgement research. The importance of this research (and their research on decision making) was shown in the award of the Nobel Prize to Kahneman. Of greatest importance, Kahneman and Tversky showed that people are surprisingly prone to systematic biases in their judgements even when experts are making judgements in their field of expertise. Their ideas and research have influenced several disciplines outside of psychology, including economics, philosophy, and political science.

We might easily imagine that Kahneman and Tversky's approach would be more applicable to less intelligent individuals than to more intelligent ones. However, the evidence suggests (perhaps surprisingly) that intelligence or cognitive ability is almost unrelated to performance on most judgement tasks. Stanovich and West (2008; see Chapter 14) found that performance on several tasks (e.g., Linda problem; framing problems; sunk-cost effect; the engineer/lawyer problem) was comparable in groups of more and less cognitively able students. These findings suggest that the heuristics-and-biases approach is generally applicable.

There are several limitations with the heuristics-and-biases approach. First, the term "heuristics" is used in many different ways by different researchers and is in danger of losing most of its meaning. Shah and Oppenheimer (2008, p. 207) argued persuasively that, "Heuristics primarily serve the purpose of reducing the effort associated with a task", which is close to Kahneman and Tversky's position. However, it has proved difficult to move from using heuristics to describe certain phenomena to providing explanations of precisely *how* effort is reduced.

Second, some errors of judgement occur because participants misunderstand the problem. For example, between 20 and 50% of participants interpret, "Linda is a bank teller", as implying that she is not active in the feminist movement. However, the conjunction fallacy is still found even when almost everything possible is done to ensure that participants do not misinterpret the problem (Sides, Osherson, Bonini, & Viale, 2002).

Third, the emphasis has been on the notion that people's judgements are biased and error-prone. However, that often seems unfair. For example, Hertwig et al. (2005) found that most people judged skin cancer to be a more common cause of death than cancer of the mouth and throat, whereas the opposite is actually the case. People make this "error" not because of inadequate thinking but simply because skin cancer has attracted considerable media coverage in recent years. We may make incorrect judgements because the available information is inadequate or because we process that information in a biased way. The heuristics-and-biases approach focuses on biased processing, but the problem is often with the quality of the available information (Juslin, Winman, & Hansson, 2007).

Fourth, many people make correct or approximately accurate judgements. This is hard to explain within the heuristics-and-biases approach, which tends to emphasise the deficiencies of human judgement although accepting that heuristics and biases can be moderately useful. Later in the chapter, we will discuss a theoretical approach (the dual-process model) that addresses this issue.

Fifth, much of the research is artificial and detached from the realities of everyday life. As a result, it is hard to generalise from laboratory findings. For example, emotional and motivational factors play a role in the real world but were rarely studied in the laboratory until recently. For example, Lerner, Gonzalez, Small, and Fischhoff (2005) carried out an online study immediately after the terrorist attacks of 11 September 2001. The participants were instructed to focus on aspects of the attacks that made them afraid, angry, or sad. The key finding was that the estimated probability of future terrorist attacks was higher in fearful participants than in sad or angry ones.

Fast and frugal heuristics

Heuristics or rules of thumb often lead us to make errors of judgement. However, Gigerenzer and his colleagues (e.g., Todd & Gigerenzer, 2007) argue that heuristics are often very valuable. Their central focus is on fast and frugal heuristics, which involve rapid processing of relatively little information. It is assumed that we possess an "adaptive toolbox" consisting of several such heuristics.

One of the key fast-and-frugal heuristics is the take-the-best heuristic or strategy. This is based on "take the best, ignore the rest". We can illustrate use of this strategy with the concrete example of deciding whether Herne or Cologne has the larger population. Suppose you start by assuming the most valid cue to city size is that cities whose names you recognise typically have larger populations than those whose names you don't recognise. However,

you recognise both names. Then you think of another valid cue to city size, namely, that cities with cathedrals tend to be larger than those without. Accordingly, since you know that Cologne has a cathedral but are unsure about Herne, you produce the answer, "Cologne". In essence, the take-the-best strategy has three components:

(1) *Search rule*: search cues (e.g., name recognition; cathedral) in order of validity.
(2) *Stopping rule*: stop after finding a discriminatory cue (i.e, the cue applies to only one of the possible answers).
(3) *Decision rule*: choose outcome.

The most researched example of the take-the-best strategy is the **recognition heuristic,** which is as follows: "If one of two objects is recognised and the other is not, infer that the recognised object has the higher value with respect to the criterion" (Goldstein & Gigerenzer, 2002, p. 76). In the example above, if you recognise the name "Cologne" but not "Herne", you guess (correctly) that Cologne is the larger city and ignore other information. Goldstein and Gigerenzer made the strong (and controversial) claim that, when individuals recognise one object but not the other, no other information influences the decision.

Why might people use the recognition and take-the-best heuristics? First, it is claimed from an evolutionary perspective that humans have to use valid cues to make certain kinds of decision. Second, these heuristics often produce accurate predictions. For example, Goldstein and Gigerenzer (2002) reported correlations of +0.60 and +0.66 in two studies between the number of people recognising a city and its population. Third, no judgement process would

KEY TERM

recognition heuristic: using the knowledge that only one out of two objects is recognised to make a judgement.

take less time or be less cognitively demanding than the recognition heuristic.

Evidence

Evidence that the recognition heuristic is important was reported by Goldstein and Gigerenzer (2002). American students were presented with pairs of German cities and decided which of the two was the larger. When only one city name was recognised, participants used the recognition heuristic 90% of the time. In another study, Goldstein and Gigerenzer told participants that German cities with football teams tend to be larger than those without football teams. When participants decided whether a recognised city without a football team was larger or smaller than an unrecognised city, participants used the recognition heuristic 92% of the time. Thus, as predicted theoretically, they mostly ignored the conflicting information about the absence of a football team.

Richter and Späth (2006) pointed out that participants in the above study may have ignored information about the presence or absence of a football team because they felt it was not strongly related to city size. They carried out a similar study in which German students decided which in each pair of American cities was larger. For some recognised cities, the students were told that it had an international airport, whereas for others they were told that it did not. The recognised city was chosen 98% of the time when it had an international airport but only 82% of the time when it did not. Thus, the recognition heuristic was often not used when the participants had access to inconsistent information. Presumably this happened because they believed that presence or absence of an international airport is a valid cue to city size.

Goldstein and Gigerenzer (2002) presented American and German students with pairs of American cities and pairs of German cities, and asked them to select the larger city in each pair. The findings were counterintuitive: American and German students performed *less* well on cities in their own country than on those in the other country. This occurred because students typically recognised both members in the pair with cities in their own country, and so they could not use the recognition heuristic.

The recognition heuristic is less important than claimed by Goldstein and Gigerenzer (2002). Oppenheimer (2003) asked participants to decide whether recognised cities known to be small were larger than unrecognised cities. The small cities were relatively close to Stanford University where the study took place and the unrecognised cities were fictitious but sounded plausible (e.g., Las Besas; Rio Del Sol). The recognition heuristic failed to predict the results: the recognised city was judged to be larger on only 37% of trials. Thus, knowledge of city size can override the recognition heuristic.

Is there *anything* special about the recognition heuristic? Pachur and Hertwig (2006) argued that there is. Retrieving the familiarity information underlying recognition occurs more rapidly and automatically than retrieving any other kind of information about an object. That gives it a "competitive edge" over other information. Pachur and Hertwig asked participants to decide which in each of several pairs of infectious diseases is more prevalent in Germany. This is a difficult test for the theory because some very rare diseases (e.g., cholera; leprosy) are almost always recognised. There were two main findings. First, the recognition heuristic was only used in 62% of cases in which it could have been used, because participants realised that recognition was not a very valid cue. Second, response times for decisions consistent with use of the recognition heuristic were 20% faster than those inconsistent with its use.

In a second experiment, Pachur and Hertwig (2006) used the same task but instructed participants to respond within 900 ms. This time pressure caused participants to produce more decisions consistent with the recognition heuristic than in the first experiment (69% versus 62%, respectively).

The take-the-best strategy is not used as often as predicted theoretically. Newell, Weston, and Shanks (2003) asked participants to choose between the shares of two fictitious companies on the basis of various cues. Only 33% of the participants conformed to all three components of the take-the-best strategy. They often failed to stop searching for information after finding a discriminatory cue. Using the same task, Newell et al. found that the take-the-best strategy was least likely to be used when the cost of obtaining information was low and the validities of the cues were unknown.

Bröder (2003) pointed out that individual differences have often been ignored. He used a task involving choosing between shares. More intelligent participants were more likely than less intelligent ones to use the take-the-best strategy when it was the best one to use.

Evaluation

People sometimes use fast-and-frugal heuristics such as the recognition heuristic and the take-the-best strategy to make rapid judgements. These heuristics can be surprisingly effective in spite of their simplicity, and it is impressive that individuals with little knowledge can sometimes outperform those with greater knowledge. Familiarity or recognition information can be accessed faster and more automatically than other kinds of information. This encourages its widespread use when individuals are under time or cognitive pressure, and explains why the recognition heuristic is used sometimes.

The approach based on fast-and-frugal heuristics has several important limitations. First, the major fast-and-frugal heuristics are used much less often than predicted theoretically (e.g., Newell et al., 2003; Oppenheimer, 2003).

Second, some heuristics are by no means as simple as Gigerenzer and others have claimed. For example, to use the take-the-best heuristic, it is necessary to organise the various cues hierarchically in terms of their validity (Newell, 2005). This is a very complex task, and there is not much evidence indicating that we have good knowledge of cue validities.

Third, when the approach is applied to decision making, it de-emphasises the importance of the decision in question. Decision making may well stop after a single discriminatory cue has been found when deciding which is the larger of two cities. However, most

women want to consider *all* the relevant evidence before deciding which of two men to marry!

Fourth, as Newell et al. (2003, p. 92) argued, "Unless we can...specify the conditions under which certain heuristics will be selected over others...the predictive and explanatory power of the fast-and-frugal approach remains questionable." As Goldstein and Gigerenzer (1999, p. 188) admitted, "There is the large question which kept us arguing days and nights....Which homunculus [tiny man inside our heads] selects among heuristics, or is there none?"

Natural frequency hypothesis

Gigerenzer and Hoffrage (1995, 1999) put forward an evolutionary account of the strengths and weaknesses of human judgements. Their account relies heavily on the notion of *natural sampling*, which is "the process of encountering instances in a population sequentially" (Gigerenzer & Hoffrage, 1999, p. 425). Natural sampling is what generally happens in everyday life. It is assumed that as a result of our evolutionary history we find it easy to work out the *frequencies* of different kinds of event. In contrast, we find it very difficult to deal with fractions and percentages.

It follows that most people ignore base rates and make other mistakes on judgement problems because these problems involve percentages and other complex statistics. The central prediction is that performance would improve greatly if the problems used natural frequencies. We will shortly discuss relevant research. Before doing so, note that some distinctions are unclear in this theoretical approach. For example, the emphasis in the theory is on the "natural" or objective frequencies of certain kinds of event. Such frequencies can undoubtedly provide potentially valuable information when making judgements. However, in the real world, we actually encounter only a sample of events, and the frequencies of various events in this sample may be selective and very different from natural or objective samples (Sloman & Over, 2003). For example, the frequencies of highly intelligent and less intelligent

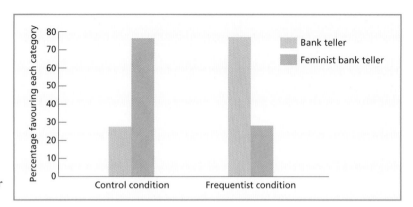

Figure 13.1 Performance on the Linda problem in the frequentist and control conditions. Data from Fiedler (1988).

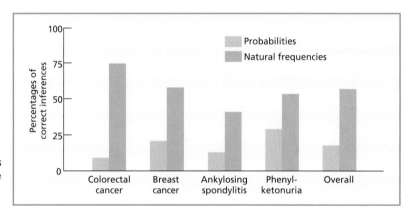

Figure 13.2 Percentage correct inferences by advanced medical students given four realistic diagnostic tasks expressed in probabilities or frequencies. From Hoffrage et al. (2000). Reprinted with permission from AAAS.

people encountered by most university students are likely to be very different from the frequencies in the general population.

It is also important to distinguish between natural frequencies and the word problems actually used in research. In most word problems, participants are simply provided with frequency information and do not have to grapple with the complexities of natural sampling.

Evidence

Judgement performance is often much better when problems are presented in the form of frequencies rather than probabilities or percentages. For example, Fiedler (1988) used the Linda problem discussed earlier. The standard version was compared to a frequency version in which participants indicated how many of 100 people fitting Linda's description were bank tellers, and how many were bank tellers

and active feminists. The percentage of participants showing the conjunction fallacy dropped dramatically with the frequency version (see Figure 13.1). Performance may have been better with the frequency version because people are more used to dealing with frequencies than with probabilities. Alternatively, it may be that the frequency version makes the problem's structure more obvious.

Hoffrage, Lindsey, Hertwig, and Gigerenzer (2000) gave advanced medical students four realistic diagnostic tasks containing base-rate information presented in a probability version or a frequency version. These experts paid little attention to base-rate information in the probability versions. However, they performed much better when given the frequency versions (see Figure 13.2).

Fiedler, Brinkmann, Betsch, and Wild (2000) tested the theoretical assumption that base rates are taken much more into account when frequencies are sampled. They used the following problem in various forms. There is an 80% probability that a woman with breast cancer will have a positive mammogram compared to a 9.6% probability that a woman without breast cancer will have a positive mammogram. The base rate of cancer in women is 1%. The task is to decide the probability that a woman has breast cancer given a positive mammogram (the correct answer is 7.8%).

Fiedler et al. (2000) did not give participants the problem in the form described above, because they were interested in people's sampling behaviour when allowed to make their own choices. Accordingly, they provided some participants with index card files organised into the categories of women with breast cancer and those without. They had to select cards, with each selected card indicating whether the woman in question had had a positive mammogram. The key finding was that participants' sampling was heavily *biased* towards women with breast cancer. As a result, the participants produced an average estimate of 63% that a woman had breast cancer given a positive mammogram (remember the correct answer is 7.8%).

Evaluation

There are two major apparent strengths of the theoretical approach advocated by Gigerenzer and Hoffrage (1995, 1999). First, it makes sense to argue that use of natural or objective sampling could enhance the accuracy of many of our judgements. Second, as we have seen, judgements based on frequency information are often superior to those based on probability information.

The natural sampling hypothesis has several limitations. First, there is often a yawning chasm between people's actual sampling behaviour and the neat-and-tidy frequency data provided in laboratory experiments. As Fiedler et al. (2000) found, the samples selected by participants can provide biased and complex information which is very hard to interpret.

Second, frequency versions of problems nearly always make their underlying structure much easier to grasp (Sloman & Over, 2003).

Thus, the improved performance found when judgement tasks are presented in frequency formats may not occur because people are naturally equipped to think about frequencies rather than about probabilities.

Third, the natural frequency hypothesis is narrowly based. Its emphasis on natural frequencies means it is unable to explain why people perform well on some judgement tasks involving probabilities (see next section). As we will see, the accuracy of judgements depends very much on whether people can make use of their intuitive causal knowledge, a factor totally ignored by the natural frequency hypothesis.

Causal models

According to the heuristics-and-biases approach and the natural frequency hypothesis, most people's judgements are generally inaccurate. These views led Glymour (2001, p. 8) to ask the question, "If we're so dumb, how come we're so smart?" Krynski and Tenenbaum (2007) addressed that question with respect to findings apparently showing that people consistently ignore (or fail to make sufficient use of) base-rate information. They argued that we possess very valuable *causal knowledge* that allows us to make successful judgements in the real world (this issue is explored in detail by Sloman, 2005). In the laboratory, however, the judgement problems we confront often fail to provide such knowledge. Many of these judgement problems make it difficult for people to match the statistical information provided with their intuitive causal knowledge.

We can see what Krynski and Tenenbaum (2007) mean by causal knowledge by discussing one of their experiments. Some of the participants were given the following judgement task (the false positive scenario), which closely resembles those used previously to show how people neglect base rates:

The following statistics are known about women at age 60 who participate in a routine mammogram screening, an X-ray of the breast tissue that detects tumours:

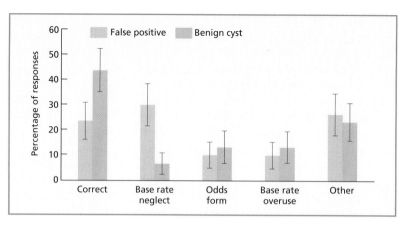

Figure 13.3 Percentages of correct responses and various incorrect responses (based on base-rate neglect, odds form, base-rate overuse, and other) with the false-positive and benign cyst scenarios. From Krynski and Tenenbaum (2007), Copyright © 2007, American Psychological Association. Reproduced with permission.

2% of women have breast cancer at the time of screening. Most of them will receive a positive result on the mammogram. There is a 6% chance that a woman without breast cancer will receive a positive result on the mammogram. Suppose a woman at age 60 gets a positive result during a routine mammogram screening. Without knowing any other symptoms, what are the chances she has breast cancer?

The base rate of cancer in the population was often neglected by participants given this task. According to Krynski and Tenenbaum (2007), this happened because having breast cancer is the *only* cause of positive mammograms explicitly mentioned in the problem. Suppose we re-worded the problem slightly to indicate clearly that there is an alternative cause of positive mammograms. Krynski and Tenenbaum did this by changing the wording of the third paragraph:

There is a 6% chance that a woman without breast cancer will have a dense but harmless cyst that looks like a cancerous tumour and causes a positive result on the mammogram.

As can be seen in Figure 13.3, there was a considerable difference in performance in the two conditions. Participants given the benign

cyst scenario were far more likely to take full account of the base-rate information than were those given the standard false positive scenario. Krynski and Tenenbaum (2007) argued that the reasonably full causal knowledge available to participants given the benign cyst scenario corresponds to real life. For example, suppose a friend of yours has a cough. You know a cough can be caused by a common cold as well as by lung cancer. You use your base-rate knowledge that far more people have colds than lung cancer to make the judgement that it is highly probable that your friend is only suffering from a cold.

We discussed Kahneman and Tversky's (1972) taxi-cab problem earlier. They found that most of their participants ignored the base-rate information about the numbers of green and blue cabs. Krynski and Tenenbaum (2007) argued that this happened because it was hard for participants to see the causal structure of the task. They devised a new version of this task. This version was very similar to the standard one except that *reasons* why the witness might have made a mistake were spelled out. Here is the crucial addition to the problem:

When testing a sample of cabs, only 80% of the Blue Co. cabs appeared blue in colour, and only 80% of the Green Co. cabs appeared green in colour. Due to faded paint, 20% of Blue Co. cabs appeared green in colour, and 20% of Green Co. cabs appeared blue in colour.

Only 8% of participants showed base-rate neglect with the faded paint version compared to 43% with the standard version. Correct answers increased from 8% with the standard version to 46% with the faded paint version. Thus, many people are very good at using base-rate information provided they understand the causal factors responsible for the statistical information they are given.

Evaluation

Krynski and Tenenbaum (2007) have identified important reasons why the judgements we make in everyday life are generally more accurate than those made with artificial problems under laboratory conditions. More specifically, they have shown that it is relatively easy to persuade people to make use of base-rate information. According to them, "People's physical, biological, and social environments are causally structured, and their intuitive theories of the world are often – but not always – sufficient to capture the most relevant structures for enabling appropriate causal Bayesian inferences" (p. 449).

There are two limitations with this theoretical approach. First, even when the underlying causal structure was made explicit, fewer than 50% of participants produced the correct answer. Thus, there is more to solving judgement problems than having access to explicit causal information. Second, and related to the first point, there are important individual differences in performance on judgement problems. However, Krynski and Tenenbaum do not identify these individual differences.

Dual-process model

Most people seem to rely heavily on heuristics or rules of thumb when making judgements. This seems somewhat puzzling given that most of these heuristics can lead to errors. Various reasons for our extensive use of heuristics have been suggested (see Hertwig & Todd, 2003). First, they have the advantage of speed, allowing us to produce approximately correct judgements very rapidly. Second, heuristics are robust in

that they can be used almost regardless of the amount of information we have available. In contrast, complex cognitive strategies are of very limited usefulness when information is sparse. Third, it may simply be that we don't like thinking hard if we can avoid it. Fourth, in a rapidly changing world it may not make much sense to devote considerable effort to making very precise judgements.

In spite of the above points, individuals do sometimes use complex cognitive processes rather than heuristics. This led various theorists (e.g., Evans & Over, 1996; Sloman, 1996) to propose dual-process models. Kahneman (2003) and Kahneman and Frederick (2002, 2005, 2007) proposed one such model, according to which probability judgements depend on processing within two systems:

- *System 1*: This system is intuitive, automatic, and immediate. More specifically, "The operations of System 1 are typically fast, automatic, effortless, associative, implicit [not open to introspection] and often emotionally charged; they are also difficult to control or modify" (Kahneman, 2003). Most heuristics are produced by this system.
- *System 2*: This system is more analytical, controlled, and rule-governed. According to Kahneman (2003), "The operations of System 2 are slower, serial [one at a time], effortful, more likely to be consciously monitored and deliberately controlled; they are also relatively flexible and potentially rule-governed."

What is the relationship between these two systems? According to Kahneman and Frederick (2002), System 1 rapidly generates intuitive answers to judgement problems. These intuitive answers are then monitored or evaluated by System 2, which may correct them. According to Kahneman and Frederick (2005, p. 274), however, we often make little or no use of System 2: "People who make a casual intuitive judgement normally know little about how their judgement came about."

Evidence

Kahneman (2003) discussed evidence relating to the dual-process model. Since System 2 is more cognitively demanding than System 1, it would be predicted that highly intelligent individuals would make more use of it than would those less intelligent. Evidence reviewed by Kahneman supported that prediction.

De Neys (2006a) carried out several experiments to test the dual-process model. Participants were presented with the Linda problem and another very similar problem involving the conjunction fallacy. Participants who obtained the correct answers (and so presumably used System 2) took almost 40% longer than those who used only System 1. This is consistent with the assumption that it takes longer to use System 2. De Neys also compared performance on the same problems performed on their own or at the same time as a demanding secondary task (tapping a complex novel sequence) involving use of the central executive. Participants performed worse on the problems when accompanied by the secondary task (9.5% correct versus 17%, respectively). This is as predicted, given that use of System 2 requires use of cognitively demanding processes.

De Neys and Glumicic (2008) tested the dual-process model in several experiments investigating base-rate neglect. There were some incongruent problems in which System 1 and System 2 processes would produce different answers. Here is an example of an *incongruent* problem:

In a study, 1000 people were tested. Among the participants there were four men and 996 women. Jo is a randomly chosen participant of this study.

Jo is 23 years old and is finishing a degree in engineering. On Friday nights, Jo likes to go out cruising with friends while listening to loud music and drinking beer.

What is most likely?
  a. Jo is a man
  b. Jo is a woman

Heuristic processing based on stereotypes (System 1 processing) would produce answer (a), whereas consideration of the base rate (System 2) would produce the correct answer (b). De Neys and Glumicic also used *congruent* problems in which the description of the person and the base-rate information both pointed to the same answer. Finally, there were some neutral problems in which the description of the person bore no obvious relationship to group membership, and so System 2 processing was needed to obtain the correct answer.

In their first experiment, De Neys and Glumicic (2008) asked their participants to think out loud while dealing with each problem. As expected, most participants failed to use base-rate information with incongruent problems. As a result, their performance was much worse with those problems than with congruent ones (under 20% versus 95%, respectively). Participants doing incongruent problems only referred to base-rate information on 18% of trials, suggesting that they generally ignored such information at the conscious level.

In their second experiment, participants were not required to think aloud during performance of the problems. As before, performance was much worse with incongruent than with congruent problems (22% versus 97%, respectively). The most interesting findings related to time taken with each type of problem (see Figure 13.4). Participants took longer to produce answers with incongruent problems than with congruent or neutral ones, whether their answers were correct or false. In addition, there was evidence that participants spent longer processing information with incongruent problems than with congruent ones.

What do the findings of De Neys and Glumicic (2008) mean? On the face of it, they seem inconsistent. When participants think aloud, there is little evidence that they consider base-rate information. However, the fact that they took longer to respond with incongruent than with congruent problems indicates that base-rate information influenced their behaviour. The most likely explanation is that base-rate information was mostly processed below the

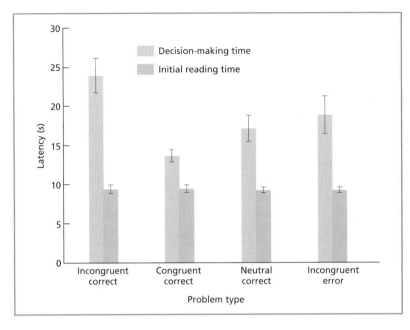

Figure 13.4 Mean times to read and make correct decisions with incongruent, congruent, and neutral problems and incorrect decisions with incongruent problems. Reprinted from De Neys and Glumicic (2008), Copyright © 2008, with permission from Elsevier.

level of conscious awareness, which is why such information was rarely referred to when participants thought aloud. In other words, participants often engaged in *implicit* processing of base-rate information when it produced a conflict with the answer suggested by heuristic processing.

Evaluation

The dual-process model has various successes to its credit. There is reasonable evidence for the existence of two different processing systems corresponding to those assumed within the model. The notion that people's judgements are typically determined by System 1 rather than by System 2 is in accord with most of the data. In addition, it provides an explanation for individual differences in judgement performance. Individuals who make extensive use of System 2 processing will perform better than those who use only System 1. Finally, note that there is much support for other versions of the dual-process model (e.g., those put forward by Evans and Over, 1996, and Sloman, 1996).

What are the limitations of the dual-process model? First, it is based on the assumption that most people rely almost exclusively on System 1.

However, De Neys and Glumicic (2007) found more evidence for processing of base-rate information than predicted by the model. Second, the model is not very explicit about the precise processes involved in judgement. For example, what is involved in monitoring and detecting problems with the answer suggested by System 1? Third, the model is basically a *serial* one, with use of System 1 preceding use of System 2. However, several theorists favour the notion of *parallel* processing, with both systems operating at the same time (see Evans, 2007, for a review). At present, there is no compelling evidence to support the serial view over the parallel one.

DECISION MAKING

Life is full of decisions. Which movie will I go to see tonight? Would I rather go out with Nancy or Sue? What career will I pursue? Who will I share a flat with next year? It is important to understand how we decide what to do. At one time, it was assumed that people behave rationally, and so select the best option. This assumption was built into normative theories, which focused on how people should make decisions while de-emphasising how they actually make them. For example, consider the views of von Neumann and Morgenstern (1947). Their utility theory was not a psychological theory of decision making. However, they suggested that it is possible that we try to maximise *utility*, which is the subjective value we attach to an outcome. When we need to choose between simple options, we assess the expected utility or expected value of each one by means of the following formula:

Expected utility = (probability of a given outcome) × (utility of the outcome)

One of the important contributions of von Neumann and Morgenstern (1947) was to treat decisions as if they were gambles. As Manktelow (1999) pointed out, this approach was subsequently coupled with Savage's (1954) mathematical approach based on using information from people's preferences to combine subjective utilities and subjective probabilities. This led to the development of subjective expected utility theory.

In the real world, various factors are generally associated with each option. For example, one holiday option may be preferable to another because it is in a more interesting area and the weather is likely to be better. However, the first holiday is more expensive and more of your valuable holiday time would be spent travelling. In such circumstances, people are supposed to calculate the expected utility or disutility (cost) of each factor to work out the overall expected value or utility of each option. In fact, people's choices and decisions are often decided by factors other than simple utility.

Decisions obviously differ enormously in their complexity. It is more difficult to decide what to do with your entire life than to decide which brand of cereal to have for breakfast. We will start with relatively simple decision making in the sense that relatively little information needs to be considered. After that, we will consider more complex decision making.

BASIC DECISION MAKING

What factors are involved in simple or basic decision making? As we will see, several theories have been put forward in the attempt to provide an answer to that question. Some theories focus mainly on cognitive factors of relevance to decision making, and we will start by considering perhaps the most influential of such theories. However, there has been an increasing acceptance that other factors are also very important. We will subsequently discuss theoretical approaches that emphasise either emotional or social factors.

Prospect theory

Much of the time we engage in risky decision making – there is uncertainty about the consequences of making a decision. As a first approximation, it seems reasonable to assume that we make decisions so as to maximise the chances of making a gain and minimise the chances of making a loss. Suppose someone offered you $200 if a tossed coin came up heads and a loss of $100 if it came up tails. You would jump at the chance (wouldn't you?), given that the bet provides an average expected gain of $50 per toss.

Here are two more decisions. Would you prefer a sure gain of $800 or an 85% probability of gaining $1000 and a 15% probability of gaining nothing? Since the expected value of the latter decision is greater than that of the former decision ($850 versus $800, respectively), you might well choose the latter alternative. Finally, would you prefer to make a sure loss of $800 or an 85% probability of losing $1000 with a 15% probability of not incurring any loss? The average expected loss is $800 for the former choice and $850 for the latter one, so you go with the former choice don't you?

The first problem was taken from Tversky and Shafir (1992) and the other two problems came from Kahneman and Tversky (1984). In all three cases, most participants did *not* make what appears to be the best choice. Two-thirds of participants refused to bet on the toss of a coin, and a majority preferred the choice with the smaller expected gain and the choice with the larger expected loss!

Kahneman and Tversky (1979, 1984) developed prospect theory in an attempt to understand such apparently paradoxical findings. Two of the main assumptions of this theory are as follows:

(1) Individuals identify a reference point generally representing their current state.

(2) Individuals are much more sensitive to potential losses than to potential gains; this is **loss aversion**. This explains why most people are unwilling to accept a 50–50 bet unless the amount they might win is about twice the amount they might lose (Kahneman, 2003).

Both of these assumptions are shown in Figure 13.5. The reference point is where the

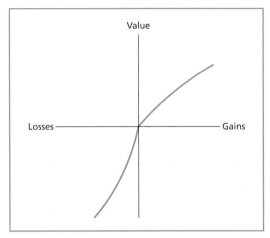

Figure 13.5 A hypothetical value function. From Kahneman and Tversky (1984). Copyright © 1984 American Psychological Association. Reproduced with permission.

line labelled losses and gains intersects the line labelled value. The positive value associated with gains increases relatively slowly as gains become greater. Thus, winning £2000 instead of £1000 does not double the subjective value of the money that has been won. In contrast, the negative value associated with losses increases relatively rapidly as losses become greater.

How does prospect theory account for the findings discussed earlier? If people are much more sensitive to losses than to gains, they should be unwilling to accept bets involving potential losses even though the potential gains outweigh the potential losses. They would also prefer a sure gain to a risky but potentially greater gain. Finally, note that prospect theory does *not* predict that people will always avoid risky decisions. If offered a chance of avoiding a loss (even if it means the average expected loss increases from $800 to $850), most people will take that chance because they are so concerned to avoid losses.

Two further predictions follow from prospect theory. When people make decisions, they

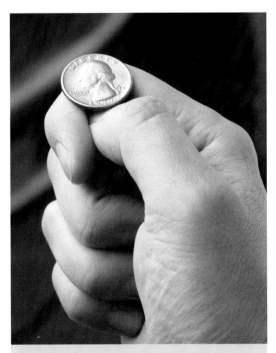

Most people are more sensitive to possible losses than to possible gains. As a result of this loss aversion, they are unwilling to bet on the toss of a coin unless the potential gains are much greater than the potential losses.

KEY TERM

loss aversion: the tendency to be more sensitive to potential losses than to potential gains.

attach *more* weight to low-probability events than those events merit according to their actual probability of occurrence. That helps to explain why people bet on the National Lottery, where the chances of winning the jackpot are approximately 1 in 14 million. In contrast, high-probability events receive *less* weight than they deserve.

Evidence

According to subjective expected utility theory and other normative theories, everyone should adhere to the **dominance principle**, according to which, "If Option A is at least as good as Option B in all respects and better than B in at least one aspect, then A should be preferred to B" (Gilhooly, 1996, p. 178). However, as predicted by prospect theory, that is not what happens. Kahneman and Tversky (1984) used a problem similar to one described above. Participants had to make two decisions, the first of which involved choosing between:

(A) a sure gain of $240
(B) a 25% probability of gaining $1000 and a 75% probability of gaining nothing.

The second decision involved choosing between:

(C) a sure loss of $750
(D) a 76% probability of losing $1000 and a 24% probability of losing nothing.

According to the dominance principle, the participants should have chosen B and C over A and D. Options B and C together offer a 25% probability of gaining $250 and a 75% probability of losing $750, whereas options A and D together offer a 24% probability of gaining $240 and a 76% probability of losing $760. In fact, 73% of the participants chose A and D, whereas only 3% chose B and C; thus, participants showed loss aversion.

Prospect theory does not focus on individual differences, but some people are much more likely than others to show loss aversion. Josephs, Larrick, Steele, and Nisbett (1992) asked individuals high and low in self-esteem to choose between two options differing in risk (e.g., a certain gain of $8 versus a 66% chance of winning $12). Those low in self-esteem were 64% more likely than those high in self-esteem to choose the sure gain in one experiment, and the difference was 78% in a replication.

In another experiment, Josephs et al. (1992) asked participants to choose one out of five gambles. The least risky gamble gave a 95% chance of winning $2.10 and the riskiest one gave a 25% chance of winning $8. The findings are shown in Figure 13.6. High self-esteem individuals were ten times more likely to select the riskiest than the least risky gamble, whereas almost twice as many low self-esteem individuals chose the least risky gamble than the riskiest one.

Why is self-esteem so important? According to Josephs et al. (1992), individuals high in self-esteem have a strong self-protective system that helps to maintain self-esteem when confronted by threat or loss. In contrast, people with low self-esteem are concerned that negative or threatening events will reduce their self-esteem.

It could be argued that most research on loss aversion is of limited applicability because the amounts of money that can be won or lost are relatively modest. However, the television game show "Deal or no deal" provides a way of testing prospect theory in a situation involving very large potential gains. Detailed examination of performance on this show provides mixed support for prospect theory (Post et al., 2008). A phenomenon resembling loss aversion is the **sunk-cost effect**, which is "a greater tendency to

KEY TERMS

dominance principle: in decision making, the notion that the better of two similar options will be preferred.
sunk-cost effect: expending additional resources to justify some previous commitment that has not worked well.

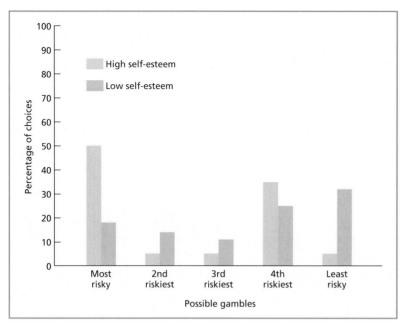

Figure 13.6 Percentages of choices of five gambles varying in riskiness for participants low and high in self-esteem. Based on data in Josephs et al. (1992).

continue an endeavour once an investment in money, effort, or time has been made" (Arkes & Ayton, 1999, p. 591). This effect is captured by the expression "throwing good money after bad". Dawes (1988) discussed a study in which participants were told that two people had paid a $100 non-refundable deposit for a weekend at a resort. On the way to the resort, both of them became slightly unwell, and felt they would probably have a more pleasurable time at home than at the resort. Should they drive on or turn back? Many participants argued that the two people should drive on to avoid wasting the $100 – this is the sunk-cost effect. This decision involves extra expenditure (money spent at the resort versus staying at home) and is less preferred than being at home!

Why did many participants make the apparently poor decision to continue with the trip? They thought it would be hard to explain to themselves and other people why they had wasted $100. As we will see later, Simonson and Staw (1992) found that the sunk-cost effect was stronger when participants thought they were going to be held accountable for their decisions.

The importance of being able to justify one's actions may help to explain why children

and various species of animal (e.g., blackbirds, mice) are much less affected than adult humans by the sunk-cost effect (Arkes & Ayton, 1999). This may seem surprising because we regard ourselves (with some justification!) as much smarter than birds and mice. However, other species do not feel the need to justify their decisions to other members of the same species.

Much research has involved the **framing effect**, in which decisions are influenced by irrelevant aspects of the situation. In a classic study, Tversky and Kahneman (1987) used the Asian disease problem. Some participants were told there was likely to be an outbreak of an Asian disease in the United States, and it was likely to kill 600 people. Two programmes of action had been proposed: Programme A would allow 200 people to be saved; programme B would have a one-third probability that 600 people would be saved and a two-thirds

KEY TERM

framing effect: the influence of irrelevant aspects of a situation (e.g., wording of the problem) on decision making.

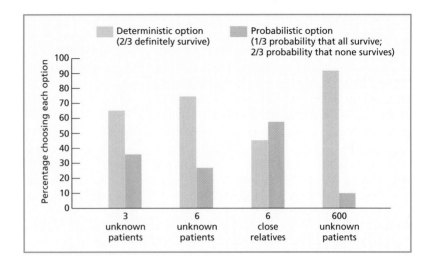

Figure 13.7 Choice of option (deterministic vs. probabilistic) as a function of number of patients and type of patient (unknown vs. close relatives). Data from Wang (1996).

probability that none of the 600 would be saved. When the issue was expressed in this form, 72% of the participants favoured programme A, although the two programmes (if implemented several times) would on average both lead to the saving of 200 lives.

Other participants in the study by Tversky and Kahneman (1987) were given the same problem, but this time it was negatively framed. They were told that programme A would lead to 400 people dying, whereas programme B carried a 1:3 probability that nobody would die and a 2:3 probability that 600 would die. In spite of the fact that the number of people who would live and die in both framing conditions was identical, 78% chose programme B.

The various findings can be accounted for in terms of loss aversion, i.e., people are motivated to avoid certain losses. However, since the problem remained basically the same whether framed positively or negatively, the prediction from subjective expected utility theory is that framing should have no effect.

According to prospect theory, framing effects should only be found when what is at stake has real value for the decision maker: loss aversion does not apply if you do not mind incurring a loss. There is much support for this prediction (e.g., Bloomfield, 2006; Wang, Simons, & Brédart, 2001). Wang et al. (2001) used a life-and-death problem involving 6 billion human

lives or 6 billion extraterrestrial lives. There was the usual framing effect when human lives were at stake, but no framing effect at all when only extraterrestrial lives were involved.

Wang (1996) showed that social and moral factors not considered by prospect theory can influence performance on the Asian disease problem. Participants chose between definite survival of two-thirds of the patients (deterministic option) or a one-third probability of all surviving and a two-thirds probability of none surviving (probabilistic option). They were told that the group size was 600, six, or three patients unknown to them, or six patients who were close relatives of the participant. The decision was greatly influenced by group size and by the relationship between the participants and the group members (see Figure 13.7). The increased percentage of participants choosing the probabilistic option with small group size (especially for relatives) probably occurred because the social context and psychological factors relating to fairness were regarded as more important in those conditions. These findings are inconsistent with utility theory. According to this theory, the participants should always have chosen the definite survival of two-thirds of the patients rather than a one-third probability of all patients surviving.

Do framing effects depend on individual differences among those making decisions?

Evidence that the answer is, "Yes", was reported by Moorman and van den Putte (2008). They used two smoking cessation messages, one with a negative frame and the other with a positive frame. The negative frame worked better among smokers whose quitting intentions were high, whereas the positive frame worked better among those whose quitting intentions were low. Thus, framing effects depend on the recipient of the message as well as on whether the message is positively or negatively framed.

According to prospect theory, people overweight the probability of rare events when making decisions. This prediction has been supported in several studies (see Hertwig, Barron, Weber, & Erev, 2004, for a review). However, Hertwig et al. argued that we should distinguish between decisions based on descriptions and those based on experience. In the laboratory, people are typically provided with a neat summary description of the possible outcomes and their associated probabilities. In contrast, in the real world, people often make decisions (e.g., to go out on a date) purely on the basis of personal experience.

Hertwig et al. (2004) compared decision making based on descriptions with decision making based on experience (i.e., personal observation of events and their outcomes). When decisions were based on descriptions, people overweighted the probability of rare events as predicted by prospect theory. However, when decisions were based on experience, people underweighted the probability of rare events, which is opposite to theoretical prediction. This happened in part because participants in the experience condition often failed to encounter the rare event at all.

Jessup, Bishara, and Busemeyer (2008) focused only on decisions based on descriptions. When no feedback was provided, participants overweighted the probability of rare events. However, the provision of feedback eliminated this effect and led to a small *underweighting* of the probability of rare events. Thus, feedback may act as a "reality check" that eliminates the bias of overweighting the probability of rare events.

Evaluation

Prospect theory provides a much more adequate account of decision making than previous normative approaches such as subjective expected utility theory. The value function (especially the assumption that people attach more weight to losses than to gains) allows us to explain many phenomena (e.g., loss aversion; sunk-cost effect; framing effects) not readily explicable by subjective expected utility theory. Even clearer evidence supporting prospect theory and disproving subjective expected utility theory has come from studies showing failures of the dominance principle.

Prospect theory has various limitations. First, Kahneman and Tversky failed to provide a detailed explicit rationale for the value function. As a result, prospect theory gives only a partial explanation. Second, the theory does not emphasise the effects of social and emotional factors on decision making (e.g., Wang, 1996; see below). Third, individual differences in willingness to make risky decisions (e.g., Josephs et al., 1992) are de-emphasised. Fourth, framing effects depend on characteristics of decision makers as well as on whether the message is positively or negatively framed (e.g., Moorman & van den Putte, 2008). Fifth, there is sometimes an underweighting of the probability of rare events (e.g., Jessup et al., 2008).

Emotional factors

In this section, we focus on the role of emotional factors in decision making. We will start by showing how our understanding of loss aversion can be increased by considering emotional factors. After that, we will discuss other decision-making biases influenced by emotion. Much of this research lies within **neuroeconomics**,

---

KEY TERM

neuroeconomics: an emerging approach in which economic decision making is understood within the framework of **cognitive neuroscience**.

in which cognitive neuroscience is used to increase our understanding of decision making in the economic environment (see Loewenstein, Rick, & Cohen, 2008, for a review).

Loss aversion

Emotions often fulfil a valuable function, but can lead us to be excessively and unrealistically averse to loss. Kermer, Driver-Linn, Wilson, and Gilbert (2006) carried out an experiment in which some participants (experiencers) played a gambling game in which on each trial a computer ranked playing-card suits from first to last. The task was to guess which suit would be ranked first, and money was won or lost depending on the computer's ranking of the selected suit. Things were arranged so that some participants finished with a profit of $4, whereas others made a loss of $4. Other participants (forecasters) watched the win or the loss version of the game. At 30-second intervals after the end of the game, experiencers rated how happy they were, and forecasters predicted how happy they would have been if they had played the game.

The findings from this first experiment are shown in Figure 13.8. Forecasters in the loss condition showed a greater change in happiness from baseline than did forecasters in the gain condition, thus showing loss aversion. However, the key finding was that experiencers in the loss condition were *not* significantly less happy than experiencers in the gain condition. Thus, people *overestimate* the intensity and duration of their negative emotional reactions to loss (compare the loss forecasters with the loss experiencers). This phenomenon (impact bias) has also been found with respect to predictions about losses such as losing a job or a romantic partner (see Kermer et al., 2006, for a review).

Kermer et al. (2006) carried out another experiment in which participants were initially given $5, and predicted how they would feel if they won $5 or lost $3 on the toss of a coin. They predicted that losing $3 would have more impact on their happiness immediately and ten minutes later than would gaining $5, a clear example of loss aversion. In fact, participants

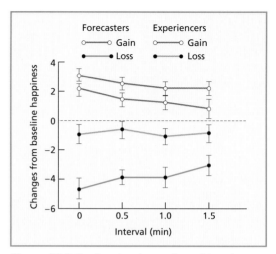

Figure 13.8 Predicted and experienced happiness after winning or losing $4 for forecasters and experiencers. From Kermer et al. (2006). Reprinted with permission of Wiley-Blackwell.

who lost felt happier than they had predicted at both time intervals, and the actual impact on happiness of losing $3 was no greater than the actual impact of gaining $5. Why did this happen? Participants who had lost $3 focused much more on the fact that they nevertheless finished with a profit of $2 than they had predicted beforehand.

De Martino, Kumaran, Seymour, and Dolan (2006) found that brain areas associated with emotion were relevant to the framing effect. Activation in the amygdala and the orbital and medial prefrontal cortex was associated with greater frame effects and so greater evidence of loss aversion. Since these areas are associated with anxiety, it is possible that anxiety caused increased loss aversion.

Wong, Yik, and Kwong (2006) argued that emotional factors are involved in the sunk-cost effect, in which good money is thrown after bad. The initial undesirable outcome (e.g., loss of money) creates negative affect (e.g., anxiety). If this negative affect is sufficiently strong, the individual will decide to withdraw from the losing situation to reduce his/her negative emotional state. It follows that individuals high in neuroticism (a personality trait characterised by high levels of negative affect) should be

Can brain damage improve decision making?

Some of the most important research within neuroeconomics was reported by Shiv et al. (2005a, 2005b). Their starting point was the assumption that emotions can make us excessively cautious and risk averse. That led them to the counterintuitive prediction that brain-damaged patients would outperform healthy participants on a gambling task provided the brain damage reduced their emotional experience.

There were three groups of participants in the study by Shiv, Loewenstein, Bechara, Damasio, and Damasio (2005a). One group consisted of patients with brain damage in areas related to emotion (amygdala, orbitofrontal cortex, and insular or somatosensory cortex). The other groups consisted of patients with brain damage in areas unrelated to emotion and healthy controls. Initially, Shiv et al. provided participants with $20. On each of 20 rounds, they decided whether to invest $1. If they did, they lost the $1 if a coin came up heads but won $1.50 if it came up tails. Participants stood to make an average gain of 25 cents per round if they invested compared to simply retaining the $1. Thus, the optimal strategy for profit maximisation was to invest on every single round.

The patients with damage to emotion regions invested in 84% of the rounds compared to only 61% for the other patient group and 58% for the healthy controls. Thus, the patients with restricted emotions performed best. Why was this? The patients with brain damage unrelated to emotion and the healthy controls were much less likely to invest following loss on the previous round than following gain. In contrast, patients with brain damage related to emotion were totally unaffected in their investment decisions by the outcome of the previous round (see Figure 13.9).

Shiv, Loewenstein, and Bechara (2005b) compared patients with damage to emotion regions, patients with substance dependence (e.g., cocaine; alcohol), and healthy controls on the gambling task. They used patients with substance dependence because they generally have

damage to parts of the brain involved in emotion. The two patient groups had a comparable level of performance, and both groups earned more money than did the healthy controls.

What can we conclude? As Shiv et al. (2005a, 2005b) argued, there is a "dark side" to emotions when it comes to decision making. An emotion such as anxiety can prevent us from maximising our profit by making us excessively concerned about possible losses and therefore excessively afraid of taking risks. However, it is not clear whether the performance of the substance-dependent patients occurred because of damage to the emotion system or because risk-takers are more likely than other people to become substance-dependent.

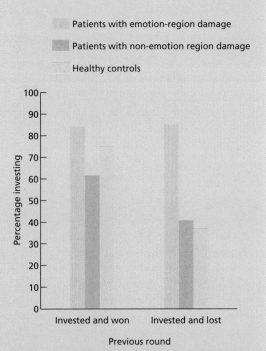

Figure 13.9 Percentage of rounds in which patients with damage to emotion regions of the brain, patients with damage to other regions of the brain, and healthy controls decided to invest $1 having won or lost on the previous round. Data from Shiv et al. (2005a).

Individuals high in neuroticism are more likely than those low in neuroticism to withdraw from an undesirable situation (e.g., losing money whilst gambling) and thus avoid the sunk-cost effect and its associated anxiety.

more likely than those low in neuroticism to withdraw from the situation and thus avoid the sunk-cost effect. That is precisely what Wong et al. found.

In sum, there is much evidence (including brain-imaging studies and studies on brain-damaged patients) that emotional factors play an important role in loss aversion. More specifically, emotional states (perhaps especially anxiety) lead individuals to become more loss averse. This research is helping to clarify why most individuals are more sensitive to losses than to gains.

We must not conclude that emotions *always* impair decision making. Seo and Barrett (2007) found using an Internet-based stock investment simulation that stock investors who experienced more intense feelings had superior decision-making performance than those with less intense feelings. Perhaps the relevant expertise of the participants made it easier for them to prevent their emotional states from biasing their decision making. Patients with damage to the ventro-medial prefrontal cortex typically have essentially intact intelligence but are very deficient in expressing and experiencing emotions (Bechara & Damasio, 2005). These patients often have very poor decision making in real life (e.g., they repeatedly make decisions that lead to negative consequences).

Omission bias and decision avoidance

There is other evidence that emotional and social factors not included within prospect theory influence decision making. Ritov and Baron (1990) told participants to assume their child had ten chances in 10,000 of dying from flu during an epidemic if he/she wasn't vaccinated. They were told the vaccine was certain to prevent the child from catching flu, but had potentially fatal side effects. Ritov and Baron found that five deaths per 10,000 was the average maximum acceptable risk participants were willing to tolerate in order to decide to have their child vaccinated. Thus, people would choose not to have their child vaccinated when the likelihood of the vaccine causing death was much lower than the death rate from the disease against which the vaccine protects!

What was going on in the study by Ritov and Baron (1990)? The participants argued they would feel more responsible for the death of their child if it resulted from their own actions rather than their inaction. This is an example of **omission bias,** in which individuals prefer inaction to action. An important factor in omission bias is anticipated regret, with the

> ### KEY TERM
>
> **omission bias:** the tendency to prefer inaction to action when engaged in risky decision making.

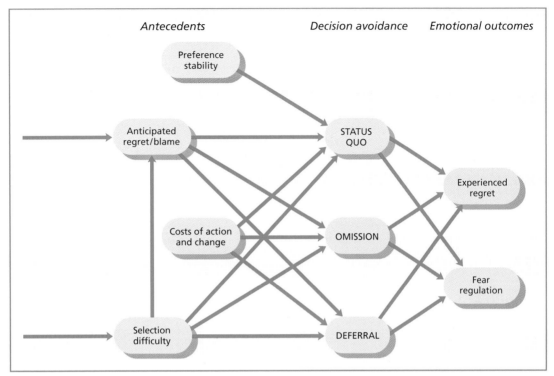

Figure 13.10 Anderson's rational–emotional model identifying factors associated with decision avoidance. From C.J. Anderson (2003). Copyright © 2003 American Psychological Association. Reproduced with permission.

level of anticipated regret being greater when an unwanted outcome has been caused by an individual's own actions. Omission bias and anticipated regret influence many real-life decisions, including those involving choices between consumer products, sexual practices, and medical decisions (see Mellers, Schwartz, & Cooke, 1998).

There have been several studies in which omission bias was not found (see Baron & Ritov, 2004, for a review). Baron and Ritov obtained evidence that may help to explain the apparently inconsistent findings. Even though there was an overall omission bias, some participants showed the opposite bias. Baron and Ritov termed this "action bias" and argued that those susceptible to it are applying the heuristic, "Don't just sit there. Do something!"

Omission bias is an example of decision avoidance caused by emotional factors. Another example is **status quo bias,** in which individuals repeat an initial choice over a series of decision situations in spite of changes in their preferences. For example, Samuelson and Zeckhauser (1988) found that in a real-life situation many people kept the same allocation of retirement funds year after year even when they would not have incurred any costs by changing.

Rational–emotional model

Anderson (2003) put forward a rational–emotional model to account for the impact of emotions on decision making (see Figure 13.10). Decision making is determined by rational factors based on inferences and outcome information, as well as experienced and anticipated emotion. The two key emotions within the

> **KEY TERM**
>
> **status quo bias:** a tendency for individuals to repeat a choice several times in spite of changes in their preferences.

model are regret (as in omission bias) and fear. Fear can be reduced when an individual decides not to make a decision for the time being. The essence of the model is as follows: "It is reasonable to assume that people make choices that reduce negative emotions" (p. 142).

The model can account for some of the phenomena discussed earlier. For example, one reason for loss aversion is the effect of anticipated regret at the possibility of making a decision that might produce losses.

Social functionalist approach

Much research designed to test subjective utility theory and prospect theory is laboratory-based. However, there are major differences between the laboratory and real life, because laboratory decisions have no interpersonal consequences. This led Tetlock (2002) to propose a social functionalist approach taking account of the social context of decision making. For example, people often behave like intuitive politicians, in that, "They are accountable to a variety of constituencies, they suffer consequences when they fail to create desired impressions on key constituencies, and their long-term success at managing impressions hinges on their skill at anticipating objections that others are likely to raise to alternative courses of action" (p. 454). Thus, people acting as intuitive politicians need to be able to justify their decisions to others.

Evidence

Simonson and Staw (1992) investigated the effects of accountability on decision making in a study on the sunk-cost effect. Participants were given information about a beer company selling light beer and non-alcoholic beer. They were asked to recommend which product should receive an additional $3 million for marketing support (e.g., advertising). They were then told that the president of the company had made the same decision, but this had produced disappointing results. Finally, they were told the company had decided to allocate $10 million of additional marketing support which could be divided between the two products.

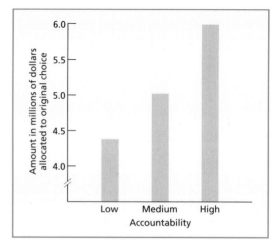

Figure 13.11 Millions of dollars allocated to original choice (sunk-cost effect) as a function of accountability. Data from Simonson and Staw (1992).

In a high-accountability condition, participants were told that information about their decisions might be shared with other students and instructors, and they were asked to give permission to record an interview about their decisions. In the low-accountability condition, participants were told that their decisions would be confidential and that there was no connection between participants' performance on the task and their managerial effectiveness or intelligence. In the medium-accountability condition, participants were told that the amount of information provided should be sufficient to allow a good decision to be made.

Simonson and Staw's (1992) findings are shown in Figure 13.11. The tendency towards a sunk-cost effect was strongest in the high-accountability condition and lowest in the low-accountability condition. Presumably, participants in the high-accountability condition experienced the greatest need to justify their previously ineffective course of action (i.e., fruitless investment in one type of beer) by increasing their commitment to it.

We might assume that medical experts would be more likely to make sound and unbiased decisions when held accountable for their actions. This assumption was disconfirmed by

Schwartz, Chapman, Brewer, and Bergus (2004). Doctors were told about a patient with osteo-arthritis for whom many anti-inflammatory drugs had proved ineffective. In the two-option condition, they chose between simply referring the patient to an orthopaedic specialist to discuss surgery or combining referral with prescribing an untried anti-inflammatory drug. In the three-option condition, there were the same options as in the two-option condition plus referral combined with prescribing a different untried anti-inflammatory drug. The doctors simply made their decisions or were made accountable for their decisions (they wrote an explanation for their decision and agreed to be contacted later to discuss it).

The doctors showed a bias in their decision making regardless of whether they were made accountable. They were *more* likely to select the referral-only option in the three-option than the two-option condition, which is contrary to common sense. This bias was significantly greater when doctors were made accountable for their decisions. What is going on here? In the three-option condition, it is very hard to justify selecting one anti-inflammatory drug over the other one. The easy way out is to select the remaining option (i.e., referral only).

Evaluation

The central assumption that most decision making is influenced by social context has attracted much support. We feel a need to justify our decisions to other people as well as to ourselves, causing us to behave like intuitive politicians. Overall, the social functionalist approach emphasises important factors de-emphasised within prospect theory.

There are some limitations with the social functionalist approach. First, important factors (e.g., our greater sensitivity to losses than to gains) are ignored. Second, there are large individual differences in the extent to which people feel the need to justify themselves to other people, but these individual differences are ignored. Third, most of the relevant research has involved laboratory tasks not making any real demands on social responsibility.

COMPLEX DECISION MAKING

So far we have focused mainly on decision making applied to fairly simple problems. In real life, however, we are often confronted by important decisions. For example, medical experts have to make diagnostic decisions that can literally be a matter of life or death (see Chapter 12). Other decisions are both important and complex (e.g., Shall I marry John?; Shall I move to Australia?). How do we deal with such decisions?

Before proceeding to discuss theory and research on decision making, an important point needs to be made. As Hastie (2001, p. 665) pointed out, "Most current decision theories are designed to account for the choice of one action at one point in time. The image of a decision maker standing at a choice point like a fork in a road and choosing one direction or the other is probably much less appropriate for major everyday decisions than the image of a boat navigating a rough sea with a sequence of many embedded choices and decisions to maintain a meandering course toward the ultimate goal." Thus, decision making in everyday life is typically much more complex than under laboratory conditions.

According to multi-attribute utility theory (Wright, 1984), a decision maker should go through the following stages:

(1) Identify attributes relevant to the decision.
(2) Decide how to weight those attributes.
(3) Obtain a total utility (i.e., subjective desirability for each option by summing its weighted attribute values).
(4) Select the option with the highest weighted total.

We can see how multi-attribute utility theory works in practice by considering someone deciding which flat to rent. First, consideration is paid to the relevant attributes (e.g., number of rooms; location; rent per week). Second, the relative utility of each attribute is calculated.

Hastie (2001) likened decision making to "...a boat navigating a rough sea with a sequence of many embedded choices and decisions to maintain a meandering course toward the ultimate goal." Thus, decision making in everyday life is often very complex; indeed, much more complex than decision making in the laboratory.

Third, the various flats being considered are compared in terms of their total utility, and the person chooses the one with the highest total utility.

Decision makers who adopt the above approach will often make the best decision provided that *all* the options are listed and the criteria are independent of each other. However, there are various reasons why people rarely adopt the above decision-making procedure in real life. First, the procedure can be very complex. Second, the set of relevant dimensions cannot always be worked out. Third, the dimensions themselves may not be clearly separate from each other.

Bounded rationality

Herb Simon (1957) put forward a much more realistic approach to complex decision making. He started by distinguishing between unbounded rationality and bounded rationality. Within models of unbounded rationality, it is assumed that all relevant information is available for use (and is used) by decision makers. The basic notion is that we engage in a process of **optimisation,** in which the best choice or decision is made. There are two problems with the notion of optimisation. First, as Klein (2001,

p. 103) pointed out, "In the majority of field settings, there is no way to determine if a decision choice is optimal owing to time pressure, uncertainty, ill-defined goals, and so forth." For example, if you found it hard to decide whether to study psychology or some other subject, you will probably never know whether you made the best decision. Second, whichever definition of optimisation we prefer, most people typically fail to select the optimal choice on a regular basis.

According to Simon (1957), we possess **bounded rationality.** This means that we produce reasonable or workable solutions to problems in spite of our limited processing ability by using various short-cut strategies (e.g., heuristics). More specifically, decision making can be "bounded" by constraints in the environment (e.g., information costs) or by constraints in the mind (e.g., limited attention;

KEY TERMS

optimisation: the selection of the best choice in decision making.
bounded rationality: the notion that people are as rational as their processing limitations permit.

limited memory). What matters is the degree of fit or match between the mind and the environment. According to Simon (1990, p. 7), "Human rational behaviour is shaped like a scissors whose blades are the structure of task environments and the computational capabilities of the actor." If we consider only one blade (i.e., the task environment or the individual's abilities), we will have only a partial understanding of how we make decisions. In similar fashion, we would be unable to understand how scissors cut if we focused on only one blade.

Simon (1978) argued that bounded rationality is shown by the heuristic known as satisficing. The essence of **satisficing** (formed from the words satisfactory and sufficing) is that individuals consider various options one at a time and select the first one meeting their minimum requirements. This heuristic isn't guaranteed to produce the best decision, but is especially useful when the various options become available at different points in time. An example would be the vexed issue of deciding who to marry. Someone using the satisficing heuristic would set a minimum acceptable level, and the first person reaching (or exceeding) that level would be chosen. If the initial level of acceptability is set too high, the level is adjusted downwards. Of course, if you set the level too low, you may spend many years bitterly regretting having used the satisficing heuristic!

Schwartz, Ward, Monterosso, Lyubomirsky, White, and Lehman (2002) distinguished between satisficers (content with making reasonably good decisions) and maximisers (perfectionists). There were various advantages associated with being a satisficer. Satisficers were happier and more optimistic than maximisers, they had greater life satisfaction, and they experienced less regret and self-blame. Thus, constantly striving to make the best possible decisions may not be a recipe for happiness.

Tversky (1972) put forward a theory of complex decision making resembling Simon's approach. According to Tversky's elimination-by-aspects theory, decision makers eliminate options by considering one relevant attribute or aspect after another. For example, someone buying a house may first of all consider the attribute of geographical location, eliminating all those houses not lying within a given area. They may then consider the attribute of price, eliminating all properties costing above a certain figure. This process continues attribute by attribute until only one option remains. The limitation with this approach is that the option selected varies as a function of the order in which the attributes are considered. As a result, the choice that is made may not be the best one.

Evidence

Payne (1976) carried out a study to see the extent to which decision makers actually use the various strategies we have discussed. Participants decided which apartment to rent on the basis of information about various attributes such as rent, cleanliness, noise level, and distance from campus, all of which were presented on cards. The number of apartments varied between two and 12 and the number of attributes between four and 12. When there were many apartments to consider, participants typically started by using a simple strategy such as satisficing or elimination-by-aspects. When only a few apartments remained to be considered, there was often a switch to a more complex strategy corresponding to the assumptions of multi-attribute utility theory.

It was assumed within multi-attribute utility theory that a given individual's assessment of the utility or preference of any given attribute remains constant. This assumption was tested by Simon, Krawczyk, and Holyoak (2004). Participants decided between job offers from two department store chains, "Bonnie's Best" and "Splendour". There were four relevant attributes (salary, holiday package, commute time, and office accommodation). Each job offer

KEY TERM

satisficing: selection of the first choice meeting certain minimum requirements; the word is formed from the words "satisfactory" and "sufficing".

was preferable to the other on two attributes and inferior on two attributes. Participants assessed their preferences. They were then told that one of the jobs was in a much better location than the other, which often tipped the balance in favour of choosing the job in the better location. The participants then re-assessed their preference for each option. Preferences for desirable attributes of the chosen job increased and preferences for undesirable attributes of that job decreased, thus disproving the assumption from multi-attribute utility theory.

Russo, Carlson, and Meloy (2006) found more evidence of non-rational decision making. Many participants were persuaded to choose an inferior restaurant (based on information they had previously provided) by the simple expedient of initially presenting positive information about it. Thus, installing the inferior restaurant as the early leading option caused subsequent information about it to be distorted.

Galotti (2007) discussed five studies concerned with important real-life decisions (e.g., students choosing a college; college students choosing their main subject). There were several findings. First, decision makers constrained the amount of information they considered, focusing on between two and five options (mean = four) at any given time. Second, the number of options considered decreased over time. Third, the number of attributes considered at any given time was between three and nine (mean = six). Fourth, the number of attributes did not decrease over time; sometimes it actually increased. Fifth, individuals of higher ability and/or more education tended to consider more attributes. Sixth, most of the decisions makers' real-life decisions were assessed as good.

What can we conclude from Galotti's (2007) study? The most striking finding is that people consistently limit the amount of information (options and attributes) they consider. This is inconsistent with multi-attribute utility theory but is precisely as predicted by Simon's (1957) notion of bounded rationality. In addition, Galotti found that the number of options considered decreased by 18% over a period of several months. A reduction is predicted by

Tversky's (1972) elimination-by-aspects theory. However, the actual reduction seems smaller than would be expected according to that theory.

We would expect experts to make better decisions on average than non-experts. Is their superior performance entirely due to greater knowledge or does their processing on decision-making tasks differ from that of non-experts? Evidence that there may be important differences in processing was discovered by Klein (1998). Experts (e.g., fire commanders; military commanders) tended to consider only one option at a time, whereas Galotti (2007) found this was rare among non-experts. Experts generally rapidly categorised even a novel situation as an example of a type of situation with which they were familiar, and then simply retrieved the appropriate decision from long-term memory.

Similar findings to those of Galotti (2007) have been found in studies on medical expertise (see Chapter 12). Perhaps surprisingly, medical experts are sometimes more prone to error than non-experts (e.g., Reyna & Lloyd, 2006; see Chapter 12). Earlier in the chapter we discussed a study by Schwartz et al. (2004) that also shows that experts' decision making can be error prone. Doctors who had to decide what should be done with a patient suffering from osteoarthritis had biased decision making. This bias was greater when they were made accountable for their decision.

Fellows (2006) addressed the issue of which parts of the brain are especially important in decision making. Patients with damage to the ventromedial frontal lobe, others with damage to other parts of the frontal lobe, and healthy controls were given the task of selecting an apartment when presented with information concerning several aspects of each one. Healthy controls and patients without damage to the ventromedial frontal lobe compared attribute information across several apartments. In contrast, patients with damage to the ventromedial frontal lobe focused their search for information around individual apartments. The findings suggest that the ability to compare information across different options (which is very important in much decision making) is impaired in these patients.

Evaluation

Most human complex decision making differs from the ideal in two major ways. First, we typically focus on only some of the available information because of our limited ability to process and remember information. Second, some aspects of our decision making can be regarded as somewhat irrational. For example, our preferences are very easily changed – they can be influenced by the options we choose and by the order in which information is presented to us. In sum, much of our decision-making behaviour is consistent with the notion of bounded rationality and is often described at least approximately by Tversky's elimination-by-aspects theory.

Unconscious thought theory

It is often assumed that conscious thinking is more effective than unconscious thinking with complex decision making, whereas unconscious thinking (if useful at all) is so with respect to simple decision making. However, Dijksterhuis and Nordgren (2006) argued that precisely the opposite is actually the case! How did they support that argument? First, they claimed that conscious thought is constrained by the limited capacity of consciousness, whereas the unconscious has considerably greater capacity. Second, "The unconscious naturally weights the relative importance of various attributes. Conscious thought often leads to suboptimal weighting because it disturbs this natural process." However, only conscious thought can follow strict rules and so provide precise answers to complex mathematical problems.

Evidence

Betsch, Plessner, Schwieren, and Gütig (2001) obtained evidence that the unconscious can successfully integrate large amounts of information. Participants were shown advertisements on a computer screen, and instructed to look carefully at them. At the same time, detailed information about increases and decreases in the prices of five hypothetical shares was presented. Participants were subsequently asked specific questions about the shares. Their performance was very poor, indicating a lack of conscious awareness of information about the shares. However, participants were able to use gut feeling to identify the best and worst shares, suggesting that unconscious processes integrated information about the shares.

Dijksterhuis (2004) used the same three conditions in three different experiments on decision making. In the control condition, participants made immediate decisions as soon as the various options had been presented. In the conscious thought condition, participants had a few minutes to think about their decision. In the unconscious thought condition, participants were distracted for a few minutes to prevent conscious thinking about the problem, and then made their decision.

The findings were similar in all three experiments, and so we will consider only one at length. Participants received detailed information about four hypothetical apartments in Amsterdam. Each apartment was described in terms of 12 attributes, and the task was to select the best apartment. Performance was best in the unconscious thought condition and worst in the control condition (see Figure 13.12). Far more of those in the unconscious thought condition than the conscious thought condition indicated they had made a global judgement (55.6% versus 26.5%, respectively). This suggests that the relatively poor performance in the conscious thought condition occurred because participants focused too much on a small fraction of the information. Since the attribute information was not visually available while they contemplated their decision, they were constrained by the limitations of memory.

We have seen that unconscious thought can lead to superior decisions to conscious thought when decision making is complex. According to unconscious thought theory, there should be an *interaction* between mode of thought and complexity of decision making. Since conscious thought has limited capacity, it is well

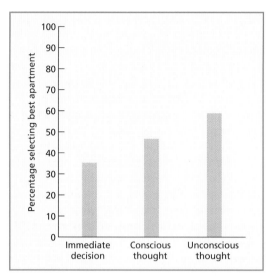

Figure 13.12 Percentage of participants selecting the best apartment as a function of condition (immediate decision; conscious thought; unconscious thought). Based on data in Dijksterhuis (2004).

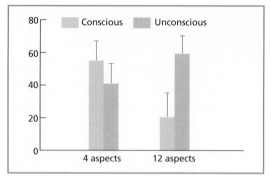

Figure 13.13 Percentage of participants choosing the most desirable car as a function of decision complexity (4 vs. 12 aspects) and mode of thought (conscious vs. unconscious). From Dijksterhuis et al. (2006). Reprinted with permission from AAAS.

suited to simple decision making but can sometimes become ineffective as decision making becomes more complex. Supportive findings were reported by Dijksterhuis, Bos, Nordgren, and van Baaren (2006). All the participants read information concerning four hypothetical cars. In the simple condition, each car was described by four attributes. In the complex condition, each car was described by 12 attributes. Participants either spent four minutes thinking about the cars (conscious thought condition) or solved anagrams for four minutes before choosing a car (unconscious thought condition).

The findings are shown in Figure 13.13. As predicted, a greater percentage of participants in the unconscious thought condition than in the conscious thought condition selected the most desirable car when the decision was complex; the opposite pattern was found when the decision was simple.

Dijksterhuis et al. (2006) decided to see whether unconscious thought theory applies in the real world. They approached shoppers coming out of two shops. One was IKEA (which sells complex products such as furniture) and the other was Bijenkorf (which sells simple products such as kitchen accessories). The shoppers were categorised as "conscious thinkers" or "unconscious thinkers" on the basis of how much thought they claimed to have put into their purchases. Subsequently, they were asked how satisfied they were with their purchases. As predicted, conscious thinkers were significantly more satisfied than unconscious thinkers with the simple Bijenkorf products. Also as predicted, unconscious thinkers were significantly more satisfied than conscious thinkers with the complex IKEA products.

Evaluation

Unconscious thought theory advances our understanding of the strengths (and limitations) of unconscious thought relative to conscious thought. The greatest advantages of unconscious thought are its very large capacity and its rapid weighting of the relative importance of different pieces of task-relevant information. However, these characteristics are disadvantageous when it is very important to attend to (and select) certain information while ignoring and discarding other information, and tasks on which the answer needs to be precise.

The evidence supports the notion that conscious thought is constrained by the limitations of attention and consciousness. However, several of Dijksterhuis' experiments undersell the usefulness of conscious thought. In his research, the time available for conscious thought was limited, and task-relevant information was frequently inaccessible during that time (e.g., Dijksterhuis, 2004). The fact that participants in the deliberate thought condition of the car-choosing study of Dijksterhuis et al. (2006) only chose the best car 25% of the time (exactly chance performance) suggests they had great problems remembering the information (Shanks, 2006).

In the real world, these constraints can be overcome by having all task-relevant information constantly accessible and by having sufficient time for it to be evaluated systematically. As Kruglanski and Orehek (2007, p. 304) pointed out, very complex problems probably require conscious thought "abetted by various capacity-enhancing devices such as writing, priming, and computer programming." For example, no one in their senses would argue that the design of a rocket to travel to the moon should be based solely on unconscious thought (Michael Doherty, personal communication)!

Dijksterhuis' approach is based on a simple distinction between conscious and unconscious thought. This is limited because there is considerable variety in the processes associated with each of these types of thought. In addition, the precise cognitive processes engaged in by participants in conscious thought conditions are unknown.

CHAPTER SUMMARY

- Introduction
  There are close relationships between the areas of judgement and decision making. Decision-making research covers all of the processes involved in deciding on a course of action. In contrast, judgement research focuses mainly on those aspects of decision making concerned with estimating the likelihood of various events. In addition, judgements are evaluated in terms of their accuracy, whereas decisions are evaluated on the basis of their consequences.

- Judgement research
  In everyday life, our estimates of the probability of something often change in the light of new evidence. In making such estimates, people (even experts) often fail to take full account of base-rate information. One reason why people fail to make proper use of base-rate information is because of their reliance on the representativeness heuristic. Our judgement errors also depend on use of the availability heuristic. According to support theory, the subjective probability of an event increases as the description of the event becomes more explicit and detailed. The take-the-best and recognition heuristics are very simple rules of thumb that are often surprisingly accurate but are used less often than predicted theoretically by Gigerenzer. An advantage of the recognition heuristic is that it can be used rapidly and automatically. Gigerenzer and Hoffrage argue that judgements are more accurate when based on natural sampling and frequencies rather than probabilities. However, people often adopt biased sampling strategies, and are inaccurate even when using frequency data. According to Krynski and Tenenbaum (2007), we possess very valuable causal knowledge that allows us to make successful judgements in the real world. According to the dual-process model, probability judgements can involve an intuitive system (System 1) that often makes use of heuristics or a more conscious and controlled system (System 2).

- Basic decision making
  According to prospect theory, people are much more sensitive to potential losses than to potential gains. As a result, they are willing to take risks to avoid losses. The theory is supported by the sunk-cost and framing effects. Prospect theory is not very explicit about the role of emotional factors in decision making. Individuals overestimate the intensity and duration of their negative emotional reactions to loss. Reduced loss aversion (and superior performance) on a gambling task is shown by patients with damage to brain areas involved in emotion. According to Anderson's rational–emotional model, decision making is influenced by anticipated regret and fear. The model helps to explain the omission and status quo biases. According to Tetlock's social functionalist approach, people often behave like intuitive politicians who need to justify their decisions to others.

- Complex decision making
  Complex decision making involves bounded rationality, meaning that we are constrained by our limited processing ability. Tversky's elimination-by-aspects theory is consistent with the notion of bounded rationality. There is evidence from major real-life decisions that people consistently limit the amount of information they consider. Medical experts process less information and make more extreme decisions than non-experts when engaged in decision making. According to Dijksterhuis' unconscious thought theory, unconscious thinking is more useful than conscious thinking with complex decision making, but the opposite is the case with simple decision making. However, conscious thinking is more valuable than the theory suggests.

FURTHER READING

- Harvey, N. (2007). Use of heuristics: Insights from forecasting research. *Thinking & Reasoning, 13*, 5–24. This article provides an interesting discussion of the major heuristics and of the circumstances in which they are typically used. Note that there are other relevant articles in this Special Issue of *Thinking & Reasoning*.
- Newell, B.R., Lagnado, D.A., & Shanks, D.R. (2007). *Straight ahead: The psychology of decision making*. Hove, UK: Psychology Press. This book gives an excellent overview of our current understanding of decision making.
- Plessner, H., Betsch, C., & Betsch, T. (eds.) (2008). *Intuition in judgement and decision making*. Hove, UK: Psychology Press. The contributors to this book focus on the heuristics and other intuitive processes that underlie many of our judgements and decisions.
- Shah, A.K., & Oppenheimer, D.M. (2008). Heuristics made easy: An effort-reduction framework. *Psychological Bulletin, 134*, 207–222. The authors make a persuasive case that effort reduction is of central importance with heuristics or rules of thumb.
- Weber, E.U., & Johnson, E.J. (2009). Mindful judgement and decision making. *Annual Review of Psychology, 60*, 53–85. This article provides a good overview of recent developments within the fields of judgement and decision making.

CHAPTER 14

INDUCTIVE AND DEDUCTIVE REASONING

INTRODUCTION

For hundreds of years, philosophers have distinguished between two different kinds of reasoning. One is **inductive reasoning**, which involves making a generalised conclusion from premises (statements) referring to particular instances. A key feature of inductive reasoning is that the conclusions of inductively valid arguments are probably (but not necessarily) true. According to Karl Popper (1968), hypotheses can never be shown to be logically true by simply generalising from *confirming* instances (i.e., induction). As the philosopher Bertrand Russell pointed out, a scientist turkey might form the generalisation, "Each day I am fed", because this hypothesis has been confirmed every day of its life. However, the generalisation provides no *certainty* that the turkey will be fed tomorrow. Indeed, if tomorrow is Christmas Eve, it is likely to be proven false.

The other kind of reasoning is deductive reasoning. **Deductive reasoning** allows us to draw conclusions that are definitely valid provided other statements are assumed to be true. For example, if we assume that Tom is taller than Dick, and that Dick is taller than Harry, the conclusion that Tom is taller than Harry is necessarily true. Deductive reasoning is related to problem solving, because people trying to solve a deductive-reasoning task have a definite goal and the solution is not obvious. However, deductive-reasoning problems differ from other kinds of problem in that they often owe their origins to systems of formal logic. The fact that most deductive-reasoning problems are based on formal logic does *not* necessarily mean people will actually use formal logic to solve them. Indeed, most people do *not* use traditional logic when presented with a problem in deductive reasoning.

Finally in this chapter, we consider informal reasoning. Increased concern has been expressed at the apparently wide chasm between everyday reasoning in the form of argumentation and the highly artificial reasoning tasks used in the laboratory. That has led to the emergence of research on informal reasoning designed to focus on the processes used in most everyday reasoning.

Bear in mind that processes over and above reasoning are used by participants given reasoning problems to solve. As Sternberg (2004, p. 444) pointed out, "Reasoning is not encapsulated [enclosed or isolated]. It is part and parcel of a wide array of cognitive functions...many cognitive processes, including visual perception, contain elements of reasoning in them".

KEY TERMS

inductive reasoning: forming generalisations (which may be probable but are not certain) from examples or sample phenomena.

deductive reasoning: reasoning to a conclusion from some set of premises or statements, where that conclusion follows necessarily from the assumption that the premises are true.

INDUCTIVE REASONING

Nearly all our reasoning in everyday life is inductive rather than deductive. Our world is full of uncertainties and unexpected events, and so most of the conclusions we draw when reasoning are subject to change over time. Here is an example of inductive reasoning based on an imaginary newspaper article (Sternberg and Ben-Zeev (2001, p. 117):

Olga, dubbed the funniest woman in the world, lives in a little village in Iceland. Olga performs in local entertainment shows, making her audience laugh for up to five hours straight. People are often forced to leave her show early, in fits of uncontrollable giggling, to prevent bodily harm.

If we assume the article was correct when written earlier today, we can put forward the following arguments with confidence:

(1)   The funniest living woman in the world today lives in Iceland.
(2)   Olga is the funniest woman in the world.

Here is a conclusion we might wish to draw:

The funniest living woman in the world tomorrow will live in Iceland.

This conclusion represents inductive reasoning, because it is only highly probable that it will turn out to be true. Olga may die in a car crash today; she may lose her voice overnight; and so on.

There are many forms of inductive reasoning. One of the main forms is analogical reasoning, in which an individual tries to solve a current problem by retrieving information about a similar problem that was successfully solved in the past (see Chapter 13). Here, we will focus on hypothesis testing, which is much used in science.

Hypothesis testing: 2–4–6 task

Karl Popper (1968) argued that there is an important distinction between confirmation and falsification. **Confirmation** involves the attempt to obtain evidence that will confirm the correctness of one's hypothesis. In contrast, **falsification** involves the attempt to falsify hypotheses by experimental tests. According to Popper, it is impossible to achieve confirmation via hypothesis testing. Even if all the evidence accumulated so far supports a hypothesis, future evidence may disprove it. In Popper's opinion, falsification separates scientific from unscientific activities such as religion and pseudo-science (e.g., psychoanalysis).

It follows from Popper's analysis that scientists should focus on falsification. However, much of the evidence suggests they seek confirmatory rather than disconfirmatory evidence when testing their hypotheses! It has also been claimed that the same excessive focus on confirmatory evidence is found in laboratory studies on hypothesis testing, to which we now turn.

Wason (1960) devised a hypothesis-testing task that has attracted much interest. Participants were told that three numbers 2–4–6 conformed to a simple relational rule. Their task was to generate sets of three numbers, and to provide reasons for each choice. After each choice, the experimenter indicated whether the set of numbers conformed to the rule the experimenter had in mind. The task was to discover the rule, which was: "Three numbers in ascending order of magnitude." The rule sounds simple, but it took most participants a long time to discover it. Only 21% of them were correct with their first attempt, and 28% never discovered the rule at all.

Why was performance so poor on the 2–4–6 problem? According to Wason (1960), most people show **confirmation bias**, i.e., they try to generate numbers conforming to their original hypothesis. For example, participants whose original hypothesis or rule was that the second number is twice the first, and the third number is three times the first number tended to generate sets of numbers consistent with that hypothesis (e.g., 6–12–18; 50–100–150). Wason argued that confirmation bias and failure to try hypothesis disconfirmation prevented participants from replacing their initial hypothesis (which was too narrow and specific) with the correct general rule.

We will shortly consider evidence relating to this issue of confirmation bias. Before doing so, however, we need to consider the distinction between confirmation and positivity (Wetherick, 1962). A positive test means the numbers you produce are an instance of your hypothesis. However, this is only confirmatory if you believe your hypothesis to be correct. Consider negative tests, in which the numbers you produce do *not* conform to your hypothesis. In that case, discovering that your set of numbers does not conform to the rule actually confirms your hypothesis!

Evidence

The main prediction following from Wason's theoretical position is that people should perform better when instructed to engage in disconfirmatory testing. The evidence is inconsistent. Poletiek (1996) found that instructions to disconfirm produced more negative tests. However, participants generally expected these negative tests to receive a "No" response, and so they actually involved confirmation.

Klayman and Ha (1987, p. 212) argued that the participants in Wason's studies were producing positive tests of their hypotheses: "You test an hypothesis by examining instances in which the property or event is expected to occur (to see if it does occur), or by examining instances in which it is known to have occurred (to see if the hypothesised conditions prevail)." The difficulty with the 2–4–6 task is that it possesses the unusual characteristic that the correct rule is much more *general* than any of the initial hypotheses participants are likely to form. As a

result, positive testing cannot lead to discovery of the correct rule and so negative testing is required. However, positive testing is often more likely than negative testing to lead to falsification of incorrect hypotheses provided that the numbers of instances conforming to the hypothesis are approximately equal to those conforming to the actual rule. For example, if the rule is "ascending by twos", then positive testing will often lead to hypothesis falsification and rule discovery.

The importance of *negative* evidence on a version of the 2–4–6 task was shown by Rossi, Caverni, and Girotto (2001). They used the reverse rule to Wason (1960), namely, "descending numbers", and participants were presented initially with the number triple 2–4–6 or 6–4–2. There was a dramatic difference in first-attempt solvers between the two conditions: 54% of those receiving 2–4–6 versus only 16% among those receiving 6–4–2. Why was there this large difference? Those presented with 2–4–6 experienced much more negative evidence via producing triples not conforming to the rule. This negative evidence forced them to revise their hypotheses and this promoted rule discovery.

Tweney et al. (1980) discovered one of the most effective ways of enhancing performance on the 2–4–6 task. Participants were told the experimenter had *two* rules in mind and it was their task to identify these rules. One of these rules generated DAX triples whereas the other rule generated MED triples. They were also told that 2–4–6 was a DAX triple. Whenever the participants generated a set of three numbers, they were informed whether the set fitted the DAX rule or the MED rule. The correct answer was that the DAX rule was any three numbers in ascending order and the MED rule covered all other sets of numbers.

Over 50% of the participants produced the correct answer on their first attempt. This

KEY TERM

confirmation bias: a greater focus on evidence apparently confirming one's hypothesis than on disconfirming evidence.

was much higher than when the 2–4–6 problem was presented in its standard version. An important reason for this high level of success was that participants could use positive testing and did not have to focus on disconfirmation of hypotheses. They could identify the DAX rule by confirming the MED rule, and so they did not have to try to disconfirm the DAX rule.

Gale and Bull (2009) argued that the use of complementary DAX and MED rules does not ensure that the DAX rule will be discovered. What matters is how easy it is for participants to identify the crucial *dimensions* of ascending versus descending numbers. They always used 2–4–6 as an exemplar of a DAX. However, participants were given 6–4–2 or 4–4–4 as an exemplar of a MED. Success in identifying the DAX rule was considerably greater when the MED exemplar consisted of descending numbers than when it consisted of identical numbers (74% versus 20%). Gale and Bull found that no participants solved the DAX rule without producing at least one descending triple, which further indicates the importance of the ascending–descending dimension.

Vallée-Tourangeau and Payton (2008) pointed out that participants in studies on the 2–4–6 problem typically only make use of an internal representation of the problem. However, in the real world, people engaged in hypothesis testing often produce external representations (e.g., diagrams; graphs) to assist them. In their study, Vallée-Tourangeau and Payton provided half of their participants with a diagrammatic representation of each set of numbers they generated. This proved very successful – the success rate on the problem was 44% compared to only 21% for those participants who tried to solve the problem under standard conditions. The provision of an external representation led participants to be less constrained in their selection of hypotheses.

Evaluation

The 2–4–6 task has proved a valuable source of information about inductive reasoning. The original notion that most people display confirmation bias is no longer accepted. One reason is because it can be misleading to describe people's strategies as biased. Another reason is because people's behaviour is often more accurately described as confirmatory or positive testing.

To what extent can we generalise findings from the 2–4–6 task? There are three main concerns on this score. First, as emphasised by Klayman and Ha (1987), the 2–4–6 task penalises positive testing because the target rule is extremely general. However, the real world does not (Ken Mantelow, personal communication).

Second, Cherubini, Castelvecchio, and Cherubini (2005) showed how easily the findings on the 2–4–6 task could be altered. They argued that people try to preserve as much information as possible in their initial hypothesis. As expected, participants given two triples such as 6–8–10 and 16–18–20 tended to produce "increasing by twos" as their first hypothesis. Of more interest, participants given two triples such as 6–8–10 and 9–14–15 tended to produce much more general hypotheses (e.g., "increasing numbers"). Thus, it is very easy to change the nature of the initial hypothesis offered by participants performing the 2–4–6 task.

Second, additional factors may come into play in the real world. For example, professional scientists often focus their research on trying to disconfirm the theories of other scientists. In 1977, the first author took part in a conference on the levels-of-processing approach to learning and memory (see Chapter 6). Almost without exception, the research presented was designed to identify limitations and problems with that approach.

Hypothesis testing: simulated and real research environments

Mynatt, Doherty, and Tweney (1977) found evidence of confirmation bias in a simulation world apparently closer to real scientific testing than the 2–4–6 task. In this computer world, participants fired particles at circles and triangles presented at two brightness levels (low and high). The world had other features, but all were irrelevant to the task (see Figure 14.1). Participants were not told that the lower-brightness shapes had a 4.2 cm invisible boundary around them that deflected particles. At the start of

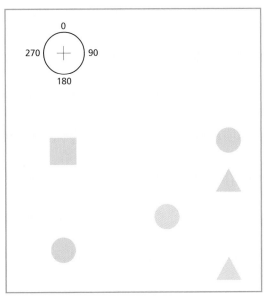

Figure 14.1 The type of display used by Mynatt et al. (1977) to study confirmation bias. Participants had to direct a particle that was fired from the upper left part of the screen, by selecting the direction of its path. The relative shading of the objects indicates the two levels of brightness at which objects were presented.

the experiment, they were shown arrangements of shapes suggesting the initial hypothesis that "triangles deflect particles".

Subsequently, participants were divided into three groups instructed to adopt a confirmatory strategy, a disconfirmatory strategy, or no particular strategy (i.e., a control group). They chose to continue the experiment on one of two screens:

(1) A screen containing similar features to those that deflected particles; on this screen, participants' observations would probably confirm their initial incorrect hypothesis.
(2) A screen containing novel features; on this screen, other hypotheses could be tested.

Mynatt et al. (1977) found that 71% of the participants chose the first screen, thus providing some evidence for a confirmation bias. Furthermore, instructions to use disconfirmatory testing did not deflect participants from this confirmation bias. Dunbar (1993) used a simulated research environment. Participants were given the difficult task of providing an explanation for the ways in which genes are controlled by other genes using a computer-based molecular genetics laboratory. The difficulty of the task can be seen in the fact that solving this problem in real life had led to the award of the Nobel Prize! The participants were led to focus on the hypothesis that the gene control was by activation, whereas it was actually by inhibition.

Dunbar (1993) found that those participants who simply tried to find data consistent with their activation hypothesis failed to solve the problem. In contrast, the 20% of participants who solved the problem set themselves the goal of explaining the discrepant findings. According to the participants' own reports, most started with the general hypothesis that activation was the key controlling process. They then applied this hypothesis in specific ways, focusing on one gene after another as the potential activator. It was typically only when all the various specific activation hypotheses had been disconfirmed that some participants focused on explaining the data not fitting the general activation hypothesis.

How closely do the above findings resemble those in real research environments? Mitroff (1974) studied geologists involved in the Apollo space programme as experts in lunar geology. They devoted most of their time to trying to confirm rather than falsify their hypotheses. However, they were not opposed to the notion of falsifying other scientists' hypotheses. Their focus on confirmation rather than falsification resembles that found in participants in simulated research environments. However, the real scientists were more reluctant than the participants in simulated research environments to abandon their hypotheses. There are probably two main reasons for this:

(1) The real scientists emphasised the value of commitment to a given position as a motivating factor.
(2) Real scientists are more likely than participants in an experiment to attribute contrary findings to deficiencies in the measuring instruments.

According to Gorman (1995), Alexander Graham Bell, in his research on the development of the telephone, showed evidence of confirmation bias – he continued to focus on undulating current and electromagnets even after good results had been obtained with liquid devices.

The issue of whether real scientists focus on confirmation or disconformation was considered by Gorman (1995) in an analysis of Alexander Graham Bell's research on the development of the telephone. Bell showed evidence of confirmation bias in that he continued to focus on undulating current and electromagnets even after he and others had obtained good results with liquid devices. For example, a liquid device was used to produce the first intelligible telephone call to Bell from his assistant, Watson, on 12 March 1876. More generally, it appears that some research groups focus on confirmation whereas others attach more importance to disconfirmation (Tweney & Chitwood, 1995).

Fugelsang, Stein, Green, and Dunbar (2004) carried out an interesting study to see how real scientists respond to falsifying evidence. The scientists were working on issues in molecular biology relating to how genes control and promote replication in bacteria, parasites, and viruses. Of 417 experimental results, over half (223) were inconsistent with the scientists' predictions. The scientists responded to 88% of these inconsistent findings by blaming problems on their method (e.g., wrong incubation temperature). In only 12% of cases did the scientists modify their theories to accommodate the inconsistent findings. Thus, the scientists showed considerable reluctance to change their original theoretical position.

Approximately two-thirds of the inconsistent findings were followed up, generally by changing the methods used. In 55% of cases, the inconsistent findings were replicated. The scientists' reactions were very different this time, with 61% of the repeated inconsistent findings being interpreted by changing some of their theoretical assumptions.

How defensible was the behaviour of the scientists studied by Fugelsang et al. (2004)? Note that almost half of the inconsistent findings were not replicated when a second study was carried out. Thus, it was reasonable for the scientists to avoid prematurely accepting findings that might be spurious.

Evaluation

It used to be believed that the optimal approach to scientific research was based on Popper's notion of falsifiability. Scientists should focus on negative evidence that might falsify their hypotheses because it is impossible to confirm the correctness of a hypothesis. It is now generally accepted that Popper's views were oversimplified and that confirmation is often appropriate (e.g., during the development of a new theory). Popper's approach is impractical because it is based on the assumption that research findings can provide *decisive* evidence falsifying a hypothesis. In fact, as we have seen, findings apparently falsifying hypotheses in molecular biology often cannot be replicated (Fugelsang et al., 2004). Such variability in findings is likely to be greater in a statistical science such as psychology.

Findings in simulated research environments have various limitations. First, the commitment that motivates real researchers to defend their own theories and try to disprove those of other researchers is lacking. Second, real scientists typically work in teams, whereas participants in simulated research environments sometimes work on their own (e.g., Dunbar, 1993). Okada and Simon (1997) found using Dunbar's (1993) genetic control task that pairs performed better than individuals. This was because they entertained hypotheses more often, considered alternative ideas more frequently, and discussed ways of justifying ideas more of the time. Thus, we cannot safely generalise from studies using individual participants. Third, the strategies used in hypothesis testing probably vary as a function of the precision of the hypotheses being tested and the reliability of the findings relevant to those hypotheses. As yet, however, these factors have not been manipulated systematically in simulated research environments.

DEDUCTIVE REASONING

Researchers have used numerous deductive reasoning problems. However, we will initially focus on conditional reasoning and syllogistic reasoning problems based on traditional systems of logic. After we have discussed the relevant research, theoretical explanations of the findings will be considered. As mentioned already, the evidence suggests that most people do not reason in a logical way on deductive-reasoning problems, which helps to explain why their performance on such problems is often relatively poor. As we will see, other factors are also involved. For example, the successful solution of deductive-reasoning problems often requires us to avoid making use of our knowledge of the world.

Conditional reasoning

Conditional reasoning (basically, reasoning with "if") has been studied to decide whether human reasoning is logical. It has its origins in propositional logic, in which logical operators such as *or, and, if . . . then, if and only if* are included in sentences or propositions. In this logical system, symbols are used to stand for sentences, and logical operators are applied to them to reach conclusions. Thus, in propositional logic we might use P to stand for the proposition, "It is raining", and Q to stand for "Nancy gets wet", and then use the logical operator

if . . . then to relate these two propositions: *if P then Q.*

The meanings of words and propositions in propositional logic differ from their meanings in natural language. For example, in this logical system, propositions can only have one of two truth values: they are either true or false. If *P* stands for "It is raining", then *P* is either true (in which case it is raining) or false (it is not raining). Propositional logic does not admit any uncertainty about the truth of *P* (where it is not really raining but is so misty you could almost call it raining).

Differences of meaning between propositional logic and ordinary language are especially great with respect to "*if . . . then*". Consider the following, which involves *affirmation of the consequent*:

> *Premises*
> If Susan is angry, then I am upset.
> I am upset.
> *Conclusion*
> Therefore, Susan is angry.

Do you accept the above conclusion as valid? Many people would, but it is not valid according to propositional logic. This is because I may be upset for some other reason (e.g., I have lost my job).

We will now consider other concrete problems in conditional reasoning, starting with the following one:

> *Premises*
> If it is raining, then Nancy gets wet.
> It is raining.
> *Conclusion*
> Nancy gets wet.

This conclusion is valid. It illustrates an important rule of inference known as *modus ponens*: "If A, then B" and also given "A", we can validly infer B.

Another major rule of inference is *modus tollens*: from the premise "If A, then B", and the premise, "B is false", the conclusion "A is false" necessarily follows. This rule of inference is shown in the following example:

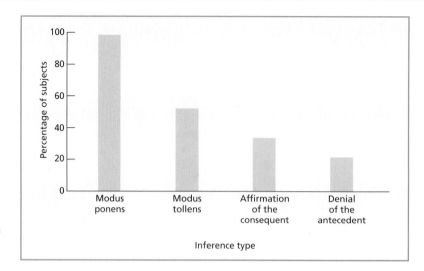

Figure 14.2 The
percentage of subjects
endorsing the various
conditional inferences from
Marcus and Rips (1979,
Experiment 2).

Premises
If it is raining, then Nancy gets wet.
Nancy does not get wet.
Conclusion
It is not raining.

People consistently perform much better with modus ponens than modus tollens.

Another inference in conditional reasoning is known as *denial of the antecedent*:

Premises
If it is raining, then Nancy gets wet.
It is not raining.
Conclusion
Therefore, Nancy does not get wet.

Many people would argue that the above conclusion is valid, but it is actually invalid. It does not have to be raining for Nancy to get wet (e.g., she might have jumped into a swimming pool).

The above conclusion is invalid in terms of traditional logic. However, in natural language, "If A, then B" often means "If and only if A, then B". Here is an example. If someone says to you, "If you mow the lawn, I will give you five dollars", then you are likely to interpret it to imply, "If you don't mow the lawn, I won't give you five dollars." Nearly 100% of the participants made the valid modus ponens

inference, but far fewer made the valid modus tollens inference (see Figure 14.2). Many people accepted the two invalid inferences, especially affirmation of the consequent. In other studies, denial of the consequent has often been accepted more often than affirmation of the consequent (Evans, Newstead, & Byrne, 1993).

We have seen that people often make mistakes in conditional reasoning. Even stronger evidence that we have only limited ability to reason logically comes from studies involving the addition of contextual information to a problem. Context effects can greatly impair performance on conditional reasoning tasks. Byrne (1989) compared conditional reasoning performance under standard conditions with a context condition: Additional argument or requirement (in brackets):

If she has an essay to write, then she
will study late in the library.
(If the library stays open, then she will
 study late in the library.)
She has an essay to write.
Therefore, ?

Byrne found that additional arguments led to a dramatic reduction in performance with modus ponens and modus tollens. Thus, we are greatly influenced by contextual information irrelevant to logical reasoning.

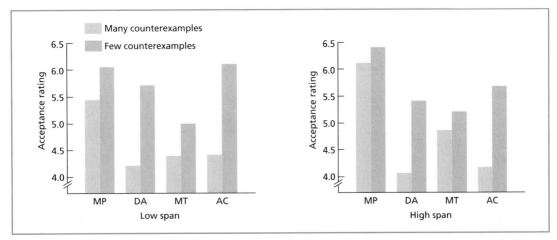

Figure 14.3 Acceptance ratings for valid syllogisms (MP = modus ponens; MT = modus tollens) and invalid syllogisms (DA = denial of the antecedent; AC = affirmation of the consequent) as a function of the number of counterexamples (few vs. many) and working memory capacity (low vs. high). From De Neys et al. (2005).

According to traditional logic, people's background knowledge should play no role in conditional reasoning. However, such knowledge typically has a major influence. De Neys, Schaeken, and d'Ydewalle (2005) argued that conditional reasoning is strongly influenced by the availability of knowledge in the form of counterexamples appearing to invalidate a given conclusion. For example, consider the above example on affirmation of the consequent. You might well be less inclined to accept the conclusion that Susan is angry if you could think of other possible reasons (counterexamples) why she might be upset. De Neys et al. used conditionals in which the number of counterexamples was low or high. The participants were either low or high in working memory capacity, a dimension closely related to intelligence.

What did De Neys et al. (2005) find? The results are shown in Figure 14.3. First, the number of available counterexamples had a major impact on performance. When there were many counterexamples, participants were less willing to accept conditional inferences whether the inferences were valid (modus ponens; modus tollens) or invalid (denial of the antecedent; affirmation of the consequent). Second, the reasoning performance of participants high in working memory capacity was better than that of those low in working memory capacity.

The findings of De Neys et al. (2005) indicate that performance on conditional reasoning tasks depends on individual differences. Bonnefon, Eid, Vautier, and Jmel (2008) explored individual differences in more detail. Their main focus was on conditional reasoning involving modus tollens, denial of the antecedent, and affirmation of the consequent. They argued that there are two processing systems individuals might use to solve conditional reasoning problems. System 1 is rapid and fairly automatic, whereas System 2 is slower and more demanding (these two systems are discussed in much more detail later in the chapter). Bonnefon et al. identified four major processing strategies on the basis of participants' performance:

(1) *Pragmatic strategy (System 1)*: This involved processing the problems as they would be processed informally during a conversation. This strategy was associated with numerous errors.

(2) *Semantic strategy (System 1)*: This involved making use of background knowledge but not of the form of argument in the problem. This strategy was associated with moderate performance.

(3) *Inhibitory strategy (System 2)*: This involved inhibiting the impact of the pragmatic strategy and background knowledge on

Figure 14.4 Rule: If there is an R on one side of the card, then there is a 2 on the other.

performance. This strategy worked well with some types of problem but not others.

(4) *Generative strategy (System 2)*: This involved combining the inhibitory strategy with use of abstract analytic processing. This strategy produced consistently good performance on all types of problem.

Summary

Various findings indicate that many people fail to think logically on conditional reasoning tasks. First, modus tollens is valid but is often regarded as invalid. Second, affirmation of the consequent and denial of the antecedent are both invalid but are sometimes seen as valid. Third, contextual information irrelevant to the validity of the conclusion nevertheless influences judgements of conclusion validity.

One of the major developments in research on conditional reasoning is the realisation that there are important individual differences in the strategies used by participants. For example, Bonnefon et al. (2008) identified four strategies, each of which was used by several participants. The ways in which the findings on conditional reasoning can be accounted for theoretically are discussed later in the chapter.

Wason selection task

The most celebrated (or notorious) task in the history of reasoning research was invented 50 years ago by the late British psychologist, Peter Wason, and is known as the Wason selection task. As Evans (2007) pointed out, this task has often been investigated by researchers primarily interested in deductive reasoning. However, it is more accurately described as a task that involves hypothesis testing using a conditional rule rather than a pure deductive-reasoning task.

In the standard version of the Wason task, there are four cards lying on a table. Each card has a letter on one side and a number on the other. The participant is told that a rule applies to the four cards (e.g., "If there is an R on one side of the cards, then there is a 2 on the other side of the card"). The task is to select *only* those cards that would need to be turned over to decide whether or not the rule is correct.

In one of the most used versions of this selection task, the four cards have the following symbols visible: R, G, 2, and 7 (see Figure 14.4), and the rule is the one just given. What is your answer to this problem? Most people select either the R card or the R and 2 cards. If you did the same, you got the answer wrong! You need to see whether any of the cards *fail* to obey the rule. From this perspective, the 2 card is irrelevant. If there is an R on the other side of it, then this only tells us the rule might be correct. If there is any other letter on the other side, then we have also discovered nothing about the validity of the rule. The correct answer is to select the cards with R and 7 on them, an answer given by only about 5–10% of university students. The 7 is necessary because it would definitely disprove the rule if it had an R on the other side.

Numerous attempts have been made to account for performance on the Wason selection task. One of the most successful was that of Evans (e.g., 1998), who identified matching bias as an important factor. **Matching bias** refers to the tendency for participants to select cards matching the items named in the rule regardless of whether the matched items are correct. There is much evidence for matching bias. For example, Ball, Lucas, Miles, and Gale (2003) used the following problems, with the percentage of participants choosing each card in brackets:

(1) Rule: If A, then 3
    Cards: A (87%), J (7%), 3 (60%), 7 (3%)
(2) Rule: If E, then not 5
    Cards: E (83%), L (23%), 2 (13%), 5 (43%)

As you can see, cards matching items in the rule were selected much more often than cards not matching items in the rule on both problems. What is striking about the findings is that selecting the number "3" in problem 1 is incorrect, whereas selecting the number "5" in problem 2 is correct. Thus, matching bias is often more important than the correctness or otherwise of the individual cards.

One likely reason why even highly intelligent individuals perform poorly on the Wason selection task is because it is abstract. Wason and Shapiro (1971) used four cards (Manchester, Leeds, car, and train) and the rule, "Every time I go to Manchester I travel by car". The correct answer (i.e., "Manchester" and "car") was given by 62% of the participants compared to only 12% given the standard abstract version of the task. However, other studies comparing concrete and abstract versions of the selection task have produced inconsistent findings (see Evans, 2002, for a review).

Stenning and van Lambalgen (2004) argued that many people have various difficulties in interpreting precisely what the selection problem is all about. First, the rule is proposed by an authoritative experimenter, which may bias participants in favour of assuming that it is very likely to be correct. Second, participants may not fully realise that they must make all their choices *before* receiving any feedback. Stenning and van Lambalgen found evidence that both of these difficulties reduced performance. Only 3.7% of participants given the standard instructions produced the correct answer. In contrast, 13% of those alerted to the possible falsity of the rule got the answer right, as did 18% of those explicitly warned that they would not receive any feedback before making all their choices.

It appears that more complex cognitive processes are required for successful performance on abstract versions of the Wason selection task than for concrete versions or deontic versions. Stanovich and West (1998) found that individual differences in cognitive ability were much more important in predicting correct solutions with the abstract selection task than either of the other two versions.

Social contract theory

The traditional Wason selection task involves an indicative rule (e.g., "If there is a *p*, then there is a *q*"). However, it is also possible to use a deontic rule (e.g., "If there is a p, then you *must* do q"). Deontic rules are concerned with detection of rule violation. They are typically easier for people to understand because the underlying structure of the problem is more explicit (e.g., the emphasis on disproving the rule). Unsurprisingly, performance on the Wason selection task is generally much better when deontic rules are used rather than indicative rules (Evans, 2007).

Cosmides (1989) proposed social contract theory to explain *why* deontic rules lead to superior performance. According to this theory, which was based on an evolutionary approach to cognition, people have rules maximising their

---

KEY TERM

matching bias: on the Wason selection task, the tendency to select those cards matching the items explicitly mentioned in the rule.

Cosmides (1989) used social contract theory to emphasise situations involving social exchange, in which two people must co-operate for mutual benefit (e.g., buying a bus ticket in order to travel).

ability to achieve their goals in social situations. Cosmides emphasised situations involving social exchange, in which two people must cooperate for mutual benefit. Of particular importance are social contracts based on an agreement that someone will only receive a benefit (e.g., travelling by train) provided they have incurred the appropriate cost (e.g., buying a ticket). Allegedly, people possess a "cheat-detecting algorithm" (computational procedure) allowing them to identify cases of cheating (e.g., travelling by train without having bought a ticket).

The main prediction from social contract theory is that people should perform especially well when the Wason selection task is phrased so that showing the rule is false involves detecting cheaters. Sperber and Girotto (2002) gave some of their participants a version of the selection task in which Paolo buys things through the Internet but is concerned he will be cheated.

For each order, he fills out a card. On one side of the card, he indicates whether he has received the item ordered, and on the other side he indicates whether he has paid for the items ordered. He places four orders, and what is visible on the four cards is as follows: "item paid for"; "item not paid for", "item received", and "item not received". Which cards does Paolo need to turn over to decide whether he has been cheated? Sperber and Girotto found that 68% of their participants made the correct choices (i.e., "item paid for"; "item not received").

Deontic versions of Wason's selection task are much easier than standard indicative versions in part because the structure of the problem is made more explicit. For example, cheating means we have fulfilled our side of the bargain but failed to receive the agreed benefit. Social contract theory may account for some findings involving cheating. However, it does not account for performance on most deontic and indicative versions of the task, and it has not been developed to explain reasoning on other tasks.

Sperber and Girotto (2002) argued that findings on Wason's selection task can be explained by their relevance theory. According to this theory, people simply engage in a comprehension process in which they evaluate the *relevance* of the four cards to the conditional rule. Worryingly for those who regard the Wason selection task as an important measure of deductive reasoning, Sperber and Girotto argued that people generally don't engage in reasoning at all!

Evaluation

A small percentage of individuals (mostly of high intelligence) obtain the correct answer on the standard Wason selection task, presumably because they use deductive reasoning. However, the great majority produce incorrect answers. This occurs because they use simple strategies like matching bias and/or because they do not understand fully what the task involves. Performance is substantially better with deontic rules than with indicative ones, because the former rules direct people's attention to the importance of disproving the rule rather than simply finding evidence consistent with it. Finally, note that Oaksford, Chater, Grainger, and Larkin (1997) put forward an alternative explanation of performance on the Wason selection task (discussed near the end of the chapter).

Syllogistic reasoning

Syllogistic reasoning has been studied for over 2000 years. A **syllogism** consists of two premises or statements followed by a conclusion. Here is an example of a syllogism: "All A are B. All B are C. Therefore, all A are C"). A syllogism contains three items (A, B, and C), with one of them (B) occurring in both premises. The premises and the conclusion each contain one of the following quantifiers: all; some; no; and some...not. Altogether, there are 64 different possible sets of premises. Each premise can be combined with eight possible conclusions to give a grand total of 512 possible syllogisms, most of which are invalid.

When you are presented with a syllogism, you have to decide whether the conclusion is valid in the light of the premises. The validity (or otherwise) of the conclusion depends *only* on whether it follows logically from the premises. The truth or falsity of the conclusion in the real world is irrelevant. Consider the following example:

Premises
All children are obedient.
All girl guides are children.
Conclusion
Therefore, all girl guides are obedient.

The conclusion follows logically from the premises. Thus, it is valid regardless of your views about the obedience of children.

Evidence

People often make errors in syllogistic reasoning, in part because of the existence of various biases. For example, there is **belief bias**: this is a tendency to accept invalid conclusions if they are believable and to reject valid conclusions when they are unbelievable. The belief-bias

effect was investigated by Klauer, Musch, and Naumer (2000). In their study on syllogistic reasoning, half the conclusions were believable (e.g., "Some fish are not trout"), whereas the others were unbelievable (e.g., "Some trout are not fish"). In addition, half of the syllogisms were valid and the remainder invalid. However, some participants were told that only one-sixth of the syllogisms were valid, whereas others were told that five-sixths were valid.

What did Klauer et al. (2000) find? First, they obtained a base-rate effect: syllogistic reasoning performance was influenced by the perceived probability of syllogisms being valid (see Figure 14.5). Second, Klauer et al. reported strong evidence for belief bias: valid and invalid conclusions were more likely to be endorsed as valid when believable than when they were unbelievable (see Figure 14.5). Both of these findings indicate that participants' decisions on the validity of syllogism conclusions were influenced by factors having nothing to do with logic.

We will see shortly that major theories of deductive reasoning have shed much light on the processes underlying belief bias. For now, we will briefly consider some of the problems caused by the differences between the meanings of expressions in formal logic and in everyday life. For example, we often assume that, "All As are Bs" means that "All Bs are As", and that, "Some As are not Bs" means that "Some Bs are not As". Ceraso and Provitera (1971) tried to prevent these misinterpretations by spelling out the premises unambiguously (e.g., "All As are Bs, but some Bs are not As"). This produced a substantial improvement in performance.

KEY TERMS

syllogism: a logical argument consisting of two premises (e.g., "All X are Y") and a conclusion; syllogisms formed the basis of the first logical system attributed to Aristotle.
belief bias: in syllogistic reasoning, the tendency to accept invalid conclusions that are believable and to reject valid conclusions that are unbelievable.

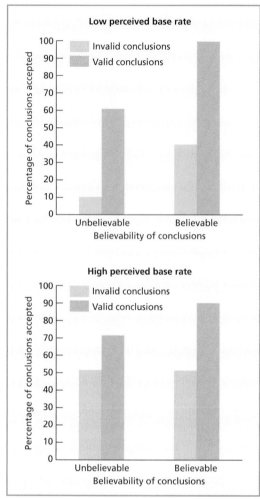

Figure 14.5 Percentage acceptance of conclusions as a function of perceived base rate (low vs. high), believability of conclusions, and validity of conclusions. Based on data in Klauer et al. (2000).

Schmidt and Thompson (2008) pointed out that "some" means "at least one and possibly all" in formal logic but it means "some but not all" in everyday usage. They found that performance on a syllogistic reasoning task improved when the meaning of "some" in formal logic was made explicit.

Summary

Most people find it hard (or impossible) to reason logically on syllogistic reasoning problems. An important reason for error-prone performance on such problems is because the meanings of various words and expressions in formal logic differ significantly from their meanings in everyday life. We turn now to theoretical accounts of the processes involved in conditional and syllogistic reasoning.

THEORIES OF DEDUCTIVE REASONING

There are more theories of deductive reasoning than you can shake a stick at. However, the theoretical approach that has been most influential over the past 20 years or so is probably the mental model theory put forward by Johnson-Laird (1983, 1999). Accordingly, that is the first theory we will consider. After that, we turn our attention to the dual-system approach that is rapidly gaining in popularity. There are several dual-system theories, but they are all based on the assumption that reasoning can involve two very different processing systems. What is of central importance to both theoretical approaches is to explain *why* nearly everyone makes many errors on deductive reasoning tasks and to provide a persuasive account of the processes underlying these errors.

Mental models

Johnson-Laird (1983, 1999) argues that individuals carrying out a reasoning task construct one or more mental models. What is a **mental model**? According to Johnson-Laird (2004, p. 170), "Each mental model represents a possibility, capturing what is common to the different ways in which the possibility could occur." For example, a tossed coin has an infinite number of trajectories, but there are only two mental models: heads; tails. In simple terms, a mental model generally represents a possible state-of-affairs in the world. Here is a concrete example:

KEY TERM

mental model: a representation of a possible state-of-affairs in the world.

Premises
The lamp is on the right of the pad.
The book is on the left of the pad.
The clock is in front of the book.
The vase is in front of the lamp.
Conclusion
The clock is to the left of the vase.

According to Johnson-Laird (1983), people use the information contained in the premises to construct a mental model like this:

book   pad   lamp
clock   vase

The conclusion that the clock is on the left of the vase clearly follows from the mental model. The fact that we cannot construct a mental model inconsistent with the conclusion indicates that it is valid.

Johnson-Laird has developed and extended his mental model theory over the years. Here are some of its main assumptions:

- A mental model describing the given situation is constructed, and the conclusions following from the model are generated.
- An attempt is made to construct alternative models that will falsify the conclusion. In other words, there is a search for counter-examples to the conclusion.
- If a counterexample model is not found, the conclusion is assumed to be valid.
- The construction of mental models involves the limited processing resources of working memory (see Chapter 6).
- Deductive reasoning problems requiring the construction of several mental models are harder to solve than problems requiring the construction of only one mental model because of the increasing demands on working memory.
- The **principle of truth**: "Individuals minimise the load on working memory by tending to construct mental models that represent explicitly only what is true, and not what is false." For example, consider the following sentence taken from Johnson-Laird, Legrenzi, and Girotto (2004):

"There is either a circle on the board or a triangle, or both." Johnson-Laird et al. argued that most people presented with that sentence would construct three mental models: (1) circle; (2) triangle; (3) circle + triangle. Note that what is false is omitted. Strictly speaking, the first mental model should include the information that it is false that there is a triangle.

In sum, Johnson-Laird (1999, p. 130) argued, "Reasoning is just the continuation of comprehension by other means." Successful thinking results from the use of appropriate mental models and unsuccessful thinking occurs when we use inappropriate mental models or fail to construct relevant mental models.

Evidence

According to the mental model approach, people's ability to construct mental models is constrained by the limited capacity of working memory. This assumption was tested by Copeland and Radvansky (2004). Participants indicated what conclusions followed validly from sets of premises, and the demands on working memory were varied by manipulating the number of mental models consistent with the premises. Eighty-six per cent of participants drew the valid conclusion when the premises only allowed the generation of one mental model. This figure dropped to 39% when two mental models were possible and to 31% with three mental models.

Copeland and Radvansky (2004) tested the hypothesis that reasoning performance depends on the limitations of working memory in a second way. They assessed participants' working memory capacity, and predicted that those with high working memory capacity would perform better than those with low working memory capacity. As predicted, there was a moderate

> **KEY TERM**
>
> **principle of truth:** the notion that we represent assertions by constructing **mental models** concerning what is true but not what is false.

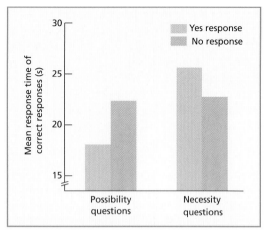

Figure 14.6 Mean response times (in seconds) for correct responses (yes and no) to possibility and necessity questions. Based on data in Bell and Johnson-Laird (1998).

correlation (+0.42) between working memory capacity and syllogistic reasoning.

It is demanding to construct a mental model. As a result, it is predicted from mental model theory that reasoning problems requiring the construction of several mental models would take longer than those requiring only one. Copeland and Radvansky (2004) found that the mean response time with one-model syllogisms was 25 seconds. This increased to 29 seconds with two-model syllogisms and to 33 seconds with three-model ones.

Bell and Johnson-Laird (1998) tested the assumption that the construction of mental models is time-consuming in a different way. They argued that a single mental model can establish that something is possible but *all* mental models must be constructed to show that something is not possible. In contrast, all mental models must be constructed to show that something is necessary, but *one* model can show that something is not necessary. Bell and Johnson-Laird used reasoning problems consisting of premises followed by a question about possibilities (e.g., "Can Betsy be in the game?") or a question about a necessity (e.g., "Must Betsy be in the game?").

According to the theory, people should respond faster to *possibility* questions when

the correct answer is "Yes" rather than "No". However, they should respond faster to *necessity* questions when the answer is "No" rather than "Yes". That is precisely what Bell and Johnson-Laird (1998) found (see Figure 14.6).

Legrenzi, Girotto, and Johnson-Laird (2003) tested the principle of truth. Participants decided whether descriptions of everyday objects (e.g., a chair) were consistent or inconsistent. Some of the descriptions were constructed so that participants would be lured into error (illusory inferences) if they adhered to the principle of truth. These illusory inferences were either that a description was consistent when it was inconsistent or inconsistent when it was consistent. Here is an example of an inference that was typically interpreted as consistent (valid) when it is actually inconsistent (invalid):

Only one of the following assertions is true: The tray is heavy or elegant, or both. The tray is elegant and portable. The following assertion is definitely true: The tray is elegant and portable.

(If the final assertion were true, that would make *both* of the initial assertions true as well. However, the problem states that only *one* is true.)

There was convincing evidence for the predicted illusory inferences (see Figure 14.7) when the principle of truth did not permit the correct inferences to be drawn. In contrast, performance was very high on control problems where adherence to the principle of truth was sufficient.

Theoretically, individuals make illusory inferences because they fail to think about what is false. They should be less susceptible to such inferences if explicitly instructed to falsify the premises of reasoning problems. Newsome and Johnson-Laird (2006) found that participants made significantly fewer illusory inferences when given such explicit instructions.

According to Johnson-Laird's theory, people search for counterexamples after having constructed their initial mental model and generated a conclusion. As a result, they will often consider

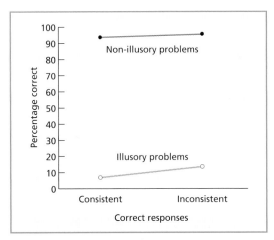

Figure 14.7 Percentage of correct responses to problems that were predicted to be susceptible (illusory problems) or not susceptible (non-illusory problems) to illusory references. Data from Legrenzi et al. (2003).

several conclusions and may construct several mental models. Newstead, Handley, and Buck (1999) compared performance on syllogisms permitting either one or multiple mental models. Theoretically, more conclusions should have been considered with the multiple-model than with the single-model syllogisms. In fact, there was no difference – 1.12 and 1.05 conclusions were considered on average with multiple- and single-model syllogisms, respectively. In a further experiment, Newstead et al. asked participants to draw diagrams of the mental models they were forming while working on syllogisms. The participants consistently failed to produce more mental models on multiple-model problems than on single-model ones.

Earlier we discussed belief bias in syllogistic reasoning. This bias involves deciding that believable conclusions are valid and unbelievable ones are invalid regardless of their actual validity. According to mental model theory, people generally accept believable conclusions but unbelievable conclusions motivate them to engage in a deeper and more time-consuming analysis. These assumptions were tested by Ball, Phillips, Wade, and Quayle (2006). Participants were presented with syllogisms that were valid or invalid and in which the conclusions were believable or

unbelievable. Eye-movement recordings indicated that participants spent longer inspecting the premises of syllogisms when the conclusion was believable than when it was unbelievable. This is exactly the opposite of the prediction from mental model theory. Inspection times were especially long when the conclusion was invalid but believable because there is considerable conflict in this condition.

Mental model theory focuses on the *general* approach taken by people faced with reasoning problems, and cannot account readily for the wide range of *specific* strategies adopted. Bucciarelli and Johnson-Laird (1999) identified the initial strategies used by people given reasoning problems by videotaping them as they used cut-out shapes to evaluate valid and invalid syllogisms. Some participants started by forming a mental model of the first premise to which they then added information based on the second premise. Other participants proceeded in the opposite direction, and still others constructed an initial mental model satisfying the conclusion and then tried to show it was wrong.

Evaluation

Mental model theory accounts for reasoning performance across a wide range of problems, and most of its predictions have been confirmed experimentally. There is convincing evidence that many errors on deductive reasoning tasks occur because people use the principle of truth and ignore what is false (e.g., Legrenzi et al., 2003). Furthermore, the notion that reasoning involves similar processes to normal comprehension is a powerful one. An important implication is that the artificial problems used in most reasoning studies may be more relevant to everyday life than is generally supposed. Finally, there is good evidence (some discussed shortly) that our reasoning ability is limited by the constraints of working memory.

There are various limitations with the theory. First, it seems to assume that people engage in deductive reasoning to a greater extent than is actually the case. It may be more accurate to argue that most people find deductive reasoning very difficult and so generally engage in less precise and less effortful forms of processing. This issue is discussed later in connection with heuristic–analytic theory.

Second, the processes involved in forming mental models are under-specified. Johnson-Laird and Byrne (1991) argued that people use background knowledge when forming mental models. However, the theory does not spell out how we decide *which* pieces of information should be included in a mental model. As a result, "It [mental model theory] offers only relatively coarse predictions about the difficulties of different sorts of inference" (Johnson-Laird, 2004, p. 200).

Third, the theory tends to ignore individual differences. For example, Ford (1995) asked people solving syllogisms to say aloud what they were thinking while working on each problem. About 40% of the participants used spatial reasoning and a further 35% used verbal reasoning.

Fourth, it is assumed that people will try to produce mental models to falsify conclusions generated from their initial mental model. However, people (especially those with low working memory capacity) sometimes construct only a single mental model and so make no systematic attempts at falsification (Copeland & Radvansky, 2004; Newstead et al., 1999).

Fifth, there is increasing evidence that two very different processing systems are used when people try to solve reasoning problems. However, the distinction between rapid and relatively automatic processes, on the one hand, and slow and effortful processes, on the other, is not spelled out explicitly in mental model theory, although it is implicit (Evans, 2008).

Dual-system theories

In recent years, several researchers have put forward dual-system theories to account for human reasoning and other aspects of higher-level cognition (see Evans, 2008, for a review). In spite of some important differences among these theories, there are several common themes. As Evans (2008) pointed out, it is often assumed that one system (sometimes termed System 1) involves unconscious processes, emerged at an early stage of evolution, involves parallel processing, and is independent of general intelligence. The other system (sometimes called System 2) involves conscious processes, emerged recently in evolutionary history, involves rule-based, serial processing, has limited capacity, and is linked to general intelligence.

One of the most developed dual-system theories was put forward by Evans (2006; see Figure 14.8). In his heuristic–analytic theory of reasoning, heuristic processes are located within System 1 and analytic processes are located within System 2. When someone is presented with a reasoning problem, heuristic processes make use of task features, the current goal, and background knowledge to construct a single hypothetical possibility or mental model. Heuristic processes as defined by Evans (2006) need to be distinguished from heuristics or rules of thumb as defined by Kahneman and Tversky (see Chapter 13).

After that, time-consuming and effortful analytic processes may or may not intervene to revise or replace this mental model. Such interventions are most likely when: (1) the task instructions tell participants to use abstract or logical reasoning; (2) participants are highly intelligent; or (3) there is sufficient time available for effortful analytic processing. Note that the analytic system engages in various cognitive processes to evaluate mental models, and should *not* be regarded simply as a system based on logic. Involvement of the analytic system often leads to improved reasoning performance, but is not guaranteed to do so. For example, conclusions that could be true but are not necessarily true are often mistakenly accepted by the analytic system because of its reliance on the satisficing principle (see below).

In sum, human reasoning (and hypothetical thinking generally) is based on the use of three principles:

(1) *Singularity principle*: only a single mental model is considered at any given time.
(2) *Relevance principle*: the most relevant (i.e., plausible or probable) mental model based on prior knowledge and the current context is considered.

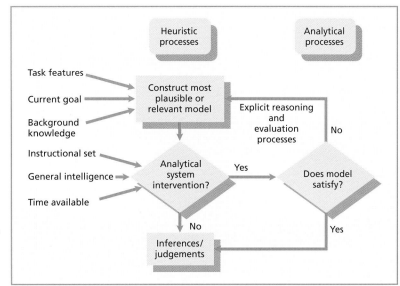

Figure 14.8 The heuristic–analytic theory of reasoning put forward by Evans (2006). From Evans (2006). Reprinted with permission of Psychonomic Society Publications.

(3) *Satisficing principle*: the current mental model is evaluated by the analytic system and accepted if adequate. Use of this principle often leads people to accept conclusions that could be true but aren't necessarily true.

Superficially, it may seem as if this heuristic–analytic theory is rather similar to Johnson-Laird's mental model theory. However, that is not actually the case. It is assumed within mental model theory that people initially use deductive reasoning which may then be affected by real-world knowledge. The sequence is basically the *opposite* in heuristic–analytic theory: people initially use their world knowledge and the immediate context in their reasoning, which may then be affected by deductive reasoning by the analytic system. In other words, deductive reasoning is regarded as much less important in heuristic–analytic theory than in mental model theory. According to Evans (2006, p. 392), "Deductive reasoning may be seen as no more than an analytic-level strategy that bright people can be persuaded to adopt by the use of special instructions."

Evidence

The heuristic system makes use of various heuristics depending on the precise nature of the reasoning problem that a reasoner is trying to solve. For example, as we saw earlier, an important heuristic used on the Wason selection task is matching bias. This bias leads people to select the cards stated in the rule regardless of their relevance.

One of the most useful phenomena for distinguishing between heuristic and analytic processes is belief bias, which was discussed earlier. This bias occurs when a conclusion that is logically valid but not believable is rejected as invalid, or a conclusion that is logically invalid but believable is accepted as valid. It is assumed that the presence or absence of this effect depends on a conflict between heuristic processes based on belief and analytic processes. More specifically, belief bias will be stronger when only heuristic processes are used than when analytic ones are also used. According to heuristic–analytic theory, analytic processes are more likely to be used (and performance will be better) when instructions stress the importance of logical reasoning. As predicted, Evans (2000) found less evidence of belief bias when the instructions emphasised logical reasoning than when they did not.

Intelligence correlates highly with working memory capacity. As a result, individuals high in working memory capacity should make more

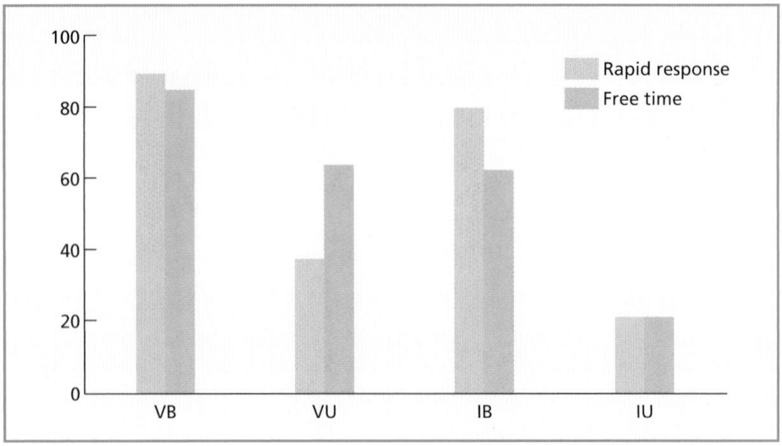

Figure 14.9 Percentage acceptance rates of four types of syllogism (VB = valid believable; VU = valid unbelievable; IB = invalid believable; IU = invalid unbelievable) in rapid response and free-time conditions. From Evans and Curtis-Holmes (2005).

extensive use of analytic processes than those low in working memory capacity. It is also predicted that the use of analytic processes while reasoning can be reduced by requiring participants to perform a demanding secondary task at the same time as the reasoning task. Both predictions were tested by De Neys (2006b). Participants low, medium, or high in working memory capacity were given a reasoning task. The task included belief-bias problems involving a conflict between validity and believability of the conclusion and which required the use of analytic processing for successful reasoning. There were also non-conflict problems that could be solved simply by using heuristic processes. The reasoning problems were presented on their own or at the same time as a secondary task low or high in its demands.

The findings of De Neys (2006b) show, as predicted, that high working memory capacity was only an advantage on conflict problems requiring the use of analytic processes. Also as predicted, a demanding secondary task impaired performance on conflict problems but not non-conflict ones.

Another prediction from heuristic–analytic theory is that the magnitude of belief bias should depend on the time available for thinking. Belief bias should be stronger when time is strictly limited and so it is difficult to use analytic processes. Evans and Curtis-Holmes (2005) used

two conditions: participants either had to respond within ten seconds or they had as much time as they wanted (free-time condition). It was expected that belief bias (rejecting unbelievable but valid conclusions and accepting believable but invalid conclusions) would be greater in the limited-time condition. However, when there was no conflict between validity and believability (i.e., valid believable conclusions and invalid unbelievable conclusions), it was expected that time pressure would have no effect on performance. As you can see in Figure 14.9, all these expectations were supported.

Ball, Lucas, Miles, and Gale (2003) recorded eye movements as people performed the Wason selection task, a study we discussed earlier. According to heuristic–analytic theory, various heuristics determine how participants allocate their attention to the four cards presented on the task. The most important heuristic is matching bias, which involves selecting cards that match items explicitly mentioned in the rule. Ball et al.'s findings supported that prediction. Another prediction from the theory is that participants should fixate selected cards for longer than non-selected cards. The reason is that participants use time-consuming analytic processes to justify their selections. The results were as predicted, with cards that tended to be selected being fixated for almost twice as long as cards that were generally not selected.

Oberauer (2006) considered the adequacy of several theories in accounting for the data from studies on conditional reasoning. There was the usual pattern of acceptance of the four major inferences: modus ponens (97%), modus tollens (57%), acceptance of the consequent (44%), and denial of the antecedent (38%). The two theories that best predicted the findings were a version of dual-process theory and a slightly modified version of mental models theory. Dual-process theory yielded somewhat better fits to the data. It also has the advantage that its general theoretical framework has been applied to several other types of human reasoning.

Evaluation

Evans' (2006) heuristic–analytic theory of reasoning has several successes to its credit. First, the overarching notion that the cognitive processes used by individuals to solve reasoning problems are essentially the same as those used in most other cognitive tasks seems to be essentially correct. For example, the use of heuristics is common in problem solving (see Chapter 12) and in judgement tasks (see Chapter 13), as well as in reasoning. Thus, the theory has wide applicability within cognitive research.

Second, most of the evidence supports the notion that thinking (including reasoning) is based on the singularity, relevance, and satisficing principles. Most of the errors that people make on reasoning problems can be explained in terms of their adherence to these principles at the expense of logic-based deductive reasoning. The theory has some advantages over mental model theory with its greater emphasis on deductive reasoning (Oberauer, 2006).

Third, there is convincing evidence for the distinction between heuristic and analytic processes, and for the notion that the latter are more effortful than the former (e.g., De Neys, 2006b). Phenomena such as belief bias and matching bias indicate the importance of heuristic processes.

Fourth, the theory accounts for some individual differences in performance on reasoning problems. For example, individuals high in working memory capacity or intelligence perform better than those low in working memory capacity or intelligence in part because they are more likely to use analytic processes.

There are various limitations with heuristic–analytic theory and the dual-process approach in general. First, it is rather an oversimplification to draw a simple distinction between implicit heuristic processes and explicit analytic processes. There is evidence that heuristic reasoning can be explicit and conscious and that analytic reasoning can be implicit and non-conscious (see Osman, 2004, for a review). Thus, there may be four kinds of process: implicit heuristic processing; implicit analytic processing; explicit heuristic processing; and explicit analytic processing. Earlier in the chapter we discussed research by Bonnefon et al. (2008), which suggested that two System 1 strategies and two System 2 strategies can be used on conditional reasoning tasks.

Second, it is assumed that there are several different kinds of analytic process (Evans, 2006), which vary in terms of how closely they approximate to logic-based deductive reasoning. However, it is not very clear precisely what these processes are or how individuals decide which analytic processes to use.

Third, it is assumed that heuristic and analytic processes interact with each other and often compete for control of behaviour. However, we do not know in detail how these different processes interact with each other.

BRAIN SYSTEMS IN THINKING AND REASONING

In recent years, there has been a substantial increase in research designed to identify the areas of the brain associated with the higher cognitive processes. Which parts of the brain are of most importance for problem solving, reasoning, and other forms of thinking? We will start by considering research on problem solving and intelligence. After that, we will focus on research on deductive and inductive reasoning.

Problem solving and intelligence

It has often been argued that the frontal lobes (one in each cerebral hemisphere) play a key role in problem solving. The frontal lobes are located in the front part of the brain and form about one-third of the cerebral cortex in humans. The posterior border of the frontal lobe with the parietal lobe is marked by the central sulcus (groove or furrow), and the frontal and temporal lobes are separated by the lateral fissure.

There is considerable evidence that the prefrontal cortex, which lies within the frontal lobes, is of special significance for various cognitive activities, including problem solving and reasoning. In humans, 50% of the entire frontal cortex consists of the prefrontal cortex. One fact suggesting that it may be of great importance for complex cognitive processing is that the prefrontal cortex is considerably larger in humans than in other mammalian species.

There is much evidence from brain-damaged patients that the frontal cortex is involved in problem solving. Owen et al. (1990) used a computerised version of the Tower of London problem, resembling the Tower of Hanoi problem discussed in Chapter 12. Patients with damage to the left frontal lobe, patients with damage to the right frontal lobe, and healthy controls did not differ in time to plan the first move. After that, however, both groups of frontal patients were much slower than the healthy controls, and required more moves to solve the problem. Goel and Grafman (1995) used a five-disc version of the Tower of Hanoi. Patients with prefrontal damage performed worse than healthy controls, even though both groups used the same strategy. These patients had special problems with complex forward planning – they did very poorly on a difficult move that required moving away from the goal.

Dagher et al. (1999) used functional neuro-imaging with the Tower of Hanoi task. Its more complex versions were associated with increased activation in the dorsolateral prefrontal cortex. Newman, Carpenter, Varma, and Just (2003) found evidence that certain brain areas may be associated with *specific* cognitive processes.

Participants performed easy, moderate, and difficult versions of the Tower of London task. The prefrontal cortex was activated during performance of all versions. However, the key findings were that *right* dorsolateral prefrontal cortex was associated with plan generation, whereas the *left* dorsolateral prefrontal cortex was associated with plan execution.

Evidence that the prefrontal cortex plays a major role in higher cognitive processes also comes from studies on intelligence. For example, Duncan et al. (2000) identified the brain regions most active when participants performed a wide range of tasks (e.g., spatial; verbal; perceptuo-motor) correlating highly with the general factor of intelligence ("g"). A specific region of the lateral frontal cortex in one or both hemispheres was highly active during the performance of virtually all the tasks. In similar fashion, Prabhakaran, Smith, Desmond, Glover, and Gabrieli (1997) used fMRI while participants performed the Raven's Progressive Matrices, which is a measure of intelligence. Brain activation levels were greatest in the dorsolateral prefrontal cortex and associated areas.

Jung and Haier (2007) reviewed 37 neuro-imaging studies in which intelligence and/or reasoning tasks had been used. On the basis of this evidence, they proposed their parieto-frontal integration theory, according to which parietal and frontal regions are of special importance in intelligence. More specifically, frontal regions associated with intelligence include the dorsolateral prefrontal cortex (BAs 6, 9, 10, 45, 46, and 47) and parietal regions including BAs 39 and 40. Additional regions associated with intelligence lie within the temporal lobes (BAs 21 and 37) and the occipital lobes (BAs 18 and 19).

Inductive and deductive reasoning

We saw earlier that there is an important distinction between inductive and deductive reasoning. To what extent do the brain areas involved in these two forms of reasoning differ? Goel and Dolan (2004) addressed this question using fMRI while participants engaged in

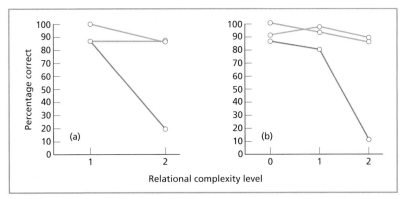

Figure 14.10 Accuracy on the test of transitive inference (a) and matrices test (b) for each group of participants. Results are shown for patients with prefrontal damage (purple lines), patients with anterior temporal damage (green lines), and normal control subjects (orange lines). From Waltz et al. (1999). Copyright © 1999 Blackwell Publishing. Reprinted with permission of Wiley-Blackwell.

deductive syllogistic reasoning and inductive reasoning. There were three main findings. First, inductive and deductive reasoning were both associated with activation in the left lateral prefrontal cortex and bilateral dorsal frontal, parietal, and occipital areas. Confirmation of the involvement of left prefrontal cortex in deductive reasoning was reported by Goel (2007). He reviewed 19 neuroimaging studies on deductive reasoning, and found that 18 of them obtained activation in that brain area.

Second, there was greater activation in the left inferior frontal gyrus (BA44) with deductive than with inductive reasoning. This part of the brain (sometimes known as Broca's area) is associated with language processing and the phonological loop of the working memory system. Its greater activation in deductive reasoning may be due to the greater involvement of syntactical processing and working memory on deductive-reasoning tasks.

Third, the left dorsolateral (BA8/9) prefrontal gyrus was more activated during induction than deduction. This is consistent with evidence from brain-damaged patients. Everyday reasoning primarily involves inductive reasoning, and patients with deficits in everyday reasoning typically have damage to the dorsolateral prefrontal cortex. Inductive reasoning tends to be influenced more by background knowledge in deductive reasoning, which may explain the involvement of dorsolateral prefrontal cortex in inductive reasoning.

We have seen that neuroimaging research implicates the prefrontal cortex as of central importance in deductive reasoning. The same conclusion follows from research on brain-damaged patients. For example, Waltz et al. (1999) argued that the prefrontal region is heavily involved in relational integration, by which they meant activities involving the manipulation and combination of the relations between objects and events. For example, consider a form of deductive reasoning known as transitive inference. Here is a transitive inference problem: Tom taller than William; William taller than Richard; William taller than Richard. The following transitive inference problem involves more complex relational integration: Bert taller than Matthew; Fred taller than Bert.

Waltz et al. (1999) tested groups of patients of similar IQs with prefrontal damage and patients with anterior temporal lobe damage. The two groups performed comparably on the simple version of the transitive inference task discussed above. However, the prefrontal patients were at a massive disadvantage on the more complex version (see Figure 14.10a).

Waltz et al. (1999) also tested the same groups of patients on a test of inductive reasoning involving matrix problems in which the appropriate stimulus to complete each pattern had to be selected. The extent to which relational integration was necessary for problem solution was manipulated. The pattern of findings was the same as with deductive reasoning (see

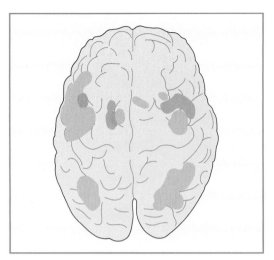

Figure 14.11 Brain areas showing increased activation with increases in relational complexity (green), increases in distortion (purple), and increases in both complexity and distortion (orange). Based on Kroger et al. (2002).

Figure 14.10b): the two groups performed comparably when little relational integration was required. However, the prefrontal patients were dramatically worse than the anterior temporal patients when the task required substantial relational integration. Thus, the prefrontal cortex seems crucial for relational integration on reasoning problems.

Kroger, Sabb, Fales, Bookheimer, Cohen, and Holyoak (2002) put forward a similar (but more specific) theory, according to which tasks of high relational complexity are associated with activation of the dorsolateral prefrontal cortex. They gave healthy participants reasoning problems varying in relational complexity adapted from an intelligence test. They also manipulated task difficulty by varying the number of distracting stimuli. Activation of the dorsolateral prefrontal cortex increased progressively with increases in relational complexity (see Figure 14.11). In contrast, increasing the amount of distraction had little effect on such activation, indicating that activation of the dorsolateral prefrontal cortex was due to relational complexity rather than simply to task difficulty.

Ramnani and Owen (2004) put forward a theory overlapping with the theoretical views of Kroger et al. (2002). They focused on the anterior prefrontal cortex (BA10), which is right at the front of the brain, and which forms part of the brain areas identified by Kroger et al. as being involved in processing relational complexity. According to Ramnani and Owen (2004, p. 190), "The aPFC [anterior prefrontal cortex] is engaged when…the integration of the results of two or more separate cognitive operations is required." Such integration resembles (but is broader than) relational integration. It seems that the anterior prefrontal cortex is the only part of the brain interconnected exclusively with other parts of the prefrontal cortex and so removed from processes concerned with perception or action. That strengthens the argument that that area integrates the outcomes of previous cognitive processes.

Evidence supporting the involvement of anterior prefrontal cortex (BA10) in deductive reasoning was reported by Monti, Osherson, Martinez, and Parsons (2007). They identified various brain regions associated with deductive reasoning but independent of brain regions associated with language processing. The two most important brain regions were the left anterior prefrontal cortex (BA10) and bilateral medial prefrontal cortex (BA8).

Goel and Dolan (2003) obtained additional evidence for the existence of two systems in reasoning. Participants received syllogisms, and decided whether the conclusions followed validly from the premises. Of most importance is what happened when the conclusion was valid but unbelievable or invalid but believable. When participants made the logically correct decision, there was activation of the right inferior prefrontal cortex (see Figure 14.12a). This presumably reflected the involvement of analytic, System 2 processes. According to Goel and Dolan (p. 19), "We conjecture that right prefrontal cortex involvement in correct response trials is detecting and/or resolving the conflict between belief and logic." When participants made the incorrect decision (and so showed belief bias), there was activation of the ventral medial prefrontal cortex (see Figure 14.12b). Such activation presumably reflects the use of heuristic, System 2 processes.

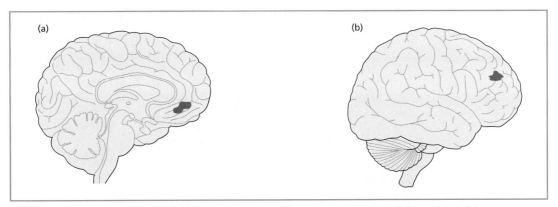

Figure 14.12 Brain activation when there was a conflict between conclusion validity and belief. Brain areas more activated when responses were correct than incorrect are shown in (a), and brain areas more activated when responses were incorrect than correct are shown in (b). Based on data in Goel and Dolan (2003).

The neuroimaging data reported in most studies indicate those brain areas that were activated during the course of a reasoning task. However, such data fail to indicate the precise stage of processing during which each brain area was activated. This omission was dealt with by Fangmeier, Knauff, Ruff, and Sloutsky (2006) in a study on deductive reasoning using material with spatial content. They used mental model theory as the basis for assuming the existence of three stages of processing, and found different brain areas associated with each stage:

(1) *Premise processing*: At this stage, there was substantial temporo-occipital activation reflecting the use of visuo-spatial processing. In related research, Knauff et al. (2003) found that there was increased activity in occipital areas when more visual features were described in reasoning problems.

(2) *Premise integration*: At this stage, there was much activation in the anterior pre-frontal cortex (e.g., BA10). This brain area is associated with executive processing and is the same area as the one found by Waltz et al. (1999) and by Kroger et al. (2002) to play a major role in deductive reasoning.

(3) *Validation*: At this stage, the posterior parietal cortex was activated, as were the areas within the prefrontal cortex (BAs 6 and 8) and the dorsal cingulate cortex. Modality-independent representations are held in the parietal cortex, and the involvement of the prefrontal cortex probably reflects the need for cognitively demanding processes during validation of the conclusion.

Overall evaluation

There is strong evidence from brain-damaged patients and from functional neuroimaging in healthy individuals that prefrontal cortex is of major importance in problem solving, intelligence, deductive reasoning, and inductive reasoning. The dorsolateral prefrontal cortex is the region of the prefrontal cortex most often activated across these types of tasks, but activation of other areas varies considerably depending on the specific task. Research by Fangmeier et al. (2006) is especially informative, because they identified the brain areas that were activated at each of three different stages of deductive reasoning. More generally, researchers are achieving increasing success in associating specific brain areas with specific cognitive processes (e.g., relational integration).

What are the limitations of research in this area? First, the findings are often less coherent than may appear from our presentation of the evidence. For example, Goel (2007, p. 435) pointed out that the findings from neuroimaging studies of deductive reasoning "might seem chaotic and inconsistent".

Second, too much research has focused on complex tasks (e.g., deductive-reasoning tasks) that undoubtedly involve several different cognitive processes. Finding that prefrontal cortex is activated during performance of such complex tasks sheds little light on *why* and *how* that happens. However, studies such as that of Fangmeier et al. (2006) show what is possible.

Third, more attention needs to be paid to individual differences in task strategies. Earlier in the chapter we discussed evidence that participants solving conditional reasoning problems adopt at least four different strategies (Bonnefon et al., 2008). The patterns of brain activation undoubtedly vary as a function of the strategy being used by any given participant. More coherent (and theoretically relevant) functional neuroimaging findings could be obtained if account were taken of individual differences in task strategy.

INFORMAL REASONING

The great majority of research on deductive reasoning is narrow and far removed from the informal reasoning of everyday life. Evans (2002, p. 991) indicated clearly the major kinds of artificiality involved in most deductive-reasoning tasks in the laboratory:

> *To pass muster, participants are required not only to disregard the problem content but also any prior beliefs they may have relevant to it. They must also translate the problem into a logical representation using the interpretations of key terms that accord with a textbook (not supplied) of standard logic (but not contemporary philosophical logic), while disregarding the meaning of the same terms in everyday discourse.*

As we have seen, most people confronted by formal deductive-reasoning tasks make exten-

sive use of informal reasoning processes (e.g., their prior knowledge and beliefs). This has led to the development of theories of deductive reasoning (e.g., Evans' heuristic–analytic theory) that emphasise people's use of informal processes such as heuristics. Such considerations strongly suggest the value of studying such processes *directly* by using informal-reasoning tasks rather than continuing to study them *indirectly* via the errors made on formal tasks (Evans & Thompson, 2004).

How similar are the processes involved in formal deductive reasoning and in informal reasoning? Here are three differences between them:

(1) Ricco (2003) found that people's ability to identify fallacies in informal reasoning did not correlate with their deductive-reasoning performance. However, Ricco (2007; discussed below) carried out more thorough research and obtained somewhat different findings.

(2) Hahn and Oaksford (2007) pointed out another important difference, using the following argument as an example: "God exists because God exists." According to classical logic, that argument is deductively valid. In the real world, however, very few people would regard it as a persuasive argument!

(3) The *content* of an argument is important in informal reasoning (and in everyday life) but is irrelevant in formal logic. For example, consider the two following arguments that seem superficially similar (Hahn & Oaksford, 2007): (a) Ghosts exist because no one has proved that they do not; (b) This drug is safe because we have no evidence that it is not. The implausibility of ghosts existing means that most people find the second argument much more acceptable than the first one.

Research on informal reasoning is still in its infancy. However, Hahn and Oaksford (2007) have carried out an impressive programme of research in this area, and we will focus mainly on that. Their theoretical approach is based on various assumptions:

(1) Most informal reasoning in everyday life occurs in the context of argumentation.

(2) Informal reasoning is *probabilistic* because it involves evaluating informal arguments. In this, it differs from formal deductive reasoning that involves *certainties*.

(3) The strength of the conclusion to an argument depends in part on the degree of prior conviction or belief.

(4) The strength of the conclusion also depends in part on the nature of new evidence relevant to it.

(5) Evidence based on positive arguments generally has more impact on the perceived strength of the conclusion than evidence based on negative arguments.

(6) The entire theoretical approach is Bayesian in that it focuses on the extent to which new information changes the probability of a given conclusion (see Chapter 13).

Evidence

As you have probably observed in everyday life, conversations involving informal reasoning often involve fallacies based on flawed reasoning. Ricco (2007) identified six of the most common informal fallacies (see Table 14.1), which you should look out for when other people disagree with you! He found that the ability to detect informal fallacies was associated with

Informal reasoning can be unduly influenced by neuroscience content

How do we decide whether the explanations of findings given by cognitive psychologists or cognitive neuroscientists are convincing? Perhaps you are most likely to be convinced when there is evidence from functional neuroimaging showing the parts of the brain that seem to be most involved. Weisberg et al. (2008) addressed this issue in a study on students taking an introductory course in cognitive neuroscience. The students were provided with a mixture of good and bad explanations for various psychological phenomena. These explanations were or were not accompanied by neuroscience evidence that was in fact irrelevant to the quality of the explanation. The students had to indicate how satisfying they found each explanation.

The findings are shown in Figure 14.13. The students were more impressed by explanations accompanied by neuroscience evidence, and this was especially the case with respect to bad explanations. This is a clear example of content having a disproportionate impact on reasoning. Why were the students so impressed by neuroscience evidence that was actually irrelevant to the quality of the explanation? An important part of the answer is that neuroscientific findings often seem more "scientific" than purely psycho-

logical ones. In the words of Henson (2005, p. 228), "Pictures of blobs on brains seduce one into thinking that we can now directly observe psychological processes." The take-home message is that you need to evaluate neuroscientific evidence as carefully as psychological evidence.

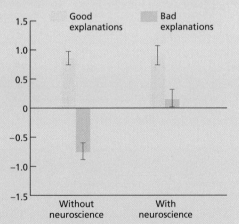

Figure 14.13 Mean ratings of good and bad explanations of scientific phenomena with and without neuroscience information. From Weisberg et al. (2008). Copyright © 2008 by the Massachusetts Institute of Technology. Reprinted with permission from MIT Press.

TABLE 14.1: Common informal fallacies (from Ricco, 2007). Copyright © 2007, with permission from Elsevier.

Fallacy	Definition
Appeal to popularity	Argues for a claim purely on the grounds that other people (without any clear expertise in the matter) accept it.
Argument from ignorance	Maintains that since we don't have evidence against some claim, the claim must be true.
False cause	Argues that there is a correlation between two things and then concludes, on that basis, that cause and effect has been shown.
Irrelevance	Attempts to support a claim by way of a reason that is not relevant to the claim.
Begging the question	Assumes as a premise what it claims to be proving. Seeks to support a conclusion by appealing to that same conclusion.
Slippery slope	Claims that an innocent-looking first step will lead to bad consequences, but doesn't provide reasons as to why or how one will lead to the other.

deductive-reasoning performance, especially the ability to overcome belief bias. Ricco concluded that some of the processes involved in deductive reasoning may be useful to the interpretation of informal arguments and thus to the identification of fallacies in those arguments.

We turn now to Hahn and Oaksford's (2007) theoretical approach. We can see how it works if we consider a study by Oaksford and Hahn (2004). Participants were given scenarios such as the following one:

Barbara:	Are you taking digesterole for it?
Adam:	Yes, why?
Barbara:	Well, because I strongly believe that it does have side effects.
Adam:	It does have side effects.
Barbara:	How do you know?
Adam:	Because I know of an experiment in which they found side effects.

This scenario presents strong prior belief (i.e., strongly believe), a positive belief (i.e., it does have side effects), and weak evidence (i.e., one experiment). There were several variations of this scenario, some of which involved a weak

prior belief, negative belief (i.e., does not have side effects), or 50 experiments rather than one. Participants decided how strongly Barbara should now believe the conclusion that the drug has side effects.

The findings are shown in Figure 14.14. All factors had the predicted effects. The strength of the argument was regarded as greater when the prior belief was positive rather than negative, when it was strong rather than weak, and when the evidence was strong rather than weak. Thus, participants' ratings of the strength of the argument took account of the strength and nature of Barbara's beliefs prior to receiving new evidence and were also influenced appropriately by the strength of the new evidence. What is also shown in Figure 14.14 is the excellent fit to the data of a model based on the Bayesian approach. In other words, people are sensitive to those factors predicted by the Bayesian approach to influence ratings of argument strength.

According to a Bayesian approach, the perceived strength of the conclusion of an argument depends in part on the probability of alternative interpretations. For example, Hahn and Oaksford (2007) presented the following scenario:

John:	I think there's a thunderstorm.
Anne:	What makes you think that?

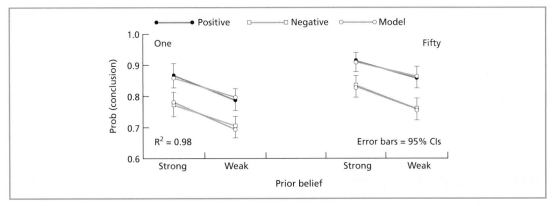

Figure 14.14 Mean acceptance ratings of arguments as a function of prior belief (weak vs. strong), amount of evidence (1 vs. 50 experiments) and whether the arguments are positive or negative. From a study by Oaksford and Hahn (2004), discussed in Hahn and Oaksford (2007). The predictions of their model are shown with green lines. From Hahn and Oaksford (2007), Copyright © 2007. American Psychological Association. Reproduced with permission.

John: I just heard a loud noise that could have been thunder.

Anne: That could have been an airplane.

John: I think it was thunder, because I think it's a thunderstorm.

Anne: Well, it has been really muggy around here today.

The probability of an alternative explanation was varied by setting the scenario in a woodland campsite or a trailer home near an airport. Participants indicated how convinced Anne should be that there was a thunderstorm. The ratings were significantly higher when the couple were in a woodland campsite than when they were near an airport.

Much evidence suggests that many people possess relatively poor informal reasoning skills. For example, Kuhn (1991) studied a wide range of people on the various sub-skills involved in informal reasoning. For each sub-skill, approximately 50% of her participants had rather limited ability. For example, over half of those participants who had opinions on controversial issues could not provide any genuine evidence to support their opinions.

How easy is it to improve people's informal reasoning? This issue was addressed by van Gelder, Bissett, and Cumming (2004) in a study on Australian university students. The students were enrolled in a 12-week course on critical thinking and spent under 100 hours involved in the course and associated practice. There were two main findings. First, most students taking the course showed a substantial improvement in informal reasoning. Second, there was a moderate correlation of +0.31 between the amount of time devoted to practice and the extent of improvement in informal reasoning. What is most striking about this study is the magnitude of the improvement for a relatively modest investment of time and effort.

Evaluation

Informal reasoning is far more important in everyday life than is deductive reasoning. Several common informal fallacies have been identified, but most people have a limited ability to detect these fallacies. Several factors (e.g., probability of alternative interpretations; strength of the prior belief) that influence the rated strength of informal arguments have been identified. In future, it will be important to establish more clearly the similarities and differences in the processes underlying performance on informal and deductive reasoning tasks. It will also be important to identify why some individuals possess much better informal-reasoning skills than others.

ARE HUMANS RATIONAL?

Much of the research discussed in this chapter and the two previous ones apparently indicates that our thinking and reasoning are often inadequate. The message seems to be that most people are simply not rational in their thinking. For example, we often ignore important base-rate information when making judgements, approximately 90% of people produce the wrong answer on the Wason selection task, and we are very prone to belief bias in syllogistic reasoning.

If we take the above findings at face value, they reveal a paradox. Most people apparently cope reasonably well with the problems and challenges of everyday life, and yet seem irrational and illogical when given thinking and reasoning problems in the laboratory. However, this overstates the differences between everyday life and the laboratory. It may well be that our everyday thinking is less rational than we believe and that our thinking and reasoning in the laboratory are less inadequate than is often supposed. So far as everyday thinking is concerned, there is evidence that many people's informal reasoning abilities are rather limited (Kuhn, 1991). Here is a concrete example. Most British people argue that it is worth spending billions of pounds to improve the safety of the rail system. However, the same people habitually travel by car rather than by train, even though travelling by car is approximately 30–50 times more dangerous than travelling by train!

What about laboratory research? There are several reasons why many of the apparent inadequacies and limitations of human thinking and reasoning under laboratory conditions should *not* be taken at face value. We will start by considering judgement and decision making. First, it is often sensible for people to make extensive use of heuristics (e.g., the representativeness heuristic; the recognition heuristic) in everyday life. Heuristics are cost-efficient, allowing us to make reasonably accurate, rapid judgements and decisions. As Maule and Hodgkinson (2002, p. 71) pointed out, "Often…people have to judge situations or objects that change over time, making it inappropriate to expend a good deal of time to make a precise judgement at any particular point in time. Under these circumstances, an approximate judgement based on a simpler, less effortful heuristic may be much more appropriate."

Second, performance on laboratory judgement and decision tasks is often poor because important information is lacking. On many judgement problems, people ignore base-rate information because its relevance has not been made explicit. When problems are re-worded so that people can use their intuitive causal knowledge to understand why base-rate information is relevant, judgement performance is much better (Krynski & Tenenbaum, 2007).

Third, many of the so-called "errors" in human judgement and decision making only appear as such when we think of people as operating in a social vacuum. As Tetlock and Mellers (2002, p. 98) pointed out, "Many effects that look like biases from a strictly individual level of analysis may be sensible responses to interpersonal and institutional pressures for accountability." For example, Camerer, Babcock, Loewenstein, and Thaler (1997) pointed out that New York cab drivers would maximise their earnings by working fewer hours when business was slack and longer hours when business was good. In fact, however, many cab drivers did precisely the opposite! The most plausible explanation of their behaviour is that they felt under pressure from their families to bring home a reasonable amount of money every day.

Many of the apparent "errors" on deductive-reasoning tasks are also less serious than they seem. Evans (1993, 2002) identified three major problems with the conclusion that poor performance on deductive-reasoning tasks means that people are illogical and irrational. First, there is the normative system problem: the system (e.g., propositional logic) used by the experimenter may differ from that used by participants. This is especially likely when participants are unfamiliar with that system.

Second, there is the interpretation problem: the participants' understanding of the problem may differ from that of the experimenter. Indeed, some participants who produce the "wrong"

If your mother says, "If you clean your room, I will give you £5", you probably conclude that you won't receive £5 if you don't do what you have been asked to do. This reasoning is fine in everyday life but not in propositional logic.

answer may actually be reasoning logically based on their interpretation of the problem! We can see the interpretation problem clearly in problems using the word "if". In propositional logic, "If A, then B", is valid except in the case of A and not-B. As mentioned earlier, "If A, then B" in everyday language often means "If and only if A, then B". If your mother says to you, "If you clean your room, I will give you £5", it strongly implies that you won't receive £5 if you don't clean your room. Thus, the affirmation of the consequent is invalid in propositional logic but can be valid in everyday life.

Third, there is the external validity problem. The deductive-reasoning tasks used in psychology experiments are artificial and often tell us little about reasoning in the real world. One way in which they are artificial is that people are not supposed to make use of any relevant background knowledge they possess. For example, the validity of conclusions does not depend at all on whether they are believable or unbelievable. It is difficult to think of real-world reasoning problems in which background knowledge is totally irrelevant. Another way in which laboratory deductive-reasoning tasks are artificial is that conclusions are definitely valid or definitely invalid. In contrast, reasoning in everyday life nearly always involves varying levels of probability rather than certainties. As Oaksford (1997, p. 260) pointed out, "Many of the errors and biases seen in people's reasoning are likely to be the result of importing their everyday probabilistic strategies into the lab."

We have seen that a strong case can be made that performance on most judgement and reasoning tasks *underestimates* people's ability to think effectively. However, we must beware the temptation to go further and claim that *all* our difficulties with such problems stem from inadequacies in the problems themselves or because the problems fail to motivate people. We will discuss four types of relevant evidence.

First, Camerer and Hogarth (1999) reviewed 74 studies concerned with the effects of motivation on thinking and reasoning. They found across several tasks that the provision of incentives rarely led to improved performance. That strongly suggests that poor motivation is not responsible for the poor judgement and reasoning exhibited by many participants in laboratory studies.

Second, there is research focusing on individual differences. Brase, Fiddick, and Harries (2006) found, with a complex judgement task involving use of base-rate information, that students from a leading university were more likely than those from a second-tier university to obtain the correct answer (40% versus 19%). Stanovich and West (1998, 2000, 2008) found that highly intelligent individuals performed better than less intelligent ones on various deductive-reasoning problems. Working memory capacity (which correlates highly with intelligence) has been found to predict performance on conditional reasoning (De Neys et al., 2005), syllogistic reasoning (Copeland & Radvansky, 2004), and belief-bias reasoning problems (De Neys, 2006b). All these findings strongly suggest that poor performance on many tasks is due in part to processing limitations. However, Stanovich and West (2008) found that intelligence was essentially unrelated to performance on several judgement tasks, including the Linda problem, framing problems, the engineer–lawyer base-rate problem, and the sunk-cost effect. Possible reasons why intelligence is more relevant on deductive-reasoning problems than judgement problems are discussed shortly.

Third, some researchers have taken steps to ensure that participants fully understand the problem. For example, Tversky and Kahneman (1983) studied the conjunction fallacy (see Chapter 13), in which many participants decided from a description of Linda that it was more likely that she was a feminist bank teller than that she was a bank teller. There was a strong (although somewhat reduced) conjunction fallacy when the category of bank teller was made explicit: "Linda is a bank teller whether or not she is active in the feminist movement."

In similar fashion, some researchers have used simplified versions of judgement tasks in which the crucial information is in the form of frequencies. Performance is typically better with such versions than with probability versions. For example, Hoffrage, Lindsey, Hertwig, and Gigerenzer (2000) found that medical students performed much better on realistic diagnostic tasks in frequency versions than probability ones. However, even with the frequency versions, only approximately 60% of the students were correct.

Fourth, we would expect experts to be much less likely than non-experts to misinterpret problems. If it were the case that most errors in thinking and reasoning are attributable to misinterpreting problems, then experts should largely avoid cognitive biases in their thinking. In fact, that is often not the case. Redelmeier, Koehler, Liberman, and Tversky (1995; Chapter 13) found that medical experts deciding on the probabilities of various diagnoses were biased by irrelevant information. Schwartz, Chapman, Brewer, and Bergus (2004) found that doctors showed biased decisions in their medical decisions, and the bias increased when they knew they were going to be held accountable for their decisions.

Theoretical considerations

Our failure to perform well on numerous problems involving judgement, decision making, and reasoning doesn't mean that our thinking is irrational. For example, Evans and Over (1997) distinguished between two types of rationality: rationality1 and rationality2. Rationality1 depends on an implicit cognitive system operating at an unconscious level, and allows us to cope effectively with the demands of everyday life. In contrast, rationality2 is involved when people "act with good reasons sanctioned by a normative theory such as formal logic or probability theory" (p. 2).

Research in the areas of judgement and reasoning has indicated that we frequently use heuristics or rules of thumb, which involve rationality1. It might be imagined that our judgements and reasoning would be much more accurate when we use effortful analytic processes which are presumably associated with rationality2. In fact, as Evans (2007) pointed out, that is often *not* the case. We often use analytic processes in a somewhat half-hearted way (conforming to the satisficing principle) that falls well short of rationality2 and leads to errors in judgement and reasoning.

Many theorists (e.g., Chater & Oaksford, 2001; Evans, 2006) go further and argue that most people rarely engage in logic-based, deductive reasoning. According to Chater and Oaksford (p. 204). "Everyday rationality is founded on uncertain rather than certain reasoning...and so probability provides a better starting point for an account of human reasoning than logic." Thus, people learn to think in probabilistic ways as a result of their everyday experience. These habitual ways of thinking continue to be used under laboratory conditions even when in some ways they seem inappropriate. As we have seen, probabilistic thinking is of central importance in informal reasoning.

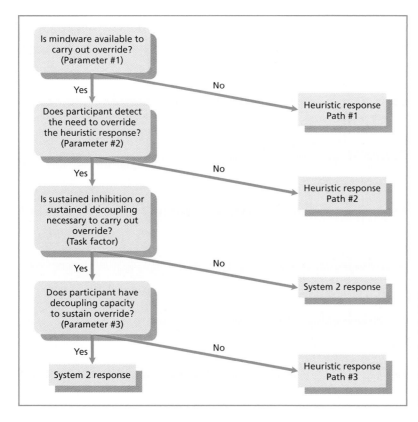

Figure 14.15 A framework for understanding individual differences in thinking biases. Three different paths used in thinking are identified. From Stanovich and West (2008). Copyright © 2008. American Psychological Association. Reproduced with permission.

Some of the basic ideas of Chater and Oaksford's approach can be seen in Oaksford's (1997) example of testing the rule, "All swans are white". According to formal logic, we should try to find swans and non-white birds. However, this can be a real problem in the real world: only a few birds are swans, and the overwhelming majority of birds are non-white. Thus, the pursuit of non-white birds may take up enormous amounts of time and effort and would be very inefficient. In the real world, it makes more sense (and is more informative) to look for white birds and see if they are swans.

The problem of testing the rule that all swans are white resembles the Wason selection task, which has the form, "If p, then q" (e.g., "If there is an R on one side of the card, then there is a 2 on the other side"). According to the probabilistic approach, people should choose q cards (e.g., 2) when the expected probability of q is low, but should choose not-q cards when the expected probability of q is high. These predictions are made on the assumption that people try to maximise information gain and those card choices achieve that goal. Oaksford et al. (1997) carried out an experiment in which the percentage of q cards was 17, 50, or 83%. As predicted, far more q cards were selected when the percentage of q cards was low than when it was high.

Why do people make errors on judgements, decision-making, and reasoning tasks? Stanovich and West (2008) provided an interesting framework within which to address that question. They adopted a two-process approach in which they assumed that successful performance typically requires that heuristic responses (such as those studied by Kahneman and Tversky) are inhibited and overridden by more precise and effortful analytic processes (see Figure 14.15). What is of most interest is the notion that there are *three* different reasons why individuals produce incorrect heuristic responses:

(1) The individual lacks the appropriate mindware (e.g., rules; strategies) to override the heuristic response (Path 1).

(2) The individual has the necessary mindware to override the heuristic response but fails to realise the need to do so (Path 2).

(3) The individual has the necessary mindware and realises that the heuristic response should be overridden, but does not have sufficient decoupling capacity to engage in the effortful analytic processing needed to avoid producing the heuristic response (Path 3).

Stanovich and West (2008) used the above theoretical framework to explain several of their own findings. They divided students into two groups on the basis of their performance on the Scholastic Aptitude Test, which is a measure of cognitive ability and intelligence. In general terms, they discovered that cognitive ability or intelligence predicted performance on deductive-reasoning tasks (e.g., Wason selection task; belief bias in syllogistic reasoning) but was almost unrelated to performance on judgement tasks (e.g., Linda problem; engineer–lawyer problem; sunk-cost effect; framing problems; omission bias). Before we proceed, note that Stanovich and West's findings do not mean that intelligence is irrelevant on judgement tasks – even the low-ability group consisted of individuals of above-average intelligence.

How can we explain the above findings? Stanovich and West (2008) argued that the fact that the great majority of people accept the correct answer when it is explained to them means that they possess the necessary mindware. With many judgement problems, no clear cues indicate that the heuristic response is probably incorrect. Thus, the main reason why people make mistakes on judgement problems is a failure to realise that the heuristic response needs to be overridden (i.e., they use Path 2).

In contrast, with many deductive-reasoning tasks (e.g., involving belief-bias), it is reasonably clear that the heuristic response needs to be overridden, but it is cognitively demanding to use analytic processes to find the right answer (e.g., Copeland & Radvansky, 2004; De Neys, 2006b; De Neys et al., 2005). Thus, they use Path 3. The implication (which seems very reasonable) is that high intelligence is of most value when high decoupling or processing capacity is needed.

What light does the research of Stanovich and West (2008) shed on human rationality? First, the finding that intelligence is almost unrelated to performance on judgement tasks suggests that poor performance on such tasks is due more to the non-obviousness of the cues pointing to the correct solution than to irrationality. Second, the finding that intelligence predicts deductive-reasoning performance suggests that more intelligent individuals may possess more rationality in some sense than less intelligent ones. However, this rationality may have little or nothing to do with logic-based thinking.

CHAPTER SUMMARY

- Inductive reasoning
  Wason argued that performance was poor on his 2–4–6 task because people show confirmation bias. In fact, it is more accurate to claim that people engage in confirmatory or positive testing. It is hard to generalise the findings from the 2–4–6 task, because it is unusual in that the correct rule is much more general than any of the initial hypotheses participants are likely to form. Some research on real scientists and participants in simulated research environments indicates that they mostly focus on confirmation rather than falsification of their hypotheses. When findings inconsistent with their theories are obtained, scientists

often blame the method they used. However, they are much more likely to change their theoretical assumptions if the inconsistent findings are obtained a second time.

- Deductive reasoning
  Conditional reasoning has its origins in propositional logic. Performance on conditional reasoning problems is typically better for the modus ponens inference than for other inferences (e.g., modus tollens). Conditional reasoning is influenced by context effects and background knowledge. Syllogistic reasoning is influenced by our world knowledge and our everyday interpretation of certain words and phrases. Performance on the Wason selection task is generally very poor, but is markedly better when the rule is deontic rather than indicative. Deductive-reasoning performance is typically error-prone, which suggests that we often fail to reason logically.

- Theories of deductive reasoning
  According to Johnson-Laird's mental model theory, people often reduce the load on working memory by constructing mental models that represent explicitly only what is true. There is good evidence for this assumption. Johnson-Laird also assumed that people search for counter-examples after having constructed their initial mental model and generated a conclusion. There is less of such searching than he assumed. The processes involved in forming mental models are under-specified in the theory. According to Evans' heuristic–analytic theory, heuristic processes are used to construct a single mental model, and effortful analytic processes may be used to revise or replace it. This theory is based on the singularity, relevance, and satisficing principles, and attaches much less importance to deductive reasoning than does mental model theory. There is much evidence for separate heuristic and analytic processes, although it is oversimplified to assume a rigid division of all processes into one category or the other. The theory provides a good account of the belief and matching biases, and also helps to explain individual differences in reasoning performance.

- Brain systems in thinking and reasoning
  Functional neuroimaging studies and those on brain-damaged patients indicate that problem-solving performance and performance on intelligence tests are both associated with activation of prefrontal cortex, especially the dorsolateral prefrontal cortex. The dorsolateral prefrontal cortex is also activated during deductive and inductive reasoning, and seems to be important for relational integration. The anterior prefrontal cortex may be involved in broader integration of information. There is some evidence that heuristic and analytic processes in deductive reasoning involve different brain areas. Fangmeier et al. (2006) have identified three major stages of deductive reasoning, and found that different brain areas are associated with each stage.

- Informal reasoning
  Since most people use informal-reasoning processes on deductive-reasoning tasks, it makes sense to study informal reasoning directly. The rated strength of an informal argument depends on the strength of the prior belief, whether that prior belief is positive or negative, the strength of the evidence, and the probability of alternative interpretations. Most people have limited informal reasoning ability, but it can be improved markedly through training.

- Are humans rational?
  There are several reasons why our apparently irrational performance on judgements tasks should not be taken at face value: heuristics are cost-efficient; important information is missing; social factors are ignored. In similar fashion, much "irrational" behaviour on deductive-reasoning tasks is due to the normative system problem, the interpretation problem, and the external validity problem. There is evidence that our everyday comprehension and probabilistic strategies are simply imported into the laboratory. Stanovich and West (2008) found that intelligence was related to performance on deductive-reasoning tasks but not judgement tasks. They argued that poor performance on deductive-reasoning tasks is due mainly to insufficient processing capacity (perhaps related to some kind of rationality). In contrast, poor performance on judgement tasks occurs because there are limited cues indicating that heuristic responses are inadequate.

FURTHER READING

- Evans, J. (2007). *Hypothetical thinking: Dual processes in reasoning and judgement.* Hove, UK: Psychology Press. Jonathan Evans provides an excellent theoretical integration of research on thinking.
- Evans, J. (2008). Dual-processing accounts of reasoning, judgement, and social cognition. *Annual Review of Psychology, 59.* This chapter gives a succinct account of several dual-processing approaches.
- Evans, J., & Frankish, K. (Eds.) (2008). *In two minds: Dual processes and beyond.* Oxford: Oxford University Press. Influential dual-process theories of reasoning and thinking are discussed by leading experts.
- Goel, V. (2007). Anatomy of deductive reasoning. *Trends in Cognitive Sciences, 11,* 435–441. The neural basis of deductive reasoning is discussed in the light of the accumulating functional neuroimaging evidence.
- Johnson-Laird, P.N. (2006). *How we reason.* Oxford: Oxford University Press. Phil Johnson-Laird provides a comprehensive account of reasoning with an emphasis on his own model.

PART V

One of the most refreshing developments within cognitive psychology in recent years has been a broadening of its horizons. In this section of the book, we will consider two of the most important manifestations of that broadening. First, there is the issue of the ways in which emotional factors are related to human cognition (Chapter 15). Second, there is the issue of consciousness (Chapter 16). It is appropriate to place these topics at the end of the book because both of them have applicability across most topics within cognitive psychology. Emotional factors influence our perception, our memory, our interpretation of language, and our decision making. So far as consciousness is concerned, distinguishing between conscious and unconscious processes is important when studying almost any aspect of human cognition.

COGNITION AND EMOTION

The origins of the notion that our emotional states are determined in part by our cognitions go back at least as far as Aristotle over two thousand years ago. Aristotle (who may have been the cleverest person who ever lived) had this to say: "Let fear, then, be a kind of pain or disturbance resulting from the imagination of impending danger" (quoted by Power & Dalgleish, 2008, p. 35). The key word in that sentence is "imagination" – how much fear we

experience depends on our expectations. Aristotle developed this point: "Those in great prosperity...would not expect to suffer; nor those who reckon they have already suffered everything terrible and are numbed as regards the future, such as those who are actually being crucified" (quoted by Power & Dalgleish, 2008, p. 35).

Aristotle emphasised the impact of cognitions on emotion. In addition, however, there is compelling evidence that emotional states influence our cognitions. As we will see in Chapter 15, emotional states have been found to influence many cognitive processes. However, it has proved hard to predict when such effects will or will not occur.

Finally, it should be noted that some research on emotion and cognition has already been discussed in this book. For example, emotional states can have a substantial effect on eyewitness testimony and autobiographical memory (Chapter 8). They have also been found to impair decision making in various ways (Chapter 13).

CONSCIOUSNESS

The topic of consciousness did not fare well during most of the twentieth century. As is well known, the behaviourists, such as John Watson, argued strongly that the concept of "consciousness" should be eliminated from psychology. He was also scathing about the value of introspection, which involves an examination and description of one's own internal thoughts. Consider, however, this quotation from Watson (1920): "The present writer has felt that a good deal more can be learned about the psychology of thinking by making subjects think aloud about definite problems, than by trusting to the unscientific method of introspection." This quotation is somewhat bizarre given that "thinking aloud" is essentially synonymous with introspection! Watson's view was that thinking aloud is acceptable because it can simply be regarded as verbal behaviour.

It is increasingly accepted that consciousness is an extremely important topic. In that connection, the first author remembers clearly a conversation with Endel Tulving in the late 1980s. Tulving said one criterion he used when evaluating a textbook on cognitive psychology was the amount of coverage of consciousness. Reference back to the fourth edition of this textbook revealed that consciousness was only discussed on two out of 525 pages of text. Accordingly, that edition clearly failed the Tulving test! The burgeoning research in consciousness was reflected in an increase to 16 pages in the fifth edition and even more in the present edition.

Cognitive psychologists in recent decades have carried out numerous studies showing the importance of unconscious processes. For example, subliminal perception and blindsight are discussed in Chapter 2, automatic processes are analysed in Chapter 5, implicit memory is dealt with in Chapter 7, and the potential importance of unconscious thinking in decision making is discussed in Chapter 13. Such research has helped to increase interest in studying consciousness – if some processes are conscious and others are unconscious, we clearly need to identify the crucial differences between them.

Finally, several of the concepts used by cognitive psychologists are clearly of much relevance to consciousness. Examples include many theoretical ideas about attention (Chapter 5), controlled processing in Shiffrin and Schneider's (1977) theory (Chapter 5), and the central executive of Baddeley's working memory system (Chapter 6).

KEY TERM

introspection: a careful examination and description of one's own inner mental thoughts.

CHAPTER 15

COGNITION AND EMOTION

INTRODUCTION

Cognitive psychology is still somewhat influenced by the computer analogy or metaphor, as can be seen in the emphasis on information-processing models. This approach does not lend itself readily to an examination of the relationship between cognition and emotion (especially the effects of emotion on cognition). This is so in part because it is hard to think of computers as having emotional states.

Most cognitive psychologists ignore the issue of the effects of emotion on cognition by trying to ensure that their participants are in a relatively neutral emotional state. However, there has been a rapid increase in the number of cognitive psychologists working in the area of cognition and emotion. Examples can be found in research on everyday memory (Chapter 8) and decision making (Chapter 13).

We discuss major topics on cognition and emotion in this chapter. First, we consider how our emotional experience is influenced not only by the current situation but also by our cognitive appraisal or interpretation of that situation. Appraisal helps to determine *which* emotion we experience and its intensity.

Second, we move on to a broader discussion of issues relating to emotion regulation. Emotion regulation is concerned with the processes (mostly deliberate) involved in managing our own emotions and so allowing us to be relatively happy and to achieve our goals.

Third, we consider the effects of emotion on cognition (e.g., what are the consequences of feeling anxious for learning and memory?). This is very different from the focus on the effects of cognition on emotion earlier in the chapter.

Fourth, we discuss various cognitive biases (e.g., a tendency to interpret ambiguous situations in a threatening way) associated with anxiety and depression in healthy individuals and clinical patients. A key issue here is whether these cognitive biases play some role in the development of anxiety and depression or whether they are merely a consequence of being anxious or depressed.

Before discussing the above four topics, we need to consider an important and controversial issue concerning the structure of emotions. There are two main schools of thought (see Fox, 2008, for an excellent review). Some theorists (e.g., Izard, 2007) argue that we should adopt a *categorical* approach, according to which there are several distinct emotions such as happiness, anger, fear, disgust, and sadness. You probably agree this approach fits your subjective experience. However, other theorists prefer a *dimensional* approach. Barrett and Russell (1998) argued for two uncorrelated dimensions of misery–pleasure and arousal–sleep. In contrast, Watson and Tellegen (1985) favoured two uncorrelated dimensions of positive affect and negative affect. In spite of the apparent differences between these two approaches, they both refer to the same basic two-dimensional space (see Figure 15.1).

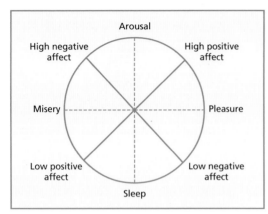

Figure 15.1 The two-dimensional framework for emotion showing the two dimensions of pleasure–misery and arousal–sleep (Barrett & Russell, 1998) and the two dimensions of positive affect and negative affect (Watson & Tellegen, 1985). Based on Barrett and Russell (1998).

There is much support for the dimensional approach. Watson and Tellegen (1985) worked out the extent to which the data from several major self-report inventories (many claiming to assess 8–12 different emotions). It emerged that about 50–65% of the variance in the data from these inventories could be accounted for in terms of the two dimensions of negative affect and positive affect. Mauss and Robinson (2009) discussed neuroimaging evidence indicating that similar patterns of activation are associated with different emotions. In addition, positive emotions are associated with relatively more left-hemisphere activation, whereas negative emotions are associated with relatively more right-hemisphere activation.

It is relatively easy to reconcile the categorical and dimensional approaches. Most emotional states can be accommodated within the two-dimensional space shown in Figure 15.1. Emotions such as happy and excited fall in the top-right quadrant, contented, relaxed, and calm are in the bottom-right quadrant, depressed and bored are in the bottom-left quadrant, and stressed and tense are in the top-left quadrant. When reading the rest of this chapter, you will see that most researchers have adopted the categorical approach. Bear

in mind that many of their findings could be re-interpreted in dimensional terms.

APPRAISAL THEORIES

Cognitive processes clearly play some role in determining *when* we experience emotional states and *what* particular emotional state we experience in any given situation. Numerous theorists have argued that the most important cognitive processes involve appraisal of the situation. Several appraisal theories have been put forward (see Power and Dalgleish, 2008, for a review). According to Roseman and Smith (2001, p. 7), "Appraisal theories claim that *appraisals start the emotion process, initiating the physiological, expressive, behavioural, and other changes that comprise the resultant emotional state.*" The most influential appraisal-based approach is that of Richard Lazarus, and so our main focus will be on his theory. However, most of the research is relevant to appraisal theories in general.

According to Lazarus's (1966, 1982) original theory, there are three forms of appraisal:

- *Primary appraisal*: an environmental situation is regarded as positive, stressful, or irrelevant to well-being.
- *Secondary appraisal*: account is taken of the resources the individual has available to cope with the situation.
- *Reappraisal*: the stimulus situation and the coping strategies are monitored, with the primary and secondary appraisals being modified if necessary.

The descriptions of these forms of appraisal seem to imply that they involve deliberate conscious processing. However, that is not necessarily the case. Lazarus (1991, p. 169) referred to "two kinds of appraisal processes – one that operates automatically without awareness or volitional control, and another that is conscious, deliberate, and volitional."

There have been two major developments in appraisal theory since the original formulation.

First, it is now assumed that each emotion is elicited by a specific and distinctive pattern of appraisal. Smith and Lazarus (1993) identified six appraisal components, two involving primary appraisal and two involving secondary appraisal:

- *Primary*: motivational relevance (related to personal commitments?).
- *Primary*: motivational congruence (consistent with the individual's goals?).
- *Secondary*: accountability (who deserves the credit or blame?).
- *Secondary*: problem-focused coping potential (can the situation be resolved?).
- *Secondary*: emotion-focused coping potential (can the situation be handled psychologically?).
- *Secondary*: future expectancy (how likely is it that the situation will change?).

According to Smith and Lazarus (1993), different emotional states can be distinguished on the basis of *which* appraisal components are involved and *how* they are involved. Anger, guilt, anxiety, and sadness all possess the primary appraisal components of motivational relevance and motivational incongruence (i.e., they only occur when goals are blocked). However, they differ in secondary appraisal components. Guilt involves self-accountability, anxiety involves low or uncertain emotion-focused coping potential, and sadness involves low future expectancy for change.

Second, most early appraisal theories (including that of Smith and Lazarus, 1993) focused on the structure of appraisal rather than the processes involved. Thus, they emphasised the *contents* of any given appraisal but largely ignored the underlying *processes* involved in producing appraisals. Smith and Kirby (2001) addressed this issue. According to their theory, various appraisal processes occur in parallel. There are three basic mechanisms (see Figure 15.2). First, there is associative processing, which involves priming and activation of memories. It occurs rapidly and automatically and lacks flexibility. Second, there is reasoning, which involves deliberate thinking and is slower and more flexible than associative processing. Third, appraisal detectors continuously monitor appraisal information coming from the associative and reasoning processes. An individual's current emotional state is

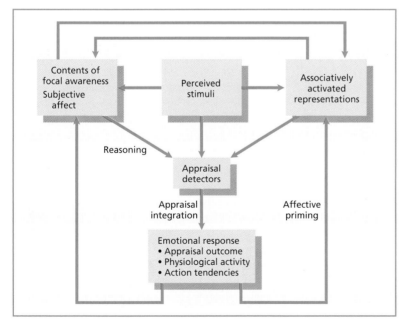

Figure 15.2 Mechanisms involved in the appraisal process. From Smith and Kirby (2001). Copyright © 2001 Oxford University Press. Reprinted with permission.

determined by the total information registered by the appraisal detectors.

Evidence

In an early study showing that emotional experience can be influenced by cognitive appraisal, participants saw various anxiety-evoking films (Speisman, Lazarus, Mordkoff, & Davison, 1964). One showed a Stone Age ritual in which adolescent boys had their penises deeply cut (ouch!), and another showed various workshop accidents. Cognitive appraisal was manipulated by varying the accompanying soundtrack. Denial was produced by indicating the incision film did not show a painful operation or that those involved in the workshop film were actors. Intellectualisation was produced in the incision film by considering matters from the perspective of an anthropologist viewing strange native customs, and in the workshop film by telling participants to consider the situation objectively. Denial and intellectualisation both produced substantial reductions in stress assessed by psychophysiological measures (e.g., heart rate) compared to a control condition with no soundtrack.

Smith and Lazarus (1993) tested the prediction that the specific appraisal components activated by a situation determine which emotion is experienced. They presented scenarios to their participants and asked them to identify with the central character. In one scenario, the central character has performed poorly in an examination and he appraises the situation. Other-accountability was produced by having him put the blame on the unhelpful teaching assistants. Self-accountability was produced by having him argue that he made many mistakes (e.g., doing work at the last minute). The appraisal manipulations generally had the predicted effects on participants' emotional states. For example, anger was more common when there was other-accountability rather than self-accountability. In contrast, guilt was more common when there was self-accountability rather than other-accountability.

Parkinson (2001) was unimpressed by the findings of Smith and Lazarus (1993). He pointed out that under 30% of the variance in emotion ratings was accounted for by the appraisal manipulations. Kuppens, van Mechelen, Smits, and de Boeck (2003) argued that one reason might be that any given emotion can be produced by various combinations of appraisals. They studied four appraisals (goal obstacle; other accountability; unfairness; and control) relevant to the experience of anger. Participants described recently experienced unpleasant situations in which one of the four appraisals was present or absent. Their ability to do this suggested that the determinants of anger are *flexible*: "None of the selected components [of appraisal] can be considered as a truly singly necessary or sufficient condition for anger" (Kuppens et al., 2003). Thus, for example, we can feel angry without the appraisal of unfairness or the presence of a goal obstacle.

We all know from personal experience that individuals differ substantially in their emotional reactions to any given situation. According to appraisal theory, these differing emotional reactions are produced by individual differences in situational appraisal. Supporting evidence was reported by Kuppens and van Mechelen (2007). They were interested in understanding why individuals differ in their characteristic levels of anger (the personality dimension of trait anger). They identified three appraisals that trigger anger: threat to self-esteem; blaming others; and feeling frustrated. As predicted, individuals high in trait anger reported higher levels of all three appraisals than those low in trait anger when presented with scenarios whether or not they involved situations likely to cause anger. Kuppens and van Mechelen concluded that anger appraisals are more easily accessible in those high in trait anger than other people.

According to Smith and Kirby (2001), appraisal can involve very rapid associative processes occurring below the level of conscious awareness. There is much supporting evidence (see next section). For example, Chartrand, van Baaren, and Bargh (2006) showed that automatic appraisal processes can influence people's emotional state. Positive (e.g., music; friends), negative (e.g., war; cancer) or neutral (e.g., building; plant) words were presented repeatedly below the level of conscious awareness. Participants receiving the negative words reported a more negative mood state than those receiving the positive words.

Much research on appraisal theory has involved the use of hypothetical scenarios. Several concerns have been expressed concerning the value of such research:

(1) Little or no genuine emotion is typically experienced with scenarios.
(2) Situations as well as appraisals often vary across emotion conditions, making it hard to disentangle the effects of appraisals from those of situations themselves.
(3) According to appraisal theory, appraisals cause emotional states rather than emotional states causing appraisals. However, most research is correlational and so fails to shed light on causality.

We start by considering the first concern. In the artificial circumstances of responding to scenarios, participants' reported situational appraisals may reflect their generalised beliefs (e.g., what they ought to think) rather than their reactions in genuinely emotional situations. Robinson and Clore (2001) argued that that may not be a major problem. Participants were either shown slides of various emotional situations (e.g., a gun a few inches away pointing directly at them; two young and apparently naked lovers kissing passionately) or were given short verbal descriptions of the slides. The kinds of appraisals and their relationship to the reported emotional states were very similar in both conditions. Thus, findings from studies using hypothetical scenarios may generalise to more emotional situations.

Bennett, Lowe, and Honey (2003) tested the applicability of appraisal theory under naturalistic conditions by asking participants to think of the most stressful event experienced over the previous four weeks. The emotional states experienced by the participants were predicted reasonably well by the cognitive appraisals they had used. Overall, the relation-ship between appraisals and emotional experience was comparable to that found by Smith and Lazarus (1993).

The second concern is that it is hard to tell whether emotional reactions occur *directly* as a response to situations or *indirectly* as a response to appraisals. Siemer, Mauss, and Gross (2007) addressed this issue in a study in which they used only a *single* situation likely to produce different appraisals in different individuals. The experimenter's behaviour towards the participants was rude, condescending, and very critical. Afterwards, participants gave emotion ratings on six emotions (guilty; shameful; sad; angry; amused; pleased) and on five appraisals (controllability; self-importance; unexpectedness; other-responsibility; self-responsibility). The key finding was that appraisals predicted the intensity of the various emotions. For example, the appraisal of personal control was negatively associated with guilt, shame, and sadness, but not anger, whereas the appraisal of other-responsibility was negatively associated with anger but no other negative emotion.

The third concern is that *correlational* evidence indicating an association between appraisals and emotions does not show that the appraisals triggered the emotion. If appraisals do cause emotions, an obvious prediction is that appraisal judgements should be made *faster* than emotion judgements. In fact, however, appraisal judgements are generally made *slower* than emotion judgements (e.g., Siemer and Reisenzein, 2007).

Siemer and Reisenzein (2007) argued that the above findings are misleading. According to their proceduralisation hypothesis: "Although emotion inferences from situational information are initially mediated by inferred appraisals, as a result of being highly practised, they have become automatised." However, when people must make *explicit* appraisal judgements, they use a more deliberate and time-consuming process, which is why appraisal judgements take longer than emotion judgements. Siemer and Reisenzein argued from appraisal theory that people must make appraisals in order to be able to make emotion judgements. If so, participants should have found it easier to make appraisal judgements about a scenario *after* making emotion judgements because emotion judgements involve accessing very similar information to that required to make appraisal judgements. That is precisely what Siemer and Reisenzein found.

Berndsen and Manstead (2007) argued that some cognitive appraisals produced in emotional situations may occur *after* a given emotion has been experienced. For example, someone might want to justify their emotion by thinking of reasons why they might feel the way they do. They tested their ideas in a study in which participants were presented with various scenarios and then rated their levels of personal responsibility and guilt. According to appraisal theory, appraisal in the form of a sense of personal responsibility should help to produce the emotion of guilt. In fact, however, Berndsen and Manstead found causality appeared to be the other way around – responsibility increased as a function of the level of guilt rather than the reverse.

More promising findings for appraisal theory were reported by Roseman and Evdokas (2004). Participants indicated a food or drink they liked or disliked very much. Appraisals were manipulated by telling participants how likely it was that they would taste that food or drink. Immediately afterwards, participants described what they were feeling. The prospect of tasting a favourite food or drink produced feelings of joy, and the prospect of not tasting a disliked food or drink produced feelings of relief. The fact that the appraisals were manipulated means that Roseman and Evdokas came closer than most previous researchers to showing that appraisals have a causal impact on emotions.

Evaluation

Appraisal is often of great importance in influencing emotional experience. Appraisal processes not only determine whether we experience emotion but also strongly influence the precise emotion experienced. As predicted, individual differences in emotional experience in a given situation can be partially explained by appraisals varying from one person to another. Smith and Kirby (2001), with their distinction between associative processes and reasoning, have clarified the processes involved in appraisal. Recent neuroimaging evidence of relevance to appraisal theory is discussed in the next section.

What are the limitations of appraisal theory? First, the assumption that appraisal of the current situation *always* plays a crucial role in determining emotional experience is too strong. For example, an individual in a neutral situation may experience intense emotion if he/she associates something in the situation with a future threat (e.g., observing someone reading a textbook reminds him/her of very important forthcoming examinations).

Second, while it is assumed theoretically that appraisal causes emotional experience, it is likely that the causality is often in the opposite direction. More generally, appraisal and emotional experience often blur into each other. As Parkinson (2001, p. 181) pointed out, "It seems likely that a willingness to endorse items describing one's helplessness and feelings of loss [appraisal] implies a tendency to agree that one is also sad and sorrowful [emotional experience]."

Third, as Parkinson and Manstead (1992, p. 146) argued, "Appraisal theory has taken the paradigm [model] of emotional experience as an individual passive subject confronting a survival-threatening stimulus." There is a danger of de-emphasising the social context in which most emotion is experienced – emotional experience generally emerges out of active social interaction.

Fourth, the distinction between automatic and deliberate or controlled appraisal processes (e.g., Smith & Kirby, 2001) is important, but there is still relatively little research devoted to clarifying *when* and *how* these processes operate. Researchers too often interpret their findings with reference to automatic appraisal processes without obtaining direct evidence that participants actually used them.

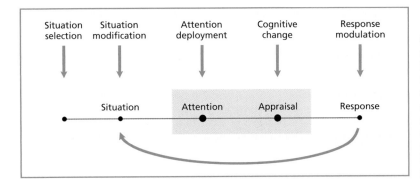

Figure 15.3 A process model of emotion regulation based on five major types of strategy (situation selection; situation modification; attention deployment; cognitive change; and response modulation). From Gross and Thompson (2007). Reproduced with permission from Guilford Press.

Fifth, as Power and Dalgleish (2008) pointed out, Lazarus failed to justify in detail the list of emotions he identified. For example, Lazarus (1991) argued that anxiety and fright are separate emotions even though they depend on rather similar patterns of appraisal and are both closely related to fear. Lazarus also claimed that envy and jealousy are separate emotions even though they overlap.

EMOTION REGULATION

Research on appraisal can be seen within the broader perspective of emotion regulation. **Emotion regulation** can be defined as, "the set of processes whereby people seek to redirect the spontaneous flow of their emotions.... The prototype of emotion regulation is a deliberate, effortful process that seeks to override people's spontaneous emotional responses" (Koole, 2009, p. 6). As Koole pointed out, there are numerous forms of emotion regulation. For example, as we have seen, we can use cognitive appraisal to modify our emotional experience. Other emotion-regulation strategies include the following: controlled breathing; progressive muscle relaxation; stress-induced eating; and distraction.

Gross and Thompson (2007) put forward a process model allowing us to categorise emotion-regulation strategies (see Figure 15.3). The crucial assumption is that emotion-regulation strategies can be used at various points in time. For example, individuals suffering from social anxiety can regulate their emotional state by

Comfort eating is a popular way of engaging emotion regulation to replace negative emotions with more positive ones.

KEY TERM

emotion regulation: the management and control of emotional states by various processes (e.g., attentional; appraisal).

avoiding potentially stressful social situations. Alternatively, they can try to modify social situations by asking a friend to accompany them. You can also use attentional deployment as an emotion-regulation strategy by, for example, having pleasant distracting thoughts when you find yourself in a stressful situation. We have already discussed at length the use of appraisal as a way of regulating emotion. Finally, there is response modulation. For example, it is commonly believed that it is best to express your angry feelings and so get them "out of your system". Alas, it turns out that expressing anger *increases* rather than decreases feelings of anger (Bushman, 2002) because it facilitates the retrieval of angry thoughts.

Attentional deployment

It is often claimed that a good way of reducing a negative mood state is via distraction or attending to something else, and there is much evidence to support that claim (see Van Dillen & Koole, 2007, for a review). *How* does distraction reduce negative affect? According to Van Dillen and Koole, the working memory system (see Chapter 6) plays a central role. Working memory, which is involved in the processing and storage of information, has limited capacity. If most of the capacity of working memory is devoted to processing distracting stimuli, then there is little capacity left to process negative emotional information.

Van Dillen and Koole (2007) tested the above working memory hypothesis. Participants were presented with strongly negative, weakly negative, or neutral photographs. After that, they performed an arithmetic task making high or low demands on working memory. Finally, they completed a mood scale. As predicted, participants' mood state following presentation of strongly negative photographs was less negative when they had just performed a task with high working memory demands than one with low demands.

Van Dillen, Heslenfeld, and Koole (2009) carried out a similar study but also assessed brain activity. The key findings related to the conditions in which negative photographs were followed by an arithmetic task making high or low demands on working memory. When the task was highly demanding, there was greater activity in the right dorsolateral prefrontal cortex, less activity in the amygdala, and less self-reported negative emotion than when the task was undemanding. These findings suggest that a demanding task activates parts of the working memory system (e.g., the dorsolateral prefrontal cortex), which leads to a dampening of negative emotion at the physiological (i.e., amygdala) and experiential (i.e., self-report) levels.

Rothermund, Voss, and Wentura (2008) identified a potentially useful strategy for emotion regulation. **Attentional counter-regulation** involves the use of attentional processes to reduce positive and negative emotional states. More specifically, what happens is that "attention allocated to information is opposite in valence (positive or negative) to the current affective–motivational state" (Rothermund et al., 2008, p. 35). Attentional counter-regulation is used when we feel the need to be cool, calm, and collected. The fact that most positive and negative events have only fairly short-term effects on our emotional states suggests that this strategy is used frequently.

Rothermund et al. (2008) obtained evidence for attentional counter-regulation. Participants were initially put into a positive or negative mood state. After that, they were given the task of naming target schematic faces in the presence of a positive or negative distracting schematic face. According to the notion of attentional counter-regulation, participants should have attended more to the positive distracting face when in a negative mood state and to the negative distracting face when in a positive

> ### KEY TERM
>
> **attentional counter-regulation:** a coping strategy in which attentional processes are used so as to minimise emotional states (whether positive or negative).

mood. That is precisely what the findings suggested.

In sum, there is considerable evidence that attentional processes can influence our emotional states. In this section, we have focused on predominantly positive effects of attentional deployment on emotional states. However, the effects are not always beneficial. Later in the chapter we discuss evidence indicating that anxious individuals often have an attentional bias (selection attention to negative stimuli) that increases their experience of anxiety.

Cognitive reappraisal

In our earlier discussion of research on cognitive appraisal, we focused mostly on behavioural studies. In recent years, however, research in this area has increasingly involved the use of functional neuroimaging, and this has clarified the role of appraisal in emotion regulation. Much of this research has focused on reappraisal, which "involves reinterpreting the meaning of a stimulus to change one's emotional response to it" (Ochsner & Gross, 2005, p. 245). A major assumption is that the emotion regulation associated with cognitive reappraisal often involves higher-level cognitive control processes within the prefrontal cortex and anterior cingulate (e.g., Ochsner & Gross, 2008).

Another major assumption is that reappraisal strategies vary in the specific processes and brain areas involved. Strategies designed to regulate emotional experience involve various cognitive processes, and the *specific* processes used vary across strategies.

Evidence

Ochsner and Gross (2008) reviewed published functional neuroimaging studies of reappraisal. They distinguished between two types of reappraisal strategy:

(1) *Reinterpretation*: this involves changing the meaning of the context in which a stimulus is presented (e.g., imagining a picture has been faked).

(2) *Distancing*: this involves taking a detached, third-person perspective.

Ochsner and Gross reported four main findings. First, regardless of which strategy was used, the prefrontal cortex and the anterior cingulate were consistently activated. These areas resemble those activated when executive processes are needed on complex, non-emotional tasks (see Chapter 6), suggesting that emotion regulation involves executive processes. What does this finding mean? There are two major possibilities. One possibility is that there is a *direct* relationship between successful cognitive reappraisal and cognitive processes within prefrontal cortex. In other words, the processes involved are primarily cognitive in nature. Another possibility is that cognitive processes within prefrontal cortex may have an *indirect* impact by reducing activity in subcortical systems associated with emotion. As we will see (third point below), the evidence strongly supports the indirect interpretation over the direct one.

Second, reappraisal strategies designed to reduce negative emotional reactions to stimuli produce reduced activation in the amygdala, which is strongly implicated in emotional responding. This finding helps to explain how reappraisal (whether based on reinterpretation or distancing) reduces self-reported negative emotional experience.

Third, the reduced amygdala activation seems to occur as a result of earlier activation in prefrontal cortex and the anterior cingulate. Wager, Davidson, Hughes, Lindquist, and Ochsner (2008) replicated and extended this finding in a study in which participants engaged in cognitive reappraisal (generating positive interpretations of aversive photographs). There were two key findings. First, successful reappraisal was associated with high levels of activity in ventrolateral prefrontal cortex combined with reduced amygdala activity. Second, successful reappraisal was also associated with high activity in ventrolateral prefrontal cortex combined with *increased* activity in nucleus accumbens, an area associated with positive affect. Thus, successful reappraisal may involve increasing positive affect as well as reducing negative affect. Note, however, that these findings are essentially correlational and cannot demonstrate causality.

We can compare the above findings to those obtained when participants engage in expressive suppression (i.e., suppressing emotionally expressive behaviour). Expressive suppression is associated with late-occurring prefrontal activation and *increased* amygdala activation over time (Ohira et al., 2006). The typical finding that expressive suppression is ineffective at reducing negative emotional experience may occur because cognitive control processes are used too late in processing – closing the stable door after the horse has bolted.

Fourth, many behavioural studies have indicated that reinterpretation and distancing can both regulate emotion effectively. However, they have not indicated whether the two strategies involve similar mechanisms. Functional neuroimaging evidence suggests somewhat different mechanisms are involved. Reinterpretation was associated with activation in the dorsal prefrontal cortex (possibly reflecting selective attention to contextual stimuli?) and areas associated with language and verbal working memory. In contrast, distancing was associated with activation in medial prefrontal cortex (possibly used to evaluate the self-relevance of images).

Evaluation

Functional neuroimaging studies have increased our knowledge of the processes underlying the effectiveness of reappraisal in reducing negative emotions. Higher cognitive control processes associated with prefrontal cortex are used rapidly, and are followed by reduced emotional responses within the amygdala. Thus, cortical and subcortical processes are both heavily involved in successful reappraisal. In addition, the cognitive processes involved in reappraisal vary as a function of the reappraisal strategy being used. More generally, functional neuroimaging evidence suggests that emotion regulation is complex and involves more different cognitive processes than previously believed.

We still need to know whether the cognitive control processes involved in emotion regulation are the same as those involved in performing complex cognitive tasks. It is also important to obtain stronger evidence that there are causal links between prefrontal activation and reduced amygdala activity. For example, it would be interesting to see whether transcranial magnetic stimulation (TMS; see Glossary) applied to prefrontal cortex prevented reappraisal strategies from reducing negative emotions.

MULTI-LEVEL THEORIES

As we have seen throughout the book, the cognitive system is complex and multi-faceted. For example, Baddeley's working memory model now consists of four different components (see Chapter 6). Accordingly, it is probable that several different cognitive processes underlie emotional experience. As discussed earlier, Smith and Kirby (2001) argued that emotional experience is influenced by associative processes and by reasoning.

The complexity of the cognitive system is one important reason why theorists are increasingly putting forward multi-level theories when identifying the key cognitive processes underlying emotion. Another reason is that such theories account for the emotional conflicts most of us experience from time to time. For example, individuals with spider phobia become very frightened when they see a spider even though they may "know" that most spiders are harmless. The easiest way of explaining such emotional conflicts is to assume that one cognitive process produces fear in response to the sight of a spider, whereas a second cognitive process provides conflicting knowledge that it is probably harmless.

LeDoux (1992, 1996) produced one of the most influential multi-level theories. He emphasised the role of the amygdala (the brain's "emotional computer") in working out the emotional significance of stimuli. According to LeDoux, sensory information about emotional stimuli is relayed from the thalamus simultaneously to the amygdala and the cortex. Of key importance, LeDoux (1992,

1996) identified two different emotion circuits in fear:

(1) A slow-acting thalamus-to-cortex-to-amygdala circuit involving detailed analysis of sensory information.
(2) A fast-acting thalamus–amygdala circuit based on simple stimulus features (e.g., intensity); this circuit bypasses the cortex.

Why do we have two emotion circuits for fear? The thalamus–amygdala circuit allows us to respond rapidly in threatening situations, and can enhance our chances of survival. In contrast, the cortical circuit produces a detailed evaluation of the emotional significance of the situation. As such, it allows us to respond appropriately to situations.

Two points need to be made at this point. First, several other theorists (e.g., Lundqvist and Öhman, 2005) have put forward theories resembling LeDoux's. Second, while LeDoux has focused primarily on fear, several other emotions also depend on somewhat separate conscious and non-conscious processing routes (Power & Dalgleish, 2008). Accordingly, we turn now to evidence concerning non-conscious emotional processing.

Non-conscious emotional processing

Processes below the level of conscious awareness can produce emotional reactions. For example, consider the following study by Öhman and Soares (1994). They presented snake and spider phobics with pictures of snakes, spiders, flowers, and mushrooms. These pictures were presented very rapidly so they could not be identified. In spite of this, the spider phobics reacted emotionally to the spider pictures, as did the snake phobics to the snake pictures. More specifically, there were greater physiological responses (in the form of skin conductance responses) to the phobia-relevant pictures. In addition, the participants experienced more arousal and felt more negative when exposed to those pictures than to the other ones.

Which parts of the brain are activated during non-conscious emotional processing? This issue was addressed by Morris, Öhman, and Dolan (1998). Participants were familiarised with two neutral faces and two angry faces, one of which was paired repeatedly with an aversive noise to produce a conditioned emotional response. After that, the participants were presented with a series of trials on which an angry face was masked by a neutral face so that they could only consciously see the neutral face. The key finding was that there was greater activation of the right amygdala to the masked conditioned angry face than the other angry face. Morris, Öhman, and Dolan (1999) extended these findings, obtaining evidence that the superior colliculus of the midbrain and the right pulvinar of the thalamus were involved, as well as the right amygdala.

In Chapter 2, we discussed patients who have suffered damage to primary visual cortex, as a result of which they lack conscious visual perception in parts of the visual field. However, they show some ability to respond appropriately to visual stimuli for which they have no conscious awareness, a phenomenon known as blindsight. Patients with blindsight have been tested to see whether they show **affective blindsight**, in which different emotional stimuli can be discriminated in the absence of conscious perception. There have been several reports indicating the existence of affective blindsight (discussed by Tamietto & de Gelder, 2008).

Pegna, Khateb, Lazeyras, and Seghier (2005) pointed out that most previous studies on affective blindsight had involved patients with lack of conscious perception in only part of the visual field. As a result, affective blindsight in these patients may have depended in part

> ## KEY TERM
>
> **affective blindsight:** the ability to discriminate between emotional stimuli in the absence of conscious perception of these stimuli; found in patients with lesions to the primary visual cortex (see **blindsight**).

on the intact parts of their visual processing system. Pegna et al. studied a 52-year-old man who was entirely cortically blind. When he was presented with a series of happy and angry faces that he could not perceive consciously, he correctly reported the emotion on 59% of trials. However, his performance was at chance when he reported whether complex scenes were positive (e.g., sports) or unpleasant (e.g., mutilation).

Pegna et al. (2005) also carried out a neuroimaging study in which the patient was presented with angry, happy, fearful, and neutral faces. There was significantly greater activation in the right amygdala with all of the emotional faces than with neutral faces, with the greatest activation occurring in response to fearful faces. These findings suggest that the patient was responding emotionally to the emotional faces.

Jolij and Lamme (2005) set out to show affective blindsight in normal individuals. They used transcranial magnetic stimulation (TMS; see Glossary) to produce a brief disruption to functioning in the occipital area of the brain that is involved in visual perception. On each trial, participants were presented with four items, three of which were neutral faces and the other of which was a happy or sad face. Their task was to report the emotional expression of the discrepant face. When the stimulus array was presented very briefly and followed by

TMS, participants were reasonably good at detecting the emotional expression even though they had no conscious perceptual experience. Surprisingly, this affective blindsight was no longer found when the visual array was presented for slightly longer. This suggests that conscious perception may block access to unconsciously perceived information. As Jolij and Lamme (p. 10751) concluded, "We might be 'blindly led by the emotions' but only when we have no other option available."

SPAARS model

We conclude this section by considering a multi-level model that takes account of the distinction between conscious and non-conscious processes in emotion. The theoretical approach in question is the Schematic, Propositional, Analogical, and Associative Representation Systems (SPAARS) model put forward by Power and Dalgleish (1997, 2008) (see Figure 15.4). The various components of the model are as follows:

- *Analogical level*: this is involved in basic sensory processing of environmental stimuli.
- *Propositional level*: this is an essentially emotion-free system that contains information about the world and the self.
- *Schematic level*: at this level, facts from the propositional level are combined with information about the individual's current goals

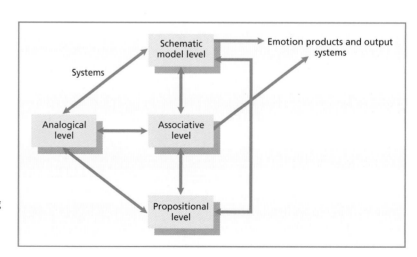

Figure 15.4 The SPAARS model of emotions showing the four representational systems. From Power and Dalgleish (1997, 2008).

to produce an internal model of the situation. This leads to an emotional response if the current goals are thwarted. There are five basic emotions: sadness, happiness, anger, fear, and disgust. Sadness occurs when a valued role or goal is lost, happiness results from a successful move towards a valued goal, anger when some agent frustrates a goal, fear when there is a physical or social threat to the self or valued goal, and disgust when something repulsive to the self and to valued goals is encountered.

- *Associative level*: at this level, emotions can be generated rapidly and automatically without the activation of relevant schematic models. The workings at this level typically occur below the level of conscious awareness, although we can become aware of the products of associative-level processes.

One of the main implications of the SPAARS model is that there are two main ways in which emotion can occur. First, it can occur as a result of thorough cognitive processing involving appraisal when the schematic level is involved. Second, it can occur automatically and without the involvement of conscious processing when the associative level is involved. Power and Dalgleish (2008, p. 153) spelled out in detail what is involved: "The process of emotion generation can become associatively driven so that it appears as if a concurrent process of appraisal is occurring even though it is not and has in fact occurred at some time in the emotional past. In other words, the accessing of the schematic model level of meaning is 'short-circuited'."

When does our emotional experience depend on the associative level? First, if we have had repeated experience with a particular object or event, this can allow us to respond emotionally via use of the associative system. Second, we are more likely to respond associatively with extreme fear or phobia to some objects (e.g., spiders; snakes) than to others that may be more dangerous (e.g., cars). According to Seligman and Hager (1972, p. 450), "The great majority of phobias are about objects of natural importance." More specifically, we are most likely to develop phobias to "objects that have threatened survival, potential predators, unfamiliar places, and the dark" (p. 465). The term **preparedness** is used to describe the tendency for members of a species to be most likely to develop phobias to certain objects as a result of their evolutionary history.

What is the role of consciousness within the SPAARS model? It would be tempting (but oversimplified) to suppose that consciousness is involved when the schematic level is involved but not when the associative level is involved. In fact, the individual's allocation of attention and inhibitory processes is also important. If someone has several models of the self as an individual with mostly positive qualities but a few more negative models of the self, the former models may inhibit conscious awareness of the latter. Alternatively, cultural factors may produce inhibition and lack of conscious awareness. For example, Power and Dalgleish (2008) pointed out that anger is disapproved of in the Malay culture, and so Malaysians endeavour to inhibit internal signs that they are starting to become angry.

Why did Power and Dalgleish (2008) claim that there are five basic emotions (sadness, anger, fear, disgust, and happiness) found in essentially all cultures? This claim was based on three kinds of research evidence, namely, studies on cognitive appraisal, studies on distinctive universal signals (especially facial expressions of emotion), and studies on distinct physiological patterns. Slightly different sets of basic emotions have emerged from these three lines of research, but the five emotions identified by Power and Dalgleish have emerged fairly consistently. Power and Dalgleish accepted that there are many other emotions, but argued that

KEY TERM

preparedness: the notion that each species develops fearful or phobic reactions most readily to objects that were dangerous in its evolutionary history.

According to Power and Dalgleish, there are only five basic emotions. However, additional emotions represent blends of two or more basic emotions (e.g., a blend of happiness and sadness produces nostalgia).

many of them are complex and represent a blend of two or more basic emotions. For example, nostalgia can be regarded as a blend of happiness and sadness.

Additional support for the notion that there are five basic emotions was reported by Power (2006). He made use of a Basic Emotions Scale in which each of the five basic emotions was represented by four conceptually related emotions. For example, anxiety was represented by the terms "anxiety", "tenseness", "worry", and "nervousness". Participants indicated how often they experienced each of the 20 emotions in the questionnaire. The data were best fitted by a model that assumed the existence of the five basic emotions as well as a higher-order factor (possibly an emotionality factor).

Evaluation

The basic assumption that there are two major routes to emotion, one of which is faster and more "automatic" than the other, is consistent with several other theories, including those of Smith and Kirby (2001) and LeDoux (1992, 1996). Two-route theories of emotion provide a more adequate account of emotion than is possible with one-route theories. Another strength of the SPAARS model is that there are reasonably strong grounds for identifying five basic emotions and for claiming that other emotions are

based on two or more of these basic ones. Finally, there is good evidence for the existence of all the main components of the model.

What are the limitations of the SPAARS model? The main one is that more research needs to be done to clarify the ways in which the various processes involved in emotion interact with each other. For example, it is likely that inhibitory processes and the allocation of attention are important. However, the precise factors determining the use of inhibitory processes or the allocation of attention remain to be determined. As a result, there are unexplained complexities in terms of processing at the schematic level. More generally, the use of functional neuroimaging could shed additional light on the nature and sequencing of processing operations in emotion.

MOOD AND COGNITION

Suppose you are in a depressed mood. How will this affect your cognitive processes? Most people find that unhappy memories spring to mind when they are depressed. They also tend to think more negatively about themselves and the world around them. More generally, *any* given mood state (negative or positive) seems to influence cognitive processing so that what we think and remember matches (or is congruent with) that mood state.

Bower's network theory

Bower (1981) and Gilligan and Bower (1984) put forward a semantic network theory to account for phenomena such as those mentioned above (see Figure 15.5). The theory as developed by Gilligan and Bower (1984) makes six assumptions:

(1) Emotions are units or nodes in a semantic network, with numerous connections to related ideas, physiological systems, events, and muscular and expressive patterns.
(2) Emotional material is stored in the semantic network in the form of propositions or assertions.

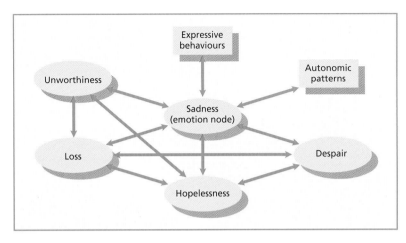

Figure 15.5 Bower's semantic network theory. The ovals represent nodes or units within the network. Adapted from Bower (1981).

(3) Thought occurs via the activation of nodes within the semantic network.

(4) Nodes can be activated by external or internal stimuli.

(5) Activation from an activated node spreads to related nodes. This assumption is crucial – it means that activation of an emotion node (e.g., sadness) triggers activation of emotion-related nodes or concepts (e.g., loss; despair) in the semantic network.

(6) "Consciousness" consists of a network of nodes activated above some threshold value.

The above assumptions lead to several testable hypotheses:

- **Mood-state-dependent memory**: memory is best when the mood at retrieval matches that at learning.
- **Mood congruity**: emotionally-toned information is learned and retrieved best when there is correspondence between its affective value and the learner's (or rememberer's) current mood state.
- *Thought congruity*: an individual's free associations, interpretations, thoughts, and judgements are thematically congruent with his/her mood state.
- *Mood intensity*: increases in intensity of mood cause increases in the activation of associated nodes in the associative network.

How do the four hypotheses relate to the six theoretical assumptions? So far as mood-state-dependent memory (typically assessed by recall) is concerned, associations are formed during learning between the activated nodes representing the to-be-remembered items and the emotion node or nodes activated because of the individual's mood state. At recall, the current mood state activates the appropriate emotion node. Activation then spreads from that emotion node to associated nodes. If the mood state at learning matches that at recall, this increases activation of the nodes of to-be-remembered items and produces enhanced recall. However, the associative links between the to-be-remembered stimulus material and the relevant emotion nodes are generally fairly weak. As a result, mood-state-dependent effects are greater when the memory test is a

Figure 15.6 Mean reaction times on the content task as a function of word content (angry vs. neutral) and word expression (angry vs. neutral). From Walz and Rapee 2003.

Mood state at learning	Mood state at recall	Predicted level of recall
Happy	Happy	High
Happy	Sad	Low
Sad	Happy	Low
Sad	Sad	High

hard one offering few retrieval cues (e.g., free recall) than when it provides strong retrieval cues (e.g., recognition memory).

Mood-state-dependent effects are also predicted by other theories. According to Tulving's encoding specificity principle (see Chapter 6), the success of recall or recognition depends on the extent to which the information available during learning is stored in memory. If information about the mood state at the time of learning is stored in memory, then being in the same mood state at the time of retrieval increases this information matching. Theoretically, this should increase recall and recognition. Mood-state-dependent effects are also consistent with the notion of transfer-appropriate processing (Morris, Bransford, & Franks, 1977). According to this notion, retrieval is more successful when the information available at the time of retrieval (including information about mood state) is relevant to the information stored in long-term memory.

Mood congruity occurs when people in a good mood learn (and remember) emotionally positive material better than those in a bad mood, whereas the opposite is the case for emotionally negative material. Gilligan and Bower (1984) argued that mood congruity depends on the fact that emotionally loaded information is associated more strongly with its congruent emotion node than with any emotion node. For example, nodes containing information about sadness-provoking events and experiences are associatively linked to the emotion node for sadness (see Figure 15.4 above). To-be-remembered material congruent with the current mood state links up with this associative network of similar information. This leads to extensive or elaborative encoding of the to-be-remembered material, and thus to

superior long-term memory. A similar process is involved during retrieval. Information congruent with an individual's mood state will be more activated than incongruent information, and so can be retrieved more easily.

Thought congruity occurs for two reasons. First, the current mood state activates the corresponding emotion node. Second, activation spreads from that emotion node to other, associated nodes containing information emotionally congruent with the activated emotion node.

Mood-state-dependent memory

Mood-state-dependent memory has typically been studied by having participants initially learn a list of words. Learning occurs in one mood state (e.g., happy or sad) and recall occurs in the same mood state or a different one (see Figure 15.6). The findings have been rather inconsistent. Ucros (1989) reviewed 40 studies, and found that there was only a moderate tendency for people to remember material better when there was a *match* between the mood at learning and that at retrieval. The effects were generally stronger when participants were in a positive mood than a negative one, probably because individuals in a negative mood are motivated to change their mood state (see discussion below).

Kenealy (1997) noted various problems with previous research. First, the level of learning was generally not assessed, and so it is not clear whether poor performance reflected deficient memory or deficient learning. Second, there was no check in some studies that the mood manipulations had been successful. Third, only one memory test was generally used, in spite of evidence suggesting that the extent of any mood-state-dependent effects on memory often depends on the nature of the memory test.

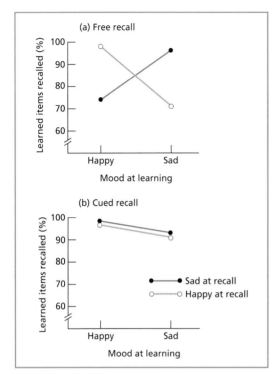

Figure 15.7 (a) Free and (b) cued recall as a function of mood state (happy or sad) at learning and at recall. Based on data in Kenealy (1997).

Kenealy (1997) addressed all these issues. Participants looked at a map and learned instructions concerning a particular route until their learning performance exceeded 80%. The following day they were given tests of free recall and cued recall (the visual outline of the map). There were strong mood-state-dependent effects in free recall but not in cued recall (see Figure 15.7). Thus, mood state can affect memory even when learning is controlled, but does so mainly when no other powerful retrieval cues are available.

How can we explain the inconsistent findings on mood-state-dependent memory? Eich (1995, p. 71) suggested the following "do-it-yourself" principle: "The more one must rely on internal resources, rather than on external aids, to generate both the target events themselves and the cues required for their retrieval, the more liable is one's memory for these events to be mood dependent." Thus, mood state

exerts less influence when crucial information (the to-be-remembered material or the retrieval cues) is explicitly presented.

Kenealy's (1997) findings fit the do-it-yourself principle – there was mood-state-dependent memory when participants generated their own cues (i.e., free recall), but not when cues were provided (i.e., cued recall). The importance of internal processes at encoding was shown by Eich and Metcalfe (1989). There were read (e.g., "river–valley") and generate (e.g., "river–v") conditions. The participants completed the second word in the latter condition during learning, and so it involved more use of internal processes. Subsequently there was free recall. Mood state (very pleasant or very unpleasant) was manipulated by having continuous music during learning and recall. The mood-state-dependent effect was *four* times greater in the generate condition than in the read condition.

Mood-state-dependent memory: dissociative identity disorder

Bower (1994) argued that research on patients with **dissociative identity disorder** (previously called multiple personality disorder) was relevant to his network theory. Such patients have two or more separate identities or personalities. Bower predicted that patients with dissociative disorder should exhibit **inter-identity amnesia**, in which each identity or personality claims amnesia for events experienced by other identities. According to Bower, inter-identity amnesia is an example of mood-state-dependent memory. Why is that? Each identity or personality has

KEY TERMS

dissociative identity disorder: a mental disorder in which the patient claims to have two or more personalities that are separate from each other.
inter-identity amnesia: one of the symptoms of **dissociative identity disorder**, in which the patient claims amnesia for events experienced by other identities.

its own characteristic mood state. As a result, a patient's mood state based on his/her current identity may differ substantially from that associated with his/her other identities, thus making memories associated with those other identities relatively inaccessible. However, Bower claimed there should be less evidence of mood-state-dependent effects such as inter-identity amnesia on tests of implicit memory (not involving conscious recollection). The stimuli relevant to implicit memory tests are "uncontrollable" or "obligatory" (Bower, 1994, p. 230), and so not subject to mood-dependent states.

Before discussing the evidence, note that there are various reasons why patients with dissociative identity disorder might apparently fail to remember information previously learned by a different personality. The information may be genuinely inaccessible or deliberately withheld. Thus, it is very useful to include a control group of healthy individuals instructed to simulate the effects of inter-identity amnesia, presumably by deliberately withholding previously learned information.

Huntjens, Peters, Woertman, van der Hart, and Postma (2007) carried out a study in which patients with dissociative identity disorder learned a list of words (List A) in one identity and then learned a second list (List B) in another identity. After adopting the second identity and before learning List B, the patients all claimed amnesia for List A. Finally, they were tested for recall of List B words and for recognition memory of both lists of words in their second identity. If the patients' claims of inter-identity amnesia were correct, there should have been no intrusions of List A words into recall of List B and no recognition of List A words on the recognition test. In fact, however, the patients showed as many List A intrusions on recall as healthy participants instructed to simulate. In addition, while they recognised more List B than List A words, they recognised 33% of List A words. The healthy simulators showed a similar pattern of results. Huntjens et al. (p. 787) concluded that patients with dissociative identity disorder "seem to be characterised by the *belief* of being unable to recall information instead of an actual retrieval inability".

Huntjens, Postma, Peters, Woertman, and van der Hart (2003) carried out an ingenious study in which apparent inter-identity amnesia could *not* be shown simply by withholding responses. Dissociative patients, healthy controls instructed to simulate inter-identity amnesia, and healthy controls not so instructed learned two lists (List A and List B). List A contained the names of vegetables, animals, and flowers, and List B contained the names of different vegetables, different animals, and articles of furniture. The first two groups learned List A in one identity and then learned List B in a different identity or a feigned identity. Finally, recall for List B was tested by free recall.

What findings would we expect? List B recall for the categories shared by both lists (i.e., vegetables and animals) should be subject to proactive interference (in which memory is disrupted by similar previous learning; see Chapter 6). However, there should be no proactive interference for the category unique to List B (articles of furniture). If patients with dissociative identity disorder have inter-identity amnesia, they should *not* show proactive interference because the information from List A would be inaccessible. In fact, all three groups showed comparable amounts of proactive interference (see Figure 15.8), indicating that memory of List A words disrupted List B recall. It is striking that Huntjens et al. (2003) only analysed the data from dissociative patients with no memory of having learned List A!

Bower's (1994) assumption that dissociative patients should not exhibit mood-state-dependent effects with implicit memory was tested by Huntjens, Postma, Woertman, van der Hart, and Peters (2005). Implicit memory was assessed using the serial reaction time task (see Chapter 6). On this task, a stimulus appears at one out of several locations on a computer screen and participants respond with the corresponding response key. The same repeating sequence of stimulus locations was used across several blocks, but participants were unaware of this. Implicit learning and memory are shown

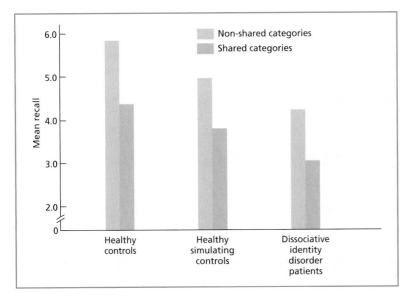

Figure 15.8 Mean recall of words from shared and unshared categories by healthy controls, healthy simulating controls, and dissociative disorder patients. Based on data in Huntjens et al. (2003).

by enhanced performance on the repeating sequence over blocks. The performance of the patients with dissociative identity disorder deteriorated when they switched identities in the middle of the experiment, suggesting there were mood-state-dependent effects and inter-identity amnesia. However, the healthy controls simulating dissociative identity disorder showed the same pattern of results, so it is entirely possible the patients were simply simulating inter-identity amnesia.

Mood congruity

A common procedure to test for mood congruity is as follows. First, a mood is induced, followed by the learning of a list or the reading of a story containing emotionally-toned material. There is then a memory test for the list or story after the participant's mood has returned to normal. Mood congruity is shown by recall being greatest when the affective value of the to-be-learned material *matches* the participant's mood state at learning. Alternatively, emotionally-toned material can be learned when the participant is in a neutral mood state. Mood congruity is shown if he/she recalls more information congruent than incongruent with his/her mood state at recall.

Bower, Gilligan, and Monteiro (1981) studied mood congruity. Participants hypnotised to feel happy or sad read a story about two college men, Jack and André. Jack is very depressed because he is having problems with his academic work, his girlfriend, and his tennis. In contrast, André is very happy, because things are going very well for him in all three areas. Participants identified more with the story character whose mood resembled their own while reading the story. In addition, they recalled more information about him.

There is more evidence of mood-congruent retrieval with positive than with negative affect. How can we explain this? The most plausible explanation is that people in a negative mood are much more likely to be motivated to change their mood. As Rusting and DeHart (2000, p. 738) expressed it, "When faced with an unpleasant emotional state, individuals may regulate their emotional states by retrieving pleasant thoughts and memories, thus reducing or reversing a negative mood-congruency effect."

Rusting and DeHart (2000, p. 738) tested the above hypothesis. Participants were presented with positive, negative, and neutral words, and wrote a sentence containing each of them. After that, there was a negative mood induction in

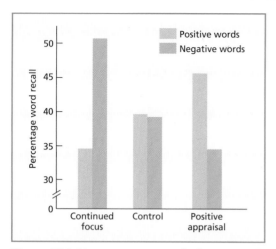

Figure 15.9 Mean percentage recall of positive and negative words as a function of condition (continued focus; control; positive re-appraisal). Based on data in Rusting and DeHart (2000).

which participants imagined experiencing distressing events. Then some participants engaged in positive reappraisal of the distressing events (e.g., "List some good things that could happen as a result of any of the negative events in the stories"). Others were told to continue to focus on negative thoughts, and the control participants were left free to choose the direction of their thoughts. Finally, everyone was given an unexpected test of free recall for all the words.

Participants in the continued focus condition showed the typical mood-congruity effect, whereas those in the positive reappraisal condition showed mood incongruity (see Figure 15.9). These effects were much stronger among participants who had previously indicated they were generally successful at regulating negative moods. Many failures to find mood-congruent effects probably occur because individuals in a negative mood are motivated to improve their mood.

Fiedler, Nickel, Muehlfriedel, and Unkelbach (2001) argued that there are two possible explanations of most mood-congruity effects. First, they may reflect a genuine memorial advantage for mood-congruent material. Second,

they may reflect a response bias, with individuals being more willing to report memories matching their current mood state even if they are not genuine. In their study, they initially presented positive and negative words. After that, participants watched an amusing film (e.g., featuring Charlie Chaplin) or a distressing film (e.g., about a man awaiting the death penalty in prison) to induce a happy or sad mood, respectively. Finally, they were given a recognition memory test in which words were presented in a degraded form so they could not be seen clearly. There was no evidence that the mood-congruity effect was due to response bias – if anything, participants were *more* cautious in responding to mood-congruent stimuli on the recognition test. Thus, mood congruity is a genuine memory effect.

According to Bower's (1981) theory, emotional nodes are activated by stimuli having the appropriate affective value and by moods having the same affective value. Lewis, Critchley, Smith, and Dolan (2005) identified those parts of the brain associated with happy and sad emotional nodes using functional magnetic resonance imaging (fMRI; see Glossary). Participants were presented with positive and negative words at study and then given a recognition-memory test when in a happy or sad mood. The subgenual cingulate (see Figure 15.10) was activated when positive stimuli were presented and was re-activated when participants were in a positive mood at test. Thus, there may be "happy" emotional nodes in this brain area. In similar fashion, the posteriolateral orbitofrontal cortex was activated when negative stimuli were presented and was re-activated when participants' mood at test was negative. This area is a likely site for "sad" emotional nodes.

Thought congruity

Thought congruity is very similar to mood congruity except that it applies outside the memory domain. Thought congruity has been studied in various ways. One method is to put participants into a positive or negative mood state before asking them to make certain judgements. Thought congruity is shown if the

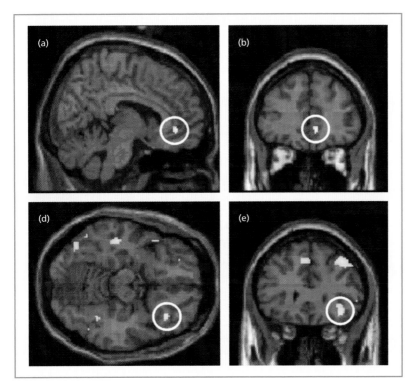

Figure 15.10 Panels A and B show activation in the right subgenual cingulate associated with positive words at learning and at retrieval. Panels D and E show activation in the left posteriolateral oribitofrontal cortex associated with negative words at learning and at retrieval. Reprinted from Lewis et al. (2005), Copyright © 2005, with permission from Elsevier.

judgements are positive or lenient among participants in a positive mood state but negative or harsh among those in a negative mood state.

Forgas and Locke (2005) provided good evidence for thought congruity. Experienced teachers were initially given a mood induction to put them into a happy or sad mood state. After that, they were given four vignettes describing workplace situations (e.g., a colleague cutting in front of you in a photocopying queue). For each vignette, the teachers made a judgement based on imagining themselves in the situation described. Mood state influenced the participants' judgements. More specifically, "Happy mood produced more optimistic and lenient causal attributions while those in a negative mood were more critical" (p. 1071).

McFarland, Buehler, von Ruti, Nguyen, and Alvaro (2007) found important individual differences in thought congruity. They distinguished between two types of attention to the self. Some people have a *ruminative* approach involving a neurotic tendency to dwell on negative aspects of the self. Others have a *reflective* approach involving an open exploratory focus on the self. All participants visualised a negative or a neutral event from the previous year. Then they rated themselves or close others. Participants who generally adopt a ruminative approach showed more evidence of thought congruity than those who generally adopt a reflective approach. Why didn't the reflective individuals show thought congruity? They tend to deal with negative mood states by engaging in mood-repair strategies such as thinking positively or watching a favourite film.

Several studies designed to test the affect infusion model (discussed next) have failed to find evidence of thought congruity. In essence, judgements requiring extensive processing are more likely to be influenced by mood state than those that can be made easily (e.g., Sedikides, 1995).

Mood intensity

There has been relatively little research on the mood intensity hypothesis. However, some relevant evidence was discussed by Eich (1995), in a review of mood-state-dependent memory. As was discussed earlier, the predicted effects of mood state on memory were obtained more often when free recall was used than recognition memory. Of relevance here, mood-state-dependent memory was found most consistently when the induced mood states were strong than when they were weak.

Evaluation

Bower's network theory has been extremely influential and opened up an entire research area. There is reasonable experimental support for most of the predicted phenomena flowing from the theory, including mood-state-dependent recall, mood congruity, and thought congruity. However, there have been many failures to obtain the predicted effects, due partly to the motivation of individuals in a negative mood to improve their mood.

There are several limitations with Bower's theoretical approach. First, it predicts that mood will influence cognitive processing more generally than actually happens. This issue is discussed in more detail shortly.

Second, as Forgas (1999, p. 597) pointed out, the theory, "is notoriously difficult to falsify....The problem of falsifiability mainly arises because in practice it is difficult to provide a complete *a priori* specification of the kind of cognitive contents likely to be activated in any particular cognitive task."

Third, the theory is oversimplified. Emotions or moods and cognitive concepts are both represented as nodes within a semantic network. However, moods typically change slowly in intensity over time whereas cognitions tend to be all-or-none, and there is rapid change from one cognition to another. As Power and Dalgleish (2008, p. 78) remarked, "A theory that gives emotions the same status as individual words or concepts is theoretically confused." Worryingly, it seems to follow from the theory that anyone who heard or read the word, "panic", many times in quick succession would become extremely anxious!

Fourth, Bower's network theory is limited in its applicability, being explicitly designed only to represent the relations among individual words. For example, we saw earlier in the chapter that emotional states can be triggered by cognitive appraisals of complex ongoing situations. It is unclear how such appraisals could be incorporated into Bower's theory.

Affect infusion model

The affect infusion model (e.g., Bower & Forgas, 2000; Forgas, 1995, 2002) resembles Bower's network theory but is broader in scope. The starting point for this model is the notion of **affective infusion**, which occurs when affective information selectively influences attention, learning, memory, decision making and judgement. At the heart of the model is the assumption that there are four processing strategies varying in the extent to which they involve affect infusion:

(1) *Direct access*: This involves the strongly cued retrieval of stored cognitive contents and is not influenced by affect infusion. For example, our retrieval of strongly held political attitudes would not be altered by changes in mood.

(2) *Motivated processing strategy*: This involves information processing being influenced by some strong, pre-existing objective (e.g., enhancing our current mood state). There is little affect infusion with this processing strategy.

(3) *Heuristic processing*: This strategy (which requires the least effort) involves using our current feelings as information influencing our attitudes. For example, if asked how satisfied we are with our lives, we might casually respond in a more positive way on a sunny day than an overcast one (Schwarz

> **KEY TERM**
>
> **affective infusion:** the process by which affective information influences various cognitive processes such as attention, learning, judgement, and memory.

Changes in mood influence many cognitive processes, but have little or no effect on the recall of strongly held political attitudes.

& Clore, 1983). There is considerable affect infusion with this strategy.

(4) *Substantive processing*: This strategy involves extensive and prolonged processing. People using this strategy select, learn, and interpret information and then relate it to pre-existing knowledge. Affect often plays a major role when this strategy is used, because it influences the information used during cognitive processing. Use of this strategy typically produces findings in line with those predicted by Bower's network theory. The notion that affect is especially likely to influence cognitive processes when individuals use substantive processing resembles Eich's (1995) "do-it-yourself" principle discussed earlier.

How does the affect infusion model differ from Bower's (1981) network theory? The effects of mood or affect on cognition are predicted to be far less widespread on the affect infusion model than on network theory. The affect infusion model assumes that mood influences processing and performance when heuristic or substantive processing are used but not when individuals use direct access or motivated processing. Only one of the four processing strategies identified within the affect infusion model (i.e., substantive processing) has the effects predicted by Bower (1981). The other three processing strategies represent an extension of network theory.

Evidence

We will briefly consider a few studies showing the use of each of the four processing strategies. Direct access is used mainly when judgements are made about familiar objects or events and so the relevant information is readily accessible in long-term memory. Salovey and Birnbaum (1989) found that mood did not influence estimates of familiar positive healthy events (e.g., those involved in maintaining health, suggesting that participants used direct access. In contrast, mood did influence estimates of unfamiliar negative health events (e.g., chances of contracting a given illness) about which participants possessed little relevant knowledge.

Forgas, Dunn, and Granland (2008) studied the effects of the direct access strategy on helping behaviour under naturalistic conditions. More and less experienced sales staff working in large department stores were exposed to a positive, negative, or neutral mood induction by someone pretending to be a customer. In the positive condition, the sales staff were told that the store looked great and the staff were very nice. In the negative condition, they were told the store looked terrible and the staff were rude. A few seconds after the mood induction, someone else who was apparently another customer asked for help in finding a book that did not exist.

What do you think happened in this study? There was a mood-congruity effect for helping behaviour only among the less experienced staff (see Figure 15.11). Thus, less experienced staff were most likely to be helpful after the positive mood induction and least likely to be helpful following negative mood induction. Forgas et al. argued that the more experienced staff used direct access processing and so were unaffected by their mood. Thus, the findings supported the affect infusion model.

Bower and Forgas (2000) argued that individuals in a bad mood often engage in motivated processing to improve their mood.

Figure 15.11 Mean positivity of employees' behavioural responses to a customer request as a function of their mood (positive; neutral; negative) and level of experience (low vs. high). From Forgas et al. (2008). Reprinted with permission of Wiley-Blackwell.

We saw some evidence of this in the studies by Rusting and DeHart (2000) and by McFarland et al. (2007). Forgas (1991) asked happy or sad participants to select a work partner. Descriptions about potential partners were provided on information cards or a computer file. Sad participants selectively searched for rewarding partners, whereas happy ones focused more on selecting task-competent partners. Thus, rather than showing mood-congruent processing, sad individuals actively tried to reduce their sad mood by selecting a supportive partner.

The strategy of heuristic processing (which requires the least amount of effort) involves using our current feelings as information influencing our attitudes. For example, Schwarz and Clore (1983) found that people expressed more positive views about their happiness and life satisfaction when questioned on a sunny day rather than on a rainy, overcast day. They felt better when the weather was fine, and this influenced their views about overall life satisfaction. However, when participants' attention was directed to the probable source of their mood (i.e., the weather) by a previous question, their mood state no longer influenced their views about life satisfaction. In those circumstances, superficial heuristic processing was no longer feasible.

Sedikides (1995) compared the effects of substantive processing and direct access. Participants made judgements about themselves involving central or peripheral self-conceptions. He argued that judgements about central self-conceptions are easily made and so should involve direct access. In contrast, judgements about peripheral self-conceptions require more extensive processing and so involve substantive processing. As predicted from the affect infusion model, mood state influenced judgements of peripheral self-conceptions but not those of central self-conceptions.

Evaluation

The theoretical assumption that affect or mood influences cognitive processing and judgements when certain processes are used (heuristic or substantive processing) has received reasonable support. Some of this support comes from studies designed to test Bower's (1981) network theory. There is also reasonable support for the additional assumption that affect or mood will not influence cognitive processing when other processes (direct access or motivated processing) are used. The affect infusion model has more general applicability than the network theory. It is also better equipped to explain non-significant effects of affect or mood on performance.

What are the limitations of the model? First, it is hard to test the model thoroughly, because there is often no direct evidence concerning the precise strategy used by individuals. Matters are complicated by Forgas's (2002) assumption that different processing strategies can be used at the same time.

Second, even if we can identify the *type* of processing strategy that participants are using on a given task, we still may not know the precise processes being used. For example, it is reasonable to assume that more extensive substantive processing is required to make unfamiliar judgements than familiar ones. However, it would be useful to know *which* substantive processes are involved in the former case.

Third, the model does not focus enough on differences in processing associated with different mood states. For example, individuals in a positive mood tend to use heuristic processing, whereas those in a negative mood use substantive processing. In one study, Chartrand et al. (2006) found that participants in a positive mood relied on superficial stereotypical information, whereas those in a negative mood engaged in more detailed non-stereotypical processing.

Fourth, the affect infusion model basically focuses on the effects of good and bad moods on processing and behaviour. This is reflected in most of the research in which happy and sad moods are compared. However, negative mood states (e.g., depressed versus anxious) often vary in their effects (see later discussion).

ANXIETY, DEPRESSION, AND COGNITIVE BIASES

Much of the research discussed in the previous section dealt with the effects of mood manipulations on cognitive processing and performance. It is also possible to focus on cognitive processing in individuals who are in a given mood state most of the time. For example, we can study patients suffering from an anxiety disorder or from depression. Alternatively, we can study healthy individuals having anxious or depressive personalities. These may sound like easy research strategies to adopt. However, a significant problem is that individuals high in anxiety also tend to be high in depression, and vice versa. This is the case in both normal and clinical

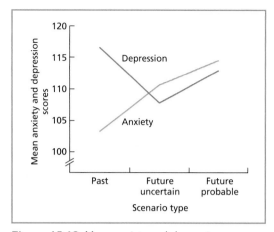

Figure 15.12 Mean anxiety and depression scores (max. = 140) as a function of scenario type (past; future uncertain; future probable) (N = 120). From Eysenck et al. (2006).

populations, and it makes it hard to disentangle the effects of the two mood states.

One of the key differences between anxiety and depression concerns the negative events associated with each emotion. More specifically, past losses are associated mainly with depression, whereas future threats are associated mainly with anxiety. For example, Eysenck, Payne, and Santos (2006) presented participants with scenarios referring to severe negative events (e.g., the potential or actual diagnosis of a serious illness). There were three versions of each scenario depending on whether it referred to a past event, a future possible event, or a future probable event. Participants indicated how anxious or depressed each event would make them. Anxiety was associated more with future than with past events, whereas the opposite was the case for depression (see Figure 15.12).

Why is it important to study cognitive processes in anxious and depressed individuals? A key assumption made by many researchers in this area (e.g., Beck & Clark, 1997; Williams, Watts, Macleod, & Mathews, 1988, 1997) is that vulnerability to clinical anxiety and depression depends in part on various cognitive biases. A second key assumption is that cognitive therapy (and cognitive-behavioural therapy) should focus on reducing or eliminating these cognitive biases as a major goal of treatment. The most important cognitive biases are as follows:

- **Attentional bias:** selective attention to threat-related stimuli presented at the same time as neutral stimuli.
- **Interpretive bias:** the tendency to interpret ambiguous stimuli and situations in a threatening fashion.
- **Explicit memory bias:** the tendency to retrieve mostly negative or unpleasant rather than positive or neutral information on a test of memory involving conscious recollection.
- **Implicit memory bias:** the tendency to exhibit superior performance for negative or threatening than for neutral or positive information on a memory test not involving conscious recollection.

It seems reasonable to assume that someone possessing most (or all) of the above cognitive biases would be more likely than other people to develop an anxiety disorder or depression. However, as you have undoubtedly discovered, things in psychology rarely turn out to be straightforward. We need to address two important issues. First, do patients with an anxiety disorder or major depression typically possess *all* of these cognitive biases or only some of them? As we will see, theorists disagree among themselves concerning the answer to that question. Second, there is the causality issue. Suppose we find that most depressed patients possess various cognitive biases. Does that mean that the cognitive biases played a role in triggering the depression, or did the depression enhance the cognitive biases? Most of what follows represents various attempts to address these two issues.

Beck's schema theory

Beck (e.g., 1976) has played a key role in the development of cognitive therapy for anxiety and depression. One of his central ideas is that some individuals have greater vulnerability than others to developing major depression or an anxiety disorder. Such vulnerability depends on the formation in early life of certain schemas or organised knowledge structures. According to Beck and Clark (1988, p. 20):

> *The schematic organisation of the clinically depressed is dominated by an overwhelming negativity. A negative cognitive trait is evident in the depressed person's view of the self, world and future.... In contrast, the maladaptive schemas in the anxious patient involve perceived physical or psychological threat to one's personal domain as well as an exaggerated sense of vulnerability.*

Beck and Clark (1988) assumed that schemas influence most cognitive processes such as attention, perception, learning, and retrieval of information. Schemas produce processing biases in which the processing of schema-consistent or emotionally congruent information is favoured. Thus, individuals with anxiety-related schemas should selectively process threatening information, and those with depressive schemas should selectively process emotionally negative information. While Beck and Clark emphasised the role of schemas in producing processing biases, they claimed that negative self-schemas would only become active and influence processing when the individual was in an anxious or depressed state. The

---

KEY TERMS

attentional bias: selective allocation of attention to threat-related stimuli when presented simultaneously with neutral stimuli.

interpretive bias: the tendency when presented with ambiguous stimuli or situations to interpret them in a relatively threatening way.

explicit memory bias: the retrieval of relatively more negative or unpleasant information than positive or neutral information on a test of **explicit memory**.

implicit memory bias: relatively better memory performance for negative than for neutral or positive information on a test of **implicit memory**.

activation of these self-schemas leads to negative automatic thoughts (e.g., "I'm a failure").

It follows from Beck's schema theory that individuals with clinical anxiety or depression should typically possess all four of the cognitive biases described above. The reason is that the schemas allegedly have pervasive influences on cognitive processing. It is worth noting that essentially the same predictions follow from Bower's (1981) network theory, with its emphasis on mood-congruity effects.

Evidence relevant to Beck's theoretical approach will be discussed in detail shortly. However, we will mention two general limitations of his approach here. First, evidence for the existence of any given schema is often based on a circular argument. Behavioural evidence of a cognitive bias is used to infer the presence of a schema, and then that schema is used to "explain" the observed cognitive bias. Thus, there is generally no direct or independent evidence of the existence of a schema.

Second, Beck implied that self-schemas in depressed individuals are almost entirely negative. If that is the case, it is hard to see how their self-schemas or self-concept become positive during the process of recovery. Brewin, Smith, Power, and Furnham (1992) found that depressed individuals described themselves in mostly negative terms when asked to describe how they felt "right now". However, and less consistent with Beck's approach, depressed individuals used approximately equal positive and negative terms when asked to describe themselves "in general".

Williams, Watts, MacLeod, and Mathews (1997)

Bower's network theory and Beck's schema theory both predict that anxiety and depression should lead to a wide range of cognitive biases. As we will see, the effects of anxiety and depression are less wide-ranging than was assumed in those theories. In addition, the pattern of biases associated with anxiety and depression differs more than was implied by those earlier theories.

The above problems with previous theoretical approaches led Williams, Watts, Macleod, and Mathews (1997) to put forward a new theory. Their starting point was that anxiety and depression fulfil different functions, and these different functions have important consequences for information processing. Anxiety has the function of anticipating danger or future threat, and so is "associated with a tendency to give priority to processing threatening stimuli; the encoding involved is predominantly perceptual rather than conceptual in nature". In contrast, if depression involves the replacement of failed goals, "then the conceptual processing of internally generated material related to failure or loss may be more relevant to this function than perceptual vigilance" (p. 315).

The approach of Williams et al. (1997) is relevant to healthy individuals having an anxious or depressive personality as well as to patients suffering from an anxiety disorder or depression. In fact, we will be focusing mainly on findings from clinical samples. However, the general pattern of results is similar within healthy populations (see Eysenck, 1997, for a review).

Williams et al. (1997) made use of Roediger's (1990) distinction between perceptual and conceptual processes. Perceptual processes are essentially data-driven, and are often relatively fast and "automatic". They are typically involved in basic attentional processes and in implicit memory. In contrast, conceptual processes are top-down, and are generally slower and more controlled than perceptual processes. They are typically involved in explicit memory (but can also be involved in attentional processes and implicit memory). Williams et al. assumed that anxiety facilitates the perceptual processing of threat-related stimuli, whereas depression facilitates the conceptual processing of threatening information. This leads to various predictions:

(1) Anxious individuals should have an attentional bias for threatening stimuli when perceptual processes are involved. Depressed individuals should have an attentional

bias when conceptual processing is involved but not when perceptual processing is involved.

(2) Anxious and depressed individuals should have an interpretive bias for ambiguous stimuli and situations.

(3) Depressed individuals should have an explicit memory bias but anxious ones should not.

(4) Anxious individuals should have an implicit memory bias but depressed ones should not provided that only perceptual processes are involved.

Experimental evidence: cognitive biases

We will shortly be discussing evidence concerning the existence of the four cognitive biases in clinically anxious and depressed groups. There are several anxiety disorders, including generalised anxiety disorder (chronic worry and anxiety about several life domains), panic disorder (frequent occurrence of panic attacks), post-traumatic stress disorder (anxiety and flashbacks associated with a previous traumatic event), and social phobia (extreme fear and avoidance of social situations). The most common form of clinical depression is major depressive disorder. It is characterised by sadness, depressed mood, tiredness, and loss of interest in various activities.

Attentional bias

Two main tasks have been used to study attentional bias (see Eysenck, 1997, for a review). First, there is the dot-probe task. In the original version of this task, two words are presented at the same time, one to an upper and the other to a lower location on a computer screen. On critical trials, one word is emotionally negative (e.g. "stupid"; "failure") and the other is neutral, and they are generally presented for 500 ms. The allocation of attention is assessed by recording speed of detection of a dot that can replace either word. It is assumed that detection latencies are shorter in attended areas. Therefore, attentional bias is indicated by a consistent tendency for detection latencies to be shorter when the dot replaces the negative word rather than the neutral one.

Attentional bias has also been studied by using the emotional Stroop task. The participants name the colour in which words are printed as rapidly as possible. Some of the words are emotionally negative whereas others are neutral. Attentional bias is shown if participants take longer to name the colours of emotionally negative words than neutral words on the assumption that the increased naming time occurs because emotionally negative words have been attended to more than neutral words. However, there has been much controversy concerning the appropriate interpretation of findings with the emotional Stroop task. For example, increased time to name the colours of emotionally negative words could be due to response inhibition or an attempt not to process the emotional word rather than to excessive attention to it (Dalgleish, 2005).

Bar-Haim, Lamy, Perganini, Bakermans-Kranenburg, and van IJzendoorn (2007) carried out a meta-analysis on studies of attentional bias in anxious individuals. They distinguished between studies involving subliminal stimuli (i.e., presented below the level of conscious awareness) and those involving supraliminal stimuli (i.e., presented above the level of conscious awareness). There was very clear evidence of attentional bias with both kinds of stimuli, with the effects being slightly (but non-significantly) greater with supraliminal stimuli. The magnitude of the attentional bias effect was broadly similar across all the anxiety disorders and normal participants high in trait anxiety (i.e., anxious personality). The only exception was that normal participants high in trait anxiety had a stronger attentional bias effect than anxious patients with subliminal stimuli. The fact that attentional bias is found with both subliminal and supraliminal stimuli suggests that various processes can be involved in producing the bias. As Bar-Haim et al. (p. 17) concluded, "The valence [emotion]-based bias in anxiety is a function of several cognitive processes, including preattentive, attentional, and postattentive processes."

Williams et al. (1997) predicted that anxious individuals attend to threat-related stimuli early in processing, but subsequently direct their attention away from threat. The studies reviewed by Bar-Haim et al. (2007) provide strong support for the first prediction. Evidence relevant to both predictions was reported by Rinck and Becker (2005). Spider-fearful individuals and non-anxious controls were presented with four pictures at the same time: a spider, a butterfly, a dog, and a cat. As predicted, the first eye fixation on the visual display was more likely to be on the spider picture with the spider-fearful participants. Also as predicted, the spider-fearful participants rapidly moved their eyes away from the spider picture. In similar fashion, Calvo and Avero (2005) found attentional bias towards harm pictures in anxious individuals over the first 500 ms after stimulus onset, but this became attentional avoidance 1500–3000 ms after onset.

Fewer studies have considered the effects of depression on attentional bias, (see Donaldson, Lam, & Mathews, 2007, for a review). The most consistent finding (or non-finding) is that depressed individuals do not show an attentional bias when the stimuli are presented subliminally, which is as predicted by Williams et al. (1997). According to their theory, however, attentional bias in depression might be found if depressed individuals had the time to process the negative stimuli conceptually. This prediction was supported by Donaldson et al. (2007), using the dot-probe task with patients suffering from major depression. These patients showed attentional bias when stimuli were presented for 1000 ms but not when they were presented for only 500 ms (see Figure 15.13).

In sum, most of the findings on attentional bias are consistent with the theoretical position of Williams et al. (1997). Anxious individuals show an attentional bias early in processing (e.g., with subliminal stimuli) but avoid threat-related stimuli later in processing. In contrast, depressed individuals do not show an attentional bias with subliminal stimuli, and are most likely to show such a bias when stimuli are presented for relatively long periods of time (e.g., Donaldson et al., 2007).

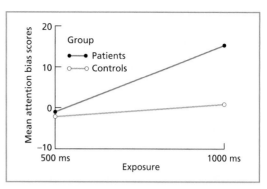

Figure 15.13 Mean attentional bias in ms for negative words in depressed patients and healthy controls as a function of stimulus-exposure duration (500 ms vs. 1000 ms). Reprinted from Donaldson et al. (2007), Copyright © 2007, with permission from Elsevier.

Interpretive bias

There is general agreement that anxious and depressed individuals possess interpretive biases. So far as anxiety is concerned, Eysenck, MacLeod, and Mathews (1987) asked normal participants with varying levels of trait anxiety to write down the spellings of auditorily presented words. Some of the words were homophones having separate threat-related and neutral interpretations (e.g., die, dye; pain, pane). There was a correlation of +0.60 between trait anxiety and the number of threatening homophone interpretations.

A potential problem with the homophone task is that participants may think of both spellings. In that case, their decisions as to which word to write down may involve response bias (e.g., selecting the spelling that is more socially desirable). Eysenck et al. (1991) assessed response bias using ambiguous sentences (e.g., "The doctor examined little Emily's growth"). Patients with generalised anxiety disorder were more likely than normal controls to interpret such sentences in a threatening fashion, and there were no group differences in response bias.

There is much evidence suggesting that depressed individuals have an interpretive bias. For example, various studies (discussed by Rusting, 1998) have made use of the Cognitive Bias Questionnaire. Ambiguous events are described briefly, with participants having to select one out of four possible interpretations of each event. Depressed patients typically select more negative interpretations than normal controls. Such findings are limited in that they rely entirely on self-report data, which are very susceptible to response bias. In other words, depressed patients may *report* negative interpretations of ambiguous events but that does not necessarily mean that their *actual* interpretations were negative.

The obvious way of dealing with the above problem is to assess interpretive bias *without* making use of self-report data. This was done by Mogg, Bradbury, and Bradley (2006), in a study on patients with major depression and on normal controls. Participants were presented with ambiguous sentences, each of which was followed by a continuation sentence matching the negative or neutral interpretation of the preceding sentence. It was assumed that depressed patients would read the continuation sentences relatively faster when they were consistent with a negative interpretation of the preceding sentence. In fact, however, the two groups did not differ, and so there was no evidence of interpretive bias associated with depression.

In sum, there is good evidence for an interpretive bias associated with anxiety. However, it is less clear that there is also an interpretive bias associated with depression. Mogg et al. (2006) pointed out that the sentences they used did not require participants to process them in a self-referential way. Thus, it may be the case that depressed individuals have an interpretive bias that is mostly limited to material that they process with respect to themselves.

Memory biases

Williams et al. (1997) concluded that explicit memory bias would be found more often in depressed than in anxious patients, whereas the opposite would be the case for implicit memory bias. We will start by considering memory biases in depression followed by anxiety. Rinck and Becker (2005) reviewed the literature, and concluded that depressed patients typically exhibit an explicit memory bias.

Murray, Whitehouse, and Alloy (1999) raised an issue concerning the interpretation of this finding. They asked normal individuals high and low in depression to perform a self-referential task ("Describes you?") on a series of positive and negative words. Then the participants provided free recall or forced recall, in which they were required to write down a large number of words. There was the typical explicit memory bias in depression with free recall but no bias at all with forced recall (see Figure 15.14). What do these findings mean? According to Murray et al. (p. 175), they "implicate an important contribution of diminished motivation and/or conservative report criterion in the manifestation of depression-related biases and deficits in recall."

Williams et al. (1997) claimed that no published studies showed implicit memory bias in depressed individuals. Since 1997, however, there have been several reports of implicit memory bias in depression (e.g., Rinck & Becker, 2005; Watkins, Martin, & Stern, 2000). The precise reasons for these mixed findings are not clear.

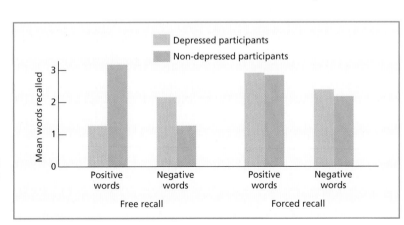

Figure 15.14 Free and forced recall for positive and negative words in individuals high and low in depression. Based on data in Murray et al. (1999).

However, Rinck and Becker's demonstration of implicit memory bias involved patients with major depressive disorder. They argued that implicit memory bias is more likely to be found in individuals with a clinical level of depression.

Williams et al. (2007) concluded that there was much more evidence for implicit memory bias than for explicit memory bias in anxious individuals. More recent research has mostly indicated that anxious patients have an implicit memory bias but suggests they also have an explicit memory bias. Coles and Heimberg (2002), in a review, concluded that patients with each of the main anxiety disorders exhibit implicit memory bias. However, the evidence was weakest for social phobia, and Rinck and Becker (2005) failed to find an implicit memory bias in social phobics.

Coles and Heimberg (2002) found clear evidence in the literature for an explicit memory bias in panic disorder, post-traumatic stress disorder, and obsessive-compulsive disorder. However, there was little support for this memory bias in generalised anxiety disorder or social phobia, and Rinck and Becker subsequently found no evidence for explicit memory bias in social phobics.

Evaluation

There is convincing evidence that anxious and depressed individuals have various cognitive biases, and such evidence suggests that it is useful to consider anxiety and depression in terms of cognitive processes. The evidence does not support predictions from Beck's schema-based theory that anxious and depressed individuals should show the *complete* range of attentional, interpretive, and memory biases. For example, depressed individuals do not seem to have an attentional bias for subliminal stimuli, and there is not much evidence that depressed patients have an implicit memory bias.

How well does the theoretical approach of Williams et al. (1997) predict the main findings? At the most general level, their assumption that the pattern of cognitive biases differs between anxious and depressed individuals has received much support. The findings relating to attentional bias mostly conform to theoretical expectation. Anxious individuals show an attentional bias when perceptual processing is involved but not when conceptual processing is involved, and depressed individuals have the opposite pattern. As predicted, interpretive bias has been found many times in anxious and depressed individuals. However, much of the evidence on depressed individuals relies heavily on self-report data, and more definitive findings are needed. As predicted, there is strong evidence that depressed individuals have an explicit memory bias and that anxious individuals have an implicit memory bias. What is less consistent with Williams et al. is the existence of explicit memory bias in patients with various anxiety disorders (Coles & Heimberg, 2002) and some evidence of implicit memory bias in depressed individuals (e.g., Rinck & Becker, 2005).

The theoretical assumption that anxious individuals display very limited conceptual or elaborative processing in explicit memory seems implausible in some ways. Worry is a form of conceptual processing and it is very common in anxious individuals. For example, Eysenck and van Berkum (1992) found that worry frequency correlated +0.65 with trait anxiety. In addition, persistent worrying is the central symptom of generalised anxiety disorder. What is needed is a better understanding of the circumstances in which anxious individuals do and do not exhibit conceptual or elaborative processing.

Causality issue: cognitive biases, anxiety, and depression

As mentioned earlier, evidence that patients with an anxiety disorder or major depressive disorder possess various cognitive biases can be interpreted in various ways. Of crucial importance is the direction of causality: do cognitive biases make individuals vulnerable to developing anxiety or depression or does having clinical anxiety or depression lead to the development of cognitive biases? Of course, it is also possible that the causality goes in both directions. This issue is important. Cognitive biases have much greater practical and theoretical significance if they help to cause clinical anxiety and depression than if they are merely the by-products of a pre-existing disorder.

Attentional bias

If attentional biases play some role in the development of anxiety disorders, then forms of therapy designed to reduce such biases might be expected to be beneficial. There is some supporting evidence (see Mobini & Grant, 2007, for a review). Adrian Wells has developed a form of attention training based on the assumption that we can only fully attend to a single stimulus or thought at any particular moment. Patients learn to improve their attentional control by carrying out exercises such as focusing successively on different stimuli. For example, social phobics can be trained to attend less to their own negative thoughts and behaviour and more to external stimuli. Attention training has proved useful in the treatment of various anxiety disorders, including social phobia and panic disorder (e.g., Wells & Papageorgiou, 1998). However, it is concerned mainly with the voluntary control of attention. As Mobini and Grant (2007) pointed out, it remains to be seen whether such training can reduce relatively automatic and involuntary attentional biases.

Experimental evidence that changing attentional biases can alter anxiety levels was reported by MacLeod, Rutherford, Campbell, Ebsworthy, and Holker (2002), in a study on healthy individuals. Some participants were trained to develop an attentional bias. This was done by altering the dot-probe task so that the target dot always appeared in the location in which the threatening word had been presented. In another group of participants, the target dot always appeared in the non-threat location. When both groups were exposed to a moderately stressful anagram task, those who had developed an attentional bias exhibited more anxiety than those in the other group.

Mathews and MacLeod (2002) discussed various studies producing results similar to those of MacLeod et al. (2002). They also investigated the effects of training healthy participants to

develop an opposite attentional bias, i.e., selectively avoiding attending to threat-related stimuli. In one of their studies, they used only healthy participants high in the personality dimension of trait anxiety. There were two groups, both of which received 7500 training trials. The training for one group was designed to produce an opposite attentional bias, but this was not the case for the control group. Only the group that developed an opposite attentional bias showed a moderate reduction in their level of trait anxiety.

Interpretive bias

The Dysfunctional Attitude Scale has often been used to assess interpretive bias in clinical studies. It assesses unrealistic attitudes such as, "My life is wasted unless I am a success" and "I should be happy all the time". Some of this research suggests that negative thoughts and attitudes are caused by depression rather than the opposite direction of causality (see Otto, Teachman, Cohen, Soares, Vitonis, & Harlow, 2007, for a review). For example, depressed patients typically have much higher scores than healthy controls on the Dysfunctional Attitude Scale. However, those who show full recovery from depressive symptoms often have scores that are nearly as low as those of healthy controls (e.g., Peselow, Robins, Block, Barsuche, & Fieve, 1990).

Reasonable evidence that negative and dysfunctional attitudes may be involved in the development of major depressive disorder was reported by Lewinsohn, Joiner, and Rohde (2001). At the outset of the study, they administered the Dysfunctional Attitude Scale to adolescents not having a major depressive disorder. One year later, Lewinsohn et al. assessed the negative life events experienced by the participants over the 12-month period. Those who experienced many negative life events had an increased likelihood of developing a major depressive disorder *only* if they were initially high in dysfunctional attitudes (see Figure 15.15). Since dysfunctional attitudes were assessed *before* the onset of major depressive disorder, dysfunctional attitudes seem to be a risk factor for developing that disorder when exposed to stressful life events.

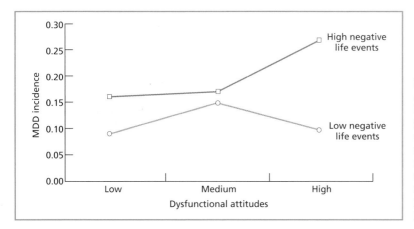

Figure 15.15 Probability of developing Major Depressive Disorder (MDD) as a function of number of life events (high vs. low) and dysfunctional attitudes (low, medium, or high). Adapted from Lewinsohn et al. (2001). Copyright © 2001 American Psychological Association. Reproduced with permission.

Supportive findings were also reported by Evans, Heron, Lewis, Araya, and Wolke (2005). They assessed negative or dysfunctional self-beliefs in women in the eighteenth week of pregnancy. Women with the highest scores for negative self-beliefs were 60% more likely to become depressed subsequently than those with the lowest scores. They even found that negative self-beliefs predicted the onset of depression three years later, which is strong evidence that negative or dysfunctional beliefs can play a role in causing depression.

Experimental evidence suggesting that changing interpretive biases has an impact on anxiety was reported by Wilson, MacLeod, Mathews, and Rutherford (2006), in a study on students. They used homographs having a threatening and a neutral meaning (e.g., stroke; fit; sink). Extensive training was provided so that one group of participants would focus on the threatening interpretations of these homographs, whereas the other group would focus on the neutral interpretations. After training, both groups were exposed to a video showing near-fatal accidents. The group trained to produce threatening homograph interpretations became more anxious than the other group during the showing of the video.

Mathews, Ridgeway, Cook, and Yiend (2007) trained healthy individuals high in trait anxiety to produce positive interpretations of various ambiguous events. This training produced a small (but significant) reduction in the parti-

cipants' level of trait anxiety. Thus, producing a positive interpretive bias can reduce anxiety just as producing a negative interpretive bias can increase anxiety.

Evaluation

There is an increasing amount of clinical and experimental research suggesting that attentional and interpretive biases can have a causal effect on an individual's anxiety or depression. Of special importance is experimental evidence showing that training attentional and interpretive biases can influence people's subsequent mood state. As Mathews (2004, p. 133) argued, "Not only can training lead to persisting alterations in encoding bias, but consequent mood changes have provided the most convincing evidence to date that such biases play a causal role in emotional vulnerability."

The causality issue is a complex one, and so no definitive conclusions can be drawn. The experimental studies seem to provide the strongest evidence that cognitive biases can alter mood state. However, these studies are clearly rather artificial, and the biases produced are unlikely to be as long-lasting as those found in clinical patients. In addition, the effects of changing biases on emotional states have typically been assessed only by means of self-report. This may provide misleading information if participants respond as they believe they are *expected* to rather than on the basis of what they actually feel.

CHAPTER SUMMARY

- Appraisal theories
  According to Lazarus' appraisal theory, emotional experience is determined by primary appraisal, secondary appraisal, and reappraisal. It has been developed to include the assumptions that each distinct emotion is elicited by a specific pattern of appraisal and that appraisal can involve automatic associative or more controlled reasoning processes. Individual differences in emotional reactions depend in part on differences in situational appraisal. While appraisal often leads to emotional experience, it is also likely that emotional experience can alter appraisals.

- Emotion regulation
  Situation selection, situation modification, attentional deployment, appraisal, and response modulation are all emotion-regulation strategies. Attentional deployment strategies include distraction (which uses some of the limited capacity of working memory) and attentional counter-regulation (which dampens positive and negative emotional states). Effective cognitive reappraisals for negative stimuli involve early prefrontal activity leading to reduced amygdala activity. However, the precise pattern of brain activity depends on the processes involved in any given form of reappraisal.

- Multi-level theories
  Multi-level theories provide explanations for the existence of emotional conflicts. LeDoux identified a slow-acting circuit in fear involving the cortex and a fast-acting one involving the amygdala but bypassing the cortex. The existence of affective blindsight in brain-damaged and healthy individuals provides evidence for non-conscious emotional processing. According to the SPAARS model, emotion can be experienced via cognitive processing at the schematic level or more automatically via the associative level. It is assumed within the model that there are five basic emotions, each of which depends on what is currently happening with respect to some valued goal. Several processes are identified with the SPAARS model, and the ways in which they interact remain unclear.

- Mood and cognition
  According to Bower's network theory, activation of an emotion node triggers activation of emotion-related nodes. The theory predicts mood-state-dependent memory, mood congruity, and thought congruity. Findings sometimes fail to support the theory because individuals in a negative mood try to improve it. The theory is oversimplified, suffers from a relative lack of falsifiability, and minimises the differences between cognitions and emotions. According to the affect infusion model, heuristic processing and substantive processing both involve affect infusion, but direct access and motivated processing do not. This emphasis on four different processing strategies is an improvement on Bower's network theory. However, the affect infusion model exaggerates the similarity of processes associated with different negative mood states.

- Anxiety, depression, and cognitive biases
  It is often assumed that vulnerability to clinical anxiety and depression depends on four cognitive biases: attentional bias; interpretive bias; explicit memory bias; and implicit memory bias. According to Beck's schema theory, individuals with clinical anxiety or

depression should typically possess all four cognitive biases. According to Williams et al., anxious individuals are more likely than depressed ones to have an attentional bias and implicit memory bias when perceptual processes are involved, whereas depressed individuals are more likely than anxious ones to have an explicit memory bias. The pattern of cognitive biases does differ between anxious and depressed individuals approximately, as predicted by Williams et al. However, anxious individuals often show an explicit memory bias, which is not predicted. Most research shows only an association between anxiety or depression and cognitive biases. However, therapeutic and experimental manipulations indicate that changes in cognitive biases can causally influence mood state.

FURTHER READING

- Davidson, R.J., Scherer, K.R., & Goldsmith, H.H. (Eds.) (2003). *Handbook of affective sciences*. New York: Oxford University Press. This edited volume contains chapters by many of the most outstanding emotion researchers in the world.
- Fox, E. (2008). *Emotion science*. New York: Palgrave Macmillan. In this excellent book, Elaine Fox discusses the relationships between emotion and cognition in detail.
- Koole, S.L. (2009). The psychology of emotion regulation: An integrative review. *Cognition and Emotion, 23*, 4–41. The author provides a broad review of the major approaches within the rapidly growing field of emotion regulation.
- Ochsner, K.N., & Gross, J.J. (2008). Cognitive emotion regulation: Insights from social cognitive and affective neuroscience. *Current Directions in Psychological Science, 17*, 153–158. An overview of the increasingly important cognitive neuroscience approach to emotion regulation is given in this article.
- Power, M., & Dalgleish, T. (2008). *Cognition and emotion: From order to disorder* (2nd ed.). Hove, UK: Psychology Press. This textbook provides an excellent account of several emotions from the cognitive perspective.

INTRODUCTION

The topic of consciousness is one of the most challenging (but most fascinating) in the whole of cognitive psychology. It has recently been the focus of a considerable amount of research. As we will see, this research has been very interesting and informative as researchers have had increasing success in grappling with important issues.

What exactly is "consciousness"? The term has been used in many different ways. It is "the normal mental condition of the waking state of humans, characterised by the experience of perceptions, thoughts, feelings, awareness of the external world, and often in humans...self-awareness" (Colman, 2001, p. 160). According to Tononi and Koch (2008, p. 253), "The most important property of consciousness is that it is extraordinarily *informative*. This is because, whenever you experience a particular conscious state, it rules out a huge number of alternative experiences."

Pinker (1997) argued that we need to consider three somewhat different issues when trying to understand consciousness:

(1) *Sentience*: This is our subjective experience or phenomenal awareness, which is only available to the individual having the experience.

(2) *Access to information*: This relates to our ability to report the content of our subjective experience but without the ability

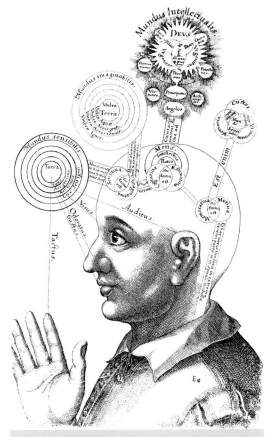

A representation of consciousness from the 17th century.

to report on the processes producing that experience.

(3) *Self-knowledge*: Of particular importance to us as individuals is the ability to have

conscious awareness of ourselves. In the words of Pinker (1997), "I cannot only feel pain and see red, but think to myself, 'Hey, here I am, Steve Pinker, feeling pain and seeing red!'"

As yet, cognitive neuroscientists and cognitive psychologists have shed little light on the issue of sentience and the origins of our subjective experience. This is what Chalmers (1995b, p. 63) famously called the "hard problem", which is "the question of how physical processes in the brain give rise to subjective experience." Chalmers (1995a, pp. 201–203) spelled out in more detail the essence of the hard problem:

> If any problem qualifies as the problem of consciousness, it is this one...even when we have explained the performance of all the cognitive and behavioural functions in the vicinity of experience – perceptual discriminations, categorisations, internal access, verbal report – there may still remain a further unanswered question: Why is the performance of these functions accompanied by experience?... Why doesn't all this information processing go on "in the dark", free of any feel?

The good news is that much progress has been made with what Chalmers (1995a, 1995b) described as "easy problems". These problems (which are only relatively easy!) relate to Pinker's (1997) access-to-information issue. They include understanding our ability to discriminate and categorise environmental stimuli, the integration of information, our ability to access our own internal states, and the deliberate control of behaviour (Chalmers, 2007). Solving most of these problems depends on developing a greater understanding of working memory (Bruce Bridgeman, personal communication).

Functions of consciousness

There has been much controversy about the functions of consciousness. According to

Humphrey (1983), the main function of consciousness is social. Humans have lived in social groups for tens of thousands of years, and so have needed to predict, understand, and manipulate the behaviour of other people. This is much easier to do if you possess the ability to imagine yourself in someone else's position. Humans developed conscious awareness of themselves, and this helped them to understand others. In the words of Humphrey (2002, p. 75), "Imagine that a new form of sense organ evolves, an 'inner eye', whose field of view is not the outside world but the brain itself."

Baars (1988, p. 347) claimed that consciousness is "the jewel in the crown" of our cognitive processing system. As such, he ascribed 18 functions to it. These functions included adaptation and learning, recruiting motor systems to organise and carry out mental and physical actions, decision making, self-monitoring, and self-maintenance. Baars (1997a, p. 7) argued that consciousness "is a facility for accessing, *disseminating, and exchanging information*, and for *exercising global co-ordination and control*." A potential limitation with this argument is that our conscious experience may not be identical to the outcomes of the cognitive processes identified by Baars (Velmans, 2009).

Controlling actions

It is often assumed that a major function of consciousness is to control our actions. Every single day of our lives, we find ourselves thinking numerous times of doing something and then doing it (e.g., "I think I'll go and get myself a coffee" is following by us finding ourselves in a cafe drinking a cup of coffee). As Wegner (2003, p. 65) pointed out, "It certainly doesn't take a rocket scientist to draw the obvious conclusion...consciousness is an active force, an engine of will."

However, accumulating evidence by researchers such as Daniel Wegner and Benjamin Libet suggests it is wrong to assume that conscious intentions cause actions (see Haggard, 2005, for a review). According to Wegner (2003), what we have is only the *illusion* of conscious or free will. Our actions are actually determined by unconscious processes. However, we typically use the evidence available to us to draw the inference that our actions are determined by our conscious intentions. More specifically, we infer that our conscious thoughts have caused our actions based on the principles of priority, consistency, and exclusivity: "When a thought appears in consciousness just before an action (priority), is consistent with the action (consistency), and is not accompanied by conspicuous alternative causes of the action (exclusivity), we experience conscious will and ascribe authorship to ourselves for the action" (Wegner, 2003, p. 67).

Evidence supporting the above point of view was reported by Wegner and Wheatley (1999). They used a 20 cm square board mounted onto a computer mouse. There were two participants at a time, both of whom placed their fingers on the same board. When they moved the board, this caused a cursor to move over a screen showing numerous pictures of small objects. Every 30 seconds or so, the participants were told to stop the cursor, and to indicate the extent to which they had consciously intended the cursor to stop where it did.

Both participants wore headphones. One participant was genuine, but the other was a confederate working for the experimenter. The genuine participant thought they were both hearing different words through the headphones. In fact, however, the confederate was actually receiving instructions to make certain movements. On crucial trials, the confederate was told to stop on a given object (e.g., cat), and the genuine participant heard the word "cat" 30 seconds before, 5 seconds before, 1 second before, or 1 second after the confederate stopped the cursor. Genuine participants wrongly believed they had caused the cursor to stop where it did when they heard the name of the object on which it stopped one or five seconds before the stop (see Figure 16.1). Thus, the participants mistakenly believed their conscious intention had caused the action. This mistaken belief can be explained in terms of the principles of priority, consistency, and exclusivity.

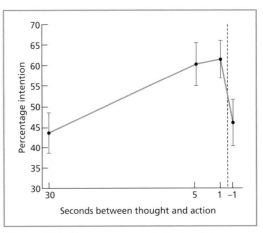

Figure 16.1 Mean percentage believing their conscious intention caused the cursor to stop where it did as a function of time between thought and action. From Wegner and Wheatley (1999). Copyright © 1999 American Psychological Association. Reproduced with permission.

Similar findings were reported by Pronin, Wegner, and McCarthy (2006) in a study on voodoo curses on American college students. Some participants encountered another person (the "victim") who was offensive. After the encounter, they stuck pins into a voodoo doll representing the victim in his presence. When the victim subsequently reported a headache, participants tended to believe that their practice of voodoo had helped to cause his symptoms. They had this belief because their negative thoughts and actions about the victim occurred shortly before his symptoms developed.

The findings reported by Wegner and Wheatley (1999) and by Pronin et al. (2006) are *not* the kiss of death for the notion that conscious intentions play an important role in determining our actions. In both studies, the set-up was very artificial, and the study by Wegner and Wheatley was also complex. By analogy, no one would argue that visual perception is hopelessly fallible simply because we make mistakes when identifying objects in a thick fog.

Very different findings casting additional doubt on the importance of conscious intentions in causing action were reported by Libet, Gleason, Wright, and Pearl (1983). Participants were asked to bend their wrist and fingers at a time of their choosing. The time at which they were consciously aware of the intention to perform the movement and the moment at which the hand muscles were activated were recorded. In addition, Libet et al. recorded event-related potentials (ERPs; see Glossary) in the brain to assess the readiness potential, which is thought to reflect pre-planning of a bodily movement. The key finding was that the readiness potential occurred 350 ms *before* participants reported having conscious awareness of the intention to bend the wrist and fingers. In turn, conscious awareness preceded the actual hand movement by about 200 ms. According to Libet (1996, p. 112), "Initiation of the voluntary process is developed unconsciously [as indexed by the readiness potential], well before there is any awareness of the intention to act."

One limitation with Libet et al.'s (1983) findings is that the readiness potential reflects very general anticipatory processes rather than any specific intention. What we need is a measure of brain activity more *directly* reflecting movement preparation. This was done by Trevena and Miller (2002). They measured lateralised readiness potential, which differs depending on whether it is the right or the left hand that is going to be moved. There were three main findings. First, they replicated Libet et al.'s (1983) finding that the readiness potential typically occurred well before participants reported conscious awareness of the decision concerning hand movement. Second, the lateralised readiness potential occurred some time *after* the readiness potential. Third, the mean onset of the lateralised readiness potential was significantly *earlier* than the mean reported decision time. Overall, these findings suggest that voluntary initiation of a hand movement generally precedes conscious awareness, but by less time than claimed by Libet et al.

There are various limitations with research based on Libet's paradigm. First, it is hard to study conscious intentions with precision, in part because "the conscious experience of intending is quite thin and evasive" (Haggard, 2005, p. 291).

Second, and related to the first point, people seem to infer the moment at which they were aware of a conscious decision from the apparent time of response. Banks and Isham (2009) used conditions in which participants either had their hand in full view or saw it at a 120-ms delay in a delayed video image. The reported decision time was 44 ms later in the latter condition than in the former. This finding suggests that the reported time of conscious decisions is influenced by what happens *after* the decision (i.e., perceived timing of their response).

Third, the Libet approach is essentially correlational, focusing on the relationship between event-related potentials and conscious awareness. What is missing is the direct *manipulation* of brain activity to observe its effects on conscious intentions. This gap has been filled in the research to which we now turn.

Brasil-Neto, Pascual-Leone, Vallsole, Coher, and Hallett (1992) asked participants to choose whether to extend the left or the right index finger. Transcranial magnetic stimulation (TMS) applied to the motor area produced a systematic tendency for participants to choose the finger on the side contralateral (on the opposite side of the body) to the site stimulated. This happened even though they were unaware that their choices had been influenced by the stimulation.

Fourth, Libet's paradigm is limited in its emphasis on only a few aspects of motor preparation within the brain and in the strength of the findings that have resulted from its use. As is discussed in the box, more compelling findings have recently been obtained using a different paradigm.

Evaluation

Different kinds of research have converged on the counterintuitive finding that at least some of our decisions are prepared preconsciously some time before we are consciously aware of having made a decision. The most convincing evidence was reported by Soon et al. (2008; see Box), whose research has the advantage of focusing on parts of the brain known to be much involved in decision making. In addition, their key finding that brain activity predicted participants' decisions seven seconds before they

Brain reading and free will

Soon, Brass, Heinze, and Haynes (2008) argued that previous research was limited because it focused on the late stages of motor preparation in the supplementary motor area rather than on earlier high-level decision processes. Accordingly, they used functional magnetic resonance imaging (fMRI; see Glossary) to assess brain activation in the prefrontal and parietal cortex before participants decided whether to make a response with their left or right index finger. Soon et al. hoped to find differences in the pattern of brain activation depending on which decision was made by participants. The findings were dramatic. The decision that participants were going to make could be predicted on the basis of brain activity in frontopolar cortex (BA10) and an area of parietal cortex running from the precuneus into posterior cingulate cortex seven seconds before they were consciously aware of their decision! In addition, activity in the supplemental and presupplemental motor areas five seconds before conscious awareness of participants' decisions predicted the timing of their responses. Thus, different brain areas are involved in working out *which* decision to make and *when* to implement it.

The findings reported by Soon et al. (2008) represent probably the strongest evidence to date that our actions may depend much less on conscious intentions than we like to think. In previous research, the time interval between certain events in the brain and participants' responses was so small that it was not very clear that conscious awareness occurred *after* the brain events. There are no such concerns with the seven-second gap reported by Soon et al. As John-Dylan Haynes (one of the researchers) concluded, "Your decisions are strongly prepared by brain activity. By the time consciousness kicks in, most of the work has already been done." However, brain activity did not *always* predict participants' subsequent decisions accurately, so it is possible that additional factors (e.g., free will) were involved on at least some trials.

The research of Soon et al. (2008) potentially raises some important ethical and legal issues relating to the whole notion of personal responsibility. As Gazzaniga (2008, p. 413) asked, "If it is simply the brain . . . that causes a person to act (even before he or she is aware of making a decision), how can we hold that person liable for his or her mental decisions?"

were aware of what decision they were going to make cannot be dismissed on the grounds of inaccurate assessment of timings.

There are three issues requiring future investigation. First, most research has involved trivial decisions (e.g., deciding which hand to move). It seems improbable that major decisions (e.g., Should I get married?; Should I move to Australia?) are prepared preconsciously.

Second, and related to the first point, most of the research is based on the assumption that people make decisions (consciously or preconsciously) and then implement them. In fact, however, much human decision making involves a lengthy process of considering and evaluating different kinds of relevant information (see Chapter 13). It seems very likely that conscious

processes are heavily involved when decision making takes long periods of time.

Third, much of the research so far has been based on an oversimplified view of intentional action. It typically depends on three different decisions: deciding *what* action to produce, deciding *when* to produce it, and deciding *whether* to produce it. This led Brass and Haggard (2008) to propose the What, When, Whether (WWW) model of intentional action, in which different brain areas are involved in the three different decisions.

Interesting evidence shedding some light on the complexities of brain processing involved in intentional action was reported by Desmurget, Reilly, Richard, Szathmari, Mottolese, and Sirigu (2009). They administered electrical stimulation to awaken patients undergoing brain surgery. Stimulation of the posterior parietal cortex caused the patients to have a strong desire to move a part of their body (and even to report that they had moved that part) in the total absence of any motor response. In contrast, stimulation of the premotor cortex triggered mouth and limb movements, but the patients denied having made those movements! Such research offers the prospect of clarifying the relationship between conscious intentions to perform actions and the triggering of such actions.

MEASURING CONSCIOUS EXPERIENCE

Much of the research on conscious experience has focused on visual consciousness – our awareness of visual objects. The main advantages of studying visual consciousness are that it is possible to control what is presented to participants and whether stimuli are or are not consciously perceived. What is the best way to assess people's visual consciousness? Overwhelmingly, the most popular answer has been that we should use behavioural measures. For example, we can ask them to provide verbal reports of their visual experience, or to make a yes/no decision concerning the presence of a target object.

In post-decision wagering, observers initially decide whether a stimulus was present and then decide how much to wager or bet on their decision (Persaud, McLeod, & Cowey, 2007). Wagers should be large and mostly successful if observers' conscious awareness is high, whereas they should be small and inaccurate if conscious awareness is lacking. Persaud et al. tested GY, a patient with blindsight (a condition in which accurate visual discriminations are made without reported conscious awareness; see Chapter 2). When GY decided whether a stimulus had been presented to his affected visual field, he was correct 70% of the time. However, he showed only a modest tendency to bet more money on correct trials than on incorrect ones, strongly suggesting that he generally lacked relevant conscious awareness. In contrast, when stimuli

were presented to GY's unaffected visual field, he consistently wagered large sums of money on his decisions.

Post-decision wagering provides a fairly natural way of assessing conscious awareness without relying on self-report measures. However, the amount wagered depends on betting strategies as well as on conscious awareness. Schurger and Sher (2008) found that most of their participants were loss averse, and so reluctant to bet large sums of money. That was so even when they were instructed as follows: "It is okay to be high all of the time – try to 'go for it' [bet high], even if you have only a vague hunch." It is possible that GY's reluctance to bet much money when he had correctly guessed that a stimulus had been presented to his affected visual field reflected his betting strategy rather than a lack of conscious awareness.

In spite of the popularity of relying on behavioural measures, the evidence obtained from using them is often hard to interpret. As Lamme (2006, p. 499) pointed out, one of the key problems is as follows: "You cannot know whether you have a conscious experience without resorting to cognitive functions such as attention, memory or inner speech." Thus, failure to report a given conscious experience may be due to failures of attention, memory, or inner speech rather than to absence of the relevant conscious experience. For example, change blindness (the failure to detect a change when two views of the same scene are presented successively) may be due mainly to the absence of attention rather than lack of relevant conscious experience (e.g., Landman, Spekreijse, & Lamme, 2003; see Chapter 4). Another example concerns split-brain patients, whose two brain hemispheres are disconnected from each other (see discussion later in this chapter). Such patients have very limited ability to provide verbal reports on objects presented to the right or non-language hemisphere. It is often unclear whether this reflects a lack of conscious experience in the right hemisphere or a deficit in right-hemisphere language abilities.

A classic example of the limitations of verbal report was shown by Sperling (1960;

see Chapter 6). He presented visual displays of three rows of four letters very briefly and found that participants could recall only four or five of them. This suggested there was very limited conscious awareness of the display. However, Sperling (1960) and Landman et al. (2003) found that this was due more to memory limitations when reporting the letters than to strict limits on conscious awareness.

Another problem with using behavioural measures to assess conscious awareness is that different measures often fail to agree. For example, consider research on subliminal perception (see Chapter 2). Observers sometimes show "awareness" of visual stimuli when asked to make forced-choice decisions about them (objective threshold) but not when asked to report their experience (subjective threshold).

The vegetative state: Behavioural versus functional neuroimaging measures of consciousness

The limitations of behavioural evidence for conscious awareness have been shown in research on the **vegetative state**, which is defined by the following criteria: "There must be no evidence of awareness of self or environment, no response to external stimuli of a kind suggesting volition or purpose, and no evidence of language comprehension or expression" (Owen & Coleman, 2008, p. 235). The vegetative state is found in brain-damaged patients who emerge from a coma and display "wakefulness without awareness". Thus, the behavioural evidence indicates very strongly that patients in the vegetative state totally lack conscious awareness.

Important research by Owen, Coleman, Boly, Davis, Laureys, and Pickard (2006) using functional neuroimaging has suggested that these patients may possess some conscious awareness. They studied a 23-year-old woman in the vegetative state as a result of a very serious road accident in July 2005. She was asked to imagine playing a game of tennis or visiting the rooms of her house starting from the front door. These two tasks were associated with different patterns of brain activity as assessed by functional magnetic resonance imaging (fMRI; see Glossary) – for example, only imagining playing tennis was associated with

activation in the supplementary motor area. Of key importance, the patterns of brain activity were very similar to those shown by healthy participants. This brain activation was not triggered automatically by the words "tennis" or "house": it lasted for the entire 30 seconds of each trial and included brain areas that do not respond automatically to familiar words.

Owen et al. (2006) carried out another test of the patient's conscious awareness. She was presented with sentences containing ambiguous words (italicised) (e.g., "The *creak* came from a *beam* in the *ceiling*"). She showed greater brain activity in the left inferior frontal region to ambiguous than to non-ambiguous words, showing that she engaged in full semantic processing of the sentences.

These findings suggest that the patient was consciously aware and purposefully following instructions (see Owen & Coleman, 2008, for a review). Of particular relevance to the current discussion, these findings suggest that functional neuroimaging sometimes provides a more valid assessment of the presence of conscious experience than behavioural measures. However, it is possible (although unlikely) that the patient's brain activity reflected unconscious but relatively sophisticated processing.

KEY TERM

vegetative state: a condition produced by brain damage in which there is wakefulness but an apparent lack of awareness and purposeful behaviour.

Neural correlates of consciousness

It is increasingly argued that we can gain a deeper understanding of consciousness by identifying the major neural correlates of consciousness. What happens is that we obtain behavioural measures of conscious awareness, and relate them to the associated patterns of brain activity. Some of the relevant research is discussed here, with other research on neural correlates of consciousness considered shortly.

Going one step further, Lamme (2006) argued that it might be preferable to define consciousness in neural terms instead of behavioural ones. He focused on visual consciousness, i.e., conscious experience of visual objects. Presentation of a visual stimulus leads to extremely rapid, essentially automatic processing at successive levels of the visual cortex, starting with early visual cortex and then proceeding to higher levels (see Chapter 2). This so-called 'feedforward sweep' is completed within about 100–150 ms. The feedforward sweep is followed by recurrent processing (also known as re-entrant processing). Recurrent processing involves feedback from higher to lower areas, producing extensive interactions between different areas. According to Lamme (2006), the relevance of all this to conscious experience is very direct – recurrent processing is accompanied by conscious experience, whereas the feedforward sweep is not.

Why does conscious experience seem to be associated with recurrent processing rather than the feedforward sweep? The simple (and honest) answer is that we do not know. However, here are three relevant considerations. First, it seems more plausible that consciousness is associated with the complexity of recurrent processing rather than the very straightforward feedforward sweep. Second, there are enormous numbers of back connections in the cerebral cortex (Tononi & Koch, 2008), making it probable that they serve some important purpose. Third, Lamme (2006) argued that we need consciousness to learn and that recurrent processing plays an important role in learning.

Evidence

When an initial visual stimulus is followed shortly afterwards by a second visual stimulus, the second stimulus often prevents conscious perception of the first. This effect is known as masking, and the issue arises as to whether **masking** is due to disruption of the feedforward sweep or of recurrent processing. Fahrenfort, Scholte, and Lamme (2007) asked participants to decide whether a given target figure (a texture-defined square) had been presented using non-masked and masked conditions. The EEG evidence indicated that feedforward processing was intact under masked conditions even when participants' target-detection performance was at chance level. In contrast, there was practically no evidence of recurrent processing in the masked condition. These findings suggest that recurrent processing can be necessary for conscious awareness, but it may well not be sufficient.

Fahrenfort, Scholte, and Lamme (2008) carried out a similar EEG study in which participants tried to detect masked visual targets. They identified an initial stage of feedforward processing followed by four stages of recurrent processing involving alternating fronto-parietal and occipital activity. The amount of feedforward activity did not correlate with target-detection performance. However, recurrent processing activity at all stages correlated highly with performance. These findings suggest that conscious experience is associated much more with recurrent processing than with feedforward processing.

The data obtained by Fahrenfort et al. (2007, 2008) are essentially correlational, and do not provide direct evidence that recurrent processing is essential for visual consciousness. The causal issue has been addressed by several researchers (e.g., Boyer, Harrison, & Ro, 2005; Corthout, Uttle, Ziemann, Cowey, & Hallett,

---

KEY TERM

masking: suppression of the perception of a stimulus (e.g., visual; auditory) by presenting a second stimulus (the masking stimulus) very soon thereafter.

1999) using transcranial magnetic stimulation (TMS; see Glossary). TMS was applied to early visual cortex (V1) at different time intervals after the presentation of a visual stimulus. Conscious perception of the stimulus was suppressed when TMS was administered about 100 ms after the stimulus, but not when it was presented less than 80 ms afterwards. What is the significance of these findings? Since feedforward reaches V1 about 35 ms after stimulus presentation, it is unlikely that TMS disrupted the feedforward sweep. It is much more likely that TMS disrupted subsequent recurrent processing starting about 100 ms after stimulus onset, suggesting that recurrent processing is needed for conscious perception.

Evaluation

The possibility of using recurrent processing as a neural index or marker of consciousness is an exciting one. As we have seen, we may fail to detect conscious awareness with behavioural measures because of problems relating to attention, memory, or language. It is possible that recurrent processing is less affected by these other cognitive functions than are most behavioural measures, but more evidence is needed before reaching any clear conclusions. In addition, there is accumulating evidence that conscious awareness is associated with recurrent processing but not with the feedforward sweep.

What are the limitations of Lamme's (2006) approach? First, it focuses explicitly on *visual* consciousness. As a consequence, it is uninformative about the processes involved when we are consciously aware of past or future events.

Second, it is unlikely that recurrent processing is *always* associated with conscious awareness. For example, there are numerous back connections between early visual cortex (V1) and visual thalamus, but it is generally assumed that the visual thalamus is not involved in conscious awareness (Tononi & Koch, 2007).

Third, recurrent processing without conscious awareness was reported by Scholte, Wittreveen, Soekreijse, and Lamme (2006). Participants focused their attention on a stream of black and white letters and reported the presence of white vowels. Sometimes additional square figures were present. These figures produced recurrent processing, but 50% of participants reported afterwards that they had not seen them. It was only when there was widespread recurrent processing that the figures were consistently seen. The interpretation of these findings is somewhat ambiguous. The failure to report seeing the figures when associated with modest amounts of recurrent processing may mean that fairly extensive recurrent processing is needed for conscious perception. Alternatively, it may be that only modest recurrent processing is needed for conscious perception, but memory failures impaired participants' ability to report their conscious experience. Another possibility is that recurrent processing needs to be accompanied by selective attention to become conscious (Max Velmans, personal communication).

BRAIN AREAS ASSOCIATED WITH CONSCIOUSNESS

There has been considerable interest in recent years in trying to locate the brain areas most associated with conscious visual awareness. Before proceeding, it must be emphasised that no one believes that simple answers will be forthcoming or that certain brain areas are *always* involved in conscious visual awareness. With that in mind, how should we proceed? What is needed is to compare patterns of brain activation associated with visual processing leading to conscious awareness with those associated with visual processing *not* leading to awareness. Several paradigms have been used for this purpose (see Kim & Blake, 2005, for a review), and three of them are discussed below.

First, there is masking (discussed above), in which a target stimulus is shortly followed by a masking stimulus that prevents conscious perception of the target stimulus. This masked condition can be compared with a non-masked condition in which the target stimulus is consciously perceived. This paradigm is effective at producing the presence or absence of conscious perception. However, the physical stimulation differs in the masked and non-masked conditions, making it hard to interpret differences in brain activation in the two conditions. This can be overcome by focusing on the masked condition and comparing brain activation when the target stimulus is or is not detected.

Second, there is **binocular rivalry**. This involves a paradigm in which two visual stimuli are presented (one to each eye) for a period of time. Observers perceive only one stimulus at any time, with the stimulus being consciously perceived alternating over time. Binocular rivalry provides an effective way of assessing brain activity associated with conscious awareness. The reason is that there are shifts in conscious content as the stimulus being perceived varies without any changes in the stimuli themselves.

Third, there are paradigms in which lack of conscious awareness is apparently due to distracted attention. Examples include inattentional blindness and change blindness (see Chapter 4). Inattentional blindness occurs when the presence of an unexpected object in a visual display is not consciously detected. Change blindness occurs when observers fail to detect some change in the visual environment. Inattentional blindness and change blindness are both phenomena that occur in everyday life and so possess ecological validity. However, it is often hard to be sure that failures to report the unexpected object or the visual change are due to failures of conscious experience rather than to limitations of attention or memory (see Chapter 4).

Evidence

We will start by considering the brain areas activated during the processing of visual stimuli that are not consciously perceived. Some evidence suggests that such processing is very limited. For example, Dehaene et al. (2001) compared brain activation during conscious perception of visually presented words with subliminal presentation (and no conscious perception) of the same words. Activation was largely confined to the visual cortex when the words were presented subliminally. However, there was widespread visual, parietal, and frontal activation when they were consciously perceived. Baars

(2002, p. 47) reviewed 13 studies in which conscious and non-conscious conditions were compared, and concluded: "Conscious perception…enables access to widespread brain sources, whereas unconscious input processing is limited to sensory regions."

In fact, several studies indicate that the processing of masked visual stimuli can be greater than implied by Baars' conclusion. For example, Rees (2007) discussed an unpublished experiment on binocular rivalry he carried out with colleagues in which observers were presented with pictures of faces and houses, one to each eye. Functional neuroimaging (fMRI) was used to assess activation in brain areas associated with face processing (the fusiform face area) and object processing (parahippocampal place area). They key finding was that it was possible to predict the identity of the suppressed (unconscious) stimulus with almost 90% accuracy by studying the brain activation pattern in those brain areas. Thus, even suppressed stimuli were processed at high levels of the visual system.

Kiefer and Brendel (2006) used a lexical decision task in which participants decided whether letter strings formed words, with the letter strings being preceded by masked stimuli that could not be perceived consciously. Some words on the lexical decision task were preceded by semantically related masked words, whereas others were preceded by semantically unrelated masked words. Kiefer and Brendel were especially interested in the N400 component of the event-related potential (ERP), which is sensitive to semantic processing. The amplitude of the N400 component to words on the lexical decision task differed significantly depending on whether the preceding masked word was semantically related to it. Thus, words not consciously perceived were nevertheless processed in terms of their meaning.

KEY TERM

binocular rivalry: this occurs when an observer perceives only one visual stimulus when two different stimuli are presented (one to each eye); the stimulus seen alternates over time.

There is further evidence that stimuli that are not consciously perceived can be processed in terms of their meaning. For example, there is the phenomenon of affective blindsight (see Chapter 15). In this phenomenon, the emotional significance of emotional stimuli (e.g., faces) is processed even though the observer has no conscious awareness of the stimuli (Pegna, Khateb, Lazeyras, & Seghier, 2005).

What conclusions can we draw? According to Rees (2007, p. 878), "All visually responsive cortical areas appear to show evidence for unconscious visual processing." However, unconscious visual processing is typically associated with a much smaller increase in activity in these areas than in conscious visual processing.

We turn now to major differences in brain activation between stimuli that are consciously perceived and those that are not. Lumer, Friston, and Rees (1998) studied binocular rivalry. Observers were presented with a red drifting grating to one eye and a green face to the other, and they pressed keys to indicate which stimulus they were perceiving. Lumer et al. used fMRI to identify the brain areas especially active immediately prior to a switch in conscious perception from one stimulus to the other. The anterior cingulate and the prefrontal cortex were among the several areas showing increased activation during shifts in conscious perception.

McIntosh, Rajah, and Lobaugh (1999) adopted the strategy of analysing brain activation data separately for those participants who did or did not become aware of some aspect of the experimental situation. They carried out a PET study on associative learning. There were two visual stimuli, and the task was to respond to one of them (the target) but not to the other. There were also two tones, one predicting that a visual stimulus would be presented and the other predicting the absence of a visual stimulus. The participants were divided into those who noticed the association between the auditory and visual stimuli (the aware group) and those who did not (the unaware group).

McIntosh et al. (1999) found that the greatest difference between the two groups in the brain activity produced by the tones was in the left prefrontal cortex (BA9; see Chapter 1). This finding suggested that this area was associated with conscious awareness of the significance of the tones. In addition, McIntosh et al. found evidence that the left prefrontal cortex forms part of a much larger neural system associated with conscious awareness including the right prefrontal cortex, bilateral superior temporal cortices, medial cerebellum, and occipital cortex.

Eriksson, Larsson, Ahlström, and Nyberg (2006) presented auditory (sounds of objects) and visual (pictures of objects) stimuli under masked conditions. They then compared brain activation on trials in which the stimulus was identified (conscious perception) with that when it was not identified (lack of conscious perception). The key finding was that activation in the lateral prefrontal cortex and the anterior cingulate cortex was associated with both auditory and visual conscious awareness. Only auditory awareness was associated with superior temporal activity and only visual awareness was associated with parietal activity. Thus, conscious awareness in the auditory and visual modalities is associated with a mixture of common and specific brain activations.

Rees (2007) reviewed findings from studies in which the focus was on brain activation associated with changes in visual awareness. There was a clear clustering of activation in the superior parietal and dorsolateral prefrontal cortex (see Figure 16.2), areas that are outside visual cortex. Of particular note, similar findings were reported across several different paradigms, including binocular rivalry, successful identification of visually masked words, and the detection of change in a visually presented object.

One of the problems in interpreting most of the evidence is that there is typically more effective information processing on trials associated with conscious awareness than on trials not associated with conscious awareness. Thus, it is sometimes hard to decide whether brain activity reflects conscious awareness rather than simply effective information processing. Lau and Passingham (2006) carried out a study on masking in which performance levels were the same for conditions associated with or

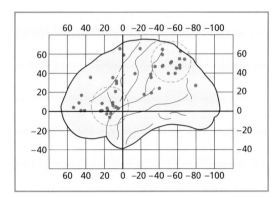

Figure 16.2 Areas of parietal and prefrontal cortex associated with changes in visual awareness (based on findings from several studies). From Rees (2007) with permission from the Royal Society.

without visual awareness. Conscious perception was associated with activation in the mid-dorsolateral prefrontal cortex (BA46) in the absence of any confounding with performance level. These findings strengthen the argument that the dorsolateral prefrontal cortex is specifically associated with conscious awareness.

The major limitation of the research discussed so far is that it is essentially correlational – visual consciousness is associated with certain patterns of brain activation. More direct evidence of the involvement of parietal and prefrontal cortex in visual consciousness can be obtained by applying transcranial magnetic stimulation (TMS) to those brain areas. Awareness of visual change was impaired when TMS was applied to the right (but not the left) dorsolateral prefrontal cortex (Turatto, Sandrini, & Miniussi, 2004). Beck, Muggleton, Walsh, and Lavie (2006) used a task in which participants detected changes between two stimuli separated by a brief interval of time. TMS applied to right (but not left) parietal cortex reduced the number of changes detected.

More evidence of the involvement of frontal and parietal cortex in visual consciousness comes from individuals with neglect or extinction (see Chapter 5). Individuals with neglect have brain damage that prevents them from detecting visual stimuli presented to the side opposite the brain damage. The brain damage is typically in the parietal cortex but sometimes also includes the frontal cortex (Driver & Mattingley, 1998). It is noteworthy that neglect patients fail to show conscious awareness of visual stimuli even when there is activation of several areas of visual cortex (Driver, Vuilleumier, Eimer, & Rees, 2001).

Extinction involves failing to detect stimuli presented to the side opposite to the brain damage when another stimulus is presented at the same time to the same side as the brain damage, and generally involves parietal damage. Extinction patients are often consciously aware of some visual stimuli, and such awareness is associated with integrated activity between visual cortical areas and undamaged parietal and prefrontal regions (Vuilleumier & Driver, 2007).

Evaluation

Visual stimuli that are not consciously perceived are often associated with modest activation of most of the visual brain areas activated during conscious visual perception. That suggests that there can be extensive processing of visual stimuli of which the observer has no conscious awareness. There is consistent evidence that visual consciousness is associated with activation in prefrontal cortex and parietal cortex, and the anterior cingulate can also be involved. Research using TMS (e.g., Beck et al., 2006; Turatto et al., 2004) has strengthened the argument that prefrontal cortex and parietal cortex are necessary for visual awareness.

What are the limitations of research in this area? First, it has focused on which brain areas are involved in visual consciousness, leaving it unclear whether the same brain areas are involved in other situations. However, relevant evidence was reported by Addis, Wong, and Schacter (2007). They asked participants to think of (and elaborate on) various past and future events (see Chapter 7), tasks requiring conscious awareness of the events in question. Several brain regions were activated during the elaboration of both past and future events, including left prefrontal cortex and parietal regions plus the medial temporal lobe. Thus, there is some overlap in the brain areas activated during visual consciousness and when consciously thinking about past and future events.

Second, it is difficult to identify the precise cognitive processes associated with activation in prefrontal cortex and parietal cortex. For example, brain activation in those brain areas occurs when observers' conscious perception switches from one stimulus to the other in binocular rivalry tasks or when a masked stimulus is identified. It is entirely possible that this brain activation reflects changes in attention as well as changes in visual awareness. In other words, the functional roles of prefrontal and parietal cortex in visual awareness are unclear. However, as is discussed later, prefrontal cortex may play an important role in integrating information from different brain areas to facilitate conscious perception.

Third, it is probably unwise to generalise to other species from the findings on humans. The development of consciousness in humans presumably occurred as a product of natural selection, with the details varying from species to species. As a consequence, the brain areas associated with consciousness in other species may well differ from those associated with consciousness in humans.

THEORIES OF CONSCIOUSNESS

Numerous theories of consciousness have been proposed over the years, and we will consider only a few of the most important ones here. In recent years, there has been a large increase in the number of theories focusing on the brain mechanisms associated with consciousness. We have already considered Lamme's theory of consciousness, according to which recurrent processing is of crucial importance to conscious awareness. Here, we will consider other major theoretical approaches.

Global workspace theory

Baars (1988) and Baars and Franklin (2003, 2007) put forward a global workspace theory.

One of the main assumptions of this theory is that we are only consciously aware of a small fraction of the information processing going on in our brain at any given moment. We generally become aware of information that is of most importance to us, for example, because it is connected to our current goals. Baars and Franklin (2007) used a theatre metaphor to clarify the nature of their global workspace theory. According to this metaphor, "Unconscious processors in the theatre audience receive broadcasts from a conscious 'bright spot' on the stage. Control of the bright spot corresponds to selective attention" (p. 957).

We will consider some of the main assumptions of global workspace theory in more detail. One major assumption is that there are very close links between consciousness and attention. For example, Baars (1997b) invited us to consider sentences such as, "We look in order to see" or "We listen in order to hear". According to Baars (1997b), "The distinction is between selecting an experience and being conscious of the selected event. In everyday language, the first word of each pair ["look", "listen"] involves attention; the second word ["see", "hear"] involves consciousness." Thus, attention resembles choosing a television channel and consciousness resembles the picture on the screen.

A second assumption is that much human information processing involves a large number of special-purpose processors that are typically unconscious. These processors are distributed in numerous brain areas, with each processor carrying out specialised functions. For example, there are brain areas specialised for different aspects of vision such as colour and motion processing (see Chapter 2).

A third assumption is that, "Conscious contents evoke widespread brain activation" (Baars & Franklin, 2007, p. 956). What happens is that consciousness is associated with *integrating* information from several special-purpose processors. Thus, unconscious processing generally involves several special-purpose processors operating in relative isolation from each other, whereas conscious processing involves integrated brain activity across large areas of the brain.

Dehaene and Naccache's theory

Dehaene and Naccache (2001) put forward a global workspace theory resembling Baars' theoretical approach but going beyond it in identifying the main brain areas associated with conscious awareness. They argued that conscious awareness depends on simultaneous activation of several distant parts of the brain. The specific brain areas involved depend in part on the content of the conscious experience. For example, conscious experience of a face involves sufficient activation in the fusiform face area (see Chapter 3), whereas conscious experience of motion involves MT+ within the middle temporal area. Transcranial magnetic stimulation (TMS) applied to that area prevented the conscious perception of motion (Walsh, Ellison, Battelli, & Cowey, 1998). Dehaene and Naccache (2001) assumed that the brain areas involved in the global workspace and conscious experience include parts of the prefrontal cortex (e.g., BA46) and the anterior cingulate, as well as various content-specific areas (see Figure 16.3). BA46 (which forms an important part of the dorsolateral prefrontal cortex) and the anterior cingulate are both much involved in problem solving (see Chapter 12) and reasoning (see Chapter 14).

This theory was developed by Dehaene, Changeux, Naccache, Sackur, and Sergent (2006). They identified three major states that can occur when a visual stimulus is presented:

(1) *Conscious state*: There is much activation in areas involved in basic visual processing, and neurons in parietal, prefrontal, and cingulate cortex associated with attention are also activated.
(2) *Preconscious state*: There is sufficient basic visual processing to permit conscious awareness but there is insufficient top-down attention.
(3) *Subliminal state*: There is insufficient basic visual processing to permit conscious awareness regardless of the involvement of attention.

In other words, conscious visual awareness requires basic visual processing (bottom-up

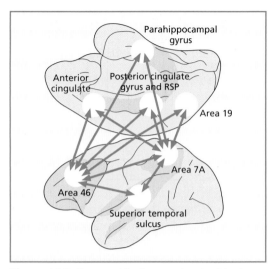

Figure 16.3 Proposed brain areas involved in the global workspace in which there are associations between the prefrontal cortex (BA46), the anterior cingulate, the parietal area, and the temporal area. From Goldman-Rakic (1988). Reprinted with permission from the *Annual Review of Neuroscience, Volume 11*. Copyright © 1988 Annual Reviews www.annualreviews.org

processing) and attention (top-down processing). There are two types of non-conscious processing, depending on whether a lack of conscious awareness is due to insufficient bottom-up or insufficient top-down processing.

Evidence: attention and consciousness

The theoretical assumption that conscious awareness depends on prior selective attention may seem reasonable, and is probably correct most of the time. However, there is increasing evidence that it is not always correct. As Lamme (2003a) pointed out, if we are consciously aware of all attended stimuli, then we might as well eliminate one of the two terms. He put forward an alternative (and controversial) viewpoint in which consciousness can *precede* attention (see Figure 16.4). According to Lamme's theory, the linkage between consciousness and attention is looser than is generally imagined. More specifically, "We are 'conscious' of many inputs but, without attention, this conscious experience cannot be reported and is quickly

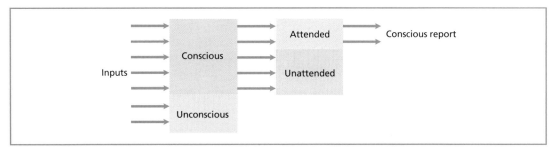

Figure 16.4 Lamme's model of visual awareness and its relation to attention. In this model, it is assumed that many visual stimuli reach consciousness but only those that are subsequently attended are reported. Reprinted from Lamme (2003), Copyright © 2003, with permission from Elsevier.

erased and forgotten" (Lamme, 2003a, p. 13). This initial, short-lived conscious experience corresponds to what Block (2007) calls "phenomenal consciousness". There is also a longer-lasting form of consciousness that depends on attention and can be used to provide a conscious report (see Figure 16.4). This corresponds to Block's (2007) "access consciousness", which involves information often used to guide action. For example, suppose you suddenly notice the steady ticking of a nearby clock. You may have previously had brief phenomenal consciousness of the ticking. However, access consciousness was required to shift your attention to the noise.

When we spend some time close to a ticking clock, we occasionally have full conscious awareness of the ticking (access consciousness). Most of the time, however, the ticking is at the periphery of awareness (phenomenal consciousness).

Koch and Tsuchiya (2007) agreed with Lamme (2003) that attention and consciousness are distinct phenomena. They argued that attention (specifically, top-down, goal-driven attention) fulfils different functions from consciousness and so cannot be regarded as the same. More specifically, top-down attention selects some aspect of the stimulus input defined by location in space, a given feature (e.g., square shape), or by an object. In contrast, the functions of consciousness "include summarising all information that pertains to the current state of the organism and its environment and ensuring this compact summary is accessible to the planning areas of the brain, and also detecting anomalies and errors, decision making, language, inferring the internal state of other animals, setting long-term goals, making recursive models and rational thought" (Koch & Tsuchiya, 2007, p. 17).

Lamme (2003) and Koch and Tsuchiya (2007) agree that consciousness without attention is possible. Koch and Tsuchiya also claim that attention without consciousness is possible. Below we focus on these two predictions.

Evidence suggesting that it is possible for conscious awareness to exist in the absence of attention was reported by Landman, Spekreijse, and Lamme (2003), in a study on change blindness discussed in Chapter 4.

Evidence from several kinds of experiment indicates that attention can influence behaviour in the absence of consciousness. For example, Jiang, Costello, Fang, Huang, and He (2006) presented pictures of male and female nudes that were completely invisible to the participants because of continuous flash suppression. In spite of their invisibility, these pictures influenced participants' attentional processes. The attention of heterosexual males was attracted to invisible female nudes, and that of heterosexual females to invisible male nudes. Gay males had a tendency to attend to the location of nude males, and gay/bisexual females' attentional preferences were between those of heterosexual males and females.

Evidence that attentional processes can influence task performance in the absence of conscious awareness was reported by Naccache, Blandin, and Dehaene (2002; see Chapter 2). Participants decided as rapidly as possible whether a target digit was greater or smaller than 5. Another digit that was invisible was presented immediately before the target digit. The two digits were congruent (i.e., both below or both above 5) or incongruent (i.e., one below and one above 5). Attention to the visual display was manipulated by having a cue present or absent.

Naccache et al. (2002) assessed the effects of the invisible digit on response times to the target digit. Information about the nature of the invisible digit (i.e., congruent or incongruent with the target digit) had no effect on uncued trials but a highly significant effect on cued trials (see Figure 16.5). Attentional processes amplified the information extracted from the

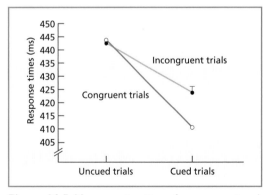

Figure 16.5 Mean reaction times for congruent and incongruent trials that were cued or uncued. From Naccache et al. (2002). Reprinted with permission of Wiley-Blackwell.

invisible digit, but did so without producing conscious awareness of that digit.

Evidence: unconscious special-purpose processors

There is plentiful evidence that considerable information processing can occur in the absence of conscious awareness. For example, consider conscious visual awareness. Much visual processing occurs in brain areas that are to some extent specialised for colour processing and motion processing (see Chapter 2). However, as Tononi and Koch (2008, p. 253) pointed out, "You cannot experience visual shapes independently of their colour, or perceive the left half of the visual field independently of the right half." These findings suggest that the outputs of the specialised visual-processing areas are initially unconscious.

The notion that much information processing occurs without conscious awareness is also supported by much of the research on brain-damaged patients we have discussed throughout this book. Examples include achromatopsia and blindsight (see Chapter 2), prosopagnosia (see Chapter 4), neglect and extinction (see Chapter 5), and amnesia (see Chapter 7).

Evidence: consciousness involves integrated brain functioning

The notion that integrated brain functioning is crucial to conscious awareness is an appealing one. One reason is because what we are consciously aware of is nearly always integrated information. For example, as Tononi and Koch (2008) indicated, it is almost impossible to perceive an object while ignoring its colour or to perceive only part of the visual field.

Earlier we discussed a study by McIntosh et al. (1999). They found that conscious visual awareness seemed to be associated with an integrated network of brain areas, including the prefrontal cortex, occipital cortex, cerebellum, and superior temporal cortex. Similar findings were reported by Rodriguez et al. (1999). Participants saw pictures that were easily perceived as faces when presented upright but which were seen as meaningless black-and-white

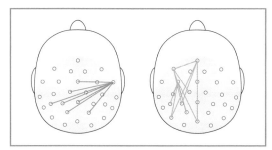

Figure 16.6 Phase synchrony (orange lines) and phase desynchrony (blue lines) in EEG 180360 ms after stimulus presentation in the no face perception (left side) and face perception (right side) conditions. Reprinted by permission from Macmillan Publishers Ltd: *Nature* (Rodriguez et al., 1999), Copyright © 1999.

shapes when presented upside-down. EEG was recorded from 30 electrodes, and the resultant data were then analysed to work out the extent to which electrical activity was in synchrony across electrodes (phase synchrony: co-ordinated activity in several different brain areas). The key findings related to brain activity at the time after picture presentation (180–360 ms) at which faces were perceived in the upright condition. There was considerable phase synchrony in this condition, especially in the area between the left parieto-occipital and frontotemporal regions (see Figure 16.6). In contrast, there was phase desynchrony rather than synchrony when no face was seen. Thus, integrated, synchronised activity across large areas of the cortex was associated with conscious awareness in the sense of coherent perception of the face. There was conscious awareness of meaningless shapes in the upside-down condition.

Melloni et al. (2007) pointed out a potential problem with the study by Rodriguez et al. (1999). There may have been much more processing (and brain activation) in the upright condition than in the upside-down condition, and this may have played a part in producing the increased phase synchrony found in the upright condition. In their study, Melloni et al. compared brain activity to words that were either consciously perceived or not consciously perceived, and found sufficient EEG activation to words not consciously perceived to suggest that they were thoroughly processed. In spite of that, *only* consciously perceived words produced synchronised neural activity across several cortical areas, including prefrontal cortex. There is an issue about causality with these findings – did synchronised neural activity *precede* and influence conscious awareness or did it occur merely as a *consequence* of conscious awareness?

Evidence: consciousness involves prefrontal, parietal, and cingulate cortex

Dehaene et al. (2006) argued that prefrontal, parietal, and cingulate cortex are brain regions of special importance to conscious awareness. We have discussed much evidence in this chapter that is generally supportive of that argument. For example, Rees (2007), in his meta-analysis, reported that changes in visual awareness were fairly consistently associated with activation of superior parietal and dorsolateral prefrontal cortex.

At the risk of repetition, we will very briefly mention three limitations of most of the research. First, functional neuroimaging has established that a brain area such as dorsolateral prefrontal cortex is associated with conscious awareness, but that does not show that it is necessarily involved. Second, there is only partial overlap in the central brain areas identified in different studies. For example, numerous studies have implicated the prefrontal cortex in conscious awareness, but the precise parts of the prefrontal cortex activated vary from study to study. Third, much is known about the neural correlates of visual awareness or consciousness but we need more research before it is clear whether the same brain areas are associated with other forms of conscious awareness.

Overall evaluation

There is reasonable support for all of the major assumptions of both global workspace theories. It is probably true that selective attention typically precedes conscious awareness, that we remain unaware of much processing within specialised processing systems, and that conscious awareness is generally associated with widespread integrated brain activity. Finally, prefrontal cortex, the anterior cingulate, and areas within the parietal cortex are more associated with consciousness than other brain areas.

What are the limitations of global workspace theories? First, there is some (admittedly controversial) evidence that conscious awareness can precede rather than follow selective attention. Second, identifying the brain areas associated with conscious awareness is not the same as having an adequate theory of consciousness. Third, the great majority of the research has considered only visual consciousness, and so the applicability of global workspace theories to other forms of conscious awareness remains to be assessed. Fourth, we still do not really know whether integrated brain functioning is more a cause or a consequence of conscious awareness. It could be argued that it is less theoretically important if it is only a consequence.

IS CONSCIOUSNESS UNITARY?

Most people believe that they have a single, unitary consciousness, although a few are in two minds on the issue. However, consider **split-brain patients**, who have few connections between the two brain hemispheres as a result of surgery. In the great majority of cases, the corpus callosum (bridge) between the two brain hemispheres was cut surgically to contain epileptic seizures within one hemisphere. The corpus callosum is a collection of 250 million axons connecting sites in one hemisphere with sites in the other. Do split-brain patients have two minds, each with its own consciousness?

Contrasting answers to the above question have been offered by experts in the field. On one side of the argument is Roger Sperry (1913–1994), who won the Nobel Prize for his influential research on split-brain patients. He was firmly of the opinion that these patients do have two consciousnesses: "Each hemisphere seemed to have its own separate and private sensations…the minor hemisphere [the right one] constitutes a second conscious entity that is characteristically human and runs along in parallel with the more dominant stream of consciousness in the major hemisphere [the left one]" (Sperry, 1968, p. 723). He regarded the left hemisphere as the dominant one because language processing typically occurs in that hemisphere.

On the other side of the argument are Gazzaniga, Ivry, and Mangun (2002). According to them, split-brain patients have only a single conscious system, based in the left hemisphere, that tries to make sense of the information available to it. This system is called the interpreter, defined as "A left-brain system that seeks explanation for internal and external events in order to produce appropriate response behaviour" (p. G-5). Cooney and Gazzaniga (2003) developed this theoretical position. They argued that the interpretive process continues to function even when provided with very limited information, as occurs with many brain-damaged patients. In their own words, "This [system] generates a causal understanding of events that is subjectively complete and seemingly self-evident, even when that understanding is incomplete" (p. 162).

Evidence

We will start by considering the subjective experience of split-brain patients. According to Colvin and Gazzaniga (2007, p. 189), "No split-brain patient has ever woken up following callostomy [cutting of the corpus callosum] and felt as though his/her experience of self had fundamentally changed or that two selves now inhabited the same body."

In order to understand the findings from split-brain patients, note that information from the left visual field goes to the right hemisphere,

---

KEY TERM

split-brain patients: these are patients in whom most of the direct links between the two hemispheres have been severed; as a result, they can experience problems in co-ordinating their processing and behaviour.

whereas information from the right visual field goes to the left hemisphere (see Chapter 2). More generally, the left half of the body is controlled by the right hemisphere and the right half of the body is controlled by the left hemisphere. It is often thought that split-brain patients have great difficulty in functioning effectively. This is *not* the case. It was not realised initially that cutting the corpus callosum caused any problems for split-brain patients, because they ensure that information about the environment reaches both hemispheres by moving their eyes around. Impaired performance in split-brain patients is produced by presenting visual stimuli briefly to only one hemisphere so there are no eye movements while the stimuli are visible.

Trevarthen (2004) discussed studies comparing the abilities of the two hemispheres in split-brain patients. The right hemisphere outperformed the left one on tasks involving visual or touch perception of complex shapes, manipulations of geometric patterns, and judgements involving hand explorations of shapes. In contrast, the left hemisphere was much better than the right hemisphere at tasks involving language. When language tasks were presented to the right hemisphere, "The subjects often gave no response. If urged to reply, they said that there might have been some weak and ill-defined event, or else they confabulated [invented] experiences, as if unable to apply a test of truth or falsity to spontaneously imagined answers to questions" (p. 875).

The fact that the right hemisphere of most split-brain patients lacks speech makes it hard to know whether it possesses its own consciousness. Accordingly, it is important to study split-brain patients with reasonable language abilities in the right hemisphere. Gazzaniga and Ledoux (1978) studied Paul S, a split-brain patient with unusually well-developed right-hemisphere language abilities. Paul S showed limited evidence of consciousness in his right hemisphere by responding appropriately to questions using Scrabble letters with his left hand. For example, he could spell out his own name, that of his girlfriend, his hobbies, his

current mood, and so on. There were some interesting differences between Paul's hemispheres. For example, his right hemisphere said he wanted to be a racing driver, whereas his left hemisphere wanted to be a draughtsman.

Gazzaniga (1992) discussed other studies on Paul S. For example, a chicken claw was presented to his left hemisphere and a snow scene to his right hemisphere. Paul S was then asked to choose relevant pictures from an array. He chose a picture of a chicken with his right hand (connected to the left hemisphere) and he chose a shovel with his left hand (connected to the right hemisphere).

Superficially, these findings are consistent with the notion that Paul S had a separate consciousness in each hemisphere. However, this seems improbable when we focus on Paul S's explanation of his choices: "Oh, that's simple. The chicken claw goes with the chicken, and you need a shovel to clean out the chicken shed" (Gazzaniga, 1992, p. 124). Gazzaniga argued that Paul S's left hemisphere was interpreting actions initiated by the right hemisphere, with the right hemisphere contributing relatively little to the interpretation. Similarly, Paul S obeyed when his right hemisphere was given the command to walk. However, his left hemisphere explained his behaviour by saying something such as that he wanted a Coke.

Gazzaniga et al. (2002) reviewed other studies on split-brain patients indicating that they have very limited right-hemisphere consciousness. For example, their right hemispheres can understand words such as "pin" and "finger", but find it very hard to decide which of six words best describes the causal relationship between them ("bleed"). According to Gazzaniga et al. (p. 680), "The left hemisphere…is constantly…labelling experiences, making inferences as to cause, and carrying out a host of other cognitive activities. The right hemisphere is simply monitoring the world."

Baynes and Gazzaniga (2000) discussed the case of VJ, a split-brain patient whose writing is controlled by the right hemisphere whereas her speech is controlled by the left hemisphere. According to Baynes and Gazzaniga (p. 1362),

"She [VJ] is the first split…who is frequently dismayed by the independent performance of her right and left hands. She is discomfited by the fluent writing of her left hand [controlled by the right hemisphere] to unseen stimuli and distressed by the inability of her right hand to write out words she can read out loud and spell." Speculatively, we could interpret the evidence from VJ as suggesting limited dual consciousness.

Uddin, Rayman, and Zaidel (2005) pointed out that the ability to recognise one's own face has often been regarded as an indication of reasonable self-awareness. They presented NG, a 70-year-old split-brain patient, with pictures representing different percentages of her own face and that of an unfamiliar face. The key finding was that she could recognise her own face equally well whether it was presented to her left or right hemisphere. Her self-recognition performance was only slightly worse than that of healthy individuals in a previous study, and suggests the existence of some basic self-awareness in both hemispheres.

The notion that the right hemisphere plays an important role in self-awareness and thus perhaps in consciousness generally has received support from studies on healthy participants. A review of neuroimaging studies by Keenan and Gorman (2007) indicated that self-awareness is generally associated with greater right hemisphere than left hemisphere activation. The limitation with such evidence is that it is only correlational. However, similar findings were reported by Guise et al. (2007) using TMS. TMS applied to the right prefrontal cortex disrupted self-perspective taking in healthy participants, whereas it had no effect on other-perspective taking. These various findings suggest that conscious experience may depend more on the right hemisphere than was assumed by Gazzaniga et al. (2002).

We turn now to Cooney and Gazzaniga's (2003) hypothesis that the left-hemisphere interpretive system often continues to interpret what is going on even in brain-damaged patients lacking access to important information. As a result, its interpretations can be very inaccurate. For example, patients with **reduplicative par-** **amnesia** believe there are multiple copies of places and people (see Bell, Halligan, & Ellis, 2006, for a review of this and other delusions). Gazzaniga (2000) studied a female patient with reduplicative paramnesia. She was studied at New York Hospital but was convinced she was at home in Freeport, Maine. When asked to explain why there were so many lifts outside the door, she replied, "Do you know how much it cost me to have those put in?"

Patients with reduplicative paramnesia have substantial difficulties in relating their stored memories with their actual experiences. There is evidence (reviewed by Feinberg and Keenan, 2005) showing that such patients are more likely to have damage to the right hemisphere than to the left one. For example, 97% of patients had right-hemisphere damage in the frontal lobe compared to only 48% who had left-hemisphere damage in that lobe. Similar findings were obtained when the focus was on the temporal or parietal lobes. These findings are consistent with the notion of a left-hemisphere interpretive system that has difficulty in accessing information stored within the right hemisphere. Alternatively, damage to the right hemisphere may interfere more directly with conscious experience.

Evaluation

Research on split-brain patients has not fully resolved the issue of whether it is possible to have two separate consciousnesses. The commonest view is that the left hemisphere in split-brain patients plays the dominant role in consciousness, because it is the location of an interpreter or self-supervisory system providing coherent (but sometimes inaccurate) interpretations of events. In contrast, the right hemisphere engages in various relatively low-level processing activities, but probably lacks its own

KEY TERM

reduplicative paramnesia: a memory disorder in which the person believes that multiple copies of people and places exist.

consciousness. This view is supported by findings showing the left hemisphere over-ruling the right hemisphere, and by the persistent failure to observe a genuine dialogue between the two hemispheres. It could also be very disruptive if each hemisphere had its own consciousness because of potential conflicts between them. However, we lack definitive evidence.

It appears that the right hemisphere exhibits self-recognition and so may exhibit some self-awareness (Keenan & Gorman, 2007; Uddin et al., 2005). Colvin and Gazzaniga (2007, p. 189) came to the following conclusion: "Left hemisphere consciousness may be considered superior to that of the right hemisphere. However, the right hemisphere has some conscious experience accessible through non-verbal means." It is possible that the contribution of the right hemisphere to conscious experience is greater than is implied by this conclusion.

CHAPTER SUMMARY

- Introduction
  In order to understand consciousness, we need to consider the nature of conscious experience, access to information in consciousness, and self-knowledge. The claimed functions of consciousness include the social one of making it easier for us to predict and understand other people, disseminate and exchange information, and exercise global control. It is often argued that a major function of consciousness is to control our actions. In fact, however, there is increasing evidence from cognitive neuroscience that some of our decisions are prepared preconsciously in the brain some time before we are consciously aware of the decision.

- Measuring conscious experience
  Conscious awareness has typically been assessed by behavioural measures (e.g., verbal reports; yes/no decisions). A major problem is that failure to report a given conscious experience may be due to failures of attention, memory, or inner speech rather than to absence of the relevant conscious experience. Lamme argued that we should focus on neural correlates of consciousness. He argued that conscious experience is associated with recurrent processing rather than the feedforward sweep, but it is unlikely that recurrent processing is *always* associated with conscious experience.

- Brain areas associated with consciousness
  Research using various paradigms (e.g., masking; binocular rivalry) has indicated that the processing of stimuli that are not consciously perceived is often associated with modest brain activation in most areas of visual cortex. However, areas within the prefrontal and parietal cortex are typically activated only during processing of stimuli that are consciously perceived. The precise functional roles of these brain regions in visual awareness are still unclear, but they may be involved in integrating information from various brain areas.

- Theories of consciousness
  According to global workspace theories, selective attention helps to determine the information of which we become aware. Another key assumption is that conscious awareness is associated with integrated, synchronous activity involving many brain areas, especially prefrontal cortex, the anterior cingulate, and parts of the parietal cortex. There is reasonable support for all the major assumptions of global workspace theories. However, there is

evidence that conscious awareness can precede rather than follow selective attention. Another issue is that it remains unclear whether activation in areas such as prefrontal cortex and anterior cingulate helps to produce conscious awareness or whether it is merely a consequence of conscious awareness.

- Is consciousness unitary?
Evidence from split-brain patients indicates that behaviour can be controlled to some extent by each hemisphere. However, the left hemisphere of split-brain patients is clearly dominant in determining conscious awareness and behaviour. Thus, the left hemisphere can be regarded as acting as an interpreter of internal and external events. In contrast, the right hemisphere of split-brain patients engages in low-level processing. It may well lack consciousness, but may have some self-awareness. The interpreter in the left hemisphere often continues to function even when deprived of important relevant information. Some evidence suggests that the right hemisphere may play an important role in consciousness.

FURTHER READING

- Baars, B.J., & Franklin, S. (2007). An architectural model of conscious and unconscious brain functions: Global Workspace Theory and IDA. *Neural Networks, 20,* 955–961. This article presents an updated version of global workspace theory, which has been one of the most influential theoretical approaches to consciousness.
- Lamme, V.A.F. (2006). Towards a true neural stance on consciousness. *Trends in Cognitive Sciences, 10,* 494–501. In this thought-provoking article, Lamme argues that it may be preferable to define visual consciousness in neural rather than behavioural terms.
- Rees, G. (2007). Neural correlates of the contents of visual awareness in humans. *Philosophical Transactions of the Royal Society B, 362,* 877–886. Geraint Rees discusses research on the brain areas that are involved in visual awareness.
- Tononi, G., & Koch, C. (2008). The neural correlates of consciousness: An update. *Annals of the New York Academy of Sciences, 1124,* 239–261. Guilio Tononi and Christof Koch provide an excellent review of consciousness from the cognitive neuroscience perspective.
- Velmans, M. (2009). How to define consciousness – and how not to define consciousness. *Journal of Consciousness Studies, 16*(5), 139–156. Max Velmans considers several well-known definitions of consciousness, and provides a thoughtful analysis of their limitations.
- Velmans, M., & Schneider, S. (Eds.) (2007). *The Blackwell companion to consciousness.* Oxford: Blackwell Publishing. This edited book contains dozens of chapters by the world's leading researchers on consciousness. The most important contemporary theories of consciousness are discussed in Part III of the book.

GLOSSARY

accommodation: one of the binocular cues to depth, based on the variation in optical power produced by a thickening of the lens of the eye when focusing on a close object.

achromatopsia: this is a condition involving brain damage in which there is little or no colour perception, but form and motion perception are relatively intact.

adaptive expertise: using acquired knowledge to develop strategies for dealing with novel problems.

affective blindsight: the ability to discriminate between emotional stimuli in the absence of conscious perception of these stimuli; found in patients with lesions to the primary visual cortex (see **blindsight**).

affective infusion: the process by which affective information influences various cognitive processes such as attention, learning, judgement, and memory.

affordances: the potential uses of an object, which Gibson claimed are perceived directly.

agrammatism: a condition in which speech production lacks grammatical structure and many function words and word endings are omitted; often also associated with comprehension difficulties.

akinetopsia: this is a brain-damaged condition in which stationary objects are perceived reasonably well but objects in motion cannot be perceived accurately.

algorithm: a computational procedure providing a specified set of steps to a solution.

allophony: an allophone is one of two or more similar sounds belonging to the same **phoneme**.

Alzheimer's disease: a condition involving progressive loss of memory and mental abilities.

anaphor resolution: working out the referent of a pronoun or noun by relating it to some previously mentioned noun or noun phrase.

anomia: a condition caused by brain damage in which there is an impaired ability to name objects.

anterior: towards the front of the brain.

anterograde amnesia: reduced ability to remember information acquired after the onset of amnesia.

Anton's syndrome: a condition found in some blind people in which they misinterpret their own visual imagery as visual perception.

aphasia: impaired language abilities as a result of brain damage.

apraxia: a neurological condition in which patients are unable to perform voluntary bodily movements.

articulatory suppression: rapid repetition of some simple sound (e.g., "the, the, the"), which uses the articulatory control process of the **phonological loop**.

artificial intelligence: this involves developing computer programs that produce intelligent outcomes; see **computational modelling**.

association: concerning brain damage, the finding that certain symptoms or performance impairments are consistently found together in numerous brain-damaged patients.

attentional bias: selective allocation of attention to threat-related stimuli when presented simultaneously with neutral stimuli.

attentional blink: a reduced ability to detect a second visual target when it follows closely the first visual target.

attentional counter-regulation: a coping strategy in which attentional processes are used so as to minimise emotional states (whether positive or negative).

autobiographical memory: memory for the events of one's own life.

autostereogram: a complex two-dimensional image that is perceived as three-dimensional when it is *not* focused on for a period of time.

availability heuristic: the assumption that the frequencies of events can be estimated accurately by the accessibility in memory.

back-propagation: a learning mechanism in **connectionist networks** based on comparing actual responses to correct ones.

base-rate information: the relative frequency of an event within a population.

belief bias: in syllogistic reasoning, the tendency to accept invalid conclusions that are believable and to reject valid conclusions that are unbelievable.

binding problem: the issue of integrating different kinds of information during visual perception.

binocular cues: cues to depth that require both eyes to be used together.

binocular disparity: the slight discrepancy in the retinal images of a visual scene in each eye; it forms the basis for **stereopsis**.

binocular rivalry: this occurs when an observer perceives only one visual stimulus when two different stimuli are presented (one to each eye); the stimulus seen alternates over time.

blindsight: the ability to respond appropriately to visual stimuli in the absence of conscious vision in patients with damage to the primary visual cortex.

BOLD: blood oxygen-level dependent contrast; this is the signal that is measured by **fMRI**.

bottom-up processing: processing that is directly influenced by environmental stimuli; see **top-down processing**.

bounded rationality: the notion that people are as rational as their processing limitations permit.

bridging inferences: inferences that are drawn to increase the coherence between the current and preceding parts of a text; also known as backward inferences.

Broca's aphasia: a form of **aphasia** involving non-fluent speech and grammatical errors.

cascade model: a model in which information passes from one level to the next before processing is complete at the first level.

categorical perception: perceiving stimuli as belonging to specific categories; found with **phonemes**.

category-specific deficits: disorders caused by brain damage in which **semantic memory** is disrupted for certain semantic categories.

central executive: a modality-free, limited capacity, component of **working memory**.

change blindness: failure to detect changes in the visual environment.

Charles Bonnet syndrome: a condition associated with eye disease involving recurrent and detailed hallucinations.

chromatic adaptation: reduced sensitivity to light of a given colour or hue after lengthy exposure.

chunk: a stored unit formed from integrating smaller pieces of information.

clause: part of a sentence that contains a subject and a verb.

co-articulation: the finding that the production of a phoneme is influenced by the production of the previous sound and preparations for the next sound; it provides a useful cue to listeners.

cognitive interview: an approach to improving the memory of eyewitness recall based on the assumption that memory traces contain many features.

cognitive neuropsychology: an approach that involves studying cognitive functioning in brain-damaged patients to increase our understanding of normal human cognition.

cognitive neuroscience: an approach that aims to understand human cognition by combining information from behaviour and the brain.

cognitive psychology: an approach that aims to understand human cognition by the study of behaviour.

colour constancy: the tendency for any given object to be perceived as having the same colour under widely varying viewing conditions.

common ground: the mutual knowledge and beliefs shared by a speaker and listener.

computational cognitive science: an approach that involves constructing computational models to understand human cognition. Some of these models take account of what is known about brain functioning as well as behavioural evidence.

computational modelling: this involves constructing computer programs that will simulate or mimic some aspects of human cognitive functioning; see **artificial intelligence**.

concepts: mental representations of categories of objects or items.

conceptual priming: a form of **repetition priming** in which there is facilitated processing of stimulus meaning.

confirmation: the attempt to find supportive or confirming evidence for one's hypothesis.

confirmation bias: a greater focus on evidence apparently confirming one's hypothesis than on disconfirming evidence.

conjunction fallacy: the mistaken belief that the probability of a conjunction of two events (A

and B) is greater than the probability of one of them (A or B).

connectionist networks: these consist of elementary units or nodes, which are connected; each network has various structures or layers (e.g., input; intermediate or hidden; output).

consolidation: a process lasting several hours or more which fixes information in **long-term memory**.

convergence: one of the binocular cues, based on the inward focus of the eyes with a close object.

converging operations: an approach in which several methods with different strengths and limitations are used to address a given issue.

covert attention: attention to an object or sound in the absence of overt movements of the relevant receptors (e.g., looking at an object in the periphery of vision without moving one's eyes).

cross-modal attention: the co-ordination of attention across two or more modalities (e.g., vision and audition).

cross-race effect: the finding that recognition memory for same-race faces is generally more accurate than for cross-race faces.

cytoarchitectonic map: a map of the brain based on variations in the cellular structure of tissues.

declarative memory: a form of long-term memory that involves knowing that something is the case and generally involves conscious recollection; it includes memory for facts (**semantic memory**) and memory for events (**episodic memory**).

deductive reasoning: reasoning to a conclusion from some set of premises or statements, where that conclusion follows necessarily from the assumption that the premises are true; see **inductive reasoning**.

deep dysgraphia: a condition caused by brain damage in which there are semantic errors in spelling and nonwords are spelled incorrectly.

deep dyslexia: a condition in which reading unfamiliar words is impaired and there are semantic reading errors (e.g., reading "missile" as "rocket").

deep dysphasia: a condition in which there is poor ability to repeat spoken words and especially nonwords, and there are semantic errors in repeating spoken words.

deliberate practice: this form of practice involves the learner being provided with informative feedback and having the opportunity to correct his/her errors.

depictive representations: representations (e.g., visual images) resembling pictures in that objects within them are organised spatially.

dichromacy: a deficiency in colour vision in which one of the three basic colour mechanisms is not functioning.

direct retrieval: involuntary recall of autobiographical memories triggered by a specific retrieval cue (e.g., being in the same place as the original event); see **generative retrieval.**

directed forgetting: impaired long-term memory resulting from the instruction to forget information presented for learning.

directed retrospection: a method of studying writing in which writers are stopped while writing and categorise their immediately preceding thoughts.

discourse: connected text or speech generally at least several sentences long.

discourse markers: spoken words and phrases that do not contribute directly to the content of what is being said but still serve various functions (e.g., clarification of the speaker's intentions).

dissociation: as applied to brain-damaged patients, normal performance on one task combined with severely impaired performance on another task.

dissociative identity disorder: a mental disorder in which the patient claims to have two ore more personalities that are separate from each other.

divided attention: a situation in which two tasks are performed at the same time; also known as multi-tasking.

domain specificity: the notion that a given module or cognitive process responds selectively to certain types of stimuli (e.g., faces) but not others.

dominance principle: in decision making, the notion that the better of two similar options will be preferred.

dorsal: superior or towards the top of the brain.

double dissociation: the finding that some individuals (often brain-damaged) do well on task A and poorly on task B, whereas others show the opposite pattern.

dysexecutive syndrome: a condition in which damage to the frontal lobes causes impairments to the **central executive** component of **working memory.**

echoic store: a sensory store in which auditory information is briefly held.

ecological validity: the extent to which experimental findings are applicable to everyday settings.

egocentric heuristic: a strategy in which listeners interpret what they hear based on their own knowledge rather than on knowledge shared with the speaker.

Einstellung: mental set, in which people use a familiar strategy even where there is a simpler alternative or the problem cannot be solved using it.

elaborative inferences: inferences that add details to a text that is being read by making use of our general knowledge; also known as forward inferences.

electroencephalogram (EEG): a device for recording the electrical potentials of the brain through a series of electrodes placed on the scalp.

Emmert's law: the size of an afterimage appears larger when viewed against a far surface than when viewed against a near one.

emotion regulation: the management and control of emotional states by various processes (e.g., attentional; appraisal).

encoding specificity principle: the notion that retrieval depends on the overlap between the information available at retrieval and the information in the memory trace.

endogenous spatial attention: attention to a given spatial location determined by voluntary or goal-directed mechanisms; see **exogenous spatial attention.**

episodic buffer: a component of **working memory** that is used to integrate and to store briefly information from the **phonological loop,** the **visuo-spatial sketchpad,** and **long-term memory.**

episodic memory: a form of long-term memory concerned with personal experiences or episodes that occurred in a given place at a specific time; see **semantic memory.**

event-related functional magnetic imaging (efMRI): this is a form of **functional magnetic imaging** in which patterns of brain activity associated with specific events (e.g., correct versus incorrect responses on a memory test) are compared.

event-related potentials (ERPs): the pattern of electroencephalograph (EEG) activity obtained by averaging the brain responses to the same stimulus presented repeatedly.

event-based prospective memory: remembering to perform an intended action when the circumstances are suitable; see **time-based prospective memory.**

executive processes: processes that organise and co-ordinate the functioning of the cognitive system to achieve current goals.

exogenous spatial attention: attention to a given spatial location determined by "involuntary" mechanisms triggered by external stimuli (e.g., loud noise); see **endogenous spatial attention.**

expertise: the specific knowledge an expert has about a given domain (e.g., that an engineer may have about bridges).

explicit memory: memory that involves conscious recollection of information; see **implicit memory.**

explicit memory bias: the retrieval of relatively more negative or unpleasant information than positive or neutral information on a test of **explicit memory.**

extinction: a disorder of visual attention in which a stimulus presented to the side opposite the brain damage is not detected when another stimulus is presented at the same time to the same side as the brain damage.

falsification: proposing hypotheses and then trying to falsify them by experimental tests; the logically correct means by which science should work according to Popper (1968); see **confirmation.**

far transfer: beneficial effects of previous problem solving on current problem solving in a dissimilar context; a form of **positive transfer.**

figurative language: forms of language (e.g., metaphor) not intended to be taken literally.

figure–ground segregation: the perceptual organisation of the visual field into a figure (object of central interest) and a ground (less important background).

flashbulb memories: vivid and detailed memories of dramatic events.

focus of expansion: this is the point towards which someone who is in motion is moving; it is the only part of the visual field that does not appear to move.

focused attention: a situation in which individuals try to attend to only one source of information while ignoring other stimuli; also known as selective attention.

formants: peaks in the frequencies of speech sounds; revealed by a **spectrograph.**

framing effect: the influence of irrelevant aspects of a situation (e.g., wording of the problem) on decision making.

Freudian slip: a motivated error in speech (or action) that reveals the individual's underlying thoughts and/or desires.

fronto-temporal dementia: a condition caused by damage to the frontal and temporal lobes in which there are typically several language difficulties.

functional magnetic resonance imaging (fMRI): a technique based on imaging blood oxygenation using an MRI machine; it provides information about the location and time course of brain processes.

functional specialisation: the assumption that each brain area or region is specialised for a specific function (e.g., colour processing; face processing).

gateway hypothesis: the assumption that BA10 in the prefrontal cortex acts as an attentional gateway between our internal thoughts and external stimuli.

generative retrieval: deliberate or voluntary construction of autobiographical memories based on an individual's current goals; see **direct retrieval.**

graphemic buffer: a store in which graphemic information about the individual letters in a word is held immediately before spelling the word.

gyri: ridges in the brain ("gyrus" is the singular).

haptic: relating to the sense of touch.

heuristics: rules of thumb that are cognitively undemanding and often produce approximately accurate answers.

hill climbing: a **heuristic** involving changing the present state of a problem into one apparently closer to the goal.

holistic processing: processing that involves integrating information from an entire object.

homophones: words having the same pronunciations but that differ in the way they are spelled.

ideomotor apraxia: a condition caused by brain damage in which patients have difficulty in carrying out learned movements.

idiots savants: individuals having limited outstanding expertise in spite of being mentally retarded.

ill-defined problems: problems in which the definition of the problem statement is imprecisely specified; the initial state, goal state, and methods to be used to solve the problem may be unclear; see **well-defined problems.**

implicit learning: learning complex information without the ability to provide conscious recollection of what has been learned.

implicit memory: memory that does not depend on conscious recollection; see **explicit memory.**

implicit memory bias: relatively better memory performance for negative than for neutral or positive information on a test of **implicit memory.**

inattentional blindness: failure to detect an unexpected object appearing in a visual display; see **change blindness.**

incubation: the finding that a problem is solved more easily when it is put aside for some time.

inductive reasoning: forming generalisations (which may be probable but are not certain) from examples or sample phenomena; see **deductive reasoning.**

infantile amnesia: the inability of adults to recall autobiographical memories from early childhood.

inhibition of return: a reduced probability of visual attention returning to a previously attended location or object.

inner scribe: according to Logie, the part of the **visuo-spatial sketchpad** that deals with spatial and movement information.

insight: the experience of suddenly realising how to solve a problem.

integrative agnosia: a form of **visual agnosia** in which patients have problems in integrating or combining an object's features in object recognition.

inter-identity amnesia: one of the symptoms of **dissociative identity disorder,** in which the patient claims amnesia for events experienced by other identities.

interpretive bias: the tendency when presented with ambiguous stimuli or situations to interpret them in a relatively threatening way.

introspection: a careful examination and description of one's own inner mental thoughts.

invariants: properties of the **optic array** that remain constant even though other aspects vary; part of Gibson's theory.

inversion effect: the finding that faces are considerably harder to recognise when presented upside down; the effect is less marked with other objects.

jargon aphasia: a brain-damaged condition in which speech is reasonably correct grammatically but there are great problems in finding the right words.

knowledge effect: the tendency to assume that others share the knowledge that we possess.

knowledge-lean problems: problems that can be solved without the use of much prior knowledge, with most of the necessary information being provided by the problem statement; see **knowledge-rich problems**.

knowledge-rich problems: problems that can only be solved through the use of considerable amounts of prior knowledge; see **knowledge-lean problems**.

Korsakoff's syndrome: amnesia (impaired long-term memory) caused by chronic alcoholism.

lateral: relating to the outer surface of the brain.

lateral inhibition: reduction of activity in one neuron caused by activity in a neighbouring neuron.

lemmas: abstract words possessing syntactic and semantic features but not phonological ones.

lesions: structural alterations within the brain caused by disease or injury.

lexical access: entering the **lexicon** with its store of detailed information about words.

lexical bias effect: the tendency for speech errors to consist of words rather than nonwords.

lexical decision task: a task in which individuals decide as rapidly as possible whether a letter string forms a word.

lexical identification shift: the finding that an ambiguous phoneme tends to be perceived so as to form a word rather than a nonword.

lexicalisation: the process of translating the meaning of a word into its sound representation during speech production.

lexicon: a store of detailed information about words, including orthographic, phonological, semantic, and syntactic knowledge.

life scripts: cultural expectations concerning the nature and order of major life events in a typical person's life.

logical inferences: inferences depending solely on the meaning of words.

long-term working memory: this is used by experts to store relevant information in long-term memory and to access it through retrieval cues in **working memory**.

loss aversion: the tendency to be more sensitive to potential losses than to potential gains.

magneto-encephalography (MEG): a non-invasive brain-scanning technique based on recording the magnetic fields generated by brain activity.

maintenance rehearsal: processing that involves simply repeating analyses which have already been carried out.

masking: suppression of the perception of a stimulus (e.g., visual; auditory) by presenting a second stimulus (the masking stimulus) very soon thereafter.

matching bias: on the Wason selection task, the tendency to select those cards matching the items explicitly mentioned in the rule.

means–ends analysis: a **heuristic** method for solving problems based on creating a subgoal to reduce the difference between the current state and the goal state.

medial: relating to the central region of the brain.

mental model: a representation of a possible state-of-affairs in the world.

metacognition: an individual's beliefs and knowledge about his/her own cognitive processes and strategies.

microspectrophotometry: a technique that allows measurement of the amount of light absorbed at various wavelengths by individual cone receptors.

mirror neuron system: a system of neurons that respond to actions whether performed by oneself or by someone else.

mixed-error effect: speech errors that are semantically and phonologically related to the intended word.

modularity: the assumption that the cognitive system consists of several fairly independent processors or modules.

monocular cues: cues to depth that can be used with one eye, but can also be used with both eyes.

mood congruity: the finding that learning and retrieval of emotional material is better when there is agreement between the learner's or rememberer's mood state and the affective value of the material.

mood-state-dependent memory: the finding that memory is better when the mood state at retrieval is the same as that at learning than when the two mood states differ.

morphemes: the smallest units of meaning within words.

motion parallax: movement of an object's image across the retina due to movements of the observer's head.

naming task: a task in which visually presented words are pronounced aloud as rapidly as possible.

near transfer: beneficial effects of previous problem solving on current problem solving; a form of **positive transfer**.

negative afterimages: the illusory perception of the complementary colour to the one that has just been fixated for several seconds; green is the complementary colour to red, and blue is complementary to yellow.

negative transfer: past experience in solving one problem disrupts the ability to solve a similar current problem.

neglect: a disorder of visual attention in which stimuli or parts of stimuli presented to the side opposite the brain damage are undetected and not responded to; the condition resembles **extinction** but is more severe.

neologisms: made-up words produced by individuals suffering from **jargon aphasia**.

neuroeconomics: an emerging approach in which economic decision making is understood within the framework of **cognitive neuroscience**.

non-declarative memory: forms of long-term memory that influence behaviour but do not involve conscious recollection; **priming** and **procedural memory** are examples of non-declarative memory.

oculomotor cues: kinaesthetic cues to depth produced by muscular contraction of the muscles around the eye.

olfaction: the sense of smell.

omission bias: the tendency to prefer inaction to action when engaged in risky decision making.

operation span: the maximum number of items (arithmetical questions + words) from which an individual can recall all the last words.

optic array: the structured pattern of light falling on the retina.

optic ataxia: a condition in which there are problems with making visually guided limb movements in spite of reasonably intact visual perception.

optic flow: the changes in the pattern of light reaching an observer when there is movement of the observer and/or aspects of the environment.

optimisation: the selection of the best choice in decision making.

orthographic neighbours: with reference to a given word, those other words that can be formed by changing one of its letters.

orthography: information about the spellings of words.

paradigm specificity: this occurs when the findings obtained with a given paradigm or experimental task are not obtained even when apparently very similar paradigms or tasks are used.

parafoveal-on-foveal effects: the finding that fixation duration on the current word is influenced by characteristics of the next word.

parallel processing: processing in which two or more cognitive processes occur at the same time; see **serial processing**.

Parkinson's disease: it is a progressive disorder involving damage to the basal ganglia; the symptoms include rigidity of the muscles, limb tremor, and mask-like facial expression.

parsing: an analysis of the syntactical or grammatical structure of sentences.

part–whole effect: the finding that it is easier to recognise a face part when it is presented within a whole face rather than in isolation.

perceptual priming: a form of repetition priming in which repeated presentation of a stimulus facilitates perceptual processing of it.

perceptual representation system: an implicit memory system thought to be involved in the faster processing of previously presented stimuli (e.g., **repetition priming**).

perceptual segregation: human ability to work out accurately which parts of presented visual information belong together and thus form separate objects.

perceptual span: the effective field of view in reading (letters to the left and right of fixation that can be processed).

phonemes: basic speech sounds conveying meaning.

phonemic restoration effect: the finding that listeners are unaware that a phoneme has been deleted from a spoken sentence.

phonological dysgraphia: a condition caused by brain damage in which familiar words can be spelled reasonably well but nonwords cannot.

phonological dyslexia: a condition in which familiar words can be read but there is impaired ability to read unfamiliar words and nonwords.

phonological loop: a component of **working memory**, in which speech-based information is held and subvocal articulation occurs.

phonological similarity effect: the finding that serial recall of visually presented words is worse when the words are phonologically similar rather than phonologically dissimilar.

phonology: information about the sounds of words and parts of words.

phrase: a group of words expressing a single idea; it is smaller in scope than a **clause**.

phrenology: the notion that each mental faculty is located in a different part of the brain and can be assessed by feeling bumps on the head.

positive transfer: past experience of solving one problem makes it easier to solve a similar current problem.

positron emission tomography (PET): a brain-scanning technique based on the detection of positrons; it has reasonable spatial resolution but poor temporal resolution.

posterior: towards the back of the brain.

pragmatics: the study of the ways in which language is used and understood in the real world, including a consideration of its intended meaning.

preformulation: this is used in speech production to reduce processing costs by saying phrases often used previously.

preparedness: the notion that each species develops fearful or phobic reactions most readily to objects that were dangerous in its evolutionary history.

priming: influencing the processing of (and response to) a target by presenting a stimulus related to it in some way beforehand.

principle of truth: the notion that we represent assertions by constructing **mental models** concerning what is true but not what is false.

problem space: an abstract description of all the possible states that can occur in a problem situation.

procedural memory/knowledge: this is concerned with knowing how, and includes the ability to perform skilled actions; see **declarative memory**.

production rules: "IF . . . THEN" or condition–action rules in which the action is carried out whenever the appropriate condition is present.

production systems: these consist of numerous "IF . . . THEN" **production rules** and a working memory containing information.

productive thinking: solving a problem by developing an understanding of the problem's underlying structure; see **reproductive thinking**.

progress monitoring: a **heuristic** used in problem solving in which insufficiently rapid progress towards solution leads to the adoption of a different strategy.

proposition: a statement making an assertion or denial and which can be true or false.

prosodic cues: features of spoken language such as stress, intonation, and duration that make it easier for listeners to understand what is being said.

prosopagnosia: a condition caused by brain damage in which the patient cannot recognise familiar faces but can recognise familiar objects.

prospective memory: remembering to carry out intended actions.

Proust phenomenon: the finding that odours are especially powerful cues for the recall of very old and emotional autobiographical memories.

pseudoword: a pronounceable nonword (e.g., "tave").

psychological refractory period (PRP) effect: the slowing of the response to the second of two stimuli when they are presented close together in time.

pure word deafness: a condition in which severely impaired speech perception is combined with good speech production, reading, writing, and perception of non-speech sounds.

rationalisation: in Bartlett's theory, the tendency in recall of stories to produce errors conforming to the cultural expectations of the rememberer.

reading span: the largest number of sentences read for comprehension from which an individual can recall all the final words more than 50% of the time.

recency effect: the finding that the last few items in a list are much better remembered than other items in immediate free recall.

receptive field: the region of the retina within which light influences the activity of a particular neuron.

recognition heuristic: using the knowledge that only one out of two objects is recognised to make a judgement.

reduplicative paramnesia: a memory disorder in which the person believes that multiple copies of people and places exist.

reminiscence bump: the tendency of older people to recall a disproportionate number of autobiographical memories from the years of adolescence and early adulthood.

repetition priming: the finding that stimulus processing is faster and easier on the second and successive presentations.

repetitive transcranial magnetic stimulation (rTMS): the administration of **transcranial magnetic stimulation** several times in rapid succession.

representativeness heuristic: the assumption that representative or typical members of a category are encountered most frequently.

repression: motivated forgetting of traumatic or other threatening events.

reproductive thinking: re-use of previous knowledge to solve a current problem; see **productive thinking**.

resonance: the process of automatic pick-up of visual information from the environment in Gibson's theory.

retinal flow field: the changing patterns of light on the retina produced by movement of the observer relative to the environment as well as by eye and head movements.

retinotopic map: nerve cells occupying the same relative positions as their respective receptive fields have on the retina.

retrograde amnesia: impaired memory for events occurring before the onset of amnesia.

retrospective memory: memory for events, words, people, and so on encountered or experienced in the past; see **prospective memory**.

routine expertise: using acquired knowledge to solve familiar problems efficiently.

saccades: fast eye movements that cannot be altered after being initiated.

savings method: a measure of forgetting introduced by Ebbinghaus, in which the number of trials for re-learning is compared against the number for original learning.

satisficing: selection of the first choice meeting certain minimum requirements; the word is formed from the words "satisfactory" and "sufficing".

schemas: organised packets of information about the world, events, or people stored in long-term memory.

segmentation problem: the listener's problem of dividing the almost continuous sounds of speech into separate **phonemes** and words.

semantic dementia: a condition in which there is widespread loss of information about the meanings of words and concepts but executive functioning is reasonably intact in the early stages.

semantic memory: a form of long-term memory consisting of general knowledge about the world, concepts, language, and so on; see **episodic memory**.

semantic priming effect: the finding that word identification is facilitated when there is priming by a semantically related word.

semantics: the meaning conveyed by words and sentences.

serial processing: processing in which one process is completed before the next one starts; see **parallel processing**.

simultanagnosia: a brain-damaged condition in which only one object can be seen at a time.

single-unit recording: an invasive technique for studying brain function, permitting the study of activity in single neurons.

size constancy: objects are perceived to have a given size regardless of the size of the retinal image.

skill acquisition: developing abilities through practice so as to increase the probability of goal achievement.

spectrograph: an instrument used to produce visible records of the sound frequencies in speech.

spillover effect: any given word is fixated longer during reading when preceded by a rare word rather than a common one.

split attention: allocation of attention to two (or more) non-adjacent regions of visual space.

split-brain patients: these are patients in whom most of the direct links between the two hemispheres have been severed; as a result, they can experience problems in co-ordinating their processing and behaviour.

spoonerism: a speech error in which the initial letter or letters of two words are switched.

spreading activation: the notion that activation of a given node (often a word) in long-term memory leads to activation or energy spreading to other related nodes or words.

status quo bias: a tendency for individuals to repeat a choice several times in spite of changes in their preferences.

stereopsis: one of the binocular cues; it is based on the small discrepancy in the retinal images in each eye when viewing a visual scene (**binocular disparity**).

striatum: it forms part of the basal ganglia of the brain and is located in the upper part of the brainstem and the inferior part of the cerebral hemispheres.

Stroop effect: the finding that naming of the colours in which words are printed is slower when the words are conflicting colour words (e.g., the word RED printed in green).

Stroop task: a task in which the participant has to name the colours in which words are printed.

subliminal perception: processing that occurs in the absence of conscious awareness.

sulcus: a groove or furrow in the brain.

sunk-cost effect: expending additional resources to justify some previous commitment that has not worked well.

surface dysgraphia: a condition caused by brain damage in which there is poor spelling of irregular words, reasonable spelling of regular words, and some success in spelling nonwords.

surface dyslexia: a condition in which regular words can be read but there is impaired ability to read irregular words.

syllogism: a logical argument consisting of two premises (e.g., "All X are Y") and a conclusion; syllogisms formed the basis of the first logical system attributed to Aristotle.

syndromes: labels used to categorise patients on the basis of co-occurring symptoms.

syntactic priming: the tendency for the syntactic structure of a spoken or written sentence to correspond to that of a recently processed sentence.

tangent point: from a driver's perspective, the point on a road at which the direction of its inside edge appears to reverse.

template: as applied to chess, an abstract schematic structure consisting of a mixture of fixed and variable information about chess pieces.

texture gradient: the rate of change of texture density from the front to the back of a slanting object.

time-based prospective memory: remembering to carry out an intended action at the right time; see **event-based prospective memory**.

top-down processing: stimulus processing that is influenced by factors such as the individual's past experience and expectations.

transcortical sensory aphasia: a disorder in which words can be repeated but there are many problems with language.

transcranial magnetic stimulation (TMS): a technique in which magnetic pulses briefly disrupt the functioning of a given brain area, thus creating a short-lived lesion; when several pulses are administered one after the other, the technique is known as repetitive transcranial magnetic stimulation (rTMS).

trial-and-error learning: a type of learning in which the solution is reached by producing fairly random responses rather than by a process of thought.

typicality effect: the finding that objects can be identified faster as category members when they are typical or representative members of the category in question.

unconscious perception: perceptual processes occurring below the level of conscious awareness.

unconscious transference: the tendency of eyewitnesses to misidentify a familiar (but innocent) face as belonging to the person responsible for a crime.

underadditivity: the finding that brain activation when two tasks are performed together is less than the sum of the brain activations when they are performed singly.

underspecification: a strategy used to reduce processing costs in speech production by producing simplified expressions.

uniform connectedness: the notion that adjacent regions in the visual environment possessing uniform visual properties (e.g., colour) are perceived as a single perceptual unit.

vegetative state: a condition produced by brain damage in which there is wakefulness but an apparent lack of awareness and purposeful behaviour.

ventral: towards the bottom of the brain.

ventriloquist illusion: the mistaken perception that sounds are coming from their apparent visual source, as in ventriloquism.

verb bias: a characteristic of many verbs that are found more often in some syntactic structures than in others.

verbal overshadowing: the reduction in recognition memory for faces that often occurs when eyewitnesses provide verbal descriptions of those faces before the recognition-memory test.

visual agnosia: a condition in which there are great problems in recognising objects presented visually even though visual information reaches the visual cortex.

visual buffer: within Kosslyn's theory, the mechanism involved in producing **depictive representations** in visual imagery and visual perception.

visual cache: according to Logie, the part of the visuo-spatial sketchpad that stores information about visual form and colour.

visual direction: the angle between a visual object or target and the front–back body axis.

visual search: a task involving the rapid detection of a specified target stimulus within a visual display.

visuo-spatial sketchpad: a component of **working memory** that is involved in visual and spatial processing of information.

voxels: these are small, volume-based units into which the brain is divided for neuroimaging research; short for volume elements.

wallpaper illusion: a visual illusion in which staring at patterned wallpaper makes it seem as if parts of the pattern are floating in front of the wall.

weapon focus: the finding that eyewitnesses pay so much attention to some crucial aspect of the situation (e.g., the weapon) that they tend to ignore other details.

well-defined problems: problems in which the initial state, goal, and methods available for solving them are clearly laid out; see **ill-defined problems**.

Wernicke's aphasia: a form of **aphasia** involving impaired comprehension and fluent speech with many content words missing.

Whorfian hypothesis: the notion that language determines, or at least influences, thinking.

word-length effect: the finding that word span is greater for short words than for long words.

word meaning deafness: a condition in which there is a selective impairment of the ability to understand spoken (but not written) language.

word superiority effect: a target letter is more readily detected in a letter string when the string forms a word than when it does not.

REFERENCES

Abramov, I., & Gordon, J. (1994). Colour appearance: On seeing red, or yellow, or green, or blue. *Annual Review of Psychology, 36*, 715–729.

Abrams, L. (2008). Tip-of-the-tongue states yield language insights: The process of turning thoughts into speech changes with age. *American Scientist, 96*, 234–239.

Achim, A.M., & Lepage, M. (2005). Dorsolateral prefrontal cortex involvement in memory post-retrieval monitoring revealed in both item and associative recognition tests. *NeuroImage, 24*, 1113–1121.

Adam, M.B., & Reyna, V.F. (2005). Coherence and correspondence criteria for rationality: Experts' estimation of risks of sexually transmitted infections. *Journal of Behavioral Decision Making, 18*, 169–186.

Addis, D.R., Wong, A.T., & Schacter, D.L. (2007). Remembering the past and imagining the future: Common and distinct neural substrates during event construction and elaboration. *Neuropsychologia, 45*, 1363–1377.

Afraz, S.-R., Kiani, R., & Esteky, H. (2006). Microstimulation of inferotemporal cortex influences face categorisation. *Nature, 442*, 692–695.

Aggleton, J.P. (2008). Understanding anterograde amnesia: Disconnections and hidden lesions. *Quarterly Journal of Experimental Psychology, 61*, 1441–1471.

Aggleton, J.P., & Brown, M.W. (1999). Episodic memory, amnesia, and the hippocampal-anterior thalamic axis. *Behavioral & Brain Sciences, 22*, 425–489.

Agnew, Z.K., Bhakoo, K.K., & Puri, B.K. (2007). The human mirror system: A motor resonance theory of mind-reading. *Brain Research Reviews, 54*, 286–293.

Aizenstein, H.J., Stenger, V.A., Cochran, J., Clark, K., Johnson, M., Nebes, R.D., & Carter, C.S. (2004). Regional brain activation during concurrent implicit and explicit sequence learning. *Cerebral Cortex, 14*, 199–208.

Aleman, A., Schutter, D.L.G., Ramsey, N.F., van Honk, J., Kessels, R.P.C., Hoogduin, J.M. et al. (2002). Functional anatomy of top-down visuo-spatial processing in the human brain: Evidence from rTMS. *Cognitive Brain Research, 14*, 300–302.

Alexander, P.A., Schallert, D.L., & Hare, U.C. (1991). Coming to terms: How researchers in learning and literacy talk about knowledge. *Review of Educational Research, 61*, 315–343.

Allen, B.P., & Lindsay, D.S. (1998). Amalgamations of memories: Intrusion of information from one event into reports of another. *Applied Cognitive Psychology, 12*, 277–285.

Allen, E.A., Pasley, B.N., Duong, T., & Freeman, R.D. (2007). Transcranial magnetic stimulation elicits coupled neural and hemodynamic consequences. *Science, 317*, 1918–1921.

Allopenna, P.D., Magnuson, J.S., & Tanenhaus, M.K. (1998). Tracking the time course of spoken word recognition using eye movements: Evidence for continuous mapping models. *Journal of Memory and Language, 38*, 419–439.

Allport, D.A., Antonis, B., & Reynolds, P. (1972). On the division of attention: A disproof of the single channel hypothesis. *Quarterly Journal of Experimental Psychology, 24*, 225–235.

Alonso, J.M., & Martinez, L.M. (1998). Functional connectivity between simple cells and complex cells in cat striate cortex. *Nature Neuroscience, 1*, 395–403.

Altenberg, B. (1990). Speech as linear composition. In G. Caie, K. Haastrup, A.L. Jakobsen, J.E. Nielsen, J. Sevaldsen, H. Sprecht et al. (Eds.), *Proceedings from the Fourth Nordic Conference for English Studies*. Copenhagen, Denmark: Copenhagen University Press.

Altmann, G.T.M. (1997). *The ascent of Babel: An exploration of language, mind, and understanding.* Oxford: Oxford University Press.

Ames, A. (1952). *The Ames demonstrations in perception.* New York: Hafner Publishing.

Anderson, C.J. (2003). The psychology of doing nothing: Forms of decision avoidance result from reason and emotion. *Psychological Bulletin, 129,* 139–167.

Anderson, E.J., Mannan, S.K., Husain, M., Rees, G., Sumner, P., Mort, D.J. et al. (2007). Involvement of prefrontal cortex in visual search. *Experimental Brain Research, 180,* 289–302.

Anderson, J.R. (1993). *Rules of the mind.* Hillsdale, NJ: Lawrence Erlbaum Associates Inc.

Anderson, J.R., & Lebiere, C. (2003). The Newell Test for a theory of cognition. *Behavioral and Brain Sciences, 26,* 587–640.

Anderson, J.R., Albert, M.V., & Fincham, J.M. (2005). Tracing problem solving in real time: fMRI analysis of the subject-paced Tower of Hanoi. *Journal of Cognitive Neuroscience, 17,* 1261–1274.

Anderson, J.R., Fincham, J.M., Qin, Y., & Stocco, A. (2008). A central circuit of the mind. *Trends in Cognitive Sciences, 12,* 136–143.

Anderson, M.C., & Green, C. (2001). Suppressing unwanted memories by executive control. *Nature, 410,* 366–369.

Anderson, M.C., & Kuhl, B.A. (in preparation). Psychological trauma and its enduring effects on memory suppression: Evidence for the plasticity of memory control.

Anderson, M.C., Ochsner, K.N., Kuhl, B., Cooper, J., Robertson, E., Gabrieli, S.W. et al. (2004). Neural systems underlying the suppression of unwanted memories. *Science, 303,* 232–235.

Anderson, R.C., & Pichert, J.W. (1978). Recall of previously unrecallable information following a shift in perspective. *Journal of Verbal Learning & Verbal Behavior, 17,* 1–12.

Anderson, S.J., Holliday, I.E., Singh, K.D., & Harding, G.F.A. (1996). Localisation and functional analysis of human cortical area V5 using magnetoencephalography. *Proceedings of the Royal Society London B, 263,* 423–431.

Andrés, P. (2003). Frontal cortex as the central executive of working memory: Time to revise our view. *Cortex, 39,* 871–895.

Antos, S.J. (1979). Processing facilitation in a lexical decision task. *Journal of Experimental Psychology: Human Perception and Performance, 5,* 527–545.

Arend, I., Rafal, R., & Ward, R. (2008). Spatial and temporal deficits are regionally dissociable in patients with pulvinar lesions. *Brain, 131,* 214–2152.

Arkes, H.R., & Ayton, P. (1999). The sunk cost and Concorde effects: Are humans less rational than lower animals? *Psychological Bulletin, 125,* 591–600.

Arnold, J.E., Eisenband, J.G., Brown-Schmidt, S., & Trueswell, J.C. (2000). The immediate use of gender information: Eyetracking evidence of the time-course of pronoun resolution. *Cognition, 76,* B13–B26.

Arzouan, Y., Goldstein, A., & Faust, M. (2007). Brainwaves are stethoscopes: ERP correlates of novel metaphor comprehension. *Brain Research, 1160,* 69–81.

Asato, M.R., Sweeney, J.A., & Luna, B. (2006). Cognitive processes in the development of TOL performance. *Neuropsychologia, 44,* 2259–2269.

Ashby, J., & Clifton, C. (2005). The prosodic property of lexical stress affects eye movements during silent reading. *Cognition, 96,* B89–B100.

Ashby, J., & Martin, A.E. (2008). Prosodic phonological representations early in visual word recognition. *Journal of Experimental Psychology: Human Perception and Performance, 34,* 224–236.

Ashida, H., Lingnau, A., Wall, M.B., & Smith, A.T. (2007). fMRI adaptation reveals separate mechanisms for first-order and second-order motion. *Journal of Neurophysiology, 97,* 1319–1325.

Assal, G., Buttet, J., & Jolivet, R. (1981). Dissociations in aphasia: A case report. *Brain and Language, 13,* 223–240.

Atkins, J.E., Fiser, J., & Jacobs, R.A. (2001). Experience-dependent visual cue integration based on consistencies between visual and haptic percepts. *Vision Research, 41,* 449–461.

Atkinson, R.C., & Shiffrin, R.M. (1968). Human memory: A proposed system and its control processes. In K.W. Spence & J.T. Spence (Eds.), *The psychology of learning and motivation, Vol. 2.* London: Academic Press.

Atkinson, R.L., Atkinson, R.C., Smith, E.E., & Bem, D.J. (1993). *Introduction to psychology* (11th Ed.). New York: Harcourt Brace.

Awh, E., & Pashler, H. (2000). Evidence for split attentional foci. *Journal of Experimental Psychology: Human Perception and Performance, 26,* 834–846.

Baars, B.J. (1988). *A cognitive theory of consciousness.* Cambridge: Cambridge University Press.

Baars, B.J. (1997a). *In the theatre of consciousness: The workspace of the mind.* New York: Oxford University Press.

Baars, B.J. (1997b). Consciousness versus attention, perception, and working memory. *Consciousness and Cognition, 5,* 363–371.

Baars, B.J. (2002). The conscious access hypothesis: Origins and recent evidence. *Trends in Cognitive Sciences*, 6, 47–52.

Baars, B.J., & Franklin, S. (2003). How conscious experience and working memory interact. *Trends in Cognitive Sciences*, 7, 166–172.

Baars, B.J., & Franklin, S. (2007). An architectural model of conscious and unconscious brain functions: Global Workspace Theory and IDA. *Neural Networks*, 20, 955–961.

Baars, B.J., Motley, M.T., & MacKay, D.G. (1975). Output editing for lexical status from artificially elicited slips of the tongue. *Journal of Verbal Learning & Verbal Behavior*, 14, 382–391.

Backus, B.T., & Haijiang, Q. (2007). Competition between newly recruited and pre-existing visual cues during the construction of visual appearance. *Vision Research*, 47, 919–924.

Baddeley, A.D. (1978). The trouble with levels: A re-examination of Craik and Lockhart's framework for memory research. *Psychological Review*, 85, 139–152.

Baddeley, A.D. (1986). *Working memory*. Oxford: Clarendon Press.

Baddeley, A.D. (1990). *Human memory: Theory and practice*. Hove, UK: Psychology Press.

Baddeley, A.D. (1996). Exploring the central executive. *Quarterly Journal of Experimental Psychology*, 49A, 5–28.

Baddeley, A.D. (1997). *Human memory: Theory and practice (revised edition)*. Hove, UK: Psychology Press.

Baddeley, A.D. (1998). The central executive: A concept and some misconceptions. *Journal of the International Neuropsychological Society*, 4, 523–526.

Baddeley, A.D. (2000). The episodic buffer: A new component of working memory? *Trends in Cognitive Science*, 4, 417–423.

Baddeley, A.D. (2001). Is working memory still working? *American Psychologist*, 56, 851–864.

Baddeley, A.D. (2007). *Working memory, thought and action*. Oxford: Oxford University Press.

Baddeley, A.D., & Andrade, J. (2000). Working memory and the vividness of imagery. *Journal of Experimental Psychology: General*, 129, 126–145.

Baddeley, A.D., Gathercole, S., & Papagno, C. (1998). The phonological loop as a language learning device. *Psychological Review*, 105, 158–173.

Baddeley, A.D., & Hitch, G.J. (1974). Working memory. In G.H. Bower (Ed.), *The psychology of learning and motivation, Vol. 8*. London: Academic Press.

Baddeley, A.D., & Wilson, B. (2002). Prose recall and amnesia: Implications for the structure of working memory. *Neuropsychologia, 40,* 1737–1743.

Baddeley, A.D., Thomson, N., & Buchanan, M. (1975). Word length and the structure of short-term memory. *Journal of Verbal Learning and Verbal Behavior*, 14, 575–589.

Baddeley, A.D., Vallar, G., & Wilson, B.A. (1987). Sentence comprehension and phonological memory: Some neuropsychological evidence. In M. Coltheart (Ed.), *Attention and performance XII: The psychology of reading* (pp. 509–529). Hove, UK: Lawrence Erlbaum Associates Inc.

Badecker, W., Straub, K. (2002). The processing role of structural constraints on the interpretation of pronouns and anaphors. *Journal of Experimental Psychology: Learning, Memory, and Cognition, 28*, 748–769.

Badre, D., & Wagner, A.D. (2007). Left ventrolateral prefrontal cortex and the cognitive control of memory. *Neuropsychologia*, 45, 2883–2901.

Badre, D., Poldrack, R.A., Pare-Blagoev, E.J., Insler, R.Z., & Wagner, A.D. (2005). Dissociable controlled retrieval and generalised selection mechanisms in ventrolateral prefrontal cortex. *Neuron*, 47, 907–918.

Bahrick, H.P. (1984). Semantic memory content in permastore: Fifty years of memory for Spanish learning in school. *Journal of Experimental Psychology: General*, 113, 1–29.

Bahrick, H.P., Bahrick, P.O., & Wittlinger, R.P. (1975). Fifty years of memory for names and faces: A cross-sectional approach. *Journal of Experimental Psychology: General*, 104(1), 54–75.

Bahrick, H.P., Hall, L.K., & Da Costa, L.A. (2008). Fifty years of memory of college grades: Accuracy and distortions. *Emotion*, 8, 13–22.

Baizer, J.S., Ungerleider, L.G., & Desimone, R. (1991). Organisation of visual inputs to the inferior temporal and posterior parietal cortex in macaques. *Journal of Neuroscience*, 11, 168–190.

Ball, L.J., Lucas, F.J., Miles, J.N.V., & Gale, A.G. (2003). Inspection times and the selection task: What do eye movements reveal about relevance effects? *Quarterly Journal of Experimental Psychology*, 56A, 1053–1077.

Ball, L.J., Phillips, P., Wade, C.N., & Quayle, J.D. (2006). Effects of belief and logic on syllogistic reasoning: Eye-movement evidence for selective processing models. *Experimental Psychology*, 53, 77–86.

Balota, D.A., Paul, S., & Spieler, D. (1999). Attentional control of lexical processing pathways during word recognition and reading. In S. Garrod & M.J. Pickering (Eds.), *Language processing*. Hove, UK: Psychology Press.

Banks, W.P., & Isham, E.A. (2009). We infer rather than perceive the moment we decide to act. *Psychological Science, 20,* 17–21.

Bar, M. (2003). A cortical mechanism for triggering top-down facilitation in visual object recognition. *Journal of Cognitive Neuroscience, 15,* 600–609.

Bar, M., Kassam, K.S., Ghuman, A.S., Boshyan, J., Schmid, A.M., Dale, A.M., et al. (2006). Top-down facilitation of visual recognition. *Proceedings of the National Academy of Sciences, 103,* 449–454.

Barbur, J.L., & Spang, K. (2008). Colour constancy and conscious perception of changes of illuminant. *Neuropsychologia, 46,* 853–863.

Bard, E.G., Anderson, A.H., Chen, Y., Nicholson, H.B.V.M., Havard, C., & Dalzel-Job, S. (2007). Let's you do that: Sharing the cognitive burdens of dialogue. *Journal of Memory and Language, 57,* 616–641.

Bar-Haim, Y., Lamy, D., Perganini, L., Bakermans-Kranenburg, N.J., & van IJzendoorn, M.H. (2007). Threat-related attentional bias in anxious and non-anxious individuals: A meta-analytic study. *Psychological Bulletin, 133,* 1–24.

Baron, J., & Ritov, I. (2004). Omission bias, individual differences, and normality. *Organizational Behavior and Human Decision Processes, 94,* 74–85.

Barr, D.J. (2008). Pragmatic expectation and linguistic evidence: Listeners anticipate but do not integrate common ground. *Cognition, 109,* 18–40.

Barrett, H.C., & Kurzban, R. (2006). Modularity in cognition: Framing the debate. *Psychological Review, 113,* 628–647.

Barrett, L.F., & Russell, J.A. (1998). Independence and bipolarity in the structure of current affect. *Journal of Personality and Social Psychology, 74,* 967–984.

Barrett, L.F., Tugade, M.M., & Engle, R.W. (2004). Individual differences in working memory capacity and dual-process theories of the mind. *Psychological Bulletin, 130,* 553–573.

Barsalou, L.W. (1988). The content and organization of autobiographical memories. In U. Neisser & E. Winograd (Eds.), *Remembering reconsidered: Ecological and traditional approaches to the study of memory.* New York: Cambridge University Press.

Barsalou, L.W. (2008). Grounded cognition. *Annual Review of Psychology, 59,* 617–645.

Barsalou, L.W., & Wiemer-Hastings, K. (2005). Situating abstract concepts. In D. Pecher and R. Zwaan (Eds.), *Grounding cognition: The role of perception and action in memory, language, and thought.* New York: Cambridge University Press.

Bartels, A., & Zeki, S. (2000). The neural basis of romantic love. *NeuroReport, 11,* 3829–3834.

Bartels, A., & Zeki, S. (2004). The chronoarchitecture of the human brain – Natural viewing conditions reveals a time-based anatomy of the brain. *Neuroimage, 22,* 419–433.

Bartlett, F.C. (1932). *Remembering.* Cambridge: Cambridge University Press.

Bartolomeo, P. (2002). The relationship between visual perception and visual mental imagery: A re-appraisal of the neuropsychological evidence. *Cortex, 38,* 357–378.

Bartolomeo, P., & Chokron, S. (2002). Orienting of attention in left unilateral neglect. *Neuroscience and Biobehavioral Reviews, 26,* 217–234.

Bartolomeo, P., Bachoud-Lévi, A.C., De Gelder, B., Denes, G., Dalla Barba, G., Brugieres, P. et al. (1998). Multiple-domain dissociation between impaired visual perception and preserved mental imagery in a patient with bilateral extrastriate lesions. *Neuropsychologia, 36,* 239–249.

Bartolomeo, P., de Schotten, M.T., & Doricchi, F. (2007). Left unilateral neglect as a disconnection syndrome. *Cerebral Cortex, 17,* 2479–2490.

Bartolomeo, P., Siéroff, E., Decaix, C., & Chokron, S. (2001). Modulating the attentional bias in unilateral neglect: The effect of the strategic set. *Experimental Brain Research, 137,* 432–444.

Bartolomeo, P. (2002). The relationship between visual perception and visual mental imagery: A reappraisal of the neuropsychological evidence. *Cortex, 38,* 357–378.

Barton, J.J.S., Press, D.Z., Keenan, J.P., & O'Connor, M. (2002). Lesions of the fusiform face area impair perception of facial configuration in prosopagnosia. *Neurology, 58,* 71–78.

Baseler, H.A., Morland, A.B., & Wandell, B.A. (1999). Topographic organization of human visual areas in the absence of input from primary cortex. *Journal of Neuroscience, 19,* 2619–2627.

Battersby, W.S., Teuber, H.L., & Bender, M.B. (1953). Problem solving behavior in men with frontal or occipital brain injuries. *Journal of Psychology, 35,* 329–351.

Bauer, P.J. (2004). Getting explicit memory off the ground: Steps toward construction of a neuro-developmental account of changes in the first two years of life. *Developmental Review, 24,* 347–373.

Baurès, R., Benguigui, N., Amorim, M.-A., & Siegler, I.A. (2007). Intercepting free falling objects: Better use Occam's razor than internalise Newton's law. *Vision Research, 47,* 2982–2991.

Bavelas, J., Gerwing, J., Sutton, C., & Prevost, D. (2008). Gesturing on the telephone: Independent effects of dialogue and visibility. *Journal of Memory and Language, 58*, 495–520.

Baynes, K., & Gazzaniga, M. (2000). Consciousness, introspection, and the split-brain: The two minds/one body problem. In M.S. Gazzaniga (Ed.), *The new cognitive neurosciences*. Cambridge, MA: MIT Press.

Baxendale, S. (2004). Memories aren't made of this: Amnesia at the movies. *British Medical Journal, 329*, 1480–1483.

Beauvois, M.-F., & Dérouesné, J. (1979). Phonological alexia: Three dissociations. *Journal of Neurology, Neurosurgery & Psychiatry, 42*, 1115–1124.

Bechara, A., & Damasio, A.R. (2005). The somatic marker hypothesis: A neural theory of economic decision. *Games and Economic Behavior, 52*, 336–372.

Beck, A.T. (1976). *Cognitive therapy and the emotional disorders*. New York: International Universities Press.

Beck, A.T., & Clark, D.A. (1988). Anxiety and depression: An information processing perspective. *Anxiety Research, 1*, 23–36.

Beck, A.T., & Clark, D.A. (1997). An information-processing model of anxiety: Automatic and strategic processes. *Behaviour Research and Therapy, 35*, 49–58.

Beck, D.M., & Kastner, S. (2005). Stimulus context modulates competition in human extrastriate cortex. *Nature Neuroscience, 8*, 1110–1116.

Beck, D.M., Muggleton, N., Walsh, V., & Lavie, N. (2006). Right parietal cortex plays a critical role in change blindness. *Cerebral Cortex, 16*, 712–717.

Becker, S. (2007). Preface to the special issue: Computational cognitive neuroscience. *Brain Research, 1202*, 1–2.

Beckers, G., & Zeki, S. (1995). The consequences of inactivating areas V1 and V5 on visual motion perception. *Brain, 118*, 49–60.

Beeke, S., Wilkinson, R., & Maxim, J. (2007). Grammar without sentence structure: A conversation analytic investigation of agrammatism. *Aphasiology, 21*, 256–282.

Behrman, B.W., & Davey, S.L. (2001). Eyewitness identification in actual criminal cases: An archival analysis. *Law and Human Behavior, 25*, 475–491.

Behrmann, M., & Bub, D. (1992). Surface dyslexia and dysgraphia: Dual routes, single lexicon. *Cognitive Neuropsychology, 9*, 209–251.

Behrmann, M., Peterson, M.A., Moscovitch, M., & Suzuki, S. (2006). Independent representation of parts and the relations between them: Evidence from integrative amnesia. *Journal of Experimental Psychology: Human Perception and Performance, 32*, 1169–1184.

Bell, A.H., & Munoz, D.P. (2008). Activity in the superior colliculus reflects dynamic interactions between voluntary and involuntary influences on orienting behaviour. *European Journal of Neuroscience, 28*, 1654–1660.

Bell, T.A., & Anderson, M.C. (in preparation). Keeping things in and out of mind: Individual differences in working memory capacity predict successful memory suppression.

Bell, V.A., & Johnson-Laird, P.N. (1998). A model theory of model reasoning. *Cognitive Science, 22*, 25–51.

Bell, V., Halligan, P.W., & Ellis, H.D. (2006). Explaining delusions: A cognitive perspective. *Trends in Cognitive Sciences, 10*, 219–226.

Benguigui, N., Ripoli, H., & Broderick, M.P. (2003). Time-to-contact estimation of accelerated stimuli is based on first-order information. *Journal of Experimental Psychology: Human Perception and Performance, 29*, 1083–1101.

Bennett, P., Lowe, R., & Honey, K.L. (2003). Appraisals, core relational themes, and emotions: A test of the consistency of reporting and their associations. *Cognition and Emotion, 17*, 511–520.

Benson, D.F., & Ardila, A. (1996). *Aphasia: A clinical perspective*. Oxford: Oxford University Press.

Benton, T.R., Ross, D.F., Bradshaw, E., Thomas, W.N., & Bradshaw, G.S. (2006). Eyewitness memory is still not common sense: Comparing jurors, judges and law enforcement to eyewitness experts. *Applied Cognitive Psychology, 20*, 115–129.

Bereiter, C., Burtis, P.J., & Scardamalia, M. (1988). Cognitive operations in constructing main points in written composition. *Journal of Memory & Language, 27*, 261–278.

Bereiter, C., & Scardamalia, M. (1987). The psychology of written composition. *Journal of Memory & Language, 27*, 261–278.

Bergman, E.T., & Roediger, H.L. (1999). Can Bartlett's repeated reproduction findings be replicated? *Memory and Cognition, 27*, 937–944.

Bergstrom, Z.M., de Fockert, J., & Richardson-Klavehn, A. (2009). Event-related potential evidence that automatic recollection can be voluntarily avoided. *Journal of Cognitive Neuroscience, 21*, 1280–1301.

Berlingeri, M., Bettini, G., Basilico, S., Silani, G., Zanardi, G., Sberna, M. et al. (2008). Anatomy of the episodic buffer: A voxel-based morphometry study in patients with dementia. *Behavioural Neurology, 19*, 29–34.

Berndt, R.S., Mitchum, C.C., Haendiges, A.N., & Sandson, J. (1997). Verb retrieval in aphas. 1. Characterising single word impairments. *Brain and Language, 56*, 69–106.

Berntsen, D. (1998). Voluntary and involuntary access to autobiographical memory. *Memory*, 6, 113–141.

Berntsen, D., & Hall, N.M. (2004). The episodic nature of involuntary autobiographical memories. *Memory and Cognition*, 32, 789–803.

Berntsen, D., & Rubin, D.C. (2002). Emotionally charged autobiographical memories across the life span: The recall of happy, sad, traumatic and involuntary memories. *Psychology and Ageing*, 17, 636–652.

Berndsen, M., & Manstead, A.S.R. (2007). On the relationship between responsibility and guilt: Antecedent appraisal or elaborated appraisal? *European Journal of Social Psychology*, 37, 774–792.

Berryhill, M.E., Phuong, L., Picasso, L., Cabeza, R., & Olson, I.R. (2007). Parietal lobe and episodic memory: Bilateral damage causes free recall of autobiographical memory. *Journal of Neuroscience*, 27, 14415–14423.

Bertamini, M., Yang, T.L., & Proffitt, D.R. (1998). Relative size perception at a distance is best at eye level. *Perception & Psychophysics*, 60, 673–682.

Beschin, N., Cocchini, G., Della Sala, S., & Logie, R.H. (1997). What the eyes perceive, the brain ignores: A case of pure unilateral representational neglect. *Cortex*, 33, 3–26.

Betsch, T., Plessner, H., Schwieren, C., & Gütig, R. (2001). I like it but I don't know why: A value-account approach to implicit attitude formation. *Personality and Social Psychology Bulletin*, 27, 242–253.

Biassou, N., Obler, L.K., Nespoulous, J.-L., Dordain, M., & Harris, K.S. (1997). Dual processing of open- and closed-class words. *Brain & Language*, 57, 360–373.

Bickerton, D. (1984). The language bioprogram hypothesis. *Behavioural and Brain Sciences*, 7, 173–221.

Biederman, I. (1987). Recognition-by-components: A theory of human image understanding. *Psychological Review*, 94, 115–147.

Biederman, I. (1990). Higher-level vision. In D.N. Osherson, S. Kosslyn, & J. Hollerbach (Eds.), *An invitation to cognitive science: Visual cognition and action*. Cambridge, MA: MIT Press.

Biederman, I., & Bar, M. (1999). One-shot viewpoint invariance in matching novel objects. *Vision Research*, 39, 2885–2899.

Biederman, I., & Gerhardstein, P.C. (1993). Recognising depth-rotated objects: Evidence for 3-D viewpoint invariance. *Journal of Experimental Psychology: Human Perception & Performance*, 19, 1162–1182.

Biedermann, B., Ruh, B., Nickels, L., & Coltheart, M. (2008). Information retrieval in tip-of-the-tongue states: New data and methodological advances. *Journal of Psycholinguistic Research*, 37, 171–198.

Biederman, I., Subramaniam, S., Bar, M., Kalocsai, P., & Fiser, J. (1999). Subordinate-level object classification re-examined. *Psychological Research*, 62, 131–153.

Bilalić, M., McLeod, P., & Gobet, F. (2008). Inflexibility of experts: Reality or myth? Quantifying the Einstellung effect in chess masters. *Cognitive Psychology*, 56, 73–102.

Binkofski, F., Dohle, C., Posse, S., Stephan, K.M., Hefter, H., Seitz, R.J. et al. (1998). Human anterior intraparietal area subserves prehension: A combined lesion and functional MRI activation study. *Neurology*, 50, 1253–1259.

Birch, H.G. (1945). The relationship of previous experience to insightful problem solving. *Journal of Comparative Psychology*, 38, 267–383.

Bishop, D.V.M. (1997). *Uncommon understanding: Development and disorders of language comprehension in children*. Hove, UK: Psychology Press.

Bjork, R.A., & Whitten, W.B. (1974). Recency sensitive retrieval processes in long-term free recall. *Cognitive Psychology*, 6, 173–189.

Blais, C., Arguin, M., & Marleau, I. (2009). Orientation invariance in visual shape perception. *Journal of Vision*, 9, 1–23.

Blake, R., & Logothetis, N.K. (2002). Visual competition. *Nature Review Neuroscience*, 3, 13–23.

Blanchette, I., & Dunbar, K. (2000). How analogies are generated: The roles of structural and superficial similarity. *Memory & Cognition*, 28, 108–124.

Blangero, A., Gaveau, V., Luaute, J., Rode, G., Salemme, R., Guinard, M., et al. (2008). A hand and a field effect in on-line motor control in unilateral optic ataxia. *Cortex*, 44, 560–568.

Blasko, D., & Connine, C. (1993). Effects of familiarity and aptness on metaphor processing. *Journal of Experimental Psychology: Learning, Memory, & Cognition*, 19, 295–308.

Block, N. (2007). Overflow, access, and attention. *Behavioral and Brain Sciences*, 30, 530–548.

Bloj, M.G., Kersten, D., & Hurlbert, A.C. (1999). Perception of three-dimensional shape influences colour perception through mutual illumination. *Nature*, 402, 877–879.

Bloomfield, A.N. (2006). Group size and the framing effect: Threats to human beings and animals. *Memory & Cognition*, 34, 929–937.

Bock, K., & Eberhard, K.M. (1993). Meaning, sound and syntax in English number agreement. *Language and Cognitive Processes*, 8, 57–99.

Boehler, C.N., Schoenfeld, M.A., Heinze, H.-J., & Hopf, J.-M. (2008). Rapid recurrent processing gates awareness in primary visual cortex. *Proceedings of the National Academy of Sciences*, 105(25), 8742–8747.

Bohannon, J.N. (1988). Flashbulb memories for the space shuttle disaster: A tale of two theories. *Cognition*, 29, 179–196.

Bohning, D.E., Shastri, A., McConnell, K.A., Nahar, Z., Lorberbaum, J.P., Roberts, D.R. et al. (1999). A combined TMS/fMRI study of intensity-dependent TMS over motor cortex. *Biological Psychiatry*, 45, 385–394.

Boland, J.E., & Blodgett, A. (2001). Understanding the constraints on syntactic generation: Lexical bias and discourse congruency effects on eye movements. *Journal of Memory and Language*, 45, 391–411.

Bolden, G.B. (2006). Little words that matter: Discourse markers "so" and "oh" and the doing of other-attentives in social interaction. *Journal of Communication*, 56, 661–688.

Boly, M., Phillips, C., Tshibanda, L., Vanhaudenhuyse, A., Schabus, M., Dange-Vu, T.T. et al. (2008). Intrinsic brain activity in altered states of consciousness: How conscious is the default mode of brain function? *Annals of the New York Academy of Sciences*, 1129, 119–129.

Bonath, B., Noesselt, T., Martinez, A., Mishra, J., Schwiecker, K., Heinze, H.J., & Hillyard, S.A. (2007). Neural basis of the ventriloquist illusion. *Current Biology*, 17, 1697–1703.

Bonnefon, J.F., Eid, M., Vautie, S., & Jmel, S. (2008). A mixed Rash model of dual-process conditional reasoning. *Quarterly Journal of Experimental Psychology*, 61, 809–824.

Booth, M.C.A., & Rolls, E.T. (1998). View-invariant representations of familiar objects by neurons in the inferior temporal visual cortex. *Cerebral Cortex*, 8, 510–523.

Bormann, T., Wallesch, C.-W., & Blanken, G. (2008). "Fragment errors" in deep dysgraphia: Further support for a lexical hypothesis. *Cognitive Neuropsychology*, 25, 745–764.

Bormann, T., Wallesch, C.-W., Seyboth, M., & Blanken, G. (2009). Writing two words as one: Word boundary errors in a German case of acquired surface dysgraphia. *Journal of Neurolinguistics*, 22, 74–82.

Bourke, P.A., Duncan, J., & Nimmo-Smith, I. (1996). A general factor involved in dual-task performance decrement. *Quarterly Journal of Experimental Psychology*, 49A, 525–545.

Bouvier, S.E., & Engel, S.A. (2006). Behavioural deficits and cortical damage loci in cerebral achromatopsia. *Cerebral Cortex*, 16, 183–191.

Bowden, E.M., & Beeman, M.J. (1998). Getting the right idea: Semantic activation in the right hemisphere may help solve insight problems. *Psychological Science*, 9, 435–440.

Bowden, E.M., & Jung-Beeman, M. (2007). Methods for investigating the neural components of insight. *Methods*, 42, 87–99.

Bowden, E.M., Jung-Beeman, M., Fleck, J., & Kounios, J. (2005). New approaches to demystifying insight. *Trends in Cognitive Sciences*, 9, 322–328.

Bower, G.H. (1981). Mood and memory. *American Psychologist*, 36, 129–148.

Bower, G.H. (1994). Temporary emotional states act like multiple personality. In R.M. Klein & B.K. Doane (Eds.), *Psychological concepts and dissociative disorders*. Hillsdale, NJ: Lawrence Erlbaum Associates Inc.

Bower, G.H., & Forgas, J.P. (2000). Affect, memory, and social cognition. In E. Eich, J.F. Kihlstrom, G.H. Bower, J.P. Forgas, & P.M. Niedenthal (Eds.), *Cognition and emotion*. Oxford: Oxford University Press.

Bower, G.H., Gilligan, S.G., & Monteiro, K.P. (1981). Selectivity of learning caused by affective states. *Journal of Experimental Psychology: General*, 110, 451–473.

Bowers, J.S. (2002). Challenging the widespread assumption that connectionism and distributed representations go hand-in-hand. *Cognitive Psychology*, 45, 413–445.

Bowers, J.S. (2009). On the biological plausibility of grandmother cells: Implications for neural network theories of psychology and neuroscience. *Psychological Review*, 116, 220–251.

Bowmaker, J.K., & Dartnall, H.J.A. (1980). Visual pigments of rods and cones in a human retina. *Journal of Physiology*, 298, 501–511.

Boyer, J.L., Harrison, S., & Ro, T. (2005). Unconscious processing of orientation and colour without primary visual cortex. *Proceedings of the National Academy of Sciences of the United States of America*, 102, 16875–16879.

Braet, W., & Humphreys, G.W. (2009). The role of re-entrant processes in feature binding: Evidence from neuropsychology and TMS on late onset illusory conjunctions. *Visual Cognition*, 17, 25–47.

Brainerd, C.J., & Mojardin, A.H. (1998). Children's spontaneous false memories for narrative statements: Long-term persistence and mere-testing effects. *Child Development*, 69, 1361–1377.

Bransford, J.D. (1979). *Human cognition: Learning, understanding and remembering*. Belmont, CA: Wadsworth.

Bransford, J.D., & Johnson, M.K. (1972). Contextual prerequisites for understanding. *Journal of Verbal Learning and Verbal Behavior*, 11, 717–726.

Bransford, J.D., & Schwartz, D.L. (1999). Rethinking transfer: A simple proposal with multiple implications. In A. Iran-Nejad & P.D. Pearson (Eds.), *Review of Research in Education*, 24, 61–101. Washington DC: American Educational Research Association.

Bransford, J.D., Barclay, J.R., & Franks, J.J. (1972). Sentence memory: A constructive versus interpretive approach. *Cognitive Psychology*, 3, 193–209.

Bransford, J.D., Franks, J.J., Morris, C.D., & Stein, B.S. (1979). Some general constraints on learning and memory research. In L.S. Cermak & F.I.M. Craik (Eds.), *Levels of processing in human memory*. Hillsdale, NJ: Lawrence Erlbaum Associates Inc.

Brandt, K.R., Gardiner, J.M., Vargha-Khadem, F., Baddeley, A.D., & Mishkin, M. (2006). Using semantic memory to boost "episodic" recall in a case of developmental amnesia. *NeuroReport*, 17, 1057–1060.

Brase, G.L., Fiddick, L., & Harries, C. (2006). Participants' recruitment methods and statistical reasoning performance. *Quarterly Journal of Experimental Psychology*, 59, 965–976.

Brasil-Neto, J.P., Pascual-Leone, A., Vallsole, J., Coher, L.G., & Hallett, M. (1992). Focal transcranial magnetic stimulation and response bias in a forced-choice task. *Journal of Neurology, Neurosurgery and Psychiatry*, 55, 964–966.

Brass, M., & Haggard, P. (2008). The What, When, Whether model of intentional action. *The Neuroscientist*, 14, 319–325.

Brédart, S., Brennen, T., Delchambre, M., McNeill, A., & Burton, A.M. (2005). Naming very familiar people: When retrieving names is faster than retrieving semantic biographical information. *British Journal of Psychology*, 96, 205–214.

Breedin, S.D., & Saffran, E.M. (1999). Sentence processing in the face of semantic loss: A case study. *Journal of Experimental Psychology: General*, 128, 547–562.

Brennan, S.E. (1990). *Seeking and providing evidence for mutual understanding*. PhD. dissertation, Department of Psychology, Stanford University.

Brewer, W.F., & Treyens, J.C. (1981). Role of schemata in memory for places. *Cognitive Psychology*, 13, 207–230.

Brewin, C.R., Smith, A.J., Power, M.J., & Furnham, A. (1992). State and trait differences in the depressive self-schema. *Behaviour Research and Therapy*, 30, 555–557.

Bridge, H., Thomas, O., Jbabdi, S., & Cowey, A. (2008). Changes in connectivity after visual cortical brain damage underlie altered visual function. *Brain*, 131, 1433–1444.

Britten, K.H. (2008). Mechanisms of self-motion perception. *Annual Review of Neuroscience*, 31, 389–410.

Britten, K.H., & van Wezel, R.J.A. (1998). Electrical microstimulation of cortical area MST biases heading perception in monkeys. *Nature Neuroscience*, 1, 59–63.

Broadbent, D.E. (1958). *Perception and communication*. Oxford: Pergamon.

Bröder, A. (2003). Decision making with the adaptive toolbox: Influence of environmental structure, personality, intelligence, and working memory load. *Journal of Experimental Psychology: Learning, Memory, and Cognition*, 29, 611–625.

Brown, R., & Kulik, J. (1977). Flashbulb memories. *Cognition*, 5, 73–99.

Brown, R.G., Jahanshahi, M., Limousin-Dowsey, P., Thomas, D., Quinn, N., & Rothwell, J.C. (2003). Pallidotomy and incidental sequence learning in Parkinson's disease. *NeuroReport*, 14, 1–4.

Brown, R.M., & Robertson, E.M. (2007). Off-line processing: Reciprocal interactions between declarative and procedural memories. *Journal of Neuroscience*, 27, 10468–10475.

Bruce, K.R., & Pihl, R.O. (1997). Forget drinking to forget: Enhanced consolidation of emotionally charged memory by alcohol. *Experimental and Clinical Psychopharmacology*, 5, 242–250.

Bruce, V., & Young, A.W. (1986). Understanding face recognition. *British Journal of Psychology*, 77, 305–327.

Bruce, V., Green, P.R., & Georgeson, M.A. (2003). *Visual perception* (4th ed.). Hove, UK: Psychology Press.

Bruce, V., Henderson, Z., Greenwood, K., Hancock, P., Burton, A.M., & Miller, P. (1999). Verification of face identities from images captured on video. *Journal of Experimental Psychology: Applied*, 5, 339–360.

Bruggeman, H., Zosh, W., & Warren, W.H. (2007). Optic flow drives human visuo-locomotor adaptation. *Current Biology*, 17, 2035–2040.

Bruner, J.S., Goodnow, J.J., & Austin, G.A. (1956). *A study of thinking*. New York: John Wiley.

Bruno, N., & Cutting, J.E. (1988). Mini-modularity and the perception of layout. *Journal of Experimental Psychology: General*, 117, 161–170.

Bruno, N., Bernadis, P., & Gentilucci, M. (2008). Visually guided pointing, the Müller–Lyer illusion, and the functional interpretation of the dorsal–ventral split: Conclusions from 33 independent studies. *Neuroscience and Biobehavioral Reviews*, 32, 423–437.

Brysbaert, M., & Mitchell, D.C. (1996). Modifier attachment in sentence parsing: Evidence from

Dutch. *Quarterly Journal of Experimental Psychology*, 49, 664–695.

Bub, D., & Kertesz, A. (1982). Deep agraphia. *Brain and Language*, 17, 146–165.

Bub, D., Cancelliere, A., & Kertesz, A. (1985). Whole-word and analytic translation of spelling to sound in a nonsemantic reader. In K.E. Patterson, J.C. Marshall, & M. Coltheart (Eds.), *Surface dyslexia: Neuropsychological and cognitive studies of phonological reading*. Hove, UK: Psychology Press.

Bucciarelli, M., & Johnson-Laird, P.N. (1999). Strategies in syllogistic reasoning. *Cognitive Science*, 23, 247–303.

Buchanan, T.W., Tranel, D., & Adolphs, R. (2006). Memories for autobiographical events following unilateral damage to medial temporal lobe. *Brain*, 129, 115–127.

Buchner, A., & Wippich, W. (1998). Differences and commonalities between implicit learning and implicit memory. In M.A. Stadler & P.A. Frensch (Eds.), *Handbook of implicit learning*. London: Sage.

Bülthoff, I., Bülthoff, H., & Sinha, P. (1998). Top-down influences on stereoscopic depth-perception. *Nature Neuroscience*, 1, 254–257.

Burgess, P.W., Dumontheil, I., Gilbert, S.J., Okuda, J., Schölvinck, & Simons, J.S. (2008). On the role of rostral prefrontal cortex (area 10) in prospective memory. In M. Kliegel, M.A. McDaniel, & G.O. Einstein (Eds.), *Prospective memory: Cognitive, neuroscience, developmental, and applied perspectives*. London: Lawrence Erlbaum Associates.

Burgess, P.W., Veitch, E., Costello, A., & Shallice, T. (2000). The cognitive and neuroanatomical correlates of multi-tasking. *Neuropsychologia*, 38, 848–863.

Burianova, H., & Grady, C.L. (2007). Common and unique neural activations in autobiographical, episodic, and semantic retrieval. *Journal of Cognitive Neuroscience*, 19, 1520–1534.

Burkhardt, P., Avrutin, S., Piñango, M.M., & Ruigendijk, E. (2008). Slower-than-usual syntactic processing in agrammatic Broca's aphasia: Evidence from Dutch. *Journal of Neurolinguistics*, 21, 120–137.

Burns, B.D. (2004). The effects of speed on skilled chess performance. *Psychological Science*, 15, 442–447.

Burns, B.D., & Wieth, M. (2004). The collider principle in causal reasoning: Why the Monty Hall dilemma is so hard. *Journal of Experimental Psychology: General*, 133, 434–449.

Burt, C.D.B., Kemp, S., & Conway, M.A. (2003). Themes, events, and episodes in autobiographical memory. *Memory & Cognition*, 31, 317–325.

Burton, A.M., Bruce, V., & Hancock, P.J.B. (1999). From pixels to people: A model of familiar face recognition. *Cognitive Science*, 23, 1–31.

Bushman, B.J. (2002). Does venting anger feed or extinguish the flame? Catharsis, rumination, distraction, anger, and aggressive responding. *Personality and Social Psychology Bulletin*, 28, 724–731.

Butterworth, B. (1985). Jargon aphasia: Processes and strategies. In S. Newman & R. Epstein (Eds.), *Current perspectives in dysphasia*. Edinburgh: Churchill Livingstone.

Butterworth, B., & Howard, D. (1987). Paragrammatisms. *Cognition*, 26, 1–37.

Buxbaum, L.J., & Saffran, E.M. (2002). Knowledge of object manipulation and object function: Dissociations in apraxic and non-apraxic subjects. *Brain and Language*, 82, 179–199.

Buxbaum, L.J., Ferraro, M., Veramonti, T., Farne, A., Whyte, J., Ladavas, E. et al. (2004). Hemispatial neglect: Subtypes, neuroanatomy, and disability. *Neurology*, 62, 749–756.

Byrd, D., & Saltzman, E. (1998). Intragestural dynamics of multiple phrasal boundaries. *Journal of Phonetics*, 26, 173–199.

Byrne, R.M.J. (1989). Suppressing valid inferences with conditionals. *Cognition*, 31, 61–83.

Cabeza, R. (2008). Role of parietal regions in episodic memory retrieval: The dual attentional processes hypothesis. *Neuropsychologia*, 46, 1813–1827.

Cabeza, R., & St. Jacques, P. (2007). Functional neuroimaging of autobiographical memory. *Trends in Cognitive Sciences*, 11, 219–227.

Cabeza, R., Prince, S.E., Daselaar, S.M., Greenberg, D.L., Budde, M., Dolcos, F. et al. (2004). Brain activity during episodic retrieval of autobiographical and laboratory events: An fMRI study using a novel photo paradigm. *Journal of Cognitive Neuroscience*, 16, 1583–1594.

Caccappolo-van Vliet, E., Miozzo, M., & Stern, Y. (2004). Phonological dyslexia: A test case for reading models. *Psychological Science*, 15, 583–590.

Caillies, S., Denhière, G., & Kintsch, W. (2002). The effect of prior knowledge on understanding from text: Evidence from primed recognition. *European Journal of Cognitive Psychology*, 14, 267–286.

Calder, A.J., & Young, A.W. (2005). Understanding the recognition of facial identity and facial expression. *Nature Reviews Neuroscience*, 6, 641–651.

Calder, A.J., Young, A.W., Keane, J., & Dean, M. (2000). Configural information in facial expression perception. *Journal of Experimental Psychology: Human Perception and Performance*, 26, 527–551.

Calvo, M.G. (2001). Working memory and inferences: Evidence from eye fixations during reading. *Memory*, 9, 365–381.

Calvo, M.G., & Avero, P. (2005). Time course of attentional bias to emotional scenes in anxiety: Gaze direction and duration. *Cognition and Emotion*, 19, 433–451.

Calvo, M.G., Castillo, M.D., & Schmalhofer, F. (2006). Strategic influence on the time course of predictive inferences in reading. *Memory & Cognition*, 34, 68–77.

Camerer, C., & Hogarth, R.B. (1999). The effects of financial incentives in experiments: A review and capital-labor-production framework. *Journal of Risk and Uncertainty*, 19, 7–42.

Camerer, C., Babcock, L., Loewenstein, G., & Thaler, R. (1997). Labour supply of New York cab drivers: One day at a time? *Quarterly Journal of Economics*, CXII, 407–441.

Campbell, R. (1983). Writing non-words to dictation. *Brain and Language*, 19, 153–178.

Campion, J., Latto, R. & Smith, Y.M. (1983). Is blindsight an effect of scattered light, spared cortex, and near-threshold vision? *Behavioral and Brain Sciences*, 6, 423–486.

Campion, N. (2004). Predictive inferences are represented as hypothetical facts. *Journal of Memory and Language*, 50, 149–164.

Canales, A.F., Gómez, D.M., & Maffet, C.R. (2007). A critical assessment of the consciousness by synchrony hypothesis. *Biological Research*, 40, 517–519.

Canessa, N., Borgo, F., Cappa, S.F., Perani, D., Falini, A., Buccino, G. et al. (2008). The different neural correlates of action and functional knowledge in semantic memory: A fMRI study. *Cerebral Cortex*, 18, 741–751.

Caramazza, A., & Coltheart, M. (2006). Cognitive neuropsychology twenty years on. *Cognitive Neuropsychology*, 23, 3–12.

Carr, T.H., Davidson, B.J., & Hawkins, H.L. (1978). Perceptual flexibility in word recognition: Strategies affect orthographic computation but not lexical access. *Journal of Experimental Psychology: Human Perception & Performance*, 4, 674–690.

Carreiras, M., & Clifton, C. (1993). Relative clause interpretation preferences in Spanish and English. *Language & Speech*, 36, 353–372.

Carvalho, J.B. (2002). Developing audience awareness in writing. *Journal of Research in Reading*, 25, 271–282.

Casasanto, D. (2008). Similarity and proximity: When does close in space mean close in mind? *Memory & Cognition*, 36, 1047–1056.

Cavaco, S., Anderson, S.W., Allen, J.S., Castro-Caldas, A., & Damasio, H. (2004).

The scope of preserved procedural memory in amnesia. *Brain*, 127, 1853–1867.

Cavanagh, P., & Mather, G. (1989). Motion: The long and short of it. *Spatial Vision*, 4, 103–129.

Ceci, S.J., & Liker, J.K. (1986). A day at the races: A study of IQ, expertise, and cognitive complexity. *Journal of Experimental Psychology: General*, 115, 255–266.

Centofanti, A.T., & Reece, J. (2006). The cognitive interview and its effect on misleading postevent information. *Psychology, Crime & Law*, 12, 669–683.

Ceraso, J., & Provitera, A. (1971). Sources of error in syllogistic reasoning. *Cognitive Psychology*, 2, 400–410.

Cermak, L.S., Lewis, R., Butters, N., & Goodglass, H. (1973). Role of verbal mediation in performance of motor tasks by Korsakoff patients. *Perceptual & Motor Skills*, 37, 259–262.

Cermak, L.S., Talbot, N., Chandler, K., & Wolbarst, L.R. (1985). The perceptual priming phenomenon in amnesia. *Neuropsychologia*, 23, 615–622.

Challis, B.H., Velichkovsky, B.M., & Craik, F.I.M. (1996). Levels-of-processing effects on a variety of memory tasks: New findings and theoretical implications. *Consciousness and Cognition*, 5, 142–164.

Chalmers, D.J. (1995a). Facing up to the problem of consciousness. *Journal of Consciousness Studies*, 3, 200–219.

Chalmers, D.J. (1995b). The puzzle of conscious experience. *Scientific American*, December, 62–68.

Chalmers, D. (2007). The hard problem of consciousness. In M. Velmans & S. Schneider (Eds.), *The Blackwell companion to consciousness*. Oxford: Blackwell.

Chamberlain, E. (2003). Review of 'Behavioural assessment of the dysexecutive syndrome (BADS)'. *Journal of Occupational Psychology*, 5, 33–37.

Channon, S., Shanks, D., Johnstone, T., Vakili, K., Chin, J., & Sinclair, E. (2002). Is implicit learning spared in amnesia? Rule abstraction and item familiarity in artificial grammar learning. *Neuropsychologia*, 40, 2185–2197.

Charness, N. (1981). Search in chess: Age and skill differences. *Journal of Experimental Psychology: Human Perception and Performance*, 7, 467–476.

Charness, N., Reingold, E.M., Pomplun, M., & Stampe, D.M. (2001). The perceptual aspect of skilled performance in chess: Evidence from eye movements. *Memory & Cognition*, 29, 1146–1152.

Charness, N., Tuffiash, M., Krampe, R., Reingold, E., & Vasyukova, E. (2005). The role of deliberate practice in chess expertise. *Applied Cognitive Psychology, 19,* 151–165.

Chartrand, T.L., van Baaren, R.B., & Bargh, J.A. (2006). Linking automatic evaluation to mood and information-processing style: Consequences for experienced affect, impression formation, and stereotyping. *Journal of Experimental Psychology: General, 135,* 7–77.

Chase, W.G., & Simon, H.A. (1973a). Perception in chess. *Cognitive Psychology, 4,* 55–81.

Chase, W.G., & Simon, H.A. (1973b). The mind's eye in chess. In W.G. Chase (Ed.), *Visual information processing.* London: Academic Press.

Chater, N., & Oaksford, M. (2001). Human rationality and the psychology of reasoning: Where do we go from here? *British Journal of Psychology, 92,* 193–216.

Cheesman, J., & Merikle, P.M. (1984). Priming with and without awareness. *Perception & Psychophysics, 36,* 387–395.

Chen, C.M., Lakatos, P., Shah, A.S., Mehta, A.D., Givre, S.J., Javitt, D.C. et al. (2007). Functional anatomy and interaction of fast and slow visual pathways in macaque monkeys. *Cerebral Cortex, 17,* 1561–1569.

Chen, L.L., & Boland, J.E. (2008). Dominance and context effects on activation of alternative homophone meanings. *Memory & Cognition, 36,* 1306–1323.

Chen, Z. (2002). Analogical problem solving: A hierarchical analysis of procedural similarity. *Journal of Experimental Psychology: Learning, Memory, and Cognition, 28,* 81–98.

Chen, Z., & Klahr, D. (1999). All other things being equal: Children's acquisition of the control of variables strategy. *Child Development, 70,* 1098–1120.

Chen, Z., & Klahr, D. (2008). Remote transfer of scientific reasoning and problem-solving strategies in children. *Advances in Child Development and Behavior, 36,* 419–470.

Chenoweth, N.A., & Hayes, J.R. (2003). The inner voice in writing. *Written Communication, 20,* 99–118.

Cherry, E.C. (1953). Some experiments on the recognition of speech with one and two ears. *Journal of the Acoustical Society of America, 25,* 975–979.

Chen, Z., Mo, L., & Honomichl, R. (2004). Having the memory of an elephant: Long-term retrieval and the use of analogues in problem solving. *Journal of Experimental Psychology: General, 133,* 415–433.

Cherubini, P., Castelvecchio, E., & Cherubini, A.M. (2005). Generation of hypotheses in Wason's 2–4–6 task: An information theory approach. *Quarterly Journal of Experimental Psychology Section A – Human Experimental Psychology, 58,* 309–332.

Chiappe, D.L., & Chiappe, P. (2007). The role of working memory in metaphor production and comprehension. *Journal of Memory and Language, 56,* 172–188.

Chin, J.M., & Schooler, J.W. (2008). Why do words hurt? Content, process, and criterion shift accounts of verbal overshadowing. *European Journal of Cognitive Psychology, 20,* 396–413.

Chincotta, D., Underwood, G., Abd Ghani, K., Papadopoulou, E., & Wresinksi, M. (1999). Memory span for Arabic numerals and digit words: Evidence for a limited-capacity visuo-spatial storage system. *Quarterly Journal of Experimental Psychology, 2A,* 325–351.

Cho, S., Holyoak, K.J., & Cannon, T.D. (2007). Analogical reasoning in working memory: Resources shared among relational integration, interference resolution, and maintenance. *Memory & Cognition, 35,* 1445–1455.

Chokron, S., Dupierrix, E., Tabert, M., & Bartolomeo, P. (2007). Experimental remission of unilateral spatial neglect. *Neuropsychologia, 45,* 3127–3148.

Chomsky, N. (1957). *Syntactic structures.* The Hague: Mouton.

Chomsky, N. (1959). Review of Skinner's "Verbal behaviour". *Language, 35,* 26–58.

Chomsky, N. (1965). *Aspects of the theory of syntax.* Cambridge, MA: MIT Press.

Chu, S., & Downes, J.J. (2000). Long live Proust: The odour-cued autobiographical memory bump. *Cognition, 75,* B41–B50.

Chu, S., & Downes, J.J. (2004). Proust re-interpreted: Can Proust's account of odour-cued autobiographical memory recall really be investigated? A reply to Jellnek. *Chemical Senses, 29,* 459–461.

Chua, R., & Enns, J. (2005). What the hand can't tell the eye: Illusion of space constancy during accurate pointing. *Experimental Brain Research, 162,* 109–114.

Chun, M.M., & Phelps, E.A. (1999). Memory deficits for implicit contextual information in amnesic subjects with hippocampal damage. *Nature Neuroscience, 2,* 844–847.

Churchland, P.S., & Sejnowski, T.J. (1991). Perspectives on cognitive neuroscience. In R.G. Lister & H.J. Weingarter (Eds.), *Perspectives on cognitive neuroscience.* Oxford: Oxford University Press.

Churchland, P.S., & Sejnowski, T. (1994). *The computational brain.* Cambridge, MA: MIT Press.

Cicerone, C.M., & Nerger, J.L. (1989). The relative number of long-wavelength-sensitive to middle wavelength-sensitive cones in the human fovea centralis. *Vision Research, 29,* 115–128.

Cipolotti, L., Shallice, T., Chan, D., Fox, N., Scahill, R., Harrison, G. et al. (2001). Long-term retrograde amnesia: The crucial role of the hippocampus. *Neuropsychologia, 39*, 151–172.

Clancy, S.A., Schacter, D.L., McNally, R.J., & Pitman, R.K. (2000). False recognition in women reporting recovered memories of sexual abuse. *Psychological Science, 11*, 26–31.

Clare, J., & Lewandowsky, S. (2004). Verbalising facial memory: Criterion effects in verbal overshadowing. *Journal of Experimental Psychology: Learning, Memory & Cognition, 30*, 739–755.

Clark, H.H., & Krych, M.A. (2004). Speaking while monitoring addressees for understanding. *Journal of Memory and Language, 50*, 62–81.

Clark, M.A., Merians, A.S., Kothari, A., Poizner, H., Macauley, B., Rothi, L.J.G., et al. (1994). Spatial planning deficits in limb apraxia. *Brain, 117*, 1093–1106.

Claus, B., & Kelter, S. (2006). Comprehending narratives containing flashbacks: Evidence of temporally organised representations. *Journal of Experimental Psychology: Learning, Memory, and Cognition, 32*, 1031–1044.

Cleeremans, A., & Jiménez, L. (2002). Implicit learning and consciousness: A graded, dynamic perspective. In R.M. French & A. Cleeremans (Eds.), *Implicit learning and consciousness: An empirical, philosophical and computational consensus in the making.* Hove, UK: Psychology Press.

Cleland, A.A., & Pickering, M.J. (2006). Do writing and speaking employ the same syntactic representations? *Journal of Memory and Language, 54*, 185–198.

Cleland, A.A., & Pickering, M.J. (2003). The use of lexical and syntactic information in language production: Evidence from the priming of noun-phrase structure. *Journal of Memory and Language, 49*, 214–230.

Clifton, C., Traxler, M.J., Mohamed, M.T., Williams, R.S., Morris, R.K., & Rayner, K. (2003). The use of thematic role information in parsing: Syntactic processing autonomy revisited. *Journal of Memory and Language, 49*, 317–334.

Coch, D., Sanders, L.D., & Neville, H.J. (2005). An event-related potential study of selective auditory attention in children and adults. *Journal of Cognitive Neuroscience, 17*, 606–622.

Coello, Y., Danckert, J., Blangero, A., & Rossetti, Y. (2007). Do visual illusions probe the visual brain? Illusions in action without a dorsal visual stream. *Neuropsychologia, 45*, 1849–1858.

Cohen, G. (2008). The study of everyday memory. In G. Cohen & M.A. Conway (Eds.), Memory in the real world (3rd. ed.) (pp. 1–19). Hove, UK: Psychology Press.

Cohen, N.J., & Squire, L.R. (1980). Preserved learning and retention of pattern-analysing skill in amnesia using perceptual learning. *Cortex, 17*, 273–278.

Coles, M.E., & Heimberg, R.G. (2002). Memory biases in the anxiety disorders: Current status. *Clinical Psychology Review, 22*, 587–627.

Colflesh, G.J.H., & Conway, A.R.A. (2007). Individual differences in working memory capacity and divided attention in dichotic listening. *Psychonomic Bulletin & Review, 14*, 699–703.

Collette, F., & Van der Linden, M. (2002). Brain imaging of the central executive component of working memory. *Neuroscience & Biobehavioral Reviews, 26*, 105–125.

Collette, F., Hogge, M., Salmon, E., & Van der Linden, M. (2006). Exploration of the neural substrates of executive functioning by functional neuroimaging. *Neuroscience, 139*, 209–221.

Collette, F., Oliver, L., Van der Linden, M., Laureys, S., Delfiore, G., Luxen, A., & Salmon, E. (2005). Involvement of both prefrontal and inferior parietal cortex in dual-task performance. *Cognitive Brain Research, 24*, 237–251.

Collins, A.M., & Loftus, E. (1975). A spreading activation theory of semantic memory. *Psychological Review, 82*, 407–428.

Collins, A.M., & Quillian, M.R. (1969). Retrieval time from semantic memory. *Journal of Verbal Learning & Verbal Behavior, 8*, 240–248.

Colman, A.M. (2001). *Oxford dictionary of psychology.* Oxford, UK: Oxford University Press.

Coltheart, M. (Ed.) (1996). *Phonological dyslexia.* Hove, UK: Lawrence Erlbaum Associates Ltd. [A special issue of *The Journal of Cognitive Neuropsychology* (1996, September).]

Coltheart, M. (2001). *Assumptions and methods in cognitive neuropsychology.* Hove, UK: Psychology Press.

Coltheart, M., Inglis, L., Cupples, L., Michie, P., Bates, A., & Budd, B. (1998). A semantic subsystem specific to the storage of information about visual attributes of animate and inanimate objects. *Neurocase, 4*, 353–370.

Coltheart, M., Rastle, K., Perry, C., Langdon, R., & Ziegler, J. (2001). The DRC model: A model of visual word recognition and reading aloud. *Psychological Review, 108*, 204–258.

Colvin, M.K., & Gazzaniga, M.S. (2007). Split-brain cases. In M. Velmans & S. Schneider (Eds.), *The Blackwell companion to consciousness.* Oxford: Blackwell.

Colvin, M.K., Dunbar, K., & Grafman, J. (2001). The effects of frontal lobe lesions of goal achievement in the water jug task. *Journal of Cognitive Neuroscience, 13*, 1129–1147.

Conci, M., Bobel, E., Matthias, E., Keller, I., Muller, H.J., & Finke, K. (2009). Preattentive surface and contour grouping in Kanizsa figures: Evidence from parietal extinction. *Neuropsychologia, 47,* 726–732.

Connine, C.M. (1990). Effects of sentence context and lexical knowledge in speech processing. In G.T.M. Altmann (Ed.), *Cognitive models of speech processing.* Cambridge, MA: MIT Press.

Conrad, C. (1972). Cognitive economy in semantic memory. *Journal of Experimental Psychology, 92,* 149–154.

Conway, A.R.A., Cowan, N., & Bunting, M.F. (2001). The cocktail party phenomenon revisited: The importance of working memory capacity. *Psychonomic Bulletin and Review, 8,* 331–335.

Conway, B.R., Moeller, S., & Tsao, Y. (2007). Specialised colour modules in macaque extrastriate cortex. *Neuron, 56,* 560–573.

Conway, M.A. (2005). Memory and the self. *Journal of Memory and Language, 53,* 594–628.

Conway, M.A., & Fthenaki, A. (2003). Disruption of inhibitory control of memory following lesions to the frontal and temporal lobes. *Cortex, 39,* 667–686.

Conway, M.A., & Pleydell-Pearce, C.W. (2000). The construction of autobiographical memories in the self-memory system. *Psychological Review, 107,* 261–288.

Conway, M.A., Anderson, S.J., Larsen, S.F., Donnelly, C.M., McDaniel, M.A., McClelland, A.G.R., et al. (1994). The function of flashbulb memories. *Memory & Cognition, 22,* 326–343.

Conway, M.A., Pleydell-Pearce, C.W., & Whitecross, S.E. (2001). The neuroanatomy of autobiographical memory: A slow cortical potential study of autobiographical memory retrieval. *Journal of Memory and Language, 45,* 493–524.

Conway, M.A., Pleydell-Pearce, C.W., Whitecross, S.E., & Sharpe, H. (2003). Neurophysiological correlates of memory for experienced and imagined events. *Neuropsychologia, 41,* 334–340.

Conway, M.A., Wang, Q., Hanyu, K., & Haque, S. (2005). A cross-cultural investigation of autobiographical memory. *Journal of Cross-Cultural Psychology, 36,* 739–749.

Cook, A.E., & Myers, J.L. (2004). Processing discourse rules in scripted narratives: The influences of context and world knowledge. *Journal of Memory and Language, 50,* 268–288.

Cooke, R., Peel, E., Shaw, R.L., & Senior, C. (2007). The neuroimaging research process from the participants' perspective. *International Journal of Psychophysiology, 63,* 152–158.

Cooney, J.W., & Gazzaniga, M.S. (2003). Neurological disorders and the structure of human consciousness. *Trends in Cognitive Sciences, 7,* 161–165.

Cooper, E.E., & Biederman, I. (1993, May). *Metric versus viewpoint-invariant shape differences in visual object recognition.* Poster presented at the Annual Meeting of the Association for Research in Vision and Ophthalmology, Sarasota, Florida.

Copeland, D.E., & Radvansky, G.A. (2004). Working memory and syllogistic reasoning. *Quarterly Journal of Experimental Psychology, 57A,* 1437–1457.

Corbetta, M., & Shulman, G.L. (2002). Control of goal directed and stimulus-driven attention in the brain. *Nature Reviews Neuroscience, 3,* 201–215.

Corbetta, M., Kincade, J.M., Ollinger, J.M., McAvoy, M.P., & Shulman, G.L. (2000). Voluntary orienting is dissociated from target detection in human posterior parietal cortex. *Nature Neuroscience, 3,* 292–297.

Corbetta, M., Patel, G., & Shulman, G.L. (2008). The re-orienting system of the human brain: From environment to theory of mind. *Neuron, 58,* 306–324.

Corkin, S. (1968). Acquisition of motor skill after bilateral medial temporal-lobe excision. *Neuropsychologia, 6,* 255–265.

Corkin, S. (1984). Lasting consequences of bilateral medial temporal lobectomy: Clinical course and experimental findings in HM. *Seminars in Neurology, 4,* 249–259.

Corkin, S. (2002). What's new with the amnesic patient HM? *Nature Reviews Neuroscience, 3,* 153–160.

Corthout, E., Uttle, B., Ziemann, U., Cowey, A., & Hallett, M. (1999). Two periods of processing in the (circum)striate visual cortex as revealed by transcranial magnetic stimulation. *Neuropsychologia, 37,* 137–145.

Cosentino, S., Chute, D., Libon, D., Moore, P., & Grossman, M. (2006). How does the brain support script comprehension? A study of executive processes and semantic knowledge in dementia. *Neuropsychology, 20,* 307–318.

Coslett, H.N., Roeltgens, D.P., Rothi, I.G., & Heilman, K.M. (1987). Transcortical sensory aphasia: Evidence for subtypes. *Brain and Language, 32,* 362–378.

Cosmides, L. (1989). The logic of social exchange: Has natural selection shaped how humans reason? Studies with the Wason selection task. *Cognition, 31,* 187–276.

Costa, A., Caramazza, A., & Sebastian-Galles, N. (2000). The cognate facilitation effect: Implications for modules of lexical access. *Journal of Experimental Psychology: Learning, Memory, and Cognition, 26,* 1283–1296.

Costello, F.J., & Keane, M.T. (2000). Efficient creativity: Constraint-guided conceptual combination. *Cognitive Science, 24,* 299–349.

Cowan, N. (2000). The magical number 4 in short-term memory: A reconsideration of mental storage capacity. *Behavioral and Brain Sciences, 24,* 87–185.

Cowan, N., Elliott, E.M., Saults, J.S., Morey, C.C., Mattox, S., Hismjatullina, A., & Conway, A.R.A. (2005). *Cognitive Psychology, 51,* 42–100.

Cowey, A. (2004). Fact, artefact, and myth about blindsight. *Quarterly Journal of Experimental Psychology, 57A,* 577–609.

Cracco, R.Q., Cracco, J.B., Maccabee, P.J., & Amassian, V.E. (1999). Cerebral function revealed by transcranial magnetic stimulation. *Journal of Neuroscience Methods, 86,* 209–219.

Craik, F.I.M. (2002). Levels of processing: Past, present . . . and future? *Memory, 10,* 305–318.

Craik, F.I.M., & Lockhart, R.S. (1972). Levels of processing: A framework for memory research. *Journal of Verbal Learning and Verbal Behavior, 11,* 671–684.

Craik, F.I.M., & Tulving, E. (1975). Depth of processing and the retention of words in episodic memory. *Journal of Experimental Psychology: General, 104,* 268–294.

Crawford, J.R., Smith, G., Maylor, E.A., Della Sala, S., & Logie, R.H. (2003). The Prospective and Retrospective Memory Questionnaire (PRMQ): Normative data and latent structure in a large non-clinical sample. *Memory, 11,* 261–275.

Cree, G.S., & McRae, K. (2003). Analyzing the factors underlying the structure and computation of the meaning of chipmunk, cherry, chisel, cheese, and cello (and many other such concrete nouns). *Journal of Experimental Psychology: General, 132,* 163–201.

Creem, S.H., & Proffitt, D.R. (2001). Grasping objects by their handles: A necessary interaction between cognition and action. *Journal of Experimental Psychology: Human Perception and Performance, 27,* 218–228.

Crisp, J., & Lambon Ralph, M.A. (2006). Unlocking the nature of the phonological-deep dyslexia continuum: The keys to reading aloud are in phonology and semantics. *Journal of Cognitive Neuroscience, 18,* 348–362.

Crutch, S.J., & Warrington, E.K. (2003). Preservation of propositional speech in a pure anomic: The importance of an abstract vocabulary. *Neurocase, 9,* 465–481.

Crystal, D. (1997). *A dictionary of linguistics and phonetics* (4th Ed.). Cambridge, MA: Blackwell.

Cubelli, R., & Della Sala, S. (2008). Flashbulb memories: Special but not iconic. *Cortex, 44,* 908–909.

Cutler, A., & Butterfield, S. (1992). Rhythmic cues to speech segmentation: Evidence from juncture misperception. *Journal of Memory and Language, 31,* 218–236.

Cutler, A., & Clifton, C. (1999). Comprehending spoken language: A blueprint of the listener. In C.M. Brown & P. Hagoort (Eds.), *The neurocognition of language*. Oxford: Oxford University Press.

Cutting, J.E., Proffitt, D.R., & Kozlowski, L.T. (1978). A biomechanical invariant for gait perception. *Journal of Experimental Psychology: Human Perception & Performance, 4,* 357–372.

Dagher, A., Owen, A.M., Boecker, H., & Brooks, D.J. (1999). Mapping the network for planning: A correlational PET activation study with the Tower of London task. *Brain, 122,* 1973–1987.

Dahan, D., Magnuson, J.S., & Tanenhaus, M.K. (2001). Time course of frequency effects in spoken-word recognition: Evidence from eye movements. *Cognitive Psychology, 42,* 317–367.

Dalgleish, T. (2005). Putting some feeling into it – the conceptual and empirical relationships between the classic and emotional Stroop tasks: Comment on Algom, Chajut, and Lev (2004). *Journal of Experimental Psychology: General, 134,* 585–591.

Dalton, A.L., & Daneman, M. (2006). Social suggestibility to central and peripheral misinformation. *Memory, 14,* 486–501.

Danckert, J., & Ferber, S. (2006). Revisiting unilateral neglect. *Neuropsychologia, 44,* 987–1006.

Danckert, J., & Rossetti, Y. (2005). Blindsight in action: What can the different sub-types of blindsight tell us about the control of visually guided actions? *Neuroscience and Biobehavioral Reviews, 29,* 1035–1046.

Danckert, J., Revol, P., Pisella, L., Krolak-Salmon, P., Vighetto, A., Goodale, M.A. et al. (2003). Measuring unconscious actions in action-blindsight: Exploring the kinematics of pointing movements to targets in the blind field of two patients with cortical hemianopia. *Neuropsychologia, 41,* 1068–1081.

Daneman, M., & Carpenter, P.A. (1980). Individual differences in working memory and reading. *Journal of Verbal Learning and Verbal Behavior, 19,* 450–466.

Daneman, M., & Merikle, P.M. (1996). Working memory and language comprehension: A meta-analysis. *Psychonomic Bulletin & Review, 3,* 422–433.

Daneman, M., Reingold, E.M., & Davidson, M. (1995). Time course of phonological activation during reading: Evidence from eye fixations. *Journal of Experimental Psychology: Learning, Memory, and Cognition, 21,* 884–898.

Danker, J.F., & Anderson, J.R. (2007). The roles of prefrontal and posterior parietal cortex in algebra problem solving: A case of using cognitive modeling to inform neuroimaging data. *NeuroImage*, 35, 1365–1377.

Davare, M., Duque, J., Vandermeeren, Y., Thonnard, J.L., & Olivier, E. (2007). Role of the ipsilateral primary motor cortex in controlling the timing of hand muscle recruitment. *Cerebral Cortex*, 17, 353–362.

Davidson, J.E., & Sternberg, R.J. (1984). The role of insight in intellectual giftedness. *Gifted Child Quarterly*, 28, 58–64.

Davis, M.H., Marslen-Wilson, W.D., & Gaskell, M.G. (2002). Leading up the lexical garden path: Segmentation and ambiguity in spoken word recognition. *Journal of Experimental Psychology: Perception and Performance*, 28, 218–244.

Dawes, R.M. (1988). *Rational choice in an uncertain world*. San Diego, CA: Harcourt Brace Jovanovich.

Dawson, M.E., & Schell, A.M. (1982). Electrodermal responses to attended and non-attended significant stimuli during dichotic listening. *Journal of Experimental Psychology: Human Perception and Performance*, 8, 315–324.

Debaere, F., Wenderoth, N., Sunaert, S., van Hencke, P., & Swinnen, S.P. (2004). Changes in brain activation during the acquisition of a new bimanual coordination task. *Neuropsychologia*, 42, 855–867.

De Bleser, R. (1988). Localisation of aphasia: Science or fiction? In G. Denese, C. Semenza, & P. Bisiacchi (Eds.), *Perspectives on cognitive neuropsychology*. Hove, UK: Psychology Press.

De Corte, E. (2003). Transfer as the productive use of acquired knowledge, skills, and motivations. *Current Directions in Psychological Science*, 12, 142–146.

Deffenbacher, K.A., Bornstein, B.H., Penroad, S.D., & McGorty, E.K. (2004). A meta-analytic review of the effects of high stress on eyewitness memory. *Law and Human Behavior*, 28, 687–706.

De Fockert, J.W., Rees, G., Frith, C.D., & Lavie, N. (2001). The role of working memory in visual selective attention. *Science*, 291, 1803–1806.

De Gelder, B., Vroemen, J., & Pourtois, G. (2001). Covert affective cognition and affective blindsight. In B. de Gelder, E. de Haan, & C.A., Heywood (Eds.), *Out of mind*. Oxford: Oxford University Press.

De Groot, A.D. (1965). *Thought and choice in chess*. The Hague: Mouton.

Dehaene, S., & Naccache, L. (2001). Towards a cognitive neuroscience of consciousness: Basic evidence and a workspace framework. *Cognition*, 79, 1–37.

Dehaene, S., Changeux, J.P., Naccache, L., Sackur, J., & Sergent, C. (2006). Conscious, preconscious, and subliminal processing: A testable taxonomy. *Trends in Cognitive Sciences*, 10, 204–211.

Dehaene, S., Naccache, L., Cohen, L., Le Bihan, D., Mangin, J., Poline, J., et al. (2001). Cerebral mechanisms of word masking and unconscious repetition priming. *Nature Neuroscience*, 4, 752–758.

Delaney, P.F., Ericsson, K.A., & Knowles, M.E. (2004). Immediate and sustained effects of planning in a problem-solving task. *Journal of Experimental Psychology: Learning, Memory, and Cognition*, 30, 1219–1234.

Delattre, M., Bonin, P., & Barry, C. (2006). Written spelling to dictation: Sound-to-spelling regularity affects both writing latencies and durations. *Journal of Experimental Psychology: Learning, Memory and Cognition*, 32, 1336–1340.

Dell, G.S. (1986). A spreading-activation theory of retrieval in sentence production. *Psychological Review*, 93, 283–321.

Dell, G.S., & Caramazza, A. (2008). Introduction to special issue on computational modeling in cognitive neuropsychology. *Cognitive Neuropsychology*, 25, 131–135.

Dell, G.S., Burger, L.K., & Svec, W.R. (1997). Language production and serial order: A functional analysis and a model. *Psychological Review*, 104, 123–147.

Dell, G.S., Oppenheim, G.M., & Kittredge, A.K. (2008). Saying the right word at the right time: Syntagmatic and paradigmatic interference in sentence production. *Language and Cognitive Processes*, 23, 583–608.

De Martino, B., Kumaran, D., Seymour, B., & Dolan, R.J. (2006). Frames, biases, and rational decision-making in the human brain. *Science*, 313, 684–687.

De Neys, W. (2006a). Automatic–heuristic and executive–analytic processing during reasoning: Chronometric and dual-task considerations. *Quarterly Journal of Experimental Psychology*, 59, 1070–1100.

De Neys, W. (2006b). Dual processing in reasoning. *Psychological Science*, 17, 428–433.

De Neys, W. & Glumicic, T. (2008). Conflict monitoring in dual process theories of thinking. *Cognition*, 106, 1248–1299.

De Neys, W., & Verschueren, N. (2006). Working memory capacity and a notorious brain teaser – The case of the Monty Hall dilemma. *Experimental Psychology*, 53, 123–131.

De Neys, W., Schaeken, W., & d'Ydewalle, G. (2005). Working memory and everyday conditional reasoning: Retrieval and inhibition of stored counterexamples. *Thinking & Reasoning*, *11*, 349–381.

Depue, B.E., Banich, M.T., & Curran, T. (2006). Suppression of emotional and nonemotional content in memory. Effects of repetition on cognitive control. *Psychological Science*, *17*(5), 441–447.

Depue, B.E., Curran, T., & Banich, M.T. (2007). Prefrontal regions orchestrate suppression of emotional memories via a two-phase process. *Science*, *317*, 215–219.

Desmurget, M., Gréa, H., Grethe, J.S., Prablanc, C., Alexander, G.E., & Grafton, S.T. (1999). Functional anatomy of nonvisual feedback loops during reaching: A positron emission tomography study. *Journal of Neuroscience*, *21*, 2919–2928.

Desmurget, M., Reilly, K.T., Richard, N., Szathmari, A., Mottolese, C., & Sirigu, A. (2009). Movement intention after parietal cortex stimulation in humans. *Science*, *324*, 811–813.

D'Esposito, M. (2007). From cognitive to neural models of working memory. *Philosophical Transactions of the Royal Society B*, *362*, 761–772.

Destrebecqz, A., Peigneux, P., Laureys, S., Degueldre, C., Del Fiorem G., Aerts, J., Luxen, A., Van der Linden, M., Cleeremans, A., & Maquet, P. (2005). The neural correlates of implicit and explicit sequence learning: Interacting networks revealed by the process dissociation procedure. *Learning and Memory*, *12*, 480–490.

Deutsch, J.A., & Deutsch, D. (1963). Attention: Some theoretical considerations. *Psychological Review*, *93*, 283–321.

DeValois, R.L., & DeValois, K.K. (1975). Neural coding of colour. In E.C. Carterette & M.P. Friedman (Eds.), *Handbook of perception*, *Vol. 5*. New York: Academic Press.

Dewar, M.T., Cowan, N., & Della Sala, S. (2007). Forgetting due to retroactive interference: A fusion of Müller and Pilzecker's (1900) early insights into everyday forgetting and recent research on retrograde amnesia. *Cortex*, *43*, 616–634.

Di Stasi, L.L., & Guardini, P. (2007). Perceiving affordances in virtual environments: Visual guidance of virtual chair climbing. *Perception*, *36* (Suppl. S), 186.

Diana, R.A., Yonelinas, A.P., & Ranganath, C. (2007). Imaging recollection and familiarity in the medial temporal lobe: A three-component model. *Trends in Cognitive Sciences*, *11*, 379–386.

Dick, F., Bates, E., Wulfeck, B., Utman, J.A., Dronkers, N., & Gernsbacher, M.A. (2001). Language deficits, localisation, and grammar: Evidence for a distributive model of language breakdown in aphasic patients and neurologically intact individuals. *Psychological Review*, *108*, 759–788.

Dijkerman, H.C., Milner, A.D., & Carey, D.P. (1998). Grasping spatial relationships: Failure to demonstrate allocentric visual coding in a patient with visual form agnosia. *Consciousness and Cognition*, *7*, 424–437.

Dijksterhuis, A. (2004). Think different: The merits of unconscious thought in preference development and decision making. *Journal of Personality and Social Psychology*, *87*, 586–598.

Dijksterhuis, A., & Nordgren, L.F. (2006). A theory of unconscious thought. *Perspectives on Psychological Science*, *1*, 95–109.

Dijksterhuis, A., Bos, M.W., Nordgren, L.F., & van Baaren, R.B. (2006). On making the right choice: The deliberation-without-attention effect. *Science*, *311*, 1005–1007.

Dinstein, I., Hasson, U., Rubin, N., & Heeger, D.J. (2007). Brain areas selective for both observed and executed movements. *Journal of Neurophysiology*, *98*, 1415–1427.

Dismukes, R.K., & Nowinski, J.L. (2006). Prospective memory, concurrent task management, and pilot error. In A. Kramer, D. Wiegmann, & A. Kirlik (Eds.), *Attention: From theory to practice*. Oxford: Oxford University Press.

Dodhia, R.M., & Dismukes, R.K. (2005). *A task interrupted becomes a prospective memory task*. Paper presented at the biennial meeting of the Society for Applied Research in Memory and Cognition, Wellington, New Zealand.

Dodson, C.S., & Krueger, L.E. (2006). I misremember it well: Why older adults are unreliable eyewitnesses. *Psychonomic Bulletin and Review*, *13*, 770–775.

Donaldson, C., Lam, D., & Mathews, A. (2007). Rumination and attention in major depression. *Behaviour Research and Therapy*, *45*, 2668–2678.

Dooling, D.J., & Christiaansen, R.E. (1977). Episodic and semantic aspects of memory for prose. *Journal of Experimental Psychology: Human Learning and Memory*, *3*, 428–436.

Doop, M., Mohr, C., Folley, B., Brewer, W., & Park, S. (2006). Olfaction and memory. In W.J. Brewer, D. Castle, & C. Partelis (Eds.), *Olfaction and the brain*. Cambridge: Cambridge University Press.

Dorman, M.F., Raphael, L.J., & Liberman, A.M. (1979). Some experiments on the sound of silence in phonetic perception. *Journal of the Acoustical Society of America*, *65*, 1518–1532.

Dosher, B.A., & Corbett, A.T. (1982). Instrument inferences and verb schemata. *Memory & Cognition, 10*, 531–539.

Douglass, A.B., & Steblay, N. (2006). Memory distortion in eyewitnesses: A meta-analysis of the post-identification feedback effect. *Applied Cognitive Psychology, 20*, 859–869.

Downing, P.E., Chan, A.W.Y., Peelen, M.V., Dodds, C.M., & Kanwisher, N. (2006). Domain specificity in visual cortex. *Cerebral Cortex, 16*, 1453–1461.

Doyon, J., Penhune, V., & Ungerleider, L.G. (2003). Distinct contribution of the cortico-striatal and cortico-cerebellar systems to motor skill learning. *Neuropsychologia, 41*, 252–262.

Driver, J., & Mattingley, J.B. (1998). Parietal neglect and visual awareness. *Nature Neuroscience, 1*, 17–22.

Driver, J., & Noesselt, T. (2008). Multisensory interplay reveals crossmodal influences on 'sensory-specific' brain regions, neural responses and judgements. *Neuron, 57*, 11–23.

Driver, J., & Spence, C. (1998). Crossmodal links in spatial attention. *Proceedings of the Royal Society London Series B, 353*, 1–13.

Driver, J., & Vuilleumier, P. (2001). Perceptual awareness and its loss in unilateral neglect and extinction. *Cognition, 79*, 39–88.

Driver, J., Vuilleumier, P., Eimer, M., & Rees, G. (2001). Functional magnetic resonance imaging and evoked potential correlates of conscious and unconscious vision in parietal extinction patients. *Nature Neuroscience, 1*, 17–22.

Duchaine, B.C. (2006). Prosopagnosia as an impairment to face-specific mechanisms: Elimination of the alternative hypotheses in a developmental case. *Cognitive Neuropsychology, 23*, 714–747.

Duchaine, B., & Nakayama, K. (2005). Dissociations of face and object recognition in developmental prosopagnosia. *Journal of Cognitive Neuroscience, 17*, 249–261.

Duchaine, B.C., & Nakayama, K. (2006). Developmental prosopagnosia: A window to context-specific face processing. *Current Opinion in Neurobiology, 16*, 166–173.

Dudukovic, N.M., Marsh, E.J., & Tversky, B. (2004). Telling a story or telling it straight: The effects of entertaining versus accurate retellings on memory. *Applied Cognitive Psychology, 18*, 125–143.

Duffy, S.A., & Pisoni, D.B. (1992). Comprehension of synthetic speech produced by rule: A review and theoretical interpretation. *Language and Speech, 35*, 351–389.

Dumay, N., Frauenfelder, U.H., & Content, A. (2002). The role of the syllable in lexical segmentation in French: Word-spotting data. *Brain and Language, 81*, 144–161.

Dunbar, K. (1993). Concept discovery in a scientific domain. *Cognitive Science, 17*, 397–434.

Dunbar, K. (2001). The analogical paradox: Why analogy is so easy in naturalistic settings, yet so difficult in the psychological laboratory. In D. Gentner, K. Holyoak, & B. Kokinov (Eds.), *Analogy: Perspectives from cognitive science* (pp. 313–334). Cambridge, MA: MIT Press.

Dunbar, K., & Blanchette, I. (2001). The in vivo/in vitro approach to cognition: The case of analogy. *Trends in Cognitive Sciences, 5*, 334–339.

Duncan, J., & Humphreys, G.W. (1989). A resemblance theory of visual search. *Psychological Review, 96*, 433–458.

Duncan, J., & Humphreys, G.W. (1992). Beyond the search surface: Visual search and attentional engagement. *Journal of Experimental Psychology: Human Perception & Performance, 18*, 578–588.

Duncan, J., & Owen, A.M. (2000). Consistent response of the human frontal lobe to diverse cognitive demands. *Trends in Neurosciences, 23*, 475–483.

Duncan, J., Bundesen, C., Olson, A., Humphreys, G., Chavda, S., & Shibuya, H. (1999). Systematic analysis of deficits in visual attention. *Journal of Experimental Psychology: General, 128*, 450–478.

Duncan, J., Seitz, R.J., Kolodny, J., Bor, D., Herzog, H., Ahmed, A. et al. (2000). A neural basis for general intelligence. *Science, 289*, 457–460.

Duncker, K. (1945). On problem solving. *Psychological Monographs, 58* (Whole No. 270).

Dunn, J.C. (2008). The dimensionality of the remember–know task: A state–trace analysis. *Psychological Review, 115*, 426–446.

Dunn, J.C., & Kirsner, K. (2003). What can we infer from double dissociations? *Cortex, 39*, 1–7.

Duvernoy, H.M. (1999). *The human brain: Surface, blood supply, and three-dimensional sectional anatomy* (2nd. ed.). New York: Springer Wien.

Eakin, D.K., Schreiber, T.A., & Sergent-Marshall, S. (2003). Misinformation effects in eyewitness memory: The presence and absence of memory impairment as a function of warning and misinformation accessibility. *Journal of Experimental Psychology: Learning, Memory, and Cognition, 29*, 813–825.

Ebbinghaus, H. (1885/1913). *Uber das Gedächtnis* (Leipzig: Dunker) [translated by H. Ruyer & C.E. Bussenius]. New York: Teacher College, Columbus University.

Eckstein, M.P., Thomas, J.P., Palmer, J., & Shimozaki, S.S. (2000). A signal-detection predicts the effects of set size on visual search accuracy for feature, conjunction, triple conjunction, and disjunction displays. *Perception & Psychophysics*, *62*, 425–451.

Egly, R., Driver, J., & Rafal, R.D. (1994). Shifting visual attention between objects and locations: Evidence from normal and parietal lesion subjects. *Journal of Experimental Psychology: General*, *123*, 161–177.

Eich, E. (1995). Searching for mood dependent memory. *Psychological Science*, *6*, 67–75.

Eich, E., & Metcalfe, J. (1989). Mood dependent memory for internal versus external events. *Journal of Experimental Psychology: Learning, Memory & Cognition*, *15*, 443–455.

Eichenbaum, H. (2001). The hippocampus and declarative memory: Cognitive mechanisms and neural codes. *Behavioural Brain Research*, *127*, 199–207.

Eimer, M., & Schröger, E. (1998). ERP effects of intermodal attention and crossmodal links in spatial attention. *Psychophysiology*, *35*, 317–328.

Eimer, M., van Velzen, J., Forster, B., & Driver, J. (2003). Shifts of attention in light and in darkness: An ERP study of supramodal attentional control and crossmodal links in spatial attention. *Cognitive Brain Research*, *15*, 308–323.

Einstein, G.O., & McDaniel, M.A. (2005). Prospective memory: Multiple retrieval processes. *Current Directions in Psychological Science*, *14*, 286–290.

Einstein, G.O., McDaniel, M.A., Thomas, R., Mayfield, S., Shank, H., Morrisette, N., & Breneiser, J. (2005). Multiple processes in prospective memory retrieval: Factors determining monitoring versus spontaneous retrieval. *Journal of Experimental Psychology: General*, *134*, 327–342.

Elder, J.H., & Goldberg, R.M. (2002). Ecological statistics of Gestalt laws for the perceptual organisation of contours. *Journal of Vision*, *2*, 324–353.

Ellis, A.W. (1984). *Reading, writing and dyslexia: A cognitive analysis*. London: Lawrence Erlbaum Associates Ltd.

Ellis, J.A., & Freeman, J.E. (2008). Ten years on: Realising delayed intentions. In M. Kliegel, M.A. McDaniel, & G.O. Einstein (Eds.), *Prospective memory: Cognitive neuroscience, developmental, and applied perspectives* (pp. 1–27). New York: Lawrence Erlbaum Associates.

Ellis, A.W., & Young, A.W. (1988). *Human cognitive neuropsychology*. Hove, UK: Psychology Press.

Ellis, A.W., Miller, D., & Sin, G. (1983). Wernicke's aphasia and normal language processing: A case study in cognitive neuropsychology. *Cognition*, *15*, 111–144.

Engbert, R., Nuthmann, A., Richter, E.M., & Kliegl, R. (2005). SWIFT: A dynamical model of saccade generation during reading. *Psychological Review*, *112*, 777–813.

Engbert, R., Longtin, A., & Kliegl, R. (2002). A dynamical model of saccade generation in reading based on spatially distributed lexical processing. *Vision Research*, *42*, 621–636.

Engel, P.J.H. (2008). Tacit knowledge and visual expertise in medical diagnostic reasoning: Implications for medical education. *Medical Teacher*, *30*, e184–e188.

Erdelyi, M.H. (1974). New look at new look: Perceptual defence and vigilance. *Psychological Review*, *81*, 1–25.

Erdelyi, M.H. (2001). Defense processes can be conscious or unconscious. *American Psychologist*, *56*, 761–762.

Erickson, T.A., & Mattson, M.E. (1981). From words to meaning: A semantic illusion. *Journal of Verbal Learning and Verbal Behavior*, *20*, 540–552.

Ericsson, K.A., & Chase, W.G. (1982). Exceptional memory. *American Scientist*, *70*, 607–615.

Ericsson, K.A., & Kintsch, W. (1995). Long-term working memory. *Psychological Review*, *102*, 211–245.

Ericsson, K.A., & Lehmann, A.C. (1996). Expert and exceptional performance: Evidence on maximal adaptations on task constraints. *Annual Review of Psychology*, *47*, 273–305.

Ericsson, K.A., Krampe, R.T., & Tesch-Römer, C. (1993). The role of deliberate practice in the acquisition of expert performance. *Psychological Review*, *100*, 363–406.

Eriksen, C.W., & St. James, J.D. (1986). Visual attention within and around the field of focal attention: A zoom lens model. *Perception & Psychophysics*, *40*, 225–240.

Eriksson, J., Larsson, A., Ahlström, K.R., & Nyberg, L. (2006). Similar frontal and distinct posterior cortical regions mediate visual and auditory perceptual awareness. *Cerebral Cortex*, *17*, 760–765.

Ernst, M.O., & Bülthoff, H.H. (2004). Merging the senses into a robust percept. *Trends in Cognitive Sciences*, *8*, 162–169.

Ervin-Tripp, S. (1979). Children's verbal turntaking. In E. Ochs & B.B. Schieffelin (Eds.), *Developmental pragmatics* (pp. 391–414). New York: Academic Press.

Evans, J. (2008). Dual-processing accounts of reasoning, judgement, and social cognition. *Annual Review of Psychology*, *59*, 255–278.

Evans, J., Heron, J., Lewis, G., Araya, R., & Wolke, D. (2005). Negative self-schemas and the onset of depression in women: Longitudinal study. *British Journal of Psychiatry*, *186*, 302–307.

Evans, J.St.B.T. (1993). Bias and rationality. In K.I. Manktelow & D.E. Over (Eds.), Rationality: Psychological and philosophical perspectives. London: Routledge.

Evans, J.St.B.T. (1998) Matching bias in conditional reasoning: Do we understand it after 25 years? *Thinking & Reasoning*, *4*, 45–82.

Evans, J.St.B.T. (2000). What could and could not be a strategy in reasoning. In W. Schaeken, G. de Vooght, A. Vandierendonck, & G. d'Ydewalle (Eds.), *Deductive reasoning and strategies*. Hove, UK: Laurence Erlbaum Associates Ltd.

Evans, J.St.B.T. (2002). Logic and human reasoning: An assessment of the deduction paradigm. *Psychological Bulletin*, *128*, 978–996.

Evans, J.St.B.T. (2006). The heuristic-analytic theory of reasoning: Extension and evaluation. *Psychonomic Bulletin & Review*, *13*, 378–395.

Evans, J.St.B.T. (2007). On the resolution of conflict in dual process theories of reasoning. *Thinking and Reasoning*, *13*(4), 321–339.

Evans, J.St.B.T., & Curtis-Holmes, J. (2005). Rapid responding increases belief bias: Evidence for the dual-process theory of reasoning. *Thinking & Reasoning*, *11*, 382–389.

Evans, J.St.B.T., & Over, D.E. (1996). Rationality in the selection tesk: Epistemic utility versus uncertainty reduction. *Psychological Review*, *103*, 356–363.

Evans, J.St.B.T., & Over, D.E. (1997). Rationality in reasoning: The problem of deductive competence. *Current Psychology of Cognition*, *16*, 3–38.

Evans, J.S.T., & Thompson, V.A. (2004). Informal reasoning: Theory and method. *Canadian Journal of Experimental Psychology*, *58*, 69–74.

Evans, J.St.B.T., Newstead, S.E., & Byrne, R.M.J. (1993). Human reasoning: *The psychology of deduction*. Hove, UK: Psychology Press.

Eysenck, M.W. (1978). Levels of processing – Critique. *British Journal of Psychology*, *69*, 157–169.

Eysenck, M.W. (1979). Depth, elaboration, and distinctiveness. In L.S. Cermak & F.I.M. Craik (Eds.), *Levels of processing in human memory*. Hillsdale, NJ: Lawrence Erlbaum Associates Inc.

Eysenck, M.W. (1997). *Anxiety and cognition: A unified theory*. Hove, UK: Psychology Press.

Eysenck, M.W., & Eysenck, M.C. (1980). Effects of processing depth, distinctiveness, and word frequency on retention. *British Journal of Psychology*, *71*, 263–274.

Eysenck, M.W., & van Berkum, J. (1992). Trait anxiety, defensiveness, and the structure of worry. *Personality and Individual Differences*, *13*, 1285–1290.

Eysenck, M.W., MacLeod, C., & Mathews, A. (1987). Cognitive functioning and anxiety. *Psychological Research*, *49*, 189–195.

Eysenck, M.W., Mogg, K., May, J., Richards, A., & Mathews, A. (1991). Bias in interpretation of ambiguous sentences related to threat in anxiety. *Journal of Abnormal Psychology*, *100*, 144–150.

Eysenck, M.W., Payne, S., & Santos, R. (2006). Anxiety and depression: Past, present, and future events. *Cognition & Emotion*, *20*, 274–294.

Fadiga, L., Craighero, L., Buccino, G., & Rizzolatti, G. (2002). Speech listening specifically modulates the excitability of tongue muscles: A TMS study. *European Journal of Neuroscience*, *15*, 399–402.

Fahenfort, J.J., Scholte, H.S., & Lamme, V.A.F. (2007). Masking disrupts re-entrant processing in human visual cortex. *Journal of Cognitive Neuroscience*, *19*, 1488–1497.

Fahrenfort, J.J., Scholte, H.S., & Lamme, V.A.F. (2008). The spatio-temporal profile of cortical processing leading up to visual perception. *Journal of Vision*, *8*, 1–12.

Faigley, L., & Witte, S. (1983). Analysing revision. *College Composition and Communication*, *32*, 400–414.

Fajen, B.R. (2008). Learning novel mappings from optic flow to the control of action. *Journal of Vision*, *8*, Article No. 12.

Fangmeier, T., Knauff, M., Ruff, C.C., & Sloutsky, V.M. (2006). fMRI evidence for a three-stage model of deductive reasoning. *Journal of Cognitive Neuroscience*, *18*, 320–334.

Farah, M.J. (1994a). Specialisation within visual object recognition: Clues from prosopagnosia and alexia. In M.J. Farah & G. Ratcliff (Eds.), *The neuropsychology of high-level vision: Collected tutorial essays*. Hillsdale, NJ: Lawrence Erlbaum Associates Inc.

Farah, M.J. (1999). Relations among the agnosias. In G.W. Humphreys (Ed.), *Case studies in the neuropsychology of vision*. Hove, UK: Psychology Press.

Farah, M.J., & McClelland, J.L. (1991). A computational model of semantic memory impairment: Modality-specificity and emergent category-specificity. *Journal of Experimental Psychology: General*, *120*, 339–357.

Farah, M.J., Wilson, K.D., Drain, M., & Tanaka, J.N. (1998). What is "special" about face perception? *Psychological Review*, *105*, 482–498.

Feinberg, T.E., & Keenan, J.P. (2005). Where in the brain is the self? *Consciousness and Cognition*, *14*, 661–678.

Fellows, L.K. (2006). Deciding how to decide: Ventromedial frontal lobe damage affects information acquisition in multi-attribute decision making. *Brain, 129*, 944–952.

Feredoes, E., Tononi, G., & Postle, B.R. (2006). Direct evidence for a prefrontal contribution to the control of proactive interference in verbal working memory. *Proceedings of the National Academy of Sciences of the United States of America, 103*, 19530–19534.

Fernandez-Duque, D., Grossi, G., Thornton, I.M., & Neville, H.J. (2003). Representation of change: Separate electrophysiological marks of attention, awareness, and implicit processing. *Journal of Cognitive Neuroscience, 15*, 491–507.

Ferreira, F. (2003). The misinterpretation of noncanonical sentences. *Cognitive Psychology, 47*, 164–203.

Ferreira, F., & Clifton, C. (1986). The independence of syntactic processing. *Journal of Memory and Language, 25*, 348–368.

Ferreira, F., & Swets, B. (2002). How incremental is language production? Evidence from the production of utterances requiring the computation of arithmetic sums. *Journal of Memory and Language, 46*, 57–84.

Ferreira, F., Bailey, K.G.D., & Ferraro, V. (2002). Good enough representations in language comprehension. *Current Directions in Psychological Science, 11*, 11–15.

Ferreira, V.S. (2008). Ambiguity, accessibility, and a division of labour for communicative success. *Psychology of Learning and Motivation, 49*, 209–246.

Ferreira, V.S., & Griffin, Z.M. (2003). Phonological influences on lexical (mis)selection. *Psychological Science, 14*, 86–90.

Fery, P., & Morais, J. (2003). A case study of visual agnosia without perceptual processing or structural descriptions' impairment. *Cognitive Neuropsychology, 20*, 595–618.

Fiedler, K. (1988). The dependence of the conjunction fallacy on subtle linguistic factors. *Psychological Research, 50*, 123–129.

Fiedler, K. (2000). Beware of samples! A cognitive–ecological sampling approach to judgement biases. *Psychological Review, 107*, 659–676.

Fiedler, K., Brinkmann, B., Betsch, T., & Wild, B. (2000). A sampling approach to biases in conditional probability judgements: Beyond base-rate neglect and statistical format. *Journal of Experimental Psychology: General, 129*, 1–20.

Fiedler, K., Nickel, S., Muehlfriedel, T., & Unkelbach, C. (2001). Is mood congruity an effect of genuine memory or response bias? *Journal of Experimental Social Psychology, 37*, 201–214.

Field, D.T., Wilkie, R.M., & Wann, J.P. (2007). Neural systems in the visual control of steering. *Journal of Neuroscience, 27*, 8002–8010.

Fierro, B., Brighia, F., Oliveri, M., Piazza, A., La Bua, V., Buffa, D., & Bisiach, E. (2000). Contralateral neglect induced by right posterior parietal rTMS in healthy subjects. *NeuroReport, 11*, 1519–1521.

Fincham, J.M., & Anderson, J.R. (2006). Distinct roles of the anterior cingulate and prefrontal cortex in the acquisition and performance of a cognitive skill. *Proceedings of the National Academy of Sciences, 103*, 12941–12946.

Fincham, J.M., Carter, C.S., van Veen, V., Stenger, V.A., & Anderson, J.R. (2002). Neural mechanisms of planning: A computational analysis using event-related fMRI. *Proceedings of the National Academy of Sciences of the United States of America, 99*, 3346–3351.

Finkenauer, C., Luminet, O., Gisle, L., El-Ahmadi, A., & van der Linden, M. (1998). Flashbulb memories and the underlying mechanisms of their formation: Toward an emotional-integrative model. *Memory & Cognition, 26*, 516–531.

Fisher, R.P. (1999). Probing knowledge structures. In D. Gopher & A. Koriat (Eds.), *Attention and performance XVII: Cognitive regulation of performance: Interaction of theory and application.* Cambridge, MA: MIT Press.

Fisher, R.P., Geiselman, R.E., & Amador, M. (1990). A field test of the cognitive interview: Enhancing the recollections of actual victims and witnesses of crime. *Journal of Applied Psychology, 74*, 722–727.

Fisher, R.P., Geiselman, R.E., Raymond, D.S., Jurkevich, L.M., & Warhaftig, M.L. (1987). Enhancing enhanced eyewitness memory: Refining the cognitive interview. *Journal of Police Science and Administration, 15*, 291–297.

Fivush, R., & Nelson, K. (2004). Culture and language in the emergence of autobiographical memory. *Psychological Science, 15*, 573–577.

Fivush, R., Gray, J.T., & Fromhoff, F.A. (1987). Two-year-olds talk about the past. *Cognitive Development, 2*, 393–409.

Flowerdew, J., & Tauroza, S. (1995). The effect of discourse markers on second language lecture comprehension. *Studies in Second Language Acquisition, 17*, 455–458.

Fodor, J. (1999). Let your brain alone. *London Review of Books, 21* (http://www.lrb.co.uk/v21/n19/fodo01_html).

Fodor, J.A. (1983). *The modularity of mind.* Cambridge, MA: MIT Press.

Fodor, J.A., & Pylyshyn, Z.W. (1981). How direct is visual perception? Some reflections on

Gibson's "ecological approach". *Cognition, 9,* 139–196.

Foerde, K., Knowlton, B.J., & Poldrack, R.A. (2006). Modulation of competing memory systems by distraction. *Proceedings of the National Academy of Sciences, 103,* 11778–11783.

Foerde, K., & Poldrack, R.A. (2009). Procedural learning in humans. In *Encyclopedia of neuroscience.* New York: Elsevier.

Folk, C.L., Remington, R.W., & Johnston, J.C. (1992). Involuntary covert orienting is contingent on attentional control settings. *Journal of Experimental Psychology: Human Perception and Performance, 18,* 1030–1044.

Ford, M. (1995). Two modes of mental representation and problem solution in syllogistic reasoning. *Cognition, 54,* 1–71.

Forgas, J.P. (1991). Mood effects on partner choice: Role of affect in social decisions. *Journal of Personality and Social Psychology, 61,* 708–720.

Forgas, J.P. (1995). Mood and judgement: The affect infusion model (AIM). *Psychological Bulletin, 117,* 39–66.

Forgas, J.P. (1999). Network theories and beyond. In T. Dalgleish & M.J. Power (Eds.), *Handbook of cognition and emotion.* Chichester, UK: Wiley.

Forgas, J.P. (2002). Towards an understanding of the role of affect in social thinking and behaviour. *Psychological Inquiry, 13,* 90–102.

Forgas, J.P., & Locke, J. (2005). Affective influences on causal inferences: The effects of mood on attributions for positive and negative interpersonal episodes. *Cognition and Emotion, 19,* 1071–1081.

Forgas, J.P., Dunn, E., & Granland, S. (2008). Are you being served? An unobtrusive experiment of affective influences on helping in a department store. *European Journal of Social Psychology, 38,* 333–342.

Forster, S., & Lavie, N. (2008). Failures to ignore entirely irrelevant distractors: The role of load. *Journal of Experimental Psychology: Applied, 14,* 73–83.

Foster, D.H., & Gilson, S.J. (2002). Recognizing novel three-dimensional objects by summing signals from parts and views. *Proceedings of the Royal Society London B, 269,* 1939–1947.

Foster, D.H., & Nascimento, S.M.C. (1994). Relational colour constancy from invariant cone-excitation ratios. *Proceedings of the Royal Society of London Series B – Biological Sciences, 257,* 115–121.

Fox, E. (2008). *Emotion science.* New York: Palgrave Macmillan.

Fox Tree, J.E. (2000). Co-ordinating spontaneous talk. In L. Wheeldon (Ed.), *Aspects of language production.* Hove, UK: Psychology Press.

Franklin, S., Turner, J., Lambon Ralph, M.A., Morris, J., & Bailey, P.J. (1996). A distinctive case of word meaning deafness? *Cognitive Neuropsychology, 13,* 1139–1162.

Frauenfelder, U.H., Segui, J., & Dijkstra, T. (1990). Lexical effects in phonemic processing: Facilitatory or inhibitory? *Journal of Experimental Psychology: Human Perception & Performance, 16,* 77–91.

Frauenfelder, U.H., Scholten, M., & Content, A. (2001). Bottom-up inhibition in lexical selection: Phonological mismatch effects in spoken word recognition. *Language and Cognitive Processes, 16,* 583–607.

Frazier, L., & Rayner, K. (1982). Making and correcting errors in the analysis of structurally ambiguous sentences. *Cognitive Psychology, 14,* 178–210.

Frazier, L., Carlson, K., & Clifton, C. (2006). Prosodic phrasing is central to language comprehension. *Trends in Cognitive Sciences, 10,* 244–249.

French, R.M., & Cleeremans, A. (2002). *Implicit learning and consciousness: An empirical, philosophical and computational consensus in the making.* Hove: Psychology Press.

Freud, S. (1915). Repression. In *Freud's collected papers, Vol. IV.* London: Hogarth.

Freud, S. (1915/1957). Repression. In *Freud's collected papers* (Vol. IV). London: Hogarth Press.

Freud, S. (1915/1963). Repression. In J. Strachey (Ed.), *Standard edition of the collected works of Sigmund Freud, Vol. 14.* London: Hogarth Press. [Originally published in 1915]

Friederici, A.D., Fiebach, C.J., Schlesewsky, M., Bornkessel, I.D., & von Cramon, D.Y. (2006). Processing linguistic complexity and grammaticality in the left frontal cortex. *Cerebral Cortex, 16,* 1707–1717.

Friedman, N.P., & Miyake, A. (2004). The relations among inhibition and interference control functions: A latent variable analysis. *Journal of Experimental Psychology: General, 133,* 101–135.

Friedman, N.P., Miyake, A., Young, S.E., DeFries, J.C., Corley, R.P., & Hewitt, J.K. (2008). Individual differences in executive functions are almost entirely genetic in origin. *Journal of Experimental Psychology: General, 137,* 201–225.

Friedman-Hill, S.R., Robertson, L.C., & Treisman, A. (1995). Parietal contributions to visual feature binding: Evidence from a patient with bilateral lesions. *Science, 269,* 853–855.

Friedrich, C.K., & Kotz, S.A. (2007). Event-related potential evidence of form and meaning coding during online speech recognition. *Journal of Cognitive Neuroscience, 19,* 594–604.

Frost, R. (1998). Toward a strong phonological theory of visual word recognition: True issues and false trails. *Psychological Bulletin, 123*, 71–99.

Fugelsang, J.A., Stein, C.B., Green, A.E., & Dunbar, K.N. (2004). Theory and data interactions of the scientific mind: Evidence from the molecular and the cognitive laboratory. *Canadian Journal of Experimental Psychology, 58*, 86–95.

Fuller, J.M. (2003). The influence of speaker roles on discourse marker use. *Journal of Pragmatics, 35*, 23–45.

Funnell, E. (1983). Phonological processes in reading: New evidence from acquired dyslexia. *British Journal of Psychology, 74*, 159–180.

Funnell, E. (1996). Response biases in oral reading: An account of the co-occurrence of surface dyslexia and semantic dementia. *Quarterly Journal of Experimental Psychology A, 49*, 417–446.

Gabrieli, J., Fleischman, D., Keane, M., Reminger, S., & Morell, F. (1995). Double dissociation between memory systems underlying explicit and implicit memory in the human brain. *Psychological Science, 6*, 76–82.

Gainotti, G. (2000). What the locus of brain lesion tells us about the nature of the cognitive defect underlying category-specific disorders: A review. *Cortex, 36*, 539–559.

Galantucci, B., Fowler, C.A., & Turvey, M.T. (2006). The motor theory of speech perception reviewed. *Psychonomic Bulletin & Review, 13*, 361–377.

Gale, M., & Bull, L.J. (2009). Exploring the determinants of dual goal facilitation in a rule discovery task. *Thinking & Reasoning, 15*, 294–315.

Gallese, V., Fadiga, L., Fogassi, L., & Rizzolatti, G. (1996). Action recognition in the premotor cortex. *Brain, 119*, 593–609.

Gallese, V., Keysers, C., & Rizzolatti, G. (2004). A unifying view of the basis of social cognition. *Trends in Cognitive Sciences, 8*, 396–403.

Galotti, K.M. (2007). Decision structuring in important real-life choices. *Psychological Science, 18*, 320–325.

Ganis, G., Thompson, W.L., & Kosslyn, S.M. (2004). Brain areas underlying visual mental imagery and visual perception: An fMRI study. *Cognitive Brain Research, 20*, 226–241.

Ganong, W.F. (1980). Phonetic categorisation in auditory word perception. *Journal of Experimental Psychology: Human Perception and Performance, 6*, 110–125.

Garnham, A., Oakhill, J., & Johnson-Laird, P.N. (1982). Referential continuity and the coherence of discourse. *Cognition, 11*, 29–46.

Garnsey, S.M., Pearlmutter, N.J., Myers, E., & Lotocky, M.A. (1997). The contributions of verb bias and plausibility to the comprehension of temporarily ambiguous sentences. *Journal of Memory and Language, 37*, 58–93.

Garrett, M.F. (1980). Levels of processing in sentence production. In B. Butterworth (Ed.), *Language production: Vol. 1. Speech and talk.* San Diego, CA: Academic Press.

Garrod, S., & Terras, M. (2000). The contribution of lexical and situational knowledge to resolving discourse roles: Bonding and resolution. *Journal of Memory and Language, 42*, 526–544.

Gaskell, M.G., & Marslen-Wilson, W.D. (1998). Mechanisms of phonological interference in speech perception. *Journal of Experimental Psychology: Human Perception and Performance, 24*, 380–396.

Gaskell, M.G., & Marslen-Wilson, W.D. (2002). Representation and competition in the perception of spoken words. *Cognitive Psychology, 45*, 220–266.

Gathercole, S.E., & Baddeley, A.D. (1993). Phonological working memory: A critical building-block for reading development and vocabulary acquisition. *European Journal of Psychology of Education, 8*, 259–272.

Gauld, A., & Stephenson, G.M. (1967). Some experiments relating to Bartlett's theory of remembering. *British Journal of Psychology, 58*, 39–50.

Gauthier, I., Behrmann, M., & Tarr, M.J. (1999). Can face recognition really be dissociated from object recognition? *Journal of Cognitive Neuroscience, 11*, 349–370.

Gauthier, I., Skudlarski, P., Gore, J.C., & Anderson, A.W. (2000). Expertise for cars and birds recruits brain areas involved in face recognition. *Nature Neuroscience, 3*, 191–197.

Gauthier, I., & Tarr, M.J. (2002). Unravelling mechanisms for expert object recognition: Bridging brain activity and behaviour. *Journal of Experimental Psychology: Human Perception and Performance, 28*, 431–446.

Gazzaniga, M.S. (1992). *Nature's mind.* London: Basic Books.

Gazzaniga, M.S. (2000). Cerebral specialisation and interhemispheric communication: Does the corpus callosum enable the human condition? *Brain, 123*, 1293–1328.

Gazzaniga, M.S. (2008). The law and neuroscience. *Neuron, 60*, 412–415.

Gazzaniga, M.S., & Ledoux, J.E. (1978). *The integrated mind.* New York: Plenum Press.

Gazzaniga, M.S., Ivry, R.B., & Mangun, G.R. (1998). *Cognitive neuroscience: The biology of the mind.* New York: W.W. Norton.

Gazzaniga, M.S., Ivry, R.B., & Mangun, G.R. (2009). *Cognitive Neuroscience: The biology of the mind* (2nd Ed.). New York: W.W. Norton.

Gebauer, G.F., & Mackintosh, N.J. (2007). Psychometric intelligence dissociates implicit and explicit learning. *Journal of Experimental Psychology: Learning, Memory, and Cognition, 33*, 34–54.

Geiselman, R.E., & Fisher, R.P. (1997). Ten years of cognitive interviewing. In D.G. Payne & F.G. Conrad (Eds.), *Intersections in basic and applied memory research*. Mahwah, NJ: Lawrence Erlbaum Associates Inc.

Geiselman, R.E., Fisher, R.P., MacKinnon, D.P., & Holland, H.L. (1985). Eyewitness memory enhancement in police interview: Cognitive retrieval mnemonics versus hypnosis. *Journal of Applied Psychology, 70*, 401–412.

Geisler, W.S., Perry, J.S., Super, B.J., & Gallogly, D.P. (2001). Edge co-occurrence in natural images predicts contour grouping performance. *Vision Research, 41*, 711–724.

Gelder, van T., Bissett, M., & Cumming, G. (2004). Cultivating expertise in informal reasoning. *Canadian Journal of Experimental Psychology, 58*, 142–152.

Geraerts, E., & McNally, R.J. (2008). Forgetting unwanted memories: Directed forgetting and thought suppression methods. *Acta Psychologica, 127*, 614–622.

Geraerts, E., McNally, R.J., Jelicic, M., Merckelbach, H., & Raymaekers, L. (2008). Linking thought suppression and recovered memories of childhood sexual abuse. *Memory, 16*, 22–28.

Geraerts, E., Schooler, J.W., Merckelbach, H., Jelicic, M., Haner, B.J.A., & Ambadar, Z. (2007). Corroborating continuous and discontinuous memories of childhood sexual abuse. *Psychological Science, 18*, 564–568.

German, T.P., & Defeyter, M.A. (2000). Immunity to functional fixedness in young children. *Psychonomic Bulletin & Review, 7*, 707–712.

Gernsbacher, M.A., Varner, K.R., & Faust, M.E. (1990). Investigating differences in general comprehension skill. *Journal of Experimental Psychology: Learning, Memory, and Cognition, 16*, 430–445.

Gibson, J.J. (1950). *The perception of the visual world*. Boston: Houghton Mifflin.

Gibson, J.J. (1966). *The senses considered as perceptual systems*. Boston: Houghton Mifflin.

Gibson, J.J. (1979). *The ecological approach to visual perception*. Boston: Houghton Mifflin.

Gick, M.L., & Holyoak, K.J. (1980). Analogical problem solving. *Cognitive Psychology, 12*, 306–355.

Giersch, A., Humphreys, G., Boucart, M., & Kovacs, I. (2000). The computation of contours in visual agnosia: Evidence for early computation prior to shape binding and figure–ground coding. *Cognitive Neuropsychology, 17*, 731–759.

Gigerenzer, G. (2007). *Gut feelings: The intelligence of the unconscious*. New York: Viking Press.

Gigerenzer, G., & Hoffrage, U. (1995). How to improve Bayesian reasoning without instruction: Frequency formats. *Psychological Review, 102*, 684–704.

Gigerenzer, G., & Hoffrage, U. (1999). Overcoming difficulties in Bayesian reasoning: A reply to Lewis and Keren (1999) and Mellers and McGraw (1999). *Psychological Review, 106*, 425–430.

Gilbert, S.J., Frith, C.D., & Burgess, P.W. (2005). Involvement of rostral prefrontal cortex in selection between stimulus-oriented and stimulus-independent thought. *European Journal of Neuroscience, 21*, 1423–1431.

Gilbert, S.J., Spengler, S., Simons, J.S., Frith, C.D., & Burgess, P.W. (2006). Differential functions of lateral and medial rostral prefrontal cortex (area 10) revealed by brain-behaviour associations. *Cerebral Cortex, 16*, 1783–1789.

Gilboa, A. (2004). Autobiographical and episodic memory – one and the same? Evidence from prefrontal activation in neuroimaging studies. *Neuropsychologia, 42*, 1336–1349.

Gilboa, A., Ramirez, J., Kohler, S., Westmacott, R., Black, S.E., & Moscovitch, M. (2005). Retrieval of autobiographical memory in Alzheimer's disease: Relation to volumes of medial temporal lobe and other structures. *Hippocampus, 15*, 535–550.

Gilboa, A., Winocur, G., Grady, C.L., Hevenor, S.J., & Moscovitch, M. (2002). A functional magnetic resonance imaging (fMRI) study of remote and recent autobiographical memory using family photographs. *Journal of Cognitive Neuroscience, Suppl. S*, B75.

Gilboa, A., Winocur, G., Grady, C.L., Hevenor, S.J., & Moscovitch, M. (2004). Remembering our past: Functional neuroanatomy of recollections of recent and very remote personal events. *Cerebral Cortex, 14*, 1214–1225.

Gilboa, A., Winocur, G., Rosenbaum, R.S., Poreh, A., Gao, F.Q., Black, S.E. et al. (2006). Hippocampal contributions to recollection in retrograde and anterograde amnesia. *Hippocampus, 16*, 966–980.

Gilhooly, K.J. (1996). *Thinking: Directed, undirected and creative* (3rd Ed.). London: Academic Press.

Gilligan, S.G., & Bower, G.H. (1984). Cognitive consequences of emotional arousal. In C. Izard, J. Kagen, & R. Zajonc (Eds.), *Emotions, cognition, and behaviour*. New York: Cambridge University Press.

Ginet, M., & Verkampt, F. (2007). The cognitive interview: Is its benefit affected by the level of witness emotion? *Memory, 15*, 450–464.

Giora, R. (1997). Understanding figurative and literal language: The graded salience hypothesis. *Cognitive Linguistics, 7*, 183–206.

Giora, R. (2002). Literal vs. figurative language: Different or equal? *Journal of Pragmatics, 34*, 487–506.

Giora, R., & Fein, O. (1999). On understanding familiar and less-familiar figurative language. *Journal of Pragmatics, 31*, 1601–1618.

Glanzer, M., & Cunitz, A.R. (1966). Two storage mechanisms in free recall. *Journal of Verbal Learning and Verbal Behavior, 5*, 351–360.

Glaser, W.R. (1992). Picture naming. *Cognition, 42*, 61–105.

Glasspool, D.W., Shallice, T., & Cipolotti, L. (2006). Towards a unified process model for graphemic buffer disorder and deep dysgraphia. *Cognitive Neuropsychology, 23*, 479–512.

Glenberg, A.M. (1987). Temporal context and recency. In D.S. Gorfein & R.R. Hoffman (Eds.), *Memory and learning: The Ebbinghaus centennial conference*. Hillsdale, NJ: Lawrence Erlbaum Associates Inc.

Glenberg, A.M., Smith, S.M., & Green, C. (1977). Type I rehearsal: Maintenance and more. *Journal of Verbal Learning & Verbal Behavior, 16*, 339–352.

Glennerster, A., Tcheang, L., Gilson, S.J., Fitzgibbon, A.W., & Parker, A.J. (2006). Humans ignore motion and stereo cues in favour of a fictional stable world. *Current Biology, 16*, 428–432.

Glover, S. (2004). Separate visual representations in the planning and control of action. *Behavioral and Brain Sciences, 27*, 3–78.

Glover, S., & Dixon, P. (2001). Dynamic illusion effects in a reaching task: Evidence for separate visual representations in the planning and control of reaching. *Journal of Experimental Psychology: Human Perception and Performance, 27*, 560–572.

Glover, S., & Dixon, P. (2002a). Dynamic effects of the Ebbinghaus illusion in grasping: Support for a planning–control model of action. *Perception and Psychophysics, 64*, 266–278.

Glover, S., & Dixon, P. (2002b). Semantics affect the planning but not control of grasping. *Experimental Brain Research, 146*, 383–387.

Glück, J., & Bluck, S. (2007). Looking back over the life span: A life story account of the reminiscence bump. *Memory & Cognition, 35*, 1928–1939.

Glucksberg, S. (2003). The psycholinguistics of metaphor. *Trends in Cognitive Sciences, 7*, 92–96.

Glushko, R.J. (1979). The organisation and activation of orthographic knowledge in reading aloud. *Journal of Experimental Psychology: Human Perception and Performance, 5*, 674–691.

Glymour, C. (2001). *The mind's arrows: Bayes nets and graphical causal models in psychology*. Cambridge, MA: MIT Press.

Gobet, F., & Clarkson, G. (2004). Chunks in expert memory: Evidence for the magical number four . . . or is it two? *Memory, 12*, 732–747.

Gobet, F., & Simon, H.A. (1996a). Templates in chess memory: A mechanism for recalling several boards. *Cognitive Psychology, 31*, 1–40.

Gobet, F., & Simon, H.A. (1996b). Recall of rapidly presented random chess positions is a function of skill. *Psychonomic Bulletin & Review, 3*, 159–163.

Gobet, F., & Simon, H.A. (1998). Expert chess memory: Revisiting the chunking hypothesis. *Memory, 6*, 225–255.

Gobet, F., & Simon, H.A. (2000). Five seconds or sixty? Presentation time in expert memory. *Cognitive Science, 24*, 651–682.

Gobet, F., & Waters, A.J. (2003). The role of constraints in expert memory. *Journal of Experimental Psychology: Learning, Memory & Cognition, 29*, 1082–1094.

Gobet, F., Voogt, A. de, & Retschitzki, J. (2004). *Moves in mind: The psychology of board games*. Hove: Psychology Press.

Godden, D.R., & Baddeley, A.D. (1975). Context dependent memory in two natural environments: On land and under water. *British Journal of Psychology, 66*, 325–331

Godden, D.R., & Baddeley, A.D. (1980). When does context influence recognition memory? *British Journal of Psychology, 71*, 99–104.

Goel, V. (2007). Anatomy of deductive reasoning. *Trends in Cognitive Sciences, 11*, 435–441.

Goel, V., & Dolan, R.J. (2003). Explaining modulation of reasoning by belief. *Cognition, 87*, B11–22.

Goel, V., & Dolan, R.J. (2004). Differential involvement of left prefrontal cortex in inductive and deductive reasoning. *Cognition, 93*, B109–B121.

Goel, V., & Grafman, J. (1995). Are the frontal lobes implicated in "planning" functions? Interpreting data from the Tower of Hanoi. *Neuropsychologia, 33*, 623–642.

Goldberg, A., Russell, M., & Cook, A. (2003). The effect of computers on student writing: A meta-analysis of studies from 1992 to 2002. *Journal of Technology, Learning, and Assessment, 2*, 1–52.

Goldberg, A.M., & Rapp, B. (2008). Is compound chaining the serial-order mechanism of spelling? A simple recurrent network investigation. *Cognitive Neuropsychology, 25,* 218–255.

Goldenburg, G., Müllbacher, W., & Nowak, A. (1995). Imagery without perception: A case study of anosognosia for cortical blindness. *Neuropsychologia, 33,* 1373–1382.

Goldinger, S.D., & Azuma, T. (2003). Puzzle-solving science: The quixotic quest for units in speech perception. *Journal of Phonetics, 31,* 305–320.

Goldman-Rakic, P.S. (1988). Topography of cognition: Parallel distributed networks in primate association cortex. *Annual Review of Neuroscience, 11,* 137–156.

Goldman, R., Schwartz, M., & Wilshire, C. (2001). The influence of phonological context on the sound errors of a speaker with Wernicke's aphasia. *Brain and Language, 78,* 279–307.

Goldrick, M. (2006). Limited interaction in speech production: Chronometric, speech error, and neuropsychological evidence. *Language and Cognitive Processes, 21,* 817–855.

Goldstein, D.G., & Gigerenzer, G. (1999). The recognition heuristic: How ignorance makes us smart. In G. Gigerenzer, P.M. Todd, & the ABC Research Group, *Simple heuristics that make us smart.* Oxford: Oxford University Press.

Goldstein, D.G., & Gigerenzer, G. (2002). Models of ecological rationality: The recognition heuristic. *Psychological Review, 109,* 75–90.

Gollwitzer, P.M., & Cohen, A.-L. (2008). Commentary: Goals and the intentions meant to fulfil them. In M. Kliegel, M.A. McDaniel, & G.O. Einstein (Eds.), *Prospective memory: Cognitive, neuroscience, developmental, and applied perspectives.* London: Lawrence Erlbaum Associates.

Gompel, van R.P.G., Pickering, M.J., Pearson, J., & Liversedge, S.P. (2005). Evidence against competition during syntactic ambiguity resolution. *Journal of Memory and Language, 52,* 284–307.

Gomulicki, B.R. (1956). Recall as an abstractive process. *Acta Psychologica, 12,* 77–94.

Goodale, M.A., & Milner, A.D. (1992). Separate visual pathways for perception and action. *Trends in Neuroscience, 15,* 22–25.

Goodale, M.A., Gonzalez, C.L.R., & Króliczak, G. (2008). Action rules: Why the visual control of reaching and grasping is not always influenced by perceptual illusions. *Perception, 37,* 355–366.

Gooding, P.A., Isaac, C.L., & Mayes, A.R. (2005). Prose recall and amnesia: More implications for the episodic buffer. *Neuropsychologia, 43,* 583–587.

Gordon, I.E. (1989). *Theories of visual perception.* Chichester, UK: Wiley.

Gorman, M.E. (1995). Hypothesis testing. In S.E. Newstead & J.St.B.T. Evans (Eds.), *Perspectives on thinking and reasoning. Essays in honour of Peter Wason.* Hove, UK: Lawrence Erlbaum Associates Ltd.

Gottfredson, L.S. (1997). Why g matters? The complexities of everyday life. *Intelligence, 24,* 79–132.

Gould, J.D. (1978). An experimental study of writing, dictating, and speaking. In J. Requin (Ed.), *Attention and performance, Vol. VII.* Hillsdale, NJ: Lawrence Erlbaum Associates Inc.

Gould, J.D. (1980). Experiments on composing letters: Some facts, some myths, and some observations. In L.W. Gregg & E.R. Sternberg (Eds.), *Cognitive processes in writing.* Hillsdale, NJ: Lawrence Erlbaum Associates Inc.

Grabner, R.H., Stern, E., & Neubauer, A. (2007). Individual differences in chess expertise: A psychometric investigation. *Acta Psychologica, 124,* 398–420.

Graesser, A.C., Millis, K.K., & Zwaan, R.A. (1997). Discourse comprehension. *Annual Review of Psychology, 48,* 163–189.

Graf, P., & Schacter, D.L. (1985). Implicit and explicit memory for new associations in normal and amnesic subjects. *Journal of Experimental Psychology: Learning, Memory, & Cognition, 11,* 501–518.

Graf, P., Squire, L.R., & Mandler, G. (1984). The information that amnesic patients do not forget. *Journal of Experimental Psychology: Learning, Memory, & Cognition, 10,* 164–178.

Grafton, S., Hazeltine, E., & Ivry, R. (1995). Functional mapping of sequence learning in normal humans. *Journal of Cognitive Neuroscience, 7B,* 497–510.

Granzier, J.J.M., Brenner, E., & Smeets, J.B.J. (2009). Reliable identification by colour under natural conditions. *Journal of Vision, 9,* 1–9.

Gray, J.A., & Wedderburn, A.A. (1960). Grouping strategies with simultaneous stimuli. *Quarterly Journal of Experimental Psychology, 12,* 180–184.

Grea, H., Pisella, L., Rossetti, Y., Desmurget, M., Tilikete, C., Grafton, S. et al. (2002). A lesion of the posterior parietal cortex disrupts on-line adjustments during aiming movements. *Neuropsychologia, 40,* 2471–2480.

Green, K.P., Kuhl, P.K., Meltzoff, A.N., & Stevens, E.B. (1991). Integrating speech information across talkers, gender, and sensory modality: Female faces and male voices in the McGurk effect. *Perception & Psychophysics, 50,* 524–536.

Greenwald, A.G. (2003). On doing two things at once: III. Confirmation of perfect timesharing when simultaneous tasks are ideomotor compatible. *Journal of Experimental Psychology: Human Perception and Performance, 29,* 859–868.

Greenwald, A.G. (2004). On doing two things at once: IV. Necessary and sufficient conditions: Rejoinder to Lien, Proctor, and Ruthruff (2003). *Journal of Experimental Psychology: Human Perception and Performance, 30,* 632–636.

Gregory, R.L. (1973). The confounded eye. In R.L. Gregory & E.H. Gombrich (Eds.), *Illusion in nature and art.* London: Duckworth.

Grice, H.P. (1967). Logic and conversation. In P. Cole & J.L. Morgan (Eds.), *Studies in syntax, Vol. III.* New York: Seminar Press.

Grice, H.P. (1975). Logic and conversation. In P. Cole & J.L. Morgan (Eds.), *Syntax and semantics, III: Speech acts.* New York: Seminar Press.

Griffin, Z.M. (2001). Gaze durations during speech reflect word selection and phonological encoding. *Cognition, 82,* B1–B14.

Grigorenko, E.L. (2009). At the height of fashion: What genetics can teach us about neurodevelopmental disabilities. *Current Opinion in Neurology, 22,* 126–130.

Grill-Spector, K., & Kanwisher, N. (2005). Visual recognition: As soon as you know it is there, you know what it is. *Psychological Science, 16,* 152–160.

Grill-Spector, K., Henson, R., & Martin, A. (2006). Repetition and the brain: Neural models of stimulus-specific effects. *Trends in Cognitive Sciences, 10,* 14–23.

Grill-Spector, K., Sayres, R., & Ress, D. (2006). High-resolution imaging reveals highly selective nonface clusters in the fusiform face area. *Nature Neuroscience, 9,* 1177–1185.

Grodzinsky, Y., & Friederici, A.D. (2006). Neuroimaging of syntax and syntactic processing. *Current Opinion in Neurobiology, 16,* 240–246.

Gross, J.J., & Thompson, R.A. (2007). Emotion regulation: Conceptual foundations. In J.J. Gross (Ed.), *Handbook of emotion regulation.* New York: Guilford Press.

Grossman, E.D., Donnelly, R., Price, R., Pickens, D., Morgan, V., Neighbor, G. et al. (2000). Brain areas involved in perception of biological motion. *Journal of Cognitive Neuroscience, 12,* 711–720.

Guasti, M.T., & Luzzatti, C. (2002). Syntactic breakdown and recovery of clausal structure in agrammatism. *Brain and Cognition, 48,* 385–391.

Guise, K., Kelly, K., Romanowski, J., Vogeley, K., Platek, S.M., Murray, E., & Keenan, J.P. (2007). The anatomical and evolutionary relationship between self-awareness and theory of mind.

Human Nature – An Interdisciplinary Biosocial Perspective, 18, 132–142.

Gunther, H., Gfoerer, S., & Weiss, L. (1984). Inflection, frequency, and the word superiority effect. *Psychological Research, 46,* 261–281.

Gupta, P., & Cohen, N.J. (2002). Theoretical and computational analysis of skill learning, repetition priming, and procedural memory. *Psychological Review, 109,* 401–448.

Gur, M., & Snodderly, D.M. (2007). Direction selectivity in V1 of alert monkeys: Evidence for parallel pathways for motion processing. *Journal of Physiology, 585,* 383–400.

Gutchess, A.H., & Park, D.C. (2006). fMRI environment can impair memory performance in young and elderly adults. *Brain Research, 1099,* 133–140.

Guttman, S.E., Gilroy, L.A., & Blake, R. (2007). Spatial grouping in human vision: Temporal structure trumps temporal synchrony. *Vision Research, 47,* 219–230.

Haart, E.G.O.-de, Carey, D.P., & Milne, A.B. (1999). More thoughts on perceiving and grasping the Müller-Lyer illusion. *Neuropsychologia, 37,* 1437–1444.

Haber, R.N., & Levin, C.A. (2001). The independence of size perception and distance perception. *Perception & Psychophysics, 63,* 1140–1152.

Haggard, P. (2005). Conscious intention and motor cognition. *Trends in Cognitive Sciences, 9,* 290–295.

Hagoort, P., & van Berkum, J. (2007). Beyond the sentence given. *Philosophical Transactions of the Royal Society B, 362,* 801–811.

Hagoort, P., Hald, L., Bastiaansen, M., & Petersson, K.M. (2004). Integration of word meaning and world knowledge in language comprehension. *Science, 304,* 438–441.

Hahn, B., Ross, T.J., & Stein, E.A. (2006). Neuroanatomical dissociation between bottom-up and top-down processes of visuospatial selective attention. *NeuroImage, 32,* 842–853.

Hahn, S., Andersen, G.J., & Saidpour, A. (2003). Static scene analysis for the perception of heading. *Psychological Science, 14,* 543–548.

Hahn, U., & Oaksford, M. (2007). The rationality of informal argumentation: A Bayesian approach to reasoning fallacies. *Psychological Review, 114,* 704–732.

Haist, F., Gore, J.B., & Mao, H. (2001). Consolidation of human memory over decades revealed by functional magnetic resonance imaging. *Nature Neuroscience, 4,* 1139–1145.

Halliday, M.A.K. (1987). Spoken and written modes of meaning. In R. Horowitz & S.J. Samuels (Eds.), *Comprehending oral and written language.* New York: Academic Press.

Han, J.J., Leichtman, M.D., & Wang, Q. (1998). Autobiographical memory in Korean, Chinese, and American children. *Developmental Psychology, 34*, 701–713.

Han, S., Humphreys, G.W., & Chen, L. (1999). Uniform connectedness and classical Gestalt principles of perceptual grouping. *Perception & Psychophysics, 61*, 661–674.

Han, S.H., & Humphreys, G.W. (2003). Relationship between connectedness and proximity in perceptual grouping. Science in *China Series C – Life Sciences, 46*, 113–126.

Handley, S.J., Capon, A., Copp, C., & Harper, C. (2002). Conditional reasoning and the Tower of Hanoi: The role of verbal and spatial working memory. *British Journal of Psychology, 93*, 501–518.

Hanley, J.R., & McDonnell, V. (1997). Are reading and spelling phonologically mediated? Evidence from a patient with a speech production impairment. *Cognitive Neuropsychology, 14*, 3–33.

Hannula, D.E., & Ranganath, C. (2008). Medial temporal lobe activity predicts successful relational memory binding. *Journal of Neuroscience, 28*, 116–124.

Hannula, D.E., Tranel, D., & Cohen, N.J. (2006). The long and the short of it: Relational memory impairments in amnesia, even at short lags. *Journal of Neuroscience, 26*, 8352–8359.

Hansen, T., Olkkonen, M., Walter, S., & Gegenfurtner, K.R. (2006). Memory modulates colour appearance. *Nature Neuroscience, 9*, 1367–1368.

Harding, A., Halliday, G., Caine, D., & Kril, J. (2000). Degeneration of anterior thalamic nuclei differentiates alcoholics with amnesia. *Brain, 123*, 141–154.

Harley, K., & Reese, E. (1999). Origins of autobiographical memory. *Developmental Psychology, 35*, 1338–1348.

Harley, T.A. (2001). *The psychology of language: From data to theory* (2nd Ed.). Hove, UK: Psychology Press.

Harley, T.A. (2004). Does cognitive neuropsychology have a future? *Cognitive Neuropsychology, 21*, 3–16.

Harley, T.A. (2008). *The psychology of language: From data to theory* (3rd ed.). Hove, UK: Psychology Press.

Harley, T.A., & Bown, H.E. (1998). What causes a tip-of-the-tongue state? Evidence for lexical neighbourhood effects in speech production. *British Journal of Psychology, 89*, 151–174.

Harm, M.W., & Seidenberg, M.S. (2001). Are there orthographic impairments in phonological dyslexia? *Cognitive Neuropsychology, 18*, 71–92.

Harm, M.W., & Seidenberg, M.S. (2004). Computing the meanings of words in reading: Co-operative division of labour between visual and phonological processes. *Psychological Review, 111*, 662–720.

Harris, M.G., & Carré, G. (2001). Is optic flow used to guide walking while wearing a displacing prism? *Perception, 30*, 811–818.

Hartley, J., Sotto, E., & Pennebaker, J. (2003). Speaking versus typing: A case-study of the effects of using voice-recognition software on academic correspondence. *British Journal of Educational Technology, 34*, 5–16.

Hartsuiker, R.J., Corley, M., & Martensen, H. (2005). The lexical bias effect is modulated by context, but the standard monitoring account doesn't fly: Related reply to Baars et al. (1975). *Journal of Memory and Language, 52*, 58–70.

Harvey, L.O. (1986). Visual memory: What is remembered? In F. Klix & H. Hagendorf (Eds.), *Human memory and cognitive capabilities*. The Hague: Elsevier.

Harvey, N. (2001). Studying judgement: General issues. *Thinking and Reasoning, 7*, 103–118.

Haskell, T.R., & MacDonald, M.C. (2003). Conflicting cues and competition in subject-verb agreement. *Journal of Memory and Language, 48*, 760–778.

Hassabis, D., Kumaran, D., Vann, S.D., & Maguire, E.A. (2007). Patients with hippocampal amnesia cannot imagine new experiences. *Proceedings of the National Academy of Sciences of the United States of America, 104*, 1726–1731.

Hastie, R. (2001). Problems for judgement and decision making. *Annual Review of Psychology, 52*, 653–683.

Hatano, G., & Inagaki, K. (1986). Two courses of expertise. In H. Stevenson, H. Azuma, & K. Hatuka (eds.), *Child development in Japan*. San Francisco, CA: W.H. Freeman.

Hauk, O., Johnsrude, I., & Pulvermüller, F. (2004). Somatotopic representation of action words in human motor and premotor cortex. *Neuron, 41*, 301–307.

Haxby, J.V., Gobbini, M.I., Furey, M.L., Ishai, A., Schouten, J.L., & Pietrini, P. (2001). Distributed and overlapping representations of faces and objects in ventral temporal cortex. *Science, 293*, 2425–2430.

Haxby, J.V., Hoffman, E.A., & Gobbini, M.I. (2000). The distributed human neural system for face perception. *Trends in Cognitive Sciences, 4*, 223–233.

Hayes, J.R. (2004). What triggers revision. In L. Allal, L. Chanquoy, & P. Largy (Eds.), *Revision of written language: Cognitive and instructional processes* (pp. 9–20). Dordrecht: Kluwer.

Hayes, J.R. (2006). New directions in writing theory. In C.A. MacArthur, S. Graham, & J. Fitzgerald (Eds.), *Handbook of writing research*. New York: Guilford Press.

Hayes, J.R., & Bajzek, D. (2008). Understanding and reducing the knowledge effect: Implications for writers. *Written Communication, 25,* 104–118.

Hayes, J.R., & Chenoweth, N.A. (2006). Is working memory involved in the transcribing and editing of texts? *Written Communication, 23,* 135–149.

Hayes, J.R., & Flower, L.S. (1986). Writing research and the writer. *American Psychologist, 41,* 1106–1113.

Hayes, J.R., Flower, L.S., Schriver, K., Stratman, J., & Carey, L. (1985). *Cognitive processes in revision* (Technical Report No. 12). Pittsburgh, PA: Carnegie Mellon University.

Hayward, W.G. (2003). After the viewpoint debate: Where next in object recognition? *Trends in Cognitive Sciences, 7,* 425–427.

Hayward, W.G., & Tarr, M.J. (2005). Visual perception II: High-level vision. In K. Lamberts & R.L. Goldstone (Eds.), *The handbook of cognition*. London: Sage.

Hazeltine, E., Teague, D., & Ivry, R. (2000). *Dual-task performance during simultaneous execution: Evidence for concurrent response selection processes.* Presented at the Annual Meeting of the Cognitive Neuroscience Society, San Francisco.

Hegarty, M., Shah, P., & Miyake, A. (2000). Constraints on using the dual-task methodology to specify the degree of central executive involvement in cognitive tasks. *Memory & Cognition, 28,* 376–385.

Hegdé, J. (2008). Time course of visual perception: Coarse-to-fine processing and beyond. *Progress in Neurobiology, 84,* 405–439.

Hegdé, J., & Van Essen, D.C. (2000). Selectivity for complex shapes in primate visual area V2. *Journal of Neuroscience, 20,* RC61.

Heider, E. (1972). Universals in colour naming and memory. *Journal of Experimental Psychology, 93,* 10–20.

Heller, D., Grodner, D., & Tanenhaus, M.K. (2008). The role of perspective in identifying domains of reference. *Cognition, 108,* 831–836.

Henson, R.A. (2005). What can functional neuroimaging tell the experimental psychologist? *Quarterly Journal of Experimental Psychology, 58A,* 193–233.

Henson, R.N.A., Burgess, N., & Frith, C.D. (2000). Recoding, storage, rehearsal and grouping in verbal short-term memory: An fMRI study. *Neuropsychologia, 38,* 426–440.

Hering, E. (1878). *Zur Lehre vom Lichtsinn.* Vienna: Gerold.

Herron, J.E., & Wilding, E.L. (2006). Brain and behavioural indices of retrieval model. *NeuroImage, 32,* 863–870.

Hertwig, R., & Todd, P.M. (2003). More is not always better: The benefits of cognitive limits. In D. Hardman & L. Macchi (Eds.), *Thinking: Psychological perspectives on reasoning, judgment and decision making*. Chichester: Wiley.

Hertwig, R., Barron, G., Weber, E.U., & Erev, I. (2004). Decisions from experience and the effect of rare events in risky choice. *Psychological Science, 15,* 534–539.

Hertwig, R., Pachur, T., & Kurzenhäuser, S. (2005). Judgements of risk frequencies: Tests of possible cognitive mechanisms. *Journal of Experimental Psychology: Learning, Memory, and Cognition, 31,* 621–642.

Heywood, C.A., & Cowey, A. (1999). Cerebral achromatopsia. In G.W. Humphreys (Ed.), *Case studies in the neuropsychology of vision*. Hove, UK: Psychology Press.

Hicks, J.L., Marsh, R.L., & Cook, G.I. (2005). Task interference in time-based, event-based, and dual intention prospective memory conditions. *Journal of Memory and Language, 53,* 430–444.

Higashiyama, A., & Adachi, K. (2006). Perceived size and perceived distance of targets viewed from between the legs: Evidence for proprioception. *Vision Research, 46,* 3961–3976.

Higham, P.A., & Tam, H. (2006). Release from generation failure: The role of study list structure. *Memory & Cognition, 34,* 148–157.

Hills, R.L., & Murray, W.S. (2000). Commas and spaces: Effects of punctuation on eye movements and sentence parsing. In A. Kennedy, R. Radach, D. Heller, & J. Pynte (Eds.), *Reading as a perceptual process*. Oxford: Elsevier.

Hirst, W., Spelke, E.S., Reaves, C.C., Caharack, G., & Neisser, U. (1980). Dividing attention without alternation or automaticity. *Journal of Experimental Psychology: General, 109,* 98–117.

Hodges, J.R., & Patterson, K. (2007). Semantic dementia: A unique clinicopathological syndrome. *Lancet Neurology, 6,* 1004–1014.

Hoffman, C., Lau, I., & Johnson, D.R. (1986). The linguistic relativity of person cognition. *Journal of Personality & Social Psychology, 51,* 1097–1105.

Hoffrage, U., Lindsey, S., Hertwig, R., & Gigerenzer, G. (2000). Communicating statistical information. *Science, 290,* 2261–2262.

Hollingworth, A. (2004). Constructing visual representations of natural scenes: The roles of short- and long-term visual memory. *Journal of Experimental Psychology: Human Perception and Performance, 30,* 519–537.

Hollingworth, A., & Henderson, J.M. (2002). Accurate visual memory for previously attended objects in natural scenes. *Journal of Experimental Psychology: Human Perception and Performance, 28,* 113–136.

Holloway, D.R., & McCutcheon, D. (2004). Audience perspective in young writers' composing and revising. In L. Allal, L. Chanquoy, & P. Largy (Eds.), *Revision of written language: Cognitive and instructional processes* (pp. 87–101). New York: Kluwer.

Holmes, V.M. (1988). Hesitations and sentence planning. *Language and Cognitive Processes, 3,* 323–361.

Holmes, V.M., & Carruthers, J. (1998). The relation between reading and spelling in skilled adult readers. *Journal of Memory and Language, 39,* 264–289.

Holmes, V.M., Malone, A.M., & Redenbach, H. (2008). Orthographic processing and visual sequential memory in unexpectedly poor spellers. *Journal of Research in Reading, 31,* 136–156.

Holtgraves, T. (1998). Interpreting indirect replies. *Cognitive Psychology, 37,* 1–27.

Holway, A.F., & Boring, E.G. (1941). Determinants of apparent visual size with distance variant. *American Journal of Psychology, 54,* 21–37.

Hopfinger, J.B., Buoncore, M.H., & Mangun, G.R. (2000). The neural mechanisms of top-down attentional control. *Nature Neuroscience, 3,* 284–291.

Horton, W.S., & Keysar, B. (1996). When do speakers take into account common ground? *Cognition, 59,* 91–117.

Hotopf, W.H.N. (1980). Slips of the pen. In U. Frith (Ed.), *Cognitive processes in spelling.* London: Academic Press.

Howard, D., & Best, W. (1996). Developmental phonological dyslexia: Real word reading can be completely normal. *Cognitive Neuropsychology, 13,* 887–934.

Howard, D.V., & Howard, J.H. (1992). Adult age differences in the rate of learning serial patterns: Evidence from direct and indirect tests. *Psychology & Aging, 7,* 232–241.

Howard, D., & Orchard-Lisle, V. (1984). On the origin of semantic errors in naming: Evidence from the case of a global aphasic. *Cognitive Neuropsychology, 1,* 163–190.

Howe. M.L., & Courage, M.L. (1997). The emergence and early development of autobiographical memory. *Psychological Review, 104,* 499–523.

Howe, M.J.A., & Smith, J. (1988). Calendar calculating in idiots savants: How do they do it? *British Journal of Psychology, 79,* 371–386.

Howe, M.L., Courage, M.L., & Edison, S.C. (2003). When autobiographical memory begins. In M. Conway, S. Gathercole, S. Algarabel, A.

Pitarque, & T. Bajo (Eds.), *Theories of memory, Vol. III.* Hove, UK: Psychology Press.

Hubel, D.H., & Wiesel, T.N. (1962). Receptive fields, binocular interaction and functional architecture in the cat's visual cortex. *Journal of Physiology, 160,* 106–154.

Hubel, D.H., & Wiesel, T.N. (1979). Brain mechanisms of vision. *Scientific American, 249,* 150–162.

Humphrey, N. (1983). *Consciousness regained: Chapters in the development of mind.* Oxford: Oxford University Press.

Humphrey, N. (2002). *The mind made flesh: Frontiers of psychology and evolution.* Oxford: Oxford University Press.

Humphreys, G.W. (1999). *Case studies in the neuropsychology of vision.* Hove, UK: Psychology Press.

Humphreys, G.W., & Riddoch, M.J. (1987). *To see but not to see: A case study of visual agnosia.* Hove, UK: Psychology Press.

Humphreys, G.W., & Riddoch, M.J. (1985). Author corrections to "Routes to object constancy". *Quarterly Journal of Experimental Psychology, 37A,* 493–495.

Humphreys, G.W., & Riddoch, M.J. (2006). Features, objects, action: The cognitive neuropsychology of visual object processing, 1984–2004. *Cognitive Neuropsychology, 23,* 156–183.

Humphreys, K., Avidan, G., & Behrmann, M. (2007). A detailed investigation of facial expression processing in congenital prosopagnosia as compared to acquired prosopagnosia. *Experimental Brain Research, 176,* 356–373.

Humphreys, G.W., Riddoch, M.J., & Quinlan, P.T. (1985). Interactive processes in perceptual organization: Evidence from visual agnosia. In M.I. Posner & O.S.M. Morin (Eds.), *Attention and performance, Vol. XI.* Hillsdale, NJ: Lawrence Erlbaum Associates Inc.

Hunt, E., & Agnoli, F. (1991). The Whorfian hypothesis: A cognitive psychological perspective. *Psychological Review, 98,* 377–389.

Hunter, J.E. (1983). *Overview of validity generalization for the U.S. Employment Service.* (USES Test Report No. 43). Washington, DC: U.S. Department of Labor, Employment, and Training Administration.

Hunter, J.E., & Schmidt, F.L. (1996). Intelligence and job performance: Economic and social implications. *Psychology Public Policy and Law, 2,* 447–472.

Huntjens, R.J.C., Peters, M.L., Woertman, L., van der Hart, O., & Postma, A. (2007). Memory transfer for emotionally valenced words between identities in dissociative identity disorder. *Behaviour Research and Therapy, 45,* 775–789.

Huntjens, R.J.C., Postma, A., Peters, M., Woertman, L., & van der Hart, O. (2003). Interidentity amnesia for neutral, episodic information in dissociative identity disorder. *Journal of Abnormal Psychology*, 112, 290–297.

Huntjens, R.J.C., Postma, A., Woertman, L., van der Hart, O., & Peters, M.L. (2005). Procedural memory in dissociative identity disorder: When can interidentity amnesia be truly established? *Consciousness and Cognition*, 14, 377–389.

Huppert, F.A., & Piercy, M. (1976). Recognition memory in amnesic patients: Effect of temporal context and familiarity of material. *Cortex*, 4, 3–20.

Hurvich, L.M., & Jameson, D. (1957). An opponent process theory of color vision. *Psychological Review*, 64, 384–390.

Iacoboni, M. (2008). The role of premotor cortex in speech perception: Evidence from fMRI and rTMS. *Journal of Physiology – Paris*, 102, 31–34.

Iacoboni, M., Molnar-Szakacs, I., Gallese, V., Buccino, G., Mazziotta, J.C., & Rizzolatti, G. (2005). Grasping the intentions of others with one's own minor neuron system. *PLOS Biology*, 3, 529–535.

Ihlebaek, C., Løve, T., Eilertsen, D.E., & Magnussen, S. (2003). Memory for a staged criminal event witnessed live and on video. *Memory*, 11, 319–327.

Indefrey, P., & Levelt, W.J.M. (2004). The spatial and temporal signatures of word production components. *Cognition*, 92, 101–144.

Indovina, I., & Macaluso, E. (2007). Dissociation of stimulus relevance and saliency factors during shifts of visuo-spatial attention. *Cerebral Cortex*, 17, 1701–1711.

Ingles, J.L., Fisk, J.D., Passmore, M., & Darvesh, S. (2007). Progressive anomia without semantic or phonological impairment. *Cortex*, 43, 558–564.

Ison, M.J., & Quiroga, R.Q. (2008). Selectivity and invariance for visual object recognition. *Frontiers in Bioscience*, 13, 4889–4903.

Isurin, L., & McDonald, J.L. (2001). Retroactive interference from translation equivalents: Implications for first language forgetting. *Memory & Cognition*, 29, 312–319.

Ittelson, W.H. (1951). Size as a cue to distance: Static localisation. *American Journal of Psychology*, 64, 54–67.

Izard, C.E. (2007). Basic emotions, natural kinds, emotion schemas, and a new paradigm. *Perspectives in Psychological Science*, 2, 260–280.

Jacobs, R.A. (2002). What determines visual cue reliability? *Trends in Cognitive Sciences*, 6, 345–350.

Jacoby, L.L., Debner, J.A., & Hay, J.F. (2001). Proactive interference, accessibility bias, and process dissociations: Valid subjective reports of memory. *Journal of Experimental Psychology: Learning, Memory, & Cognition*, 27, 686–700.

Jacoby, L.L., Bishara, A.J., Hessels, S., & Toth, J.P. (2005). Aging, subjective experience, and cognitive control: Dramatic false remembering by older adults. *Journal of Experimental Psychology: General*, 134, 131–148.

Jacquemot, C., Dupoux, E., & Bachoud-Lévi, A.C. (2007). Breaking the mirror: Asymmetrical input and output codes. *Cognitive Neuropsychology*, 24, 3–22.

Jakobson, L.S., Archibald, Y.M., Carey, D.P., & Goodale, M.A. (1991). A kinematic analysis of reaching and grasping movements in a patient recovering from optic ataxia. *Neuropsychologia*, 29, 803–809.

James, W. (1890). *Principles of psychology*. New York: Holt.

James, T.W., Culham, J., Humphrey, G.K., Milner, A.D., & Goodale, M.A. (2003). Ventral occipital lesions impair object recognition but not object-directed grasping: An fMRI study. *Brain*, 126, 2463–2475.

Jared, D. (2002). Spelling-sound consistency and regularity effects in word naming. *Journal of Memory and Language*, 46, 723–750.

Jared, D., Levy, B.A., & Rayner, K. (1999). The role of phonology in the activation of word meanings during reading: Evidence from proof-reading and eye movements. *Journal of Experimental Psychology: General*, 128, 219–264.

Jansma, J.M., Ramsey, N.F., Slagter, H.A., & Kahn, R.S. (2001). Functional anatomical correlates of controlled and automatic processing. *Journal of Cognitive Neuroscience*, 13, 730–743.

Jared, D. (2002). Spelling – Sound consistency and regularity effects in word naming. *Journal of Memory and Language*, 46, 723–750.

Jax, S.A., Buxbaum, L.J., & Moll, A.D. (2006). Deficits in movement planning and intrinsic co-ordinate control in ideomotor apraxia. *Journal of Cognitive Neuroscience*, 18, 2063–2076.

Jefferies, E., Sage, K., & Lambon Ralph, M.A. (2007). Do deep dyslexia, dysphasia, and dysgraphia share a common phonological impairment? *Neuropsychologia*, 45, 1553–1570.

Jenkins, J.J. (1979). Four points to remember: A tetrahedral model of memory experiments. In L.S. Cermak & F.I.M. Craik (Eds.), *Levels of processing in human memory* (pp. 429–446). Hillsdale, NJ: Erlbaum.

Jessup, R.K., Bishara, A.J., & Busemeyer, J.R. (2008). Feedback produces divergence from prospect theory in descriptive choice. *Psychological Science, 19,* 1015–1020.

Jiang, Y., Costello, P., Fang, F., Huang, M., & He, S. (2006). A gender- and sexual orientation-dependent spatial attentional effect of invisible images. *Proceedings of the National Academy of Sciences of the United States of America, 103,* 17048–17052.

Johansson, G. (1973). Visual perception of biological motion and a model for its analysis. *Perception & Psychophysics, 14,* 201–211.

Johansson, G. (1975). Visual motion perception. *Scientific American, 232,* 76–89.

Johansson, G., von Hofsten, C., & Jansson, G. (1980). Event perception. *Annual Review of Psychology, 31,* 27–64.

Johnson, J.A., & Zatorre, R.J. (2006). Neural substrates for dividing and focusing attention between simultaneous auditory and visual events. *NeuroImage, 31,* 1673–1681.

Johnson, J.A., Strafella, A.P., & Zatorre, R.J. (2007). The role of the dorsolateral prefrontal cortex in bimodal divided attention: Two transcranial magnetic stimulation studies. *Journal of Cognitive Neuroscience, 19,* 907–920.

Johnson, M.K., Hashtroudi, S., & Lindsay, D.S. (1993). Source monitoring. *Psychological Bulletin, 114,* 3–28.

Johnson-Laird, P.N. (1983). *Mental models.* Cambridge: Cambridge University Press.

Johnson-Laird, P.N. (1999). Deductive reasoning. *Annual Review of Psychology, 50,* 109–135.

Johnson-Laird, P.N. (2004). Mental models and reasoning. In J.P. Leighton & R.J. Sternberg (Eds.), *The nature of reasoning.* Cambridge: Cambridge University Press.

Johnson-Laird, P.N., & Byrne, R.M.J. (1991). *Deduction.* London: Psychology Press.

Johnson-Laird, P.N., Legrenzi, P., & Girotto, V. (2004). How we detect logical inconsistencies. *Current Directions in Psychological Science, 13,* 41–45.

Jolij, J., & Lamme, V.A.F. (2005). Repression of unconscious information by conscious processing: Evidence for affective blindsight induced by transcranial magnetic stimulation. *Proceedings of the National Academy of Sciences, 102,* 10747–10751.

Jonides, J., Lewis, R.L., Nee, D.E., Lustig, C.A., Berman, M.G., & Moore, K.S. (2008). The mind and brain of short-term memory. *Annual Review of Psychology, 59,* 193–224.

Jörgens, S., Biermann-Ruben, K., Kurz, M.W., Flugel, C., Kurz, K.D., Antke, C., et al. (2008). Word deafness as a cortical auditory processing deficit: A case report with MEG. *Neurocase, 14,* 307–316.

Josephs, R.A., Larrick, R.P., Steele, C.M., & Nisbett, R.E. (1992). Protecting the self from the negative consequences of risky decisions. *Journal of Personality and Social Psychology, 62,* 26–37.

Jost, A. (1897). Die Assoziationsfestigkeit in ihrer Abhängigkeit von der Verteilung der Wiederholungen. *Zeitschrift für Psychologie, 14,* 436–472.

Jung, R.E., & Haier, R.J. (2007). The parieto-frontal integration theory (P-FIT) of intelligence: Converging neuroimaging evidence. *Behavioral and Brain Sciences, 30,* 135–154.

Juslin, P., Winman, A., & Hansson, P. (2007). The *naïve* intuitive statistician: A naïve sampling model of intuitive confidence intervals. *Psychological Review, 114,* 678–703.

Just, M.A., & Carpenter, P.A. (1992). A capacity theory of comprehension. *Psychological Review, 99,* 122–149.

Just, M.A., Carpenter, P.A., Keller, T.A., Emery, L., Zajac, H., & Thulborn, K.R. (2001). Interdependence of non-overlapping cortical systems in dual cognitive tasks. *NeuroImage, 14,* 417–426.

Kaakinen, J., & Hyönä, J. (2007). Perspective effects in repeated reading: An eye movement study. *Memory & Cognition, 35,* 1323–1336.

Kaakinen, J.K., Hyönä, J., & Keenan, J.M. (2003). How prior knowledge, WMC, and relevance of information affect eye fixations in expository text. *Journal of Experimental Psychology: Learning, Memory, and Cognition, 29,* 447–457.

Kahneman, D. (1973). *Attention and effort.* Englewood Cliffs, NJ: Prentice Hall.

Kahneman, D. (2003). A perspective on judgment and choice: Mapping bounded rationality. *American Psychologist, 58,* 697–720.

Kahneman, D., & Chajczyk, D. (1983). Tests of the automaticity of reading: Dilution of Stroop effects by colour-irrelevant stimuli. *Journal of Experimental Psychology, 9,* 497–509.

Kahneman, D., & Frederick, S. (2002). Representativeness revisited: Attribute substitution in intuitive judgements. In T. Gilovich, T.D. Griffin, & D. Kahneman (Eds.), *Heuristics and biases: The psychology of intuitive judgement.* Cambridge: Cambridge University Press.

Kahneman, D., & Frederick, S. (2005). A model of heuristic judgement. In K.J. Holyoak and R.G. Morrison (Eds.), *The Cambridge handbook of thinking and reasoning.* Cambridge: Cambridge University Press.

Kahneman, D., & Frederick, S. (2007). Frames and brains: Elicitation and control of response tendencies. *Trends in Cognitive Sciences, 11,* 45–46.

Kahneman, D., & Tversky, A. (1972). Subjective probability – Judgement of representativeness. *Cognitive Psychology, 3*, 430–454.

Kahneman, D., & Tversky, A. (1973). On the psychology of prediction. *Psychological Review, 80*, 237–251.

Kahneman, D., & Tversky, A. (1979). Prospect theory: An analysis of decision under risk. *Econometrica, 47*, 263–291.

Kahneman, D., & Tversky, A. (1984). Choices, values and frames. *American Psychologist, 39*, 341–350.

Kalat, J.W. (2001). *Biological psychology* (7th Ed.). Pacific Grove: Brooks/Cole.

Kampf, M., Nachson, I., & Babkoff, H. (2002). A serial test of the laterality of familiar face recognition. *Brain and Cognition, 50*, 35–50.

Kandel, E.R., Schwartz, J.H., & Jessell, T.M. (2005). *Principles of neural science (4th. Ed.).* New York: McGraw-Hill.

Kandel, E.R., Kupferman, I., & Iverson, S. (2000). Learning and memory. In E.R. Kandel, J.H. Schwartz, & T.M. Jessell (Eds.), *Principles of neural sciences* (pp. 1227–1246). New York: McGraw-Hill.

Kane, M.J., & Engle, R.W. (2000). Working-memory capacity, proactive interference, divided attention: Limits on long-term memory retrieval. *Journal of Experimental Psychology: Learning, Memory, and Cognition, 26*, 336–358.

Kane, M.J., Brown, L.H., McVay, J.C., Silvia, P.J., Myin-Germeys, I., & Kwapil, T.R. (2007). For whom the mind wanders and when – An experience-sampling study of working memory and executive control in daily life. *Psychological Science, 18*, 614–621.

Kanizsa, G. (1976). Subjective contours. *Scientific American, 234*, 48–52.

Kanwisher, N., & Yovel, G. (2006). The fusiform face area: A cortical region specialised for the perception of faces. *Philosophical Transactions of the Royal Society B – Biological Sciences, 361*, 2109–2128.

Kanwisher, N., McDermott, J., & Chun, M.M. (1997). The fusiform face area: A module in human extrastriate cortex specialised for face perception. *Journal of Neuroscience, 9*, 605–610.

Kaplan, G.A., & Simon, H.A. (1990). In search of insight. *Cognitive Psychology, 22*, 374–419.

Kapur, N. (1999). Syndromes of retrograde amnesia: A conceptual and empirical synthesis. *Psychological Bulletin, 125*, 800–825.

Karnath, H.O., & Perenin, M.T. (2005). Cortical control of visually guided reaching: Evidence from patients with optic ataxia. *Cerebral Cortex, 15*, 1561–1569.

Karney, B.R., & Frye, N.E. (2002). But we've been getting better lately: Comparing prospective and retrospective views of relationship development. *Journal of Personality and Social Psychology, 82*, 222–238.

Kastner, S. (1999). Increased activity in human visual cortex during directed attention in the absence of visual stimulation. *Neuron, 22*, 751–761.

Kaufer, D., Hayes, J.R., & Flower, L.S. (1986). Composing written sentences. *Research in the Teaching of English, 20*, 121–140.

Kaup, B., Lüdtke, J., & Zwaan, R.A. (2006). Processing negated sentences with contradictory predicates: Is a door that is not open mentally closed? *Journal of Pragmatics, 38*, 1033–1050.

Kaup, B., Yaxley, R.H., Madden, C.J., Zwaan, R.A., & Lüdtke, J. (2007). Experiential simulations of negated text information. *Quarterly Journal of Experimental Psychology, 60*, 976–990.

Kay, J., & Ellis, A.W. (1987). A cognitive neuropsychological case study of anomia: Implications for psychological models of word retrieval. *Brain, 110*, 613–629.

Kay, K.N., Naselaris, T., Prenger, R.J., & Gallant, J.L. (2008). Identifying natural images from human brain activity. *Nature, 452*, 352–355.

Kazmerski, V.A., Blasko, D.G., & Dessalegn, B.G. (2003). ERP and behavioural evidence of individual differences in metaphor comprehension. *Memory & Cognition, 31*, 673–689.

Keane, M. (1987). On retrieving analogues when solving problems. *Quarterly Journal of Experimental Psychology, 39A*, 29–41.

Keane, M.M., Gabrieli, J.D.E., Mapstone, H.C., Johnson, K.A., & Corkin, S. (1995). Double dissociation of memory capacities after bilateral occipital-lobe or medial temporal-lobe lesions. *Brain, 118*, 1129–1148.

Keenan, J.P., & Gorman, J. (2007). The causal role of the right hemisphere in self-awareness: It is the brain that is selective. *Cortex, 43*, 1074–1082.

Kellogg, R.T. (1988). Attentional overload and writing performance: Effects of rough draft and outline strategies. *Journal of Experimental Psychology: Learning, Memory, & Cognition, 14*, 355–365.

Kellogg, R.T. (1994). *The psychology of writing.* Oxford: Oxford University Press.

Kellogg, R.T. (1995). *Cognitive psychology.* Thousand Oaks, CA: Sage.

Kellogg, R.T. (1996). A model of working memory in writing. In C.M. Levy & S.E. Ransdell (Eds.), *The science of writing: Theories, methods, individual differences and applications* (pp. 57–71). Mahwah, NJ: Erlbaum.

Kellogg, R.T. (2001a). Long-term working memory in text production. *Memory & Cognition, 29*, 43–52.

Kellogg, R.T. (2001b). Competition for working memory among writing processes. *American Journal of Psychology*, *114*, 175–191.

Kellogg, R.T. (2008). Training writing skills: A cognitive developmental perspective. *Journal of Writing Research*, *1*, 1–26.

Kellogg, R.T., & Mueller, S. (1993). Performance amplification and process restructuring in computer-based writing. *International Journal of Man–Machine Studies*, *39*, 33–49.

Kellogg, R.T., Olive, T., & Piolat, A. (2007). Verbal, visual, and spatial working memory in written language production. *Acta Psychologica*, *124*, 382–297.

Kelly, A.M.C., & Garavan, H. (2005). Human functional neuroimaging of brain changes associated with practice. *Cerebral Cortex*, *15*, 1089–1102.

Kelly, S.W. (2003). A consensus in implicit learning? *Quarterly Journal of Experimental Psychology*, *56A*, 1389–1391.

Kempton, W. (1986). Two theories of home heat control. *Cognitive Science*, *10*, 75–91.

Kenealy, P.M. (1997). Mood-state-dependent retrieval: The effects of induced mood on memory reconsidered. *Quarterly Journal of Experimental Psychology*, *50A*, 290–317.

Kennedy, A., & Pynte, J. (2008). The consequences of violations to reading order: An eye-movement analysis. *Vision Research*, *48*, 2309–2320.

Kennedy, A., Pynte, J., & Ducrot, S. (2002). Parafovealon-foveal interactions in word recognition. *Quarterly Journal of Experimental Psychology*, *55A*, 1307–1338.

Keren, G., & Teigen, K.H. (2004). Yet another look at the heuristics and biases approach. In D. Koehler & N. Harvey (Eds.), *Blackwell handbook of judgment and decision making.* Oxford: Blackwell.

Kermer, D.A., Driver-Linn, E., Wilson, T.D., & Gilbert, D.T. (2006). Loss aversion is an affective forecasting error. *Psychological Science*, *17*, 649–653.

Kershaw, T.C., & Ohlsson, S. (2004). Multiple causes of difficulty in insight: The case of the nine-dot problem. *Journal of Experimental Psychology: Learning, Memory, & Cognition*, *30*, 3–13.

Keysar, B., & Henly, A.S. (2002). Speakers' overestimation of their effectiveness. *Psychological Science*, *13*, 207–212.

Keysar, B., Barr, D.J., Balin, J.A., & Brauner, J.S. (2000). Taking perspective in conversation: The role of mutual knowledge in comprehension. *Psychological Science*, *11*, 32–38.

Kiefer, N., & Brendel, D. (2006). Attentional modulation of unconscious "automatic" processes: Evidence from event-related potentials in a masking priming paradigm. *Journal of Cognitive Neuroscience*, *18*, 184–198.

Kilpatrick, F.P., & Ittelson, W.H. (1953). The size–distance invariance hypothesis. *Psychological Review*, *60*, 223–231.

Kim, C.Y., & Blake, R. (2005). Psychophysical magic: Rendering the visible 'invisible'. *Trends in Cognitive Sciences*, *9*, 381–388.

Kim, P.Y., & Mayhorn, C.B. (2008). Exploring students' prospective memory inside and outside the lab. *American Journal of Psychology*, *121*, 241–254.

Kimchi, R., & Hadad, B.S. (2002). Influence of past experience on perceptual grouping. *Psychological Science*, *13*, 41–47.

Kimchi, R., & Peterson, M.A. (2008). Figure-ground segmentation can occur without attention. *Psychological Science*, *19*, 660–668.

Kingdom, F.A.A. (2003). Colour brings relief to human vision. *Nature Neuroscience*, *6*, 641–644.

Kintsch, W. (1988). The role of knowledge in discourse comprehension: A construction–integration model. *Psychological Review*, *95*, 163–182.

Kintsch, W. (1992). A cognitive architecture for comprehension. In H.L. Pick, P. van den Broek, & D.C. Knill (Eds.), Cognition: Conceptual and methodological issues. Washington, DC. American Psychological Association.

Kintsch, W. (1998). *Comprehension: A paradigm for cognition.* New York: Cambridge University Press.

Kintsch, W. (2000). Metaphor comprehension: A computational theory. *Psychonomic Bulletin & Review*, *7*, 257–266.

Kintsch, W., & Keenan, J.M. (1973). Reading rate and retention as a function of the number of propositions in the base structure of sentences. *Cognitive Psychology*, *5*, 257–274.

Kintsch, W., Welsch, D., Schmalhofer, F., & Zinny, S. (1990). Sentence memory: A theoretical analysis. *Journal of Memory and Language*, *29*, 133–159.

Klauer, K.C., Musch, J., & Naumer, B. (2000). On belief bias in syllogistic reasoning. *Psychological Review*, *107*, 852–884.

Klauer, K.C., & Zhao, Z. (2004). Double dissociations in visual and spatial short-term memory. *Journal of Experimental Psychology: General*, *133*, 355–381.

Klayman, J., & Ha, Y.-W. (1987). Confirmation, disconfirmation, and information in hypothesis testing. *Psychological Review*, *94*, 211–228.

Klein, G. (1998). *Sources of power: How people make decisions.* Cambridge, MA: MIT Press.

Klein, G. (2001). The fiction of optimization. In G. Gigerenzer & R. Selten (Eds.), *Bounded rationality: The adaptive toolbox.* Cambridge, MA: MIT Press.

Klein, I., Dubois, J., Mangin, J.-F., Kherif, F., Flandin, G., Poline, J.-B., Denis, M., Kosslyn, S.M., Lebihan, D. (2004). Retinotopic organisation of visual mental images as revealed by functional magnetic resonance imaging. *Cognitive Brain Research, 22,* 26–31.

Kliegl, R. (2007). Toward a perceptual-span theory of distributed processing in reading: A reply to Rayner, Pollatsek, Drieghe, Slattery, and Reichle (2007). *Journal of Experimental Psychology: General, 136,* 530–537.

Knauff, M., Fangmeier, T., Ruff, C.C., & Johnson-Laird, P.N. (2003). Reasoning, models, and images: Behavioural measures and cortical activity. *Journal of Cognitive Neuroscience, 15,* 559–573.

Knoblich, G., Ohlsson, S., Haider, H., & Rhenius, D. (1999). Constraint relaxation and chunk decomposition in insight. *Journal of Experimental Psychology: Learning, Memory, & Cognition, 25,* 1534–1555.

Knoblich, G., Ohlsson, S., & Raney, G.E. (2001). An eye movement study of insight problem solving. *Memory & Cognition, 29,* 1000–1009.

Knowlton, B.J., & Foerde, K. (2008). Neural representations of non-declarative memories. *Current Directions in Psychological Science, 17,* 107–111.

Knowlton, B.J., Ramus, S.J., & Squire, L.R. (1992). Intact artificial grammar learning in amnesia: Dissociation of category-level knowledge and explicit memory for specific instances. *Psychological Science, 3,* 172–179.

Koch, C., & Tsuchiya, N. (2007). Attention and consciousness: Two distinct brain processes. *Trends in Cognitive Sciences, 11,* 16–22.

Koehler, J.J. (1996). The base rate fallacy reconsidered: Descriptive, normative, and methodological challenges. *Behavioral & Brain Sciences, 19,* 1–17.

Koffka, K. (1935). *Principles of Gestalt psychology.* New York: Harcourt Brace.

Köhler, W. (1925). *The mentality of apes.* New York: Harcourt Brace & World.

Köhler, S., & Moscovitch, M. (1997). Unconscious visual processing in neuropsychological syndromes: A survey of the literature and evaluation of models of consciousness. In M.D. Rugg (Ed.), *Cognitive Neuroscience.* Hove, UK: Psychology Press.

Köhnken, G., Milne, R., Memon, A., & Bull, R. (1999). The cognitive interview: A meta-analysis. *Psychology of Crime Law, 5,* 3–27.

Konen, C.S., & Kastner, S. (2008). Two hierarchically organised neural systems for object information in human visual cortex. *Nature Neuroscience, 11,* 224–231.

Koole, S. (2009). The psychology of emotion regulation: An integrative review. *Cognition & Emotion, 23,* 4–41.

Koriat, A., & Goldsmith, M. (1996). Memory metaphors and the real-life/laboratory controversy: Correspondence versus storehouse conceptions of memory. *Behavioral & Brain Sciences, 19,* 167–188.

Kosslyn, S.M. (1994). *Image and brain: The resolution of the imagery debate.* Cambridge, MA: MIT Press.

Kosslyn, S.M. (2005). Mental images and the brain. *Cognitive Neuropsychology, 22,* 333–347.

Kosslyn, S.M., & Thompson, W.L. (2003). When is early visual cortex activated during visual mental imagery? *Psychological Bulletin, 129,* 723–746.

Kosslyn, S.M., Pascual-Leone, A., Felician, O., Camposano, S., Keenan, J.P., Thompson, W.L. et al. (1999). The role of Area 17 in visual imagery: Convergent evidence from PET and rTMS. *Science, 284,* 167–170.

Kounios, J., Frymiare, J., Bowden, E., Fleck, J., Subramaniam, K., Parrish, T., & Jung-Beeman, M. (2006). The prepared mind: Neural activity prior to problem presentation predicts subsequent solution by sudden insight. *Psychological Science, 17,* 882–890.

Kourtzi, Z., & Kanwisher, N. (2000). Activation in human MT/MST by static imagaes with implied motion. *Journal of Cognitive Neuroscience, 12,* 48–55.

Kourtzi, Z., Krekelberg, B., & van Wezel, R.J.A. (2008). Linking form and motion in the primate brain. *Trends in Cognitive Sciences, 12,* 230–236.

Kozlowski, L.T., & Cutting, J.E. (1977). Recognising sex of a walker from a dynamic point-light display. *Perception & Psychophysics, 21,* 575–580.

Kraft, J.M., & Brainard, D.H. (1999). Mechanisms of colour constancy under nearly natural viewing. *Proceedings of the National Academy of Sciences, USA, 96,* 307–312.

Kraljic, T., & Brennan, S.E. (2005). Prosodic disambiguation of syntactic structure: For the speaker or for the addressee? *Cognitive Psychology, 50,* 194–231.

Krams, M., Rushworth, M., Deiber, M.P., Frackowiak, R., & Passingham, R. (1998). The preparation, execution, and suppression of copied movements in the human brain. *Experimental Brain Research, 120,* 386–398.

Krauss, S., & Wang, X.T. (2003). The psychology of the Monty Hall problem: Discovering psychological mechanisms for solving a tenacious brain teaser. *Journal of Experimental Psychology: General, 132,* 3–22.

Krawczyk, D.C., Morrison, R.G., Viskontas, I., Holyoak, K.J., Chow, T.W., Mendez, M.F., et al. (2008). Distraction during relational reasoning: The role of prefrontal cortex in interference control. *Neuropsychologia, 46*, 2020–2032.

Kroger, J.K., Sabb, F.W., Fales, C.L., Bookheimer, S.Y., Cohen, M.S., & Holyoak, K.J. (2002). Recruitment of anterior dorsolateral prefrontal cortex in human reasoning: A parametric study of relational complexity. *Cerebral Cortex, 12*, 477–485.

Króliczak, G., Heard, P., Goodale, M.A., & Gregory, R.L. (2006). Dissociation of perception and action unmasked by the hollow-face illusion. *Brain Research, 1080*, 9–16.

Kruglanski, A.W., & Orehek, E. (2007). Partitioning the domain of social inference: Dual mode and systems models and their alternatives. *Annual Review of Psychology, 58*, 291–316.

Krupinsky, E.A., Tillack, A.A., Richter, L., Henderson, J.T., Bhattacharyya, A.K., Scott, K.M., et al. (2006). Eye-movement study and human performance using telepathology and differences with experience. *Human Pathology, 37*, 1543–1556.

Krynski, T.R., & Tenenbaum, J.B. (2007). The role of causality in judgement under uncertainty. *Journal of Experimental Psychology: General, 136*, 430–450.

Kuchenbecker, J.A., Sahay, M., Tait, D.M., Neitz, M., & Neitz, J. (2008). Topography of the long- to middle-wavelength sensitive cone ratio in the human retina assessed with a wide-field colour multi-focal electroretinogram. *Visual Neuroscience, 25*, 301–306.

Kuhl, B.A., Kahn, I., Dudukovic, N.M., & Wagner, N.M. (2008). Overcoming suppression in order to remember: Contributions from anterior cingulated and ventrolateral prefrontal cortex. *Cognitive Affective and Behavioral Neruroscience, 8*, 211–221.

Kuhn, D. (1991). *The skills of argumentation.* Cambridge: Cambridge University Press.

Kuhn, G., Amlani, A.A., & Rensink, R.A. (2008). Towards a science of magic. *Trends in Cognitive Sciences, 12*, 349–354.

Kuiper, K. (1996). *Smooth talkers.* Mahwah, NJ: Lawrence Erlbaum Associates Inc.

Kulatunga-Moruzi, C., Brooks, L.R., & Norman, G.R. (2004). Using comprehensive feature lists to bias medical diagnosis. *Journal of Experimental Psychology: Learning, Memory and Cognition, 30*, 563–572.

Kundel, H.L., Nodine, C.F., Conant, E.F., & Weinstein, S.P. (2007). Holistic component of image perception in mammogram interpretation: Gaze-tracking study. *Radiology, 242*, 396–402.

Künnapas, T.M. (1968). Distance perception as a function of available visual cues. *Journal of Experimental Psychology, 77*, 523–529.

Kuppens, P., & van Mechelen, I. (2007). Interactional appraisal models for the anger appraisals of threatened self-esteem, other-blame, and frustration. *Cognition and Emotion, 21*, 56–77.

Kuppens, P., van Mechelen, I, Smits, D.J.M., & De Boeck, P. (2003). The appraisal basis of anger: Specificity, necessity and sufficiency of components. *Emotion, 3*, 254–269.

Kurtz, K.J., & Loewenstein, J. (2007). Converging on a new role for analogy in problem solving and retrieval: When two problems are better than one. *Memory & Cognition, 35*, 334–341.

Kusunoki, M., Moutoussis, K., & Zeki, S. (2006). Effect of background colours on the tuning of colour-selective cells in monkey area V4. *Journal of Neurophysiology, 95*, 3047–3059.

Kvavilashvili, L., & Ellis, J. (2004). Ecological validity and twenty years of real-life/laboratory controversy in memory research: A critical (and historical) review. *History and Philosophy of Psychology, 6*, 59–80.

Kvavilashvili, L., & Fisher, L. (2007). Is time-based prospective remembering mediated by self-initiated rehearsals? Role of incidental cues, ongoing activity, age, and motivation. *Journal of Experimental Psychology: General, 136*, 112–132.

LaBar, K.S., et al. (2005). *The phenomenology of autobiographical recall: Neural correlates of emotional intensity and reliving.* Abstract from programme of the Society for Neuroscience online (http://sfn.scholarone.com).

LaBerge, D. (1983). The spatial extent of attention to letters and words. *Journal of Experimental Psychology: Human Perception & Performance, 9*, 371–379.

LaBerge, D., & Buchsbaum, J.L. (1990). Positron emission tomography measurements of pulvinar activity during an attention task. *Journal of Neuroscience, 10*, 613–619.

Lachter, J., Forster, K.I., & Ruthruff, E. (2004). Forty-five years after Broadbent: Still no identification without attention. *Psychological Review, 111*, 880–913.

Lacquaniti, F., Carozzo, M., & Borghese, N. (1993). The role of vision in tuning anticipatory motor responses of the limbs. In A. Berthoz (Ed.), *Multisensory control of movement.* Oxford: Oxford University Press.

Ladefoged, P. (2001). *Vowels and consonants: An introduction to the sounds of languages.* Oxford: Blackwell.

Lai, C.S.L., Fisher, S.E., Hurst, J.A., Vargha-Khadem, E., & Monaco, A.P. (2001). A forkhead-domain gene is mutated in a severe speech and language disorder. *Nature, 413*, 519–523.

Laird, D.A. (1935). What can you do with your nose? *Scientific Monthly, 41*, 126–130.

Laloyaux, C., Destrebecqz, A., & Cleeremans, A. (2006). Implicit change identification: A replication of Fernandez-Duque and Thornton (2003). *Journal of Experimental Psychology: Human Perception and Performance, 32*, 1366–1379.

Lambon Ralph, M.A., Moriarty, L., & Sage, K. (2002). Anomia is simply a reflection of semantic and phonological impairments: Evidence from a case-series study. *Aphasiology, 16*, 56–82.

Lamme, V.A.F. (2003). Why visual attention and awareness are different. *Trends in Cognitive Sciences, 7*, 12–18.

Lamme, V.A.F. (2006). Towards a true neural stance on consciousness. *Trends in Cognitive Sciences, 10*, 494–501.

Land, E.H. (1977). The retinex theory of colour vision. *Scientific American, 237*, 108–128.

Land, E.H. (1986). Recent advances in retinex theory. *Vision Research, 26*, 7–21.

Land, M.F., & Lee, D.N. (1994). Where we look when we steer. *Nature, 369*, 742–744.

Landman, R., Spekreijse, H., & Lamme, V.A.F. (2003). Large capacity storage of integrated objects before change blindness. *Vision Research, 43*, 149–164.

Larsen, J.D., Baddeley, A., & Andrade, J. (2000). Phonological similarity and the irrelevant speech effect: Implications for models of short-term memory. *Memory, 8*, 145–157.

Latour, P.L. (1962). Visual threshold during eye movements. *Vision Research, 2*, 261–262.

Lau, H.C., & Passingham, R.E. (2006). Relative blindsight in normal observers and the neural correlate of visual consciousness. *Proceedings of the National Academy of Sciences, 103*, 18763–18768.

Laurent, J.-P., Denhières, G., Passerieux, C., Iakimova, G., & Hardy-Baylé, M.-C. (2006). On understanding idiomatic language: The salience hypothesis assessed by ERPs. *Brain Research, 1068*, 151–160.

Lavie, N. (1995). Perceptual load as a necessary condition for selective attention. *Journal of Experimental Psychology: Human Perception and Performance, 21*, 451–648.

Lavie, N. (2005). Distracted and confused? Selective attention under load. *Trends in Cognitive Sciences, 9*, 75–82.

Lazarus, R.S. (1966). *Psychological stress and the coping process*. New York: McGraw Hill.

Lazarus, R.S. (1982). Thoughts on the relations between emotion and cognition. *American Psychologist, 37*, 1019–1024.

Lazarus, R.S. (1991). *Emotion and adaptation*. Oxford: Oxford University Press.

Leake, J. (1999). Scientists teach chimpanzees to speak English. *Sunday Times*.

LeDoux, J.E. (1992). Emotion as memory: Anatomical systems underlying indelible neural traces. In S.-A. Christianson (Ed.), *The handbook of emotion and memory: Research and theory*. Hillsdale, NJ: Lawrence Erlbaum Associates Inc.

LeDoux, J.E. (1996). *The emotional brain: The mysterious underpinnings of emotional life*. New York: Simon & Schuster.

Lee, A.C.H., Graham, K.S., Simons, J.S., Hodges, J.R., Owen, A.M., & Patterson, K. (2002). Regional brain activations differ for semantic features but not for categories. *NeuroReport, 13*, 1497–1501.

Lee, D.N. (1976). A theory of visual control of braking based on information about time-to-collision. *Perception, 5*, 437–459.

Lee, H.W., Hong, S.B., Seo, D.W., Tae, W.S., & Hong, S.C. (2000). Mapping of functional organisation in human visual cortex: Electrical cortical stimulation. *Neurology, 54*, 849–854.

Leek, E.C. Reppa, I., & Tipper, S.P. (2003). Inhibition of return for objects and locations in static displays. *Perception & Psychophysics, 65*, 388–395.

Legrenzi, P., Girotto, V., & Johnson-Laird, P.N. (2003). Models of consistency. *Psychological Science, 14*, 131–137.

Lehle, C., Steinhauser, M., & Hubner, R. (2009). Serial or parallel processing in dual tasks: What is more effortful? *Psychophysiology, 46*, 502–509.

Leichtman, M.D., Wang, Q., & Pillemer, D.B. (2003). Cultural variations in interdependence and autobiographical memory: Lessons from Korea, China, India, and the United States. In R. Fivush & C.A. Haden (Eds.), *Autobiographical Memory and the Construction of a Narrative Self: Developmental and Cultural Perspectives* (pp. 73–98). Mahwah, NJ: Lawrence Erlbaum Associates.

Lenneberg, E.H. (1962). Understanding language without ability to speak: A case report. *Journal of Abnormal and Social Psychology, 65*, 419–425.

Lennie, P. (1998). Single units and visual cortical organisation. *Perception, 27*, 889–935.

Leonards, U., Sunaert, S., Van Hecke, P., & Orban, G.A. (2000). Attention mechanisms in visual search – an fMRI study. *Journal of Cognitive NeuroScience, 12*, 61–75.

Leopold, D.A., & Logothetis, N.K. (1999). Multi-stable phenomena: Changing views in perception. *Trends in Cognitive Sciences, 3*, 254–264.

Lerner, J.S., Gonzalez, R.M., Small, D.A., & Fischhoff, B. (2005). Effects of fear and and anger on perceived risks of terrorism: A national field experiment. In S. Wessely & V.N. Krasnov (Eds.), *Psychological responses to the new terrorism: A NATO–Russia dialogue*. Amsterdam: IOS Press.

Levelt, W.J.M. (1989). *Speaking: From intention to articulation*. Cambridge, MA: MIT Press.

Levelt, W.J.M., Roelofs, A., & Meyer, A.S. (1999a). A theory of lexical access in speech production. *Behavioral and Brain Sciences, 22*, 1–38.

Levelt, W.J.M., Schriefers, H., Vorberg, D., Meyer, A.S., Pechmann, T., & Havinga, J. (1991). Normal and deviant lexical processing: Reply to Dell and O'Seaghda (1991). *Psychological Review, 98*, 615–618.

Levin, D.T., & Simons, D.J. (1997). Failure to detect changes to attended objects in motion pictures. *Psychonomic Bulletin and Review, 4*, 501–506.

Levin, D.T., Drivdahl, S.B., Momen, N., & Beck, M.R. (2002). False predictions about the detectability of visual changes: The role of beliefs about attention, memory, and the continuity of attended objects in causing change blindness blindness. *Consciousness and Cognition, 11*, 507–527.

Levine, D.N., Calvanio, R., & Popovics, A. (1982). Language in the absence of inner speech. *Word, 15*, 19–44.

Levy, B.J., & Anderson, M.C. (2008). Individual differences in the suppression of unwanted memories: The executive deficit hypothesis. *Acta Psychologica, 127*, 623–635.

Levy, C.M., & Ransdell, S.E. (1995). Is writing as difficult as it seems? *Memory & Cognition, 23*, 767–779.

Levy, C.M., & Ransdell, S. (2001). Writing with concurrent memory loads. In T. Olive & C.M. Levy (Eds.), *Contemporary tools and techniques for studying writing*. Dordrecht: Kluwer Academic Publishers.

Levy, D.A., Stark, C.E.L., & Squire, L.R. (2004). Intact conceptual priming in the absence of declarative memory. *Psychological Science, 15*, 680–686.

Levy, J., Pashler, H., & Boer, E. (2006). Central interference in driving: Is there any stopping the psychological refractory period? *Psychological Science, 17*, 228–235.

Lewinsohn, P.M., Joiner, T.E., Jr., & Rohde, P. (2001). Evaluation of cognitive diathesis–stress models in predicting major depressive disorder in adolescents. *Journal of Abnormal Psychology, 110*, 203–215.

Lewis, M., & Brooks-Gunn, J. (1979). Toward a theory of social cognition: The development of self. *New Directions for Child Development, 4*, 1–20.

Lewis, P.A., Critchley, H.D., Smith, A.P., & Dolan, R.J. (2005). Brain mechanisms for mood congruent memory facilitation. *NeuroImage, 25*, 1214–1223.

Liberman, A.M., Cooper, F.S., Shankweiler, D.S., & Studdert-Kennedy, M. (1967). Perception of the speech code. *Psychological Review, 74*, 431–461.

Liberman, A.M., Delattre, P.C., & Cooper, F.S. (1952). The role of selected stimulus variables in the perception of the unvoiced stop consonants. *American Journal of Psychology, 65*, 497–516.

Libet, B. (1996). Neural processes in the production of conscious experience. In M. Velmans (Ed.), *The science of consciousness: Psychological, neuropsychological and clinical reviews*. London: Routledge.

Libet, B., Gleason, C.A., Wright, E.W., & Pearl, D.K. (1983). Time of conscious intention to act in relation to onset of cerebral activity (readiness potential): The unconscious initiation of a freely voluntary act. *Brain, 106*, 623–642.

Lichten, W., & Lurie, S. (1950). A new technique for the study of perceived size. *American Journal of Psychology, 63*, 280–282.

Lichtenstein, S., Slovic, P., Fischhoff, B., Layman, M., & Coombs, J. (1978). Judged frequency of lethal events. *Journal of Experimental Psychology: Human Learning and Memory, 4*, 551–578.

Lieberman, P. (1963). Some effects of semantic and grammatical context on the production and perception of speech. *Language & Speech, 6*, 172–187.

Lief, H., & Fetkewicz, J. (1995). Retractors of false memories: The evolution of pseudo-memories. *The Journal of Psychiatry & Law, 23*, 411–436.

Lien, M.C., Ruthruff, E., & Johnston, J.C. (2006). Attentional limitations in doing two tasks at once – The search for exceptions. *Current Directions in Psychological Science, 15*, 89–93.

Likova, L.T., & Tyler, C.W. (2008). Occipital network for figure/ground organisation. *Experimental Brain Research, 189*, 257–267.

Lindholm, T., & Christianson, S.-A. (1998). Intergroup biases and eyewitness testimony. *Journal of Social Psychology, 138*, 710–723.

Lindsay, D.S., Allen, B.P., Chan, J.C.K., & Dahl, L.C. (2004). Eyewitness suggestibility and source similarity: Intrusions of details from one event into memory reports of another event. *Journal of Memory and Language, 50*, 96–111.

Lindsay, R.C.L., & Harvie, V. (1988). Hits, false alarms, correct and mistaken identifications:

The effects of method of data collection on facial memory. In M. Grunberg, P. Morris, & R. Sykes (Eds.), *Practical Aspects of Memory: Current Research and Issues, Vol. 1: Memory in Everyday Life* (pp. 47–52). Chichester, UK: Wiley.

List, A., & Robertson, L.C. (2007). Inhibition of return and object-based attentional selection. *Journal of Experimental Psychology: Human Perception and Performance, 33*, 1322–1334.

Liu, G., Chua, R., & Enns, J.T. (2008). Attention for perception and action: Task interference for action planning, but not for online control. *Experimental Brain Research, 185*, 709–717.

Lockhart, R.S., & Craik, F.I.M. (1990). Levels of processing: A retrospective commentary on a framework for memory research. *Canadian Journal of Psychology, 44*, 87–112.

Loewenstein, G., Rick, S., & Cohen, J.D. (2008). Neuroeconomics. *Annual Review of Psychology, 59*, 647–672.

Loftus, E.F., & Palmer, J.C. (1974). Reconstruction of automobile destruction: An example of the interaction between language and memory. *Journal of Verbal Learning & Verbal Behavior, 13*, 585–589.

Loftus, E.F., Loftus, G.R., & Messo, J. (1987). Some facts about "weapons focus". *Law and Human Behavior, 11*, 55–62.

Logan, G.D. (1988). Toward an instance theory of automatisation. *Psychological Review, 95*, 492–527.

Logan, G.D., Taylor, S.E., & Etherton, J.L. (1996). Attention in the acquisition and expression of automaticity. *Journal of Experimental Psychology: Learning, Memory, & Cognition, 22*, 620–638.

Logan, G.D., Taylor, S.E., & Etherton, J.L. (1999). Attention and automaticity: Toward a theoretical integration. *Psychological Research, 62*, 165–181.

Logie, R.H. (1995). *Visuo-spatial working memory*. Hove, UK: Psychology Press.

Logie, R.H. (1999). State of the art: Working memory. *The Psychologist, 12*, 174–178.

Logie, R.H., & van der Meulen, M. (2009). Fragmenting and integrating visuo-spatial working memory. In J.R. Brockmole (Ed.), *Representing the Visual World in Memory*. Hove, UK: Psychology Press.

Logie, R.H., Baddeley, A.D., Mane, A., Donchin, E., & Sheptak, R. (1989). Working memory and the analysis of a complex skill by secondary task methodology. *Acta Psychologica, 71*, 53–87.

Logie, R.H., Cocchini, G., Della Sala, S., & Baddeley, A. (2004). Is there a specific capacity for dual task co-ordination? Evidence from Alzheimer's Disease. *Neuropsychology, 18*, 504–513.

Logie, R.H., Venneri, A., Della Sala, S., Redpath, T.W., & Marshall, I. (2003). Brain activation and the phonological loop: The impact of rehearsal. *Brain and Cognition, 53*, 293–296.

Logothetis, N.K. (2007). The ins and outs of fMRI signals. *Nature Neuroscience, 10*, 1230–1232.

Logothetis, N.K., Pauls, J., Augath, M., Trinath, T., & Oelterman, A. (2001). Neurophysiological investigation of the basis of the fMRI signal. *Nature, 412*, 150–157.

López-Moliner, J., Field, D.T., & Wann, J.P. (2007). Interceptive timing: Prior knowledge matters. *Journal of Vision, 11*, 1–8.

Lorteije, J.A.M., Kenemans, J.C., Jellema, T., van der Lubbe, R.H.J., Lommers, M.W., & van Wright, R.J.A. (2007). Adaptation to real motion reveals direction-selective interactions between real and implicit motion processing. *Journal of Cognitive Neuroscience, 19*, 1231–1240.

Losier, B.J.W., & Klein, R.M. (2001). A review of the evidence for a disengagement deficit following parietal lobe damage. *Neuroscience and Biobehavioral Reviews, 25*, 1–13.

Lucas, M. (1999). Context effects in lexical access: A meta-analysis. *Memory & Cognition, 27*, 385–398.

Luchins, A.S. (1942). Mechanisation in problem solving. The effect of Einstellung. *Psychological Monographs, 54*, 248.

Luchins, A.S., & Luchins, E.H. (1959). *Rigidity of behaviour*. Eugene, OR: University of Oregon Press.

Luck, S.J. (1998). Neurophysiology of selective attention. In H. Pashler (Ed.), *Attention*. Hove, UK: Psychology Press.

Lumer, E.D., Friston, K.J., & Rees, G. (1998). Neural correlates of perceptual rivalry in the human brain. *Science, 280*, 1930–1934.

Lundqvist, D., & Öhman, A. (2005). Emotion regulates attention: The relation between facial configurations, facial emotion, and visual attention. *Visual Cognition, 12*, 51–84.

Luo, J., & Knoblich, G. (2007). Studying insight problem solving with neuroscientific methods. *Methods, 42*, 77–86.

Luo, Q., Perry, C., Peng, D. Jin, Z., Xu, D., Ding, G., & Xu, S. (2003). The neural substrate of analogical reasoning: An fMRI study. *Cognitive Brain Research, 17*, 527–534.

Luo, X., Kenyon, R., Kamper, D., Sandin, D., & DeFanti, T. (2007). The effects of scene complexity, stereovision, and motion parallax on size constancy in a virtual environment. *IEEE Virtual Reality, Proceedings* (pp. 59–66).

Luria, A.R. (1976). *Cognitive development: Its cultural and social foundations*. Cambridge, MA: Harvard University Press.

Lustig, C., & Hasher, L. (2001). Implicit memory is not immune to interference. *Psychological Bulletin*, 127, 618–628.

Lustig, C., & Hasher, L. (2001). Implicit memory is not immune to interference. *Psychological Bulletin*, 127, 618–628.

Lustig, C., Konkel, A., & Jacoby, L.L. (2004). Which route to recovery? Controlled retrieval and accessibility bias in retroactive interference. *Psychological Science*, 15, 729–735.

Macaulay, D., & Eich, E. (2002). Implications of the affect infusion model: Conjecture and conflict. *Psychological Inquiry*, 13, 68–70.

MacDermot, K.D., Bonora, E., Sykes, N., Coupe, A.M., Lai, C.S., Vernes, S.C., et al. (2005). Identification of FOXP2 truncation as a novel cause of developmental speech and language deficits. *American Journal of Human Genetics*, 76, 1074–1080.

MacDonald, M.C., Pearlmutter, N.J., & Seidenberg, M.S. (1994). Lexical nature of syntactic ambiguity resolution. *Psychological Review*, 101, 676–703.

MacGregor, J.N., Ormerod, T.C., & Chronicle, E.P. (2001). Information processing and insight: A process model of performance on the nine-dot and related problems. *Journal of Experimental Psychology: Learning, Memory, and Cognition*, 27, 176–201.

Mack, A. (2003). Inattentional blindness: Looking without seeing. *Current Directions in Psychological Science*, 12, 180–184.

Mack, M.L., Gauthier, I., Sadr, J., & Palmeri, T.J. (2008). Object detection and basic-level categorization: Sometimes you know it is there before you know what it is. *Psychonomic Bulletin & Review*, 15, 28–35.

Mackay, D.G., James, L.E., Taylor, J.K., & Marian, D.E. (2007). Amnesic HM exhibits parallel deficits and sparing in language and memory: Systems versus binding theory accounts. *Language and Cognitive Processes*, 22, 377–452.

Mackintosh, N.J. (1998). *IQ and human intelligence*. Oxford: Oxford University Press.

MacLeod, C., Rutherford, E., Campbell, L., Ebsworthy, G., & Holker, L. (2002). Selective attention and emotional vulnerability: Assessing the causal basis of their association through the experimental manipulation of attentional bias. *Journal of Abnormal Psychology*, 111, 107–123.

Macoir, J., & Bernier, J. (2002). Is surface dysgraphia tied to semantic impairment? Evidence from a case of semantic dementia. *Brain and Cognition*, 48, 452–457.

MacPherson, S.E., Della Sala, S., Logie, R.H., & Wilcock, G.K. (2007). Specific AD impairment in concurrent performance of two memory tasks. *Cortex*, 43, 858–865.

Madison, P. (1956). Freud's repression concept: A survey and attempted clarification. *International Journal of Psychoanalysis*, 37, 75–81.

Magnuson, J.S., Tanenhaus, M.K., & Aslin, R.N. (2008). Immediate effects of form-class constraints on spoken word recognition. *Cognition*, 108, 866–873.

Maier, N.R.F. (1931). Reasoning in humans II: The solution of a problem and its appearance in consciousness. *Journal of Comparative Psychology*, 12, 181–194.

Majerus, S., Poncelet, M., Elsen, B., & van der Linden, M. (2006). Exploring the relationship between new word learning and short-term memory for serial order recall, item recall, and item recognition. *European Journal of Cognitive Psychology*, 18, 848–873.

Malone, D.R., Morris, H.H., Kay, M.C., & Levin, H.S. (1982). Prosopagnosia: A double dissocation between the recognition of familiar and unfamiliar faces. *Journal of Neurology, Neurosurgery, & Psychiatry*, 45, 820–822.

Malpass, R.S. (2006). A policy evaluation of simultaneous and sequential lineups. *Psychology, Public Policy, and Law*, 12, 394–418.

Mandel, D.R. (2005). Are risk assessments of a terrorist attack coherent? *Journal of Experimental Psychology: Applied*, 11, 277–288.

Mandler, G. (1980). Recognizing – the judgment of previous occurrence. *Psychological Review*, 87, 252–271.

Manktelow, K.I. (1999). *Reasoning and thinking*. Hove, UK: Psychology Press.

Manns, J.R., Hopkins, R.O., & Squire, L.R. (2003). Semantic memory and the human hippocampus. *Neuron*, 38, 127–133.

Marcus, S.L., & Rips, L.J. (1979). Conditional reasoning. *Journal of Verbal Learning & Verbal Behavior*, 18, 199–233.

Marian, V., & Kaushanskaya, M. (2007). Language context guides memory content. *Psychonomic Bulletin & Review*, 14, 925–933.

Marian, V., & Neisser, U. (2000). Language-dependent recall of autobiographical memories. *Journal of Experimental Psychology: General*, 129, 361–368.

Marques, J.F., Canessa, N., Siri, S., Catricala, E., & Cappa, S. (2008). Conceptual knowledge in the brain: fMRI evidence for a featural organization. *Brain Research*, 1194, 90–99.

Marr, D. (1982). *Vision: A computational investigation into the human representation and processing of visual information*. San Francisco, CA: W.H. Freeman.

Mars, F. (2008). Driving around bends with manipulated eye-steering co-ordination. *Journal of Vision*, 8, 1–11.

Marsh, E.J. (2007). Retelling is not the same as recalling – Implications for memory. *Current Directions in Psychological Science*, 16, 16–20.

Marsh, E.J., & Tversky, B. (2004). Spinning the stories of our lives. *Applied Cognitive Psychology*, 18, 491–503.

Marsh, R.L., & Hicks, J.L. (1998). Event-based prospective memory and executive control of working memory. *Journal of Experimental Psychology: Learning, Memory & Cognition*, 24, 336–349.

Marsh, R.L., Hicks, J.L., & Landau, J.D. (1998). An investigation of everyday prospective memory. *Memory & Cognition*, 26, 633–643.

Marshall, J. (2006). Jargon aphasia: What have we learned? *Aphasiology*, 20, 387–410.

Marshall, J., Robson, J., Pring, T., & Chiat, S. (1998). Why does monitoring fail in jargon aphasia? *Brain and Language*, 63, 79–107.

Marshall, J.C., & Halligan, P.W. (1988). Blindsight and insight in visuo-spatial neglect. *Nature*, 336, 766–767.

Marshall, J.C., & Halligan, P.W. (1994). The yin and yang of visuo-spatial neglect: A case study. *Neuropsychologia*, 32, 1037–1057.

Marslen-Wilson, W. (1984). Function and process in spoken word recognition – A tutorial review. *Attention and Performance*, 10, 125–150.

Marslen-Wilson, W.D. (1990). Activation, competition, and frequency in lexical access. In G.T.M. Altmann (Ed.), *Cognitive models of speech processing: Psycholinguistics and computational perspectives*. Cambridge, MA: MIT Press.

Marslen-Wilson, W.D., & Tyler, L.K. (1980). The temporal structure of spoken language comprehension. *Cognition*, 6, 1–71.

Marslen-Wilson, W., & Warren, P. (1994). Levels of perceptual representation and process in lexical access – Words, phonemes, and features. *Psychological Review*, 101, 653–675.

Martin, A., & Caramazza, A. (2003). Neuropsychological and neuroimaging perspectives on conceptual knowledge: An introduction. *Cognitive Neuropsychology*, 20, 195–221.

Martin, A., & Chao, L.L. (2001). Semantic memory and the brain: Structure and processes. *Current Opinion in Neurobiology*, 11, 194–201.

Martin, R.C. (2003). Language processing: Functional organisation and neuroanatomical basis. *Annual Review of Psychology*, 54, 55–89.

Martin, R.C., Miller, M., & Vu, H. (2004). Lexical-semantic retention and speech production: Further evidence from normal and brain-damaged participants for a phrasal scope of planning. *Cognitive Neuropsychology*, 21, 625–644.

Martinez, A., Anllo-Vento, L., Sereno, M.I., Frank, L.R., Buxton, R.B., Dubowitz, D.J., et al. (1999). Involvement of striate and extrastriate visual cortical areas in spatial attention. *Nature Neuroscience*, 4, 364–369.

Martone, M., Butters, N., Payne, M., Becker, J.T., & Sax, D.S. (1984). Dissociations between skill learning and verbal recognition in amnesia and dementia. *Archives of Neurology*, 41, 965–970.

Marzi, C.A., Girelli, M., Natale, E., & Miniussi, C. (2001). What exactly is extinguished in unilateral visual extinction? *Neuropsychologia*, 39, 1354–1366.

Marzi, C.A., Smania, N., Martini, M.C., Gambina, G., Tomelleri, G., Palamara, A., et al. (1997). Implicit redundant-targets effect in visual extinction. *Neuropsychologia*, 34, 9–22.

Mason, R.A., & Just, M.A. (2004). How the brain processes causal inferences in text. *Psychological Science*, 15, 1–7.

Massaro, D.W. (1994). Psychological aspects of speech perception: Implications for research and theory. In M.A. Gernsbacher (Ed.), *Handbook of psycholinguistics*. San Diego, CA: Academic Press.

Mather, G. (2009). *Foundations of sensation and perception*. Hove, UK: Psychology Press.

Mathews, A. (2004). On the malleability of emotional encoding. *Behaviour Research and Therapy*, 42, 1019–1036.

Mathews, A., & MacLeod, C. (2002). Induced processing biases have causal effects on anxiety. *Cognition and Emotion*, 16, 331–354.

Mathews, A., Ridgeway, V., Cook, E., & Yiend, J. (2007). Inducing a benign interpretational bias reduces trait anxiety. *Journal of Behavior Therapy and Experimental Psychiatry*, 38, 225–236.

Mattingley, J.B., Davis, G., & Driver, J. (1997). Pre-attentive filling-in of visual surfaces in parietal extinction. *Science*, 275, 671–674.

Mattys, S.L. (2004). Stress versus coarticulation: Toward an integrated approach to explicit speech segmentation. *Journal of Experimental Psychology: Human Perception and Performance*, 30, 397–408.

Mattys, S.L., & Liss, J.M. (2008). On building models of spoken-word recognition: When there is as much to learn from natural "oddities" as artificial normality. *Perception & Psychophysics*, 70, 1235–1242.

Mattys, S.L., White, L., & Melhorn, J.F. (2005). Integration of multiple speech segmentation cues: A hierarchical framework. *Journal of Experimental Psychology: General*, 134, 477–500.

Maule, A.J., & Hodgkinson, G.P. (2002). Heuristics, biases and strategic decision making. *The Psychologist*, 15, 69–71.

Mauss, I., & Robinson, M. (2009). Measures of emotion: A review. *Cognition & Emotion*, 23, 209–237.

Mayer, R.E. (1990). Problem solving. In M.W. Eysenck (Ed.), *The Blackwell dictionary of cognitive psychology*. Oxford, UK: Blackwell.

Maylor, E.A., Carter, S.M., & Hallett, E.L. (2002). Preserved olfactory cuing of autobiographical memories in old age. *Journal of Gerontology Series B – Psychological Sciences*, 57, P41–P46.

Mazyn, L.I.N., Savelsbergh, G.J.P., Montagne, G., & Lenoir, M. (2007). Planning and on-line control of catching as a function of perceptual-motor constraints. *Acta Psychologica*, 126, 59–78.

McCandliss, B.D., Cohen, L., & Dehaene, S. (2003). The visual word form area: Expertise for reading in the fusiform gyrus. *Trends in Cognitive Sciences*, 7, 293–299.

McCarthy, R., & Warrington, E.K. (1984). A two-route model of speech production. *Brain*, 107, 463–485.

McClelland, J.L. (1991). Stochastic interactive processes and the effect of context on perception. *Cognitive Psychology*, 23, 1–44.

McClelland, J.L., & Elman, J.L. (1986). The TRACE model of speech perception. *Cognitive Psychology*, 18, 1–86.

McClelland, J.L., & Rumelhart, D.E. (1981). An interactive activation model of context effects in letter perception. Part 1. An account of basic findings. *Psychological Review*, 88, 375–407.

McClelland, J.L., Rumelhart, D.E., & The PDP Research Group (1986). *Parallel distributed processing: Vol. 2. Psychological and biological models*. Cambridge, MA: MIT Press.

McCloskey, M. (2001). The future of cognitive neuropsychology. In B. Rapp (Ed.), *The handbook of cognitive neuropsychology: What deficits reveal about the human mind* (pp. 593–610). Philadelphia: Psychology Press.

McCloskey, M.E., & Glucksberg, S. (1978). Natural categories: Well defined or fuzzy sets? *Memory & Cognition*, 6, 462–472.

McDaniel, M.A., Robinson-Riegler, B., & Einstein, G.O. (1998). Prospective remembering: Perceptually driven or conceptually driven processes? *Memory & Cognition*, 26, 121–134.

McDonald, J.L. (2008). Differences in the cognitive demands of word order, plural, and subject-verb agreement constructions. *Psychonomic Bulletin & Review*, 15, 980–984.

McDonald, S.A., & Shillcock, R.C. (2003). Eye movements reveal the on-line computation of lexical probabilities during reading. *Psychological Science*, 14, 648–652.

McElree, B., & Carrasco, M. (1999). Temporal dynamics of visual search: A speed–accuracy analysis of feature and conjunction searches. *Journal of Experimental Psychology: Human Perception & Performance*, 25, 1517–1539.

McElroy, T., Seta, J.J., & Waring, D.A. (2007). Reflections of the self: How self-esteem determines decision framing and increases risk taking. *Journal of Behavioral Decision Making*, 20, 223–240.

McEvoy, S.P., Stevenson, M.R., & Woodward, M. (2007). The contribution of passengers versus mobile phone use to motor vehicle crashes resulting in hospital attendance. *Accident Analysis and Prevention*, 39, 1170–1176.

McFarland, C., Buehler, R., von Ruti, R., Nguyen, L., & Alvaro, C. (2007). The impact of negative moods on self-enhancing cognitions: The role of reflective versus ruminative mood orientations. *Journal of Personality and Social Psychology*, 93, 728–750.

McGlinchey-Berroth, R., Milber, W.P., Verfaellie, M., Alexander, M., & Kilduff, P.T. (1993). Semantic processing in the neglected visual field: Evidence from a lexical decision task. *Cognitive Neuropsychology*, 10, 79–108.

McGlone, M.S., & Manfredi, D. (2001). Topic–vehicle interaction in metaphor comprehension. *Memory & Cognition*, 29, 1209–1219.

McGregor, S.J., & Howes, A. (2002). The role of attack and defence semantics in skilled players' memory for chess positions. *Memory & Cognition*, 30, 707–717.

McGurk, H., & MacDonald, J. (1976). Hearing lips and seeing voices. *Nature*, 264, 746–748.

McIntosh, A.R., Rajah, M.N., & Lobaugh, N.J. (1999). Interactions of prefrontal cortex in relation to awareness in sensory learning. *Science*, 284, 1531–1533.

McIntyre, J., Zago, M., Berthoz, A., & Lacquaniti, F. (2001). Does the brain model Newton's laws? *Nature Neurosciences*, 4, 693–694.

McKay, A., Davis, C., Savage, G., & Castles, A. (2008). Semantic involvement in reading aloud: Evidence from a nonword training study. *Journal of Experimental Psychology: Learning, Memory & Cognition*, 34, 1495–1517.

McKeefry, D.J., Burton, M.P., Vakrou, C., Barrett, B.T., & Morland, A.B. (2008). Induced deficits in speed perception by transcranial magnetic stimulation of human cortical areas V5/MT and V3A. *Journal of Neuroscience*, 28, 6848–6857.

McKone, E. (2004). Isolating the special component of face recognition: Peripheral identification and a Mooney face. *Journal of Experimental Psychology: Learning, Memory and Cognition*, 30, 181–197.

McKone, E., Kanwisher, N., & Duchaine, B.C. (2007). Can generic expertise explain special processing for faces? *Trends in Cognitive Sciences*, 11, 8–15.

McKoon, G., & Ratcliff, R. (1992). Inference during reading. *Psychological Review*, 99, 440–466.

McLaughlin, K., Remy, M., & Schmidt, H.G. (2008). Is analytic information processing a feature of expertise in medicine? *Advances in Health Sciences Education*, 13, 123–128.

McLeod, P. (1977). A dual-task response modality effect: Support for multiprocessor models of attention. *Quarterly Journal of Experimental Psychology*, 29, 651–667.

McMullen, P.A., Fisk, J.D., Phillips, S.J., & Mahoney, W.J. (2000). Apperceptive agnosia and face recognition. *Neurocase*, 6, 403–414.

McNamara, T.P. (1992). Priming and constraints it places on theories of memory and retrieval. *Psychological Review*, 99, 650–662.

McQueen, J.M. (1991). The influence of the lexicon on phonetic categorisation: Stimulus quality in word-final ambiguity. *Journal of Experimental Psychology: Human Perception & Performance*, 17, 433–443.

McVay, J.C., & Kane, M.J. (2009). Conducting the train of thought: Working memory capacity, goal neglect, and mind wandering in an executive-control task. *Journal of Experimental Psychology: Learning, Memory, and Cognition*, 35, 196–204.

Meacham, J.A., & Singer, J. (1977). Incentive in prospective remembering. *Journal of Psychology*, 97, 191–197.

Meister, I.G., Wilson, S.M., Deblieck, C., Wu, A.D., & Iacoboni, M. (2007). The essential role of premotor cortex in speech perception. *Current Biology*, 17, 1692–1696.

Mellers, B.A., Schwartz, A., & Cooke, A.D.J. (1998). Judgement and decision making. *Annual Review of Psychology*, 49, 447–477.

Melloni, L., Molina, C., Pena, M., Torres, D., Singer, W., & Rodriguez, E. (2007). Synchronisation of neural activity across cortical areas correlates with conscious perception. *Journal of Neuroscience*, 27, 2858–2865.

Mendoza, J.E., Elliott, D., Meegan, D.V., Lyons, J.L., & Welsh, T.N. (2006). The effect of the Müller–Lyer illusion on the planning and control of manual aiming movements. *Journal of Experimental Psychology: Human Perception and Performance*, 32, 413–422.

Merikle, P.M., Smilek, D., & Eastwood, J.D. (2001). Perception without awareness: Perspectives from cognitive psychology. *Cognition*, 79, 115–134.

Metcalfe, J., & Weibe, D. (1987). Intuition in insight and noninsight problem solving. *Memory & Cognition*, 15, 238–246.

Meulemans, T., & Van der Linden, M. (2003). Implicit learning of complex information in amnesia. *Brain and Cognition*, 52, 250–257.

Meyer, A.S., & Damian, M.F. (2007). Activation of distractor names in the picture-picture interference paradigm. *Memory & Cognition*, 35, 494–503.

Meyer, D.E., & Schvaneveldt, R.W. (1971). Facilitation in recognising pairs of words: Evidence of a dependence between retrieval operations. *Journal of Experimental Psychology*, 90, 227–234.

Meyer, D.E., & Schvaneveldt, R.W. (1976). Meaning, memory structure, and mental processes. *Science*, 192, 27–33.

Michael, G.A., & Buron, V. (2005). The human pulvinar and stimulus-driven attentional system. *Behavioral Neuroscience*, 119, 1353–1367.

Michel, F., & Henaff, M.A. (2004). Seeing without the occipito-parietal cortex: Simultagnosia as a shrinkage of the attentional visual field. *Behavioural Neurology*, 15, 3–13.

Miller, G.A. (1956). The magic number seven, plus or minus two: Some limits on our capacity for processing information. *Psychological Review*, 63, 81–93.

Miller, G.A., & McNeill, D. (1969). Psycholinguistics. In G. Lindzey & E. Aronson (Eds.), *The handbook of social psychology, Vol. 3*. Reading, MA: Addison-Wesley.

Milner, A.D., & Goodale, M.A. (1995). *The visual brain in action*. Oxford: Oxford University Press.

Milner, A.D., & Goodale, M.A. (1998). The visual brain in action. *Psyche*, 4, 1–14.

Milner, A.D., & Goodale, M.A. (2006). *The visual brain in action* (2nd ed.). Oxford: Oxford University Press.

Milner, A.D., & Goodale, M.A. (2008). Two visual systems re-viewed. *Neuropsychologia*, 46, 774–785.

Milner, A.D., Dijkerman, H.C., McIntosh, R.D., Rossetti, Y., & Pisella, L. (2003). Delayed reaching and grasping in patients with optic ataxia. *Progress in Brain Research*, 142, 225–242.

Milner, A.D., Perrett, D.I., Johnston, R.S., Benson, P.J., Jordan, T.R., Heeley, D.W., et al. (1991). Perception and action in "visual form agnosia". *Brain*, 114, 405–428.

Milner, B. (1962). Les troubles de la mémoire accompagnant des lésions hippocampiques bilaterales. In P. Passouant (Ed.), *Physiologie de l'hippocampe*. Paris: Centre des Recherches Scientifiques.

Mirman, D., McClelland, J.L., Holt, L.L., & Magnuson, J.S. (2008). Effects of attention on the strength of lexical influences on speech perception: Behavioural experiments and computational mechanisms. *Cognitive Science, 32,* 398–417.

Mitchell, D.B. (2006). Nonconscious priming after 17 years. *Psychological Science, 17,* 925–929.

Mitroff, I. (1974). *The subjective side of science.* Amsterdam: Elsevier.

Miyake, A., Friedman, N.P., Emerson, M.J., Witzki, A.H., Howerter, A., & Wager, T. (2000). The unity and diversity of executive functions and their contributions to complex "frontal lobe" tasks: A latent variable analysis. *Cognitive Psychology, 41,* 49–100.

Mobini, S., & Grant, A. (2007). Clinical implications of attentional bias in anxiety disorders: An integrative review. *Psychotherapy: Theory, Research, Practice, Training, 44,* 450–462.

Mogg, K., Bradbury, K.E., & Bradley, B.P. (2006). Interpretation of ambiguous information in clinical depression. *Behaviour Research and Therapy, 44,* 1411–1419.

Molholm, S., Martinez, A., Shpanker, M., & Foxe, J.J. (2007). Object-based attention is multisensory: Co-activation of an object's representations in ignored sensory modalities. *European Journal of Neuroscience, 26,* 499–509.

Monti, M.M., Osherson, D.N., Martinez, M.J., & Parsons, L.M. (2007). Functional neuroanatomy of deductive inference: A language-independent distributed network. *NeuroImage, 37,* 1005–1016.

Montoya, A., Pelletier, M., Menear, M., Duplessis, E., Richer, F., & Lepage, M. (2006). Episodic memory impairment in Huntington's disease: A meta-analysis. *Neuropsychologia, 44,* 1984–1994.

Moorman, M., & van den Putte, B. (2008). The influence of message framing, intention to quit smoking, and nicotine dependence on the persuasiveness of smoking cessation messages. *Addictive Behaviors, 33,* 1267–1275.

Moors, A., & De Houwer, J. (2006). Automaticity: A theoretical and conceptual analysis. *Psychological Bulletin, 132,* 297–326.

Morawetz, C., Holz, P., Baudewig, J., Treue, S., & Dechent, P. (2007). Split of attentional resources in human visual cortex. *Visual Neuroscience, 24,* 817–826.

Moray, N. (1959). Attention in dichotic listening: Affective cues and the influence of instructions. *Quarterly Journal of Experimental Psychology, 11,* 56–60.

Morris, C.D., Bransford, J.D., & Franks, J.J. (1977). Levels of processing versus transfer appropriate processing. *Journal of Verbal Learning and Verbal Behavior, 16,* 519–533.

Morris, J.S., Öhman, A., & Dolan, R.J. (1998). Conscious and unconscious emotional learning in the human amygdala. *Nature, 393,* 467–470.

Morris, J.S., Öhman, A., & Dolan, R. (1999). A sub-cortical pathway to the right amygdala mediating "unseen" fear. *Proceedings of the National Academy of Science, USA, 96,* 1680–1685.

Morrison, D.J., Bruce, V., & Burton, A.M. (2003). Understanding provoked overt recognition in prosopagnosia. *Visual Cognition, 8,* 47–65.

Morrison, R.G. (2005). Thinking in working memory. In K.J. Holyoak & R.G. Morrison (Eds.), *Cambridge handbook of thinking and reasoning.* Cambridge: Cambridge University Press.

Morrison, R.G., Holyoak, K.J., & Truong, B. (2001). Working-memory modularity in analogical reasoning. In J.D. Moore & K. Stenning (Eds.), *Proceedings of the Twenty-third Annual Conference of the Cognitive Science Society.* Mahwah, NJ: Lawrence Erlbaum Associates Inc.

Moscovitch, M. (2008). Commentary: A perspective on prospective memory. In M. Kliegel, M.A. McDaniel, & G.O. Einstein (Eds.), *Prospective memory: Cognitive, neuroscience, developmental, and applied perspectives.* New York: Lawrence Erlbaum Associates.

Moscovitch, M., Nadel, L., Winocur, G., Gilboa, A., & Rosenbaum R.S. (2006). The cognitive neuroscience of remote episodic, semantic and spatial memory. *Current Opinion in Neurobiology, 16,* 179–190.

Moscovitch, M., Winocur, G., & Behrmann, M. (1997). What is special about face recognition? Nineteen experiments on a person with visual object agnosia and dyslexia but normal face recognition. *Journal of Cognitive Neuroscience, 9,* 555–604.

Most, S.B., Simons, D.J., Scholl, B.J., Jimenez, R., Clifford, E., & Chabris, C.F. (2001). How not to be seen: The contribution of similarity and selective ignoring to sustained inattentional blindness. *Psychological Science, 12,* 9–17.

Motley, M.T. (1980). Verification of "Freudian slips" and semantic prearticulatory editing via laboratory-induced spoonerisms. In V.A. Fromkin (Ed.), *Errors in linguistic performance: Slips of the tongue, ear, pen, and hand.* New York: Academic Press.

Motley, M.T., Baars, B.J., & Camden, C.T. (1983). Experimental verbal slip studies: A review and an editing model of language encoding. *Communication Monographs, 50,* 79–101.

Mottaghy, F.M. (2006). Interfering with working memory in humans. *Neuroscience, 139,* 85–90.

Moutoussis, K., & Zeki, S. (1997). Functional segregation and temporal hierarchy of the visual perceptive systems. *Proceedings of the Royal Society of London Series B – Biological Sciences, 264,* 1407–1414.

Mueller, S.T., Seymour, T.L., Kieras, D.E., & Meyer, D.E. (2003). Theoretical implications of articulatory duration, phonological similarity, and phonological complexity in verbal working memory. *Journal of Experimental Psychology: Learning, Memory, and Cognition, 29,* 1353–1380.

Müller, N.G., Bartelt, O.A., Donner, T.H., Villringer, A., & Brandt, S.A. (2003). A physiological correlate of the "zoom lens" of visual attention. *Journal of Neuroscience, 23,* 3561–3565.

Murray, C. (1998). *Income inequality and IQ.* Washington, DC: American Enterprise Institute.

Murray, J.D., & Burke, K.A. (2003). Activation and encoding of predictive inferences: The role of reading skill. *Discourse Processes, 35,* 81–102.

Murray, L.J., & Ranganath, C. (2007). The dorsolateral prefrontal cortex contributes to successful relational memory encoding. *Journal of Neuroscience, 27,* 5515–5522.

Murray, L.A., Whitehouse, W.G., & Alloy, L.B. (1999). Mood congruence and depressive deficits in memory: A forced-recall analysis. *Memory, 7,* 175–196.

Muter, P. (1978). Recognition failure of recallable words in semantic memory. *Memory & Cognition, 6,* 9–12.

Mynatt, C.R., Doherty, M.E., & Tweney, R.D. (1977). Confirmation bias in a simulated research environment. *Quarterly Journal of Experimental Psychology, 29,* 85–95.

Naccache, L., Blandin, E., & Dehaene, S. (2002). Unconscious masked priming depends on temporal attention. *Psychological Science, 13,* 416–424.

Nairne, J.S. (2002a). Remembering over the short-term: The case against the standard model. *Annual Review of Psychology, 53,* 53–81.

Nairne, J.S. (2002b). The myth of the encoding–retrieval match. *Memory, 10,* 389–395.

Nairne, J.S., Whiteman, H.L., & Kelley, M.R. (1999). Short-term forgetting of order under conditions of reduced interference. *Quarterly Journal of Experimental Psychology, 52A,* 241–251.

Nascimento, S.M.C., De Almeida, V.M.W., Fiadeiro, R.T., & Foster, D.H. (2004). Minimum-variance cone-excitation ratios and the limits of relational colour constancy. *Visual Neuroscience, 21,* 337–340.

Nassi, J.J., & Callaway, E.M. (2006). The parvocellular LGN provides a robust disynaptic input to the visual motion area MT. *Neuron, 50,* 319–327.

Nassi, J.J., & Callaway, E.M. (2009). Parallel processing strategies of the primate visual system. *Nature Reviews Neuroscience, 10,* 360–372.

Nee, D.E., Jonides, J., & Berman, M.G. (2007). Neural mechanisms of proactive interference-resolution. *Neuroimage, 38(4),* 740–751.

Neely, J.H. (1977). Semantic priming and retrieval from lexical memory: Roles of inhibitionless spreading activation and limited capacity attention. *Journal of Experimental Psychology: General, 106,* 226–254.

Neisser, U. (1978). Memory: What are the important questions? In M.M. Gruneberg, P.E. Morris & R.N. Sykes (Eds.), *Practical Aspects of Memory* (pp. 3–24). London: Academic Press.

Neisser, U. (1996). Remembering as doing. *Behavioral & Brain Sciences, 19,* 203–204.

Neisser, U., & Becklen, P. (1975). Selective looking: Attending to visually superimposed events. *Cognitive Psychology, 7,* 480–494.

Newell, A., & Simon, H.A. (1972). *Human problem solving.* Englewood Cliffs, NJ: Prentice Hall.

Newell, A., Shaw, J.C., & Simon, H.A. (1958). Elements of a theory of human problem solving. *Psychological Review, 65,* 151–166.

Newell, B.R. (2005). Re-visions of rationality? *Trends in Cognitive Sciences, 9,* 11–15.

Newell, B.R., & Shanks, D.R. (2003). Take-the-best or look at the rest? Factors influencing "one-reason" decision making. *Journal of Experimental Psychology: Learning, Memory, and Cognition, 29,* 53–65.

Newell, B.R., Weston, N.J., & Shanks, D.R. (2003). Empirical tests of a fast and frugal heuristic: Not everyone "takes-the-best". *Organizational Behavior and Human Decision Processes, 91,* 82–96.

Newman, S.D., Carpenter, P.A., Varma, S., & Just, M.A. (2003). Frontal and parietal participation in problem solving in the Tower of London: fMRI and computational modelling of planning and high-level perception. *Neuropsychologia, 41,* 1668–1682.

Newman, S.D., Keller, T.A., & Just, M.A. (2007). Volitional control of attention and brain activation in dual-task performance. *Human Brain Mapping, 28,* 109–117.

Newsome, M.R., & Johnson-Laird, P.N. (2006). How falsity dispels fallacies. *Thinking & Reasoning, 12,* 214–234.

Newstead, S.E., Handley, S.J., & Buck, E. (1999). Falsifying mental models: Testing the predictions of theories of syllogistic reasoning. *Memory & Cognition, 27,* 344–354.

Nickels, L., Biedermann, B., Coltheart, M., Saunders, S., & Tree, J.J. (2008). Computational modelling of phonological dyslexia – How does the DRC model fare? *Cognitive Neuropsychology*, 25, 165–183.

Nieuwenstein, M.R., Potter, M.C., & Theeuwes, J. (2009). Unmasking the attentional blink. *Journal of Experimental Psychology: Human Perception & Performance*, 35, 159–169.

Nieuwland, M.S., & van Berkum, J.J.A. (2006). When peanuts fall in love: N400 evidence for the power of discourse. *Journal of Cognitive Neuroscience*, 18, 1098–1111.

Nijboer, T.C.W., McIntosh, R.D., Nys, G.M.S., Dijkerman, H.C., & Milner, A.D. (2008). Prism adaptation improves voluntary but not automatic orienting in neglect. *Neuroreport*, 19, 293–298.

Nissen, M.J., Willingham, D., & Hartman, M. (1989). Explicit and implicit remembering: When is learning preserved in amnesia? *Neuropsychologia*, 27, 341–352.

Norman, D.A. (1980). Twelve issues for cognitive science. *Cognitive Science*, 4, 1–32.

Norman, G., Young, M., & Brooks, L. (2007). Non-analytical models of clinical reasoning: The role of experience. *Medical Education*, 41, 1140–1145.

Norman, G.R., Brooks, L.R., & Allen, S.W. (1989). Recall by expert medical practitioners and novices as a record of processing attention. *Journal of Experimental Psychology: Learning, Memory, and Cognition*, 15, 1166–1174.

Norman, J. (2002). Two visual systems and two theories of perception: An attempt to reconcile the constructivist and ecological approaches. *Behavioral and Brain Sciences*, 25, 73–144.

Norris, D., McQueen, J.M., & Cutler, A. (2003). Perceptual learning in speech. *Cognitive Psychology*, 47, 204–238.

Norris, D., McQueen, J.M., Cutler, A., & Butterfield, S. (1997). The possible-word constraint in the segmentation of continuous speech. *Cognitive Psychology*, 34, 191–243.

Novick, L.R., & Sherman, S.J. (2003). On the nature of insight solutions: Evidence from skill differences in anagram solution. *Quarterly Journal of Experimental Psychology*, 56A, 351–382.

Nyberg, L., Marklund, P., Persson, J., Cabeza, R., Forkstam, C., Petersson, K.M., & Ingvar, M. (2003). Common prefrontal activations during working memory, episodic memory, and semantic memory. *Neuropsychologia*, 41, 371–377.

Nyffeler, T., Pflugshaupt, T., Hofer, H., Baas, U., Gutbrod, K., von Wartburg, R., et al. (2005). Oculomotor behaviour in simultanagnosia: A longitudinal case study. *Neuropsychologia*, 43, 1591–1597.

O'Craven, K., Downing, P., & Kanwisher, N. (1999). fMRI evidence for objects as the units of attentional selection. *Nature*, 401, 584–587.

O'Rourke, T.B., & Holcomb, P.J. (2002). Electrophysiological evidence for the efficiency of spoken word processing. *Biological Psychology*, 60, 121–150.

O'Shea, R.P., Blackburn, S.G., & Ono, H. (1994). Contrast as a depth cue. *Vision Research*, 34, 1595–1604.

Oaksford, M. (1997). Thinking and the rational analysis of human reasoning. *The Psychologist*, 10, 257–260.

Oaksford, M., & Hahn, U. (2004). A Bayesian approach to the argument from ignorance. *Canadian Journal of Experimental Psychology*, 58, 75–85.

Oaksford, M., Chater, N., Grainger, B., & Larkin, J. (1997). Optimal data selection in the Reduced Array Selection Test (RAST). *Journal of Experimental Psychology: Learning, Memory, and Cognition*, 23, 441–458.

Oatley, K., & Djikic, M. (2008). Writing as thinking. *Review of General Psychology*, 12, 9–27.

Oberauer, K. (2006). Reasoning with conditionals: A test of formal models of four theories. *Cognition*, 53, 238–283.

Ochsner, K.N., & Gross, J.J. (2005). The cognitive control of emotion. *Trends in Cognitive Sciences*, 9, 242–249.

Ochsner, K.N., & Gross, J.J. (2008). Cognitive emotion regulation: Insights from social cognitive and affective neuroscience. *Current Directions in Psychological Science*, 17, 153–158.

Ohira, H., Nomura, M., Ichikawa, N., Isowa, T., Iidaha, T., Sato A. et al. (2006). Association of neural and physiological responses during voluntary emotion suppression. *Neuroimage*, 29, 721–733.

Ohlsson, S. (1992). Information processing explanations of insight and related phenomena. In M.T. Keane & K.J. Gilhooly (Eds.), *Advances in the psychology of thinking*. London: Harvester Wheatsheaf.

Öhman, A., & Soares, J.J.F. (1994). "Unconscious anxiety": Phobic responses to masked stimuli. *Journal of Abnormal Psychology*, 103, 231–240.

Okada, T., & Simon, H.A. (1997). Collaborative discovery in a scientific domain. *Cognitive Science*, 21, 109–146.

Okuda, J., Fujii, T., Ohtake, H., Tsukiura, T., Yamadori, A., Frith, C.D., & Burgess, P.W. (2007). Differential involvement of regions of rostral prefrontal cortex (Brodmann area 10) in time- and event-based prospective memory. *International Journal of Psychophysiology*, 64, 233–246.

Olive, T. (2004). Working memory in writing: Empirical evidence from the dual-task technique. *European Psychologist*, 9, 32–42.

Olive, T., & Kellogg, R.T. (2002). Concurrent activation of high- and low-level production processes in written composition. *Memory & Cognition*, 30, 594–600.

Olive, T., & Piolat, A. (2002). Suppressing visual feedback in written composition: Effects on processing demands and co-ordination of the writing processes. *International Journal of Psychology*, 37, 209–218.

Olivers, C.N.L. (2007). The time course of attention: It is better than we thought. *Current Directions in Psychological Science*, 16, 11–15.

Olivers, C.N.L., van der Stigchel, S., & Hulleman, J. (2007). Spreading the sparing: Against a limited-capacity account of the attentional blink. *Psychological Research*, 71, 126–139.

Olson, A.C., Romani, C., & Halloran, L. (2007). Localising the deficit in a case of jargon aphasia. *Cognitive Neuropsychology*, 24, 211–238.

Oppenheimer, D.M. (2003). Not so fast! (and not so frugal!): Re-thinking the recognition heuristic. *Cognition*, 90, B1–B9.

Oppenheimer, D.M. (2004). Spontaneous discounting of availability in frequency judgement tasks. *Psychological Science*, 15, 100–105.

Orban, G.A., Fize, D., Peuskens, H., Denys, K., Nelissen, K., Sunaert, S. et al. (2003). Similarities and differences in motion processing between the human and macaque brain: Evidence from fMRI. *Neuropsychologia*, 41, 1757–1768.

Osman, M. (2004). An evaluation of dual-process theories of reasoning. *Psychonomic Bulletin & Review*, 11, 988–1010.

Osman, M., Wilkinson, L., Beigi, M., Castaneda, C.S., & Jahanshahi, M. (2008). Patients with Parkinson's disease learn to control complex systems via procedural as well as non-procedural learning. *Neuropsychologia*, 46, 2355–2363.

Ost, J., Vrij, A., Costall, A., & Bull, R. (2002). Crashing memories and reality monitoring: Distinguishing between perceptions, imaginations and 'false memories'. *Applied Cognitive Psychology*, 16, 125–134.

Otto, M.W., Teachman, B.A., Cohen, L.S., Soares, C.N., Vitonis, A.F., & Harlow, B.L. (2007). Dysfunctional attitudes and episodes of major depression: Predictive validity and temporal stability in never-depressed, depressed, and recovered women. *Journal of Abnormal Psychology*, 116, 475–483.

Overgaard, M., Fehl, K., Mouridsen, K., Bergholt, B., & Cleermans, A. (2008). Seeing without seeing? Degraded conscious vision in a blindsight patient. *Public Library of Science One*, 3, e3028.

Owen, A.M., & Coleman, M.R. (2008). Functional neuroimaging of the vegetative state. *Nature Reviews Neuroscience*, 9, 235–243.

Owen, A.M., Coleman, M.R., Boly, M., Davis, M.H., Laureys, S., & Pickard, J.D. (2006). Detecting awareness in the vegetative state. *Science*, 313, 1402–1402.

Owen, A.M., Downes, J.J., Sahakian, B.J., Polkey, C.E., & Robbins, T.W. (1990). Planning and spatial working memory following frontal lobe lesions in man. *Neuropsychologia*, 28, 1021–1034.

Pachur, T., & Hertwig, R. (2006). On the psychology of the recognition heuristic: Retrieval primacy as a key determinant of its use. *Journal of Experimental Psychology: Learning, Memory, and Cognition*, 32, 983–1002.

Page, M.P.A. (2006). What can't functional neuroimaging tell the cognitive psychologist? *Cortex*, 42, 428–443.

Palmer, J., Verghese, P., & Pavel, M. (2000). The psychophysics of visual search. *Vision Research*, 40, 1227–1268.

Palmer, S., & Rock, I. (1994). Rethinking perceptual organisation: The role of uniform connectedness. *Psychonomic Bulletin & Review*, 1, 29–55.

Palmer, S.E. (1975). The effects of contextual scenes on the identification of objects. *Memory & Cognition*, 3, 519–526.

Palmer, S.E., & Kimchi, R. (1986). The information processing approach to cognition. In T. Knapp & L.C. Robertson (Eds.), *Approaches to cognition: Contrasts and controversies*. Hillsdale, NJ: Lawrence Erlbaum Associates Inc.

Papagno, C., Valentine, T., & Baddeley, A.D. (1991). Phonological short-term memory and foreign language learning. *Journal of Memory & Language*, 30, 331–347.

Pappas, Z., & Mack, A. (2008). Potentiation of action by undetected affordant objects. *Visual Cognition*, 16, 892–915.

Park, H., & Rugg, M.D. (2008a). The relationship between study processing and the effects of cue congruency on retrieval: fMRI support for transfer appropriate processing. *Cerebral Cortex*, 18, 868–875.

Park, H., & Rugg, M.D. (2008b). Neural correlates of successful encoding of semantically and phonologically mediated inter-item associations. *Neuroimage*, 43, 165–172.

Park, H., Quinlan, J., Thornton, E., & Reder, L.M. (2004). The effect of midazolam on visual search: Implications for understanding amnesia. *Proceedings of the National Academy of Sciences of the United States of America*, 101, 17879–17883.

Parker, A.J. (2007). Binocular depth perception and the cerebral cortex. *Nature Reviews Neuroscience, 8,* 379–391.

Parkinson, B. (2001). Putting appraisal in context. In K.R. Scherer, A. Schorr, & T. Johnstone (Eds.), *Appraisal processes in emotion: Theory, methods, research.* Oxford: Oxford University Press.

Parkinson, B., & Manstead, A.S.R. (1992). Appraisal as a cause of emotion. In M.S. Clark (Ed.), *Review of personality and social psychology (Vol. 13).* New York: Sage.

Pashler, H. (1993). Dual-task interference and elementary mental mechanisms. In D.E. Meyer & S. Kornblum (Eds.), *Attention and performance* (Vol. XIV). London: MIT Press.

Pashler, H., Johnston, J.C., & Ruthruff, E. (2001). Attention and performance. *Annual Review of Psychology, 52,* 629–651.

Pastötter, B., Hanslmayr, S., & Bäuml, K.-H. (2008). Inhibition of return arises from inhibition of response processes: An analysis of oscillatory beta activity. *Journal of Cognitive Neuroscience, 20,* 65–75.

Patterson, K., Nestor, P.J., & Rogers, T.T. (2007). Where do you know what you know? The representation of semantic knowledge in the human brain. *Nature Reviews Neuroscience, 8,* 976–987.

Payne, J. (1976). Task complexity and contingent processing in decision making: An information search and protocol analysis. *Organizational Behavior and Human Performance, 16,* 366–387.

Pearson, J., Clifford, C.W.G., & Tong, F. (2008). The functional impact of mental imagery on conscious perception. *Current Biology, 18,* 982–986.

Pegna, A.J., Khateb, A., Lazeyras, F., & Seghier, M.L. (2005). Discriminating emotional faces without primary visual cortices involves the right amygdala. *Nature Neuroscience, 8,* 24–25.

Peissig, J.J., & Tarr, M.J. (2007). Visual object recognition: Do we know more now than we did 20 years ago? *Annual Review of Psychology, 58,* 75–96.

Penolazzi, B., Hauk, O., & Pulvermüller, F. (2007). Early semantic context integration and lexical access as revealed by event-related brain potentials. *Biological Psychology, 74,* 374–388.

Perenin, M.-T., & Vighetto, A. (1988). Optic ataxia: A specific disruption in visuomotor mechanisms. 1. Different aspects of the deficit in reaching for objects. *Brain, 111,* 643–674.

Peretz, I., Kolinsky, R., Trano, M., et al. (1994). Functional dissociations following bilateral lesions of auditory cortex. *Brain, 117,* 1283–1301.

Perre, L., & Ziegler, J.C. (2008). On-line activation of orthography in spoken word recognition. *Brain Research, 1188,* 132–138.

Perry, C. (2003). Priming the rules of spelling. *Quarterly Journal of Experimental Psychology Section A – Human Experimental Psychology, 56,* 515–530.

Perry, C., Ziegler, J.C., & Zorzi, M. (2007). Nested incremental modelling in the development of computational theories: The CDP+ model of reading aloud. *Psychological Review, 114,* 273–315.

Persaud, N., & Cowey, A. (2008). Blindsight is unlike normal conscious vision: Evidence from an exclusion task. *Consciousness and Cognition, 17,* 1050–1055.

Persaud, N., & McLeod, P. (2008). Wagering demonstrates subconscious processing in a binary exclusion task. *Consciousness and Cognition, 17,* 565–575.

Persaud, N., McLeod, P., & Cowey, A. (2007). Post-decision wagering objectively measures awareness. *Nature Neuroscience, 10,* 257–261.

Peru, A., & Avesani, R. (2008). To know what it is for, but not how it is: Semantic dissociations in a case of visual agnosia. *Neurocase, 14,* 249–263.

Peselow, E.D., Robins, C., Block, P., Barsuche, F., & Fieve, R.R. (1990). Dysfunctional attitudes in depressed patients before and after clinical treatment and in normal control subjects. *American Journal of Psychiatry, 147,* 439–444.

Peters, D.P. (1988). Eyewitness memory in a natural setting. In M.M. Gruneberg, P.E. Morris, & R.N. Sykes (Eds.), *Practical aspects of memory: Current research and issues: Vol. 1. Memory in everyday life.* Chichester: Wiley.

Petersen, S.E., Corbetta, M., Miezin, F.M., & Shulman, G.L. (1994). PET studies of parietal involvement in spatial attention: Comparison of different task types. *Canadian Journal of Experimental Psychology, 48,* 319–338.

Peterson, C. (2002). Children's long-term memory for autobiographical events. *Developmental Review, 22,* 370–402.

Peterson, L.R., & Peterson, M.J. (1959). Short-term retention of individual verbal items. *Journal of Experimental Psychology, 58,* 193–198.

Peterson, M.S., Kramer, A.F., Wang, R.F., Irwin, D.E., & McCarley, J.S. (2001). Visual search has memory. *Psychological Science, 12,* 287–292.

Pezdek, K. (2003). Event memory and autobiographical memory for the events of September 11, 2001. *Applied Cognitive Psychology, 17,* 1033–1045.

Philipose, L.E., Gottesman, R.F., Newhart, M., Kleinman, J.T., Herschkovits, E.H., Pawlak, M.A., Marsh, E.B., Davis, C., Heidler-Gary, J., & Hillis, A.E. (2007). Neural regions essential for reading and spelling of words and pseudowords. *Annals of Neurology, 62*(5), 481–492.

Pickel, K.L. (1999). The influence of context on the "weapon focus" effect. *Law and Human Behavior, 23,* 299–311.

Pickering, M.J., & Ferreira, V.S. (2008). Structural priming: A critical review. *Psychological Bulletin, 134,* 427–459.

Pickering, M.J., & Garrod, S. (2004). Toward a mechanistic psychology of dialog. *Behavioral and Brain Sciences, 27,* 169–226.

Pickering, M.J., & Garrod, S. (2007). Do people use language production to make predictions during comprehension? *Trends in Cognitive Sciences, 11,* 105–110.

Pickering, M.J., & Traxler, M.J. (1998). Plausibility and recovery from garden-paths: An eye-tracking study. *Journal of Experimental Psychology: Learning, Memory, & Cognition, 24,* 940–961.

Pillemer, D.B. (1998). What is remembered about early childhood events? *Clinical Psychology Review, 18,* 895–913.

Pillemer, D.B., Goldsmith, L.R., Panter, A.T., & White, S.H. (1988). Very long-term memories of the first year in college. *Journal of Experimental Psychology: Learning, Memory, & Cognition, 14,* 709–715.

Pinard, M., Chertkow, H., Black, S., & Peretz, I. (2002). A case study of pure word deafness: Modularity in auditory processing? *Neurocase, 8,* 40–55.

Pinker, S. (1984). *Language learnability and language development.* Cambridge, MA: Harvard University Press.

Pinker, S. (1997). *How the mind works.* New York: W.W. Norton.

Pisella, L., Binkofski, F., Lasek, K., Toni, I., & Rossetti, Y. (2006). No double-dissociation between optic ataxia and visual agnosia: Multiple sub-streams for multiple visuo-manual integrations. *Neuropsychologia, 44,* 2734–2748.

Pisoni, D.B., & Tash, J. (1974). Reaction times to comparisons within and across phonetic categories. *Perception & Psychophysics, 15,* 285–290.

Pitt, M.A. (1995). The locus of the lexical shift in phoneme identification. *Journal of Experimental Psychology: Learning, Memory, and Cognition, 21,* 1037–1052.

Plaut, D.C., McClelland, J.L., Seidenberg, M.S., & Patterson, K. (1996). Understanding normal and impaired word reading: Computational principles in quasi-regular domains. *Psychological Review, 103,* 56–115.

Pobric, G., Jefferies, E., & Lambon Ralph, M.A. (2007). Anterior temporal lobes mediate semantic representation: Mimicking semantic dementia by using rTMS in normal participants. *Proceedings of the National Academy of Sciences, 104,* 20137–20141.

Poldrack, R.A., & Gabrieli, J.D.E. (2001). Characterising the neural mechanisms of skill learning and repetition priming: Evidence from mirror reading. *Brain, 124,* 67–82.

Poldrack, R.A., Sabb, F.W., Foerde, K., Tom, S.M., Asarnow, R.F., Bookheimer, S.Y., & Knowlton, B.J. (2005). The neural correlates of motor skill automaticity. *Journal of Neuroscience, 25,* 5356–5364.

Poldrack, R.A., Selco, S.L., Field, J.E., & Cohen, N.J. (1999). The relationship between skill learning and repetition priming: Experimental and computational analyses. *Journal of Experimental Psychology: Learning, Memory, and Cognition, 25,* 208–235.

Poletiek, F.H. (1996). Paradoxes of falsification. *Quarterly Journal of Experimental Psychology, 49A,* 447–462.

Polka, L., Rvachew, S., & Molnar, M. (2008). Speech perception by 6-to-8-month-olds in the presence of distracting sounds. *Infancy, 13,* 421–439.

Pollatsek, A., Bolozky, S., Well, A.D., & Rayner, K. (1981). Asymmetries in the perceptual span for Israeli readers. *Brain & Language, 14,* 174–180.

Pollatsek, A., Reichle, E.D., & Rayner, K. (2006). Tests of the E-Z Reader model: Exploring the interface between cognition and eye-movement control. *Cognitive Psychology, 52,* 1–56.

Pomerantz, J.R. (1981). Perceptual organisation in information processing. In M. Kubovy & J.R. Pomerantz (Eds.), *Perceptual organisation.* Hillsdale, NJ: Lawrence Erlbaum Associates Inc.

Popper, K.R. (1968). *The logic of scientific discovery.* London: Hutchinson.

Posner, M.I. (1980). Orienting of attention. The VIIth Sir Frederic Bartlett lecture. *Quarterly Journal of Experimental Psychology, 32A,* 3–25.

Posner, M.I., & Cohen, Y. (1984). Components of visual orientating. In H. Bouma & D.G. Bouwhuis (Eds.), *Attention and performance X* (pp. 531–556). Hillsdale, NJ: Lawrence Erlbaum Associates Inc.

Posner, M.I., & Petersen, S.E. (1990). The attention system of the human brain. *Annual Reviews of Neuroscience, 13,* 25–42.

Posner, M.I., Rafal, R.D., Choate, L.S., & Vaughan, J. (1985). Inhibition of return: Neural basis and function. *Cognitive Neuropsychology, 2,* 211–228.

Post, T., Van Den Assem, M., Baltrussen, G., & Thaler, R. (2008). Deal or no deal? Decision making under risk in a large-payoff game show. *American Economic Review, 98,* 38–71.

Power, M., & Dalgleish, T. (1997). *Cognition and emotion: From order to disorder*. Hove, UK: Psychology Press.

Power, M., & Dalgleish, T. (2008). *Cognition and emotion: From order to disorder (2nd ed.)*. Hove, UK: Psychology Press.

Power, M.J. (2006). The structure of emotion: An empirical comparison of six models. *Cognition & Emotion*, 20, 694–713.

Poynor, D.V., & Morris, R.K. (2003). Inferred goals in narrative: Evidence from self-paced reading, recall, and eye movements. *Journal of Experimental Psychology: Learning, Memory, and Cognition*, 29, 3–9.

Prabhakaran, V., Smith, J.A.L., Desmond, J.E., Glover, G., & Gabrieli, J.D.E. (1997). Neural substrates of fluid reasoning: A fMRI study of neocortical activation during performance of the Raven's Progressive Matrices Test. *Cognitive Psychology*, 33, 43–63.

Prat, C.S., Keller, T.A., & Just, M.A. (2007). Individual differences in sentence comprehension: A functional magnetic resonance imaging investigation of syntactic and lexical processing demands. *Journal of Cognitive Neuroscience*, 19, 1950–1963.

Prime, D.J., & Ward, L.M. (2004). Inhibition of return from stimulus to response. *Psychological Science*, 15, 272–276.

Prince, S.E., Tsukiura, T., & Cabeza, R. (2007). Distinguishing the neural correlates of episodic memory encoding and semantic memory retrieval. *Psychological Science*, 18, 144–151.

Pronin, E., Wegner, D.M., & McCarthy, K. (2006). Everyday magical powers: The role of apparent mental causation in the overestimation of personal influence. *Journal of Personality and Social Psychology*, 91, 218–231.

Pulvermüller, F., Hauk, O., Nikulin, V.V., & Ilmoniemi, R.J. (2005). Functional links between motor and language systems. *European Journal of Neuroscience*, 21, 793–797.

Pylyshyn, Z. (2003a). Return of the mental image: are there really pictures in the brain? *Trends in Cognitive Sciences*, 7(3), 113–118.

Pylyshyn, Z. (2003b). *Seeing and visualizing: It's not what you think*, Cambridge, MA: The MIT Press.

Pylyshyn, Z.W. (2000). Situating vision in the world. *Trends in Cognitive Science*, 4, 197–207.

Pylyshyn, Z.W. (2002). Mental imagery: In search of a theory. *Behavioral and Brain Sciences*, 25, 157–238.

Qin, Y.L., Carter, C.S., Silk, E.M., Stenger, V.A., Fissell, K., Goode, A., & Anderson, J.R. (2004). The change of the brain activation patterns as children learn algebra equation solving. *Proceedings of the National Academy of Sciences of the United States of America*, 101, 5686–5691.

Quinlan, P.T. (2003). Visual feature integration theory: Past, present, and future. *Psychological Bulletin*, 129, 643–673.

Quinlan, P.T., & Wilton, R.N. (1998). Grouping by proximity or similarity? Competition between the Gestalt principles in vision. *Perception*, 27, 417–430.

Quiroga, R.Q., Reddy, L., Kreiman, G., Koch, C., & Fried, I. (2005). Invariant visual representation by single neurons in the human brain. *Nature*, 435, 1102–1107.

Radeau, M., Morais, J., Mousty, P., & Bertelson, P. (2000). The effect of speaking rate on the role of the uniqueness point in spoken word recognition. *Journal of Memory and Language*, 42, 406–422.

Radvansky, G.A., & Copeland, D.E. (2001). Working memory and situation model updating. *Memory & Cognition*, 29, 1073–1080.

Rafal, R., Smith, J., Krantz, A., Cohen, A., & Brennan, C. (1990). Extrageniculate vision in hemianopic humans: Saccade inhibition by signals in the blind field. *Science*, 250, 118–121.

Rafal, R.D., & Posner, M.I. (1987). Deficits in human visual spatial attention following thalamic lesions. *Proceedings of the National Academy of Science*, 84, 7349–7353.

Raichle, M.E. (1997). Brain imaging. In M.S. Gazzaniga (Ed.), *Conversations in the cognitive neurosciences*. Cambridge, MA: MIT Press.

Raichle, M.E., & Snyder, A.Z. (2007). A default model of brain function: A brief history of an evolving idea. *NeuroImage*, 37, 1083–1090.

Raizada, R.D.S., & Poldrack, R.A. (2007). Selective amplification of stimulus differences during categorical processing of speech. *Neuron*, 56, 726–740.

Ramachandran, V.S. (1988). Perception of shape from shading. *Nature*, 331, 163–166.

Ramnani, N., & Owen, A.M. (2004). Anterior prefrontal cortex: Insights into function from anatomy and neuroimaging. *Nature Reviews Neuroscience*, 5, 184–194.

Rapp, B., Epstein, C., & Tainturier, M.-J. (2002). The integration of information across lexical and sublexical processes in spelling. *Cognitive Neuropsychology*, 19, 1–29.

Rapp, B., & Goldrick, M. (2000). Discreteness and interactivity in spoken word production. *Psychological Review*, 107, 460–499.

Rapp, D.N., & Kendeou, P. (2007). Revising what readers know: Updating text representations during narrative comprehension. *Memory & Cognition*, 35, 2019–2032.

Rapcsak, S.Z., Beeson, P.M., Henry, M.L., Leyden, A., Kim, E., Rising, K. et al. (2009). Phonological dyslexia and dysgraphia: Cognitive mechanisms and neural substrates. *Cortex*, 45, 575–591.

Rastle, K., & Brysbaert, M. (2006). Masked phonological priming effects in English: Are they real? Do they matter? *Cognitive Psychology*, 53, 97–145.

Ratcliff, R., & McKoon, G. (1978). Priming in item recognition: Evidence for the propositional structure of sentences. *Journal of Verbal Learning and Verbal Behavior*, 20, 204–215.

Raymer, A.M. (2001). Acquired language disorders. *Topics in Language Disorders*, 21, 42–59.

Rayner, K., Li, X.S., & Pollatsek, A. (2007). Extending the E-Z Reader model of eye movement control to Chinese readers. *Cognitive Science*, 31, 1021–1033.

Rayner, K., & Pollatsek, A. (1989). *The psychology of reading*. London: Prentice Hall.

Rayner, K., & Sereno, S.C. (1994). Eye movements in reading: Psycholinguistic studies. In M.A. Gernsbacher (Ed.), *Handbook of psycholinguistics*. New York: Academic Press.

Reber, A.S. (1967). Implicit learning of artificial grammars. *Journal of Verbal Learning and Verbal Behavior*, 6, 855–863.

Reber, A.S. (1993). *Implicit learning and tacit knowledge: An essay on the cognitive unconscious*. Oxford, UK: Oxford University Press.

Reber, P.J., Knowlton, J.R., & Squire, L.R. (1996). Dissociable properties of memory systems: Differences in the flexibility of declarative and nondeclarative knowledge. *Behavioral Neuroscience*, 110, 861–871.

Redelmeier, C., Koehler, D.J., Liberman, V., & Tversky, A. (1995). Probability judgement in medicine: Discounting unspecified alternatives. *Medical Decision Making*, 15, 227–230.

Reder, L.M., Park, H., & Kieffaber, P.D. (2009). Memory systems do not divide on consciousness: Re-interpreting memory in terms of activation and binding. *Psychological Bulletin*, 135, 23–49.

Rees, G. (2007). Neural correlates of the contents of visual awareness in humans. *Philosophical Transactions of the Royal Society B – Biological Sciences*, 362, 877–886.

Rees, G., Wojciulik, E., Clarke, K., Husain, M., Frith, C., & Driver, J. (2000). Unconscious activation of visual cortex in the damaged right hemisphere of a parietal patient with extinction. *Brain*, 123, 82–92.

Reese, C.M., & Cherry, K.E. (2002). The effects of age, ability, and memory monitoring on prospective memory task performance. *Aging, Neuropsychology, and Cognition*, 9, 98–113.

Reeves, A.J., Amano, K., & Foster, D.H. (2008). Colour constancy: Phenomenal or projective? *Perception & Psychophysics*, 70, 219–228.

Reicher, G.M. (1969). Perceptual recognition as a function of meaningfulness of stimulus material. *Journal of Experimental Psychology*, 81, 274–280.

Reichle, E.D., Pollatsek, A., Fisher, D.L., & Rayner, K. (1998). Toward a model of eye movement control in reading. *Psychological Review*, 105, 125–157.

Reichle, E.D., Rayner, K., & Pollatsek, A. (2003). The E-Z Reader model of eye-movement control in reading: Comparisons to other models. *Behavioral and Brain Sciences*, 26, 445–526.

Reingold, E.M. (2004). Unconscious perception and the classic dissociation paradigm: A new angle? *Perception & Psychophysics*, 66, 882–887.

Rensink, R.A. (2002). Change detection. *Annual Review of Psychology*, 53, 245–277.

Rensink, R.A., O'Regan, J.K., & Clark, J.J. (1997). To see or not to see: The need for attention to perceive changes in scenes. *Psychological Science*, 8, 368–373.

Repovš, G., & Baddeley, A. (2006). The multi-component model of working memory: Explorations in experimental cognitive psychology. *Neuroscience*, 139, 5–21.

Reverberi, C., Toraldo, A., D'Agostini, S., & Skrap, M. (2005). Better without (lateral) frontal cortex? Insight problems solved by frontal patients. *Brain*, 128, 2882–2890.

Reyna, V.F., & Lloyd, F.J. (2006). Physician decision making and cardiac risk: Effects of knowledge, risk perception, risk tolerance, and fuzzy processing. *Journal of Experimental Psychology: Applied*, 12, 179–195.

Ribot, T. (1882). *Diseases of memory*. New York: Appleton.

Ricco, R.B. (2003). The macrostructure of informal arguments: A proposed model and analysis. *Quarterly Journal of Experimental Psychology: Human Experimental Psychology*, 56A, 1021–1051.

Ricco, R.B. (2007). Individual differences in the analysis of informal reasoning fallacies. *Contemporary Educational Psychology*, 32, 459–484.

Richmond, J., & Nelson, C.A. (2007). Accounting for change in declarative memory: A cognitive neuroscience perspective. *Developmental Review*, 27, 349–373.

Richter, T., & Späth, P. (2006). Recognition is used as one cue among others in judgement and decision making. *Journal of Experimental Psychology: Learning, Memory, and Cognition*, 32, 150–162.

Riddoch, G. (1917). Dissociations of visual perceptions due to occipital injuries, with especial reference to appreciation of movement. *Brain*, *40*, 15–57.

Riddoch, M.J., & Humphreys, G.W. (2001). Object recognition. In B. Rapp (Ed.), *The handbook of cognitive neuropsychology: What deficits reveal about the human mind*. Hove, UK: Psychology Press.

Riddoch, M.J., Humphreys, G.W., Akhtar, N., Allen, H., Bracewell, R.M., & Scholfield, A.J. (2008). A tale of two agnosias: Distinctions between form and integrative agnosia. *Cognitive Neuropsychology*, *25*, 56–92.

Riddoch, M.J., Humphreys, G.W., Hickman, J.C., Daly, A., & Colin, J. (2006). I can see what you are doing: Action familiarity and affordance promote recovery from extinction. *Cognitive Neuropsychology*, *23*, 583–605.

Rinck, M., & Becker, E.S. (2005). A comparison of attentional biases and memory biases in women with social phobia and major depression. *Journal of Abnormal Psychology*, *114*, 62–74.

Rinck, M., & Weber, U. (2003). Who when where: An experimental test of the event-indexing model. *Memory & Cognition*, *31*, 1284–1292.

Rips, L.J., Shoben, E.J., & Smith, E.E. (1973). Semantic distance and the verification of semantic relations. *Journal of Verbal Learning and Verbal Behavior*, *12*, 1–20.

Rittle-Johnson, B. (2006). Promoting transfer: Effects of self-explanation and direct instruction. *Child Development*, *77*, 1–15.

Ritov, J., & Baron, J. (1990). Reluctance to vaccinate: Omission bias and ambiguity. *Journal of Behavioral Decision Making*, *3*, 263–277.

Rizzo, M., Nawrot, M., Sparks, J., & Dawson, J. (2008). First and second-order motion perception after focal human brain lesions. *Vision Research*, *48*, 2682–2688.

Rizzolatti, G., & Craighero, L. (2004). The mirror-neuron system. *Annual Review of Neuroscience*, *27*, 169–192.

Roberson, D., Davies, I., & Davidoff, J. (2000). Colour categories are not universal: Replications and new evidence from a stone-age culture. *Journal of Experimental Psychology: General*, *129*, 369–398.

Robertson, E.M., Théoret, H., & Pascual-Leone, A. (2003). Studies in cognition: The problems solved and created by transcranial magnetic stimulation. *Journal of Cognitive Neuroscience*, *15*, 948–960.

Robertson, S.I. (2001). *Problem solving*. Hove, UK: Psychology Press.

Robinson, M.D., & Clore, G.L. (2001). Simulation, scenarios, and emotional appraisal: Testing the convergence of real and imagined reactions to emotional stimuli. *Personality and Social Psychology Bulletin*, *27*, 1520–1532.

Robbins, T.W., Anderson, E.J., Barker, D.R., Bradley, A.C., Fearnyhough, C., Henson, R., Hudson, S.R., & Baddeley, A. (1996). Working memory in chess. *Memory & Cognition*, *24*, 83–93.

Robson, J., Pring, T., Marshall, J., & Chiat, S. (2003). Phoneme frequency effects in jargon aphasia: A phonological investigation of non-word errors. *Brain and Language*, *85*, 109–124.

Rock, I., & Palmer, S. (1990). The legacy of Gestalt psychology. *Scientific American*, December, 48–61.

Rock, P.B., Harris, M.G., & Yates, T. (2006). A test of the tau-dot hypothesis of braking control in the real world. *Journal of Experimental Psychology: Human Perception and Performance*, *32*, 1479–1484.

Rodriguez, E., George, N., Lachaux, J., Martinerie, J., Renault, B., & Varela, F.J. (1999). Perception's shadow: Long-distance synchronization of human brain activity. *Nature*, *397*, 430–433.

Roediger, H.L. (1990). Implicit memory: Retention without remembering. *American Psychologist*, *45*, 1043–1056.

Roediger, H.L. (2008). Relativity of remembering: Why the laws of memory vanished. *Annual Review of Psychology*, *59*, 225–254.

Roediger, H.L., & Karpicke, J.D. (2006a). Test-enhanced learning: Taking memory tests improves long-term retention. *Psychological Science*, *17*, 249–255.

Rogers, B.J., & Graham, M.E. (1979). Motion parallax as an independent cue for depth perception. *Perception*, *8*, 125–134.

Rogers, T.T., Hocking, J., Noppeney, U., Mechelli, A., Gorno-Tempini, M.L., Patterson, K., & Price, C.J. (2006). Anterior temporal cortex and semantic memory: Reconciling findings from neuropsychology and functional imaging. *Cognitive, Affective, & Behavioral Neuroscience*, *6*, 201–213.

Rogers, T.T., Lambon Ralph, M.A., Garrard, P., Bozeat, S., McClelland, J.L., Hodges, J.R., & Patterson, K. (2004). Structure and deterioration of semantic memory: A neuropsychological and computational investigation. *Psychological Review*, *111*, 205–235.

Roorda, A., & Williams, D.R. (1999). The arrangement of the three cone classes in the living human eye. *Nature*, *397*, 520–522.

Rosch, E.H. (1973). Natural categories. *Cognitive Psychology*, *4*, 328–350.

Rosch, E.H., & Mervis, C.B. (1975). Family resemblances: Studies in the internal structure of categories. *Cognitive Psychology*, *7*, 573–605.

Roseman, I.J., & Evdokas, A. (2004). Appraisals cause experienced emotions: Experimental evidence. *Cognition & Emotion*, 18, 1–28.

Roseman, I.J., & Smith, C.A. (2001). Appraisal theory: Overriew, assumptions, varieties, controversies. In K.R. Scherer, A. Schorr, & T. Johnstone (Eds.), *Appraisal processes in emotion: Theory, methods, research*. Oxford: Oxford University Press.

Rosenbaum, R.S., Köhler, S., Schacter, D.L., Moscovitch, M., Westmacott, R., Black, S.E., Gao, F., & Tulving, E. (2005). The case of KC: Contributions of a memory-impaired person to memory theory. *Neuropsychologia*, 43, 989–1021.

Ross, D.F., Ceci, S.J., Dunning, D., & Toglia, M.P. (1994). Uncsoncious transference and mistaken identity: When a witness misidentifies a familiar but innocent person. *Journal of Applied Psychology*, 79, 918–930.

Rossetti, Y., & Pisella, L. (2002). Several "vision for action" systems: A guide to dissociating and integrating dorsal and ventral functions. In W. Prinz & B. Hommel (Eds.), *Common mechanisms in perception and action: Attention and performance*. Oxford: Oxford University Press.

Rossetti, Y., Rode, G., Pisella, L., Boisson, D., & Perenin, M.T. (1998). Prism adaptation to a rightward optical deviation rehabilitates left hemispatial neglect. *Nature*, 395, 166–169.

Rossi, S., Caverni, J.P., & Girotto, V. (2001). Hypothesis testing in a rule discovery problem: When a focused procedure is effective. *Quarterly Journal of Experimental Psychology*, 54, 263–267.

Rossi, S., Pasqualetti, P., Zito, G., Vecchio, F., Capps, S.F., Miniussi, C., et al. (2006). Prefrontal and parietal cortex in human episodic memory: An interference study by repetitive transcranial magnetic stimulation. *European Journal of Neuroscience*, 23, 793–800.

Rossion, B., Caldara, R., Seghier, M., Schuller, A.M., Lazeyras, F., & Mayer, E. (2003). A network of occipito-temporal face-sensitive areas besides the right middle fusiform gyrus is necessary for normal face processing. *Brain*, 126, 2381–2395.

Rothermund, K., Voss, A., & Wentura, D. (2008). Counter-regulation in affective attentional biases: A basic mechanism that warrants flexibility in emotion and motivation. *Emotion*, 8, 34–46.

Rottenstreich, Y., & Tversky, A. (1997). Unpacking, repacking, and anchoring: Advances in support theory. *Psychological Review*, 104, 406–415.

Rousselet, G.A., Thorpe, S.J., & Fabre-Thorpe, M. (2004). How parallel is visual processing in the ventral pathway? *Trends in Cognitive Sciences*, 8, 363–370.

Roussey, J.-Y., & Piolat, A, (2008). Critical reading effort during text revision. *European Journal of Cognitive Psychology*, 20, 765–792.

Roy, D.F. (1991). Improving recall by eyewitnesses through the cognitive interview: Practical applications and implications for the police service. *The Psychologist*, 4, 398–400.

Rubin, D.C., Berntsen, D., & Hutson, M. (2009). The normative and the personal life: Individual differences in life scripts and life story events among US and Danish undergraduates. *Memory*, 17, 54–68.

Rubin, D.C., Rahhal, T.A., & Poon, L.W. (1998). Things learned in early childhood are remembered best. *Memory & Cognition*, 26, 3–19.

Rubin, D.C., & Wenzel, A.E. (1996). One hundred years of forgetting: A quantitative description of retention. *Psychological Bulletin*, 103, 734–760.

Rubin, D.C., Wetzler, S.E., & Nebes, R.D. (1986). Autobiographical memory across the life span. In D.C. Rubin (Ed.), *Autobiographical memory*. Cambridge: Cambridge University Press.

Rudner, M., Fransson, P., Ingvar, M., Nyberg, L., & Ronnberg, J. (2007). Neural representation of binding lexical signs and words in the episodic buffer of working memory. *Neuropsychologia*, 45, 2258–2276.

Ruff, C.C., Blankenburg, F., Bjoertomt, O., Bestmann, S., Freeman, E., Haynes, J.-D., et al. (2006). Concurrent TMS-fMRI and psychophysics reveal frontal influences on human retinotopic visual cortex. *Current Biology*, 16, 1479–1488.

Rugg, M.D., Johnson, J.D., Park, H., & Uncapher, M.R. (2008). Encoding–retrieval overlap in human episodic memory: A functional neuroimaging perspective. In W. Sossin, J.C. Lacaille, V. Castellucci, & S. Belleville (eds.), *Essence of memory*. Oxford: Elsevier.

Rumelhart, D.E. & and McClelland, J.L. (1986). *Parallel distributed processing: Explorations in the microstructure of cognition (Vol. 1)*. Cambridge, MA: MIT Press.

Rumelhart, D.E., & McClelland, J.L. (1986). On learning the past tenses of English verbs. In D.E. Rumelhart, J.L. McClelland, & The PDP Research Group (Eds.), *Parallel distributed processing, Vol. 2* (pp. 216–271). Cambridge, MA: MIT Press.

Rumelhart, D.E., McClelland, J.L., & The PDP Research Group (Eds.) (1986). *Parallel distributed processing, Vol. 1: Foundations*. Cambridge, MA: MIT Press.

Rumelhart, D.E., & Ortony, A. (1977). The representation of knowledge in memory. In R.C. Anderson, R.J. Spiro, & W.E. Montague (Eds.), *Schooling and the acquisition of knowledge*. Hillsdale, NJ: Lawrence Erlbaum Associates Inc.

Runeson, S., & Frykholm, G. (1983). Kinematic specifications of dynamics as an informational basis for person-and-action perception: Expectation, gender recognition, and deceptive intention. *Journal of Experimental Psychology: General*, 112, 585–615.

Rushton, S.K. (2008). Perceptually guided action: A step in the right direction. *Current Biology*, 18, R36–R37.

Rushton, S.K., Harris, J.M., Lloyd, M.R., & Wann, J.P. (1998). Guidance of locomotion on foot uses perceived target direction rather than optic flow. *Current Biology*, 8, 1191–1194.

Rushton, S.K., & Wann, J.P. (1999). Weighted combination of size and disparity: A computational model for timing a ball catch. *Nature Neuroscience*, 2, 186–190.

Rushworth, M.F.S., Ellison, A., & Walsh, V. (2001). Complementary localisation and lateralisation of orienting and motor attention. *Nature Neuroscience*, 4, 656–661.

Russo, J.E., Carlson, K.A., & Meloy, M.G. (2006). Choosing an inferior alternative. *Psychological Science*, 17, 899–904.

Rusting, C.L. (1998). Personality, mood, and cognitive processing of emotional information: Three conceptual frameworks. *Psychological Bulletin*, 124, 165–196.

Rusting, C.L., & DeHart, T. (2000). Retrieving positive memories to regulate negative mood: Consequences for mood-congruent memory. *Journal of Personality and Social Psychology*, 78, 737–752.

Ryan, J.D., Althoff, R.R., Whitlow, S., & Cohen, N.J. (2000). Amnesia is a deficit in relational memory. *Psychological Science*, 11, 454–461.

Sachez, C.A., & Wiley, J. (2006). An examination of the seductive details effect in terms of working memory capacity. *Memory & Cognition*, 34, 344–355.

Sacks, H., Schegloff, E.A., & Jefferson, G. (1974). A simplest systematics for the organisation of turn-taking in conversation. *Language*, 50, 696–735.

Saint-Cyr, J.A., Taylor, A.E., & Lang, A.E. (1988). Procedural learning and neostriatal dysfunction in man. *Brain*, 111, 941–959.

Saffran, E.M., Schwartz, M.F., & Marin, O.S.M. (1980a). Evidence from aphasia: Isolating the components of a production model. In B. Butterword (Ed.), *Language production, Vol. 1*. London: Academic Press.

Saffran, E.M., Schwartz, M.F., & Marin, O.S.M. (1980b). The word order problem in agrammatism: II. Production. *Brain & Language*, 10, 249–262.

Sala, J.B., Rämä, P., & Courtney, S.M. (2003). Functional topography of a distributed neural system for spatial and nonspatial information maintenance in working memory. *Neuropsychologia*, 41, 341–356.

Saling, L.L., & Phillips, J.G. (2007). Automatic behaviour: Efficient not mindless. *Brain Research Bulletin*, 73, 1–20.

Salovey, P., & Birnbaum, D. (1989). Influence of mood on health-related cognitions. *Journal of Personality and Social Psychology*, 57, 539–551.

Samuel, A.G. (1981). Phonemic restoration: Insights from a new methodology. *Journal of Experimental Psychology: General*, 110, 474–494.

Samuel, A.G. (1987). The effect of lexical uniqueness on phonemic restoration. *Journal of Memory and Language*, 26, 36–56.

Samuel, A.G. (1997). Lexical activation produces potent phonemic percepts. *Cognitive Psychology*, 32, 97–127.

Samuel, A.G., & Kat, D. (2003). Inhibition of return: A graphical meta-analysis of its time course and an empirical test of its temporal and spatial properties. *Psychonomic Bulletin & Review*, 10, 897–906.

Samuelson, W., & Zeckhauser, R.J. (1988). Status quo bias in decision making. *Journal of Risk and Uncertainty*, 1, 7–59.

Sanocki, T., Bowyer, K.W., Heath, M.D., & Sarkar, S. (1998). Are edges sufficient for object recognition? *Journal of Experimental Psychology: Human Perception & Performance*, 24, 340–349.

Santhouse, A.M., Howard, R.J., & ffytche, D.H. (2000). Visual hallucinatory syndromes and the anatomy of the visual brain. *Brain*, 123, 2055–2064.

Sato, H., Patterson, K., Fushimi, T., Maxim, J., & Bryan, K. (2008). Deep dyslexia for kanji and phonological dyslexia for kana: Different manifestations from a common source. *Neurocase*, 14, 508–524.

Sato, K., & Matsushima, K. (2006). Effects of audience awareness on procedural text writing. *Psychological Reports*, 99, 51–73.

Savage, L.J. (1954). *The foundations of statistics*. New York: Dover.

Savelsbergh, G.J.P., Pijpers, J.R., & van Santvoord, A.A.M. (1993). The visual guidance of catching. *Experimental Brain Research*, 93, 148–156.

Savelsbergh, G.J.P., Whiting, H.T.A., & Bootsma, R.J. (1991). Grasping tau. *Journal of Experimental Psychology: Human Perception & Performance*, 17, 315–322.

Saygin, A.P. (2007). Superior temporal and premotor brain areas necessary for biological motion perception. *Brain*, 130, 2452–2461.

Schacter, D.L., & Addis, D.R. (2007). The cognitive neuroscience of constructive memory: Remembering the past and imagining the future. *Philosophical Transactions of the Royal Society B*, 362, 773–786.

Schacter, D.L., Addis, D.R., & Buckner, R.L. (2004). Remembering the past to imagine the future: The prospective brain. *Nature Reviews Neuroscience*, 8, 657–661.

Schacter, D.L., Alpert, N.M., Savage, C.R., Rauch, S.L., & Albert, M.S. (1996). Conscious recollection and the human hippocampal formation: Evidence from positron emission tomography. *Proceedings of the National Academy of Science, USA*, 93, 321–325.

Schacter, D.L., & Church, B.A. (1995). Implicit memory in amnesic patients: When is auditory priming spared? *Journal of the International Neuropsychological Society*, 1, 434–442.

Schacter, D.L., Church, B.A., & Bolton, E. (1995). Implicit memory in amnesic patients: Impairment of voice-specific impairment priming. *Psychological Science*, 6, 20–25.

Schacter, D.L., & Tulving, E. (1994). What are the memory systems of 1994? In D.L. Schacter & E. Tulving (Eds.), *Memory systems*. Cambridge, MA: MIT Press.

Schacter, D.L., Wagner, A.D., & Buckner, R.L. (2000). Memory systems of 1999. In E. Tulving & F.I.M. Craik (Eds.), *The Oxford handbook of memory*. New York: Oxford University Press.

Schacter, D.L., Wig, G.S., & Stevens, W.D. (2007). Reductions in cortical activity during priming. *Current Opinion in Neurobiology*, 17, 171–176.

Schank, R.C. & Abelson, R.P. (1977). *Scripts, plans, goals and understanding*. Hillsdale, NJ: Lawrence Erlbaum Associates Inc.

Scharlau, I. (2004). Evidence for split foci of attention in a priming paradigm. *Perception & Psychophysics*, 66, 988–1002.

Scharlau, I. (2007). Perceptual latency priming: A measure of attentional facilitation. *Psychological Research*, 71, 678–686.

Schendan, H.E., Searl, M.M., Melrose, R.J., & Stern, C.E. (2003). An fMRI study of the role of the medial temporal lobe in implicit and explicit sequence learning. *Neuron*, 37, 1013–1025.

Schindler, I., McIntosh, R.D., Cassidy, T.R., Birchall, D., Benson, V., Ietswaart, M., & Milner, A.D. (2009). The disengage deficit in hemispatial neglect is restricted to between-object shifts and is abolished by prism adaptation. *Experimental Brain Research*, 192, 499–510.

Schmidt, J.R., & Thompson, V.A. (2008). "At least one" problem with "some" formal reasoning paradigms. *Memory and Cognition*, 36, 217–229.

Schmolesky, M.T., Wang, Y., Hanes, D.P., Thompson, K.G., Leutgeb, S., Schall, D., et al. (1998). Signal timing across the macaque visual system. *Journal of Neurophysiology*, 79, 3272–3278.

Schneider, W., & Shiffrin, R.M. (1977). Controlled and automatic human information processing: 1. Detection, search, and attention. *Psychological Review*, 84, 1–66.

Scholte, H.S., Wittreveen, S.C., Soekreijse, H., & Lamme, V.A.F. (2006). The influence of inattention on the neural correlates of scene segregation. *Brain Research*, 1076, 106–115.

Schooler, J.W., & Engstler-Schooler, T.Y. (1990). Verbal overshadowing of visual memories: Some things are better left unsaid. *Cognitive Psychology*, 22, 36–71.

Schott, B.H., Henson, R.N., Richardson-Klavehn, A., Becker, C., Thoma, V. et al. (2005). Redefining implicit and explicit memory: The functional neuroanatomy of priming, remembering, and control of retrieval. *Proceedings of the Natural Academy of Sciences of the USA*, 102, 1257–1262.

Schott, B.H., Richardson-Klavehn, A., Henson, R.N.A., Becker, C., Heinze, H.J., & Duzel, E. (2006). Neuroanatomical dissociation of encoding processes related to priming and explicit memory. *Journal of Neuroscience*, 26, 492–800.

Schrater, P.R., Knill, D.C., & Simoncelli, E.P. (2001). Perceiving visual expansion without optic flow. *Nature*, 410, 816–819.

Schriver, K. (1984). *Revised computer documentation for comprehension: Ten lessons in protocol-aided revision* (Tech. Rep. No. 14). Pittsburgh, PA: Carnegie Mellon University.

Schumacher, E.H., Seymour, T.L., Glass, J.M., Fencsik, D.E., Lauber, E.J., Kieras, D.E. et al. (2001). Virtually perfect time sharing in dual-task performance: Uncorking the central cognitive bottleneck. *Psychological Science*, 12, 101–108.

Schurger, A., & Sher, S. (2008). Awareness, loss aversion, and post-decision wagering. *Trends in Cognitive Sciences*, 12, 209–210.

Schwartz, B., Ward, A., Monterosso, J., Lyubomirsky, S., White, K., & Lehman, D.R. (2002). Maximising versus satisficing: Happiness is a matter of choice. *Journal of Personality and Social Psychology*, 83, 1178–1197.

Schwartz, B.L., & Hashtroudi, S. (1991). Priming is independent of skill learning. *Journal of Experimental Psychology: Learning, Memory, and Cognition*, 17, 1177–1187.

Schwartz, J.A., Chapman, G.B., Brewer, N.T., & Bergus, G.B. (2004). The effects of accountability on bias in physician decision making: Going from bad to worse. *Psychonomic Bulletin & Review*, 11, 173–178.

Schwartz, S., Vuilleumier, P., Hutton, C., Marouta, A., Dolan, R.J., & Driver, J. (2005). Modulation of fMRI responses by load at fixation during task-irrelevant stimulation in the peripheral visual field. *Cerebral Cortex*, 15, 770–786.

Schwarz, N., & Clore, G.L. (1983). Mood, misattribution and judgements of well-being: Informative and directive functions of affective states. *Journal of Personality and Social Psychology*, 45, 513–523.

Scoville, W.B., & Milner, B. (1957). Loss of recent memory after bilateral hippocampal lesions. *Journal of Neurology, Neurosurgery, & Psychiatry*, 20, 11–21.

Sears, C.R., Campbell, C.R., & Lupker, S.J. (2006). Is there a neighbourhood frequency effect in English? Evidence from reading and lexical decision. *Journal of Experimental Psychology: Human Perception and Performance*, 32, 1040–1062.

Sedikides, C. (1995). Central and peripheral self-conceptions are differentially influenced by mood – Test of the differential sensitivity hypothesis. *Journal of Personality and Social Psychology*, 14, 244–270.

Segal, S.J., & Fusella, V. (1970). Influence of imaged pictures and sounds on detection of visual and auditory signals. *Journal of Experimental Psychology*, 83, 458–464.

Seghier, M.L., Lee, H.L., Schofield, T., Ellis, C.L., & Price, C.J. (2008). Inter-subject variability in the use of two different neuronal networks for reading aloud familiar words. *NeuroImage*, 42, 1226–1236.

Seidenberg, M.S., & McClelland, J.L. (1989). A distributed, developmental model of word recognition and naming. *Psychological Review*, 96, 523–568.

Sejnowski, T.J., & Rosenberg, C.R. (1987). Parallel networks that learn to pronounce English text. *Complex Systems*, 1, 145–168.

Sekuler, R., & Blake, R. (2002). *Perception* (4th Ed.). New York: McGraw-Hill.

Sellen, A.J., Lowie, G., Harris, J.E., & Wilkins, A.J. (1997). What brings intentions to mind? An *in situ* study of prospective memory. *Memory*, 5, 483–507.

Seligman, M.E.P., & Hager, J.L. (1972). *Biological boundaries of learning*. New York: Appleton-Century-Crofts.

Senghas, A., Kita, S., & Özyürek, A. (2004). Children creating core properties of language: Evidence from an emerging sign language in Nicaragua. *Science*, 305, 1779–1782.

Seo, M.-G., & Barrett, L.F. (2007). Being emotional during decision making: good or bad? An empirical investigation. *Academy of Management Journal*, 50, 923–940.

Sereno, A.B., Briand, K.A., Amador, S.C., & Szapiel, S.V. (2006). Disruption of reflexive attention and eye movements in an individual with a collicular lesion. *Journal of Clinical and Experimental Neuropsychology*, 28, 145–166.

Sereno, S.C., Brewer, C.C., & O'Donnell, P.J. (2003). Context effects in word recognition: Evidence for early interactive processing. *Psychological Science*, 14, 328–333.

Sereno, S.C., Rayner, K., & Posner, M.I. (1998). Establishing a time-line of word recognition: Evidence from eye movements and event-related potentials. *NeuroReport*, 9, 2195–2200.

Sergent, J., & Signoret, J.L. (1992). Varieties of functional deficits in prosopagnosia. *Cerebral Cortex*, 2, 375–388.

Serrien, D.J., Ivry, R.B., & Swinnen, S.P. (2007). The missing link between action and cognition. *Progress in Neurobiology*, 82, 95–107.

Service, E. (2000). Phonological complexity and word duration in immediate recall: Different paradigms answer different questions: A comment on Cowan, Nugent, Elliott, and Geer. *Quarterly Journal of Experimental Psychology Section A: Human Experimental Psychology*, 53, 661–665.

Shah, A.K., & Oppenheimer, D.M. (2008). Heuristics made easy: An effort–reduction framework. *Psychological Bulletin*, 134, 207–222.

Shallice, T. (1991). From neuropsychology to mental structure. *Behavioral & Brain Sciences*, 14, 429–439.

Shallice, T., & Warrington, E.K. (1970). Independent functioning of verbal memory stores: A neuropsychological study. *Quarterly Journal of Experimental Psychology*, 22, 261–273.

Shallice, T., & Warrington, E.K. (1974). The dissociation between long-term retention of meaningful sounds and verbal material. *Neuropsychologia*, 12, 553–555.

Shanks, D.R. (2005). Implicit learning. In K. Lamberts & R. Goldstone (Eds.), *Handbook of cognition* (pp. 202–220). London: Sage.

Shanks, D.R. (2006). Complex choices better made unconsciously? *Science*, 313, 760.

Shanks, D.R., Rowland, L.A., & Ranger, M.S. (2005). Attentional load and implicit sequence learning. *Psychological Research*, 69, 369–382.

Shanks, D.R., & St. John, M.F. (1994). Characteristics of dissociable human learning systems. *Behavioral & Brain Sciences*, 17, 367–394.

Shelton, J.R., & Weinrich, M. (1997). Further evidence of a dissociation between output phonological and orthographic lexicons: A case study. *Cognitive Neuropsychology*, 14, 105–129.

Shiffrin, R.M., & Schneider, W. (1977). Controlled and automatic human information processing: II. Perceptual learning, automatic attending, and a general theory. *Psychological Review*, 84, 127–190.

Shimojo, S., & Ichikawa, S. (1989). Intuitive reasoning about probability – Theoretical and experimental analyses of the problem of 3 prisoners. *Cognition, 32,* 1–24.

Shintel, H., & Keysar, B. (2007). You said it before and you'll say it again: Expectations of consistency in communication. *Journal of Experimental Psychology: Learning, Memory, and Cognition, 33,* 357–369.

Shiv, B., Loewenstein, G., & Bechara, A. (2005b). The dark side of emotion in decision-making: When individuals with decreased emotional reactions make more advantageous decisions. *Cognitive Brain Research, 23(1),* 85–92.

Shiv, B., Loewenstein, G., Bechara, A., Damasio, H., & Damasio, A.R. (2005a). Investment behaviour and the negative side of emotion. *Psychological Science, 16,* 435–439.

Shrager, Y., Levy, D.A., Hopkins, R.O., & Squire, L.R. (2008). Working memory and the organization of brain systems. *Journal of Neuroscience, 28,* 4818–4822.

Shriver, E.R., Young, S.G., Hugenberg, K., Bernstein, M.J., & Lanter, J.R. (2008). Class, race, and the face: Social context modulates the cross-race effect in face recognition. *Personality and Social Psychology Bulletin, 34(2),* 260–274.

Shulman, G.L., Ollinger, J.M., Akbudak, E., Conturo, T.E., Snyder, A.Z., Petersen, S.E., & Corbetta, M. (1999). Areas involved in encoding and applying directional expectations to moving objects. *Journal of Neuroscience, 19,* 9480–9496.

Shuren, J.E., Hammond, C.S., Maher, L.M., Roth, L.J.G., & Heilman, K.M. (1995). Attention and anosognosia – The case of a jargonaphasic patient with unawareness of language deficit. *Neurology, 45,* 376–378.

Sides, A., Osherson, D., Bonini, N., & Viale, R. (2002). On the reality of the conjunction fallacy. *Memory & Cognition, 30,* 191–198.

Siegert, R.J., Taylor, K.D., Weatherall, M., & Abernethy, D.A. (2006). Is implicit sequence learning impaired in Parkinson's disease? A meta-analysis. *Neuropsychology, 20,* 490–495.

Siemer, M., & Reisenzein, R. (2007). The process of emotion inference. *Emotion, 7,* 1–20.

Siemer, M., Mauss, I., & Gross, J.J. (2007). Same situation – different emotions: How appraisals shape our emotions. *Emotion, 7,* 592–600.

Sigala, N. (2004). Visual categorization and the inferior temporal cortex. *Behavioural Brain Research, 149,* 1–7.

Sigman, M., & Dehaene, S. (2008). Brain mechanisms of serial and parallel processing during dual-task performance. *Journal of Neuroscience, 28,* 7585–7598.

Silvanto, J. (2008). A re-evaluation of blindsight and the role of striate cortex (V1) in visual awareness. *Neuropsychologia, 46,* 2869–2871.

Simcock, G., & Hayne, H. (2002). Breaking the barrier? Children fail to translate their preverbal memories into language. *Psychological Science, 13,* 225–231.

Simion, F., Regolin, L., & Bulf, H. (2008). A predisposition for biological motion in the newborn baby. *Proceedings of the National Academy of Sciences of the United States of America, 105,* 809–813.

Simon, D., Krawczyk, D.C., & Holyoak, K.J. (2004). Construction of preferences by constraint satisfaction. *Psychological Science, 15,* 331–336.

Simon, H.A. (1957). *Models of man: Social and rational.* New York: Wiley.

Simon, H.A. (1966). Scientific discovery and the psychology of problem solving. In H.A. Simon (Ed.), *Mind and Cosmos: Essays in contemporary science and philosophy.* Pittsburgh, PA: University of Pittsburgh Press.

Simon, H.A. (1974). How big is a chunk? *Science, 183,* 482–488.

Simon, H.A. (1978). Rationality as a process and product of thought. *American Economic Association, 68,* 1–16.

Simon, H.A. (1990). Invariants of human behaviour. *Annual Review of Psychology, 41,* 1–19.

Simon, H.A., & Gilmartin, K. (1973). Simulation of memory for chess positions. *Cognitive Psychology, 5,* 29–46.

Simons, D.J., & Chabris, F. (1999). Gorillas in our midst: Sustained inattentional blindness for dynamic events. *Perception, 28,* 1059–1074.

Simons, D.J., & Levin, D.T. (1997). Change blindness. *Trends in Cognitive Science, 1,* 261–267.

Simons, D.J., & Rensink, R.A. (2005). Change blindness: Past, present, and future. *Trends in Cognitive Sciences, 9,* 16–20.

Simons, J.S., Peers, P.V., Hwang, D.Y., Ally, B.A., Fletcher, P.C., & Budson, A.E. (2008). Is the parietal lobe necessary for recollection in humans? *Neuropsychologia, 46,* 1185–1191.

Simonson, I., & Staw, B.M. (1992). De-escalation strategies: A comparison of techniques for reducing commitment to losing courses of action. *Journal of Applied Psychology, 77,* 419–426.

Sinai, M.J., Ooi, T.L., & He, Z.H. (1998). Terrain influences the accurate judgement of distance. *Nature, 395,* 497–500.

Singer, M. (1994). Discourse inference processes. In M.A. Gernsbacher (Ed.), *Handbook of psycholinguistics.* San Diego, CA: Academic Press.

Sio, U.N., & Ormerod, T.C. (2009). Does incubation enhance problem solving? A meta-analytic review. *Psychological Bulletin, 135,* 94–120.

Sirigu, A., & Duhamel, J.R. (2001). Motor and visual imagery as two complementary but neutrally dissociable mental processes. *Journal of Cognitive Neuroscience, 13,* 910–919.

Sirigu, A., Zalla, T., Pillon, B., Grafman, J., Agid, Y., & Dubois, B. (1995). Selective impairments in managerial knowledge following prefrontal cortex damage. *Cortex, 31,* 301–316.

Skinner, E.I., & Fernandes, M.A. (2007). Neural correlates of recollection and familiarity: A review of neuroimaging and patient data. *Neuropsychologia, 45,* 2163–2179.

Slezak, P. (1991). Can images be rotated and inspected? A test of the pictorial medium theory. *Program of the Thirteenth Annual Conference of the Cognitive Science Society,* 55–60.

Slezak, P. (1995). The 'philosophical' case against visual imagery. In T. Caelli, P. Slezak, & R. Clark (Eds.), *Perspectives in cognitive science: Theories, experiments and foundations* (pp. 237–271). New York: Ablex.

Sloboda, J.A., Davidson, J.W., Howe, M.J.A., & Moore, D.G. (1996). The role of practice in the development of performing musicians. *British Journal of Psychology, 87,* 287–309.

Sloman, S. (2005). *Causal models: How people think about the world and its alternatives.* Oxford: Oxford University Press.

Sloman, S.A., & Over, D.E. (2003). Probability judgment: From the inside and out. In D.E. Over, *Evolution and the psychology of thinking.* Hove, UK: Psychology Press.

Sloman, S.A. (1996). The empirical case for two systems of reasoning. *Psychological Bulletin, 119,* 3–22.

Smith, A.T., Wall, M.B., Williams, A.L., & Singh, K.D. (2006). Sensitivity to optic flow in human cortical areas MT and MST. *European Journal of Neuroscience, 23,* 561–569.

Smith, C.A., & Kirby, L.D. (2001). Toward delivering on the promise of appraisal theory. In K.R. Scherer, A. Schorr, & T. Johnstone (Eds.), *Appraisal processes in emotion: Theory, methods, research.* Oxford, UK: Oxford University Press.

Smith, C.A., & Lazarus, R.S. (1993). Appraisal components, core relational themes, and the emotions. *Cognition & Emotion, 7,* 233–269.

Smith, E.E., & Jonides, J. (1997). Working memory: A view from neuroimaging. *Cognitive Psychology, 33,* 5–42.

Smith, E.E., & Kosslyn, S.M. (2007). *Cognitive Psychology: Mind and Brain.* Upper Saddle River, NJ: Pearson/Prentice Hall.

Smith, G., Della Sala, S., Logie, R.H., & Maylor, E.A. (2000). Prospective and retrospective memory in normal ageing and dementia: A questionnaire study. *Memory, 8,* 311–321.

Smith, M. (2000). Conceptual structures in language production. In L. Wheeldon (Ed.), *Aspects of language production.* Hove, UK: Psychology Press.

Smith, M., & Wheeldon, L. (2004). Horizontal information flow in spoken sentence production. *Journal of Experimental Psychology: Learning, Memory, & Cognition, 30,* 675–686.

Smith, R.E. (2003). The cost of remembering to remember in event-based prospective memory: Investigating the capacity demands of delayed intention performance. *Journal of Experimental Psychology: Learning, Memory, and Cognition, 29,* 347–361.

Smith, R.E., & Bayen, U.J. (2005). The effects of working memory resource availability on prospective memory: A formal modelling approach. *Experimental Psychology, 52,* 243–256.

Smith, R.E., Hunt, R.R., McVay, J.C., & McConnell, M.D. (2007). The cost of event-based prospective memory: Salient target events. *Journal of Experimental Psychology: Learning, Memory, and Cognition, 33,* 734–746.

Smyth, M.M., Morris, P.E., Levy, P., & Ellis, A.W. (1987). *Cognition in action.* Hove, UK: Psychology Press.

Snedeker, J., & Trueswell, J. (2003). Using prosody to avoid ambiguity: Effects of speaker awareness and referential context. *Journal of Memory and Language, 48,* 103–130.

Snodgrass, M., Bernat, E., & Shevrin, H. (2004). Unconscious perception at the objective detection threshold exists. *Perception & Psychophysics, 66,* 888–895.

Snow, J.C., & Mattingley, J.B. (2006). Goal-driven selective attention in patients with right hemisphere lesions: How intact is the ipsilesional field? *Brain, 129,* 168–181.

Snowden, J., Griffiths, H., & Neary, D. (1994). Semantic dementia: Autobiographical contribution to preservation of meaning. *Cognitive Neuropsychology, 11,* 265–288.

Solomon, K.O., & Barsalou, L.W. (2001). Representing properties locally. *Cognitive Psychology, 43,* 129–169.

Solomon, S.G., & Lennie, P. (2007). The machinery of colour vision. *Nature Reviews Neuroscience, 8,* 276–286.

Soon, C.S., Brass, M., Heinze, H.J., & Hayes, J.D. (2008). Unconscious determinants of free decisions in the human brain. *Nature Neuroscience, 11,* 543–545.

Southwood, M.H., & Chatterjee, A. (2001). The simultaneous activation hypothesis: Explaining recovery from deep to phonological dyslexia. *Brain and Language, 76,* 18–34.

Spearman, C.E. (1927). *The abilities of man: Their nature and measurement.* London: Macmillan.

Speisman, J.C., Lazarus, R.S., Mordkoff, A.M., & Davison, L.A. (1964). Experimental reduction of stress based on ego-defence theory. *Journal of Abnormal Psychology*, 68, 367–380.

Spelke, E.S., Hirst, W.C., & Neisser, U. (1976). Skills of divided attention. *Cognition*, 4, 215–230.

Spence, C. (2008). Cognitive neuroscience: Searching for the bottleneck in the brain. *Current Biology*, 18, R965–R968.

Spence, C., & Driver, J. (1996). Audiovisual links in endogenous covert spatial attention. *Journal of Experimental Psychology: Human Perception and Performance*, 22, 1005–1030.

Spencer, R.M., & Weisberg, R.W. (1986). Context-dependent effects on analogical transfer. *Memory & Cognition*, 14, 442–449.

Sperber, D., & Girotto, V. (2002). Use or misuse of the selection task? Rejoinder to Fiddick, Cosmides, and Tooby. *Cognition*, 85, 277–290.

Sperber, D., & Wilson, D. (1986). *Relevance.* Cambridge, MA: Harvard University Press.

Sperling, G. (1960). The information that is available in brief visual presentations. *Psychological Monographs*, 74 (Whole No. 498), 1–29.

Sperry, R.W. (1968). Hemisphere deconnection and unity in conscious awareness. *American Psychologist*, 23, 723–733.

Spieler, D.H., & Griffin, Z.M. (2006). The influence of age on the time course of word preparation in multiword utterances. *Language and Cognitive Processes*, 21, 291–321.

Spiers, H.J., Maguire, E.A., & Burgess, N. (2001). Hippocampal amnesia. *Neurocase*, 7, 357–382.

Spivey, M.J., Tanenhaus, M.K., Eberhard, K.M., & Sedivy, J.C. (2002). Eye movements and spoken language comprehension: Effects of visual context on syntactic ambiguity resolution. *Cognitive Psychology*, 45, 447–481.

Sun, R. (2007). The importance of cognitive architectures: An analysis based on CLARION. *Journal of Experimental & Theoretical Artificial Intelligence*, 19, 159–193.

Stanovich, K.E., & West, R.F. (1998). Individual differences in rational thought. *Journal of Experimental Psychology: General*, 127, 161–188.

Stanovich, K.E., & West, R.F. (2000). Individual differences in reasoning: Implications for the rationality debate? *Behavioral and Brain Sciences*, 23, 645–665.

Stanovich, K.E., & West, R.F. (2008). On the relative independence of thinking biases and cognitive ability. *Journal of Personality and Social Psychology*, 94, 672–695.

Staresina, B.P., & Davachi, L. (2006). Differential encoding mechanisms for subsequent associative recognition and free recall. *Journal of Neuroscience*, 26, 9162–9172.

Steblay, N.M. (1997). Social influence in eyewitness recall: A meta-analytic review of line-up instruction effects. *Law and Human Behavior*, 21, 283–298.

Steblay, N.M., Dysart, J., Fulero, S., & Lindsay, R.C.L. (2001). Eyewitness accuracy rates in sequential and simultaneous line-up presentations: A meta-analytic comparison. *Law and Human Behavior*, 25, 459–474.

Stein, B.E., & Meredith, M.A. (1993). *The merging of the senses.* Cambridge, MA: MIT Press.

Steinhauer, K., & Friederici, A.D. (2001). Prosodic boundaries, comma rules, and brain responses: The closure positive shift in ERPs as a universal marker for prosodic phrasing in listeners and readers. *Journal of Psycholinguistic Research*, 11, 305–323.

Steinvorth, S., Corkin, S., & Halgren, E. (2006). Ecphory of autobiographical memories: An fMRI study of recent and remote memory retrieval. *Neuroimage*, 30, 285–298.

Stenning, K., & van Lambalgen, M. (2004). A little logic goes a long way: Basing experiment on semantic theory in the cognitive science of conditional reasoning. *Cognitive Science*, 28, 481–529.

Sternberg, R.J. (2004). What do we know about the nature of reasoning? In J.P. Leighton & R.J. Sternberg (Eds.), *The nature of reasoning.* Cambridge: Cambridge University Press.

Sternberg, R.J., & Ben-Zeev, T. (2001). *Complex cognition: The psychology of human thought.* Oxford: Oxford University Press.

Stoerig, P., & Cowey, A. (1997). Blindsight in man and monkey. *Brain*, 120, 535–559.

Strayer, D.L., & Drews, F.A. (2007). Cell-phone induced driver distraction. *Current Directions in Psychological Science*, 16, 128–131.

Strayer, D.L., & Johnston, W.A. (2001). Driven to distraction: Dual-task studies of simulated driving and conversing on a cellular telephone. *Psychological Science*, 12, 462–466.

Stuss, D.T., & Alexander, M.P. (2007). Is there a dysexecutive syndrome? *Philosophical Transactions of the Royal Society B*, 362, 901–1015.

Styles, E.A. (1997). *The psychology of attention.* Hove, UK: Psychology Press.

Sugase, Y., Yamane, S., Ueno, S., & Kawano, K. (1999). Global and fine information coded by single neurons in the temporal visual cortex. *Nature*, 400, 869–872.

Sulin, R.A., & Dooling, D.J. (1974). Intrusion of a thematic idea in retention of prose. *Journal of Experimental Psychology*, 103, 255–262.

Sullivan, L. (1976). Selective attention and secondary message analysis: A reconsideration of Broadbent's filter model of selective attention. *Quarterly Journal of Experimental Psychology*, 28, 167–178.

Summerfield, J.J., Hassabis, D., & Maguire, E.A. (2009). Cortical midline involvement in autobiographical memory. *Neuroimage*, 44, 1188–1200.

Sun, R. (2007). The importance of cognitive architectures: An analysis based on CLARION. *Journal of Experimental and Theoretical Artificial Intelligence*, 19, 159–193.

Sun, R., Zhang, X., & Mathews, R. (2009). Capturing human data in a letter-counting task: Accessibility and action-centredness in representing cognitive skills. *Neural Networks*, 22, 15–29.

Sussman, H.M., Hoemeke, K.A., & Ahmed, F.S. (1993). A cross-linguistic investigation of locus equations as a phonetic descriptor for place of articulation. *Journal of the Acoustical Society of America*, 94, 1256–1268.

Svoboda, E., McKinnon, M.C., & Levine, B. (2006). The functional neuroanatomy of autobiographical memory: a meta-analysis. *Neuropsychologia*, 44, 2189–2208.

Sweller, J., & Levine, M. (1982). Effects of goal specificity on means–ends analysis and learning. *Journal of Experimental Psychology: Learning, Memory, and Cognition*, 8, 463–474.

Swets, B., Desmet, T., Clifton, C., & Ferreira, F. (2008). Underspecification of syntactic ambiguities: Evidence from self-paced reading. *Memory & Cognition*, 36, 201–216.

Tainturier, M.J. (1996). Phonologically-based errors and their implications in the specification of phonology to orthography conversion processes. *Brain And Cognition*, 32, 148–151.

Tainturier, M.-J., & Rapp, B. (2001). The spelling process. In B. Rapp (Ed.), *The handbook of cognitive neuropsychology*. Hove, UK: Psychology Press.

Tainturier, M.-J., Schiemenz, S., & Leek, E.C. (2006). Separate orthographic representations for reading and spelling? Evidence from a case of preserved lexical reading and impaired lexical spelling. *Brain and Language*, 99, 40–41.

Talarico, J.M., & Rubin, D.C. (2003). Confidence, not consistency, characterises flashbulb memories. *Psychological Science*, 14, 455–461.

Tamietto, M., & de Gelder, B. (2008). Affective blindsight in the intact brain: Neural interhemispheric summation for unseen fearful expressions. *Neuropsychologia*, 46, 820–828.

Tanenhaus, M.K., Spivey-Knowlton, M.J., Eberhard, K.M., & Sedivy, J.C. (1995). Integration of visual and linguistic information in spoken language comprehension. *Science*, 268, 1632–1634.

Tarr, M.J., & Bülthoff, H.H. (1995). Is human object recognition better described by geon structural descriptions or by multiple views? Comment on Biederman and Gerhardstein (1993). *Journal of Experimental Psychology: Human Perception & Performance*, 21, 1494–1505.

Tarr, M.J., & Bülthoff, H.H. (1998). Image-based object recognition in man, monkey and machine. *Cognition*, 67, 1–20.

Tarr, M.J., Williams, P., Hayward, W.G., & Gauthier, I. (1998). Three-dimensional object recognition is viewpoint-dependent. *Nature Neuroscience*, 1, 195–206.

Tartter, V. (1986). *Language processes*. New York: Holt, Rinehart & Winston.

Terry, H.R., Charlton, S.G., & Perrone, J.A. (2008). The role of looming and attention capture in drivers' braking responses. *Accident Analysis and Prevention*, 40, 1375–1382.

Tetlock, P.E. (1991). An alternative metaphor in the study of judgement and choice: People as politicians. *Theory and Psychology*, 1, 451–475.

Tetlock, P.E. (2002). Social functionalist frameworks for judgement and choice: Intuitive politicians, theologians, and prosecutors. *Psychological Review*, 109, 451–471.

Tetlock, P.E., & Mellers, B.A. (2002). The great rationality debate. *Psychological Science*, 13, 94–99.

Thomas, J.C. (1974). An analysis of behaviour in the hobbits–orcs problem. *Cognitive Psychology*, 6, 257–269.

Thomson, D.M., & Tulving, E. (1970). Associative encoding and retrieval: Weak and strong cues. *Journal of Experimental Psychology*, 86, 255–262.

Thornton, I.M., Rensink, R.A., & Shiffrar, M. (2002). Active versus passive processing of biological motion. *Perception*, 31, 837–853.

Thorndike, E.L. (1898). Animal intelligence: An experimental study of the associative processes in animals. *The Psychological Review Monograph Supplements*, 2, No. 4 (Whole No. 8).

Thornton, T.L., & Gilden, D.L. (2007). Parallel and serial processes in visual search. *Psychological Review*, 114, 71–103.

Thorpe, S., Fize, D., & Marlot, C. (1996). Speed of processing in the human visual system. *Nature*, 381, 520–522.

Tian, Y., & Yao, D. (2008). A study on the neural mechanism of inhibition of return by the event-related potential in the Go/No go task. *Biological Psychology*, 79, 171–178.

Todd, P.M., & Gigerenzer, G. (2007). Environments that make us smart. *Current Directions in Psychological Science*, 16, 167–171.

Tollestrup, P.A., Turtle, J.W., & Yuille, J.C. (1994). Actual victims and witnesses to robbery and fraud: An archival analysis. In D.F. Ross, J.D. Read, & M.P. Toglia (Eds.), *Adult eyewitness testimony: Current trends and developments*. New York: Wiley.

Tononi, G., & Koch, C. (2008). The neural correlates of consciousness: An update. *Annals of the New York Academy of Sciences, 1124*, 239–261.

Townsend, J.T. (1990). Serial vs. parallel processing: Sometimes they look like Tweedledum and Tweedledee but they can (and should) be distinguished. *Psychological Science, 1*, 46–54.

Tranel, D., Damasio, A.R., Damasio, H., & Brandt, J.P. (1994). Sensori-motor skill learning in amnesia: Additional evidence for the neural basis of non-declarative memory. *Learning and Memory, 1*, 165–179.

Trappery, C. (1996), A meta-analysis of consumer choice and subliminal advertising. *Psychology & Marketing, 13*, 517–530.

Tree, J.J., & Kay, J. (2006). Phonological dyslexia and phonological impairment: An exception to the rule? *Neuropsychologia, 44*, 2861–2873.

Treisman, A.M. (1960). Contextual cues in selective listening. *Quarterly Journal of Experimental Psychology, 12*, 242–248.

Treisman, A.M. (1964). Verbal cues, language, and meaning in selective attention. *American Journal of Psychology, 77*, 206–219.

Treisman, A.M. (1988). Features and objects: The fourteenth Bartlett memorial lecture. *Quarterly Journal of Experimental Psychology, 40A*, 201–237.

Treisman, A.M. (1992). Spreading suppression or feature integration? A reply to Duncan and Humphreys (1992). *Journal of Experimental Psychology: Human Perception & Performance, 18*, 589–593.

Treisman, A.M. (1993). The perception of features and objects. In A. Baddeley & L. Weiskrantz (Eds.), *Attention: Selection, awareness, and control*. Oxford: Clarendon Press.

Treisman, A.M., & Davies, A. (1973). Divided attention to ear and eye. In S. Kornblum (Ed.), *Attention and performance, Vol. IV*. London: Academic Press.

Treisman, A.M., & Gelade, G. (1980). A feature integration theory of attention. *Cognitive Psychology, 12*, 97–136.

Treisman, A.M., & Riley, J.G.A. (1969). Is selective attention selective perception or selective response: A further test. *Journal of Experimental Psychology, 79*, 27–34.

Treisman, A.M., & Sato, S. (1990). Conjunction search revisited. *Journal of Experimental Psychology: Human Perception & Performance, 16*, 459–478.

Tresilian, J.R. (1999). Visually timed action: Time out for "tau"? *Trends in Cognitive Sciences, 3*, 301–310.

Trevena, J.A., & Miller, J. (2002). Cortical movement preparation before and after a conscious decision to move. *Consciousness and Cognition, 11*, 162–190.

Trevarthen, C. (2004). Split-brain and the mind. In R. Gregory (Ed.), *The Oxford companion to the mind* (2nd Ed.). Oxford: Oxford University Press.

Triesch, J., Ballard, D.H., Hayhoe, M.M., & Sullivan, B.T. (2003). What you see is what you need. *Journal of Vision, 3*, 80–94.

Triesch, J., Ballard, D.H., & Jacobs, R.A. (2002). Fast temporal dynamics of visual cue integration. *Perception, 31*, 421–434.

Trojano, L., & Grossi, D. (1995). Phonological and lexical coding in verbal short-term memory and learning. *Brain & Cognition, 21*, 336–354.

Trueswell, J.C., Tanenhaus, M.K., & Garnsey, S.M. (1994). Semantic influences on parsing: Use of thematic role information in syntactic disambiguation. *Journal of Memory and Language, 33*, 285–318.

Tsal, Y. (1983). Movement of attention across the visual field. *Journal of Experimental Psychology: Human Perception and Performance, 9*, 523–530.

Tsao, D.Y., Freiwald, W.A., Tootell, R.B.H., & Livingstone, M.S. (2006). A cortical region consisting entirely of face-selective cells. *Science, 311*, 670–674.

Tsutsui, K., Taira, M., & Sakata, H. (2005). Neural mechanisms of three-dimensional vision. *Neuroscience Research, 51*, 221–229.

Tuckey, M.R., & Brewer, N. (2003a). How schemas affect eyewitness memory over repeated retrieval attempts. *Applied Cognitive Psychology, 7*, 785–800.

Tuckey, M.R., & Brewer, N. (2003b). The influence of schemas, stimulus ambiguity, and interview schedule on eyewitness memory over time. *Journal of Experimental Psychology: Applied, 9*, 101–118.

Tuffiash, M., Roring, R.W., & Ericsson, K.A. (2007). Expert performance in SCRABBLE: Implications for the study of the structure and acquisition of complex skills. *Journal of Experimental Psychology: Applied, 13*, 124–134.

Tulving, E. (1972). Episodic and semantic memory. In E. Tulving & W. Donaldson (Eds.), *Organisation of memory*. London: Academic Press.

Tulving, E. (1979). Relation between encoding specifity and levels of processing. In L.S. Cermak & F.I.M. Craik (Eds.), *Levels of processing in human memory*. Hillsdale, NJ: Lawrence Erlbaum Associates Inc.

Tulving, E. (2002). Episodic memory: From mind to brain. *Annual Review of Psychology*, *53*, 1–25.

Tulving, E., & Psotka, J. (1971). Retroactive inhibition in free recall: Inaccessibility of information available in the memory trace. *Journal of Experimental Psychology*, *87*, 1–8.

Tulving, E., Schacter, D.L., & Stark, H.A. (1982). Priming effects in word-fragment completion are independent of recognition memory. *Journal of Experimental Psychology: Learning, Memory, & Cognition*, *17*, 595–617.

Turatto, M., Sandrini, M., & Miniussi, C. (2004). The role of the right dorsolateral prefrontal cortex in visual change awareness. *Neuroreport*, *15*, 2549–2552.

Turella, L., Pierno, A.C., Tubaldi, F., & Castiello, U. (2009). Mirror neurons in humans: Consisting or confounding evidence? *Brain & Language*, *108*, 10–21.

Tversky, A. (1972). Elimination by aspects: A theory of choice. *Psychological Review*, *79*, 281–299.

Tversky, A., & Kahneman, D. (1974). Judgement under uncertainty: Heuristics and biases. *Science*, *185*, 1124–1131.

Tversky, A., & Kahneman, D. (1983). Extensional versus intuitive reasoning: The conjunction fallacy in probability judgement. *Psychological Review*, *91*, 293–315.

Tversky, A., & Kahneman, D. (1987). Rational choice and the framing of decisions. In R. Hogarth & M. Reder (Eds.), *Rational choice: The contrast between economics and psychology*. Chicago: University of Chicago Press.

Tversky, A., & Koehler, D.J. (1994). Support theory: A nonextensional representation of subjective probability. *Psychological Review*, *101*, 547–567.

Tversky, A., & Shafir, E. (1992). The disjunction effect in choice under uncertainty. *Psychological Science*, *3*, 305–309.

Tweney, R.D., & Chitwood, S.C. (1995). Scientific reasoning. In S. Newstead & J.St.B.T. Evans (Eds.), *Perspectives on thinking and reasoning: Essays in honour of Peter Wason* (pp. 241–260). Hove, UK: Lawrence Erlbaum Associates Ltd.

Tweney, R.D., Doherty, M.E., Worner, W.J., Pliske, D.B., Mynatt, C.R., Gross, K.A. et al. (1980). Strategies for rule discovery in an inference task. *Quarterly Journal of Experimental Psychology*, *32*, 109–123.

Tyler, H.R. (1968). Abnormalities of perception with defective eye movements (Balint's syndrome). *Brain and Cognition*, *12*, 195–204.

Tyler, L.K., & Moss, H.E. (1997). Imageability and category-specificity. *Cognitive Neuropsychology*, *14*, 293–318.

Uchikawa, K., Uchikawa, H., & Boynton, R.M. (1989). Partial colour constancy of isolated surface colours examined by a colour-naming method. *Perception*, *18*, 83–91.

Ucros, C.G. (1989). Mood state-dependent memory: A meta-analysis. *Cognition & Emotion*, *3*, 139–167.

Uddin, L.Q., Rayman, J., & Zaidel, E. (2005). Split-brain reveals separate but equal self-recognition in the two cerebral hemispheres. *Consciousness and Cognition*, *14*, 633–640.

Ullman, S. (2007). Object recognition and segmentation by a fragment-based hierarchy. *Trends in Cognitive Sciences*, *11*, 58–64.

Umiltà, C. (2001). Mechanisms of attention. In B. Rapp (Ed.), *The handbook of cognitive neuropsychology*. Hove, UK: Psychology Press.

Umiltà, M.A., Kohler, E., Gallese, V., Fogassi, L., Fadiga, L., Keysers, C., Rizzolatti, G. (2001). I know what you are doing: A neurophysiological study. *Neuron*, *31*, 155–165.

Underwood, G. (1974). Moray vs. the rest: The effect of extended shadowing practice. *Quarterly Journal of Experimental Psychology*, *26*, 368–372.

Underwood, B.J., & Postman, L. (1960). Extra-experimental sources of interference in forgetting. *Psychological Review*, *67*, 73–95.

Unterrainer, J.M., Rahm, B., Kaller, C.P., Ruff, C.C., Speer, J., Krause, B.J., Schwarzwald, R., Hautzel, H., & Halsbad, H. (2004). When planning fails: Individual differences and error-related brain activity in problem solving. *Cerebral Cortex*, *14*, 1390–1397.

Vaina, L.M. (1998). Complex motion perception and its deficits. *Current Opinion in Neurobiology*, *8*, 494–502.

Vaina, L.M., Cowey, A., LeMay, M., Bienfang, D.C., & Kinkinis, R. (2002). Visual deficits in a patient with "kaleidoscopic disintegration of the visual world". *European Journal of Neurology*, *9*, 463–477.

Valentine, T., Pickering, A., & Darling, S. (2003). Characteristics of eyewitness identification that predict the outcome of real line-ups. *Applied Cognitive Psychology*, *17*, 969–993.

Vallar, G., & Papagno, C. (1995). Neuropsychological impairments of short-term memory. In A.D. Baddeley, B.A. Wilson, & F.N. Watts (Eds.), *Handbook of memory disorders*. Chichester: Wiley.

Vallar, G., & Papagno, C. (2002). Neuropsychological impairments of verbal short-term memory. In A.D. Baddeley, M.D. Kopelman, & B.A. Wilson (Eds.), *Handbook of memory disorders* (2nd Ed, pp. 249–270.). Chichester: Wiley.

Vallee-Tourangeau, F., & Payton, T. (2008). Graphical representation fosters discovery in the 2-4-6 task. *Quarterly Journal of Experimental Psychology, 61,* 625–640.

Van den Berg, A.V., & Brenner, E. (1994). Why two eyes are better than one for judgements of heading. *Nature, 371,* 700–702.

Van Dillen, L.F., & Koole, S.L. (2007). Clearing the mind: A working memory model of distraction from negative mood. *Emotion, 7,* 715–723.

Van Dillen, L.F., Heslenfeld, D.J., & Koole, S.L. (2009). Turning down the emotional brain: an fMRI study of the effects of cognitive load on the processing of affective images. *Neuroimage, 45,* 1212–1219.

Van Doorn, H., van der Kamp, J., & Savelsbergh, G.J.P. (2007). Grasping the Müller-Lyer illusion: The contributions of vision for perception in action. *Neuropsychologia, 45,* 1939–1947.

Van Gelder, T., Bissett, M., & Cumming, G. (2004). Cultivating expertise in informal reasoning. *Canadian Journal of Experimental Psychology, 58,* 142–152.

Van Gompel, R.P.G., & Pickering, M.J. (2001). Lexical guidance in sentence processing: A note on Adams, Clifton, and Mitchell (1998). *Psychonomic Bulletin & Review, 8,* 851–857.

Van Gompel, R.P.G., Pickering, M.J., Pearson, J., & Liversedge, S.P. (2005). Evidence against competition during syntactic ambiguity resolution. *Journal of Memory and Language, 52,* 284–307.

Van Gompel, R.P.G., Pickering, M.J., & Traxler, M.J. (2000). Unrestricted race: A new model of syntactic ambiguity resolution. In A. Kennedy, R. Radach, D. Heller, & J. Pynte (Eds.), *Reading as a perceptual process.* Oxford: Elsevier.

Van Gompel, R.P.G., Pickering, M.J., & Traxler, M.J. (2001). Reanalysis in sentence processing: Evidence against constraint-based and two-stage models. *Journal of Memory and Language, 43,* 225–258.

Van Harreveld, F., Wagenmakers, E.J., & van der Maas, H.L.J. (2007). The effects of time pressure on chess skill: An investigation into fast and slow processes underlying expert performance. *Psychological Research, 71,* 591–597.

Van Orden, G.C. (1987). A rows is a rose: Spelling, sound and reading. *Memory and Cognition, 14,* 371–386.

Van Petten, C., Coulson, S., Rubin, S., Plante, E., & Parks, M. (1999). Time course of word identification and semantic integration in spoken language. *Journal of Experimental Psychology: Learning, Memory, and Cognition, 25,* 394–417.

Van Turennout, M., Hagoort, P., & Brown, C.M. (1998). Brain activity during speaking: From syntax to phonology in 40 milliseconds. *Science, 280,* 572–574.

Vanderberg, R., & Swanson, H.L. (2007). Which components of working memory are important in the writing process? *Reading and Writing, 20,* 721–752.

Vandenberghe, M., Schmidt, N., Fery, P., & Cleeremans, A. (2006). Can amnesic patients learn without awareness? New evidence comparing deterministic and probabilistic sequence learning. *Neuropsychologia, 44,* 1629–1641.

Vanrie, J., Béatse, E., Wagemans, J., Sunaert, S., & van Hecke, P. (2002). Mental rotation versus invariant features in object perception from different viewpoints: An fMRI study. *Neuropsychologia, 40,* 917–930.

Vargha-Khadem F., Gadian, D.G., & Mishkin, M. (2002). Dissociations in cognitive memory: The syndrome of developmental amnesia. In *Episodic memory: new directions in research* 2002 (pp.153–163). New York: Oxford University Press.

Vargha-Khadem, F., Gadian, D.G., Watkins, K.E., Connelly, A., Van Paesschen, W., & Mishkin, M. (1997). Differential effects of early hippocampal pathology on episodic and semantic memory. *Science, 277,* 376–380.

Vecera, S.P., Flevaris, A.V., & Filapek, J.C. (2004). Exogenous spatial attention influences figure-ground assignment. *Psychological Science, 15,* 20–26.

Veilleumier, P., Schwartz, S., Clark, K., Husain, M., & Driver, J. (2002). Testing memory for unseen visual stimuli in patients with extinction and spatial neglect. *Journal of Cognitive Neuroscience, 14,* 875–886.

Velmans, M. (2009). How to define consciousness – and how not to define consciousness. *Journal of Consciousness Studies, 16*(5), 139–156.

Verfaellie, M., Koseff, P., & Alexander, M.P. (2000). Acquisition of novel semantic information in amnesia: Effects of lesion location. *Neuropsychologia, 38,* 484–492.

Viggiano, M.P., Giovannelli, F., Borgheresi, A., Feurra, M., Berardi, N., Pizzorusso, T., Zaccara, G., & Cincotta, M. (2008). Disruption of the prefrontal cortex function by rTMS produces a category-specific enhancement of the reaction times during visual object identification. *Neuropsychologia, 46,* 2725–2731.

Vigliocco, G., Antonini, T., & Garrett, M.F. (1997). Grammatical gender is on the top of Italian tongues. *Psychological Science, 8,* 314–317.

Vingerhoets, G., Vermeule, E., & Santens, P. (2005). Impaired intentional content learning but spared incidental retention of contextual information in non-demented patients with Parkinson's disease. *Neuropsychologia, 43,* 675–681.

Virji-Babul, N., Cheung, T., Weeks, D., Kerns, K., & Shiffrar, M. (2008). Neural activity involved in the perception of human and meaningful object motion. *Neuroreport*, *18*, 1125–1128.

Virtue, S., Parrish, T., & Jung-Beeman, M. (2008). Inferences during story comprehension: Cortical recruitment affected by predictability of events and working memory capacity. *Journal of Cognitive Neuroscience*, *20*, 2274–2284.

Vitu, F., McConkie, G.W., Kerr, P., & O'Regan, J.K. (2001). Fixation location effects on fixation durations during reading: An inverted optimal viewing position effect. *Vision Research*, *41*, 3511–3531.

Vogels, R., Biederman, I., Bar, M., & Lorincz, A. (2001). Inferior temporal neurons show greater sensitivity to non-accidental than to metric shape differences. *Journal of Cognitive Neuroscience*, *13*, 444–453.

Von Neumann, J., & Morgenstern, O. (1947). *Theory of games and economic behaviour.* Princeton, NJ: Princeton University Press.

Von Wright, J.M., Anderson, K., & Stenman, U. (1975). Generalisation of conditioned G.S.R.s in dichotic listening. In P.M.A. Rabbitt & S. Dornic (Eds.), *Attention and performance, Vol. V.* London: Academic Press.

Vousden, J.I., & Maylor, E.A. (2006). Speech errors across the lifespan. *Language and Cognitive Processes*, *21*, 48–77.

Vuilleumier, P., & Driver, J. (2007). Modulation of visual processing by attention and emotion: Windows on causal interactions between human brain regions. *Philosophical Transactions of the Royal Society B – Biological Sciences*, *362*, 837–855.

Vuilleumier, P., Armony, J.L., Clarke, K., Husain, M., Driver, J., & Dolan, R.J. (2002). Neural response to emotional faces with and without awareness: Event-related fMRI in a parietal patient with visual extinction and spatial neglect. *Neuropsychologia*, *40*, 2156–2166.

Vul, E., & Pashler, H. (2007). Incubation benefits only after people have been misdirected. *Memory & Cognition*, *35*, 701–710.

Wade, N.J., & Swanston, M.T. (2001). *Visual perception: An introduction* (2nd Ed.). Hove, UK: Psychology Press.

Wade, A.R., Brewer, A.A., Rieger, J.W., & Wandell, B.A. (2002). Functional measurements of human ventral occipital cortex: Retinopy and colour. *Philosophical Transactions: Biological Sciences*, *357*, 963–973.

Wagenaar, W.A. (1986). My memory: A study of autobiographical memory over six years. *Cognitive Psychology*, *18*, 225–252.

Wager, T.D., Davidson, M.L., Hughes, B.L., Lindquist, M.A., & Ochsner, K.N. (2008). Prefrontal-subcortical pathways mediating successful emotion regulation. *Neuron*, *59*, 1037–1050.

Wagner, A.D., Maril, A., Bjork, R.A., & Schacter, D.L. (2001). Prefrontal contributions to executive control: fMRI evidence for functional distinctions within lateral prefrontal cortex. *Neuroimage*, *14*, 1337–1347.

Wagner, A.D., Schacter, D.L., Rotte, M., Koutstaal, W., Maril, A., Dale, A.M., Rosen, B.R., & Buckner, R.L. (1998). Building memories: Remembering and forgetting of verbal experiences as predicted by brain activity. *Science*, *281*, 188–191.

Wagner, A.D., Shannon, B.J., Kahn, I., & Buckner, R.L. (2005). Parietal lobe contributions to episodic memory retrieval. *Trends in Cognitive Sciences*, *9*, 445–453.

Wagner, U., Gais, S., Haider, H., Verleger, R., & Born, J. (2004). Sleep inspires insight. *Nature*, *427*, 352–355.

Wallas, G. (1926). *The art of thought.* London: Cape.

Walsh, V., Ellison, A., Battelli, L., & Cowey, A. (1998). Task-specific impairments and enhancements induced by magnetic stimulation of human visual area V5. *Proceedings of the Royal Society of London Series B – Biological Sciences*, *265*, 537–543.

Waltz, J.A., Knowlton, B.J., Holyoak, K.J., Boone, K.B., Mishkin, F.S., de Menezes Santos, M. et al. (1999). A system for relational reasoning in human prefrontal cortex. *Psychological Science*, *10*, 119–125.

Walz, P.G., & Rapee, R.M. (2003). Disentangling schematic and conceptual processing: A test of the Interactive Cognitive Subsystems framework. *Cognition & Emotion*, *17*, 65–81.

Wandell, B.A., Dumoulin, S.O., & Brewer, A.A. (2007). Visual field maps in human cortex. *Neuron*, *56*, 366–383.

Wang, X.T. (1996). Domain-specific rationality in human choices: Violations of utility axioms and social contexts. *Cognition*, *60*, 31–63.

Wang, X.T., Simons, F., & Brédart, S. (2001). Social cues and verbal framing in risky choice. *Journal of Behavioral Decision Making*, *14*, 1–15.

Ward, J. (2006). *The student's guide to cognitive neuroscience.* Hove, UK: Psychology Press.

Ward, R., Danziger, S., Owen, V., & Rafal, R. (2002). Deficits in spatial coding and feature binding following damage to spatiotopic maps in the human pulvinar. *Nature Neuroscience*, *5*, 99–100.

Warren, R.M., & Warren, R.P. (1970). Auditory illusions and confusions. *Scientific American*, *223*, 30–36.

Warren, W.H., & Hannon, D.J. (1988). Direction of self-motion is perceived from optical flow. *Nature*, 336, 162–163.

Warrington, E.K., & Shallice, T. (1984). Category specific semantic impairments. *Brain*, 107, 829–853.

Wason, P.C. (1960). On the failure to eliminate hypotheses in a conceptual task. *Quarterly Journal of Experimental Psychology*, 12, 129–140.

Wason, P.C., & Shapiro, D. (1971). Natural and contrived experience in reasoning problems. *Quarterly Journal of Experimental Psychology*, 23, 63–71.

Watkins, P.C., Martin, C.K., & Stern, L.D. (2000). Unconscious memory bias in depression: Perceptual and conceptual processes. *Journal of Abnormal Psychology*, 109, 282–289.

Watson, J.B. (1920). Is thinking merely the action of language mechanisms? *British Journal of Psychology*, 11, 87–104.

Watson, D., & Tellegen, A. (1985). Toward a consensual structure of mood. *Psychological Bulletin*, 98, 219–235.

Weber, A., & Cutler, A. (2004). Lexical competition in non-native spoken-word recognition. *Journal of Memory and Language*, 50, 1–25.

Wegner, D.M. (2003). The mind's best trick: How we experience conscious will. *Trends in Cognitive Sciences*, 7, 65–69.

Wegner, D.M., & Wheatley, T. (1999). Apparent mental causation: Sources of the experience of will. *American Psychologist*, 54, 480–492.

Weisberg, D.S., Keil, F.C., Goodstein, J., Rawson, E., & Gray, J.R. (2008). The seductive allure of neuroscience explanations. *Journal of Cognitive Neuroscience*, 20, 470–477.

Weiskrantz, L. (1980). Varieties of residual experience. *Quarterly Journal of Experimental Psychology*, 32, 365–386.

Weiskrantz, L. (2002). Prime-sight and blindsight. *Consciousness and Cognition*, 11, 568–581.

Weiskrantz. L. (2004). Blindsight. In R.L. Gregory (Ed.), *Oxford companion to the mind*. Oxford: Oxford University Press.

Weiskrantz, L., Warrington, E.K., Sanders, M.D., & Marshall, J. (1974). Visual capacity in the hemianopic field following a restricted occipital ablation. *Brain*, 97, 709–728.

Weisstein, N., & Wong, E. (1986). Figure–ground organisation and the spatial and temporal responses of the visual system. In E.C. Schwab & H.C. Nusbaum (Eds.), *Pattern recognition by humans and machines, Vol. 2*. New York: Academic Press.

Welford, A.T. (1952). The psychological refractory period and the timing of high speed performance. *British Journal of Psychology*, 43, 2–19.

Wells. A., & Papageorgiou, C. (1998). Social phobia: Effects of external attention on anxiety, negative beliefs, and perspective taking. *Behavior Therapy*, 29, 357–370.

Wells, G.L., & Olson, E.A. (2003). Eyewitness testimony. *Annual Review of Psychology*, 54, 277–295.

Werker, J.F., & Tees, R.C. (1992). The organisation and reorganisation of human speech perception. *Annual Review of Neuroscience*, 15, 377–402.

Wertheimer, M. (1923/1955). Gestalt theory. In W.D. Ellis (Ed.), *A source book of Gestalt psychology* (pp. 1–16). London: Routledge & Kegan Paul.

Wesp, R., Cichello, P., Gracia, E.B., & Davis, K. (2004). Observing and engaging in purposeful actions with objects influences estimates of their size. *Perception & Psychophysics*, 66, 1261–1267.

Westmacott, R., Black, S.E., Freedman, M., & Moscovitch, M. (2004). The contribution of autobiographical significance to semantic memory: Evidence from Alzheimer's disease, semantic dementia, and amnesia. *Neuropsychologia*, 42, 25–48.

Wetherick, N.E. (1962). Eliminative and enumerative behaviour in a conceptual task. *Quarterly Journal of Experimental Psychology*, 14, 246–249.

Wheaton, L.A., & Hallett, M. (2007). Ideomotor apraxia: A review. *Journal of the Neurological Sciences*, 260, 1–10.

Wheeler, M.A., Stuss, D.T., & Tulving, E. (1997). Toward a theory of episodic memory: The frontal lobes and autonoetic consciousness. *Psychological Bulletin*, 121, 331–354.

White, S.J. (2008). Eye-movement control during reading: Effects of word frequency and orthographic familiarity. *Journal of Experimental Psychology: Human Perception and Performance*, 34, 205–223.

Whithaus, C., Harrison, S., & Midyette, J. (2008). Keyboarding compared with handwriting on a high-stakes assessment: Student choice of composing medium, raters' perceptions and text quality. *Assessing Writing*, 13, 4–25.

Whorf, B.L. (1956). *Language, thought, and reality: Selected writings of Benjamin Lee Whorf*. New York: Wiley.

Wickelgren, W.A. (1968). Sparing of short-term memory in an amnesic patient: Implications for strength theory of memory. *Neuropsychologia*, 6, 235–244.

Wickens, C.D. (1984). Processing resources in attention. In R. Parasuraman & D.R. Davies (Eds.), *Varieties of Attention*. London: Academic Press.

Wickens, C.D. (2002). Multiple resources and performance prediction. *Theoretical Issues in Ergonomic Science, 3,* 159–177.

Wig, G.S., Grafton, S.T., Demos, K.E., & Kelley, W.M. (2005). Reductions in neural activity underlie behavioural components of repetition priming. *Nature Neuroscience, 8,* 1228–1233.

Wilkie, R.M., & Wann, J.P. (2002). Driving as night falls: The contribution of retinal flow and visual direction to the control of steering. *Current Biology, 12,* 2014–2017.

Wilkie, R.M., & Wann, J.P. (2003). Controlling steering and judging heading: Retinal flow, visual direction, and extraretinal information. *Journal of Experimental Psychology: Human Perception and Performance, 29,* 363–378.

Wilkie, R.M., & Wann, J.P. (2006). Judgements of path, not heading, guide locomotion. *Journal of Experimental Psychology: Human Perception and Performance, 32,* 88–96.

Wilkie, R.M., Wann, J.P., & Allison, R.S. (2008). Active gaze, visual look-ahead, and locomotor control. *Journal of Experimental Psychology: Human Perception and Performance, 34,* 1150–1164.

Wilkinson, L., & Jahanshahi, M. (2007). The striatum and probabilistic implicit sequence learning. *Brain Research, 1137,* 117–130.

Wilkinson, L., & Shanks, D.R. (2004). Intentional control and implicit sequence learning. *Journal of Experimental Psychology: Learning, Memory, & Cognition, 30,* 354–369.

Willander, J., & Larsson, M. (2006). Smell your way back to childhood: Autobiographical odour memory. *Psychonomic Bulletin and Review, 13,* 240–244.

Williams, J.M.G., Watts, F.N., MacLeod, C., & Mathews, A. (1988). *Cognitive psychology and emotional disorders.* Chichester, UK: Wiley.

Williams, J.M.G., Watts, F.N., MacLeod, C.M., & Mathews, A. (1997). *Cognitive psychology and emotional disorders* (2nd. Ed.). Chichester: Wiley.

Wilson, B.A., Alderman, N., Burgess, P.W., Emslie, H., & Evans, J.J. (1996). *Behavioral Assessment of the Dysexecutive Syndrome.* Bury. St. Edmunds, UK: Thames Valley Test Company.

Wilson, E.J., MacLeod, C., Mathews, A., & Rutherford, E.M. (2006). The causal role of interpretive bias in anxiety reactivity. *Journal of Abnormal Psychology, 115,* 103–111.

Wilson, S.M., Saygin, A.P., Sereno, M.I., & Iacoboni, M. (2004). Listening to speech activates motor areas involved in speech production. *Nature Neuroscience, 7,* 701–702.

Winawer, J., Witthoft, N., Frank, M.C., Wade, A.R., & Boroditsky, L. (2007). Russian blues reveal effects of language on colour discrimination. *Proceedings of the National Academy of Sciences of the United States of America, 104,* 778–785.

Windmann, S. (2004). Effects of sentence context and expectation on the McGurk illusion. *Journal of Memory and Language, 50,* 212–230.

Winningham R.G., Hyman I.E. Jr, & Dinnel, D.L. (2000). Flashbulb memories? The effects of when the initial memory report was obtained. *Memory, 8,* 209–216.

Winston, J.S., Vuilleumier, P., & Dolan, R.J. (2003). Effects of low-spatial frequency components of fearful faces on fusiform cortex activity. *Current Biology, 13,* 1824–1929.

Witt, J.K., Linkenauger, S.A., Bakdash, J.Z., & Proffitt, D.R. (2008). Putting to a bigger hole: Golf performance relates to perceived size. *Psychonomic Bulletin & Review, 15,* 581–585.

Wixted, J.T. (2004). The psychology and neuroscience of forgetting. *Annual Review of Psychology, 55,* 235–269.

Wixted, J.T. (2005). A theory about why we forget what we once knew. *Current Directions in Psychological Science, 14,* 6–9.

Woike, B., Gershkovich, I., Piorkowski, R., & Polo, M. (1999). The role of motives in the content and structure of autobiographical memory. *Journal of Personality and Social Psychology, 76,* 600–612.

Wojciulik, E., Kanwisher, N., & Driver, J. (1998). Modulation of activity in the fusiform face area by covert attention: An fMRI study. *Journal of Neuropsysiology, 79,* 1574–1579.

Wolfe, J.M. (1998). Visual search. In H. Pashler (Ed.), *Attention.* Hove, UK: Psychology Press.

Wolfe, J.M. (2003). Moving towards solutions to some enduring controversies in visual search. *Trends in Cognitive Sciences, 7,* 70–76.

Wolfe, J.M., Horowitz, T.S., Van Wert, M.J., Kenner, N.M., Place, S.S., & Kibbi, N. (2007). Low target prevalence is a stubborn source of errors in visual search tasks. *Journal of Experimental Psychology: General, 136,* 623–638.

Wong, K.F.E., Yik, M., & Kwong, J.Y.Y. (2006). Understanding the emotional aspects of escalation of commitment: The role of negative affect. *Journal of Applied Psychology, 91,* 282–297.

Wong, P.C.M., Nusbaum, H.C., & Small, S.L. (2004). Neural bases of talker normalisation. *Journal of Cognitive Neuroscience, 16,* 1173–1184.

Woollams, A.M., Lambon Ralph, M.A., Plaut, D.C., & Patterson, K. (2007). SD-squared: On the association between semantic dementia and surface dyslexia. *Psychological Review, 114,* 316–339.

Wright, D.B., & Loftus, E.F. (2008). Eyewitness memory. In G. Cohen & M.A. Conway (Eds.), *Memory in the real world* (3rd ed.). Hove, UK: Psychology Press.

Wright, D.B., & Stroud, J.N. (2002). Age differences in line-up identification accuracy: People are better with their own age. *Law and Human Behavior, 26,* 641–654.

Wright, G. (1984). *Behavioral decision theory.* Harmondsworth: Penguin.

Wylie, G.R., Foxe, J.J., & Taylor, T.L. (2007). Forgetting as an active process: An fMRI investigation of item-method-directed forgetting. *Cerebral Cortex, 18,* 670–682.

Yang, Z.H., Zhao, X.Q., Wang, C.X., Chen, H.Y., & Zhang, Y.M. (2008). Neuroanatomic correlation of the post-stroke aphasias studied with imaging. *Neurological Research, 30,* 356–360.

Yantis, S. (2008). The neural basis of selective attention: Cortical sources and targets of attentional modulation. *Current Directions in Psychological Science, 17,* 86–90.

Yasuda, K., Watanabe, O., & Ono, Y. (1997). Dissociation between semantic and autobiographic memory: A case report. *Cortex, 33,* 623–638.

Yates, M. (2005). Phonological neighbours speed visual word processing: Evidence from multiple tasks. *Journal of Experimental Psychology: Learning, Memory, and Cognition, 31,* 1385–1397.

Yates, M., Friend, J., & Ploetz, D.M. (2008). Phonological neighbours influence word naming through the least supported phoneme. *Journal of Experimental Psychology: Human Perception and Performance, 34,* 1599–1606.

Yilmaz, E.H., & Warren, W.H. (1995). Visual control of braking: A test of the "tau-dot" hypothesis. *Journal of Experimental Psychology: Human Perception and Performance, 21,* 996–1014.

Young, A.W., Hay, D.C., & Ellis, A.W. (1985). The faces that launched a thousand slips: Everyday difficulties and errors in recognising people. *British Journal of Psychology, 76,* 495–523.

Young, A.W., Hellawell, D., & Hay, D.C. (1987). Configurational information in face perception. *Perception, 16,* 747–759.

Young, A.W., Hellawell, D., & de Haan, E. (1988). Cross-domain semantic priming in normal subjects and a prosopagnosic patient. *Quarterly Journal of Experimental Psychology, 40,* 561–580.

Young, A.W, McWeeny, K.H., Hay, D.C., & Ellis, A.W. (1986). Matching familiar and unfamiliar faces on identity and expression. *Psychological Research, 48,* 63–68.

Young, A.W., Newcombe, F., de Haan, E.H.F., Small, M., & Hay, D.C. (1993). Face perception after brain injury: Selective impairments affecting identity and expression. *Brain, 116,* 941–959.

Yovel, G., & Kanwisher, N. (2004). Face perception: Domain specific, not process specific. *Neuron, 44,* 889–898.

Yue, X.M., Tjan, B.S., & Biederman, I. (2006). What makes faces special? *Vision Research, 46,* 3802–3811.

Zago, M., McIntyre, J., Senot, P., & Lacquaniti, F. (2008). Internal models and prediction of visual gravitational motion. *Vision Research, 48,* 1532–1538.

Zeki, S. (1983). Colour coding in the cerebral cortex: The reaction of cells in monkey visual cortex to wavelengths and colour. *Neuroscience, 9,* 741–756.

Zeki, S. (1992). The visual image in mind and brain. *Scientific American, 267,* 43–50.

Zeki, S. (1993). *A vision of the brain.* Oxford: Blackwell.

Zeki, S. (2005). The Ferrier Lecture 1995. Behind the seen: The functional specialization of the brain in space and time. *Philosophical Transactions of the Royal Society B, 360,* 1145–1183.

Zeki, S.M. (1991). Cerebral akinetopsia (visual motion blindness): A review. *Brain, 114,* 811–824.

Zeki, S., Watson, J.D.G., Lueck, C.J., Friston, K.J., Kennard, C., & Frackowiak, R.S.J. (1991). A direct demonstration of functional specialisation in human visual cortex. *Journal of Neuroscience, 11,* 641–649.

Zeki, S.M., & Marini, L. (1998). Three cortical stages of colour processing in the human brain. *Brain, 121,* 1669–1685.

Zevin, J.D., & Balota, D.A. (2000). Primary and attentional control of lexical and sublexical pathways during naming. *Journal of Experimental Psychology: Learning, Memory, and Cognition, 26,* 121–135.

Zevin, J.D., & Seidenberg, M.S. (2006). Simulating consistency effects and individual differences in nonword naming: A comparison of current models. *Journal of Memory and Language, 54,* 145–160.

Zhang, D., Zhang, X.C., Sun, X.W., Li, Z.H., Wang, Z.X., He, S., & Hu, W.P. (2004). Cross-modal temporal order memory for auditory digits and visual locations: An fMRI study. *Human Brain Mapping, 22,* 280–289.

Zihl, J., von Cramon, D., & Mai, N. (1983). Selective disturbance of movement vision after bilateral brain damage. *Brain, 106,* 313–340.

Zoccolan, D., Kouh, M., Poggio, T., & DiCarlo, J.J. (2007). Trade-off between object selectivity and tolerance in monkey inferotemporal cortex. *Journal of Neuroscience, 27,* 12292–12307.

Zwaan, R.A. (1994). Effects of genre expectations on text comprehension. *Journal of Experimental*

Psychology: Learning, Memory, & Cognition, 20, 920–933.

Zwaan, R.A. (2008). Time in language, situation models, and mental simulation. *Language Learning, 58,* 13–26.

Zwaan, R.A., & Madden, C.J. (2004). Updating situation models. *Journal of Experimental Psychology: Learning, Memory, and Cognition, 30,* 283–288.

Zwaan, R.A., & Radvansky, G.A. (1998). Situation models in language comprehension and memory. *Psychological Bulletin, 123,* 162–185.

Zwaan, R.A., Stanfield, R.A., & Yaxley, R.H. (2002). Language comprehenders mentally represent the shapes of objects. *Psychological Science, 13,* 168–171.

Zwaan, R.A., & van Oostendorp, U. (1993). Do readers construct spatial representations in naturalistic story comprehension? *Discourse Processes, 16,* 125–143.

Zwitserlood, P. (1989). The locus of the effects of sentential–semantic context in spoken-word processing. *Cognition, 32,* 25–64.

AUTHOR INDEX

SUBJECT INDEX